THE OXFORD HANDBOOK OF

COGNITIVE
SOCIOLOGY

THE OXFORD HANDBOOK OF

COGNITIVE SOCIOLOGY

Edited by

WAYNE H. BREKHUS

and

GABE IGNATOW

OXFORD

UNIVERSITY PRESS

Oxford University Press is a department of the University of Oxford. It furthers
the University's objective of excellence in research, scholarship, and education
by publishing worldwide. Oxford is a registered trade mark of Oxford University
Press in the UK and certain other countries.

Published in the United States of America by Oxford University Press
198 Madison Avenue, New York, NY 10016, United States of America.

Library of Congress Cataloging-in-Publication Data
Names: Brekhus, Wayne, editor. | Ignatow, Gabe, editor.
Title: The Oxford handbook of cognitive sociology / edited by
Wayne H. Brekhus and Gabe Ignatow.
Description: New York : Oxford University Press, [2019]
Identifiers: LCCN 2018045600 (print) | LCCN 2018046613 (ebook) |
ISBN 9780190273392 (updf) | ISBN 9780190945480 (epub) |
ISBN 9780190273385 (hardcover)
Subjects: LCSH: Social psychology. | Sociology. | Cognitive psychology.
Classification: LCC HM1033 (ebook) | LCC HM1033 .O937 2019 (print) |
DDC 302—dc23
LC record available at https://lccn.loc.gov/2018045600

1 3 5 7 9 8 6 4 2

Printed by Sheridan Books, Inc., United States of America

Contents

PART II PERSPECTIVES FROM OTHER FIELDS

PART III METHODS OF COGNITIVE SOCIOLOGY

PART IV THE SOCIOLOGY OF PERCEPTION AND ATTENTION

PART V SOCIOCULTURAL FRAMES OF MEANING, METAPHOR, AND ANALOGY

PART VI CATEGORIES, BOUNDARIES, AND IDENTITIES

PART VII TIME AND MEMORY

List of Contributors

Nina Bandelj is Professor of Sociology, Associate Vice Provost for Faculty Development, and Co-director of the Center for Organizational Research at the University of California, Irvine. Her research examines the social, cultural, and emotional influences on economic phenomena, globalization, and postsocialism. She is the coauthor or coeditor of six books, most recently, *Money Talks: Explaining How Money Really Works* (with F. Wherry and V. Zelizer).

Brittany Pearl Battle is Assistant Professor of Sociology at Wake Forest University. Her work examines the child support system and the consequences of state intervention in the family, specifically exploring the influence of norms of morality and deservingness in the use of shame, the conceptualization of parenthood and family, and the criminal justice and economic consquences of involvement with the system. She is a Ford Foundation Dissertation Fellow and American Sociological Association Minority Fellowship Program recipient.

Wayne H. Brekhus is Professor of Sociology at the University of Missouri. His research interests include the cultural sociology of cognition, the sociology of identities, social markedness and unmarkedness, and developing sociological theory. He is the author of *Culture and Cognition: Patterns in the Social Construction of Reality*; *Peacocks, Chameleons, Centaurs: Gay Suburbia and the Grammar of Social Identity*, and *Sociologia dell'inavvertito* (translated into Italian by Lorenzo Sabetta). He is currently writing a book on the sociology of identities.

Karen A. Cerulo is a Professor of Sociology at Rutgers University. She is pastVice President of the Eastern Sociological Society and the current editor of *Sociological Forum*, the flagship journal of the Eastern Sociological Society. Her articles appear in a wide variety of journals, annuals, and collections. She also is the author of *Never Saw It Coming: Cultural Challenges to Envisioning the Worst, Deciphering Violence: The Cognitive Order of Right and Wrong*, and *Identity Designs: The Sights and Sounds of a Nation*—winner of the Culture Section of the American Sociological Association's Best Book Award, 1996. She also coauthored *Second Thoughts: Seeing Conventional Wisdom through the Sociological Eye*, and edited a collection titled *Culture in Mind: Toward a Sociology of Culture and Cognition*. Cerulo served as the chair of the American Sociological Association's Culture Section (2009 through 2010), and she functions as the section's network coordinator, and the director of the Culture and Cognition Network. In 2013, she was named the Robin M. Williams Jr. Lecturer by the Eastern Sociological Society, and she also won that organization's 2013 Merit Award.

Paul Chilton is Professor Emeritus of Linguistics at Lancaster University, United Kingdom, with a multidisciplinary research background. He is currently a visiting academic in the Centre for Applied Linguistics, at the University of Warwick, where he formerly taught and published in the field of French Renaissance studies. At the time of the collapse of the Cold War, he was researching the discourse of international conflict in the Centre for International Security and Arms Control, at Stanford, producing the book *Security Metaphors*. Having returned to linguistic theorizing, he recently published *Language, Space, and Mind*. Turning to a neglected area of human experience where language is crucial, he has coedited, with Monika Kopytowska, an interdisciplinary collection of papers on *Religion, Language, and the Human Mind*.

Thomas DeGloma is Associate Professor of Sociology at Hunter College and the Graduate Center of the City University of New York (CUNY). He specializes in the areas of culture, cognition, memory, symbolic interaction, and sociological theory. His research interests also include the sociology of time, knowledge, autobiography, identity, and trauma. DeGloma's book, *Seeing the Light: The Social Logic of Personal Discovery* (2014), which received the 2015 Charles Horton Cooley Book Award from the Society for the Study of Symbolic Interaction, explores the stories people tell about life-changing discoveries of "truth" and illuminates the ways that individuals and communities use autobiographical stories to weigh in on salient moral and political controversies. DeGloma has also published articles in *Social Psychology Quarterly*, *Sociological Forum*, *Symbolic Interaction*, and the *American Journal of Cultural Sociology*, along with chapters in various edited volumes. He is currently working on his second book, which explores the phenomenon of anonymity and the impact of anonymous actors in various social situations and interactions. He served as President of the Society for the Study of Symbolic Interaction (2017–2018) and Secretary of the Eastern Sociological Society (2016–2019).

David Eck is Assistant Professor of Philosophy at Cañada College in Redwood City, California. His teaching and research interests concern the social dimensions of knowledge, with an emphasis on the relationship between cognitive science and social epistemology. His other writing includes "Social Coordination in Scientific Communities" in *Perspectives on Science* and "Prioritizing Otherness: The Line between Vacuous Individuality and Hollow Collectivism" (with Alexander Levine) in *Sociality and Normativity for Robots*.

Margaret Frye is an Assistant Professor in the Department of Sociology at the University of Michigan. Her research connects cultural understandings and behavioral outcomes during the transition to adulthood in sub-Saharan Africa.

Asia Friedman is Associate Professor of Sociology at the University of Delaware. Dr. Friedman is a cultural sociologist with a primary research focus on the cognitive and sensory underpinnings of the social construction process. More specifically, each of her core projects is concerned with understanding how individuals make mental distinctions in contexts of ambiguity and complexity. She also examines how sensory perception works to support cultural distinctions as a mechanism to simplify and resolve competing meanings. Through this work, she aims to advance thinking on what it means to claim that something is "socially constructed," particularly a material entity such as the human body. Although her approach is rooted in cultural and cognitive sociology and sensory studies, the questions about the social construction process that most interest her have applicability to a wide range of other substantive topics, allowing her to engage in debates in the sociology of gender, the sociology of the body, the sociology of race, medical sociology, and sociological theory. In each case, she uses an analysis of social patterns of thought and sensory perception to bring productive new questions to ongoing conversations in the field. Her first book, *Blind to Sameness: Sexpectations and the Social Construction of Male and Female Bodies* (2013), which won the 2016 Distinguished Book Award from the Sex and Gender Section of the American Sociological Association, draws on more than sixty interviews with two very different populations—blind people and transgender people—to answer questions about the relationships between gender, biology, and visual perception.

Amir Goldberg is Associate Professor of Organizational Behavior at the Stanford Graduate School of Business, where he is also the Codirector of the Computational Culture Lab. His research focuses on measuring and modeling culture in market, organizational and national contexts. These research projects all share an overarching theme: the desire to understand the social mechanisms that underlie how people construct meaning, and consequently pursue action. His work has been published in *American Journal of Sociology*, *American Sociological Review*, *Management Science*, and *Review of Financial Studies*.

Igor Grossmann is Associate Professor of Psychology at the University of Waterloo. He is a behavioral scientist exploring the interplay of sociocultural factors for wisdom in the face of daily stressors. His interdisciplinary work uses a range of methods, including big data analytics, psychophysiology, diary surveys, and behavioral experiments.

Daina Cheyenne Harvey is an Associate Professor in the Department of Sociology and Anthropology, and by courtesy Environmental Studies, at the College of the Holy Cross. He researches and teaches in the fields of social disruption, risk, climate, culture and cognition, suffering, urban marginality, and the environmental precariat. He is currently writing a book tentatively titled *Anthropocene Demos: Neoliberal Disorder and the Long-Term Lessons of Hurricane Katrina*. This book explores the concepts of urban fragility and ecological citizenship as a way to understand democratic exclusion in the anthropocene. It focuses on the experiences of residents of the Lower Ninth Ward in rebuilding their community. His recent work has appeared in *Sociological Forum*, *Urban Studies*, *Symbolic Interaction*, *Humanity and Society*, and *Local Environment*.

Gabe Ignatow is Professor of Sociology and Director of Graduate Studies at the University of North Texas. His research interests are mainly in the areas of sociological theory, cognitive social science and digital research methods, and his most recent books include *An Introduction to Text Mining* and *Text Mining: A Guidebook for the Social Sciences*, both coauthored with Rada Mihalcea.

Erin F. Johnston is the Jim Johnson Postdoctoral Fellow in the Graduate School of Education at Stanford University. Her research focuses on experiences of personal transformation, and seeks to illuminate how the process of self-change unfolds in relation to the cultural resources made available in different organizational contexts. She has written about the rhetorical conventions underlying Pagan practitioners' narratives of conversion (*Sociological Forum*, 2013), the aspirational nature of identity in spiritual communities (*Religions*, 2016), and about how novices learn to overcome failures and obstacles in the process of learning new spiritual disciplines by drawing on shared interpretive resources (*Qualitative Sociology*, 2017). Erin's current book project, *Learning to Practice, Becoming Spiritual: Spiritual Disciplines as Projects of the Self*, draws on her fieldwork in two communities—an integral yoga studio and a Catholic prayer house—to reveal how these organizations enable the formation of new spiritual selves in and through the process of apprenticeship. Her latest research project examines the dynamics of identity formation among emerging adults on structured "gap year" programs.

Zoltán Kövecses is Professor Emeritus in the Department of American Studies at Eötvös Loránd University. His research interests include metaphor, metonymy, emotion language, American English and culture, and the relationship between metaphorical conceptualization and context. His major publications include *Metaphor and Emotion* (2000), *American English: An Introduction* (2000), *Metaphor: A Practical Introduction* (2002/2010), *Metaphor in Culture* (2005), *Language, Mind, and Culture* (2006), and *Where Metaphors Come From* (2015).

Dmitry Kurakin is a Leading Research Fellow at the Centre for Fundamental Sociology and the Director of the Centre for Cultural Sociology and Anthropology of Education at the National Research University Higher School of Economics (Moscow, Russia). He is also a Faculty Fellow at the Center for Cultural Sociology at Yale University. He works in the fields of sociological theory, Durkheimian cultural sociology, focusing particularly on the theories of the sacred, cultural sociology of the body, and cultural sociology of education. He has published widely on these topics.

Vanina Leschziner is an Associate Professor in the Department of Sociology at the University of Toronto. Her main areas of interest are sociological theory, cultural sociology, culture and cognition, organizational theory, and sociology of valuation and evaluation. Her book *At the Chef's Table: Culinary Creativity in Elite Restaurants*, based on research with elite chefs in New York and San Francisco, analyzes the creative work of chefs to explain the logics of action and social dynamics of cultural creation. She has published research on social cognition, organizational dynamics, and field theory, in *Sociological Theory*, *Theory and Society*, and *Sociological Forum*, among other publications.

Omar Lizardo is the LeRoy Neiman Term Chair Professor in the Department of Sociology at the University of California, Los Angeles. His areas of research interest include the sociology of culture, social networks, the sociology of emotion, social stratification, cognitive social science, and organizational theory. He is currently a member of the editorial advisory board of *Social Forces*, *Theory and Society*, *Poetics*, *Sociological Forum*, *Journal for the Theory of Social Behaviour*, and *Journal of World Systems Research*, and, with Rory McVeigh and Sarah Mustillo, he is one of the current coeditors of the *American Sociological Review*.

John Levi Martin is the Florence Borchert Bartling Professor of Sociology at the University of Chicago. He is the author of *Social Structures*, *The Explanation of Social Action*, *Thinking through Theory*, *Thinking through Methods*, and *Thinking through Statistics*, as well as articles on methodology, cognition, social networks, and theory. He is currently working on the history of the theory of social action.

Terence E. McDonnell is an Associate Professor of Sociology at the University of Notre Dame. He is a cultural sociologist who studies the meaning of objects, art, and media in everyday life. He is the author of *Best Laid Plans: Cultural Entropy and the Unraveling of AIDS Media Campaigns*. His research has appeared in the *American Journal of Sociology*, *Sociological Theory*, *Theory and Society*, *Poetics*, *Qualitative Sociology*, and *Social Problems*.

Andrew Miles is an Assistant Professor of Sociology at the University of Toronto. His work lies at the intersection of the sociology of culture, social psychology, and moral and cognitive psychology. His research focuses on the social development of different moral cultures, and the role moral constructs play in predicting behavior. He also studies how cognitive processes affect action, and has an abiding love for learning and teaching quantitative methods.

Sanaz Mobasseri is an Assistant Professor of Organizational Behavior at Boston University's Questrom School of Business. Her research investigates how organizational and social network processes shape gender and race differences amongst employees in the workplace. She does this by examining the roles of culture, cognition, and emotion in organizations using field experimental and computational research methodologies.

Jamie L. Mullaney is Professor of Sociology and Associate Provost for Faculty Affairs at Goucher College. In addition to numerous journal articles, she is the author of two books: *Everyone is NOT Doing It* (2006) and *Paid to Party: Working Time and Emotion in Direct Home Sales* (with Janet Hinson Shope, 2012). Her research interests and projects largely focus around issues of time, emotion, and identity.

Stephanie Peña-Alves is a doctoral candidate in the Department of Sociology at Rutgers University with research foci in the areas of culture, cognition, language, space, and boundaries. Her current work revolves around the cognitive sociology of access and, within that, the theoretical links between the built environment, language, culture, and thought. In particular, she is interested in tracing the ways boundary objects and in-out relations operate at multiple levels of analysis and abstraction.

Diane M. Rodgers is an Associate Professor at Northern Illinois University. Her book *Debugging the Link between Social Theory and Social Insects* examines social insect analogies that were shared between entomologists and social scientists during the nineteenth and early twentieth centuries. These analogies were co-constructed and created a legitimating loop that naturalized Western conceptions of race, class, and gender structural hierarchies. Emerging from this critical analysis, subsequent articles by Rodgers have explored the shift from hierarchical social insect analogies to contemporary self-organizing models. Rodgers's research interests are science and technology studies, social theory, and social movements. Her work has appeared in *The Sociological Quarterly*; *Symbolic Interaction*; *Bulletin of Science, Technology and Society*; *Organization: The Critical Journal of Organization, Theory, and Society*; *Humanity and Society*; *Minerva*; *Origin(s) of Design in Nature*; *History of the Human Sciences*; and *Sociological Spectrum*.

Henri C. Santos is a Post-doctoral Fellow in Behavioral Science at Geisinger Health System. His research explores how people make consequential decisions in a changing world. On an individual level, he studies expertise, intellectual humility, and wisdom, particularly in the context of healthcare. On a societal level, he investigates cultural change in individualism-collectivism over time.

Markus Schroer is Professor of Sociology at Philipps-Universität Marburg. His research interests include sociological theory, cultural sociology, sociology of space, city and architecture, sociology of knowledge, sociology of the body, visual sociology, history of sociology, social diagnosis of time, and sociology of artifacts.

Lynette Shaw is currently a Postdoctoral Scholar with the Michigan Society of Fellows and an Assistant Professor of Complex Systems at the University of Michigan. Her main area of research involves theorizing and modeling the emergence of social construction dynamics from individual level cognitive processes. Her other primary area of research lies at the intersection of computational social science and economic sociology and focuses on the social construction of value around new digital currencies such as Bitcoin and Ethereum.

Hana Shepherd is Assistant Professor of Sociology at Rutgers University. She studies culture and cognition, social networks, and organizations. She is interested in how social processes at different levels of analysis contribute to social change. She uses diverse methods such as network analysis, lab and field-based experiments, interviews, and archival research. Her recent projects include a year-long field experiment in fifty-six middle schools that used theories from social norms embedded in social networks to change school-level behavioral patterns. Her current projects examine organizational context and network structure, and comparative studies of how organizations implement new law in schools and in local labor law enforcement offices.

Benjamin H. Snyder is Assistant Professor of Sociology at Williams College, where he teaches and conducts research on temporality, morality, and economic life. He is the author of *The Disrupted Workplace: Time and the Moral Order of Flexible Capitalism*.

John Sonnett is Associate Professor of Sociology at the University of Mississippi. His research interests include culture, music, climate change, race and racism, and research methods. His work has been published in *Global Environmental Change*, *Poetics*, *Public Understanding of Science*, and *Sociological Forum*, among other outlets.

Sameer B. Srivastava is an Associate Professor and Harold Furst Chair in Management Philosophy and Values at UC Berkeley's Haas School of Business, where he is also the codirector of the Computational Culture Lab. His research unpacks the complex interrelationships among the culture of social groups, the cognition of individuals within these groups, and the connections that people forge within and across groups. Much of his work is set in organizational contexts, where he uses computational methods to examine how culture, cognition, and networks independently and jointly relate to career outcomes. His work has been published in outlets such as *American Journal of Sociology*, *American Sociological Review*, *Management Science*, and *Organization Science*.

Jacob Strandell is currently an Assistant Professor at Uppsala University in Sweden. Before this, he worked primarily at the University of Copenhagen (Denmark), where he also attained his PhD degree with a dissertation titled "Culture-Cognition Interaction: Bridging Cultural Sociology and Cognitive Science." Dr. Strandell's work has since specialized in the relationship between psychology and sociology, and more specifically cognition and culture, to overcome the arbitrary divide and illusionary incompatibility between the two.

Piet Strydom, an ethical exile from the apartheid regime, retired from the Department of Sociology, School of Sociology and Philosophy, University College Cork, Ireland, in 2011, is still associate editor of the *European Journal of Social Theory*. His research interests range from critical theory, social theory, and cognitive sociology, through the philosophy and history of social science, to substantive areas such as rights, risk, cosmopolitanism, environment, and the human mind. Besides many pieces in anthologies, encyclopedias and journals, major publications include *Contemporary Critical Theory and Methodology*; *New Horizons of Critical Theory: Collective Learning and Triple Contingency*; *Risk, Environment and Society*; and *Discourse and Knowledge*. He also edited *Philosophies of Social Science* (with Gerard Delanty) as well as special issues of the *European Journal of Social Theory* and the *Irish Journal of Sociology*.

Ron Sun is Professor of Cognitive Science and Computer Science at Rensselaer Polytechnic Institute. His research interests center around the study of cognition, especially in the areas of cognitive architectures, human reasoning and learning, cognitive social simulation, and hybrid connectionist-symbolic models. He published many papers in these areas, as well as ten books, including *Anatomy of the Mind* and

Cambridge Handbook of Computational Psychology. For his paper on integrating rule-based and connectionist models for accounting for human everyday reasoning, he received the David Marr Award from Cognitive Science Society. For his work on human skill learning, he received the Hebb Award from International Neural Network Society. He was the founding co-editor-in-chief of the journal *Cognitive Systems Research*, and also serves on the editorial boards of many other journals. He chaired a number of major international conferences. He is a fellow of IEEE, APS, and other societies, and he was president of International Neural Network Society 2011–2012.

Chana Teeger is an Assistant Professor in the Department of Methodology at the London School of Economics and Political Science and a senior research associate of the Department of Sociology at the University of Johannesburg. She works on issues around inequality, race, education, and collective memory. Her work has appeared in venues such as the *American Sociological Review, Social Forces*, and *Sociology of Education*. She is currently working on a book manuscript that examines how the history of apartheid is being taught to, and understood by, young South Africans.

Stephen Turner is Distinguished University Professor in Philosophy at the University of South Florida. He has written extensively on the history and philosophy of social science, including extensive writings on Max Weber and Emile Durkheim and on the history of statistics, as well as on cognitive science, including *Brains/Practices/Relativism: Social Theory after Cognitive Science* and *Understanding the Tacit*, as well as his recent *Cognitive Science and the Social: A Primer*. He has also recently coedited *The Sage Handbook of Political Sociology* (with William Outhwaite) and *The Calling of Social Thought: Rediscovering the Work of Edward Shils* (with Christopher Adair-Toteff).

Stephen Vaisey is Professor of Sociology and Director of the Worldview Lab at the Kenan Institute for Ethics at Duke University. The main goal of his research is to understand moral and political worldviews: what they are, where they come from, and what they do.

Michael E. W. Varnum is an Assistant Professor in the Department of Psychology at Arizona State University. Dr. Varnum's primary research focuses on how ecology shapes patterns of cultural variation and cultural change. His work incorporates theory from evolutionary psychology, behavioral ecology, and cultural psychology, and methods ranging from econometrics to neuroscience.

Kelcie L. Vercel is an Assistant Professor of Sociology at Augsburg University in Sioux Falls, South Dakota. Her research investigates identity and meanings of home in intimate relationships and market interactions.

Vered Vinitzky-Seroussi is a Professor of Sociology at the Hebrew University of Jerusalem. Her main field is collective memory and commemoration, and she is currently working on home museums and the sociology of atmosphere (together with Irit Dekel). She is the coeditor (together with Jeffrey Olick and Daniel Levy) of *The*

Collective Memory Reader. Her other work has appeared in places such as The University of Chicago Press and the *American Sociological Review.*

J. Patrick Williams is an Associate Professor of Sociology at Aalborg University in Denmark and an Associate Professor of Sociology at Nanyang Technological University, Singapore. He has many research publications on the experiences of individuals who self-identify as subcultural and is particularly interested in the social construction of subcultural authenticities. He is an associate editor of the journal *Deviant Behavior* and has edited and authored several books, including *Authenticity in Culture, Self, and Society* (2009) and *Subcultural Theory: Traditions and Concepts* (2011). He is currently working on a new, interdisciplinary collection of studies related to identity andauthenticity.

Eviatar Zerubavel is Board of Governors and Distinguished Professor of Sociology at Rutgers University. He is the author of *Patterns of Time in Hospital Life: A Sociological Perspective* (1979), *Hidden Rhythms: Schedules and Calendars in Social Life* (1981), *The Seven-Day Circle: The History and Meaning of the Week* (1985), *The Fine Line: Making Distinctions in Everyday Life* (1991), *Terra Cognita: The Mental Discovery of America* (1992), *Social Mindscapes: An Invitation to Cognitive Sociology* (1997), *The Clockwork Muse: A Practical Guide to Writing Theses, Dissertations, and Books* (1999), *Time Maps: Collective Memory and the Social Shape of the Past* (2003), *The Elephant in the Room: Silence and Denial in Everyday Life* (2006), *Ancestors and Relatives: Genealogy, Identity, and Community* (2011), *Hidden in Plain Sight: The Social Structure of Irrelevance* (2015), and *Taken for Granted: The Remarkable Power of the Unremarkable* (2018). In 2000–2001 he served as chair of the Culture Section of the American Sociological Association. In 2003 he was awarded a Guggenheim Fellowship. He is currently writing a book on formal theorizing.

Christoffer J. P. Zoeller is a PhD candidate in Sociology at the University of California–Irvine. He is interested in economic sociology and institutional theory, with a historical focus on economic policy in the neoliberal era.

CHAPTER 1

··

COGNITIVE SOCIOLOGY AND THE CULTURAL MIND

debates, directions, and challenges

··

WAYNE H. BREKHUS AND GABE IGNATOW

EDITING a volume showcasing contemporary contributors to cognitive sociology is a challenging enterprise because debates over the parameters of cognitive sociology, and over how best to understand the ways culture and cognition interact, are ongoing. As coeditors of this volume, coming from different theoretical orientations within cognitive sociology, we take our task to be to illuminate debates, directions, and challenges within this field. One theoretical tension that informs ongoing debates is a contrast between cognitive cultural sociology approaches and interdisciplinary cognitive social science approaches. Our aim here is to present cognitive sociology in a pluralistic manner, emphasizing tensions and differences, but also commonalities, across schools of thought within cognitive sociology. The contributors to this volume come from a range of theoretical perspectives and methodological approaches. In this introduction we first discuss the development of cognitive sociology as a specific area of inquiry. We then discuss different theoretical traditions and controversies as well as emerging efforts to synthesize competing approaches.

Sociology has had a long-standing interest in the relationship between culture, social structure, and thought, extending as far back as classical theorists such as Durkheim, Weber, Simmel, and Marx. But cognitive sociology as a dedicated area of inquiry is a more contemporary development. The term "cognitive sociology" appears as early as 1974 in Cicourel's collection of essays titled *Cognitive Sociology: Language and Meaning in Social Interaction*. Cicourel was interested in how speech and language are intricately embedded in a sociocultural context, and in such matters as how children learn social structure and meaning from adults through the socialization of language and intergenerational interaction. While Cicourel used the term "cognitive sociology," the more programmatic use of "cognitive sociology" to define a body of sociological inquiry began to coalesce in the late 1990s with Eviatar Zerubavel's (1997) *Social Mindscapes: An Invitation to Cognitive Sociology* and Paul DiMaggio's (1997) "Culture and Cognition." Zerubavel and DiMaggio emphasized similar cognitive sociological applications and processes such as perception/attention, social classification, identity, and collective memory (DiMaggio also included logics of action), while differing in their programmatic goals. Zerubavel advances a distinctively sociological approach that recognizes and highlights sociocultural variation and cognitive pluralism between the extremes of cognitive individualism and cognitive universalism, while DiMaggio advances an integrative, interdisciplinary approach that draws on cognitive psychology and calls for greater incorporation of psychology into sociological analysis.

The respective visions of Zerubavel and DiMaggio reflect a tension between a more cognitive cultural sociological approach and a more interdisciplinary neuropsychological cognitive social science approach. For Zerubavel, cognitive sociology involves studying human thinking as socially patterned and influenced, for example, by the culture, subculture, organizational culture, interactional setting, or social networks in which one is contextually situated. Whereas Zerubavel's cognitive sociology emphasizes highlighting cultural differences in category knowledge, for DiMaggio, cognitive sociology involves studying the mechanisms by which cultural processes enter into individual minds and shape the microfoundations of social action (see also Ignatow 2007:117). This distinction between these two cognitive sociology programs continues to be reflected in current theoretical and methodological debates. Cognitive cultural sociologists who more closely follow Zerubavel's program are interested in cultural variation and analyzing general patterns of cognition across aggregate social and cultural categories, while neuropsychologically informed interdisciplinary cognitive social scientists who more closely follow DiMaggio's tradition are interested in the processes by which individuals process information, make intuitive judgments, and act on their sensory and social environments. For those who follow in DiMaggio's tradition, sociology is an interdisciplinary contributor to cognitive social science that exists downstream from and draws on the insights of cognitive science. Zerubavel and other sociologists employing a cultural cognitive sociology approach view sociology as a distinctive discipline that is an equal partner to cognitive neuroscience.

Karen Cerulo (2002) further took up the challenge of advancing a sociology of culture and cognition in her edited volume *Culture in Mind: Toward a Sociology of Culture and Cognition*. Cerulo emphasized cognitive processes such as attention, classification, representation, and memory, and considered the ways that sociocultural conditions interact with neurocognitive processes to influence cognitive experience. She advances a cultural cognitive pluralist approach, noting that "each contributor treats cognitive patterns as neither general to the species nor specific to the individual" (p. 3), and thus engages with an intermediate cognitivist position that highlights cognitive difference and distinction. While sharing Zerubavel's cognitive pluralism, Cerulo also shares with DiMaggio an interest in more directly incorporating cognitive neuroscience into sociology. This latter interest continues to take further shape in Cerulo's more recent and continuing efforts to mine the intersections of cognitive sociology and neuroscience (Cerulo 2010, 2014, this volume).

In a special issue of the *European Journal of Social Theory* on social theory after the cognitive revolution, Piet Strydom (2007) maps the tremendous epistemological diversity of types of cognitive sociological theorizing, calling attention to significant variation along such dimensions as strong or weak cognitivism, infraindividualism (processes in the organism below the level of the individual), methodological individualism, social cognition, and distributed cognition. Strydom (2007:347–8) demonstrates, for example, that social cognition approaches rooted in classical psychology regard cognition as a basic, largely automatic process involving little or no reflection, while distributed cognition approaches advance a heterodox view of cognition as significantly contextual and as a "process in which collective knowledge is jointly produced and acquired in the plural in a particular context." Ranging from infraindividual explanations to macrocultural explanations and from strongly naturalistic to strongly humanistic approaches, Strydom's mapping demonstrates the significant scope of cognitive sociological theorizing.

Efforts to define cognitive sociology or the sociology of culture and cognition arising from these programmatic attempts by Zerubavel, DiMaggio, Cerulo, and Strydom are ongoing and raise a range of questions about how culture enters cognition, how we think and act as culturally cognitive actors, what is sociological about cognition, which methods we use to access culture and cognition, what are cognitive neuroscience's contributions to sociology, and what are sociology's contributions to the social science of human cognition. These ongoing debates often stem from different theoretical origins that inform cognitive sociological approaches.

1.1 Theoretical Traditions: Cultural, Social, and Embodied Approaches and Origins

Brekhus (2015:4–9) identifies three general orientational strands of cognitive sociology, ranging from the macrocultural, to the intermediate-social, to the individual practical-actor and represented respectively by sociological theoretical traditions associated with Durkheim (cultural), Goffman (social), and Bourdieu (embodied). These strands relate to the different cognitive sociological visions of Zerubavel, whose approach emerges from the Durkheimian and Goffmanian traditions, and DiMaggio, who emphasizes a more Bourdieusian approach. Ranging on a continuum from the macrocultural, to the social, to the individual, to the infraindividual, contemporary cognitive approaches draw from a variety of theoretical traditions. These traditions include the large-scale cultural sociologies of Durkheim, the social constructionist theorists of Berger and Luckmann, and interactionist social approaches that draw from Goffman and from symbolic interactionism, and embodied individual and infraindividual approaches that intersect with recent work in cognitive neuroscience and cognitive psychology and draw on Bourdieu's *habitus*, as well as on Dewey's understanding of the alternation of habit and conscious processing, and Wacquant's work on embodiment. Within these varying theoretical approaches, cognitive sociologists analyze cognitive processes such as attention and inattention, perception, automatic and deliberate cognition, cognition and social action, stereotypes, categorization, classification, judgment, symbolic boundaries, meaning-making, metaphor, embodied cognition, morality and religion, identity construction, narrative, time sequencing, and memory. This diversity of theoretical perspectives to understanding the relationship between culture and cognition entails lively discussion, conflicting orientations, and controversies about the best way to access the cultural in the cognitive. Many current debates are tied to competing origins of contemporary cognitive sociological theorizing and to different epistemological assumptions and methodological approaches associated with these contrasting theoretical traditions. These debates across cognitive traditions continue to lead to critique, definition, and refinement of theoretical assumptions and sociological methods in the field. We briefly discuss these varying origin strands as a starting point for understanding current conversations and controversies in the field.

The early foundations for the study of culturally and socially mediated thinking can be observed in social constructionist and sociology of knowledge approaches to sociology. Durkheim's interest in "collective representations" and "social facts" represent early sociological interest in the ways that culture organizes social thinking. In Durkheim's view there is a strong relationship between individual representations (states of cognition) and collective representations (culture), and people think largely as social and cultural beings. Durkheim's classical sociological approach emphasizing cultural and historical variation in human thought, provides the foundations of a sociological and anthropological perspective that emphasizes cultural, social, and historical variation. Durkheim's macrocultural approach to human thinking is emblematic of classical sociological interest in how humans think as members of specific cultures and are therefore influenced by the collectivities to which they belong. Other classical theorists also took an interest in the role of the individual's position within a culture or a social structure, in shaping human thinking. Marx, for instance, in noting that people think differently based on their economic position in the social structure, implied the important role of social standpoint and social position within a culture and an economy as it influences human thinking. Simmel (1964:140–43) saw individuals and their thinking as shaped by their intersecting mix of affiliations and thus saw identities and thought as intersectional. Berger and Luckmann's (1966) influential treatise on the social construction of reality further emphasizes the social and intersubjective nature of human knowledge and human thinking. These foundational classical theorists provide a lens for understanding the intersubjective and culturally variable elements of human thought and for understanding human beings as social and cultural thinkers rather than unique individual thinkers or biological universal thinkers. The idea that we think primarily as cultural beings, rather than as a generic biological species or as unique individuals, is central to the intermediate cognitive sociology approaches of contemporary cognitive sociological theorists (e.g., Zerubavel 1997; Brekhus 2007), who view thought as mediated through one's cultural context and sociomental affiliations.

While the macrocultural approaches of Durkheim and of social constructionist theorists such as Berger and Luckmann shape theoretical presuppositions for the ways many cultural sociologists think about culture and thinking, researchers gathering local empirical data have often prioritized more meso- and micro-level analyses of specific cultural groups and social interactions. Goffman's various emphases on sociocultural and contextual frames of meaning, interactional settings and audiences, and socializing and resocializing organizations and institutions, has brought the cultural down to smaller units of analysis such as subcultures, organizations, and interactional settings. These units of analysis for interpreting the social, unlike entire societies or cultures as the unit of analysis, lend themselves well to middle-range studies of a particular social movement, subculture, organization, or community, and align well with contemporary qualitative sociological methods such as ethnographies or in-depth interviews. Goffman's cognitive sociology focused on culture in its interactional and institutional forms, shaping significant strands of research in the cultural elements of cognition, framing, social attention and inattention, and identity. Goffman examined primary frameworks, schemata of interpretation, frames, the strategic deployment of identity, attention and interaction, and a variety of processes that can be interpreted in interactional and cultural settings and has thus served as an orienting theorist for works on social mindscapes, group styles of cognition and interaction, social movement framing and other cognitive cultural interactive processes. Whereas Goffman brought the cultural down to the social interactional level, Bourdieu has brought the cultural down to the level of human practical action and the embodied social actor.

For Bourdieu (1990), culture is located not in the shared cultural symbols, language, socialization, conscious values, and collective representations of societies but in the everyday, mostly unconscious and habitual routines of institutions and individuals. Bourdieu's approach views specific bodily experiences as an essential aspect of the structure and processing of cognition; this approach varies from cognitive sociological understandings that see culture as largely a system of abstract symbols that people process through mind with little association to direct bodily sensory experience (Lizardo 2015). Lizardo (this volume) identifies the distinction between "hard" and "soft" embodiment as an important one that Bourdieu brings to understanding cognition. The embodied turn in cognitive sociology also draws from theoretical traditions of other French psychological sociologists such as Mauss (see Ignatow this volume), from the American pragmatism of Dewey (1930) (see Martin this volume), and from Wacquant (1998, 2004) who focused on the embodied nature of cognition in emphasizing the corporeal dispositions of practical and moral behavior in boxers (see Vaisey and Frye this volume). Wacquant also studied the embodied metaphors of boxers and thus additionally informs a cognitive sociological interest in embodied metaphor. A greater focus on embodied cognition, from sociologists in this tradition, redirects cultural and cognitive sociology's heavy focus on disembodied information, cool cognition, and cultural schemas (Ignatow 2007:119). A central development arising out of the embodied tradition is the idea that people process information using dual-process thinking, where some thought is conscious and reflective, while much thought is automatic, deeply embodied, habitual, and intuitive.

In the remainder of this introduction we highlight (1) cultural cognitive sociological perspectives as they relate to aggregate cognitive processes of attention, meaning and metaphor, categories and identity, and time and memory; (2) embodied perspectives as they relate to social action and the embodied challenge to classical cultural approaches; and (3) cultural sociological counterchallenges and responses to the embodied critique and the theoretical and methodological ideas rising out of these debates, including attempts to synthesize the cultural and the cognitive poles. These issues inform cognitive sociology and help to frame the wide range of contributions in this volume. We start with the cultural cognitive focus on cultures of perception and attention, distributed cognition, and the collective sociocultural aspects of thinking.

1.2 CULTURES OF PERCEPTION AND ATTENTION: CULTURAL VARIATION, DISTRIBUTED COGNITION, AND THE SOCIOCULTURAL MIND

For sociologists interested in cultural variation in what we think, the processes of perception, attention, meaning, identity, and memory as they relate to cultural, subcultural, and organizational patterns and differences have been of particular interest. In discussing scientific knowledge, Fleck (1979:38–51) refers to the "thought collective" or "thought community" as an aggregate thought style of an entire interactive community who follow similar norms of focusing and who direct their thought and social attention in similar ways. We think within cultures, communities, and social networks and we often think in similar ways to those around us. Relevance and irrelevance are social (Zerubavel 1993). What people see and pay attention to and what they do not see and do not attend to, are influenced by their cultural, subcultural, occupational, ideological, and organizational frames for viewing reality.

Brekhus (1996, 1998, 2000, 2015) analyzes cognitive asymmetry in cultural frameworks of attention between the "socially marked" and the "socially unmarked," noting that the linguistic contrast between the "marked" and the "unmarked" closely follows the visual psychology contrast between "figure" and "ground"; this extends beyond visual perception to social perception between marked items that are regarded as socially specialized and relevant and unmarked items that are socially taken-for-granted and ignored as largely unimportant and irrelevant. Building from Goffman (1963, 1974, 1986), who focused on the interactional rules of attention and inattention and from linguistics (see Waugh 1982), these concepts of the marked and the unmarked highlight the culturally cognitive dimensions of attention and inattention that shape how people perceive reality in socioculturally patterned ways. Brekhus emphasizes that different cultures and groups mark and unmark reality in different ways; the marked refers to those elements of social reality that people, as social actors, accentuate and focus on as "socially specialized," while the unmarked refers to those aspects that they routinize, take-for-granted, and ignore as "socially generic." What people highlight and what they ignore is highly influenced by their sociocultural standpoint—a point further emphasized in the sociology of boundaries and identities. While the conceptual distinction between marked items that are heavily focused on, and unmarked items that are taken-for-granted is a generic analytic one, significant differences in what generates attention and inattention are culture and social. The cognitive asymmetry between how people actively attend to the socially marked and how they routinely ignore the socially unmarked relates to perception, attention, meaning, identity, memory, and other cognitive processes.

Illustrating a cultural perceptual asymmetry in recognizing sex differences and sex similarities, Friedman (2013) highlights how in the contemporary United States, the predominating culture marks, highlights, and notices "sexual difference" between men and women, while ignoring the many routine ways that men and women are alike, similar, and overlapping in their characteristics. She contrasts this dominant cultural perceptual understanding of sex, with two "thought communities," transgender people and blind people, who perceive sex differently. Transgender people have a heightened awareness of attributes associated with male and female bodies, while blind people describe a very different universe of sex cues that they use to attribute sex relative to the cues used by sighted people. FTM transgender individuals noted the cultural contextual nature of sex perception in that they were almost always read as "male" in small towns, but were often read as "butch-female" in larger metropolitan areas (Friedman 2013:64). Friedman (this volume) introduces the notion of "cultural blindness" illustrating how our social and cultural perspectives and backgrounds shape our perceptual attention and our perceptual blind spots and blind fields.

Cerulo (2006) highlights a cultural perceptual "positive asymmetry" in the United States wherein across a wide range of realms including intimate relationships, life events, work and play, driving, and group and organizational decision-making, most people have a well-articulated, clear vision of positive outcomes, but a blurred, fuzzy, or even nonexistent vision for potential worst case outcomes. Cerulo (2006:8) ties this to brain processes of graded membership and asymmetry (the tendency for the brain to emphasize the ideal example of any concept) that are transformed to a cultural process of positive asymmetry (the tendency to emphasize examples of best and most positive cases). Cerulo draws on multiple realms to demonstrate that this is both a common perceptual tendency in the United States and that it is also embedded into the specific cultures of several organizations. Highlighting groupthink, risky shift, and failures of bystander intervention, as three areas where positive asymmetry becomes a collective perception issue, Cerulo (2006:54–57) shows how context and culture influence cognition.

Hutchins (2006) has emphasized the importance of organizational cultures and the context-dependent nature of cognition through the idea of "distributed cognition."

Distributed cognition is a perspective that involves analyzing how cognitive processes normally associated with the individual mind can be present in a group of individuals (Hutchins 2001:2068; see also Hutchins 2014). This perspective is employed to examine how cognition is coordinated in the contexts in which people interact with one another such as their organizational and cultural environments. Hutchins (2014) views human cognition as occurring within cultural-cognitive ecosystems. The idea of a collective mind can be broadly applied to the distribution of cognitive processes across members of a group, which become socially patterned, so that members will come to share similar thought processes, perceptual norms of focusing, and attention styles.

Vaughan (2002) has compared the distributed cognitions of different organizations and the ways they structure attention and inattention among their members. In her analysis of the *Challenger* launch decision and shuttle disaster, Vaughan shows how the organizational influences on cognition led *Challenger* launch decision-makers to foreground the routine and attend to the culture of production. This organizational framing of production emphasized the routine and de-emphasized technological uncertainty as something to be taken for granted rather than heavily attended. By contrast, air traffic controllers are trained into an organizational frame that aggressively attends to anomalies and small deviations, and centers as marked, rather than dismisses as routine and unmarked, even minor issues of technological uncertainty. Organizationally distributed and mediated cognition is shaped by socialization, training, interactions, and incentive structures that channel the ways members perceptually foreground what is socially significant and what remains in the background as routine, mundane, and unmarked.

Spain (2018) applies cognitive sociology's insights on the perceptual asymmetry between the marked and the unmarked to risk and threat assessment in the global security community. He demonstrates that the organizationally mediated focus for threat assessment experts is to mark dramatic and unusual technological dangers and to heavily articulate, prepare for, and devote resources to combat these spectacular but highly unlikely threats, while devoting proportionately less attention and resources to updating ordinary holes in aging infrastructure that address more mundane, less exciting, but far more probable damaging threats. He notes, for example, that while cyber security experts were focused on preventing elaborate apocalyptic scenarios of cyber doom from superhackers, the Office of Personnel and Management (OPM) information network was breached by suspected Chinese hackers who took advantage of mundane gaps in a decaying federal information technology base, to compromise the personnel records of 21.5 million people including personal information used for sensitive national-security background checks.

Daipha (2010) analyzes the attention structure and distributed cognition of meteorologists, demonstrating that while the folk ideology of weather forecasters is that "everyone does it differently," the forecasters develop only small differences within widely shared, contextually situated practices of perception and decision-making; thus, for example, shared practices of seasonal perception wherein winter forecasters analyze the holistic picture of large-scale meteorological conditions, while summer forecasters develop a laser-focus that attentively marks the telltale target of a "hook echo," are part of the shared attention and perception styles of the organization.

Meaning, analogy, classification, and value are also culturally and socially mediated and of interest to those who study distributed cognition and cultural variation. Bandelj and Zoeller (this volume) demonstrate the many ways that economic thinking is cultural and contextual and has social meanings beyond "rational" economic ideas and strictly functional economic values. They and others (e.g., Wherry 2008; Zelizer 1994) emphasize the social meaning of money, demonstrating that decisions about how money gets distributed, spent, and valued are dependent on the cultural classification of that money as a direct award, a salary, a gift, a bonus, or another kind of compensation. Rodgers (2008, this volume) highlights the ways that thinking is organized by cultural context and standpoint in demonstrating the close relationship between social insect analogies that humans use and the human organization of the social systems the humans live in. For example, entomologists from colonial powers perceived and named the ants that indigenous populations had called "ants of visitation" because they regularly visited to clear dwellings of pests, "army ants" (Rodgers 2008:128). What indigenous people understood as periodic visits, the entomologists analogically defined and perceived as militarily organized invasion and colonization.

Cultural categorization and value extends to the meaning of social categories, boundaries, and identities. People perform identities and roles, which often express moral and social value, at different times across different settings (Brekhus 2015; Moore 2017:200) and these identities are associated with patterns of cultural and subcultural markedness and social attention. Within cultural sociology there has been a growing interest in identity in the plural cognitivist actor (Raphael 2017). A cognitively pluralist view of identity emphasizes the dynamic and strategic deployment of identity across different settings and the managing of competing statuses that draw different levels of cultural attention and social value from others. Brekhus (2015:111–46) emphasizes examining the strategic organization of socioculturally marked and unmarked attributes in negotiating identity multidimensionality, constructing identity authenticity, and manifesting identity mobility or fluidity. Because the plural cognitivist actor has multiple marked and unmarked social attributes that shape their social location and thus their social standpoints and the varying thought communities that they belong to, cultural cognitive sociologists explore the intersectionality of complex multifaceted identities. Emphasizing the role of intersecting cultural, interactional, and cognitive processes in the strategic deployment of identities across time and space they explore authenticity debates, and changes in identity across social networks, time, and space (see Brekhus 2003). Perceptions of authenticity are cultural rather than universal (see Williams this volume). People construct their own authenticity and attribute insider and outsider status to others based on social and cultural standards of perception and valuation. DeGloma and Johnston (this volume) explore the mobility of identities that change dramatically during the life course (see also DeGloma 2014). They demonstrate that the narrative scripts that people who articulate identity transformations use, follow similar formal patterns associated with varying cultural valuations. Zerubavel (2018) analyzes how the words people in a culture use (and do not use) have implications for social attention and for marked and unmarked identities. Social normalcy and cultural power are reinforced through the declarative culture of language and thus, for example, marking "Black History Month" or "women's history" also reinscribes the unremarkable sociocultural taken-for-granted normality of white men's history. Zerubavel highlights the strategic deployment of identity, both in its more automatic reproductions of unmarked social advantage, and in more deliberative, consciously declarative attempts to challenge unmarkedness. In this volume, Zerubavel outlines semiotic subversion as a strategy, often linked to marginalized identities, to mark and accentuate that which is typically cognitively unattended.

Memory and time are also processes that can be studied as culturally patterned cognition. Collective and collected memories shared by different members of a group, community, generation, or region are socially organized in ways that accentuate some events and ignore other events. Forgetting and ignoring events are also a collective phenomenon. This does not mean, of course, that there is a single emergent "social mind" but rather that, as Schwartz (2009:123) puts it, "remembering and forgetting are distributed unevenly among different communities, groups, and individuals." Schwartz (2009) shows, for instance, in the story of what people in the United States remember and forget about Rosa Parks that the common narrative construction of Rosa Parks as a lone heroine who refused to give up her seat on the bus is about both the social marking and commemorating of her single heroic act, and the organizing of inattention to her previous longstanding civil rights activism and to the work of other activists who resisted bus segregation before her. Vinitzky-Seroussi and Teeger (2010, this volume) analyze the role of collective silence in reinforcing collective remembering and forgetting. The remembrance of time, as Ricoeur (1984, 1988) has demonstrated is often event-centered and punctuated by marked events and shaped by organizational and cultural expectations, rather than chronologically centered. The experience of the movement of time in organizations is shaped by the organizational rhythms (Fine 1990; Snyder 2012) and temporal structures (see Snyder this volume).

1.3 Embodied Cognition: Cognitive Mechanics and the Neuropsychology Challenge to Cultural Sociology

In contrast to the more classical cultural sociology focus on the cultural organization and sociocultural variation of collective cognition, a growing number of cognitive sociologists have begun to focus on the neurocognitive mechanics of cognition and its relationship to practical social action. Extending from DiMaggio's (1997) interest in greater engagement with cognitive neuropsychology to explore the mechanisms through which culture enters cognition, these cognitive scholars emphasize bodily sensory experience of individuals as fundamental to the relationship between culture and cognition (see Ignatow 2007).

The varying orienting strands of cognitive sociology from the more cultural anthropological approaches of Durkheim and social constructionists, to the social interactional approaches of Goffman, to the embodied, sensory, practical action approaches of

Bourdieu and Wacquant, underlie different perceptions of how culture enters into cognition. On one end of a continuum, foundational/classical theorists of culture and cognition influenced by the cultural sociology of Durkheim and the structural anthropology of Levi-Strauss, prioritize language, symbols, and socialization as key elements of culture that shape how individuals within a culture think. In this view, internalizing external symbols and concepts provided by language is an important part of learning and human experience. Theorists in this tradition emphasize cultural and subcultural variation and see a strongly anthropological, social constructionist, and culturally pluralist view of cognition. At the other end, embodied theorists of cognition, influenced by the approach of Bourdieu and the more psychological anthropology of Bloch (1987), reject the classical view of culture and socialization. Embodied theorists emphasize that cognition is "inherently 'grounded' in the nonarbitrary features of human bodies as they relate to the material environment" (Lizardo 2015:576). Scholars in this tradition take a less culturally constructed, more universalist neurocognitive view of human thinking, seeing the relevance of culture as primarily how it shapes the sensory experiences and environments of practical actors. The emphasis here is not on highlighting cultural variation in category knowledge (e.g., Zerubavel) but understanding the mechanisms by which social and cognitive processes affect one another (e.g., DiMaggio).

In "Culture, Cognition and Embodiment," Lizardo (2015) provides a detailed critique of the classical cultural sociological approach and articulates an embodied approach to understanding culture. Moving away from linguistic and symbolic forms of sociology, embodied cognitive theorists draw from developmental psychology and cognitive neuroscience, viewing culture as largely expressed and located in the individual through sensory perception, bodily schemas, and practical action. Bourdieu's (1977) view of habitus as the unconscious schemas that we form and act on through bodily, life, and sensory experience, shapes the sensory-informed approach of embodied cognitive sociologists. They embrace an interdisciplinary cognitive social science that draws significantly from developmental psychology, cognitive science, robotics, and the philosophy of mind and action to highlight the sensory nature of the human cultural mind. A major aspect of this approach is to understand culture as incoherent in its use by individual actors and to see basic bodily operations as structuring cognition independent of a coherent culture or cultural system. That is, while culture is not irrelevant, it enters the mind in fragmented ways through the built environment and the social environments that shape individuals' sensory apparatus.

In advancing a more neuropsychologically informed view of human cognition, cognitive sociologists within the embodied tradition offer a challenge to cultural sociology which has undertheorized both sensory bodily experience and the mechanics of cognitive processes. In addition to theoretical issues, they point to methodological advances. DiMaggio (2002:275) indicates that many questions that are metatheoretical for cultural sociologists are tested empirically by cognitive sociologists. Ignatow (2014) argues for the central importance of engaging with cognitive neuropsychology for developing contributions to sociological and cognitive methods, not just theory. Methodological advances that allow measures of individual cognitive processes are an important contribution and align with the theoretical aims of an embodied, non-amodal, cognitive sociology (see Ignatow 2007).

Culture's fragmented role in thought and action, Lizardo (2015) argues, cannot be explained with cultural anthropological models that implicitly assume that individuals internalize entire cultural systems; rather the habitus of repeated embodied simulations reproduced through the unconscious track of the human brain best explains the deep implicit level in which culture operates on our human thoughts. Martin (2010) similarly suggests that culture is not a holistic entity but a complex combination of mental acts and processes (see also Moore 2017:196). In contrast to classical cultural sociological views of humans as internalizing large chunks and coherent fabrics of shared intersubjective culture, this view emphasizes the largely unconscious and fragmented role of culture. Humans largely think, in this view, at an unconscious level with little agency or cultural reflection or deliberation on their values and beliefs. Scholars in this tradition emphasize that we need to observe culture, not at the surface level of declarations, conscious deliberations, and language, but at the deep intuitive and automatic level of bodily responses, snap judgments, and unconscious dispositions; culture in action is found not on the surface, but embodied, deep within the individual's subconscious (e.g., Vaisey 2009). Important to this view is the cognitive neuropsychological "dual-process model" of thinking that suggests that our cognition is divided between two tracks of thinking: one fast, hot, automatic, and unconscious, and the other slow, cool, reflexive/deliberative, and conscious.

The most influential of these dual-process models within cognitive sociology has been Haidt's model (2001, 2005), which emphasizes that automatic cognition is the central track on which most of our thinking happens and that this track is parallel and separate from our conscious track. Vaisey (2009:1683) imports Haidt's metaphor of human thought as operating like a rider on an elephant, where conscious thought and deliberative reasoning is the rider and intuitive practical consciousness is the elephant that is largely in charge. In this dual-process view of cognition, actors are primarily driven by their unconscious, automatic use of fragmented and inconsistent culturally available schemas. The explanation for social action is found not in conscious, declarative culture and values, but in internalized knowledge stored in unconscious cognitive schemas.

While it provides a needed correction to socialization models of internalizing culture whole, some scholars question whether Haidt's dual-process model with its rigid separation of automatic and deliberative paths is the best dual-process model for sociology (see Leschziner this volume; Moore 2017; Vila-Henninger 2015). Moore (2017) characterizes the Haidt dual-process model, imported into sociology through Vaisey's (2009) influential analysis, as an either/or model of thinking where System 1 (automatic/intuitive) thinking takes precedence in nearly all decision-making and System 2 (deliberative/reflective) thinking appears in interviews, justifications, and accounts. Yet, cognitive and social psychologists, he argues, have shown that both cognitive modes operate simultaneously and cannot be so easily segmented into separate individual domains. Leschziner (this volume) allows that Vaisey drew significant attention to the need to reorient sociology to reconsider some of its most enduring ideas about how culture shapes action, but contends that local context appears to have a more significant role in shaping cognition than the dominant sociological dual-process model implies. Shepherd (2011:123) similarly argues that the Vaisey/Haidt view of automatic cognitive processes as deeply internalized schematic processes, lacks attention to the important features of supraindividual culture that affect the availability, acquisition, and activation of cognitive representations.

Lizardo et al. (2016:290) point out that most of the debate over dual-process models is not about the existence of different cognitive modes but about their relative degree of independence and interaction. Sociological uses of dual-process models are increasingly being refined to incorporate greater consideration of the interaction of cognitive processes and the importance of cultural context.

Vila-Henninger (2015) identifies a significant body of research in cognitive neuroscience supporting a more moderate "default interventionist" approach where System 1 intuitive thinking makes an initial decision that can be overridden by System 2 reflective thinking especially in difficult, disruptive, or norm violating situations. Psychologists Evans and Stanovich (2013) advocate a default interventionist model, arguing that reasoning and decision-making are often rapid and automatic, but in situations where decisions are perceived as consequential, people are more inclined to resist efficient cognitive miserly processing and to override default intuition with reflective thinking.

Moore (2017:200) shows that the relationship between System 1 and System 2 processing has implications for how we make sense of the ways people express identity, noting that some performances of the self are performed automatically but that System 2 (declarative culture) is also involved in the presentation of situated moral identities and suggests that studying identity performances in line with both fast, nondeclarative and slow, declarative processes is important to capture the entire picture.

Leschziner and Green (2013) demonstrate that across two different fields (high cuisine chefs and gay enclave men) individuals regularly combine Type 1 (automatic processing and nondeclarative culture) and Type 2 (deliberative processing and declarative culture) processing in a wide range of tasks, heavily depending on Type 1 processing when engaged in purposeful action, and relying on Type 2 processing when dedicated to routine activities. In culinary fields, for example, chefs early in their careers rely heavily on Type 1 processing because they have yet to embody culinary conventions and actions as part of their everyday habitus to the point of experiencing these conventions as institutions (Leschziner and Green 2013:132).

1.4 DEBATES OVER METHOD AND UNIT OF ANALYSIS

Debates over whether to emphasize more the cultural/social bases or the neurological/infraindividual processes of cognition and on whether or not the underlying conception of cognition is more primarily focused on deliberate/declarative or automatic/intuitive cognition are also tied to methodological issues of observing culture and measuring cognition. Vaisey has argued (2009:1688–89) that fixed-response surveys are better methods for understanding how people make judgments and meaning, than open-ended interviews because survey respondents rely more on intuition and cognitive efficiency than deliberation when responding to surveys, and this form of response is closer to the automatic cognition we use in everyday decision-making processes. Jerolmack and Khan (2014) argue that much cultural sociology, particularly in relation to culture and cognition, suffers from a widespread assumption that verbal methods are the best way to assess how culture operates as people act on cognitive processes such as schemas, frames, and repertoires. They suggest studying the activation of schemas where they happen rather than in accounts. They share Vaisey's criticism of interviews, but argue that surveys also gather accounts, rather than observations, of action. Ethnography and participant observation, they suggest, observe meaning-making in situ and over time rather than in the single contrived temporal moment of a survey or interview; as such, they contend that ethnography is best suited to analyze how unconscious cognitive dispositions can shape behavior, stating that "through sustained participation in the lives of her subjects, the ethnographer can actually witness and even experience the formation and/or activation of dispositions or schemas" (Jerolmack and Khan 2014:196).

Pugh (2013) argues that Vaisey's and other dual-process cognitive sociologists' (e.g., Martin 2010) criticisms of interviews are misguided in assuming that interviews can only access justifications and that these criticisms employ a limited and misleading interpretation of the range of kinds of information available in interviews, especially in-depth interviews. Pugh creates a typology of four types of information available in in-depth interviews: the honorable, the schematic, the visceral, and meta-feelings, each with their own important analytic uses for understanding how individuals use culture. All four kinds of interview data reflect on culture and each illustrate different points in the process of how culture shapes action (Pugh 2013:52). Pugh argues that cognitive sociologists who dismiss interviews imply that interviews only gathers honorable kinds of data, but that this does not fairly account for the many ways that good in-depth interview strategies go beyond mere accounts of what people say to look at how they say it and to ask for specific examples that go beyond impression management and surface-level belief statements.

Lizardo (this volume) suggests that in-depth interviews, discourse, and text analysis can be used to capture soft-embodiment phenomena (embodied meaning, externalization), while hard embodied culture attuned to measuring gestures, comportments, and ways of acting is suited for sensitized ethnography (e.g., Wacquant 2004, 2006).

McDonnell and Vercel (this volume) challenge the assertion that interview methods only access people's discursive consciousness and do little to reveal their unconscious cognitive processes (also see McDonnell 2014). They argue for "productive methods"— methods that observe people creating a cultural object to draw out moments of shared automatic cognition and resonance. As an alternative to simplifying the world for respondents with fixed choices, McDonnell (2014:248) argues that researchers should find productive methods where the bulk of selection is done by the actor rather than the researcher, suggesting that, "by asking people to produce an object, and then observing the process of decision making, deliberation, and discussion, cultural processes become legible" (McDonnell 2014:248). By integrating focus group interviews with productive methods such as drawing, automatic cognition can be made visible without severely limiting response options in advance as surveys do; in the act of drawing, social actors put culture into action by selecting, arranging, and translating reality, and they do so in ways that the researcher can observe both deliberate and automatic responses (McDonnell 2014:253).

Besides methodological debates, cultural sociologists have also criticized the neuro-cognitive trend for its emphasis on the individual as the unit of analysis. Swidler (2008), in response to Vaisey (2008), argues that a microfocus on how cognitive models operate in the heads of individuals moves the scope of analysis away from the social contexts, institutions, situations, and structures where social action occurs. Swidler argues that cultural meanings are organized at the collective and social, rather than the individual level, and suggests that the sociological gold comes in understanding the social rather than the individual or infraindividual. Thus, for example, while dual-process cognition can explain the automatic moral revulsion most individuals in the United States have to eating dogs, the sociological interest may come in studying how the collective institution of pet ownership affects cognition within a specific sociocultural context (Swidler 2008:617–18). For Swidler, without some substantive notion of what structures determine where the intuitive judgments come from, asserting that there are such judgments deep in the unconscious does not address the cultural role in shaping action. Pugh (2013:46) similarly argues that the fact that people have strong intuitive responses that guide their action, still leaves one longing for understanding the role culture plays in shaping these intuitions. Pugh argues that the focus on the deep motivations and infra-individual mechanics for action underemphasizes the broadly social contexts in which such action takes place.

Vaisey (2014) responds to these criticisms, arguing that where something is measured does not necessarily indicate what is being measured. Although cultural meanings are organized collectively, for instance, they are not always deployed collectively and thus understanding individual differences in deploying cultural capacities and observing net effects among individuals can provide cultural information.

Norton (2018) warns that cognitive sociologists should be wary of moving so far in the direction of individualism "that they isolate themselves from analytical and theoretical concepts that are essential for conceptualizing the complex interactional fields that define scales of analysis larger than the individual." He argues that much of what is sociologically significant about meaning is determined in relations and interactions between actors and in cultural systems, not in the heads of actors, and that, as such, situations and not individual actors should be the sociologist's primary unit of analysis (see also Norton 2014). Zerubavel and Smith (2010) argue for the importance of studying individuals in the context of their dyadic interactions, social networks, groups, and thought communities, noting, for example, that impression formation is socially distributed cognition.

Cognitive cultural sociologists argue that larger social and cultural institutions and contexts are necessary units of analysis because the cultural elements of cognition are collectively organized. For embodied cognitive sociologists, by comparison, the individual is the primary unit of analysis for analyzing cognition and its relationship to culture, because it is the embodied individual actor responding to sensory input that ultimately thinks and acts. Acting in the spirit of DiMaggio's (1997) call for greater engagement with cognitive neuropsychology, many cognitive sociologists continue to move toward a greater interdisciplinary focus on cognitive processes in individuals. At the same time, cultural sociologists interested in sociocultural variation and collective cognition maintain an interest in focusing on larger cultural institutions (Swidler 2008), group-level cultural repertoires (Lamont et al. 2017), and the social normative dimensions of cognition (Zerubavel and Smith 2010). There are also growing attempts at synthesizing more strongly cultural and more strongly cognitive analyses.

1.5 Challenges for Cultural Cognitive Analysis: Synthesizing the Neurocognitive and the Cultural

Debates over dual-process thinking, the conditions under which what kinds of cognitive processing predominate, and over the best methods for accessing the cultural in the cognitive, have opened up cognitive sociology to further study the role of social context in shaping social action. Sociologists focused on dual-process cognition have brought sociology into greater interdisciplinary engagement with cognitive neuroscience and have required sociologists to account for how people process information and use culture. Sociologists focused on cultural variation and on socially distributed cognition have emphasized the importance of cultural context and reasserted the importance of the social in shaping the mental. While scholars continue to make epistemological cases for their point along the divide between cultural sociology approaches and interdisciplinary cognitive neuroscience approaches, there are also growing attempts to bridge this divide, even among strong partisans and proponents of both the more strongly cultural and the more highly cognitive approaches.

Norton (2018:1) articulates the divide in stating,

> there lies an unfortunate gulf between cognitive and systemic concepts of culture. Both the investigation of intersubjective cultural systems (from the big—religion, law—to the small—interaction orders) and of the cognitive dimensions of culture (from the small—social cognition, individual motivation—to the smaller—patterns of neuronal activation) are active areas of research, but between them lies a theoretical haze that makes their relationship uncertain.

Norton concedes that the real limits on individual human cognitive capacity identified by Lizardo and Strand (2010), Martin (2010) and other cognitively focused sociologists require cultural sociologists to acknowledge the consensus in cognitive science that much cognitive activity happens outside our conscious awareness. Norton (2018:23) argues for reconciling the idea of cognitive limits and cultural complexity noting that "structural analysis at scales from cultural systems to interaction orders is a good way to order the cultural complexity of the social world, just as cognitive cultural analysis at scales from the cognitive dimensions of interaction to patterns of neuronal activity is a good way to approach the specific formulations of culture that define human cognition and the proximate semiotic circumstances of action." Norton advocates a shared territory of cognitive and systems concepts of culture.

Related to debates over units of analysis are debates between a more cognitive universalist and a more cognitive pluralist sociocultural variation approach. Lamont et al. (2017) advocate bridging cultural sociology and cognitive psychology in three contemporary research programs: (1) poverty studies focused on scarcity and cognitive bandwidth, (2) dual-process research on moral judgements, and (3) implicit association tests (IATs) of biases. They note that in all three areas, researchers explain judgments and behaviors focused on *universal* cognitive processes, and that this focus on universal processes of individual thinking often ignores the *group- and collective-level* repertoires that shape cognitive processes.

Cognitive psychology, they argue, would benefit from a stronger engagement with the sociocultural context of cognition. Cognitive bandwidth research, for instance, demonstrates that the poor are shaped by scarcity that taxes cognitive bandwidth and leads to nonoptimal decisions, but this research assumes a natural universal prioritization of multiple scarce resources and does not investigate sociocultural variation in perceptions of scarcity (Lamont et al. 2017:867). Dual-process research, they contend, shows two modes of cognition associated with distinct types of moral judgment, but assumes Western moral schemas as universal and generic rather than culturally specific. And IATs demonstrate implicit biases in automatic cognition that are not captured in deliberative self-reports, but do not examine the cultural repertoires that shape ideas about social groups or the cultural meanings of differential associations and whether such meanings are tied to image salience or image evaluation. They argue for incorporating these cognitive psychology findings about human thinking while moving beyond the implicit assumption of a "natural" set of cultural referents to demonstrate cultural variation shaped by complex sociocultural pathways.

Lizardo (2017) builds on significant debates in cognitive sociology to challenge the declarative culture bias in cultural sociology and to highlight the need to take nondeclarative competencies such as skills, habits, and nonverbal styles seriously. In doing so, he identifies the important dual-process distinction between nondeclarative culture (our habits, dispositions, routine practices, intuitive, and undeclared forms of cultural action) and declarative culture (those forms of culture more strongly linked to verbal declaration and linguistic-like acquisition). In many contexts, nondeclarative culture is the most relevant cultural mechanism to explain an action or outcome and sociologists need to be attuned to intuitive Type 1 nondeclarative processes and to the intersection of declarative and nondeclarative culture where much of the analytic action happens (Lizardo 2017).

Lizardo links the analytic distinction between declarative and nondeclarative culture with the unit of analysis differentiation between personal culture (made manifest at the level of the individual) and public culture (externalized in the form of public symbols, discourse, and institutions). Personal culture in its declarative forms includes values, attitudes, orientations, worldviews, and ideologies and includes in its nondeclarative forms skills, dispositions, schemata, prototypes, and associations. Public culture includes codes, frames, vocabularies, classifications, narratives, and models. Lizardo (2017:97) develops an analytic vocabulary for understanding "the weak within person coupling of declarative and nondeclarative culture" and suggests that further understanding of the origins and consequences of this weak coupling will put analysts in a better position to theorize how both dimensions of personal culture relate to public systems of cultural institutions, codes, and symbols. Lizardo argues for an analytic specification between declarative and nondeclarative culture tied to an empirically grounded account of the ways persons acquire culture, as a way to link cultural and cognitive approaches and to be especially attuned to the intersection of declarative and nondeclarative culture and to linking both of these with public culture.

Strandell (this volume) highlights the declarative or explicit culture (reflective) and the nondeclarative or implicit culture (intuitive) elements of influential cultural socio-logical theories to demonstrate that dual-process reasoning is common, though not actively acknowledged, within cultural theorizing. Raising sociological questions about conditions under which implicit culture operates in relative independence of explicit culture, those under which structural change does occur, and how explicit and implicit culture relate to one another at the individual level, he suggests the need to explore in more detail how and when these two forms of culture interact with each other.

Although not specifically using the terms of declarative and nondeclarative culture, Shapira and Simon (2018) examine processes by which carrying gun owners are social-ized into learned sociocultural schemas about how to think about guns, and disciplined by their embodied practices to experience guns as a part of their identity. Gun carriers become part of a sociocultural thought community and morally identify as "carrying gun owners" who first feel conscious and declarative about carrying guns as moral action, but through self-training, eventually develop this as part of their routine embod-ied habitus.

Shaw (this volume) proposes agent-based modeling as a computational method that allows researchers to simulate how macro-level cultural phenomena arise from micro-level interactions. Developing this as a cognitive sociological method for clarifying how individual cognition can give rise to collective cultural processes and social constructions has the potential to allow sociologists to reconcile the nonrational microfoundations of nondeclarative culture with macro-level declarative public culture, and thus to bridge the cognitive dimensions of culture with intersubjective cultural systems.

The increasing attempts to combine insights from interdisciplinary neuroscience approaches and cultural sociology approaches are likely to shape and to analytically inform cognitive sociology as it continues to expand and develop further as a field of intellectual inquiry. In this volume, we highlight the contributions, controversies, and insights of the exciting enterprise of cognitive sociology.

1.6 BRIEF OVERVIEW OF THE BOOK

In the space that follows we provide a brief guide to the sections and chapters in this volume. Readers will find multiple paths for engaging with cognitive sociology. These chapters range from the theoretical to the methodological and from programmatic essays to more performative and illustrative ones. The volume is organized into seven parts. The early parts, "I. Theoretical Foundations"; "II. Perspectives from Other Fields"; and "III. Methods of Cognitive Sociology," address key theoretical, interdisciplinary, and methodological developments related to cognitive sociology; while the later parts, "IV. The Sociology of Perception and Attention"; "V. Sociocultural Frames of Meaning, Metaphor, and Analogy"; "VI. Categories, Boundaries, and Identities"; and "VII. Time and Memory," highlight sociological contributions to interpreting and understanding the culturally cognitive process of attention, meaning, identity, and time. Readers interested in the debates and controversies that continue to forge cognitive sociology and its relationship to cognitive science will want to begin with the first three parts. Those interested in the socioculturally organized nature of cognitive processes of perception, meaning, identity, and memory/time will find the later sections noteworthy.

In "Part I: Theoretical Foundations," we emphasize contributions and debates in cognitive sociology through twelve chapters from fourteen contributors with a wide-ranging mix of complementary and competing ideas about the nature of cognitive sociology. This section emphasizes key contemporary traditions, debates, and directions in the field of cognitive sociology. In the opening chapter Eviatar Zerubavel lays out the foundations for a distinctively sociological view of thinking that takes as our charge understanding the sociocultural dimensions of the ways we think. Zerubavel emphasizes that we think neither as atomized individuals nor as generic biological humans, but as members of specific thought communities with specific sociocognitive practices.

Piet Strydom highlights the importance of an intersecting critical theory and cognitive sociology, arguing that an integral cognitive sociology is needed to secure critical sociology's multilevel analysis and praxis-oriented critical capacity.

Omar Lizardo articulates Bourdieu's cognitive sociology project, making the case for Bourdieu as a theorist of embodied cognition. Lizardo emphasizes that understanding the "hard" and "soft" embodiment of culture allows us to further forward an empirically grounded Bourdieusian cognitive sociology.

Karen Cerulo advocates an interdisciplinary approach to the interaction of mind, body, and environment, wherein sociologists employ embodied cognition theories. Whereas cognitive scientists are primarily focused on the processes by which such interactions occur, Cerulo argues that sociologists bring necessary attention to sociocultural variations and patterns, which are integral elements to conceptualization, perception, and meaning-making.

Stephen Vaisey and Margaret Frye use Wacquant's *Body and Soul* as a case study for examining dual-process cognition. Showing that Wacquant's experiences of learning both the rules, hierarchies, and beliefs (Type 2 discursive cognition or explicit learning) and learning the bodily routines and postures that make up the skill of boxing through implicit learning or Type 1 automatic cognition, they advance the analytic utility of preserving dualism for a Bourdieusian cognitive sociology.

John Levi Martin responds to Vaisey and Frye, making an argument about the limits and potentials of a carnal embodied sociology of the habitus. Martin argues that while recognizing the development of a habitus or "a capacity to respond to the environment without need of mediation of concepts" (a key observation of Bourdieusian and dual-process cognitivists) is important, sociologists will need to make a distinction between elements of the habitus inaccessible and accessible to consciousness. The latter provides the promise for a rigorous embodied empirical field theory that can make sociological contributions to the science of cognition by looking at interindividual differences and the social patterning of subjectivity.

Gabe Ignatow articulates the contributions of the French tradition of psychological society to cognitive sociology, building from the contributions of Mauss, Bourdieu, and Wacquant, to discuss the methodological and conceptual evolution of Bourdieu's habitus for contemporary cognitive sociology. He surveys several theoretical and methodological innovations related to these developments.

David Eck and Stephen Turner contrast two approaches in the cognitive sciences: the standard model of the computational mind, and the 4Es of cognition: the embedded, embodied, extended, and enactive movements. They argue that the first model holds sway over most social theories (including those of Durkheim, Weber, Parsons, and early Bourdieu) and that this leads to explanations centered on the social. The latter model of society as an extended cognitive system, they argue, shows that the mind-body is no longer a calculating machine, but a plastic product of routines and technologies, and thus the scaffolding of routines and technologies rather than the "social" become the primary explanatory burdens for cognition and social action.

Vanina Leschziner examines the ways that sociologists have used dual-process models of cognition, demonstrating that many researchers have emphasized the primacy of automatic Type 1 cognitive processing and how this shapes action, and a smaller group of researchers have examined Type 1 and Type 2 processing together and how they shape cognition and action. She argues that the primary sociological dual-process model has prompted a heavy focus on Type 1 processing and this has had the consequence of de-emphasizing social context. Leschziner offers the promise of the latter types of research as a bridge to a more contextual social understanding of cognitive processing and action.

Jacob Strandell highlights the dual-processing reasoning implicit in sociological theories, demonstrating what parts of these theories focus on explicit culture (reflective Type 2 processing) and what parts focus on implicit culture (intuitive Type 1 processing) as a way of bridging vocabularies between sociology and psychological dual-process models. He argues for an integrative dual-process model of culture, complimentary with Leschziner's call for examining Type 1 and Type 2 processing together.

The cognitive linguist Zoltán Kövecses brings the role of different contexts into conceptual metaphor theory by emphasizing how the situational, discourse, and cognitive-conceptual context regulate the conceptualization of the world and contribute to metaphorical creativity. In emphasizing context-induced metaphorical creativity, he provides a context-sensitive approach to metaphor that breaks from more cognitive universalist approaches that do not consider the relevance of context.

John Sonnett advances an interdisciplinary cognitive sociology of priming and framing by identifying eight dimensions of communication and cognition that can be used to reflect on and design sociological studies of priming and framing using observational data.

Given the growing interest within cognitive sociology for an interdisciplinary cognitive social science, we provide in "Part II: Perspectives from Other Fields" the perspectives of several contributors in fields that can inform an interdisciplinary cognitive sociology. The cognitive linguist Paul Chilton provides an overview of strands of cognitive linguistics research that have a bearing on the structure and processes of society including the importance of dialogue, and thus, early socialization in language acquisition. He outlines the approaches of cognitive frame theory, conceptual metaphor theory, and the role of spatial cognition and relates the social and linguistic aspects of language to cognitive neuroscience.

The psychologists Henri Santos, Igor Grossman, and Michael Varnum examine differences in cognition based on social class, demonstrating research, ranging broadly from archival data to functional magnetic resonance imaging (fMRI), on how social class differences affect a variety of cognitive processes. These relate to differences in environment and social standpoint and point to the cultural contextual nature of cognition. They suggest a particularly important area of study is how people react to transitions in social class position and to shifting definitions and trends in social class.

The cognitive scientist and computer scientist Ron Sun examines the multiple qualitatively different systems of the human mind and the interaction between implicit and explicit processes of learning. Sun argues that while many studies focus on one or the other, the evidence suggests a strong implicit-explicit interaction with few situations in which only one type of learning is engaged. He discusses both top-down learning (assimilating explicit knowledge into implicit form) and bottom-up learning (gaining explicit knowledge through extracting implicit knowledge) and argues that the latter is more fundamental and underemphasized. These insights from cognitive science are likely to be of interest to cognitive sociologists interested in further theorizing and empirically studying dual-process cognition.

From business, management, and organizational behavior, Sanaz Mobasseri, Amir Goldberg, and Sameer Srivastava develop a framework for measuring the cognitive and behavioral dimensions of enculturation between individuals and social groups to examine cultural fit and the relationship between cognitive and behavioral fit. They explore this issue of cultural fit across three substantive domains: organizations, education, and immigration and argue that rather than focus on either cognitive or behavioral manifestations of cultural fit, it is important to study both together.

In "Part III: Methods of Cognitive Sociology," we highlight different methods for cognitive sociological analysis. Widely used sociological methods such as surveys, interviews, and ethnography are also important to studying cognition, but here we focus largely on innovative methods specifically intended to advance cognitive sociological analysis. Terence McDonell and Kelcie Vercel introduce "productive methods" as a methodological strategy for accessing culture in cognition. Productive methods require research participants to collectively create a cultural object that solves a problem. McDonell and Vercel present productive methods as a rigorous approach that gets at nondiscursive culture by capturing process, context, emotion, and embodied schema. The group setting, they argue, also allows for assessment of which schemata are cultural and which are more idiosyncratic.

Andrew Miles evaluates a wide range of methods for analyzing Type 1 (automatic) cognition. Arguing that theoretical innovations about deliberative and automatic cognition are more developed than sociologists' empirical ability to test these, he summarizes and articulates the potential of several different methods designed to access Type 1 cognitive processes.

Hana Shepherd centers the question of culture and context in implicit cognition by reviewing methods that can connect the ways individuals store culture with their social, physical, and cultural environments. These methods, Shepard argues, can contribute theoretically by allowing greater precision in our understandings of how individuals acquire and deploy habitus, and potentially move us from conceptualizing mechanisms by which individuals take primacy, to studying situations and contexts primarily. As such, these methods and their approach may contribute both to theories of culture and theories of action.

Jamie Mullaney discusses social pattern analysis as a theory-building sociological method that prioritizes analytic form over specific content details, and allows researchers to compare generic cognitive processes such as attention, classification, and identity across different substantive domains and levels of analysis. The important dimensions of this approach are not its thick description within cases, but the analytic generalizability across different substantive cases and levels. Mullaney emphasizes, in particular, social pattern analysis's utility for understanding the sociology of identities.

Lynette Shaw advances the computational method of agent-based modeling (ABM) as a theory-building method to link cognitive individual processes to emergent macro collective processes. This approach models the nonrational microfoundations of emergent social and cultural phenomena. The benefits Shaw articulates include analytic leverage, generality, precision, and the development of new connections to existing fields of research. This modeling technique, while methodologically distinct from social pattern analysis, shares with social pattern analysis a minimization of within case thick description, in favor of between case generalizability and comparison.

In "Part IV: The Sociology of Perception and Attention," we highlight cognitive sociologists who examine the sociocultural elements of attention and inattention.

Markus Schroer argues that understanding attention is central to understanding the social. Schroer advances the contours of a programmatic sociology of attention that recognizes a distinction between voluntary and involuntary attention and the modern subject's oscillation between being able to bestow their attention willingly and being forced to organize their attention. Schroer identifies modernization, individualization, mediatization, and technicalization as sociological explanations for attention becoming a scarce resource.

Daina Harvey analyzes the social construction of risk, examining the dynamics of risk perception, risk communication, and risk responsibility through a sociology of culture and cognition lens. Harvey uses ethnographic data on how New Orleans residents managed risk through strategies of chunking for cognitive consistency and simplicity, immersion, and the formation of community approaches, to demonstrate the utility of a cultural cognitive approach to risk and to demonstrate how risk is a collective construction.

Asia Friedman outlines a cultural cognitive sociology of inattention elaborating the generic concepts of "cultural blind spots" and "blind fields" and examining their relation to cognitive process of habituation and focusing. Friedman highlights several analytical strategies for revealing blind spots and recognizing the taken-for-granted, unmarked, habitual, and unfocused elements of social reality.

In "Part V: Sociocultural Frames of Meaning, Metaphor, and Analogy," contributors examine social meaning through cultural sociological perspectives on the sociocultural relevance of cognition. Dmitry Kurakin articulates a neo-Durkheimian approach, arguing for a culture-cognition relations understanding of emotionally charged cultural categories and metaphors, suggesting that culture is governed by configurations of emotionally charged "sacred" and "profane" categories, created and recreated in human interactions.

Nina Bandelj and Christoffer Zoeller examine cognition and social meaning in economic sociology, reviewing research on cognitive embeddedness and frameworks of meaning, institutional logics, and classifications and categories that influence the cultural meaning of economics and money. They argue that cognitive frameworks are linked to culture and social networks and that economic sociology should take on a sharper more explicitly cognitive focus and draw more directly from advances in the sociology of cognition.

Diane Rodgers examines sociocultural frames of meaning and analogy and the dynamic and contextual qualities of analytic reasoning by tracing the influence of a culture's own social and political organization on the metaphors its entomologists apply to insect behavior. Stephanie Peña-Alves analyzes sociocultural frames of meaning and metaphor in door metaphors, theorizing the ways culture shapes metaphorical projection of a concrete object onto abstract target realms.

In "Part VI: Categories, Boundaries, and Identities," contributors examine the sociocultural processes of attention to and valuation of social categories, boundaries, and identities, and the strategic uses of identity in boundary maintenance and category valuation.

Eviatar Zerubavel examines upending the routine, taken-for-grantedness of culturally unmarked categories and identities through processes of semiotic subversion. In emphasizing the negotiation of unmarkedness, Zerubavel illustrates the politics of cognition in art, comedy, academia, and everyday life.

Brittany Battle analyzes the sociocognitive organization of morally deserving and undeserving categories and identities through the cultural frames and filters underlying normative ideas of poverty, welfare, and the family.

J. Patrick Williams analyzes the framing of identity authenticity, emphasizing the significance of essentialism, categories, and boundaries in framing authenticity. Employing a symbolic interactionist perspective, he highlights the intersection of cognitive, cultural, and interactional processes in perceiving, constructing, and enacting authentic identities.

Thomas DeGloma and Erin Johnston examine the self-identity process of cognitive migrations—transformative identity changes and radical shifts in worldview. They identify three forms of cognitive migrations: awakenings, self-actualizations, and ongoing quests, and demonstrate that these cognitive migrations are manifested as narrative autobiographical identity work.

In "Part VII: Time and Memory," contributors analyze the cognitive reckoning of time and memory. Benjamin Snyder demonstrates how organizations influence individuals' experience of time by scaffolding temporal cognition through timescapes and time maps. Vered Vinitzky-Seroussi and Chana Teeger examine collective memory, analyzing specifically the role of overt and covert silences in structuring what we collectively remember and what we collectively forget.

References

Berger, Peter L., and Thomas Luckmann. 1966. *The Social Construction of Reality: A Treatise in the Sociology of Knowledge*. Garden City, NY: Doubleday.

Bloch, Maurice. 1987. "From Cognition to Ideology." pp. 21–48 in *Power and Knowledge: Anthropological and Sociological Approaches, Proceedings of a Conference Held at the University of St. Andrews in December 1982*, edited by R. Fardon. Edinburgh: Scottish Academic Press.

Bourdieu, Pierre. 1977. *Outline of a Theory of Practice*. Cambridge and New York: Cambridge University Press.

Bourdieu, Pierre. 1990. *The Logic of Practice*. Stanford, CA: Stanford University Press.

Brekhus, Wayne H. 1996. "Social Marking and the Mental Coloring of Identity: Sexual Identity Construction and Maintenance in the United States." *Sociological Forum* 11(3):497–522.

Brekhus, Wayne H. 1998. "A Sociology of the Unmarked: Redirecting Our Focus." *Sociological Theory* 16(1):34–51.

Brekhus, Wayne H. 2000. "A Mundane Manifesto." *Journal of Mundane Behavior* 1(1):89–105.

Brekhus, Wayne H. 2003. *Peacocks, Chameleons, Centaurs: Gay Suburbia and the Grammar of Social Identity*. Chicago: University of Chicago Press.

Brekhus, Wayne H. 2007. "The Rutgers School: A Zerubavelian Culturalist Cognitive Sociology." *European Journal of Social Theory* 10(3):448–64.

Brekhus, Wayne H. 2015. *Culture and Cognition: Patterns in the Social Construction of Reality*. Cambridge and Malden, MA: Polity.

Cerulo, Karen A. 2002. *Culture in Mind: Toward a Sociology of Culture and Cognition*. New York: Routledge.

Cerulo, Karen A. 2006. *Never Saw It Coming: Cultural Challenges to Envisioning the Worst.* Chicago: University of Chicago Press.

Cerulo, Karen A. 2010. "Mining the Intersections of Cognitive Sociology and Neuroscience." *Poetics* 38(2):115–32.

Cerulo, Karen A. 2014. "Continuing the Story: Maximizing the Intersections of Cognitive Science and Sociology." *Sociological Forum* 29(4):1012–19.

Cicourel, Aaron Victor. 1974. *Cognitive Sociology: Language and Meaning in Social Interaction.* New York: Free Press.

Daipha, Phaedra. 2010. "Visual Perception at Work: Lessons from the World of Meteorology." *Poetics* 38(2):151–65.

DeGloma, Thomas. 2014. *Seeing the Light: The Social Logic of Personal Discovery.* Chicago: University of Chicago Press.

Dewey, John. 1930. *Human Nature and Conduct: An Introduction to Social Psychology.* New York: Modern Library.

DiMaggio, Paul. 1997. "Culture and Cognition." *Annual Review of Sociology* 23(1):263–87.

DiMaggio, Paul. 2002. "Why Cognitive (and Cultural) Sociology Needs Cognitive Psychology." pp. 274–82 in *Culture in Mind: Toward a Sociology of Culture and Cognition*, edited by K. A. Cerulo. New York: Routledge.

Evans, Jonathan St. B. T., and Keith E. Stanovich. 2013. "Dual-Process Theories of Higher Cognition: Advancing the Debate." *Perspectives on Psychological Science* 8(3):223–41.

Fine, Gary Alan. 1990. "Organizational Time: Temporal Demands and the Experience of Work in Restaurant Kitchens." *Social Forces* 69(1):95–114.

Fleck, Ludwik. 1979. *Genesis and Development of a Scientific Fact.* Chicago: University of Chicago Press.

Friedman, Asia. 2013. *Blind to Sameness: Sexpectations and the Social Construction of Male and Female Bodies.* Chicago and London: University of Chicago Press.

Goffman, Erving. 1963. *Behavior in Public Places: Notes on the Social Organization of Gatherings.* New York: Free Press.

Goffman, Erving. 1974. *Frame Analysis: An Essay on the Organization of Experience.* New York: Harper & Row.

Goffman, Erving. 1986. *Encounters: Two Studies in the Sociology of Interaction.* New York and London: Macmillan; Collier Macmillan.

Haidt, Jonathan. 2001. "The Emotional Dog and Its Rational Tail: A Social Intuitionist Approach to Moral Judgment." *Psychological Review* 108(4):814–34.

Haidt, Jonathan. 2005. *The Happiness Hypothesis: Finding Modern Truth in Ancient Wisdom.* New York: Basic Books.

Hutchins, Edwin. 2001. "Cognition, Distributed." pp. 2068–72 in *International Encyclopedia of the Social & Behavioral Sciences.* Vol. 3, edited by N. J. Smelser and P. B. Baltes. Amsterdam: Elsevier.

Hutchins, Edwin. 2006. *Cognition in the Wild.* Cambridge, MA: MIT Press.

Hutchins, Edwin. 2014. "The Cultural Ecosystem of Human Cognition." *Philosophical Psychology* 27(1):34–49.

Ignatow, Gabriel. 2007. "Theories of Embodied Knowledge: New Directions for Cultural and Cognitive Sociology?" *Journal for the Theory of Social Behaviour* 37(2):115–35.

Ignatow, Gabe. 2014. "Ontology and Method in Cognitive Sociology." *Sociological Forum* 29(4):990–94.

Jerolmack, Colin, and Shamus Khan. 2014. "Talk Is Cheap: Ethnography and the Attitudinal Fallacy." *Sociological Methods and Research* 43(2):178–209.

Lamont, Michèle, Laura Adler, Bo Yun Park, and Xin Xiang. 2017. "Bridging Cultural Sociology and Cognitive Psychology in Three Contemporary Research Programmes." *Nature Human Behaviour* 1(12):866–72.

Leschziner, Vanina, and Adam Isaiah Green. 2013. "Thinking about Food and Sex Deliberate Cognition in the Routine Practices of a Field." *Sociological Theory* 31(2):116–44.

Lizardo, Omar. 2015. "Culture, Cognition and Embodiment." pp. 576–81 in *International Encyclopedia of the Social and Behavioral Sciences*, edited by J. D. Wright. Amsterdam: Elsevier.

Lizardo, Omar. 2017. "Improving Cultural Analysis: Considering Personal Culture in Its Declarative and Nondeclarative Modes." *American Sociological Review* 82(1):88–115.

Lizardo, Omar, and Michael Strand. 2010. "Skills, Toolkits, Contexts and Institutions: Clarifying the Relationship between Different Approaches to Cognition in Cultural Sociology." *Poetics* 38(2):205–28.

Lizardo, Omar, Robert Mowry, Brandon Sepulvado, Dustin S. Stoltz, Marshall A. Taylor, Justin Van Ness, and Michael Wood. 2016. "What Are Dual Process Models? Implications for Cultural Analysis in Sociology." *Sociological Theory* 34(4):287–310.

Martin, John Levi. 2010. "Life's a Beach but You're an Ant, and Other Unwelcome News for the Sociology of Culture." *Poetics* 38(2):229–44.

McDonnell, Terence E. 2014. "Drawing Out Culture: Productive Methods to Measure Cognition and Resonance." *Theory and Society* 43(3–4):247–74.

Moore, Rick. 2017. "Fast or Slow: Sociological Implications of Measuring Dual-Process Cognition." *Sociological Science* 4:196–223.

Norton, Matthew. 2014. "Mechanisms and Meaning Structures." *Sociological Theory* 32(2):162–87.

Norton, Matthew. 2018. "Meaning on the Move: Synthesizing Cognitive and Systems Concepts of Culture." *American Journal of Cultural Sociology.* https://dx.doi.org/10.1057/s41290-017-0055-5.

Pugh, Allison J. 2013. "What Good Are Interviews for Thinking about Culture? Demystifying Interpretive Analysis." *American Journal of Cultural Sociology* 1(1):42–68.

Raphael, Michael W. 2017. "Cognitive Sociology." Retrieved March 12, 2018. http://www.oxfordbibliographies.com/display/id/obo-9780199756384-0187.

Ricoeur, Paul. 1984. *Time and Narrative.* Chicago: University of Chicago Press.

Ricoeur, Paul, Kathleen MacLaughlin, and David Pellauer. 1988. *Time and Narrative.* Vol. 3. Chicago: University of Chicago Press.

Rodgers, Diane M. 2008. *Debugging the Link Between Social Theory and Social Insects.* Baton Rouge: Louisiana State University Press.

Schwartz, Barry. 2009. "Collective Forgetting and the Symbolic Power of Oneness: The Strange Apotheosis of Rosa Parks." *Social Psychology Quarterly* 72(2):123–42.

Shapira, Harel, and Samantha J. Simon. 2018. "Learning to Need a Gun." *Qualitative Sociology* 41(1):1–20.

Shepherd, Hana. 2011. "The Cultural Context of Cognition: What the Implicit Association Test Tells Us about How Culture Works." *Sociological Forum* 26(1):121–43.

Simmel, Georg. 1964. *Conflict and the Web of Group-Affiliations.* New York: Free Press.

Snyder, Benjamin. 2012. "Dignity and the Professionalized Body: Truck Driving in the Age of Instant Gratification." *Hedgehog Review* 14(3):8–20.

Spain, Wes. 2018. "Curious Incidents: Dogs That Haven't Barked." pp. 52–70 in *Strategic Latency: Red, White and Blue: Managing the National and International Security Consequences of*

Disruptive Technologies, edited by Z. S. Davis and M. Nacht. Livermore, CA: Center for Global Security Research, Lawrence Livermore National Laboratory.

Strydom, Piet. 2007. "Introduction: A Cartography of Contemporary Cognitive Social Theory." *European Journal of Social Theory* 10(3):339–56.

Swidler, Ann. 2008. "Comment on Stephen Vaisey's 'Socrates, Skinner, and Aristotle: Three Ways of Thinking about Culture in Action.'" *Sociological Forum* 23(3):614–18.

Vaisey, Stephen. 2008. "Socrates, Skinner, and Aristotle: Three Ways of Thinking about Culture in Action." *Sociological Forum* 23(3):603–13.

Vaisey, Stephen. 2009. "Motivation and Justification: A Dual-Process Model of Culture in Action." *American Journal of Sociology* 114(6):1675–715.

Vaisey, Stephen. 2014. "Is Interviewing Compatible with the Dual-Process Model of Culture?" *American Journal of Cultural Sociology* 2(1):150–58.

Vaughan, Diane. 2002. "Signals and Interpretive Work: The Role of Culture in a Theory of Practical Action." pp. 28–54 in *Culture in Mind: Toward a Sociology of Culture and Cognition*, edited by K. A. Cerulo. New York: Routledge.

Vila-Henninger, Luis Antonio. 2015. "Toward Defining the Causal Role of Consciousness: Using Models of Memory and Moral Judgment from Cognitive Neuroscience to Expand the Sociological Dual-Process Model." *Journal for the Theory of Social Behaviour* 45(2):238–60.

Vinitzky-Seroussi, Vered, and Chana Teeger. 2010. "Unpacking the Unspoken: Silence in Collective Memory and Forgetting." *Social Forces* 88(3):1103–22.

Wacquant, Loïc. 1998. "The Prizefighter's Three Bodies." *Ethnos* 63(3):325–52.

Wacquant, Loïc. 2004. "Following Pierre Bourdieu into the Field." *Ethnography* 5(4):387–414.

Wacquant, Loïc. 2006. *Body and Soul: Notebooks of an Apprentice Boxer*. Oxford: Oxford University Press.

Waugh, Linda R. 1982. "Marked and Unmarked: A Choice between Unequals in Semiotic Discourse." *Semiotica* 38:299–318.

Wherry, Frederick F. 2008. "The Social Characterizations of Price: The Fool, the Faithful, the Frivolous, and the Frugal." *Sociological Theory* 26(4):363–79.

Zelizer, Viviana A. 1994. *The Social Meaning of Money*. New York: Basic Books.

Zerubavel, Eviatar. 1993. "Horizons: On the Sociomental Foundations of Relevance." *Social Research* 60(2):397–413.

Zerubavel, Eviatar. 1997. *Social Mindscapes: An Invitation to Cognitive Sociology*. Cambridge, MA: Harvard University Press.

Zerubavel, Eviatar. 2018. *Taken for Granted: The Remarkable Power of the Unremarkable*. Princeton, NJ: Princeton University Press.

Zerubavel, Eviatar, and Eliot R. Smith. 2010. "Transcending Cognitive Individualism." *Social Psychology Quarterly* 73(4):321–25.

PART I

THEORETICAL FOUNDATIONS

....

CHAPTER 2

COGNITIVE SOCIOLOGY

between the personal and the universal mind

....

EVIATAR ZERUBAVEL

WHY does adding a slice of cheese turn a "hamburger" into a "cheeseburger," whereas adding some ketchup does not turn it into a "ketchupburger"? Why is Barack Obama considered a black man whose mother was white rather than a white man whose father was black? And why is the term "openly gay" far more widely used than its nominally equivalent lexical counterpart "openly straight"? Answering such questions calls for a *sociology of thinking*.[1]

2.1 THE SOCIOLOGY OF THINKING

....

When we think about thinking, we often envision an individual thinker. Such an image is a product of *cognitive individualism* (Downes 1993), an epistemological paradigm inspired by John Locke's empiricist vision of a blank mind (tabula rasa) on which the world impresses itself experientially through our senses.

While still dominating our popular vision of thinking, however, such a personalized view is for the most part dismissed by modern science. Very few scholars today still envision an individual thinker whose thoughts are products of his or her own unique personal experience and idiosyncratic outlook on the world, instead calling attention to the nonpersonal foundations of our thinking. Inspired by Immanuel Kant's rationalist vision of innate mental faculties that precede our sensory experience and actually condition the way we mentally process it, most cognitive scientists reject Locke's vision of an a priori empty mind, thereby also shifting their scholarly attention from individuals to humans.

As a result, it is our cognitive commonality as human beings rather than our uniqueness as individual thinkers that is at the heart of the study of thinking today, and cognitive scientists downplay our cognitive idiosyncrasies, instead highlighting what we share in common as humans. Such *cognitive universalism* in fact represents the dominant modern vision of how we think.

That certainly enhances cognitive scientists' understanding of the universal foundations of human cognition. It is their concern with our cognitive commonality, after all, that helps neuroscientists, psychologists, and linguists identify universal patterns in the way we process information, activate mental schemas, make decisions, solve problems, generate sentences, and access our memory. Yet while embracing universalism provides cognitive scientists access to the way we are mentally "hardwired," it rarely addresses the nonuniversal mental "software" we use when we think. Their almost exclusive concern with our cognitive commonality as human beings prevents them from exploring, for example, the difference between the ancient and modern Greek visions of the universe or between the ways liberals and conservatives view climate change, gun laws, immigration, and abortion.

It is hardly surprising, therefore, that major aspects of our cognition are ignored by cognitive science. Most cognitive scientists, for example, ignore cross-cultural and historical differences in the way we think. Few of them would consider exploring, for instance, the difference between the ways in which gender is conceptualized in Sweden and in Yemen, in which Buddhists and Presbyterians envision God, or in which most people viewed disease five hundred years ago and today.

There are three levels at which one can study cognition, given the fact that we think as individuals, as human beings, and as social beings. Whereas cognitive individualism addresses only the first level, cognitive universalism confines itself to the second. Yet as Emile Durkheim first observed (1912/1995:12–18), we do not really have to choose between these two epistemological paradigms. In addressing the third level, *cognitive sociology*[2] thus calls attention to what they often leave unexplored between them.

Whereas cognitive individualism can shed light on the particular mnemonic techniques I use to remember my e-mail password, and cognitive universalism can best explain how past information is stored in my brain, only a sociology of memory can account for how I remember Copernicus or Julius Caesar. And while a psychology of perception is clearly necessary for understanding how we disembed visual figures from their surrounding background, only a sociology of perception can address our tendency to notice the differences rather than the similarities between male and female bodies (Friedman 2013).

In calling attention to the *social* dimension of cognition, cognitive sociology reminds us that *we think not just as individuals and as human beings but also as social beings*, products of particular social environments that affect the way we mentally interact with the world. In probing the social underpinnings of the mental, it thus sheds light on traditionally neglected aspects of our thinking.

2.2 Thought Communities

Effectively recognizing that we do not think just as individuals, cognitive sociology calls attention to the *similar* manner in which different people reckon time or classify things as well as to their *common* visions and memories. Rejecting the individualistic image of the utterly original solitary thinker, it reminds us that if a ten-year-old child today knows that the earth is round and the world is made up of atoms, it is because she happens to live in the *twenty*-first rather than the first century. It also reminds me that it is not as an individual but as a product of a particular social environment that I dismiss religious accounts of natural disasters, and that the way I think about death is remarkably similar to the way many other Westerners today think about it.

Recognizing our *cognitive commonality* entails realizing that perceiving Monet's paintings as "Impressionist" has less to do with our senses than with the pronouncedly *impersonal* as well as *collective* categories into which we are socialized to force our personal experience. It likewise entails realizing that we also think about things that we have not experienced personally. Engraved in my mind are the ideas of Isaac Newton, whom I never met, as well as the memory of the voyage of Ferdinand Magellan, which took place more than four centuries before I was born. In other words, I experience things not only personally, through my own senses, but also impersonally, through my mental membership in various *thought communities*.[3]

This certainly attests to the major role of *language* in social life. Whereas perception alone would confine me to a strictly sensory experience of the world, language allows me to bypass my senses and also access reality conceptually (Durkheim 1912/1995:433–40; Durkheim 1914/1973). Unlike the utterly personal nature of sensory perception, when I use words like "mediocrity" or "authenticity" I am using unmistakably impersonal ideas that did not originate in my own mind. In fact, as Karl Mannheim put it,

> it is not…isolated individuals who do the thinking, but men in certain groups who have developed a particular style of thought…Strictly speaking it is incorrect to say that the single individual thinks. Rather it is more correct to insist that he participates in thinking further what other men have thought before him.
>
> (Mannheim 1929/1936:3)

Indeed, it is the impersonal nature of language that enables us to transcend our subjectivity. Whereas my senses confine me to my own personal experience, language allows me to also "share" others' thoughts.[4]

Such *intersubjectivity* (Schutz 1932/1967:97–138; Schutz 1973:10–15, 112, 150–83, 312–29) constitutes the distinctive focus of cognitive sociology. Rejecting cognitive individualism, it thus ignores the inner, strictly personal world of individuals, essentially confining itself to the impersonal "social mindscapes" (Zerubavel 1997) we *share in common*.

2.3 COGNITIVE CONVENTIONS

Such mindscapes, however, are by no means universal. What we cognitively share in common we do not just as human beings but also as social beings—as feminists, as engineers, as baby boomers, as Jews.

While avoiding the strictly personal, cognitive sociologists are careful not to mistake the merely impersonal for the truly universal. Thus, while rejecting cognitive individualism, they do not go to the other extreme and embrace cognitive universalism. While some aspects of our cognition are either personal or universal, many others are neither.

Avoiding both cognitive individualism and universalism, cognitive sociology reminds us that while we certainly think both as individuals and as humans, what goes on in our minds is also affected by the particular thought communities to which we belong. Such communities (religious, generational, occupational, ideological) are considerably smaller than humanity at large.

Furthermore, the mindscapes we share in common are neither naturally nor logically inevitable. Many of them, in fact, are utterly *conventional*.

As we try to avoid the strictly subjective, we need not go all the way to the other extreme and regard everything that is not subjective as therefore necessarily objective. In other words, we should refrain from attributing inevitability to what is ultimately conventional (Zerubavel 2016). Although much of our thinking transcends our subjectivity, it is often grounded in our common social experience rather than in Nature or some absolute standard of Reason or Logic.

Cognitive sociology helps us avoid the epistemic pitfall of regarding the merely conventional as if it were part of the natural order by calling attention to that which is not subjective yet not entirely objective either. Between the subjective inner world of the individual and the objective physical world out there lies an intersubjective social world that is quite distinct from both of them (Berger and Luckmann 1966/1967). Unlike the former, it transcends our subjectivity and can therefore be commonly shared by an entire thought community. Yet in marked contrast to the latter, it is *neither naturally nor logically inevitable*.

This intersubjective social world is quite distinct from the subjective world of the individual as well as from the objective world of Nature and Logic. It is a world where time is reckoned according to neither the sun nor our inner sense of duration but in accordance with conventional time-reckoning systems like clock time (Zerubavel 1982) and the calendar, and in which the way we trace our descent is based on neither our own personal choice nor any natural or logical necessity (Zerubavel 2011:59–69).

Refraining from mistaking intersubjectivity for objectivity has some major methodological implications. Since the social world is taken for granted by those who inhabit it, the more we study different social worlds from the one we come to regard as a given, the easier it is to recognize the social nature of both.

Cognitive sociology helps promote greater awareness of our *cognitive diversity* as members of different thought communities. The more we become aware of such diversity, the less likely we are to regard the particular way in which we mentally process the world as naturally or logically inevitable.

Just as it resists cognitive individualism by calling attention to the similar way in which different individuals often perceive, attend to, or classify things, cognitive sociology also challenges cognitive universalism by highlighting major *differences* in the way members of different thought communities do that (see, e.g., Zerubavel 1991/1993:62–70). It thus demonstrates that *many of our cognitive habits are not so different as to be utterly idiosyncratic yet also not so similar as to be universal.*

Hence the need for a *comparative* approach to cognition that highlights our cognitive diversity as members of different thought communities. By featuring such diversity, it helps rid us of the illusion that all humans think alike.

The most striking evidence of our cognitive diversity as members of different thought communities are culturally specific *cognitive traditions.* The contrast between the Western and Navajo styles of propositional reasoning (Hamill 1990:73–101), for example, attests to our cognitive diversity as members of different cultures. So do culturally specific traditions of attending (Masuda and Nisbett 2001; Nisbett 2003; Zerubavel 2015:54–55) and marking (Zerubavel 2018:21–26).

Embracing a comparative approach to cognition, cognitive sociology also calls attention to the considerable cognitive diversity within the same culture. Most spectacular in this regard are intracultural historical changes, such as the significant shifts in Americans' attention to people's age, gender, race, and sexual orientation over the past few decades. Such generation-specific cognitive traditions are but one instance of the considerable cognitive diversity among different social groups within any given culture, as evidenced by the profound differences between mathematicians' and detectives' traditions of mental focusing (see also Zerubavel 2015:56–57, 65–68) or between the way mystics and astronomers envision the universe.

Their sensitivity to cognitive diversity also leads cognitive sociologists to become more aware of the *politics of cognition* (see, e.g., Zerubavel 1991/1993:67–70; 1997:44, 98–99; 2003:103–10; 2011:77–103; 2015:57; 2018:29–59, 63–68). The fact that the very definition of art, justice, or obscenity is often contested reminds us that the way we happen to organize the world in our minds is by no means inevitable. Just as instructive are *cognitive battles* over contested memories. The fact that many such mnemonic battles (Zerubavel 1997:97–99; 2003:109–10) are between social camps rather than just individuals (see, e.g., DeGloma 2015), of course, indicates that they are more than just personal. Yet the very fact that they even exist reminds us that the way we mentally process the past is by no means universal.

2.4 COGNITIVE NORMS

Cognitive sociology also calls attention to *cognitive deviants*[5] who focus their attention (Zerubavel 2015:81–82), categorize things, or reason somewhat differently from the rest of their thought community. Such *cognitive deviance* reminds us that the way we mentally process the world is neither naturally nor logically inevitable. More specifically, it implies the existence of *cognitive norms* that affect as well as constrain the way we think.

It is pronouncedly social *attentional norms*, for instance, that lead us to disregard certain parts or aspects of our surroundings as mere "background" (Zerubavel 2015:59–63). By the same token, it is unmistakably social *norms of remembrance* that tell us what we should remember and what we may, or even must, forget (Zerubavel 1997:84–89; 2011:10, 65, 67). Various *rules* of comparing and classifying play a similar role in the way we think.

Mental acts such as perceiving, attending, and remembering, in other words, are unmistakably social acts bound by not just physiological but also *normative constraints*. Ignoring or forgetting something thus often presupposes some *social pressure* to exclude it from our attention or memory.

By the same token, it is society that determines what we consider "reasonable" or regard as "making no sense." And it usually does so by exerting on us tacit pressure that we may not even notice (Durkheim 1912/1995:16–17; Fleck 1935/1979:100–101). As a result of such pressure, I come to perceive sounds I hear as "classical music" or "jazz," and to reckon time in conventional terms such as "ten to six," "Thursday," and "2015" even when I am all by myself.

2.5 COGNITIVE SOCIALIZATION

Like any other social norm, cognitive norms are something we *learn*. In other words, we learn how to focus our attention, reckon time, generalize, and reason in a socially appropriate manner.

By the same token, we learn to view things as "similar" to or "different" from one another. After all, when classifying people, food products, or films, we consider only some of the differences among them relevant, ignoring "minor" ones that "make no difference" (Zerubavel 1991/1993:16–17, 62–64; 1996). Yet which differences are considered significant is something we learn. *Separating the relevant from the irrelevant is therefore not just a logical but also a normative matter.*

We likewise learn to notice the fine mental lines separating "friends" from mere "acquaintances" and the "sane" from the "insane." (Yet like the contours of our celestial constellations, we notice such lines only after we learn that we should expect to see them there!) In the same way, we also learn to distinguish "alcoholic" from "nonalcoholic" drinks and ignore the moral plight of the cockroaches we so casually poison.

Unlike adults, young children do not notice yet the fine mental lines separating sociologists from psychologists, Sunnis from Shiites, or the "normal" from the "perverse." Nor do they notice yet the conventional mental frames separating the "real" world from the worlds of fiction, fantasy, and play. Young children who have not learned yet how to focus their attention in a socially appropriate manner, thereby attending to what we are supposed to disregard, likewise remind us that ignoring the "irrelevant" is something we learn to do (Zerubavel 2015:89–93).

Yet the difference between children's and adults' cognition is a result of their being at different stages of their cognitive development not just as human beings but also as social beings. Learning to reckon the time in terms of "Thursday" or "2015" is part of our *socio*cognitive development. That is also true of the process of learning to ignore "the background" and remember Plato, Shakespeare, and Attila the Hun.

It is the process of *cognitive socialization* that enables us to enter the intersubjective social world and learn to think in a socially appropriate manner. As we become socialized and learn to view the world through the mental lenses of our thought communities, we come to assign objects the same meaning that they have for others around us and to remember and ignore the same things that they do. Only then do we actually "enter" the social world.

While some of our cognitive socialization is explicit (which accounts for cognitive differences between people with different amounts of formal schooling [see, e.g., Luria 1976]), much of it is tacit. When a young boy returns from a long day with his mother downtown and hears her telling the rest of their family what they did there, he is also getting a tacit lesson in what is conventionally considered relevant (and therefore memorable) and irrelevant (and thus forgettable), which is part of the process of learning how to attend as well as how to remember in a socially appropriate manner.

Consider also the way we learn conventional distinctions. While such socialization is sometimes explicit, as when we formally learn the difference between fruits and vegetables, much of it is tacit. By noting that some people come to her house only as part of a larger group while others also come by themselves, a young girl tacitly learns the subtle cultural distinctions between various degrees of intimacy. In a similar vein, by noting when people close doors and when they leave them open, a young boy also learns the social distinction between private and public. Wearing certain clothes only on holidays likewise helps introduce both of them to the equally elusive conventional distinction between the ordinary and the special.

Such tacit socialization is also part of the process of learning a language. As they learn to address some people as *tu* and others as *usted*, for example, young Spanish speakers are also being tacitly sensitized to the cultural distinction between formal and informal relations. By the same token, learning that desks are grammatically considered masculine whereas sofas are considered feminine tacitly introduces young Hebrew speakers to gender distinctions in general.

2.6 COGNITIVE PLURALISM

The process of cognitive socialization underscores the considerable amount of control society has over what we attend to, what we remember, or how we interpret our experiences. Usually taken for granted, such *cognitive control* (Genieys and Smyrl 2008:11, 22, 27, 171; see also Zerubavel 1997:17; DeGloma 2007) is therefore one of the most insidious aspects of social control. In fact, it often assumes the form of *cognitive hegemony* (Spence 1978:9, 173, 183, 219–20; Zerubavel 2018:58–59).

Yet members of thought communities are not simply cognitive clones of one another, which ought to remind us that how we think is by no means utterly determined by society. Ironically, that is due to the fact that each of us is actually a member of more than just a single thought community (Fleck 1935/1979: 45, 110), thereby actually inhabiting multiple social worlds at the same time (Rommetveit 1985:186). Such *cognitive pluralism* is in fact a major feature of modern life.

The roots of modern cognitive pluralism are partly structural. Greater social mobility produces modern affiliation patterns that involve membership in more than just a single social group (Simmel 1908a/1964).[6] As a result, *most people today belong to multiple thought communities.*

To appreciate the cognitive implications of the modern web of our sociomental affiliations, consider, for example, the social structure of our memory. After all, the modern individual belongs to multiple *mnemonic communities* (Zerubavel 1997:90, 96–99), and there is hardly any overlap between his memories as a Catholic, as a criminal lawyer, and as a basketball fan.

Cognitive pluralism is also a byproduct of the considerable functional differentiation within modern society. In an increasingly specialized world, we inhabit more specialized thought communities (Holzner 1968:122–42; Schutz and Luckmann 1973:299–318). One would not expect the cognitive skills of a police officer, for example, to resemble those of a car mechanic, an accountant, or a chess player.

Yet the roots of modern cognitive pluralism are also partly ideological. The decline of religion's cognitive hegemony has led to a proliferation of "thought styles" (Mannheim 1929/1936:3; Fleck 1935/1979) that are often quite different from one another (see also Mannheim 1929/1936:33–34). Equally significant in this regard has been the modern rejection of traditionalism and valorization of originality. In sharp contrast to traditional systems of education, where individuals are essentially expected to cognitively reproduce what their predecessors have thought before them, modern education promotes a pronouncedly skepticist spirit of free inquiry (Durkheim 1897/1966:157–70).[7] People who five centuries ago would have been burned alive for refusing to think like everyone else around them actually win awards today precisely because of their unabashed display of originality.

*   *   *   *

Over the past thirty-nine years,[8] inspired by the pioneering works of Durkheim, Mannheim, Fleck, and Schutz, I have become increasingly committed to highlighting the distinctly sociological character of cognitive sociology. In other words, I have become far more interested in trying to export the sociological gospel to what has come to be known as "cognitive science" than in trying to import the cognitive-scientific gospel to sociology—an equally exciting project launched by Paul DiMaggio (1997, 2002). Rather than try to intellectually situate cognitive sociology as part of a more integrative approach to cognition that also draws on cognitive universalism, I have come to believe that the sociology of thinking also deserves to be appreciated on its own merit. It is my attempt to display such appreciation that thus constitutes my "big-picture" contribution to this volume.

NOTES

1. This term was introduced by Ludwik Fleck (1936/1986:80, 98, 105). See also Fleck (1947/1986:150–51).
2. This term was first used as the title of a collection of Aaron Cicourel's (1974) essays on language and social interaction.
3. This term was introduced by Fleck (1935/1979:45, 103). See also 38–51, 98–111 for his discussion of "thought collectives." For a classic analysis of thought communities, see Mannheim (1929/1936).
4. Berger and Luckmann (1966/1967:36–41); Schutz and Luckmann (1973:233–5, 249–50). See also Mead (1934:42–134). For an early statement on "shared cognition," see Durkheim (1893/1984:38–39). See also Moscovici (1982); Resnick (1991).
5. See also Fleck (1935/1979:99) on cognitive "heretics."
6. On the cognitive implications of social mobility, see also Simmel (1908a/1950); Sorokin (1927/1964:509–15).
7. As for the possible danger of *cognitive anomie*, see also Durkheim (1893/1984:294–301).
8. As a teacher, my interest in cognitive sociology dates back to 1980, the first time I taught a course explicitly titled "Cognitive Sociology" at the University of Pittsburgh.

REFERENCES

Berger, Peter L., and Thomas Luckmann. 1966/1967. *The Social Construction of Reality: A Treatise in the Sociology of Knowledge*. Garden City, NY: Doubleday Anchor.

Cicourel, Aaron. 1974. *Cognitive Sociology: Language and Meaning in Social Interaction*. New York: Free Press.

DeGloma, Thomas. 2007. "The Social Logic of 'False Memories': Symbolic Awakenings and Symbolic Worlds in Survivor and Retractor Narratives." *Symbolic Interaction* 30:543–65.

DeGloma, Thomas. 2015. "The Strategies of Mnemonic Battle: On the Alignment of Autobiographical and Collective Memories in Conflicts over the Past." *American Journal of Cultural Sociology* 3:156–83.

DiMaggio, Paul. 1997. "Culture and Cognition." *Annual Review of Sociology* 23:263–87.

DiMaggio, Paul. 2002. "Why Cognitive (and Cultural) Sociology Needs Cognitive Psychology." pp. 274–81 in *Culture in Mind: Toward a Sociology of Culture and Cognition*, edited by Karen A. Cerulo. New York: Routledge.

Downes, Stephen M. 1993. "Socializing Naturalized Philosophy of Science." *Philosophy of Science* 60:452–68.

Durkheim, Emile. 1893/1984. *The Division of Labor in Society*. New York: Free Press.

Durkheim, Emile. 1897/1966. *Suicide: A Study in Sociology*. New York: Free Press.

Durkheim, Emile. 1912/1995. *The Elementary Forms of Religious Life*. New York: Free Press.

Durkheim, Emile. 1914/1973. "The Dualism of Human Nature and Its Social Conditions." pp. 149–63 in *Emile Durkheim: On Morality and Society*, edited by Robert N. Bellah. Chicago: University of Chicago Press.

Fleck, Ludwik. 1935/1979. *Genesis and Development of a Scientific Fact*. Chicago: University of Chicago Press.

Fleck, Ludwik. 1936/1986. "The Problem of Epistemology." pp. 79–112 in *Cognition and Fact: Materials on Ludwik Fleck*, edited by Robert S. Cohen and Thomas Schnelle. Dordrecht: D. Reidel.

Fleck, Ludwik. 1947/1986. "To Look, To See, To Know." pp. 129–51 in *Cognition and Fact: Materials on Ludwik Fleck*, edited by Robert S. Cohen and Thomas Schnelle. Dordrecht: D. Reidel.

Friedman, Asia. 2013. *Blind to Sameness: Sexpectations and the Social Construction of Male and Female Bodies*. Chicago: University of Chicago Press.

Genieys, William, and Marc Smyrl. 2008. *Elites, Ideas, and the Evolution of Public Policy*. New York: Palgrave Macmillan.

Hamill, James F. 1990. *Ethno-Logic: The Anthropology of Human Reasoning*. Urbana: University of Illinois Press.

Holzner, Burkart. 1968. *Reality Construction in Society*. Cambridge, MA: Schenkman.

Luria, Alexander R. 1976. *Cognitive Development: Its Cultural and Social Foundations*. Cambridge, MA: Harvard University Press.

Mannheim, Karl. 1929/1936. *Ideology and Utopia: An Introduction to the Sociology of Knowledge*. New York: Harvest.

Masuda, Takahiko, and Richard E. Nisbett. 2001. "Attending Holistically versus Analytically: Comparing the Context Sensitivity of Japanese and Americans." *Journal of Personality and Social Psychology* 81:922–34.

Mead, George H. 1934. *Mind, Self, and Society: From the Standpoint of a Social Behaviorist*. Chicago: University of Chicago Press.

Moscovici, Serge. 1982. "The Phenomenon of Social Representations." pp. 3–70 in *Social Representations*, edited by Robert M. Farr and Serge Moscovici. Cambridge: Cambridge University Press.

Nisbett, Richard E. 2003. *The Geography of Thought: How Asians and Westerners Think Differently… and Why*. New York: Free Press.

Resnick, Lauren B. 1991. "Shared Cognition: Thinking as Social Practice." pp. 1–20 in *Perspectives on Socially Shared Cognition*, edited by Lauren B. Resnick et al. Washington: American Psychological Association.

Rommetveit, Ragnar. 1985. "Language Acquisition as Increasing Linguistic Structuring of Experience and Symbolic Behavior Control." pp. 183–204 in *Culture, Communication, and Cognition: Vygotskian Perspectives*, edited by James V. Wertch. Cambridge: Cambridge University Press.

Schutz, Alfred. 1932/1967. *The Phenomenology of the Social World*. Evanston, IL: Northwestern University Press.

Schutz, Alfred. 1973. *Collected Papers, Vol.1*. The Hague: Martinus Nijhoff.

Schutz, Alfred, and Thomas Luckmann. 1973. *The Structures of the Life-World*. Evanston, IL: Northwestern University Press.

Simmel, Georg. 1908a/1950. "The Stranger." pp. 402–8 in *The Sociology of Georg Simmel*, edited by Kurt H. Wolff. New York: Free Press.

Simmel, Georg. 1908b/1964. "The Web of Group Affiliations." pp. 127–95 in *Conflict and the Web of Group Affiliations*. New York: Free Press.

Sorokin, Pitirim A. 1927/1964. *Social and Cultural Mobility*. New York: Free Press.

Spence, Larry D. 1978. *The Politics of Social Knowledge*. University Park: Pennsylvania State University Press.

Zerubavel, Eviatar. 1982. "The Standardization of Time: A Sociohistorical Perspective." *American Journal of Sociology* 88:1–23.

Zerubavel, Eviatar. 1991/1993. *The Fine Line: Making Distinctions in Everyday Life*. Chicago: University of Chicago Press.

Zerubavel, Eviatar. 1996. "Lumping and Splitting: Notes on Social Classification." *Sociological Forum* 11:421–33.

Zerubavel, Eviatar. 1997. *Social Mindscapes: An Invitation to Cognitive Sociology*. Cambridge, MA: Harvard University Press.

Zerubavel, Eviatar. 2003. *Time Maps: Collective Memory and the Social Shape of the Past*. Chicago: University of Chicago Press.

Zerubavel, Eviatar. 2011. *Ancestors and Relatives: Genealogy, Identity, and Community*. New York: Oxford University Press.

Zerubavel, Eviatar. 2015. *Hidden in Plain Sight: The Social Structure of Irrelevance*. New York: Oxford University Press.

Zerubavel, Eviatar. 2016. "The Five Pillars of Essentialism: Reification and the Social Construction of an Objective Reality." *Cultural Sociology* 10:69–76.

Zerubavel, Eviatar. 2018. *Taken for Granted: The Remarkable Power of the Unremarkable*. Princeton, NJ: Princeton University Press, 2018.

CHAPTER 3

CRITICAL THEORY AND COGNITIVE SOCIOLOGY

PIET STRYDOM

To honor my brief of having to write on the theme of critical theory and cognitive sociology requires taking up an autobiographical perspective, both my own and my generation's, in order to briefly retrace the trajectory of this relation from the viewpoint of my current understanding of cognitive sociology. The integral version of cognitive sociology presented here is closely associated with critical theory. It originally emerged against the background of the intellectual constellation of the late 1960s and early 1970s in which critical theory occupied a central position, and it gradually unfolded in parallel with the development of the latter in a context partially shaped by the cognitive revolution.

The intellectual constellation of the time provided Karl-Otto Apel and Jürgen Habermas, the leading second-generation critical theorists, with the opportunity to reinvent critical theory and simultaneously, albeit unintentionally, to lay the basic parameters of a dovetailing cognitive sociology. Having emerged from the inspiring contributions of these two renowned authors, the intuition of this sociology gradually assumed form and continued to be deeply influenced by the development and revision of their thought, particularly the latter's who is the younger of the two and also a sociologist. In the course of its articulation, it was further shaped by various contributions of the younger generation in the context of the international debate around critical theory in general and Habermas's work in particular. From my own perspective, the current version forms part of a program going back at least to the late 1970s and early 1980s to enhance Apel's and Habermas's decidedly normative approach by a social-scientific complement of a cognitive nature. In the course of time, the aim of this long-standing program became clear—namely, a fully rounded cognitive sociology, an integral version, as it were, that is able to interrelate the sociocultural and naturalistic dimensions in a manner that complements critical theory. This necessitated the correction of two problems in the extant contributions: first, articulating the cognitive aspects of the sociocultural world so as to avoid a lingering sense of opacity; and, second, incorporating naturalism brought in by Habermas in a weak or soft version, but left undeveloped by him and completely ignored by those following him closely.

Accordingly, this chapter is divided into two parts. The first identifies both earlier and later prompts and starting points that emerged in the course of the intellectual development of critical theory for the formulation and development of a complementary cognitive sociology. The second part focuses on the major sociocultural and weak naturalistic dimensions that needed extrapolation, conceptual clarification, and integration to form an integral cognitive sociology enhancing critical theory's analytical and defining critical capacity.

3.1 PROMPTS AND STARTING-POINTS

The cognitive motif had by no means been absent from classical critical theory, as is apparent from the writings of Lukács, Adorno, Marcuse, and Benjamin, but it was only in the wake of the cognitive revolution of the late 1950s that this largely subterranean dimension began to receive the attention which allowed the hesitant and gradual emergence of cognitive sociology in the late 1970s and 1980s.[1] The starting point of this development is to be found in an innovation of Apel's and Habermas's elaboration of it.

1. By reconciling Kant and Heidegger, uncovering the convergence between Wittgenstein and Heidegger, on that basis criticizing Winch and Gadamer and, finally, systematizing this set of relations by recourse to the Left-Hegelians Marx and Peirce, especially the latter's pragmaticism and semiotic theory of signs, Apel (1980, 1981) struck on his characteristic "transcendental-pragmatic" epistemology. At its core is the distinction between the constitution of meaning—the Heideggerian-Wittgensteinian moment—and reflection on validity—the Kantian moment—which are interrelated in the medium of signs, language, or communication carried by the human communication community as it subject—the Marxian-Peircean moment. At this point it was clear that critical theory required a *medium quo* rather than the usual *medium quod* theory of knowledge and that it would be able to fulfill its function of the critique of the constitution of meaning or the construction of society only on the basis of reflection on the validity of the latter. Crucial to note is that it is this particular model, which effectively captures the cognitive metaproblematic, that from the start served as the intuitive impetus toward the development of a corresponding multilevel cognitive sociology, but it first had to await supporting contributions and insights before it could take off. Here Habermas enters.

2. Habermas's (1984, 1987) interest in social theory besides epistemology enabled him to fill a lacuna in Apel's account left by the lack of a differentiated theory of the constitution of meaning at the core of the theory of language. For this he drew on Chomsky's theory of language and, especially, Searle's so-called Berkeley approach, which pitted a linguistic theory forming part of the theory of action—so-called speech act theory—against the narrow computational conception of cognitivism then predominant in the context of the cognitive revolution. Corresponding to Apel's distinction between meaning and validity, he focused on the relation between the different kinds of—constative, regulative and expressive—speech acts and their respective rational or validity bases

represented by objective truth, social or moral rightness and subjective truthfulness. From this emerged Habermas's (1979) own distinct version of "formal-pragmatics," which served as a framework for the development of his social theory. Most centrally, it covered the relation within the lifeworld between action and discourse, a relation allowing for the potentialities of the lifeworld to be identified, articulated, and realized. While activities depending on competences normally proceed on taken-for-granted assumptions, once they break down, become questionable or problematized, reflective discourse can bring their formal presuppositions to bear on them in a way that leads to their correction, refinement, and further development. Visible here is the impact of ethnomethodology's cognitive notion of the rational properties of interaction processes on the upgrading of his phenomenological concept of lifeworld from being the merely taken-for-granted domain of meaning to also the repository of unavoidable cognitive presuppositions which can be discursively mobilized and given effect in social life. This conception played an important role in Habermas's analysis of the evolutionary unfolding of society, itself informed by the cognitive sociologist-psychologist Piaget, and provided a basis for the identification of societal problems and the critique of emergent unjustifiable social conditions.

To the reader of Habermas's writings from the late 1960s to the early 1980s it was apparent that he had been influenced quite decisively by the cognitive revolution—a perception strengthened by the publications of contemporaneous sociologists like Nowotny, Cicourel, Goffman, and in particular Knorr-Cetina's and Cicourel's suggestion of a cognitive turn in sociology. But what drew attention and focused the issue of his conception of the cognitive was an anomaly in his presentation stemming from the treatment of the concept in both a narrow and a broad sense—a practice observable right up to his late work. One and only one of the three modes of communication—constative speech acts—was specified as being "cognitive," while he simultaneously nevertheless submitted that all three "validity claims have a cognitive character...a rational basis...[which renders them]...cognitively testable" (Habermas 1979:63). This meant that the formally presupposed validity concepts of truth, rightness, and truthfulness, and not truth alone, are all cognitive magnitudes. More deeply, this anomaly was compounded by the contradiction between his pragmatist view that validity could be explicated only in terms of validity claims, which itself led to a conflation of validity with constitution, and his demand that a theory of the formal presuppositions of action was necessary. In my own case, the awareness of these tensions proved to be a persistent impetus toward clarifying the sense of the cognitive and developing a corrective sociology.

Once Habermas translated his formal-pragmatic framework into the idiom of social theory, a step in the direction of a possible cognitive sociology became apparent. Both his programs for the reconstruction of historical materialism and for the theory of communicative action, originally published in 1976 and 1981, respectively, made an innovative conceptual and theoretical contribution that resonated widely. Inspired by cognitive theorists, he adopted a genetic-structuralist theory with competence and structural components, linked through speech-act-based communicative and learning processes, and incorporating historical and evolutionary temporalities. Despite the decisive cognitive influence, however, the conceptualization was largely couched in crypto-cognitive terms and, therefore, at most delivered a methodologically conceived "reconstructive sociology" trained on the normative problematic. Thus the scene was set for the next generation.

3. Habermas's writings of the period unmistakably communicated an invitation to pursue the cognitive suggestions. Although obvious to his cognitively awakened reader, the third generation following his writings closely nevertheless did not, at least not yet, exhibit an awareness of the possibility for such a development beyond the texts. Habermas's focus on "normative structures" in particular acted as a barrier to such a departure. While adopting his communication paradigm, they focused critically on his theory of developmental-logical sociocultural evolution and implicated matters such as the constitution of society, social movements, collective learning, and so forth.[2] These concerns would furnish some of the scholars with starting points for the inclusion of selected cognitive aspects, especially under the inspiration of European discourse analysis and American social movement studies, both of which were shaped by the cognitive revolution. The former focused on the central role of cognitive structuring of communication processes and by way of the concepts of "frames" and "framing" the latter allowed the kind of interpretative *Rahmen* or *Muster* familiar in phenomenology and hermeneutics to became much more pointedly conceptualized in cognitive terms.

Three contemporaneous examples of the solidification of certain cognitive suggestions in Habermas's writings stand out—Miller and Eder in particular, but also Eyerman and Jamison, none of whom, however, went all the way to a cognitive sociology. Drawing on Piaget, Miller (1986) showed in his sociological learning theory that Habermas's presentation of social constitution lacked an adequate account of the cognitive structuring of communication processes—according to his late work (Miller 2002), a dimension best conceptualized in systems-theoretical terms. Employing Habermas's early distinction among technical, interpretive, and emancipatory cognitive interests, Eyerman and Jamison (1991) conceptualized social movements as processes of cognitive or knowledge-producing praxis, but despite seeing such praxis as feeding into the larger cognitive map of society, they overlooked the significance of the metacultural dimension—that is, Apel's and Habermas's quasi-transcendental validity—by reducing it to different historical types of knowledge articulated by social movements. In research he directed in 1991–1993 on the framing and communication of environmental problems in Europe and formally reported in 1996, Eder started from Habermas's later theory of communicative action instead, and developed what may be considered the broad outlines of a cognitive sociology which, however, was not presented as such. The main limitation was that the cognitive component was treated not as the defining feature, but simply as subserving public discourse analysis. In later work, Eder indeed did conceive the Habermasian communication-theoretical approach as "cognitivist" (1999:211) and as implicitly containing "cognitive sociology" (2007), but it lacked sufficient substantiation. Despite his innovative and meaningful contribution, he never really embraced the idea of cognitive sociology, while also maintaining an ambivalent relation to critical theory.[3] In the wake of the mentioned authors' contributions, the nagging question remained as to how Apel's and Habermas's concern with validity, rather than being neglected, could and should be given social-theoretical effect.

The suggestions of a possible cognitive sociology in the writings of Apel, Habermas, and other authors, but in particular the issues raised and the problems left unresolved, are what motivated my attempt since the mid-1980s at a more systematic pursuit of this goal. It first of all required attending to aspects such as cognitive processes and cognitive structure formation at different levels[4] as well as the introduction of new concepts such as the "cognitive order of society" and "triple contingency" (Strydom 1996, 2000, 1999). To have remained at that level, however, would have been tantamount to reproducing the most basic limitation of the cognitive sociology latent in the writings of the third generation. Their self-confinement to the sociocultural dimension, undoubtedly partly conditioned by Habermas's stance during his middle period of 1981–1999, occluded the need to incorporate also the naturalistic dimension. Between 1965 and 1976, Habermas maintained a naturalistic reference, as exhibited by his concern with the evolution of the human species and its form of life, but subsequently it was seemingly left by the wayside, only to be reasserted much later under the title of "weak naturalism" (1999:32; 2003:22). Already in 1979, Apel (1984) revived the distinction between first and second nature, which is crucial to critical theory, as is borne out by early critical theorists such as Lukács, Adorno, and Marcuse. This concern signals that the development of a cognitive sociology suitable to critical theory needs to avoid a one-sided sociocultural or cultural emphasis by adopting a balanced two-pronged sociocultural and naturalistic approach that simultaneously also specifies the bridging principle between the two. This leads beyond the recollection of the historical background of the current proposal.

3.2 Toward an Integral Cognitive Sociology

The second part of this chapter is devoted to indications of an integral cognitive sociology with a view to correcting its continuing conspicuous absence in critical theory. The first subsection deals with the sociocultural world and in the second attention shifts to the question of weak naturalism.

3.2.1 Sociocultural World: Cognitive Structures and Dynamics

1. The principal problem in the writings of the second and third generations of critical theorists relevant to cognitive sociology is the conflation of dimensions that must be distinguished and kept in mind when considering the dynamic processes involved in

the constitution and organization of the social life. Needless to say, this conflation has to be undone if a coherent and articulated cognitive sociology were to be formulated. The following critical observations on the key theorists are intended to set the scene for introducing the conceptual correction necessary for arriving at such a sociological stance in relation to the sociocultural world.

Despite having drawn the founding distinction between constitution and validity, Apel consistently advanced the argument that validity could be realized through constitution in social life. For example, he treated the validity concept of truth as an ideal value that could be attained by a consensus among participants. As such, the concept plays the role of a regulative principle that directs and guides the process leading to the consensus. This argument, however, short-circuits the flow of cognitive properties. Rather than maintaining the distinction between constitution and validity, it effectively reduces the high-level abstract structuring validity concept to the particular situationally defined ideal value that the constitutive activities pursue and, in turn, directs and guides those very activities within the parameters laid down by the validity concept.

For almost three decades, Habermas followed Apel closely, until the late 1990s, when he finally became convinced that the collapse of truth into consensus leading to an "epistemic concept of truth" was untenable. What had to be countenanced was that epistemic truth involves knowledge of a specific matter belonging to a particular context, unlike the abstract validity concept that is presupposed beyond all contexts. The source of the mistake he quite wrongly ascribed to Peirce, on whom Apel had originally drawn. But what is remarkable is that, despite having seen through the error, Habermas frequently nevertheless continued conflating the two levels. Throughout his writings, for example, truth, rightness, and truthfulness are treated as validity claims, as though there was no difference between claims qua actions and their rational basis or conceptual conditions. And even after the revision of 1999, his new distinction between the validity concept of truth and ideal rational acceptability serving as the ideal value pursued by the discursive process about a particular validity claim did not deter him from conflating the distinct roles played by truth and rational acceptability or veridicity as orientation complexes. What needs to be stressed is that truth is a conceptual condition that structurally enables the discursive process from on high by laying down its broad parameters, while the ideal of rational acceptability orients a situated justificatory discourse testing a specific claim regarding a particular matter in a concrete context. The conflation of these two distinct levels, the "unconditional" or "absolute" nonepistemic validity concept of truth beyond the context and the epistemic achievement concept within the context, shows up graphically in Habermas's problematic account of the paradox endemic in any justificatory discourse and of the irredeemable fallibility of any and every truth claim (Strydom 2018).

In what can be interpreted as his outline of an effective, if not actually intended, cognitive sociology, Eder (1996) began from cognitive competences and in an exemplary fashion covered factual, moral and ethical cognitive framing devices, the construction by a plurality of agents of competing identity and actor frames, corresponding strategies of communicating frames in public discourse, the master frame emerging from the resulting frame competition and, finally, descriptive, prescriptive, and expressive rule systems regulating the discursively mediated process. To the cognitively awakened eye, the inherent ambiguity of the concept of "rules" or "rule systems," originally exposed by Apel, stood out, but three years later a modicum of disambiguation followed, when Eder renounced following Habermas's predilection to "idealize." He accordingly characterized his approach, in an endnote called "cognitivist" (1999:211), as focused on immanent "rules" operating in "a narratively based shared world." In a late essay on the cognitive sociology implicit in Habermas,[5] it by contrast at first seemed as though "cognitive rules" were plausibly elevated above "norms" (Eder 2007:394) in line with Habermas's conception of the "cognitive foundations of communicative action" in the sense of conceptual conditions, but this turned out not to be the case. Despite denouncing the mistaken view of learning directly leading to evolution, Eder nevertheless opened himself to the criticism of continuing to conflate different levels of cognitive structures by aligning cognitive foundations and regulative logic with Habermas's problematic notion of "the ideal speech situation."

2. The distinction between dimensions necessary for definitively dissipating the critical theorists' conflation and, thus, for the formulation of a consistent and articulated cognitive sociology can be backed by recourse to mathematics and philosophy. In the more than 2,000-year-long mathematical-philosophical tradition borne by mathematicians, scientists, philosophers, and logicians such as Aristotle, Galileo, Newton, Leibniz, Kant, Cauchy, and Peirce, a most basic distinction had been established and validated. It is the distinction that in mathematics is drawn between the "convergent series" and "divergent series" (Dantzig 2007:150–51) and in philosophy the one Leibniz (1965:235–6), under the influence of Galileo, introduced between "truths of fact" and "truths of reason," which proved decisive for Kant (1968:321) who, correspondingly, distinguished "the *descending* series" from "the *ascending* series."

Since each of these series represents an infinite process, both mathematics and philosophy are particularly concerned with their limits. Mathematically, the convergent series' limit is called pi (π), in the sense of a finite or specific ideal value toward which the series tends yet is unable ever to reach—π having the conventional value of 3.14159, but actually being indeterminate, since on calculating it the number of digits after the decimal point is endless. Similarly in philosophy, Kant (1968:321) defined the descending series as lying "on the side of the conditioned" and representing "potential" manifest in an endless "*process of becoming*." As regards the limit of this series, comparable to the value of π, toward which the process tends yet never reaches, Kant mentioned "models" and "examples" (1968:486) that can never be fully realized, and to hold that it could be perfectly emulated would be tantamount to an "illusion" (Kant 1956:152).

Mathematically, the divergent series does not tend toward a finite yet ideal limit like π, but is one in which the addition of more and more numbers leads to a total that outgrows any boundary one might try to set. This exponentially accumulating series with its projected sought-after totality, its infinite ideal limit, corresponds to Aristotle's (2015:Book III, Part 6) "actual" or "complete infinity." Philosophically, Kant (1968:321) defined the ascending series as lying "on the side of the conditions" that are always already "presupposed" so that the series is "given *in its completeness.*" Although recognizing that we could not comprehend this series in its totality, he (1968:322; Kant 1972:93) insisted that it must nevertheless have such a totality that we, consequently, must imaginatively project as a totality given in its completeness if we were to be able to make inferences and judgments. It is this infinite ideal limit of the accumulative series that he captured by his transfinite or transcendental notion of "*idea* or concept of reason" (Kant 1968:314) as a logically possible and necessary idealization.

Now, from a cognitive perspective the above-mentioned two series are of great interest. Cognitive sociologically, the mathematical-philosophical convergent or descending series is equivalent to the ongoing historical process of the constitution or construction of society, which constantly generates structures like personalities, identities, groups, organizations, institutions and cultural phenomena of all sorts, and, finally, knowledge and technologies mediating the relation to nature. By contrast, the divergent or ascending series is equivalent to the evolutionary process, which from time to time stabilizes whatever structures become selected and emerge from the historical process. However, the cognitive interest in the respective limits of these two series is greater still. In fact, the distinction between the two different limits—the constantly receding unattainable finite ideal value of π or models and examples, and the imaginatively presupposed infinite ideal totality or idealized ideas of reason—provides the necessary means whereby the critical theorists' conflation can be finally dissipated and the door opened for a cognitive sociology complementary to critical theory.

Sociologically, both types of limits are cognitive structures in the form of cultural phenomena, but they differ in that they occupy distinct levels and fulfill unique functions. On the one hand, the infinite ideal limit or complete totality of conditions refers to our necessary and unavoidable presuppositions without which it is impossible not just to investigate any object domain but also to create and organize society and cultivate ethical subjects. Most immediately, it is available as the conceptual conditions that have become evolutionarily stabilized, make social life possible, index all its contents, and structure it.[6] They occupy the metaconventional metacultural level of the human sociocultural form of life that includes such concepts or principles as Habermas's truth, rightness, and truthfulness. It is here that we encounter the cognitive-sociologically important "cognitive order of society," as I have proposed to call it. On the other hand, the finite ideal limit or Kant's unrealizable models or examples are equivalent to the multiplicity of conventional cultural models that regulate or direct and guide orientations and constitutive or constructive activities at the historical dimension within particular situational contexts. Although largely of a semantic, pragmatic, and symbolic kind, they also have a cognitive component insofar as they are made possible, indexed, and structured by the cognitive order. As should become clear if it is not yet, the assumption here is that the cognitive order is a universal feature of the human sociocultural form of life as such, for example, in line with Jackendoff's (1999:74–75) view of the "conceptual conditions of social organization [which provide] a skeleton of issues around which cultures are built," while cultural models are relative refractions in different cultures or societies of that order.

Undoing the critical theorists's conflation mathematical-philosophically thus eventuates in the basic theoretical distinction between the context-transcendent cognitive order and context-immanent cultural models that must be borne in mind throughout cognitive sociological analyses. In the cases of both Apel and Habermas, despite the latter's advance beyond the former, the confusion of metacultural principles with cultural models, for example truth with directing and guiding finite ideals, should be studiously avoided. Likewise in Eder's case, every vestige of the permutations of this conflation should be eliminated from cognitive sociological thought.

3. To make this vital theoretical distinction more palpable and intelligible, Figure 3.1 presents the three major dimensions of the sociocultural world—the objective, the social, and the subjective—in terms of their respective convergent and divergent axes and concomitant distinct limits represented by cognitive order principles and cultural models. Buttressing this dividing line, the figure also includes the corresponding distinctions between the transcendent and immanent, between validity and meaning, and between cognitive universality and semantic-pragmatic-symbolic generality. From the

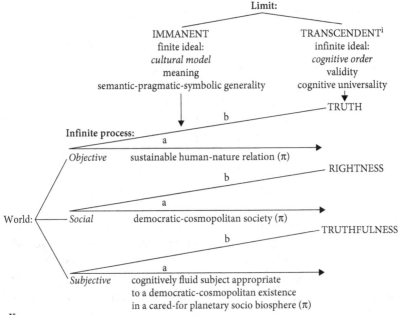

Key:
a = convergent or decreasing series: historical constitutive process indefinitely tending toward a finite limit value
b = divergent or increasing series: long-term process of structural accumulation and evolutionary stabilization of universally presupposed rational potentials representing the conceptual conditions of society
π = π-like cultural model directing and guiding the constitutive process within the parameters laid down by the conceptual conditions but never fully realizable
i = Immanent transcendence expresses the cognitive meta-problematic (Strydom 2011) and thus reproduces the constitution-validity distinction.

FIGURE 3.1 Cognitive-sociological parameters of the sociocultural form of life.

vanishing number of actually operative cultural models, only three contemporarily relevant and perhaps most urgent high-level ones are selected for exemplary purposes. And the cognitive order of course consists of many more concepts or principles than the three major domain-circumscribing ones—truth, rightness, and truthfulness—mentioned, as discussed later.

The thrust of eliminating the conflation of dimensions is not just the acknowledgment of the distinction between immanent cultural models and the transcendent cognitive order. This distinction is indeed most important. Crucial for cognitive sociology, however, is the clarification also of the cognitive order itself. While presupposing the generative efficacy of the historical constitutive process, it consists of evolutionarily stabilized self-organizing presupposed principles that represent the conceptual conditions of the sociocultural form of life. Lacking clarification of these conditions, cognitive-sociological analysis is impossible, since recourse to them is an absolutely necessary element of such analysis. Despite the critical theorists' appeal to them—for example, invoking truth, rightness, and truthfulness, or their equivalents—which indeed confirms their importance for critical theory, none of them has attempted to bring out the cognitive order, not to mention specifying it. Habermas has contributed by far the most, but what there is in his writings lacks systematization due to reluctance on his part (Strydom 2015a). This neglect can be corrected, however, without falling into bad metaphysics or giving up altogether on pragmatism. Metaphysics is occluded by the fact that the cognitive order is the outcome of evolution thus far, both the natural evolution of the cognitively fluid, metarepresentational mind of *Homo sapiens sapiens*[7] and the sociocultural evolution that stabilized the metacultural conceptual conditions. And instead of stopping short or, what amounts to the same thing, extending formal-pragmatic worlds too far, as does Habermas, it should be recognized that they rest on corresponding cognitive objective, social, and subjective domains secured by the extended mind, which itself presupposes language, mathematics, and logic.

The cognitive order of society can for current purposes be characterized as in Table 3.1. Listed is a selection of the most important cognitive order concepts or principles, which took form over millennia and eventually became explicated in the wake of the scientific revolution and, once evolutionarily stabilized, became associated with the names of classical figures.[8] The cognitive presuppositions of truth, rightness, and truthfulness that Habermas emphasizes are only three—albeit domain-defining ones—among a whole range of others, all of which are amenable eventually to being sorted into the threefold framework of cognitive objective, social, and subjective domains.

Sociologically conceived, the conceptual conditions that found society are the meta-conventional metacultural cognitive order that embraces what may be regarded as the design principles of society or the blueprints for constructing a possible world in the sense of being like the linguistic or genetic code. In the constitutive process borne by action and communication, a value- and norm-laden yet emergent selection and more or less balanced combination or composition of differently emphasized cognitive order principles from the objective, social, and subjective domains are made in order to construct more specific cognitive structures necessary for problem-solving and world-creation.

Table 3.1 The Cognitive Order of Society

Century	Representative	Field	Cognitive Order
12th	the Troubadours	endeutics	needs
12th	Capellanus	intimacy	love
15th	Brunelleschi	technology	effectiveness
16th	Machiavelli	power	control
	Bodin	state	sovereignty
	Beza & Mariana	politics	the people
16th–17th	Galileo	nature	formalization
17th	Bacon	knowledge	instrumentality
	Descartes	*cogito*	self-reflection
	Newton	science	mastery
	Hobbes	coercive law	legality
	Locke	civil society	negative freedom
	Bayle	conscience	critique/reflexive freedom
18th	Smith	economy	efficiency
	Montesquieu	civil society	constitutionalism
	Rousseau	civil society	solidarity/social freedom
	Sieyès	civil society	legitimacy
	Payne	rights	equality
	Kant	culture:	
		pure reason	truth
		practical reason	right/justice
		judgment	truthfulness/ appropriateness
	Rousseau	education	learning
19th	Kierkegaard	the self	authenticity/aesthetic freedom
19th	Marx	society	association

The outcomes are variable cognitively shaped semantic-pragmatic-symbolic forms or frames such as actor and collective identities and, especially important, a variety of cultural models for the regulation of orientations, actions, practices, and so forth. The human rights cultural model presented in Figure 3.2 serves as an example of the cognitive order's structuring role.[9]

The cognitive order as a set of presupposed conceptual conditions is enabling in that it provides a space of reasoning containing a whole range of possible reasons from which a selection could be made through inference by choosing between binarily coded positive preference values and their negatives. Simultaneously, however, it also indexes the context by imposing a space of placement in which every relevant item is assigned a particular position that opens the possibility of different interpretations of its status. Finally, the cognitive order's structuring impact on the formation of a cultural model depends on the selective combination of a number of the concepts or principles it houses, as depicted in Figure 3.2. The coded cognitive core of the model, which lends it validity, is symbolically packaged in a way that includes both semantic meanings

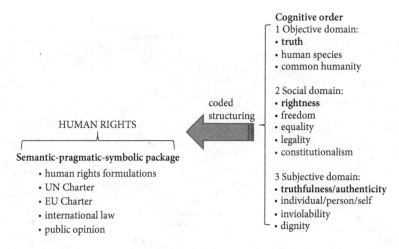

FIGURE 3.2   Cognitive order shaping of a cultural model.

and pragmatic scripts. The semantic component renders the model expressible and communicable, while the pragmatic component prescribes courses of action by offering directions and guidance. The symbolic package encapsulates the intersubjectively comprehensible consilience attained by the cognitive schematic formation and makes publicly visible the collective acceptance, consensus, achieved recognition, and validity of the cultural model, which nevertheless allows a variety of different interpretations.

4. To shed more light on this complex set of relations with which cognitive-sociological analysis is typically confronted, it is necessary to highlight the implied dynamics from a cognitive perspective (e.g., Strydom 2015b). Figure 3.3 captures some of the most important aspects relevant in the present context.[10]

The cognitive dynamics of interest to cognitive sociology involve, to begin with, two major countervailing processes—an historical constructive process following the arrow of time and a shaping, indexing, structuring process pushing against the flow of time. The constructive process, first, presupposes the human cognitive endowment, especially latent or tacit cognitive capacities and competences, and is borne by a plurality of cognitively equipped agents, both actors and their public audience, who differ as to their positions, orientations, engagements, actions, and thus cognitive frames, yet in a given situation interrelate through differently interpreted common presuppositions, interaction, discourse, competition, conflict, learning, and cooperation. Through their interrelations the actors and audience together transform all sorts of information into meanings and thereby generate a variety of cognitive properties from which a selection could be made by the use of different cognitive modes of inference, such as abduction (adopting a perspective), induction (referring to objects) and deduction (drawing on concepts). Second, the structuring process presupposes the availability of reflexively presupposed cognitive structures beyond the situation taking the form of the evolutionary stabilized self-organizing cognitive order, which embraces a wide range of structural information,

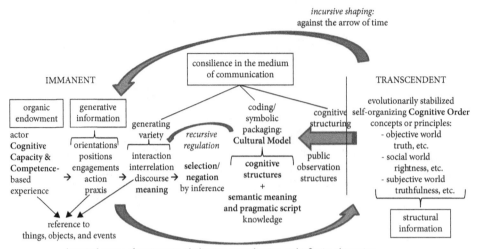

FIGURE 3.3 Cognitive dynamics.

concepts, or principles serving as the conditions of social life. While dependent on the historical process for its origination, reproduction, and evolutionary modification, the cognitive order incursively shapes the sociocultural world by enabling it as something specifically sociocultural, indexing its contents and allowing for the variable cognitive structuring of individual minds, actor frames, orientations, actions, communications, public audience frames, resonances, relations, and the emergent socially relevant meanings and frames or cognitive schemata.

Wherever there is a trace of rationality, it is the cognitive order that lends cognitive form to phenomena from the macro to the micro level, but of special interest to cognitive sociology is consilience—that is, the outcome of the countervailing processes meeting and, in the communication medium, giving rise to a synthesis of cognitive structures, knowledge, and meanings deriving from a number of disparate sources. Such a consilience is achieved by two complementary procedures, both of which involve selection and hence negation, what is called coding from the perspective the cognitive order and symbolic packaging from that of the process of meaning-creating practices or transformative praxis. The most significant emergent outcome takes the form of a cultural model that consists of a variety of inputs generated in the constructive process, on the one hand, and relevant properties of the cognitive order that structure and give form to a selection of the constructive inputs, on the other. It thus envelops cognitive structures as well as semantic meanings and pragmatic directions for possible actions and relations. Once cultural models of this kind are available, they play a decisive role not only in generally transmitting structuring force by recursively regulating lower levels such as orientations, actions, communications, and so forth, but especially also in regulating particular, oftentimes temporary, achievements such as agreements about common problems and burning issues or longer-term arrangements such as the founding of organizations and institutions. Such achievements exclude neither persistent rational disagreements nor their initial generation by transformative interventions spearheaded by latent forces or disclosures that had been overlooked, misrecognized, excluded, suppressed, discriminated against, and so forth.

Instances of consilience such as these are among the prime objects of cognitive sociology, but for critical theory the decisive questions concern the formation and role of such composite structures—that is, whether not just reason but "impure reason" (McCarthy 1994:8) substructures their composition; whether they function not just as justifiable cultural models but also as deformed, reified, misleading ones; and, further, whether they contain potentials and as yet unrealized possibilities amenable to disclosure. This is where critical theory's "political epistemology" (Marinopoulou 2017), which presupposes a negative or subtractive ontology and is activated through critical cognitive sociology enters. Methodologically, this approach can fruitfully investigate and diagnose neither the formation of cultural models nor social situations recursively regulated by cultural models unless recourse is had to the incursive impact and structuring effect of the relevant cognitive order principles. Only in the light of such context-transcendent cognitive structures, which are reconciled with the situation by extrapolating the competence-based framed meanings emerging from the actions and communication of those involved, could actual immanent rationality deficits be critically exposed as well as unacknowledged potential rationality surpluses pointing beyond the situation be identified—irrespective whether these surpluses are preserved in dormant human cognitive capacities, one the one hand, or in unexploited linguistic, logical, mathematical, and informational redundancy behind the cognitive order, on the other. For this purpose, it adopts critical theory's characteristic methodological procedure of reconstruction.[11]

Reconstruction makes normative—both negative exposing and positive disclosing—critique possible, but far from being content with these, critical theory seeks to provide also an action- and praxis-oriented explanation and critique of the factors, forces, or processes that generate normatively criticizable situations and obfuscation of potentials and possibilities. Rather than adopting the conventional sociological approach of simply fixing on material power relations and productive forces, for example, the state, science, technology, industrialism, and capitalism, its cognitive-sociological complement requires that also the cognitive structures defining, directing, and guiding such relations and forces, both transcendent principles and immanent cultural models, be taken into account insofar as they operate as real generative mechanisms responsible for deformation or obfuscation (e.g., Strydom 2002).

What is missing from critical theory, however, is the pursuit of the further relation, the one between the sociocultural world and nature. Promising to correct this deficit is the notion of "weak naturalism" that Habermas introduced but left undeveloped and, astonishingly, is ignored by the younger—including both the third and fourth—generations. To forge the full cognitive character of critical theory's explanatory critique it is necessary, therefore, to take weak naturalism seriously beyond the exclusive focus on the sociocultural world. Above all, acknowledging the link between society and nature is imperative if an integral cognitive sociology were to be established.

3.2.2 Weak Naturalism: Elementary Social Forms Between First and Second Nature

The thesis of weak naturalism posits that there is a relation of continuity between nature and the human sociocultural form of life in both an ontological and a cognitive sense, but qualifies it epistemologically.

1. Ontologically, continuity means that there is an intact evolutionary link between the natural historical processes which two million years ago gave rise to the *Homo* line, on the one hand, and the sociocultural form of life of *Homo sapiens sapiens*, which emerged between 60,000 and 30,000 years ago, on the other. Humans and their form of life are an inherent part of nature. Nature has ontological primacy insofar as it gives rise to, provides the natural conditions for, and generally shapes the human sociocultural form of life. Over time, the sociocultural form of life emerged from nature, generally resembling nature, so that even today still in the form of a global capitalist-industrial society it remains in an important respect firmly rooted in nature and basically shaped by it. In this context, however, ontological priority has to be properly understood. As distinct from strict or strong naturalism, which entails a reduction of the sociocultural world to an epiphenomenon of nature, following Habermas (1999, 2003, 2005, 2007) a weak form of naturalism is adopted here. According to this conception, a set of mutually implicating relations holds between nature and the sociocultural world. They form a unity insofar as they are evolutionarily continuous and nature shapes the general character of the sociocultural world, yet they are distinct insofar as they represent different dimensions of reality. Nature enjoys ontological primacy by making the sociocultural world possible and affording it opportunities to develop and articulate itself, but the latter generates and articulates itself through a variety of practices structured, given direction, and guided by ideas which for humans define the order of nature rather than belong to nature. In turn, the continuity with nature is both reinforced and refracted insofar as sociocultural constructs work back on the forms to which natural mechanisms give rise in the first instance.

Although forming part of nature, the sociocultural dimension as defining the order of nature at any particular point in time enjoys epistemological primacy. This is the case for ordinary practices, but all the more so for sociology, which accounts for the fact that the sociocultural world rightly claims the larger part by far of sociologists' attention. It is the domain of human activities that are structured by ideas such as truth, rightness, and authenticity which open potentialities for practices to generate and internally differentiate the sociocultural world and even to transform both it and the face of the earth. Yet, even given its epistemological primacy, it is nevertheless appreciated that this world is to a certain degree still open to the impact of its natural substrate and inheritance and, therefore, both susceptible to being augmented and vulnerable to being limited and confined by it.[12]

2. Continuity between nature and the sociocultural world is not just ontological, however, but also of a cognitive kind. In this respect, cognitive sociology has to learn from the cognitive sciences, including neuroscience, evolutionary biology, developmental and evolutionary psychology, anthropology, and archaeology. Under particular conditions and constraints of reality, the process of evolution not only gave rise to the brain but also, over a period of approximately six millions years before the present, allowed it to enlarge from 500 cm^3 to the approximately 1700 cm^3 of contemporary humans (Van Gelder 2005; Wilson 2012). Based on this physical structure embedded in its environment, the human mind concomitantly evolved from a number of specific—social, physical, biological, technical, and incipient musical-linguistic—modules, cognitive domains or intelligences that lacked the interconnections underpinning the "cognitively fluid" (Mithen 1998) or "cognitively flexible" (Cross 2001) mind of *Homo sapiens sapiens*. The latter is characterized by a metarepresentational module (Sperber 2000) enabling the fully reflexive combination of all the previously isolated modules. This acquisition of the "Human Revolution" (Stringer 2012:116), a veritable cultural explosion, provided a starting point for social and cultural learning processes that are at the center of the creation and organization of the sociocultural form. Since natural historical processes provide emergent properties that, as evolutionarily stabilized structures, make possible social forms allowing social and cultural learning processes and the development and articulation of the sociocultural form of life, they can be regarded as themselves being cognitively significant (Habermas 2003). It can thus be assumed that their cognitive import carries over into the cognitive processes characteristic of the sociocultural world.

Now, it is not just the process of evolution in the sense of hominization, encephalization, and phylogenesis that is ontologically and cognitively significant, however, since there is a whole range of more specific natural processes and their corresponding forms that underpin and are reflected in the sociocultural form of life. Many years ago, Park (1936), for instance, proposed the study of processes falling in the domain of "human ecology," and in the intervening period a manifest concern is observable with processes such as group membership, alliance formation, play, competition, rivalry, dominance, subordination, conflict, reconciliation, and cooperation (e.g., Bateson 1973; Goffman 1974; Hirschfeld 2001; Jackendoff 2004; Conein 2005; Kaufmann and Clément 2007). These are all processes humans share with their *Homo* ancestors as well as with contemporary primates. To such ontologically significant ecological processes Piaget (1983) added a range of cognitively significant coordination processes which, despite qualitative differences, we likewise have in common with our predecessors and primate neighbors. Among them are attending, comparing, counting, relating, combining, ordering, interacting, evaluating, and judging.

The importance of these two sets of processes resides in the fact that they provide both primates and humans with elementary social and practical forms (Kaufmann and Clément 2007) that are categorially graspable.[13] What primates are able to grasp only by means of preverbal categories (Conein 2005), humans elaborate in the linguistic, logical, and mathematical media in the form of categories that quite precisely capture the ecological and coordination processes and their corresponding forms. The significance of the elementary forms, in turn, is that they are the vehicles or bridges that secure the continuity between nature and the human sociocultural form of life.[14] In addition, indeed crucially, the extended human competence given with language, logic, and mathematics allows for the extrapolation of these elementary social forms and the construction and elaboration of their implications into the most defining features of the human sociocultural form of life. Group membership serves as an excellent example of such construction and elaboration (e.g., Jackendoff 2004). On the one hand, group membership is a natural or innate property shared by primates, archaic *Homo sapiens*, *Homo sapiens*, and *Homo sapiens sapiens*, but in the case of the latter, on the other, in-group and intergroup cooperation is a learned sociocultural achievement going well beyond the underlying form provided by natural mechanisms and intuitive experiential cognition. It is precisely due to this particular nature of theirs that such elementary forms become a major concern of a cognitive sociology that not only starts from critical theory but also seeks to activate the full range of its critical capacity.

3. The notion of weak naturalism and, especially, elementary forms raise the question of the relation between what may be called first and second nature. "First nature" refers most basically to φύσις, *natura*, or *natura naturans*, in the sense of both a creative, productive, and serendipitous force and a law of inheritance in accordance with which the sociocultural world generally resembles its original source.[15] Second nature, by contrast, refers to the sociocultural world as a second or quasi-reality building on and potentially stretching beyond the resemblance imparted to it by first nature. The concern with second nature as such has a long, albeit submerged, history in the tradition of critical theory, with authors like Lukács, Marcuse, and Adorno, but also Apel (1984) and Habermas (1987, 2005), employing the expression while being acutely aware that second nature—the core subject matter of the social sciences—is an inherently ambivalent phenomenon. Now, it is this peculiar quality of the sociocultural form of life, best grasped in cognitive terms, that should be at the center of critical-theoretical investigation. What the critical theorists did not pursue was this ambivalence in terms of the relation of second to first nature.

As regards its ambivalent quality (Apel 1984), the sociocultural form of life is on the one hand composed of common-sense, habits, and conventions, among which are personality structures, social practices, institutions, social systems, and cultural models. They represent a whole range of historically developed and sedimented quasi-nature that—as should be stressed—derive originally from, yet remaining rooted in, the elementary forms generated and shaped by ecological and coordination processes. Through the elementary forms, nature not only makes sociocultural life possible, affording it opportunities and substructuring it so as to make it resemble nature. Simultaneously, natural mechanisms and intuitive experiential cognition also lay down elementary parameters, delimiting the sociocultural world and thus restricting and confining it in multiple ways. For example, social forms deriving from processes such as dominance, subordination, and conflict shared with primates not only continue to live on and exert themselves in social life, but they often become fixed by distorted or reified cultural models that ensure their odious efficacy in the structuring of personalities, social practices, relations, organizations, institutions, and systems.

On the other hand, however, humans have proved able, at least to some by no means negligible degree, to free themselves from the fetters of such natural primitives and the limits they impose on sociocultural forms. Through learning and enlightenment of some sort, they succeeded in emancipating themselves psychologically, socially, institutionally, and culturally from natural mechanisms and intuitive cognition. In felicitous cases, they were thus able to construct and communicatively articulate meaningful sociocultural forms, perhaps most spectacularly recognizing emergent ideas of reason, universal principles or metacultural cognitive structures which, in an incursive feedback loop, call up actors and inspire practices that articulate and transform the sociocultural world, at times for the better. For example, humans learned to emancipate themselves sufficiently to formulate such cognitive order principles as truth, efficiency, right, justice, freedom, equality, solidarity, truthfulness, and authenticity and, on that basis, to co-responsibly generate knowledge and construct constitutional democracies of different kinds and international regimes of civil, social, cultural, and human rights—however inadequate these might still be at present. We owe the establishment of both the metacultural cognitive order and the corresponding cultural models enabling emancipated practices to such unique human achievements.

4. Earlier, it was argued that in negatively exposing the deformations of undesirable and unjustifiable social situations and positively disclosing their unacknowledged potentialities, critical theory employs its characteristic methodological procedure of reconstruction to extrapolate the situational sense of the relevant cognitive order principles from human capacities and competences and the understandings and meanings generated by the actors and their audience. The reconstructively confirmed principles provide not only a measure for both an exposing and disclosing normative critique of the situation, however, but also a basis for the explanation and critique of the role real mechanisms such as material power relations and productive forces play in causing problematic social conditions. If this describes the principal methodological thrust of critical theory in its focus on the sociocultural world, then it is only half the story from the viewpoint of a complementary integral cognitive sociology. While the link to nature is indeed asserted by the thesis of weak naturalism, in critical theory it has not been substantiated, not to mention its cognitive significance adequately recognized. From a cognitive-sociological perspective, the elementary social forms deriving from evolutionarily shaped mechanisms on the side of nature are as important to critical theory as the presupposed cognitive order principles on the sociocultural side. These elementary forms not only link nature and the sociocultural world, but they also lie behind many a fault line running through the inherently ambivalent sociocultural form of life and, hence, behind the prevailing quasi-natural, historically sedimented personality structures, habits, practices, conventions, and cultural models that are still to a significant extent caught in the constraining web of natural mechanisms and intuitive cognition.

It is generally recognized that the behavior of any animal or human is partly influenced by its genetic make-up and partly by its developmental environment, partly by nature and partly by nurture. The relative weighting of these two forces varies markedly not only between species but also between different aspects of behavior within a single species (Mithen 1998). As regards humans, certain practices are much more prone to remain caught up, often unnecessarily, in elementary social forms deriving from nature than others that attain higher degrees of emancipation and freedom within the sociocultural world. Such attainment requires learning, and according to Bateson (1973:278), "The broad history of the evolution of learning seems to have been a slow pushing back of genetic determinism to levels of higher logical type." This lucid grasp of the shift from nature to the sociocultural world—perhaps the most basic social-scientific law—can be taken not only as confirmation of the necessity of weak naturalism as an essential presupposition of critical theory enhanced by cognitive sociology but also as pointing to its primary task of explanatory critique aimed at advancing learning by pushing back the limits nature imposes on the sociocultural form of life. It is inadequate, for example, to tackle unjustifiable domination strictly in its sociocultural context if this social pathology is rooted in primate dominance, the fetters of which need to be pushed back still further than thus far. Similarly, those persistent problematic practices in modern society regulated by at least partly distorted and reified cultural orientation complexes that indisputably contribute disproportionately to the global risk of climate change, for example, cannot be transformed without critically tracing them also to their roots in elementary natural social forms (e.g., Strydom 2015c). The efficacy of critical theory's explanatory critique in many if not all cases hinges on this naturalistic detour.

3.3 Conclusion

Critical theory stands in need of an integral cognitive sociology. First, it requires cognitive sociology to give depth to its reconstructively based, normatively critical analysis of the sociocultural world in both exposing and disclosing registers. Only a cognitive sociology in command of the cognitive order of the sociocultural form of life is capable of fulfilling this task, since it alone allows critical theory to open up that part of the world that is yet to be imagined and realized by human beings. To do this to the fullest extent possible, however, critical theory secondly requires a cognitive sociology adept at dealing appropriately with naturalism to meet the demands of the explanatory critique of deep-seated mechanisms necessary to impel and reinforce the kind of learning that secures the civilizing distance of the sociocultural form of life from nature. But to critically disclose and make visible the unacknowledged potentials harbored by organically endowed human capacities and elementary social forms once again calls for an articulated conception of the cognitive order.

Lacking the support of such a double-edged integral cognitive sociology, critical theory would be unable simultaneously to conserve the founding act of the human revolution of 60,000–30,000 years ago and to continue critically contributing to the development of the spectacular sociocultural achievements of the past three or so millennia. While critical theory urgently requires this type of cognitive sociology, it is apparent in the light of this civilizational demand that, conversely, contemporary cognitive sociology is as much in need of being complemented by a critical theoretical approach.

Notes

1. Some critical theorists reject—albeit erroneously—the cognitive approach, for example Honneth (Strydom 2012a).
2. For critical overviews of this wide literature, see Strydom (1987a, 1987b/2009, 1990, 1992, 1993).
3. A critical evaluation is presented in Strydom (2013).
4. See note 2 for relevant literature.
5. Eder wrote this essay at my request for a special issue of the *European Journal of Social Theory* on types of cognitive sociology after the cognitive revolution—on which see Strydom (2007).
6. Rather than just linguistic, these conditions also include logic and mathematics as well as the implicated informational redundancy.
7. The cognitive archaeologist Mithen (1998) consistently uses this designation to refer to the contemporary version of the human species.
8. The origin of the cognitive order can be traced to the cultural revolution of 60,000–30,000 years ago (Mithen 1998; Wilson 2012; Stringer 2012), while its beginnings are observable at the latest in the first millennium BCE.
9. Strydom (2012b) offers the example of the formation of a cosmopolitan cultural model.
10. For the—indeed cognitively significant—negative or subtractive ontological dimension complementing the positive presentation in Figure 3.3, which is left in the background in the present context, see in general Adorno (1970) and for specifics Strydom (2017b).
11. For an account of contemporary critical theory and its methodology, see Strydom (2011).
12. A graphic example of the mutual implication of nature and the sociocultural world is the new period of the "Anthropocene," including global warming and climate change, on which see Strydom (2015c, 2017a).
13. The treatment of this issue obviously invokes Durkheim's classical inquiry in his last great work, but goes back behind his conception of elementary forms, avoids his ambivalence about the relation between society and nature, and is more systematic about the cognitive dimension.
14. Kaufmann and Clément (2007:50) regard "universal social forms that characterize primary forms of life" as the "ontological 'missing link'" between nature and culture—for example, between "individual organisms and collective symbolic representations"—rather than mental states or physical objects, as is widely assumed by naturalists.
15. Peirce (1998:121) draws the distinction between nature as a force and as a law.

References

Adorno, Theodor W. 1970. *Negative Dialektik*. Frankfurt: Suhrkamp.

Apel, Karl-Otto. 1980. *Towards a Transformation of Philosophy*. London: Routledge & Kegan Paul.

Apel, Karl-Otto. 1981. *Charles S. Peirce: From Pragmatism to Pragmaticism*. Amherst, MA: University of Massachusetts Press.

Apel, Karl-Otto. 1984. *Understanding and Explanation: A Transcendental-Pragmatic Perspective*. Cambridge, MA: MIT Press.

Aristotle. 2015. *Physics*. Adelaide: University of Adelaide.

Bateson, Gregory. 1973. *Steps to an Ecology of Mind*. Frogmore, UK: Paladin.

Conein, Bernard. 2005. *Les sens sociaux*. Paris: Economica.

Cross, Ian. 2001. "Music, Cognition, Culture and Evolution." *Annals of the New York Academy of Sciences* 930:28–42.

Dantzig, Tobias. 2007. *Number*. London: Plume.

Eder, Klaus. 1996. *The Social Construction of Nature*. London: SAGE.

Eder, Klaus. 1999. "Societies Learn and Yet the World Is Hard to Change." *European Journal of Social Theory* 2(2):195–215.

Eder, Klaus. 2007. "Cognitive Sociology and the Theory of Communicative Action." *European Journal of Social Theory* 10(3):389–408.

Eyerman, Ron, and Andrew Jamison. 1991. *Social Movements: A Cognitive Approach*. Cambridge: Polity.

Goffman, Erving. 1974. *Frame Analysis*. New York: Harper & Row.

Habermas, Jürgen. 1979. *Communication and the Evolution of Society*. London: Heinemann.

Habermas, Jürgen. 1984. *The Theory of Communicative Action*. Vol. 1. London: Heinemann.

Habermas, Jürgen. 1987. *The Theory of Communicative Action*. Vol. 2. Cambridge: Polity.

Habermas, Jürgen. 1999. *Wahrheit und Rechtfertigung*. Frankfurt: Suhrkamp.

Habermas, Jürgen. 2003. *Truth and Justification*. Cambridge: Polity.

Habermas, Jürgen. 2005. *Zwischen Naturalismus und Religion*. Frankfurt: Suhrkamp.

Habermas, Jürgen. 2007. "The Language Game of Responsible Agency and the Problem of Free Will." *Philosophical Explorations* 10(1):13–50.

Hirschfeld, Lawrence. 2001. "On a Folk Theory of Society." *Personality and Social Psychology Review* 5(2):107–17.

Jackendoff, Ray. 1999. *Languages of the Mind*. Cambridge, MA: MIT Press.

Jackendoff, Ray. 2004. "Toward a Cognitive Science of Culture and Society." Pinkel Lecture, University of Pennsylvania. Retrieved December 13, 2013. http://www.ircs.upenn.edu/pinkel/lectures/jackendoff/index.shtml.

Kant, Immanuel. 1956. *Critique of Practical Reason*. New York: Bobbs-Merrill.

Kant, Immanuel. 1968. *Critique of Pure Reason*. London: Macmillan.

Kant, Immanuel. 1972. *Critique of Judgement*. New York: Hafner.

Kaufmann, Laurence, and Fabrice Clément. 2007. "How Culture Comes to Mind." *Intellectica* 2:46–75.

Leibniz, Gottfried Wilhelm. 1965. *The Monadology and Other Philosophical Writings*. London: Oxford University Press.

Marinopoulou, Anastasia. 2017. *Critical Theory and Epistemology*. Manchester: Manchester University Press.

McCarthy, Thomas. 1994. "Philosophy and Critical Theory: A Reprise." pp. 5–100 in *Critical Theory*, edited by D. C. Hoy and T. McCarthy. Oxford: Blackwell.

Miller, Max. 1986. *Kollektive Lernprozesse*. Frankfurt: Suhrkamp.

Miller, Max. 2002. "Some Theoretical Aspects of Systemic Learning." *Sozialer Sinn* 3:379–421.

Mithen, Steven. 1998. *The Prehistory of the Mind*. London: Phoenix.

Park, Robert. 1936. "Human Ecology." *American Journal of Sociology* 42:1–15.

Peirce, Charles Sanders. 1998. *The Essential Peirce*. Vol. 2. Bloomington: Indiana University Press.

Piaget, Jean. 1983. *Meine Theorie der geistigen Entwicklung*. Frankfurt: Fischer.

Sperber, Dan., ed. 2000. *Metarepresentations*. Oxford: Oxford University Press.

Stringer, Chris. 2012. *The Origin of Our Species*. London: Penguin.

Strydom, Piet. 1987a. "Collective Learning: Habermas's Concessions and Their Theoretical Implications." *Philosophy and Social Criticism* 13(3):265–81.

Strydom, Piet. 1987b/2009. "The Construction of Collective Identity: The South African Liberation Movement as a Collective Learning Process, 1882–1987." pp. 197–215 in *New Horizons of Critical Theory: Collective Learning and Triple Contingency*. New Delhi: Shipra.

Strydom, Piet. 1990. "Habermas and New Social Movements." *Telos* 85:156–64.

Strydom, Piet. 1992. "The Ontogenetic Fallacy: The Immanent Critique of Habermas's Developmental-Logical Theory of Evolution." *Theory, Culture and Society* 9(3):65–93.

Strydom, Piet. 1993. "Sociocultural Evolution or the Evolution of Practical Reason: Eder's Critique of Habermas." *Praxis International* 13(3):304–22.

Strydom, Piet. 1996. "The Cognitive Order of Modernity: The 'Scaffolding of Modernity' or the Rights Frame?" Unpublished paper, Centre for European Social Research, University College Cork. https://ucc-ie.academia.edu/P/Strydom.

Strydom, Piet. 1999. "Triple Contingency: The Theoretical Problem of the Public in Communication Societies." *Philosophy and Social Criticism* 25(2):1–25.

Strydom, Piet. 2000. *Discourse and Knowledge*. Liverpool: Liverpool University Press.

Strydom, Piet. 2002. *Risk, Environment and Society*. Buckingham: Open University Press.

Strydom, Piet. 2007. "Introduction: A Cartography of Contemporary Cognitive Social Theory." *European Journal of Social Theory* 10(3):339–56.

Strydom, Piet. 2011. *Contemporary Critical Theory and Methodology*. London: Routledge.

Strydom, Piet. 2012a. "Cognition and Recognition: On the Problem of the Cognitive in Honneth." *Philosophy and Social Criticism* 38(6):591–607.

Strydom, Piet. 2012b. "Toward a Global Cosmopolis? On the Formation of a Cosmopolitan Cultural Model." *Irish Journal of Sociology* 20(2):28–50.

Strydom, Piet. 2013. "The Counterfactual Imagination Punctuated by Triple Contingency: On Klaus Eder's Theory of the New Public Sphere." pp. 56–74 in *Rethinking the Public Sphere through Transnationalizing Processes*, edited by A. Salvatore, O. Schmidtke, and H.-J. Trenz. Houndmills, UK: Palgrave Macmillan.

Strydom, Piet. 2015a. "The Latent Cognitive Sociology in Habermas: Extrapolated from 'Between Facts and Norms.'" *Philosophy and Social Criticism* 41(3):273–91.

Strydom, Piet. 2015b. "Critical Theory of Justice: On Forst's 'Basic Structure of Justification' from a Cognitive Sociological Perspective." *Philosophical Inquiry* 39(2):110–33.

Strydom, Piet. 2015c. "Cognitive Fluidity and Climate Change: A Critical-Theoretical Approach to the Current Challenge." *European Journal of Social Theory* 18(3):236–56.

Strydom, Piet. 2017a. "The Sociocultural Self-Creation of a Natural Category: Social-Theoretical Reflections on Human Agency under the Temporal Conditions of the Anthropocene." *European Journal of Sociology* 20(1):61–79.

Strydom, Piet. 2017b. "Critical Theory's Negative or Subtractive Ontology: Seminar Theses." Presented at the Critical Theory and Cognitive Sociology Seminar, Harbour View, Kilbrittain, Co. Cork, Ireland, December 20. https://ucc-ie.academia.edu/P/Strydom.

Strydom, Piet. 2018. "The Problem of Limit Concepts in Habermas." *Philosophical Inquiry* 42(1–2):168–89.

Van Gelder, Nico. 2005. "The Integration of Body and Mind." *Current Sociology* 53(2):323–54.

Wilson, Edward O. 2012. *The Social Conquest of Earth*. New York: Liveright.

CHAPTER 4

PIERRE BOURDIEU AS COGNITIVE SOCIOLOGIST

OMAR LIZARDO

INTRODUCTION

It is now well established that Pierre Bourdieu's overall oeuvre can be interpreted, in its essence, as a form of cognitive sociology (Lizardo 2004). Yet, given the broad scope of what the notion of cognition is taken to refer to across the human and social sciences (Wilson 2004; Zerubavel this volume), the question of *what kind* of cognitive sociology Bourdieu was proffering can become a subject for debate (Lizardo 2011, 2012). In this chapter, I argue that if Bourdieu is taken up to be a theorist of the relationship between the "social" and the "cognitive"—as he characterized it himself (Bourdieu 1996b:1–3)— then there is only one way in which we can interpret his conception of the latter notion, and that is as a form of *embodied* cognition (Clark 1997; Lizardo and Strand 2010; see also Cerulo this volume; Ignatow this volume; Martin this volume).

   Put succinctly, embodied cognition approaches are distinct in viewing the bodily structure and the particular experiences the body affords as an *essential* aspect (both in terms of structure and process) of the activities that have usually been labeled "cognitive." These include perception, categorization, morality, social interaction, and reasoning among others (Lakoff and Johnson 1999). The thesis of embodied cognition stands opposed to "classical" approaches in cognitive science and artificial intelligence developed in the 1950s and 1960s that viewed cognition as essentially a form of "computation" conceptualized as the manipulation and "processing" of abstract symbols with no natural connection to the body and the world (Dreyfus 1992). Within this latter paradigm, the mind was only contingently embodied in the brain, and its operations could be described as a "physical symbol system" of which (universal) computers were also an instance (Newell 1980). Embodied or "enactive" cognitive neuroscience is now considered one of the most promising strands of work in the field (Chemero 2011; Hutto and Myin 2013; Wheeler 2005). It is also the one that displays the most promise of unifying the cognitive neurosciences with all the other human and social sciences (Wilson 2004). In these respects, Bourdieu's approach can be considered having been not only eminently on the right track and ahead of his time, but also a still relatively underexplored source of fundamental insights into the relation of culture, action, and cognition.

The notion of embodiment or embodied cognition itself, is polysemous, carrying distinct meanings across different areas of inquiry (Rohrer 2010; Wilson 2002). Thus, even if we are to agree that Bourdieu's cognitive sociology belongs within embodied cognitive science, we still need to make clear what we mean by embodiment. In what follows, I differentiate some related (but analytically distinct) meanings of embodiment, as these may help us specify exactly how Bourdieu is a cognitive sociologist. I then consider one recently documented empirical phenomenon relevant to the embodiment discussion as it relates to Bourdieu: What has been referred to as "the hard embodiment of culture." This represents an impressive empirical vindication (outside of sociology and anthropology) of the basic principles of embodied cognitive sociology developed by Bourdieu. I close by outlining the conceptual and empirical challenges (focusing on contemporary cultural theory in sociology) that come from considering the possibility that what has traditionally been referred to as "culture" may come to be "internalized" by actors in particularly "hard" and "soft" embodied ways.

4.1 EMBODIMENT IN CONTEMPORARY SOCIAL ANALYSIS

Theoretical reflections on "embodiment" are now ubiquitous in the human, social, and cognitive sciences (Lizardo 2015). In the social sciences, a concern with embodiment has influenced areas as disparate as studies of science and technology, cultural and cognitive sociology, organizational analysis, interactionist theory, ethnography, the sociology of emotions, the sociology of gender, and the sociology of religion. The basic impulse that holds together these disparate appeals to the notion of embodiment is a rejection of classical and postclassical (symbolist and structuralist) models of enculturation and action. In this respect, the developmental arc of Bourdieu's basic notions (e.g., habitus, practice, field) can be read as a protracted movement away from disembodied structuralist accounts of cultural meaning as an abstract relation between absent differences and towards an embodied and embedded view of cognition, perception as grounded in bodily action (Lizardo 2011).

4.1.1 Senses of Embodiment

(a) *The embodiment of cultural meaning.* Sometimes embodiment theorists have in mind a particular approach to the analysis of (linguistic) meaning. For instance, in Lakoff and

Johnson's (1980) influential conceptual metaphor theory, the notion of embodiment is brought in to explain the asymmetric dependence of certain metaphors on core domains of experience. For instance, MORE IS UP ("inflation rates have shot to the sky") or STATES ARE LOCATIONS ("my career has stalled at this juncture"). Because the domain of verticality or locomotion in space are fundamental to our experience as embodied beings, this explain why metaphors drawn from these source domains are systematically recruited to conceptualize more abstract realms of experience but not the other way around.

Recent attempts (e.g., by the cognitive psychologist Lawrence Barsalou [1999]) to move beyond "amodal" theories of meaning (the notion that knowledge is stored in long-term memory in a format separate from the sensory modalities) can also be thought as relying on the notion of the embodiment of conceptual meaning (Ignatow 2007). This naturally extends to a consideration of the embodiment of lexical, grammatical, and linguistic meaning as is characteristic of modern cognitive linguistics (Rohrer 2010).

This notion of embodiment undoubtedly played a central role in Bourdieu's cognitive sociology. For instance, Bourdieu's discussion of the "practical metaphors" governing the spatial and visual texture of the Kabyle household (Bourdieu 1970), is essentially an anticipation of the Lakoff-Johnson conception of embodiment as a way to move beyond the "digital" (disembodied) conception of meaning developed in Levi-Straussian structuralism (Bourdieu 1996a:314–315). In Bourdieu's account, the Kabyle household is organized around a set of bodily grounded oppositions activated during routine practical action such as left-right, front-back, and so on (Bloch 1986), some of which are inscribed to the very spatial (e.g., east/west) orientation of the various regions of the house. These, along with the calendrical rhythms associated with the various activities (e.g., sleeping, cooking, entertaining guests), come to be experientially correlated with certain qualities (dark/light, inside/outside, dry/moist). These are inclusive of the typical presence of members of each gender in each region, which come to attach "gendered" meanings to these qualities and spaces, thus resulting in more "abstract" correspondences (e.g., male: dry: female: wet).

(b) The embodiment of subjectivity. Here the notion of embodiment is a platform with which to move beyond certain long-standing aporias in the analysis of mind, reason, and subjectivity that come from the Western rationalist (Platonic and Descartesian) and critical-rationalist (Kantian/Hegelian) traditions. The basic idea here (particularly powerful in contemporary feminist philosophy) is that the notion of a disembodied subject independent of bodily sensations, experience, perspective, and emotion is a fiction. Embodiment provides an escape from the "view from nowhere" conception of subjectivity, providing instead a platform from which to theorize the subject as an inherently perspectival phenomenon.

Following the lead of such thinkers as Heidegger and Merleau-Ponty, persons are conceived as fundamentally embodied subjects endowed with the rootedness, particularity, and finitude that such a condition entails. Philosophical accounts of embodiment are sometimes brought into dialogue with classical sources in social theory (e.g., Marx, Weber, Durkheim) in order to either point to the drawbacks that come from the inheritance of pernicious philosophical postulates by the classical theorists, or to point to their prescient attempts to escape from those postulates. In this respect, Bourdieu's somewhat underappreciated (perhaps due to the its particular relevance to the French context) critique of the Sartrean notion of the self (or "I") as a "pure" a-substantial center of consciousness that is only *contingently* embodied is strongly rooted in this "philosophical" account of cognition as *inherently* embodied inspired by Merleau-Ponty (Crossley 2001).

(c) The embodiment of sociocultural activity. Alternatively, analysts may use the notion of embodiment as a sensitizing concept that is brought to the field to enrich situated descriptions of concrete empirical settings. This may happen in various forms, from recent symbolic interactionist attempts to link long-standing concerns with the development of meaning via significant symbols with the concrete challenges and opportunities that come from considering the role of the lived body in this process (Waskul and Vannini 2006), to more recent attempts (exemplified in Loïc Wacquant's (2004b) call to "follow Bourdieu to the field") to enrich analytical ethnography with first-person accounts of the acquisition of practical dispositions (both "cognitive" and "motor"). Both traditions use the notion of embodiment to provide richer accounts of lived experience in the field (which may involve dramatic cognitive, emotive, and physical transformations). Wacquant's "carnal sociology" (2004a), therefore, can be considered an extension and radicalization of the embodied cognition account of mind and activity first developed in Bourdieu's fieldwork among the Kabyle and later extended to the understanding of taste and cognition in the France of his time (Bourdieu 1984, 1996b).

(d) The external embodiment of cognition. This perspective is more common in social scientific studies of science and technology including the study of interactions between persons, artifacts, and lived environments. In addition to being "embodied" in the (lived) physical body of persons, knowledge and experience also comes to be embodied in a variety of extrapersonal sites. Here a concern with embodiment links to a sensitivity to materiality as an important dimension of social and cultural life (McDonnell 2016). Here "embodiment" is a catch-all phrase to denote most forms of the cognitive externalization of meaning and action, and the problem of interfacing physical bodies with externalized aids to knowledge, perception, and experience (prototypically scientific instruments). This sense of embodiment is muted (but not absent) in Bourdieu's work, probably due to the residual concern with the structural analysis of discursive and symbolic systems that characterized the majority of his empirical work (Lizardo 2011).

(e) The embodiment of the cognitive unconscious. This sense of embodiment, more common in the cognitive than in the social sciences (see, for instance, Lakoff and Johnson's [1999] work on embodiment in philosophical discourse) acquires more relevance in social and cultural analysis via the influence of practice theory. This is the strongest sense in which Bourdieu's work can be considered a form of cognitive sociology, since for Bourdieu, the cognitive unconscious was the actual repository of collective representations in the Durkheimian sense (Lizardo 2004).

Here, the body (and embodiment) is the site of the "internalization of exteriority" so that environmental conditionings are transformed into active dispositions pre-adapted to the world and operating in an implicit state (Strand and Lizardo 2015). Embodiment plays a key role here because what is from another perspective seen as rooted in representational abstractions (e.g., values, beliefs) are conceived here as rooted in fundamental comportments of the body (Lizardo 2009). Enculturation, then resolves itself in the conditioning of the body to generate the subjective attitudes that are required in each situation (Lizardo 2017; Strauss and Quinn 1997). This sense of embodiment provides a rare avenue of dialogue between cultural analysts in anthropology and sociology, and cognitive scientific work concerned with theorizing implicit and unconscious phenomena (Cerulo 2015; Wacquant 2013). This may range from cognitive-emotive appreciative, moral, and cognitive dispositions, to "procedural" competences embodied as know-how and skill (Downey 2014; Pálsson 1994).

4.1.2 Making Sense of Embodiment

This brief (and by design selective) consideration of the various usages of the notion of embodiment in the contemporary social and cultural sciences provides us with a platform to differentiate between different analytical deployments of the notion as it pertains to our consideration of Bourdieu's cognitive sociology. I consider the consequences (if any) these different conceptions of embodiment have for how we understand the process via which persons become "encultured," with the caveat that Bourdieu's own version of cognitive sociology did not itself conceive of the internalization of experience as "enculturation" (Lizardo 2011). The reason for this choice is that while "culture" as an analytic category may not have been useful to Bourdieu, it is nonnegotiable in the contemporary landscape of the social and human sciences (Lizardo 2017). The question to ask therefore, is the extent to which the basic premises of Bourdieu's own cognitive sociology, built as they are on a particular commitment to some of the notions of embodiment discussed earlier, pose "trouble" for traditional conceptions of culture and enculturation dominant in the social sciences today.

My argument is that business as usual in contemporary cultural analysis faces a bigger challenge depending on which (combination) of the senses of embodiment we adopt. The differences in emphasis across these conceptions are important because they in part determine both the phenomena conceived as relevant in a given empirical setting and the empirical material we as analysts (and our methods) will be sensitive to. For instance, a theorist who does not see linguistic meaning as embodied in sense *(a)*, from Section 4.1.1, will miss the plethora of conceptual metaphors whose source domain is embodied even when her subjects express them overtly (Ignatow 2007, 2009, 2016). In the same way, an analyst blind to the embodiment of culture in the cognitive unconscious will perforce overestimate the influence of explicit (e.g., linguistic) factors (Lizardo 2017).

Mostly, while "philosophical" conceptions of embodiment have had a salutary role in reorienting cultural analysis, they have not changed the basic parameters of contemporary research in the social and cultural sciences in a fundamental way. The problem is that in taking "embodiment" as a constitutive category rather than as an empirically specifiable phenomenon, philosophically oriented embodiment theories err on the side of overgeneralization. This may account for the lack of bite of Bourdieu's critique of Sartre as a point of departure for discussions of embodiment in contemporary social and cultural theory.

Both embodiment of meaning and phenomenological accounts have fared better precisely because they stick closer to their respective empirical settings (Uhlmann 2000). Lakoff and Johnson's work on conceptual metaphor has launched a veritable revolution in the contemporary study of language and meaning; the embodied-phenomenology turn in ethnography has revitalized qualitative fieldwork across a variety of areas, moving the analyst from mere participant observation to "observant participation" (see, for instance, the work of Desmond [2007], Wacquant [2004a], Mears [2011], Winchester [2008], and Pagis [2010]—among others—in the United States).

Externalized embodiment accounts (as in the classic work of the anthropologist Edwin Hutchins [1995]) have also brought the field forward, but are less directly related to the central problem of internalization and enculturation in cultural analysis. Because they rely on externalized, materially manifested meaning, externalization theorists do not have to worry about the hard problem of enculturation and internalization (Collins 2010). In many respects, the traditional observational tools of the social sciences (ethnography and the in-depth interview) have always been more calibrated to capture processes of meaning externalization than they have the more covert process of "internalization" and enculturation.

The more we move away from embodiment as an acknowledgment of the broad experiential limits and potentialities opened by our status as embodied subjects (senses *b*, *c*, and *d* from Section 4.1.1), and more toward embodiment as the bodily substrate of meaning and experience (senses *a*, and *e* from Section 4.1.1) the more problematic is a consideration of meaning as rooted in bodily experience and the body as the repository of the cognitive unconscious from standard accounts of the link between culture and action in social theory.

4.2 Bourdieu and the Hard Embodiment of Culture

There is now a systematic body of evidence across the social and cognitive sciences showing that (1) persons come to embody (via direct experience) forms of "personal culture" (Lizardo 2017; Strauss and Quinn 1997); (2) that this stock of personal culture can be systematically activated, retrieved and used in context (Higgins and Brendl 1995); (3) that, once activated, personal culture can have a powerful influence on subsequent cognition, emotion, judgment, and action across settings (Barsalou et al. 2003); and (4) the activation of this culture happens not via linguistic or symbolic elicitation or interpretation mechanisms but via direct manipulation (e.g., changes in posture) of states of the body. I refer (following the psychologists Dov Cohen and Angela Yeung (2009)) to this culture as having been subjected to "hard embodiment." As Cohen and Yeung make clear, the hard embodiment phenomenon was directly presaged and first articulated in Bourdieu's discussion of internalization in *Logic of Practice*.

In cognitive psychology, the phenomenon of hard embodiment of culture was first hinted at in (now well-established) research establishing the sensitivity of the personal use of high-level cognitive and affective processes to seemingly "irrelevant" states of the body. The deployment of seemingly "abstract" concepts and ideas seems to have a strong dependence on the "state of the body" of the person at the time in which those concepts are being put to use. These bodily states carry a form of "analog" meaning that may elicit semantically compatible (or interfere with semantically incompatible) cognitions and emotions (Glenberg and Gallese 2012).

Thus, persons forced to nod while attempting to process a persuasive message under time pressure are more likely to agree with the speaker; persons made to carry a heavy object when listening to a message give higher estimates of its importance (e.g., "weight"); persons forced to hold a pen between their teeth (eliciting a forced smile) report a more positive mood afterward; persons who are forced to puff their chest and open their arms are more likely to report feelings of exaltation and pride; when asked to recognize "powerful" words under time pressure, persons find it easier to do it when the words are presented in the upper part of the computer screen than when they are forced to look at the lower part, and so on (see Gallagher 2005, for a review).

Essentially the notion of hard embodiment extends this embodied elicitation mechanism toward more complex elements usually studied under symbolic approaches to culture: namely, belief and value systems (Lizardo 2009). The basic idea is that, rather than being first acquired via the direct internalization of elaborate symbolic representations, belief and value systems are first inculcated via the routine enactments of bodily comportments and only later elaborated in terms of high level symbolic representations. This is precisely the mechanism that Bourdieu (1990) proposed when interpreting his ethnographic data from the Kabyle in *Logic of Practice* (and as first codified in Mauss's classic essay on "techniques of the body" [1973]; see also Ignatow this volume). Routine enactments include specific ways of "sitting, standing, walking, eating, praying, gazing, hugging, relaxing, washing, and so on" (Cohen and Leung 2009:1279; see also Leung et al. 2011). In this way, the "strong" senses of embodiment discussed earlier can readily understand how cognition can be embodied within a sociocultural context (Schubert and Semin 2009).

The discovery of hard embodiment of culture shows that the body functions precisely as described in Bourdieu's cognitive sociology: As a "living memory pad" (Bourdieu 1990:68); the substrate of the cognitive unconscious where culture is embodied in a particularly durable way (in the sense *e* from Section 4.1.1). There is a systematic nonarbitrary link between the meaning (encoded in "analog" or "iconic" form) in the bodily posture and the abstract high-level meaning (or emotional quality) elicited by that posture. A classic example of this connection is the link between power and the above/below axis in "vertical classification" discussed in early work by Schwartz (1981) in sociology and corroborated experimentally in a series of studies by Schubert (2005) in psychology. The elicitation of hard-embodied culture may be expanded and made even more complex by embedding routine enactments in externalized forms of embodiment (sense *d* from Section 4.1.1), thus recruiting artifacts (with their specific affordances) and constructing (and changing) specific material environments that predispose persons towards particular cognitive and emotional states consistent with abstract belief and value systems. For instance, Bourdieu's (1991) classic discussion of the situated use of the *skeptron* to both display (to others) and *elicit* (in self) feelings of the authority of the spoken word is an example of this latter version of the effect.

In this way, the notion of hard-embodiment links most directly to senses *(a)* and *(e)* from Section 4.1.1, related to the embodiment of cultural meaning. Postures (standing tall versus slouching), ways of doing things (energetically or lethargically, with sweeping or fine-grained movements) and position in physical space (standing above or below; sitting at the "head" of the table) carry experiential, primary, embodied meaning (Schubert 2005; Toren 1999). For instance, partaking of the same substance (via ingestion), non-negotiably leads to the conception we share a common substance. In this respect, most instances of constituting "communal" relations are "hard embodied" in rituals sharing this aspect (Fiske 2004). These "hard-embodied" meanings then feed into those encoded in more complex ideological systems requiring more explicit symbolic representation. The direction of meaning construction is asymmetric, in the sense that relatively disembodied realms of meaning (e.g., abstract philosophical principles) must recruit this hard-embodied culture for semantic specification (via conceptual metaphors and analogies) and not the other way around (Lakoff and Johnson 1999).

The key lesson is that when the things that social scientists refer to as "culture" are learned via hard embodiment, complex orientations can be elicited via the habitual incitement to adopt specific bodily postures during the performance of typical everyday routines by socialization agents. In this way, routine enactments prepare the ground for the activation, retrieval, and access of more complex cognitive emotive complexes, including beliefs, ideologies, worldviews, and cosmologies. These may include gender-based ideologies (Uhlmann and Uhlmann 2005), or more complex "value" complexes (Hitlin and Piliavin 2004). In this respect the proposition that "complex sentiments may be embodied, in the sense that the physical movements of our body promote or predispose us to adhere to certain mindsets, and these mindsets can be associated with relatively complex and nuanced judgments about the world and moral behavior" (Cohen and Leung 2009:1279) has gone from theoretical speculation to well-supported thesis.

For instance, Cohen and Leung show that a classic cultural pattern in the functionalist tradition, namely the universalism-particularism distinction, can be hard-embodied. In a study designed to tap how the availability of these different cultural schemas depended on certain patterns of embodiment researchers asked both Anglo-American and Asian American participants to respond to a series of ethical dilemmas that involved accessing either universalistic or particularistic cultural patterns. Researchers found that when participants were asked to embody a physical posture of rectitude (holding your chin above a string placed at the required height) while answering the questionnaire both Anglo- and Asian American participants were more likely to provide answers consistent with universalism. However, when asked to provide answers embodying a more "relational" posture (e.g., hugging a pillow) Asian Americans but not Anglo-Americans were more likely to provide answers consistent with particularism (Cohen and Leung 2009:1283).

The group-specificity of this result suggests, as argued earlier, that embodiment can only evoke preexisting moral codes rather than drawing on disorganized bits of culture. Anglos have access to predominantly universalistic patterns while Asian Americans have access to both particularistic and universalistic criteria as equally legitimate platforms for moral reasoning. Similar culture-specific evocations of complex moral attitudes via routine embodiments have been observed for such cultural complexes as ideas of honor and masculinity, and notions of moral purity and impurity (Cohen and Leung 2009: 1281–2, 1283–5) The evocation of complex cultural codes and moral sentiments via embodiment manipulations stands in unequivocal contradiction to the claim culture does not influence action via the generation of psychological (dispositional) proclivities (Swidler 1986:283).

From this perspective, one of Bourdieu's most misunderstood books, *Masculine Domination* (2001), can be interpreted as proposing the hypothesis that the primary way in which patriarchal gender "ideology" is encoded is via the hard-embodiment mechanism (Uhlmann 2000; Uhlmann and Uhlmann 2005). For instance, Bourdieu notes how a particular form of female subordination is encoded in the angle and direction of the eye gaze that women in Middle East and North Africa (MENA) region societies are expected (and come to habitually) hold (low and toward the ground; never meeting the gaze of other men directly and seldom looking up). Once hard-embodied, gendered culture can affect self-identity via routine pathways (well-honed habitual comportments) bypassing self-reflection. Thus, persons come to perceive themselves acting in certain patterned ways (e.g., with self-assurance or subordinate tentativeness) rather than acting in particular ways because they are being guided by higher level reflective principles (which may be dissociated from the routine comportments and the cultural associations they activate (Lizardo 2017)).

4.3 BOURDIEU AND THE SOFT EMBODIMENT OF CULTURE

Ideologies may not only be "hard embodied"; they can also be subject to "soft embodiment" (Leung and Cohen 2007). The key difference between hard and soft embodiment is that in the latter, culture comes to be embodied not via the "online" direct manipulation of bodily posture or the handling of material artifacts but via the "offline" *embodied simulation* (Niedenthal et al. 2005) of the typical experiences we have as embodied subjects (e.g., like looking at the world through a point of view). Soft embodiment phenomena lie behind the various embodiment effects shown in the processing of conceptual metaphors and sequencing effects in grammatical and idiomatic constructions (Glenberg and Robertson 2000; Ignatow 2007).

Gender ideologies, as Bourdieu (2001) intimated in *Masculine Domination*, may also be subject to soft embodiment. For instance, Uhlmann and Uhlmann (2005:95) review linguistic evidence regarding word ordering in conventional linguistic constructions involving two adjectives or prepositions (e.g., "up and down," "front and back," "good and bad," "here and there," etc.). The basic finding is that the first element in the pair is almost always the term associated either with the physical or psychological "egocentric" point of view of the speaker (a typical soft-embodiment effect among Westerners (Leung and Cohen 2007)). In locational terms that means that prepositional phrases depicting a point in space (or time) "close" to the subject will tend to come first ("today and tomorrow" rather than "tomorrow and today"), and for valued adjectives the positive valued (which has been associated with the "self" among Westerners) will come first ("good and bad" rather than "bad and good").

To show how gender ideology goes below discourse, Uhlmann and Uhlmann (2005) hypothesize that the precedence accorded to men in the larger culture should be homologous to that accorded to the self in linguistic constructions. They go to review corpus data showing the overwhelming prevalence of the same effect for gendered pairs; thus "boys and girls," "men and women," and "husband and wife," are more conventionally sanctioned than the reverse. This suggests (except for domestic or familial contexts) that the primacy of men over women (e.g., the conceptual construction of men as primary, prototypical persons and women as deviations) is coded not only as explicit complex ideologies but also as simple patterns of conventionalization in linguistic constructions.

The work of Cerulo (1998) provides convergent evidence of the soft embodiment of *moral prominence* in innocent sequencing patterns in language. While not initially couched in these terms, her findings are thoroughly compatible with, and in fact can be considered a prime example of, the soft-embodiment phenomenon. As Cerulo shows, the typical sequencing of an active-voice sentence involves the initial mention of an actor doing something to an object. This (typical) sequencing assigns prominence to the actor in relation to the object. This means that when third parties have to report on an event in which a morally privileged actor is the object of the action of a morally devalued actor, they must use a mechanism to override this typical arrangement: the passive construction (which reverses order by making the object of the sentence first in the sequence). Cerulo (1998:40–41) provides various examples of this soft embodiment phenomenon. These occur whenever violence is inflicted by a morally dubious actor on a set of morally worthy victims. She insightfully proposed that the reason these sentences are organized in this way has all to do with the assignment of cognitive priority to the patient: "victim sequences prioritize the characteristics of those whom violence strikes" (Cerulo 1998:40). She also noted that these types of sequences are "prototypical" for the case of "deviant" violence narratives.

In what Cerulo refers to as "performer sequences" violent acts that the conceptualizer presumes are morally justified—"normal violence" (Cerulo 1998:43)—in the eyes of his or her audience are presented using the (prototypical for events) active voice. Under these circumstances, we should expect reporters to not deviate from the prototypical active construction. Consistent with this hypothesis, Cerulo shows that performer sequences are almost invariably active voice constructions. The soft-embodiment account naturally explains why this should be the case: in the active voice construction cognitive prominence falls naturally on the agent (not the patient) of the interaction symbolized by the verb in the finite clause. Because actors who do "bad things to bad people" (with the depiction of violent acts) are unproblematically conceptualized as being "good" they can be raised to cognitive prominence without resulting in any tension between the exogenous moral position of the actor and their prominent position in the linguistic construction. In this respect, moral prominence in discourse is subject to "soft embodiment" in the same way as it is subject to "hard embodiment" in the elicitation and enactment of purification rituals that involve literal washing of the body (Cohen and Leung 2009:1283–4).

4.4 IMPLICATIONS OF BOURDIEU'S (EMBODIED) COGNITIVE SOCIOLOGY

The existence of hard and soft embodiment of cultural phenomena has important implications for research and theory in cultural analysis in the social sciences. First, it is not enough to say one is taking an "embodied" or "embodiment" approach. It is important to specify what type of embodied approach one is attempting to deploy. As we have seen, some versions of embodiment imply weaker commitments when taken in isolation (e.g., embodied meaning, externalization); these are compatible with the existence of "soft" embodiment phenomena. Other approaches (e.g., cognitive unconscious, possibly coupled to phenomenological and embodied-meaning approaches) imply stronger empirical and theoretical commitments. Some long-standing cultural theories in sociology (e.g., structuralism and classical social phenomenology) cannot predict or even accommodate the existence of hard embodiment phenomena, especially the elicitation of complex cognitive, emotional, and even ideological mindsets from the simple manipulation of the body (Bourdieu 1990). In this respect, the biggest challenge (and promise) of Bourdieu's (embodied) cognitive sociology can be found here.

A key difference concerns the relative usefulness of the traditional battery of analytic methods in social science in the face of these issues. For soft-embodiment phenomena, traditional social scientific methods, ranging from the in-depth interview to discourse and text analysis, can be calibrated to capture the traces of embodied cognition in meaning construction, especially those left behind in the spoken or written word (Ignatow 2009). It is when researchers attempt to capture traces of hard-embodied culture that things get more problematic. Because culture that is hard-embodied requires the researcher to be attuned to the analog meaning of gestures, comportments, and ways of acting, observational strategies that keep the research "close to the action" (such as ethnography) are ideal (Wacquant 2004b). However, ethnography without the aid of proper cognitive theory will not be sufficient; researchers need to go to the field already sensitized to the nature of the sociocultural processes they will look for (Timmermans and Tavory 2012), otherwise their attention will be predictably drawn to the standard linguistically mediated symbols (Wacquant 2013).

I close by providing some generative examples of how analysts (properly sensitized) can uncover hard-embodied culture in the field.

4.4.1 Study Novices

One approach is to examine the conceptions of relative novices to the culture. Because culture patterns, to become hard-embodied, require repetition and practice, and this practice is seldom accompanied by overt interpretations or detailed exegesis, we should find that relative novices in the process of internalizing correspondences between specific bodily comportments and higher-order belief and values should be particularly transparent about this linkage.

The anthropologist Christina Toren (1999) suspected that conceptions of rank and hierarchy and their connection to higher-order belief systems that justify them are built up from routine comportments around ritual occasions, in particular everyday meals and the drinking of kava (beer made from the root vegetable) during special ceremonies. To verify this hypothesis, Toren asked a convenience sample of Fijian children ranging from five to eleven years old to examine a prepared drawing and provide the identity of unlabeled figures sitting around a table during the kava drinking ritual and during meals in the household (in effect eliciting "iconic" representations). She also asked them to provide their own drawings identifying where different persons (mother, father, chief, etc.) would be seated in similar circumstances.

Toren finds that by the age of six, Fijian children can reproduce the structural correspondence between gender and rank hierarchy and the above/below spatial axis of seating arrangements (it is a behavioral rule that men sit toward the "top" or head of the table—that is, the side of the table that points away from the main entrance to the house—and women and younger children sit toward the "bottom"), with younger children producing less ranking gradations than do older children (Toren 1999:88–90). Toren concludes from these data that "an understanding of above/below in terms of its polar extremes occurs just before school age" (Toren 1999:94). For these children the position of mother below "is the anchor for situations within the household... for prepared drawings of meals, all children chose the figure below to be mother.... By contrast, the figure said to be above was either father, father's elder brother, father's father, mother's brother or a 'guest.'"

4.4.2 Get Creative With Methods

Another approach is to expand the range of methodological tools, including the incorporation of video recording for capturing the hard-embodied bodily techniques that could easily be lost to the naked eye of the ethnographer. For instance, the anthropologist N. J. Enfield (2005) shows that personal knowledge regarding the central analytic object of structuralist anthropology, namely kinship, is hard-embodied in "analog" motor schemes. Drawing on data from videotaped interviews of residents of Laos, Enfield shows that when prompted by the interviewer to explicitly verbalize the culturally accepted relations between different kinship roles, people use spatial bodily orientation along the right-left and up-down axes and gestures designed to show positions at locations "drawn" in the space immediately in the front of the informant's body to show the relative position of occupants of different positions in their kinship system. Thus, rather than being stored as amodal, abstract, categories, the "rules" of kinship exist as directly embodied sets of perceptual and motor skills, expressed as "bodily gymnastics" (Bourdieu 1990).

4.4.3 Take Embodiment Into the Field

Finally, Wacquant (2004a) provides an example of the fruitfulness of combining a phenomenological approach to embodiment in the field with a theoretical sensitivity for the body as the substrate of the cognitive unconscious (senses *c* and *e* from Section 4.1.1). Here we get a rich description of the dynamics via which culture (in this case that of the boxing gym) becomes hard-embodied. This was particularly evident in the pedagogical style of the trainer who refused to believe boxing could be learned from books or by imitating static "pictures." The problem is that "[y]ou don't get a sense of movement. Boxin's movement....In a book everything's standin' still" (Wacquant 2004a:101). The capacity to understand and "grasp" the meaning and telos of action by other agents at an implicit, bodily level, without recourse to an explicit "theory of mind" of other agents, coupled with the capacity to "mirror" the action of others and engage in implicit imitation of the bodily techniques of others, provide a different perspective of what it means to be "socialized" into the "culture" of a collectivity (see also Downey 2014). Some of these mechanisms were presaged in Bourdieu's (1990) own theoretical reflections regarding the "implicit pedagogy" that was necessary for full enculturation into a social group.

REFERENCES

Barsalou, Lawrence W. 1999. "Perceptual Symbol Systems." *The Behavioral and Brain Sciences* 22(4):577–609; discussion 610–60.

Barsalou, Lawrence W., Paula M. Niedenthal, Aron K. Barbey, and Jennifer A. Ruppert. 2003. "Social Embodiment." *Psychology of Learning and Motivation* 43:43–92.

Bloch, Maurice. 1986. "From Cognition to Ideology." pp. 21–48 in *Knowledge and Power: Anthropological and Sociological Approaches*, edited by R. Fardon. Edinburgh: Scottish University Press.

Bourdieu, Pierre. 1970. "La maison Kabyle, ou Le monde renversé." in *Echanges et communications: Mélanges offerts à Claude Levi-Strauss à l'occasion de son 60éme anniversaire*, edited by Jean Pouillon and Pierre Maranda. Paris: Mouton.

Bourdieu, Pierre. 1984. *Distinction: A Social Critique of the Judgement of Taste*. Cambridge, MA: Harvard University Press.

Bourdieu, Pierre. 1990. *The Logic of Practice*. Stanford, CA: Stanford University Press.

Bourdieu, Pierre. 1991. *Language and Symbolic Power*. Harvard University Press.

Bourdieu, Pierre. 1996a. *The Rules of Art: Genesis and Structure of the Literary Field*. Stanford, CA: Stanford University Press.

Bourdieu, Pierre. 1996b. *The State Nobility: Elite Schools in the Field of Power*. Stanford, CA: Stanford University Press.

Bourdieu, Pierre. 2001. *Masculine Domination*. Stanford, CA: Stanford University Press.

Cerulo, Karen A. 1998. *Deciphering Violence: The Cognitive Structure of Right and Wrong*. New York: Routledge.

Cerulo, Karen A. 2015. "The Embodied Mind: Building on Wacquant's Carnal Sociology." *Qualitative Sociology* 38(1):33–38.

Chemero, Anthony. 2011. *Radical Embodied Cognitive Science*. Cambridge, MA: MIT Press.

Clark, Andy. 1997. *Being There: Putting Brain, Body, and World Together Again*. Cambridge, MA: MIT Press.

Cohen, Dov, and Angela K. Y. Leung. 2009. "The Hard Embodiment of Culture." *European Journal of Social Psychology* 39(7):1278–89.

Collins, Harry. 2010. *Tacit and Explicit Knowledge*. Chicago: University of Chicago Press.

Crossley, Nick. 2001. "The Phenomenological Habitus and Its Construction." *Theory and Society* 30(1):81–120.

Desmond, Matthew. 2007. *On the Fireline*. Chicago: University of Chicago Press.

Downey, Greg. 2014. "'Habitus in Extremis': From Embodied Culture to Bio-Cultural Development." *Body and Society* 20(2):113–17.

Dreyfus, Hubert L. 1992. *What Computers Still Can't Do: A Critique of Artificial Reason*. Cambridge, MA: MIT Press.

Enfield, Nick J. 2005. "The body as a cognitive artifact in kinship representations: Hand gesture diagrams by speakers of Lao." *Current Anthropology* 46(1):51–81.

Fiske, Alan P. 2004. "Four Modes of Constituting Relationships: Consubstantial Assimilation; Space, Magnitude, Time, and Force; Concrete Procedures; Abstract Symbolism." pp. 61–146 in *Relational Models Theory: A Contemporary Overview*, edited by Nick Haslam. New York: Routledge.

Gallagher, Shaun. 2005. *How the Body Shapes the Mind*. Oxford: Oxford University Press.

Glenberg, Arthur M., and Vittorio Gallese. 2012. "Action-Based Language: A Theory of Language Acquisition, Comprehension, and Production." *Cortex: A Journal Devoted to the Study of the Nervous System and Behavior* 48(7):905–22.

Glenberg, Arthur M., and David A. Robertson. 2000. "Symbol Grounding and Meaning: A Comparison of High-Dimensional and Embodied Theories of Meaning." *Journal of Memory and Language* 43(3):379–401.

Higgins, E. Tory, and C. Miguel Brendl. 1995. "Accessibility and Applicability: Some 'Activation Rules' Influencing Judgment." *Journal of Experimental Social Psychology* 31(3):218–43.

Hitlin, Steven, and Jane Allyn Piliavin. 2004. "Values: Reviving a Dormant Concept." *Annual Review of Sociology* 30(1):359–93.

Hutchins, Edwin. 1995. *Cognition in the Wild*. Cambridge, MA: MIT Press.

Hutto, Daniel D., and Erik Myin. 2013. *Radicalizing Enactivism: Basic Minds without Content*. Cambridge, MA: MIT Press.

Ignatow, Gabe. 2016. "Theoretical Foundations for Digital Text Analysis." *Journal for the Theory of Social Behaviour* 46(1):104–20.

Ignatow, Gabriel. 2007. "Theories of Embodied Knowledge: New Directions for Cultural and Cognitive Sociology?" *Journal for the Theory of Social Behaviour* 37(2):115–35.

Ignatow, Gabriel. 2009. "Culture and Embodied Cognition: Moral Discourses in Internet Support Groups for Overeaters." *Social Forces: A Scientific Medium of Social Study and Interpretation* 88(2):643–69.

Lakoff, George, and Mark Johnson. 1999. *Philosophy in the Flesh: The Embodied Mind and Its Challenge to Western Thought*. New York: Basic Books.

Leung, Angela K., Lin Qiu, Laysee Ong, and Kim-Pong Tam. 2011. "Embodied Cultural Cognition: Situating the Study of Embodied Cognition in Socio-Cultural Contexts." *Social and Personality Psychology Compass* 5(9):591–608.

Leung, Angela K. Y., and Dov Cohen. 2007. "The Soft Embodiment of Culture: Camera Angles and Motion through Time and Space." *Psychological Science* 18(9):824–30.

Lizardo, Omar. 2009. "Is a 'Special Psychology' of Practice Possible? From Values and Attitudes to Embodied Dispositions." *Theory and Psychology* 19(6):713–27.

Lizardo, Omar. 2004. "The Cognitive Origins of Bourdieu's Habitus." *Journal for the Theory of Social Behaviour* 34(4):375–401.

Lizardo, Omar. 2011. "Pierre Bourdieu as a Post-Cultural Theorist." *Cultural Sociology* 5(1):25–44.

Lizardo, Omar. 2012. "The Three Phases of Bourdieu's U.S. Reception: Comment on Lamont." *Sociological Forum* 27(1):238–44.

Lizardo, Omar. 2015. "Culture, Cognition and Embodiment." pp. 576–81 in *International Encyclopedia of the Social and Behavioral Sciences*, edited by James D. Wright. New York: Elsevier.

Lizardo, Omar. 2017. "Improving Cultural Analysis: Considering Personal Culture in Its Declarative and Nondeclarative Modes." *American Sociological Review* 82(1):88–115.

Lizardo, Omar, and Michael Strand. 2010. "Skills, Toolkits, Contexts and Institutions: Clarifying the Relationship between Different Approaches to Cognition in Cultural Sociology." *Poetics* 38(2):205–28.

Mauss, Marcel. 1973. "Techniques of the Body." *Economy and Society* 2(1):70–88.

McDonnell, Terence E. 2016. *Best Laid Plans: Cultural Entropy and the Unraveling of AIDS Media Campaigns*. Chicago: University of Chicago Press.

Mears, Ashley. 2011. *Pricing Beauty: The Making of a Fashion Model*. Berkeley: University of California Press.

Newell, Allen. 1980. "Physical Symbol Systems." *Cognitive Science* 4(2):135–83.

Niedenthal, Paula M., Lawrence W. Barsalou, Piotr Winkielman, Silvia Krauth-Gruber, and François Ric. 2005. "Embodiment in Attitudes, Social Perception, and Emotion." *Personality and Social Psychology Review: An Official Journal of the Society for Personality and Social Psychology* 9(3):184–211.

Pagis, Michal. 2010. "From Abstract Concepts to Experiential Knowledge: Embodying Enlightenment in a Meditation Center." *Qualitative Sociology* 33(4):469–89.

Pálsson, Gísli. 1994. "Enskilment at Sea." *Man* 29(4):901–27.

Rohrer, Tim. 2010. "Embodiment and Experientialism." in *The Oxford Handbook of Cognitive Linguistics*, edited by Dirk Geeraerts and Hubert Cuykens. New York: Oxford University Press.

Schubert, Thomas W. 2005. "Your Highness: Vertical Positions as Perceptual Symbols of Power." *Journal of Personality and Social Psychology* 89(1):1–21.

Schubert, Thomas W., and Gün R. Semin. 2009. "Embodiment as a Unifying Perspective for Psychology." *European Journal of Social Psychology* 39(7):1135–41.

Schwartz, Barry. 1981. *Vertical Classification: A Study in Structuralism and the Sociology of Knowledge*. Chicago: University of Chicago Press.

Strand, Michael, and Omar Lizardo. 2015. "Beyond World Images: Belief as Embodied Action in the World." *Sociological Theory* 33(1):44–70.

Strauss, Claudia, and Naomi Quinn. 1997. *A Cognitive Theory of Cultural Meaning*. New York: Cambridge University Press.

Swidler, Ann. 1986. "Culture in action: Symbols and strategies." *American Sociological Review* 51(2):273–86.

Timmermans, Stefan, and Iddo Tavory. 2012. "Theory Construction in Qualitative Research: From Grounded Theory to Abductive Analysis." *Sociological Theory* 30(3):167–86.

Toren, Christina. 1999. *Mind, Materiality, and History: Explorations in Fijian Ethnography* New York: Routledge.

Uhlmann, Allon. 2000. "Incorporating Masculine Domination: Theoretical and Ethnographic Elaborations." *Social Analysis: The International Journal of Social and Cultural Practice* 44(1):142–61.

Uhlmann, Allon J., and Jennifer R. Uhlmann. 2005. "Embodiment below Discourse: The Internalized Domination of the Masculine Perspective." *Women's Studies International Forum* 28(1):93–103.

Wacquant, Loïc. 2013. "Homines in Extremis: What Fighting Scholars Teach Us about Habitus." *Body and Society* 20(2):3–17.

Wacquant, Loïc J. D. 2004a. *Body and Soul: Notebooks of an Apprentice Boxer*. New York: Oxford University Press.

Wacquant, Loïc J. D. 2004b. "Following Pierre Bourdieu into the Field." *Ethnography* 5(4):387–414.

Waskul, Dennis D., and Phillip Vannini. 2006. "Introduction: The Body in Symbolic Interaction." Body/*Embodiment: Symbolic Interaction and the Sociology of the Body*.

Wheeler, Michael. 2005. *Reconstructing the Cognitive World: The Next Step*. Cambridge, MA: MIT Press.

Wilson, Margaret. 2002. "Six Views of Embodied Cognition." *Psychonomic Bulletin and Review* 9(4):625–36.

Wilson, Robert A. 2004. *Boundaries of the Mind: The Individual in the Fragile Sciences— Cognition*. New York: Cambridge University Press.

Winchester, Daniel. 2008. "Embodying the Faith: Religious Practice and the Making of a Muslim Moral Habitus." *Social Forces: A Scientific Medium of Social Study and Interpretation* 86(4):1753–80.

CHAPTER 5

....

EMBODIED COGNITION
sociology's role in bridging mind,
brain, and body

....

KAREN A. CERULO

THINKING...how exactly does it occur? The question is age old, and answers abound. Some—including neurologists, cognitive psychologists, evolutionary biologists, and computer scientists—attend almost exclusively to neural operations; they tie the structure and function of the brain to representational processes involved in attending, perceiving, classifying, and remembering. Others—cognitive sociologists, cultural anthropologists, and social psychologists—argue that mind takes priority over the brain; these scholars explore the sociocultural patterns that inform what we attend to or ignore; how we classify people, places, objects, or events; and what we remember or forget within our social interactions.

In recent years, a third approach to thinking has emerged—an expansive, interdisciplinary view of cognition. Theories of "embodied cognition" bridge brain and mind. The body is central to this bridging project. Embodied cognition theories state that how we apprehend, process, make meaning and remember the world involves the sentient—what our bodies feel, see, hear, smell, taste and touch. Moreover, thinking is inseparable from the environments in which our bodies collect such information. Thus the brain alone cannot explain how we think, and thought is not merely the product of cultural patterns and rules. Rather, thinking emerges from a fully entwined system including neural operations, corporeal experience, and the context in which they are embedded.

In this chapter, I explore the roots of embodied cognition theory and I trace its rather recent entry into the sociological literature. I move on to summarize the growing number of empirical sociological works informed by embodied cognition theory. In so doing, I touch on the methodological debates surrounding work in this area. I conclude the chapter by suggesting ways in which sociology can forward the embodied cognition project.

5.1 The Roots of Embodied
Cognition Theories

When cognitive science emerged as a distinct field of study,[1] "cognitivism" (the study of the mind's representational structures) and "computationalism" (the study of how the brain processes those structures) dominated the field. Cognitivist and computational writings of the period centered wholly on nonobservable neural processes; researchers had little regard for the role of the body beyond the fact that it housed the brain.

Theories of embodied cognition developed in direct opposition to this stance, commanding serious attention in the late 1980s. In this approach to thinking, meaning-making is quite distinct from the processes described in abstract representational models. Rather, meaning-making is deeply entwined in the body's experience with surrounding environments. Consider the example of food. If you were bred on the American diet, you likely have memories of consuming hamburgers. Your understanding of hamburgers is not the product of a mental computation. Rather, it involves hamburgers you have tasted, salivated over, or smelled in the past; the sight of rounded meat patties; their texture; your efforts in chewing them; and your digestion of the meat. Also important to your thinking is where, when, and with whom you ate the food and the ways in which that environment altered your encounter with the meat. Your understanding of hamburgers rests in your corporeal experience, the contexts in which you had that experience, and the neural processing of that experience.

But does this mean that we cognate or comprehend only things we directly experience? Not according to the theory. We can, for example, cognate and make meaning of foods never consumed. Consider something like roasted crickets (at least, within American cuisine). To think about and understand roasted crickets, we link our visual systems to the language of roasted crickets. In essence, we take previously experienced ideas about what crickets look like, and we combine them with our understanding of the action of roasting. We form new visual combinations by which to experience roasted crickets and give them meaning. Embodied cognition theorists refer to this as "embodied simulation." (We will return to this idea shortly.)

The elements of embodied cognition theory are not altogether new. Recall that in *Phenomenology of Perception* (1945/1962) and later in *The Visible and the Invisible* (1964/1968), Merleau-Ponty rejected all forms of mind-body dualism. He presented mind and body as part of an integrated system, and the body as "our general medium for having a world" (1945/1962:146). For Merleau-Ponty, perception is grounded in the body's location and experience—in its "being in the world" (1945/1962:82). The body is both subject and object; it is inhabited space, with space defined in relation to the body and its motor possibilities. When we think of the body in this way, perception and other forms of thought take on a new character. Merleau-Ponty's actors do not perceive the world as disembodied agents, abstracted from the sites of action, merely observing it from afar and computing its properties. Rather, perception involves our flesh and blood in situations; it is contingent on inhabiting situations, on environmental beckoning to respond to or manipulate situations.

The psychologists Francisco Varela, Evan Thompson, and Eleanor Rosch revisited Merleau-Ponty's work some forty-five years later, combining it with burgeoning ideas in cognitive science and Buddhist meditative philosophy. Like Merleau-Ponty, they argue that information does not exist ready-made in the world; human beings do not have a priori innate categories nor does cognition revolve around representation (1991:140). Rather, our thinking and our consciousness develop from the "enactment" of a world—the structural coupling of bodies with environments, the sensorimotor involvement with our world. Varela and colleagues use experimental studies on color vision to illustrate their point. In reviewing this research—particularly research on optical illusions—they demonstrate that color perception is dependent on the physiology of viewers in concert with viewers' environments. "Colors are not 'out there' independent of our perceptual and cognitive capacities," and "colors are not 'in here' independent of our surrounding biological and cultural world. Color categories are experiential and belong to our shared biological and cultural world" (1991:172). We see colors, make sense of them, relative to where we encounter them, what is adjacent to them, how they are illuminated, our recurrent patterns of perception, and so forth. There could, perhaps, be no better example of these ideas than the "Great Dress Debate of 2015." Recall that a woman posted a picture of a dress to Tumblr and asked for people's opinions on the garment's colors. Viewers split into two camps—one seeing the dress as blue and black and the other seeing it as white and gold. (Mahler [2015] offers more details.) The debate became a social media "happening," triggering copious research. To understand the variable reactions to the dress, Schlaffke et al. (2015) showed that one must simultaneously consider not simply the dress but the environmental illumination of the dress, the physical condition of viewers' eyes, and the ways in which brains processes those factors. Object, environment, body, or brain cannot, independently, provide an answer to the conundrum; all simultaneously impact viewers' assessments of color.

Currently, the philosopher/robotics expert Andy Clark (1997, 2010; Clark and Chalmers 1998) is the greatest proponent of embodied cognition theories, and he hopes to enrich these ideas. Using the term "active externalism" (Clark and Chalmers 1998:7), Clark argues for a basic change in the brain's very "job description." Brains cannot be understood as computer-like, for we encounter far too many stimuli in our daily environmental exposures. Brains would "bottleneck" under such stress, making it impossible to continually compute blueprints for immediate action. For Clark, the workings of brains are much simpler, (a view shared by Damasio [2008], Eagleman [2012], and others). Brains are the "locus of inner *structures* that act as operators upon the world via their role in determining action" (1997:47); they coordinate physical movement and control and exploit environmental structures. But brain activity does not surpass that of body or environment in cognition. Rather, brains interface with body and environment, forming a cognitive system. Indeed for Clark, environments are as important to thought as brains because environments drive cognition. "If we remove the external component of the system, behavioral competence will drop, just as it would if we removed part of our brain" (1998:8–9).

What do Clark's ideas look like in practice? How do they differ from cognitivist/computational models? Andrew Wilson (2012) compares two contemporary robots—Honda's "Asimo" and Boston Dynamic's "Big Dog"—to illustrate the distinctions. Both robots are highly sophisticated; however, Asimo relies on cognitivist/computational knowledge for operation while Big Dog emerges from embodied cognition. Comparing the performance of both robots—that is, their ability to think, move and respond like humans—brings the two theoretical approaches to life. (See Asimo in action at https://www.youtube.com/watch?v=0Yrto7TJ7zI and Big Dog at https://www.youtube.com/watch?v=cNZPRsrwumQ.)

In performance, one can see that Asimo falls short—its movements are awkward and inefficient. Why? According to Wilson, "All the work of generating and controlling Asimo's walking is happening in Asimo's head, and his legs don't provide any help at all." Computational needs also make the robot unstable. "If you allow Asimo to execute his prepared programme in a safe environment, he typically does just fine. If, however, there is anything complicated in his world, or if he miscalculates by just a tiny bit, then he fails." For Wilson, constant computing in lieu of sensory and environmental input proves detrimental. "All the hard work of making Asimo go happens in his central processers; his body just happens to come along for the ride." Contrast this with Big Dog. This robot has a smaller "brain center" than Asimo and is not reliant on the constant computations that Asimo must execute. Rather, Big Dog's movements materialize from "active externalism" (à la Clark)—the interface of brain, body, and environment. This includes the robot's highly flexible legs, the character of the surface the robot is moving on, and any environmental forces that act on the robot while it moves. Big Dog's sensory system tells it "how" it needs to move, how to respond to its environment, to balance, correct, and control force and pressure in its motion. Its brain simply provides the instructions for executing the moves. Big Dog's embodied cognition results in a fast, efficient, responsive robot with almost humanlike reactions. When the robot is knocked off balance, it does not fail as does Asimo. Its body works in tandem with the environment to restore balance. Thus Wilson concludes "Asimo *mentally represents* his abilities, while Big Dog *embodies* its abilities. Big Dog doesn't need any complex computational machinery to produce stable, robust performance, and, if Asimo is anything to go by, such machinery might just get in its way."

5.1.1 Mechanisms of Embodied Cognition

What mechanisms enable the structural coupling of brain, body, and environment? The linguist George Lakoff and philosopher Mark Johnson identify language—metaphors in particular—as critical to the process. In *Metaphors We Live By* (1980) and follow-up works (e.g., Brockman 1999; Johnson 1989; Lakoff 1990, 2014; Lakoff and Johnson 1999), they argue that sensorimotor and perceptual systems are pivotal to the cognitive content: "Every understanding that we can have of the world, ourselves, and others can only be framed of concepts shaped by our bodies... areas maximally in touch with the reality of our environments." Metaphors translate the neural aspects of sensorimotor activity to the abstract concepts that underpin thinking. In this way, metaphors allow "sensory motor experiences to structure conceptualizations of subjective experience and judgement" (Lakoff and Johnson 1999:555–6).

Lakoff, Johnson, and others often illustrate their ideas via spatial concepts, arguing that issues of up, down, front, back, side-to-side, and so forth, inform our metaphorical descriptions, intended meanings, and comprehension of experience. Thus stocks prices "rise and fall." In negotiations we take "two steps back and one forward." Faced with adversity, our spirits "fall" and obstacles "arise." We "move on," "retreat," or "stand our ground." For Lakoff and Johnson (1990:69), "schemas that structure our bodily experience preconceptually have a basic logic. Preconceptual structural correlations in experience motivate metaphors that map that logic into abstract domains. Thus, what has been called abstract reason has a bodily basis in our everyday physical functioning."

Some of Lakoff and Johnson's ideas have been supported in the laboratory. For example, Eerland et al. (2011) suggest that body posture can influence conceptualizations of amounts or quantities. They invoke a conceptual tool called a "mental number line," arguing that when we consider quantities, we typically "represent numbers along a line with smaller numbers on the left and larger numbers on the right." In experimental testing, Eerland and colleagues asked subjects to estimate quantities while leaning to the right or left. In line with the mental number line, they found subjects leaning to the left underestimated quantities while those leaning to the right overestimated quantities. Cooperrider and Núñez (2009) explored the role of the body in conceptualizations of time. Studying gestures in a laboratory setting, they found that American English speakers conceptualize time as moving from left to right across the body. Similarly, Miles et al. (2010) showed that mental time travel—for example, thinking about the past or future— may be metaphorically "represented in the sensory motor systems that regulate human movement" (2010:222). In the laboratory, subjects were asked to envision moments from their past and moments that might occur in their future. Subjects engaged in retrospection more often leaned backward while those engaged in prospection more often leaned forward. The past was experienced as behind subjects and the future ahead of them. Embodiment also proved critical to thoughts about inclusion and exclusion. Zhong and Leonardelli (2008) asked people to think about times when they were left out or incorporated in a group or activity. They also asked subjects to estimate room temperature during these cognitions. Subjects actually felt the experience of inclusion and exclusion, reporting a cold room when remembering exclusion and a warm room when recalling inclusion. (For related studies, see, e.g., Bargh et al., 1996; Dijkstra, Eerland et al. 2014; Lee and Schwarz, 2010; Schubert, 2005; Stepper and Strack, 1993; Strack et al., 1988; Wells and Petty, 1980; Williams et al. 2000.)

As mentioned earlier, "embodied simulation" constitutes another mechanism that enables the structural coupling of brain, body, and environment. In the mid-1990s, three research teams (Bailey et al. 1997; Barsalou 1999; Rizzolatti et al. 1996) proposed the *embodied simulation hypothesis*, suggesting that we understand language not via computational processes but by mentally simulating the experiences that language describes.[2]

"We create mental experiences of perception and action in the absence of their external manifestation." We "see" without the sights actually being there; we perform without actually moving (Bergen 2012:14).

What does simulation look like in practice? Imagine the way your favorite candy bar tastes...or how the sun feels on a summer day. Picture yourself grabbing your car's steering wheel and swerving to avoid a darting squirrel. Imagine the smell of your mother's favorite perfume. Tests of the embodied simulation hypothesis show that most of us not only picture these experiences—we feel them. We taste the flavor and texture of chocolate or nuts even though we are not now eating them. We sense the sun's heat on our skin even though it may be winter. We feel the jolt of a swerving car even though we are safely seated at our desk. We feel our mother's presence and the good (or bad) way her scent made us feel. In each example, we use past experience to consciously, even intentionally, create a powerful mental image—one that we can re-experience. But perhaps the most important part of this discovery lies here. "Embodied simulation makes use of the same parts of the brain that are dedicated to directly interacting with the world...simulation creates echoes in our brains of previous experiences, attenuated resonances of brain patterns that were active during previous perceptual and motor experiences" (Bergen 2012:14). Clarke takes the argument one step further: "Cognition exists as a spatio-temporally extended process not limited by the tenuous envelope of skin and skull.... The kinds of internal representations and computations we employ are selected so as to complement the complex social and ecological settings in which we must act. Thus we ignore or downplay such wider settings at our peril" (1997:221).

But what of things that do not exist—how do we simulate these? Bergen contends that language plays a pivotal role here. "You should be able to make sense of language about not only things that exist in the real world, like polar bears, but also things that don't actually exist, like, say, flying pigs. When words are combined—whether or not the things they refer to exist in the real world—language users make mental marriages of their corresponding mental representations" (2012:17).[3]

5.2 WHERE DOES SOCIOLOGY FIT IN?

Sociologists have been slow to embrace theories of embodied cognition. Pierre Bourdieu was among the first modern theorists to entertain these ideas. Bourdieu introduced the concept "habitus"—a "system of durable transposable dispositions...principles which generate and organize practices and representation that can be objectively adapted to their outcomes without presupposing a conscious aiming at ends or an express mastery of the operations necessary in order to attain them" (1990:52). Via habitus, Bourdieu promoted a tripartite approach to cognition. He argued that mental structures are formed through action and corporeal experience and exist relative to a "field" or contextual environment.

To be sure, the body lives in Bourdieu. He writes of it as a "living memory pad" on which a "whole cosmology" is written during childhood socialization (1990:68). Yet Bourdieu's body never seemed on equal footing with mind and field. The anthropologist Gregory Downey (2008) writes, "the habitus gets discussed with much reference to 'the body' and no clear explanation of any physiology or plausible discussion of how habits might affect perception or subjectivity." Thus the theory retains elements of cognitivist models; indeed, early applications of Bourdieu in cognitive sociology addressed issues and questions rooted in the cognitivist arena.

As sociologists continue to interpret Bourdieu, the meaning of habitus is moving toward tenets of embodied cognition. Lizardo (2004:394), for example, urges sociologists to rethink the origins of habitus, embedding them in Piaget's "genetic structuralism." This shift could place mind, body and field on equal footing:

> we need to think of two temporalities and ontological orders when considering Bourdieu. One temporality is *developmental* and manifested in the specific materiality of the human body and the life-course history of dispositions stored in the psycho-motor and cognitive-motivational system (*habitus*), while the other is *historical* and manifested as durable objectified institutions and symbolic orders (*field*).

Ignatow also suggests ways to expand the meaning of habitus, arguing, "culture's effects on social life can be more readily identified if cognitive schemas, which Bourdieu treats as part of the habitus, are understood to be embodied and when discourses are seen as containing bodily information that interacts with the habitus" (2009:643).

Loïc Wacquant (2004, 2015) has been especially vocal in advocating for a sociology of embodied cognition. He frames the project as a "carnal sociology" built on three specific foundational elements. First, as prescribed by Merleau-Ponty, carnal sociology divorces itself from mind-body dualism and visions of the agent as "an active mind mounted on an absent, inert, dumb body." Second, building on Bourdieu, carnal sociology demands the reconceptualization of structure, treating it as "dynamic webs of forces inscribed upon and infolded deep within the body" rather than external webs of possibilities and constraints. Finally, carnal sociology breaks with computational models of thought and prioritizes practical knowledge acquired through action (2015:2). For Wacquant, thinking actors must also be treated as more than wielders of symbols. Rather, actors are "sentient" (capable of feeling awareness), "suffering" (enduring in the face of anguish, stress, and pain), "skilled" (possessing a capacity for action and competence), "sedimented" (with skills inextricably tied to engagement with the world), and "situated" (with thoughts informed by one's unique location in physical and social space). Carnal sociology defines cognition as "situated activity growing out of a tangled dance of body, mind, activity and world" (2015:3).

Victoria Pitts-Taylor brings a feminist perspective to sociological considerations of embodied cognition. Like others, (see, e.g., Cerulo 2010, 2016; Franks 2010; Turner 2007; Vaisey 2008), Pitts-Taylor suggests that we avoid the universality that cognitive science imposes on embodied cognition. "Because bodies are differently located in the social world, and social hierarchies affect the experiences of body-subjects, embodiment is as much a site of difference as it is a site of commonality" (2016:45). Thus, sociologists working in this area must call attention to "discrepancies and dissonances in how minded bodies and worlds fit together" (2016:46; see also Clough 2007; Pitts-Taylor 2014).

5.2.1 Moving Sociology Forward

Theories of embodied cognition are gaining a foothold in sociology, but these theories require empirical verification. Here, sociologists have been slow to act. Cognitive science has tested its hypotheses in extensive laboratory studies. At present, sociology (as well as communications and social psychology) lags behind.

Among sociologists, there has been some controversy regarding appropriate methods for studying embodied cognition. Some see ethnography as uniquely suited to the task. The sociologist must "submit himself to the fire of action in situ … and put his own organism, sensibility and incarnate intelligence at the epicenter of the array of material and symbolic forces that he intends to dissect" (Wacquant 2004:4,viii). Others advocate for "interpretive interviewing"—directed dialogue that allows subjects to describe, narrate, and analyze their experiences in certain situations. This technique promises researchers a roadmap of subjects' thought processes (e.g., Pugh 2013). Still others contend that focus groups capture "minds at work" as subjects "air, reflect and reason their views aloud" with both researchers and other group members (e.g., Cerulo 2000, 2018; McDonnell 2016). Some favor experimental research, particularly when one can monitor subjects' physiological responses to situations and challenges that surround their actions (e.g., Biocca 2014). And still others argue for discourse analysis. Since our embodied experiences are present in language—especially metaphor—studying text and discourse can show us much about how thinking ensues (e.g., Ignatow 2015).

Here, I wish to circumvent debates about the single "appropriate" strategy for studying thought as these arguments slow our progress. Multiple approaches to embodied cognition can only benefit the field, providing a fascinating mosaic of evidence by which to assess sociological elements of thinking. To jumpstart this effort, I raise several themes deserving our attention. Sociologists have initiated study in these fields, but further work is required.

5.2.2 Presence

The communications scholar Frank Biocca and his team at The Media, Interface and Network Design (M.I.N.D.) Labs are generating compelling work on presence. The researchers use avatars and virtual reality environments to study the relationship between embodiment—the feeling of being situated in one's own body, and the cognitive experience of presence—a "psychological state in which the virtuality of the experience is unnoticed" (Lee 2004).

For these researchers, presence has multiple dimensions. "Spatial presence" addresses a sense of physical involvement in virtual environments (Regenbrecht and Schubert 2002); "telepresence" refers to feelings of "being there"(Lee 2004); "social presence" captures feelings of closeness and connectedness to remote others or feelings of immersion in interpersonal interactions (Biocca 1998; Blascovich 2002); "copresence" addresses the ability to interact with others, touch others, and jointly manipulate environments (Durlach and Slater 2000); and "self-presence" occurs when individuals feel they inhabit their avatars and do not distinguish between avatars and their physical body (Eastwick and Gardner 2008; Hofer et al. 2017).

In certain experiments, researchers manipulate elements such as sensory stimulation, avatar mobility, and avatar representativeness to increase feelings of embodiment and maximize one's sense of presence in virtual settings. These subjects report inhabiting their avatars; they have physiological responses to the environments in which their avatars operate; they can lose a sense of connectedness to their physical bodies. Such findings have implications for cognition. "With increasing embodiment we expect increasing levels of psychophysiological responses to virtual environments. The brain's relationship to the body is highly malleable; therefore it is possible to convince the brain that it will suffer the consequences of actions within the virtual environments" (Costa et al. 2013; see also Lombard et al. 2015). Indeed, Biocca (1998, 2014) argues that increasing embodiment may permanently affect our body schemas, eventually making it difficult to control what crosses over from virtual reality to natural reality.

Similar findings emerge in ethnographic studies of presence. In *See Like a Rover*, Janet Vertesi observed scientists working on the "Mars Exploration Rover Project." She tracked a progression of actions—talk, gestures, practices—by which scientists "developed an intuitive sensibility to what the Rover might see, think, or feel on a given day." Vertesi watched scientists become intimately attached to the Rovers, to see the robots as members of their team, and eventually, to seemingly "step into" or inhabit the Rovers' bodies:

> When the Rovers are healthy or sick, human team members may exude energy or tense up. Jude explained to me that when something is not right with the Rover, "We feel it in our bodies." ... The intensity of the embodied experience is such that team members regularly compare the experience of operating Rovers on Mars to simply "being there."

Vertesi's scientists moved from "seeing" like Rovers to "being" Rovers. Their bodies and minds merged with the physicality of Rovers, creating an embodied connection that influenced planning, action and decision-making (2009:285–7; see also Vertesi 2015:chapter 6).

These works are important for they address presence established in interaction. This fundamentally social experience requires further investigation. For example, do feelings of presence change based on the sameness/difference between subject and other, the scope of the interaction, or the tasks at hand? What role do variable contexts play in feelings of presence? Such issues represent exciting research opportunities tailor made for the sociological eye.

5.2.3 Position, Location, and Cognition

Closely tied to studies of presence are links between cognition, position (the physical characteristics and relationships between objects, words, and bodies), and location (the cognitive schemas triggered by position) (Griswold et al. 2013:6). In this domain, Wendy Griswold and colleagues studied art museum exhibits to understand the importance of the body and materiality to meaning-making. The researchers found that position initiates the meaning-making surrounding artworks, as position constrains or enables perception. The environments in which artworks are displayed, whether or not these settings allow for close inspection, reflection, or clear observation; how objects are labeled; how environments capture and sustain attention to the art—all such elements impact perception possibilities in systematic ways. "Position guides location and location guides meaning-making," writes Griswold (Griswold et al. 2013:360), as mind, body, and environment interact to make meaning. Sophia Acord (2010) studied art curators and found similar connections, writing, "Curators build successful installations through their physical orientations to artworks" (2010:447).

In another arena, Adam and Galinsky (2012) use experimental work to show how the position and location of clothing—here, lab coats—influences perception and meaning-making. Researchers determined how subjects "located" lab coats, finding strong associations to attentiveness and carefulness. The experiments also explored how the positioning of lab coats altered subjects' performance in various contexts. Hajo and Galinsky (2012) found that wearing lab coats increased subjects' selective attention and increased care. Simply seeing such coats in the experimental context was insufficient to alter performance. Performance effects occurred only when individuals were positioned inside the coats.

Work on position and location strongly supports the embodied cognition project. Moreover, sociological concerns with contextual variation, practice, and meaning-making make our discipline uniquely suited to further explore these links.

5.2.4 Subjectivity

Nick Yee and colleagues at the Palo Alto Research Center use experimental work to explore embodied cognition and subjectivity. In studying exchange, for example, Yee and Bailenson (2007) found that avatar appearance influenced subjects' self-perceptions. Those given taller avatars were more likely to negotiate from a position of power in online trading tasks; those given shorter avatars tended to accept asymmetrical trades. The researchers also found that the attractiveness of avatars impacted participants' self-confidence and comfort with intimacy. Those with attractive avatars were most intimate with strangers, mirroring findings on the role of physical attractiveness in physically copresent settings. Bailenson et al. (2002) report related findings. In experimental settings, they found that the physical behavior of highly detailed avatars felt so real to participants that, just as in "material" environments, they were able to complete tasks with less verbal communication than subjects in sparse virtual environments. The highly realistic avatars provided the capacity for nonverbal signals that effectively enhanced verbal information, (see also Taylor 2002). These patterns prove especially strong for people who established a psychological connection with their avatars versus those who felt only loosely or not at all connected to their avatars (Ratan and Dawson 2016).

Subjectivity takes many forms. Winchester (2008, 2016) used ethnography to study the development of religious subjectivity via embodied religious practices—namely, ritual prayer, body covering, and fasting. He illustrated the creation of a new "moral habitus" in his subjects—"a thoroughly embodied and practical form of moral subjectivity." According to Winchester, converts did not see these embodied practices as emerging from a moral schema internalized prior to action. Rather, practices such as prayer, body covering, fasting, and so forth helped construct a moral self—one produced through the interaction of environment, body, and mind (2008:1755; see also Pagis 2010).

Subjectivity is ripe for additional sociological inquiry. Self-perception in changing contexts, in performance and practice, in action and thought are central to the sociological agenda and must be further studied with simultaneous attention to mind, body, and environment.

5.2.5 Inscription

Habitus is a key sociological contribution to the embodied cognition project. But how is habitus inscribed? Loïc Wacquant spent three years at the *Woodlawn Gym*. By living the life of a boxer, eventually entering the ring, he demonstrated the development of a boxer's "habitus." In Wacquant's experiences, we see firsthand the folly of bifurcating mind and body, the rational and emotional, thought and action. Wacquant shows that "once in the ring, it is the body that learns and understands, sorts and stores information, finds the correct answer in its repertory of possible actions and reactions and, in the end, becomes the veritable 'subject'... of pugilistic practice" (2004:99). Such findings have important implications for theories of embodied cognition; they show that learned actions must be inscribed on the body before they can be stored as mental categories invoked to invisibly guide future action. Wacquant unpacks that inscription process. He shows that inscription relies on the structuring of the boxing setting, the action pace, intercorporeality, and the roles and relative status and power of all involved.

Phaedra Daipha also documents habitus inscription in her ethnography of meteorology forecasting. Daipha itemizes the wide-ranging practices used in weather forecasting. Much of this work involves highly sophisticated technologies. Yet, equally important are times when meteorologists leave their workstations to study the weather outside. Meteorologists must inhabit weather in addition to simply observing it via indicators and computer screens. These observations show that "expert problem solving, and expert cognition more broadly, is an inherently embodied process. The mind is thoroughly constituted by bodily activity, even in the compulsively artificial and aseptic environment of a laboratory" (2015:796–7).

Mathew Desmond's ethnography of firefighters documents not only the inscription process but also its transportability. He studies how the "general *habitus* of self-described 'country boys'" (the product of social embodiment) is transformed into a more focused, more specific "firefighters *habitus*," (the product of organizational contexts in which action occurs). Desmond explains:

> Crewmembers' practical knowledge of the woods, their embodied outdoorsmanship acquired through a rural upbringing—the way a hand grips an axe, the way a foot mounts a trail—is directly bound up with their core sense of self, their masculinity and identity, for that which is "learned by body" is not something that one has, like knowledge that can be brandished, but something that one is ... crewmembers gravitate "naturally" to the ranks of firefighting because the country-masculine *habitus* seeks out a universe in which it can recognize itself, an environment in which it can thrive. For the men at Elk River, the decision to fight fire was not a bold leap into a brave new world, but rather, a mild step into familiar territory.   (2006:396, 411)

This approach has been applied in a variety of ethnographic studies, including blind people's negotiations of sighted spaces (Måseide and Grøttland 2015), bike messengers' negotiations of urban spaces (Kidder 2009), body techniques and identity among mixed martial arts fighters (Spencer 2009), the internalization of audiences by ballet dancers (Kleiner 2009), athletes' adaptations to competing when debilitated by disease (Allen-Collinsen and Owten 2014), or differences in knowledge construction among academics (Peterson 2015). In these varied arenas, we learn how the mind connects with the body and the body absorbs from the environment. Moreover, we witness the process from the distinct perspective of sociology—one atuned to contextual variation and evolving performance.

5.2.6 Embodied Simulation

Embodied simulation suggests that cognition and meaning-making occurs not via computational processes but by mentally simulating the experiences that language and other stimuli describe. Karen Cerulo (2015, 2018) explored this process with regard to olfactory stimuli and meaning-making. In a series of focus groups, Cerulo asked subjects to smell three perfumes, each targeting a different sort of buyer. She asked study participants to describe each perfume's composition, the manufacturers' desired buyer (including age, occupation, race, socioeconomic status) and the setting for which the perfume was designed (i.e., daytime/workplace; evening/romance; leisure, etc.). Study participants were quite adept at identifying fragrance components and intended markets. How were decisions made? Subjects did not compute their descriptions of the perfumes— they felt them. They inhabited memories of people and places triggered by these smells. Subjects reported feeling the presence of people wearing similar scents, the feel and texture of the places in which the scent was experienced—often with intense, emotional results. Once "inside" the memories, subjects also simulated potential applications of the scents. In essence, individuals physically "relived" olfactory moments as they processed and brought meaning to them. This exercise often involved racializing, genderizing, or attributing age to scents based on the context in which the smells were initially experienced.

Embodied simulation proves important to people's experience of visual stimuli as well. Adriano D'Aloia analyzed viewers' reactions to the characters in the film *Gravity*. He shows how effective camerawork motivates moviegoers to both see characters while internally "*acting out* and simulating the intentional actions performed by the characters," including feelings of celestial motion, emptiness, and being adrift (2015:191).

Studies of embodied simulation illustrate the connections between emotions and cognition. Hansson and Jacobsson (2014), for example, showed that embodied simulation guides animal activists' feelings of empathy. The most effective activists report developing empathy for animal rights only after they relived past experiences with animals. Others relived past experiences with abused or suffering humans and generalized that memory to animals' dire conditions. According to one subject: "If I picture myself in the situation of the animals, I feel such a pain in my body that I can't just ignore that feeling." "Feeling" the pain proves more powerful to thought and subsequent action than mental computations of suffering.

Sociologists have been nearly silent in discussions of embodied simulation. Yet, a full understanding of this process—how it unfolds in varying contexts, among those located in different social categories, how the process is influenced by interactional dynamics— beckons scrutiny through a sociological lens.

5.2.7 Embodied Metaphor and Discourse Analysis

Like simulation, embodied metaphors can drive cognition. Gabriel Ignatow (2009) advocates for discourse analysis—particularly on embodied metaphors versus abstract language—to better understand the process. In one study, Ignatow analyzed online posts from two Internet support groups—each addressing compulsive overeating. One group self-identified as religious, the other as secular. Ignatow found systematic differences in the groups' use of embodied metaphors versus abstract language. Specifically, metaphor use was not random or haphazard but systematically tied to embodied cognitive structures integral to groups' moral cultures. (In line with moral doctrine, for example, the religious group favored embodied metaphors of cleanliness.) Ignatow also found embodied metaphor use resulted in stronger social bonding effects than abstract language use. Ignatow's findings "imply that culture's effects on social bonding can be identified more readily when culture structures are conceived as embodied cognitive structures, rather than as purely mental or behavioral patterns, that operate both within the individual habitus and at the level of small-group discourse" (2009:14).

John Schuster and colleagues (2011) took a similar approach, studying hypertension patients' use of embodied metaphors to capture causes of their disease. Study participants thought of their bodies as machines and used "breakdown" metaphors to understand hypertension's onset. In a similar vein, Rees and colleagues (2007) explored patients' use of embodied metaphors to describe the doctor–patient relationship. Subjects described doctors as "up there" or "central" and patients as "down here" or "peripheral" in describing doctor–patient interactions.

Others have found that embodied metaphor use casts light on people's perception of time. Recall that among Americans and western Europeans, the future is envisioned as "in front of us" and the past as "behind us" (Lakoff and Johnson 1980). However, this pattern is not culturally universal. Subjects in the Andes, for example, reverse these directions. Andes subjects locate the future behind them because it is unknown, and therefore, cannot be seen. In contrast, they locate the past in front of them because it is known and thus can be seen (Nunez and Sweetser 2006).

Studies such as these are important because they help us understand how people, through language, conceptualize their position in interactions, the unfolding of their problems, and the role of body and environment in the conceptualization process. But beyond simply understanding conceptualization, sociologists must further address the sites and patterns of systematic sociocultural variation within the process.

5.3 Where to Go From Here?

Embodied cognition theories address an issue of interest to contemporary cultural and cognitive sociologists—the interaction of mind, body, and environment. But as this chapter shows, cognitive scientists are almost solely focused on the processes by which such interaction occurs. Attention to sociocultural variations and patterns—elements so integral to conceptualization, perception or meaning-making—are largely missing from their discussions. Sociologists must enthusiastically enter this dialogue. We bring a unique intellectual lens that will enrich and enhance embodied cognition models, and if we wait any longer to join the discussion, those from other disciplines will define the parameters of such issues for us.

In recent decades, sociologists have rallied *for* considering the differences within groups and *against* treating members of a particular group as identical. At the same time, the sociological mission involves the ability to move beyond individuals and consider patterns at the group and collective level. By expanding theories of embodied cognition, sociologists could pursue both missions. Consider, for example, the process of embodied simulation. Cognitive scientists study the process itself, viewing it as a general phenomenon common to all bodies and minds. Yet, cognitive scientists acknowledge that, as a process, embodied simulation may not unfold identically across individuals. Bergen (2012:18–19) illustrates via the concept "flying pigs." Flying pigs do not exist in the concrete world and must be simulated to be understood. For some, flying pigs take on the guise of flying superheroes—"Superswines" equipped with capes, unitards, and identity logos. For others, flying pigs are imagined as Pegasus-like entities—majestic animals with broad commanding wings. For still others, flying pigs are conceived as cupid-like—cute, mischievous, and porky. The beauty of simulation, according to Bergen, is that it acknowledges individual variation via simulation products. At the same time, it argues for universalism at the level of process.

Simply acknowledging variation is insufficient to fully understanding embodied cognition. We must pinpoint how sameness and difference in thought processes are established. Thus, while it is important to acknowledge the role of environment and context in cognition, we must also consider how individuals perceive and define contexts, their substance, boundaries, functions, who is included and excluded from a context, and the differing access within them to people with variant characteristics, status, and power. Similarly, to fully understand the role of body, one must understand not only the process of inscription but also variations in outcome. The body does not read and store all stimuli in its path. There is a selection process at work in inscription that is closely tied to the norms, values, and practices of the inscription context. The workings of the brain raise similar issues. While fMRIs can illustrate brain activity, we must also study how that activity is experienced by the individual. As Pitts-Taylor notes (2014, 2016), cognitive scientists sometimes make neural differences real even when no behavioral outcomes exist. Understanding the "break" that occurs between attention and retention, between apprehension and response, requires a sociological eye:

> Embodiment can be understood as marked by inequality; affected by race, class, gender, and other patterns of social difference; enmeshed in suffering and violence, as easily as it can be viewed as a common thread that unites. Embodiment is not exactly the same for everyone, and simulation cannot guarantee sociality or empathy. The potential for conflict, misunderstanding, and violence should not be set aside, nor acknowledged only as clinical pathology, but rather understood as part of embodied reality in contexts of persistent inequality.
>
> (Pitts-Taylor 2016:92; see also Frank 2010)

To be sure, sociologists are beginning to forge new ground in embodied cognition studies. However, the mission must be expanded. Toward that end, sociologists should briefly pause from theorizing embodied cognition and begin to broadly test the ideas that existing theories present. As this chapter reveals, empirical work in this area is scant. To successfully expand a sociological presence, we must embrace all methodological approaches to embodied cognition—including findings generated in laboratories, interviews, focus groups, field observations, and discourse analyses. Only patient empirical inquiry, in all its forms, can bring sociology to the center of dialogue on embodied cognition—a perspective sorely needed in any inquiry on thought.

NOTES

1. In the 1950s, computer scientists, linguists, neuroscientists, and psychologists joined in a common quest to better understand how thinking occurs.
2. In animals, we call tools of simulation "mirror neurons." Some feel that mirror neurons are distinct to animals, but most cognitive scientists agree that similar representational

architectures or "mirroring mechanisms" operate in the human brain. See, for example, Bergen (2012), Gallese (2010), Gallese et al. (2004).

3. For a more extensive review of cognitive science work on embodied cognition, see, for example, Spackman and Yanchar (2013).

REFERENCES

Acord, Sophia Krzys. 2010. "Beyond the Head: The Practical Work of Curating Contemporary Art." *Qualitative Sociology* 33(4):447–67.

Adam, Hajo, and Adam D. Galinsky. 2012. "Enclothed Cognition." *Journal of Experimental Social Psychology* 48(4):918–25.

Allen-Collinson, Jacquelyn, and Helen Owton. 2014. "Take a Deep Breath: Asthma, Sporting Embodiment, the Senses and 'Auditory Work.'" *International Review for the Sociology of Sport* 49(5):592–608.

Bailenson, Jeremy N., Andrew C. Beall, and Jim Blascovich. 2002. "Gaze and Task Performance in Shared Virtual Environments." *Journal of Visualization and Computer Animation* 5(13):313–20.

Bailey, David, Jerome Feldman, Srini Narayanan, and George Lakoff. 1997. "Modeling Embodied Lexical Development." pp. 19–24 in *Proceedings of the 19th Cognitive Science Society Conference*, edited by M. G. Shafto and P. Langley. Hillsdale: Lawrence Erlbaum Associates.

Bargh John A., Mark Chen, and Lara Burrows. 1996. "Automaticity of Social Behavior: Direct Effects of Trait Construct and Stereotype Activation on Action." *Journal of Personality and Social Psychology* 71(2):230–44.

Barsalou, Lawrence W. 1999. "Perceptual Symbol Systems." *Behavioral and Brain Sciences* 22(4):577–660.

Bergen, Benjamin K. 2012. *Louder than Words: The New Science of How the Mind Makes Meaning*. New York: Basic.

Biocca, Frank. 1998. "The cyborg's dilemma: Progressive embodiment in virtual environments." *Human Factors in Information Technology* 13(1):113–44.

Biocca, Frank. 2014. "Connected to My Avatar." *Social Computing and Social Media* 8531:421–9. New York: Springer International.

Blascovich, Jim. 2002. "Social Influence within Immersive Virtual Environments." pp. 127–45 in *The Social Life of Avatars*, edited by R. Schroeder. London: Springer.

Bourdieu, Pierre. 1990. *The Logic of Practice*. London: Polity Press.

Brockman, John. 1999. "'Philosophy in the Flesh' A Talk with George Lakoff [3.9.99]." *The Third Culture*. http://edge.org/3rd_culture/lakoff/lakoff_p1.html.

Cerulo, Karen A. 2000. "The Rest of the Story: Sociocultural Patterns of Story Elaboration." *Poetics* 28:21–45.

Cerulo, Karen A. 2010. "Mining the Intersections of Cognitive Sociology and Neuroscience." *Poetics* 38(2):115–32.

Cerulo, Karen A. 2015. "The Embodied Mind: Building on Wacquant's Carnal Sociology." *Qualitative Sociology* 38(1):33–38.

Cerulo, Karen A. 2016. "Cognition and Cultural Sociology: The Inside and Outside of Thought." pp. 116–130 in *Sage Handbook of Cultural Sociology*, edited by D. Inglis. London: SAGE.

Cerulo, Karen A. 2018. "Scents and Sensibility: Olfaction, Sense-making and Meaning Attribution." *American Sociological Review* 83(2):361–89.

Clark, Andy. 1997. *Being There: Putting Brain, Body, and World Together Again*. Cambridge, MA: MIT Press.

Cerulo, Karen A. 2010. *Supersizing the Mind: Embodiment, Action, and Cognitive Extension*. New York: Oxford University Press.

Clark, Andy, and David Chalmers. 1998. "The Extended Mind." *Analysis* 58(1):7–19.

Clough, Patricia T. 2007. "Introduction." pp. 1–33 in *The Affective Turn: Theorizing the Social*, edited by P. Clough. Durham, NC: Duke University Press.

Cooperrider, Kensy, and Rafael Núñez. 2009. "Across Time, across the Body: Transversal Temporal Gestures." *Gesture* 9(2):181–206.

Costa, Mark R., Sung Yeun Kim, and Frank Biocca. 2013. "Embodiment and Embodied Cognition." pp. 333–42 in *Virtual Augmented and Mixed Reality. Designing and Developing Augmented and Virtual Environments*, edited by R. Shumaker and S. Lackey. Berlin/Heidelberg: Springer.

D'Aloia, Adriano. 2015. "The Character's Body and the Viewer: Cinematic Empathy and Embodied Simulation in the Film Experience." pp. 187–99 in *Embodied Cognition and Cinema*, edited by M. Coegnarts and P. Kravagna. Leuven, Belgium: Leuven University Press.

Daipha, Phaedra. 2015. "From Bricolage to Collage: The Making of Decisions at a Weather Forecast Office." *Sociological Forum* 30(3):787–808.

Damasio, Antonio. 2008. *Descartes' Error: Emotion, Reason and the Human Brain*. New York: Random House.

Desmond, Matthew. 2006. "Becoming a Firefighter." *Ethnography* 7(4):387–421.

Downey, Greg. 2008. "Beyond Bourdieu's 'Body': Giving Too Much Credit?" *Neuroanthropology* (Jan. 20). http://neuroanthropology.net/2008/01/20/beyond-bourdieus-body-giving-too-much-credit/.

Durlach, Nat, and Mel Slater. 2000. "Presence in Shared Virtual Environments and Virtual Togetherness." *Presence* 9(2):214–17.

Dijkstra, Katinka, Anita Eerland, Josjan Zijlmans, and Lysanne S. Post. 2014. "Embodied Cognition, Abstract Concepts, and the Benefits of New Technology for Implicit Body Manipulation." *Frontiers in Psychology* 5:757–65.

Eagleman, David. 2012. *Incognito: The Secret Lives of the Brain*. New York: Vintage.

Eerland, Anita, Tulio M. Guadalupe, and Rolf A. Zwaan. 2011. "Leaning to the Left Makes the Eiffel Tower Seem Smaller: Posture-Modulated Estimation." *Psychological Science* 22(12):1511–14.

Eastwick, Paul W., and Wendi L. Gardner. 2008. "Is It a Game? Evidence for Social Influence in the Virtual World." *Social Influence* 4(1):18–32.

Franks, David. 2010. *Neurosociology: The Nexus between Neuroscience and Social Psychology*. New York: Springer.

Gallese, Vittorio. 2010. "Embodied Simulation and Its Role in Intersubjectivity." pp. 78–92 in *The Embodied Self. Dimensions, Coherence and Disorders*, edited by T. Fuchs, H. C. Sattel, and P. Henningsen. Stuttgart: Schattauer.

Gallese, Vittorio, Christian Keysers, and Giacomo Rizzolatti. 2004. "A Unifying View of the Basis of Social Cognition." *Trends in Cognitive Sciences* 8(9):396–403.

Griswold, Wendy, Gemma Mangione, and Terence E. McDonnell. 2013. "Objects, Words, and Bodies in Space: Bringing Materiality into Cultural Analysis." *Qualitative Sociology* 36(4):343–64.

Hansson, Niklas, and Kerstin Jacobsson. 2014. "Learning to Be Affected: Subjectivity, Sense, and Sensibility in Animal Rights Activism." *Society and Animals* 22(3):262–88.

Hofer, Matthias, Andreas Hüsser, and Sujay Prabhu. 2017. "The effect of an avatar's emotional expressions on players' fear reactions: The mediating role of embodiment." *Computers in Human Behavior* 75(5):883–90.

Ignatow, Gabriel. 2009. "Culture and Embodied Cognition: Moral Discourses in Internet Support Groups for Overeaters." *Social Forces* 88(2):643–69.

Ignatow, Gabriel. 2015. "Theoretical Foundations for Digital Text Analysis." *Journal for the Theory of Social Behaviour* 46(1):104–20.

Johnson, Mark. 1989. "Embodied Knowledge." *Curriculum Inquiry* 19(4):361–77.

Kidder, Jeffrey L. 2009. "Appropriating the City: Space, Theory, and Bike Messengers." *Theory and Society* 38(3):307–28.

Kleiner, Sibyl. 2009. "Thinking with the Mind, Syncing with the Body: Ballet as Symbolic and Nonsymbolic Interaction." *Symbolic Interaction* 32(3):236–59.

Lakoff, George. 1990. *Women, Fire, and Dangerous Things: What Categories Reveal about the Mind*. Chicago: University of Chicago Press.

Lakoff, George. 2014. *The All New Don't Think of an Elephant!: Know Your Values and Frame the Debate*. Claremont, NH: Chelsea Green.

Lakoff, George, and Mark Johnson. 1980. *Metaphors We Live By*. Chicago: University of Chicago Press.

Lakoff, George, and Mark Johnson. 1999. *Philosophy in the Flesh: The Embodied Mind and Its Challenge to Western Thought*. New York: Basic Books.

Lee, Kwan Min. 2004. "Presence, Explicated." *Communication Theory* 14(1):27–50.

Lee, Spike W. S., and Norbert Schwarz. 2010. "Washing Away Postdecisional Dissonance." *Science* 328(5979):709.

Lizardo, Omar. 2004. "The Cognitive Origins of Bourdieu's *Habitus*." *Journal for the Theory of Social Behaviour* 34(4):375–401.

Lombard, Matthew, Frank Biocca, Jonathan Freeman, Wijnand IJsselsteijn, and Rachel J. Schaevitz. 2015. *Immersed in Media: Telepresence Theory, Measurement and Technology*. New York: Springer.

Mahler, Jonathan. 2015. "The White and Gold (No, Blue and Black!) Dress That Melted the Internet." *New York Times* (February 27). http://www.nytimes.com/2015/02/28/business/a-simple-question-about-a-dress-and-the-world-weighs-in.html?_r=0.

Måseide, Per, and Håvar Grøttland. 2015. "Enacting Blind Spaces and Spatialities: A Sociological Study of Blindness Related to Space, Environment and Interaction." *Symbolic Interaction* 38(4):594–610.

McDonnell, Terence E. 2016. *Best Laid Plans: Cultural Entropy and the Unraveling of AIDS Media Campaigns*. Chicago: University of Chicago Press.

Merleau-Ponty, Maurice. 1945/1962. *Phenomenology of Perception*. Translated by Colin Smith. New York: Humanities Press, and London: Routledge & Kegan Paul.

Merleau-Ponty, Maurice. 1964/1968. *The Visible and the Invisible, Followed by Working Notes*. Translated by Alphonso Lingis. Evanston, IL: Northwestern University Press.

Miles, Lyndon K., Louise K. Lind, and C. Neil Macrae. 2010. "Moving through Time." *Psychological Science* 21(2):222–3.

Núñez, Rafael E., and Eve Sweetser. 2006. "With the Future Behind Them: Convergent Evidence from Aymara Language and Gesture in the Crosslinguistic Comparison of Spatial Construals of Time." *Cognitive Science* 30(3):401–50.

Pagis, Michal. 2010. "Producing Intersubjectivity in Silence: An Ethnographic Study of Meditation Practice." *Ethnography* 11(2): 309–28.

Peterson, David. 2015. "All That Is Solid Bench-Building at the Frontiers of Two Experimental Sciences." *American Sociological Review* 80(6):1201–25.

Pitts-Taylor, Victoria. 2014. "Cautionary Notes on Navigating the Neurocognitive Turn." *Sociological Forum* 29(4):995–1000.

Pitts-Taylor, Victoria. 2016. *The Brain's Body: Neuroscience and Corporal Politics.* Durham, NC: Duke University Press.

Pugh, Allison J. 2013. "What Good Are Interviews for Thinking about Culture and Quest: Demystifying Interpretive Analysis." *American Journal of Cultural Sociology* 1(1):42–68.

Ratan, Rabindra A., and Michael Dawson. 2016. "When Mii Is Me: A Psychophysiological Examination of Avatar Self-Relevance." *Communication Research* 43(8):1065–93.

Rees, Charlotte E., Lynn V. Knight, and Clare E. Wilkinson. 2007. "Doctors Being Up There and We Being Down Here: A Metaphorical Analysis of Talk about Student/Doctor–Patient Relationships." *Social Science and Medicine* 65(4):725–37.

Regenbrecht, Holger, and Thomas Schubert. 2002. "Real and Illusory Interactions Enhance Presence in Virtual Environments." *Presence: Teleoperators and Virtual Environments* 11(4):425–34.

Rizzolatti, Giacomo, Luciano Fadiga, Vittorio Gallese, and Leonardo Fogassi. 1996. "Premotor Cortex and the Recognition of Motor Actions." *Cognitive Brain Research* 3(2):131–41.

Schlaffke, Lara, Anne Golisch, Lauren M. Haag, Melanie Lenz, Stefanie Heba, Silke Lissek, et al. 2015. "The Brain's Dress Code: How 'The Dress' Allows to Decode the Neuronal Pathway of an Optical Illusion." *Cortex* 73:271–5.

Schubert Thomas W. 2005. "Your Highness: Vertical Positions as Perceptual Symbols of Power." *Journal of Personality and Social Psychology* 89(1):1–21.

Schuster, John, Erik Beune, and Karien Stronks. 2011. "Metaphorical Constructions of Hypertension among Three Ethnic Groups in the Netherlands." *Ethnicity and Health* 16(6):583–600.

Spackman, Jonathan S., and Stephen C. Yanchar. 2013. "Embodied Cognition, Representationalism, and Mechanism: A Review and Analysis." *Journal of the Theory of Social Behavior* 44(1):46–79.

Spencer, Dale C. 2009. "Habit (us), Body Techniques and Body Callusing: An Ethnography of Mixed Martial Arts." *Body and Society* 15(4):119–43.

Stepper Sabine, and Fritz Strack. 1993. "Proprioceptive Determinants of Emotional and Nonemotional Feelings." *Journal of Personality and Social Psychology* 64(2):211–20.

Strack Fritz, Leonard L. Martin, and Sabine Stepper. 1988. "Inhibiting and Facilitating Conditions of the Human Smile: A Nonobtrusive Test of the Facial Feedback Hypothesis." *Journal of Personality and Social Psychology* 54(5):768–77.

Taylor, T. L. 2002. "Living Digitally: Embodiment in Virtual Worlds." pp. 40–62 in *The Social Life of Avatars: Presence and Interaction in Shared Virtual Environments,* edited by R. Schroeder. London: Springer/Verlag.

Turner, Stephen. 2007. "Social Theory as a Cognitive Neuroscience." *European Journal of Social Theory* 10(3):357–74.

Vaisey, Stephen. 2008. "Socrates, Skinner, and Aristotle: Three Ways of Thinking about Culture in Action1." *Sociological Forum* 23(3):603–13.

Varela, Francisco, Evan Thompson, and Eleanor Rosch. 1991. *The Embodied Mind: Cognitive Science and Human Experience.* Cambridge, MA: MIT Press.

Vertesi, Janet. 2009. "Seeing Like a Rover": Images in Interaction on the Mars Exploration Rover Mission." Dissertation. Cornell University, Ithaca, New York.

Vertesi, Janet. 2015. *Seeing Like a Rover: How Robots, Teams, and Images Craft Knowledge of Mars*. Chicago: University of Chicago Press.

Wacquant, Loïc. 2004. *Body and Soul: Notebooks of an Apprentice Boxer*. New York: Oxford.

Wacquant, Loïc. 2015. "For a Sociology of Flesh and Blood." *Qualitative Sociology* 38(1):1–11.

Wells Gary L. and Richard E. Petty. 1980. "The Effects of Overt Head Movement on Persuasion: Compatibility and Incompatibility of Responses." *Basic and Applied Social Psychology* 1:219–30.

Williams, Kipling D., Christopher K. T. Cheung, and Wilma Choi. 2000. "Cyberostracism: Effects of Being Ignored over the Internet." *Journal of Personality and Social Psychology* 79(5):748–62.

Wilson, Andrew D. 2012. "A Tale of Two Robots" *Psychology Today* (June 28). https://www.psychologytoday.com/blog/cognition-without-borders/201206/tale-two-robots.

Winchester, Daniel. 2008. "Embodying the Faith: Religious Practice and the Making of a Muslim Moral Habitus." *Social Forces* 86(4):1753–80.

Winchester, Daniel. 2016. "A Hunger for God: Embodied Metaphor as Cultural Cognition in Action." *Social Forces* 95(2):585–606.

Yee, Nick, and Jeremy Bailenson. 2007. "The Proteus Effect: The Effect of Transformed Self-Representation on Behavior." *Human Communication Research* 33(3):271–90.

Zhong, Chen-Bo, and Geoffrey J. Leonardelli. 2008. "Cold and Lonely: Does Social Exclusion Literally Feel Cold?" *Psychological Science* 19(9):838–42.

CHAPTER 6

....

THE OLD ONE-TWO

preserving analytical dualism
*in cognitive sociology**

....

STEPHEN VAISEY AND MARGARET FRYE

AMONG contemporary microsociologists, three related beliefs are increasingly common. The first is that sociology suffers from the lack of a coherent "theory of action." On this view, sociologists differ from, for example, economists (who have expected utility maximization) or personality psychologists (who have traits) because we rely on a troublingly ad hoc mix of norms, sanctions, social influence, power seeking, and crypto-rational instrumentalism to explain human conduct (see Campbell 1996; Smith 2003). The second belief is that sociologists should pay more attention to research in the cognitive sciences (used here broadly to include psychology, neuroscience, and related disciplines) to outline a set of cognitively realistic principles that can inform the construction of a better theory of action (see, e.g., DiMaggio 1997; Lizardo 2007; Vaisey 2009). The third belief is that the theoretical tradition of Pierre Bourdieu can serve as a bridge between sociology and the cognitive sciences that will facilitate better answers to questions about why people do the things they do (Lizardo 2004; Ignatow 2009; Vaisey 2009).

We share these three beliefs, though we hasten to add that the dialogue between cognitive science and microsociology has barely begun. Even among the subset of cognitive sociologists who agree that the "Bourdieusian bridge" is especially promising, fundamental issues remain underexplored. A particular danger at this stage is that superficial similarities between positions can mask disagreements (or potential disagreements) on issues that are important for conducting and interpreting empirical research.

In our view, a particularly important issue surrounding the Bourdieu–cognitive science fusion—and the one we explore in the chapter—is how to conceive of the various binary oppositions subsumed under the rubric of "dual-processing" models of cognition (Vaisey 2009). Though not all research in this domain can be subsumed under a unitary "System 1–System 2" framework, most psychologists and neuroscientists recognize a wide variety of contrasts that map roughly onto an analytical distinction between "fast, automatic, or unconscious" processes on the one hand and "slow, effortful, or conscious" processes on the other (see Evans 2008:270; Kahneman 2011). One source of the affinity between Bourdieusian sociology and the contemporary cognitive sciences is that both are principled reactions to the faulty "Cartesian" conception of mind as perfectly rational and separable from the body (Bourdieu and Wacquant 1992:5, 20, 26, 49; Willmott 1999; Uleman 2007). Both recognize the ubiquity and importance of unconscious, embodied cognition; in fact, Bourdieu's (e.g., 1977, 1990) notion of *habitus* is surprisingly compatible with emerging conceptions of the "cognitive unconscious" (Hassin et al. 2007; Lizardo 2009).

But unless we simply want to exchange the *terms* "habitus" for "cognitive unconscious" when we cross the interdisciplinary bridge, we need to work toward specifying more precisely the character of this compatibility. Like many of our colleagues (e.g., Lizardo 2004, 2009; Ignatow 2007, 2009), we are quite optimistic about bringing together cognitive science and the Bourdieusian tradition and we hope our argument is interpreted with this in mind. Our concern is that the Bourdieusian distaste for "dualisms" risks rendering this cross-pollination less fruitful than it might otherwise be. We argue that there are two basic responses to faulty mind-body dualism. The first option, taken by the Bourdieusian tradition, is simply to reject it. The second option is to preserve what is of value in this classical dualism by better specifying it. Our thesis here is that respecification is preferable to rejection on both theoretical and empirical grounds. We attempt to argue for this claim while demonstrating that it is compatible with the aims and commitments of Bourdieusian sociology.

We proceed as follows: first, we outline rejection and respecification as possible reactions to mind-body dualism and argue that the latter is a preferable option. Second, we use excerpts from Loïc Wacquant's seminal book, *Body and Soul: Notebooks of an Apprentice Boxer*, to demonstrate the usefulness of our analytic reformulation. *Body and Soul* provides an ethnographic account of Wacquant's years spent becoming a boxer at a gym on the South Side of Chicago. We rely on this book because it is one of the most clearly articulated cases for mind-body holism in cultural sociology and because it contains both theoretical explanation and a deep engagement with empirical data. Further, as an "apprenticeship ethnography" (Lizardo et al. 2016:294), *Body and Soul* is an excellent case study for examining the dual-process model, because it describes Wacquant's experiences learning both the rules, hierarchies, and beliefs that circulate within the Woodlawn gym (through a process known as *explicit* learning, associated with Type 2 cognition) and the bodily routines and postures that make up the skill of boxing (through a process known as *implicit* learning, associated with Type 1 cognition). This allows us to engage with both the theoretical logic and its application to a concrete case.

We hope to show that distinguishing between "practical" and "discursive" cognition (or, more accurately, between Type 1 and Type 2 cognitions [Evans 2008:270–71]) and considering their interplay over time can shed additional light on the social processes Wacquant identifies. We conclude by considering how a properly (that is, analytically) dualistic model of cognition might be grafted into a Bourdieusian sociology in ways that will benefit both research traditions.

6.1 Dealing with Descartes: Two Responses to the Flaws of Mind-Body Dualism

A strong distinction between body and mind is a dominant and recurring feature of the Western philosophical tradition. Mind-body dualism is most often associated with René Descartes, who claimed that mind "was a substance whose whole essence or nature is simply to think, and which does not require any place, or depend on any material thing, in order to exist" (Descartes, quoted in Hatfield 2008). This is not to say that Descartes rejected the importance of the body or did not consider some of what we today might call "automatic cognitions." For example, he argued,

> [A] very large number of the motions occurring inside us do not depend in any way on the mind.... When people take a fall, and stick out their hands so as to protect their head, it is not reason that instructs them to do this; it is simply that the sight of the impending fall reaches the brain and sends the animal spirits into the nerves in the manner necessary to produce this movement even without any mental volition, just as it would be produced in a machine.   (quoted in Hatfield 2008)

Despite such acknowledgments, Descartes saw the mind-body divide as fundamental. There is no need here to expound here on the limitations of this view; in this context it is enough to say that a great deal of research has shown that even the highest-order mental processes are dependent in crucial ways on the "embodied mind" (see, e.g., Lakoff and Johnson 1999; Ignatow 2007, 2010).

Although the embodied nature of mind is now rarely—if ever—explicitly denied, a great deal of research in sociology proceeds *as if* Descartes's dualism were correct (see related discussions in, e.g., Wrong 1961; Shilling 1997; Wilmott 1999; Ignatow 2007). But as scholars living at a time in which the embodiment of mind is firmly established, our question must not be *whether* to reject Descartes's strict mind-body dualism but rather what to put in its place. There appear to be two basic answers. The first is to reject Descartes's dualism as a false dichotomy. This is the path Bourdieu and Wacquant take, although we will argue in the conclusion that categorical rejection is not a necessary part of Bourdieusian theory. The second is to recognize that while body and mind are *physically* inseparable, we can nevertheless treat "mind" (Descartes's higher level, "Type 2" cognitions) and "body" (lower level, "Type 1" cognitions) as *analytically* distinguishable.

6.1.1 Dualism Denied

As a matter of theoretical commitment, it is not difficult to establish that Bourdieu and Wacquant regard body-mind holism as a key principle (see also Ignatow 2010). In their collaborative book, *Invitation to Reflexive Sociology*, the first sentence of Wacquant's summary of the Bourdieusian approach avers that it is "based on a non-Cartesian social ontology that *refuses to split* subject and object, intention and cause, *materiality and symbolic representation*" (Bourdieu and Wacquant 1992:5, emphasis added). Bourdieu himself makes a similar claim, stating that his theory "reject[s] all the conceptual dualisms upon which nearly all post-Cartesian philosophies are based: subject and object, *material and spiritual*, individual and social, and so on" (Bourdieu and Wacquant 1992:122). While more dualisms are involved here than mind-body, rejecting this particular dualism is clearly a key theoretical commitment.

A firm dedication to mind-body holism persists in *Body and Soul* (2004). Using boxing as a case because of what it "can teach us about the logic of any practice" (16), Wacquant begins his account with the claim that becoming a boxer is a process of "appropriat[ing] ... a set of corporeal mechanisms and mental schemata so intimately imbricated that they *erase the distinction* between the physical and spiritual," a process so deeply embodied that it "*erases the boundary* between reason and passion [and] *explodes the opposition* between action and representation" (17, emphasis added). Following Marcel Mauss, who is an early founder of the Bourdieu-Wacquant tradition (see Ignatow, this volume), Wacquant advances a "theor[y] of social action" that regards human conduct as "physio-psycho-sociological assemblages of series of acts ... more or less habitual or more or less ancient in the life of the individual" (17). Wacquant's rejection of mind-body dualism (which includes rejecting corollary oppositions like reason and passion, representation and action) could not be clearer, nor could it be given greater theoretical emphasis.

In the strict ontological sense, Wacquant is completely justified in his holistic position. All forms of thinking, judging, reasoning, perceiving, learning, and so on are equally "embodied" in the sense Descartes rejected because they all "depend on [the] material thing" called the body (including particularly, though not exclusively, the brain). Even the "highest" forms of reasoning—such as philosophizing—are dependent in crucial ways on "lower" processes (Lakoff and Johnson 1999; Evans 2008:271). We now know beyond a reasonable doubt that no rigid ontological separation of mind and body is, in fact, possible (see Ignatow 2007).

6.1.2 Defending (Analytical) Dualism

In an analytic sense, however, rejecting these distinctions seems to us to go too far. Though we must dismiss the idea that there is no such thing as pure, disembodied consciousness, it does not follow that we must reject the fact that some cognitions are *more* "mind-like" in the traditional sense—conscious, reasoned, propositional, or "platform independent"—while others are more "body-like"—unconscious, passionate, procedural, or "platform dependent" (see Clark 2008:43; Evans 2008:270; Kahneman 2011). Indeed, this is the whole thrust behind dual-processing models in cognitive science.

Nor would we be justified in declaring this analytic distinction "merely" analytic; although there are not discrete neurological systems for different types of cognition, they do draw on different elements of the brain and body disproportionately (see Evans and Stanovich 2013 for a recent overview).

What are the advantages of keeping these systems analytically distinct in our research? The tension between holism and dualism here resembles similar tensions around other classic polarities in social theory, such as structure and agency, structure and culture, micro and macro, among others (Archer 1995; Martin 2003). Though the potential pitfalls of generic holism have been discussed at greater length elsewhere (see, e.g., Archer 1995), we discuss only two here that seem particularly salient to the "mind-body" issue.

First, Mauss, Bourdieu, and Wacquant are correct in their assertions that action is the result of "physio-psycho-sociological" processes and that strategies of action are "more or less habitual" (Wacquant 2004:17). While we agree, we would like to put the emphasis on the disjunctive "or" in "more *or* less." That is, a particular form of knowledge or action associated with a particular social actor (or set of social actors) may properly be considered more habitual and "embodied" *or* less habitual and "embodied," depending on the phenomenon in question. Though a holistic approach tends to downplay these differences (precisely because it decides *not* to see them), we argue that it is worth paying attention to them because they can lead to additional insight into social processes.

Second, a holism that is "*at once* corporeal and mental" (Wacquant 2004:16) does not provide theoretical leverage on examining how the "corporeal" and the "mental" can influence each other sequentially over time via analytically distinct types of processes. If—as asserted by holism—all learning is always *simultaneously* corporeal and mental, then we cannot ask whether and when learning processes become more "mental" and less "corporeal," or vice versa.

6.1.3 An Analytic Typology of Cognitive Socialization

By combining an analytical dualism that distinguishes between "practical" (i.e., embodied, unconscious, Type 1) and "discursive" (i.e., propositional, conscious, Type 2) forms of cognition (Vaisey 2009) with a consideration of temporality, we can form a typology that may shed light on different dynamics of "cognitive socialization" in naturalistic settings (Zerubavel 1997; Lizardo 2009). Our simplified typology distinguishes between (1) social knowledge that starts and continues as practical knowledge; (2) social knowledge that begins discursively and gradually becomes practical; (3) social knowledge that is formed as practical knowledge but that its holders attempt to articulate discursively; and (4) social knowledge that remains primarily at the level of discursive consciousness. These processes, represented in Figure 6.1, are analytically distinct (like Weber's [1978] types of action) and are characterized by different causal dynamics, as we show in what follows.

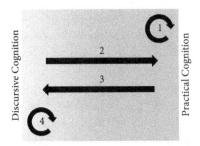

FIGURE 6.1 Four analytic types of cognitive socialization.

Note: the directions of the arrows represent the passage of time. The four types are: (1) social knowledge that starts and continues as practical knowledge; (2) social knowledge that beginsdiscursively and gradually becomes practical; (3) social knowledge that is formed as practicalknowledge but that its holders attempt to articulate discursively; and (4) social knowledge thatremains primarily at the level of discursive consciousness.

6.2 THE DIVIDENDS OF DUALISM: A BRIEF LOOK AT *BODY AND SOUL*

To illustrate the value of this typology for analyzing the logic of social practices, we analyze a variety of episodes from Wacquant's *Body and Soul*. Revisiting this book with these four "ideal-typical" modes of action in mind demonstrates how an analytically dualist approach to cognition can reveal subtle distinctions that are hard to detect using a holist approach.

6.2.1 Staying in the Practical Realm: The Comprehension of the Body

The first mode of action occurs when actors remain at the level of practical cognition throughout the acquisition of a practice. Three types of cognitive socialization described in *Body and Soul* in which actors seem to remain at the practical, automatic level of cognition are the cultivation of boxing skills through repetitive drills and exercise routines, mimetic copying of the movements of others, and reflexive responses during sparring.

Floorwork, or the sequence of drills that is repeated by all boxers in the gym, "day after day, week after week, with only barely perceptible variations" (2004:60), constitutes the core of the training regimen for boxers. Through seemingly endless cycles of shadowboxing, simulated boxing, bag punching, rope jumping, and strength training, boxers cultivate a "comprehension of the body" wrought through the repeated gestures and postures, which remains independent of conscious awareness. Wacquant writes:

> There *is a comprehension of the body that goes beyond—and comes prior to—full visual and mental cognizance.* Only the permanent carnal experimentation that is

training, as a coherent complexus of "incorporating practices," can enable one to acquire this practical mastery of the practical rules of pugilism, *which precisely satisfies the condition of dispensing with the need to constitute them as such in consciousness.*

(2004:69, emphasis added)

Here all learning is rooted in the comprehension of the body: bodily movements evolve into symbolic schemas and abstract concepts, as a child develops "higher order" knowledge from a set of "lower order" sensorimotor schemas (see Lizardo 2009). Gallagher (1998) refines Piaget's concept of the body schema, which he describes as "the body's nonconscious appropriation of habitual postures and movements, its incorporation of various significant parts of the environment into its own experiential organization" (226; see also Gallagher 2005). Gallagher distinguishes *body schemas*, which are "preintentional" and "never fully represented in consciousness" from *body image*, in which the body constitutes the "object or content of intentional consciousness" (1998:226). Despite being nonconscious, body schemas are not passive or reflexive: the body "*actively organizes*" stimuli according to the circumstances and intentions of the individual (1998:235). As Lizardo et al. (2016) note, practical or embodied learning is in cognitive science understood to be slow learning, and indeed Wacquant describes these drills as monotonous and repetitious.

Beyond the mere repetition of sequences of movements at the individual level, boxing gyms also cultivate practical knowledge through mimesis: a fighter is constantly surrounded by other bodies in motion, who act as visual models of the proper execution of each gesture. As Wacquant describes:

> This continuous visual and auditory reinforcement generates a state of "collective effervescence"... which has the effect of facilitating the assimilation of gestures by prodding participants to *drop their inhibitions, to "let go" of their bodies*, to whip up their energy.   (2004:116)

We can see that the synchronicity of the training routines often enables fighters to remain at the level of automatic cognition, without the interference of deliberate, conscious thought. Bourdieu (1990) speaks of a "practical mimesis" that is "opposed to both memory and knowledge and tend[s] to take place below the level of consciousness [and] has nothing in common with an *imitation* that would presuppose a conscious effort to reproduce a gesture, an utterance, or an object" (73). As Lizardo astutely points out, mirror neurons are a possible mechanism allowing somatic knowledge to "'jump' from person to person" mimetically (2009:717). They appear to light up when an animal *sees, hears,* and *executes* an action (2009). Just as Bourdieu and Wacquant have argued, witnessing others complete a sequence of action allows an individual to develop familiarity with that sequence of movements in much the same way as if she were executing the actions herself.

The third example of action that remains at the practical level in *Body and Soul* is the cultivation of reflexes during sparring. As Wacquant describes, sparring alters perception, as the boxer learns to filter out distractions and focus on the movements of his opponent (87), and instills in the fighter a "cultivated instinct," where the body "computes and judges for him, instantaneously, without the mediation—and the costly delay that it would cause—of abstract thinking, prior representation, and strategic calculation" (97). This is an exceptionally clear example of Bourdieu's "practical sense," which is "instilled by the childhood learning that treats the body as a living memory pad, an automaton that 'leads the mind unconsciously along with it'" (1990:68). With the body operating as an automaton, skills and capabilities apprehended *practically* shape future behaviors much as instincts do, through mechanisms that remain imperceptible and inoperable to the conscious mind. Bourdieu writes, "What is 'learned by body' is not something that one has, like knowledge that can be brandished, but something that one is" (1990:73).

6.2.2 From Discourse to Practice: Verbal Instructions and Regulation of Sparring

All bodily knowledge, however, is not produced through practice alone. In several instances, the Woodlawn boxers move from the discursive realm to the practical realm, primarily when attempting to master a specific posture or movement. In his fieldnotes, Wacquant acknowledges the difference between this mode of transmission and the "carnal experimentation" described in the previous section. For example, in the short passage recounting how both coach DeeDee and fellow boxer Anthony attempt to instruct him on how to block an opponent's jab, there are at least six instances of verbal instructions given to Wacquant. Wacquant writes how "It's embarrassing to have this movement, seemingly so simple, explained to me again.... I think I'm starting to grasp the mechanics better, but it's *hard to go from mental comprehension to physical realization*" (123, emphasis added). The text here suggests that Wacquant the ethnographer recognizes the separation between mental and practical understanding that he is committed to denying in a more theoretical mode. The difficulty Wacquant faces in going from the practical to the discursive realm is also consistent with research from cognitive science; as Lizardo et al. (2016:17) write, "if learners of a complex motor skill attempt to consciously focus on their movements or even verbalize rules for task completion, this can hinder the acquisition of the skill."

Elsewhere in the narrative, DeeDee is trying to help Wacquant with his left hook. After repeated verbal descriptions of how the move should be executed, DeeDee runs out of patience and "grudgingly resigns himself to calling on the reflex of self-defense," announcing that he will tell Wacquant's sparring partner to teach him "*with his left hook*, if you don't wanna listen." Wacquant responds: "That's the best way to learn, right?" DeeDee replies: "No, it ain't the best way, *it's the hard way*. I rather you learn it on your own when I tell you, not by getting your face beat up" (103, emphasis in original). In this passage, both Wacquant and DeeDee are explicitly comparing the deliberate mode of verbal instruction with the "reflexive," automatic mode of bodily experience.

Likewise, another episode shows Wacquant's sparring partner freezing the action in order to verbally communicate instructions on the technique of a move. As he describes in his fieldnotes:

> I move on Ashante right away and badger him with quick jabs, which he parries. *He stops me in my tracks to tell me,* "If you're coming at me, keep yo' han's up or I'monna deck you." Thanks for the advice, which I take into account by swiftly raising my guard. I resume my march forward.   (88, emphasis added)

The fact that Ashante chose to intervene in the middle of a match to relate this piece of advice demonstrates once again that boxers recognize the distinction between practical and discursive transmission of knowledge about boxing techniques. It seems from these examples that they deliberately choose between these two modes depending on the level of specificity of the information being expressed, in terms of the movements of the body. When the fighter needs advice about a particular move or an isolated part of the body, the discursive mode is preferred, while the practical mode is better for transmitting a "feel for the game" and for cultivating fluency in the sequences of moves required for success in the ring.

In addition to providing instructions for how to execute the techniques of boxing, the discursive mode often precedes the automatic mode in order to ensure the fighters' safety. This is particularly true during sparring matches, where boxer and coach must negotiate with each other to ensure that the sparring matches produce the optimal amount of exposure to combat while minimizing the risk of serious injury.

In the same passage describing the sparring match between Wacquant and Ashante, Wacquant describes the fighters' exchange during the break in between the second and third round: "[Ashante said] 'Tha's good Louie, you're doing good, you're punching har' today, keep it up.' [Wacquant replied] 'Yeah, the only problem is I'm not sure I can hold out for another round at this pace'" (90). Here, Wacquant is warning Ashante that his strength is waning, that he will be more vulnerable in the next round, so Ashante should lighten up or he may get hurt. And sure enough, when the fighting commences, Ashante lets up considerably and "pretends to be boxing but is only hitting me superficially" (90).

This discursive underpinning of sparring matches is also carried out on the sidelines, where the coach must monitor each fighter's progress to ensure that the delicate balance between exposure and risk is maintained. If a fighter oversteps the boundaries of the sparring match, the coach must intervene and verbally reprimand him. Wacquant gives an example, again discussing his experiences sparring with Ashante:

> On 29 June 1989, I am dumbfounded to learn that Ashante complained to DeeDee that I hit too hard and that he is forced to respond by firing back solid shots right in the mug. "He told me he can't hav fun witchu no more, you hit too hard. You've made enough progress now, he gotta be careful to not let you land your punches or you can hurt him."   (84–85)

As part of the practice of boxing, deliberate, intentional actions are sometimes required in order to ensure the safety of the practical, bodily actions in the ring.

The experiences Wacquant reports are in perfect agreement with the latest cognitive research on learning, which has learned that knowledge and goals "acquired reflectively through System 2 can, through repeated activation, be installed into rigid implicit processing mechanisms—a kind of automation of thought" (Evans 2008:261). In other words, not everything has to be learned "the hard way."

6.2.3 Practical to Discursive: "Corrective Face-Work"

The fighters portrayed in *Body and Soul* sometimes try to "make sense" verbally of rules and codes that are unspoken. In these instances, the boxers are moving from the practical mode of cognition, in which their judgments and decisions are automatic and subconscious, to the discursive, in which they, mindfully and intentionally, attempt to construct "post hoc" explanations of their actions and judgments (compare Haidt 2001; Wilson 2002). In the following passage, Wacquant describes how boxers resort to an "official explanation" to justify the unquestioned practical knowledge that only DeeDee should sit in a certain chair:

> The high swivel armchair... is strictly reserved for the master of the premises. The official explanation is that DeeDee does not want anyone else to sit in it on grounds that they would stain it with their sweat. But the prohibition applies also to those who come dressed in civilian clothes and do not train.... *The hygienic excuse cannot hide the social reason behind this taboo*: the armchair materializes DeeDee's place and function in the gym.   (2004:40, emphasis added)

In this passage, Wacquant compares the "social reason," which is tacitly accepted by all but explicitly mentioned by none, to the "official explanation" that boxers offer when questioned. This official explanation does not adequately explain the full extent of the taboo on the chair, yet it survives in the discourse of the gym. The fighters "just know" that they should not sit in the chair, but when asked to explain it, they attempt to construct a rational explanation for their moral judgments, an explanation which, constructed after the fact, turns out to be patchy and easily refuted by observing the practice itself (see Haidt 2001; Cushman et al. 2006; Vaisey 2009).

In another example of "post hoc" justification, Wacquant describes how, when a boxer flounders in a fight and threatens the hierarchy of the gym, other fighters quickly come to his aid and offer excuses to justify his actions:

> Every time a boxer steps into the ring... he puts a fraction of his symbolic capital at stake: the slightest failing or slip-up... brings immediate embarrassment to the fighter, as well as to his gym-mates who hasten to assist his "corrective face-work" so as to restabilize the fuzzy and labile status order of the gym. Boxers have at their disposal a variety of socially validated excuses for this purpose, ranging from minor

health hassles…to imaginary injuries…to the alibi most readily called upon…a breach of the sacrosanct code of sexual abstinence.   (79)

The term "corrective facework" is reminiscent of the rationales offered by the adult respondents in Swidler (2003) to explain their romantic love. Swidler describes how these individuals were choosing the most situationally appropriate justifications from a repertoire of cultural tropes to "make sense" of their actions for themselves and others. Like the boxers in *Body and Soul*, who select from "a variety of socially validated excuses," Swidler's respondents also chose from a "medley" of rationales; she writes, "If what one wants to do is support and justify a given way of life, having a variety of rationales available should strengthen one's position. If one argument fails, there are plenty of others available" (2003:30).

6.2.4 Exclusively Discursive Behavior: "Rules Is Rules"

While the Woodlawn boxers share an implicit, intuitive moral code, they also answer to a series of explicit, clearly defined *rules*, many of which have only a distant, hypothetical connection to the sport of boxing. Wacquant reports how Mickey Rosario, a trainer at another gym in New York, instructs a new recruit to his gym:

> Ok, first thing you got to know is the rules. We don't allow no cursing here. We don't allow no fighting, except in the ring. I ain't here to waste your time and you ain't here to waste mine. I don't smoke and I don't drink and I don't chase womens.…Rules is rules, no argument. You understand?   (2004:57)

Though Wacquant states that "initiation into boxing is an *initiation without explicit norms*" (2004:102, emphasis in original), the prohibitions listed in the passage just cited are earlier contrasted with a "series of lesser and often implicit rules" (2004:55), clearly implying that at least some rules are explicit and deliberately communicated to the fighters as a vital part of their apprenticeship. One fighter describes his experience attempting to follow the rules of the gym, "You know, *dedication,* when you gotta really dig deep down inside of you and go for what you want—you gotta say like well no women this month, you know, an' no hamburgers" (2004:67, emphasis in original). This fighter's language speaks of the conscious intentionality of his attempt to follow these rules: he talks to himself and tries to suppress his desire in order to display his dedication to the sport. (Presumably no amount of embodied expertise would make avoiding sex or hamburgers completely "natural.")

While some of these prohibitions could potentially be linked to the sport of boxing in terms of maintaining physical strength and mental focus during training periods, others are inarguably pedantic: coach DeeDee "will not allow the expression 'to fight' to be used in lieu of 'to box' (or 'to spar' for sparring sessions)" (2004:55). With no practical significance, these rules are consciously learned, deliberately followed, and verbally communicated. Such strict regulations serve to separate the "island of order and virtue" that is the gym from the surrounding disorder of the ghetto. By splitting hairs, the men at the gym signify their membership in a community where the unbridled passions of the street have no place.

6.3 CONCLUDING DISCUSSION

We want to clarify our intentions behind choosing to explicate this typology using examples from Wacquant's *Body and Soul*. We realize that by doing so, we run the risk of being interpreted as trying to pick apart Wacquant's analysis and reveal holes or false-hoods. This is far from our real objective, which is to build on—not criticize—his superb analysis of life in the gym. Leaving aside Wacquant's explicit denials of the dualism between the "mental" and "corporeal," we see abundant evidence that he fruitfully—if implicitly—relied on some version of this analytic tension in his explanation of the process of becoming a boxer. In any case, we freely acknowledge our limited under-standing of the sorts of scenes described in the book, since we relied solely on Wacquant as a source and "enter[ed] the pugilistic universe only through the mediation of the written word" (Wacquant 2004:70).

Despite these potential pitfalls, we chose to sketch our typology using examples from *Body and Soul* because we hoped that this would demonstrate that refining and specify-ing the duality between Type 1 and Type 2 cognition is fundamentally compatible with a Bourdieusian approach to sociological research.[1] We chose Wacquant's book because it seamlessly combines theoretical reasoning and empirical observation, enabling us to make our argument concrete. We understand and agree with Wacquant's desire to estab-lish distance from the exaggerated ontological dualisms of the Western philosophical tradition, but we firmly believe that respecifying the "mind-body" dualism in this manner adds valuable tools to the Bourdieusian repertoire that can help us to learn even more about "the logic of any practice."

We saw that Wacquant's actors rely on two analytically distinct types of cognition when learning both the postures of boxing as well as the rules of the pugilistic universe. They use Type 1 cognition, with their bodies acting as "automatons," to gain a "feel for the game," to understand the flow and rhythm of the ring. Yet when trying to develop competencies around more specific movements, they begin in the discursive realm, explicitly describing the sequence of movements and the placement of each part of the body before such gestures slowly become bodily knowledge, accessible through auto-matic processes directly. In terms of the code of rules and expectations, boxers also use two modes of cognition. There are some rules that remain unspoken, that just "make sense" intuitively as boxers become part of the gym community. In contrast, other rules seem to make little sense at all on a practical level; they are imparted through verbal admonishments and advice, and appear to convey and uphold the order of the gym amid the disorder of the street.

The goal of our argument has been to suggest that an important item on the agenda for the ongoing dialogue between cognitive scientists and microsociologists is how to replace Descartes's flawed mind-body dualism. Although we agree that strict mind-body dualism should be laid to rest, we believe that replacing this dichotomy with a holistic theory risks making it harder for researchers to see analytic distinctions that make a real difference. Thus, we have argued that sociologists should replace the old dualism with a new, improved one that incorporates cognitive science regarding differences between habitual, embodied cognition and intentional, discursive cognition. This will help microsociologists and cognitive scientists be in the best possible position to understand, enrich, and improve each other's work.

NOTES

* We thank Gabe Ignatow and Omar Lizardo for a stimulating discussion that improved this chapter.
1. See also Vaisey and Lizardo (2010) for an example of combining analytical dualism and Bourdieusian sociology in a study of social network formation.

REFERENCES

Archer, Margaret S. 1995. *Realist Social Theory: The Morphogenetic Approach*. New York: Cambridge University Press.

Bourdieu, Pierre. 1977. *Outline of a Theory of Practice*. New York: Cambridge University Press.

Bourdieu, Pierre. 1990. *The Logic of Practice*. Stanford, CA: Stanford University Press.

Bourdieu, Pierre, and Loic J. D. Wacquant. 1992. *An Invitation to Reflexive Sociology*. Chicago, IL: University of Chicago Press.

Campbell, Colin. 1996. *The Myth of Social Action*. New York: Cambridge University Press.

Clark, Andy. 2008. "Embodiment and Explanation." pp. 41–58 in *Handbook of Cognitive Science: An Embodied Approach*, edited by Paco Calvo and Toni Gomila. San Diego, CA: Elsevier.

Cushman, Fiery, Liane Young, and Marc Hauser. 2006. "The Role of Conscious Reasoning and Intuition in Moral Judgment." *Psychological Science* 17(12): 1082–9.

DiMaggio, Paul. 1997. "Culture and Cognition." *Annual Review of Sociology* 23:263–87.

Evans, Jonathan St. B. T. 2008. "Dual-Processing Accounts of Reasoning, Judgment, and Social Cognition." *Annual Review of Psychology* 59:255–78.

Evans, Jonathan St B. T., and Keith E. Stanovich. 2013. "Dual-Process Theories of Higher Cognition: Advancing the Debate." *Perspectives on Psychological Science* 8 (3): 223–41.

Gallagher, Shaun. 1998. "Body Schema and Intentionality." pp. 225–45 in *The Body and the Self*, edited by José Bermudez, Anthony Marcel, and Naomi Elian. Cambridge, MA: MIT Press.

Haidt, Jonathan. 2001. "The Emotional Dog and Its Rational Tail: A Social Intuitionist Approach to Moral Judgment." *Psychological Review* 108:814–34.

Hassin, Ran, James S. Uleman, and John A. Bargh, eds. 2007. *The New Unconscious*. New York: Oxford University Press.

Hatfield, Gary. 2008. "René Descartes." In *The Stanford Encyclopedia of Philosophy*, edited by Edward N. Zalta. http://plato.stanford.edu/entries/descartes/ (Accessed June 21, 2010).

Ignatow, Gabriel. 2007. "Theories of Embodied Knowledge: New Directions for Cultural and Cognitive Sociology?" *Journal for the Theory of Social Behaviour* 37:115–35.

Ignatow, Gabriel. 2009. "Why the Sociology of Morality Needs Bourdieu's Habitus." *Sociological Inquiry* 79:98–14.

Ignatow, Gabriel. 2010. "Morality and Mind-Body Connections." pp. 411–24 in *Handbook for the Sociology of Morality*, edited by Steven Hitlin and Stephen Vaisey. New York: Springer.

Kahneman, Daniel. 2011. *Thinking, Fast and Slow*. New York: Farrar, Straus and Giroux.

Lakoff, George, and Mark Johnson. 1999. *Philosophy in the Flesh: The Embodied Mind and Its Challenge to Western Thought*. New York: Basic Books.

Lizardo, Omar. 2004. "The Cognitive Origins of Bourdieu's Habitus." *Journal for the Theory of Social Behaviour* 34:375–401.

Lizardo, Omar. 2007. "Mirror Neurons, Collective Objects and the Problem of Transmission: Reconsidering Stephen Turner's Critique of Practice Theory." *Journal for the Theory of Social Behaviour* 37:319–50.

Lizardo, Omar. 2009. "Is a "Special Psychology" of Practice Possible? From Values and Attitudes to Embodied Dispositions." *Theory Psychology* 19:713–27.

Lizardo, Omar, Robert Mowry, Brandon Sepulvado, Dustin S. Stoltz, Marshall A. Taylor, Justin Van Ness, and Michael Wood. 2016. "What Are Dual Process Models? Implications for Cultural Analysis in Sociology." *Sociological Theory* 34(4): 287–310.

Martin, John Levi. 2003. "What Is Field Theory?" *American Journal of Sociology* 109:1–49.

Shilling, Chris. 1997. "The Undersocialized Conception of the Embodied Agent in Modern Sociology." *Sociology* 31:737–64.

Smith, Christian. 2003. *Moral, Believing Animals: Human Personhood and Culture*. New York: Oxford University Press.

Swidler, Ann. 2003. *Talk of Love: How Culture Matters*. Chicago: University of Chicago Press.

Uleman, James S. 2007. "Introduction: Becoming Aware of the New Unconscious." pp. 3–15 in *The New Unconscious*, edited by Ran Hassin, James S. Uleman, and John A. Bargh. New York: Oxford University Press.

Vaisey, Stephen. 2009. "Motivation and Justification: A Dual-Process Model of Culture in Action." *American Journal of Sociology* 114:1675–715.

Vaisey, Stephen, and Omar Lizardo. 2010. "Can Cultural Worldviews Influence Network Composition?" *Social Forces* 88:1595–618.

Wacquant, Loïc J. D. 2004. *Body and Soul: Notebooks of an Apprentice Boxer*. New York: Oxford University Press.

Weber, Max. 1978. *Economy and Society*. Berkeley, CA: University of California Press.

Willmott, Robert. 1999. "Structure, Agency and the Sociology of Education: Rescuing Analytical Dualism." *British Journal of Sociology of Education* 20:5–21.

Wilson, Timothy D. 2002. *Strangers to Ourselves: Discovering the Adaptive Unconscious*. Cambridge, MA: Harvard University Press.

Wrong, Dennis H. 1961. "The Oversocialized Conception of Man in Modern Sociology." *American Sociological Review* 26:183–93.

Zerubavel, Eviatar. 1997. *Social Mindscapes: An Invitation to Cognitive Sociology*. Cambridge, MA: Harvard University Press.

CHAPTER 7

CAN CARNAL SOCIOLOGY BRING TOGETHER BODY AND SOUL?

or, who's afraid of christian wolff?

JOHN LEVI MARTIN

Through bodily and linguistic discipline (which often entails a temporal discipline), objective structures are incorporated into the body and the "choices" constituting a certain relation to the world are internalized in the form of durable patternings not accessible to consciousness nor even, in part, amenable to will (automatisms, facilitation).

> —Pierre Bourdieu, "The Economics of Linguistic Exchange," p. 662

The principles em-bodied in this way are placed beyond the grasp of consciousness, and hence cannot be touched by voluntary, deliberate transformation, cannot even be made explicit.

> —Pierre Bourdieu, *Outline of a Theory of Practice*, p. 94

The schemes of the habitus, the primary forms of classification, owe their specific efficacy to the fact that they function below the level of consciousness and language, beyond the reach of introspective scrutiny or control by the will.

> —Pierre Bourdieu, *Distinction*, p. 466

One could endlessly enumerate the values given body, made body, by the hidden persuasion of an implicit pedagogy which can instill a whole cosmology, through injunctions as insignificant as "sit up straight" or "don't hold your knife in your left hand," and inscribe the most fundamental principles of the arbitrary content of a culture in seemingly innocuous details of bearing or physical and verbal manners, so putting them beyond the reach of consciousness and explicit statement.

> —Pierre Bourdieu, *The Logic of Practice*, p. 69

> [E]verything that native insertion into a nation and a state buries in the innermost depths of minds and bodies, in a quasi-natural state, or in other words far beyond the reach of consciousness.
>
> —Pierre Bourdieu, Preface to *The Suffering of the Immigrant*, p. xiv

THE cognitive turn in sociology has spawned a great deal of excitement, and has been taken as having implications for the sorts of research that we do (Martin 2010; Pugh 2013; Vaisey 2009, 2014). Here we seem to be tagging along after psychologists who had done quite well for themselves, first in claiming to be a science by banishing minds altogether from their study and intead concentrating on behavior, and then, once the heavy machinery was developed for the study of brains, making an about-face, and returning cognition to the center of their field. There is nothing wrong with following others, if they are headed in the right direction, but we are certain to be a bit confused, for, as we do so, and see the oasis of cognition just up ahead, we encounter an advance party of our own who have turned back, declaring that the oasis is a mirage!

These are the Bourdieusians, who reject the focus on the cognitive as such, insisting that it is the body that does the work previously credited to the mind. More specifically, it is the body's whole way of being, its burnt-in dispositions, that does the patterned response to recognized (and misrecognized) patterns in the world. And Loïc Wacquant in particular has made the strong argument that for this reason, a sociology that uses the sociologist's own body as measuring instrument can reflexively handle the sorts of problems that are currently of interest to cognitive sociologists, by doing what he calls a "carnal sociology."

In this chapter, I try to make an argument about the limits and potentials of carnal sociology as a technique of field theoretic investigation into the nature of embodied dispositions, or habitus. First, I consider the utility of a focus on the habitus as a way of making a specifically sociological contribution to cognition, as well as whether it can be studied via reflexive awareness. Here I suggest that Bourdieu assumed the inaccessibility of habitus to conscious awareness for reasons more to do with intellectual history than psychology. Second, I argue that, even if Bourdieu was not exactly correct in some of his ideas regarding the inaccessibility of habitus to conscious investigation, it does indeed make sense that there will be embodied practices that will resist efforts at any deliberate attempt at reflexive explication beyond the mere restatement of the embodied nature of habitus. Third, I argue that Loïc Wacquant's *Body and Soul* (hence B&S) demonstrates these limits even as it portrays the nature of the process of embodiment. But this does not mean that a carnal sociology cannot be the avenue of the production of key data that are required by any serious social science. And the fourth point thus is that such a carnal sociology is most useful when the focus is not on the body itself, but the social objects this body confronts. Fifth, I argue that indeed it makes sense that a specifically sociological approach to such a carnal cognitive sociology will be a field theoretic one. Finally, I argue that the line of reasoning here suggests the necessity for a large number of replications by researchers inserted into the field at different points.

7.1 BOURDIEU AND COGNITIVE SOCIOLOGY

There are, it seems to me, two different ways in which sociologists now can and should grapple with questions of cognition. The first is as consumers of work done by cognitive scientists and their kin; here, without becoming swept up in momentary fads, we want to make sure that our own various theories do not require substantive claims about cognitive processing that are unlikely to be true. The second is to make specifically *socio-logical* contributions to our understanding of cognition. This latter task requires working to the special strengths and insights of our field, as opposed to that of the psychological sciences; while they tend to focus on the generic individual, we look at interindividual differences and the social patterning of subjectivity, as well as the relation between intra-individual psychic processes and interpersonal processes. Here, we are unlikely to use methods similar to those of cognitive scientists; however, we must beware of conducting the same old sorts of research we always do, and simply attaching irresponsible claims about unobserved cognitive processes to it.

In this light, some sociologists think that the general approach of Pierre Bourdieu is as good a starting place as we have for such a sociological investigation of the pattern-ings of cognition. Here, I believe that Bourdieu's contributions to cognitive sociology are both underestimated and overestimated. Regarding the latter, American sociologists frequently credit Bourdieu with boldly discovering ideas that were well worked out in William James's (1890/1950) work on psychology, or those having to do with the alter-nation of habit and conscious processing that are the core of Dewey's (1922/1930) psychol-ogy (see Martin 2018). On the other hand, Bourdieu is often imagined to have plucked from sheer imagination the notion of *habitus*, and attached a pretentious Latin term, when in fact he here takes a well-worked out philosophical concept that has a clear existential referent—it is each's way of being, understood in terms of interactions with an environment, and something that is probably as solid and unambiguous a concept as one can hope to come across in sociology. Thus rather than being some arbitrary "black box" inserted in between the two sociological notions such as "structure" and "agency" or whatever absurd dualisms sociologists prefer to treat as more concrete than human bodies (a point that has been justly made by Wacquant [2013]), the problem with habitus is that however obvious the habitus is in terms of regularities in bodily *doings*, the *implications* for cognitive sociology are quite ambiguous.

Indeed, I suspect that the very integration of Bourdieu's social psychology with his epistemology and theory of science, however aesthetically pleasing it may be, easily produces, as opposed to dispelling, confusion. There are two ways of thinking in philo-sophical psychology, dualist and nondualist. Dualist theories tend to be false, and nondualist unspecifiable. A common philosophical truism is that "all monisms are the same," and much wisdom lies therein. The minute we try to say something specific about *our* version of monism, something that isn't true of all of them, we find that we are, by implication, accepting a dualism. And if we have conditioned ourselves with an aversion reaction to all dualisms, we may refuse to take the step of necessary clarification. That does not mean that there may not be *specific* dualisms that can and should be overcome, perhaps even that between the soul and the body. But it does mean that we can rashly seek to support our arguments on this specific issue by calling down excoriations against dualism in general, and thinking that because one dualism is false, all are.

In this way, the more ungainly approach of Dewey, which attempts to overcome the great epistemic dualisms, but recognizes psychological dualisms, has much to commend it, and it is significant that the most exciting work building on the Bourdieusian system (espec. Leschziner and Green 2013) attempts to push it in a more Deweyan direction. In particular, there is a methodological question about the monistic interpretation; if the mind does not simply control the levers of the body, can a mind, through participant observation, produce reliable and valid conclusions about the nature of action? Like Vaisey and Frye (this volume) I want to consider this question using Wacquant's *Body and Soul*, but I suspect that the issues are ones that are harder to resolve than do they.

7.2 Unconsciously Structuring the Unconscious Structures

I opened with a set of wonderful citations indicating that Bourdieu basically saw the answer to the question of whether we can, via reflexivity, produce knowledge of the habitus, as no. One way of defending this pessimistic view is a principled quasi-Nietzschean one: the brain is a survival organ, humans evolved language as part of their will to survive, but one unhappy side effect of this was consciousness, a capacity to becloud and obfuscate, to spin out the sorts of tomfoolery for which the educated have an inexhaustible appetite. The mind cannot come to correct conclusions about what bodies do because the mind's job is precisely the opposite—asking it to produce science would be like asking the *People's Daily* for investigative journalism.

We know that Bourdieu did not accept this vision, as he was convinced that at least social science, with its bird's-eye view, could play a praiseworthy role in the process of collective enlightenment. But a more optimistic view has been put forward by Bourdieu's student Loïc Wacquant, which is that through exposing the body to field effects, and monitoring the development of habitus, the sociologically trained observer can produce sociological knowledge and make the unconscious the subject of reflexive conscious investigation.

There is much to commend in this approach. First, it promises a reasonably fast road to a cognitive sociology. Such a fast road was largely abandoned when psychologists gave up their faith that the mind was, at least potentially, the sort of self-reflective consciousness whose processes could be transparent to itself. The excesses of the denial of self-insight to ordinary humans pushed by behaviorism and Freudianism may have obscured the validity of the underlying argument: whatever foundation the phenomenological experience of thinking is built upon is not itself thinking, and it seems to be unobservable *by* thinking. But if, like Wacquant, we take a functional view of the cognizing body, we may indeed be able to use reflective bodily experience to track the development of corpora-cognitive structure. Yes, it is the body that processes information from the environment, but the observer can triangulate various sources of information to describe the process of bodily structuration.

Second, contrary to Bourdieu's statements, there is no obvious reason to believe that the habitus is not, to some extent, accessible to consciousness. If you know that you hate eggplant, and that you specifically detest it because it is fleshy, rubbery, tumescent, bruise-purple, and altogether too much like a sea-dwelling invertebrate (perhaps an armless octopus), then you already know *something* about your habitus! I believe that Bourdieu's conviction that the habitus cannot be brought to consciousness comes from the fact that he remained tied to aspects of the Lévi-Straussian program that actually did not logically fit his emerging understanding of the nature of practice. This accounts for both this idea of the inaccessibility of habitus to reflective thought and his (moderated and critical) appropriation of aspects of psychoanalysis.

We all know the creation myth of Bourdieu's understanding of habitus—struggling after his fieldwork in Kabylia to make Lévi-Straussian sense of the culture before him, Bourdieu realizes that culture cannot be understood in abstract, tabular form; rather, it is something that is used for practical purposes (see, e.g., Bourdieu 1992/1996:179; 1997/2000:56). The classic structuralist account was frustrated by anomalies: for example, that although in general, man:woman :: dry:wet, because man:woman :: fertilizer: fertilized :: rain:land :: wet:dry, we seem to find that wet:dry :: dry:wet. But with a rethinking, these anomalies turned into a strong finding making possible a new sort of cognitive anthropology, one in which the unconscious logical structures of Lévi-Strauss are replaced by the habitus.

The habitus, says Bourdieu, is a structuring structure, but it is also a structured structure. This is all very well and good, and indeed follows necessarily from the idea of habitus. Or at least it necessarily follows that it is structured, and that it structures. But why is it a structure? Unfortunately, the word "structure" is used variably in the social and behavioral sciences, with some definitions narrow (such as Piaget's [1971] that a structure is a self-regulating set of transformations), some sloppy (structure is the opposite of agency), some misleading (any sort of regularity is structure) and some innocuously empty (as when in everyday life we refer to anything existent as a structure, especially if it is artificial—e.g., "at this point the suspect individual proceeded to run behind a large structure").

Given this variation, we find some plausible definitions of structure according to which it makes a great deal of sense to say that habitus is a structure. For example, a habitus has much in common with a "character structure" as spoken of by Wilhelm Reich (1949:459)—an integrated way of being that includes both psychological reactions and ways of holding the body ("the sum total of the relationship between the orgonotic energy system and the sensory-motor system which has to perceive the plasmatic currents" etc.). But Bourdieu tended to assume a sort of Lévi-Straussian psychological structure (though neither the sort of psychology nor the sort of structure that Lévi-Strauss invoked), something that could be seen as a "matrix of division" as well as a set of dispositions (the more obvious way of describing a habitus). That is, because habitus coordinates alignments with key binaries such as heavy/light, coarse/refined, cold/warm, it could be imagined as a fundamental orientating module that was involved not simply in classificatory reactions but also in perceptual comprehension. Although it seems clear that Bourdieu did not want to conceptualize habitus thusly, it also seems clear that he was sorely tempted to do so and that this temptation sometimes won out. And it seems that it was in large part for this reason that he conceived habitus as inaccessible to consciousness[1]—not so much because this is true of many cognitive processes, but because this was serving the same functional role as other ideas of "deep" structures. It could not be seen if it is that through which we see.

Now one of the frustrating things about commentary on Bourdieu, at least in the United States, is that it has, both pro and con, tended toward a strange fundamentalism. If Bourdieu studies reproduction (which he did at one time), he must be saying that *everything* is reproduced and nothing ever changes. If he says that certain actions or reactions that might subjectively be perceived as nonstrategic can be shown to be objectively strategic, he must be saying that *all* actions by *all* people *all the time* are strategic. If he studies action that is coordinated by unconscious embodied structures, he must be saying that *all* action is unconscious, and so on, which would be very foolish. Consciousness probably is good for *something*, otherwise why have it? Thus the mere fact of Bourdieu's concentration on "unconscious" structures (those that are not only nonconscious but also inaccessible to consciousness) in no way implies that his parsing of corporeal and cognitive faculties is incompatible with reflective conscious examinations of certain nonconscious processes. Still, if we attempt to formulate an understanding of the psychology of action compatible with Bourdieu's findings, we might come up against some difficulties inherent in the way in which Bourdieu described the unconscious nature of habitus.

In particular, I think we should worry that Bourdieu allowed himself to use the language of a pseudo-Durkheimian "grid of perception" understanding of habitus, one supported by lingering Lévi-Straussian ideas of cognitive structures as necessarily below the threshold of consciousness—a substrate, even a substructure, in which consciousness worked and played but of which it was never aware.[2] In contrast, Wacquant's work— precisely because it involved attacks on his body more than his mind—led him back to a conception of the habitus more fundamentally related not only to that previously proposed by Mauss but more in keeping with previous understandings of habitus (and habit) as an embodied way of being (see Martin 2011b:257). Further, this led Wacquant to reject the assumption that the formation and nature of habitus is not accessible to reflective consciousness. His approach is therefore of special interest to cognitive sociologists who take Bourdieu's intervention seriously.

7.3 Experience and Statements About Experience

And yet, that Wacquant's conception seems more empirically defensible does not, unfortunately, demonstrate that a carnal ethnography is able to retrieve information about the habitus that other methods cannot. In making this argument, I will use "carnal ethnography" to refer to the case in which a researcher exposes his or her body not simply to contact, but to precisely those sorts of experiences that shape habitus as a means of an investigation of embodied cognition (e.g., Desmond 2007). Also, I will make a simple distinction between experience (for example, the experience of being smacked upside the head) and propositions *about* experience such as "I focused on his right and he got me with his left."[3] There is no reason to think that there are no cases in which we find members of the second class (propositions about) that we consider valid—that is, that they map onto the first class (experience itself) as accurate descriptions (and not, say, simply practically effective principles). However, a closer inspection of Wacquant's work demonstrates the difficulties in using ethnography to distinguish consistently between (1) reflexive awareness of the formation of a set of propositions about experience and (2) reflexive awareness of the actual experience and the shaping of habitus by that experience.

First, I am afraid that it is not only that we are not ready to banish all dualisms: we currently need to better distinguish between three different ones. The first, which I have just laid out, is the difference between experience and propositions about experience. The second is that between declarative knowledge (such as "if the exhaust is black, the fuel mixture is too rich") and nondeclarative knowledge (such as knowing how to ride a motorcycle) (for an interesting approach building on this, see Lizardo 2017). The third is between two modes of neural system functioning, the ambiguous System 1 and System 2. As Leschziner (this volume; also see Vila-Henninger 2015; Moore 2017) has emphasized, our usage of the last dualism in sociology has often tended to be a bit casual and opportunistic, blending with one or both of the previous dualisms. But none of these are the same,[4] and certainly, none can be seamlessly mapped onto the divide between the Body and the Soul!

To avoid confusion, we should always seek to hug the data as closely as we can. Let me give a great example. In a fascinating comparative carnal ethnography of how biologists and First Nations (Native American) fishermen think of and interact with clams, Chantelle Marlor (2009, 2010) apprenticed herself to both. Slowly she learned how to "read" a beach as a whole (when digging), quite different from how she learned to divide it into quadrants for sampling (when working with scientists); she learned how to feel the difference between a clam and a rock at the end of her pitchfork, and she learned how to get a sense of where clams were likely to be. In this sense, she began to develop much of the habitus of the clam diggers, at least regarding this one activity.

But she also asked the clam diggers not only about the process of digging but also about clams, about wildlife, about oceanography, initially imagining that the oldest expert informants would provide traditional knowledge perhaps missed by Western scientists. She found, however, that theories of clams varied from one informant to another. This was, she realized, not surprising, as they rarely talked about these matters to one another (there was, unlike with the scientists, no institutional structure for the winnowing out of different interpretations and the formation of portable claims). Thus experts might converge on where they chose to dug, having the insightful ability to use the visible to make extrapolations to that which is not visible—the best diggers would choose to dig in the same place, and Marlor could find herself "seeing" where the clams were. But the experts might disagree on their theories of what made this place the best— some argued that clams were sedentary, and others believed them motile. As a result, there was a difference between the results of her ethnography that came from her reflexive awareness of the process of her own learning regarding the process of clam digging, and the results that came from the discussions with others—even though she herself accepted as valid some of these propositions about clam digging, and some about clam biology and ecology.

Most important, the theories of the clam's life and ways held by the diggers was something quite different from a simple translation of habitual behavior to consciousness, or a shift to a serial processing to solve problems where habitus fails (both of which undoubtedly sometimes occurred). And neither of these was the same as the verbal expression of rules of practical activity. Certainly, the diggers did not believe that such propositions should be treated as unproblematic reflexive knowledge—valuing taciturnity over volubility, they tended to assume that other people's verbal expressions were "bullshit." This is of course a hypothesis that we would not want to overgeneralize, but is rarely one that we should reject out of hand before conducting our research. In particular, it is easy for those pushing Bourdieu's monism toward dualism to treat verbal formulae less critically than they should.

One of the great breakthroughs in sociological analysis—one going back to Mills (1940)—is the realization that norms and rules are not something that lie *behind* and guide action (that ever menacing "structure" that forces us to preserve ourselves with "agency," like Luke Skywalker using steel beams to prevent a garbage compactor from flattening him). Norms and rules are things that participants make reference to *in* action (Wieder 1974).[5] They are important data for our explanations—they are not explanations of data (Martin 2011b).

This means that we need to carefully separate the data that a carnal ethnographer gathers from experience, from those that are gathered via talk. When we reconsider Wacquant's work, we find that much (though by no means all) of the analysis of the formation of habitus seems to pertain to propositions about boxing, and not boxing itself. Given that Wacquant actually was part of a social structure that had a clear authority figure (DeeDee) in the domain of such propositions, it may have been difficult for him to distinguish between one informant's theory of the process and the process. Further, it may well be that the second-person instructions that the authority figure gives may differ by his theory of the nature of the novice. "The skilled boxer," Aristotle said (*Nicomachean Ethics* 1180b10–13), "does not prescribe to all the same kind of fighting." And even if we do know these prescriptions, it may be that we do not know where there is a substitution of propositions about experience for experience itself because we make this substitution precisely where we lack other forms of discursive access to experience. For although there is no reason to simply assume that any and all processes of the shaping of habitus are *inaccessible* to conscious processing, there is also no reason to assume that such processes in general *are* accessible, that we preserve traces of them in memory, or that training and/or deliberate focus increases the accuracy of reflection regarding such processes.

Wacquant (2011:87) claims that his work "disclos[es] the production and assembly of the cognitive categories, bodily skills and desires which together define the competence and appetence specific to the boxer." If this is interpreted to mean that he discloses the *fact* of this production and assembly, and indeed "what it is like" to undergo said production and assembly, we should have no quibbles—and indeed, this is what I believe Wacquant intends by this statement. (Elsewhere [1995a:72] he speaks of the process of the formation of the pugilistic habitus as "an imperceptible embodiment of the mental and corporeal schemata immanent in pugilistic practice that admits of no discursive mediation or systemization.") But successful accomplishment of the task of showing *that* there is such production does not necessarily help give us an analytic account of this production—just as knowing what it is like to have your heart race is not the same thing as showing how the blood circulates.

Indeed, the limits of any direct access to the process of the experience of habitus formation is well illustrated in B&S. We generally recognize that we do not have this sort of access to our habit formation if only because we find ourselves using external senses to monitor the operation of our embodied neural system. Thus a talented violinist can *hear* how she is holding her body; Wacquant too hears if he is punching correctly (2004:64). If indeed the Cartesian division between the body and the mind, between action and representation, has been totally demolished (cf. 2004:17), no one remembered to tell the mind about this.

Wacquant illustrates this lack of accessibility to the habitus formation in his frequent use of "robot," "machine," and "engine" metaphors to describe his actions in training (e.g., 2004:65, 66, 95). His feeling of dissociation from the body is itself a variable experience, and the range of this variation an important datum. But this means that the virtue of an approach like that of B&S cannot be based on unmediated access to habitus-forming experiences and the ability of the reflexively oriented participant to bring these to discursive consciousness. And I believe that Wacquant fundamentally agrees, as seen in his resistance to the characterization of B&S as "auto-ethnography," as well as his pointing to the difficulty in discerning the process of the development of such skills (70). But then it may be less clear what might be the relation between the undergone experiences and the written book. Here it may help to go a bit more slowly regarding the relation between experiences and propositions about experiences, even as they are encountered in participant observation. I will argue that works such as B&S *do* have the capacity to help provide an analytic account of the production of habitus, and hence to shed light on issues central to cognitive sociology, but not via reflexivity.

7.4 THE LIMITS OF REFLEXIVITY

Some occurrences of our mental processing seem available to us upon inspection; other parts are harder to reach in this manner. It was for this reason that Christian Wolff (1679–1754) (1733:453ff) proposed a dual science of psychology, one part (empirical psychology) the more conventional introspectionism of his day, and the other, a "rational psychology" to deal with the aspects of things beyond experience—thus replicating within the mind the division between the sensible and intelligible worlds (on Wolff's claim to invent rational psychology, see Dyck 2009:251). Wolff's solution did not survive Kant's critique (on which, below), but perhaps we must reconsider a similar sort of a division when it comes to an experiential investigation of habitus.

In B&S, Wacquant both illustrates and to some degree transforms Bourdieu's understanding of habitus. Certainly, Wacquant supports the main outlines of Bourdieu's (or anyone's) idea of habitus as an embodied set of dispositions, but the Lévi-Strauss is gone and Mauss is back. Given the tendency in America for sociologists to imagine that the habitus is a generic "theoretical" element intervening in some path diagram, simply providing a vivid description of habitus as lived is an important contribution. But precisely in illustrating the embodied nature of habitus, Wacquant comes up against the limits of reflexivity.

Wacquant speaks eloquently regarding how the practical mastery of the techniques, the "practical rules" of boxing, "satisfies the condition of dispensing with the need to constitute them as such in consciousness" (2004:69). But this points to the outstanding question of the relation between the acquisition of these techniques and the discursive elaboration, for example, in the form of verbally presenting the techniques as "rules." Now the question before us is twofold—first, is the process of developing practical mastery equivalent to internalizing and embodying the rule (which I shall call "automation") in all cases? Second, to what extent can one's own experiencing of the learning via the development of rules of practice lead to useful (scientific or nonscientific) statements about the process of development?

Regarding the first, there is no reason to deny that many cases of habitus formation involve the automation of behavioral sequences that are first guided by rules acquired through verbal instructions. For example, when learning to ride a motorcycle, one may be told, "look where you want to go—don't stare ahead of you and for God's sake, don't look at your front wheel!" The novice may repeat this under her breath and occasionally correct herself when she finds herself staring at her front wheel or looking straight ahead on a turn. But there will come a day when the rule never occurs to her. It has been automated in the organism.

Now for cases like this, we find that it may not be necessary for a researcher to *experience* the automating in order to be able to give as complete a description as possible, for this consists only of two elements, first, the rule (which is easily expressed in propositional form), then the fact of automation (which nobody will deny). But we know that not all practical mastery works via automation of once-verbal rules. Many people learn to ride bicycles without being told anything other than "keep your hands on the bars and your feet on the pedals" and "if you can't stop, head for the bushes" (that coupled with the untruth, "I won't let go," were all the instruction I got). We might imagine that in these cases, the only way that someone can bring the formation of such practical skills to consciousness is undergoing them reflexively, or reflecting on them after the fact.

However, there seems little reason for faith that this reflection is always possible.[6] For example, many bicyclists, when learning about countersteering (that one moves the bars to the left in order to initiate a right turn) insist that they do no such thing, even after profound reflection, though physicists will insist that they do, even if this procedure is initiated by a shift in weight. Further, there are also cases in which we have no reason to believe that we correctly preserve memories as to how we do things, so that an honest reflection can produce incorrect conclusions, because what the memory retrieves as stored sequence is a narrative theory of the bodily movements, and not the movements themselves.[7]

Finally, there may be cases when the verbal instruction given to a novice is quite incorrect, but functions to get the novice into a position in which some other sorts of learning may kick in. Thus even when we have verbal instructions from experts at the beginning (a rule) and successful embodied practice at the end, it is not necessarily the case that the embodied action bears any relation to the verbalized rules. For example, when my family and friends took turns learning how to operate a new two-wheeled skateboard with a torsion bar, the verbal explanations of those who "got it" varied greatly from "you push your leading foot forwards and backwards" to "you swing your hips" to "you flap your feet alternatingly" to "you have to be a snake in the grass." In fact, any initial theory of operation that led to a transverse motion was equally useful so long as a person who made one set of motions eventually learned through the negative reinforcement of crashes to compensate with opposing motions. One could insist that a novice begin hula-hooping by moving hips back and forth or from side to side—either could generate the motion that leads to a systemic response of circular reactions and eventually the smooth hula hoop motion.

Interestingly, Thomas Aquinas (*Truth* Qu. 10, Art 9; 1953:49ff) made precisely this point, when he considered the question of whether our knowledge of habits lay within the soul. Although his language is somewhat different from ours, he first emphasized that our knowledge of habits could not come from the habits (the essence of such habits) themselves, because habits lack the active nature that could transform the potential character of the intellect (that which *can* understand) to an actual understanding. He argued that "Knowledge of habits, as that of the soul, is twofold. One knowledge is that by which one knows whether he has a habit. The other is that by which one knows what a habit is." He argued that cognitive habits were the source of the act by which we perceived the habit, but this could not be said for affective habits. I am not sure that we would accept his argument for the former, but even so, knowledge *that* we have a habit does not imply knowledge of *how* we have come to hold it.

Thus things are perhaps a bit more worrisome than even Vaisey and Frye (this volume) might suggest, for there are cases in which the seemingly straight arrow between one realm and another is misleading. We may see cases in which there is a discursive instruction expressed, one that garners general acceptance of its validity, and is accepted by the learner ("keep your hands up, or I will deck you"), and then a later nonconscious habit (hands are always up) without in all cases being able to see the latter as an internalization of the former.

Of course, there certainly are times when the continuity of experience suggests at least some validity to a discursive representation. For example, in B&S there are cases in which we do get information on a serial process of adaption of the body; for example, how an initially restricted field of view opens up and becomes organized (Wacquant 2004:75, 87). But in general we lack confidence that a verbal description runs in parallel to the body's practical rules; we may accept that the habitus is the source of that pre-established harmony—an idea formulated by Leibniz to account for the parallel unfolding of the physical and the mental realms, body and soul, when one could not (he was confident) affect the other—that accounts for the otherwise puzzling aspects of social interaction, without assuming that we can account for its establishment in anything other than the most general terms.

But we are unlikely to be long satisfied with a verbal formula (such as "pre-established harmony"—one often recycled by Bourdieu) simply because it keeps the specter of Descartes at bay.[8] The problem Descartes (1637/2001:100) struggled with was how the body could affect the soul and vice versa, given the fundamental distinction between the two substances. Christian Wolff (1733:478) restated Leibniz's response to Descartes as follows: "Now as the soul has its own [distinct] power, through which it represents the world to itself, while all physical [*natürliche*] alterations of the body are grounded in *its* own essence and nature, it is easy to see that the soul has its actions and the body its simultaneous alterations, without it being either that the soul acts on the body, the body on the soul, or that God directs this through His unmediated action ... and in such a way we come to the explanation which Leibniz gave of the community of the body with the soul and termed the 'pre-established harmony' or agreement."[9]

It was Wolff's formulation that was the orthodoxy in the philosophical world in which Immanuel Kant came of age. Already, Johan Nicolas Tetens (1777:156) had undermined the faith that any introspective road to data on our mental processes existed—there was no more reason to believe that our internal sensations of our feelings mapped onto their objects in a one to one fashion than when it came to our external sensations. "This realization," he wrote, "throws an impenetrable darkness over the core of our mental processes [*Seelenäusserungen*]." Intellectual operations could not be guaranteed to reach facts of inner sensation. Kant emerged as a vital thinker when he rejected the Wolffian orthodoxy *in toto* and allowed the realms of the sensible and the intelligible to, once again, go their separate ways.[10] However, after devoting his first and second critiques to problems centering on these two seemingly different worlds of phenomena and noumena, he proposed (Kant 1790/1987) a crucial mediating role in the faculty of judgment, especially our capacity to intuit lawful regularities in the world even where we lacked formal concepts that could be used to defend the objectivity of such synthetic judgments: that is, our aesthetic capacity. (Interestingly, Wacquant himself makes this connection 1995b:507; a somewhat less brief discussion can be found in Martin 2011a.)

To account for how we can correctly orient to the qualitative aspects of objects around us (to recognize them as beautiful, say) when we cannot defend this through the understanding (we cannot *prove* that Beethoven's second symphony is beautiful), Kant had to propose that we must treat the world as if it were made for us. But as Bourdieu argued (as do other theorists of habit), we can also expect such a harmony of our powers and the world if we are made for the world—if we are the sorts of beasts that can become those sorts of beasts that can make sense of the world around us. Further, this process would (as I go on to show) be crucial to the development of any field theory. Thus carnal sociology, should it be able to shed light on habitus formation, would be of the greatest interest and importance to a general sociological theory of cognizing actors.

7.5 SCIENCE AND SENSIBILITY

> I'd rather be a lightning rod than a seismograph.
>
> —Ken Kesey

I began by noting that the cognitive turn in sociology need not be restricted to our housekeeping, in which we throw away theories that have implausible conjectures regarding cognitive functioning, but also may lead us to attempt to develop specifically sociological accounts of actors' cognizing. If all goes well, these will increasingly involve attempts to describe regularities in the social patterning of cognitive processes.[11] If we are to follow the Bourdieusians and to try to have our contribution to a science of cognition be a largely (though not necessarily entirely) phenomenological one, then it makes sense that such investigations will appear conformable to field theory, since a patterned distribution of responses to the world is at least one version of what we mean by "field" (in addition to others, such as organizational definitions). Thus the Bourdieusian approach to making a contribution to cognitive sociology—and not necessarily only this—implies the construction of a field theory of action.

No field theory of action can do without an understanding of habitus and its formation, for it is precisely this process that makes us the sorts of things that are amenable to field effects. (I derive the following argument with greater specificity in Martin 2011b; here I present a catechistic version.) One of the most fundamental questions for any social science pertains to the nature of the arising of forms of social organization; one commonly proposed form of such organization is the "field." What is a field? It is an organized set of vectors. What is a vector? It is a push or pull of a certain magnitude in a certain direction. What sorts of vectors are found in social life? They are the phenomenological experiences of attraction, repulsion, indifference, and so on, to the different social objects that confront us. These are the aspects of cognitive process that present themselves as data amenable to sociological analysis. Whence the origin of these experiences? As far as we can tell, these are the subjective correlates of intersubjectively valid qualities of the objects that are available to direct intuition. Thus, just as on a hot summer day, a glass of lemonade says "drink me," so too the Republican party says "oppose me" and the Golden Gloves tournament says "try me"—at least to some. Then is a field theory a possible avenue for the investigation of aesthetics in Kant's terms, one that might lie precisely at the intersection of the realms held together only by fiat in Wolff's system? And would this be a cognitive sociology? It would seem so.

We thus need to understand how fields form and develop, and not reduce field theory into a set of catch phrases and data-reduction techniques that can be thrown at any case. Because a field induces motion in objects due to an interaction between field state at any position and certain properties of objects, a key question is always how an object becomes that-sort-of-thing that is amenable to a field effect. This is related to the physical processes known as "hysteresis," in which (paradigmatically) there is some sort of unsettling and reforming of local domains in response to the field in question (cf. Lizardo and Strand 2011). There is every reason to think that something closely analogous happens with us, and for millennia this unsettling phenomenon of the unsettling (and resettling) of character has been grappled with in terms of the formation of "habit" and "habitus." Thus carnal ethnography is one of the most fundamental avenues for social scientific exploration.

It is, however, extremely difficult to explain *how* one's body has changed, how automatic processes develop, and so on. In part because of the very fact of a transformation of our way of being in the world, we often find it confusing to make sense of how things seemed *before* a process of enculturation and cultural development. How *did* one learn to appreciate cigars, or wine? We can tell a few stories involving disastrous first encounters, but that does little for a systematic and scientific study of the development of habitus. Far more successful would be data produced not on what it means to taste wine (for knowing about wine has very little to do with knowing about knowing about wine), but on what *wines taste like*. A researcher who dutifully kept track of her tastes and appreciations over the course of learning about wines (first informally as a maturing young adult and then perhaps through later explicit schooling) would produce data that could be used to chart the introduction of a sequence of overlayed distinctions similar to that produced by Boyd (1969) in his speculative reconstruction of the development of kinship structures.

The strict duality of the habitus as disposition and the qualitative experience of bodies suggests, then, that the way in which a carnal sociology can contribute to cognitive sociology is through the description of the qualitative experience of things in the field. And Wacquant has highlighted the importance of this aspect of a carnal sociology, saying that he placed himself "in the local vortex of action in order to acquire through practice…the dispositions of the boxer with the aim of elucidating the magnetism proper to the pugilistic cosmos" (2005:462). That is, he recognizes that he is in a unique position to describe the transformation of someone over whom the boxing field has no hold to someone who can be powerfully pulled and pushed by it.

We only have a few glimpses of this—what the Golden Gloves tournament means for Wacquant, for one, and why he could find the prospects of trying to continue as a prize-fighter sufficiently alluring that he could contemplate, if only in fantasy, abandoning the gratifying and luxurious life of a graduate student at the University of Chicago. We also have data, unfortunately not preserved in paper, in the wave of excitement that passes over Wacquant when he speaks of certain aspects of boxing, or when he falls into a brief bit of shadow boxing (before faculty meetings! [personal observation]). But this is also something that he has described in his works (e.g., 2004:88; 1995b:491, 519)—that the field effect is not simply one of cultivation but also of captivation, and that we never experience anything realer than being caught up in what Bourdieu has perhaps unfortu-nately called the *illusio* of a field.

I am quite happy to call this capacity embodied—as all thoughts and sentiments are, in a way. But it does not seem to be embodied in the same way as is the knowledge of how to balance on a bicycle. If asked about how one rides a bicycle, we are likely to feel unable to say much and if we do say something, we may well be wrong. But if asked what the allure of boxing is, or why one wine is better than another, we have something to say because we have somewhere to look. We can *describe* the qualities of the objects of our phenomenological experience—although these qualities are (or so they say) really aspects of an interaction between the object and us, we experience them as outside and so we have something to say. It is this sort of habitus formation that, it seems, can be profitably investigated by a carnal ethnography (and I believe this is why Wacquant both emphasizes the inaccessibility of certain practices to verbal specification while he also asks fighters to describe what boxing is to them).

Documenting and analyzing this process is itself an important aspect of any serious social science, and certainly is a sine qua non for a rigorous field investigation. Yet there is a second part, perhaps the more daunting one, in a field analysis, which is to chart out the complete organization of that set of vectors—felt impulses to do one thing in one position and another in a different position—that constitutes a field. We can no more reproduce this field from a single ethnographer's experience than oceanographers could chart out the nature of the circulation of the currents of the oceans by dropping in a single cork.

7.6 PUT A CORK IN IT; BETTER, MANY CORKS

Although a full treatment exceeds the bounds of this chapter, we must recognize that one of the puzzles of our incorporation of carnal ethnography is the same as our problem with ethnography in general—it has an ambivalent position in a generalizing science.

The pressure on ethnographers to either confess their second-class status as mere hypothesis-generators, or to overgeneralize from a case, can lead them to extremes that are unfairly debasing or implausibly grandiose. There is no reason to think that knowledge about cases—about *specific* cases—is not social scientific knowledge, nor that it does not support *inference* (which is not the same as mechanical *generalizability*; here see Desmond [2014:573]).

However, I think that there *is* a serious generalization problem with ethnography, one that is not about generalization *across* cases but *within*, and it is recognized by all good ethnographers. The "group" is a set of individuals who are different, and even the same person is one way at one time and a different way at another. For this reason, good ethnographers work on talking to multiple informants, and seeing people at different times of day and in different social configurations, and so on. But the problem is only aggravated for a carnal ethnography, where the ethnographer cannot do that—cannot try on different bodies.

And even worse, the techniques that allow an ethnographer to communicate legitimate research findings tend to push us deeper in the direction of problematic generalization. All explanation worthy of the term carries with it some form of intuitive understanding, the sort of thing that only a human can do. When it comes to a reflexive project of making one's own cognitive formation processes an object of scientific knowledge, this means establishing an intersubjective concordance where the reader or listener vicariously re-experiences the analytically described sequence of events. One forceful technique for doing so that I find becoming very attractive to carnal ethnographers is to substitute the second person for the first when describing their understanding of the regularities of experience. "Throwing a jab," Wacquant tells us, requires "properly placing your feet, hips, shoulders and arms; you must 'pump' your left arm out to your adversary..." (69). In this context, the second person works quite well: the statements are hypothetical and didactic, just the sort of thing that Wacquant might have been told as a novice. But the same rhetorical device is used for general interpretations of the experience of others, indeed, experiences which Wacquant himself has not shared: for example, in his meditation on what boxing means to his poorer colleagues: "You bracket for a moment a life that you no longer even find unfair, because you're so used to it, so weary of it..." (238; also 240).

Now Wacquant uses this literary device, it must be admitted, not to claim homogeneity of experience (he [78n65; also 1995b:490] notes the variation across gyms and persons) but more to allow the reader to vicariously share in what Wacquant believes to be a modal experience. However, there can be a slippage here between the experience and the proposition about, a slippage made by informants and subjects as well. In the case of the two-wheeled skateboard, I insisted that I had the correct formula: "You have to be a snake in the grass." Others, however, who had mastered the technique politely informed me that they actually did *not* need to be a snake in the grass, that what I said made no sense to them, and that my proffered rule was "stupid." Now if, however, I were trying to describe my own experience to others in print, I might well say "You have to be a snake in the grass" as a way of communicating this most vividly. But a reader would be wrong were she to interpret this as a rigid hypothetical imperative. Because we are different, and we do not always know how.

Now Wacquant was not maintaining that there is a single way to formulate the nature of what boxing is, and what it means, to urban boxers. Indeed, he has emphasized the opposite (1995b:491). But there remains a fundamental methodological problem: a single carnal ethnography can reach the phenomenological validity of field effects, and perhaps this is the only way to do so. To generalize, however, seems to require either substituting others' talk about experience for others' experience, or substituting one's own experience for others' experience. (And most worrisome, there may be a reconstruction in which one's own experience, what others say, and what one thinks of others, are fused in an ad hoc manner to create an attributed interiority that is impossible to verify.) What does this mean for the task of a scientific explanation? Is this avenue inherently limited? Should ethnographers confess the inadequacy of having only their own experiences (and others' propositions about experience), and conclude that they have nothing to offer cognitive psychology? I think not—making oneself an instrument (a lightning rod, in Kesey's striking terminology) means that one should feel no more apologetic for one's singularity than should any person answering a survey or any rat running a maze (or Kurt Koffka and Wolfgang Köhler being the main subjects of their teacher Max Wertheimer's experiments!). The problem is not singularity of any individual, but the lack of multiple singularities, many persons.

A field theoretic explanation does not look for "generalization" as commonly done via the subsumption of a case into a set of functionally equivalent cases, and so there is no reason to demand that Wacquant's experience be the same as another researcher's. Indeed, were it so, then we have wasted this researcher's time and should have chosen someone different. For the vectors of a field not only are organized, they are differential. Unless we explore the areas of turbulence and the brackish backwaters along with the main current, we will not really understand this organization. Thus it seems to me to follow that replication is needed here more than in any other place.

I suspect that many ethnographers are still struggling with how to understand contradictions based on revisits, and many secretly yearn for some aspects of the day when one could count on one's site being forever off limits to competitors, either because others were off finding their own sites, or because colonization was eradicating the civilizations being studied so quickly that revisiting was impossible. While there is wide agreement that the experiences of culture are fractured and distributed (though a few still cannot imagine any explanation for why a cranky old man's experience in, say, Samoa would be any different from that of a charming young woman other than "fakery"), it still seems hard for ethnographers to accept this variation not as something that should be explained on the basis of exogenous divisions, but as the fundamental variation necessary for an investigation of social fields. Just as a yearly social survey would not keep asking a question that had 100 percent agreement (such as do you disapprove of cannibalism), so ethnographers should not bother investigating aspects of experience that do not vary across persons.

The validity of Wacquant's experience is no way lessened because it was his, and because someone (we may guess) gifted with slightly different reflexes or body tone might have had a completely different trajectory through the field than that charted in B&S, as might Wacquant himself had he started five years earlier or five years later. The dispersion in experiences across persons is not what field theory fears as disproof, it is what it systemizes and hence explains. While not all of those persons need themselves be researchers—important research can be conducted by researchers who follow the habitus-formation process of subjects who, for whatever reason, are internally motivated to do the difficult work of reporting their experience of social objects—it seems to me that a set of researchers, each with their own experiences, and also their own theoretical agendas, who work together, could make remarkable progress in terms of a theory of social cognition.

To conclude, carnal sociology *can* be a gateway to a rigorous scientific study of habitus by measuring the differential pull of social objects—the duality of a particular "libido" and the qualitative nature of these objects is the core of any field theoretic explanation. Wacquant seems to be correct—there are aspects of habitus-formation beyond conscious access, but also aspects that can be elucidated by a reflexive ethnographer with enough energy to keep field notes, and these latter aspects pertain to the developing qualitative experience of objects in the field, most notably, the prize itself. But if the acculturated body is in love with the stakes of the field, the course of true love never did run smooth. B&S shows us that (should it be doubted) a carnal sociology *can* elucidate aspects of the habitus but—following classic structuralist logic—it will only be the variations across cases that contain the meaning of the field. Hence only by strewing researchers across the field—researchers with different backgrounds and different degrees of luck—can we trace out the turbulences and vortexes that exist in any field worth fighting in and over.

ACKNOWLEDGMENTS

I am grateful to Loïc Wacquant and Wayne Brekhus for comments and for encouragement.

NOTES

1. I recognize that in later work, especially *Masculine Domination*, Bourdieu was likely to introduce a qualification: here he speaks of "schemes of perception and appreciation *not readily* accessible to consciousness" (1998/2001:95, emphasis added), I think because he did not want his ideas understood as disproved by the mere existence of consciousness raising. Further, I should acknowledge that in the opening quotation taken from the *Outline* earlier, Bourdieu is really speaking not of habitus in general, but the most fundamental cultural orientations. Finally, I recognize that Bourdieu had other theoretical reasons, ones turning on the need to oppose folk sociologies, to push for a "principle of non-consciousness" (Bourdieu, Chamboredon, and Passeron 1991:16).

2. "I therefore claim to show, not how men think in myths, but how myths operate in men's minds without their being aware of the fact" (Lévi-Strauss 1964/1969:12).

3. Lizardo (2009) has previously made a very similar point, also using *Body and Soul* as exemplar.

4. For example, there may (on the one hand) be the experience correlative to serial (conscious) processing and then (on the other hand, and perhaps later) propositions formulated *about* serial processing, and these may be different from one another. This complicates, or so I believe, the account given by Vaisey and Frye (this volume).

5. Of course, it is not that they are nowhere else: Illinois statute 720 ILCS 550 holds that any person possessing no more than 10 grams of cannabis (subject to various exceptions) is guilty of breaking a civil law and subject to a moderate fine. But whether such a law is invoked emerges from the particularities of police–civilian interactions, or police budgeting decisions. The general sociologist, still groggy from Durkheimianism, may tend to associate "laws" with social values and norms, a "Ten Commandments" view of law (even though most Americans would only hold themselves to somewhere between three and five of these). An interesting corrective would be to randomly search through the statutes of the state in which you dwell.

6. Oakeshott (1962:62) "We acquire habits of conduct, not by constructing a way of living upon rules or precepts learned by heart and subsequently practiced, but by living with people who habitually behave in a certain manner: we acquire habits of conduct in the same way as we acquire our native language."

7. An analogous distortion is illustrated in a discussion in B&S of one boxer who retells being hit so hard that he lost consciousness, but continued to box for quite some time, successfully, in this unconscious state (2004:96). It is far more likely that his impairment(s) had to do not with consciousness, but with long-term memory formation. His absence of memory and the gap in self-narrative, however, leads him to conclude that his self was absent during this time, and hence that "he" was unconscious. A similar experience of a rugby player was described by Bartlett (1932/1995:233).

8. And even then, only partially: "In fact, Leibniz was a Cartesian, by virtue of his very struggle to free himself from the influence of Descartes" (Bourdieu 2017:101).

9. Descartes had proposed that the mind could affect the body without violation of the laws of physics if it conserved the amount of momentum but *redirected* it. Wolff (1733:478) here repeats Leibniz's (1715/1991:264 §80;1710/1985:156 §61) critique that Descartes did not understand that for purposes of conservation it is not only the magnitude but the direction of motion that matters—that is, momentum is a vector, not a scalar, and a vector can only be affected by another vector.

10. From his inaugural dissertation: "But I fear that the illustrious Wolff by means of this (for him merely logical) distinction between the sensitive and the intellectual may to the great detriment of philosophy have quite destroyed the noblest enterprise of antiquity, the determining of the nature of phenomena and noumena, and turned men's minds from these investigations to what are frequently but logical minutiae" (Kant 1986; 1770/1986: II.7; 395; p.157).

11. If all goes badly, we will simply ape psychological social psychologists by sticking people in expensive machines and presenting them with various stimuli, a fine first step, but not a viable long-term strategy for sociology.

REFERENCES

Aquinas, Thomas. 1953. [Disputed Questions on] *Truth*. Translated by James V. MvGlynn, S. J. Vol. 2. Chicago: Henry Rengery.

Aristotle. 2011. *Nicomachean Ethics*. Translated by Robert C. Bartlett and Susan D. Collins. Chicago: University of Chicago Press.

Bartlett, Sir Frederic C. 1932/1995. *Remembering: A Study in Experimental and Social Psychology*. Cambridge: Cambridge University Press.

Bourdieu, Pierre. 1972/1977. *Outline of a Theory of Practice*. Translated by Richard Nice. Cambridge: Cambridge University Press.

Bourdieu, Pierre. 1977. "The Economics of Linguistic Exchanges." *Social Science Information* 16:645–68.

Bourdieu, Pierre. 1979/1984. *Distinction: A Social Critique of the Judgment of Taste*. Translated by Richard Nice. Cambridge, MA: Harvard University Press.

Bourdieu, Pierre. 1980/1990. *The Logic of Practice*. Stanford: Stanford University Press.

Bourdieu, Pierre. 1992/1996. *The Rules of Art*. Translated by Susan Emanuel. Stanford: Stanford University Press.

Bourdieu, Pierre. 1997/2000. *Pascalian Meditations*. Translated by Richard Nice. Stanford: Stanford University Press.

Bourdieu, Pierre. 1998/2001. *Masculine Domination*. Translated by Richard Nice. Stanford: Stanford University Press.

Bourdieu, Pierre. 2004. "Preface." in *The Suffering of the Immigrant*, edited by A. Sayad. Cambridge: Polity.

Bourdieu, Pierre. 2017. *Manet: A Symbolic Revolution*. Translated by Peter Collier and Margaret Rigaud-Drayton. Cambridge: Polity Press.

Bourdieu, Pierre, Jean-Claude Chamboredon, and Jean-Claude Passeron. 1968/1991. *The Craft of Sociology*. Translated by Richard Nice. New York: Walter De Gruyter.

Boyd, John Paul. 1969. "The Algebra of Group Kinship." *Journal of Mathematical Psychology* 6(1):139–67.

Descartes, Rene. 1637/2001. *Discourse on Method, Optics, Geometry, and Meteorology*. Translated by Paul J. Olscamp. Rev. ed. Indianapolis, IN: Hackett.

Desmond, Matthew. 2007. *On the Fireline*. Chicago: University of Chicago Press.

Desmond, Matthew. 2014. "Relational Ethnography." *Theory and Society* 43:547–79.

Dewey, John. 1922/1930. *Human Nature and Conduct: An Introduction to Social Psychology*. New York: Modern Library.

Dyck, Corey W. 2009. "The Divorce of Reason and Experience: Kant's Paralogisms of Pure Reason in Context." *Journal of the History of Philosophy* 47(2):249–75.

James, William. 1890/1950. *The Principles of Psychology*. New York: Dover Publications.

Kant, Immanuel. 1770/1986. *On the Form and Principles of the Sensible and the Intelligible World (Inaugural Dissertation)*. Translated and edited by John Handyside and Lewis White Beck. pp. 145–92 in *Kant's Latin Writings*, edited by Lewis White Beck. New York: Peter Lang.

Kant, Immanuel. 1790/1987. *Critique of Judgment*. Translated by Werner S. Pluhar. Indianapolis, IN: Hackett.

Leibniz, Gottfried Wilhelm. 1710/1985. *Theodicy*. Translated by E. M. Huggard. La Salle, IL: Open Court.

Leibniz, Gottfried Wilhelm. 1715/1991. *Monadology*. Translated by Nicholas Rescher. Pittsburgh: University of Pittsburgh Press.

Leschziner, Vanina, and Adam Isaiah Green. 2013. "Thinking about Food and Sex: Deliberate Cognition in the Routine Practices of a Field." *Sociological Theory* 31(2):116–44.

Lévi-Strauss, Claude. 1964/1969. *The Raw and the Cooked*. Translated by John and Doreen Weightman. New York: Harper and Row.

Lizardo, Omar. 2009. "Is a 'Special Psychology' of Practice Possible?" *Theory and Psychology* 19(6):713–27.

Lizardo, Omar. 2017. "Improving Cultural Analysis: Considering Personal Culture in Its Declarative and Nondeclarative Modes." *American Sociological Review* 82(1):88–115.

Marlor, Chantelle. 2009. *Ways of Knowing: Epistemology, Ontology, and Community among Ecologists, Biologists and First Nations Clam Diggers*. PhD Dissertation. New Brunswick, NJ: Rutgers, State University of New Jersey.

Marlor, Chantelle. 2010. "Bureaucracy, Democracy and Exclusion: Why Indigenous Knowledge Holders Have a Hard Time Being Taken Seriously." *Qualitative Sociology* 33(4):513–31.

Martin, John Levi. 2010. "Life's a Beach but You're an Ant, and Other Unwelcome News for the Sociology of Culture." *Poetics* 38:228–43.

Martin, John Levi. 2011a. "Immanuel Kant: A Grammar for the Relation between Cognition and Action." pp. 279–88 in *Sociological Insights of Great Thinkers*, edited by Christofer Edling and Jens Rydgren. Santa Barbara: Praeger.

Martin, John Levi. 2011b. *The Explanation of Social Action*. New York: Oxford University Press.

Martin, John Levi. 2018. "Bourdieu's Unlikely Contribution to the Human Sciences." pp. 435–453 in *The Oxford Handbook of Pierre Bourdieu*, edited by Thomas Medvetz and Jeffrey Sallaz.

Mills, C. Wright. 1940. "Situated Actions and Vocabularies of Motive." *American Sociological Review* 5: 904–31.

Moore, Rick. 2017. "Fast or Slow: Sociological Implications of Measuring Dual-Process Cognition." *Sociological Science* 4:196–223. http://dx.doi.org/10.15195/v4.a9.

Oakeshott, Michael. 1962. *Rationalism and Other Essays*. New York: Basic Books.

Piaget, Jean. 1971. *Structuralism*. Translated and edited by Chaninah Maschler. London: Routledge and Kegan Paul.

Pugh, Allison J. 2013. "What Good Are Interviews for Thinking About Culture? Demystifying Interpretive Analysis." *American Journal of Cultural Sociology* 1(1):42–68.

Reich, Wilhelm. 1949. *Character Analysis*. 3rd ed. Translated by Theodore P. Wolfe. New York: Noonday Press.

Strand, Michael, and Omar Lizardo. 2015. "Beyond 'World Images': Belief as Embodied Action in the World." *Sociological Theory* 33(1):44–70.

Tetens, Johann Nicolas. 1777. Philosophische Versuche über die menschliche Natur und ihre Entwicklung. Vol. Two. Leipzig, Weidmanns.

Vaisey, Stephen. 2009. "Motivation and Justification: A Dual-Process Model of Culture in Action." *American Journal of Sociology* 114(6):1675–715.

Vaisey, Stephen. 2014. "Is Interviewing Compatible with the Dual-Process Model of Culture?" *American Journal of Cultural Sociology* 2(1):150–58.

Vila-Henninger, Luis Antonio. 2015. "Toward Defining the Causal Role of Consciousness: Using Models of Memory and Moral Judgment from Cognitive Neuroscience to Expand the Sociological Dual-Process Model." *Journal for the Theory of Social Behaviour* 45(2):238–60.

Wacquant, Loïc J. D. 1995a. "Pugs at Work: Bodily Capital and Bodily Labour among Professional Boxers." *Body and Society* 1(1):65–93.

Wacquant, Loïc J. D. 1995b. "The Pugilistic Point of View: How Boxers Think and Feel about Their Trade." *Theory and Society* 24(4):489–535.

Wacquant, Loïc. 1998. "The Prizefighter's Three Bodies." *Ethnos* 63(3–4):325–52.

Wacquant, Loïc. 2004. *Body and Soul: Notebooks of an Apprentice Boxer*. New York: Oxford University Press.

Wacquant, Loïc. 2005. "Carnal Connections on Embodiment, Apprenticeship and Membership." *Qualitative Sociology* 28(4):441–71.

Wacquant, Loïc. 2011. "Habitus as Topic and Tool: Reflections on Becoming a Prizefighter." *Qualitative Research in Psychology* 8(1):81–92.

Wacquant, Loïc. 2013. "Homines in Extremis: What Fighting Scholars Teach Us about Habitus." *Body and Society* 20(2):3–17.

Wieder, D. L. 1974. *Language and Social Reality*. The Hague: Mouton.

Wolff, Christian, Freiherr von. 1733. *Vernünfftige Gedancken von Gott, der Welt, und der Seele des Menschen, auch allen Dingen Überhaupt, den Liebhabern der Wahrheit Mitgetheilet*, Fifth Edition. Frankfurt and Leipzig: Pohln. und. Churfürstl.

CHAPTER 8

COGNITIVE SOCIOLOGY AND FRENCH PSYCHOLOGICAL SOCIOLOGY

GABE IGNATOW

8.1 Introduction: A French Connection

THE present volume can be seen as an extension of a tradition of sociological interest in the study of *cognos* and *psyche* that dates at least to Marcel Mauss, Émile Durkheim's nephew and collaborator. In the 1920s Mauss served for several years as president of the Societé de Psychologie. He developed his unique understanding of what sociological and psychological science had to offer one another, and a particular conception of *habitus*, in a series of lectures delivered to the *Societé* in the 1920s and 1930s (Mauss, 1923; 1925/1966; 1935/1979). After these lectures, *habitus* mostly disappeared from world sociology until the late 1960s, when Pierre Bourdieu reintroduced the concept in a study on gothic architecture and Scholastic thought. Bourdieu refined the *habitus* idea in several of his later works, and though he drew heavily on the cognitive psychology of his time (Lizardo 2004), he never addressed psychologists directly in his published work. More recently, Loïc Wacquant's ethnographic projects have taken *habitus* in new directions, and in so doing have strengthened several points of weakness in Bourdieu's formulation.

In this chapter I consider this Mauss–Bourdieu–Wacquant lineage of psychological sociology from several vantage points. First I consider the intellectual and institutional contexts in which these sociologists encountered ideas from psychology. I next discuss how the idea of *habitus* has evolved from Mauss through Bourdieu to Wacquant. Finally, I consider the influence of French psychological sociology on contemporary American sociology, with particular reference to theoretical positions developed by Lizardo (2007, 2009a, 2009b) and Vaisey (2009; Vaisey and Frye, this volume). I conclude with a consideration of possible avenues for future development of the Mauss–Bourdieu–Wacquant tradition of psychologically informed sociology.

8.2 Changing Institutional and Intellectual Contexts

There are several striking commonalities in the intellectual biographies of the major figures in French psychological sociology. All three sociologists encountered foreign cultures in military settings abroad: Mauss spent four years serving in World War I attached to British and Australian divisions, and even fought alongside Australian aboriginal soldiers (Fournier 1994/2006:176–9). Bourdieu's early work on Kabyle society was based on his years of military service in Algeria (Bourdieu 1979). And Wacquant performed two years of civilian service at a research center in New Caledonia (a French island in the South Pacific), where he studied the indigenous Kanak population (Wacquant 2009:138).

All three sociologists worked in intellectual *milieux* that encouraged interdisciplinarity. Where Durkheim, concerned for the survival of sociology as a discipline, had equivocated on the role psychological factors should play in sociological explanation,[1] Mauss was able to discuss publicly the contributions psychology and physiology could potentially make to sociology, and vice versa (Mauss 1924/1966; 1927/2005:34; Fournier 1994/2006:222–3). In a 1927 essay he even suggested that Durkheim himself, had he lived longer, would have called on the next generation of sociologists to welcome contributions from psychology and related disciplines (Mauss 1927/2005:34). Like Mauss, Bourdieu operated in an academic environment that was relatively conducive to interdisciplinary social science. During Bourdieu's intellectual coming of age, the French academic field was heavily influenced by structuralism, a movement that "allowed psychologists, linguists, anthropologists, and sociologists to speak a common theoretical language for almost two decades" (Lizardo 2009a:715; also Dosse 1999; Schurmans and Bronckart 1999). Finally, with Mauss and Bourdieu, Wacquant has managed to engage with psychologists (and cognitive scientists and neurobiologists) with little apparent concern for the borders separating academic disciplines.

While the academic settings in which Mauss, Bourdieu, and Wacquant each operated were relatively conducive to cross-disciplinary forays, Anglophone sociology has been less consistently hospitable to ideas from psychology, and this has affected the reception of French psychological sociology in the English-speaking academic world. In the United States in particular, psychology and cognitive neuroscience have appeared to sociologists to be much more hostile to sociology than has been the case in France, due to the popularity of, first, behaviorism, and then sociobiology and evolutionary psychology. Setting aside the question of the scientific merits of these movements, it is clear that their popularity outside of academia, and the imperialistic stances their standard bearers have occasionally taken toward sociology and the social sciences as a whole, have poisoned the psychology well for many sociologists. As a consequence, American sociologists interested in appropriating ideas from psychology have faced an uphill battle against both the traditional self-definition of sociology as the study of higher-order social phenomena, and outmoded nature-nurture and realism-constructionism dualisms. As we will see later in this chapter, in spite of this unfortunate history there is today reason to be optimistic about the prospects of sophisticated new forms of sociology that are benefiting from insights afforded by psychology and cognitive neuroscience.

8.3 MAUSS TRACKS

> That is why Durkheim, the pupil of Wundt and Ribot, Espinas, Ribot's friend, and the rest of us, the followers of these teachers, have always been ready to accept the advances of psychology. For only the latter, besides our own elaborations, provides us with the necessary concepts, the useful words which denote the most numerous facts and connote the clearest and most essential ideas.
>
> —Mauss (1935/1979:12–13)

World War I marked the end of the golden age of Durkheimian sociology in France. Durkheim's son André perished in the war, as did many of his students (Fournier 1994/2006:177–8). Durkheim himself died a few years later, but his nephew Marcel Mauss fought for four years, survived, and was highly decorated for his service. Following the war, Mauss completed and published many of his uncle's unfinished works, and would later gain fame for *The Gift*, his 1923–1924 classic on exchange in archaic societies.

During the 1920s and 1930s Mauss was widely recognized as Durkheim's successor as leader of the French school of sociology (Fournier 1994/2006:273), and it was during this period that Mauss began to focus on sociology's relations with psychology and physiology. He came to advocate a "psychophysiological" (Mauss 1935/1979:27), or "socio-psycho-biological" (1935/1979:122) holistic sociology. In four lectures delivered to the Societé de Psychologie between 1923 and 1934, Mauss argued for a rapprochement between sociology and psychology, and discussed topics ranging from mind–body linkages to inhibitions, delirium, dreams, and hallucinations. Mauss did not align himself with Freudian psychoanalysis, but rather with psychiatry and French neurology: though he stated that psychoanalytic concepts "have an enormous capacity to advance and endure," he feared psychoanalysts' "excesses" and "exaggerations" (Mauss 1924/1966:284). In his 1924 address Mauss discussed the practical relationship between sociology and psychology, as well as four specific psychological phenomena: mental or nervous health or debility, psychosis, the notion of symbol, and the notion of instinct. The objective of his 1926 lecture was to convince psychologists of the psychological reality of higher-order social facts, and thus to "take further Durkheim's very fine and profound study of the relation between the individual and the social in the case of suicide" (1935/1979:13). He detailed cases where death was caused by the idea that it was the necessary consequence of a sin, such as a crime against the totem. He discussed "thanatomania," a phenomenon consisting of "a violent negation of the life instinct by the social instinct." And he reviewed studies by Hertz and others that analyzed the physical effects on the individual of the idea of death suggested by the collectivity in Australia, New Zealand, and Polynesia.

Mauss's term for social facts that act on the physical body, introduced in his 1934 lecture, was "techniques du corps" (1935/1979:104). Body techniques are "the ways in which from society to society men know how to use their bodies" (97)—"special habits" (99) of each society that could come to light only with comparative observation. His examples were numerous: differences in the gaits of French and American women, English and French soldiers' methods of wielding a spade and marching, English and French children's postures at the dinner table, and how different generations of Frenchmen had been taught to run and swim (98–101). In his lecture Mauss discussed his choice of the term "*habitus*" to describe these social idiosyncrasies. These "special habits" (99) of each society were of a "social nature" (101), but were not a matter of metaphysical principles or collective memory. Rather, *habitus* was a product of social habits that "vary especially between societies, educations, proprieties and fashions, prestiges. In them we should see the techniques and work of collective and individual *practical reason* rather than, in the ordinary way, merely the soul and its repetitive faculties" (101, emphasis added).

Mauss's comparative observations led him to promote a holistic sociology in which "the triple consideration of the body, the mind and the social environment must go together" (Mauss 1935/1979:31). He "concluded that it was not possible to have a clear idea of all these facts about running, swimming, etc., unless one introduced a triple consideration instead of a single consideration, be it mechanical and physical...or on the contrary psychological or sociological. It is the triple viewpoint, that of the 'total man', that is needed" (101). Mauss contended that ordinary people were different both from intellectuals and from intellectuals' theoretical models of ordinary people: the "complete non-compartmentalized" person is the "indivisible, measurable but not dissectible being that we meet in our moral, economic and demographic statistics" (26). He gave the example of rhythmic music, in which "rhythms and symbols bring into play not just the aesthetic or imaginative faculties of man but his whole body and his soul simultaneously" (27). These were not, in Mauss's view, uncommon occurrences, but examples of an ontological reality: "In society itself when we study a special fact it is with the total psycho-physiological complex that we are dealing" (27).

Mauss's vision of a psychological sociology put forward in his 1920s–1930s lectures is reflected in recent trends in cognitive neuroscience, psychology, and cognitive sociology as presented in this volume. Where Mauss had argued that the "three elements" (the physiological, psychological, and social) were "indissolubly mixed together" (1935/1979:102), cognitive neuroscientists and psychologists have shown that this is literally the case. Neuroscientists have developed models of reasoning in which human rationality is built not just "on top of the apparatus of biological regulation but also from in and with it" (Damasio 1994:128), while cognitive scientists have explored how thought is rooted in bodily and sensory experience (e.g., Prinz 2002; Barsalou 1999) Cognition, reasoning, and memory are understood to be embodied phenomena that operate with, and through, perceptual (vision, touch, taste, smell, hearing) and emotional bodily systems (see Ignatow [2007] for a review). While the holistic psychological sociology Mauss proposed in his 1920s–1930s lectures appears to have been remarkably prescient, a downside of his approach is that he did not provide a template for how to perform psychologically informed sociology. He expressed a desire for psychologists to take seriously social facts, and for sociologists to embrace ideas from psychology, but he did not suggest any methods that would allow either group to follow his lead. And his own methods, if we can call them that, were mostly comparative observation, archival research, and armchair theory.

8.4 BOURDIEU'S REDEPLOYMENT OF *HABITUS*

> Merging with psychology, though with a kind of psychology undoubtedly quite different from the most widely accepted image of this science, such an exploration of the cognitive structures that agents bring to bear in their practical knowledge of the social worlds thus structured. Indeed there exists a correspondence between social structures and mental structures, between the objective divisions of the social world . . . and the principles of vision and division that agents apply to them.
>
> —Bourdieu (1989/1996:1, qtd. in Lizardo 2004:3)

Pierre Bourdieu first revived *habitus* in his 1967 reinterpretation of the art historian Erwin Panofsky's analysis of gothic architecture and Scholastic thought in the Middle Ages, and he refined the idea afterward in several of his major works. Along with the ideas of power field and forms of capital, *habitus* is widely regarded as one of Bourdieu's most important theoretical objects. For Bourdieu, *habitus* is composed of systems of "durable, transposable dispositions, structured structures predisposed to function as structuring structures, that is, as principles which generate and organize practices and representations that can be objectively adapted to their outcomes without presupposing a conscious aiming at ends or an express mastery of the operations necessary in order to attain them" (Bourdieu 1990:53). *Habitus* can potentially serve as a theoretical bridge between sociology and psychology (see Vaisey and Frye this volume), because it is a theoretical device that incorporates two levels of analysis in one conceptual framework (see Lizardo 2004): at the micro level, a person's bodily and cognitive habits; and at the meso level, the other people, practices, and institutions with which she interacts.

A second analytic advantage of *habitus* is how thoroughly it synthesizes bodily and cognitive elements. For Bourdieu, *habitus* comprises a large number of bodily phenomena, including the actor's posture and bearing, demeanor, accent, eating conventions, and aesthetic preferences (Bourdieu 1984:466), and it also comprises cognitive schemas, which Bourdieu conceives as qualitatively different from, if at times directed by, these bodily phenomena. Bourdieu, like Mauss, suggested that "practical belief" is less a "state of mind" than a "state of the body" (1990:68–69), and that

> every social order systematically takes advantage of the disposition of the body and language to function as depositories of deferred thoughts that can be triggered off at a distance in space and time by the simple effect of re-placing the body in an overall posture which recalls the associated thoughts and feelings, in one of the inductive states of the body which, as actors know, give rise to states of mind.   (Bourdieu 1990:69)

I have argued elsewhere (Ignatow 2009a) that, though he claims to do so, Bourdieu does not quite escape what Wacquant has termed his "neo-Kantian cognitivism" (Wacquant 2009:149). While Bourdieu sees bodily postures as capable of triggering cognition, elsewhere in *The Logic of Practice* he states that cognitive schemas are stored in memory without any bodily or emotional content (cf. Strauss and Quinn 1997:47). The "countless practical metaphors" that are the basis of practical sense are "probably as devoid of perception and feeling as the algebraist's dull thoughts" (Bourdieu 1990:69). But algebraists' thoughts are quite not as dull as Bourdieu suggests, as even the most abstract mathematical thought is grounded in bodily operations (Lakoff and Nunez 2000). Though Bourdieu emphasizes the sway of the body *over* cognition, his formulation reinforces an artificial binary of two elements that are in practice "indissolubly mixed together" (Mauss 1935/1979:102). As a result of the lingering Cartesianism/cognitivism in Bourdieu's development of *habitus*, there is little room for emotion in the body-cognition dialectic that he constructed (see Strauss and Quinn 1997:47; cf. Vaisey and Frye, this volume).

A second limitation of Bourdieu's development of *habitus* is his disregard of morality (Sayer 2005). Bourdieu showed little interest in ethical matters, except for a passing reference to ethical dispositions in *Practical Reason* (Bourdieu 1998). In a discussion of the domestic family, Bourdieu wrote of forces of "dilapidation and dispersion" threatening the family, and of "the ethical dispositions that incline its members to identify the particular interests of individuals with the collective interests of the family" (1998:70). Sayer has been particularly forceful in arguing that morality represents a major lacuna for Bourdieu:

> Much of our normative orientation to the world is at the level of dispositions and emotions, indeed not only aesthetic but ethical dispositions can be part of the habitus, acquired through practice as intelligent dispositions which enable us often to react appropriately to situations instantly.... In order to understand our normative orientation to the world we therefore need to avoid the dualisms of fact and value, reason and emotion, and acknowledge that while emotions and values are fallible they are not irrational or "merely subjective", but are often perceptive and reasonable judgements about situations and processes.   (Sayer 2007:91)

Habitus is one of Pierre Bourdieu's most influential theoretical objects, and it represents a major extension of ideas developed in Mauss's lectures on bodily techniques. But Bourdieu's particular take on *habitus* has its limitations, a few of which have been pointed out here. Still, as we will see, a number of scholars (e.g., Atkinson 2016; Crossley

2001; Winchester 2008; Ignatow 2009b) have further developed and refined *habitus* and have used the concept in new ways to address theoretical and substantive concerns.

8.5 AN INTIMATE IMBRICATION: WACQUANT'S CARNAL SOCIOLOGY

> [T]o become a boxer is to appropriate through progressive impregnation a set of corporeal mechanisms and mental schemata so intimately imbricated that they erase the distinction between the physical and the spiritual, between what pertains to athletic abilities and what belongs to moral capacities and will. The boxer is a *live gearing* of the body and the mind that erases the boundary between reason and passion.
>
> —Wacquant (2004:17)

With Mauss and Bourdieu, Loïc Wacquant has sought to explicate *habitus*, the "workings of a sociocultural competency residing in prediscursive capacities" (Wacquant 2005:445). While much of the scholarly discussion of Wacquant's work thus far has concerned itself with his methods of embodied ethnography, here I concentrate on some of the theoretical innovations to *habitus* developed through his ethnographic explorations.

Wacquant makes frequent reference to Mauss, and explicitly places his own work within the Durkheimian lineage. He writes approvingly of the holistic approach Mauss advocated in his lectures to psychologists, and concurs with Mauss "when he speaks of 'the physio-psycho-sociological assemblages of series of acts . . . more or less habitual or more or less ancient in the life of the individual and in the history of the society' that are 'assembled by and for social authority' " (Mauss 1950/1979:101, qtd. in Wacquant 2004:17). Citing Mauss, he refers to "[t]hese elements of an anthropology of boxing as 'biologic-sociological phenomenon' " that "invite us to move beyond the traditional distinctions between body and mind, instinct and idea, the individual and the institution" (2004:149). Wacquant criticizes "disembodied" sociological analysis that foregrounds cognition and backgrounds emotion, "[b]ecause the tendency to *over-intellectualize* social action leads to grievous analytical mistakes" (Wacquant 1998:329). His account of how boxers view their own bodies is thus "deliberately cast so as to foreground the bodily doings and feelings of fighters in their natural surrounding of the gym" (1998:329). In this way his study of boxing resembles Mauss's detailed discussions of techniques of swimming and running from his 1934 lecture to the Societé de Psychologie (Mauss 1935/1979), techniques that differ across national societies, and that changed drastically even during Mauss's lifetime (see also Wacquant 1995:88).

Wacquant's sociology is claimed to be more *visceral* than is Bourdieu's, and it is also, not unrelatedly, more concerned with *morality* than Bourdieu ever was. His boxing ethnography sounds Durkheimian themes that are absent from Bourdieu's thought, emphasizing as he does the normative dimensions of life in the gym, a setting that "is to boxing what the church is to religion: the 'moral community,' the 'solidary system of beliefs and practices' that makes it possible and constitutes it as such" (2004:100). With Durkheim, his concern is with a "practical, enacted ethics—as opposed to the discursive, principal morality that concerns philosophers and moral theorists" (1998:346). He discusses the "corporeal and moral dispositions" (2004:44) that are needed if boxers are to successfully learn their sport, the "endless and thankless preparation, inseparably physical and moral" (Wacquant 2004:6), and prizefighters' "professional ethic of sacrifice" (1998:325) that requires them to subjugate their desires for food, sex, and comradery. Wacquant suggests that boxers

> offer us but an exaggerated, idiosyncratic instantiation of a generic social process. They show *how we learn morality: with and through our bodies*, by attaching deeply felt, visceral, "prepredicative" reactions of disgust or attraction, rejection or assent, sympathy or antipathy, to definite classes of events, actions, and circumstances; by reshaping our inner sensual and emotive registers according to shared rules creating a sphere of recognition and therefore of collective existence.   (1998:346)

A third area in which Wacquant's conception of *habitus* differs from Bourdieu's, and one that builds on both his anti-Cartesianism and his recognition of the central significance of morality in social life, is his analysis of *metaphor*. He finds that boxers use a variety of metaphors to describe both their positions within the boxing field and their own bodies. Their consciousness of their economic exploitation is expressed in morally loaded idioms of prostitution, slavery, and animal husbandry (Wacquant 2001:182): they see themselves as "Whores, Slaves and Stallions" in relation to their promoters and matchmakers. Prizefighters regard their bodies as a "*machine or engine* that constantly needs to be 'tuned up' and taken care of in the proper way" (330). Military metaphors of *weaponry and armory* are reflected in the boxing vernacular and in nicknames (331), and boxers often employ a radically instrumentalist conception in which the body is seen as a *tool*, an instrument of work: "It's my tool, it's my money-maker"; "it's your object, it's your ultimate object of survival"; "I wasn't takin' time to sharpen, sharpen the saw...you saw and you saw and you saw and it's become dull!" (Wacquant 2001:333). Other metaphors explain the effects of sexual activity on boxing ability: leakage of bodily fluids, including "blood from the spine," and sperm: "It's like lettin' water out of a faucet....It's like takin' a cork out" (1998:56–57).

This brief sketch of a portion of Wacquant's work reveals that he has made at least three major theoretical innovations to Bourdieu's development of the *habitus* concept: his even more emphatic anti-Cartesianism; his recognition of the central importance of morality in social life; and his attention to metaphor as a window into subjective meaning. However, in spite of these innovations, Wacquant's embodied sociology suffers to some degree from the same latent Cartesianism that characterizes Bourdieu's treatment of *habitus*, though with a different set of implications. Wacquant does not transcend neo-Kantian cognitivism to the degree that he claims, and instead in his work the pendulum has swung from Cartesian cognitivism to a hyperbolically carnal conception of the person. As a consequence, there is a risk that an emphatically and self-consciously "carnal sociology" will be a short-term trend within sociology (see Eliasoph 2005), or a tool used by small numbers of ethnographers rather than, as Wacquant claims it to be (and as I for one think it should be), a template for a new kind of sociology.

8.6 New Theoretical Connections

In its anti-neo-Kantianism and anti-Cartesianism, the Mauss–Bourdieu–Wacquant tradition of psychological sociology is antithetical to main currents in American sociology. In this vein one can contrast American sociologists' interest in Mauss's *Gift* with their lack of familiarity with his lectures to psychologists. Then there is the initial American appropriation of Bourdieu's work (Wacquant 1993), which treated Bourdieu as

> primarily a macrostructural conflict theorist, who has been able to deploy certain strands of Durkheimian and Weberian theory in order to develop a species of "generalized materialism.... This focus on Bourdieu as essentially a theorist of class has brought with it a subsequent hyper-emphasis on the more "mesolevel" aspects of Bourdieu's work...but has resulted in the theoretical neglect and denigration of...the idea of the habitus.   (Lizardo 2004:3)

Despite these distorted reception patterns (see Wacquant 1989), the French tradition of psychological sociology does hold a special attraction to a small minority of American sociologists, and there have been several exciting recent developments at the intersection of sociological theory and psychology, cognitive science, and neuroscience that have incorporated ideas rooted in this tradition. In what follows, I consider two prominent recent theoretical projects informed by the French tradition: Vaisey's "dual-process model" of culture, and Lizardo's arguments for the relevance of neuroscience research on mirror neurons to sociological practice theory.

8.6.1 Vaisey's Dual-Process Model

Vaisey's (2009) "dual-process" model of culture in action is an effort to integrate sociological practice theory (including both Bourdieu's and Swidler's versions), sociological value theory (Hitlin and Piliavin 2004), and intuitionist psychology (e.g., Haidt 2001; Rozin et al. 1999). His argument, in brief, is that it is both sociologically parsimonious and psychologically realistic to conceptualize culture as operating within individuals simultaneously through two systems. The first is a system of intuitions that is "fast, automatic, and largely unconscious," while the second is a cognitive system that is "slow, deliberate, and largely conscious" (Vaisey 2009:1683; see also DiMaggio 2002). The first system is for "practical consciousness," which allows people to operate in ordinary situations without having to constantly re-evaluate their goals and strategies. The second is the basis of "discursive moral consciousness," people's consciously stated values and beliefs. Vaisey argues that this dual-process model is a "heuristic encapsulation of decades of research" (1684) that has substantial implications for sociology. First, he suggests that this model casts doubt on the value of using interview methods to study culture, because such methods "engage with discursive consciousness alone" (1687) and therefore give scholars "little leverage on unconscious cognitive processes." In contrast, because fixed-response survey questions are more akin to solving everyday practical problems, they may tap into practical consciousness, which "has to *make* (as opposed to *discuss*) many such decisions each day" (1688–89): "When we hear a survey question, we simply have to pick the response our practical consciousness prefers, the response that 'feels right' or 'sounds right' to us" (1689).

Vaisey's analysis of survey data from the National Study of Youth and Religion demonstrates that people are often unable to articulate reasons for their moral judgments and decisions (see also Haidt 2001), but that moral schemas that are a part of practical consciousness are nevertheless generative of future behavior. In my view, a dual-process model can make sense of findings from experiments (Haidt 2001) and forced-choice survey items. In both cases, many respondents cannot produce reasons for their decisions (at least, not reasons that meet academic standards for clarity and logical coherence), and this suggests that they do not have conscious access to a repository of propositional information that informs moral decisions, nor do they have the ability to produce, on the spot, a linguistic representation of the mental schemas that generate their moral decisions.

There are at least two questions that can be asked of this model. The first is whether people's inability to account for their reasons for doing things implies that those reasons are driven by an id-like, pre- or nonlinguistic circumscribed brain region (one sociologists may choose to call practical consciousness). There is both experimental and ethnographic evidence to suggest that this view is mistaken because, first, bodily and emotional capacities are implicated in discursive consciousness (see Ignatow 2007, 2009a). Second, cognitive and linguistic information is part of practical reason. Storbeck and Robinson's (2004) experimental studies of semantic and affective priming make this latter point. They suggest that affective priming depends on prior semantic analysis (see also Storbeck et al. 2006; Storbeck and Clore 2007). While there are different areas of the brain for producing affect and for higher-order linguistic and abstract cognitive processes, it is not possible to psychologically prime the former (practical consciousness, in Vaisey's terminology) without *first* activating parts of the brain dedicated to object identification and categorization (known as area LOC: see Tovee 1998) and semantic processing. The results from studies of affective information processing are "rather dramatic in suggesting that affective analysis is typically dependent, or parasitic, on some prior semantic analysis" (Storbeck and Robinson 2004:92). Respondents to Vaisey's survey, and subjects in Haidt and his colleagues' experiments, may claim to make moral decisions based on what "feels right" or "sounds right" (Vaisey 2009:1689), but these sorts of responses do not imply that people answer questions *directly* from practical consciousness. It is impossible to speak, or even to *feel*, "from the gut" alone (see Pizarro and Bloom 2003; also Denzin's 2007 critique of Wacquant on this point). Rather, as Storbeck and Robinson put it, people "cannot determine how they feel about an object until they know what it is" (2004:92).

Tavory's (2010) ethnographic study of members of an orthodox Jewish community in Los Angeles includes a critique of what he terms Vaisey's "knee jerk" model of moral judgments. The Orthodox Jews of Tavory's study live in a "secular and 'transgressive'" neighborhood filled with objects and situations they view as defiling (e.g., "Moe's," a non-Kosher hot dog stand). But members of this tight-knit community do not react to morally charged objects and situations via practical consciousness alone, or practical consciousness temporally followed by discursive moral consciousness. Rather, the two work in parallel, emotional reactions being interwoven with discursive social categorization processes:

> The relation between emotional valence and action is not a knee-jerk reaction. Members' actions toward the same object differ, even though the moral valence of the object is not contested. To continue with the mundane example of walking by Moe's, members perform different actions to connote their positions vis a vis the moral threat. Most members simply ignore the threat, treating it as if it does not exist at all. They avert their eyes and look at the opposite side of the street, concentrate on the pavement, or look to a distant point on the horizon. Indeed, on two separate occasions, members talked amongst themselves about the ways they ignored Moe's—what one member called, in jest, the "oh, look at the birdies" attitude.   (Tavory 2010)

Many objects are mildly contaminating, and yet their moral valences do not "translate in knee-jerk fashion into action." Instead, the bulk of Tavory's ethnography describes the many ways members reflexively *use* their own reactions to these objects (the hot dog stand, light switches on the Sabbath) to establish and maintain their status in the community.

To make the point another way, one can ask whether it is apt to model Wacquant's prizefighters through Vaisey's dualist model, when Wacquant has shown that prizefighters make moral judgments of themselves and other through elaborate social metaphors (of fighters as whores, slaves, and stallions), and not through quick, hot knee-jerk reactions followed by slow, cool contemplation. Thus, while Vaisey's model provides a valuable corrective to the Cartesianism/cognitivism implicit in Swidler's version of practice theory, it may be misleading if it leads researchers to think in terms of a Cartesian (cold and hot, mind and body) dualism rather than in terms of the more subtle dualism of implicit versus explicit forms of cognition (see Sun this volume).

8.6.2 Lizardo's "Special Psychology"

> What takes place is a prestigious imitation. The child, the adult, imitates actions which have succeeded and which he has seen successfully performed by people in whom he has confidence and who have authority

over him. The action is imposed from without, from above, even if it is an exclusively biological action, involving his body. The individual borrows the series of movements which constitute it from the action executed in front of him or with him by others.

—Mauss (1935/1979:101–2)

Like Vaisey, Lizardo (2004, 2007, 2009a, 2009b) has brought contemporary research from psychology and cognitive neuroscience to bear on questions of social theory. His concern is with "mimeticism" (Wacquant 2004) or "embodied simulation" (Gallese 2003), the human capacity to quickly and often unconsciously imitate the movements of others. Lizardo argues that research on the human mirror neuron system (MNS), a specialized yet flexible "neurocognitive structure primarily charged with forming fairly abstract representations of *practical action upon objects in the world performed by other actors*" (Lizardo 2007:330), supports Bourdieusian practice theory, and especially Bourdieu's notions of "bodily generalization" (Bourdieu 1984:175; 1990:89) and *habitus*. Mirror neurons, Lizardo suggests, may be the basis of both action imitation and action understanding, and the MNS "can be seen as one possible substrate of not only the practical capacities *productive of action* . . . but those which are in charge of the practical *representation, coding and comprehension of the practical action of self and others*" (Lizardo 2007:330). Like Bourdieu and Wacquant, Lizardo cites Mauss on "bodily techniques" (Lizardo 2007, 2009a), and his employment of Wacquant's ethnographic work in the service of his psychologically informed practice theory (Lizardo 2009a) locates his work in the tradition of psychological sociology as it is presented in this chapter (see also Lizardo 2009b).

In my view, Lizardo's position is basically correct (cf. Turner 2007). But its potential sociological contribution is as of yet unclear, for several reasons. The first is that his position is developed in a double negative fashion: it takes the form of a psychologically informed defense of practice theory that is in effect a critique of Stephen Turner's critique of practice theory (Turner 2002). This arms sympathetic readers with stouter psychological support for *habitus* and practice theory generally, but it hardly seems too much to ask for a template for, or empirical example of, "behavioral realist" (Lizardo 2009b) sociology that somehow builds on contemporary knowledge of the MNS. Lizardo brings psychological research to bear on sociological theory, but that same research ought to be able to contribute to new forms of empirical sociological research as well.

A second limitation of Lizardo's framework is that his interest in social mimesis restricts his consideration of bodily capacities other than those of "vision, hearing (and possible tactile) stimulation," capacities that are claimed to come into play in the process of socialization (Lizardo 2009a:722). This results in a half-embodied sociology that leaves out affect, taste, and smell. Even if these three bodily capacities are less central to social mimesis than are vision, hearing, and feel (though it is not clear why this should be the case), they must surely play a role in embodied forms of sociology, as they do in Wacquant's and others' ethnographic work.

8.7 Conclusions

The French tradition of psychological sociology is not the only sociological tradition to incorporate ideas from psychology and cognitive neuroscience. But it is arguably the most influential and most fruitful, and, as I have argued here and elsewhere (Ignatow 2009a, 2009b), it should be familiar to sociologists if for no other reason that that its main tenets, such as its anti-Cartesianism and concern with morality, and its major concepts such as bodily techniques and *habitus*, find support in recent psychological and cognitive neuroscientific research on embodied cognition, moral judgments, and affective information processing. Thus these are exciting times for scholars who are sympathetic to the French tradition of psychological sociology. Institutional resistance to cross-disciplinary forays is not especially daunting, at least in comparison to sociology in the classical era or the heyday of sociobiology in the 1970s. Sociological interest in Mauss, Bourdieu, and Wacquant appears to be on the rise, and sociologists are developing new research methods for exploring the workings of *habitus*. We are, perhaps, living through the early days of a new kind of cognitive sociology in which *habitus* is a guiding theoretical object.

NOTE

1. Durkheim was very well versed in the psychology of his day, and biological and psychological factors do come into play in several places in his sociology, such as in the idea of *anomie* in his earlier work, and "collective effervescence" in his later work on religion.

REFERENCES

Atkinson, Will. 2016. *Beyond Bourdieu*. Cambridge: Polity.

Barsalou, Lawrence W. 1999. "Perceptions of perceptual symbols." *Behavioral and brain sciences* 22(4):637–660.

Bourdieu, Pierre. 1979. "The Kabyle House or the World Inversed." pp. 133–53 in *Algeria 1960*. Cambridge: Cambridge University Press.

Bourdieu, Pierre. 1984. *Distinction: A Social Critique of the Judgment of Taste*. Cambridge, MA: Harvard University Press.

Bourdieu, Pierre. 1989/1996. *The State Nobility*. Translated by Lauretta C. Clough. Cambridge: Polity Press.

Bourdieu, Pierre. 1990. *The Logic of Practice*. Stanford, CA: Stanford University Press.

Bourdieu, Pierre. 1998. *Practical Reason*. Stanford, CA: Stanford University Press.

Bourdieu, Pierre. 2000. *Pascalian Meditations*. Stanford, CA: Stanford University Press.

Bourdieu, Pierre, and Loïc. Wacquant. 1992. *An Invitation to Reflexive Sociology*. Chicago: University of Chicago Press.

Crossley, Nick. 2001. "The Phenomenological Habitus and Its Construction." *Theory and Society* 30:81–120.

Damasio, Antonio. 1994. *Descartes' Error: Emotions, Reason, and the Human Brain.* New York: G. P. Putnam's Sons.

Danna-Lynch, Karen. 2009. "Objects, Meanings, and Role-Identities: The Practices That Establish Association in the Case of Home-Based Employment." *Sociological Forum* 24(1):76–103.

Denzin, Norman. 2007. "Book Review of *Body & Soul: Notebooks of an Apprentice Boxer.*" *Cultural Sociology* 1(3):429–30.

DiMaggio, Paul. 2002. "Why Cognitive (and Cultural) Sociology Needs Cognitive Psychology." pp. 274–81 in *Culture in Mind: Toward a Sociology of Culture and Cognition*, edited by Karen Cerulo. New York: Routledge.

Dosse, Francois. 1999. *History of Structuralism.* Vol. 1. Minneapolis: University of Minnesota Press.

Eliasoph, Nina. 2005. "Theorizing from the Neck Down." *Qualitative Sociology* 28(2):159–69.

Fournier, Marcel. 1994/2006. *Marcel Mauss: A Biography.* Translated by Jane Marie Todd. Princeton, NJ: Princeton University Press.

Gallese, Vittorio. 2003. "The Manifold Nature of Interpersonal Relations: The Quest for a Common Mechanism." *Philosophical Transactions of the Royal Society of London, B* (358):517–28.

Haidt, Jonathan. 2001. "The Emotional Dog and Its Rational Tail." *Psychological Review* 108:814–34.

Hitlin, Steven, and Jane Allyn Piliavin. 2004. "Current Research, Methods, and Theory of Values." *Annual Review of Sociology* 30:359–93.

Ignatow, Gabe. 2007. "Theories of Embodied Knowledge: New Directions for Cultural and Cognitive Sociology?" *Journal for the Theory of Social Behavior* 37(2):1–21.

Ignatow, Gabe. 2009a. "Why the Sociology of Morality Needs Bourdieu's *Habitus.*" *Sociological Inquiry* 79(1):98–114.

Ignatow, Gabe. 2009b. "Culture and Embodied Cognition: Moral Discourses in Internet Support Groups for Overeaters." *Social Forces* 88(2):643–69.

Lakoff, George, and Núñez, Rafael E. 2000. Where mathematics comes from: How the embodied mind brings mathematics into being. *AMC* 10:12.

Lizardo, Omar. 2004. "The Cognitive Origins of Bourdieu's Habitus." *Journal for the Theory of Social Behavior* 34(4):375–401.

Lizardo, Omar. 2007. "Mirror Neurons, Collective Objects and the Problem of Transmission: Reconsidering Stephen Turner's Critique of Practice Theory." *Journal for the Theory of Social Behaviour* 37(3):319–50.

Lizardo, Omar. 2009a. "Is a 'Special Psychology' of Practice Possible? From Values and Attitudes to Embodied Dispositions." *Theory and Psychology* 19(6):713–27.

Lizardo, Omar. 2009b. "Formalism, Behavioral Realism, and the Interdisciplinary Challenge in Sociological Theory." *Journal for the Theory of Social Behavior* 39(1):39–79.

Mauss, Marcel. 1923. "Address to the Société de Psychologie." *Journal de Psychologie.* In Mauss, *Oeuvres.* Paris: Éditions de Minuit.

Mauss, Marcel. 1966. *Sociologie et Anthropologie* [Sociology and Anthropology]. Paris: PUF.

Mauss, Marcel. 1924/1966. "Rapports réels et pratiques de la psychologie et de la sociologie." *Journal de Psychologie Normale et Pathologique.* pp. 281–310 in *Sociologie et anthropologie*, 3rd ed. Paris: PUF.

Mauss, Marcel. 1927/2005. "Sociology: Its Divisions and Their Relative Weightings." pp. 31–89 in *The Nature of Sociology: Two Essays*, edited by Mauss, Marcel, William Jeffrey, and Mike Gane. New York: Durkheim Press/Berghahn Books.

Mauss, Marcel. 1935/1979. *Sociology and Psychology: Essays*. Translated by Ben Brewster. London: Routledge & Kegan Paul.

Mauss, Marcel. 2005. Sociology: Its divisions and their relative weightings. *The Nature of Sociology*, 31–89.

Pizarro, David, and Paul Bloom. 2003. "The Intelligence of the Moral Intuitions: Comment on Haidt 2001." *Psychological Review* 110(1):193–96.

Prinz, Jesse. 2002. *Furnishing the Mind: Concepts and Their Perceptual Bases*. Cambridge, MA: MIT Press.

Rozin, Paul, Laura Lowery, Sumio Imada, and Jonathan Haidt. 1999. "The CAD Triad Hypothesis: A Mapping between Three Moral Emotions (Contempt, Anger, Disgust) and Three Moral Codes (Community, Autonomy, Divinity)." *Journal of Personality and Social Psychology* 76(4):574.

Sayer, Andrew. 2005. *The Moral Significance of Class*. Cambridge: Cambridge University Press.

Sayer, Andrew. 2007. "Class, Moral Worth and Recognition." pp. 88–102 in *(Mis)recognition, Social Inequality and Social Justice*, edited by Terry Lovell, Nancy Fraser and Pierre Bourdieu. New York: Oxford University Press.

Schurmans, Marie Noëlle, and Jean-Paul Bronckart. 1999. "Pierre Bourdieu - Jean Piaget. habitus, schemes et construction du psychologique." pp. 153–75 in *Le travail sociologique de Pierre Bourdieu*, edited by B. Lahire. Paris: La Découverte.

Storbeck, Justin, and Gerald L. Clore. 2007. "On the Interdependence of Cognition and Emotion." *Cognition and Emotion* 21(6):1212–37.

Storbeck, Justin, and Michael Robinson. 2004. "Preferences and Inferences in Encoding Visual Objects: A Systematic Comparison of Semantic and Affective Priming." *Personality and Social Psychology Bulletin* 30(1):81–93.

Storbeck, Justin, Michael Robinson, and Mark McCourt. 2006. "Semantic Processing Precedes Affect Retrieval: The Neurological Case for Cognitive Primacy in Visual Processing." *Review of General Psychology* 10(1):41–55.

Strauss, Claudia, and Naomi Quinn. 1997. *A Cognitive Theory of Cultural Meaning*. Cambridge: Cambridge University Press.

Tavory, Iddo. 2010. "Everyday Morality: Street Danger and Moral Density in a Jewish Orthodox Community." Unpublished manuscript, Department of Sociology, The New School University.

Tovée, Martin. 1998. "The Speed of Thought." pp. 143–52 in *The Speed of Thought*. Berlin: Springer.

Turner, Stephen. 2002. *Brains/Practices/Relativism*. Chicago: University of Chicago Press.

Turner, Stephen. 2007. "Mirror Neurons and Practices: A Response to Omar Lizardo." *Journal for the Theory of Social Behavior* 37(3):351–71.

Vaisey, Stephen. 2009. "Motivation and Justification: A Dual-Process Model of Culture in Action." *American Journal of Sociology* 114(6):1675–715.

Wacquant, Loïc. 2009. "Habitus as Topic and Tool: Reflections on Becoming a Fighter." in *Ethnographies Revisited*, edited by William Shaffir, Antony Puddephatt, and Steven Kleinknecht. New York: Routledge.

Wacquant, Loïc. 1989. "Towards a Reflexive Sociology: A Workshop with Pierre Bourdieu." *Sociological Theory* 7(1):26–63.

Wacquant, Loïc. J. 1993. "Bourdieu in America: Notes on the transatlantic importation of social theory" pp. 235–62 in *Bourdieu: Critical Perspectives*, edited by C. Calhoun, E. LiPuma, and M. Postone. Chicago: University of Chicago Press.

Wacquant, Loïc. 1995. "Pugs at Work: Bodily Capital and Bodily Labor among Professional Boxers." *Body and Society* 1-1 (March 1995):65–94.

Wacquant, Loïc. 1998. "The Prizefighter's Three Bodies." *Ethnos* 63(3):325–52.

Wacquant, Loïc. 2001. "Whores, Slaves and Stallions: Languages of Exploitation and Accommodation among Boxers." *Body and Society* 7(2–3):181–94.

Wacquant, Loïc. 2004. *Body & Soul: Ethnographic Notebooks of an Apprentice Boxer.* London: Oxford University Press.

Wacquant, Loïc. 2005. "Carnal Connection: On Embodiment, Membership, and Apprenticeship." *Qualitative Sociology* 28(4):441–71.

Winchester, Daniel. 2008. "Embodying the Faith: Religious Practice and the Making of a Muslim Moral Habitus." *Social Forces* 86(4):1753.

CHAPTER 9

··

COGNITIVE SCIENCE
AND SOCIAL THEORY

··

DAVID ECK AND STEPHEN TURNER

THE impact of cognitive science, social neuroscience, and research on cognitive development on social theory has been limited by a mismatch or disconnection between the ground-up, mechanism-driven perspectives developed in these areas and the top-down perspective of social science, which begins with descriptions of social phenomena that need explanation and looks for mechanisms that fit the apparent explanations. In this chapter we are concerned with the bottom-up approach. We discuss the implications for social theory of various competing cognitive science approaches, and reconsider some of the issues between them in light of their different implications for social phenomena.

The basic landscape of cognitive science can be summarized in the following manner. The original and core approach to modeling the mind in terms of the brain brought together a set of basic ideas, more or less organized around a common strategy: to identify the functional conditions necessary for the production of particular mental processes, and to reconstruct these as elements of a process that could be represented by flowcharts. These elements included reasoning understood as concept manipulation, memory, perception, motor skills, representation, pattern recognition, language, the ability to orient in space, and over time added such things as facial recognition—and, notably, the understanding of other minds, the understanding encoded in folk psychology, that is to say the ideas behind the ordinary way in which people speak and think about the beliefs and intentions of others.

There are two puzzling phenomena that have dominated the literature, and have tended to support the standard model: language and theory of mind. The considerations, however, are very indirect. Language proficiency and the capacity to think about others as thinking beings with thoughts distinct from and different from one's own both arrive at a certain, young, developmental point, and arrive, so to speak, all at once. They do not have the same slow incremental development that one would expect if they were like ordinary learning about the world through trial and error and empirical feedback.

In the case of ordinary learning, it would seem, intelligence would matter to the pace of what was learned; the data that were being given through life experiences varied and would presumably produce variant outcomes, and the process would be slow and incremental. However, it seems that none of the features of ordinary learning matter much if at all: children learn language and come to speak and understand syntactically or in terms of linguistic rules "naturally" or without instruction, come to conform to these elaborate unconscious rules at a certain developmental stage and only at that stage, and exhibit remarkable uniformity, in contrast to the diversity of the results of ordinary learning. These facts lend themselves to the idea that there are pregiven modules, that is to say innate neural structures, common to all people that are activated at a particular developmental stage. We will have more to say about modularity shortly.

9.1 BOXOLOGY

Modules or innate structures are appealed to in order to explain not only the apparently odd way in which language use and theory of mind use appear developmentally but also their "fast" or automatic character. But the thing being explained requires its own specification, which is typically represented as a flowchart in which arrows are drawn between boxes representing components of these processes and the arrows representing (usually unspecified) causal and information-transforming processes. The boxes are functional units, parts of what is taken to be the minimal set of unitized processes that make up the cognitive conditions for the possibility of some phenomenon (Nichols and Stitch 2003:10).

The choice of the functional units reflects two constraints. First, there is experimental evidence from psychology about the phenomenon in question. One might have, for example, evidence of the specific details of the memory capacities of ants returning to a nest as revealed by experiments. Second, there are considerations of economy and simplicity. There should be no more boxes than are needed as "conditions for the possibility" to account for the total phenomenon. The "account" is functional, not physical. The point is to have boxes representing every necessary subprocess that figures into the capacity in question as the experimental evidence has defined it.

What is it that the boxes stand in for? There are of course inputs and outputs that are represented by arrows, and something that happens in the boxes. What happens, however, is a problem. The problem is this: in treating these depictions as explanations, we are in effect explaining brain processes by positing a little human-like operative, a homunculus, in the brain performing the relevant tasks in a manner similar to conscious explicit thought. There certainly are not such things. But the boxes help define the explanatory problem, and enable us to take an additional step: breaking the tasks down into a series of boxes that do not require full-fledged homunculi. Consider, for instance, Daniel Dennett's portrayal:

> without saying how it is to be accomplished (one says, in effect: put a little man in there to do the job). If we then look closer at the individual boxes we see that the

function of each is accomplished by subdividing it via another flowchart into still smaller, more stupid homunculi. Eventually this nesting of boxes within boxes lands you with homunculi so stupid...that they can be, as one says, "replaced by a machine." One discharges fancy homunculi from one's scheme by organizing armies of such idiots to do the work.   (Dennett 1978:123–4)

Less colorfully, "They try to explain mindreading (or some other complex cognitive capacity) by positing functionally characterized underlying mechanisms with capacities that are simpler than the capacity they are trying to explain" (Nichols and Stich 2003:11). In reducing a cognitive capacity to successively simpler underlying processes, the standard model's mechanism-driven perspective implies that combinatorial processes operating on representations play a primary role.

The temptation is to think of the thing that happens in the boxes in computational terms, and specifically in terms of rules. The inputs are conveniently thought of as things that are already in some sense representational, and the processes in the boxes as something that is done with the representations, which involves combining the representations and making them into something different, perhaps a different representation, or a command to a part of the body to act, or, in the case of perception taking raw inputs and turning them into a representation that can be stored as a memory or matched with a stored memory. Nichols and Stich put it this way:

the representational account of cognition...maintains that beliefs, desires, and other propositional attitudes are relational states. To have a belief or a desire with a particular content is to have a representation token with that content stored in the functionally appropriate way in the mind. So, for example, to believe that Socrates was an Athenian is to have a representation token whose content is *Socrates was an Athenian* stored in one's "Belief Box," and to desire that it will be sunny tomorrow is to have a representation whose content is *It will be sunny tomorrow* stored in one's "Desire Box."   (Nichols and Stich 2003:14–15; italics in the original)

They note, "Many advocates of the representational account of cognition also assume that the representation tokens subserving propositional attitudes are linguistic or quasi-linguistic in form" (Nichols and Stich 2003:15). Fodor makes the reasoning behind this explicit: what he calls "compositionality is at the heart of the productivity and systematicity of thought, but also because it determines the relation between thoughts and concepts. The key to the compositionality of thoughts is that they have concepts as theory constituents" (Fodor 2008:18), and further, "only something language-like can have a logical form" (Fodor 2008:18). It is difficult to see what the alternative is, given this construction of the problem. The bias toward thinking in terms of representations is overwhelming, in part because it is only representations that can be readily thought of as undergoing combinatorial processes.

"Readily thought of," however, implicitly means thought of in terms more or less familiar from folk psychology. The homunculus problem is simply an extreme case of imagining the inner workings of the mind in familiar human terms. The combinations or representations in question are modeled on explicit reasoning, or explicit reasoning as formalized in computer programming. And this is a particular issue in relation to our understanding of other people. We seem to have implicit mindreading capacities, demonstrated by experiments, such as the famous false belief experiments to be discussed shortly. And these capacities seem to be the basis of social interaction: we could not easily imagine a social world without the employment of these capacities, routinely and as a part of every relationship between people.

We discursively reason about other minds in terms of notions like belief and motivation and this raises the question of whether the ToM (theory of mind) implied by the usage is true. One reason for thinking it is true, that is to say whether the mind really works in a way that has elements that more or less correspond to the concepts of folk psychology, like belief and desire, and therefore, the correct starting point both for accounts of the brain's role in mindreading and social explanation is the very fact of the ubiquity of the relevant concepts. So pervasive is the role of mindreading in our lives that Jerry Fodor has remarked that if the ordinary person's understanding of the mind should turn out to be seriously mistaken, it would be "the greatest intellectual catastrophe in the history of our species" (Fodor 1987:xii). But for our ToM, as depicted functionally in flowcharts and boxes, to be true, there needs to be something corresponding to its elements, or some of its elements, in the brain itself.

Modularity provides an answer to the question of what the boxes might correspond to. But modules explain at a different level of analysis: they are not physical features of the brain, but they are organizational features, with defined operational properties. Their major properties are defined differently by different users of the term, but among them is that they are fast, and they are highly specialized operations with simple outputs and are "informationally encapsulated" meaning that they operate on their own kind of informational inputs only, and their processes are mandatory. These may correspond to the functional units represented as boxes in flow charts—but they may not. There is no reason in principle for functionalists to think that any particular neural structure is necessary for the capacity. The reason for supposing that there are modules comes from other considerations: how the capacity appears in the course of child development, and the fact that they are "fast," which implies that they are products of evolution and are innate (Cosmides and Tooby 1994:86).

Thinking of the mind as modular thus solves certain crucial problems about speed, the speed needed to perform complex cognitive tasks, and also enables us to think about these dedicated components as both complex and simple at the same time: complex in that they perform complex calculations quickly; simple in that as components of a process they can be treated as simple mechanical devices.

On the surface, this solution works. But it presents a picture of the human mind that is difficult to reconcile with some aspects of social science knowledge, while fitting in a rough way with others, and, as it turns out, difficult to reconcile with the physical properties of the brain and neural processes. We know, for example, that affect or emotion plays a significant role in reasoning, but it is difficult to see how this role can be modeled as computation. The issues, as they relate to social science in particular, are exemplified by the idea of ToM, though many of the same issues arise in connection with language, which has its own "folk" grammatical ideas, which vary by culture even more dramatically than folk psychologies do. We also know that there are mechanisms, such as mirror neurons, that operate in ways that do not correspond to the mental operations allowed for in folk psychology. Theory of mind is the "social" topic that fits the standard computational model most closely. It is "social" because complex human social interaction involves assessing the beliefs and motives of other people. If the condition for the possibility of doing this is possessing a "theory"—implicit in the narratives of action in terms of which people understand and explain one another—then this theory has a foundational role in accounting for social action. A long tradition of social phenomenology engaged with the presuppositions of understanding other minds reasoned in the same way (Schutz 1932/1967). This fits, though imperfectly, into the biexperimental results involving "false belief" that impressed a generation of researchers and spawned a large literature.

The findings were this: only at about four years of age could children correctly answer questions about where someone would look for an object if it had been moved from its original place without their knowledge. This was interpreted as meaning that children developed a ToM only after four, or to put it in modularity terms, activated their ToM module only at this age. The modularity interpretation was understood to fit the experimental results perfectly, in part because it was also claimed, based on a small cross-cultural sample, that all humans developed the same ToM. Learning and difference was therefore beside the point—nothing was learned; something was activated that was already there, universally. The conclusion was that an infant does not have a ToM yet, but an inbuilt capacity to have one that gets activated at a certain age, and which, once activated, allows them to solve particular problems that they could not solve before it was activated. There is, however, no account of how this activation happens. Indeed, the modularity hypothesis refers such questions to evolutionary explanations, on the grounds that only evolution could produce such complex capacities.

But these claims need to come with a warning. We do not have an argument other than plausibility and the lack of alternatives for believing in the results of boxology, or in modules. There is a sense in which this is simply a sign of our limitations and the limitations of folk psychology: without it, we cannot make sense of the actual processes of thought, because folk psychology is *how* we make sense of thought, indeed, how we define it. How any of this works in the brain is unknown, and indeed there is a substantial explanatory gap between what we would like to explain (thought, actual speech, consciousness, and the qualities of human experience) and the neuroscience mechanisms we have an understanding of (Horgan 1999).

This is not to say that there is no empirical basis for these claims. As noted earlier, these accounts are constrained by experimental results in psychology: if there is a demonstrated capacity, such as the homing capacity of an ant and its capacity for self-correcting spatial orientation, a functionalist model of this capacity must include the necessary subroutines. There is, however, a physical side to the reasoning. Ideally, the boxes, which represent modularized capacities, should correspond to *something* in the brain. The brain is a variegated organ, which has been mapped into different regions that are known, especially as a result of lesion or cognitive deficit studies, to be associated with particular activities or competencies. Ideally, a box should correspond to a cluster of neurons that activate in the appropriate point in the sequence of the boxed processes. Because at least some cognitive processes can be replicated in conditions in which brain activity can be measured, such as fMRI machines, it is technically possible to determine where and in what order brain activity occurs—up to a certain resolution. It is a bonus for boxology if these capacities can be localized in the brain, and the fact that many capacities, such as phoneme recognition, can be localized, serves as a general warrant for the strategy of boxology.

Boxology arguments depend very heavily on considerations of plausibility. Localizing enhances plausibility. But the two are logically distinct: "Positing a 'box' which represents a functionally characterized processing mechanism or a functionally characterized set of mental states does not commit a theorist to the claim that the mechanism or the states are spatially localized in the brain, any more than drawing a box in a flow chart for a computer program commits one to the claim that the operation that the box represents is spatially localized in the computer" (Nichols and Stich 2003:11). This is an important point for what follows. Nevertheless, this bonus, when it can be obtained, for example by localizing certain kinds of thoughts or mental processes, plays an important role.

The standard model's evidential appeal to plausibility, however, is troublesome given other considerations that undermine its plausibility. The modular account depends very heavily on its being universal, on everyone having the same module to activate, and on the modules being primordial products of evolution, and thus freed from any requirement to make sense of how they are acquired, which would be the case if they varied culturally. The claim is made that ToM is robust at least across several modern cultures. But although the basics of ToM, such as recognition of goal directedness, do seem universal, ToM terms are not universal. Epistemic language varies widely, and even the distinction between true and false belief does not appear in some languages (Needham 1972). Some cultures regard talk about another person's beliefs and mental contents as deeply inappropriate and treat their minds as opaque (Robbins and Rumsey 2008; Robbins 2008; Schiefflin 2008). And there are a number of other variations in explicit ToM talk between cultures.

What are the implications for social theory of the standard model? They are familiar from Hobbes, rational choice theory, and analytic sociology, for the most part, but the image of the human is arrived at in a somewhat different way, with somewhat different elements. What is common to all of these social theoretical conceptions is an image of man as a kind of calculator whose calculations and the actions that are produced by them are explained by their desires and beliefs. Differences in desires and beliefs explain differences in action. Cultural differences are the product of differences in desires and beliefs. Differences in desires and beliefs are understood as the product of data—of what is fed into the calculating mind. Other people have no special status, other than as sources of this data, objects of desires and fears, and as obstacles to action. But people also have a ToM and can make inferences about the beliefs and desires of others, and this is at the core of the mutual calculations that make up social action and determine institutional arrangements.

The model extends and relies on folk psychology, the folk psychology of belief and desire. The tyranny of this model over social theory results from the implication that social relations are structured by beliefs, desires, and the actions they produce, and by the rational choices that are implied by the combinations of beliefs and desires. Obviously to some extent they are, and there are some contexts in which this form of explanation is sufficient. But other contexts are by definition impervious to this form: those involving the tacit, embodiment, and the frames in which beliefs become intelligible, and the causes of desire. Norms, to the extent that they are not explicit and encapsulated in beliefs, and are tacit, are excluded. And consequently much of what we would call culture—that which operates at the level of perceptual structuring—is also excluded.

However, the standard computational model of the mind is quite elastic: it can be expanded to account for any functional capacity. One could, for example, take something described in symbolic interactionist terms, such as significant gesturing, redescribe it in functional capacity terms, and then break it down into the modular components necessary for the exercise of this capacity. Or one might enhance this model by giving a functional account of joint action or collective action and positing the necessary modules for these capacities. Or one can take a Parsonsian account of norms, and endow the mind with a functional capacity for norm-detection and responsiveness to norms that fits with this account of norms. In this sense, the computationalist model of mind does not come into direct conflict with the various conventional accounts of "the social," and indeed fits them very well.

Indeed, the sheer elasticity of the standard model thus seems to make it impervious to empirical refutation, and potentially consistent with any possible social theory. But the alternatives to the standard model lead in some different directions, and point to some important limitations to the strategy of positing modules that is central to its explanations. More importantly, they point to alternative explanations that do not rely on fixed evolutionary cognitive structures and are potentially better at accounting for diversity and change. The limitations of the standard model may be seen, however, in connection with the distinction between slow and fast thinking made famous by Daniel Kahneman (2011). The basic idea behind this distinction is this: we normally function by thinking by way of short-cuts or heuristics that are not part of our conscious thinking or inferential process, and which have some biases when compared to pure rational choice or to the results we might obtain by slow, explicit thinking, which would allow us to articulate reasons and inferences and reflect on them.

The relevance of the distinction between fast and slow is this: the standard way to explain the existence of modules is to claim that they are the product of long evolutionary processes and that the functional origins are lost in deep time. The problem with the account is this: if we explain fast thinking by the existence of modules, and slow thinking—the kind we can reconstruct or articulate explicitly—by training and linguistic competence, which is language-specific, we are faced with a conundrum about the things that seem also to fall into the category of fast and difficult to articulate thinking but which are *not* the product of evolution.

What might this category include? The list would involve, as suggested above, everything that is tacit and embodied, which would include such things as habitus, practices, and the kinds of skills that chess masters and other experts have, of acting, thinking, or performing at a high level of proficiency without thinking of rules. It would also include what are sometimes called reactive attitudes (Strawson 1962/2003), the immediate feelings that are generated in response to an offending act, a wrong, and so forth. Such things as our immediate negative response to the appearance of free-riding, for example, a topic much discussed in the neuroeconomics literature, would also fall into this category.

9.2 The Cognitive Science Alternatives

There has been no shortage of critiques of cognitive science's dominant computationalist paradigm. In an attempt to clarify and elucidate this motley landscape, Richard Menary (2010) refers to the 4Es of cognition: the embedded, embodied, extended, and enactive movements. These movements form the rhetorical center of challenges to computationalism, though it is worth stressing that there are numerous theoretical frameworks—not all of which begin with the letter E—that overlap, cross-cut, or even fall outside the range of the 4Es. Missing from Menary's list, for instance, is the ecological approach based on Gibsonian psychology and Mark Bickhard's (2009a, 2009b, 2010, 2011, n.d.) interactivism. One of the chief obstacles to developing the social aspects of the 4Es, as suggested by this preliminary glance, is the heterogeneity of the literature.

With that said, there are substantive convergences among the 4E movements. Most basic among these is that all of 4E theory finds the computationalist paradigm's treatment of the individual–environment relationship to be woefully inadequate. When put in positive terms, the critique suggests as an alternative a focus on what is called embeddedness or situatedness. A second point of convergence among the contender theories is the methodological significance of dynamical systems theory for modeling embeddedness.

Dynamical systems theory is a mathematical framework for modeling complex systems. Complex systems change over time, possess interacting components that exhibit emergent behavior, and, as collectively implied by these two traits, the system's emergent behavior does not result from a controlling component agent (Chemero and Richardson 2014:116). Unlike component-dominant systems—where the function of components can be identified in isolation from each other—the behavior of interaction-dominant systems is "the result of interactions between system components, agents, and situational factors, with these intercomponent or interagent interactions altering the dynamics of the component elements, situational factors, and agents themselves" (118). The individual–environment relationship is thus the most important frame of analysis because agents and the function of their components cannot be understood in abstraction from particular interactive contexts. Embeddedness and dynamical systems theory serve as the most general framework for the 4E movements. Given this general framework, we turn now to the many competing conceptions of embodiment developed therein.

Embodiment is also central theme of the 4E movement, and comes in weak and strong forms. The ecological movement of Gibsonian psychology presents a strong form and, according to Michaels and Palatinus (2014), places general constraints on any account of embodiment. It is important to note that some theorists use "ecology" interchangeably with "embeddedness," which is consistent with Michaels and Palatinus's claim to generality. The key concept of Gibsonian psychology—what makes it appealing to dynamical modeling and, for others, the general framework for embodiment—is its theory of affordances. Gibson (1977) describes affordances as "what it [the environment] offers the animal, what it provides or furnishes, either for good or ill" (127). Donald A. Norman added the notion that affordances are products of human perception, in the sense that the environment affords only that which is perceived as a use (1988/2013). Norman further distinguished real and perceived affordances (1999). This led to the view that perceived affordances are not properties of the environment or of the organism; rather, they are objective features or *relata* between the environment and the organism. Organisms directly respond to perceived affordances rather than mind-independent features of an objective environment: the world we live in is a world of perceived affordances, affordances for us, rather than a world of inherent properties. This intrinsic link between perception and embodiment departs significantly from the standard model, implying a nonrepresentational account of cognition. In the next section, we examine affordances in a broader light, focusing on the environment–individual relationship rather than the associated antirepresentationalism.

Although antirepresentationalism is a common position within the 4E literature, a strong conception of embodiment does not necessarily eliminate representations from primitive forms of perception. Pursuing this line of enquiry, however, does require a radically different concept to substitute for the work done by representation. Bickhard's interactivism advances such an account: the lesson to be learned from Gibsonian affordances, on this view, is not that organisms directly perceive information in their environment—thereby eliminating representations from primitive forms of perception—but rather that representational content in its most primitive form is an organism's anticipation of environmental interactions, which is indexed to an organism's internal bodily states (Bickhard and Richie 1983; Bickhard 2009a).

Enactivism—the most influential account of strong embodiment—has been largely interpreted as antirepresentationalist. This is clearest with Daniel Hutto and Erik Myin's (2013) radical enactive cognition hypothesis, whose primary goal is to eliminate any notion of representations at the level of basic cognition. But even within the enactive movement there has been a great deal of theoretical diversity. The radical enactive cognition hypothesis is aligned with the sensorimotor contingency theory (O'Regan and Noë 2001), which is only one of two major strands of enactivism (Torrance 2006). In contrast to the sensorimotor contingency theory's central tenet—namely, that bodily movement constitutes cognition of the world—the strand of enactivism associated with Varela, Rosch, and Thompson (1991) begins with a more general perspective on cognitive agency and perception, which allows for a wider range of positions. The Varela-inspired strand asserts the primacy of processes—treating organisms, cognition, and, ultimately, social interaction as all different types of emergent processes rather than substances with objective physical properties. One development from these ideas is De Jaegher, Di Paolo, and Gallagher's concept of participatory sense-making—an enactivist account of social interaction (De Jaegher 2009; De Jaegher et al. 2010).

The movement that has gained most attention from theorists outside of cognitive science, including social science, is the idea of the extended mind. According to theories of extended cognition, there has been a general evolutionary trend of organisms becoming more efficient cognizers via offloading burdensome tasks onto the environment. Clark (2008) refers to this general type of activity as "scaffolding" one's environment. Organisms who offload thereby figure out how to do more within relatively stable biological constraints and, as a result, have a better chance of survival. Clark (1993) previously dubbed this adaptationist sketch the "007 principle": organisms tend to know only as much as they need to. But adaptationism arguably comes at a dear price. One concern—seen previously in connection with the standard model's modules—is that the adaptationism burdens extended theories of cognition with just-so evolutionary histories. But in contrast to special purpose modular mechanisms, Clark is at pains to characterize the evolutionary trajectory implied by extended theories as one of ever increasing plasticity (e.g., Clark 2001). Another concern is highlighted by phenomeno-logically informed accounts of *social* interaction. The concern is as follows: adaptationism is *anti*social, reducing all intersubjective relationships to forms of exploitative resource maximization. Other people—like an individual's own body—are reduced to being "operating profiles" within larger functional processes.

Despite these concerns the extended movement has been the most popular of the 4Es among social scientists, in particular social scientists working with representationalist models of cognition (e.g., Harrison and Ross [2010] on neuroeconomics). This is in large part because the extended movement retains major aspects of the standard model: there are representations at the basic level of cognition and, more importantly, all cognition is computation. What the dominant paradigm fails to appreciate, on this view, is simply the pervasive offloading of representations onto the environment, a process occurring on both evolutionary and ontogenetic timescales. Given the commonalities between the standard model and extended theories of cognition and the latter's popularity, it is worth questioning whether the 4Es offer any novel insights for social theory.

9.3 RECONSTRUCTING SOCIAL THEORY

How do these movements bear on social theory? The term "extended mind" suggests something more radical than it might appear. Clark's key example is innocuous enough:

There is a documented case (from the University of California's Institute for Nonlinear Science) of a California spiny lobster, one of whose neurons was deliberately damaged and replaced by a silicon circuit that restored the original functionality: in this case, the control of rhythmic chewing....now imagine a case in which a person (call her Diva) suffers minor brain damage and loses the ability to perform a simple task of arithmetic division using only her neural resources. An external silicon circuit is added that restores the previous functionality. Diva can now divide just as before, only some small part of the work is distributed across the brain and the silicon circuit: a genuinely mental process (division) is supported by a hybrid bio-technological system. That alone, if you accept it, establishes the key principle of Supersizing the Mind.   (Clark 2009)

The key principle, in short, is the substitutability of some other means for a mental or at least partly mental process.

In the literature the total process is called an algorithm, and a procedure or object that produces the same result is said to be the same algorithm. The term "same," here, and the designation of the functional process represented by the "algorithm" itself are not well defined, and the results are different depending on how fine-grained the descriptions of the processes are (Milkowski 2013:67). They can be readily extended from very simple perceptual processes to large action sequences, such as a human being going home from work, which can be performed in a large variety of ways, using a large variety of devices, but getting the same result. These may include such mental content as the memory of what bus to take, knowledge of the routines of public transport, map-like memory, and much more. Different content, analogous to different computer code for the "same" algorithm, would be involved if the person walked home or drove a car. But the result would be the "same."

If we think of the notion of affordances more broadly, we can enrich our picture of the extended mind, and show its relation to social theory. Perception is perception of affordances. Affordances are distributed in the environment. The relationship between perceiver and environment, rather than the environment taken by itself, consists of objective features. The objective features of the relationship, in turn, ground specific capacities.

Scaffolding is a term that originally referred, in the work of Lev Vygotsky "to the help and support that adults provide children in order for them to learn and develop complex cognitive abilities" (Estany and Martinez 2014:103). Thus scaffolding is a means to the transformation of mind and mental capacities itself. It has been extended in its meaning to include the tools we have which substitute for cognitive abilities, for example, "scaffolding as a source of capacities that complement those provided by the biological brain, such as a note pad; and language as scaffolding that allows us to freeze a thought or idea in words" (Estany and Martinez 2014:103). The idea is closely related to affordances: affordances are like the convenient handles of a tool, but are the handles given, so to speak, by the natural facts of our interactions with the environment. But as Donald Norman stressed, affordances can be created artificially, like tools, and serve as scaffolding—as a source of advanced or novel capacities and self-transformation.

The routines of the social world, like the educational practices that were the original concern of the psychological theorists of scaffolding, are such creations.

Connecting scaffolding to the routines of the social world, and thus to the institutions that are made up of these routines, and that constitute our social environment, allows for the following: to live in a society is simply to live in an extended cognitive system— where there are alternative means to goals, but only for some goals, through substitutability, and living in this system transforms our own minds.

The effect of this simple idea on the traditional concerns of social theory is remarkable. The traditional problem of social theory was set by the model of the individual who had to come into, and created, society. The explanatory problem was to account for the evident differences between societies. As Durkheim taught, these differences could not be explained by general principles of psychology: those principles held for all people; what needed to be explained was what was different, and varied between "societies." The presumption was that the explanation was to be found in "the social" itself, in something about the content of the social. It was assumed that "the social" and its specific content, such as norms, was produced out of social interaction alone.

This idea produced a standard discourse, in which theorists tried to conceive of this content—always a kind of theoretical abstraction—in different ways: Parsons's idea of a central value system was one; Bourdieu's notions of habitus and field is another; "culture" is yet another; so is "power," hegemonic power, and so forth; other theoretical traditions focused on the process of social interaction itself, or on the legitimating beliefs that sustained institutions. This generated a distinctive discourse involving the notion of "emphasis." Theorists criticized one another for "overemphasizing" one or another of these supposed contents of the social: culture, or power, or socialization, or whatever the unfashionable emphasis of the time was. In this discourse Weber "emphasized" action and belief, Durkheim and his heirs "emphasized" collective mental structures, like culture or habitus, and rational choice theorists emphasized problems of collective rationality.

The idea of society as an extended cognitive system, consisting of scaffolding of routines and substitutable technologies, such as the note pad, removes the explanatory burden from "the social." To understand the differences between societies, and to understand change, is to understand the ways in which routines and technology substitute for capacities and create capacities for action. Nothing special has to emanate from the posited space of "the social." The enactivist concept of participatory sense-making buttresses this insight, highlighting interactive dynamics between individuals that are endogenous to the encounters themselves, which do not presuppose a previously existent social domain (cf. Steiner and Stewart 2009). The way we act differently from the way people act in another society is largely determined by the affordances and scaffolding available to us: what is, in effect, convenient to do, or convenient to believe. This is a profound thought: and it can be made more profound if we think about the ways in which the affordances available to us shape our selves.

It also has deep implications for the traditional account of the social: it takes over the explanatory burden of such questions as "what holds society together" and shifts them from the abstractions familiar from social theory, and indeed from the supposed realm of "the social" itself, and places these burdens on the facts of scaffoldings and the affordances they provide. The answer to the question of what makes people in different societies behave differently is that they have different options for substitution, and different scaffolding, with different affordances. In this sense, the critics of Clark are correct: the effect of the argument is precisely to displace explanations in terms of "the social."

The embedding, enactivist, and ecological arguments, as well as the embodiment argument, can work in concert with this new account of "society," but face, so to speak, in the opposite direction: not from the individual toward her extensions, but from the extensions to the individual. A paradigm of these outward-inward directional arguments is the claim that practices, that is to say the continual and repeated enactment of particular routines, shape the mind, and the body (Roepstorff et al. 2010). Embedding generalizes this kind of argument, to say that even within the self or mind, or as a constitutive part of any content, there is the incorporation or embodiment of habit, which is produced by the external things with which we engage. Thus the mind-body is no longer a calculating machine, but a plastic product of the world it interacts with, and of the interactions themselves. The effect of this is to dissolve the individual and also to dissolve the social and the intersubjective as categories, and to eliminate, on the grounds of interchangeability, nature-culture, object-human distinctions, as well.

This picture may seem very strange, but there are close parallels in science studies: the idea of distributed cognition (Giere 2007; Latour 1987), in which the agent is surrounded by actants, objects and nonhumans understood as having their own limited agency, and discussions of where knowledge is located which point to the recognition that knowledge may reside in routines, objects, instruments (Turner 2007) and the like, as well as in people's heads. There are also classical parallels: Weber made the point that persisting conduct could result from persisting intentions, but it could also result from such things as contagion (Turner and Factor 1994:34). Omar Lizardo has recently argued that Bourdieu in his early work already had a kind of view of the psychological implantation of frameworks as a result of the material environment. He suggests,

> The key point to keep in mind is that for Bourdieu "a child brought up in a Berber house by Berber parents picks up Berber notions, just because the material nature of the house, as well as the behavior of the people with whom he interacts [itself constrained by the material nature of the house], contains in itself the specific history of the Berbers." Therefore, "the [material] environment is not neutral but is itself culturally constructed." (Lizardo 2010:6)

Lizardo also suggests that Bourdieu changed his views on habitus in the 1990s, and moved away from "the remnants of the structuralist inspired 'encoding-decoding' model of aesthetic appreciation that still survives in that early work" (Lizardo 2010:17) in such a way that "the 'semiological' conceptualization of culture as a system of elements connected by arbitrary relations of significance is reduced to a minimum in favor of culture as a system of action and perception that is acquired in a tacit state through tacit mechanisms" (Lizardo 2010:19). The mechanisms involve, as Lizardo quotes Ingold, "the kind of practice mastery that we associate with skill—a mastery that we carry in our bodies and that is refractory to formulation in terms of any system of mental rules and representations" (Ingold 2000:162, quoted in Lizardo 2010:9). Although it is questionable whether Bourdieu finally breaks free of the notion of a system of representations, the change in emphasis is evident.

In the new view we have been outlining here, agency does not vanish, but the agent becomes a person in a world which already has a plethora of, so to speak, handles, handholds, and footholds, which do not "constrain" her so much as endow her and others—differentially—with capacities or powers. In this picture it is not the rational choices of the agent that explains social differences, but the embedded character of all choice. This approach is what Damasio would call anti-Cartesian (1994): it characterizes as an error the attribution of something like the conscious thought of folk psychology, such as decision-making and rational choice, to something that in cognitive terms is in fact executed by reliance on others, on habit, on devices, or on the scaffolding provided by routines.

This is a clue: we are predisposed by our folk psychology and by preverbal mechanisms to overintentionalize action, a notion familiar from attribution theory. But differences in behavior may be produced by something else—affordances and scaffolding. The point of the idea of the extended mind, or more prosaically, substitutability, together with considerations of embodiment, embedding, enactivism, and interactivism, is just this. Where the standard model adds to its explanations through boxology—or epicycles—these accounts at least point the way to the possibility of making empirical questions about substitutability and its effects out of what had formerly been theoretical speculation. And this is especially important in relation to the hypothetical domain of mysterious causes called "the social," which we can now see as a byproduct of a particular model of the individual, common to Cartesianism, Hobbes, and the computational model of mind.

References

Bickhard, Mark H. 2009a. "The Interactivist Model." *Synthese* 166(3):547–91.

Bickhard, Mark H. 2009b. "Interactivism: Introduction to the Special Issue." *Synthese* 166(3):449–51. http://dx.doi.org/10.1007/s11229-008-9371-1.

Bickhard, Mark H. 2010. "Interactive Knowing: The Metaphysics of Intentionality." pp. 207–29 in *Theory and Applications of Ontology: Philosophical Perspectives*, edited by R. Poli and J. Dordrecht: Springer.

Bickhard, Mark H. 2011. "Does Process Matter? An Introduction to the Special Issue on Interactivism." *Axiomathes* 21:1–2.

Bickhard, Mark. N.d. "Interactivism: A Manifesto." http://www.lehigh.edu/~mhbo/InteractivismManifesto.pdf.

Bickhard, Mark H., and D. Michael Richie. 1983. *On the Nature of Representation: A Case Study of James Gibson's Theory of Perception*. New York: Praeger Press.

Chemero, Anthony, and Michael J. Richardson. 2014. "Dynamical Systems Approaches to Cognition." pp. 39–50 in *Routledge Handbook of Embodied Cognition*, edited by L. Shapiro. Abingdon: Routledge.

Clark, Andy. 1993. *Associative Engines: Connectionism, Concepts and Representational Change.* Cambridge, MA: MIT Press.

Clark, Andy. 2001. "Visual Experience and Motor Action: Are the Bonds Too Tight?" *Philosophical Review* 110:4.

Clark, Andy. 2008. *Supersizing the Mind: Embodiment, Action, and Cognitive Extension.* Oxford: Oxford University Press.

Clark, Andy. 2009. Letters Page, March 26. *London Review of Books.*

Cosmides, Leda, and John Tooby. 1994. "Origins of Domain-Specificity: The Evolution of Functional Organization." pp. 85–116 in *Mapping the Mind: Domain-Specificity in Cognition and Culture,* edited by L. Hirschfeld and S. Gelman. New York: Cambridge University Press.

Damasio, Antonio. 1994. *Descartes' Error: Emotion, Reason and the Human Brain.* London: Picador.

De Jaegher, Hanne. 2009. "Social Understanding through Direct Perception? Yes, By Interacting." *Consciousness and Cognition* 18:535–42.

De Jaegher, Hanne, Ezequiel Di Paolo, and Shaun Gallagher. 2010. "Can Social Interaction Constitute Social Cognition?" *Trends in Cognitive Sciences* 14(10):442–7.

Dennett, Daniel. 1978. "Artificial Intelligence as Philosophy and Psychology." pp. 109–26 in *Brainstorms: Philosophical Essays on Mind and Psychology.* Cambridge, MA: MIT Press.

Estany, Anna, and Sergio Martínez. 2014. "'Scaffolding' and 'Affordance' as Integrative Concepts in the Cognitive Sciences." *Philosophical Psychology* 27(1):98–111.

Fodor, Jerry. 1987. *Psychosemantics.* Cambridge, MA: MIT Press.

Fodor, Jerry. 2008. *LOT 2: The Language of Thought Revisited.* Oxford: Oxford University Press.

Gibson, James. J. 1977. "The Theory of Affordances." pp. 67–82 in *Perceiving, Acting, and Knowing: Toward and Ecological Psychology,* edited by Robert Shaw and John Bransford. Mahwah, NJ: Erlbaum.

Giere, Ronald. 2007. "Distributed Cognition without Distributed Knowing." *Social Epistemology* 21(3):313–20.

Harrison, Glenn and Don Ross. 2010. "The Methodologies of Neuroeconomics." *Journal of Economic Methodology* 17(2):185–96.

Horgan, John. 1999. "Neuroscience's Explanatory Gap." pp. 15–46 in *The Undiscovered Mind: How the Human Brain Defies Replication, Medication, and Explanation.* New York: The Free Press.

Hutto, Daniel, and Eric Myin. 2013. *Radicalizing Enactivism: Radical Minds without Content.* Cambridge, MA: MIT Press.

Ingold, Tim. 2000. *The Perception of the Environment: Essays on Livelihood, Dwelling and Skill.* Abingdon: Routledge.

Kahneman, Daniel. 2011. *Thinking, Fast and Slow.* New York: Farrar, Strauss, Giroux.

Latour, Bruno. 1987. *Science in Action: How to Follow Scientists and Engineers through Society.* Milton Keynes: Open University Press.

Lizardo, Omar. 2010. "Pierre Bourdieu as a Post-Cultural Theorist." *Cultural Sociology* 5(1):1–22.

Menary, Richard. 2010. *The Extended Mind.* Cambridge, MA: MIT Press.

Michaels, Claire, and Zsolt Palatinus. 2014. "A Ten Commandments for Ecological Psychology." pp. 19–28 in *Routledge Handbook of Embodied Cognition,* edited by L. Shapiro. Abingdon: Routledge.

Miłkowski, Marcin. 2013. *Explaining the Computational Mind.* Cambridge, MA: The MIT Press.

Needham, Robert. 1972. *Belief, Language, and Experience*. Chicago: University of Chicago Press.

Nichols, Shaun and Stephen P. Stich. 2003. *Mindreading: An Integrated Account of Pretense, Self-Awareness, and Understanding Other Minds*. Oxford: Clarendon Press.

Norman, Donald A. 1988/2013. *Design of Everyday Things*. Rev. and exp. ed. New York: Basic Books. London: MIT Press. First published as *The Psychology of Everyday Things*.

Norman, Donald A. 1999. "Affordances, Conventions, and Design." *Interactions* 6(3):38–43.

O'Regan, J. Kevin, and Alva Noë. 2001. "A Sensorimotor Account of Vision and Visual Consciousness." *Behavioral and Brain Sciences* 24:939–1031.

Robbins, Joel. 2008. "On Not Knowing Other Minds: Confession, Intention, and Linguistic Exchange in a Papua New Guinea Community." *Anthropological Quarterly* 81(2):421–9.

Robbins, Joel, and Alan Rumsey. 2008. "Introduction: Cultural and Linguistic Anthropology and the Opacity of Other Minds." *Anthropological Quarterly* 81(2):407–20.

Roepstorff, Andreas, Jörg Niewöhner, and Stefan Beck. 2010. "Enculturing Brains through Patterned Practices." *Neural Networks* 23:1051–59.

Schiefflin, Bambi B. 2008. "Speaking Only Your Own Mind: Reflections on Talk, Gossip and Intentionality in Bosavi (PNG)." *Anthropological Quarterly* 81(2):431–41.

Schutz, Alfred. 1932/1967. *The Phenomenology of the Social World*. Translated by George Walsh and Frederick Lehnert. Evanston, IL: Northwestern University Press.

Steiner, Pierre, and John Stewart. 2009. "From Autonomy to Heteronomy (and Back): The Enaction of Social Life." *Phenomenology and the Cognitive Sciences* 8:527–50.

Strawson, Peter 1962/2003. "Freedom and Resentment." *Proceedings of the British Academy* 48:1–25. Reprinted, pp. 72–93 in *Free Will*, edited by Gary Watson. Oxford: Oxford University Press.

Torrance, Steve. 2006. "In Search of the Enactive: Introduction to Special Issue on Enactive Experience." *Phenomenology and the Cognitive Sciences* 4:357–68.

Turner, Stephen. 2007. "Political Epistemology, Expertise, and the Aggregation of Knowledge." *Spontaneous Generations: A Journal for the History and Philosophy of Science* 1(1):36–47.

Turner, Stephen, and Regis A. Factor. 1994. *Max Weber: The Lawyer as Social Thinker*. London: Routledge.

Varela, Francisco, Evan Thompson, and Eleanor Rosch. 1991. *The Embodied Mind*. Cambridge, MA: MIT Press.

CHAPTER 10

....

DUAL-PROCESS MODELS
IN SOCIOLOGY

....

VANINA LESCHZINER

IN the ongoing quest to find new analytical or methodological tools to explicate social action, cultural sociologists have most recently turned to the dual-process models developed by cognitive and social psychologists (Chaiken and Trope 1999; D'Andrade 1995; Evans 2010; Evans and Stanovich 2013; Haidt 2001; Lizardo et al. 2016; Moore 2017; Strauss and Quinn 1997; Vaisey 2009; Vila-Henninger 2015). Designed to explain the two basic types of cognitive processing—one autonomous and the other requiring controlled attention (Evans and Stanovich 2013), dual-process models became a natural partner for sociological theories of action, with their interest in parsing dispositional and deliberative types of action (e.g., Bourdieu 1980/1990; Joas 1996; Swidler 2003). In effect, the sociological literature on dual-process models has grown exponentially in the past few years (see Lizardo et al. 2016:288), with cultural and cognitive sociologists increasingly engaging with the fundamentals of the models (Leschziner 2015; Leschziner and Green 2013; Lizardo et al. 2016; Lizardo and Strand 2010; Martin 2010; Patterson 2014; Pugh 2013; Vaisey 2009; Vila-Henninger 2015), and sociologists beyond these areas applying the models across a wide range of subfields (e.g., Auyero and Swistun 2008; Rivers et al. 2017; Srivastava and Banaji 2011).

The sociological literature on dual-process models has challenged some of the central tenets in cultural sociology, chief among which are how much culture we share, the extent to which shared culture is internalized, and how culture shapes action (see Brekhus 2015:172; DiMaggio 1997; Lizardo 2017). This challenge stems from the premise that much of action is unconscious, and that motivations and justifications are often inconsistent, which calls into question the validity of individuals' accounts to explain social action (Lizardo 2017; Lizardo and Strand 2010; Martin 2010; Vaisey 2009).[1] From this perspective, the explanation of action is not to be found in conscious, declarative knowledge, but rather in internalized knowledge stored in cognitive schemas, and accessed through what sociologists call automatic cognition (cf. Vaisey 2009), and will be here referred to as Type 1 processing. Deliberate cognition, or what will be here called Type 2 processing, is only thought to drive action when Type 1 processing is not effective because it is not well matched with the external conditions of action (cf. DiMaggio 1997).[2] The two cognitive processes together constitute a dual-process model.

Sociologists have highlighted, in particular, the similarities between the premises of dual-process models and Bourdieu's (1977, 1980/1990) practice theory, with its emphasis on the dispositional nature of perception and action, or the habitus (Lizardo 2004, 2007; Lizardo and Strand 2010; Vaisey 2009).[3] The consistency between dual-process models and Bourdieu's practice theory (but also Giddens's [1984] structuration theory) is arguably one of the reasons why dual-process models have gained such popularity in sociology. In contrast, the sociological literature on dual-process models typically presents Swidler's (1986, 2003) toolkit theory as the more limited perspective to explain action given its focus on individuals' discursive accounts of their actions, and relative disregard for unconscious processes (Lizardo and Strand 2010; Vaisey 2009).[4]

The sociological literature constitutes but a small part of the vast body of work on dual-process models, which spans disciplines as varied as cognitive neuroscience, medicine, cognitive science, and cognitive and social psychology (e.g., Chaiken and Trope 1999; Djulbegovic et al. 2012; Evans 2003, 2008; Kahneman 2011; Lieberman 2007; Nisbett et al. 2001), but this chapter focuses on the sociological implications of dual-process models. The focus is on how sociologists have interpreted dual-process models, how they have incorporated them into sociological theory, and the kinds of empirical investigations of dual-process models that have been conducted.[5]

The chapter begins with a brief outline of the fundamentals of dual-process models, addressing current knowledge in cognitive and social psychology. It then examines the premises that sociologists have borrowed from dual-process models to analyze cognition and action. After establishing the foundations and implications of what has come to be known as the sociological dual-process model, I review sociological research that applies dual-process models. This literature is divided into two distinct groups, separated along sharp epistemological, methodological, and analytical lines. The first group I review is a largely consistent body of work that follows from the premises of the sociological dual-process model, as first outlined by Vaisey (2009). The literature in this group emphasizes the primacy of Type 1 processing, and relies mostly on survey and experimental data—and also network data—to investigate how this form of cognition shapes action. The second group I review developed, to some extent, in response to the sociological dual-process model, and comprises a more diverse body of work. This body of work examines Type 1 and Type 2 processing, and sometimes the relationship between them. It typically uses interview and ethnographic data to capture the processes that shape cognition and action, rather than measuring the outcomes of a type of cognition on action, as the literature in the first group does. The chapter concludes with remarks about the critiques raised against dual-process models, along with their potential contributions to sociological analysis.

10.1 DUAL-PROCESS MODELS IN COGNITIVE AND SOCIAL PSYCHOLOGY

Dual-process models constitute a diverse body of work in cognitive and social psychology, where scholars disagree about their central principles, including the attributes of the two processing types, and whether the two types operate separately or in tandem (Chaiken and Trope 1999; Evans 2007, 2008; Evans and Stanovich 2013; Smith and DeCoster 2000). Such diversity is, however, not reflected in the sociological literature, where one especially dualistic model has become standard (cf. Haidt 2001, 2005; Vaisey 2009), and the whole body of dual-process models is typically presented as relatively homogeneous and noncontroversial (Lizardo et al. 2016). Sociologists generally cite dual-process theories of social cognition, which not only evince wide variance but also have little in common with dual-process theories of reasoning and decision-making (Evans 2008:268).[6] Whereas the former were developed in the 1980s (Chaiken 1980; Petty and Cacioppo 1981) to explain phenomena such as consciousness and free will, and their moral implications, the latter were preoccupied with the cognitive evolution of the mind (Epstein and Pacini 1999; Evans and Over 1996; Reber 1993; Stanovich 1999).

Cognitive and social psychologists do agree on some basic characteristics, chief among which is the principle that there are two different types of cognitive processing, one being autonomous (Type 1) and the other requiring controlled attention (Type 2), a distinction supported by significant empirical findings (Evans 2008:256; Evans and Stanovich 2013:224–6; Kahneman and Shane 2002; Stanovich 1999).[7] Whereas the former type is typically characterized as unconscious, fast, and automatic, the latter is described as conscious, slow, and deliberative (Evans 2008:256), though these distinctions have been questioned in recent scholarship (see Evans and Stanovich 2013).[8] Most dual-process theories are consistent with the idea that Type 2 processing is rule-based and sequential, but they disagree about whether Type 1 processing is based on associative, functionally parallel neural networks (Evans 2008:261). Because there are many systems of implicit cognitive processes, and scholars write about different implicit systems, there is generally less agreement on the characteristics of Type 1 than Type 2 processing (Evans 2007:336; 2008:263; Glöckner and Witteman 2010; Wilson 2002).

Recent research in social cognitive neuroscience has provided support for the basic dual-model of cognition. In particular, scholars have found two neurological systems—the X-system and the C-system—that are associated with reflexive and reflective cognitive processes, respectively (Lieberman 2003; Lieberman, Jarcho, and Satpute 2004: see also Evans 2008:270). The X-system, constituted by areas in the brain dedicated to associative learning (including the amygdala, basal ganglia, and lateral temporal cortex), is connected with Type 1 processes. The C-system, consisting of areas that have to do with explicit learning and executive control (including the cingulate cortex, prefrontal cortex, and the medial-temporal lobe), is therefore connected with Type 2 processes.[9]

From a more theoretical perspective, the fundamentals of a dual-process model of cognition had already been formulated in the early twentieth century. Dewey (1922/2002) offered an extensive theorization of habit and deliberation in his book *Human Nature and Conduct*, which bear the basic attributes associated with Type 1 and Type 2 cognition, respectively. The relationship between the two processing types has also been traced back to another pragmatist theory, namely Mead's (1934/1967) theory of the mind (Smith and DeCoster 2000:116). Smith and DeCoster (2000) point out that the social world first influences the mind through Type 2 cognition, and thereby shapes the more personal Type 1 cognition. Thus, intersubjectively shared ideas encoded in language and learned through symbolic processing (e.g., cookies are unhealthy) become embodied over time and turn into associative knowledge (e.g., cookies feel heavy on my stomach). This means that an idea learned from others eventually acquires the same phenomenological quality as a subjectively experienced gut reaction (Smith and DeCoster 2000:123), therefore that the social world shapes all types of cognition (Smith and DeCoster 2000:129). Smith and DeCoster are thus unambiguous about the inherent relationship between Type 1 and Type 2 processing, as well as about the sociological implications of dual-process models.[10] Such implications did not escape the attention of sociologists for too long, though it took some time until interest in dual-process models gathered sufficient momentum to have a significant impact on sociological scholarship.

10.2 The Origins of the Sociological Dual-Process Model

DiMaggio first introduced these models to sociology in his 1997 *Annual Review of Sociology* article "Culture and Cognition," a seminal piece for the area of culture and cognition. In this article, DiMaggio encouraged sociologists to reach out to cognitive and social psychology to improve the explanation of how culture shapes action, and highlighted several findings from psychology, including the brain's propensity to process new information automatically, retain most of it, and store it as correct (see Gilbert 1991). To the extent that actors absorb all sorts of information from random sources, and keep ideas that may be inconsistent with one another, DiMaggio (1997:267–8) argued that there is a strong reason to view culture not as a latent variable transmitted through socialization (cf. Parsons 1937/1968) but as an inconsistent set of representations, skills, and strategies of action (cf. Swidler 1986).

DiMaggio explained that cognition is constituted by two modes, one being automatic—implicit, unconscious, nonverbalized, and fast—and the other deliberate—explicit, conscious, verbalized, and slow (D'Andrade 1995).[11] Automatic cognition operates through the unconscious use of culturally available schemas, "knowledge structures that represent objects or events and provide default assumptions about their characteristics, relationships, and entailments under conditions of incomplete information"

(DiMaggio 1997:269). Schemas are not just representations of knowledge but also knowledge processors, for they organize disparate bits of information into units and fill in for missing information (D'Andrade 1992; DiMaggio 1997; Mandler 1984; Rumelhart et al. 1986). DiMaggio (1997:269–72) noted that schemas are efficient (if also error-prone) and therefore the default cognitive mechanism, only replaced by the linear processing associated with deliberate cognition under special conditions.

It was not until the publication of Vaisey's article "Motivation and Justification: A Dual-Process Model of Culture in Action" in the *American Journal of Sociology* in 2009 that the use of dual-process models took off in sociology.[12] Unlike DiMaggio's (1997) broader agenda, Vaisey (2009; see also Vaisey 2008a, 2008b) launched a pointed critique of Swidler's (1986) toolkit theory of action, and relied on dual-process models to do so.[13] Drawing on Haidt's (2001, 2005) particular dual-process model (wherein Type 1 and Type 2 processing are sharply dissociated from each other), Vaisey argued that the explanation of action does not lie in the deliberative discourses highlighted in Swidler's work (1986, 2003), but in the deeply ingrained values that motivate action through automatic (i.e., nondiscursive) cognitive processes.[14]

In a general sense, dual-process models are hardly new in sociology. Sociological theory has long shed light on the existence of conscious and subconscious processes that shape thinking and action (e.g., Durkheim 1912/1995; Marx [1845] 1965; Weber 1920/1992), and the theoretical program of American pragmatism, in particular Dewey (1922/2002), revolves precisely around the nature of habitual and deliberative types of cognition and action (see also Mead 1934/1967).[15] To be sure, practice theory (e.g., Bourdieu 1977, 1980/1990; Giddens 1984) is predicated on the mechanisms of these two types of cognition and action, and indebted to the insights of pragmatism (see Lizardo and Strand 2010; Martin 2011; Strand and Lizardo 2015). For practice theory, as well as for the sociological dual-process model, subconscious and fast cognitive processes, developed through repeated practical action, make up the bulk of cognition (i.e., Bourdieu's *habitus*, or Giddens's *practical consciousness*). These processes are only overridden by conscious thought when they prove ineffective, an instance thought to occur when the actor is faced with a novel or difficult scenario, or when she is especially motivated to act deliberately (DiMaggio 1997:271–2).[16] In short, the argument that actors are chiefly driven by deeply internalized schemas, and only resort to deliberate thought under special circumstances, articulated in Vaisey's sociological dual-process model (Vaisey 2009: 1687), has dramatically shaped the sociological literature.[17]

Indeed, the last decade has seen a fair amount of research consistent with the analytical and methodological premises of the sociological dual-process model. This research tends to draw on a variety of cognitive disciplines to explain the workings of the brain, and favors survey, experimental, and network data to measure the effects of Type 1 processing on action. Another body of work developed—to some extent—in response to this. This line of research is typically concerned with the workings of both Type 1 and Type 2 processing, and seeks to unpack the sociocultural underpinnings of cognition and action. To do so, this literature generally uses interview and ethnographic data. Beyond analytical or methodological divides, perhaps the most significant difference between the two groups is that cognitive processing is an explanans in the former group, and an object of study in the latter. In what follows I review the two bodies of literature. Because the literature in the first group evinces a high consistency with the goals and premises of the sociological dual-process model, and the second body of work is more analytically disparate, more space is devoted to the latter.

10.3 DUAL-PROCESS MODELS IN SOCIOLOGICAL RESEARCH: COGNITIVE PROCESSING AS EXPLANANS

Maintaining that implicit culture (Bourdieu 1979/1984, 1980/1990, 1997/2000) bears a more significant role in motivating action than declarative knowledge (Lizardo 2017; see also Giddens 1984; Swidler 1986, 2003), scholars in this group use dual-process models to buttress their arguments, and demonstrate the influence of Type 1 processing on action (cf. Vaisey 2009).[18] This body of work does not investigate cognitive processing itself, but rather takes cognitive processing as a premise and measures its effect on action.

Vaisey and Lizardo (2010), for instance, borrow the principles of dual-process models to measure the relationship between cultural worldviews and social network composition. Specifically, they investigate the effect of implicit cultural worldviews (i.e., broad orientations toward moral evaluations processed through Type 1 cognition) on the choice and formation of friendship ties. Through panel data from the National Study of Youth and Religion, they analyze the role of behaviors such as the use of controlled substances, getting in trouble at school, and community volunteering, on future network composition. They find strong evidence that what predicts future network composition is not any of these behaviors, or previous networks, but moral orientations toward the behaviors. Vaisey and Lizardo (2010:1611) argue that embodied culture operates as a relational filter, and explains the evolution of social networks over time. What is more, contrary to traditional assumptions about the causal role of networks on culture (Emirbayer and Goodwin 1994), they find that network composition has no influence on cultural worldviews.

With similar research questions and approach, Hoffmann (2014) uses longitudinal data from the National Survey of Youth and Religion to study the relationship among moral schemas, religiousness, behavior, and social networks. To Vaisey and Lizardo's (2010) causal relationship between cultural schemas and network composition, Hoffmann adds an examination of how cultural schemas affect behavior and, in turn, how these two affect social network composition. He finds a positive association between behavior and social network composition, given that drug users tend to form relationships with other drug users (Hoffmann 2014:203). Furthermore, he argues that this is not a simple causal relationship, but rather that cultural schemas (i.e., perceptions of what is right or wrong, and evaluations of rule-breaking, which operate through Type 1 processing) are reciprocally associated with religiousness and marijuana use, and that changes in networks have significant implications for behavior such as marijuana use (Hoffmann 2014:202; see Mische 2011). While Hoffmann (2014) challenges Vaisey and Lizardo (2010) by showing that the causal effect of Type 1 processing on network composition cannot sufficiently account for the complex relationship among cultural schemas, behavior, and social networks, neither authors provide evidence of cognitive processing (i.e., cultural schemas are assumed to be internalized and operate through Type 1 processing), or a theorization of the processes in question that involves cognition.

Similar to these authors, Srivastava and Banajia (2011) also examine the effect of Type 1 processing on behavior, culture, and networks, but add analysis of the role of identity to it. They draw on the sociological dual-process model to study how individuals' self-concepts affect their proclivity to make connections with colleagues across organizational boundaries and collaborate. Maintaining that implicit self-concepts (Type 1 processing) are a better predictor of behavior than explicit self-concepts (Type 2 processing), given that the latter might simply be discourses expressed to align with prescribed norms (Srivastava and Banaji 2011:210, 227–8), Srivastava and Banajia study the effect of collaborative self-concepts on collaborative behavior in an organizational context wherein collaboration is viewed positively.[19] Through quantitative and network data from a biotechnology firm, the authors find that individuals with implicit collaborative self-concepts are more likely to make connections with, and be recruited by, organizationally distant colleagues and collaborate with them than those without such self-concept, and that explicit self-concepts are not associated with these behaviors.

Miles (2015:680, 699) intervenes in debates about dual-process models by pointing out that sociologists have been more focused on the process of how culture motivates action than in which kinds of culture motivate it. Miles thus sets out to demonstrate that values motivate action with primary survey data and secondary data from the European Social Survey. Interested in how Type 1 processing shapes action, he designed an online experiment to ask respondents to work on cognitively demanding tasks (memorizing long numbers) so as to inhibit Type 2 processing and test the effect of their prosocial values on behavior (giving their lottery tickets to non-ticket-holders). He finds that when cognitively impaired and unable to assess the pros and cons of prosocial behavior, individuals tend to act on their prosocial values and give the tickets away, but may decide against it when they are able to make those assessments. Miles (2015:699) concludes that values influence behavior through Type 1 processing, and that they likely do so across all types of contexts.

Somewhat similarly to Miles, Martin and Desmond (2010) are also interested in explaining which kind of culture shapes behavior, and how it does so. Martin and Desmond examine how ideological views shape how actors process new information, and argue that political ideology provides actors with a set of information and ideas that enable them to process new stimuli through Type 1 cognition and bypass Type 2 processing. This is not because political ideologies endow individuals with values, but rather with social ontologies, beliefs about the nature of the world (Martin and Desmond 2010:8). Martin and Desmond use data from the Race and Politics Survey, an experiment that modifies parts of a hypothetical policy, and supplement it with surveys with the same respondents, in order to study cognitive processes and constellations of ideas. Their findings show that stronger ideological positions (whether on the left or the right) lead actors to interpret events in light of their pre-existing beliefs, and be less prone to deliberation (Martin and Desmond 2010:9). Weaker or less consistent ideological beliefs, by contrast, demand a wider variety of knowledge and more deliberation to interpret new information, so actors are more likely to use Type 2 processing. This research, along with the literature reviewed previously, has been instrumental in refining the understanding of how culture shapes action. Nonetheless, such understanding has been largely limited to the effects of Type 1 processing on action. This body of work has yielded little knowledge about Type 2 processing, or about how cognition works.

10.4 Dual-Process Models in Sociological Research: Cognitive Processing and Context

The influence of the sociological dual-process model has led to a growing emphasis on the investigation of the effects of Type 1 processing across varied areas of study, as the previous section has shown. Meanwhile, research on Type 2 processing, on the relationship between the two types of cognition, and on the ways in which context shapes cognitive processing, has been more parsimonious. Given the higher diversity of this body of research, and its implications for the interdisciplinary conversation around the mind that has been promoted by cognitive sociologists (Cerulo 2010; Lizardo 2014; Turner 2007), a lengthier review is provided, organized around different emphases within this body of work.

10.4.1 Context and Cognitive Processing in Action

In response to the growing literature on the sociological dual-process model, some scholars began to call attention to the role of context, pointing out that even Type 1 processing is more contextually dependent than the sociological dual-process model allows for (Shepherd 2011).[20] Shepherd (2011:123) makes a specific call for the study of supraindividual culture that informs the availability, activation, and acquisition of cognitive patterns. In line with an argument now well accepted in cultural sociology that culture inheres not in individuals or situations, but in the interactions between the two (DiMaggio 1997; Eliasoph and Lichterman 2003), scholars are emphasizing the need to examine such interactions in order to explain cognitive patterns (Moore 2017; Shepherd 2011).

Vila-Henninger (2015) argues that the sociological dual-process model and practice theory (cf. Bourdieu 1977, 1980/1990) are effective for showing how cultural ends shape action through subconscious schemas, but that neither approach accounts for how Type 2 processing informs decision-making, or how Type 1 and Type 2 processing interact.[21] Vila-Henninger (2015) thus sets out to fill this gap by empirically teasing out when Type 2 processing alone shapes decision-making, when it overrides Type 1 processing, and when the two processing types operate together. This can only be accomplished, he notes (Vila-Henninger 2015:241–2), if sociologists move beyond the narrow understanding of dual-process models that has become the norm, an understanding originated in Bourdieu's (1977, 1980/1990) theory and sustained by Vaisey (2009) and those who have adopted the sociological dual-process model. He maintains that motives are subconsciously generated, as this model would have it, but only take form as motivations, therefore only drive action, when combined with sequence knowledge and social perceptual knowledge (Vila-Henninger 2015:252). Contra a fundamental tenet of the sociological dual-process model, this implies that motivations may well be conscious, even if to varying degrees.[22]

Moore (2017) also critiques the sociological dual-process model's sharp separation between Type 1 and Type 2 processing, citing evidence from cognitive science and cognitive psychology that the two occur in tandem more frequently than is typically acknowledged by sociologists. In light of the paucity of knowledge about what cognitive processes are used in what situations, Moore (2017) sets out to answer this question through a study of individuals' self-concepts as religious (evangelicals) or atheist, and their views on religion, relying on participant observation, in-depth interviews, and field experiments. He measures cognitive processing through timed response data, and finds that evangelicals are quicker to associate positive words with both Christianity and religion, and slower to associate negative words with them, despite the fact that their professed views on Christianity and religion are separated by a sharp boundary (i.e., whereas Christianity is positive, religion is viewed negatively for being an artificial construct). This indicates positive dispositional beliefs about religion as well as Christianity, and that evangelicals require effort to override those beliefs in order to undergird their self-concepts as biblically based Christians (Moore 2017:197, 217–8). Moore (2017:199) finds that Type 1 and Type 2 processing are often used in combination, and that Type 2 processing is indeed more common in decision-making than is typically shown in sociology. Unlike much research on the sociological dual-process model, Moore takes cognitive processing as an empirical question and, in turn, an indicator of identities and beliefs.

Danna-Lynch (2010) shares this interest in cognitive processing and social identities, but focuses on how context shapes the enactment of social roles. Actors switch between various roles on a daily basis (e.g., from being a mother, to an employee, and friend) and need to determine which role they should be playing in any given situation. To do so, they engage in what Danna-Lynch (2010:181) calls "mental weighing" so as to assign significance to motivational cues. Through in-depth interviews with working parents across a range of occupations, Danna-Lynch (2010:169) finds that when actors have the time and ability to interpret contextual cues through Type 2 processing, they assign weight consciously and switch roles in a controlled and determined manner, through "voluntary pushes." When actors face unanticipated situations and are urged to respond quickly, through Type 1 processing, they feel impelled to switch roles through less controlled "involuntary pulls." In short, Danna-Lynch (2010:181) suggests that the process of mental weighing provides evidence of how actors take different viewpoints and resort to different logics of action to respond to context (see also Danna-Lynch 2007, 2009).

Friedman (2016:439) makes an intervention in the dual-process model literature by pointing out that cognitive processing is generally modeled after the workings of the visual sense (e.g., Kahneman 2011), which has limited our understanding of cognition. To fill this gap, she investigates differences in cognitive processing through in-depth interviews with blind persons about how they perceive and attribute race. Friedman (2016:456) notes that the visual perception of race typically occurs through Type 1 processing, given that visual indicators of race are taken for granted unless there is ambiguity. By contrast, the nonvisual perception of race is always filled with uncertainty and ambiguity, and requires active interaction (not just copresence), so Type 2 processing is most likely in this context (Friedman 2016:450–51).

McDonnell (2014) makes a strong case for what he calls productive methods, that is, having research subjects create cultural products collectively so as to capture the two cognitive processes and observe how culture shapes action. McDonnell argues that, contrary to the predetermined responses elicited through surveys (Vaisey 2009), which measure outcome and assume it was achieved through Type 1 processing, productive methods measure both types of cognition, and cognitive processing as well as outcome, given that respondents are asked to create, represent, and interpret meaning over a specific task. As focus group respondents created AIDS campaign posters in Ghana, McDonnell (2014:272) found that they relied on quick judgments, heightened emotions (see McDonnell et al. 2017), and discursive deliberation. McDonnell notes that these data provide evidence of how individuals use available symbols and combine Type 1 and Type 2 processing. More generally, through this research McDonnell aims to show the processes whereby ideas motivate action. To do so, he goes beyond the authors reviewed above both in methodological and theoretical terms, for he develops methods to capture the specificities of cognitive processes in action, and offers a theorization of the relationship between cognition, context, and action (see McDonnell 2016).

10.4.2 Locality and Cognitive Processing

Starting from the common critique that context plays a more important role shaping cognition than has been acknowledged by the sociological dual-process model, a number of scholars have zeroed in on the ways in which the particular characteristics of local context shape cognitive processing. For instance, Mische (2014) shares McDonnell's interest in collective deliberation processes, but examines how a local context shapes actors' projections about the future, which she captures through narratives, performances, and attitudes. Cautioning that the sociological emphasis on habits and schemas has limited our knowledge about deliberation, she points to the analytical tools of contemporary American pragmatism to analyze conscious deliberation about the future (Mische 2014:441). Through data on the Rio+20 debates, she shows that sites ripe with tension and uncertainty demand cognitive work, which can lead to reflective learning and creative reformulation and, in turn, to changing lines of action (Mische 2014:457). Contra Vaisey's (2009) argument about the primacy of deep-seated moral schemas and Type 1 processing, Mische (2014:443) argues that reflective, tentative, imaginative cognitive processes—not captured through surveys—are more common than has been acknowledged.

Interest in the relationship between cognition and uncertainty, and how it unfolds given the characteristics of a particular context, has also motivated Auyero and Swistun's (2008; see also Auyero and Swistun 2007, 2009) research on the perceptions of environmental hazard among residents in an Argentine shantytown. Contrary to Mische, however, they investigate habitual action, and shed light on the processes whereby routine action constrains actors' capacity to think critically, and accurately perceive risk (Cerulo 2006; Vaughan 1990, 1996). They show how routine actions and interactions work to blind residents to the increasing environmental risk in their area, reproducing uncertainty and confusion. Auyero and Swistun (2008:375) call this "relational anchoring," as mental schemas are shaped by available information and anchored in reference points, but are also affected by powerful actors' attempts to veil a given issue through the reinforcement of routine practices.

Rivers et al. (2017:74) also study the relationship between cognition and locality. While they take a different perspective from the literature reviewed earlier, their findings are consistent with Auyero and Swistun's (2008). Interested in criminology and race, Rivers et al. combine research on neighborhood effects and on the motivations of racialized actors to engage in crime, thus supplementing a structural explanation with analysis of cognition and decision-making. Drawing on Swidler (1986) and Kahneman (2011), they suggest that the structural conditions of disadvantaged neighborhoods generate cultural practices that foster Type 1 processing for quick and easy problem-solving and decision-making, instead of the strategies based on Type 2 cognition that are more likely among residents of more advantaged neighborhoods, who are in better conditions to think deliberately before acting (Rivers et al. 2017:76, 84). Rivers et al. (2017:90) suggest that values (whether structurally determined or individually held) are not the primary explanatory factor of differences in crime across groups, but rather cognitive patterns, which develop in response to problematic scenarios and difficult tasks.

Another scholar interested in the relationship between cognition and locality, Harvey (2010) studies how a physical space's level of complexity affects cognitive processing. Harvey (2010:186) finds that spaces with simpler and more predictable designs (e.g., small convenience stores with clearly marked aisles) trigger Type 1 processing, whereas more complex structures (e.g., disorganized libraries or bookstores) elicit Type 2 processing (Harvey 2010:186). That physical space shapes cognitive processing (see Goldhagen 2017) has implications for culture, Harvey (2010:200) suggests, because it can lead to faster or slower apprehension of cultural messages.

The findings on the role of locality on cognition reviewed above might appear in tension with one another. However, this is less because the findings are at odds with each other than because the scholars examined different processes, or distinct mechanisms through which locality shapes cognition and action. In this way, Mische (2014) shows that a context ripe with tension and uncertainty requires deliberation, thus encouraging Type 2 processing, and Auyero and Swistun (2008) show the other side of the same phenomenon, namely that a routine context discourages Type 2 processing. Much in line with these authors, Harvey (2010) shows that simpler and more predictable physical spaces trigger Type 1 processing, while more complex spaces demand Type 2 processing. For their part, Rivers et al. (2017) argue that the conditions of a disadvantaged neighborhood foster Type 1 processing, but this is because they call for quick responses to conflict, which become habitual over time, whereas Type 2 processing is more likely in advantaged neighborhoods, where those conditions are low or absent. If these findings appear contradictory, it is also because some authors examine cognition, whereas others investigate action, but cognition and action become conflated in research and confounded in the analysis, as is often the case in the literature on culture and cognition more generally (Lizardo et al. 2016:297–8).

10.4.3 Beyond a Dualistic Cognitive Model

In addition to attention to the role of context in shaping cognition, and to the relationship between Type 1 and Type 2 processing, some critiques of the sociological dual-process model have zeroed in on the limitations of an overly dualistic view of cognition for explaining particular kinds of actions. Winchester (2016), for instance, joins others in the critique of the sociological dual-process model's sharp dichotomy between the two processing types but, rather than reject the dichotomy, he proposes a pluralistic and practice-oriented approach that recognizes that cognition may sometimes be dualistic, and others holistic (Winchester 2016:601), therefore that the sociological dual-process model is useful for explaining the former but not the latter. With data from an ethnographic study of religious conversion to Eastern Orthodox Christianity in the United States, Winchester (2016:592) examines the relationship between the bodily aspects of conversion, such as the practice of fasting, and discursive interpretations. He finds that individuals correlate abstract religious concepts with experiential gestalts gained through fasting by means of what is referred to as "embodied metaphor" (Winchester 2016:601). Winchester (2016:590) draws on cognitive linguistics to account for holistic cognition, and suggests that metaphorical cognition helps create associations between practical perception and discursive conceptualization.

Leschziner (2015; see also Leschziner and Green 2013) offers a different critical intervention in the dual-process models literature. With data from in-depth interviews with chefs and observation of their work in their restaurant kitchens, she analyzes the cognitive and conative processes whereby individuals create new products and delineate careers in an organizational field (Leschziner 2015). Leschziner shows that individuals combine different types of cognition and action across a variety of tasks and external conditions in ways that are not captured by the dualism characteristic of the sociological dual-process model (Leschziner 2015; Leschziner and Green 2013). She thus proposes a model to explain cognition and action that points to three paths (Leschziner 2015:119–20). One path of action relies on Type 2 processing to accomplish purposeful action; another path involves little to no Type 2 processing or conscious experience of the action; and the last one is phenomenologically experienced as motivated action (therefore not autonomous) yet not reliant on Type 2 processing but on intuitions experienced as a sense of what feels right (Leschziner 2015:119). Leschziner (2015; see also Leschziner and Green 2013) shows the ways in which actors regularly combine Type 1 and Type 2 processing across all sorts of tasks, heavily relying on Type 1 processing when engaged in purposeful action, and on Type 2 processing when dedicated to routine activities.

10.5 Concluding Remarks

Following the publication of Vaisey's (2009) article, with its critique of Swidler's (1986) toolkit theory and reliance on Haidt's (2001, 2005) dual-process model, a sharply dualistic process model became the norm in the sociological literature on culture and cognition. The sociological dual-process model thus began to take form, based on the assumption that there is a clear separation between Type 1 and Type 2 processing—that is, that thinking occurs *either* through Type 1 *or* Type 2 processing, and that the former drives most cognition and decision-making (cf. Vaisey 2009). The epistemological and methodological implications that follow from this view, proposed by Vaisey (2008a, 2008b, 2009; Vaisey and Miles 2014) and taken up by several others (e.g., Bonikowski 2016; Ignatow 2014) are that Type 1 processing is paramount to the explanation of action, and that it can only be captured through fixed response survey questions, because interviews elicit Type 2 processing, and therefore the post hoc justifications of action that are at the core of Swidler's (1986, 2003, 2008) theory, but not necessarily motivations for action.[23]

Vaisey's (2009) article attracted a wide and enthusiastic reception (see Lizardo et al. 2016:288), largely because its critique of some of the central arguments in cultural sociology was novel and bold and led sociologists to question key assumptions, not least of which is the fundamental understanding of how culture shapes action. The reexamination of taken-for-granted assumptions, including the nature of motivations and justifications, was thus a positive outcome of the publication of Vaisey's article. A less positive outcome, however, was that it produced a highly limited—if not distorted—understanding of cognition and action that went on to shape the sociological dual-process model. Ironically, this sociological model bracketed out the role of social interaction and environment. And, while it is more heavily grounded on interdisciplinary knowledge of cognition (especially cognitive psychology and cognitive neuroscience) than other sociological literature, it has effectively offered little evidence of cognitive processing, or a strong sociological theorization of cognition.

This model has faced growing criticism for its clear-cut representation of the two types of cognition, and its methodological stance against the validity of interview data for the study of cognition and action (Leschziner and Green 2013; McDonnell 2014; Moore 2017; Pugh 2013; Vila-Henninger 2015).[24] As was illustrated in the literature reviewed previously, sociologists have begun to counter the sociological dual-process model, based on an overall agreement that the two types of cognition are more inherently associated than has been recognized in the sociological literature, and that qualitative methods are valuable for the study of both Type 1 and Type 2 processing (Leschziner 2015; Leschziner and Green 2013; Moore 2017; Pugh 2013; Vila-Henninger 2015; Winchester 2016). This body of literature coheres around the examination of cognitive processes, and the use of qualitative methods to examine those processes in action. Beyond these general characteristics, however, this body of work is less cohesive than the former, given that it is driven by a wider range of questions, analytical approaches, and phenomena under study. Thus, the literature has, by and large, not produced cumulative knowledge, which has limited its potential for building an explanatory framework of social cognition. The seemingly contradictory findings from research on the relationship between locality and cognition reviewed earlier are but one clear example of this—an aggregate of research on the same phenomenon, based on different research questions and approaches that, by not establishing an engaged dialogue with existing knowledge on the topic, fails to produce an overall understanding of how locality shapes cognition.

The use of dual-process models in sociology—including the two distinct bodies of work reviewed in this chapter—has not been without criticism. Chief among the critiques is the argument that cognitive schemas pertain to individual-level processes, and that the study of cognitive processes fails to capture the profoundly social ways in which culture shapes thought and action (e.g., Lamont and Swidler 2014; Norton 2014; Swidler 2008). Though this is a fundamental critique of the study of cognition, some of its arguments are echoed in the positions of cognitively inclined sociologists who are critical of the sociological dual-process model. This is especially evident in the argument that the overly dualistic conceptualization of cognition is (at least in part) the product of relatively decontextualized research on individual cognitive processes (Brekhus 2015; Jerolmack and Khan 2014; Leschziner and Green 2013; Pugh 2013; Swidler 2008; Vila-Henninger 2015).

In all, the critiques point to the role of social context in shaping thought and action, and the limitations of methodologies designed to access the cognitive processing of isolated individuals, whether in experimental conditions or surveys. These critiques emphasize the significance of Type 2 processing on decision-making and action, as well as its inherent connection with Type 1 processing.[25] To the extent that research on the sociological dual-process model investigates the effects of Type 1 processing on action in artificial conditions—isolated actors, outside their regular environments, responding to extra-ordinary situations—it cannot weigh in on the relationship of Type 1 to Type 2 processing, or how social context shapes cognition (Leschziner and Green 2013:135). Starting with pragmatist insights into how actors rely on and respond to attributes of their environment in cognition and action (cf. Dewey 1922/2002; but also Mead 1934/1967), a wide range of social science literature has shown the various ways in which the social and physical environment shapes cognition (Hutchins 1995; Lave 1988; Rosch 1978), so investigating stimulus-response patterns beyond real-world conditions can do little to advance sociological knowledge on cognition.

In their review of the literature on dual-process models, Lizardo et al. (2016:296–7: see also Lizardo 2017) argue that these models urge sociologists to understand that culture cannot be reduced to a single dimension (e.g., values, beliefs, habits), but rather that it is constituted by explicit knowledge as well as nondeclarative forms of culture.[26] Dual-process models are instrumental for explaining how actors store and use culture for cognition and action, but Lizardo et al. (2016:297–8) point out that sociological research on dual-process models often conflates cognition and action, making claims about culture in action (Vaisey 2009) with data on the processing—not the use—of cultural knowledge. The "generic focus on automatic and deliberate cognition" (Lizardo et al. 2016:297) that has characterized sociological research on dual-process models has certainly facilitated this elision, whereby cognition and action are conflated into one of two possible modes.

Though the sociological study of dual-process models has grown rapidly in the past few years, it is arguably still in its infancy. Progress in the area will require more empirical investigations of a variety of cognitive processes and the context of action, wherein actors use both Type 1 and Type 2 processing, and engage in both habitual and creative action (Elsbach and Breitsohl 2016; Leschziner and Green 2013). This would help sociological theory move away from the perennial oscillation between the pole of conscious thought and instrumental action (cf. Parsons 1937/1968; see Lizardo et al. 2016) and that of subconscious cognition and dispositional action (cf. Bourdieu 1977, 1979/1984, 1980/1990; see also Vaisey 2009), and thereby develop a more balanced and nuanced conceptualization of cognition and action, and their multiple and complex interrelationships.

NOTES

1. For the debate around these issues between Vaisey and Swidler, see Vaisey (2008a, 2008b) and Swidler (2008).
2. For the sake of consistency, I will generally use these terms, regardless of those used in the literature I review. The most widely used terms in sociology are "automatic cognition" and "deliberate cognition," while some also use the notions of "fast cognition" and "slow cognition," or "System 1" and "System 2."
3. The parallels between Bourdieu's theory and dual-process models of cognition had already been identified in cognitive anthropology (see D'Andrade 1995; Strauss and Quinn 1997).

4. On the more positive side, it has been suggested that Swidler's theory (1986, 2003) does indeed prove useful, even if only for particular situations (Lizardo and Strand 2010). The theory, as the argument goes, lends itself to the explanation of cases wherein the conditions of action prove problematic or novel, such that individuals are led to think and act deliberately (Lizardo and Strand 2010; Swidler 2008; Vaisey 2008a, 2008b, 2009).

5. There is a significant body of literature that has arguments consistent with the premises of dual-process models, but does not engage with these models (e.g., DiMaggio and Powell 1983, 1991; Heimer 2001; Vaughan 2002). This chapter is solely concerned with literature that engages with these models.

6. Evans and Stanovich (2013:223–4) suggest that dual-process theories of social cognition have the largest amount of labels and theories of all dual-process theories. In Evans's (2008:268) own words, "The proposal of new accounts or at least new labels for dual processes in social cognition has reached near epidemic proportions, causing some reaction in terms of a unimodel that instead emphasizes multiple parameters known to influence social judgments (Kruglanski et al. 2003)."

7. "Type 1" and "Type 2" are the most neutral terms among the varied terminology used in dual-process models. They have been advocated by Evans and Stanovich (2013:224–6), who previously used the labels "System 1" and "System 2," because they denote qualitatively distinct forms of cognitive processing, without implying that either of them is constituted by a single kind of cognitive or neural system.

8. Evans and Stanovich (2013) argue that the only consistent defining features of Type 1 and Type 2 processes are that the former are autonomous and do not require controlled attention (or, in other words, working memory), and the latter are characterized by cognitive decoupling—that is, the capacity to distinguish supposition from belief, and to conduct mental simulation to make choices—and require working memory. Cognitive and social psychologists have made a few arguments that are of particular relevance for the sociological literature on dual-process models: Type 1 and Type 2 processing can both have conscious and unconscious cognitive processes; Type 1 and Type 2 processing may both be rule-based (a feature often associated only with Type 2); processing cannot be easily distinguished between automatic and controlled/intentional (Evans and Stanovich 2013:227; see also Bargh 2005; Evans 2006, 2010; Wegner 2002).

9. Evans (2008:270) suggests that this research offers the strongest evidence in support of some kind of dual distinction in cognition, along with research conducted with experimental and psychometric methods (Evans and Stanovich 2013:224, 232–5).

10. The sociological implications of dual-process models are put in particularly evocative terms by Clark (1997:53, cited in Smith and DeCoster (2000:116)): "[O]ur behavior is often sculpted and sequenced by a special class of complex external structures: the linguistic and cultural artifacts that structure modern life, including maps, texts, and written plans. Understanding the complex interplay between our on-board and online neural resources and these external props and pivots is a major task confronting the sciences of embodied thought."

11. It bears noting that DiMaggio (1997) introduced the principles of dual-process models but did not actually discuss or even mention "dual-process models."

12. For citation data of the reception of Vaisey's article, see Lizardo et al. (2016:288).

13. Furthermore, whereas DiMaggio (1997) framed his ideas in support of Swidler's toolkit theory, Vaisey (2009) sought to do precisely the opposite—to demonstrate the fundamental flaws of this theory for explaining action.

14. The type of dual-process model proposed by Haidt (2001, 2005) has been criticized in the cognitive and social psychology literature for its dualistic representation of the role of Type 1 and Type 2 processing on decision-making (see Evans 2008; Forbes and Jordan 2010; Kruglanski and Orehek 2007; for a sociological critique, see Brekhus 2015:180; Vila-Henninger 2015:4).

15. For a different perspective that bears many parallels to Dewey's ideas, see Margolis's (1987) formulation of a dual-process model of cognition. Drawing neither on pragmatism nor dual-process models in cognitive or social psychology, Margolis also theorizes about the existence of two different types of cognition that are inherently interrelated because they both rely on existing patterns (i.e., pattern recognition in Margolis's terms, or habits in Dewey's terminology).

16. For an earlier and extensive elaboration of these ideas, see Dewey (1922/2002).

17. Vaisey (2009:1705) notes that social interaction matters for the formation of cultural schemas and ensuing actions, but this is not something he examines. Arguably, this bracketing has shaped much research on the sociological dual-process model (especially the first body of research reviewed in what follows).

18. Although authors in this group typically rely on Bourdieu's (1977, 1980/1990) theory, they sometimes draw on Giddens (1984), especially his notions of practical consciousness and discursive consciousness.

19. Much in line with the sociological dual-process model, Srivastava and Banajia (2011) view Type 1 processing as a predictor of behavior, and Type 2 processing as largely post hoc justifications.

20. Shepherd (2011:123) points out that evidence from social psychology shows that Type 1 processing is more contextually dependent than it has been typically recognized in sociology (see Evans 2007).

21. Vila-Henninger (2015:246–7) notes that the sociological dual-process model's overemphasis on the weight of Type 1 processing on decision-making is not supported by cognitive neuroscience research.

22. Vila-Henninger (2015:252) suggests that the process of interpretation and framing of a situation relies on Type 1 and Type 2 processing, and that the two interact. It follows, for him, that the process is conscious because the actor actively evaluates and interprets the situation, makes judgments about possible outcomes, and chooses a course of action.

23. Moore (2017:199) notes that the way sociologists write about dual-process models creates the impression that there is a neat mapping of dual processes onto sociological methods, such that Type 1 processing is involved in responses to survey questions, and Type 2 processing in answers to in-depth interview questions.

24. Vaisey (2014) himself moderated his initial position by acknowledging that the relationship between the two cognitive types is not as clear-cut as he originally argued, and that interviews are more valuable for studying cognition and action than he originally proposed (Vaisey 2009).

25. Vila-Henninger (2015:15; see also Brekhus 2015:180–81) points out that studies of brain activity show that conscious and unconscious processes interact (i.e., activity in the prefrontal cortex, the temporal lobes, and subcortical neural areas). This interaction is shown to be itself a conscious process, as the actor makes assessments, interpretations, judgments, and decisions (Vila-Henninger 2015:15).

26. For an extensive elaboration of the distinction between declarative and nondeclarative forms of culture, see Lizardo (2017).

References

Auyero, Javier, and Debora Swistun. 2007. "Confused because Exposed: Towards an Ethnography of Environmental Suffering." *Ethnography* 8:123–44.

Auyero, Javier, and Debora Swistun. 2008. "The Social Production of Toxic Uncertainty." *American Sociological Review* 73:357–79.

Auyero, Javier, and Debora Swistun. 2009. "Tiresias in Flammable Shantytown: Toward a Tempography of Domination." *Sociological Forum* 24:1–21.

Bargh, John A. 2005. "Bypassing the Will: Toward Demystifying the Nonconscious Control of Social Behavior." pp. 37–58 in *The New Unconscious*, edited by Ran R. Hassin, Uleman James S., and John A. Bargh. New York: Oxford University Press.

Bonikowski, Bart. 2016. "Nationalism in Settled Times." *Annual Review of Sociology* 42:427–49.

Bourdieu, Pierre. 1977. *Outline of a Theory of Practice*. Cambridge: Cambridge University Press.

Bourdieu, Pierre. 1979/1984. *Distinction: A Social Critique of the Judgment of Taste*. Cambridge, MA: Harvard University Press.

Bourdieu, Pierre. 1980/1990. *The Logic of Practice*. Stanford, CA: Stanford University Press.

Bourdieu, Pierre. 1997/2000. *Pascalian Meditations*. Stanford, CA: Stanford University Press.

Brekhus, Wayne. 2015. *Culture and Cognition: Patterns in the Social Construction of Reality*. Cambridge, UK; Malden, MA: Polity Press.

Cerulo, Karen. 2006. *Never Saw It Coming: Cultural Challenges to Envisioning the Worst*. Chicago; London: University of Chicago Press.

Cerulo, Karen. 2010. "Mining the Intersections of Cognitive Sociology and Neuroscience." *Poetics* 38:115–32.

Chaiken, Shelly. 1980. "Heuristic versus Systematic Information Processing and the Use of Source versus Message Cues in Persuasion." *Journal of Personality and Social Psychology* 39:752–66.

Chaiken, Shelly, and Yaacov Trope. 1999. *Dual-Process Theories in Social Psychology*. New York: Guilford Press.

Clark, Andy. 1997. *Being There: Putting Brain, Body, and World Together Again*. Cambridge, MA: MIT Press.

D'Andrade, Roy. 1992. "Schemas and Motivation." pp. 23–44 in *Human Motives and Cultural Models*, edited by Roy D'Andrade and Claudia Strauss. Cambridge: Cambridge University Press.

D'Andrade, Roy. 1995. *The Development of Cognitive Anthropology*. Cambridge: Cambridge University Press.

Danna-Lynch, Karen. 2007. "Modeling Role Enactment: Linking Role Theory and Social Cognition." *Journal for the Theory of Social Behaviour* 37:379–99.

Danna-Lynch, Karen. 2009. "Objects, Meanings, and Role Identities: The Practices That Establish Association in the Case of Home-Based Employment." *Sociological Forum* 24:76–103.

Danna-Lynch, Karen. 2010. "Culture and Cognition in the Performance of Multiple Roles: The Process of Mental Weighing." *Poetics* 38:165–83.

Dewey, John. 1922/2002. *Human Nature and Conduct*. New York: The Modern Library.

DiMaggio, Paul. 1997. "Culture and Cognition." *Annual Review of Sociology* 23:263–87.

DiMaggio, Paul, and Walter Powell. 1983. "The Iron Cage Revisited: Institutional Isomorphism and Collective Rationality in Organizational Fields." *American Sociological Review* 48:147–60.

DiMaggio, Paul, and Walter Powell. 1991. "Introduction." pp. 1–38 in *The New Institutionalism in Organizational Analysis*, edited by Paul DiMaggio and Walter Powell. Chicago; London: University of Chicago Press.

Djulbegovic, Benjamin, Iztok Hozo, Jason Beckstead, Athanasios Tsalatsanis, and Stephen G. Pauker. 2012. "Dual Processing Model of Medical Decision-Making." *BMC Medical Informatics and Decision Making* 12:1–13.

Durkheim, Emile. 1912/1995. *The Elementary Forms of Religious Life*. New York: The Free Press.

Eliasoph, Nina, and Paul Lichterman. 2003. "Culture in Interaction." *American Journal of Sociology* 108:735–94.

Elsbach, Kimberly, and Heiko Breitsohl. 2016. "A Dual-Mode Framework of Organizational Categorization and Momentary Perception." *Human Relations* 69:2011–39.

Emirbayer, Mustafa, and Jeff Goodwin. 1994. "Network Analysis, Culture, and the Problem of Agency." *American Journal of Sociology* 99:1411–54.

Epstein, Seymour, and Rosemary Pacini. 1999. "Some Basic Issues Regarding Dual-Process Theories from the Perspective of Cognitive-Experiential Theory." pp. 462–82 in *Dual-Process Theories in Social Psychology*, edited by Shelly Chaiken and Yaacov Trope. New York: Guilford Press.

Evans, Jonathan St. B. T. 2003. "In Two Minds: Dual Process Accounts of Reasoning." *Trends in Cognitive Sciences* 7:454–9.

Evans, Jonathan St. B. T. 2006. "Dual System Theories of Cognition: Some Issues." pp. 202–7 in *Proceedings of the 28th Annual Meeting of the Cognitive Science Society*. Hillsdale, NJ: Erlbaum.

Evans, Jonathan St. B. T. 2007. "On the Resolution of Conflict in Dual-Process Theories of Reasoning." *Thinking and Reasoning* 13:321–9.

Evans, Jonathan St. B. T. 2008. "Dual-Processing Accounts of Reasoning, Judgment, and Social Cognition." *Annual Review of Psychology* 59:255–78.

Evans, Jonathan St. B. T. 2010. *Thinking Twice: Two Minds in One Brain*. Oxford: Oxford University Press.

Evans, Jonathan St. B. T., and David E. Over. 1996. *Rationality and Reasoning*. Hove, UK: Psychology Press.

Evans, Jonathan St. B. T., and Keith E. Stanovich. 2013. "Dual-Process Theories of Higher Cognition: Advancing the Debate." *Perspectives in Psychological Science* 8:223–41.

Forbes, Chad E., and Grafman Jordan. 2010. "The Role of the Human Prefrontal Cortex in Social Cognition and Moral Judgment." *Annual Review of Neuroscience* 33:299–324.

Friedman, Asia. 2016. "'There Are Two People at Work That I'm Fairly Certain Are Black': Uncertainty and Deliberative Thinking in Blind Race Attribution." *Sociological Quarterly* 57:437–61.

Giddens, Anthony. 1984. *The Constitution of Society: Outline of a Theory of Structuration*. Berkeley: University of California Press.

Gilbert, Daniel. 1991. "How Mental Systems Believe." *American Psychologist* 46:107–19.

Glöckner, Andreas, and Cilia Witteman. 2010. "Beyond Dual-Process Models: A Categorisation of Processes underlying Intuitive Judgement and Decision Making." *Thinking and Reasoning* 16:1–25.

Goldhagen, Sarah Williams. 2017. *Welcome to Your World: How the Built Environment Shapes Our Lives*. New York: Harper Collins.

Haidt, Jonathan. 2001. "The Emotional Dog and Its Rational Tail: A Social Institutionist Approach to Moral Judgment." *Psychological Review* 108:814–34.

Haidt, Jonathan. 2005. *The Happiness Hypothesis: Finding Modern Truth in Ancient Wisdom*. New York: Basic Books.

Harvey, Daina. 2010. "The Space for Culture and Cognition." *Poetics* 38:184–203.

Heimer, Carol. 2001. "Cases and Biographies: An Essay on Routinization and the Nature of Comparison." *Annual Review of Sociology* 27:47–76.

Hoffmann, John P. 2014. "Religiousness, Social Networks, Moral Schemas, and Marijuana Use: A Dynamic Dual-Process Model of Culture and Behavior." *Social Forces* 93:181–208.

Hutchins, Edwin. 1995. *Cognition in the Wild*. Cambridge, MA: MIT Press.

Ignatow, Gabriel. 2014. "Ontology and Method in Cognitive Sociology." *Sociological Forum* 29:990–4.

Jerolmack, Colin, and Shamus Khan. 2014. "Talk Is Cheap: Ethnography and the Attitudinal Fallacy." *Sociological Methods and Research* 43:178–209.

Joas, Hans. 1996. *The Creativity of Action*. Chicago: University of Chicago Press.

Kahneman, Daniel. 2011. *Thinking Fast and Slow*. New York: Farrar, Straus and Giroux.

Kahneman, Daniel, and Frederick Shane. 2002. "Representativeness Revisited: Attribute Substitution in Intuitive Judgment." pp. 49–81 in *Heuristics and Biases: The Psychology of Intuitive Judgment*, edited by Thomas Gilovich, Dale Griffin, and Daniel Kahneman. Cambridge: Cambridge University Press.

Kruglanski, Arie W., Woo Young Chun, Hans Peter Erb, Antonio Pierro, Lucia Mannetti, and Scott Spiegel. 2003. "A Parametric Unimodel of Human Judgment: Integrating Dual-Process Frameworks in Social Cognition from a Single-Mode Perspective." pp. 137–61 in *Social Judgments: Implicit and Explicit Processes*, edited by Joseph P. Forgas, Kipling D. Williams, and William Von Hippel. New York: Cambridge University Press.

Kruglanski, Arie W., and Edward Orehek. 2007. "Partitioning the Domain of Social Inference: Dual Mode and Systems Models and Their Alternatives." *Annual Review of Psychology* 58:291–316.

Lamont, Michèle, and Ann Swidler. 2014. "Methodological Pluralism and the Possibilities and Limits of Interviewing." *Qualitative Sociology* 37:153–71.

Lave, Jean. 1988. *Cognition in Practice: Mind, Mathematics, and Culture in Everyday Life*. New York: Cambridge University Press.

Leschziner, Vanina. 2015. *At the Chef's Table: Culinary Creativity in Elite Restaurants*. Stanford, CA: Stanford University Press.

Leschziner, Vanina, and Adam Isaiah Green. 2013. "Thinking about Food and Sex: Deliberate Cognition in the Routine Practices of a Field." *Sociological Theory* 31:116–44.

Lieberman, Matthew D. 2003. "Reflective and Reflexive Judgment Processes: A Social Cognitive Neuroscience Approach." pp. 44–67 in *Social Judgments: Implicit and Explicit Processes*, edited by Joseph P. Forgas, Kipling D. Williams, and William Von Hippel. New York: Cambridge University Press.

Lieberman, Matthew D. 2007. "Social Cognitive Neuroscience: A Review of Core Processes." *Annual Review of Psychology* 58:259–89.

Lieberman, Matthew D., Johanna M. Jarcho, and AJay B. Satpute. 2004. "Evidence-Based and Intuition-Based Self-knowledge: An fMRI Study." *Journal of Personality and Social Psychology* 87:421–35.

Lizardo, Omar. 2004. "The Cognitive Origins of Bourdieu's Habitus." *Journal for the Theory of Social Behaviour* 34:375–401.

Lizardo, Omar. 2007. "'Mirror Neurons,' Collective Objects and the Problem of Transmission: Reconsidering Stephen Turner's Critique of Practice Theory." *Journal for the Theory of Social Behaviour* 37:319–50.

Lizardo, Omar. 2014. "Beyond the Comtean Schema: The Sociology of Culture and Cognition Versus Cognitive Social Science." *Sociological Forum* 29:983–9.

Lizardo, Omar. 2017. "Improving Cultural Analysis: Considering Personal Culture in Its Declarative and Nondeclarative Modes." *American Sociological Review* 82:88–115.

Lizardo, Omar, Robert Mowry, Brandon Sepulvado, Dustin S. Stoltz, Marshall A. Taylor, Justin Van Ness, et al. 2016. "What Are Dual Process Models? Implications for Cultural Analysis in Sociology." *Sociological Theory* 34:287–310.

Lizardo, Omar, and Michael Strand. 2010. "Skills, Toolkits, Contexts and Institutions: Clarifying the Relationship between Different Approaches to Cognition in Cultural Sociology." *Poetics* 38:205–28.

Mandler, Jean. 1984. *Stories, Scripts, and Scenes: Aspects of Schema Theory*. Hillsdale, NJ: Erlbaum.

Margolis, Howard. 1987. *Patterns, Thinking, and Cognition: A Theory of Judgment*. Chicago; London: University of Chicago Press.

Martin, John Levi. 2010. "Life's a Beach but You're an Ant, and Other Unwelcome News for the Sociology of Culture." *Poetics* 38:229–44.

Martin, John Levi. 2011. *The Explanation of Social Action*. New York: Oxford University Press.

Martin, John Levi, and Matthew Desmond. 2010. "Political Position and Social Knowledge." *Sociological Forum* 25:1–26.

Marx, Karl. 1845/1965. *The German Ideology*. London: Lawrence & Wishart.

McDonnell, Terence E. 2014. "Drawing Out Culture: Productive Methods to Measure Cognition and Resonance." *Theory and Society* 43:247–74.

McDonnell, Terence E. 2016. *Best Laid Plans: Cultural Entropy and the Unraveling of AIDS Media Campaigns* Chicago: University of Chicago Press.

McDonnell, Terence E., Christopher A. Bail, and Iddo Tavory. 2017. "A Theory of Resonance." *Sociological Theory* 35:1–14.

Mead, George H. 1934/1967. *Mind, Self, and Society: From the Standpoint of a Social Behaviorist*. Chicago: University of Chicago Press.

Miles, Andrew. 2015. "The (Re)genesis of Values: Examining the Importance of Values for Action." *American Journal of Sociology* 80:680–704.

Mische, Ann. 2011. "Relational Sociology, Culture, and Agency." pp. 80–98 in *Sage Handbook of Social Network Analysis*, edited by Scott J. Carrington. Thousand Oaks, CA: SAGE.

Mische, Ann. 2014. "Measuring Futures in Action: Projective Grammars in the Rio+20 Debates." *Theory and Society* 43:437–64.

Moore, Rick. 2017. "Fast or Slow: Sociological Implications of Measuring Dual-Process Cognition." *Sociological Science* 4:196–223.

Nisbett, Richard E., Kaiping Peng, Incheol Choi, and Ara Norenzayan. 2001. "Culture and Systems of Thought: Holistic versus Analytic Cognition." *Psychological Review* 108:291–310.

Norton, Matthew. 2014. "Mechanisms and Meaning Structures." *Sociological Theory* 32:162–87.

Parsons, Talcott. 1937/1968. *The Structure of Social Action: A Study in Social Theory with Special Reference to a Group of Recent European Writers*. New York: Free Press.

Patterson, Orlando. 2014. "Making Sense of Culture." *Annual Review of Sociology* 40:1–30.

Petty, Richard E., and John T. Cacioppo. 1981. *Attitudes and Persuasion: Classical and Contemporary Approaches*. Dubuque, IA: Brown.

Pugh, Allison J. 2013. "What Good Are Interviews for Thinking about Culture? Demystifying Interpretive Analysis." *American Journal of Cultural Sociology* 1:42–68.

Reber, Arthur S. 1993. *Implicit Learning and Tacit Knowledge*. Oxford: Oxford University Press.

Rivers, Louie, III, Carole Gibbs, and Raymond Paternoster. 2017. "Integrating Criminological and Decision Research Theory: Implications for Understanding and Addressing Crime in Marginalized Communities." *Deviant Behavior* 38:74–93.

Rosch, Eleanor. 1978. "Principles of Categorization." pp. 27–48 in *Cognition and Categorization*, edited by Eleanor Rosch and Barbara Lloyd. Hillsdale, NJ: Erlbaum.

Rumelhart, David E., Geoffrey E. Hinton, and Ronald J. Williams. 1986. "Learning Representations by Back-Propagating Errors." *Nature* 323:533–6.

Shepherd, Hana. 2011. "The Cultural Context of Cognition: What the Implicit Association Test Tells Us about How Culture Works." *Sociological Forum* 26:121–43.

Smith, E. R., and J. DeCoster. 2000. "Dual-Process Models in Social and Cognitive Psychology: Conceptual Integration and Links to Underlying Memory Systems." *Personality and Social Psychology Review* 4:108–31.

Srivastava, Sameer B., and Mahzarin R Banaji. 2011. "Culture, Cognition, and Collaborative Networks in Organizations." *American Sociological Review* 76:207–33.

Stanovich, Keith E. 1999. *Who Is Rational? Studies of Individual Differences in Reasoning.* Mahwah, NJ: Erlbaum.

Strand, Michael, and Omar Lizardo. 2015. "Beyond World Images: Belief as Embodied Action in the World." *Sociological Theory* 33:44–70.

Strauss, Claudia, and Naomi Quinn. 1997. *A Cognitive Theory of Cultural Meaning.* Cambridge: Cambridge University Press.

Swidler, Ann. 1986. "Culture in Action: Symbols and Strategies." *American Sociological Review* 51:273–86.

Swidler, Ann. 2003. *Talk of Love: How Culture Matters.* Chicago; London: University of Chicago Press.

Swidler, Ann. 2008. "Comment on Stephen Vaisey's 'Socrates, Skinner, and Aristotle: Three Ways of Thinking about Culture in Action.'" *Sociological Forum* 23:614–18.

Turner, Stephen. 2007. "Social Theory as a Cognitive Neuroscience." *European Journal of Social Theory* 10:357–74.

Vaisey, Stephen. 2008a. "Reply to Ann Swidler." *Sociological Forum* 23:619–22.

Vaisey, Stephen. 2008b. "Socrates, Skinner, and Aristotle: Three Ways of Thinking about Culture in Action." *Sociological Forum* 23:603–13.

Vaisey, Stephen. 2009. "Motivation and Justification: A Dual-Process Model of Culture in Action." *American Journal of Sociology* 114:1675–715.

Vaisey, Stephen. 2014. "Is Interviewing Compatible with the Dual-Process Model of Culture?" *American Journal of Cultural Sociology* 2:150–58.

Vaisey, Stephen, and Omar Lizardo. 2010. "Can Cultural Worldviews Influence Network Composition?" *Social Forces* 88:1595–618.

Vaisey, Stephen, and Andrew Miles. 2014. "Tools from Moral Psychology for Measuring Personal Moral Culture." *Theory and Society* 43(3–4):311–32.

Vaughan, Diane. 1990. "Autonomy, Interdependence, and Social Control: NASA and the Space Shuttle Challenger." *Administrative Science Quarterly* 35:225–57.

Vaughan, Dianne. 1996. *The Challenger Launch Decision: Risky Technology, Culture, and Deviance at NASA.* Chicago: University of Chicago Press.

Vaughan, Dianne. 2002. "Signals and Interpretive Work. The Role of Culture in a Theory of Practical Action." pp. 28–54 in *Culture in Mind. Toward a Sociology of Culture and Cognition*, edited by Karen Cerulo. New York; London: Routledge.

Vila-Henninger, Luis Antonio. 2015. "Toward Defining the Causal Role of Consciousness: Using Models of Memory and Moral Judgment from Cognitive Neuroscience to Expand the Sociological Dual-Process Model." *Journal for the Theory of Social Behaviour* 45:238–60.

Weber, Max. 1920/1992. *The Protestant Ethic and the Spirit of Capitalism*. Translated by Talcott Parsons. London and New York: Routledge.

Wegner, Daniel M. 2002. *The Illusion of Conscious Will*. Cambridge, MA: MIT Press.

Wilson, Timothy D. 2002. *Strangers to Ourselves: Discovering the Adaptive Unconscious*. Cambridge, MA: Harvard University Press.

Winchester, Daniel. 2016. "A Hunger for God: Embodied Metaphor as Cultural Cognition in Action." *Social Forces* 95:585–606.

CHAPTER 11

BRIDGING THE VOCABULARIES OF DUAL-PROCESS MODELS OF CULTURE AND COGNITION

JACOB STRANDELL

HUMAN beings are uniquely capable of rational deliberation, hypothetical thinking, and consequential decision-making, abilities that have allowed our species to evolve cultures, build advanced societies, and produce scientific knowledge. Our capacity to reason reflectively is perhaps most evident in scientific articles or formal political debates, where words are carefully and intentionally chosen, and logical coherence is institutionally demanded. Yet despite the pervasive belief in the rational individual in contemporary Western societies, people's actions are usually not guided by deliberate rationality. More often than not, intuition, affective states, and heuristics guide our behavior and experiences, and the vast majority of cognitive processes are not rational deliberations but occur automatically, outside our conscious awareness and without basis in logic or fact (Bargh 1997; J. Evans and Stanovich 2013).

Philosophers and psychologists have studied this duality of the human mind for centuries, often in entirely dissociated traditions using incommensurable vocabularies (see J. Evans and Frankish 2009). Throughout the history of psychology, nonconscious, automatic, or intuitive cognitive processes have often played a key role in research paradigms. Freud introduced the psychoanalytic idea that subconscious drives, desires, and repressed motives influence most of what people do, while the conscious and rational parts of the mind rationalize this behavior with morally and socially acceptable rationales. Behaviorist psychologists rejected the (scientific) importance of subjective meaning and instead emphasized nonconscious and automatic processes, such as conditioning, as better explanations of human behavior. In the second half of the twentieth century, cognitive scientists developed a notion of nonconscious cognitive processes responsible for a multitude of basic functions of the mind (Khilstrom 1987; Reber 1993). Countless studies have since verified how automatic processes, tacit knowledge, implicit attitudes, heuristics, and biases influence human behavior outside of conscious awareness.

Contemporary dual-process theories of cognition are attempts at detailing the duality of the human mind (J. Evans 1989; Wason and Evans 1975). These theories distinguish between two fundamentally different types of cognitive processes: one fast, effortless, automatic, and largely nonconscious, and another that is slower and cognitively demanding, but deliberative and conscious. Dual-process theories have proven useful for a wide range of research topics, including learning (Reber 1993; Sun, Slusarz, and Terry 2005), social cognition (Smith and Collins 2009; Smith and DeCoster 2000), judgment and decision-making (Kahneman and Frederick 2002), and reasoning (J. Evans 2003, 2007; Stanovich 2011). However, sociological use of dual-process reasoning to describe the micromechanisms of culture have been limited, although in recent years, sociological interest have increased significantly (see, for example, Lizardo and Strand 2010; Lizardo et al. 2016; Vaisey 2009). Consequently, sociological theory and research remain largely ignorant of dual-process models of cognition and their implications for how we understand the workings of culture.

This chapter provides some of the groundwork toward integrating dual-processing insights from cognitive science with cultural theories. It aims to give the reader insight into state-of-the-art cognitive dual-process models from the perspective of cognitive scientists—in particular those of Evans and Stanovich (J. Evans 2008, 2011; J. Evans and Stanovich 2013)—before proceeding to make direct comparisons with established cultural theories. Dual-process reasoning has existed in psychology since at least William James, but Jonathan Evans formally suggested the first dual-process theory in 1975. Since then, Evans has been one of the main proponents of dual-process reasoning and has together with Stanovich argued strongly for its validity over other variations (see J. Evans and Stanovich 2013). The approach of Evans and Stanovich holds particular potential for the sociological study of culture, in part because their terminology is relatively easy to translate into sociological terms, but also because their model and research tell us something about how explicit and implicit elements of culture interacts. I argue that many cultural theories already rest on dual-process reasoning and that there is therefore much to gain if we can develop accessible integrated language for a dual-process model of culture compatible with the dual-process models of cognitive science.

11.1 DUAL-PROCESS MODELS OF COGNITION

While most dual-process theorists agree on a fundamental distinction between two types of cognitive processes—one that is fast, nonconscious, and automatic, and one that is often slow, conscious, and deliberative—a wide range of different terminologies has been used to label the two types of processes (J. Evans 2008). Some researchers have

Table 11.1 Common Terminology in Dual-Process Models of Cognition (adapted from Evans 2008)

Intuitive Processes	Reflective Processes
Type 1	Type 2
System 1	System 2
Implicit	Explicit
Automatic	Controlled
Heuristic	Systematic
Impulsive	Reflective
Associative	Rule-based
Holistic	Analytic
Old mind	New mind

tried to pinpoint the defining characteristics of each process, using labels such as automatic/deliberative or holistic/analytic processes, while others have chosen to speak in more abstract terms about two types or systems (see Table 11.1). The fact that many different terms exist indicates that this duality is a widely recognized aspect of human experience, yet one that is remarkably difficult to pin down with precision. To be able to access the broad literature on dual-process models, it is important to realize that while these terms refer to the same basic duality of the mind, they nonetheless have different theoretical implications (see J. Evans 2008; J. Evans and Stanovich 2013 for some discussion).

Attempting to characterize the two processes using one of their common characteristics, such as "automatic" or "heuristic," has proven difficult, because there are exceptions to almost all characteristics attributed to either process, as we shall see later. Other terminologies are problematic because they commit to different assumptions about the underlying mechanisms of the two processes. The common distinction between System 1 and System 2, for example, implies there is a single neurocognitive system responsible for either cognitive process, but multiple cognitive systems are involved in all intuitive or reflective processing.[1] Evans and Stanovich (J. Evans 2008; J. Evans and Stanovich 2013) therefore argue for simply talking about two *types* of processes in dual-process models, designated Type 1 and Type 2. J. Evans (2011) has also argued for the accuracy of the more accessible terms "intuitive" versus "reflective" processes, which are used throughout this chapter.

In dual-process research, a broad range of common characteristics has been ascribed to each process, as shown in Table 11.2. However, while these common characteristics neatly divide into two categories, they are *typical correlates* and not *defining features* necessary for either process type (J. Evans and Stanovich 2013). Intuitive processes tend to be fast, nonconscious, and automatic, while reflective processes tend to be slow and controlled, and operate in a rule-like fashion, but there are many exceptions to these tendencies as well as situations in which the processes interact. For example, people may learn to apply quick heuristic rules in conscious and deliberate thinking. Similarly,

Table 11.2 Clusters of Typical Features Correlating with Each Process Type in Dual-Process Models (adapted from Evans and Stanovich 2013)

Intuitive Processes (Type 1)	Reflective Processes (Type 2)
Fast	Slow
High capacity	Capacity limited
Parallel	Serial
Nonconscious	Conscious
Biased	Normative
Contextualized	Abstract
Automatic/autonomous	Controlled/deliberative
Associative	Rule-based
Experience-based decision-making	Consequential decision-making
Independent of cognitive ability	Correlated with cognitive ability

although intuitive processes are associative in nature, they can operate in a systematic and rule-like fashion through training.

Despite the sometimes-overlapping characteristics of reflective and intuitive processes, a large mass of research supports the divide between two distinct types of cognitive processes. The crux has been to pinpoint the defining feature of either process type. In correspondence with empirical evidence, Evans and Stanovich have argued the defining difference is that intuitive processes are autonomous from working memory, while reflective processes rely on working memory (J. Evans 2007, 2008; J. Evans and Stanovich 2013). Experimental evidence has repeatedly shown that if working memory capacity is suppressed, for example by asking participants to keep a string of numbers in mind while answering questions, their reasoning abilities decline and their answers show systematic belief biases (J. Evans and Stanovich 2013). Working memory refers to the restricted cognitive capacity to keep a limited amount of information active in the mind at a given moment, and is a concept closely related to "controlled attention" and even "consciousness" (J. Evans 2008, 2011).

Our working memory enables the uniquely human capacities for hypothetical thinking and cognitive decoupling (J. Evans 2007; Stanovich 2011). People with higher working memory capacity can work with more hypothetical information not present in the current environment and can make more complex manipulations of this information to, for example, predict probable future scenarios. The ability of working memory to maintain abstract or hypothetical information active in consciousness is also what allows the brain to override automatic reactions to environmental stimuli, as it provides alternative information for us to respond to. We can, for example, use an abstract imperative such as "you should not generalize" to override an intuition based on a stereotype. Working memory capacity also allows us to imagine alternative scenarios, run thought experiments, consider their consequences, evaluate our own beliefs, manipulate abstract information, and think in multiple steps ahead. Working memory is, however, a highly limited resource, capable of attending only one hypothesis at a time with effort, which is why automatic and intuitive processes that are capable of multiple fast parallel processes are much more efficient at most everyday tasks.

11.1.1 Process Interaction

The distinction between two fundamental types of cognitive processes is now uncontroversial and well studied. However, a more complex question with greater importance for sociologists is how the two process types interact in everyday life. Understanding the conditions under which one process is dominant is imperative for understanding how culture affects people and their behavior, as well as the mechanisms by which culture is attained and reproduced.

Multiple intuitive processes are always continually active, independently of reflective cognition, and often inaccessible through direct introspective reflection. These intuitive processes include such basic processes as, for example, body movement control, basic perception and object recognition, affective reactions, and associative learning by conditioning. Social information is likely to be heavily mediated by intuitive processes because of the sheer amount of information that requires rapid parallel processing in social interactions, including assessing, interpreting, and evaluating roles, motives, histories, body language, facial expressions, tone of voice, relationships, emotions, and so on, some of which may be managed automatically by neurocognitive systems such as the mirror neuron system (Spunt and Lieberman 2013). Processes such as these are likely to be responsible for the reproduction of overt and implicit elements of cultural practices (Lizardo 2007).

However, people can also intuitively learn to use and predict complex systems and abstract logics without necessarily being able to reflectively account for this (Berry and Dienes 1993; J. Evans 2008; Reber 1993; Sun et al. 2005). Automatic intuitive processes are also involved in processing emotions, implicit attitudes, implicit self-evaluative cognition, and social perception and stereotyping (Epstein 1994; Hassin, Uleman, and Bargh 2005; Lieberman 2003; Smith and DeCoster 2000; Zeigler-Hill and Myers 2011). The relative independence of automatic or intuitive processes is further accentuated by people often using reflective processing to rationalize, explain, or justify their actions post hoc, thereby remaining unaware of how intuitive processes influence their behavior (Nisbett and Wilson 1977; Evans and Over 1996; Vaisey 2009; Wason and Evans 1975; Wilson 2002; Wilson and Dunn 2004). The relative independence of intuitive processes does not mean that they are not entirely unaffected by reflective processes, however. People may not be able to directly control their intuitive reactions, inferences, emotions, and so on, but it is possible to shape intuitive processing through long-term training (Sun et al. 2005).

The dual-process theorists interested in judgment and decision-making have primarily focused on the question of when one process is dominant in decisions. Evans and Stanovich argue for a default-interventionist model of decision-making, in which intuitive processes provide quick, automatic default responses in all situations unless reflective processes intervene and inhibit the initial intuitive response (J. Evans 2008, 2011; J. Evans and Stanovich 2013). These default intuitive responses are generally accepted, however, as most cognitive processes in daily functioning are intuitive processes that may be subject to mental heuristics, including stereotyping and belief bias. Reflective processes are rarely involved because they are inefficient (in the sense that they are slow), resource-limited (in the sense that working memory can only attend to one hypothesis at a time) and require mental effort. As the effortless intuitive response is rapid and allows us to function efficiently in most of our everyday life, reflective processes are reserved for special circumstances. Research has shown that several factors contribute to reaching the critical degree of effort needed for reflective processes to intervene and inhibit intuition. These can be divided into two categories, motivational factors, and cognitive resources, as overviewed in Table 11.3.

This default-interventionist model has many important implications for sociologists, one of which is the importance of context. Cognitive sociologists have already stressed the importance of context for culture and behavior, as cognitive science research suggests that contextual cues from the physical environment or ongoing interaction work like a scaffold for how culture is put into action (DiMaggio 1997; Lizardo 2015; Lizardo and Strand 2010). Because people possess a multitude of flexible schemas that can be used in many ways and in several situations, schemas alone underdetermine action, and environmental input plays a bigger role than we previously thought in perception, interpretation, and action (see Shepherd 2011). However, the default-interventionist model suggests that context influences not only *what* we experience, think, or do, but also *how* we do it, by influencing the dominant process-type involved in the interaction. For example, in a busy, demanding, social environment, under time pressure or when subject to ongoing social interaction, people are much more likely to rely on fast, automatic, intuitive processing compared to when time and space are given to solve a problem in an

---

Table 11.3 Factors Determining When Reflective Processing Overrides Intuitive Processing

Motivational Factors

- Contextual or instructional cues to think critically, pragmatically, or deductively.
- Individual or cultural dispositions, for example toward analytical thinking (cf. Nisbett et al. 2001).
- Intuitive metacognitive "feelings of rightness," confidence in the default response (Thompson 2009; Thompson et al. 2013).

Cognitive Resources

- Available time (time pressure suppresses the slower reflective processes).
- Competing tasks (competing tasks suppress the limited capacity of working memory).
- Individual variations in working memory capacity (De Neys et al. 2005a, 2005b).
- Variations in "mindware," the set of mental tools and capacities acquired throughout life (see Stanovich 2009).

environment that encourages critical thinking. Further, sociologists must be aware of, and consider, that different social groups may be equipped with different "mindware" from different experiences, which influences how they rely on different cognitive processes. Finally, sociologists can capitalize on these insights by carefully constructing methodologies that inhibit or encourage reflective processing, similar to the experimental methods used to study dual processes and intuitive cognition (Hunzaker 2014; Miles this volume; Shepherd this volume; Vaisey 2009, 2013).

11.2 DUAL-PROCESS MODELS OF CULTURE

As culture relies on cognition to be reproduced through human actions, it is not surprising that dual-process theories have recently garnered the interest of cognitive sociologists interested in culture (see, for example, Cerulo 2010; DiMaggio 1997; Lizardo and Strand 2010; Vaisey 2009; Vaisey and Frye this volume). The work of these researchers has shown the utility of dual-process models for sociological problems, but much work remains to make dual-process models accessible to sociologists in general. There are two main challenges to the integration of cognitive dual-process models: (1) the lack of an accessible interdisciplinary language; and (2) the lack of a broader recognition of dual-process reasoning in cultural theory.

Dual-process reasoning is by no means new to the sociology of culture: distinctions have long been made between explicit, propositional, or language-based cultural processes on the one hand and implicit, affective, or practice-based processes on the other (Sewell 2005). However, these have not been integrated into a formalized dual-process model of culture, as new theoretical work in cultural sociology has tended to highlight one aspect of culture while critiquing another, instead of attempting to build cumulative models. This part of the chapter shows that comparable dual-process reasoning is common in the concepts of influential cultural theories and there is, therefore, good common ground integrating insights from the dual-process models of cognition.

11.2.1 Explicit (or Reflective) Culture: Ideologies, Repertoires, Explanations, and Justifications

In cultural theory, some authors and traditions have emphasized the explicit aspects of culture and argued that culture primarily shapes the rationales used to reflectively explain or justify actions, with little or no relevance for the actual, implicit, or intuitive motivations behind people's actions. Thus, in this view, the real causes of social action must be found elsewhere than in people's attempts at sense-making. In early Marxist theory, for example, *ideology* was used to refer to explicit cultural phenomena consisting of the ideas and discourses that explained and justified the world, a world that was primarily determined by material, economic, and historical conditions (Marx and Engels 1932). Cultural ideologies, thus, maintained the status quo by obscuring the true, implicit, mechanisms of society, keeping them from entering people's awareness. Hegemonic ideology was treated as a set of explicit cultural ideas that maintains the implicit reproduction of a system of power relations below the surface of conscious awareness. The hegemonic ideology of capitalist societies was seen as a means to maintain "false consciousness," that is, the mental ignorance and obedience of the working class, and ensuring the continued dominance of the bourgeoisie (Engels 1863/1968). While in some ways having real consequences, ideology was nonetheless perceived as a secondary function to other, more fundamental, mechanisms such as the means and relations of production.

Many other theorists outside the Marxist tradition have also seen culture as primarily a way of talking about or making sense of things, rather than as something with direct influence on people's actions or desires. Mills (1940), for example, is a classic example of a theorist who argued that culture provides people with *vocabularies of motives* used to explain action. A more recent example of a similar perspective on explicit cultural rationales is Boltansky and Thévenot's (1991/2006) *On Justification*, which argues that justifications are of critical importance to social interaction not only in the strict moral sense (i.e., justifying an action) but also to command respect or argue for the value or importance of something (i.e., justifying someone's or something's status). Collectively, these theorists now fall under the umbrella of *repertoire theories*, a view that culture consists of sets of loosely interrelated and often contradictory repertoires of explicit rationales, used primarily to explain, justify, or rationalize actions irrespective of the actual psychological mechanisms behind the action (Lizardo and Strand 2010; Vaisey 2009). The repertoire of motives that people use can be seen as part of a larger cultural ideology of acceptable motivations for actions, such as, for example, rational or individualistic explanations in neoliberal societies. Repertoires, justifications, or vocabularies of motives are similar to, and likely mediated primarily by, reflective cognitive processes because they are propositional or rule-like logics, which are consciously available and used in a more or less deliberate way to explain, justify, or rationalize things that may already have happened because of other, less explicit, social or psychological mechanisms.

The perhaps more important contribution to contemporary repertoire theories and the ongoing debate around dual-process theories is Swidler's (1986, 2001) *toolkit theory*. Swidler's 2001 book *Talk of Love* presents empirical material consisting of interviews with Americans on the topic of love and marriage. Here, Swidler notes that people are remarkably bad at giving coherent and consistent accounts of their decisions and actions—even for seemingly important things, such as the choice of partner and the decision to marry. From this observation, Swidler concludes that the rationales for their actions that people offer when asked cannot be what motivated the action in the first place. While this conclusion can be questioned (Pugh 2013; Vaisey 2009), Swidler's observations indicate that people's rationales are disconnected from the actual action, and seemingly chosen from a "tool kit" of available rationales when asked. These cultural toolkits consist of a range of cultural resources from which people can pick and choose, as they "trim their philosophies to fit their action commitments" (2001:148). Consequently, the values and ideals people talk about as if they were guiding their behavior are not stable internalized motivators of action but parts of the repertoires from which people draw to construct acceptable accounts post hoc. Much like explicit ideologies, vocabularies of motive, or justifications, and the social use of repertoires resembles the cognitive sense-making and rationalization achieved mentally through reflective processes.

11.2.2 Implicit (or Intuitive) Culture: Practices, Dispositions, and Motivations

In contrast to the theories emphasizing explicit elements of culture, other cultural theories have argued that culture operates primarily through implicit or intuitive mechanisms, which correspond to those of intuitive cognitive processes. These theorists have stressed unconscious, automatic, or habitual aspects of culture as influencing our behavior in profound ways, and often argue that culture is deeply internalized in the sense that it psychologically modifies the actors' intuitive dispositions and motivations to act in certain ways.

Unconscious processes have, for example, played a central role in later and more psychoanalytically influenced takes on Marxist theory (Althusser 1969; Gramsci 1990; Lukes 2005; Žižek 1989). To these thinkers, ideology does not simply consist of explicit ideas or rationales of justification, but is, rather, an unconscious system of power operating through the representations that govern how people relate to society and themselves. Explicit cultural elements such as rationales consequently come after, or from, ideology. Similarly to its earlier mentioned counterpart, however, unconscious hegemonic ideology is assumed to support reproducing a society stratified by class positions, but in this case by motivating actors to intuitively reproduce their own positions.

A more recent example of intuitive cultural influence is Bourdieu's (1977, 1990) practice theory and *habitus* concept, which, with the help of cognitive anthropologists and sociologists, has found much support in cognitive science. The habitus is conceptualized as a set of intuitive dispositions to experience the world and act in a certain way shaped over time by recurring experiences in one's social environment. There is a strong resemblance between this habitus concept and the cognitive schema, and several cognitive sociologists and anthropologists have, consequently, explicitly compared the habitus to a collection of implicit schemas (D'Andrade 1995; Lizardo and Strand 2010; Quinn and Strauss 1997). Like cognitive schemas or scripts, the habitus enables the actor to navigate a familiar environment through intuitive "default responses" that have been built up from experience. Like schemas, the habitus is also transposable and flexible, in the sense that it can be used to understand and respond to similar experiences in other contexts than that in which it was originally learned, thus providing improvised or even creative solutions to new problems (Bourdieu 1990). Thus, the habitus deeply modifies the actor and shapes how the actor experiences the social world, and it can do so through intuitive cognitive processes entirely independent of reflective cognition or explicit cultural repertoires, logics, or meanings.

Among other contemporary theories emphasizing how intuition plays a key role in cultural reproduction is *affect control theory*, an unmistakably cognitive take on inter-actionist theory (see, for example, Robinson et al. 2006). The theory states that explicit (cognitive/cultural) concepts, referred to as *labels*, such as identities or actions, have associated affective meanings (scales ranging from good to bad or powerful to power-less). Furthermore, people strive to maintain the affective meaning evoked when situations are defined using labels. If the affective meanings produced by a definition do not align with an individual's expectation, they are emotionally motivated to redefine the situation or act in a way that conforms to their affective sentiments. For example, if a teacher receives an unexpected personal compliment from a student, which creates a psychological dissonance between expectation and experience, motivating the teacher to realign the affective meaning evoked by the situation to conform to expectations, for example by reinterpreting the student as ingratiating. The theory thus relies on intuitive cognitive processes and implicit affective cultural meanings to explain people's behavior.

Recently, the perspective of embodied cognition has provided cognitive sociologists with another framework for understanding how culture is reproduced through intuitive cognitive processes (see, e.g., Cerulo this volume). Accordingly, it is argued from this perspective that it is embodied schemas that provide the bricks and mortar for how people experience and understand the world, not abstract linguistic or symbolic systems.

11.2.3 Explicit and Implicit Aspects of Culture

Some cultural theories involve not only dual-process assumptions but also more elabo-rate dual-process reasoning that contrasts explicit and implicit elements of culture. For example, Geertz's (1973) distinction between *cultural ideologies* and cultural *common sense* is a distinction between explicit, or reflective, cultural meanings and logics on the one hand, and implicit or intuitively reproduced meanings on the other, which seem-ingly may operate in relative independence of each other (i.e., ideologies may continue to assert one thing even while common sense suggests another).

Even Merton's (1949) functionalism relies on a form of cultural dual-process reasoning—if read as a cultural theory (e.g., Young 2003). Merton distinguished between the *manifest* and *latent* functions of social phenomena such as institutions, where manifest functions were considered the overt, *conscious*, and *deliberate* functions, while latent functions were the *unconscious* or *unintended* social consequences or effects. The similarities between the functions and the cognitive process types are striking, although similarities such as these should not be read as if they are the same thing, but rather, as if reflective cognition reproduces the manifest functions of social structures, while intuitive cognition maintains the latent functions (for example, by motivating people to reproduce a stereotype without their being able to account for why that makes sense).

In contemporary sociological theory, Giddens's (1984) structuration theory rests on a distinction between *discursive* and *practical consciousness*, a clear-cut form of dual-process reasoning that closely resembles the dual-process models of cognition. Likely mediated by intuitive cognition, practical consciousness refers to "all things which actors know tacitly about how to 'go on' in the contexts of social life without being able to give them discursive expression" (Giddens 1984:xxiii). Such practical knowledge is, in Giddens's theory, essentially nonreflective, nonconscious, and nonlinguistic, but nonetheless of critical importance for everyday behavior. Discursive consciousness, in contrast, is verbalizable and consists of knowledge that can be used reflectively and deliberatively in, for example, sense-making and interpretation of behavior, and likely mediated by reflective cognition.

The close resemblance between Giddens's concepts and the dual-process theories of cognition led Stephen Vaisey (2009) to use Giddens's terminology in direct comparison with reflective and intuitive cognition in his seminal paper on the prospect of a dual-process model of culture (see also Lizardo and Strand 2010). Vaisey did not only make a theoretical comparison between the contributions of Giddens and the dual-process models of cognition, however, but also used survey and interview data to empirically show why we need a dual-process model of culture. The survey data showed that people do have preferences for moral logics that are stable over several years and that an unreflected preference for one of four moral orientations predicted behavior almost three years later. Yet in interviews, participants could not give consistent and uncontradictory explanations for their moral preferences. The latter observation is in line with the conclusions and arguments of repertoire theorists such as Swidler (1986, 2001), who argue that people make up rationales as they go, but the fact that people have stable and seemingly causally influential preferences for moral logics, but are unable to reflectively account for these, shows that people internalize intuitive dispositions as well as construct post hoc rationales.

Despite being largely absent from the endeavors of cognitive sociology, variations of discourse theory remain highly influential in cultural sociology and many other disciplines studying culture, such as cultural studies. A dual-process model of culture can, however, provide a framework for integrating discourse theory, because discourse theory already rests on dual-process assumptions. "Discourse" should not be understood here in the sense it is used by Giddens (1984), as primarily an explicit cultural element synonymous with language, but as it is used in discourse theories to denote *meaning- or knowledge-structures expressed through language* (Laclau and Mouffe 1985). While the explicit syntactic structure of an articulation may be studied using discourse analysis, what is often of interest are the implications and presuppositions of a statement, what Foucault (1972) sometimes referred to as the underlying order of culture, episteme, or *unconscious rules* of discourse. These underlying elements of discourse are intuitive, yet crucial to our understanding of the articulated statement (see, for example, Van Dijk 2014; Laclau and Mouffe 1985; Malcolm and Sharifian 2002). Consider, for example, the famous quote of Horace saying, "What coasts know not our blood?" It is not difficult to understand that Horace reflects on the extensive spread of the Roman Empire across the Mediterranean, Europe, and the Middle East, yet our understanding of the quote relies not on the explicitly articulated words, grammar, or dictionary definitions, but on implicit, cultural knowledge. The explicit articulation itself is, given grammatical and dictionary knowledge alone, not meaningful; coasts do not have knowledge of things, and what would it possibly mean to literally "know someone's blood"? To understand it presupposes historical knowledge of the expansion of the Roman Empire and requires an intuitive understanding of the metaphorical use of the words "coasts," "know," and "blood." A dual-process framework can clarify how discourse consists of both explicit elements (articulations, statements) and implicit meaning structures. Some researchers have even suggested the use of the notion of cognitive schemas to refer to the implicit or intuitive elements of discourses (much ass schemas have been suggested as the cognitive basis of the habitus). These researchers argue that these schemas are implicit and often nonlinguistic knowledge structures underlying and structuring explicit articulations of discourse (Van Dijk 2014; Malcolm and Sharifian 2002).

Although Giddens's (1984) distinction between discursive consciousness and practical consciousness has been used in discussions of dual-process models of culture this far (e.g., Lizardo and Strand 2010; Vaisey 2009), finding alternative terminology would be preferable. The discourse/practice divide is a problematic analog for reflective/intuitive cognition in the interest of both inter- and intradisciplinary integration. For example, as just argued, "discourse" is in discourse theory not used to denote linguistic or propositional cultural elements, but meaning structures in a broad sense. The terminology of Giddens is, therefore, incompatible with discourse theory, and if we want cognitive sociology to be "larger and more inclusive" (Danna 2014:1001), it is necessary to employ a vocabulary that is more accessible and inclusive. A larger obstacle to interdisciplinary bridging is that the terms "discourse" and "practice" are parts of a jargon with a long discipline-specific history, and are therefore inaccessible to those unfamiliar with cultural theory, including many cognitive scientists. Similarly, the term "consciousness" is problematic because it is used in a way specific to some social theoretical traditions, which constitutes another semantic obstacle to engaging in dialogue with disciplines where "consciousness" has a different meaning, such as psychology or neurology.[2] I therefore suggest that a more accessible terminology may simply be *explicit* (or *reflective*) and *implicit* (or *intuitive*) aspects of culture. Table 11.4 below provides a comparative overview of dual-process reasoning present in the cultural theories discussed, using the explicit/implicit divide. Using this terminology, explicit culture refers to the elements of culture primarily processed by reflective cognition, while implicit culture tends to be intuitively processed.

11.2.4 Toward an Integrated Dual-Process Framework

As we have seen thus far, dual-process reasoning is commonly present in some of the most influential cultural theories. There is, therefore, solid common ground for cognitive

Table 11.4 Overview of Dual-Process Reasoning in Cultural Theories

	Explicit Culture (Reflective)	Implicit Culture (Intuitive)
Geertz (1973)	Ideology	Common sense
Marxist theory	Ideology as superstructure	Unconscious ideology
Swidler (1986, 2001)	Cultural toolkits	Strategies of action
Giddens (1984)	Discursive consciousness	Practical consciousness
Vaisey (2009)	Justification	Motivation
Bourdieu (1977, 1990)	Official representations	Habitus
Mills (1940)	Vocabularies of motive	
Merton (1949)	Manifest functions	Latent functions
Discourse theory (e.g., Laclau and Mouffe 1985; also Malcolm and Sharifian 2002)	Articulations	Implicit meaning structures (Schemas)
Boltansky and Thévenot (1991/2006)	Economies of worth/ Justifications	
Lizardo and Strand (2010)	Repertoires	Practices
Affect control theory (Robinson et al. 2006)	Labels	Affective meanings

sociology to bridge dual-process insights from cognitive science with the dual-process reasoning already present in cultural sociology. The next step in the effort to bridge vocabularies is to compare how the concepts used for cultural dualities fit with those of dual-processing models of cognition. Besides recognizing how different cultural theories and their concepts are commensurable with each other and rely on shared cognitive microfoundations, comparing them and their conceptualizations of culture is a step toward developing a unified basic dual-process model of culture. Much as cognitive dual-process models have identified common correlates of the two process types, we can derive a preliminary set of common features of explicit and implicit aspects of culture by drawing on the descriptions of the concepts of the cultural theories discussed (see Table 11.5).

If we recognize that cultural reproduction relies on a cognitive microfoundation and that cognitive processes can be divided into two distinct types, it may seem straightforward to simply adopt the dual-process models of cognition into culture research. However, culture is not only cognition but is defined by being reproduced through social interactions and concrete instantiations. Culture is, therefore, more complex than cognition because it involves additional mechanisms and cannot accurately be described in terms of cognitive processes alone. Consequently, while dual-process models tell us much about how culture influences actions, more work is required in clearly defining the explicit and implicit aspects of culture and their relations to their cognitive counterpart. Therefore, we cannot simply import the reflective/intuitive divide to describe all forms of culture, as cognition is but a part of cultural reproduction. A text is, for example, not reflective, but it may be understood using reflective cognition.

Table 11.5 Common Characteristics of Explicit and Implicit Culture and Cognition

	Cultural Characteristics	Cognitive Characteristics
Explicit (reflective)	Verbalizable (conceptual or symbolic)	Deliberative
	Sense-making	Slow
	Justification and explanation	Limited capacity
	Propositional	Conscious
	Labeling	Rule-based/Reasoning
	Articulated discourse	Requires working memory
		Dependent on cognitive ability
Implicit (intuitive)	Nonlinguistic	Automatic/Autonomous
	Motivational	Fast
	Implicit knowledge	High-capacity
	Institutionalized practices	Nonconscious
	Dispositions and preferences	Associative
	Affective meaning	Independent of cognitive ability

11.3 Interactions in a Dual-Process Model of Culture

The most important implication of a dual-process model of culture, which suggests that culture comes in two distinct and different forms, is that sociologists must explore in detail how and when the two forms of culture interact with each other. Being able to clarify the relationship between the two, and the conditions under which they interact is also the main analytical advantage of using a dual-process model in empirical research. The relationship between explicit and implicit culture is far from straightforward, however. While the two forms of culture often interact, and/or regulate each other, they are also capable of operating in relative independence of each other. Explicit cultural elements may even be supported by unrecognized intuitive processes. Further, when they do interact, the interaction may be indirect, such as when intuitive cognition evokes an emotion without reflective awareness of what caused the emotion. This raises three key questions for cognitive sociologists to clarify:

1. Under what social conditions does implicit culture operate in relative independence of explicit culture? Implicit cultural elements may, under some circumstances, be reproduced without being recognized by corresponding explicit rationales (Lizardo 2007; Swidler 2001; Vaisey 2009). Explicit cultural rationales may even obscure and support the implicit reproduction of contradictory or antagonistic logics or behavior. This may even be the default condition, as most behavior is driven by intuitive and automatic cognitive processes while reflective processes intervene only when necessary, such as when being asked to explain or justify one's behavior (Bargh 1997; J. Evans and Stanovich 2013). But even then people seemingly construct post hoc rationales of intuitively driven actions, which seems to maintain a disconnect between the two (Swidler 2001; Vaisey 2009). For example, Eldén (2012) showed that Swedish couples understand and explain their relationship behavior (such as division of household chores or strategies for dealing with problems) using an individualized and gender egalitarian narrative (e.g., referring to individual preferences) while at the same time reproducing traditional gender norms through their actual practices. The individualized, nongendered, discourse-making sense of practices as autonomous choices, therefore, obscured the reproduction of traditional social structures through implicit mechanisms. Explicit cultural rationales may even obscure and support the implicit reproduction of contradictory or antagonistic logics or behavior (see for example Strandell 2018).

2. *Under what conditions does institutional change occur?* Another critical question for cognitive sociologists is to consider when explicit and implicit cultural elements interact and, consequently, cause change to implicit cultural elements that would otherwise be reproduced uninterrupted. Drawing on the cognitive dual-process model of J. Evans and Stanovich (2013) and their default-interventionist model of cognition, we can assume that implicit culture is reproduced independently of explicit culture or reflective cognition by default unless a critical degree of *social motivation and resources* is present. If this is the case, then cognitive sociologists must map out this process and the relevant conditions, resources, and sources of motivation necessary to force change. An example of a process leading to intervention by explicit culture is what Foucault called "problematization," in which implicit discourse becomes the object of explicit metadiscourse such as irony or critical debate, revealing previous presuppositions and destabilizing them (Foucault 1996). Such problematizations may be forced when a conflict between implicit and explicit culture becomes evident and difficult to ignore, such as when old rationales can no longer justify traditional institutions.

Likewise, researchers concerned with the interaction of repertoires and practices (or the lack thereof) have begun to consider the societal and structural circumstances under which one type of culture remains causally dominant (Lizardo and Strand 2010; Swidler 1986; Vaisey 2009). These researchers argue that under socially and institutionally stable, or "settled," conditions, intuitive cultural elements such as habitual practices tend to be most influential for actions, while also being taken for granted and relatively unrecognized as being culturally shaped. In contrast, during institutionally unstable times, explicit or ideological cultural elements may play a bigger causal role when previously intuitive practices become unfit for the new conditions, which forces explicit debate that draws on ideology or knowledge to institutionalize new practices (see Lizardo and Strand 2010 for an extended argument).

3. *How do explicit and implicit culture relate to each other on an individual level?* A dual-process model of culture suggests that cognitive sociologists must consider how explicit elements of culture translate into implicit elements, and vice versa, on an individual level. This question may appear more relevant for disciplines studying intraindividual cognitive processes, but to understand how culture durably affects people, it is necessary for us to take part in and develop this knowledge. To better understand this, we can, for

example, draw on established research from cognitive science and psychology to study learning processes (see Vaisey and Frye this volume). This also pertains to the larger question of what role, if any, explicit meanings, logics, and knowledge play in structuring people's experiences, emotions, and actions. Some researchers, such as discourse theorists and constructionists, have traditionally argued that explicit cultural elements fundamentally shape people while other researchers, such as repertoire or embodied theorists, have questioned the causal importance of explicit culture (e.g., Lizardo 2015; Swidler 1986, 2001).

It seems that a middle ground is supported by the cognitive dual-process theories, however, as reflective cognition can become automated and intuitive, but only indirectly and over time through repeated use (J. Evans 2008; Sun et al. 2005).[3] In other words, deliberately using an explicit logic, such as a certain discourse ("I should not generalize"), to override your default intuitive processes (say, a stereotype) may eventually shift one's default intuitive response toward that explicit logic. The crux is, of course, that deliberatively intervening in default intuitive processes frequently is effortful and requires sufficient motivation and resources (J. Evans and Stanovich 2013). The question, then, is perhaps not so much *if* explicit culture matters, but more a question of *when* explicit culture shapes intuitive cognition, how it is *transformed*, what *form* it takes, and in what *ways* it influences experience and action.

Thus far we have seen that dual-process reasoning is common in influential cultural theories and there is substantial common ground with the dual-process models of cognition. Conceptual translation work remains a main obstacle to full integration, however, as well as clarifying the defining characteristics and mechanisms distinguishing a cultural dual-process model. A dual-process model of culture can already provide us with a powerful analytical framework, new methodological tools,[4] access to important insights from cognitive science, and an integrative intra- and interdisciplinary vocabulary. However, a dual-process model also introduces new questions, challenges, and opportunities for understanding our research object.

NOTES

1. Some dual-process accounts take the dual-systems account one step further, and argue that the different brain regions involved in the two process types developed at two different stages in our evolutionary history (Epstein 1994; Over and Evans 1996; Reber 1993; Stanovich 2004).
2. In sociology, consciousness is often used to denote knowledge or awareness of something external, such as social relations, while in psychology it refers to the part of the mind one is aware of in contrast to unconscious aspects; in neurology, consciousness is the state or phenomenon of awareness, in contrast to the state of unconsciousness, as in lacking any awareness at all.
3. Furthermore, associative cognitive networks responsible for implicit knowledge are capable of learning complex and abstract logics, as well as behaving *as if* governed by rules (G. Evans 2015).
4. See for example Miles this volume and Shepherd this volume.

REFERENCES

Althusser, Louis. 1969. *For Marx*. Translated by Allen Lane. London: Penguin Press.

Bargh, John. 1997. "The Automaticity of Everyday Life." *Advances in Social Cognition* 10:1–61.

Berry, Dianne C., and Zoltan Dienes. 1993. *Implicit Learning*. Hove, UK: Erlbaum.

Boltanski, Luc, and Laurent Thévenot. 1991/2006. *On Justification: Economies of Worth*. Princeton, NJ: Princeton University Press.

Bourdieu, Pierre. 1977. *Outline of a Theory of Practice*. Edited by E. Gellner, J. Goody, S. Gudeman, M. Herzfeld, and J. Parry. Cambridge: Cambridge University Press.

Bourdieu, Pierre. 1990. *The Logic of Practice*. Cambridge: Polity Press.

Cerulo, Karen. 2010. "Mining the Intersections of Cognitive Sociology and Neuroscience." *Poetics* 38(2):115–32.

D'Andrade, Roy G. 1995. "The Growth of Schema Theory." pp. 122–49 in *The Development of Cognitive Anthropology*. Cambridge: Cambridge University Press.

Danna, Karen. 2014. "The Study of Culture and Cognition." *Sociological Forum* 29(4):1001–6.

De Neys, Wim, Walter Schaeken, and Géry. D'Ydewalle. 2005a. "Working Memory and Counterexample Retrieval for Causal Conditionals." *Thinking and Reasoning* 11:123–50.

De Neys, Wim, Walter Schaeken, and Géry. D'Ydewalle. 2005b. "Working Memory and Everyday Conditional Reasoning: Retrieval and Inhibition of Stored Counterexamples." *Thinking and Reasoning* 11:349–81.

DiMaggio, Paul. 1997. "Culture and Cognition." *Annual Review of Sociology* 23(25):263–87.

Eldén, Sara. 2012. "Scripts for the 'Good Couple': Individualization and the Reproduction of Gender Inequality." *Acta Sociologica* 55(1):3–18.

Engels, Friedrich. 1863/1968. *Marx and Engels Correspondence*. Edited by D. Torr. New York: International.

Epstein, Seymour. 1994. "Integration of Cognitive and Psychodynamic Unconscious." *American Psychologist* 49:709–24.

Evans, Garrett Nolan. 2015. "Two Projects in Theoretical Neuroscience : A Convolution-Based Metric for Neural Membrane Potentials and A Combinatorial Connectionist Semantic Network Method." PhD dissertation. Penn State University.

Evans, Jonathan St. B. T. 1989. *Bias in Human Reasoning: Causes and Consequences*. Brighton, UK: Erlbaum.

Evans, Jonathon St. B. T. 2003. "In two minds: dual-process accounts of reasoning." *Trends in Cognitive Sciences* 7(10):454–9.

Evans, Jonathan St. B. T. 2007. *Hypothetical Thinking: Dual Processes in Reasoning and Judgement*. Hove, UK: Psychology Press.

Evans, Jonathan St. B. T. 2008. "Dual-Processing Accounts of Reasoning, Judgment, and Social Cognition." *Annual Review of Psychology* 59:255–78.

Evans, Jonathan St. B. T. 2011. "Dual-Process Theories of Reasoning: Contemporary Issues and Developmental Applications." *Developmental Review* 31(2–3):86–102.

Evans, Jonathan St. B. T., and K. Frankish. 2009. "The Duality of Mind: An Historical Perspective." pp. 1–30 in *In Two Minds: Dual Processes and Beyond*, edited by J. S. B. T. Evans and K. Frankish. Oxford: Oxford University Press.

Evans, Jonathan St. B. T., and David. E. Over. 1996. *Rationality and Reasoning*. Hove, UK: Psychology Press.

Evans, Jonathan St. B. T., and K. E. Stanovich. 2013. "Dual-Process Theories of Higher Cognition: Advancing the Debate." *Perspectives on Psychological Science* 8(3):223–41.

Foucault, Michel. 1972. *The Archaeology of Knowledge*. London: Tavistock Publications.

Foucault, Michel. 1996. *Foucault Live: Collected Interviews, 1961–1984*. Edited by S. Lotringer. New York: Semiotext(e).

Geertz, Clifford. 1973. *The Interpretation of Cultures*. New York: Basic Books.

Giddens, Anthony. 1984. *The Constitution of Society: Outline of the Theory of Structuration*. Cambridge: Polity Press.

Gramsci, Antonio. 1990. "Culture and Ideological Hegemony." in *Culture and Society: Contemporary Debates*. Cambridge: Cambridge University Press.

Hassin, Ran R., J. S. Uleman, and John A. Bargh. 2005. *The New Unconscious*. Oxford: Oxford University Press.

Hunzaker, Mary Beth Fallin. 2014. "Making Sense of Misfortune Cultural Schemas, Victim Redefinition, and the Perpetuation of Stereotypes." *Social Psychology Quarterly* 77(2):166–84.

Kahneman, Daniel, and Shane Frederick. 2002. "Representativeness Revisited: Attribute Substitution in Intuitive Judgements." pp. 49–81 in *Heuristics and Biases: The Psychology of Intuitive Judgement*, edited by T. Gilovich, D. Griffin, and D. Kahneman. Cambridge: Cambridge University Press.

Khilstrom, John F. 1987. "The Cognitive Unconscious." *Science* 237:1445–52.

Laclau, Ernesto, and Chantal Mouffe. 1985. *Hegemony and Socialist Strategy*. 2nd ed. New York: Verso Books.

Lieberman, Matthew D. 2003. "Reflective and Reflexive Judgement Processes: A Social Cognitive Neuroscience Approach." pp. 44–67 in *Social Judgements: Implicit and Explicit Processes*, edited by J. P. Forgas, W. K. R., and W. von Hippel. New York: Cambridge University Press.

Lizardo, Omar. 2007. "Mirror Neurons' Collective Objects and the Problem of Transmission: Reconsidering Stephen Turner's Critique of Practice Theory." *Journal for the Theory of Social Behaviour* 37(3):319–50.

Lizardo, Omar. 2015. "Culture, Cognition and Embodiment." *International Encyclopedia of the Social and Behavioral Sciences* 5:576–81.

Lizardo, Omar, Robert Mowry, Brandon Sepulvado, Dustin S. Stoltz, Marshall A. Taylor, Justin Van Ness et al. 2016. "What Are Dual Process Models? Implications for Cultural Analysis in Sociology." *Sociological Theory* 34(4): 287–310.

Lizardo, Omar, and Michael Strand. 2010. "Skills, Toolkits, Contexts and Institutions: Clarifying the Relationship between Different Approaches to Cognition in Cultural Sociology." *Poetics* 38(2):205–28.

Lukes, Steven. 2005. *Power: A Radical View*. 2nd ed. London: Macmillan.

Malcolm, Ian G., and Farzad Sharifian. 2002. "Aspects of Aboriginal English Oral Discourse: An Application of Cultural Schema Theory." *Discourse Studies* 4(2):169–81.

Marx, Karl, and Friedrich Engels. 1932. *The German Ideology*. Moscow: The Marx-Engels institute.

Merton, Robert King. 1949. *Social Theory and Social Structure*. New York: Free Press.

Mills, Charles Wright. 1940. "Situated Actions and Vocabularies of Motive." *American Sociological Review* 5(6):904–13.

Nisbett, Richard, Kaiping Peng, Incheol Choi, and Ara Norenzayan. 2001. "Culture and Systems of Thought: Holistic vs Analytic Cognition." *Psychological Review* 108:291–301.

Nisbett, Richard E., and Timothy D. Wilson. 1977. "Telling More than We Know: Verbal Reports on Mental Processes." *Psychological Review* 84:231–95.

Pugh, Allison J. 2013. "What Good Are Interviews for Thinking about Culture? Demystifying Interpretive Analysis." *American Journal of Cultural Sociology* 1(1):42–68.

Quinn, Naomi, and Claudia Strauss. 1997. *A Cognitive Theory of Cultural Meaning*. Cambridge: Cambridge University Press.

Reber, Arthur S. 1993. *Implicit Learning and Tacit Knowledge*. Oxford: Oxford University Press.

Robinson, Dawn T., Lynn Smith-Lovin, and Allison Wisecup. 2006. "Affect Control Theory." pp. 179–202 in *Handbook of the Sociology of Emotions*, edited by J. Turner and J. Stets. Boston: Springer Press.

Sewell, William H., Jr. 2005. *Logics of History: Social Theory and Social Transformation*. Chicago: Chicago University Press.

Shepherd, Hana. 2011. "The Cultural Context of Cognition: What the Implicit Association Test Tells Us about How Culture Works." *Sociological Forum* 26(1):121–43.

Smith, Eliot R., and Elizabeth C. Collins. 2009. "Dual-Process Models: A Social Psychological Perspective." pp. 187–216 in *In Two Minds: Dual Processes and Beyond*, edited by Jonathan. St. B. T. Evans and Keith Frankish. Oxford: Oxford University Press.

Smith, Eliot R., and Jamie DeCoster. 2000. "Dual-Process Models in Social and Cognitive Psychology: Conceptual Integration and Links to Underlying Memory Systems." *Personality and Social Psychology* 4(2):108–31.

Spunt, Robert P., and Matthew D. Lieberman. 2013. "The Busy Social Brain: Evidence for Automaticity and Control in the Neural Systems Supporting Social Cognition and Action Understanding." *Psychological Science* 24(1):80–6.

Stanovich, Keith E. 2004. *The Robot's Rebellion: Finding Meaning in the Age of Darwin*. Chicago: Chicago University Press.

Stanovich, Keith E. 2009. *What Intelligence Tests Miss: The Psychology of Rational Thought*. New Haven, CT, and London: Yale University Press.

Stanovich, Keith E. 2011. *Rationality and the Reflective Mind*. New York: Oxford University Press.

Strandell, Jacob. 2018. "Increasing marriage rates despite high individualization: Understanding the Role of Internal Reference in Swedish Marriage Discourse." *Cultural Sociology* 12 (1): 75–95.

Sun, Ron, Paul Slusarz, and Christh Terry. 2005. "The Interaction of the Explicit and the Implicit in Skill Learning: A Dual-Process Approach." *Psychological Review* 112(1):159–92.

Swidler, Ann. 1986. "Culture in Action: Symbols and Strategies." *American Sociological Review* 51(2):273–86.

Swidler, Ann. 2001. *Talk of Love: How Culture Matters*. Chicago: University of Chicago Press.

Thompson, Valerie A. 2009. "Dual-Process Theories: A Metacognitive Perspective." pp. 171–96 in *In Two Minds: Dual Processes and Beyond*, edited by J. S. B. T. Evans and K. Frankish. Oxford: Oxford University Press.

Thompson, Valerie, Jamie Turner, and Gordon Pennycock. 2013. "Intuition, Reason, and Metacognition." *Cognitive Psychology* 63(3):107–47.

Vaisey, Stephen. 2009. "Motivation and Justification: A Dual-Process Model of Culture in Action." *American Journal of Sociology* 114(6):1675–715.

Vaisey, Stephen. 2013. "Is Interviewing Compatible with the Dual-Process Model of Culture?" *American Journal of Cultural Sociology* 2(1):150–58.

Van Dijk, Teun. 2014. *Discourse and Knowledge: A Sociocognitive Approach*. United Kingdom: Cambridge University Press.

Wason, Peter C., and Jonathan St. B. T. Evans. 1975. "Dual-Processes in Reasoning?" *Cognition* 3:141–54.

Wilson, Timothy D. 2002. *Strangers to Ourselves*. Cambridge, MA: Belknap.

Wilson, Timothy D., and Elizabeth W. Dunn. 2004. "Self-Knowledge: Its Limits, Value, and Potential for Improvement." *Annual Review of Psychology* 55:492–518.

Young, Jock. 2003. "Merton with Energy, Katz with Structure." *Theoretical Criminology* 7(3):388–414.

Zeigler-Hill, Virgil, and Erin M. Myers. 2011. "An Implicit Theory of Self-Esteem: The Consequences of Perceived Self-Esteem for Romantic Desirability." *Evolutionary Psychology: An International Journal of Evolutionary Approaches to Psychology and Behavior* 9(2):147–80.

Žižek, Slavoj. 1989. *The Sublime Object of Ideology*. London: Verso Books.

CHAPTER 12

....

METAPHORICAL
CREATIVITY
the role of context

....

ZOLTÁN KÖVECSES

WHERE do we recruit novel and unconventional conceptual materials from when we speak, think, and act metaphorically? This question has been partially answered by several scholars in the cognitive linguistic literature. In this chapter I hope to answer the question more fully than it was done previously and thus provide a more complete account of metaphorical creativity. By metaphorical creativity I mean the production and use of conceptual metaphors and/or their linguistic manifestations that are novel or unconventional in particular discourse contexts. Metaphorical creativity in discourse can involve a variety of distinct forms. In *Metaphor in Culture* (2005), I distinguished two types: creativity that is based on the source domain and creativity that is based on the target. "Source-related" creativity can be of two kinds: "source-internal" and "source-external" creativity. Source-internal creativity involves cases that Lakoff and Turner (1989) describe as elaboration and extending, where unused source-internal conceptual materials are used to comprehend the target. For example, given the conventional DEATH IS SLEEP metaphor, we find in Hamlet's soliloquy "To die to sleep? Perchance to dream!," where dreaming is an extension of the source domain (Lakoff and Turner 1989). "Source-external" cases of creativity operate with what I called the "range of the target" phenomenon, in which a particular target domain receives new, additional source domains in its conceptualization (Kövecses 2005). For instance, Ning Yu (1998) notes that the concept of HAPPINESS is conceptualized by means of the metaphor HAPPINESS IS FLOWERS IN THE HEART that is additional to other, more conventional source domains that are present both in Chinese and English. The type of creativity in discourse that is based on the target was also described by Kövecses (2005). In target-based creativity, elements of a target domain that are not part of the routine mappings between a source and a target "select" elements from a source domain otherwise not conventionally participating in the mappings. One such case is when the expression *fire-exit* is used metaphorically in connection with the target domain of EUROPEAN UNION (see Musolff 2001; Kövecses 2005).

According to Lakoff and Turner (1989), metaphorical creativity in poetry is the result of four common conceptual devices that poets use in manipulating otherwise shared conceptual metaphors. These include the devices of elaboration, extension, questioning, and combining (Lakoff and Turner 1989). However, other scholars have shown that these cognitive devices, or strategies, exist not only in poetic language but also in more ordinary forms of language use, such as journalism (see, e.g., Jackendoff and Aaron 1991; Semino 2008). Moreover, it has been noticed that not all cases of the creative use of metaphor in poetry are the result of the four cognitive devices just mentioned. Turner and others proposed that in many cases literature and poetry make use of what he and Fauconnier call "(conceptual) blends," in which various elements from two or more spaces, domains, or frames, can be conceptually fused, or integrated (see, e.g., Turner 1996; Fauconnier and Turner 2002). In addition, Landau (2017) provides a good overview of work on metaphorical creativity in social psychology.

In a way all of these accounts share the view that metaphorical creativity builds on conceptual relationships (sets of mappings) between two domains—a source and a target (see Lakoff and Johnson 1980, 1999; Kövecses 2010a). But a fuller account a metaphorical creativity requires more. There are many examples that do not simply involve new mappings between well-established source and target domains. I argued in previous publications (especially Kövecses 2010a, 2010b, 2015) that many cases of creativity cannot be explained unless we pay close attention to the role of context in our account.

12.1 How Do Metaphors Emerge?

Before we turn to the crucial role of context in metaphorical creativity, we need to briefly survey the ways in which metaphors arise. We can find out if we try to answer the following question: On what basis do we pair target concepts with particular source concepts to form a conceptual metaphor with a set of source-to-target mappings? In this section, I discuss four ways that can be distinguished.

First, the choice of a particular source to go with a particular target can also be motivated by some embodied experience (Lakoff and Johnson 1980, 1999; Grady 1997a, 1997b; Kövecses 2010a). For example, the correlation between the increase in the intensity of an activity or a state, on the one hand, and the production of body heat, on the other, is inevitable for the kinds of bodies that we have. This correlation forms the basis of a conceptual metaphor: INTENSITY IS HEAT. Since INTENSITY is an aspect of many concepts, the source domain of heat will apply to many concepts, such as ANGER, LOVE, LUST, WORK, ARGUMENT, and so forth. In general, many conceptual metaphors (i.e., source and target pairings) are motivated by such bodily correlations in experience.

Second, in a large number of other cases, the basis of combining a source with a target concept is some kind of real or assumed similarity, often a set of similar structural relations (see, e.g., Gentner 1983; Holyoak and Thagard 1996; Glucksberg and Keysar 1993). For example, we can find shared generic-level structure in such domains as HUMAN LIFETIME and the LIFE-CYCLE OF PLANTS. This case is of course the highly conventional metaphor: THE HUMAN LIFETIME IS THE LIFE-CYCLE OF A PLANT. Humans have the ability to recognize shared generic-level structure in distinct domains.

Third, metaphorical conceptualization can work jointly with the construal operation of schematization. Take the conceptualization of the biblical notion of HEAVEN (Kövecses 2011). It is metaphorically viewed as a number of different physical places that share the property of "being ideal." That is, the source domains of the concept of HEAVEN are all places where (eternal) life is good and pleasant—free of pain, sorrow, injustice, and so forth. The target concept of HEAVEN thus appears to be a schematically ideal place; hence the metaphor HEAVEN IS AN IDEAL PHYSICAL PLACE. The particular and specific nature and qualities of the places in the source domains are in a way "bleached out" with only the schematic idealization remaining. That is to say, we can think of this schematic idealization as heaven. In other words, the target domain seems to be an idealized schematization of a variety of particular and specific source domains. In such cases, we can suggest that the target is a schematization of the various source domains relating to the target domain. The nature of this process of schematization is essentially metonymic. The sources are specific instances of the target; this is the generic-level metonymy A PARTICULAR INSTANCE OF A CATEGORY FOR THE WHOLE CATEGORY. We can put this in the present example as PARTICULAR PLACES THAT ARE PLEASANT TO BE IN (STAND) FOR HEAVEN. Since such places and heaven share only the property of "being ideal," we can construe the basically metonymic relationship as a metaphor. The specific instances that share the feature become the schematized target domain of a number of different but related source domains (i.e., the different source domains share a high-level feature). I believe that this is a metonymy-based process, but its end result functions as a metaphor, such as the various specific-level versions of HEAVEN IS AN IDEAL PHYSICAL PLACE.

Fourth, the cognitive operations at our disposal produce a particular conceptual system informed by and based on embodiment. But conceptual systems emerge as a result of contextual factors as well. Both the cognitive operations and the conceptual systems function under the pressure of a vast range of contextual factors. Simply put, the cognitive operations and the resulting conceptual systems function in context. The conceptual system and the context in which it emerges are in continuous interaction. The cognitive operations we use are universal in the sense that all (normal) human beings are capable of performing them. Much of the embodiment on which conceptual systems are based is universal (but see Casasanto 2009). Despite the universality of the (availability of) operations and the universality of embodiment, the conceptual systems vary considerably both cross-culturally and within cultures, with individual variation as a limiting case. This is possible because the contexts are variable and in different contexts people often use differential operations. In addition, the prominence of certain cognitive operations may be greater or smaller across groups of people. The changeability of contexts and that of cognitive operations as affected by differential contexts leads to differential conceptual systems.

The significance of context in shaping the conceptual system is also noted by Barsalou (1999), who states:

> Variable embodiment allows individuals to adapt the perceptual symbols in their conceptual system to specific environments. Imagine that different individuals consume somewhat different varieties of the same plants because they live in different locales. Through perceiving their respective foods, different individuals develop somewhat different perceptual symbols to represent them. As a result, somewhat different conceptual systems develop through the schematic symbol formation process, each tuned optimally to its typical referents.   (Barsalou 1999:598)

Here Barsalou talks about "different locales," a kind of context that I call the "physical environment" (Kövecses 2005, 2010b). As we will see, in addition to the physical environment, I recognize the influence of several other contextual factors. I use the term "context" very broadly, to include both the linguistic and the nonlinguistic context.

Let me illustrate this broad conception of context with just one example. It involves the topic of the discourse. This has to do with what we know about the major entities participating in the discourse in a long article about the American cyclist Lance Armstrong in the January 25–27 issue of the American newspaper *USA Today*. The article is about Armstrong's confessions concerning his doping and that his confessions up to that point had not been sufficient to redeem himself and clean up the sport of cycling. Several experts who were interviewed thought that additional steps must be taken by Armstrong to achieve this. One specialist in crisis management said this in an interview: "To use an analogy from the Tour de France, he's still in the mountain stage, and will be for some time" (2013, *USA Today*, 6W Sports, Weekly International Edition). What we have here is that the specialist has extensive knowledge about the topic of the discourse, which is Armstrong's doping scandal. That knowledge includes that as a cyclist Armstrong participated in several Tour de France events and that this race has several "mountain stages." In other words, the topic of the discourse primed the speaker to choose a metaphor to express a particular idea; namely, that, in order to come completely clean, Armstrong has a long and difficult way to go. This idea was expressed by the *mountain stage* metaphor, which is based on the mapping "impediment to motion à difficulty of action (making full confession and being forgiven)" in the ACTION IS MOTION conceptual metaphor.

As this example and numerous others indicate (see, e.g., Kövecses 2010b, 2015), the immediate (or local) context can induce the emergence of novel metaphors in particular communicative situations. The emergence of the metaphor takes place in a local, immediate situation in the course of the online production and comprehension of the metaphor.

12.2 TYPES OF CONTEXT AND KINDS OF CONTEXTUAL FACTORS

If we examine the use of metaphors in discourse in detail, we can see that they are influenced by a large variety of contextual factors. The specific contextual factors that produce metaphors can be grouped into four large categories: situational context, discourse context, conceptual-cognitive context, and bodily context (see Kövecses 2015). All four of these context types can be broken down into various kinds of specific contextual factors.

Before we begin to look at these, it is useful to make a distinction. In my book *Metaphor in Culture* (Kövecses 2005), I distinguish two large sets of factors that seem to play a role in metaphor variation: those that have to do with *differential experience* and those that have to do with *differential "cognitive styles."* The contextual factors that I summarize in this section have to do with differential experience. The factors subsumed under differential experience consist of some *contentful knowledge* (i.e., one that has conceptual content) that reflects (direct or indirect) experiences of the world. These reflect experiences that can trigger the use of particular metaphors. In order for conceptualizers to produce and comprehend metaphors they need to be able to resort to the experiences that are used in the metaphors. These experiences provide the common ground that allow conceptualizers to produce and comprehend contextually induced, or generated, metaphors in discourse.

The factors under cognitive styles, by contrast, reflect particular *ways* in which experiences of the world need to be presented, given the prevalent cognitive conventions and preferences of a language community. Such issues as at which level a metaphorical idea is presented (schematicity), how it should be framed (framing), to what degree it should be conventionalized (conventionalization), which aspect of the body it should involve or profile (experiential focus), and others, are *presentational* in nature. In general, the former set of factors respond to the question of "what" can prompt or prime the use of certain metaphors, whereas the latter set to the question of "how" metaphorical conceptualization needs to be presented in a language community. The factors listed under differential cognitive style function as constraints on the speaker-conceptualizer only, who is to follow the cognitive conventions of the language community. The hearer (comprehender) is not constrained in this way.

We can now turn to the four types of context mentioned previously (situational, discourse, conceptual-cognitive, bodily) and the specific kinds of contextual factors they subsume. Throughout the discussion I rely heavily on my book *Where Metaphors Come From* (Kövecses 2015).

12.2.1 Situational Context

The situational context comprises a variety of different contextual factors. Most commonly it can be thought of as the physical environment, the social situation, and the cultural context.

12.2.1.1 *Physical Environment*

The *physical environment* can shape metaphorical meaning making. The physical environment includes the flora, the fauna, the landscape, the temperature, the weather, perceptual properties of the situation, and so on. For example, it is a common observation that American English metaphors relating to the physical environment are characteristically different from those of other English-speaking countries (see, e.g., Kövecses 2000). The small-scale, local environment, such as the visible events in or the perceptual properties of a situation, can also make their influence felt in shaping metaphors. Physical events and their consequences are well demonstrated by a statement made by the American journalist who traveled to New Orleans to do an interview with the American musician Fats Domino two years after the devastation wreaked by Hurricane Katrina, when the city of New Orleans was still struggling with many of the consequences of the hurricane. The journalist comments:

> The 2005 hurricane capsized Domino's life, though he's loath to confess any inconvenience or misery outside of missing his social circle.
>
> (*USA Today*, September 21, 2007, Section 6B)

The metaphorical statement "The 2005 hurricane *capsized* Domino's life" is based on the general metaphor LIFE IS A JOURNEY and its more specific version LIFE IS A SEA JOURNEY. The SEA JOURNEY source domain is chosen probably because of the role of the sea in the hurricane. More importantly, it should be noted that the verb *capsize* is used (as opposed to, say, *run aground*), though it is not a conventional linguistic manifestation of either the general JOURNEY or the more specific SEA JOURNEY source domains. I suggest that this verb is selected by the journalist as a result of the then (still) visible consequences in New Orleans of the hurricane as a devastating physical event. The physical setting thus possibly triggers the extension of an existing conventional conceptual metaphor and causes the speaker/conceptualizer to choose an unconventional metaphorical expression that best fits that setting.

12.2.1.2 *Social Situation*

The *social situation* consists of social aspects of life that typically center around notions such as gender, class, politeness, work, education, social organizations, social structure, and others. All of these can play a role in metaphorical conceptualization. For example, Kolodny (1975, 1984) shows that American men and women developed very different metaphorical images for what they conceived of as the frontier in America. While the women commonly thought of America as a "garden to be cultivated," men conceptualized it as "virgin land to be taken." (For several more examples, see Kövecses 2005.)

12.2.1.3 *Cultural Context*

The *cultural context* involves both the global context (the shared knowledge represented in the conceptual system) and the local context (the specific knowledge in a given communicative situation) (see also what follows). An example of how the global context can affect metaphorical conceptualization can be seen in the way different concepts can produce differential metaphors in different cultures and languages, such as the metaphors for anger: ANGER IS HEAT (OF FLUID OR SOLID) in a large number of languages such as English and Hungarian, whereas in Chinese the metaphor can also involve GAS as its source domain—as a result of the influence of Yin and Yang theory (see Yu 1998). The more immediate local context can play a similar role in the production of metaphors (see Kövecses 2010a).

12.2.2 Discourse Context

The discourse context involves the surrounding discourse, the previous discourses on the same topic, and the dominant forms of discourse related to a particular subject matter.

12.2.2.1 *Surrounding Discourse*

The *surrounding discourse* is simply the linguistic context—often referred to as "cotext." Viewed from the perspective of the producer of discourse, the speaker, elements of the preceding discourse (either by the speaker/conceptualizer 1 or the hearer/conceptualizer 2) can influence the choice of metaphors, as was shown in an example taken from *The Times* by Kövecses (2010): "which helped to tilt the balance—and Mr Hain—over the edge." In this case, the contextually induced metaphor arises from the elliptical use of the verb *tilt* in the phrase *tilt Mr Hain over the edge*. It is the presence of *tilt* in the immediate cotext that leads to the second use of the metaphor.

The metaphorical expression *tilt the balance* is a conventional one and is a linguistic example of the metaphor UNCERTAINTY IS BALANCE (OF THE SCALES) (and CERTAINTY IS LACK OF BALANCE (OF THE SCALES)). In the metaphor, making a choice (i.e., eliminating uncertainty) corresponds to tilting the balance. The second expression, *tilt someone over the edge*, is much less conventional than the first. In the second expression the relevant conceptual metaphor is LOSS OF RATIONAL/MORAL CONTROL IS LOSS OF PHYSICAL CONTROL, such as PHYSICAL FALL (INTO A (DEEP) HOLE). The cause of the loss of rational/moral control is the same as the cause that made the commission involved in the Hain case just mentioned arrive at a decision—namely, "showing 'contempt' for the law." There are many linguistic expressions that could be used to convey the idea "to cause someone to fall down (into a hole)," including *push, drive, force, jolt, nudge, poke, prod, propel, shove, press, butt,* and so on. Of these, the most conventional ones are certainly *push* and *drive*; both of which occur in the idiom *push/drive someone over the edge.* However, in the discourse the author uses *tilt,* which is an additional but somewhat unmotivated possibility to express the idea of causing someone to physically fall down (into a hole). What makes it acceptable and natural, though, is that it fits the metaphor (no matter how unconventionally), on the one hand, and that it is elicited by the word used in the previous linguistic metaphor, on the other. This means that the phonetic shape of an expression in discourse can function as an elicitor of a metaphorically used expression in the same discourse, provided that the condition of fitting the required conceptual metaphor is also met.

12.2.2.2 *Previous Discourses on the Same Topic*

The metaphors used in previous discourses on the same topic as the current discourse can also introduce new metaphors into the discourse. This can take a variety of forms ranging from elaborating, extending, questioning, negating, reflecting on, ridiculing, to otherwise taking advantage of a metaphor previously introduced. For example, an MP in the British Parliament responded to the then–prime minister Tony Blair, who said that he does not have a reverse gear (i.e., he can only go forward), by means of making the following statement: "but when you're on the edge of a cliff it is good to have a reverse gear" (example taken from Semino 2008). This was a humorous twist induced by the prior discourse on the PROGRESS IS MOTION FORWARD conceptual metaphor.

12.2.2.3 *Dominant Forms of Discourse and Intertextuality*

Certain forms of discourse can acquire dominant status in a community. When this happens, the metaphor used in or based on this discourse can become widespread both temporally (historically) and spatially (cross-culturally). For example, the discourse of Christianity commonly gives rise to the use of metaphors in the Christian world.

12.2.3 Conceptual-Cognitive Context

This type of context consists of a variety of different kinds, including the following: the metaphorical conceptual system, knowledge about the elements of discourse, ideology, knowledge about past events, and interests and concerns.

12.2.3.1 *Metaphorical Conceptual System*

Concepts can stand in a metaphorical relationship with one another (e.g., LIFE IS A JOURNEY, ARGUMENT IS WAR) in long-term memory. Given such metaphorical relationships between concepts, their presence or absence in the metaphorical conceptual system may lead to the production and comprehension of particular metaphors. A metaphorical conceptual system can function as context in this sense. Given an intended metaphorical meaning, we can search the conventional metaphorical conceptual system for the best choice of metaphor. This happens in cases where a conventionalized metaphorical meaning is expressed via a conventional linguistic metaphor, with a matching target element activating the corresponding mapping in an existing conceptual metaphor (e.g., the meaning "supporting an argument" by means of the word "defend" in the ARGUMENT IS WAR conceptual metaphor).

12.2.3.2 *Knowledge about Elements of the Discourse*

Conceptualizers often rely on the knowledge they have about the main elements of the discourse: about the speaker, hearer, and topic. For example, I have noticed that in many newspaper articles knowledge about the topic as a contextual factor can lead to the creation of new metaphors (Kövecses 2010). We have seen an example for this earlier, involving the cyclist Lance Armstrong. As the next example, let us take a case that involves the famous British soccer player David Beckham. In an article, a journalist remarked:

> Beckham is 32. He has not played top-class football since November. Los Angeles Galaxy are sardines not sharks in the ocean of footy.
>
> (Comment section of *The Times*, January 30, 2008, p. 14)

The journalist makes a recommendation to Fabio Capello, the then new Italian head coach of the English team, that he should play David Beckham against Switzerland in an upcoming game at Wembley Stadium, despite the fact that Beckham had not played top-class football for several months at the time. If Beckham is given a chance to play, he will have played on the English national team 100 times, and this would be a nice way of saying good-bye to him as regards his career on the national team. The author of the article explains that he or she is aware that Beckham is not fully prepared for this last game on the national team. The interesting issue for us is to see how the author arrived at the novel metaphors according to which the American soccer team, the Los Angeles Galaxy, "are *sardines* not *sharks* in the *ocean* of footy"? In all probability, it is the author's knowledge about David Beckham, the main topic of the discourse, that gives rise to the metaphors. The author (together with us) knows that Beckham plays for the Los Angeles Galaxy, a team located in Los Angeles, which, in turn, is a city on the Pacific Ocean, and the Pacific Ocean contains sardines and sharks. In somewhat more technical language, we could say that the frame for Beckham as a football player includes the name of the team that he plays for and the place where the team is located, which in turn evokes the frame of the Pacific Ocean. The frame for the Pacific Ocean in turn involves the various kinds of fish that live in that ocean.

12.2.3.3 *Ideology*

Ideology can also be a formative factor in the use of metaphors in discourse. One's ideology concerning major social and political issues may govern the choice of metaphors (as work by, for instance, Goatly 2007, shows). A good example of this is George Lakoff's

(1996) study of American politics, where conservatives tend to use THE NATION IS A STRICT FATHER FAMILY metaphor, while liberals prefer THE NATION IS A NURTURANT PARENT FAMILY version of the generic metaphor THE NATION IS A FAMILY.

12.2.3.4 *Knowledge about Past Events*

Being aware of past events and states (i.e., items both in short-term and long-term memory) shared by the conceptualizers may also lead to the emergence of specific metaphors in discourse. A special case of this involves a situation in which the speaker assumes that the hearer has a particular mental state. Such memories of events can belong to the life of a community or an individual. It has been often observed that the memory of historical events can lead to the production (and comprehension) of certain metaphors (see, e.g., Deignan 2003; Kövecses 2005). Different historical contexts can create differential preferences for particular LIFE metaphors among Hungarians and Americans (see Kövecses 2005). The particular events in a specific communicative situation preceding an act of metaphorical conceptualization may also produce similar effects.

12.2.3.5 *Interests and Concerns*

People are commonly prompted to use particular metaphors (more precisely, metaphorical source domains) in real communicative situations relative to their interests and concerns about the world (see Kövecses 2005). Entire groups and individuals can be said to have certain characteristic interests or concerns that may affect the way they make meaning metaphorically. For example, since Americans are claimed to be dynamically oriented, rather than passive, in their attitude to life, and, relatedly, are sports-loving in general, it is not surprising that they use a large number of sports metaphors. Similarly, if a person has some kind of professional interest, that person is likely to draw metaphors from his or her sphere of interest (see Kövecses 2005).

12.2.4 Bodily context

A particular state of the body can produce particular metaphorical conceptualizations in specific cases, such as a poet's or writer's illness. Elsewhere, I showed how Dickinson's choice of metaphors may have been influenced by her optical illness (see Kövecses 2010b, 2015). Moreover, individual bodily specificities can have an influence on which metaphors are used by particular people. For example, Casasanto (2009) found that left-handers prefer to use the MORAL IS LEFT, as opposed to the MORAL IS RIGHT metaphor. Such metaphors contrast with the metaphors that evolve on the basis of the general (universal) properties of the human body (i.e., the primary metaphors, as proposed by Grady [1997a, 1997b] and Lakoff and Johnson [1999]). In recent work (Kövecses 2015), I argue that we can take the body as a further aspect of the context—among the several others listed above. On this view, the body—especially those aspects of it that are activated in the ongoing situation—can influence the choice of metaphors. The body is not only responsible for the production of hundreds of conceptual metaphors through the many correlations in subjective and sensory-motor experience (cf. Grady 1997a, 1997b; Lakoff and Johnson 1999) but also it can prime the use of particular metaphors in more immediate, local contexts (see, e.g., Gibbs 2006; Gibbs and Colston 2012). In other words, the body can lead to the production of metaphors in discourse in the same way as the other contextual factors previously mentioned can. This change in our view of the status of the body would imply that the idea according to which the body and context that were seen as being in diametrical opposition would have to be abandoned and that it would have to be recognized that the body can produce metaphors locally as well, not only globally and universally.

12.3 LOCAL AND GLOBAL CONTEXT

As we have seen, within the varied set of contextual factors that I have briefly introduced, two general types of context can be distinguished: local and global. The *local context* involves the specific knowledge conceptualizers have about some aspect of the immediate communicative situation. Thus, the local context implies specific knowledge that attaches to the conceptualizers in a specific communicative situation. It corresponds, at least roughly, to Clark's (1996) personal common ground. By contrast, the *global context* consists of the conceptualizers' general knowledge concerning the nonimmediate situation that characterizes a community. It implies knowledge shared by an entire community of conceptualizers. Thus, the notion is close to Clark's (1996) communal common ground. The distinction between global and local context is mostly of a theoretical nature. In many actual communicative situations, there is no sharp dividing line between the two types of context.

Figure 12.1 summarizes the various kinds and types of contextual factors, as discussed previously:

The figure is somewhat misleading in that it presents the four major context types as having rigid boundaries. In reality, the context types overlap and metaphorical conceptualization in particular communicative situations commonly involves more than one context type.

12.4 CONCLUSIONS

As we have seen in the paper and in other publications (such as Kövecses, 2010b, 2015), there is a considerable number of cases that indicate that context is not simply an aid to comprehending novel metaphors but also is very much a creator and shaper of novel metaphors. The various types of context prompt speakers to use unconventional and even

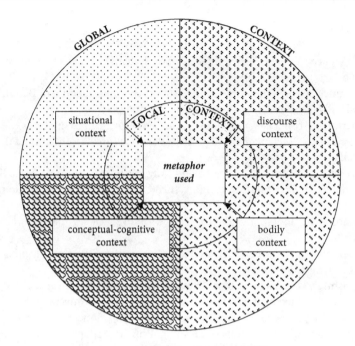

FIGURE 12.1 Summary of contextual factors.

unique metaphors. If we examine metaphorical conceptualization in natural discourse, we find robust evidence for this claim. Interestingly enough, though, researchers in conceptual metaphor theory did not pay much attention to this phenomenon. The "standard" version of conceptual metaphor theory (where conceptual metaphors are seen as being constituted by stable sets of mappings between a source and a target domain based on correlations in bodily experience) should recognize the importance of context if it aspires to account for a large segment of metaphorical creativity.

My claim is that in addition to the well-studied conceptual metaphors and metaphorical analogies used to convey meanings and achieve rhetorical effects in discourse, conceptualizers are also very much aware and take advantage of the various factors that make up the (local and global) context in which metaphorical conceptualization takes place. In some cases, the contextual factors will simply lead to the emergence and use of well-worn, conventional metaphorical expressions, but in others they may lead conceptualizers to choose genuinely novel or unconventional metaphorical expressions. The core idea is that we try to be coherent not only with universal embodiment but also with most of the factors that regulate the conceptualization of the world, such as, in addition to the body, the situational, discourse, and cognitive-conceptual context. Many context-induced metaphorical expressions appear to be novel and unconventional. This is because the (immediate) context of discourse varies from one occurrence of discourse to another, and with it the conceptual and linguistic metaphors that are based on the context will also vary. I suggest that accepting this idea would greatly expand our ability to systematically account for many hitherto unaccounted-for cases of metaphorical creativity.

REFERENCES

Barsalou, Lawrence W. 1999. "Perceptual Symbol Systems." *Behavioral and Brain Sciences* 22:577–660.

Casasanto, Daniel. 2009. "Embodiment of Abstract Concepts: Good and Bad in Right- and Left-Handers." *Journal of Experimental Psychology* 138(3):351–67.

Clark, Herbert. 1996. *Using Language*. New York: Cambridge University Press.

Deignan, Alice. 2003. "Metaphorical Expressions and Culture: An Indirect Link." *Metaphor and Symbol* 18(4): 255–71.

Fauconnier, Gilles, and Mark Turner. 2002. *The Way We Think*. New York: Basic Books.

Gentner, Dedre. 1983. Structure-Mapping: A Theoretical Framework for Analogy. *Cognitive Science* 7:155–70.

Gibbs, Raymond W. 2006. *Embodiment and Cognitive Science*. New York: Cambridge University Press.

Gibbs, Raymond W., and Herbert Colston. 2012. *Interpreting Figurative Meaning*. New York: Cambridge University Press.

Glucksberg, Sam, and Boaz Keysar. 1993. "How Metaphors Work." pp. 401–24 in *Metaphor and Thought*, 2nd ed., edited by A. Ortony. New York: Cambridge University Press.

Goatly, Andrew. 2007. *Washing the Brain*. Amsterdam: Benjamins.

Grady, Joseph E. 1997a. "Foundations of Meaning: Primary Metaphors and Primary Scenes." PhD dissertation, University of California at Berkeley.

Grady, Joseph E. 1997b. "*Theories are Buildings* Revisited." *Cognitive Linguistics* 8:267–90.

Holyoak, Keith, and Paul Thagard. 1996. *Mental Leaps: Analogy in Creative Thought*. Cambridge, MA: MIT Press.

Jackendoff, Ray, and David Aaron. 1991. "More than Cool Reason: A Field Guide to Poetic Metaphor by George Lakoff and Mark Johnson." *Language* 67(2):320–28.

Kolodny, Annette. 1975. The Lay of the Land: Metaphor as Experience and History in American Life and Letters. Chapel Hill: The University of North Carolina Press.

Kolodny, Annette. 1984. The Land Before Her: Fantasy and Experience of the American Frontiers, 1630–1860. Chapel Hill: The University of North Carolina Press.

Kövecses, Zoltán. 2000. *American English. An Introduction*. Peterborough, Canada: Broadview Press.

Kövecses, Zoltán. 2005. *Metaphor in Culture: Universality and Variation*. Cambridge: Cambridge University Press.

Kövecses, Zoltán. 2010a. *Metaphor: A Practical Introduction*. New York: Oxford University Press.

Kövecses, Zoltán. 2010b. "A New Look at Metaphorical Creativity in Cognitive Linguistics." *Cognitive Linguistics* 21(4):663–97.

Kövecses, Zoltán. 2011. "The Biblical Story Retold: A Cognitive Linguistic Perspective." pp. 325–54 in *Cognitive Linguistics. Convergence and Expansion*, edited by Mario Brdar, Stefan Th. Gries, and Milena Zic Fuchs. Amsterdam: John Benjamins.

Kövecses, Zoltán. 2015. *Where Metaphors Come From: Reconsidering Context in Metaphor*. New York: Oxford University Press.

Lakoff, George. 1996. *Moral Politics*. Chicago: University of Chicago Press.

Lakoff, George, and Mark Johnson. 1980. *Metaphors We Live By*. Chicago: University of Chicago Press.

Lakoff, George, and Mark Johnson. 1999. *Philosophy in the Flesh*. New York: Basic Books.

Lakoff, George, and Mark Turner. 1989. *More than Cool Reason: A Field Guide to Poetic Metaphor*. Chicago: University of Chicago Press.

Landau, Mark. 2017. *Conceptual Metaphor in Social Psychology*. New York: Routledge.

Langacker, Ronald. 1987. *Foundations of Cognitive Grammar*. Vol. 1. Stanford, CA: Stanford University Press.

Musolff, Andreas. 2001. "Political Imagery of Europe: A House without Exit Doors?" *Journal of Multilingual and Multicultural Development* 21(3):216–29.

Semino, Elena. 2008. *Metaphor in Discourse*. Cambridge: Cambridge University Press.

Turner, Mark. 1996. *The Literary Mind*. New York: Oxford University Press.

Yu, Ning. 1998. *The Contemporary Theory of Metaphor: A Perspective from Chinese*. Amsterdam: John Benjamins.

CHAPTER 13

....

PRIMING AND FRAMING

dimensions of communication and cognition

....

JOHN SONNETT

CULTURAL sociology has begun to incorporate more detailed models of cognition into its theories (Brekhus 2015; Patterson 2014), and various subfields of sociology are starting to give more attention to cognition. One area that is particularly promising for further uptake of cognitive science are studies employing the concept of *framing*. This concept has wide currency across social science disciplines, and within sociology is featured most prominently in the study of media and communication (Gamson et al. 1992) and social movements (Benford and Snow 2000), two areas that are closely related (Earl et al. 2004; Earl and Garrett 2017). Growing from a seminal article on frame alignment (Snow et al. 1986), prominent sociological studies of framing include analyses of mobilization around political and economic protests (Gerhards and Rucht 1992), nuclear disarmament (Benford 1993), patronage seeking (McLean 1998), homelessness (Cress and Snow 2000), abortion (Ferree 2003), racial exclusion (McVeigh, Myers, and Sikkink 2004), equal employment laws (Pedriana 2006), and many other issues.

In contrast, the concept of *priming* is not used much in sociology, despite a growing body of work in other disciplines. Priming and framing are closely related concepts that have been subject to much debate in the interdisciplinary literature from psychology, communication studies, and political science. Priming is often said to focus on what information is presented and framing on how information is presented, although these elements overlap in actual communication practices. Priming has received some attention in sociological social psychology (Corsaro and Molinari 2000; Dippong 2015; Ford 1997; Harrison and Michelson 2015; Quillian 2008) and other areas of the discipline (Danna-Lynch 2010; DiMaggio et al. 2013; Perrin and McFarland 2011; Shepherd 2011; Sonnett et al. 2015; Vila-Henninger 2015), but far less than framing.

In this chapter, I first review interdisciplinary theoretical debates about priming and framing. In response to the question, "Do we need to be more intentional in our efforts to build on the work from related fields of inquiry?" (Snow et al. 2014:38), my answer is, "Yes," so I primarily focus attention on studies outside of sociology. Some interdisciplinary scholars define framing in a way that encompasses both the what and the how of communication, while others subsume framing under agenda-setting theory as second-order priming effects, while yet others advocate separating priming and framing theories because they have different assumptions. Adding to the conceptual disagreements are differences in methodology, especially between experimental and observational approaches, which structure the possibilities for internal and external validity. I aim to show how debates from other disciplines about the relationship between priming and framing can enrich sociological studies, and I specify dimensions of communication and cognition that can help clarify the use of these concepts.

13.1 THE WHAT AND HOW OF COMMUNICATION?

The concepts of priming and framing rely on different metaphors to describe communication. Priming is based on a temporal and sequential metaphor where something comes before the next thing, as in priming a pump or an engine. This gives it the sense of defining the "what" of communication, because it involves the choice of what topic or content will be presented first. For example, experimental subjects exposed to stereotypical portrayals of African Americans in comedy sketches (versus neutral portrayals) were subsequently more likely to negatively evaluate an African American accused of assault (Ford 1997). Framing is based on a spatial and visual metaphor, for example, the frames placed around pictures or the arrangement of artworks in a gallery. This gives framing the sense of shaping "how" something is communicated, because it sets a context around communicative content. For example, Ferree (2003) shows how abortion is often framed as a matter of choice and individual rights in the United States, whereas in Germany a protectionist framing emphasizes the state's role in protecting women from coercion.

Psychological research using these concepts has developed largely separately. For priming, most studies come out of research on memory systems, where priming describes the cueing and activation of mental modules (Collins and Loftus 1975). Framing has multiple disciplinary roots, but among cognitively oriented studies it has been most widely used to conceptualize factors affecting decisions and evaluations (Tversky and Kahneman 1981). What the literatures share, however, is a reliance on experimental methods. This commonality has allowed researchers to specify and test hypotheses with precision; however, experiments also suffer limitations of external validity. This affects the usefulness of experiments for understanding the wider contexts in which communication takes place, including structures of social power (Carragee and Roefs 2004; Vliegenthart and van Zoonen 2011).

Priming has been studied using observational data, under the conceptual umbrella of agenda setting (McCombs and Shaw 1972; McCombs 2004), but this work has made little impact in sociology. In contrast, framing has been widely studied using observational methods. The most important theoretical source for sociologists is Goffman's (1974) *Frame Analysis*, especially as applied to media studies (Gitlin 1980) and social movements research (Snow et al. 1986). Although Goffman's work bears little relation to experimental studies of framing, it has been useful for thinking about the kinds of observational data that sociologists typically collect. These observational methods avoid the problems of external validity that limit experiments, but they suffer from lack of control over conditions, and this weakness of internal validity may be one source for persistent problems of conceptualization (Benford 1997).

Conceptual confusion about framing is not limited to sociology, and a variety of approaches have been used to try to clarify the theoretical terrain. Entman (1993) attempted to clarify framing theory in a way that encompassed both the what and the how of communication, what he called salience and selection. This attempted synthesis was not without its critics, who have argued to retain a multiparadigmatic approach (D'Angelo 2002) where framing is a bridge between different styles of research (Reese 2007). Others have explicitly argued that framing theory encompasses priming effects, arguing that "the two terms can be used interchangeably" (Chong and Druckman 2007b:115), and have delineated differences between framing that creates new beliefs, makes existing beliefs more accessible, or makes beliefs applicable to new issues.

Theoretical synthesis has also come from work on agenda setting, which has expanded from "first-order" agendas of what to think about, to "second-order" agendas of message attributes, that is, how to think about agenda items (McCombs 2004). In this perspective, framing can be subsumed under agenda setting (McCombs and Ghanem 2001) because there can be no attitude toward an object without first having an object to describe (Kim and McCombs 2007:300). However, Borah's (2011) meta-analysis of communication journals indicates that few studies emphasize this equivalence between framing and second-order agenda setting. The definition of priming in this literature comes from Iyengar and Kinder (1987), who argued that priming affects the standards by which attitude objects are judged (see McCombs 2004:122). However, critics have argued that research on agenda setting uses a definition of priming that does not match that used in psychology (Chong and Druckman 2007b:115). More recent work on agenda setting has sought to update the cognitive foundations of the theory by examining differences between explicit and implicit processes (Arendt and Brantner 2015).

A third approach to conceptual clarification is the effort to better delineate the cognitive mechanisms behind priming and framing, in the hope of specifying their scope. Price and Tewksbury (1997:176) drew on knowledge activation theory (Collins and Loftus 1975) to differentiate two cognitive processes: applicability, meaning "the salient attributes of a message evoke and activate certain constructs, which then have an increased likelihood of use in evaluations made in response to the message," and accessibility, which is "residual activation potential, making [concepts] likely to be activated and used in subsequent evaluations" (Price and Tewksbury 1997:197). Scheufele and Tewksbury (2007) build on this distinction to argue that agenda setting is based on memory models and accessibility, where processing time and attention is what matters, whereas framing is based on interpretive schemas and their applicability or appropriateness for how we think about an issue (see also Nelson et al. 1997). Scheufele and Iyengar (2017:625) further argue that priming should be seen as "schema-independent" and therefore a universal effect across audiences, but they hedge on this claim by stating, "political sophistication or levels of preexisting knowledge" may moderate this effect. Other researchers have confirmed that such schema-related preexisting knowledge matters (Slothuus 2008), and have therefore argued that the availability of knowledge should be considered a separate cognitive mechanism alongside applicability and accessibility (Chong and Druckman 2007a).

Various empirical studies have worked at the intersections of agenda setting, priming, and framing theories to compare the different mechanisms. Iyengar and Simon (1993) described these three effects in a study after the first Persian Gulf war: agenda setting was indicated by survey data reporting that the Gulf crisis was considered the most important problem by respondents, priming was indicated by the increased salience of foreign policy (as opposed to other political issues) in evaluating President Bush once the crisis began, and framing effects were indicated by a positive relationship between viewing television news (which was supportive of the war) and expressed support for the war. More recently, Dillman Carpentier (2014:531) drew on experimental studies to show a difference between agenda setting as "perceived importance" and priming as "top-of-mind awareness." Shehata and Falasca (2014) studied opinions of government policy before and after the 2008 financial crisis and proposed that accessibility and applicability should be considered a two-step process of priming.

Despite efforts at theoretical clarification and empirical adjudication, there remains a distinct absence of theoretical consensus, prompting calls to abandon the framing concept altogether (Cacciatore et al. 2016). In the next section, I build on this suggestion by specifying dimensions of communication and cognition that are relevant to debates about priming and framing. Rather than attempting a theoretical subsummation, separation, or synthesis, I argue that various approaches to priming and framing can themselves be broken into component parts and analyzed along multiple dimensions of difference. This clarification of theoretical and methodological dimensions in the debate might help researchers be more reflexive in conceptualizing their studies.

A note on terminology: many have noted the distinction between "framing" as a verb and "frame" as a noun, and the former is often given theoretical primacy while the latter is used in discussions of measurement. When Borah (2011:249) examined "framing" versus "frames" in the communication literature, she found very few studies examining production processes. A similar observation has been made about the sociological literature: "It is still the case that a significant portion of framing research examines frames as the artifacts of framing processes while devoting comparatively little attention to uncovering the process itself" (Snow et al. 2014:37). In the following discussion, I use verb forms to emphasize that it is communicative action that we are studying, even when that action is reified and embedded within cultural objects. I also use the term "framing" where possible, because it is more commonly used than "priming."

A second prefatory note: in what follows, I focus on what have been termed "generic frames" rather than issue-specific frames (de Vreese 2005). One particularly sharp criticism of "sociological" studies of framing is the profusion of issue-specific frames and lack of attention to general features of the frames being studied (Scheufele and Iyengar 2017). In communication journals, Borah (2011:249) found that 49 percent of framing studies used only unique frames, that is, frames defined with reference to a specific subject of investigation and without attention to features that may be relevant across topics and contexts. Therefore, Borah's (2011:256) concluding questions on this point are a useful reminder: "Does the examination of the issue-specific frames help in methodological development of frame analysis? How does the unique set of frames associate with already developed generic frames in the literature?" In the next section, I outline a set of dimensions that can help identify generic features of framing.

13.2 Dimensions of Communication and Cognition

Many studies in cognitive sociology begin by applying distinctions derived from cognitive science, such as automatic and deliberative cognition (Vaisey 2009), "hot" and emotionally charged versus "cool" and dispassionate cognition (DiMaggio 2002), or amodal versus embodied theories of knowledge (Ignatow 2007). Most are then interested in "continuing the story" of cognition (Cerulo 2014) beyond the experimental settings that cognitive scientists tend to employ to investigate cognition "in the wild" (cf. Hutchins 1995). My goal in constructing the following dimensions of communication and cognition is to provide a toolkit for reflecting on and designing studies of framing and priming using observational data, in the hope of going beyond theorizing and toward methodological contributions (Ignatow 2014). These dimensions are specified as conceptual pairs linked by "and" rather than "or," to signify that both elements are important and that the most complete studies will incorporate both, at least in theory if not in empirical measurements. I introduce each dimension with questions to highlight the potential issues that they address.

13.2.1 Where Is Framing? Cultural Objects and Individual Cognition

This dimension addresses the question of where framing is to be found, in meaning-carrying cultural objects such as media texts of various sorts, or in the minds of individuals encountering these cultural objects. Cultural objects are "shared significance embodied in form" which are "tangible or can be put into words" (Griswold 1987:4). Distinguishing objects from minds helps to clarify the places we might look for evidence of framing, and builds on widely accepted distinctions in the literature. For example, Scheufele (1999) distinguishes media frames in communication content and individual frames in audience cognition, and argues that explanations of framing should focus on linking these two. Druckman (2001) conceptualizes frames in communication versus frames in thought, and identifies the influence of the former on the latter as framing effects. This distinction also forms the basis of Borah's (2011:254) first research question in her coding of communication articles about framing, which she answers by coding data collection methods, with content or text analysis indicating frames in communication (over 60 percent of articles), and experiments (almost 20 percent of articles) or surveys indicating frames in thought. Many sociological studies focus on one or the other part of this conceptual pair, but in such cases, researchers should be careful to theorize the intersection between cultural objects and the people interacting with them—whether producers or receivers of communication.

13.2.2 Who Does Framing? Producers and Receivers of Communication

Studies of individual cognition vary on what type of individuals they investigate. Social movement studies often focus on movement actors who produce frames and their connection to wider movement mobilization (Snow et al. 2014). Media studies often examine elite strategic communicators who interact with news institutions in the creation of news reports, and their relationships to public opinion (Entman 2004). Other examples of pairing content analysis with public opinion data include studies of agenda setting during elections (Arendt and Brantner 2015; Kim and McCombs 2007) and Gamson and Modigliani's (1989) classic study of media discourse and public opinion about nuclear power. A range of actors often stand between producers and receivers of communication messages, most importantly journalists and other mediators of public information (Shoemaker and Reese 2013). Where production and reception processes are not directly observed, field theory can be used to highlight how media outlets are positioned within structures of political and economic power, including relations composing the journalistic field itself (Benson and Saguy 2005). For example, specialized media like *Earth Island Journal*, *Oil & Gas Journal*, or *Science Magazine* can only be successful over time if there is some connection between the content produced and audience expectations (Sonnett 2010). Whether data is collected directly on both producers and receivers of communication, this is an important dimension to conceptualize in studies of framing.

13.2.3 How Is Framing Done? Visual and Verbal Communication

Many studies of framing use newspaper data and focus on language-based communication (Earl et al. 2004), and while this was already problematic in the twentieth-century television-saturated environment, the changing media landscape continues to shift toward visual modes of communication (Earl et al. 2017). Framing and priming studies can be distinguished by the typical modes of communication investigated, with framing largely based on verbal data while priming studies more often examine verbal and visual designs. For example, visual research on implicit racial bias on television has identified priming effects in crime news (Gilliam and Iyengar 2000), political campaign ads (Mendelberg 2001; Valentino et al. 2002), and on-screen nonverbal behaviors (Weisbuch et al. 2009). Whereas verbal racial cues occur when nonracial words with "racial associations" are used, implicit visual cues occur when seemingly race-neutral language is paired with "negative images of the target group" (Mendelberg 2008:110), as in television news representations of African Americans after Hurricane Katrina (Sonnett et al. 2015). Researchers interested in framing have started to make connections to the literature on visual communication (Geise and Baden 2014), and some have called for use of technologies that can manipulate aspects of images, such as skin tone or facial features, for experiments (Scheufele and Iyengar 2017). More observational research on the visual aspects of framing is also needed.

13.2.4 What Is the Context of Framing?
Cultural and Social Contexts

Both producers and receivers of communication, and the cultural objects that carry meaning between them, operate within larger contexts. Griswold (2013) identifies this context as the "social world," which includes larger systems of social stratification that surround communication activities. Along with cultural objects, producers, and receivers, the social world is the fourth part of Griswold's "cultural diamond" methodological framework for the sociology of culture. A similar model of the political framing process is offered by Entman et al. (2009:176), but they name the larger context "culture," which for them includes "schemas commonly found in the minds of a society's individuals, and the stock of frames present in the system's communications." Both social and cultural contexts are important for situating the actors and objects of study within the full range of factors shaping their communication processes. Theorizing often aims to generalize beyond specific contexts, but to do this, contexts need to be specified conceptually. Differentiating such social and cultural contexts helps connect studies of framing and priming to larger themes in cultural sociology and the sociology of knowledge.

13.2.5 How Do Priming and Framing Shape Cognition?
Accessibility and Applicability

One of the fundamental distinctions between priming and framing is argued to be the mechanisms by which they influence audiences (Scheufele and Iyengar 2017; Cacciatore et al. 2016; Chong and Druckman 2007b). For priming, there are two senses in which messages are said to make thoughts more accessible. The first derives from studies of agenda setting, and assumes a connection between the repetition of topics in the media and the relative importance of those topics for audiences. The dependent variable is usually a question about what a respondent thinks is the "most important" issue facing the country. This definition is used by Iyengar and Kinder (1987), who are credited with bringing the concept of priming into the study of political communication. However, this definition is different than what is usually meant in the psychology literature, which focuses on a much shorter time span. There, accessibility means a consideration has been made temporarily salient in working memory, and therefore will affect subsequent considerations, and this is understood as a component of automatic cognitive processing (Druckman 2001). In contrast, the success of a framing effect is said to be dependent on the perceived applicability or appropriateness of a concept in the mind of a message receiver, and this involves a matching process between media content and individual cognition that involves conscious deliberation (Chong and Druckman 2007a:109). Beyond the distinction between accessibility and applicability, a third effect can be considered a scope condition for the first two: whether considerations are available (Chong and Druckman 2007a:108), meaning whether a message receiver has any relevant knowledge which might be made either accessible or applicable, and this is a factor that can moderate framing effects (Slothuus 2008). All three of these concepts are relevant for studies seeking to understand the "resonance" of framing activities.

13.2.6 How Does Framing Shape Cognition?
Equivalency and Emphasis Framing

This conceptual distinction is most informative for differentiating sociological approaches to framing from the more experimentally based literature in political communication (Scheufele and Iyengar 2017:624). Druckman (2001) bases this distinction on the widely accepted definition of attitudes as involving two components: weight and evaluation. The weight element involves the salience of a consideration, while evaluation is measured as positive or negative valence toward the topic in question. Equivalency framing corresponds to an emphasis on evaluation, and emphasis framing to salience or selection of relevant topics to give weight to. Equivalency refers to different ways of presenting the exact same content, as in the commonplace of a glass half-full versus a glass half-empty, or a choice between "5% unemployment or 95% employment" (Druckman 2001:228). Emphasis, on the other hand, refers to substantively different frames for a common phenomenon, for example, framing news of a KKK rally as an issue of free speech or as an issue of public order (Nelson et al. 1997). Some major distinctions in what might be called emphasis framing include diagnostic, prognostic, and motivational frames (Snow and Benford 1988), episodic and thematic frames (Iyengar 1991), and substantive and procedural frames (Entman 2004). Each of these typologies is potentially useful because they identify generic features of framing that can be linked to other dimensions of communication and cognition.

13.2.7 How Does Priming Shape Cognition?
Affective and Cognitive Priming

One of the primary distinctions in cognitive sociology is between hot and cool cognition (DiMaggio 2002; Metcalfe and Mischel 1999). The metaphor juxtaposes "hot" emotion-laden thought to "cool" rational thought, emphasizing that emotions are the major differentiating variable. However, an important underlying dimension is affect, the positive or negative valence of cognition. Zajonc (1980) first proposed the affective primacy hypothesis, showing that the reaction of liking or disliking comes temporally prior to cognitive functions such as recognition and feature identification. This finding is the basis for later work in moral psychology proposing that cognition is like an elephant and a rider, with the intuitive elephant as the dominant force (Haidt 2012:387). A prominent application of this finding in social psychology is in the development of the Implicit Association Test (IAT) to measure affective reactions to different social categories (Greenwald et al. 1998; Shepherd 2011; Haidt 2012:67). In relation to theories of framing, affective primacy can be equated with the accessibility of cognitions, but conceptually the focus on affect helps to clarify the valenced aspect of cognitive accessibility. Affective valence begins with "a minimum of cognitive participation" (Murphy and Zajonc 1993:724) but with a clear positive or negative reaction, which can then be developed into more specific attitudes in subsequent reasoning. Therefore, judgments about the applicability or appropriateness of frames are the slower and "cooler" rider of the affective elephant. Automatic cognition is not limited to affect, and may involve categorization and other cognitive processes, but affect is the crucial feature that priming studies highlight. To the extent that the framing literature is largely premised on the study of cool deliberative cognition, studies of affective priming offer a useful corrective in emphasizing the importance of automatic affective intuitions.

13.2.8 How to Measure Priming and Framing?
Direct and Indirect Measures

Much of the interdisciplinary literature on priming and framing uses experimental methods, and while some studies pair content analysis with surveys, there is a continuing need to innovate methods for studying implicit communicative and cognitive processes with observational data. These methods must often use indirect measures so that the measurement process does not trigger conscious and deliberative thinking. Many implicit measures are available in psychology (Fazio and Olson 2003), and some sociological studies have successfully borrowed methods such as the IAT from cognitive psychology (Srivastava and Banaji 2011). Other recent psychological studies have also introduced creative methods for investigating concepts of interest to sociologists. For example, mobile media devices open up possibilities for studying how social "connection habits" are primed by technical, spatial, or mental cues (Bayer et al. 2016:7). Implicit self-esteem can be measured with responses to common pronouns such as I, me, we, and us; by choosing and evaluating random letters from the alphabet; or by evaluating words associated with ethnic identity and culture (Verkuyten 2005). In sociology, debates about how in-depth interviews relate to cognition (Pugh 2013; Vaisey 2014) can be seen as an outgrowth of the growing interest in indirect measures. Vaisey (2009) argues that fixed-choice survey questions are good measures of automatic processing, because they rarely engage cognition beyond practical consciousness. However, open-ended questions can also provide indirect measures when they are worded and sequenced in a way that does not trigger processes of deliberative judgment. For example, a study of music genre evaluations can first ask respondents their favorite and least favorite musical artists, and then ask them to classify these artists by genre (Sonnett 2016). Other qualitative approaches include focus group research that taps automatic cognition by having participants draw campaign posters, and then "attending to the process of *how*" the groups did their drawing (McDonnell 2014:253). There are many possibilities for observational measurement of automatic cognition, and further innovations in this area will help specify the cognitive dimensions of priming and framing in sociological studies.

13.3 CONCLUSION

Debates over the proper conceptualization and measurement of priming and framing are likely to continue. Besides the dimensions reviewed in this chapter, many other considerations are also relevant, for example, synchronic and diachronic study designs (Matthes and Schemer 2012), and mediators and moderators of relationships among variables (Chong and Druckman 2007b; Baron and Kenny 1986). What I hope to have contributed in this chapter is a clarification of some of the main dimensions of communication and cognition along which interdisciplinary studies of priming and framing converge and diverge. Whether future studies use one or the other or neither concept, giving attention to issues raised in these interdisciplinary debates can help clarify both theoretical and methodological approaches to cognitively oriented sociology.

REFERENCES

Arendt, Florian, and Cornelia Brantner. 2015. "Toward an Implicit Cognition Account of Attribute Agenda Setting." *International Journal of Communication* 9:2735–56.

Baron, Reuben M., and David A. Kenny. 1986. "The Moderator–Mediator Variable Distinction in Social Psychological Research: Conceptual, Strategic, and Statistical Considerations." *Journal of Personality and Social Psychology* 51(6):1173–82.

Bayer, Joseph B., Scott W. Campbell, and Rich Ling. 2016. "Connection Cues: Activating the Norms and Habits of Social Connectedness." *Communication Theory* 26(2): 128–49.

Benford, Robert D. 1993. "Frame Disputes within the Nuclear Disarmament Movement." *Social Forces* 71(3):677–701.

Benford, Robert D. 1997. "An Insider's Critique of the Social Movement Framing Perspective." *Sociological Inquiry* 67(4):409–30.

Benford, Robert D., and David A. Snow. 2000. "Framing Processes and Social Movements: An Overview and Assessment." *Annual Review of Sociology* 26:611–39.

Benson, Rodney, and Abigail C. Saguy. 2005. "Constructing Social Problems in an Age of Globalization: A French-American Comparison." *American Sociological Review* 70(2):233–59.

Borah, Porismita. 2011. "Conceptual Issues in Framing Theory: A Systematic Examination of a Decade's Literature." *Journal of Communication* 61(2):246–63.

Brekhus, Wayne H. 2015. *Culture and Cognition: Patterns in the Social Construction of Reality.* Malden, MA: Polity.

Cacciatore, Michael A., Dietram A. Scheufele, and Shanto Iyengar. 2016. "The End of Framing as We Know it…and the Future of Media Effects." *Mass Communication and Society* 19(1):7–23.

Carragee, Kevin M., and Wim Roefs. 2004. "The Neglect of Power in Recent Framing Research." *Journal of Communication* 54(2):214–33.

Cerulo, Karen A. 2014. "Continuing the Story: Maximizing the Intersections of Cognitive Science and Sociology." *Sociological Forum* 29(4):1012–19.

Chong, Dennis, and James N. Druckman. 2007a. "A Theory of Framing and Opinion Formation in Competitive Elite Environments." *Journal of Communication* 57(1):99–118.

Chong, Dennis, and James N. Druckman. 2007b. "Framing Theory." *Annual Review of Political Science* 10:103–26.

Collins, Allan M., and Elizabeth F. Loftus. 1975. "A Spreading-Activation Theory of Semantic Processing." *Psychological Review* 82(6):407–28.

Corsaro, William A., and Luisa Molinari. 2000. "Priming Events and Italian Children's Transition from Preschool to Elementary School: Representations and Action." *Social Psychology Quarterly* 63(1):16–33.

Cress, Daniel M., and David A. Snow. 2000. "The Outcomes of Homeless Mobilization: The Influence of Organization, Disruption, Political Mediation, and Framing." *American Journal of Sociology* 105(4):1063–104.

D'Angelo, Paul. 2002. "News Framing as a Multiparadigmatic Research Program: A Response to Entman." *Journal of Communication* 52(4):870–88.

Danna-Lynch, Karen. 2010. "Switching Roles: The Process of Mental Weighing." *Poetics* 38(2):166–84.

Dillman Carpentier, Francesca R. 2014. "Agenda Setting and Priming Effects Based on Information Presentation: Revisiting Accessibility as a Mechanism Explaining Agenda Setting and Priming." *Mass Communication and Society* 17(4):531–52.

DiMaggio, Paul. 2002. "Why Cognitive (and Cultural) Sociology Needs Cognitive Psychology." pp. 274–81 in *Culture in Mind*, edited by Karen A. Cerulo. New York: Routledge.

DiMaggio, Paul, Manish Nag, and David Blei. 2013. "Exploiting Affinities between Topic Modeling and the Sociological Perspective on Culture: Application to Newspaper Coverage of US Government Arts Funding." *Poetics* 41(6):570–606.

Dippong, Joseph. 2015. "Priming Effects and Performance Expectations in Mixed-Sex Task Groups." *Social Psychology Quarterly* 78(4):387–98.

Druckman, James N. 2001. "The Implications of Framing Effects for Citizen Competence." *Political Behavior* 23(3):225–56.

Earl, Jennifer, and R. Kelly Garrett. 2017. "The New Information Frontier: Toward a More Nuanced View of Social Movement Communication." *Social Movement Studies* 16(4): 479–93.

Earl, Jennifer, Andrew Martin, John D. McCarthy, and Sarah A. Soule. 2004. "The Use of Newspaper Data in the Study of Collective Action." *Annual Review of Sociology* 30:65–80.

Entman, Robert M. 1993. "Framing: Toward Clarification of a Fractured Paradigm." *Journal of Communication* 43(4):51–58.

Entman, Robert M. 2004. *Projections of Power: Framing News, Public Opinion, and US Foreign Policy*. Chicago: University of Chicago Press.

Entman, Robert M., Jörg Matthes, and Lynn Pellicano. 2009. "Nature, Sources, and Effects of News Framing." pp. 175–90 in *Handbook of Journalism Studies*, edited by Karin Wahl-Jorgensen and Thomas Hanitzsch. New York: Routledge.

Fazio, Russell H., and Michael A. Olson. 2003. "Implicit Measures in Social Cognition Research: Their Meaning and Use." *Annual Review of Psychology* 54:297–327.

Ferree, Myra Marx. 2003. "Resonance and Radicalism: Feminist Framing in the Abortion Debates of the United States and Germany." *American Journal of Sociology* 109(2):304–44.

Ford, Thomas E. 1997. "Effects of Stereotypical Television Portrayals of African-Americans on Person Perception." *Social Psychology Quarterly* 60(3):266–75.

Gamson, William A., David Croteau, William Hoynes, and Theodore Sasson. 1992. "Media Images and the Social Construction of Reality." *Annual Review of Sociology* 18:373–93.

Gamson, William A., and Andre Modigliani. 1989. "Media Discourse and Public Opinion on Nuclear Power: A Constructionist Approach." *American Journal of Sociology* 95(1):1–37.

Geise, Stephanie, and Christian Baden. 2015. "Putting the Image Back into the Frame: Modeling the Linkage between Visual Communication and Frame-Processing Theory." *Communication Theory* 25(1):46–69.

Gerhards, Jürgen, and Dieter Rucht. 1992. "Mesomobilization: Organizing and Framing in Two Protest Campaigns in West Germany." *American Journal of Sociology* 98(3):555–96.

Gilliam, Franklin D., Jr., and Shanto Iyengar. 2000. "Prime Suspects: The Influence of Local Television News on the Viewing Public." *American Journal of Political Science* 44(3):560–73.

Gitlin, Todd. 1980. *The Whole World Is Watching: Mass Media in the Making and Unmaking of the New Left*. Berkeley: University of California Press.

Goffman, Erving. 1974. *Frame Analysis: An Essay on the Organization of Experience*. Cambridge, MA: Harvard University Press.

Greenwald, Anthony G., Debbie E. McGhee, and Jordan LK Schwartz. 1998. "Measuring Individual Differences in Implicit Cognition: The Implicit Association Test." *Journal of Personality and Social Psychology* 74(6):1464–80.

Griswold, Wendy. 1987. "A Methodological Framework for the Sociology of Culture." *Sociological Methodology* 17:1–35.

Griswold, Wendy. 2013. *Cultures and Societies in a Changing World*. 4th ed. Los Angeles: SAGE.

Haidt, Jonathan. 2012. *The Righteous Mind: Why Good People Are Divided by Politics and Religion*. New York: Vintage Books.

Harrison, Brian F., and Melissa R. Michelson. 2015. "God and Marriage: The Impact of Religious Identity Priming on Attitudes toward Same-Sex Marriage." *Social Science Quarterly* 96(5):1411–23.

Hutchins, Edwin. 1995. *Cognition in the Wild*. Cambridge, MA: MIT Press.

Ignatow, Gabe. 2014. "Ontology and Method in Cognitive Sociology." *Sociological Forum* 29(4):990–94.

Ignatow, Gabriel. 2007. "Theories of Embodied Knowledge: New Directions for Cultural and Cognitive Sociology?" *Journal for the Theory of Social Behaviour* 37(2):115–35.

Iyengar, Shanto. 1991. *Is Anyone Responsible? How Television Frames Political Issues*. Chicago: University of Chicago Press.

Iyengar, Shanto, and Donald R. Kinder 1987. *News That Matters: Television and American Opinion*. Chicago: University of Chicago Press.

Iyengar, Shanto, and Adam Simon. 1993. "News Coverage of the Gulf Crisis and Public Opinion: A Study of Agenda-Setting, Priming, and Framing." *Communication Research* 20(3):365–83.

Kim, Kihan, and Maxwell McCombs. 2007. "News Story Descriptions and the Public's Opinions of Political Candidates." *Journalism and Mass Communication Quarterly* 84(2):299–314.

Matthes, Jörg, and Christian Schemer. 2012. "Diachronic Framing Effects in Competitive Opinion Environments." *Political Communication* 29(3):319–39.

McCombs, Maxwell. 2004. *Setting the Agenda: The Mass Media and Public Opinion*. Malden, MA: Polity Press.

McCombs, Maxwell, and Salma I. Ghanem. 2001. "The Convergence of Agenda Setting and Framing." pp. 67–81 in *Framing Public Life: Perspectives on Media and Our Understanding of the Social World*, edited by Stephen D. Reese, Oscar H. Gandy Jr., and August E. Grant. Mahwah, NJ: Lawrence Erlbaum.

McCombs, Maxwell E., and Donald L. Shaw. 1972. "The Agenda-Setting Function of Mass Media." *Public Opinion Quarterly* 36(2):176–87.

McDonnell, Terence E. 2014. "Drawing Out Culture: Productive Methods to Measure Cognition and Resonance." *Theory and Society* 43(3–4):247–74.

McLean, Paul D. 1998. "A Frame Analysis of Favor Seeking in the Renaissance: Agency, Networks, and Political Culture." *American Journal of Sociology* 104(1):51–91.

McVeigh, Rory, Daniel J. Myers, and David Sikkink. 2004. "Corn, Klansmen, and Coolidge: Structure and Framing in Social Movements." *Social Forces* 83(2):653–90.

Mendelberg, Tali. 2001. *The Race Card: Campaign Strategy, Implicit Messages, and the Norm of Equality*. Princeton, NJ: Princeton University Press.

Mendelberg, Tali. 2008. "Racial Priming Revived." *Perspectives on Politics* 6(1):109–23.

Metcalfe, Janet, and Walter Mischel. 1999. "A Hot/Cool-System Analysis of Delay of Gratification: Dynamics of Willpower." *Psychological Review* 106(1):3–19.

Murphy, Sheila T., and Robert B. Zajonc. 1993. "Affect, Cognition, and Awareness: Affective Priming with Optimal and Suboptimal Stimulus Exposures." *Journal of Personality and Social Psychology* 64(5):723–39.

Nelson, Thomas E., Rosalee A. Clawson, and Zoe M. Oxley. 1997. "Media Framing of a Civil Liberties Conflict and Its Effect on Tolerance." *American Political Science Review* 91(3):567–83.

Nelson, Thomas E., Zoe M. Oxley, and Rosalee A. Clawson. 1997. "Toward a Psychology of Framing Effects." *Political Behavior* 19(3):221–46.

Patterson, Orlando. 2014. "Making Sense of Culture." *Annual Review of Sociology* 40:1–30.

Pedriana, Nicholas. 2006. "From Protective to Equal Treatment: Legal Framing Processes and Transformation of the Women's Movement in the 1960s." *American Journal of Sociology* 111(6):1718–61.

Perrin, Andrew J., and Katherine McFarland. 2011. "Social Theory and Public Opinion." *Annual Review of Sociology* 37:87–107.

Price, Vincent, and David Tewksbury. 1997. "News Values and Public Opinion: A Theoretical Account of Media Priming and Framing." *Progress in Communication Sciences* 13:173–212.

Pugh, Allison J. 2013. "What Good Are Interviews for Thinking about Culture: Demystifying Interpretive Analysis." *American Journal of Cultural Sociology* 1(1):42–68.

Quillian, Lincoln. 2008. "Does Unconscious Racism Exist?" *Social Psychology Quarterly* 71(1):6–11.

Reese, Stephen D. 2007. "The Framing Project: A Bridging Model for Media Research Revisited." *Journal of Communication* 57(1):148–54.

Scheufele, Dietram A. 1999. "Framing as a Theory of Media Effects." *Journal of Communication* 49(1):103–22.

Scheufele, Dietram A., and Shanto Iyengar. 2017. "The State of Framing Research: A Call for New Directions." pp. 619–32 *Oxford Handbook of Political Communication*, edited by Kate Kenski and Kathleen Hall Jamieson. New York: Oxford University Press.

Scheufele, Dietram A., and David Tewksbury. 2007. "Framing, Agenda Setting, and Priming: The Evolution of Three Media Effects Models." *Journal of Communication* 57(1):9–20.

Shehata, Adam, and Kajsa Falasca. 2014. "Priming Effects during the Financial Crisis: Accessibility and Applicability Mechanisms behind Government Approval." *European Political Science Review* 6(4):597–620.

Shepherd, Hana. 2011. "The Cultural Context of Cognition: What the Implicit Association Test Tells Us about How Culture Works." *Sociological Forum* 26(1):121–43.

Shoemaker, Pamela J., and Stephen D. Reese. 2013. *Mediating the Message in the 21st Century: A Media Sociology Perspective*. New York: Routledge.

Slothuus, Rune. 2008. "More than Weighting Cognitive Importance: A Dual-Process Model of Issue Framing Effects." *Political Psychology* 29(1):1–28.

Snow, David A., and Robert D. Benford. 1988. "Ideology, Frame Resonance, and Participant Mobilization." *International Social Movement Research* 1(1):197–217.

Snow, David, Robert Benford, Holly McCammon, Lyndi Hewitt, and Scott Fitzgerald. 2014. "The Emergence, Development, and Future of the Framing Perspective: 25+ Years since 'Frame Alignment.'" *Mobilization: An International Quarterly* 19(1):23–46.

Snow, David A., E. Burke Rochford Jr., Steven K. Worden, and Robert D. Benford. 1986. "Frame Alignment Processes, Micromobilization, and Movement Participation." *American Sociological Review* 51(4):464–81.

Sonnett, John. 2010. "Climates of Risk: A Field Analysis of Global Climate Change in US Media Discourse, 1997–2004." *Public Understanding of Science* 19(6):698–716.

Sonnett, John. 2016. "Ambivalence, Indifference, Distinction: A Comparative Netfield Analysis of Implicit Musical Boundaries." *Poetics* 54:38–53.

Sonnett, John, Kirk A. Johnson, and Mark K. Dolan. 2015. "Priming Implicit Racism in Television News: Visual and Verbal Limitations on Diversity." *Sociological Forum* 30(2):328–47.

Srivastava, Sameer B., and Mahzarin R. Banaji. 2011. "Culture, Cognition, and Collaborative Networks in Organizations." *American Sociological Review* 76(2):207–33.

Tversky, Amos, and Daniel Kahneman. 1981. "The Framing of Decisions and the Psychology of Choice." *Science* 211(4481):453–8.

Vaisey, Stephen. 2009. "Motivation and Justification: A Dual-Process Model of Culture in Action." *American Journal of Sociology* 114(6):1675–715.

Vaisey, Stephen. 2014. "Is Interviewing Compatible with the Dual-Process Model of Culture?" *American Journal of Cultural Sociology* 2(1):150–8.

Valentino, Nicholas A., Vincent L. Hutchings, and Ismail K. White. 2002. "Cues That Matter: How Political Ads Prime Racial Attitudes during Campaigns." *American Political Science Review* 96(1):75–90.

Verkuyten, Maykel. 2005. "The Puzzle of High Self-Esteem among Ethnic Minorities: Comparing Explicit and Implicit Self-Esteem." *Self and Identity* 4(2):177–92.

Vila-Henninger, Luis Antonio. 2015. "Toward Defining the Causal Role of Consciousness: Using Models of Memory and Moral Judgment from Cognitive Neuroscience to Expand the Sociological Dual-Process Model." *Journal for the Theory of Social Behaviour* 45(2):238–60.

Vliegenthart, Rens, and Liesbet van Zoonen. 2011. "Power to the Frame: Bringing Sociology Back to Frame Analysis." *European Journal of Communication* 26(2):101–15.

de Vreese, Claes H. 2005. "News Framing: Theory and Typology." *Information Design Journal + Document Design* 13(1):51–62.

Weisbuch, Max, Kristin Pauker, and Nalini Ambady. 2009. "The Subtle Transmission of Race Bias via Televised Nonverbal Behavior." *Science* 326(18):1711–14.

Zajonc, Robert B. 1980. "Feeling and Thinking: Preferences Need No Inferences." *American Psychologist* 35(2):151–75.

PART II
··
PERSPECTIVES FROM OTHER FIELDS
··

CHAPTER 14

....

COGNITIVE LINGUISTICS

....

PAUL CHILTON

14.1 INTRODUCTION

....

COGNITIVE sociology and social cognition differ in their frames of reference, the former adhering to classic sociological theorizing (Durkheim, Weber, Goffman, Bourdieu, Cicourel), the latter formulated in experimental psychology, more specifically social psychology. The present chapter hovers on the border, and leans toward the scientific and empirical paradigm. The core assumption, however, is that whichever disciplinary perspective is adopted, the human capacity for language and language use is centrally integrated both with cognitive (and affective) processes grounded in the evolved physical structures of the human brain, and with the interactions among brains (and the bodies they are part of) in various observable kinds of social structure and process.

Among other things research in social cognition concerns itself with how information about—or perhaps better, knowledge of—society is processed, stored, and communicated. By "society" here we need to understand both social structures (microstructures and macrostructures) and social processes (again, on micro- and various macro-levels). Much work in this domain has been done within psychology and the cognitive sciences. Within those research agendas there is, speaking generally, an important neglected area—communication and in particular linguistic communication. This is partly a matter of academic disciplines—linguistics has its own often highly technical agendas. However, linguistics too has developed its own interests in the obvious social embeddedness of language-in-use, specifically in the linguistics subdisciplines of pragmatics, discourse analysis, and sociolinguistics. In these disciplines also, at least until relatively recently, the neighboring disciplines—those of psychology and cognitive science—have been neglected. That is, they were long studied without reference to the study of the human mind, and vice versa. This is a fairly crude generalization, but I believe it is nonetheless the case that much still needs to be done to promote serious scientific collaboration among the linguistic and the psychological and the cognitive research activities. This chapter focuses on one major development in linguistics that does take the psychological and mental spheres seriously—cognitive linguistics (CL), where the working assumption is that the human language ability is derived from and intertwined with other cognitive and affective processes of the mind-brain. It also respects the fact that human language is not just for processing and storing information and knowledge but is a socially situated and interactive phenomenon that must also be reflected in its biological evolution and cultural development (see, e.g., Knight 1998).

14.2 LANGUAGE, MIND, AND SOCIETY

It has become clear to many scholars over recent decades that human language, the uses of human language, the workings of the human mind, and many dimensions of human societies are both interwoven and interdependent. The traditional divisions of academic fields have tended to obscure this fact and made it difficult for researchers in one field to fully grasp developments in a neighboring one. This section attempts a brief overview of linguistics and cognitive linguistics and their inherent interconnections with social and psychological sciences.

14.2.1 Linguistics

It is important to be clear from the start what the discipline of linguistics is. It is the scientific study of the phenomenon human language and should not be confused with approaches in literary criticism, media studies, cultural studies, or in poststructuralist or postmodernist writings such as those of Kristeva, Foucault, and Derrida, or with Marxist and post-Marxist speculations about language such as those of Laclau and Mouffe. Nor should linguistically informed discourse analysis, including the sociologically informed work, be confused with such approaches.

The earliest systematic descriptive formulations are attributed to Pāṇini (4th century BCE), who formulated descriptive rules of Sanskrit morphology. Modern descriptive linguistics emerged in the eighteenth and nineteenth centuries with the work of scholars such as William Jones, Wilhelm von Humboldt, Rasmus Rask, Jacob Grimm, and Karl Verner—who discovered law-like regularities in the sound changes of European languages. The classic example is Grimm's Law, in effect, an empirical hypothesis derived from data and testable against data. Linguistics has ever since been a scientific discipline in that sense.

Since human language is a highly complex phenomenon, various specialized subdisciplines have developed—including branches investigating the physiology and physics of speech sounds, the study of grammatical structure (syntax), and the study of meaning (semantics). Language in relation to society is studied under two broad disciplinary headings. Pragmatics deals with interaction between and among individuals, particularly with respect to the phenomenon of in situ meaning production. Sociolinguistics deals with variation within and between speech communities, including the variables of age, gender, socioeconomic class, and ethnic identity. Some researchers include pragmatics in sociolinguistics. It is important to note that linguistics now overlaps with other scientific disciplines interested in human language—psychology, neuroscience, and evolutionary biology. All linguistics subdisciplines would regard themselves as working like any other natural or social science—making explanatory models subject to logical consistency and consistency with empirical data.

14.2.2 Cognitive Linguistics

Perhaps the most known and most influential linguistics paradigm of the twentieth and early twenty-first century has been that of generative grammar, primarily associated with Noam Chomsky. This approach proposed an algorithmic format that "generates" all and only the "grammatical" sentences of a natural human language (this is not of course about "correct" or "proper" grammar). It is an appealingly elegant model and has gone through many variants. Chomsky has proposed further that the human mind possesses an autonomous language module, that is, one that is not a product of other cognitive systems and that possibly arose by chance mutation. Generative grammar does not claim to account for the phenomenon of meaning or to model "external" linguistic facts such as its observably tight connection with social structure and behavior. Although generative linguistics has been linked with the "cognitive revolution," this is only the case in the sense that Chomsky and his associates focus on linguistic knowledge—defined as unconscious knowledge of the grammar of a language, a grammar describable in the format of generative grammar. Jackendoff, however, who has worked within the generative paradigm, sees syntax as closely interacting with meaning (Jackendoff 1996).

Cognitive linguistics accepts that available evidence indicates that the language ability of humans is not autonomous, but involves massive neural connections across the brain, even though the left hemisphere has an evolved specialization (broadly, the classic Broca's and Wernicke's areas) for language and language use. It proposes that lexical items involve multiple connections with many different parts of the brain, including those that deal with emotions. The term "cognitive" should not be taken in the narrow sense of "knowledge." Grammatical structures do not simply "interface with" semantic systems, as in generative syntax, but are themselves meaningful, that is, paired with conceptualizations (Langacker 1987, 1991, 2002, 2008; Goldberg 1995). Cognitive linguists also argue for a continuum of meaningful units from morphemes, through words to grammatical constructions (see especially Goldberg 1995; Croft 2001; Croft and Cruse 2004).

14.2.3 Language, Cognition, and Society

Research in social cognition now has to acknowledge that the detailed scientific investigation of language needs to be included in its purview. This is self-evident in the observable characteristics of human social behavior. It has become unavoidable with advances in neuroscience. The evidence now shows that human linguistic ability and social ability share neural connections and brain regions. For example, Bzdok et al. (2016) show in their survey that the left parietal lobe is a zone of convergence for both abilities, and there are also massively distributed connections for both abilities across the brain. Intuitively, the overlapping of linguistic and social circuitry is not surprising. Understanding language requires understanding the basic social phenomenon that we call dialogue, and this includes seeking to understand the mind and intentions of one's interlocutor, or what psychologists and others call "theory of mind" (see Baron-Cohen 1991). Dunbar et al. (1997) and Dunbar (2004) say language evolved for the exchange of socially relevant information, and Tomasello (1999; Tomasello et al. 2005) emphasizes the possibility that it evolved to facilitate group cooperation and the emergence of societies in general. Gallese (2003) and Decety and Somerville (2003) show that representations of self and other are processed in specific brain regions, namely, the right inferior parietal cortex, which is homologous to the language area in the left hemisphere, and the prefrontal cortex.

While cognitive linguists generally agree that human language has socially related structure and origin, there has been little attempt to theorize this. An exception is William Croft, a researcher into lexical and grammatical structure as well as the historical development of languages, who draws extensively on the work of the psychologist Herbert Clark (e.g., Clark 1996). Croft 2009 emphasizes the need for CL to incorporate in its core theory the fact that human language is inherently sociocognitive and not merely cognitive: "grammatical structures and processes in the mind are instances of general social cognitive abilities" (Croft 2009:398). The most important of the latter in his view are joint action, coordination, and convention. Joint action is pertinent because human communication not only is a means of coordinating actions involving groups of individuals, but also is *in itself* a kind of action that requires joint attention. Similarly, like all forms of goal-directed cooperative acts, communicating via language requires finely tuned meshing of numerous subactions, that is, coordination.

One implication of Croft's point is that human language is fundamentally dialogic, and has "design" features that reflect that. Such coordination further requires, or is facilitated by, mutually shared background knowledge, for example, about salient objects, locations, and practices in the environment. To be more detailed, we should also include shared beliefs, values, and attitudes. Such shared background is tantamount to what linguists and others call "context," viewed as a continually updated mental structure, and capable of being sufficiently recognized among sufficiently cooperating individuals. This is also where convention comes in, understood as a group's shared knowledge about behavioral regularities, partly arbitrary, that relate to a group's tacit or explicit agreement about how to do things. A language is one such specialized system of conventions, again given sufficient overlap, agreement, and cooperativity.

In CL the notion of "construal," a term also used within social psychology (see section 14.3.4.1), is important in understanding the processes of meaning-making that human language enables (see Lee 2001; Croft and Cruse 2004). In a broad sense of the term, the human mind is cognitively construing situations continuously—what to focus on, what has just happened, what is going to happen, how to act, and so forth—and this is not a specifically linguistic process. We are continuously "making sense of" the situation we are in. However, *communicating about* situations, or better, communicating about one's cognitive construals of situations, requires us to say something specific about the linguistic processes involved, and CL attempts to do that. The first point to make is that the conventional meanings of words and grammatical constructions is underdetermined so far as the needs of the communicative moment are concerned. In the moment by moment processing of language a speaker/hearer is engaging in continual inferencing on the basis of the linguistic input, following principles of relevance. Relevance can be defined, as in relevance theory, as the cognitive trade-off between processing effort and cognitive payoff (Sperber and Wilson 1995). The second point is that, additionally, human languages provide, by way of their lexical and grammatical choices, alternative construals of situations, which means that different choices from the language system can influence the conceptualizations presented and received. Consider a simple example: *the track rises steeply out of the valley* versus *the track drops steeply into the valley*. You may say that these sentences describe the same objective situation. But in reading these two sentences you may also experience a sense of viewing the scene that is evoked from different positions. Many such effects arise in the using of language, and are related to the conventionally established meanings of words and constructions interacting with our general cognitive systems. The point in the present chapter is that social situations are particularly susceptible to alternate conceptualization in the course of language-based human communication.

14.2.4 Societal Discourse Analysis and Cognition

It is important to distinguish between the related domains of *language* and *discourse*, sometimes confused in social science writing. Simply put, language is the knowledge of a language and how to use it that is stored in long-term memory, while discourse is an instance of the use in situ of a human language. Discourse requires, in addition to the activation of long-term memory, the use of working memory, short-term memory, and episodic memory (Baddeley and Hitch 1974; Baddeley 2000). The term "discourse" is of course also used to refer to relatively stable systems of thought, expressible in language use, which are also referred to in sociological, literary, and philosophical literature as worldviews, ideologies, and so forth. When the term "discourse" is used in this chapter, it means "an instance of the use *in situ* of a language."

Many discourse analysts work without reference to the cognitive sciences; some use non-cognitive models of language (e.g., the most popular form of systemic functional grammar), elaborations of argumentation theory and rhetoric, or some form of post-structuralist hermeneutic. There is, however, a growing network of discourse analysts who are primarily concerned with social processes and structures, and who also work within a cognitive framework.[1]

Van Dijk's work is one influential example, although it does not draw on CL. His earliest work was on cognitive mechanisms of discourse processing in collaboration with the cognitive psychologist, Walter Kintsch (Kintsch 1974, 1988; Kintsch and van Dijk 1978; van Dijk and Kintsch 1983). This line of research proposed that a personal mental model of situations is the cognitive basis for the interpretation and production of discourse, of its coherence, and of social (inter-) action in general. This cognitive approach is carried through in van Dijk's (1998) comprehensive study of ideology, which departs from the existing sociological approaches ("false consciousness," for example), redefining ideology as the basic social cognition of (ideological) groups, controlling more specific social attitudes (e.g., on immigration, abortion, or capital punishment), which control personal mental models, which control discourse. In van Dijk (1998, 2008, 2009, 2014) we have an outline of a theory of communicative context that is compatible with cognitive approaches, for example that of Clark (followed by Croft), and with the use in CL of notions of schema, semantic frames, cognitive categories, and social convention. In this account the making of sense in ongoing language use is dependent on *context models*, representing the ongoing individual interpretation of the relevant properties of the communicative situation (e.g., time, place, and participants in various roles). For van Dijk context is a dynamic cognitive structure, continually updated, that includes a large amount of knowledge of social structure and process, from the micro-level of face-to-face interaction to social institutions, culture-relative beliefs, and political ideologies. This knowledge must also include the speaker's knowledge of what their interlocutors are likely also to know. Van Dijk postulates a distinct mental "device" (the "K-device") that manages this requirement.

In his 2014 monograph van Dijk outlines a theory of discourse processing that includes an account of what the philosophically problematic notion of "knowledge" consists of, and how it contributes (necessarily) to discourse itself. However, this work does not engage with the findings either of cognitive science in general or of cognitive linguistics in particular, and while it represents a marked advance in the study of discourse, it does not enter into the connections between linguistic structures and the cognitive (and affective) systems of the brain-mind. Knowing the words and grammatical constructions of a language is, after all, a kind of knowledge, one unique to humans. Even so, to a considerable extent van Dijk's broad principles converge with those of independent CL work and indeed have much that needs to be absorbed into the CL framework, despite their lack of formal and psychological (and neurological) detail. Van Dijk's application of his cognitive theory of context and discourse processing has included many examples of actual discourse relating to and arising in racism, gender, and political institutions. However, it is arguable that there is a gap between the cognitive context modeling and the detail of linguistic utterances—the semantics of words and grammatical structures together with their links to the cognitive systems of which context models are a part.

This is where CL is beginning to bridge the gap, by providing detailed theories and data that can be applied to the analysis of discourse data in social contexts. The remainder of this chapter is given to summarizing some of the cognitive-linguistic theories and methods that are being applied in the study of *discourse*. Strictly speaking, one should say in the study of society, but it is important make clear that society is very largely composed of interactive linguistic communication; discourse is, precisely, the uses of human languages "in" society.

14.3 COGNITIVE LINGUISTIC APPROACHES TO DISCOURSE

The following sections can do no more that give an outline of the various applications of CL that have been attempted, and are being developed, in the investigation of discourse (cf. Hart and Lukeš 2007). This is an evolving field, both in the theoretical investigation of the many linkages between the brain's language systems and its cognitive and other systems, and in the application of these results in the investigation and critique of the social dimension of the human mind.

14.3.1 Frames, Construals, and Grammatical Constructions

Much of CL has focused on the intriguing phenomenon of "meaning" as it is experienced when humans use language, whether spoken, written, or signed. Cognitive linguistics departs from accounts of meaning (e.g., truth-conditional semantics) which hold that meaning resides in a relation between a linguistic sign and a referent in some real or possible world. This is a limited view of meaning, though it may be seen as part of the story. A word or a sentence can be meaningful to a situated speaking subject, even if it is false or too vague to have an identifiable referent. Moreover, truth-conditional semantics has no account of socially significant features of language, such as imperatives, interrogatives, and forms that express possibility, obligation, and other attitudes toward spoken content. Perhaps most importantly, CL acknowledges that linguistic meanings are not fixed and code-like, but conventionalized schemata that are filled in, or "construed" in situations of use. Furthermore, the schematic content of words stored in long-term memory include cultural understandings and attitudes.

The concept of "frame" now plays an important part across a range of disciplines, including computer science, artificial intelligence, and cognitive science (pioneered by Minsky 1975; Schank and Abelson 1977), social science (pioneered by Goffman 1974), and cognitive linguistics (for key papers, see Lehrer and Kittay 1992), drawing on both the last two currents. In CL the concept of frame focuses on the phenomenon of meaning at both the lexical and grammatical level. Fillmore's frame semantics (1968, 1982, 1985) proposes that many word meanings can only be understood in terms of a structured larger concept with which they cohere. For example, "waiter" only makes sense if one knows the cultural concept of restaurant, which also contains concepts paired with words such as "food," "eat," "table," and "serve."

Grammatical constructions are treated in a similar way, that is, as conceptualizations consisting of specific roles associated with actions and states. Consider the verb "sell." Its meaning and use is fundamentally tied in with basic social knowledge, reflected in the grammatical structure into which it can enter in English, namely *A sell B to C for D* (currency), where *A* is a seller, *B* a commodity, *C* a buyer, *D* an amount of currency, and "sell" is conceptualized as a transfer of *B* to *C* and *D* to *A*. This may be obvious, but it is quite different from traditional semantics, since it is based on social knowledge. Note that languages often have converses, which enable alternative perspectives: *Jenny sold the house to Ben; Ben bought the house from Alice*. And notice that roles do not always need to be made explicit (the examples just given omit *D*)—since the underlying known frame supplies them and their referent may be known by the speakers in the context. It is possible to simply say *Jenny sold*; the verb is still understood in terms of its conceptual frame. This is true also when verbs are nominalized: *the sale was completed*.

It should be clear from these examples, and from many others that have been examined, that one of the major tasks of grammatical constructions is to provided alternative "views" of the situations that are objectively similar, or, to put it in the terms of traditional semantics, situations can be expressed in terms of different sentences all of which have the same propositional formulae. In *she came into the room* and *she went into the room*, we have the same objective event. The phenomenology is different however, since in the first since the reader "feels" they are in the room, in the second outside the room. In fact, "point of view" switching of this kind is frequently found in the mental construal operations that are stimulated by grammatical choices.

Similarly, shifting focus of attention is often apparently the reason for choosing one rather than another grammatical construction to refer to a particular event. We can see this in a pair of words like *buy* and *sell*. Word frames cluster together to produce meaning in the mind. The commercial transaction frame for *buy* and *sell* is likely to be linked in the socialized subject to more specialized cultural frames such as "shopping," "marketing," "estate agency," "finance," and so forth. At the micro-level of individual interaction, then, fine linguistic detail is a part of cooperativity (and its potential collapse), since humans are sensitive to such cognitive alignments, and these have both social and political consequences.

Frames are linked with emotional structures of the brain. All words have meaning because they stimulate specific neural networks, and clusters in various brain regions, sometimes widely distributed (Pulvermuller 2013).[2] A good example is the word "threat" and related danger words. Isenberg et al. (1999) asked participants in their experiment to read a list of randomly ordered danger or threat words mixed in with words of neutral valence while their brain activity was measured by a neural imaging technique (positron emission tomography). The results suggested that emotionally negative word meanings activate the emotional circuitry of the brain, in particular the amygdala (Isenberg et al. 1999). Later experiments indicate that the dedicated language-processing areas of the brain (around the left perisylvian fissure) have dedicated sub-areas, and nearby cortical areas, specifically responding to written threat words as distinct from neutral words (Weisholtz et al. 2015). This raises at least the possibility that language centers evolved in relation to danger calls. Now, for social cognitive science, signaling danger to conspecifics is fundamental. And the linguistic signaling of danger affects the whole of social life, from signaling concrete environmental dangers to abstract discourse concerning national and international security. In general, language-related findings of this kind are of considerable significance for researchers in social cognition both when it comes to understanding the social brain-mind and when it comes to analyzing social discourse in all its manifestations.

This example points us to the hypothesis that linguistic meanings are simply a certain kind of cultural filtering and stabilizing of nonlinguistic cognitive brain mechanisms, particularly those having to do with perception, spatial awareness, and locomotion. Spatial conceptualization does in fact appear to be particularly important in linguistic conceptualization, and not only at the level of reference to locations and spatial relationships (Bloom et al.1996; Levinson 2003). The latter are clearly reflected in spatial prepositions *in, on, under*, and so forth, which primarily capture the relative positions of concrete objects—but not only, since one can be "in" a social group even if the individuals in it are not spatially bounded, "under" a commander, or more abstractly still "under" an obligation.[3] Neuroimaging corroborates these linguistic findings—that is, that spatial cognition underlies certain kinds of social cognition (Yamakawa et al. 2009; Yamazaki 2009; see also section 14.3.4).

Since CL argues that linguistic meanings are conceptualizations, it has also been argued that the same nonlinguistic conceptualizations are the source of meaning in visual communications, for example, cartoons (Forceville 2006, 2014; Abdel-Rheem 2017) and that like language they too follow general cognitive principles proposed in relevance theory (Sperber and Wilson 1995), which state that any communication comes with presumed relevance to the hearer and is computed as a function of processing effort and cognitive effect. In practical discourse, conceptual framing, by selectively activating culturally shared frames, steers the intended communication and its interpretation. This should make cognitive frame theory of central interest to social scientists in the study of rhetorical effects found in, for example advertising, politics, ideology, and religion (Fauconnier and Turner 2002; Coulson 2003, 2006, 2008).

In a series of papers, Hart (2013a, 2013b, 2014, 2015) has been interested in the basic event-models, in the form of image schemata, invoked by alternative language usages in press reports about political protests. In one case study, he investigated the use of transitive versus reciprocal verbs in reports of violence at political protests. These were analyzed as invoking an asymmetrical, one-sided action schema versus a neutral, bi-directional one, respectively. Ideologically, the transitive verns as opposed to the reciprocal verbs assign agency in significantly different ways.

In another paper (Hart 2015), Hart was concerned with a grammar of point of view (PoV) operating over image schemata. This grammar was derived from studies in multimodal discourse analysis (e.g., Kress and van Leeuwen 1996) but drawing on an embodied understanding of language Hart showed how the PoV parameters modeled in a visual grammar show up in language too. It can be shown that the grammar of PoV is instantiated across a range of grammatical constructions, with certain constructions having as part of their meaningful base a PoV specification in three dimensions—anchor, angle, and distance. The main argument of the paper was that if PoV functions in language as well as images, and if PoV in images carries particular ideological connotations as has been suggested in multimodal semiotics, then those ideological connotations will also be part of language usages with equivalent PoV specifications. This was all also illustrated with reference to press reports of political protest. In one further paper (Hart 2016), Hart showed experimentally how differences in event schemata and PoVs affected blame allocation and perception of aggression in discourses concerning political protest.

14.3.2   Conceptual Frames and Metaphor

The phenomenon of meaning that we experience in using language involves image schemata in the way we have just suggested—but not only image schemata. I use here the term "conceptual frame" to denote more elaborate cognitive assemblages that include cultural knowledge and, possibly, image schemata.

We need also here to consider the notion of "category." In philosophy language one way of defining meaning was in terms of classical (nonfuzzy) categories: the meaning of a word is given by the necessary and sufficient conditions that determine its membership of a category. The psychologist Eleanor Rosch established that, so far as human psychology is concerned, categories have internal "radial" structure, with a central prototype concept and interlinked peripheral members (see, e.g., Rosch 1978). This includes, of course, social categories like *mother*, *family*, as shown in detail by George Lakoff (1987). These categories are subjective, relative and variable, and the particular structure in play in any one brain at any one time has knock-on effects for the cognitive (and affective) processes in which they may be involved in mental processing, including the mental processing of language.

Lakoff is probably best known known as a theorist who, with the philosopher Mark Johnson, laid the foundations of conceptual metaphor theory (Lakoff and Johnson 1980), as well as developing the theory of conceptual categories, image schemata and their role in the lexical and grammatical structure of languages. However, he has from the start applied these analytical ideas to language as it is found in social and political contexts. In *Moral Politics* (1996) he applies conceptual frame theory in conjunction with conceptual metaphor theory (CMT), arguing that the different political mindsets of conservatives and liberals in the United States, in the sense in which those terms are understood in that country, can be characterized in terms of different conceptual frames (or "models" as he calls them in this book). Thus conservatives are said to think predominantly in terms of a "strict father" model, liberals in terms of a "nurturant parent" model. These different conceptual frames of the family are then claimed to be projected metaphorically, and normatively, onto society at large, leading to very different trains of thought and action. In this and other similar writings Lakoff makes it clear what his own political and social values are (Lakoff 2004, 2006, 2008).

The summaries in the last two paragraphs concern the ways in which mental categories and conceptual frames are projected onto social and political experience and impact patterns of thought. At the center of this approach is the theoretical concept of "metaphor," as understood in CL. The claim is that metaphor is a basic cognitive operation of the human mind. What it does is bring two mental domains together and facilitate the elaboration of thought, though not deterministically. The theoretical machinery is simple: there is a mental "source domain" that is relatively well understood and taken for granted and a "target domain" that is more vaguely or abstractly conceptualized. Elements of the former are "mapped" (in the logico-mathematical sense of that term) onto the latter. In the examples of the strict father and the nurturant parent, the metaphor is: SOCIETY IS A FAMILY. A family is a relatively familiar cultural conceptual frame, but varies in its content; society is the more abstract target domain. Three points are important in regard to conceptual metaphor. First, it is cognitively fundamental in the sense that cross-domain links appear to operate our cognitive systems, and to be "embodied" in the sense that the sensorimotor cortex is active not only in perception and action but also when humans think about and process abstractions such as "length" of time and social "distance" (Casasanto and Boroditsky 2008; Casasanto et al. 2010; Parkinson et al. 2014). Second, when we use language metaphor is found in varying degrees of explicitness and speaker awareness, ranging from entrenched idioms such as those just mentioned to elaborated analogies stretching over several sentences. Third, the inputs to the source domain of metaphors vary in cognitive type as well as content: they can be fundamental embodied image schemata such as CONTAINER and PATH, and they can be detailed conceptual frames that may include image schemata but are derived from experience (fire, water, wind...) or are variable cultural artifacts (dwellings, vehicles...), activities (rituals, warfare...), and social roles and institutions (mothers, families...).

Conceptual blending theory (Fauconnier and Turner 2002) builds on and is compatible with CMT, though different from it in the following respects. It is essentially a model of online cognitive processes, rather than a model of stable input frames and mappings. Its input spaces can be multiple, the mappings may flow both ways. In addition to a minimum of two input spaces CBT postulates a generic space that contains the abstract conceptual commonality of the inputs, and, crucially, a blend space in which conceptual structure emerges selectively from the inputs. Clearly, such a process is applicable in our understanding of dynamic social processes. Hart (2008, 2010, 2011) for instance, analyzes discourse about nation and immigration using conceptual blending theory. Systematic work of this type has not so far been extensive, however.

The classic conceptual metaphor apparatus has now been applied numerous times by researchers whose main concern is social discourse as it manifests itself in various domains of human activity, and across a variety of sociocultural locations, languages, and historical periods. Some studies claim to examine the embedded conceptualizations of whole cultures and their languages (Kövecses 2000, 2005, 2006; Goatly (2007).

Lakoff (1996a, 1996b), as we have seen, seeks to explain in cognitive terms the ideological structures of two whole groups, politically defined, in the society of the United States. Santa Ana (2002) addressed the metaphorical choices in anti-immigration (specifically, anti-Latino) discourse in the late twentieth century.

The scope is sometimes much larger. Musolff (2010) addresses metaphorical thought structures of major historical importance, the "body politic" metaphor as it manifests itself in national-socialist discourse of the 1930s (cf. also Chilton 2005), and subsequently of the metaphorical patterns in political discourse around the formation of the European Union (Musolff 2004). The cognitive structures and discourses of the Cold War, cutting across the national boundaries of the West, were analyzed in terms of the container image schema and its metaphorical transformations over a period of about forty years (Chilton 1996; Chilton and Lakoff 1995). While many such studies are sociopolitical, the investigation of even more large-scale sociocognitive phenomena are being investigated with CMT tools. Examples include ideology (Dirven et al. 2003; Goatly 2006, 2007; Koller 2014b), collective identity (Koller 2014a), and gender and sexuality (Koller 2015). Religious discourse is also coming under cognitive-linguistic scrutiny: many of the papers in Chilton and Kopytowska (2017) apply CMT to several different world religions. But in parallel the CMT-analytic approach also has to focus in on particular social sectors and genres, as is proposed and illustrated in Semino (2008, 2017) and Deignan et al. (2013), for example. The focus may be highly specific, as in the investigation of metaphor use in specialized medical situations (Semino et al. 2017; Semino et al. 2018), or in business contexts (Koller 2013), or it may combine broad and narrow focus (Koller 2004).

The principle behind most of these studies, and others like them that cannot be enumerated here, is the following. The linguistic utterances expressed in public media of various sorts exhibit patterns of thinking that can, at least, in part be analyzed (and perhaps explained) in terms of prevailing metaphors and the inferential mental processes that they support. In some studies authors focus on the claimed persuasive function of metaphors (Charteris-Black 2005; Boeynaems et al. 2017), as indeed did classical rhetoric, though it is important to note that in CMT "persuasion" is generally understood as analogical reasoning within a metaphorical frame (see, e.g., Musolff [2016] on political metaphor analysis). Some studies (e.g., Charteris-Black 2017) start with a particular source domain (e.g., fire) and investigate its mapping in various target domains.

Many studies are also "critical," in the sense that they presuppose an ethical stance that is, at least for the most part, made explicit. This is also true of van Dijk's work, which is not experimental or CL-based (though it is both cognition-based and language-based). These studies are for the most part executed in systematic and closely reasoned ways. The methodology has been defined and systematized by the use of large text corpora and software that establish statistically significant frequencies in the use of lexical items specified as identifying conceptual metaphors (Charteris-Black 2004; Steen et al. 2010).

There remains the question whether it can be asserted that such studies amounted to a *demonstration* that metaphor actually influenced overall patterns of sociopolitical cognition and consequent behaviors. However, the application of CMT to discourse has also entered the experimental stage. Response elicitation is one method that constrains some of the plausible but untested claims of many critical discourse analyses (see Gibbs and Steen 1999; Boeynaems et al. 2017). A number of experiments target particular metaphors. Landau et al. (2009) primed experimental participants by having them read a science article about the dangers of airborne bacteria—in effect, sensitizing them to the risk of bodily penetration by foreign bodies. When subsequently presented with a text about immigration that personified the United States—in effect, using the COUNTRY IS A BODY metaphor—the participants were found more likely to express more negative immigration attitudes. This constitutes evidence for numerous exploratory studies, based on language data, that have examined the "body politic" metaphor in thinking about political entities. A similar finding emerges from a series of experiments by Thibodeau and Boroditsky (2011), where the effects were examined of alternative framing metaphors—namely CRIME IS A DISEASE vs. CRIME IS A WILD BEAST, with respect to attitudes toward crime prevention. Even minimally expressed metaphors were found to significantly influence attitudes. Hart (2017) reports a parallel experiment in which participants were presented with more authentic texts—mock-ups of newspaper headlines and reports—that utilized the metaphor CIVIL DISORDER IS FIRE, a metaphor known to be conventionalized in such news stories. The stimulus texts were designed to compare the effects of visual images as against verbal ones (i.e., metaphors) and literal ones. "The results showed that [visual] images of fire in multimodal news texts and fire metaphors in the absence of competing [visual] images both achieve framing effects in legitimating police use of water cannon." Ongoing experimental work seeks to refine such studies by investigating the detailed conditions under which metaphor can be shown to influence thought, as proposed by Steen et al. (2014) in their review of Thibodeau and Boroditsky (2013). Cognitive linguistics postulates common neural structures underlying vision and language. Accordingly, analyses of multimodal texts are increasingly multimodal. That is, metaphor can be visual as well as verbal, in for example, news reporting in which manifestations of the metaphor [AN INDUSTRIAL] STRIKE IS WAR (Hart 2017; on visual metaphor, see also Forceville 2006).

14.3.3 Image Schemata

Image schemata are simple conceptual structures that derive from the interaction of the human organism with its environment, and that recur in the semantics of natural human language. This hypothesis was formulated in philosophy by Johnson (1987) and Lakoff (1987; see also Desclés n.d.), and their existence in the brain is now well supported by experiment (Mandler 2004) and by neuroimaging (see Rohrer 2005). Image schemata are not necessarily static; they are also patterns of action, such as grasping, walking, throwing, and the like. They are integrated patterns, a part of which can induce pattern completion, that is, inference. The central point here is that the basis of meaning, including social meaning, is inscribed in the sensorimotor systems of human bodies interacting with one another; they are formed during both prenatal and postnatal development. Not all meaning is image-schematic, but much of it is, and in any case all meaning is constituted by patterns of neural networks distributed in and between different areas of the brain. Image schemata are lexical items and modulated by context; they also provide the source domains for conceptual metaphor.

I concentrate here on two particular image schemata, CONTAINER AND PATH. These are image schema that are of particular importance in social conceptualization, social actions, ideologies, and policies of many kinds of discourse application (cf. Chilton 1996). We may tend to think of schemata in the abstract, but they are anatomically and neurologically grounded, as an evolutionary outcome of the interaction of organisms and environment.

This embodiment of semantics is important but in practical discourse research we need to have an equally well motivated abstract methodology. As in the case of orientational conceptualization and deixis (on which, see section 14.3.4.2), basic geometrical concepts and diagrams make sense because they themselves are grounded in the spatial experience of the human body. Since Johnson (1987) diagrams have been used in image schema semantics. Image schema diagrams are of various types—CONTAINER is essentially topological, PATH is essentially a translation vector. All can, however, be combined conceptually, since they all model different ways in which space is experienced.

Figure 14.1 combines two image schema models. The labeled ellipse is a diagrammatic model of CONTAINER, labeled with the English words that actually fire the neural circuits that constitute it and whose meanings are dependent on it. The two labeled arrows are the diagrammatic form of PATH that can be regarded as (geometric) vectors (the full deictic space theory (DST) makes use of vectors also: see section 14.3.4.2). The basic diagram for path is source-path-goal in the direction of the arrow. However, it seems that the path schemata stored in memory and used in language are likely to be more detailed. The path vector is a translation vector: indicating direction and distance of travel. But in discursive use, the source and goal are specified as a location and the moving point as an actor that may be self or other, within the deictic space. Crucially, self (S) may be inside a container location moving out (evoked by lexemes *exit, go out* or even *leave, quit, depart,* etc.), and a distal actor in the deictic space (O), may be conceptualized as *outside* S's containing space *coming in, entering, intruding, penetrating,* and so forth. It is not necessary to examine all the permutations here. But it is worth noting that a separate schema may well be constituted by two vectors in opposite directs, with S located at both source of vector 1 and goal of vector 2, both vectors combined in a deictic space, which of course includes temporal directionality. This is a composite image schema that grounds notions such as "two way" street, and all concepts of *return*. This composite schema is of fundamental importance in social discourse, incidentally, because it provides the embodied basis of the concept *home,* in addition to other kinds of social knowledge and affect: "home" (cf. "home base") is the location to which one habitually returns.

It is particularly important for what follows in section 14.4 to note that motion of an object or agent in the direction of S is probably linked to numerous neural circuits, most significantly those representing the containing boundary of peripersonal space. If peripersonal space (and its discursively constructed extension to the social group) is

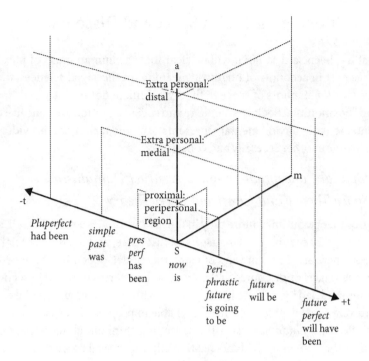

FIGURE 14.1 CONTAINER and PATH image schemas.

approached or transgressed, there is a neural response linked to the amygdala, which is responsible for processing fear and danger and the attendant hormonal responses. We have already mentioned brain-imaging evidence that words related to danger (e.g., "threat," "kill," and the like) trigger amygdala activity (Isenberg et al. 1999; Weisholtz et al. 2015). Discourses that activate penetration of the self's container—whether biological peripersonal space or the borders of S's territory—may stimulate the same biological fear response. It is a testable hypothesis.

Now it is this conceptual neurocognitive background that motivates another humanly vital area of behavior, conceptualization, linguistic lexicalization and discursive action—the area evoked by words such as "safe," "secure," "security," and "protect." In fact, the very meaning of these words *requires* the activation of the container concepts. However, containers can have an emotionally negative value: inside a container, you might feel confined, imprisoned. This kind if container concept depends not only on the internal point of view but also on bodily systems responding to pressure and skin contact—that is, to vector forces that impinge on the container surface. So, CONTAINER is emotionally ambiguous; it can be good or bad. It is bad if there is pressure whose source is from outside, or whose boundary is a force blocking S's path out from inside. It is good if its boundary is blocking Other's pressure on the boundary in the direction of S.

To sum up, the hypothesis is that language-discourse processing in necessarily social contexts draws on multiple neural networks that constitute conceptual schemata of this kind.

14.3.4 Positioning the Self in Space and Discourse

From what has been said so far, it will be clear that the human grasp of physical space plays a large part in accounts of linguistic meaning. In the social sciences, there is also increasing use of metaphors of space in theory—think of notions of social "space," "distance," and "positioning." Social psychology and social cognition are concerned with the study of interactive behavior, mental representations and feelings of individual humans in relation to one another severally and collectively.

14.3.4.1 *Spatial Conceptualization of Abstract Domains: Deictic Space Theory and Construal Level Theory*

Deictic space theory, outlined more fully in the next section, is a model of self-and-other relations as they are manifest in language and discourse, and of course social structure and process. There are different ways of using the model, depending on whether one is orienting to language or discourse in the sense of these terms outlined in section 14.2.4). The relations modeled by DST are hypothesized to involve space and spatial conceptualization to a very large degree. It seems reasonable to propose that spatial cognition and attendant affect are *fundamental*, in the sense that thinking about society and social relations uses the human individual's relationship to physical space as a source domain for conceptualization, and given that social emotions are dependent on spatial cognition. But more than that: actually being "in," and "moving around in," society is rooted in physical and physiological activity. In general terms, both thinking about society and acting "in" it involve cognitive operations using metaphorical mapping (in the CMT sense) from the spatial domain to the more abstract social one. Such operations are not only cognitive: they come with affect and values, since relative spatial distance between self and others, and between one group and others, is bound up with physical contact of different types, threat perception, and fear-attraction responses. The kinds of cognitive cross-over and affect involvement referred to here are well attested in the neurological and psychological literature, both empirical and theoretical, even if the full complexity is far from being mapped.

There are parallel lines of research in cognitive and social psychology that are consistent with this approach, and with DST. In particular, ideas developed by Yaakov Trope in his construal level theory (CLT), one kind of distance is defined as "hypothetical distance," and this appears to be similar to the linguistically defined egocentric scale of epistemic modality postulated in DST. The "hypotheticality" scale in CLT is empirically evidenced. Experiments and brain imaging demonstrate the congruence of spatial conceptualization and "hypotheticality": *sure* is closer, *maybe* is distant (Bar-Anan et al. 2006; Bar-Anan et al. 2007; Tamir and Mitchell 2011). Deictic space theory postulates an equivalent but more detailed scale, proposing that the extreme distal end of this scale (axis) is equivalent to the cognitively unreal and also to linguistically expressed negation—both of which are termed "irrealis" (as opposed to "realis" in DST).[4] Though not explicit on this point, CLT does seem to imply a realis/irrealis conceptualization: "Perhaps hypotheticality, the distinction between real and imagined objects and between probable and improbable events, is least prominent and acquired at an older age, compared to other distance dimensions" (Trope and Liberman 2010:444). As suggested here, within the epistemic domain, the cognitively metaphorical meaning of proximity to self as opposed to distance from self, may be developed relatively late in the child. There are differences also between CLT and DST, despite their common ground. One has to do with the conceptualization of time. Trope and Liberman (2010:444) say, "The various distance dimensions may differ in other respects. Time is unidimensional and uncontrollable. We incessantly travel from the past to the future and have no control over time." True, for physical time, but psychologically human selves orient "back" toward the past and "forward" toward the future. This is why the *t*-axis in DST is bidirectional. The DST model selects only direction and distance from spatial conceptualization—because those are the fundamental features that are used in the linguistic conceptualization of time and modality also. This does not imply, of course, that other characteristics of spatial cognition (topological relations such as containment, gravitational orientation, for instance) are irrelevant to other aspects of linguistic conceptualization: it is just that we need several approaches, models, or modes, to grasp the diverse structures of linguistic meanings.

Construal level theory also incorporates valence (in other terms, affect, evaluation) into the meaning of spatial distance under the different construals: "Another important difference among the distances is their relation to valence. Whereas social distance decreases positivity (e.g., ingroups are perceived as more positive than outgroups), temporal distance typically increases positivity (people are more positive about the more distant future)" (Trope and Liberman 2010: 444). When the DST model is applied to discourse, such differential effects are equally expected, although pragmatic contextual factors, both verbal and situational, would be expected to be heavily involved in interlocutor construal.

The "positioning" metaphor is ubiquitous in social research of many kinds, theoretical and applied. As we have noted, such metaphors point to the fundamental and varied use of spatial cognition in stable conventional lexicons, in their development over time, and in the ongoing use of language (discourse) that we constantly engage in as a species. But what we are observing here is not "mere" rhetorical ornament, turns of phrase, or handy tools for thinking, but something more basic to human organisms. Parkinson et al. (2014) have shown that there is a common cortical zone (the right inferior parietal lobule, in which egocentric distance of objects is processed—not just physical spatial distance but also what we metaphorically call distance, namely, temporal distance), and, of particular relevance here, Parkinson and Wheatley (2013) argue specifically that cognition of spatial distance is evolutionarily exapted for social "distance." It has also been shown that the left homologous region is concerned with *both* language and social cognition (Bzdok et al. 2016). The likelihood is that both left and right parietal lobules are involved in language (or more accurately in our terms, discourse). The spatial correlation was predictable on the basis of linguistic data of the kind first discussed by Lakoff and Johnson (1980), for example, *in the near/distant future/past; close friend, a distant relative,* and so forth. It is also worth noting that this location (the lower parietal lobules) is engaged in both language and social cognition as are the nearby superior temporal lobules, in particular the posterior area known as Wernicke's area that is predominantly engaged in language comprehension and what we might call meaning making or making sense.

14.3.4.2 *Elements of Deictic Space Theory*

Deictic space theory, as presented in Chilton (2014), draws on the psychologically oriented linguistic theories of Bühler (1990 [1934]) and has also been influenced by French theorists in the tradition of Benveniste (1966) and Culioli (1991 1999. All these theorists insist on the centrality of deictic engagement in the inferring of meaning. Deictic space theory finds corroboration in work within cognitive psychology (Trope and colleagues, as already noted, and MacWhinney 2005). In neuroscience, imaging evidence points to the involvement of specific brain regions in the processing of deixis and point of view shift. For example, in the case of the pronouns *I* and *you,* right anterior insula and precuneus are active (Mizuno et al. 2011). Shifts in narrative comprehension involve the right temporal gyrus, precuneus, and the posterior/middle cingulate in both cerebral hemispheres (Whitney et al. 2009).

Differently than Trope and Liberman, DST develops a theoretical three-dimensional space. This is a space in the geometric, Cartesian sense, which has the ability to model, in an abstract but rigorous way, the characteristics of three fundamental features of linguistic meaning and communication. The three dimensions (Cartesian axes) stand for metaphorical projections from spatial cognition, as explained in what follows. This geometric space is deictic because the Cartesian origin (intersection of the axes) is taken to stand for the self. Conceptualizations expressed in language in sentence form are defined in this space by means of natural geometric vectors with coordinates on these axes.

Both CLT and DST, then, take orientation of self in experienced space-time as their starting point and integrate it with the self's experiences of and judgments about what is real and "irreal." The advantage of this model is that it is the basis for modeling highly abstract concepts, without losing touch with their bodily basis, and also linking them to linguistic and other semiotic input from a context. Figure 14.2 presents the basic diagram for the abstract deictic space. It is a conceptual space not a physical one. It is the conceptual space that language systems use to represent many kinds of conceptualizations by way of words, parts of words, and grammatical constructions—conceptualizations that need not be literally to do with spatial objects at all but that are derived from our brain's representation of physical objects. In the diagram the point where the three axes converge, *viz.* the geometric origin (S), is the experiential self, the *I* who represents to itself the world around it in terms of three conceptual dimensions.[5]

The vertical axis in Figure 14.2 was originally considered spatial (and labeled "*d*-axis," distance axis; see Chilton 2005). However, although focusing within the visual field is the prototypical example, we can focus attention on the nonvisual and nonspatial too— on particular thoughts in our stream of consciousness, or sounds in our environment.

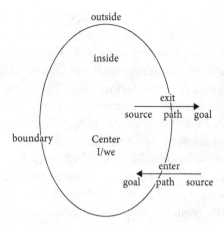

FIGURE 14.2 The fundamental deictic space.

In nonspatial consciousness, spatiovisual metaphors are often used to refer to the phenomenon of attention. Psychologists often speak of the "spotlight" of attention, the "beam" of attention, or the "zoom lens" model. Deictic space theory proposes to think of attention in terms of foreground and background. If we concentrate on something in the "forefront" of our attention, the rest is in the background. In terms of Figure 14.2, an entity on the a-axis is "closer" to S, analogously to spatial perception, where anything that comes into our peripersonal space is likely to command greater attention.

The t-axis is intended to model the subjective bidirectionality of time. Analogously to the a-axis, events on t are subjectively "closer" to S or more "remote," whether S is "looking back" into the past or "forward" into the future, from the deictic center t_0. The t-axis represents the way human minds think of time via metaphor—as extending in two directions, into the future (abstracted from planning and anticipation systems of the brain) and into the past (abstracted from memory systems).[6]

The m-axis (modal axis) is a case of spatial projection into a highly abstract conceptual domain, and seems to reflect the same phenomena as Trope and Liberman's hypotheticality scale. This axis represents our sense of what is most real (true), generally that which is closest to us, *present* and *here*, literally and metaphorically within our grasp. What is more distant is progressively less real, more uncertain epistemically, and ultimately "irreal." So, the m-axis is a scale from what is here, now, and real to what is from S's perspective not real at all. Geometrically, the m-axis, like the a-axis, is a half-line for good reasons. Bidirectionality does not make sense in either case; this is simply the way the geometric space has to model the properties of the human cognitive space that has these three fundamental dimensions—attentive awareness, temporal awareness, and awareness that some events and entities are actual, merely possible, impossible, or non-existent. The m-axis includes concepts linguistically expressed by, for example, modal verbs; however, there are many kinds and degrees of epistemic reality and irreality that have not been specified in DST.[7]

In sum, we have relative degrees of distance from self on axes of attention, temporal ordering and epistemic judgment. These are abstractions, used by language and other semiotic systems, for building complex ideas and communicating them. Deictic space theory models the meanings of sentences in terms of relationships between entities that are labeled on the a-axis as closer or further away. The relationships are modeled by vectors—giving the direction of, for example, an entity's motion or force. Sentences modeling events always have an anchor coordinate on the *t*-axis, sentences modeling general assertions being anchored at t = 0. Sentences indicate an epistemic status too: *John married Mary* versus *John might have married Mary* versus *John didn't marry Mary*. The first of these sentences would be anchored at the m = 0 point, the second at the midpoint on *m*, and the third at *m*'s endpoint, where the irrealis plane is anchored. Many complex sentences involve switches of epistemic status that can be transparently shown in a DST diagram. For example, *John wanted to marry Mary*—where "John wanted" is anchored at some point on past *t* relative to the speaker S, but "to marry Mary" is at *m*'s midpoint, because S is not saying, and the hearer cannot guess (at least from the sentence) whether John ever did marry her. The sentence *John must not marry Mary* involves not only the epistemic representation "John might marry Mary" but also a special modeling feature to model the deontic force of "must" (Chilton 2011). Simple though such examples seem, they show that communicating the sort of social information that humans are interested in can be cognitively quite complex.

It is important to stress that the outline and examples just presented focus on the structure of language viewed independently of discourse, that is, situated language use (again, see section 14.2.4). An earlier version of DST (Chilton 2004) and later work, notably by Cap (2010, 2013, 2014), Kopytowska (2013, 2015), and Kaal (2012, 2015) apply the DST three-dimensional deictic space model to various kinds of social, political, and media discourse, locating linguistically indicated material that is larger than the sentence within a deictic space. Their approach uses the same basic idea of a three-dimensional conceptual space, with the self (which can be a collective *we* as well as an individual *I*) at the geometric center, and with direction and distance being key to the overall representation. It is an approach that formalizes the notion of self and other, found in more informal social and psychological analyses, is formalized. This discourse-oriented application of DST defines two of the axes differently than in the language faculty-oriented approach of Chilton (2014). The time axis remains the same, but the attention or *a*-axis (cognitive foregrounding/backgrounding) of Chilton (2014) is instead understood as standing for literal geographical distance, or perceived (and metaphorical) personal, social, or political space and distance. The third axis in the discourse-oriented DST is not epistemic, as in Chilton (2014), but axiological, that is, to do with value as perceived by the self S (see Cap 2010).

These different developments of the basic DST framework need not be seen as contradictory. Spatial cognitions such as distance are recruited for axiological meanings as much as they are for epistemic ones, for example. There are more than three conceptual domains that find expression in, and are in all likelihood neurally linked to spatial cognitions, and it follows that in principle the deictic space is multidimensional. We have noted that the fact that existing DST models, of whatever kind, currently have three dimensions is a convenience, and the differing labeling of the axes a reflection of particular research interests.

14.4 CONCLUSION

In this chapter I have tried to introduce to a transdisciplinary readership some of the ways in which research in CL might contribute to and benefit from work in social cognition. I have aimed to give glimpses of established work while offering some new ideas and avenues for further work. Both research traditions explore the workings of the human mind, and both recognize that the mind is social. Cognitive linguistics emphasizes the embodied nature of mind, and consequently of language. Equally, social knowledge and behavioral competence is mental and also embodied. The role of spatial experience in particular leaves its mark, in the various ways discussed. From time to time in this chapter I have referred to the neuroscientific level of description, and ultimately it should be the aim of the cognitive sciences, linguistic and social, to relate their theories and empirical findings to the neural level. Many loose ends and unexplored paths remain for future collaborative research.

NOTES

1. In many cases discourse analysts, whatever their methods, are concerned also with the *critique* of social discourse. That is, they critique discourse as desirable or undesirable on the basis of principles and values. The latter should be stated explicitly.
2. It is important to note that the discursive context further modulates word meaning, often in major ways. If the context is a spoken one then affective prosody stimulates right-hemispheric homologues of the usually left-hemispheric language areas around the Sylvian fissure.
3. It should be noted that spatial prepositions differ across languages, and there is evidence that the conceptualizations influence behavior depending on the language one is speaking.
4. The terms "realis mood" and "irrealis mood" are used in linguistics to refer to meanings, sometimes morphologically marked, that a speaker presents as matters of fact or not as matters of fact, respectively. The indicative versus the subjunctive verb forms in Romance languages are examples of the linguistic reflex of this cognitive distinction.
5. In this theoretical model, that is. Of course, the self's mental representations involve many more dimensions. There is no *theoretical* reason to limit the modeling dimensions to three, but three is obviously easier to handle and also possibly natural.
6. Whether the direction in relation to the body is conventionally up-down, front-back, back, back-front, and so forth, varies across languages. In English, we speak of the past being behind us and the future in front; speakers of Aymara do the reverse. The left-right orientation of the t-axis in the diagrams is not significant in itself but the bidirectionality centered on self is.
7. Modal verbs often also express deontic meanings. In this version of DST, m is epistemic; on deontic models in DST, see Chilton (2011).

REFERENCES

Abdel-Raheem, Ahmed. 2017. "Decoding Images: Toward a Theory of Pictorial Framing." *Discourse and Society* 28(4):327–52.

Baddeley, Alan. 2000. "The Episodic Buffer: A New Component of Working Memory?" *Trends in Cognitive Science*. 4:417–23.

Baddeley, Alan, and Graham Hitch. 1974. "Working Memory." pp. 47–89 in *The Psychology of Learning and Motivation: Advances in Research and Theory*, Vol. 8, edited by G. H. Bower. New York: Academic Press.

Bar-Anan, Yoav, Nira Liberman, and Yaakov Trope. 2006. "The Association between Psychological Distance and Construal Level: Evidence from an Implicit Association Test." *Journal of Experimental Psychology: General* 135(4):609–22.

Bar-Anan, Yoav, Nira Liberman, Yaakov Trope, and Daniel Algom. 2007. "Automatic Processing of Psychological Distance: Evidence from a Stroop Task." *Journal of Experimental Psychology: General* 136:610–22.

Baron-Cohen, Simon. 1991. "Precursors to a Theory of Mind: Understanding Attention in Others." pp. 233–51 in *Natural Theories of Mind: Evolution, Development and Simulation of Everyday Mindreading*, edited by A. Whiten. Oxford: Basil Blackwell.

Benveniste, Émile. 1966. *Problèmes de linguistique générale*. Paris: Gallimard.

Bloom, Paul, Mary A. Peterson, Lynn Nadel, and Merrill F. Garrett. 1996. *Language and Space*. Cambridge, MA: The MIT Press Ltd.

Boeynaems, Amber, Christian Burgers, Elly A. Konijn, and Gerard J. Steen. 2017. "The Effects of Metaphorical Framing on Political Persuasion: A Systematic Literature Review." *Metaphor and Symbol* 32(2):118–34.

Bühler, Karl. 1990 [1934]. *The Theory of Language: The Representational Function of Language*. Translated by D. F. Goodwin. Amsterdam: Benjamins.

Bzdok, Danilo, Gesa Hartwigsen, Andre Reid, Angela R. Laird, Peter T. Fox, and Simon B. Eickhoff. 2016. "Left Inferior Parietal Lobe Engagement in Social Cognition and Language." *Neuroscience and Biobehavioral Reviews* 68:319–34.

Cap, Piotr. 2010. "Axiological Aspects of Proximization." *Journal of Pragmatics* 42(2):492–7.

Cap, Piotr. 2013. *Proximization: The Pragmatics of Symbolic Distance Crossing*. Amsterdam: John Benjamins.

Cap, Piotr. 2014. "Applying Cognitive Pragmatics to Critical Discourse Studies: A Proximization Analysis of Three Public Space Discourses." *Journal of Pragmatics* 70:16–30.

Casasanto, Daniel, and Lera Boroditsky. 2008. "Time in the Mind: Using Space to Think about Time." *Cognition* 106:579–93.

Casasanto, Daniel, Olga Fotakopoulou, and Lera Boroditsky. 2010. "Space and Time in the Child's Mind: Evidence for a Cross-Dimensional Asymmetry." *Cognitive Science* 34:387–405.

Charteris-Black, Jonathan. 2004. *Corpus Approaches to Critical Metaphor Analysis*. Basingstoke: Palgrave Macmillan.

Charteris-Black, Jonathan. 2005. *Politicians and Rhetoric: The Persuasive Power of Metaphor*. Basingstoke: Palgrave.

Charteris-Black, Jonathan. 2017. *Fire Metaphors: Discourses of Awe and Authority*. London: Bloomsbury.

Chilton, Paul. 1996. *Security Metaphors: Cold War Discourse from Containment to Common House*. New York: Peter Lang.

Chilton, Paul. 2004. *Analysing Political Discourse: Theory and Practice*. London: Routledge.

Chilton, Paul. 2005. "Manipulation, Memes and Metaphors: The Case of *Mein Kampf*." pp. 15–43 in *Manipulation and Ideologies in the Twentieth Century*, edited by L. de Saussure, and P. Schulz. Amsterdam: Benjamins.

Chilton, Paul. 2011. "The Conceptual Structure of Deontic Meaning: A Model Based on Geometrical Principles." *Language and Cognition* 2(2):191–220.

Chilton, Paul. 2014. *Language, Space and Mind: The Conceptual Geometry of Linguistic Meaning*. Cambridge: Cambridge University Press.

Chilton, Paul, and Monika Kopytowska, eds. 2017. *Religion, Language and the Human Mind*. New York: Oxford University Press.

Chilton, Paul, and George Lakoff. 1995. "Foreign Policy by Metaphor." pp. 37–60 in *Language and Peace*, edited by C. Schäffner and A. I. Wenden. Aldershot: Ashgate.

Clark, Herbert H. 1996. *Using Language*. Cambridge: Cambridge University Press.

Coulson, Seana. 2003. "Reasoning and Rhetoric: Conceptual Blending in Political and Religious Rhetoric." pp. 59–88 in *Research and Scholarship in Integration Processes*, edited by E. Oleksy and B. Lewandowska-Tomaszczyk. Lodz: Lodz University Press.

Coulson, Seana. 2006. "Conceptual Blending in Thought, Rhetoric, and Ideology." pp. 187–210 in *Cognitive Linguistics: Current Applications and Future Perspectives*. Amsterdam and Philadelphia: John Benjamins.

Coulson, Seana. 2008. "Framing and Blending in Persuasive Discourse." pp. 33–42 in *Frames, Corpora, and Knowledge Representation*, edited by R. R. Favretti. Bologna: Bononia University Press.

Croft, William. 2001. *Radical Construction Grammar*. Oxford: Oxford University Press.

Croft, William. 2009. "Toward a Social Cognitive Linguistics." pp. 395–420 in *New Directions in Cognitive Linguistics*, edited by V. Evans and S. Pourcel. Amsterdam: John Benjamins.

Croft, William, and D. Alan Cruse. 2004. *Cognitive Linguistics*. Cambridge: Cambridge University Press.

Culioli, Antoine. 1991. *Pour une linguistique de l'énonciation*. Vol. 1. *Opérations et représentations*. Paris: Ophrys.

Culioli, Antoine. 1999. *Pour une linguistique de l'énonciation*. Vol. 2 *Formalisations et opérations de repérage*. Paris: Ophrys.

Decety, Jean, and Jessica A. Sommerville. 2003. "Shared Representations between Self and Other: A Social Cognitive Neuroscience View." *Trends in Cognitive Sciences* 7:527–33.

Deignan, Alice, Jeannette Littlemore, and Elena Semino. 2013. *Figurative Language, Genre and Register*. Cambridge: Cambridge University Press.

Desclés, Jean-Pierre. n.d. Schèmes sémantico-cognitifs et représentations lexicales. http://lalic.paris-sorbonne.fr/PAGESPERSO/Descles/.

Dirven, René, Roslyn Frank, and Martin Pütz, eds. 2003. *Cognitive Models in Language and Thought: Ideology, Metaphors and Meanings*. Berlin: W. de Gruyter.

Dunbar, Robin. I. M. 2004. "Gossip in Evolutionary Perspective." *Review of General Psychology* 8(2):100–110.

Dunbar, Robin I. M., Neil D. C. Duncan, and Anna Marriott. 1997. "Human Conversational Behavior." *Human Nature* 8(3):231–46.

Fauconnier, Gilles, and Mark Turner. 2002. The Way We Think. New York: Basic Books.

Fillmore, Charles J. 1968. "The Case for Case." pp. 1–90 in *Universals of Linguistic Theory*, edited by E. Bach, and R. T. Harms. New York: Holt, Rinehart & Winston.

Fillmore, Charles J. 1982. "Frame Semantics." pp. 111–37 in *Linguistics in the Morning Calm*, edited by Linguistics Society of Korea. Seoul: Hanshin Publishing.

Fillmore, Charles J. 1985. "Frames and the Semantics of Understanding." *Quaderni di Semantica* 6:222–54.

Forceville, Charles. 2006. "Non-Verbal and Multimodal Metaphor in a Cognitivist Framework: Agendas for Research." pp. 379–402 in *Cognitive Linguistics: Current Applications and Future Perspectives*, edited by G. Kristiansen, M. Achard, R. Dirven, and F. Ruiz de Mendoza Ibàñez. Berlin: Mouton de Gruyter.

Forceville, Charles. 2014. "Relevance Theory as a Model for Multimodal Communication." pp. 51–70 in *Visual Communication*, edited by D. Machin. Berlin: Mouton de Gruyter.

Gallese, Vittorio. 2003. "The Manifold Nature of Interpersonal Relations: The Quest for a Common Mechanism." *Philosophical Transactions of the Royal Society of London. Series B, Biological Sciences* 358(1431):517–28.

Gibbs, Raymond W., and Gerard J. Steen, eds. 1999. *Metaphor in Cognitive Linguistics: Selected Papers from the 5th International Cognitive Linguistics Conference, Amsterdam, 1997*. Amsterdam: Benjamins.

Goatly, Andrew. 2006. "Ideology and Metaphor." *English Today* 22(3):25–39.

Goatly, Andrew. 2007. *Washing the Brain: The Hidden Ideology of Metaphor*. Amsterdam: Benjamins.

Goffman, Erving. 1974. *Frame Analysis and Communication: An Essay on the Organization of Experience*. Cambridge, MA: Harvard University Press.

Goldberg, Adele. 1995. A Construction Grammar Approach to Argument Structure. Chicago: University of Chicago Press.

Hart, Christopher. 2008. "Critical Discourse Analysis and Metaphor: Toward a Theoretical Framework." *Critical Discourse Studies* 2(5):91–106.

Hart, Christopher. 2010. *Critical Discourse Analysis and Cognitive Science: New Perspectives on Immigration Discourse*. Basingstoke: Palgrave.

Hart, Christopher. 2011. "Moving beyond Metaphor in the Cognitive Linguistic Approach to CDA: Construal Operations in Immigration Discourse." pp. 171–92 in *Critical Discourse Studies in Context and Cognition*, edited by C. Hart. Amsterdam: John Benjamins.

Hart, Christopher. 2013a. "Event-Construal in Press Reports of Violence in Political Protests: A Cognitive Linguistic Approach to CDA." *Journal of Language and Politics* 12(3):400–23.

Hart, Christopher. 2013b. "Constructing Contexts through Grammar: Cognitive Models and Conceptualisation in British Newspaper Reports of Political Protests." pp. 159–84 in *Discourse in Context*, edited by J. Flowerdew. London: Continuum.

Hart, Christopher. 2014. *Discourse, Grammar and Ideology: Functional and Cognitive Perspectives*. London: Bloomsbury.

Hart, Christopher. 2015. "Viewpoint in Linguistic Discourse: Space and Evaluation in News Reports of Political Protests." *Critical Discourse Studies* 12(3):238–60.

Hart, Christopher. 2016. "Event-Frames Affect Blame Assignment and Perception of Aggression in Discourse on Political Protests: An Experimental Case Study in Critical Discourse Analysis." *Applied Linguistics*, amw017, https://doi.org/10.1093/applin/amw017.

Hart, Christopher. 2017. "Metaphor and Intertextuality in Media Framings of the 1984–85 British Miners' Strike: A Multimodal Analysis." *Discourse and Communication* 11(1):3–30.

Hart, Christopher. 2017. "Riots Engulfed the City: An Experimental Study Investigating the Legitimating Effects of Fire Metaphors in Discourses of Disorder." *Discourse and Society*. http://dx.doi.org/10.1177/0957926517734663.

Hart, Christopher, and Dominik Lukeš, eds. 2007. *Cognitive Linguistics in Critical Discourse Analysis: Application and Theory*. Newcastle: Cambridge Scholars Publishing.

Isenberg, N., D. Silbersweig, A. Engelien, S. Emmerich, K. Malavade, B. Beattie, et al. 1999. "Linguistic Threat Activates the Human Amygdala." *Proceedings of the National Academy of Sciences USA* 96:10456–9.

Jackendoff, Ray. 1996. "Conceptual Semantics and Cognitive Linguistics." *Cognitive Linguistics* 7(1):93–129.

Johnson, Mark. 1987. *The Body in the Mind: The Bodily Basis of Meaning, Imagination, and Reason.* Chicago: University of Chicago.

Kaal, Bertie. 2012. "Worldviews: The Spatial Ground of Political Reasoning in Dutch Election Manifestos." *CADAAD* 6(1):1–22.

Kaal, Bertie. 2015. "How 'Real' are Time and Space in Politically Motivated Worldviews?" *Critical Discourse Studies* 12(3):330–46.

Kintsch, Walter. 1974. *The Representation of Meaning in Memory.* Hillsdale, NJ: Erlbaum.

Kintsch, Walter. 1988. "The Use of Knowledge in Discourse Processing: A Construction-Integration Model." *Psychological Review* 95:163–82.

Kintsch, Walter, and Teun van Dijk. 1978. "Toward a Model of Text Comprehension and Production." *Psychological Review* 85(5):363–94.

Knight, Chris. 1998. "Introduction: Grounding Language Function in Social Cognition." pp. 9–16 in *Approaches to the Evolution of Language*, edited by J. R. Hurford, M. Studdert-Kennedy, and C. Knight. Cambridge: Cambridge University Press.

Koller, Veronika. 2004. *Metaphor and Gender in Business Media Discourse: A Critical Cognitive Study.* Basingstoke: Palgrave.

Koller, Veronika. 2013. "Deliberate Conventional Metaphor in Images: The Case of Corporate Branding Discourse." *Metaphor and Symbol* 3(28):131–47.

Koller, Veronika. 2014a. "Applying Social Cognition Research to Critical Discourse Studies: The Case of Collective Identities." pp. 147–65 in *Contemporary Critical Discourse Studies*, edited by C. Hart, and P. Cap. London: Bloomsbury.

Koller, Veronika. 2014b. "Cognitive Linguistics and Ideology." pp. 234–52, in *The Bloomsbury Companion to Cognitive Linguistics*, edited by J. Littlemore, and J. Taylor, London: Bloomsbury.

Koller, Veronika. 2015. "Sexuality and Metaphor." In *The International Encyclopedia of Human Sexuality*, edited by P. Whelehan, and A. Bolin. Hoboken, NJ: Wiley-Blackwell.

Kopytowska, Monika. 2013. "Blogging as the Mediatization of Politics and a New Form of Social Interaction." pp. 379–421 in *Analyzing Genres in Political Communication*, edited by P. Cap, and U. Okulska. Amsterdam: John Benjamins.

Kopytowska, Monika. 2015. "Ideology of 'Here and Now': Mediating Distance in Television News." *Critical Discourse Studies* 12(3):347–65.

Kövecses, Zoltán. 2000. *Metaphor and Emotion: Language, Culture, and Body in Human Feeling.* Cambridge: Cambridge University Press.

Kövecses, Zoltán. 2005. *Metaphor in Culture: Universality and Variation.* Cambridge and New York: Cambridge University Press.

Kövecses, Zoltán. 2006. *Language, Mind, and Culture.* Oxford and New York: Oxford University Press.

Kress, Gunther R., and Theo van Leeuwen. 1996. *Reading Images: The Grammar of Visual Design.* London: Routledge.

Lakoff, George. 1987. *Women, Fire and Dangerous Things: What Categories Tell Us about the Nature of Thought.* Chicago: University of Chicago Press.

Lakoff, George. 1996a. *Moral Politics: How Conservatives and Liberals Think.* Chicago: University of Chicago Press.

Lakoff, George. 1996b. *Moral Politics: What Conservatives Know That Liberals Don't*. Chicago: University of Chicago Press.

Lakoff, George. 2004. *Don't Think of an Elephant: Know Your Values and Frame the Debate*. White River Junction, VT: Chelsea Green.

Lakoff, George. 2006. *Thinking Points: Communicating Our American Values and Vision*. New York: Farrar, Straus and Giroux.

Lakoff, George. 2008. *The Political Mind: Why You Can't Understand 21st Century Politics with an 18th Century Brain*. New York: Viking.

Lakoff, George, and Mark Johnson. 1980. *Metaphors We Live By*. Chicago: University of Chicago Press.

Landau, Mark. J., Daniel Sullivan, and Jeff Greenberg. 2009. "Evidence That Self-Relevant Motives and Metaphoric Framing Interact to Influence Political and Social Attitudes." *Psychological Science* 20(11):1421–6.

Langacker, Ronald W. 1987. *Foundations of Cognitive Grammar: Volume I. Theoretical Prerequisites*. Stanford, CA: Stanford University Press.

Langacker, Ronald W. 1991. *Foundations of Cognitive Grammar: Volume II. Descriptive Application*. Stanford, CA: Stanford University Press.

Langacker, Ronald W. 2002. *Concept, Image, and Symbol: The Cognitive Basis of Grammar*, 2nd ed. Berlin: Mouton de Gruyter.

Langacker, Ronald W. 2008. *Cognitive Grammar: A Basic Introduction*. Oxford: Oxford University Press.

Lee, David. 2001. *Cognitive Linguistics. An Introduction*. Oxford: Oxford University Press.

Lehrer, Adrienne, and Eva Kittay, eds. 1992. *Frames, Fields and Contrasts: New Essays in Semantic and Lexical Organisation*. Hillsdale, NJ: Erlbaum.

Levinson, Stephen C. 2003. *Space in Language and Cognition*. Cambridge: Cambridge University Press.

MacWhinney, Brian. 2005. "The Emergence of Grammar from Perspective." pp. 198–223 in *Grounding Cognition: The Role of Perception and Action in Memory, Language and Thinking*, edited by D. Pecher, and R. A. Zwaan. Cambridge: Cambridge University Press.

Mandler, Jean M. 2004. *The Foundations of Mind: Origins of Conceptual Thought*. Oxford: Oxford University Press.

Minsky, Marvin. 1975. "A Framework for Representing Knowledge." pp. 211–77 in *The Psychology of Computer Vision*, edited by P. H. Winston. New York: McGraw Hill.

Mizuno, Akiko, Yanni Liu, Diane L. Williams, Timothy A. Keller, Nancy J. Minshew, and Marcel Adam Just. 2011. "The Neural Basis of Deictic Shifting in Linguistic Perspective-Taking in High-Functioning Autism." *Brain* 134(8):2422–35.

Musolff, Andreas. 2004. *Metaphor and Political Discourse: Analogical Reasoning in Debates about Europe*. Basingstoke: Palgrave.

Musolff, Andreas. 2010. *Metaphor, Nation and the Holocaust: The Concept of the Body Politic*. New York and Oxford: Routledge.

Musolff, Andreas. 2016. *Political Metaphor Analysis: Discourse and Scenarios*. London: Bloomsbury.

Parkinson, Carolyn, Shari Liu, and Thalia Wheatley. 2014. "A Common Cortical Metric for Spatial, Temporal, and Social Distance." *Journal of Neuroscience* 34(5):1979–87.

Parkinson, Carolyn, and Thalia Wheatley. 2013. "Old Cortex, New Contexts: Re-Purposing Spatial Perception for Social Cognition." *Frontiers in Human Neuroscience* 7:645.

Pulvermüller, Friedemann. 2013. "How Neurons Make Meaning: Brain Mechanisms B. Hampe and J. Grady (eds), for Embodied and Abstract Semantics." *Cognitive Sciences* 17(9):458–70.

Rohrer, Tim. 2005. "Image Schemata in the Brain." pp. 165–96 in *From Perception to Meaning: Image Schemas in Cognitive Linguistics*, edited by B. Hampe, and J. Grady. Berlin: Mouton de Gruyter.

Rosch, Eleanor. 1978. "Principles of Categorization." pp. 27–48 in *Cognition and Categorization*, edited by E. Rosch, and B. B. Lloyd. Hillsdale: NJ: Erlbaum.

Santa Ana, Otto. 2002. *Brown Tide Rising: Metaphors of Latinos in Contemporary American Public Discourse*. Austin: University of Texas Press.

Schank, Roger C., and Robert P. Abelson. 1977. *Scripts, Plans, Goals and Understanding*. Hillsdale, NJ: Erlbaum.

Semino, Elena. 2008. *Metaphor in Discourse*. Cambridge: Cambridge University Press.

Semino, Elena. 2017. "Images and the Dynamics of Pain Consultations." *Lancet* 10075(389): 1186–7.

Semino, Elena, Zsofia Demjen, and Jane Demmen. 2018. "An Integrated Approach to Metaphor and Framing in Cognition, Discourse and Practice, with an Application to Metaphors for Cancer." *Applied Linguistics* 39(5): 625–45.

Semino, Elena, Zsofia Demjen, Jane Demmen, Veronika Koller, Sheila Payne, Andrew Hardie, et al. 2017. "The Online Use of Violence and Journey Metaphors by Patients with Cancer, as Compared with Health Professionals: A Mixed Methods Study." *BMJ Supportive and Palliative Care* 7(1):60–6. http://spcare.bmj.com/content/7/1/60.

Sperber, Dan, and Deirdre Wilson. 1995. *Relevance Theory: Communication and Cognition*, 2nd ed. Oxford: Blackwell.

Steen, Gerard. J., Aletta G. Dorst, J. Berenike Herrmann, Anna Kaal, Tina Krennmayr, and Trijntje Pasma. 2010. *A Method for Linguistic Metaphor Identification*. Amsterdam: Benjamins.

Steen, Gerard. J., W. Gudrun Reijnierse, and Christian Burgers. 2014. "When Do Natural Language Metaphors Influence Reasoning? A Follow-Up Study to Thibodeau and Boroditsky (2013)." *PloS ONE* 9:e113536.

Tamir, Diana, and Jason P. Mitchell. 2011. "The Default Network Distinguishes Construals of Proximal versus Distal Events." *Journal of Cognitive Neuroscience* 23(10):2945–55.

Thibodeau, Paul. H, and Lera Boroditsky. 2011. "Metaphors We Think With: The Role of Metaphor in Reasoning." *PLoS ONE* 6 (2):e16782.

Thibodeau, Paul H., and Lera Boroditsky. 2013. "Natural Language Metaphors Covertly Influence Reasoning." *PLoS ONE* 8 (1):e52961.

Tomasello, Michael. 1999. *The Cultural Origins of Human Cognition*. Cambridge, MA: Harvard University Press.

Tomasello, Michael, Malinda Carpenter, Josep Call, Tanya Behne, and Henrike Moll. 2005. "Understanding and Sharing Intentions: The Origins of Cultural Cognition." *Behavioral and Brain Sciences* 28(5):675–91.

Trope, Yaakov, and Nira Liberman. 2010. "Construal-Level Theory of Psychological Distance." *Psychological Review* 117(2):440–63.

van Dijk, Teun A. 1998. *Ideology: A Multidisciplinary Approach*. London: SAGE.

van Dijk, Teun A. 2008. *Discourse and Context: A Sociocognitive Approach*. Cambridge: Cambridge University Press.

van Dijk, Teun A. 2009. *Society and Discourse: How Social Contexts Influence Text and Talk.* Cambridge: Cambridge University Press.

van Dijk, Teun A. 2014. *Discourse and Knowledge: A Sociocognitive Approach.* Cambridge: Cambridge University Press.

van Dijk, Teun A., and Walter Kintsch. 1983. *Strategies of Discourse Comprehension.* New York: Academic Press.

Weisholtz, Daniel S., James C. Root, Tracy Butler, Oliver Tüscher, Jane Epstein, Hong Pan, et al. 2015. "Beyond the Amygdala: Linguistic Threat Modulates Perisylvian Semantic Access Cortices." *Brain and Language* 151:12–22.

Whitney, Carin, Walter Huber, Juliane Klann, Susanne Weis, Sören Krach, and Tilo Kircher. 2009. "Neural Correlates of Narrative Shifts during Auditory Story Comprehension." *Neuroimage* 47:360–6.

Yamakawa, Yoshinori, Ryota Kanai, Michikazu Matsumura, and Eiichi Naito. 2009. "Social Distance Evaluation in Human Parietal Cortex." *PLoS ONE* 4(2):e4360.

Yamazaki, Yumiko, Teruo Hashimoto, and Atsushi Iriki. 2009. "The Posterior Parietal Cortex and Non-Spatial Cognition." *F1000 Biology Reports* 1:74.

....

CHAPTER 15

CLASS, COGNITION, AND CULTURAL CHANGE IN SOCIAL CLASS

....

HENRI C. SANTOS, IGOR GROSSMANN, AND MICHAEL E. W. VARNUM

WHILE social scientists have long been interested in the nature of social class, psychologists have recently begun to examine how social class shapes psychological experience. In this overview, we discuss how people from different social classes differ in terms of their values, basic neural processes, and higher level reasoning. We then explore the dynamic nature of social class, looking at the effect of the upper class on the working class, transitions between social classes, and historical trends that impact societal norms and behaviors. We end with reflections on the complexity of studying the effects of social class.

Across multiple decades and fields of study, social class has been defined in different ways. The early definitions of "class" focused on one's position in the workforce (Durkheim 1984; Marx and Engels 1848), distinguishing between those who owned the means of production and those that worked under them. Other social scientists looked at differences in lifestyle across social classes. For instance, members of the upper class were associated with refined habits and aesthetic tastes, such as the appreciation of sports like gymnastics, which emphasizes training for its own sake, as compared to contact sports, which prepare the body for manual labor (Bourdieu 1984). Drawing from these definitions, psychologists have examined social class as a form of culture (Cohen and Varnum 2016; Grossmann and Huynh 2013; Kraus and Keltner 2013). People with different levels of socioeconomic status (measured by looking at markers like educational attainment or having a white- vs. blue-collar job) are immersed in social environments, which consist of different practices, rules, and values. These experiences lead people to construct a certain class identity, which is subjectively ranked above or below other groups in society (Kraus et al. 2012). Based on this definition, psychologists have typically studied social class by comparing relatively higher-class individuals (e.g., college-educated adults) with relatively lower- or working-class individuals (e.g., adults who did not attend college).

15.1 Social Class Differences

In the following part of this chapter, we compare differences psychologists have documented between people of different social class. We first examine differences in attitudes and values. Next, we discuss some underlying differences in basic cognitive processing and neural responses. We conclude by discussing differences in higher-order cognition and prosociality.

15.1.1 Values, Attitudes, and Beliefs

Building on the psychological definition of social class, researchers argue that an important difference across social class is how people represent the self in relation to others (Grossmann and Varnum 2011; Kraus et al. 2012). Individuals vary in how they see themselves as unique and distinct from other people (i.e., independent self-representation) or closely connected to others (i.e., interdependent self-representation; Markus and Kitayama 1991). Those with independent self-representations are largely self-focused—they are more likely to emphasize personal goals, attitudes, and feelings. In contrast, those with interdependent self-representations are largely other-focused—they are influenced more strongly by the concerns of close others and pay greater attention to social expectations (Triandis 1995).

These self-representations arise from differences in one's environmental circumstances, such as one's cultural background or standing in society. From the outset, working-class individuals have less status and resources, which limits their opportunities (e.g., job instability, unsafe neighborhoods). Thus, they are more likely than upper-class individuals to pay attention to their external environment and focus on their relationships with other people. In contrast, upper-class people have fewer external constraints and are more likely to focus on their own internal states, goals, and emotions (for a review, see Kraus et al. 2012). In support of this view, surveys and experiments in psychology and related fields suggest that higher social class is associated with independent (as opposed to interdependent) self-representations in the United States and in several non-Western societies (Grossmann and Varnum 2011; Hamamura et al. 2013; Inkeles 1975; Kohn et al. 1990; Ma and Schoeneman 1997).

Independent and interdependent self-representations shape how people think, feel, and act in the world (Markus and Kitayama 1991). In particular, these self-representations are closely linked to the values and beliefs systems that individuals from different groups hold (Triandis 1993; Varnum et al. 2010). For instance, people with independent self-representations prioritize values like freedom, choosing one's own goals, and living a varied life. In contrast, those with interdependent self-representations endorse values like belongingness, respect for one's elders, and social harmony (Gardner et al. 1999; Grossmann and Na 2014).

Supporting the claim that higher social class is associated with self-focused representations and values, researchers have observed that individuals with higher social class are more likely to see themselves at the center of their social network. They also tend to describe themselves using personal traits (e.g., "I am smart") as opposed to focusing on relationships (e.g., "I am a parent"). Moreover, data from three large, national surveys in the United States suggest that higher-class individuals believe they can independently make an impact in the world, being less influenced by other people and external factors (Lachman and Weaver 1998). In line with this observation, American adults with higher social class are also more likely to demonstrate illusory superiority (Varnum 2015). Outside psychology, other social scientists have also discussed this cultural variation in values. For instance, Mortimer et al. (1984) observed differences in child-rearing practices based on occupational status. Specifically, people with high-status occupations are more likely to emphasize self-direction with their children, whereas working-class parents place greater value on conformity.

We also see these values manifested in how people choose and use cultural products. For example, in a large, national survey in the United States, higher-class individuals reported preferring cultural products—like types of music—that endorse self-expression rather than self-management (Snibbe and Markus 2005). Consider how Led Zeppelin's "Stairway to Heaven" promotes the pursuit of personal goals with lyrics like, "She's buying a stairway to heaven," which stands in contrast to The Beatle's "Let It Be," that encourages self-control and acceptance of what is happening in one's life. Aside from musical preferences, higher-class individuals prefer to pick gifts out for themselves rather than having one selected for them (Stephens et al. 2011). They also prefer unique products, disliking a gift more if a friend also received the same kind of item (Stephens et al. 2007). These examples highlight the values of independence and personal control among higher-class individuals. In summary, evidence from people's self-descriptions, beliefs, and consumer behavior suggest that higher-class individuals are more self-focused in comparison to working-class individuals.

15.1.2 Basic Processes and Neurological Bases

Recently, researchers have extended the exploration of how class affects the way we think by using powerful neuroscience techniques. Such techniques are useful not only because they provide more proximate access to the neural activity that produces mental phenomena, but also because they are less susceptible to socially desirable responses, and provide information about the specific mental processes that are responsible for the downstream effects captured by traditional methods. These techniques also can detect differences in mental activity in the absence of overt behavioral responses.

A growing body of behavioral and self-report evidence suggests that people who are lower in social standing may be more socially attuned than those of higher social class (Kraus et al. 2012). A series of recent neuroscience studies has shed additional light on how social class may affect the extent to which we are attuned to others. For example, using functional magnetic resonance imaging (fMRI) on samples of American college and high school students, Muscatell and colleagues (2012) have shown that lower social class is associated with greater activation in brain areas involved in understanding the mental states of other people (e.g., prefrontal cortex and precuneus) when presented with images of others paired with social information. This finding suggests that working-class people may devote more cognitive resources to processing social information and that they may encode such information more deeply. This greater attunement to others is also seen at a more basic level. In another study, Varnum and colleagues (2016) have shown that lower social class among college students was correlated with greater activation of the mirror neuron system (measured by stronger Mu-suppression in electroencephalogram [EEG] tests) when viewing another person's motor movements. This finding suggests that the neural systems of working-class people may be more reactive to others' actions. Further, a recent event-related potential (ERP) investigation among college students found that lower social class was associated with stronger frontocentral P2 responses to images of others in pain (Varnum et al. 2015). This study suggests that those from lower socioeconomic status (SES) backgrounds may experience stronger feelings of empathy for others, and given the timing of this effect, it suggests that it may be the result of fairly early and automatic attentional processes. Taken together these studies provide strong support for the notion that working-class people are more socially attuned and that such attunement may be fairly automatic and visceral.

Finally, psychologists theorize that differences in the cognitive processes of working-class individuals stem from being in an unpredictable environment (Kraus et al. 2012). These circumstances encourage these individuals to pay greater attention to external constraints and to the greater context of a particular situation. In support of this idea, working-class individuals showed a stronger activation of the amygdala in response to faces expressing anger, suggesting that they were more reactive to threat (Gianaros et al. 2008; Muscatell et al. 2012). In addition, evidence from a recent ERP study with college students suggests that whereas those from higher-class backgrounds appear to engage in spontaneous trait inference, this process is absent among those from lower-class backgrounds (Varnum et al. 2012). This result means that higher-class individuals are more likely to attribute people's behavior to their internal dispositions instead of first considering any situational contributors to behavior. These findings shed additional light on how fairly early cognitive and affective processes are also affected by one's social class standing.

15.1.3 Reasoning and Prosociality

Social class differences have also been observed in higher order cognitive processes and their downstream behavioral consequences. In particular, as higher-class individuals have less external constraints, value self-direction, and prefer personal control of the world, they are more likely to think in what researchers consider to be an analytic cognitive style, which involves isolating an object to analyze it and paying less attention to the background environment. This pattern of thought stands in contrast to a holistic cognitive style, where people pay more attention to different aspects of the environment and how they relate to each other (Nisbett et al. 2001). For example, when looking at sets of pictures, university students whose parents went to college (i.e., higher social class), were more likely to notice when the foreground of an image is different. In contrast, first-generation university students (i.e., lower social class) were more likely to notice background changes (Grossmann and Varnum 2011).

When applied to social interactions, the independent self-representation of higher-class individuals promotes greater focus on internal rather than external states. That is, higher-class individuals are more likely to explain behaviors in terms of that person's characteristics and dispositions. On the other hand, lower-class individuals pay more attention to the context, and think about external factors that might influence a person's behavior (Kraus et al. 2012). For example, seeing coworkers arrive late to a meeting could be attributed to the internal characteristics of the person (e.g., they are irresponsible) or to an external explanation (e.g., they were delayed by traffic).

Even though higher-class individuals are more likely to attribute people's actions to their personality, it does not mean they make more accurate evaluations of those around them. As a result of their relatively more inward focus, higher-class individuals would be less likely to pay attention to their social environment. This would affect their ability to perceive how other people think and feel. For instance, research among university employees and students in the United States found that lower-class individuals were more accurate at judging the emotions of other individuals (Kraus et al. 2010). Lower class individuals, in contrast, were more likely to pay attention to the context of the situation, and this helped them make more accurate emotional judgments.

One important consequence of these social processes is prosocial behavior. In partic-ular, Piff and colleagues (2010) found in both students and a nationwide sample adults in the United States that individuals who are higher in SES make fewer contributions to charity, share less in economic games, and are less inclined to help those in need. They are also more likely to behave unethically to increase self-interest, for instance by cheating. Keltner and colleagues (2014) argue that these behaviors reflect an upper-class preference for independence over social connection. This tendency is in contrast to people from lower-class backgrounds, who spend more time taking care of people (Argyle 1994) and are embedded in social networks that rely on reciprocal aid (Lamont 2010).

These findings suggest that upper-class environments promote less consideration of the external, social context and a prioritization of self-serving interests over another's welfare. This could also influence how people reason and make predictions. Since upper-class individuals think in an analytic, narrow fashion, they assume a single, linear trajectory when making predictions about the future. In contrast, lower-class individu-als consider multiple contextual factors when thinking about cause and effect, which means they are more likely to accept the possibility of change and contradiction in their predictions (i.e., dialecticism; Nisbett et al. 2001). For example, university students were asked to plot societal trends like economic growth. Higher-class individuals were more likely to predict linear trends compared to those from lower-class backgrounds (Grossmann and Varnum 2011).

Another possibility is that higher-class individuals may be more likely to reason in a fashion that biases them toward self-centered concerns and focal arguments. As a result, these individuals might ignore the larger context and opinions of other people, even if such opinions may be correct. To test this proposition, recent work by Brienza and Grossmann (2017) using a large, online sample from across the United States tested whether social class was associated with differences in wise reasoning, that is, the use of unbiased and pragmatic thought, which includes recognition of limits of one's knowledge, recognition that the world is changing and in flux, and the ability to integrate different perspectives (Grossmann and Kross 2014; Grossmann et al. 2013; Grossman et al. 2010). In support of this proposition, researchers observed that individuals from states with a greater percentage of blue-collar workers were more likely to show signs of intellectual humility, recognition of the world being in flux and change, and integration of different perspectives, when reflecting on recently experienced interpersonal conflicts. On an individual level, online and in-lab studies showed that lower self-reported social class was associated with wiser reasoning. Overall, these findings suggest that lower social class is associated with a greater attention to the situation and the external states, which may be functional for working-class individuals, enabling them to be more vigilant and less biased in their reasoning. These tendencies affect how they interact with other people, to what degree they pursue prosocial actions, and how wisely they deal with conflicts with others.

15.2 DYNAMICS AND SOCIAL CHANGE

To fully understand how social class affects psychological experience, it is informative to examine changes in social class and its associated psychosocial processes. Social class does not exist in a vacuum, as the class norms and societal norms could influence each other. Social class is also not permanent. On an individual level, lower-class individuals could transition from one social class to another—for example by going to college or moving to a more affluent neighborhood. Further, social class and the values associated with it are not static. Rather, they can be thought of as dynamic and constantly changing (Kashima 2014). For instance, a country could become more economically developed over time, which would also affect its cultural values. In the following part of this chapter, we explore how social class can change across different levels of analysis.

15.2.1 Dynamics between Different Levels of Social Class

Although individuals across social class have different psychological experiences, they are not isolated from people from other social classes. One view held by many social scientists is that the upper classes dictate the cultural values and practices of the rest of society (Bourdieu and Passeron 1977; Gramsci and Rosengarten 1994). Under this perspective, the ideas and customs of higher-class individuals are viewed as the general cultural norm, and working-class individuals try to emulate them (Gramsci and Rosengarten 1994). Similarly, Bourdieu (Bourdieu and Passeron 1977; Bourdieu 1984) argues that the upper classes spread their values, practices, and cognitive tendencies through cultural institutions, like education. According to this view, the culture of the upper classes should be the dominant culture in a particular society, and we should expect higher-class members to exemplify the values held by that society. An alternative view has been proposed by twentieth-century Marxist sociologists, who suggested that control over the means of production and associated working conditions promote psychological differences between social classes (e.g., Mortimer et al. 1984; Schooler et al. 2004) To test these competing ideas, Grossmann and Varnum (Grossmann and Varnum 2011) examined how social class affects psychological processes in societies that differ in their default cultural orientation toward independence versus interdependence (i.e., the United States and Russia, respectively). They found that regardless of the country's independence or interdependence, social class differences predicted differences in cognitive styles in the same way, such that higher SES was linked to more independent self-construal in both countries. Hamamura et al. (2013) also observed similar effects of class in China. These studies suggest that the upper classes are not reinforcing the dominant cognitive styles of the particular country and that psychological effects of social class are mainly driven by the environmental affordances that higher versus lower classes bring with them.

15.2.2 Transitions Across Social Class

Another area of interest has been in how people can make successful transitions from one social class to another. Social scientists have been interested in improving the lives of lower-class individuals, and many have focused on how to improve their environment—from early educational opportunities (e.g., Love et al., 2005) to improving physical surroundings (Wilson and Kelling 1982). However, simply moving to a more affluent neighborhood can backfire, for instance, leading to more delinquent behaviors (Stephens, Markus, et al. 2012). It is thus important not just to consider the environment of people in lower social classes but also to take into account their individual characteristics, paying attention to how they might transition when moving to a new environment. In particular, since working-class individuals have values that focus on others (vs. the self), they might struggle when transitioning to a more affluent environment that endorses rather self-focused values (Stephens, Fryberg, et al. 2012).

Looking at the case of education, American universities have recently been working to promote socioeconomic diversity on their campuses (Bowen et al. 2005; Housel and Harvey 2005). However, attracting and retaining first-generation university students (e.g., students whose parents did not attend university) is difficult, with a substantially smaller percentage of first-generation students completing their degree compared to other students (Warburton, Bugarin, and Nuñez 2001). To explain this attrition, psychologists argue that the independent norms of American universities clash with the interdependent values that many first-generation students hold (Stephens, Fryberg, et al. 2012). For instance, the American educational system promotes self-discovery (vs. acquiring knowledge from authority figures; Tweed and Lehman 2002) and individual motivation (Greenfield 1997). Because of this mismatch, working-class students who enter this new, more self-focused environment feel discomfort, and as a result perform more poorly in school. These findings suggest that although people can move up in social class, researchers need to consider the struggles involved in this transition.

15.2.3 Societal Shifts in Social Class

With the advance of the twenty-first century, an emerging body of research across a wide range of variables suggests that advanced economies are promoting more independent and self-focused norms. For instance, looking at the personal relationships, the divorce rate has risen in the United States and Japan over the last fifty years (Hamamura 2012). Other studies have documented shifts in personality (e.g., increasing narcissism) and growing use of individualistic themes in books (e.g., personal choice), all of which point to rising individualism in the United States (Greenfield 2013; Twenge and Foster 2010). For example, one of the key characteristics of the independent self-representation is an emphasis on uniqueness (Markus and Kitayama 1991); Figure 15.1 shows that the preference for unique baby names in the United States has increased from 1970 to 2010.

Accompanying this shift in values are similar changes in social class and educational attainment. For instance, the percentage of people who finished at least one year of college has been increasing over the past seventy years (see Figure 15.1). Recent research suggests that as the US population becomes more educated and fills more white-collar jobs, it becomes more individualistic, as seen in smaller households, a greater percentage of unique baby names, and increased themes of individualism in books (Grossmann and Varnum 2015). Additionally, time-lagged analysis showed that over 150 years, these socioeconomic changes preceded shifts in individualism, which suggests a causal relationship between these variables.

These patterns are not limited to the United States. Researchers have observed similar patterns in Japan (Hamamura 2012), China (Hamamura and Xu 2015; Zeng and Greenfield 2015), and Mexico (Garcia et al. 2015; Greenfield et al. 2003); in each country economic development accompanied changes in individualistic practices (e.g., learning with less input from teachers), family structure (e.g., living alone), and values (e.g., emphasizing independence for children). Similarly, our recent work examining national survey and census data across seventy-eight countries found that increases in income, education, occupational prestige, and urbanization in the last sixty years accompanies increases in individualistic family structures and values (Santos et al. 2017; see Figure 15.2).

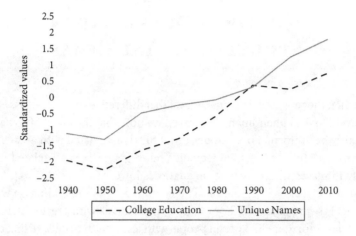

FIGURE 15.1

> *Note.* Information on naming practices among babies obtained from the US Social Security Administration by researchers (Grossmann and Varnum 2015), with uniqueness calculated by subtracting the percentage of children receiving names among the top 20 names in the year of their birth from 100 percent. Information on educational attainment collected from the Integrated Public Use Microdata Series (Minnesota Population Center 2015), with the percentage of respondents who reported completing at least one year of college. Standardized values for both are shown here.

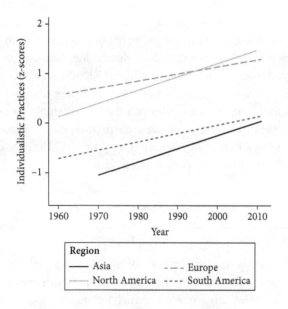

FIGURE 15.2

> *Note.* Information on family structures (e.g., living alone, smaller household, fewer children), collected from the Integrated Public Use Microdata Series (Minnesota Population Center 2015), with higher scores indicating more individualistic family structures (values represent a standardized composite score). Countries were grouped into cultural regions that were examined in previous work (Inglehart and Baker 2000).

15.3 Open Questions in Studying Social Class

Taken together, the reported findings suggest that differences in social class affect a wide range of psychological phenomena. However, we note that the effect of social class may not necessarily be uniform. For example, lower SES is associated with greater prosociality in regions with higher income inequality, but higher SES is associated with greater prosociality in places where income inequality is lower (Côté et al. 2015). Further, the association of social class with unethical behavior may vary depending on what marker of social class is being observed. For example, individuals with greater financial wealth (i.e., higher class) are more likely than people with less wealth to believe that cheating on taxes is justified, but so do people with temporary as opposed to permanent employment (i.e., lower class; Trautmann et al. 2013). We conducted additional analyses on longitudinal cross-cultural data finding that social class has a weaker effect on individualism in some cultural regions (e.g., Europe and South America) compared to others (see Figure 15.2). These questions challenge researchers to take a closer look at social class, considering both internal (e.g., personal resources) and external (e.g., community environment) factors (Stephens, Markus, et al. 2012).

Furthermore, the broad shifts in social class bring into question the whole meaning of the term. Are more people rising in affluence and independence around the globe? And are the relative differences between groups changing or remaining static? The widespread effects of modernization could reduce distinctions between social classes (Flynn 2007). And people across different times are inconsistent in how they define class (Hout 2008). For instance, while most individuals are able to identify class differences at the extremes (e.g., family incomes of $20,000 vs. $100,000), a significant number of people find themselves at the boundary, by having some markers of higher social class but lacking others (e.g., having a university degree but low income). The next few decades could thus see shifts in how people characterize social class.

15.4 Conclusion

Cognitive processes and values vary across social class. Compared to those in the working class, upper-class individuals are more likely to have independent self-representation and values. They also think in a more analytic manner and are less prosocial and wise. These findings are based on evidence from a rich and diverse body of research using methods ranging from archival analysis to fMRI. Social class also has important effects at the level of society. Societies across the globe are shifting toward greater self-centeredness and individualism, and these shifts appear to be the aligned with changes in socioeconomic structures such as mean-level occupation and education. Given these unfolding changes, it is more important than ever to pay attention to how people react to transitions and shifting definitions in social class.

REFERENCES

Argyle, Michael. 1994. *The Psychology of Social Class.* London: Routledge.

Bourdieu, Pierre. 1984. *Distinction: A Social Critique of the Judgement of Taste.* Cambridge, MA: Harvard University Press.

Bourdieu, Pierre, and Jean-Claude Passeron. 1977. *Reproduction in Education, Society, and Culture.* Beverly Hills, CA: SAGE.

Bowen, William, Martin Kurzewil, and Eugene Tobin. 2005. *Equity and Excellence in American Higher Education.* Charlottesville: University of Virginia Press.

Brienza, Justin P., and Igor Grossmann. 2017. "Social Class and Wise Reasoning about Interpersonal Conflicts across Regions, Persons and Situations." *Proceedings of the Royal Society Biological Sciences* 284(1869):1–9.

Cohen, Adam B., and Michael E. W. Varnum. 2016. "Beyond East vs. West: Social Class, Region, and Religion as Forms of Culture." *Current Opinion in Psychology* 8:5–9.

Côté, Stéphane, Juilan House, and Robb Willer. 2015. "High Economic Inequality Leads Higher-Income Individuals to Be Less Generous." *Proceedings of the National Academy of Sciences of the United States of America* 112(52):15838–43.

Durkheim, Emile, and George Simpson. 2012. *The Division of Labor in Society: Being a Translation of His De la Division du Travail Social, With an Estimate of His Work.* Mansfield Centre, CT: Martino Publishing.

Flynn, James R. 2007. *What Is Intelligence? Beyond the Flynn Effect.* New York: Cambridge University Press.

Garcia, Camilo, Natanael Rivera, and Patricia M. Greenfield. 2015. "The Decline of Cooperation, the Rise of Competition: Developmental Effects of Long-Term Social Change in Mexico." *International Journal of Psychology* 50(1):6–11.

Gardner, Wendi L., Shira Gabriel, and Angela Y. Lee. 1999. "'I' Value Freedom, but 'We' Value Relationships: Self-Construal Priming Mirrors Cultural Differences in Judgment." *Psychological Science* 10:321–6.

Gianaros, Peter J., Jeffrey A. Horenstein, Ahmad R. Hariri, Lei K. Sheu, Stephen B. Manuck, Karen A. Matthews, et al. 2008. "Potential Neural Embedding of Parental Social Standing." *Social Cognitive and Affective Neuroscience* 3:91–6. http://www.pubmedcentral.nih.gov/articlerender.fcgi?artid=2311502&tool=pmcentrez&rendertype=abstract.

Gramsci, Antonio, and Frank Rosengarten. 1994. *Letters from Prison.* New York: Columbia University Press.

Greenfield, Patricia M. 1997. "You Can't Take It with You: Why Ability Assessments Don't Cross Cultures." *American Psychologist* 52:1115–24.

Greenfield, Patricia M. 2013. "The Changing Psychology of Culture from 1800 through 2000." *Psychological Science* 24:1722–31.

Greenfield, Patricia M., Ashley E. Maynard, and Carla P. Childs. 2003. "Historical Change, Cultural Learning, and Cognitive Representation in Zinacantec Maya Children." *Cognitive Development* 18:455–87.

Grossmann, Igor, and Alex C. Huynh. 2013. "Where Is the Culture in Social Class?" *Psychological Inquiry* 24(2):112–19.

Grossmann, Igor, and Ethan Kross. 2014. "Exploring Solomon's Paradox: Self-Distancing Eliminates the Self-Other Asymmetry in Wise Reasoning about Close Relationships in Younger and Older Adults." *Psychological Science* 25(8):1571–80.

Grossmann, Igor, and Jinkyung Na. 2014. "Research in Culture and Psychology: Past Lessons and Future Challenges." *Wiley Interdisciplinary Reviews: Cognitive Science* 5:1–14.

Grossmann, Igor, Jinkyung Na, Michael E. W. Varnum, Shinobu Kitayama, and Richard E. Nisbett. 2013. "A Route to Well-Being: Intelligence versus Wise Reasoning." *Journal of Experimental Psychology: General* 142(3):944–53.

Grossmann, Igor, Jinkyung Na, Michael E. W. Varnum, Denise C. Park, and Richard E. Nisbett. 2010. "Reasoning about Social Conflicts Improves into Old Age." *Proceedings of the National Academy of Sciences of the United States of America* 107(16):7246–50.

Grossmann, Igor, and Michael E. W. Varnum. 2011. "Social Class, Culture, and Cognition." *Social Psychological and Personality Science* 2(1):81–9.

Grossmann, Igor, and Michael E. W. Varnum. 2015. "Social Structure, Infectious Diseases, Disasters, Secularism, and Cultural Change in America." *Psychological Science* 26:311–24.

Hamamura, Takeshi. 2012. "Are Cultures Becoming Individualistic? A Cross-Temporal Comparison of Individualism-Collectivism in the United States and Japan." *Personality and Social Psychology Review* 16(1):3–24.

Hamamura, Takeshi, Qinmei Xu, and Yushen Du. 2013. "Culture, Social Class, and Independence-Interdependence: The Case of Chinese Adolescents." *International Journal of Psychology* 48(3):344–51.

Hamamura, Takeshi, and Yi Xu. 2015. "Changes in Chinese Culture as Examined through Changes in Personal Pronoun Usage." *Journal of Cross-Cultural Psychology* 46(7):930–41.

Housel, Theresa H., and Vickie L. Harvey, eds. 2009. *The Invisibility Factor: Administrators and Faculty Reach out to First-Generation College Students*. Boca Raton: BrownWalker Press.

Hout, Michael. 2008. "How Class Works: Objective and Subjective Aspects of Class since the 1970s." pp. 25–64 in *Social Class: How Does It Work?*, edited by A. Lareau and D. Conley. New York: Russel Sage Foundation.

Inglehart, Ronald F., and Wayne E. Baker. 2000. "Modernization, Cultural Change, and the Persistence of Traditional Values." *American Sociological Review* 65(1):19–51.

Inkeles, Alex. 1975. "Becoming Modern: Individual Change in Six Developing Countries." *Ethos* 3:323–42.

Kashima, Yoshihisa. 2014. "How Can You Capture Cultural Dynamics?" *Frontiers in Psychology* 5:1–16.

Keltner, Dacher, Aleksandr Kogan, Paul K. Piff, and Sarina R. Saturn. 2014. "The Sociocultural Appraisals, Values, and Emotions (SAVE) Framework of Prosociality: Core Processes from Gene to Meme." *Annual Review of Psychology* 65:425–60.

Kohn, Melvin L., Atsushi Naoi, Carrie Schoenbach, Carmi Schooler, and Kazimierz M. Slomczynski. 1990. "Position in the Class Structure and Psychological Functioning in the United States, Japan, and Poland." *American Journal of Sociology* 95:964.

Kraus, Michael W., Stéphane Côté, and Dacher Keltner. 2010. "Social Class, Contextualism, and Empathic Accuracy." *Psychological Science : A Journal of the American Psychological Society/APS* 21:1716–23.

Kraus, Michael W., and Dacher Keltner. 2013. "Social Class Rank, Essentialism, and Punitive Judgment." *Journal of Personality and Social Psychology* 105(2):247–61.

Kraus, Michael W., Paul K. Piff, Rodolfo Mendoza-Denton, Michelle L. Rheinschmidt, and Dacher Keltner. 2012. "Social Class, Solipsism, and Contextualism: How the Rich Are Different from the Poor." *Psychological Review* 119:546–72.

Lachman, Margie. E., and Suzanne. L. Weaver. 1998. "The Sense of Control as a Moderator of Social Class Differences in Health and Well-Being." *Journal of Personality and Social Psychology* 74:763–73.

Lamont, Michèle. 2010. "Looking Back at Bourdieu." pp. 127–41 in *Cultural Analysis and Bourdieu's Legacy: Settling Accounts and Developing Alternatives*. London: Routledge.

Love, John M., Ellen Eliason Kisker, Christine Ross, Jill Constantine, Kimberly Boller, Rachel Chazan-Cohen et al. 2005. "The Effectiveness of Early Head Start for 3-Year-Old Children and Their Parents: Lessons for Policy and Programs." *Developmental Psychology* 41(6):885–901.

Ma, Vaunne, and Thomas J. Schoeneman. 1997. "Basic and Applied Social Psychology Individualism Versus Collectivism: A Comparison of Kenyan and American Self-Concepts." *Basic and Applied Social Psychology* 19:261–73.

Markus, Hazel R., and Shinobu Kitayama. 1991. "Culture and the Self: Implications for Cognition, Emotion, and Motivation." *Psychological Review* 98(2):224–53.

Marx, Karl, and Friedrich Engels. 1848. *The Communist Manifesto*. Moscow: Foreign Languages Publishing House.

Minnesota Population Center. 2015. "Integrated Public Use Microdata Series." http://international.ipums.org/international/.

Mortimer, Jeylan T., Melvin L. Kohn, and Carmi Schooler. 1984. "Work and Personality: An Inquiry into the Impact of Social Stratification." *Contemporary Sociology* 13:356.

Muscatell, Keely A., Sylvia A. Morelli, Emily B. Falk, Baldwin M. Way, Jennifer H. Pfeifer, Adam D. Galinsky, et al. 2012. "Social Status Modulates Neural Activity in the Mentalizing Network." *NeuroImage* 60:1771–7.

Nisbett, Richard E., Kaiping Peng, Incheol Choi, and Ara Norenzayan. 2001. "Culture and Systems of Thought: Holistic vs. Analytic Cognition." *Psychological Review* 108(2):291–310.

Piff, Paul K., Michael W. Kraus, Stéphane Côté, Bonnie Hayden Cheng, and Dacher Keltner. 2010. "Having Less, Giving More: The Influence of Social Class on Prosocial Behavior." *Journal of Personality and Social Psychology* 99:771–84.

Santos, Henri C., Michael E. W. Varnum, and Igor Grossmann. 2017. "Global Increases in Individualism." *Psychological Science* 28(9):1228–39.

Schooler, Carmi, Mesfin Samuel Mulatu, and Gary Oates. 2004. "Functioning, and Self-Directed Orientation in Older Workers : Findings and Implications for Individuals and Societies 1." *American Journal of Sociology* 110(1):161–97.

Snibbe, Alana Conner, and Hazel Rose Markus. 2005. "You Can't Always Get What You Want: Educational Attainment, Agency, and Choice." *Journal of Personality and Social Psychology* 88:703–20.

Stephens, Nicole M., Stephanie A. Fryberg, and Hazel Rose Markus. 2011. "When Choice Does Not Equal Freedom: A Sociocultural Analysis of Agency in Working-Class American Contexts." *Social Psychological and Personality Science* 2:33–41.

Stephens, Nicole M., Stephanie A. Fryberg, Hazel Rose Markus, Camille S. Johnson, and Rebecca Covarrubias. 2012. "Unseen Disadvantage: How American Universities' Focus on Independence Undermines the Academic Performance of First-Generation College Students." *Journal of Personality and Social Psychology* 102:1178–97.

Stephens, Nicole M., Hazel R. Markus, and Stephanie A. Fryberg. 2012. "Social Class Disparities in Health and Education: Reducing Inequality by Applying a Sociocultural Self Model of Behavior." *Psychological Review* 119(4):723.

Stephens, Nicole M., Hazel Rose Markus, and Sarah S. M. Townsend. 2007. "Choice as an Act of Meaning: The Case of Social Class." *Journal of Personality and Social Psychology* 93(5):814–30.

Trautmann, Stefan T., Gijs Van De Kuilen, and Richard J. Zeckhauser. 2013. "Social Class and (Un) Ethical Behavior : A Framework , With Evidence from a Large Population Sample." *Psychological Science* 8(5):487–97.

Triandis, Harry. C. 1993. "Collectivism and Individualism as Cultural Syndromes." *Cross-Cultural Research* 27:155–80.

Triandis, Harry C. 1995. *Individualism and Collectivism: New Directions in Social Psychology*. Boulder, CO: Westview Press.

Tweed, Roger G., and Darrin R. Lehman. 2002. "Learning Considered within a Cultural Context: Confucian and Socratic Approaches." *American Psychologist* 57:89–99.

Twenge, Jean M., and Joshua D. Foster. 2010. "Birth Cohort Increases in Narcissistic Personality Traits among American College Students, 1982–2009." *Social Psychological and Personality Science* 1(1):99–106.

Varnum, Michael E. W. 2015. "Higher in Status, (Even) Better-than-Average." *Frontiers in Psychology* 6:496.

Varnum, Michael E. W., Chris Blais, and Gene A. Brewer. 2016. "Social Class Affects Mu- Suppression during Action Observation." *Social Neuroscience* 11(4):449–54.

Varnum, Michael E. W., Chris Blais, Ryan S. Hampton, and Gene A. Brewer. 2015. "Social Class Affects Neural Empathic Responses." *Culture and Brain* 3:122–30.

Varnum, Michael E. W., Igor Grossmann, Shinobu Kitayama, and Richard E. Nisbett. 2010. "The Origin of Cultural Differences in Cognition: Evidence for the Social Orientation Hypothesis." *Current Directions in Psychological Science* 19(1):9–13.

Varnum, Michael E. W., Jinkyung Na, Asuka Murata, and Shinobu Kitayama. 2012. "Social Class Differences in N400 Indicate Differences in Spontaneous Trait Inference." *Journal of Experimental Psychology. General* 141:518–26.

Warburton, Edward C., Rosio Bugarin, and Anne-Marie Nuñez. 2001. *Bridging the Gap: Academic Preparation and Postsecondary Success of First-Generation Students*. Washington, DC: U.S. Department. of Education, Office of Educational Research and Improvement, National Center for Education Statistics.

Wilson, James Q., and George L. Kelling. 1982. "Broken Windows: The Police and Neighborhood Safety." *Atlantic Monthly*, March 1, 1982, 29–38.

Zeng, Rong, and Patricia M. Greenfield. 2015. "Cultural Evolution over the Last 40 Years in China: Using the Google Ngram Viewer to Study Implications of Social and Political Change for Cultural Values." *International Journal of Psychology* 50:47–55.

CHAPTER 16

COGNITIVE DICHOTOMIES, LEARNING DIRECTIONS, AND THE COGNITIVE ARCHITECTURE

RON SUN

ARE there multiple qualitatively different systems within the human mind? Are there different processes of learning and performance that have radically different character- istics? If so, what are these? How do they differ from each other? How do they interact and integrate with each other? There have been various speculations in this regard, often centered on two contrasting systems (or sometimes more) within the human mind. In this chapter, I review arguments in favor of two-system views, and discuss the interaction and integration of the two systems, in particular in the forms of different learning direc- tions that go from one system to the other. I also outline the overall cognitive architecture that encompasses and structures these aspects.

16.1 COGNITIVE DICHOTOMIES

There have been some very early ideas concerning the duality (the two systems) of the human mind that dated back before the inception of cognitive science. For instance, Martin Heidegger's distinction—the preontological versus the ontological—is an abstract version of such a duality (Heidegger 1927/1962). His view was roughly that, because the essential way of being is existence in the world, an individual always embodies an understanding of its being through such existence. This embodied understanding consists of skills, reactions, and know-hows, without an explicit "ontology," and is thus "preontological" (implicit). On that basis, an individual may also achieve an explicit ("ontological") understanding, especially through making the implicit understanding explicit. That is, an individual can turn preontological understanding into ontological understanding (Heidegger 1927/1962; Dreyfus 1992).

William James's distinction of empirical thinking and true reasoning is also worth mentioning. According to James (1890), "empirical thinking" is associative, made up of sequences of "images" that are suggested by one another. It is "reproductive," because it replicates in some way past experience, instead of producing new ideas. Empirical thinking relies on overall comparisons and similarity among various concrete situations, and therefore may lose sight of critical information. On the other hand, "true reasoning" is achieved by abstracting attributes. It is "productive," because it is capable of producing novel ideas through abstraction. True reasoning breaks up direct links between thought and action and provides means for reasoning about consequences of an action without actually performing it.

The modern idea of two cognitive systems in the human mind (implicit and explicit) that are separate for representing or learning different types of knowledge can be traced back to early work in experimental psychology, for example, the work on classical and instrumental conditioning (without conscious awareness). Since then, much more work has been done and the characteristics and the interactions of the two systems have been investigated. Let us look into some of that more recent work.

First, the distinction of implicit and explicit processes has been argued in the implicit memory literature (e.g., Roediger 1990; Schacter 1987). The early work on amnesic patients showed that these patients might have intact implicit memory while their explicit memory was severely impaired. Warrington and Weiskrantz (1970), for example, demonstrated that when using implicit measures, amnesic patients' memory was as good as normal subjects; but when using explicit measures, their memory was far worse than normal subjects. The "explicit measure" used included free recall and recognition, while the "implicit measures" used included word-fragment naming and word completion. It was argued that the implicit measures reflected unconscious (implicit) processes (amnesic patients were usually unaware that they knew the materials; Warrington and Weiskrantz 1970). Such results demonstrating dissociations between implicit and explicit measures have been replicated in a variety of circumstances.

Second, Jacoby (e.g., Jacoby 1983) demonstrated that implicit and explicit measures might be dissociated among normal subjects as well. Three study conditions were used: generation of a word from a context, reading aloud a word in a meaningful context, and reading aloud a word out of context. The explicit measure used was recognition (from a list of words), while the implicit measure was perceptual identification (from fast presentations of words). The results showed that, using the explicit measure, generated words were remembered the best and words read out of context were remembered the least. However, using the implicit measure, the exact opposite pattern was found. Other dissociations were also found from other manipulations (see, e.g., Roediger 1990; Schacter 1987). Toth et al. (1994) devised an inclusion-exclusion procedure for assessing implicit and explicit contributions, which also provided strong indications of dissociation.

Third, the distinction of implicit and explicit processes has also been empirically demonstrated in the implicit learning literature (Reber 1989; Berry and Broadbent 1988). In particular, Reber demonstrated early on (in the 1970s and 1980s) that subjects could memorize letter strings that followed certain patterns and after that discriminated valid from invalid novel strings without conscious awareness of the basis for their judgments (Reber 1989). Similar work has been carried out by Broadbent and others in similar or different experimental settings (e.g., Berry and Broadbent 1988). For example, dynamic process control tasks involve learning of a relation between the input and the output variables of a controllable system, through interacting with the system. Although subjects often did not recognize the underlying relations explicitly, they nevertheless reached a certain level of performance in these tasks (e.g., Berry and Broadbent 1988). In all, these tasks shared the characteristic of implicit learning processes being involved to a significant extent (Seger 1994; Sun 2002).

Generally speaking, explicit processing may be described, mechanistically (computationally), as being based on rules in some way, while implicit processing is more associative (Sun 2002). Explicit processing may involve the manipulation of symbols, while implicit processing involves more instantiated knowledge that is more holistically associated (Sun 1994, 2002; Reber 1989). While explicit processes require attention, implicit processes often do not (Reber 1989). Explicit processes may compete more for resources than implicit processes. Summaries of empirical evidence in support of these differences can be found in, for example, Reber (1989), Seger (1994), and Sun (2002). Some more general claims, which have been controversial, were that implicit processes occur without conscious awareness at all, that such processes occur completely automatically (i.e., without involving limited cognitive resources), and that such processes involve abstracting the underlying structure of the stimuli. Empirical (psychological) results have shown that while the notion of implicit processes is well established, specific claims often need qualifications to take into account complex interactions between implicit and explicit processes (more later on this; Sun et al. 2005).

Now turn to the distinction between procedural and declarative processes, which has been advocated by many (although some details vary across different proposals). Procedural processes involve knowledge that is specifically concerned with actions (and action sequences) in various circumstances, that is, how to do things. Declarative processes involve knowledge that is not specifically concerned with actions but more about objects, persons, events, and so on, in more generic terms (i.e., the "what," not the "how"). The major factor that distinguishes procedural and declarative processes is the action-centeredness or the lack thereof—in other words, the procedural versus non-procedural nature.

Evidence in support of this distinction includes many studies of skill acquisition in both high-level and low-level skill domains (e.g., Anderson 1983; Kanfer and Ackerman 1989; Anderson and Lebiere 1998). These studies included both experimental work on human subjects, as well as modeling/simulation and other work aimed at theoretical interpretations. This distinction provides useful insight in interpreting a range of data and phenomena. For instance, Anderson (1983) used this distinction to account for changes in performance resulting from extensive practice, based on data from a variety of skill-learning studies. According to Anderson, the initial stage of skill development is characterized by the acquisition of declarative knowledge. The learner must explicitly attend to this knowledge in order to perform a task. Through practice, procedures develop that may accomplish the task without declarative knowledge.

We need to examine the relation between the procedural-declarative distinction and the implicit-explicit distinction. In Anderson (1983), declarative knowledge was assumed to be consciously accessible (i.e., explicit): subjects could report on and manipulate such knowledge. Procedural knowledge was not: it led to actions without explicit accessibility. Thus, in Anderson (1983), the two dichotomies were merged into one.

On the other hand, in Anderson and Lebiere (1998), each individual piece of knowledge, be it procedural or declarative, involved both subsymbolic and symbolic representation. Symbolic representation was used for denoting semantic labels and structural components of each concept, while subsymbolic representation was used for expressing its activation and other numerical factors. One interpretation was that the symbolic representation was explicit while the subsymbolic representation was implicit (either for declarative knowledge, or for both declarative and procedural knowledge). This view constituted another take on the relationship between the two dichotomies.

According to the first view, the difference in action-centeredness (i.e., the procedural versus nonprocedural nature) seems the main factor in distinguishing the two types of knowledge, while accessibility (i.e., implicitness versus explicitness) is a secondary factor. Sun (2012) argues that this view unnecessarily confounds two aspects: action-centeredness and accessibility, and can be made clearer by separating the two dimensions. Action-centeredness does not necessarily go with implicitness (inaccessibility), as shown by, for example, the experiments of Stanley et al. (1989), Willingham et al. (1989), or Sun et al. (2001). Likewise, non-action-centeredness does not necessarily go with explicitness (accessibility) either, as shown by conceptual priming and other implicit memory experiments (e.g., Schacter 1987; Moscovitch and Umilta 1991) or by experiments demonstrating implicit information (e.g., Hasher and Zacks 1979; Nisbett and Wilson 1977). Some might choose to group all implicit memory (including semantic, associative, and conceptual priming) under procedural memory, but such views confound the notion of "procedural." In light of the above, these two dimensions need to be separated.

The alternative view that each individual piece of knowledge (either procedural or declarative, or both) involves both an implicit and an explicit part is also problematic. Such a view entails a close coupling between implicit and explicit processes, which is highly questionable. The underlying assumption that every piece of knowledge (either declarative or procedural, or both) has an explicit part contradicts the fact that some knowledge may be completely implicit (e.g., Lewicki et al. 1987). This raises the question of whether such a tight coupling or a more separate organization, for example, having these two types of knowledge in separate memory stores (Sun 2002, 2016), makes better sense.

As a more natural, more intuitively appealing alternative to those views, Sun (2012) proposed the separation of the two dichotomies—treating them as logically separate from (i.e., orthogonal to) each other (see also Sun et al. 2009). Arguments in favor of this view can be found in the existing literature. For example, based on empirical data,

Willingham (1998) argued that motor skills (a type of procedural process) consisted of both implicit and explicit processes. Rosenbaum et al. (2001) argued based on empirical data that intellectual skills and perceptual-motor skills alike were made up of implicit and explicit knowledge. In other words, procedural (action-centered) processes, ranging from high-level intellectual skills to perceptual-motor skills, may be divided into implicit and explicit processes.

Similarly, declarative (non-action-centered) processes may also be divided in a like manner (Tulving and Schacter 1990). There is no reason to believe that all implicit knowledge is procedural. Some implicit knowledge may be declarative (non-action-centered). As mentioned before, conceptual priming and other implicit memory experiments demonstrated that. In terms of functional consideration, having separate implicit and explicit declarative memory stores may allow different tasks to be tackled simultaneously in these separate memory stores (e.g., while reasoning explicitly about one task, letting intuition work on another). Sun (1994) and Sun and Zhang (2006) showed that through dividing declarative memory into explicit and implicit modules, many reasoning data could be naturally accounted for. Furthermore, Helie and Sun (2010) showed that this division accounted well for creative problem solving (which otherwise would be difficult to account for).

On this view, procedural and declarative knowledge reside separately in procedural and declarative memory stores respectively, which are representationally different (Sun et al. 2009; Sun 2012). Procedural knowledge (in procedural memory; Sun 2002, 2016) may be represented by either action rules (explicit) or action neural networks (implicit), both of which are centered on situation-action mappings. Declarative knowledge (in declarative memory; Sun 2002, 2016), on the other hand, may be represented by either associative rules (explicit) or associative neural networks (implicit), in both of which knowledge is represented in a non-action-centered way.

In a similar fashion but orthogonally, implicitness/explicitness is also distinguished by representation. Implicit knowledge may be represented using connectionist distributed representation (such as in a hidden layer of a Backpropagation neural network), which is less accessible to an individual possessing it (Sun 1994, 2002), while explicit knowledge may be represented using symbolic-localist representation, which is relatively more accessible. Implicit and explicit knowledge thus reside in different memory stores with different representations. Moreover, in this way, the two dichotomies are separate from each other—that is, there are both implicit and explicit procedural memory stores, and both implicit and explicit declarative memory stores.

16.2 Interactions and Learning Directions

Furthermore, on the basis of the aforementioned distinction between implicit and explicit learning, the interaction between implicit and explicit learning is worth examining. Sun et al. (2001, 2005) focused on the very process of that interaction and proposed the notion that learning can go from implicit learning and implicit knowledge to explicit learning and explicit knowledge, which was termed bottom-up learning or implicit-to-explicit explicitation (see also Stanley et al. 1989). This style of learning is distinct from the more commonly recognized way of learning going from explicit knowledge to implicit knowledge: that is, top-down learning or, as it has been termed before, assimilation or implicitation (or even "proceduralization," which, unfortunately, confounds the issue of implicit versus explicit learning with the issue of procedure versus declarative learning).

In general, the relation between implicit and explicit processes during learning includes top-down learning (explicit learning first and implicit later), bottom-up learning (implicit learning first and explicit later), and parallel learning (simultaneous or separate implicit and explicit learning). However, bottom-up learning may be more essential (Sun et al. 2001; Sun 2002). There have been various indications and arguments for bottom-up learning, including (1) philosophical arguments, such as Heidegger (1927/1962) and Dewey (1958), in which the primacy of direct interaction with the world in a mostly implicit way initially is emphasized, and (2) psychological evidence of the acquisition and the delayed explication of implicit knowledge. Let us look into some psychological findings below.

As reviewed in Sun (2002), it has been found that in skill learning, subjects' ability to verbalize is often independent of their performance (Berry and Broadbent 1988). Furthermore, performance typically improves earlier than explicit knowledge that can be verbalized by subjects (Stanley et al. 1989). For instance, in a process control task, although the performance of subjects quickly rose to a high level, their verbal knowledge improved more slowly: subjects could not provide usable verbal knowledge until near the end of their training (Stanley et al. 1989). This phenomenon has also been demonstrated in artificial grammar learning (Reber 1989). Another study of bottom-up learning was carried out by Sun et al. (2001) using a complex minefield navigation task. In all of these tasks, it appears relatively easier to acquire implicit skills than explicit knowledge and hence the delay in the development of explicit knowledge. The delay indicates that explicit learning may be triggered by implicit learning. Explicit knowledge may be in a way "extracted" from implicit skills. (However, in some other tasks, explicit and implicit knowledge appear to be more closely associated.)

In the context of discovery tasks, Bowers et al. (1990) showed evidence of the explication of implicit knowledge. When subjects were given patterns to complete, they initially showed implicit recognition of what a proper completion might be, although they did not have explicit recognition of a correct completion. The implicit recognition improved over time until an explicit recognition was achieved. Siegler and Stern (1998) also showed in an arithmetic problem that children's strategy changes often occurred several trials earlier than their explicit recognition of strategy changes. Stanley et al. (1989), Seger (1994), and Sun et al. (2001) suggested that because explicit knowledge lagged behind but improved along with implicit knowledge, explicit knowledge could be viewed as obtained from implicit knowledge.

Several developmental theorists considered a similar delayed explication process. Karmiloff-Smith (1986) suggested that developmental changes involved "representational redescription." In children, first low-level implicit representations of stimuli were formed. Then when more knowledge was accumulated and stable behavior patterns developed, through a redescription process, more abstract representations were formed that transformed low-level representations and made them more explicit. This redescription process was repeated a number of times, and a verbal form of representation emerged. Mandler (1992) proposed another kind of redescription. From perceptual stimuli, relatively abstract "image-schemas" were extracted that coded several basic types of movements. Then, on top of such image-schemas, concepts were formed using information therein. In a similar vein, Keil (1989) viewed conceptual representations as composed of an associative component and a theory component. Developmentally, there was a shift from associative to theory-based representations. These ideas and the empirical data on which they were based testify to the ubiquity of the implicit-to-explicit transition.

In the other direction, top-down learning usually occurs when explicit knowledge is available or when it is relatively easy to learn such knowledge (compared with learning corresponding implicit knowledge). Explicit knowledge, learned or directly received from external sources, is then assimilated into an implicit form. For example, learning to play chess would be a good illustration. One often first learns the basic rules of chess as well as some essential guidelines as to what to do in prototypical situations. One may then develop more complex and more nuanced knowledge that may be largely implicit. See, for example, the detailed discussions in Dreyfus and Dreyfus (1987) on such a process.

16.3 OVERALL COGNITIVE ARCHITECTURE

To fit all these pieces (various dichotomies and various directions) together and to account for their detailed processes and mechanisms, a comprehensive model of the human mind (known as a "cognitive architecture" in the cognitive science parlance) has been developed (named Clarion; see Sun 2002, 2016), which provides detailed mechanistic explanations of these distinctions. This model has since been used to account for a large variety of empirical data related to the cognitive dichotomies and learning directions discussed earlier.

In particular, to account for bottom-up and top-down learning, this cognitive architecture provides detailed mechanistic (computational) explanations of bottom-up learning and top-down learning (based, in part, on machine learning algorithms for reinforcement learning and rule learning; see Sun 2002 for details). These mechanisms accurately account for empirical data related to implicit learning, bottom-up learning, and top-down learning (Sun 2002, 2016).

A quick sketch of the Clarion cognitive architecture is in order. Clarion consists of a number of subsystems (Sun 2016): the action-centered subsystem (the ACS), the non-action-centered subsystem (the NACS), the motivational subsystem (the MS), and the metacognitive subsystem (the MCS). The role of the ACS is to control actions (regardless of whether the actions are for external physical movements or for internal mental operations), using procedural knowledge. The role of the NACS is to use declarative knowledge for information and inferences of various kinds. The role of the MS is to provide underlying motivations for perception, action, and cognition (in terms of providing impetus and feedback). The role of the MCS is to monitor and regulate the operations of the other subsystems dynamically (Sun 2016).

Each of these interacting subsystems consists of two "levels" of representations (i.e., a dual-representational structure), as discussed earlier (and theoretically posited in Sun 2002). Generally speaking, in each subsystem, the "top level" encodes explicit knowledge with associated explicit processes (using symbolic-localist representations), while the "bottom level" encodes implicit knowledge with associated implicit processes (using connectionist distributed representations; Rumelhart et al. 1986). The two levels interact, for example, by cooperating in action decision-making through integration of the action recommendations from the two levels of the ACS respectively, as well as by cooperating in learning through bottom-up and top-down learning processes (in the ACS or in the NACS; Sun et al. 2001, 2005). See Figure 16.1 for a sketch of Clarion.

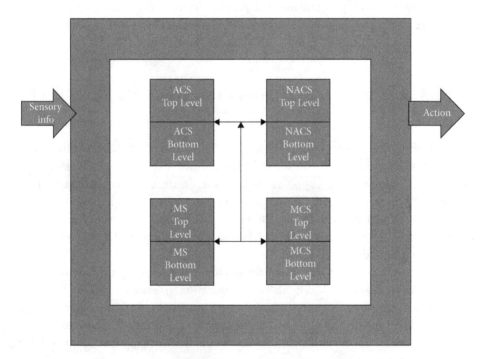

FIGURE 16.1 The subsystems of the Clarion cognitive architecture. The major information flows are shown with arrows. ACS stands for the action-centered subsystem. NACS stands for the non-action-centered subsystem. MS stands for the motivational subsystem. MCS stands for the metacognitive subsystem. See the text for more explanations.

An important characteristic of Clarion is that it embodies the belief that cognition is activity-based, action-oriented, and embedded in the world (Sun 2002, 2016). Therefore, for example, the principle regarding reasoning in Clarion is: action first (in the ACS) and reasoning in the service of action (in the NACS). Another important characteristic of Clarion is its focus on the cognition–motivation–environment interaction (Sun 2016), as opposed to dealing only with cognition in its narrow sense. In what follows, we examine two of the subsystems in more detail, which will illustrate some of these points (see Sun 2002, 2016 for further details).

16.3.1 Action-Centered Subsystem

The ACS captures the action decision-making of an individual when interacting with the world, involving procedural knowledge (Sun 2002, 2012).

In the ACS, the process for action selection is essentially as follows: Observing the current (observable) state of the world, the two levels within the ACS (implicit or explicit) make their action decisions in accordance with their respective procedural knowledge, and their outcomes are "integrated." Thus, a final selection of an action is made and the action is then performed. The action changes the world in some way. Comparing the changed state of the world with the previous state somehow, the person learns. The cycle then repeats itself.

Thus, the overall action decision-making may be described as follows:

1. Observe the current input state x.
2. Compute in the bottom level the "value" of each of the possible actions (a_i's) associated with the current input state x: $Q(x, a_1)$, $Q(x, a_2)$, ..., $Q(x, a_n)$. Stochastically choose one action according to these values.
3. Find out all the possible actions at the top level ($b_1, b_2, ..., b_m$), based on the current input state x (which goes up from the bottom level) and the existing rules in place at the top level. Stochastically choose one action.
4. Choose an action, by stochastically selecting the outcome of either the top level or the bottom level.
5. Perform the action, and observe the next input state y and (possibly) the reinforcement r.
6. Update implicit knowledge at the bottom level in accordance with an appropriate learning algorithm (e.g., Q-learning; more later), based on the feedback information.
7. Update explicit knowledge at the top level using an appropriate learning algorithm (e.g., the RER algorithm; more later).
8. Go back to Step 2.

In this subsystem, the bottom (implicit) level is implemented using neural networks involving distributed representations (Rumelhart et al. 1986), and the top level is implemented using symbolic-localist representations.

For the bottom level, the input state (x) consists of the sensory input (environmental or internal), the current goal, and the working memory. All that information is important in deciding on an action. The input state is represented as a set of microfeatures. The output of the bottom level is the action choice, also represented as a set of microfeatures.

At the top level, "chunk" nodes are used for denoting concepts. A chunk node connects to its corresponding microfeatures at the bottom level (represented by a set of separate nodes, constituting a distributed representation in the bottom level). At the top level, action rules connect chunk nodes representing conditions to chunk nodes representing actions. If the condition of an action rule is met, then the corresponding action is recommended.

At the bottom level, with neural networks encoding implicit knowledge, actions are selected based on their values, which are the outputs of the neural networks. A Q value is an evaluation of the "quality" of an action in a given input state: $Q(x, a)$ indicates how desirable action a is in state x. At each step, given input state x, the Q values of all the actions (i.e., $Q(x, a)$ for all a's) are computed in parallel. Then the Q values are used to decide stochastically on an action to be performed, through a Boltzmann distribution of Q values (i.e., a softmax function):

$$p(a \mid x) = e^{Q(x,a)/\tau} / \sum_i e^{Q(x,a_i)/\tau}$$

where τ (temperature) controls the degree of randomness of action decision-making, and i ranges over all possible actions. (This is known as Luce's choice axiom; see Watkins 1989.)

For learning implicit knowledge at the bottom level (i.e., the Q values), the Q-learning algorithm (Watkins 1989), which is a reinforcement learning algorithm, may be used (e.g., as implemented in Backpropagation neural networks). Q values are gradually tuned through successive updating, which enables reactive sequential behavior to emerge through trial-and-error interaction with the world (Watkins 1989; Sun et al. 2001). At a result of such learning, the Q values come to represent, roughly, the maximum cumulative reinforcement that can be received from the current point on, where reinforcement represents the fulfillment of needs and achievement of goals (as decided by the MS and the MCS; Sun 2016).

For learning explicit action rules at the top level with a bottom-up learning process, the *rule-extraction-refinement* algorithm (RER) uses information from the bottom level in learning rules at the top level.

The basic idea of RER is as follows (Sun et al. 2001): if an action implicitly decided by the bottom level is successful, then one extracts an explicit rule that corresponds to the action selected by the bottom level and adds the rule to the top level. Then, in subsequent interaction with the world, one verifies the extracted rule by considering the outcome of applying the rule: if the outcome is not successful, then the rule should be revised and made more specific; if the outcome is successful, the rule may be generalized to make it more universally applicable.

Based on this idea, the following is done within each action cycle of the ACS:

1. Update the rule statistics.
2. Check the current criterion for rule extraction, generalization, and specialization:
    2.1. If the result is successful according to the current rule extraction criterion, and there is no rule matching the current state and action, then perform extraction of a new rule. Add the extracted rule to the top level of the ACS.
    2.2. If the result is unsuccessful according to the current specialization criterion, then revise all the rules matching the current state and action through specialization:
        2.2.1. Remove these rules from the top level.
        2.2.2. Add the specialized versions of these rules into the top level.
    2.3. If the result is successful according to the current generalization criterion, then revise the rules matching the current state and action through generalization:
        2.3.1. Remove these rules from the top level.
        2.3.2. Add the generalized versions of these rules to the top level.

These operations and their associated criteria are guided by various statistical measures. Further details of bottom-up learning and its variations can be found in Sun et al. (2001) and Sun (2002). One can find empirical and theoretical arguments in favor of this kind of algorithm in, for example, Bruner et al. (1956), Dominowski (1972), Sun et al. (2001), and so on.

On the other hand, top-down learning goes in the opposite direction (Sun 2002). Once explicit knowledge is established at the top level (e.g., through externally provided information), it can be assimilated into the bottom level. This often occurs during the novice-to-expert transition in instructed learning settings (Dreyfus and Dreyfus 1987; Anderson and Lebiere 1998). The assimilation process, termed "top-down learning" (as opposed to "bottom-up learning"), can be carried out using the same implicit learning mechanisms sketched earlier (e.g., reinforcement learning algorithms).

For stochastic selection of the outcomes of the two levels, at each step, with probability P_{BL}, the outcome of the bottom level is used. Likewise, with probability P_{RER}, the outcome from the RER rule set is used. Other components, if exist, may also be included in the stochastic selection. There exists some psychological evidence for such intermittent use of rules (Sun et al. 2001).

16.3.2 Non-Action-Centered Subsystem

The NACS is for dealing with declarative, or non-action-centered, knowledge (Sun 2012, 2016). It stores such knowledge in a dual representational form (the same as in the ACS): that is, in the form of explicit "associative rules" (at the top level), and in the form of implicit "associative memory" (at the bottom level). Its operation is under the control of the ACS (thus it is in the service of action decision-making).

At the bottom level of the NACS, associative memory neural networks encode implicit declarative knowledge. Associations are formed by mapping an input to an output (e.g., Rumelhart et al. 1986).

At the top level of the NACS, explicit declarative knowledge is stored. As in the ACS, chunk nodes (denoting concepts) at the top level are linked to microfeatures at the bottom level. Additionally, at the top level, links between chunk nodes encode explicit associative rules (which may be learned in a variety of ways; Sun 2016).

As in the ACS, top-down or bottom-up learning may take place in the NACS, either to extract explicit knowledge at the top level from implicit knowledge in the bottom level, or to assimilate explicit knowledge of the top level into implicit knowledge at the bottom level.

With the interaction of its two levels, the NACS carries out rule-based, similarity-based, and constraint-satisfaction-based reasoning. The overall operation of the NACS is as follows:

1. A directive is received by the NACS to initiate reasoning on a specified input.
2. Bottom-up and top-down activation propagate the input to both levels of the NACS.
3. Associative reasoning is performed simultaneously at both levels:
    3.1. Associative memory networks propagate activations at the bottom level.
    3.2. Associative rules activate chunk nodes at the top level.
4. Activations of the two levels are integrated at the top level.
5. At a set time limit or when no further conclusions can be inferred, the NACS returns chunks that were inferred. Otherwise, the process is reiterated (e.g., using the results of the previous iteration as inputs).

Further details of the NACS can be found in Sun (2016) or Helie and Sun (2010).

16.4 INTERPRETATIONS
OF EMPIRICAL DATA

We may view existing computational models and simulations of various processes—implicit, explicit, procedural, declarative, bottom-up, or top-down—as a form of theoretical interpretation (in particular, concerning their mechanistic or algorithmic details). In that case, we may look into the following example illustrating the interaction of implicit and explicit processes and bottom-up learning.

The human data of Stanley et al. (1989) were typical of human performance in process control tasks and demonstrated the interaction between explicit and implicit processes. In their experiments, human subjects were instructed to control the outputs of a simulated system by choosing their inputs into the system (from a set of available inputs). The outputs of the system were determined from the inputs provided by the subjects, through a certain relationship. However, this relationship was not known to the subjects. Subjects gradually learned to control the outputs of the system through trial and error. Many of them also developed some explicit knowledge of the relationship. Various experimental manipulations of learning settings placed differential emphases on explicit and implicit learning.

Specifically, two versions of process control tasks were used. In the person version, each subject interacted with a computer simulated "person" whose behavior ranged from "very rude" to "loving" (over a total of twelve levels), and the task was to maintain the behavior of the simulated person at "very friendly" by controlling his/her own behavior (which could also range over the twelve levels, from "very rude" to "loving"). In the sugar factory version, each subject interacted with a simulated factory to maintain a particular production level (out of a total of twelve possible levels), through adjusting the size of the workforce (which also had twelve levels). In either case, the behavior of the simulated system was determined by $P = 2 * W - P_1 + N$, where P was the current system output, P_1 was the previous system output, W was the input from a subject to the system, and N was noise. Noise (N) was added to the output of the system, so that there was a chance of being up or down one level (a 33 percent chance, respectively).

There were four groups of subjects. The control group was not given any instruction to help performance and not asked to verbalize during performance. The "original" group was asked to verbalize after each block of ten trials. Other groups of subjects were given explicit instructions in various forms. To the "memory training" group, a series of twelve correct input/output pairs was presented. To the "simple rule" group, a simple rule ("always select the response level half way between the current production level and the target level") was given. All the subjects were trained for 200 trials (20 blocks of 10 trials).

Statistical analysis was done based on "score," defined as the average number of on-target responses per trial block (where the exact target value plus/minus one level was considered on target). The analysis showed that the score of the original group was significantly higher than that of the control group. It also showed that the scores of the memory training group and the simple rule group were also significantly higher than that of the control group. See Table 16.1.[1]

Some explanation is in order. First, the performance in this task involved mostly procedural processes and, moreover, mostly implicit procedural processes, judging from many experiments in the past (e.g., Berry and Broadbent 1988; Mathews et al. 2011). Bottom-up learning occurred on the basis of implicit learning (as explained earlier). Second, the memory training and the simple rule condition led to more involvement of explicit processes, because of the emphasis placed on explicit knowledge in these conditions. Third, verbalization also increased the involvement of explicit processes, because verbalization necessarily placed more emphasis on explicit (verbalizable) knowledge. Fourth, increased involvement of explicit processes led to better performance. More detailed analysis may be found in Sun et al. (2007).

Table 16.1 The human data from Stanley et al. (1989). Each cell indicates the average number of on–target responses per trial block. The exact target value plus/minus one level was considered on target

	Sugar Task	Person Task
control	1.97	2.85
original	2.57	3.75
memory training	4.63	5.33
simple rule	4.00	5.91

The simulation setup for this task (based on Clarion) was as follows (see Sun et al. 2007 for further details). The ACS was mainly responsible in this task, because this task relied on procedural processes. In the bottom level of the ACS, a four-layered neural network implemented Q-learning with Backpropagation. Reinforcement was determined by the outcome from the to-be-controlled system, based on the distance between the target value and the actual outcome. At the top level, bottom-up learning of rules acquired explicit knowledge.

For capturing each of the experimental conditions, few parameter values were adjusted. To model the effect of verbalization (in the "original" group), bottom-up rule learning thresholds were adjusted so as to increase rule learning activities at the top level. The hypothesis was that verbalization tended to increase explicit activities, especially rule learning activities. To capture explicit instructions, given knowledge was wired up at the top level: In the memory training condition, each of the twelve explicit examples was wired up at the top level as rules. In the simple rule condition, the explicit rule was wired up at the top level.

For each group, a total of 100 simulation runs were conducted, representing 100 simulated "subjects." Each run lasted 20 blocks, for a total of 200 trials, exactly the same as in the human experiments.[2]

The simulation with this setup (including variations in bottom-up learning) captured all the observed effects in the human data (Sun et al. 2007). First, the simulation captured the effect of verbalization in the human data, as shown by Table 16.2. Statistical tests compared the simulated "original" group with the simulated control group, which showed a significant performance improvement due to verbalization, analogous to the human data. The simulation also captured the effect of explicit instructions (also shown in Table 16.2). Statistical tests compared the simulated memory training and the simulated simple rule group with the simulated control group, which showed significant improvements of these two groups over the simulated control group, analogous to the human data. Overall, the interpretations as embodied by the simulation setup above were shown to capture well the human data and thus to be highly plausible.

Many other examples of simulations and interpretations of empirical data may be found in Sun (2002, 2016).

Table 16.2 The simulation of Stanley et al. (1989). Each cell indicates the average number of on-target responses per trial block

Human Data

	Sugar Task	Person Task
control	1.97	2.85
original	2.57	3.75
memory training	4.63	5.33
simple rule	4.00	5.91

Model Data

	Sugar Task	Person Task
control	1.92	2.62
original	2.77	4.01
memory training	4.45	5.45
simple rule	4.80	5.65

16.5 DISCUSSION

Implicit learning (and implicit cognitive processes in general) has been gaining recognition in recent decades (Reber 1989; Sun 2002). However, although both implicit and explicit learning have been investigated empirically, the interaction between implicit and explicit learning (such as bottom-up learning) and the importance of this interaction have been less widely recognized. The interaction has traditionally been downplayed in empirical research (with a few exceptions, of course). Research has been focused on showing the lack of explicit learning in various settings and on the controversies stemming from such claims. Similar oversight is also evident in computational models of implicit learning (with a few exceptions).

Despite the relative scarcity of studies of the implicit–explicit interaction, it has become evident that it is difficult to find a situation in which only one type of learning is engaged. Various indications of the implicit–explicit interaction can be found scattered in the literature. For instance, in addition to Stanley et al. (1989), Ahlum-Heath and DiVesta (1986), Sun et al. (2001), and many others also found that verbalization led to better performance. However, as Sun et al. (2001) showed, verbalization might also hamper implicit learning, especially when too much verbalization induced an overly explicit learning mode.

Similarly, as shown by Berry and Broadbent (1988), Reber et al. (1980), Stanley et al. (1989), and many others, verbal instructions given prior to skill learning could facilitate or hamper performance. One type of instruction was to encourage subjects to perform explicit search for regularities that might aid in performance. Reber et al. (1980) found that, depending on ways in which stimuli were presented, explicit search might help or hamper performance. Another type of instruction was explicit how-to instruction that told subjects specifically how a task should be performed, including providing information concerning regularities. As discussed earlier, Stanley et al. (1989) found that such instructions helped to improve performance significantly.

In a way, such empirical results indicated the possibility of synergy between implicit and explicit procedural processes, in the sense that under proper circumstances, the interaction of implicit and explicit procedural processes led to better overall performance (Sun et al. 2005; Sun 2002). Similar effects exist in declarative processes as well (Helie and Sun 2010).

A particularly important form of the implicit-explicit interaction, as stated before, is bottom-up and top-down learning. A major finding from the recent exploration of bottom-up and top-down learning is that learning can occur in either direction (or both): (1) learning can occur through trial-and-error implicitly, without explicit knowledge to begin with; implicit skills may be acquired before explicit knowledge emerges; explicit knowledge may in fact be learned through the mediation of already acquired implicit knowledge (i.e., through extracting implicit knowledge in a sense); and (2) learning can also occur through acquiring explicit knowledge first and then, with practice, assimilating explicit knowledge into implicit forms. Bottom-up learning refers to learning implicit knowledge first and then learning explicit knowledge on that basis (i.e., through extracting implicit knowledge). Top-down learning refers to learning explicit knowledge first and then learning implicit knowledge on that basis (i.e., assimilating explicit knowledge into an implicit form). These two forms of learning have been extensively explored, for example, in Sun (2002, 2016).

The significance of stressing the distinction of the two learning directions lies in the fact that bottom-up learning has been very much a neglected topic (even its very existence was ignored in cognitive science for a long time; Sun et al. 2001), while top-down learning has been overemphasized. Given the culturally created systems of schooling, apprenticeship, and other forms of guided (or instructed) learning, top-down learning is quite prevalent in human society. However, bottom-up learning is more fundamental. It is more fundamental in two senses: the ontological sense and the ontogenetic sense.

Ontologically, explicit knowledge needs to be obtained in the first place before it can be imparted to people (e.g., to enable top-down learning). Therefore, bottom-up learning, which creates new explicit knowledge, is more fundamental. Only after bottom-up learning (or other types of learning) created explicit knowledge, can top-down learning be possible. Ontogenetically, there seem to be some empirical indications that children learn sensory-motor skills (as well as knowledge concerning concepts) implicitly first, and then acquire explicit knowledge on that basis (see Sun et al. 2001 for a review of the relevant psychological literature). Therefore, bottom-up learning is also more important ontogenetically (i.e., developmentally).

Of course, instead of bottom-up learning, it is possible that one can learn explicit knowledge directly. One reason why bottom-up learning has been emphasized here is because it has not been sufficiently emphasized in the literature in the past. Furthermore, a cognitive advantage that comes with bottom-up learning, as opposed to directly learning explicit knowledge, is the reduction of the "computational" cost of learning. For one thing, employing this two-stage approach may be a more efficient way of learning explicit knowledge (in a "computational" sense), because, guided by implicit knowledge, the search space for explicit knowledge is narrowed down and an on-line incremental search can then be more easily performed (as has been demonstrated through modeling and simulation using Clarion; Sun 2002). This fact may, in part, explain why evolution has chosen this approach. There have been human data that indicate that humans do engage in bottom-up learning (see, e.g., Stanley et al. 1989; Sun et al. 2001; Sun et al. 2005; Sallas et al. 2007). So, bottom-up learning is cognitively realistic.

The research on these two learning directions may have some practical applications. For example, it may have implications for educational practice (Sun et al. 2007). Most educational settings focus on directly teaching explicit knowledge rather than opportunities for developing experiential, that is, mostly implicit, knowledge first and then bottom-up learning on that basis. While this may be beneficial for some subject matters, others may require learning complex skills and knowledge (e.g., a convoluted system or some ill-structured categories) that are better learned (at least initially) through repeated experience. In general, repeated practice, memorization of examples, laboratory exploration, and so on may help to promote implicit learning and consequently bottom-up learning on that basis, while classroom lectures and textbooks often promote learning of explicit knowledge first and top-down learning on that basis. While the importance of explicit knowledge is evident, the significance of implicit learning/knowledge and bottom-up learning in education should not be downplayed either.

Current research in this area includes investigation of the interaction and integration of implicit and explicit knowledge in complex skill learning through bottom-up and top-down learning. Psychological experiments with human subjects are being conducted that explore different ways for, and different effects of, the interaction and integration of implicit and explicit knowledge through bottom-up and top-down learning (e.g., Sallas et al. 2007). They also explore different methods of facilitating bottom-up and top-down learning in order to enhance skill acquisition. In relation to such research, cognitive architectures (in particular, Clarion) are being further developed for capturing the fine details of bottom-up and top-down learning. Through exploring a variety of empirical data, a unified and comprehensive cognitive architecture may be attained, which may shed light on plausible mechanisms and processes of bottom-up and top-down learning, as well as the interaction and integration of implicit and explicit processes in general. The contribution of such ongoing research lies in coming up with useful theories that explain a wide range of human data in terms of bottom-up and top-down learning and in terms of the interaction and integration of implicit and explicit cognitive processes in general.

NOTES

1. Note that subjects performed somewhat better in the person task compared with the sugar factory task. Subjects might have brought in their prior knowledge of interacting with other people in the real world into their performance of the person task.
2. To capture the fact that subjects performed better in the person task compared with the sugar factory task (presumably due to the fact that subjects brought their prior knowledge of interacting with other people in the real world into their performance of this task), some pretraining was conducted prior to performing the person task.

REFERENCES

Ahlum-Heath, Mary, and DiVesta, Francis. 1986. "The Effect of Conscious Controlled Verbalization of a Cognitive Strategy on Transfer in Problem Solving." *Memory and Cognition* 14:281–5.

Anderson, John R. 1983. *The Architecture of Cognition*. Cambridge, MA: Harvard University Press.

Anderson, John R., and Lebiere, Christian. 1998. *The Atomic Components of Thought*. Mahwah, NJ: Erlbaum.

Berry, Dianne, and Donald Broadbent. 1988. "Interactive Tasks and the Implicit-Explicit Distinction." *British Journal of Psychology* 79:251–72.

Bowers, Kenneth, Glenn Regehr, Claude Balthazard, and Kevin Parker. 1990. "Intuition in the Context of Discovery." *Cognitive Psychology* 22:72–110.

Bruner, Jerome, Jacqueline J. Goodnow, and George A. Austin. 1956. *A Study of Thinking*. New York: Wiley.

Dewey, John. 1958. *Experience and Nature*. New York: Dover.

Dominowski, Roger. 1972. "How Do People Discover Concepts?" pp. 257–88 in *Theories in Cognitive Psychology: The Loyola Symposium*, edited by R. L. Solso. Potomac, MD: Erlbaum.

Dreyfus, Hubert. 1992. *Being-In-The-World*. Cambridge, MA: MIT Press.

Dreyfus, Hubert, and Stuart Dreyfus. 1987. *Mind over Machine: The Power of Human Intuition*. New York: Free Press.

Hasher, Lynn, and Rose T. Zacks. 1979. "Automatic and Effortful Processes in Memory." *Journal of Experimental Psychology: General* 108:356–8.

Heidegger, Martin. 1927/1962. *Being and Time*. New York: Harper and Row.

Helie, Sèbastien, and Ron Sun. 2010. "Incubation, Insight, and Creative Problem Solving: A Unified Theory and a Connectionist Model." *Psychological Review* 117(3):994–1024.

James, William. 1890. *The Principles of Psychology*. New York: Dover.

Jacoby, Larry. 1983. "Perceptual Enhancement: Persistent Effects of an Experience." *Journal of Experimental Psychology: Learning, Memory, and Cognition* 9(1):21–38.

Kanfer, Ruth, and Phillip L. Ackerman 1989. "Motivation and Cognitive Abilities: An Integrative/Aptitude-Treatment Interaction Approach to Skill Acquisition." *Journal of Applied Psychology* 74(4):657–90.

Karmiloff-Smith, Annette. 1986. "From Meta-Processes to Conscious Access: Evidence from Children's Metalinguistic and Repair Data." *Cognition* 23:95–147.

Keil, Frank. 1989. *Concepts, Kinds, and Cognitive Development*. Cambridge, MA: MIT Press.

Lewicki, Pawel, Maria Czyzewska, and Hunter Hoffman. 1987. "Unconscious Acquisition of Complex Procedural Knowledge." *Journal of Experimental Psychology: Learning, Memory and Cognition* 13(4):523–30.

Mandler, Jean M. 1992. "How to Build a Baby." *Psychological Review* 99(4):587–604.

Mathews, Robert C., Jonathan Tall, Sean M. Lane, and Ron Sun. 2011. "Getting It Right Generally, but Not Precisely: Learning the Relation between Multiple Inputs and Outputs." *Memory and Cognition* 39(6):1133–45.

Moscovitch, Morris, and Carlo Umilta. 1991. "Conscious and Unconscious Aspects of Memory: A Neuropsychological Framework of Modules and Central Systems." In *Perspectives on cognitive neuroscience*, edited by R. Lister and H. Weingartner. New York: Oxford University Press.

Nisbett, Richard, and Timothy Wilson. 1977." Telling More than We Can Know: Verbal Reports on Mental Processes." *Psychological Review* 84(3):231–59.

Reber, Arthur. 1989. "Implicit Learning and Tacit Knowledge." *Journal of Experimental Psychology: General* 118(3):219–35.

Reber, Arthur, Saul M. Kassin, Selma Lewis, and Gary Cantor. 1980. "On the Relationship between Implicit and Explicit Modes in the Learning of a Complex Rule Structure." *Journal of Experimental Psychology: Human Learning and Memory* 6:492–502.

Roediger, Henry L. 1990. "Implicit Memory: Retention without Remembering." *American Psychologist* 45(9):1043–56.

Rosenbaum, David A., Richard A. Carlson, and Rick O. Gilmore. 2001. "Acquisition of Intellectual and Perceptual-Motor Skills." *Annual Review of Psychology* 52:453–70.

Rumelhart, David, James McClelland, and PDP Research Group. 1986. *Parallel Distributed Processing: Explorations in the Microstructures of Cognition.* Cambridge, MA: MIT Press.

Sallas, Bill, Robert Mathews, Sean Lane, and Ron Sun. 2007. "Developing Rich and Quickly Accessed Knowledge of an Artificial Grammar." *Memory and Cognition* 35(8):2118–33.

Schacter, Daniel. 1987. "Implicit Memory: History and Current Status." *Journal of Experimental Psychology: Learning, Memory, and Cognition* 13:501–18.

Seger, Carol Augart. 1994. "Implicit Learning." *Psychological Bulletin* 115(2):163–96.

Siegler, Robert, and Elsbeth Stern. 1998. "Conscious and Unconscious Strategy Discovery: A Microgenetic Analysis." *Journal of Experimental Psychology: General* 127(4):377–97.

Stanley, William B., Robert C. Mathews, Ray Buss, and Susan Kotler-Cope. 1989. "Insight without Awareness: On the Interaction of Verbalization, Instruction and Practice in a Simulated Process Control Task." *Quarterly Journal of Experimental Psychology* 1215:553–77.

Sun, Ron. 1994. *Integrating Rules and Connectionism for Robust Commonsense Reasoning.* New York: Wiley.

Sun, Ron. 2002. *Duality of the Mind.* Mahwah, NJ: Erlbaum.

Sun, Ron. 2012. "Memory Systems within a Cognitive Architecture." *New Ideas in Psychology* 30:227–40.

Sun, Ron. 2016. *Anatomy of the Mind.* New York: Oxford University Press.

Sun, Ron, Robert C. Mathews, and Sean M. Lane. 2007. "Implicit and Explicit Processes in the Development of Cognitive Skills: A Theoretical Interpretation with Some Practical Implications for Science Education." pp. 1–26 in *Educational Psychology Research Focus*, edited by E. Vargios. Hauppauge, NY: Nova Science.

Sun, Ron, Edward Merrill, and Todd Peterson. 2001. "From Implicit Skills to Explicit Knowledge: A Bottom-Up Model of Skill Learning." *Cognitive Science* 25(2):203–44.

Sun, Ron, Paul Slusarz, and Chris Terry. 2005. "The Interaction of the Explicit and the Implicit in Skill Learning: A Dual-Process Approach." *Psychological Review* 112(1):159–92.

Sun, Ron, and Zhang, Xi. 2006. "Accounting for a Variety of Reasoning Data within a Cognitive Architecture." *Journal of Experimental and Theoretical Artificial Intelligence* 18(2):169–91.

Sun, Ron, Xi Zhang, and Robert Mathews. 2009. "Capturing Human Data in a Letter Counting Task: Accessibility and Action-Centeredness in Representing Cognitive Skills." *Neural Networks* 22:15–29.

Sun, Ron, Xi Zhang, Paul Slusarz, and Robert C. Mathews. 2007. "The Interaction of Implicit Learning, Explicit Hypothesis Testing Learning, and Implicit-to-Explicit Knowledge Extraction." *Neural Networks* 20(1):34–47.

Toth, Jeffrey, Eyal M. Reingold, and Larry Jacoby, 1994. Toward a redefinition of implicit memory: Process dissociations following elaborative processing and self-generation. *Journal of Experimental Psychology: Learning, Memory, and Cognition* 20(2):290–303.

Tulving, Endel, and Daniel L. Schacter, 1990. "Priming and Human Memory Systems." *Science* 247:301–5.

Warrington, Elizabeth K., and Weiskrantz, Lawrence. 1970. "Amnesic Syndrome: Consolidation or Retrieval?" *Nature* 228:628–30.

Watkins, Chris. 1989. "Learning with Delayed Rewards." PhD thesis, Cambridge University, Cambridge, UK.

Willingham, Daniel B. 1998. "A Neuropsychological Theory of Motor Skill Learning." *Psychological Review* 105(3):558–84.

Willingham, Daniel B., Mary Jo Nissen, and Peter Bullemer. 1989. "On the Development of Procedural Knowledge." *Journal of Experimental Psychology: Learning, Memory, and Cognition* 15:1047–60.

CHAPTER 17

WHAT IS CULTURAL FIT?

from cognition to behavior (and back)

SANAZ MOBASSERI, AMIR GOLDBERG,
AND SAMEER B. SRIVASTAVA

How people fit into social groups is a core topic of investigation across a range of social science disciplines including sociology, social psychology, political science, and economics. Although the concept of fitting in bears many different names—for example, assimilation, enculturation, integration, socialization, acculturation, adaptation, or social belonging—it is fundamentally about how people construct similarities and navigate differences between themselves and social groups. Specifically, we conceptualize fitting in as the process of thinking and acting in ways that are aligned with the thoughts and behavioral expectations of members of a social group.

The process of fitting in and its consequences have been studied across multiple domains, including education, immigration, and organizations. Sociologists of education have investigated the many ways in which school environments—for example, those with a culture of bullying or characterized by racial or socioeconomic segregation—affect whether and how students fit in and how they consequently perform (Arum 2000; Carter and Welner 2013; Reardon and Owens 2014; Jack 2016). On a larger scale, the social forces of urbanization, industrialization, and global migration have motivated research into whether, how, and when immigrants assimilate to new locales (Park and Burgess 1921; Gordon 1964; Alba and Nee 2003). Separately, organizational scholars have examined how congruence between values, norms, and beliefs of employees and an organization as a whole can affect the coordination of activity and thereby influence individual and organizational success (Van Maanen 1975; Chatman 1991; Srivastava et al. 2018). Although these literatures examine distinct social phenomena and have thus developed along parallel, mostly disconnected, trajectories, they share an underlying focus on the dynamics and consequences of cultural fit.

In this chapter, we synthesize findings from these literatures to develop an overarching framework for conceptualizing and measuring the level of cultural fit and the dynamics of enculturation between an individual and a social group. In particular, we distinguish between the *cognitive* and *behavioral* aspects of cultural fit, which previous work has tended to either examine in isolation or to conflate. Reviewing the literature through this lens enables us to identify the strengths and limitations of such unitary—that is, primarily cognitive or primarily behavioral—approaches. We then develop a theoretical framework that integrates the two perspectives and demonstrates the value of more closely interrogating the congruence, incongruence, and interplay between cognitive and behavioral cultural fit. We turn next to identifying promising theoretical pathways that can link the two perspectives. We conclude by discussing the implications of pursuing these conceptual routes for research methods and provide some illustrative examples of such work.

17.1 CULTURAL FIT: COGNITIVE AND BEHAVIORAL MANIFESTATIONS

Cultural fit can only be understood in reference to "culture": a system of meanings and behavioral norms shared by members of a group (DiMaggio 1997; Small et al. 2010; Patterson 2014). Our parsimonious definition of culture highlights two fundamental dimensions that delineate the sources and implications of cultural fit: cognition and behavior. The cognitive dimension refers to the mental representations, beliefs, and values that individuals draw on to make sense of their everyday experiences. The behavioral dimension relates to the norms and expectations that circumscribe individuals' actions.

To make these abstract definitions more tangible, consider differences between national cultures. Asian and Western cultures, for example, are said to differ systematically in how individuals understand themselves and their relationships with others. Whereas Westerners tend to espouse an independent and individualistic self-construal, Asians tend to think of the self as inherently interdependent with others (Markus and Kitayama 1991). Concomitantly, Asian and Western cultures promote different behavioral norms when it comes to personal disclosure, privacy, and the pursuit of self- versus group-oriented goals.

Drawing on these foundations, we propose that cultural fit should be understood as comprising both cognitive and behavioral components. We define *cognitive cultural fit* as the degree of similarity between an individual's set of mental representations, beliefs, and values, and those espoused by group members. By *behavioral cultural fit* we mean the individual's degree of compliance with the group's normative behavioral expectations. We can thus characterize individuals by the extent to which they have achieved cognitive and behavioral cultural fit, as illustrated in Figure 17.1.[1]

An American immigrating to China, to continue our (admittedly oversimplified) example, might exhibit high cognitive cultural fit if she adopts an interdependent self-construal and might demonstrate high behavioral cultural fit by conforming to normative expectations—for example, complying with requests from mere acquaintances to

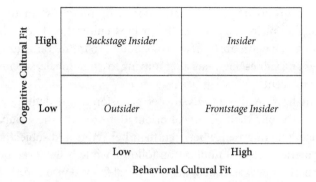

FIGURE 17.1 Framework—Two dimensions of cultural fit.

exchange sensitive information about work responsibilities and remuneration that might be considered rude or intrusive in her home country. As even this primitive example highlights, cognitive and behavioral cultural fit are distinct and separable. The American in China might accede to the request to share sensitive information but still consider it to be at odds with her independently construed private self; conversely, she might adopt an interdependent self-construal but still be habituated to refrain from asking acquaintances about the sensitive details of their work.

The distinction between cognition and behavior affords two important advantages. First, cognitive and behavioral cultural fit have different consequences for others' perceptions of the individual. While cognition is generally private, behavior is easier for others to observe. Goffman's (1959) dramaturgic analogy helps to make this distinction tangible. Individuals make inferences about others' backstage cognition by observing their frontstage behavior. These inferences are themselves mediated by the observer's own backstage cognition. If cognition and behavior are not aligned, then individuals might develop incorrect perceptions of their own and others' cultural fit. Furthermore, these perceptions might be inconsistent across group members. Such inconsistencies in members' perceptions can lead to schisms within the group or to dysfunction more broadly.

Second, the analytical distinction between cognition and behavior allows us to identify four ideal types of cultural fit, as illustrated in Figure 17.1. Whereas most of the literature conceives of cultural fit as a gradient ranging from being an outsider to being an insider, our framework also pays attention to individuals with incongruent levels of cognitive and behavioral cultural fit. The *frontstage insider* exhibits high behavioral cultural fit but is cognitively distant from other group members. This behavior may be strategic, for example, when organizational members purposively don façades to get ahead in their careers, but it can also be unintentional, such as when a newcomer to a group is pressured into adopting normatively compliant behaviors before she has the time to think of herself as being part of the group or when a group member reluctantly upholds a norm due to an incorrect impression of its popularity (Centola et al. 2005). Conversely, the *backstage insider* is cognitively similar to her peers but behaviorally inconsistent with group norms. This situation can emerge when the individual in question is not skillful in deciphering the group's cultural code or when habituated counternormative behaviors are difficult to abandon. An immigrant, for example, might adapt her beliefs and values but, years after moving to a new locale, still find it difficult to speak without an accent.

Our conceptualization also affords greater precision in the definition of the *insider* and the *outsider*. Despite their divergent orientations toward the group, both insiders and outsiders exhibit congruence between their behaviors and subjective experiences. An important methodological implication follows: while behavioral measures of cultural fit can be used as proxies for cognitive cultural fit (and vice versa) for insiders and outsiders, focusing on just observable behaviors or only self-reported feelings of fit would lead to incomplete and potentially even inaccurate assessments of fit for individuals who are backstage or frontstage insiders. Compliance with a firm's conversational norms, for example, is likely to be a poor indicator of cultural fit for the frontstage insider, just as self-reported fit with the organization's prevailing values and norms is likely to be an inaccurate measure of cultural fit for the backstage insider. Purely cognitive or purely behavioral measures are most likely to be informative only for the subset of individuals whose cognitive fit is aligned with their behavioral fit.

17.2 MAPPING PRIOR WORK ON THE SPECTRUM FROM COGNITION TO BEHAVIOR

Previous work tends to conceptually and methodologically privilege either the cognitive or the behavioral dimension of cultural fit or to conflate the two. To understand the commonalities, strengths, and limitations of research on fitting in across the domains of education, immigration, and organizations, we assemble prior work along a continuum that ranges from primarily cognitive to primarily behavioral. Figure 17.2 below depicts this spectrum and arrays along it the methods most commonly used in these literatures.

17.2.1 Primarily Cognitive Approaches

A critical component of fitting in is its subjective experience—what people think and perceive about themselves in relation to their social groups. Each of the three literatures—education, immigration, and organizations—has highlighted different aspects of this subjective experience.

Research in the sociology of education has focused, for example, on how students feel they fit into the "mainstream" (often middle-class, white) culture that prevails in many schools or into the specific culture (e.g., sports- or drama- or service-oriented) of their own school; the extent to which they have similar attitudes, preferences, tastes, and

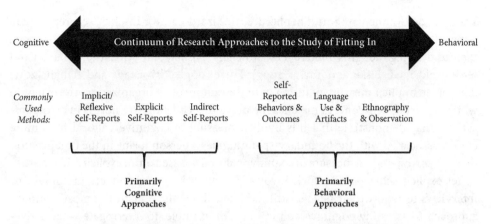

FIGURE 17.2 Continuum of research approaches to the study of fitting in.

styles as their peers; and the degree to which they are valued by teachers, administrators, and other students (Bourdieu and Passeron 1970; Bourdieu 1977; Willis 1977; Bowles et al. 2009). Social psychological research on education has more specifically called attention to students' sense of social belonging—defined as a "need for frequent, nonaversive interactions within an ongoing relational bond" (Baumeister and Leary 1995:497; Walton and Cohen 2007, 2011; Yeager and Walton 2011; Stephens et al. 2014).

Within immigration research, the subjective experience of assimilation has been conceptualized as achieving shared "peoplehood" or similarity (Park and Burgess 1921).[2] Other work in this tradition has instead thought of fitting in as the perceived match between a person's self-presentation and the distinguishing characteristics of the social group into which that person seeks to assimilate (Gordon 1964; Alba and Nee 2003). More recently, Schacter (2016) introduced the notion of "symbolic belonging," which considers how both immigrants and natives think about and relate to each other.

Organizational research has similarly highlighted the process of socializing into groups within an organization and the organization as a whole. Building on Schein's (1985) theory of organizational culture, which highlights the importance of assumptions shared by organizational members, extant research has explored how values, norms, and beliefs held by members are related to group and organizational culture. These shared assumptions affect how members coordinate activities and engage in work that supports or does not support the organization's goals and success (Chatman and O'Reilly 2016). In this literature, cultural fit is often thought of as shared patterns of meaning among group members (Martin and Siehl 1983), shared sets of symbols and myths within an organization (Ouchi 1981), or shared attitudes and practices (Tellis et al. 2009).

Three of the most common methods for studying cognitive cultural fit are: implicit, explicit, and indirect self-reports. Building on the insight that there are two distinct modes of thinking—automatic and deliberative—implicit self-reports gather information about the former: what a person thinks about the self in relation to the social group in more rapid, involuntary, and less conscious cognition (Chen and Bargh 1997;

Vaisey 2009; Kahneman 2011; Shepherd 2011; Lizardo 2016). Implicit self-reports are especially useful when people are less aware of, or otherwise lack the capacity to report, their underlying thoughts, preferences, or beliefs (Nisbett and Wilson 1977; Banaji and Greenwald 1994; Fiske and Taylor 2007). For example, Srivastava and Banaji (2011) develop an implicit measure of fitting in to the culture of an organization: the extent to which a person's self-concept matches the prevailing collaborative norms in an organization. They demonstrate that this implicit measure of cognitive cultural fit is more closely associated with the boundary-spanning ties a person forms in the organization than is a corresponding measure of cognitive cultural fit based on an explicit self-report.

Yet explicit self-reports, which involve directly asking respondents in surveys or interviews to report their beliefs, attitudes, and thoughts, remain the most common approach to assessing cognitive cultural fit. For example, to interrogate what native-born US citizens think it means for immigrants to achieve "symbolic belonging," Schacter (2016:988) presents respondents with a survey containing various hypothetical profiles of potential new neighbors and directly asks: "In general, how similar is [Neighbor] to you?"; "In terms of culture, how much in common does [Neighbor] have with most Americans?"; and "If [Neighbor] moved to your block, how interested would you be in becoming friends?" Self-reports of cognitive cultural fit can also be found in organizational research. For example, Judge and Cable (1997) ask job seekers to report on their direct perception of fit with the culture of the organizations to which they are applying and examine how this measure relates to their attraction to the organization.

Like implicit measures, indirect self-reports offer researchers the benefit of collecting data from participants without revealing the relationship between their responses and the intended use of this data. This approach helps to alleviate concerns about social desirability bias, which can distort the accuracy of explicit self-reports. In organizational research, one of the most widely used indirect approaches to assessing cultural fit is the Organizational Culture Profile (OCP). The OCP measures fit by correlating an individual's self-reported preferences for a work environment with the aggregated perceptions of the environment made by organizational leaders (O'Reilly et al. 1991). The key to this measure is that respondents are not directly asked to state whether or how they fit in. Instead, data about their preferences are collected independently from others' assessments of the organization's prevailing culture. In a sense, the OCP is more behavioral than an explicit self-report because the aggregate views of the prevailing culture— the culture people are fitting into—are informed by people's actual behavior. Yet the first component of the OCP—a person's own values and preferences—is still primarily cognitive.

Implicit, explicit, and indirect self-reports yield measures of fitting in that have certain advantages. First, they illuminate the subjective experience of cultural fit, which is itself worthy of study and which has been shown to have consequences for individual and group outcomes (Chatman and O'Reilly 2016). Second, the instruments used to collect these measures can be tailored to the setting to reveal the content of group culture, the hierarchy of affiliations people have with different social groups, and the extent to which they fit in within and across these groups. For example, a student might fit in well with the academic culture of a school but less well with its athletic culture. Similarly, a new immigrant might resonate with the entrepreneurial culture of a destination country but be at odds with its family culture. Finally, such measures allow for comparisons across individuals, thus revealing which cultural dimensions are strongly shared and thus most salient to the process of fitting in.

These virtues of primarily cognitive approaches to measuring cultural fit are counterbalanced by some key limitations. First, people may have varying interpretations of survey or interview questions, which may lead to mismeasurement of cultural features and of how people fit in. Although both implicit and indirect self-reports are less susceptible to social desirability bias than explicit self-reports (Wittenbrink and Schwarz 2007), none of these approaches is entirely immune to the problem. For example, respondents may claim to value collaboration but nevertheless be inclined not to pursue it in practice (Srivastava and Banaji 2011). Second, it is typically not feasible to administer self-reports on a frequent basis. Thus, self-reports provide mostly static pictures of how people assimilate into social groups. Third, the flipside of a core benefit of self-reports—their ability to highlight different facets of cultural content—is that the categories of cultural content are typically defined by researchers or a handful of informants who may not comprehend the categories that matter to group members. Finally, not everyone chooses to respond to surveys or participate in interviews. Moreover, response rates to surveys are in a period of steady decline (Baker et al. 2010). Although various techniques exist to try to account for nonresponse bias (e.g., Wooldridge 2002), self-reports typically yield not only static but also incomplete portraits of social integration into groups.

17.2.2 Primarily Behavioral Approaches

Behavioral data are often considered the gold standard in social science research. Scholars of education, immigration, and organizations have each emphasized a distinct set of behaviors that serve as markers of individuals fitting in.

Education research has examined cultural fit as enacted behaviors that align with an institution's dominant, "mainstream," or "common" cultural ideal type (Darder 1991; Carter 2005). This work has drawn heavily on Bourdieu's (1984) theory of cultural capital to examine the resources that enable or constrain people in conforming to these expectations (Bourdieu 1984; Carter 2005; Lareau and Weininger 2008; Armstrong and Hamilton 2013). For example, prior work has considered the tensions that black students can face between conforming to the ideal type of intelligent student while not coming across as "acting white" (Fordham and Ogbu 1986; Carter 2005). Similarly, marginal class backgrounds shape the behavioral strategies students draw on in daily life, such as asking for help from teachers, leaning on a community (versus relying on themselves), or building relationships with peers (Calarco 2011; Stephens et al. 2012; Jack 2014; Rivera 2016).

In immigration research, cultural fit has often been examined with respect to the concrete choices that immigrants and their children make relative to those made by native populations—for example, where people choose to live, what language and dialect they adopt, and whom they decide to marry (Waters and Jimenez 2005). Similarly, Alba and Nee's (2003:11) definition of assimilation considers not only the declining salience of an ethnic distinction but also "its corollary cultural and social differences." The latter can be detected in concrete behaviors such as family rituals that are practiced on important occasions even when ethnic distinctions have otherwise receded to background.

In organizational research, cultural fit is typically conceptualized as the individuals' acting in ways that conform to normative expectations defined by the shared beliefs, assumptions, and values of organizational members (Kanter 1977/1993; Schein 1985; Kunda 2009). Although this work has often conceptualized cultural fit in concrete behavioral terms—for example, the correspondence between an individual's propensity to engage in team-oriented, rather than individually focused, work and the organization's normative focus on teamwork—it has typically measured the cognitive aspects of fitting in and implicitly assumed a high degree of correspondence between cognition and behavior.

Across these literatures, the three most commonly used methods for assessing behavioral cultural fit are: (1) reported behaviors (including but not limited to self-reports) and outcomes; (2) analyses of language use and other behavioral artifacts; and (3) participant observation. Examples of the first can be found in education research, which studies behaviors that can easily be aggregated across schools—for example, whether students graduate, how they perform on standardized tests, and the grades they earn in school. Such outcomes are often archived in databases such as Common Core Data, The National Longitudinal Study of Adolescent to Adult Health ("Add Health"), High School and Beyond, or other databases collected and managed by the National Center for Educational Statistics (Coleman et al. 1966; Lucas 1999; Card and Rothstein 2007). Economists studying assimilation use reports of occupational choices and earnings to examine the degree of convergence between immigrants and native groups. These studies have employed cross-sectional or longitudinal survey data on reported behaviors—for example, from the Census or Social Security records (Chiswick 1978; Borjas 1985; Lubotsky 2007; Abramitzky et al. 2016).

Immigration researchers have also considered the names people choose to give to their children as a marker of assimilation. Names facilitate the study of immigrant assimilation because the choice of a name represents the trade-off that immigrant parents face between preserving their native naming traditions or naming their children in ways that promote assimilated identities, which can increase their chance of success in a new country. Goldstein and Stecklov (2016), for example, distinguish given from last names as a means to differentiate between origin- and ethnicity-based mechanisms of labor market discrimination. They find that American-sounding first names help second-generation immigrants achieve occupational success.

In addition to direct and indirect reports on behaviors or outcomes, a growing body of work relies on people's use of language to assess cultural fit. Recent scholarship has measured cultural fit in terms of the topics, such as sports talk, that enable some people to fit in and that keep others from doing so (Turco 2010; McFarland et al. 2013), as well as the linguistic style they use when communicating with group members. For example, Srivastava and colleagues (2018) derive a measure of cultural fit using a corpus of e-mail messages exchanged among employees in a midsized firm and demonstrate that this measure produces distinct "enculturation trajectories" for employees who quit, who leave involuntarily, and who stay in the organization. Goldberg et al. (2016) further demonstrate that the consequences of cultural fit for individual attainment depend on a person's position in the network structure: those in positions of brokerage that connect them to otherwise disconnected groups fare substantially better when they have high levels of fit, while individuals ensconced in dense networks derive advantage by exhibiting cultural nonconformity in their language style.

The proliferation of digital trace data (Salganik in press) have provided researchers with access to other kinds of behavioral artifacts that can be associated with enculturation. For example, education technology platforms can indicate how students are integrating into classes by tracking online behaviors such as the number of online discussions a student has with their peers and the time spent on these peer discussions (Coetzee et al. 2015). Similarly, mobile phone data such as students' phone calls, text messaging, face-to-face interactions, and mobility patterns, have also been used to measure dimensions of behavioral cultural fit, such as who students choose to communicate with, how often they choose to communicate, and the spatial distribution of their contacts (Yang et al. 2016).

Even with the advent of these new forms of data, perhaps the richest forms of behavioral data still come from ethnography and participant observation. Notable examples include Kunda's (2009) account of the culture of a high-tech engineering firm, Lareau's (2002) work on how parents transmit to their children the cultural resources needed to fit into schools, and Hondagneu-Sotelo's (2003) study of the role of gender in immigrant assimilation.

Behavioral approaches to assessing cultural fit have some obvious advantages over more cognitive approaches. First, they provide arguably more objective indicators of fit, given that how people report thinking about their fit with a social group may not correspond to how they act in response to the group. Indeed, observing how people vary in their conformity to the norms of different social groups can help uncover their implicit hierarchy of group affiliations. Second, behavioral approaches are generally better suited to understanding interactional dynamics that give rise to cultural fit because they can easily be observed by other group members. Finally, certain behavioral approaches employed over a period of time—for example, analyses of archived electronic communications—can help uncover the dynamics of enculturation at a level of granularity that is typically infeasible with more cognitive approaches.

Yet researchers who use behavioral measures of cultural fit can only draw indirect inferences about the thoughts, beliefs, and motivations that give rise to normatively compliant or nonconforming behavior. The subjective experience of fitting in is itself important to study yet has thus far remained largely outside the reach of researchers who only employ behavioral measures. In addition, with only behavioral indicators of cultural fit, researchers cannot examine how thoughts and actions about the individual in relation to a social group can be mutually constitutive. Finally, some approaches to assessing behavioral cultural fit—for example, ethnography and participant observation—are difficult to scale to large social groups, require significant investments of time, and rely heavily on the subjective interpretations of individual observers, which may or may not correspond to the interpretations that other observers would have of the same setting.

17.3 THEORETICAL PATHWAYS BETWEEN COGNITIVE AND BEHAVIORAL FIT

Across the diverse contexts of education, immigration, and organizations, research on cultural fit has tended to take either a primarily cognitive or a primarily behavioral approach. Given that both approaches have strengths and limitations, we see great potential in work that investigates the interplay between the two. Two interrelated over-arching questions are particularly pertinent. First, to what extent is congruence—or lack thereof—between one's levels of behavioral and cognitive cultural fit related to individual and group outcomes? For example, how do backstage and frontstage insiders fare compared to insiders and outsiders and how does their membership in these categories affect the group? Second, how do cognitive and behavioral cultural fit shape one another? How do others' perceptions and behaviors toward a person, for example, affect cognitive cultural fit and in turn produce behaviors that influence others' subjective experiences?

To make initial progress on this agenda, we propose four conceptual pathways that represent promising theoretical linkages between the cognitive and behavioral aspects of cultural fit. The first, which draws inspiration from Goffman's (1959) insights about impression management, is *strategic decoupling*, which references purposive choices people make to act toward social group members in ways that do not correspond to how they think about the group. The second pathway, which we term *unintentional decoupling*, refers to instances when cognition and behavior can become decoupled but not because the person actively chooses or wants to sever the link. For example, people may know how one should behave in a social group but may simply lack the capacity or skills to enact that behavior. Or they may face structural constraints—for example, the inability to coordinate actions with others—that keep them from acting in ways they know they should act.

Although they are not able to distinguish between its strategic and unintentional forms, Doyle et al. (2017) develop an approach that highlights a linguistic manifestation of decoupling. Using a directed measure of linguistic alignment applied to a corporate e-mail corpus, they distinguish between the internalization of linguistic norms related to pronoun use (e.g., "I" versus "we"), as measured by base rates of word usage over the first six months of new employees' adjustment to a new organization, and self-regulation, as indicated by how their use of these pronouns changes in response to colleagues' use of these terms in an e-mail thread. They propose that the former is more likely to reflect taken-for-granted dispositions rather than mere perfunctory normative compliance. For example, base rates of "we" usage tend to increase on entry and to decline before exit. By contrast, self-regulation represents departures from a person's baseline tendency in response to others, and these deviations may represent acts of strategic decoupling.

Examining how cognitive and behavioral fit can be decoupled leads naturally to questions about their *interaction effects*—that is, the conditions under which the two forms of fit act as complements or substitutes in producing consequential outcomes. For example, are there contexts in which the alignment of thoughts and actions can accelerate assimilation and more quickly realize the benefits of group membership or conversely hasten a person's exclusion and eventual exit from the group? Are there settings in which increases in one kind of fit decrease the efficacy of having the other kind of fit? And are there contexts in which cognitive and behavioral have no interaction effect and instead operate independently on outcomes of interest? If all three types of social contexts exist, what are the distinguishing features of these contexts?

Multiple group memberships are a fourth, and perhaps the most challenging yet promising, avenue for connecting cognitive and behavioral cultural fit to each other and to social outcomes of interest. It has long been recognized that people identify with, are characterized by, and maintain memberships to multiple groups simultaneously, with different self-conceptions being situationally activated (Markus and Nurius 1986; Markus and Wurf 1987; Banaji and Prentice 1994; Lahire 2011). Multiple group membership is a chronic challenge of cultural alignment when individuals intersect groups that impose different normative expectations and institutionalized belief and value systems (Friedland and Alford 1991; Bourdieu 2000; Stark 2011; DiMaggio and Goldberg 2017).

The concept of cultural fit conventionally implies movement from one group to the other, but in many cases, people may seek to fit in to multiple social groups simultaneously: children in the schoolyard often seek entry into distinct, sometimes rivalrous play groups; in a new locale, immigrants often wish to socialize with native groups but also stay tethered to other recent immigrants from their country of origin; and employees are frequently trying to integrate into their own department but also forge alliances and coalitions with colleagues in other departments who share common interests. Similarly, when people experience social mobility they necessarily intersect cultural domains, potentially importing norms and beliefs from one domain to the other, for example, when working class boys complete their education and obtain jobs in finance or when upwardly mobile black Caribbeans gain entry into the white-dominated middle class (Rollock et al. 2011; Friedman 2016).

In cases of either stable or fluid intersectionality, the interplay between cognitive and behavioral fit is likely to be particularly complex. For example, when people seek to affiliate with multiple groups, do they find it easier or harder to decouple the two forms of fit? What are the consequences of cognitive and behavioral fit with multiple groups on one's thoughts, feelings, and social identity? For example, how do people navigate the experience of being frontstage insiders with respect to one group and backstage insiders with respect to others? Are people more likely to engage in unintentional or strategic decoupling in such situations? How does the hierarchy of group affiliations manifest in cognition versus behavior? Similarly, can cognitive and behavioral fit be substitutes for each other with respect to one social group and be complements to each other in the context of another social group? Does fitting into one group necessarily crowd out one's ability to fit into another?

17.4 METHODOLOGICAL IMPLICATIONS

To fully map and construct these pathways between cognitive and behavioral fit, researchers will increasingly need to bring together the tools and methods that have, until now, been used to study each form of fit independently. This is not just a call for more mixed methods research. Rather, we anticipate that significant insights will be uncovered through approaches, including but not limited to computational and field experimental methods, that can uncover systematic relationships between the two (cf. Salganik in press) and that can identify how they are causally linked.

Lu et al. (2019) provide an illustration of the former. They collect data from an OCP, an indirect self-report, and e-mail data from an organization. The OCP provides a snapshot of how accurately individuals perceive the organization's culture (based on how close or far their perception of the current culture is from the "typical" perception of their peers) and how they perceive their own fit (based on how close or far their preferred culture is from their perception of the current culture). Lu and colleagues (2017) then use machine learning techniques to train an algorithm to identify the "linguistic signature" of these two types of fit. They use the linguistic signatures to impute perceptual accuracy and perceived fit scores and propagate the imputed scores back in time based on historical e-mail data. Using this technique, they transform the OCP completed at one point in time into a longitudinal assessment, enabling them to examine the dynamic interplay between perceptions of culture and of fitting in and behavior that is or is not normatively compliant with group expectations.

Examples of the latter—field experiments that identify the causal relationships between cognition and behavior—can be found in educational psychology research. For example, field experiments have produced tangible behavioral changes that signal greater fit—as indicated by grade point averages, grades, and test scores—through cognitive manipulations—how students think about themselves in relation to their academic environment (Yeager and Walton 2011; Stephens et al. 2014; Walton and Cohen 2007).

Other work in this vein manipulates students' beliefs about prevailing norms to change behavior in ways that foster the inclusion of all students (Tankard and Paluck 2016; Paluck and Shafir 2016). For example, Paluck and Shepherd (2012) influenced students' perceptions of norms about harassment in schools by identifying well-connected students, whom they label "social referents," and training them on new behavioral expectations that emphasize tolerance instead of harassment. Subtly changing these beliefs resulted in fewer reported cases of harassment, more public support for antiharassment campaigns, and fewer cases of disciplinary action against students engaged in harassment.

17.5 Conclusion

Whether in the context of education, immigration, or organizations, where there are social groups, there will be group cultures and individuals who, to varying degrees, seek to fit into those cultures. Whereas prior work has thought about fitting in as a continuum of group membership ranging from outsider to insider status, we instead propose that that there are two analytically and theoretically distinct components of cultural fit: cognitive and behavioral. These dimensions help us to more sharply define what it means to be an outsider or an insider and also identify two other types of cultural fit: the frontstage insider and the backstage insider.

The many different strands of research on fitting in share a common feature: they focus on either the cognitive or the behavioral manifestations of cultural fit but pay insufficient attention to how they relate to one another whether contemporaneously or over time. The methods commonly used to study fitting in are similarly bifurcated into those that primarily uncover cognitive cultural fit and those that primarily reveal behavioral manifestations of cultural fit, often implicitly assuming that both relate to a singular underlying construct: cultural fit. To help remedy the imbalance, we propose four conceptual pathways that link the cognitive and behavioral aspects of cultural fit and identify how research methods will need to be better integrated for researchers to be able to traverse these pathways. Completing these and other yet-to-be-defined circuits from cognition to behavior—and back—promises to yield fresh insights about the cultural fit between individuals and the social groups to which they belong.

Acknowledgments

We thank Wayne Brekhus, Jenny Chatman, Gabe Ignatow, Tony Jack, Tomás Jiménez, and Van Tran for valuable feedback on prior drafts. The usual disclaimer applies.

Notes

1. For simplicity, we begin by conceptualizing cognitive and behavioral fit with respect to one particular social group. Yet, as we discuss in greater detail below, people often seek to fit into multiple social groups and can achieve varying levels of cognitive and behavioral fit across these reference groups. Although immigration and education research sometimes focuses on a social group's "distance" from a dominant or mainstream culture, we focus instead on how individuals think of themselves and act in accordance with the norms of any given social group, without making normative assumptions about whether people "ought to" fit into that group.

2. We focus our review on research that examines the determinants and consequences of individual-level assimilation, although we recognize that immigration research has also considered how individual mobility over time and across generations can lead to the integration of entire social groups into society.

REFERENCES

Abramitzky, Ran, Leah Platt Boustan, and Katherine Eriksson. 2016. "Cultural Assimilation During the Age of Mass Migration." Working Paper. Cambridge, MA: National Bureau of Economic Research.

Alba, Richard, and Victor Nee. 2003. *Remaking the American Mainstream: Assimilation and Contemporary Immigration.* Cambridge, MA: Harvard University Press.

Armstrong, Elizabeth A., and Laura T. Hamilton. 2013. *Paying for the Party.* Cambridge, MA: Harvard University Press.

Arum, Richard. 2000. "Schools and Communities: Ecological and Institutional Dimensions." *Annual Review of Sociology* 26:395–418.

Baker, Reg, Stephen J. Blumberg, J. Michael Brick, Mick P. Couper, Melanie Courtright, J. Michael Dennis, et al. 2010. "Research Synthesis AAPOR Report on Online Panels." *Public Opinion Quarterly* 74(4):711–81.

Banaji, Mahzarin R., and Anthony G. Greenwald. 1994. "Implicit Stereotyping and Prejudice." *The Psychology of Prejudice: The Ontario Symposium* 7:55–76. Hillsdale, NJ: Erlbaum.

Banaji, Mahzarin R., and Deborah A. Prentice. 1994. "The Self in Social Contexts." *Annual Review of Psychology* 45(1):297–332.

Baumeister, Roy F., and Mark R. Leary. 1995. "The Need to Belong: Desire for Interpersonal Attachments as a Fundamental Human Motivation." *Psychological Bulletin* 117(3):497–529.

Borjas, George J. 1985. "Assimilation, Changes in Cohort Quality, and the Earnings of Immigrants." *Journal of Labor Economics* 3(4):463–89.

Bourdieu, Pierre. 1977. *Outline of a Theory of Practice.* Cambridge, UK: Cambridge University Press.

Bourdieu, Pierre. 1984. *Distinction: A Social Critique of the Judgement of Taste.* London: Routledge.

Bourdieu, Pierre. 2000. *Pascalian Meditations.* Stanford, CA: Stanford University Press.

Bourdieu, Pierre, and Jean-Claude Passeron. 1970. *Reproduction in Education, Culture, and Society.* London: Sage.

Bowles, Samuel, Herbert Gintis, and Melissa Osborne Groves, eds. 2009. *Unequal Chances: Family Background and Economic Success.* Princeton, NJ: Princeton University Press.

Calarco, Jessica McCrory. 2011. "'I Need Help!': Social Class and Children's Help-Seeking in Elementary School." *American Sociological Review* 76(6):862–82.

Card, David, and Jesse Rothstein. 2007. "Racial Segregation and the Black-White Test Score Gap." *Journal of Public Economics* 91(11):2158–84.

Carter, Prudence L. 2005. *Keepin' It Real: School Success beyond Black and White.* New York: Oxford University Press.

Carter, Prudence L., and Kevin G. Welner. 2013. *Closing the Opportunity Gap: What America Must Do to Give Every Child an Even Chance.* New York: Oxford University Press.

Centola, Damon, Robb Willer, and Michael Macy. 2005. "The Emperor's Dilemma: A Computational Model of Self-Enforcing Norms." *American Journal of Sociology* 110(4):1009–40.

Chatman, Jennifer A. 1991. "Matching People and Organizations: Selection and Socialization in Public Accounting Firms." *Administrative Science Quarterly* 36(3):459–84.

Chatman, Jennifer A., and Charles A. O'Reilly. 2016. "Paradigm Lost: Reinvigorating the Study of Organizational Culture." *Research in Organizational Behavior* 36:199–224.

Chen, Mark, and John A. Bargh. 1997. "On the Automaticity of Self-Fulfilling Prophecies: The Nonconscious Effects of Stereotype Activation on Social Interaction." *Journal of Experimental Social Psychology* 33:541–60.

Chiswick, Barry R. 1978. "The Effect of Americanization on the Earnings of Foreign-Born Men." *Journal of Political Economy* 86(5):897–921.

Coetzee, Derrick, Seongtaek Lim, Armando Fox, Bjorn Hartmann, and Marti A. Hearst. 2015. "Structuring Interactions for Large-Scale Synchronous Peer Learning." *Proceedings of the 18th ACM Conference on Computer Supported Cooperative Work & Social Computing* 1139–52. Vancouver, BC, Canada: Association for Computer Machinery.

Coleman, James Samuel, and Department of Health USA. 1966. *Equality of Educational Opportunity*. Vol. 2. Washington, DC:US Department of Health, Education, and Welfare, Office of Education.

Darder, Antonia. 1991. *Culture and Power in the Classroom: A Critical Foundation for Bicultural Education*. Westport, CT: Bergin and Garvey.

DiMaggio, Paul. 1997. "Cultural and Cognition." *Annual Review of Sociology* 23:263–88.

DiMaggio, Paul, and Amir Goldberg. 2017. "Searching for Homo Economicus: Institutional Boundaries and Americans' Construals of Attitudes Toward Markets." Stanford University Working Paper.

Doyle, Gabriel, Amir Goldberg, Sameer B. Srivastava, and Michael C. Frank. 2017. "Alignment at Work: Using Language to Distinguish the Internalization and Self-Regulation Components of Cultural Fit in Organizations." In Proceedings of the 55th Annual Meeting of the Association for Computational Linguistics (ACL).

Fiske, Susan T., and Shelley Taylor. 2007. *Social Cognition: From Brains to Culture*. New York: McGraw-Hill.

Fordham, Signithia, and John U. Ogbu. 1986. "Black Students' School Success: Coping with the "Burden of 'Acting White.'" " *Urban Review* 18(3):176–206.

Friedland, Roger, and Robert Alford. 1991. "Bringing Society Back In: Symbols, Practices, and Institutional Contradictions." pp. 232–67 in *The New Institutionalism in Organizational Analysis*, edited by Woody W. Powell and Paul J. DiMaggio. Chicago: University of Chicago Press.

Friedman, Sam. 2016. "Habitus Clivé and the Emotional Imprint of Social Mobility." *Sociological Review* 64(1):129–47.

Goffman, Erving. 1959. *The Presentation of Self in Everyday Life*. Garden City, NY: Doubleday.

Goldberg, Amir, Sameer B. Srivastava, V. Govind Manian, William Monroe, and Christopher Potts. 2016. "Fitting In or Standing Out? The Tradeoffs of Structural and Cultural Embeddedness." *American Sociological Review* 81(6):1190–222.

Goldstein, Joshua R., and Guy Stecklov. 2016. "From Patrick to John F.: Ethnic Names and Occupational Success in the Last Era of Mass Migration." *American Sociological Review* 81(1):85–106.

Gordon, Milton M. 1964. *Assimilation in American Life: The Role of Race, Religion, and National Origins*. New York: Oxford University Press.

Hondagneu-Sotelo, Pierrette. 2003. *Gender and US Immigration: Contemporary Trends*. Berkeley: University of California Press.

Jack, Anthony Abraham. 2014. "Culture Shock Revisited: The Social and Cultural Contingencies to Class Marginality." *Sociological Forum* 29(2):453–75.

Jack, Anthony Abraham. 2016. "(No) Harm in Asking: Class, Acquired Cultural Capital, and Academic Engagement at an Elite University." *Sociology of Education* 89(1):1–19.

Judge, Timothy A., and Daniel M. Cable. 1997. "Applicant Personality, Organizational Culture, and Organization Attraction." *Personnel Psychology* 50(2):359–94.

Kahneman, Daniel. 2011. *Thinking, Fast and Slow.* New York: Macmillan.

Kanter, Rosabeth Moss. 1977/1993. *Men and Women of the Corporation.* New York: Basic Books.

Kunda, Gideon. 2009. *Engineering Culture: Control and Commitment in a High-Tech Corporation.* Philadelphia, PA: Temple University Press.

Lahire, Bernard. 2011. *The Plural Actor.* Cambridge: Polity Press.

Lareau, Annette. 2002. "Invisible Inequality: Social Class and Childrearing in Black Families and White Families." *American Sociological Review* 67:747–76.

Lareau, Annette, and Elliot B. Weininger. 2008. "Class and the Transition to Adulthood." pp. 118–51 in *Social Class: How Does It Work?* Stanford, CA: Stanford University Press.

Lizardo, Omar. 2016. "Why 'Cultural Matters' Matter: Culture Talk as the Mobilization of Cultural Capital in Interaction." *Poetics: Journal of Empirical Research on Culture, the Media, and the Arts* 58:1–17.

Lu, Richard, Jennifer A. Chatman, Amir Goldberg, and Sameer B. Srivastava. 2019. "Situated Cultural Fit: Value Congruence, Perceptual Accuracy, and the Interpersonal Transmission of Culture." University of California, Berkeley, Working Paper.

Lubotsky, Darren. 2007. "Chutes or Ladders? A Longitudinal Analysis of Immigrant Earnings." *Journal of Political Economy* 115(5):820–67.

Lucas, Samuel R. 1999. *Tracking Inequality: Stratification and Mobility in American High Schools.* New York: Teachers College Press.

Markus, Hazel R., and Shinobu Kitayama. 1991. "Culture and the Self: Implications for Cognition, Emotion, and Motivation." *Psychological Review* 98(2):224–53.

Markus, Hazel R., and Paula Nurius. 1986. "Possible Selves." *American Psychologist* 41(9):954.

Markus, Hazel R., and Elissa Wurf. 1987. "The Dynamic Self-Concept: A Social Psychological Perspective." *Annual Review of Psychology* 38(1):299–337.

Martin, Joanne, and Caren Siehl. 1983. "Organizational Culture and Counterculture: An Uneasy Symbiosis." *Organizational Dynamics* 12(2):52–64.

McFarland, Daniel A., Daniel Ramage, Jason Chuang, Jeffrey Heer, Christopher D. Manning, and Daniel Jurafsky. 2013. "Differentiating Language Usage through Topic Models." *Poetics* 41(6):607–25.

Nisbett, Richard E., and Timothy D. Wilson. 1977. "Telling More Than We Can Know: Verbal Reports on Mental Processes." *Psychological Review* 84(3):231.

O'Reilly, Charles A., Jennifer Chatman, and David F. Caldwell. 1991. "People and Organizational Culture: A Profile Comparison Approach to Assessing Person-Organization Fit." *Academy of Management Journal* 34(3):487–516.

Ouchi, William G. 1981. *Theory Z: How American Business Can Meet the Japanese Challenge.* New York, NY: Avon Books.

Paluck, Elizabeth Levy, and Eldar Shafir. 2016. "The Psychology of Construal in the Design of Field Experiments." Working Paper.

Paluck, Elizabeth Levy, and Hana Shepherd. 2012. "The Salience of Social Referents: A Field Experiment on Collective Norms and Harassment Behavior in a School Social Network." *Journal of Personality and Social Psychology* 103(3):89915.

Park, Robert Ezra, and Ernest Watson Burgess. 1921. *Introduction to the Science of Sociology*. Chicago: University of Chicago Press.

Patterson, Orlando. 2014. "Making Sense of Culture." *Annual Review of Sociology* 40:1–30.

Reardon, Sean F., and Ann Owens. 2014. "60 Years after *Brown*: Trends and Consequences of School Segregation." *Annual Review of Sociology* 40:199–218.

Rivera, Lauren A. 2016. *Pedigree: How Elite Students Get Elite Jobs*. Princeton, NJ: Princeton University Press.

Rollock, Nicola, David Gillborn, Carol Bincent, and Stephen Ball. 2011. "The Public Identities of the Black Middle Classes: Managing Race in Public Space." *Sociology* 45(6):1078–93.

Salganik, Matthew J. 2017. *Bit by Bit: Social Research in the Digital Age*. Princeton, NJ: Princeton University Press.

Schacter, Ariela. 2016. "From 'Different' to 'Similar': An Experimental Approach to Understanding Assimilation." *American Sociological Review* 81(5):981–1013.

Schein, Edgar H. 1985. *Organizational Culture and Leadership: A Dynamic View*. San Francisco: Jossey-Bass.

Shepherd, Hana. 2011. "The Cultural Context of Cognition: What the Implicit Association Test Tells Us about How Culture Works." *Sociological Forum* 26(1):121–43.

Small, Mario Luis, David J. Harding, and Michele Lamont. 2010. "Reconsidering Culture and Poverty." *Annals of the American Academy of Political and Social Science* 629:6–27.

Srivastava, Sameer B., and Mahzarin R. Banaji. 2011. "Culture, Cognition, and Collaborative Networks in Organizations." *American Sociological Review* 76(2):207–33.

Srivastava, Sameer B., Amir Goldberg, V. Govind Manian, and Christopher Potts. 2018. "Enculturation Trajectories and Individual Attainment: An Interactional Language Use Model of Cultural Dynamics in Organizations." *Management Science* 64(3):1348–64.

Stark, David. 2011. *The Sense of Dissonance: Accounts of Worth in Economic Life*. Princeton, NJ: Princeton University Press.

Stephens, Nicole M., Stephanie A. Fryberg, Hazel Rose Markus, Camille Johnson, and Rebecca Covarrubias. 2012. "Unseen Disadvantage: How American Universities' Focus on Independence Undermines the Academic Performance of First-Generation College Students." *Journal of Personality and Social Psychology* 102(6):1178–97.

Stephens, Nicole M., MarYam G. Hamedani, and Mesmin Destin. 2014. "Closing the Social-Class Achievement Gap: A Difference-Education Intervention Improves First-Generation Students' Academic Performance and All Students' College Transition." *Psychological Science* 25(4):1–11.

Tankard, Margaret E., and Elizabeth Levy Paluck. 2016. "Norm Perception as a Vehicle for Social Change." *Social Issues and Policy Review* 10(1):181–211.

Tellis, Gerard J., Jaideep C. Prabhu, and Rajesh K. Chandy. 2009. "Radical Innovation across Nations: The Preeminence of Corporate Culture." *Journal of Marketing* 73(1):3–23.

Turco, Catherine J. 2010. "Cultural Foundations of Tokenism: Evidence from the Leveraged Buyout Industry." *American Sociological Review* 75(6):894–913.

Vaisey, Stephen. 2009. "Motivation and Justification: A Dual-Process Model of Culture in Action." *American Journal of Sociology* 114(6):1675–715.

Van Maanen, John. 1975. "Breaking In: Socialization to Work." pp. 67–130 in *Handbook of Work, Organization, and Society*, edited by Robert Dubin. Chicago: Rand-McNally.

Walton, Gregory M., and Geoffrey L. Cohen. 2007. "A Question of Belonging: Race, Social Fit, and Achievement." *Journal of Personality and Social Psychology* 92(1):82–96.

Walton, Gregory M., and Geoffrey L. Cohen. 2011. "A Brief Social-Belonging Intervention Improves Academic and Health Outcomes of Minority Students." *Science* 331(6023):1447–51.

Waters, Mary C., and Tomás R. Jiménez. 2005. "Assessing Immigrant Assimilation: New Empirical and Theoretical Challenges." *Annual Review of Sociology* 31:105–25.

Willis, Paul E. 1977. *Learning to Labor: How Working Class Kids Get Working Class Jobs*. New York: Columbia University Press.

Wittenbrink, Bernd, and Norbert Schwarz. 2007. "Introduction." pp. 1–16 in *Implicit Measures of Attitude*, edited by Bernd Wittenbrink and Norbert Schwarz. New York: Guilford Press.

Wooldridge, Jeffrey M. 2002. "Inverse Probability Weighted M-Estimators for Sample Selection, Attrition, and Stratification." *Portugese Economic Journal* 1:117–39.

Yang, Yang, Omar Lizardo, Dong Wang, Yuxiao Dong, Aaron D. Striegel, David Hachen, et al. 2016. "Gender Differences in Communication Behaviors, Spatial Proximity Patterns, and Mobility Habits." *arXiv preprint arXiv:1607.06740*.

Yeager, David S., and Gregory M. Walton. 2011. "Social-Psychological Interventions in Education: They're Not Magic." *Review of Educational Research* 81(2):267–301.

PART III

METHODS OF COGNITIVE SOCIOLOGY

CHAPTER 18

PRODUCTIVE METHODS IN THE STUDY OF CULTURE AND COGNITION

TERENCE E. MCDONNELL
AND KELCIE L. VERCEL

IN this chapter, we present one methodological strategy for drawing out and measuring cognitive processes in social research—productive methods (McDonnell 2014). Productive methods build on methodological advances in the areas of participatory research, arts-based research, creativity research, visual methods, and focus group research, and capitalize on the advantages of attending to embodiment, emotion, and interaction. Productive methods require research participants to work together to create a cultural object, some *thing* that did not exist prior to the research. By "cultural object" we take Griswold's broad definition of "shared significance embodied in form" (1986:5). Observing this collaboration and production process, and comparing the process with the product, gives the researcher access to difficult-to-obtain data, including implicit and nondiscursive cognition and cultural schemas. We believe productive methods offer one solution to the widely acknowledged challenge of studying and measuring cognition.

The perennial methodological challenge of studying cognition is the problem of externalization. Before we can understand how shared cognitive processes shape behavior, we first need to make people's cognitive processes visible. We have to draw out those "implicit" "internal" cognitive processes, making them "explicit," in order to observe and measure them. The problem this poses is that the externalized expressions or outputs of internal phenomena are necessarily different from the processes that produce them. In this sense, we do not measure cognition, only the traces produced by cognitive processes.

Why is this important? If we cannot directly measure cognitive processes, we need to think carefully about what our methods can tell us about cognition. Many of our methods focus on outcomes of cognitive processes and then use those outcomes to impute the processes. The problem with relying only on outcomes is that different internal cognitive processes might yield the same outcome. If we can only observe and measure the externalized outcome, it is often difficult to know whether people arrive at the outcome by the same or different internal cognitive processes. What matters methodologically, then, is how we make visible and measure the cognitive process that led to the outcome, rather than only observing the outcome.

Recent methodological debates in sociological circles raise critical questions about what data we collect and what it can tell us about culture and cognition. Vaisey (2009) suggests interviews primarily capture discursive consciousness and ex post facto justifications of action but cannot access unconscious cognitive processes (which more accurately predict action, according to Vaisey). Instead, Vaisey argues that forced-choice surveys effectively reveal patterns in people's practical moral consciousness by forcing respondents to quickly make a choice. Critics suggesting that "talk is cheap" argue that verbal methods like interviews fail to capture cognitive frames that influence action, but also that the surveys Vaisey advocates fall victim to an "attitudinal fallacy" (Jerolmack and Khan 2014).[1] Jerolmack and Khan instead call for ethnographic observation to reveal cognitive frameworks in action. While ethnographic work may give more access to process than forced-choice surveys or interviews, elaborating on such processes often requires some mind-reading of intentions. To make sense of actions, the observer must perform interpretive work to read schemas and cognitive processes into those actions. Witnessing repeated actions in similar situations may give an ethnographer confidence in their interpretations, but they still need to infer the motives and cognitive processes driving these actions. The difficulty is that cognitive processes need to be imputed from actions (i.e., observed behavior or survey choices) and then *transformed* into schemas (Latour and Woolgar 1986; Becker 2007). By relying on interpretive work to make sense of observed outcomes, both fixed-choice surveys and ethnographic methods struggle to differentiate between the multiple cognitive paths that may lead to the same observable outcome.

Objects offer another site of analysis that can fall prey to using outcomes as proxies for process. If cognition is really an "extended mind" (Clark and Chalmers 1998), that mind is instantiated in a world of objects. Objects, though, are imperfect instantiations. They are "unruly" (Dominguez Rubio 2014), "act back" (Pickering 1995), and "afford" different meanings and uses (Gibson 1979; DeNora 2000). Because objects are much less stable than we typically acknowledge, it is difficult to confidently impute the cognitive process that led to the object. In this way, analyzing the content of objects for their cognitive and cultural remains similarly biases our understanding of cognitive processes, falling prey to the same problems as ethnographic approaches. However, if we could capture how cognitive schema are extended and externalized into objects, we could have more confidence in our understanding of the cognitive processes that lead to the resulting objects. By observing the production process, then, we could confidently identify the cognitive-cultural scaffolding that made the object ultimately produced possible.

Drawing out cognitive *processes* is a more difficult task, one that requires methodological creativity and triangulation. More than just observing outcomes, we need to make measurable more levels of data, over time, by forcing the cognitive processes out into the open through *externalization*. Pugh (2013) points an important way forward through her use of interview data in examining emotions, rather than only discourse. By collecting four kinds of data during interviews—what she calls "the honorable, the schematic, the visceral, and meta-feelings"—she argues that interviews can reveal how cognition, culture, emotion, and action are linked. Tracing the interplay between what people say and how they appear to feel as they say it can give us important insight into the cognitive process. Pugh goes further to suggest how interviewer methods reveal and embrace contradictions of cognitive processes and dig deeper than the ideal "presentations of self" people display (Goffman 1959).

Productive methods (McDonnell 2014) pursue a parallel course. By capturing both the process and the product of cognitive work, productive methods draw from the best of these methodological insights. Productive methods (1) ask people to make an object, (2) require participants to work collectively in a group to solve a problem, (3) permit observation of multiple kinds of information (e.g., discourse, emotional highs and lows, etc.), and (4) compare the process of production with the actual product. Productive methods systematically draw our cognitive processes out into the open through their collective approach and their emphasis on externalizing cognition into cultural objects. They do this by forcing participants to make choices, observing the discursive, emotional, and behavioral dimensions of this decision-making process, and producing objects that encapsulate the product of that cognitive work. In what follows, we develop the idea of productive methods, demonstrate how productive methods can overcome some of the problems introduced thus far, and describe productive methods' potential for measuring culture and cognition.

18.1 Productive Methods

The first principle of productive methods is the production of a cultural object. Observing people making something reveals the process of that making. When making an object, people make numerous cognitive decisions: "trying on" schemas, dismissing some, and choosing others. Some choices come easily, and others require more work. Watching this process improves on some of the methodological challenges confronting other cognitive methods, in that it can reveal a great deal more about how culture is activated than imputing cognitive processes through the ultimate choice, action, or product.

Second, productive methods require that participants *work collectively* to solve a problem. Working collectively helps to draw out internal cognitive processes in ways individual interviews cannot. Tasked with working together to solve a problem through the making of an object, participants must *articulate* what they are thinking so as to coordinate. If an individual performed the same task alone, the work could be done entirely internally, and therefore hidden from researchers' view. Collaborative tasks also make visible when participants *shared* (or did not share) cognitive schemas, allowing researchers to discern which schemas are widely shared and taken for granted.

Such work is important. Recognizing when schemas are personalistic versus shared can reveal a great deal about when and how culture matters. Which schemas are well-worn, widely shared, and taken for granted? Which schemas are less stable, requiring effort to transpose to new problems? Pragmatist theory views people as "problem solvers" with cognition and emotion serving as guides to solutions (Gross 2009). Cognition is put to work when people face problem situations. In order to witness people undergoing cognitive processes, engaging habit and deliberation, we need to observe people in problem situations. Doing so allows observations of the relations *between* habit and deliberation, and conscious and unconscious cognitive processes. The kinds of problem situations a group interview can create are wide ranging, and depend on the research question.

As Pugh has suggested about in-depth interviews, we need to "go beyond what people say to how they say it" (2013:54). Observing groups as they make an object that solves a problem produces multiple layers of information that can reveal cognitive processes and schemas. People talk about possible ideas and solutions, producing discourse. People also use their bodies to express acceptance, disgust, frustration, and excitement by nodding or shaking heads, raising voices, sitting forward in seats—all externalized, observable indicators of emotional states, coherence, or disagreement that do not require participants to have reflexive metacognitive self-observation. Emotional highs and lows can be incredibly revealing, suggesting when the group is motivated to act or frustrated by their inability to find a cognitive fit. Timing also matters—people may come to agreement quickly or slowly through reflection and deliberation, which can tell us much about whether Type 1 or Type 2 processes are at work (Evans 2003; Lizardo et al. 2016). They also produce the object itself, which has content and form, yielding patterns worthy of explanation. In addition to the object produced, following the process of creation also reveals schema that were considered but ultimately discarded, and grants insight into these choices. The key to productive methods is to capture as much information as possible and leverage that information to glean insights about the cognitive processes and schemas the group members relied on to come to a solution.

Once this data is collected, it is important to consider how the ultimate object was selected, translated, and arranged (Becker 2007). Which schemas did the group embody in that object? How did they represent it? How do these ideas interact? The ultimate representation of these schemas can reveal unconscious associations that are not typically verbalized. Comparing the product to the process that created it can reveal a great deal about which schemas are widely shared or taken for granted, and which are contested. Looking at how the final product is arranged can be enlightening. For instance, a drawing might reveal some symbols as larger or more centrally positioned, which might give insight into how the group understands the relation between schemas.

18.1.1 What Productive Methods Are Not

Productive methods may seem like the focus group interviews commonly used by cultural sociologists and media studies scholars (Liebes and Katz 1990; Kitzinger 1994; Shively 1992; Press and Cole 1999). While both methods use objects and group interviews, the agenda is different. Focus group interviews using objects typically show a group an object (e.g., a TV show, a Hollywood movie) and then ask participants questions about how they interpret that object. The focus here is consumption, and the act of interpreting an object. The object and the questions the researcher asks about it in part shape respondents' answers. In this way, focus group interviews elicit attitudes about the object and the themes it presents (e.g., Press and Cole's [1999] work on abortion), media effects (e.g., Kitzinger [1994] on AIDS campaigns), or the boundaries of an interpretive community (e.g., Liebes and Katz [1990] on how Americans interpret *Dallas* versus Israelis or Japanese). Alternatively, productive methods emphasize collective production of an object and problem solving. In so doing, they put cognition to work and encourage consensus, revealing how people use *shared* (rather than idiosyncratic or personalistic) schemas to solve problems.

Productive methods also share some similarities with the use of experimental vignettes in that they use objects to get at cognitive schemas and biases. Like media-based focus groups, vignettes prompt participants to consider the content of the object, thus channeling cognition along paths of interest to the researcher. Experimental vignette studies expose people to hypothetical situations through vignettes, usually one-on-one rather than in groups, and ask how they would respond to that situation. Researchers then vary the vignette content to systematically test how different but similar stories activate different cognitive schemas and interpretations. Such vignette studies often are survey studies that do not capture enough levels of information to understand the process of meaning making. For instance, Pager and Quillian (2005) use vignettes describing potential job candidates, varying race but not credentials, and then look to see whether employers would be willing to consider this hypothetical candidate for a job. In this way, we know the outcome, but not anything about the employers' thought process. Survey studies are very good at capturing patterns of cognitive biases in the aggregate, but tell us little about cognitive processes or the act of meaning making (Phelan et al. 2013; Schram et al. 2009; Horne et al. 2013; Pager and Quillian 2005). Some vignette studies use qualitative methods like interviews to capture responses (Hughes 1998), which get closer to the goals of productive methods, especially when group interviews are used. Using group discussion may draw out cognitive processes more, but vignettes overly constrain them. Researchers dramatically narrow the possible responses and cognitive processes through the construction of the vignette, priming people to think in some ways and not others. This is exactly why vignettes are systematically altered—to cue some cognitive schema and not others. Alternatively, productive methods try to get out of the way of people's cognitive processes. By giving people a problem to solve, rather than asking them to respond hypothetically, productive methods put people in a situation that may be more true to everyday life. We could imagine ways in which vignettes might be made to align with the tenets of productive methods, like having groups complete an unfinished vignette and writing a story that imagines what happens next.

The key difference between productive methods and these other "object-based" methods is their focus on consumption, rather than production. The act of collectively making something that solves a problem, rather than just responding to an object, better activates and makes visible cognitive processes that undergird meaning making.

18.1.2 Exemplars of Productive Methods

In his study of HIV/AIDS-prevention media campaigns, McDonnell (2014 and 2016) makes clear the value of using productive methods. McDonnell gave focus groups of Ghanaians paper, colored pencils, and a problem: make a poster with a message about AIDS that your community needs to hear. Once prompted with this task, the group brainstormed ideas, deliberated about what message they needed to communicate and how to represent it, and then produced the poster. McDonnell found that this method revealed moments of automatic and deliberative cognitive processing. For instance, one focus group came to quick consensus that they should draw a skeleton, suggesting that this image was ready at hand. The association of AIDS and skeletons was offered without hesitation—suggesting it resulted from automatic, practical consciousness (DiMaggio 1997; Vaisey 2009). The rest of the group accepted this without reflection or criticism, suggesting this symbolic link was taken for granted. Looking across focus groups confirms how widely shared the skeletons and skulls and crossbones were, as these were the most commonly drawn symbols. Once the skeleton was drawn, the group realized they had to come to some consensus around what the poster was "about."

After some deliberation about their community's needs and what the poster was to be about, the group decided the poster should use the skeleton for a "before and after" poster, displaying a healthy person without HIV changing into a dead, skeletal person with HIV. While this idea seemed to offer a resonant solution for incorporating the skeleton into a message, they soon realized their quick placement of the skeleton on the left side of the paper stuck them with an "after, before" structure. This suggests that before deciding a message or how they could help the community, they were so committed to skeletons that it got in the way of what they ultimately felt they should do. This offers evidence for the power of *automatic, practical cognition* and Vaisey's (2009) account of how deliberation justifies choices made out of participants' practical consciousness.

These focus groups also revealed moments when *deliberative cognition* and the experience of *resonance* motivated people toward a solution. Another group faced the problem of how to represent the effects of the disease while acknowledging its invisibility and avoiding stigma. One person in the group wanted to depict someone with AIDS symptoms so severe that people would "run from" them, using fear as a tactic to encourage people to avoid HIV. In response, another participant suggested that such a depiction might cause psychological harm to people with HIV and lead others to fear and stigmatize them. This created a problem for the group to solve. The creative solution that emerged out of this deliberation was to use the color red to depict HIV-positive stick figures and green to depict HIV-negative. This way, the stick figures would be asymptomatic and HIV could remain invisible, but the infected person could be marked by color. The solution of using red (which Ghanaians strongly associate with HIV) clearly resonated, as the group expressed heightened emotions and excitement—raising voices and sitting up in their seats—and thus motivated the group to collaborate on how they could use red in their poster to solve this problem. Importantly, these methods also revealed how groups came to similar choices but through different paths. Comparing across groups it became apparent that red was a common solution for how to represent AIDS. While some groups went right for the red pencil as if out of habit and practical consciousness, the example of this last group demonstrated how red became a resonant solution emerging from deliberation. In this way, multiple pathways to the same outcome became visible.

Juliene Boehme (2014) adopted what we would categorize as a "productive" method in her project on "unknown objects." To understand how people put cultural knowledge to work, she gave groups of people unfamiliar objects (though these objects were preexisting tools designed for a particular purpose, not invented for the project) and asked them to come to some consensus about the purpose of the object. Video-recordings show participants pick up the object, look at it, move it around to get all the angles, mimic possible uses, make hypotheses, reject others, begin circling in on some viable possibilities, and ultimately come to some consensus about a guess. What gets produced, then, is an account of what the object is meant to do. Like McDonnell's drawing approach, Boehme's method also elicits moments of frustration and excitement, indicative of moments throughout the cognitive processes. By picking bizarre objects that do not easily fit people's available cognitive schemas, she forces people out of easy, automatic modes of cognition. By "making strange," her approach is particularly good for studying processes of deliberation and resonance, but likely undermines habitual cognitive processes.

In her study of homebuying couples, Vercel (unpublished) uses productive methods to research the meanings of home and the homebuying process. Building on studies that asked participants to rank descriptors of their homes and possessions on survey instruments, she asks individuals and couples to rank a set of home descriptors (e.g., "spacious," "comfortable") from most desirable or important in a home to least desirable or important within an interview setting. When *individuals* performed this activity, they typically engaged in silent reflection, shuffling and reordering the words until they were satisfied with their ranking. In order to uncover their rationale for ranking the descriptors in a particular order, she needed to probe for explanations, which mostly led to brief and straightforward responses. However, when she asked *couples* to collaborate and rank the descriptors together, richer—and previously hidden—meanings and motivations emerged through the couple's interaction and negotiation. Descriptors were relegated to the bottom of the list not simply because they were less desirable, but because they clashed with how one or both members of the couple imagined their lives in their future home. For example, one couple had to resolve their desire for a home that could provide for a variety of needs—multiple children, home office space, a guest room to support their aspirations to be a welcoming and hospitable family—and their desire for a smaller home. Another couple explained that they were not seeking a "new" house, but also recognized that their schedules, particularly the husband's work as a pilot, precluded taking on any major renovations. Couples' histories were also revealed as they produced this ranking: multiple men described previous housing experiences in which they did not feel safe in their neighborhoods or homes, and as such, insisted that "safe" be ranked near the top of the list. Above and beyond identifying what cultural values people have, or whether people's cultural schemas lead them to biased interpretations, productive methods can reveal how people navigate when and how to express those preferences when facing people with competing values.

All of these productive methods meet the criteria set above: people work collectively to make an object that solves a problem, permitting the researcher access to multiple kinds of information and comparisons between the process of production and the ultimate product. What participants produce together to solve the problem could be any number of tasks. We have discussed AIDS campaign drawings, a shared understanding of an object's purpose, and a rank ordered list, but this just scratches the surface of the possibilities of objects to produce. Asking a group to write a story together, draw a map (Lynch 1960), or make a collage of images are other possibilities. How different kinds of objects may yield different kinds of insights is an essential consideration when adopting productive methods for a study. These approaches vary on a number of characteristics: (1) the degree to which the object produced constrains the process; (2) their capacity to elicit different kinds of cognition; and (3) links between emotion and cognition.

Vercel constrains participants a bit more than McDonnell or Boehme by preselecting the list of descriptors. Alternatively, Boehme and McDonnell could have constrained groups more by suggesting a list of possible uses for the unfamiliar object or narrowing the focus of the AIDS campaign to condom promotion. These are important choices, given that they may shape the kinds of information about cultural and cognitive processes attained and shape the comparability of groups. For instance, Vercel might have taken a more open-ended approach by asking couples to draw the exteriors and interiors of their "dream homes." This may have increased the variation in her data and made her data too noisy. People's desire for a hot tub, an English garden, cedar shake roof, shag carpet, or Formica countertops, or Venetian blinds may be too much to make commensurate. Ranking a set list of house qualities permits a cleaner and more systematic comparison between couples, but may ultimately miss cultural preferences that do not fit in the categories she provides. The ranking approach may then engage deliberative cognition more than automatic, especially when couples do not already align. When ranking metrics conflict, that may create problem situations that encourage couples to negotiate over and identify solutions, which may in turn reveal moments of resonance, or small-group dynamics. But, this likely better captures the constraints that shape how people buy homes—the weighing of qualities, negotiation processes between couples, considerations of competing preferences—rather than a dream home scenario that is left unconstrained. It seems there is a balance to be struck between structuring comparisons across groups and capturing a range of cognitive schemas. Such are the choices one has to make when designing a study.

Different kinds of productive methods may engage different kinds of schemas. For instance, when people engage physically with an object in Boehme's study, they activate sensory-motor schemas. The way the object "feels" in one's hand, the weight of the object, the texture of the surface, then inform the kinds of things one can "do" with it. Through their actions, participants question whether the object might be used to dig, or hammer, or slice, or press by engaging these sensory-motor schemas—moving the object in these familiar ways to see if it "feels right." A purpose for the object, then, emerges from the act of picking up the object and engaging with it, trying on different schemas through tactile engagement. In this sense, productive methods can draw sensory motor schema out into the open, making them available for systematic study. *Doing*, rather than just thinking, activates routinized and powerful schema that may be unavailable in survey data.

While the images drawn by McDonnell's participants also activated embodied sensory motor schema and made visible tacit knowledge and habitus (Bourdieu 1990; Ignatow 2007; Lizardo and Strand 2010; Mukerji 2014; Polanyi 1966; Sennett 2008)— revealing differences in drawing skill—these schema were less relevant to the research question. Certainly, these capacities mediated to some degree what could be represented, but variation in drawing skill did not dramatically undermine their capacity to get their ideas across. Had the research question been "How does a person's ability to draw shape their capacity to communicate meaning?" such variation would be essential to capture, and productive methods offers a good approach. Watching Boehme's participants working with the unknown objects, it is clear they rely on sensory motor feedback to assess whether the object fit the schema they are "trying on." The exercise appears to evoke questions like "Is this too heavy to be shovel?" or "does this handle have enough length to work as a meat tenderizer?" Trying to compare how this unfamiliar object feels similarly (or differently) in the hand compared to other tools revealed to participants a great deal about schematic fit.

These diverse approaches to productive methods vary in the degree to which they reveal the emotional dimensions of cognition. The techniques of productive methods, then, make important methodological contributions to recent work that bridges insights from cognitive sociology and the sociology of emotions (Danna Lynch 2009; Eliasoph and Lichterman 2003; Ignatow 2007; Strauss and Quinn 1997). Both McDonnell and Boehme's research capture the emotional highs that indicate resonance, contrasted with the emotional lows that appear when participants are frustrated by the lack of an "easy at hand" solution. In these cases, cognitive fit or misfit precede emotions. Emotions intersect cognition differently in Vercel's case, in that her approach draws out how emotions can mediate which cognitive schemas are deployed. Interacting with their spouses, couples engage in emotion work as preferences conflict or align (Hochschild 1979). This emergent emotion work influences how they produce the shared ranking, mediating cognitive processing and meaning, suppressing or encouraging some kinds of compromises and not others. Using tests for individual preferences before encouraging a shared list permits the measurement of how interaction and emotion work move people away from their predisposed schematic orientations.

18.2 BENEFITS OF PRODUCTIVE METHODS

Productive methods build on the insights provided by methodological advances in the areas of participatory research, arts-based research, creative methods, visual methods, and focus group research. Researchers in these areas have argued for the unique advantages they offer. By building on these innovations and combining their benefits, productive methods offer a strategy for accessing several kinds of data that are generally difficult to obtain, including implicit and nondiscursive cognition and cultural schemas. In what follows, we review the benefits of these methods, situate productive methods as a distinctive methodological strategy among existing methods, and describe the analytical payoff of using productive methods.

One distinctive characteristic of productive methods is that research participants are required to produce a cultural object. Researchers employing similar methods have noted the range of benefits that accompany this type of activity. When researchers ask subjects to create an object—whether through drawing, building, filming, or taking photographs—participants are able to express thoughts, experiences, and perspectives that they do not articulate during interviews or on surveys. One notable application of this is when the topic of research is sensitive or related to trauma. Health researchers have used methods like photovoice, photo elicitation, and drawing to enable participants to access experiences and emotions that are difficult to discuss (Guillemin and Drew 2010). Photovoice, a method that was initiated within community-based health research (Wang and Burris 2004), asks individuals to document their experiences or environment through photography. Photovoice has spread beyond the community-based and participatory research communities to others employing visual methods, and is often used in combination with photo elicitation, a method in which participants respond to photographs in an interview setting (Harper 2002).

When researchers ask participants to take photographs or video footage of their social worlds and neighborhoods, participants have the opportunity to shape the direction of the research. Many have argued that this importantly shifts the balance of power, and gives voice to the research participants (Wang and Burris 2004; Wang and Pies 2004; Wang 2006; Kindon 2003; Auyero and Swistun 2007). When the community or population being studied is vulnerable or marginalized, this consideration of the influence of the researcher is even more relevant. This is one of the reasons that these types of methods are particularly common in studies with children and youth (e.g., Auyero and Swistun 2007; Guillemin and Drew 2010; Bragg and Buckingham 2008; Niesyto 2000). While some scholars have questioned the degree to which these methods truly empower participants (Buckingham 2009), the methods avoid the trap of top-down, researcher-imposed conceptual schemes.

In addition to helping participants express sensitive experiences and opinions, those using visual methods, arts-based methods and creative methods have pointed to the capacity for these methods to access different discourses (Bragg and Buckingham 2008; Buckingham and Bragg 2004), experiential rather than analytical knowledge (McNiff 2012; Liamputtong and Rumbold 2008), unique emotions and memories (Harper 2002), and tacit or embodied knowledge (Sweetman 2009; Boehme 2014; Gauntlett and Holzwarth 2006).

In addition to eliciting different types of data from respondents, asking participants to create cultural objects—as when drawing (McDonnell 2014), building (Gauntlett and Holzwarth 2006), or making a video (Noor 2007)—helps to clarify cultural meanings.

Translating ideas or experiences into a material object necessarily means leaving out some possible meanings and including others. When researchers ask participants to create something, they can observe how participants make these decisions, and how they choose between contradictory or divergent meanings (Noor 2007).

There are also particular benefits that accrue to researchers when participants engage in collective activities. Collective activities reveal group boundaries and norms that remain hidden in individual interviews and survey research (Kitzinger 1994; Colucci 2007). Group interaction gives researchers access to cultural scripts and schemas (Cerulo 2000). Interaction and discussion among group members as they collaborate yield moments of resonance and dissonance, revealed through emotional displays and nonverbal communication (McDonnell 2014; Kitzinger 1990, 1994). As research with mock juries has demonstrated, observing group interaction yields insight into how group deliberation can alter individuals' perceptions and judgments, and mitigate biases (Miller et al. 2011; Ellison and Munro 2008).

Productive methods harness the benefits both of the creation of a cultural object and of observing group interaction, and by combining the two, access additional methodological payoffs. Many creative and participatory methods require individuals to produce cultural objects independently (Guillemin and Drew 2010), even if the objects are later discussed in a group setting or with the researcher (Catalani and Minkler 2010; Auyero and Swistun 2009; Sampson-Cordle 2001; Schratz and Steiner-Loffler 1998; Niesyto 2000; Wang and Pies 2004). Creating objects *together* forces participants to choose between meanings, to defend their points of view, making implicit culture explicit (Wuthnow and Witten 1988; McDonnell 2014, Vercel unpublished). Objects have a limited number of qualities and meanings. Because the finished form of objects requires the participants to choose one set of meanings, there will be debate about what should be included, and researchers may observe how participants choose among conflicting meanings (Noor 2007). These decisions are hidden when researchers observe individuals creating objects independently.

While many researchers have indicated that creative methods compel participants to contemplate a topic more thoroughly than they might in response to an interview question, resulting in a more reflective and rich response (e.g., Gauntlett and Holzwarth 2006), requiring participants to create a cultural object in a group setting allows researchers to observe automatic, as well as deliberative, cognition (McDonnell 2014). As participants collaborate and negotiate to make group decisions, researchers may observe moments of spontaneous consensus and emotional swell, revealing resonant and salient cultural meanings. They may also gain access to participants' practical knowledge in addition to their formal responses—as when members of the group who are known to one another call each other out on what they "really" think about something or what they "actually" do in a given situation (Kitzinger 1994).

Performing an activity like creating an object foregrounds group interaction, highlighting one of the most potentially fruitful aspects of focus groups, and one that is left out of the analysis of much focus group data (as noted in Kitzinger 1994, and demonstrated in Cerulo 2000), when individuals' responses are emphasized. Some focus group researchers have noted the benefit of asking participants to engage in activities together, though this is often described as one of many strategies to deploy within focus groups, rather than as a distinct method of inquiry (e.g., Colucci 2007). Nonetheless, these examples of group collaboration point to the potential fruitfulness of productive methods, and their capacity to help researchers uncover different, implicit, and emotionally charged data. This is apparent when group members work together to create political campaigns (Krueger and Casey 2000); when they collaborate to compile lists, rankings, or labels for different topics and cultural images; and when they build stories, analogies, and collages (Colucci 2007).

18.3 CONCLUSION

Recent work in cognitive sociology has relied on large-scale survey approaches to capture cognition (Vaisey 2009; Miles 2015). Despite the important insights this body of work has produced, these approaches often cannot fully capture the importance of process, context, emotion, and embodied schemas. On the other hand, while traditional qualitative methods like interviews, content analysis, and ethnography are better suited for capturing these understudied elements, they are not as well suited for studying cognition systematically. We have argued that productive methods offer a rigorous qualitative alternative for measuring cognition. Productive methods ask people to work collectively to make a cultural object that solves a problem, permitting researchers an opportunity to observe multiple levels of analysis and compare process and product. Because productive methods permit the measurement of cognitive process and outcome, they improve on methods that intuit process from outcomes. In addition, group settings make visible which schemas are cultural, and which are idiosyncratic. For these and many reasons, we believe productive methods are an important addition to our toolkit of methodological techniques.

That said, no method is perfect. Like all methods, productive methods have important limitations. Sample size and generalizability is certainly an issue. In our minds, problems with generalizability can be countered through mixed-methods approaches that use productive methods in combination with quantitative approaches. Once processes and outcomes are identified, they may be testable at a larger scale using more efficient survey-based or vignette techniques. Another potential downside of productive methods is the possibility of group effects. Are there unique processes happening in each specific group, or might there be ways that power differences (the presence of authority figures in the group, or gendered inequalities between couples) inflect the process and outcomes? While these are certainly possible, identifying commonalities across multiple groups with different dynamics can help differentiate between cultural features and unique effects emerging from group dynamics (McDonnell 2014, 2016). One might also question whether productive methods generate a laboratory effect that will not translate to "real" situations. This is something that requires additional study, and can be tested by using mixed-qualitative methods that combine productive and ethnographic methods to see whether cognitive processes that emerge when making an object translate to similarly shaped situations in everyday life. While not a methodological critique, it is also worth noting that recruiting for and facilitating this type of group research might not be feasible for every researcher or realistic for every study. Productive methods do not require costly materials—paper and pencil might often suffice—but they do require recruitment, access to an appropriate space for the group to meet, and research skills in facilitating and analyzing group research. The point being, productive methods do not offer a one-size-fits-all approach, but complement the range of other available methods.

NOTE

1. In reply, Vaisey (2014) challenges the grounds of the "attitudinal fallacy" finding evidence to suggest that attitudes are good predictors of behavior, and argues against the privileging of one method over others.

REFERENCES

Auyero, Javier, and Debora Swistun. 2007. "Amidst Garbage and Poison: An Essay on Polluted Peoples and Places." *Contexts* 6(2):46–51.

Auyero, Javier, and Débora Alejandra Swistun. 2009. *Flammable: Environmental Suffering in an Argentine Shantytown*. New York: Oxford University Press.

Becker, Howard S. 2007. *Telling about Society*. Chicago: University of Chicago Press.

Boehme, Juliane. 2014. "From Unknown to Known Objects: Cultural Knowledge in Action." Paper presented at the International Sociological Association Meetings, July 17, Yokohama Japan.

Bourdieu, Pierre. 1990. *The Logic of Practice*. Stanford, CA: Stanford University Press.

Bragg, Sara, and David Buckingham. 2008. "'Scrapbooks' as a Resource in Media Research with Young People." pp. 114–31 in *Doing Visual Research with Children and Young People*, edited by P. Thomson. London: Routledge.

Buckingham, David. 2009. "'Creative' Visual Methods in Media Research: Possibilities, Problems and Proposals." *Media, Culture, and Society* 31(4):633–52.

Buckingham, David, and Sarah Bragg. 2004. *Young People, Sex and the Media*. New York: Palgrave Macmillan.

Catalani, Caricia, and Meredith Minkler. 2010. "Photovoice: A Review of the Literature in Health and Public Health." *Health Education and Behavior* 37(3):424–51.

Cerulo, Karen A. 2000. "The Rest of the Story: Sociocultural Patterns of Story Elaboration." *Poetics* 28:21–45.

Clark, Andy, and David J. Chalmers. 1998. "The Extended Mind." *Analysis* 58:7–19.

Colucci, Erminia. 2007. "'Focus Groups Can Be Fun': The Use of Activity-Oriented Questions in Focus Group Discussions." *Qualitative Health Research* 17(10):1422–33.

Cornwall, Andrea, and Rachel Jewkes. 1995. "What Is Participatory Research?" *Social Science and Medicine* 41(12):1667–76.

Danna Lynch, Karen. 2009. "Objects, Meanings, and Role Identities: The Practices That Establish Association in the Case of Home-Based Employment." *Sociological Forum* 24(1):76–103.

DeNora, Tia. 2000. *Music in Everyday Life*. Cambridge: Cambridge University Press.

DiMaggio, Paul. 1997. "Culture and Cognition." *Annual Review of Sociology* 23:263–87.

Dominguez Rubio, Fernando. 2014. "Preserving the Unpreservable: Docile and Unruly Objects at MOMA." *Theory and Society* 43(6):617–45.

Eliasoph, Nina, and Paul Lichterman. 2003. "Culture in Interaction." *American Journal of Sociology* 108(4):735–94.

Ellison, Louise, and Vanessa E. Munro. 2008. "Reacting to Rape: Exploring Mock Jurors' Assessments of Complainant Credibility." *British Journal of Criminology* 49(2):202–19.

Evans, Jonathan St. B.T. 2003. "In Two Minds: Dual-Process Accounts of Reasoning." *Trends in Cognitive Sciences* 7(10):454–9.

Gauntlett, David. 2004. "Using New Creative Visual Research Methods to Understand the Place of Popular Media in People's Lives." Paper presented at IAMCR, Audience and Reception Studies Section.

Gauntlett, David, and Peter Holzwarth. 2006. "Creative and Visual Methods for Exploring Identities." *Visual Studies* 21(1):82–91.

Gibson, James J. 1979. *The Ecological Approach to Visual Perception*. Hillsdale, NJ: Erlbaum.

Goffman, Erving. 1959. *The Presentation of Self in Everyday Life*. New York: Anchor Books.

Griswold, Wendy. 1986. *Renaissance Revivals: City Comedy and Revenge Tragedy in the London Theatre, 1576–1980*. Chicago: University of Chicago Press.

Gross, Neil. 2009. "A Pragmatist Theory of Social Mechanisms." *American Sociological Review* 74(3):358–79.

Guillemin, Marilys, and Sarah Drew. 2010. "Questions of Process in Participant-Generated Visual Methodologies." *Visual Studies* 25(2):175–88.

Harper, Douglas. 2002. "Talking about Pictures: A Case for Photo Elicitation." *Visual Studies* 17(1):13–26.

Hochschild, Arlie Russell. 1979. "Emotion Work, Feeling Rules, and Social Structure." *American Journal of Sociology* 85(3):551–75.

Horne, Christine, F. Nii-Amoo Dodoo, and Naa Dodua Dodoo. 2013. "The Shadow of Indebtedness: Bridewealth and Norms Constraining Female Reproductive Autonomy." *American Sociological Review* 78(3):503–20.

Hughes, Rhidian. 1998. "Considering the Vignette Technique and Its Application to a Study of Drug Injecting and HIV Risk and Safer Behavior." *Sociology of Health and Illness* 20(3):381–400.

Ignatow, Gabriel. 2007. "Theories of Embodied Knowledge: New Directions for Cultural and Cognitive Sociology?" *Journal for the Theory of Social Behaviour* 37(2):115–35.

Jerolmack, Colin, and Shamus Khan. 2014. "Talk Is Cheap: Ethnography and the Attitudinal Fallacy." *Sociological Methods and Research* 43(2):178–209.

Kindon, Sara. 2003. "Participatory Video in Geographic Research: A Feminist Practice of Looking?" *Area* 35(2):142–53.

Kitzinger, Jenny. 1990. "Audience Understandings of AIDS Media Messages: A Discussion of Methods." *Sociology of Health and Illness* 12(3):319–35.

Kitzinger, Jenny. 1994. "The Methodology of Focus Groups: The Importance of Interaction between Research Participants." *Sociology of Health and Illness* 16(1):103–21.

Krueger, Richard A., and Mary Anne Casey. 2000. *Focus Groups: A Practical Guide for Applied Research*. Singapore: SAGE.

Latour, Bruno, and Steve Woolgar. 1986. *Laboratory Life: The Construction of Scientific Facts.* Princeton, NJ: Princeton University Press.

Liamputtong, Pranee, and Jean Rumbold. 2008. *Knowing Differently: Arts-Based and Collaborative Research Methods.* New York: Nova Science.

Liebes, Tamar, and Elihu Katz. 1990. *The Export of Meaning: Cross-Cultural Readings of Dallas.* London: Oxford University Press.

Lizardo, Omar, Robert Mowry, Brandon Sepulvado, Dustin S. Stoltz, Marshall A. Taylor, and Justin Van Ness. 2016. "What Are Dual Process Models? Implications for Cultural Analysis in Sociology." *Sociological Theory* 34(4):287–310.

Lizardo, Omar, and Michael Strand. 2010. "Skills, Toolkits, Contexts and Institutions: Clarifying the Relationship between Different Approaches to Cognition in Cultural Sociology." *Poetics* 38(2):205–28.

Lynch, Kevin. 1960. *The Image of the City.* Cambridge, MA: MIT Press.

McDonnell, Terence E. 2014. "Drawing Out Culture: Productive Methods to Measure Cognition and Resonance." *Theory and Society* 43(3–4):247–74.

McDonnell, Terence E. 2016. *Best Laid Plans: Cultural Entropy and the Unraveling of AIDS Media Campaigns.* Chicago: University of Chicago Press.

McNiff, Shaun. 2012. "Opportunities and Challenges in Art-Based Research." *Journal of Applied Arts and Health* 3(1):5–12.

Miles, Andrew. 2015. "The (Re)Genesis of Values: Examining the Importance of Values for Action." *American Sociological Review* 80(4):680–704.

Miller, Monica K., Jon Maskaly, Morgan Green, and Clayton D. Peoples. 2011. "The Effects of Deliberations and Religious Identity on Mock Jurors' Verdicts." *Group Processes and Intergroup Relations* 14(4):517–32.

Mukerji, Chandra. 2014. "The Cultural Power of Tacit Knowledge: Inarticulacy and Bourdieu's Habitus." *American Journal of Cultural Sociology* 2(3):348–75.

Niesyto, Horst. 2000. "Youth Research on Video Self-productions: Reflections on a Social-aesthetic Approach." *Visual Sociology* 15(1):135–53.

Noor, Habiba. 2007. "Assertions of Identities through News Production." *European Journal of Cultural Studies* 10(3):374–88.

Pager, Devah, and Lincoln Quillian. 2005. "Walking the Talk? What Employers Say versus What They Do." *American Sociological Review* 70:355–80.

Phelan, Jo C., Bruce G. Link, and Naumi M. Feldman. 2013. "The Genomic Revolution and Beliefs about Essential Racial Differences: A Backdoor to Eugenics?" *American Sociological Review* 78(2):167–91.

Pickering, Andrew. 1995. *The Mangle of Practice: Time, Agency and Science.* Chicago: University of Chicago Press.

Polanyi, Michael. 1966. *The Tacit Dimension: Towards a Post-Critical Philosophy.* London: Routledge.

Press, Andrea L., and Elizabeth. R. Cole. 1999. *Speaking of Abortion: Television and Authority in the Lives of Women.* Chicago: University of Chicago Press.

Pugh, Alison J. 2013. "What Good are Interviews for Thinking about Culture? Demystifying Interpretive Analysis." *American Journal of Cultural Sociology* 1(1):42–68.

Sampson-Cordle, Alice V. 2001. "Exploring the Relationship between a Small Rural School in Northeast Georgia and Its Community." PhD dissertation, University of Georgia, Athens.

Schram, Sanford F., Joe Soss, Richard C. Fording, and Linda Houser. 2009. "Deciding to Discipline: Race, Choice, and Punishment at the Frontlines of Welfare Reform." *American Sociological Review* 74(3):398–422.

Schratz, Michael, and Ulrike Steiner-Löffler. 1998. "Pupils Using Photographs in School Self-Evaluation." pp. 235–51 in *Image-based Research: A Sourcebook for Qualitative Researchers*, edited by J. Prosser. London: Taylor & Francis.

Sennett, Richard. 2008. *The Craftsman*. New Haven, CT: Yale University Press.

Shively, JoEllen. 1992. "Cowboys and Indians: Perceptions of Western Films among American Indians and Anglos." *American Sociological Review* 57(6): 725–34.

Strauss, Claudia, and Naomi Quinn. 1997. *A Cognitive Theory of Cultural Meaning*. New York: Cambridge University Press.

Sweetman, Paul. 2009. "Revealing Habitus, Illuminating Practice: Bourdieu, Photography and Visual Methods." *Sociological Review* 57(3):491–511.

Vaisey, Stephen. 2009. "Motivation and Justification: A Dual Process Model of Culture in Action." *American Journal of Sociology* 114:1675–715.

Vaisey, Stephen. 2014. "The 'Attitudinal Fallacy' Is a Fallacy: Why We Need Many Methods to Study Culture." *Sociological Methods Research* 43(2):227–31.

Vercel, Kelcie L. Unpublished research. "Choosing a Home: Family Decision-Making and the Meaning of Home."

Wang, Caroline, and Mary Ann Burris. 2004. "Photovoice: Concept, Methodology, and Use for Participatory Needs Assessment." *Health Education and Behavior* 24(3):369–87.

Wang, Caroline C. 2006. "Youth Participation in Photovoice as a Strategy for Community Change." *Journal of Community Practice* 14(1–2):147–61.

Wang, Caroline C., and Cheri A. Pies. 2004. "Family, Maternal, and Child Health through Photovoice." *Maternal and Child Health Journal* 8(2):95–102.

Wuthnow, Robert, and Marsha Witten. 1988. "New Directions in the Study of Culture." *Annual Review of Sociology* 14: 49–67.

CHAPTER 19

AN ASSESSMENT OF METHODS FOR MEASURING AUTOMATIC COGNITION

ANDREW MILES

SOCIOLOGISTS have long recognized that impulse, habit, and other forces beyond the conscious mind shape human thought and behavior (Durkheim 1982; Weber 1920). Most recently, this idea has resurfaced in the form of dual-process models imported from the cognitive sciences. While varying in the details, these models agree that cognitive processes are of two general types (Lizardo et al. 2016). The first—referred to generically as Type 1 processes—tend to execute rapidly and automatically, require little effort, and are often unconscious (or preconscious), while the second—Type 2 processes—are slow, controlled, effortful, and conscious (Evans 2008). Enthusiasm has been particularly high for Type 1 processes, which provide a strong cognitive foundation for (and validation of) treasured sociological constructs like Giddens's practical consciousness and Bourdieu's *habitus* (Bourdieu 1990; Giddens 1984), and suggest avenues for addressing thorny theoretical issues like how internal and external elements of culture are implicated in producing action (Lizardo and Strand 2010; Vaisey 2009). However, theoretical treatments have outstripped empirical work, in part because ideas about Type 1 processes have proven more portable than the methods for measuring them.

This chapter evaluates methods that have been advanced for measuring Type 1 cognition, with the goal of bringing the most useful, well-validated, and promising measures into sociology. I begin by discussing general principles for capturing Type 1 processes, and then apply these principles to evaluate how well existing measures accomplish this task. Along the way, I provide practical guidance for implementing the best measures, and suggestions for improving measures in cases where the link to Type 1 cognition is unclear.

Given space constraints, I focus on measures that purport to capture constructs and topics that are of interest to sociologists. Foremost among these are various forms of evaluations and motivating constructs, including attitudes, values, moral worldviews, and identities (e.g., Burke and Stets 2009; Gauchat 2012; Miles 2015; Srivastava and Banaji 2011; Vaisey 2009). Sociologists have also shown a recurring interest in habits and practices that occur largely without conscious effort (Bourdieu 1990; Dewey 1922; Gross 2009; Joas 1996; Lizardo 2009, 2012), and in schemas, or interconnected networks of cognitively represented cultural elements that facilitate the interpretation of (and acting in) the social world (Boutyline 2017; D'Andrade 1992; DiMaggio 1997; Goldberg 2011; Martin and Desmond 2010; Rivera 2012). Finally, action theorists have repeatedly raised the question of the extent to which behavior is driven by deliberate versus habitual/practical/unconscious processes, suggesting a need for a valid way of comparing these types of cognition (Bourdieu 1990; Giddens 1984; Gross 2009; Joas 1996; Vaisey 2009). I examine measurement strategies for each of these topics below.[1]

19.1 General Considerations for Measuring Type 1 Processes

Before examining specific measures, we must consider two issues that crosscut different measurement approaches. These are the nature of automatic cognition, and the use of forced-choice measures.

19.1.1 A Template for Measuring Type 1 Processes

Type 1 processes have been described in many ways, including rapid, effortless, and unconscious (Evans 2008:257). A number of scholars, however, argue that their defining characteristic is automaticity (Evans 2012; Stanovich and Toplak 2012). Automaticity means that "the execution of . . . processes is mandatory when their triggering stimuli are encountered, and they are not dependent on input from high-level control systems" (Stanovich and Toplak 2012:7). Thus a person entering an office space is likely to immediately recognize chairs, desks, and other familiar objects without having to consciously remember what they are. In fact, a person does not have the choice to *not* recognize them—the recall is automatic. Automatic execution tends to happen quickly, without conscious awareness, and requires little effort, so these features are likely to be present whenever Type 1 cognition is occurring, suggesting that they are good *indicators* of automaticity, but do not constitute definitive evidence of automatic processing—Evans (2012) refers to them as "typical or common correlates" (123). Automaticity is only guaranteed when intentional cognitive control is absent.

This understanding of Type 1 processing means that measurement approaches that focus exclusively on common indicators of automaticity increase the likelihood of capturing Type 1 cognition, but cannot rule out alternative processes. Rapid response, for instance, suggests automatic processing, but can also be accomplished through well-practiced, conscious application of rules. However, alternative explanations disappear to the extent that respondents do not have control over their responses (Gawronski and De Houwer 2014). The level of intentional control thus provides a benchmark for evaluating different measurement strategies, and—as we shall see— weakens the claim of some measures that purport to tap Type 1 cognition. Given the centrality of automaticity to Type 1 cognition, I use the terms "automatic" and "Type 1" interchangeably throughout the remainder of this chapter.

19.1.2 Forced Choice Measures

Scholars have used forced choice (FC) survey items to measure several types of automatic cognition, so I address FC items here to set the stage for later discussions (Goldberg 2011; Vaisey 2009; Verplanken and Orbell 2003). Forced choice items have many advantages: they are familiar, easy to use, quick to administer, and can be adapted to measure many types of constructs. Unfortunately, FC items also suffer from a number of weaknesses that severely restrict their ability to serve as effective measures of Type 1 processes.

Forced choice items are explicit measures, meaning that respondents are aware of what is being assessed. This opens the door to reflection and intentional control of responses. Of course, individuals can answer FC items quickly, with little effort or attention, relying on their gut feelings to select "the response that 'feels right' or 'sounds right' to [them]" (Vaisey 2009), all of which should facilitate automatic processing. However, nothing in the design of the standard FC item *requires* this type of response, so researchers cannot be sure that Type 1 processing is occurring. Rather, researchers can only judge whether automatic processing is *likely* based on additional information about the data collection environment, the features of the FC questions, and the characteristics of individual respondents.

Fazio and Olson (2003) argue that the level of deliberation used in answering FC items depends on individuals having both the motivation and the opportunity to think carefully, and that removing either produces greater reliance on automatic processes. The good news is that either of these can, in theory, be manipulated to better isolate Type 1 processes (e.g., by distracting respondents, see Miles 2015, for an example).[2] However, many researchers do not have the control over the data-collection process needed to make this a feasible option, and must determine levels of opportunity and motivation post hoc. Opportunity for deliberation might differ based on how the survey is administered (e.g., in a controlled environment vs. online), while motivation is likely to vary from person to person, and from question to question in response to social desirability and related concerns.

The extent to which FC measures tap automatic cognition also depends on the type of information being requested, with individuals relying more on their intuitions when asked to provide subjective information (e.g., preferences or feelings) than when asked to recall events or report information with objectively correct answers (e.g., income;

Gawronski and LeBel 2008; Smith and Nosek 2011). Additionally, individual differences in thinking styles, working memory, and past experience relying on intuitions may affect the extent to which respondents use Type 1 and Type 2 cognition (Akinci and Sadler-Smith 2013; Conner et al. 2007; Epstein et al. 1996; Evans 2010; Friese et al. 2008; Hofmann et al. 2008). Automatic processes are also more influential when cognitive resources are depleted, as might happen when remembering complex information during a survey (Friese et al. 2008). Cognitive depletion is often situational, but might become chronic to the extent that individuals vary in their life circumstances and/or capacities to manage them.

The foregoing suggests that FC responses almost always represent an unknown mixture of Type 1 and Type 2 processes. Consequently, using FC items as measures of automatic cognition requires making strong and often untestable assumptions about survey environments, individual motivations, and the capacities of respondents. This, in turn, generates uncertainty about which type of cognition is being measured. Forced choice items therefore cannot be recommended as measures of automatic processes.

To summarize, there are several considerations that can be used to evaluate how likely it is that a measure captures automatic processes. The most important is whether the measurement approach restricts intentional cognitive control over responses. A weaker indicator of automaticity is that the measure relies on one of the common correlates of automaticity, such as rapid response. Similarly, automaticity is more likely—but not guaranteed—if a measurement strategy reduces the motivation for careful thought. Finally, use of FC items in unmodified form introduces uncertainty about whether automatic processes are being measured. The following sections apply these criteria to evaluate different measures that aim to capture automatic cognition.

19.2 Measures of Evaluations and Motivating Structures

By far the most common way to measure evaluative and motivating constructs like attitudes, values, morality, and identities is a FC survey (e.g., Burke and Stets 2009:222–30; DiMaggio et al. 1996; Miles 2015; Ottoni-Wilhem and Bekkers 2010; Vaisey 2009). However, given the problems with using FC items to measure automatic processes, I restrict my attention here to a class of measures known as implicit measures. In contrast to explicit measures, implicit measures are characterized by a lack of awareness among respondents about what is being measured, and consequently are more likely to capture the lack of intentionality and cognitive control that is central to Type 1 processing. There are many different implicit measures (Fazio and Olson 2003; Gawronski and De Houwer 2014), but I focus on two common, well-validated, and psychometrically reliable ones—the Implicit Association Test (IAT) and the Affect Misattribution Procedure (AMP) (Greenwald et al. 1998; Hahn and Gawronski n.d.; Payne et al. 2005).[3] Both were originally designed to tap attitudes but have since been adapted to measure constructs such as identities, self-esteem, and cultural beliefs.[4]

19.2.1 Implicit Association Test

The IAT is a computerized task that measures associations between concepts. It rests on a connectionist understanding of human cognition in which concepts are assumed to activate one another more quickly to the extent that they are more closely related in memory (Greenwald et al. 1998). Faster responses are taken as evidence that concepts are strongly related and that activating one will automatically activate the other. For example, a positive attitude toward blacks would produce a rapid connection between the concepts "black" and "good," while a stereotype linking Asians to math ability would facilitate linking "Asian" with "math."

In the IAT, respondents are shown items belonging to two sets of contrasting categories, and must rapidly sort the items into the correct categories. Each item appears in the middle of the screen, along with contrasting category labels on either side of the screen, as shown in Figure 19.1. Respondents categorize items using keystrokes, pressing one key if the item belongs to a category listed on the right, and a different key if it belongs to a category on the left. In the arrangement depicted in Figure 19.1, for example, respondents would press the "right" key if the item displayed is either a white face or an item from the "bad" category, and press the "left" key if the item is either a black face or a "good" item. The task immediately advances to the next item once a response is entered. If respondents make an error, a red X appears below the item and they must press the correct key to proceed. Each classification attempt is referred to as a "trial," and multiple trials are grouped together into blocks. Typically, the IAT consists of seven blocks, with category labels shown in different configurations in each block (see Table 19.1). In our example, that means that "black" (or "white") would be paired with "good" in some blocks, and with "bad" in other blocks.

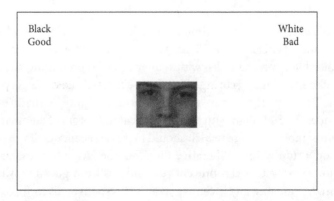

FIGURE 19.1 Screen layout for the IAT.

Table 19.1 Ordering of IAT Blocks

Block	Left Key	Right Key	Trials	
1	Black	White	20	
2	Good	Bad	20	
3	Black	White	20	
	Good	Bad		
4	Black	White	40	randomly present blocks
	Good	Bad		2–4 or blocks 5–7 first
5	Bad	Good	40	
6	Black	White	20	
	Bad	Good		
7	Black	White	40	
	Bad	Good		

Note: Using 40 trials in block 5 and counterbalancing blocks 3 and 4 with 6 and 7 across respondents mitigates order effects (Lane et al. 2007; Nosek et al. 2005).

In a connectionist framework, responses should be faster to the extent that categories are more closely associated in the respondent's mind. The crucial information is therefore how long respondents take to categorize items given the way that the category labels are paired. A person with strong negative feelings toward blacks, for example, should sort items into categories more quickly when "black" and "bad" are paired then when "white" and "bad" are paired, so systematically faster times on black/bad trials can be used to gauge racial prejudice. Response times are combined into a single score called D that reflects differences in response tendencies under each configuration of categories (Greenwald et al. 2003):[5]

$$D = \frac{\dfrac{\bar{t}_3 - \bar{t}_6}{s_{3,6}} + \dfrac{\bar{t}_4 - \bar{t}_7}{s_{4,7}}}{2} \tag{1}$$

where $\bar{t}_x$ is the average response time for block x and $s_{x,z}$ is the standard deviation from blocks x and z (Greenwald et al. 2003).[6] In our example, D represents automatic preference for whites versus blacks, with higher scores representing stronger positive evaluations of whites. Other scoring algorithms exist, but most are very similar (e.g., Srivastava and Banaji 2011) or improve the D score only slightly (Richetin et al. 2015).

How well does the IAT align with our theoretical indicators of automatic processes? The IAT requires rapid response, which should increase reliance on Type 1 cognition by limiting the opportunity for deliberative thought. The IAT also presents a face-valid cover story for the task that can prevent respondents from guessing what is actually being measured, removing any incentive to adjust responses. Even if respondents are made aware of the purpose of the IAT, it is not clear how they can "fool" the test without a deep understanding of how it works (e.g., Fiedler and Bluemke 2005; Stieger et al. 2011). In fact, if respondents follow task instructions and sort the items as quickly as they can, a connectionist understanding of cognition suggests that they *cannot* misrepresent their attitudes because they lack direct control over how quickly their brains are able to make connections between the items and the categories. The IAT, then, very likely captures automatic cognition because it minimizes the opportunity, motivation, and ability to engage in deliberative thought.

How useful is the IAT as a measure? Evaluations suggests that it has good internal reliability ($\bar{\alpha}$ = 0.79, Hofmann et al. 2005) but low test-retest reliability ($\bar{\alpha}$ = 0.50, Lane et al. 2007, see also Gawronski et al. 2017). Nonetheless, it generally relates to other constructs in theoretically predicted ways, though correlations among the IAT and other implicit measures purporting to tap the same constructs are often quite low, possibly due to measurement error or differences in test formats that lead to measuring different facets of the constructs (Lane et al. 2007; Payne et al. 2008). Of particular note, the IAT consistently predicts behaviors, judgments, and even physiological responses ($\bar{r}$ = 0.27), and may have particular utility in socially sensitive domains such as race (Greenwald et al. 2009; Greenwald et al. 2015; c.f., Oswald et al. 2013).

IAT scores vary based on the features of the response environment, which can be interpreted either as a problem in measuring stable cognitive structures or as providing insight into the situation-specific nature of cognition, and hence might be seen variously as a flaw or a feature of the method (Blair 2002; Han et al. 2010; Nosek and Hansen 2008; Shepherd 2011).[7] At the very least, it suggests the need to think carefully about potential influences on IAT responses such as question ordering and the administration context (Gawronski et al. 2017). Olson and Fazio (2004) demonstrate that extrapersonal influences can also be minimized by personalizing the IAT—for example, replacing the "good" and "bad" categories with "I like" and "I don't like" when measuring attitudes (see also Han et al. 2010).

The IAT has been widely used to measure attitudes, but nothing in its measurement approach restricts it to these constructs (Lane et al. 2007). In fact, the IAT can be adapted to capture associations between *any* mental constructs. Researchers have used IATs to measure self-concepts (Devos et al. 2012; Knowles and Peng 2005; Srivastava and Banaji 2011), self-esteem (Greenwald and Farnham 2000), and sexual attraction to children (Babchishin et al. 2013), as well as automatic associations between gender and science (Nosek et al. 2009), blacks and violence (Glaser and Knowles 2008), and body type and shame (Clerkin et al. 2014). IATs can also be adapted to measure a variety of other tacit assumptions, worldviews, and stereotypes that are likely to be of interest to sociologists. To illustrate, Table 19.2 gives examples of IAT categories that could be used to measure associations between characteristics and different social groups.[8] In theory, the IAT could similarly be adapted to measure action tendencies, though to my knowledge this has not been tested. For example, contrasting categories of "help vs. not help" with "stranger vs. friend" could measure the strength of intuitions about helping familiar and unfamiliar people.

Scholars have adapted the IAT in various ways to increase its utility, often to allow it to assess a single construct rather than paired constructs (e.g., blacks *or* whites rather than

Table 19.2 IAT Category Labels for Measuring Characteristics of Social Groups

Group characteristic	1st set of Categories (Characteristics)	2nd set of Categories (Social Groups)
poverty	poor vs. rich	Black vs. White
intelligence	intelligent vs. unintelligent	Asian vs. Black
morality	moral vs. immoral	Republican vs. Democrat
work ethic	lazy vs. hard-working	poor vs. middle-class
friendliness	friendly vs. hostile	police vs. doctors

blacks *vs.* whites; single category IAT, Karpinski and Steinman 2006; go/no-go association task, Nosek and Banaji 2001; single attribute IAT, Penke et al. 2006). Of particular note is the Brief IAT (BIAT). The BIAT retains the paired constructs format of the IAT, but is less complex and generally takes less time while retaining many of the IAT's psychometric properties, including internal consistencies that generally exceed 0.75, test-retest reliabilities averaging 0.63, and the ability to relate to other variables in theoretically predicted ways (Bar-Anan and Nosek 2014; Nosek et al. 2014; Sriram and Greenwald 2009). Researchers interested in the BIAT should refer to Sriram and Greenwald (2009) and Nosek and colleagues (2014) for design details and recommended scoring procedures.

19.2.2 Affect Misattribution Procedure

The AMP is a relatively recent addition to the corpus of implicit measures, but one that is already well validated and widely used by psychologists (Payne and Lundberg 2014). Rather than inferring evaluations from response times for paired categories as the IAT does, the AMP relies on direct evaluative ratings, giving it a simple interpretation. The AMP is also flexible—it can be used to measure single or paired constructs, as described below.

The implementation of the AMP is straightforward (Payne et al. 2005). Respondents are shown in quick succession a series of primes—words or images related to the concept of interest—and neutral images—pictures that are unlikely to provoke a reaction. The key assumption is that primes generate a positive or negative affective response that carries through and influences ratings of the neutral images. Because respondents are instructed to rate just the neutral images, this carryover effect represents a misattribution of the true source of the affect.

Figure 19.2 depicts a single trial. Here, a prime is displayed (Hillary Clinton), followed by a blank screen, then a neutral image (Chinese pictograph) that respondents are instructed to rate.[9] The neutral image is replaced by a visual mask that remains on the screen until subjects respond. Subjects typically rate images by pressing one of two keys (e.g., press "I" if the image is more pleasant than average, press "E" if it is less pleasant), though the task can be adapted to work with a Likert-type rating scale (Payne et al. 2008).

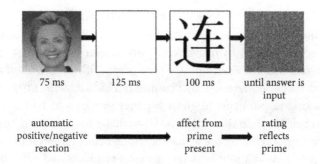

FIGURE 19.2 Sequence of the affect misattribution procedure.

Single attitude scores are calculated by examining the proportion of "pleasant" responses associated with each category of primes (e.g., pictures of Hillary Clinton). Alternately, a difference score can be computed to show relative preference for one category versus another, much as in the IAT (e.g., Hillary Clinton vs. Donald Trump). This is accomplished by taking the difference between the proportion of pleasant responses given following primes from each of the two categories (Payne et al. 2005).[10] In either case, current recommendations are to use all responses without modification, except for removing respondents who clearly did not follow task instructions (e.g., by pressing a single key throughout the task, Payne and Lundberg 2014).

Does the AMP capture automatic processes? As in the IAT, the rapid pace of the AMP should reduce opportunities for deliberate, controlled responding. More importantly, primes are expected to generate affective reactions that carry through and influence the ratings of neutral images, contrary to the intentions of respondents (see Figure 19.2, Hahn and Gawronski forthcoming; Payne and Lundberg 2014). In fact, most AMPs warn participants in advance that the primes might affect their responses, and explicitly instruct them to guard against this. This means that systematic influences of the primes occur despite deliberate attempts to control them, strongly supporting the idea that the AMP captures automatic processes.

The AMP also generally demonstrates good measurement properties. A recent meta-analysis calculated an average reliability of $\alpha = 0.81$, and found that reliability increases linearly with the number of trials. Notably, predicted reliability exceeded 0.70 with as few as 20 trials (Payne and Lundberg 2014, see Figure 19.2), which would make the AMP very fast to administer (1–2 minutes).[11] Test-retest reliability is lower, ranging from 0.33 to 0.73 (Bar-Anan and Nosek 2014; Gawronski et al. 2017; Payne and Lundberg 2014). Another meta-analysis found that the AMP predicted behavior ($r = 0.35$) and was positively correlated with explicit attitude measures ($r = 0.36$), but only under conditions that discouraged deliberation (Cameron et al. 2012). It is also noteworthy that the AMP asks respondents for evaluative judgments directly rather than inferring them from reaction times, making it clearer what it measures (Payne and Lundberg 2014).

Like the IAT, the AMP can be adapted to measure constructs other than attitudes, though this is not yet common. Several studies have demonstrated that altering task instructions allows other cognitive constructs to be misattributed in the same way that the traditional task allows the misattribution of affect. For example, Sava et al. (2012) measured personality by using descriptive adjectives as primes and instructing respondents to rate whether each Chinese pictograph "fit" them. Imhoff and colleagues (2011) captured sexual preferences by priming individuals with images of males and females and asking respondents to guess whether pictographs had a sexual meaning (see also Gray et al. 2014). In theory, the AMP could be adapted to capture any number of cultural meanings, including those that have long been of interest to sociologists. For example, automatic associations between material products and elite culture could be measured by using images of art, apparel, and other goods as primes, and asking respondents to guess whether Chinese pictographs have meanings associated with being rich or poor, represent the names of people who are socially prominent or not, and so on. Similarly, gender beliefs could be assessed by using pictures of men and women as primes and asking respondents to guess whether pictographs are related to attributes like power or competency, or to domains like work and home life.

19.3 MEASURES OF HABIT

Sociologists have used the term "habit" to cover a broad range of physical, emotional, and mental regularities that have little in common except that they are repeated and relatively automatic (e.g., Dewey 1922; Gross 2009). In this view, automatically processed evaluations, motivations, and cultural schemas are all habits. Because these are discussed elsewhere in this chapter, I restrict my attention here to behavioral habits, which is also consistent with the psychological literature that I draw on. Even in this restricted sense of the term, habits figure prominently in sociological theories including Giddens's (1984) structuration theory, pragmatist theories of behavior (Gross 2009; Joas 1996), and practice theories of culture and action (Bourdieu 1990; Lizardo 2009, 2012), suggesting a fertile field of application for habit measures.

Habits can be usefully divided into two components: automatic *impulses* that prompt action when relevant cues are encountered in the environment, and *behaviors* that require little conscious monitoring to execute (Gardner 2015). These are referred to as habitual instigation and habitual execution, respectively (Gardner et al. 2016). As an example, the ping of an incoming message can prompt a worker to check her e-mail (habitual instigation), at which point she follows a set of simple, largely automated actions to open the e-mail program (habitual execution). This distinction—often absent in both psychological and sociological treatments of habit—is both theoretically and practically useful (Gardner et al. 2016). Theoretically, it allows for more nuanced understandings of how habit might feature in behavioral models, recognizing, for instance, that impulse need not lead to action. Practically, it provides a framework for determining what existing measures of habit are actually measuring.

19.3.1 Self-Report Habit Index

Almost all measures of habit are administered using FC questionnaires. The most common is the Self-Report Habit Index (SRHI), which is designed to tap the "experience of habit" and "the underlying cognitive association" that it depends on by focusing on three aspects of automaticity: lack of awareness, lack of control, and mental efficiency (Gardner 2015; Orbell and Verplanken 2015; Verplanken and Orbell 2003). Each of its twelve items begins with the stem "[Behavior X] is something..." followed by a phrase describing some aspect of habit (e.g., "I do without thinking," "I do frequently"). The SRHI has high internal reliability ($\alpha > 0.85$), correlates moderately strongly with behavior ($r = 0.44$, Gardner et al. 2011), and can easily be adapted to incorporate specific contexts. Although the SRHI was designed without reference to the distinction between instigation and execution, a recent study suggests that the SRHI predominately measures habitual instigation, though the scale can be adapted to target habitual execution as well (Gardner et al. 2016).

Despite its wide use and adaptability, the SRHI has a number of shortcomings that limit its ability to serve as an effective measure of habit. First, it assumes that individuals can accurately report on automaticity-related experiences, such as how much thought performing a given behavior requires (Gardner 2015; Orbell and Verplanken 2015), yet evidence suggests that individuals often do a poor job of recalling routine behaviors and the circumstances that gave rise to them (Hagger et al. 2015). Furthermore, describing how an action occurs requires recall and analysis of past experiences, a process that necessarily recruits deliberative cognition. This means that opportunity for deliberation cannot be circumscribed to increase reliance on automatic processes, and leaves open the possibility that the SRHI reflects conscious editing, particularly for behaviors subject to social desirability concerns. Researchers using the SRHI therefore cannot be certain that they are getting an accurate measure of the automatic processes that underlie habitual behavior.

19.3.2 Implicit Measures of Habit

Concerns about the SRHI and related measures have led a number of scholars to turn to implicit measures that more directly assess the rapid cue-response associations that initiate habitual behavior (Gardner 2015; Hagger et al. 2015; Labrecque and Wood 2015; cf. Orbell and Verplanken 2015). These measures assume that habit strength—or more precisely, the strength of the habitual instigation impulse—is directly tied to the amount of time it takes to think of a particular behavior when presented with a relevant cue, with faster times indicating stronger habits. As an example, Danner and colleagues (2011) asked respondents to list typical and atypical ways of pursuing common goals (e.g., eating lunch), thus creating a repository of goal-relevant behaviors (e.g., making a sandwich, going out to eat). Respondents were then shown the goals one at a time, followed by a relevant or irrelevant behavior, and asked to respond as quickly as possible whether the behavior could be used to achieve the goal. Habit strength was measured as the speed with which respondents correctly identified goal-relevant behaviors.[12]

Implicit measures of habit can make a strong claim to capturing automatic processes for the same reasons the IAT can—they rely on the speed with which brains trace mental associations, a process over which respondents have no direct control. To date, however, the use of implicit measures of habit is limited. This is due in part to the challenge of designing tasks that appropriately capture habit cues, which can vary from person to person—a kitchen might cue snacking for some people, while for others a work cubicle is the primary culprit (Orbell and Verplanken 2015). Consequently, implicit measures of habit often need to use personally relevant habit cues, making them more complex and burdensome to administer (see Neal et al. 2012, for an example).

Implicit measures also do not capture habitual execution. Although past work suggests that habitual instigation better predicts behavior (Gardner et al. 2016), habitual execution is also likely to interest sociologists because fluency in social behaviors directly affects individuals' ability to enact identities and interact successfully with others, skills that affect outcomes ranging from employment to mental health (Bourdieu 1984; Goffman 1959; Ilic et al. 2012; Miles 2014; Rivera 2012). Measuring habitual execution requires observing behaviors in conditions where deliberate thought is difficult or unlikely. One possibility would be to ask respondents to engage in a behavior while performing a cognitively demanding task and examining the fluency with which they execute the behavior.

Implicit measures of habitual instigation can be difficult to implement and, to my knowledge, measures of habitual execution do not yet exist. However, these challenges can be surmounted, and the payoff for doing so is likely to be substantial. With measures of both habitual impulse and execution, scholars will be well positioned to give empirical form to influential theoretical constructs like Giddens's practical consciousness and Bourdieu's *habitus*, both of which rely heavily on the idea habit (Bourdieu 1990; Giddens 1984). Researchers can also examine how instigation and execution interact to produce—or fail to produce—adaptive behaviors related to health, social interaction, and in other domains. Such investigations will help reveal the micro-level processes that give rise to consequential macro-level patterns.

19.4 Measures of Cultural Schemas

Schemas are organized mental representations that guide perception, facilitate understanding, and shape action, and are generally considered to be processed automatically (e.g., D'Andrade 1992; DiMaggio 1997; Goldberg 2011; Vaisey 2009). Schemas are perhaps the most widely used construct imported from the cognitive sciences, a fact that is not surprising when one considers that schemas can be seen as an overarching category that subsumes many other internalized phenomena: attitudes can be seen as the association between objects and evaluations, self-concepts as organized mental representations of the self, and habits as default patterns of response. Despite this wide theoretical coverage, most attempts at measuring schemas have focused on how people organize information about the social world. I review three types of schema measures below.

19.4.1 Relational and Correlational Class Analysis

Goldberg's (2011) relational class analysis (RCA) uses patterns of response similarity among individuals to uncover cultural schemas. Cultural schemas refer to mental representations that are shared by individuals in a given culture or subculture. Relational class analysis computes measures of relationality between all individuals, where relationality means that two individuals share a similar logic of responses, even if they differ in the absolute value of those responses (see Goldberg (2011) for mathematical details). For example, two people with opposing views on every measure of immigration would be seen as highly similar because the pattern of their responses is the same—either uniformly high or uniformly low. These individuals do not agree about immigration, but both organize information about it in the same way. Because schemas are defined as organized mental representations, relationality scores can be used to identify individuals who share cultural schemas.

Boutyline's (2017) correlational class analysis (CCA) is a modification of RCA. Using Goldberg's work as a starting point, Boutyline demonstrates that schemas can be formally defined as patterns of responses that can be made equivalent through linear transformations. He therefore replaces RCA's relationality measure with the absolute value of Pearson's correlation coefficient, which captures linear relationships between variables. His simulations suggest that this change improves the accuracy of the RCA algorithm, both in cases where connections between elements are constructed to be linear (which matches the theoretical basis for his approach), and when they are constructed to be nonlinear (which does not).[13]

Both RCA and CCA share a number of notable features and two limitations for identifying automatically processed cultural schemas.[14] Both techniques allow researchers to identify groups of people who share schemas, or in other words the cultural "class" that people belong to. These can be used to determine how widespread (or niche) different cultural schemas are, and to answer questions about the origins of different schematic representations and their effects on various outcomes. The pattern of responses within a given cultural class can also be examined to reveal the structure of its shared schema, including which elements are central and peripheral. These features make RCA and CCA valuable tools in answering questions about the origins, structure, and consequences of cultural schemas.

The first limitation shared by RCA and CCA is that they are usually applied to survey data. Surveys lend themselves well to easily measuring the wide range of cultural constructs necessary to map cultural schemas, but FC measures are not guaranteed to capture automatic cognition, as argued earlier. This means that analysts cannot assume that the schemas detected using RCA or CCA are processed automatically unless they are also willing to assume that all of the survey measures used were completed under conditions amenable to Type 1 processing. In many instances these assumptions will be untenable, and in most they will be untestable. Fortunately, there is nothing in the machinery of either method that requires that it be applied to survey data. Both RCA and CCA could be applied to attitudes and beliefs measured by IATs, AMPs, or other techniques that better capture automatic processes.[15] Collecting enough of these data for analysis might be challenging, but the payoff would be increased confidence that the measures actually reflect the operation of automatic processes.

The second limitation is that RCA and CCA do not measure schemas directly, but infer them from patterns of responses across individuals. That is, we must assume that the reason responses form the patterns they do is because people share cognitive representations, but this is not directly measured. This would be true even if RCA and CCA were applied to non-survey data—it is inherent in the method. This does not necessarily invalidate these techniques—after all, shared schemas are a plausible explanation of similarities in response patterns—but it does suggest a need for validation by comparison to a direct measure of schemas at the individual level, such as the concept association task described next.

19.4.2 Concept Association Task

A particularly promising measure of cultural schemas is the concept association task (CAT) recently developed by Hunzaker (2017, chapter 4). In this task, respondents are shown concepts related to a given topic two at a time and asked to indicate whether they are related (see Figure 19.3). Prior to beginning the task, respondents are told that concepts might be related because "one causes the other" or because "they commonly go together for some other reason," prompting them to think about relationality in broad

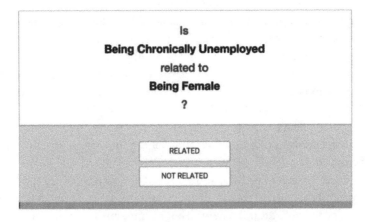

FIGURE 19.3 Task screen for the concept association task.

terms (12). To increase reliance on automatic processing, respondents are instructed to respond rapidly and using their initial instinct. All possible pairwise combinations of concepts are rated in this way, excluding logically incoherent pairs.

The CAT is time consuming (averaging 33 minutes to rate 490 concept pairs, for instance),[16] but the payoff is data on the entire network of conceptual associations that can be analyzed using any of the myriad network methods designed to detect central or structurally equivalent concepts, isolate groups (i.e., subcultural understandings), and so on. These data are direct measures of individual-level associations, which means that they can be used to detect cultural patterns, as RCA and CCA do, but also to probe individual variation in schematic representations. Additionally, the CAT can be adapted to capture associations between any set of concepts, but this places the onus on the researcher to accurately identify the concepts that apply to a given topic. Although this determination could be made post hoc, suggesting a "let's include it and see if it matters" approach, this will be generally unworkable in practice, because each new concept must be paired with all other concepts, which substantially increases the response burden on participants.[17]

The CAT instructs participants to rely on instinct and to respond rapidly, both of which should facilitate capturing automatic processes. Motivation to consciously control responses is likely to be low, given that respondents are instructed to state whether concepts are related (but not why), and because it is not obvious from the task instructions how the data will be used. These features alone, however do not guarantee automatic processing, because they do not necessarily capture unintentional or uncontrolled responding. To address this, data from the task can be supplemented with response times for each concept pair.[18] These might be used to identify and remove individuals who are likely to have deliberated on their answers (as suggested by high response times), or incorporated directly into analyses. In a network analysis, for instance, response times could be used as weights on the ties between concepts. Using the same logic as for IAT data, response times should be largely uncontrollable and reflect the strength of cognitive associations. Therefore, using response times in analyses would increase the probability that results reflect the operation of automatic processes. Response time data could be made even more useful by modifying the task to allow respondents to respond using keystrokes rather than mouse-clicks. This would increase the speed of responses and make it harder for deliberative processes to intervene.

19.4.3 Schema Inconsistency Measures

Schema inconsistency measures are based on the premise that events that violate cultural expectations seem unusual or bizarre to respondents, and so unexpectedness can be used to trace the contours of cultural schemas (Hunzaker 2016). Schemas about social status, for example, can be revealed by examining how unusual it seems to see different social groups in dominant positions. Would it be stranger to see a black man giving advice to a white man, or vice versa?

Hunzaker (2016) offers a measure of schema inconsistency drawn from affect control theory (ACT). Affect control theory sees emotions and behaviors as arising from differences between cultural expectations (schemas) and what is happening in a situation—or in other words, from schema inconsistency. For this reason, the ACT measure of this difference, known as deflection, can be used as a measure of schema inconsistency. Deflection can be thought of as an affective or intuitive sense for how unusual an event seems—it would be unremarkable to see a mother talking to her child, for instance (low deflection), but extremely unusual to see a mother beating her child (high deflection). The deflection expected from observing simple events of the form actor–behavior–object is almost always calculated using an online and freely available program known as Interact. The details of how Interact calculates deflection are rooted deeply in ACT and therefore beyond the scope of this chapter (see Heise 2007, for details); what is important for our purposes is that Interact relies on dictionaries of FC measures and standard equations derived from previous research to make its calculations. Interact therefore gives the deflection we would expect on average in a given population, not deflection at the individual level.

An alternative is to measure schema (in)consistency by directly asking respondents how unusual or typical different scenarios seem. Using this approach, Hunzaker (2016a) found that mean ratings of cultural consistency correlated highly with standard deflection measures across twenty scenarios ($|r| = 0.72$), but also showed substantial variation at the individual level, indicating heterogeneity in cultural schemas (see Figure 1 in Hunzaker 2016a). Although Hunzaker used this technique to validate ratings generated by Interact, direct ratings have much to recommend them in their own right. Direct ratings of schema (in)consistency are flexible—they can be used to find aggregate patterns, as Interact does, or to probe individual and subcultural variation. They also allow for descriptions of events that are more detailed and complex than is currently possible in Interact.

Do these measures of schema (in)consistency capture automatic processes? Both deflection and direct ratings of schema (in)consistency rely on self-report data, which means there is no built-in control over deliberate responding. Rating how unusual a particular scenario seems might rely on initial reactions, consistent with automatic processing, but might also result from a deliberate search of relevant memories and logical reasoning. Because deflection is calculated based on dictionaries of existing data, little more can be done to increase its reliance on automatic processes. Direct ratings could be improved by asking individuals to rely on their first impressions when responding, and to answer as quickly as possible. These modifications should reduce both the intention and opportunity to engage in conscious reflection, but—as with the CAT—cannot guarantee Type 1 processing.

An AMP format might also be adopted to circumvent respondents exercising intentional control over their answers. For instance, images or short descriptions of scenarios could be used as primes (e.g., "lazy poor"), with respondents asked to rate how usual or unusual the neutral images are. As with the traditional AMP, such an approach would be able to lay strong claim to tapping automatic processes. However, the efficacy of an AMP-approach to measuring schema-inconsistency remains to be tested.

19.5 COMPARING AUTOMATIC AND CONTROLLED COGNITION

Many questions of interest to sociologists and other social scientists are about the relative contributions of automatic and controlled cognition. Is racial prejudice intentional or not? How thoughtful are people about which cultural products they consume? Do people make important decisions rationally, or intuitively? Our first instinct might be to address these questions by comparing measures of deliberate and automatic cognition, but this will generally give an equivocal answer. This is because the measures of choice for deliberative cognition—FC items—also tap automatic cognition, and some measures that purport to tap automatic cognition can be affected by deliberation. Furthermore, measures of each type usually differ in ways that have nothing to do with cognition, such as how they are structured, which introduces noise into estimates (Payne et al. 2008).

One approach to resolving this dilemma is to use a process dissociation technique. Process dissociation refers to procedures that obtain separate estimates of automatic and controlled (i.e., deliberate) influences on a single outcome, using a single task. Because both estimates are derived from the same task, they are not confounded by measurement differences and give cleaner estimates of the underlying processes. This procedure was originally developed to understand memory, but has since been applied to social cognition and decision making (Jacoby et al. 1993; Payne and Bishara 2009; Yonelinas and Jacoby 2012).

Dissociating automatic from controlled influences requires observing conditions in which the two forms of cognition work in harmony—called inclusion conditions—and in opposition—called exclusion conditions. Differences between conditions in the probability of acting in accordance with one's intentions can be leveraged to obtain estimates of the contributions of each type of cognition to the outcome. For example, in a study of racial stereotypes, Payne (2001) asked respondents to quickly identify tools and weapons after being primed with black or white faces. Stereotypical associations between blacks and violence means that a black prime followed by a weapon creates an inclusion condition in which respondents might accurately identify the weapon either because they consciously recognize the weapon, or because their automatic reaction when seeing the black prime predisposes them to expect a weapon. In contrast, when a tool follows a black face, respondents' automatic reactions work against correct identification, creating an exclusion condition.

More formally, the probability of a "weapon" response in an inclusion condition is determined by the level of a person's control (C) over their response, or if control fails (1–C), by the strength of their automatic reaction (A)[19]:

$$P(\text{inclusion}) = C + A(1 - C)$$

In an exclusion condition, a "weapon" response will only occur if control fails, and automatic processes guide the response:

$$P(\text{exclusion})A(1-C)$$

These equations can be solved to obtain estimates of C and A:

$$C = P(\text{inclusion}) - P(\text{exclusion}) \tag{2}$$

$$A = P(\text{exclusion}) / (1 - C) \tag{3}$$

C and A can be interpreted as the influence of controlled and automatic processes on correctly identifying weapons.

Process dissociation can be used to capture automatic and controlled influences on any behavior for which inclusion and exclusion conditions can be created. The simplest way to do this is to design a task that captures a behavior, but varies intentions to perform that behavior, typically through instructions to participants. However, this will only work for behaviors that can be performed in controlled environments, such as voting, petition signing, resource allocation, and so forth. A more involved—but potentially more powerful—approach would be to follow respondents over time as they move through inclusion and exclusion conditions in a natural environment. For example, researchers could assess cultural consumption habits by observing the rate at which respondents consume cultural products like television programs for a week (inclusion condition), and then their consumption rate during a week in which they are instructed to avoid these activities (exclusion condition). The probabilities of consumption in each condition could then be used to calculate automatic (A) and controlled (C) influences on cultural consumption. Such a procedure could be applied to study influences on any number of consequential behaviors, such as social media use, health behaviors, interpersonal engagement, or housework.

Researchers using process dissociation techniques should be aware of a few considerations. First, because process dissociation requires observing inclusion and exclusion conditions, results will only be valid if respondents genuinely alter their behavioral intentions across conditions. This might not present much of a problem for short, artificial tasks, but might prove troublesome for tasks that stretch over several hours or days and occur in natural settings.[20] Second, researchers need to ensure that all extraneous influences on behavior are comparable across exclusion and inclusion conditions so that differences between them can be attributed to differences in intentions. This should be fairly straightforward in a laboratory, and might be approximated in a natural setting by collecting data during "typical" time periods in which one day is unlikely to vary in any meaningful way from another. Third, tasks should be designed to minimize floor and ceiling effects in both the inclusion and exclusion conditions (i.e., never performing or always performing a behavior). This makes it possible to use formulas 2 and 3 to

Table 19.3 Summary of Automatic Cognition Measures

Method	Taps Automatic Cognition?	Can be Modified to Better Tap Automatic Cognition?	Uses	Estimated Administration Time*†
Forced Choice (FC)	Uncertain	Yes	myriad (e.g., evaluations, habits, cultural associations)	often < 1 minute
Evaluations and Motivations				
Implicit Association Test (IAT)	Yes	–	evaluations (e.g., attitudes), self-concepts, cultural associations	4–6 minutes[b,c] (200 trials)
Brief Implicit Association Test (BIAT)	Yes	–	evaluations (e.g., attitudes), self-concepts, cultural associations	3–4 minutes[a,b] (96 trials)
Affect Misattribution Procedure (AMP)	Yes	–	evaluations (e.g., attitudes), self-concepts, cultural associations	3–5 minutes[a,b,c] (120 trials)
Habit				
SRHI	Uncertain	No	habitual instigation (can be modified for habitual execution)	1 minute[a]
Implicit measures of habit	Yes	–	habitual instigation	5 minutes[a]
Schemas				
Relational Class Analysis	Uncertain (if using FC items)	Yes	cultural associations	n/a
Correlational Class Analysis	Uncertain (if using FC items)	Yes	cultural associations	n/a
Concept Association Task	Likely	Yes	cultural associations	30 minutes (for 32 concepts)[b]
Schema Inconsistency Measures	Uncertain	Yes	cultural associations	< 1 minute
Comparing Automatic and Controlled Cognition				
Process dissociation	Yes	–	total automatic and controlled influences on behavior	varies

Notes: * Approximated from [a] = published accounts, [b] = personal communications with study authors, and [c] = personal experience.
† Reducing the number of trials will reduce the administration time for all implicit measures, but this will also reduce measurement reliability.

calculate C and A (Yonelinas and Jacoby 2012). Finally, researchers should recognize that process dissociation reveals *all* controlled and automatic influences on a given behavior, without revealing which types of constructs are involved. Process dissociation can thus provide evidence that automatic processing occurs, but sheds no light on whether it operates through attitudes, identities, perceptions, habits, or some combination of these constructs.

19.6 Conclusion

Recognition of the differences between deliberative and automatic cognition has greatly enriched sociological theory, but to date theoretical innovations have outstripped sociologists' empirical ability to test them. This chapter is an effort to give sociologists the tools they need to begin measuring automatic cognition so that theoretical claims can be evaluated in the crucible of rigorous empirical analysis. My focus has been intentionally selective—focusing on measures that are likely to be widely useful—and practical, outlining how measures work, how to use them, and how they can be improved. Table 19.3 presents a summary of key results. My hope is that scholars will apply and, as necessary, improve the measures presented here so that research in this important area can continue to progress.

Notes

The author thanks Hana Shepherd, Mary Beth Fallin Hunzaker, and Shyon Baumann for comments on earlier versions of this chapter.

1. See (Lizardo et al. 2016) for examples of other cultural domains that feature Type 1 processing.
2. Miles (2015) asked respondents to perform a survey-based task while remembering a random eight-digit number, and argued that this inhibited their ability to deliberate and forced a greater reliance on automatic processes. In theory, this approach could also be used to increase reliance on Type 1 processing while completing an FC item, thereby increasing the proportion of automaticity relative to deliberation captured by the measure. To my knowledge, the effectiveness of this technique has not been tested.
3. Gawronski and De Houwer (2014) review an extensive list of implicit measures.
4. The IAT and AMP can be implemented using commercial software packages like Inquisit, or free programs including FreeIAT and WebIAT. Both classes of products provide options for administering these tests online, so researchers are not restricted to local, lab-based samples.
5. Current best practice is to first remove trials with response times of 10,000 ms or above (trials where respondents might have become distracted), and delete subjects for whom 10 percent of more of trials are less than 300 ms (individuals who were not paying attention to the task; Greenwald et al. 2003).
6. The formula given here is the equal-weight average of D scores calculated from the initial and repeated blocks of trials.

7. Context-sensitivity could also contribute to the low test-retest reliability of the IAT (Gawronski et al. 2017).

8. These categories are for illustration only. To my knowledge, they have not been used in IAT measures, and have not been validated.

9. The presentation times shown in Figure 19.2 are those often used with college-aged samples. Shorter or longer durations can be used and still produce valid results. See Payne et al. (2005), particularly experiments 3 and 4, and Payne and Lundberg (2014), who recommend longer durations for studies of the general population.
   Note that Chinese pictographs are only neutral primes for individuals who cannot read Chinese or any language related to it.

10. Single attitude scores can suffer from individual biases toward giving a "pleasant" response, regardless of the prime. This can be corrected by measuring the bias directly (e.g., proportion of "pleasant" responses following neutral primes) and then using it as a control in analyses (Payne et al. 2005). Comparative attitudes do not suffer from this problem, as stable individual differences in "pleasant" responding are subtracted out when constructing the difference score.

11. Given that additional trials take approximately 1 second each, Payne and Lundberg (2014) recommend using at least 100 trials for the standard two-category task.

12. This type of approach could be adapted to measure any type of habit cue. To capture the behaviors cued by different situations, for instance, goal cues could be replaced with situations, and respondents asked to determine as quickly as possible whether different behaviors are appropriate in each context.

13. Statistical routines for both RCA and CCA are freely available as R packages.

14. See Baumann and de Laat (2012) for a discussion of using media representations to measure cultural schemas.

15. Currently, applying RCA to continuous measures would require converting them to an ordinal scale.

16. I obtained this average response time in private correspondence with Hunzaker.

17. A more efficient strategy would be to use RCA or CCA to identify cultural schemas and the elements that are associated with them, and then use the CAT on this restricted set of items to determine how well the cultural schemas are reflected in individual cognition.

18. Response times were collected by Hunzaker, but because they are not used in analyses I treat them here as separate from the method.

19. These equations assume that automatic and controlled processes are independent. Yonelinas and Jacoby (2012) summarize evidence for this claim.

20. Note, though, that temporary changes in intention (i.e., rationalization) might reasonably be seen as the result of strong automatic influences in a particular situation, and therefore consistent with the process dissociation approach.

References

Akinci, Cinla, and Eugene Sadler-Smith. 2013. "Assessing Individual Differences in Experiential (Intuitive) and Rational (Analytical) Cognitive Styles." *International Journal of Selection and Assessment* 21(2):211–21.

Babchishin, Kelly, Kevin Nunes, and Chantal Hermann. 2013. "The Validity of Implicit Association Test (IAT) Measures of Sexual Attraction to Children: A Meta-Analysis." *Archives of Sexual Behavior* 42(3):487–99.

Bar-Anan, Yoav, and Brian Nosek. 2014. "A Comparative Investigation of Seven Indirect Attitude Measures." *Behavior Research Methods* 46(3):668–88.

Baumann, Shyon, and Kim de Laat. 2012. "Socially Defunct: A Comparative Analysis of the Underrepresentation of Older Women in Advertising." *Poetics* 40(6):514–41.

Blair, Irene. 2002. "The Malleability of Automatic Stereotypes and Prejudice." *Personality and Social Psychology Review* 6(3):242–61.

Bourdieu, Pierre. 1984. *Distinction: A Social Critique of the Judgement of Taste*. Cambridge, MA: Harvard University Press.

Bourdieu, Pierre. 1990. *The Logic of Practice*. Stanford, CA: Stanford University Press.

Boutyline, Andrei. 2017. "Improving the Measurement of Shared Cultural Schemas with Correlational Class Analysis: Theory and Method." *Sociological Science* 4:353–93.

Burke, Peter J., and Jan E. Stets. 2009. *Identity Theory*. New York: Oxford University Press.

Cameron, C. Daryl, Jazmin L. Brown-Iannuzzi, and B. Keith Payne. 2012. "Sequential Priming Measures of Implicit Social Cognition: A Meta-Analysis of Associations with Behavior and Explicit Attitudes." *Personality and Social Psychology Review* 16(4):330–50.

Clerkin, Elise M., Bethany A. Teachman, April R. Smith, and Ulrike Buhlmann. 2014. "Specificity of Implicit-Shame Associations: Comparison across Body Dysmorphic, Obsessive-Compulsive, and Social Anxiety Disorders." *Clinical Psychological Science* 2(5):560–75.

Conner, Mark, Marco Perugini, Rick O'Gorman, Karen Ayres, and Andrew Prestwich. 2007. "Relations between Implicit and Explicit Measures of Attitudes and Measures of Behavior: Evidence of Moderation by Individual Difference Variables." *Personality and Social Psychology Bulletin* 33(12):1727–40.

D'Andrade, Roy G. 1992. "Schemas and Motivation." pp. 23–44 in *Human Motives and Cultural Models*, edited by R. G. D'Andrade and C. Strauss. New York: Cambridge University Press.

Danner, Unna N., Henk Aarts, Esther K. Papies, and Nanne K. de Vries. 2011. "Paving the Path for Habit Change: Cognitive Shielding of Intentions against Habit Intrusion." *British Journal of Health Psychology* 16(1):189–200.

Devos, Thierry, Que-Lam Huynth, and Mahzarin R. Banaji. 2012. "Implicit Self and Identity." pp. 155–79 in *Handbook of Self and Identity*, edited by M. R. Leary and J. P. Tangney. New York: Guilford Press.

Dewey, John. 1922. *Human Nature and Conduct : An Introduction to Social Psychology*. New York: H. Holt.

DiMaggio, Paul. 1997. "Culture and Cognition." *Annual Review of Sociology* 23(1):263–87.

DiMaggio, Paul, John Evans, and Bethany Bryson. 1996. "Have Americans' Social Attitudes Become More Polarized?" *American Journal of Sociology* 102(3):690.

Durkheim, Émile. 1982. *The Rules of Sociological Method*. 2nd ed. Edited by S. Lukes. New York: The Free Press.

Epstein, Seymour, Rosemary Pacini, Veronika Denes-Raj, and Harriet Heier. 1996. "Individual Differences in Intuitive-Experiential and Analytical-Rational Thinking Styles." *Journal of Personality and Social Psychology* 71(2):390–405.

Evans, Jonathan St. B. T. 2008. "Dual-Processing Accounts of Reasoning, Judgment, and Social Cognition." *Annual Review of Psychology* 59:255–78.

Evans, Jonathan St. B. T. 2010. "Intuition and Reasoning: A Dual-Process Perspective." *Psychological Inquiry* 21(4):313–26.

Evans, Jonathan St B. T. 2012. "Spot the Difference: Distinguishing between Two Kinds of Processing." *Mind and Society* 11(1):121–31.

Fazio, Russell H., and Michael A. Olson. 2003. "Implicit Measures in Social Cognition Research: Their Meaning and Use." *Annual Review of Psychology* 54(1):297–327.

Fiedler, Klaus, and Matthias Bluemke. 2005. "Faking the IAT: Aided and Unaided Response Control on the Implicit Association Tests." *Basic and Applied Social Psychology* 27(4):307–16.

Friese, Malte, Wilhelm Hofmann, and Michaela Wänke. 2008. "When Impulses Take Over: Moderated Predictive Validity of Explicit and Implicit Attitude Measures in Predicting Food Choice and Consumption Behaviour." *British Journal of Social Psychology* 47(3):397–419.

Gardner, Benjamin. 2015. "A Review and Analysis of the Use of 'Habit' in Understanding, Predicting and Influencing Health-Related Behaviour." *Health Psychology Review* 9(3):277–95.

Gardner, Benjamin, L. Alison Phillips, and Gaby Judah. 2016. "Habitual Instigation and Habitual Execution: Definition, Measurement, and Effects on Behaviour Frequency." *British Journal of Health Psychology* 21(3):613–30.

Gardner, Benjamin, Gert Jan De Bruijn, and Phillippa Lally. 2011. "A Systematic Review and Meta-Analysis of Applications of the Self-Report Habit Index to Nutrition and Physical Activity Behaviours." *Annals of Behavioral Medicine* 42(2):174–87.

Gauchat, Gordon. 2012. "Politicization of Science in the Public Sphere: A Study of Public Trust in the United States, 1974 to 2010." *American Sociological Review* 77(2):167–87.

Gawronski, Bertram, and Jan De Houwer. 2014. "Implicit Measures in Social and Personality Psychology." pp. 283–310 in *Handbook of Research Methods in Social and Personality Psychology*, edited by H. T. Reis and C. M. Judd. New York: Cambridge University Press.

Gawronski, Bertram, and Etienne P. LeBel. 2008. "Understanding Patterns of Attitude Change: When Implicit Measures Show Change, but Explicit Measures Do Not." *Journal of Experimental Social Psychology* 44(5):1355–61.

Gawronski, Bertram, Mike Morrison, Curtis E. Phills, and Silvia Galdi. 2017. "Temporal Stability of Implicit and Explicit Measures: A Longitudinal Analysis." *Personality and Social Psychology Bulletin* 43(3):300–12.

Giddens, Anthony. 1984. *The Constitution of Society*. Berkeley: University of California Press.

Glaser, Jack, and Eric D. Knowles. 2008. "Implicit Motivation to Control Prejudice." *Journal of Experimental Social Psychology* 44(1):164–72.

Goffman, Erving. 1959. *The Presentation of Self in Everyday Life*. New York: Anchor Books.

Goldberg, Amir. 2011. "Mapping Shared Understandings Using Relational Class Analysis: The Case of the Cultural Omnivore Reexamined." *American Journal of Sociology* 116(5):1397–436.

Gray, Kurt, Chelsea Schein, and Adrian F. Ward. 2014. "The Myth of Harmless Wrongs in Moral Cognition: Automatic Dyadic Completion from Sin to Suffering." *Journal of Experimental Psychology: General* 143(4):1600–615.

Greenwald, Anthony G., T. Andrew Poehlman, Eric Luis Uhlmann, and Mahzarin R. Banaji. 2009. "Understanding and Using the Implicit Association Test: III. Meta-Analysis of Predictive Validity." *Journal of Personality and Social Psychology* 97(1):17–41.

Greenwald, Anthony G., Mahzarin R. Banaji, and Brian A. Nosek. 2015. "Statistically Small Effects of the Implicit Association Test Can Have Societally Large Effects." *Journal of Personality and Social Psychology: Attitudes and Social Cognition* 108(4):553–61.

Greenwald, Anthony G., and Shelly D. Farnham. 2000. "Using the Implicit Association Test to Measure Self-Esteem and Self-Concept." *Journal of Personality and Social Psychology* 79(6):1022–38.

Greenwald, Anthony G., Debbie E. McGhee, and Jordan L. K. Schwartz. 1998. "Measuring Individual Difference in Implicit Cognition: The Implicit Association Test." *Journal of Personality and Social Psychology* 74(6):1464–80.

Greenwald, Anthony G., Brian A. Nosek, and Mahzarin R. Banaji. 2003. "Understanding and Using the Implicit Association Test: I. An Improved Scoring Algorithm." *Journal of Personality and Social Psychology* 85(2):197–216.

Gross, Neil. 2009. "A Pragmatist Theory of Social Mechanisms." *American Sociological Review* 74(3):358–79.

Hagger, Martin S., Amanda L. Rebar, Barbara Mullan, Ottmar V. Lipp, and Nikos L. D. Chatzisarantis. 2015. "The Subjective Experience of Habit Captured by Self-Report Indexes May Lead to Inaccuracies in the Measurement of Habitual Action." *Health Psychology Review* 9(3):296–302.

Hahn, Adam, and Bertram Gawronski. Forthcoming. "Implicit Social Cognition." in *The Stevens' Handbook of Experimental Psychology and Cognitive Neuroscience*, edited by J. T. Wixted. Malden, MA: Wiley.

Han, H. Anna, Sandor Czellar, Michael A. Olson, and Russell H. Fazio. 2010. "Malleability of Attitudes or Malleability of the IAT." *Journal of Experimental Social Psychology* 46(2):286–98.

Heise, David R. 2007. *Expressive Order: Confirming Sentiments in Social Actions*. New York: Springer.

Hofmann, Wilhelm, Bertram Gawronski, Tobias Gschwendner, Huy Le, and Manfred Schmitt. 2005. "A Meta-Analysis on the Correlation between the Implicit Association Test and Explicit Self-Report Measures." *Personality and Social Psychology Bulletin* 31(10):1369–85.

Hofmann, Wilhelm, Tobias Gschwendner, Malte Friese, Reinout W. Wiers, and Manfred Schmitt. 2008. "Working Memory Capacity and Self-Regulatory Behavior: Toward an Individual Differences Perspective on Behavior Determination by Automatic versus Controlled Processes." *Journal of Personality and Social Psychology* 95(4):962–77.

Hunzaker, M. B. Fallin. 2016. "Cultural Sentiments and Schema-Consistency Bias in Information Transmission." *American Sociological Review* 81(6):1223–50.

Hunzaker, M. B. Fallin. 2017. "Cultural Cognition and Bias in Information Transmission." Duke University. https://dukespace.lib.duke.edu/dspace/handle/10161/14405.

Ilic, Marie, Jost Reinecke, Gerd Bohner, Röttgers Hans-Onno, Thomas Beblo, Martin Driessen, et al. 2012. "Protecting Self-Esteem from Stigma: A Test of Different Strategies for Coping with the Stigma of Mental Illness." *International Journal of Social Psychiatry* 58(3):246–57.

Imhoff, Roland, Alexander F. Schmidt, Johanna Bernhardt, Andreas Dierksmeier, and Rainer Banse. 2011. "An Inkblot for Sexual Preference: A Semantic Variant of the Affect Misattribution Procedure." *Cognition & Emotion* 25(4):676–90.

Jacoby, Larry L., Jeffrey P. Toth, and Andrew P. Yonelinas. 1993. "Separating Conscious and Unconscious Influences of Memory: Measuring Recollection." *Journal of Experimental Psychology: General* 122(2):139–54.

Joas, Hans. 1996. *The Creativity of Action*. Chicago: University of Chicago Press.

Karpinski, Andrew, and Ross B. Steinman. 2006. "The Single Category Implicit Association Test as a Measure of Implicit Social Cognition." *Journal of Personality and Social Psychology* 91(1):16–32.

Knowles, Eric, and Kaiping Peng. 2005. "White Selves: Conceptualizing and Measuring a Dominant-Group Identity." *Journal of Personality and Social Psychology* 89(2):223–41.

Labrecque, Jennifer S., and Wendy Wood. 2015. "What Measures of Habit Strength to Use? Comment on Gardner (2015)." *Health Psychology Review* 7199(July):1–17.

Lane, Kristin A., Mahzarin R. Banaji, Brian A. Nosek, and Anthony G. Greenwald. 2007. "Understanding and Using the Implicit Association Test: IV What We Know (So Far) about the Method." *Implicit Measures of Attitudes* 97(1):59–102.

Lizardo, Omar. 2009. "Is a 'Special Psychology' of Practice Possible? From Values and Attitudes to Embodied Dispositions." *Theory and Psychology* 19(6):713–27.

Lizardo, Omar. 2012. "Embodied Culture as Procedure: Rethinking the Link between Personal and Objective Culture." *Studies across Disciplines in the Humanities and Social Sciences* 12:70–86.

Lizardo, Omar, and Michael Strand. 2010. "Skills, Toolkits, Contexts and Institutions: Clarifying the Relationship between Different Approaches to Cognition in Cultural Sociology." *Poetics* 38(2):205–28.

Lizardo, Omar, Robert Mowry, Brandon Sepulvado, Marshall A. Taylor, Justin Van Ness, and Michael Wood. 2016. "What Are Dual Process Models ? Implications for Cultural Analysis in Sociology." *Sociological Theory* 34(4):287–310.

Martin, John Levi, and Matthew Desmond. 2010. "Political Position and Social Knowledge." *Sociological Forum* 25(1):1–26.

Miles, Andrew. 2014. "Addressing the Problem of Cultural Anchoring: An Identity-Based Model of Culture in Action." *Social Psychology Quarterly* 77(2):210–27.

Miles, Andrew. 2015. "The (Re)genesis of Values: Examining the Importance of Values for Action." *American Sociological Review* 80(4):680–704.

Neal, David T., Wendy Wood, Jennifer S. Labrecque, and Phillippa Lally. 2012. "How Do Habits Guide Behavior? Perceived and Actual Triggers of Habits in Daily Life." *Journal of Experimental Social Psychology* 48(2):492–8.

Nosek, Brian A., and Mahzarin R. Banaji. 2001. "The Go/No-Go Association Task." *Social Cognition* 19(6):625–64.

Nosek, Brian A., Yoav Bar-Anan, N. Sriram, Jordan Axt, and Anthony G. Greenwald. 2014. "Understanding and Using the Brief Implicit Association Test: Recommended Scoring Procedures." *PLoS ONE* 9(12):e110938.

Nosek, Brian A., and Jeffrey J. Hansen. 2008. "The Associations in Our Heads Belong to Us: Searching for Attitudes and Knowledge in Implicit Evaluation." *Cognition and Emotion* 22(4):553–94.

Nosek, Brian A., Frederick L. Smyth, N. Sriram, Nicole M. Lindner, Thierry Devos, Alfonso Ayala, et al. 2009. "National Differences in Gender–Science Stereotypes Predict National Sex Differences in Science and Math Achievement." *Proceedings of the National Academy of Sciences of the United States of America* 106(26):10593.

Nosek, Brian, Anthony Greenwald, and Mahzarin Banaji. 2005. "Understanding and Using the Implicit Association Test: II. Method Variables and Construct Validity." *Personality and Social Psychology Bulletin* 31(2):166–80.

Olson, Michael A., and Russell H. Fazio. 2004. "Reducing the Influence of Extrapersonal Associations on the Implicit Association Test: Personalizing the IAT." *Journal of Personality and Social Psychology* 86(5):653–67.

Orbell, Sheina, and Bas Verplanken. 2015. "The Strength of Habit." *Health Psychology Review* 9(3):311–17.

Oswald, Frederick L., Gregory Mitchell, Hart Blanton, James Jaccard, and Philip E. Tetlock. 2013. "Predicting Ethnic and Racial Discrimination: A Meta-Analysis of IAT Criterion Studies." *Journal of Personality and Social Psychology: Attitudes and Social Cognition* 105(2):171–92.

Ottoni-Wilhelm, Mark, and Rene Bekkers. 2010. "Helping Behavior, Dispositional Empathic Concern, and the Principle of Care." *Social Psychology Quarterly* 73(1):11–32.

Payne, B. Keith. 2001. "Prejudice and Perception: The Role of Automatic and Controlled Processes in Misperceiving a Weapon." *Journal of Personality and Social Psychology* 81(2):181–92.

Payne, B. Keith, and Anthony J. Bishara. 2009. "An Integrative Review of Process Dissociation and Related Models in Social Cognition." *European Review of Social Psychology* 20(1):272–314.

Payne, B. Keith, Melissa A. Burkley, and Mark B. Stokes. 2008. "Why Do Implicit and Explicit Attitude Tests Diverge? The Role of Structural Fit." *Journal of Personality and Social Psychology* 94(1):16–31.

Payne, B. Keith, Clara Michelle Cheng, Olesya Govorun, and Brandon D. Stewart. 2005. "An Inkblot for Attitudes: Affect Misattribution as Implicit Measurement." *Journal of Personality and Social Psychology* 89(3):277–93.

Payne, Keith, and Kristjen Lundberg. 2014. "The Affect Misattribution Procedure: Ten Years of Evidence on Reliability, Validity, and Mechanisms." *Social and Personality Psychology Compass* 8(12):672–86.

Penke, Lars, Jan Eichstaedt, and Jens B. Asendorpf. 2006. "Single-Attribute Implicit Association Tests (SA-IAT) for the Assessment of Unipolar Constructs: The Case of Sociosexuality." *Experimental Psychology* 53(4):283–91.

Richetin, Juliette, Giulio Costantini, Marco Perugini, and Felix Schönbrodt. 2015. "Should We Stop Looking for a Better Scoring Algorithm for Handling Implicit Association Test Data? Test of the Role of Errors, Extreme Latencies Treatment, Scoring Formula, and Practice Trials on Reliability and Validity: e0129601." *PLoS One* 10(6).

Rivera, Lauren A. 2012. "Hiring as Cultural Matching: The Case of Elite Professional Service Firms." *American Sociological Review* 77(6):999–1022.

Sava, Florin A., Laureniu P. Maricuoiu, Silvia Rusu, Irina MacSinga, Delia Virga, Clara Michelle Cheng, et al. 2012. "An Inkblot for the Implicit Assessment of Personality: The Semantic Misattribution Procedure." *European Journal of Personality* 26(6):613–28.

Shepherd, Hana. 2011. "The Cultural Context of Cognition: What the Implicit Association Test Tells Us about How Culture Works." *Sociological Forum* 26(1):121–43.

Smith, Colin Tucker, and Brian A. Nosek. 2011. "Affective Focus Increases the Concordance between Implicit and Explicit Attitudes." *Social Psychology* 42(4):300–13.

Sriram, Natarajan, and Anthony G. Greenwald. 2009. "The Brief Implicit Association Test." *Experimental Psychology* 56(4):283–94.

Srivastava, Sameer B., and Mahzarin R. Banaji. 2011. "Culture, Cognition, and Collaborative Networks in Organizations." *American Sociological Review* 76(2):207–33.

Stanovich, Keith E., and Maggie E. Toplak. 2012. "Defining Features versus Incidental Correlates of Type 1 and Type 2 Processing." *Mind and Society* 11(1):3–13.

Stieger, Stefan, Anja S. Goritz, Andreas Hergovich, and Martin Voracek. 2011. "Intentional Faking of the Single Category Implicit Association Test and the Implicit Association Test." *Psychological Reports* 109(1):219–30.

Vaisey, Stephen. 2009. "Motivation and Justification: A Dual-Process Model of Culture in Action." *American Journal of Sociology* 114(6):1675–715.

Verplanken, Bas, and Sheina Orbell. 2003. "Reflections on Past Behavior: A Self-Report Index of Habit Strength." *Journal of Applied Social Psychology* 33(6):1313–30. Retrieved November 18, 2016 from http://journals.scholarsportal.info/detailsundefined.

Weber, Max. 1920. *Economy and Society*. Edited by G. Ross and C. Wittich. Berkeley: University of California Press.

Yonelinas, Andrew, and Larry Jacoby. 2012. "The Process-Dissociation Approach Two Decades Later: Convergence, Boundary Conditions, and New Directions." *Memory and Cognition* 40(5):663–80.

CHAPTER 20

METHODS FOR STUDYING THE CONTEXTUAL NATURE OF IMPLICIT COGNITION

HANA R. SHEPHERD

CULTURE as shared understandings of concepts, objects, people, behaviors, and ways of interacting with others is the result of dynamic, relational processes. These processes that support the formation of culture in the sense of shared meanings, and the way that culture shapes action, depend on the interaction between culture at the individual level, including culture as implicit cognition, and forms of culture that exist publicly, independent of individuals. This contention relies on two key premises. The first is that implicit cognition (which goes by a variety of other labels, such as "automatic cognition" or "unconscious processing" or "automatic processing" or "implicit associations," see Evans [2008]) is an important aspect of how we might understand how culture is stored and processed by individuals, and thus how it operates to shape behavior. The second premise is that processes of implicit cognition are fundamentally dependent on the social, physical, and cultural environmental of an individual in two senses: first, in the sense of the immediate, relatively short-term patterns of *activation* derived from immediate situation and context, and second, in the sense of the chronic patterns of exposure that inscribe learning as relatively durable sets of cognitive associations, what I refer to as *acquisition*. I provide a brief justification for these premises and then turn to a discussion of some methods that can help us develop our theoretical arguments about culture based on these premises.

20.1 PREMISE ONE: IMPLICIT COGNITION IS CENTRAL TO HOW CULTURE IS STORED AND PROCESSED AT AN INDIVIDUAL LEVEL

Implicit cognition is a key feature of culture, as measured on the individual level. Within the field of social cognition, researchers often distinguish between cognitive structures that store information about previous experiences (e.g., schemas, stereotypes, attitudes, scripts), and cognitive processes involved in building and using those stored representations (e.g., attention, interpretation, inference) (see Bodenhausen and Morales 2013).[1] Sociologists can think about implicit cognition in two ways that map onto this distinction: as a way that information is stored that can be inaccessible to conscious awareness and thus not something that individuals can report on in interviews or in everyday talk (what Schacter [1987] labeled nondeclarative or implicit memory), and as processes that occur automatically, without cognitive control; require few mental resources; and may occur in parallel with other processes (e.g., Evans 2008). When I refer to implicit cognition, I am referring to both automatic processing and implicit memory. In this chapter, I use the term "implicit cognitive representations" to refer to information stored implicitly, and "implicit cognitive processes" to refer to cognitive processes that operate beneath conscious awareness.

Given that much of human cognition occurs beneath awareness or conscious control, an interest in the role of cognition in culture requires an interest in the role of *implicit cognition* in culture. Scholars drawing on cognition to understand culture have acknowledged the central place of implicit cognition (e.g., DiMaggio 1997; Lizardo 2017; Patterson 2014; Shepherd 2011; Vaisey 2009). For example, Lizardo (2017) distinguishes between elements of culture that are personal—located in individuals or assessed at the individual level—and elements that are public (supraindividual), where the personal elements are further divided into declarative and nondeclarative forms. Nondeclarative elements of culture are those to which individuals do not have conscious access. These nondeclarative cultural forms—implicit cognition—are a key element of culture and cultural analysis.

20.2 PREMISE TWO: THE ACTIVATION AND ACQUISITION OF IMPLICIT COGNITION DEPENDS ON THE ENVIRONMENT

Implicit cognition depends on the social, physical, and cultural environmental of an individual. In the rest of the chapter, I use "context" as shorthand for these multiple elements of the external environment that are relevant to implicit cognition. These elements include patterns of social co-presence and interaction, sets of social roles and group norms, physical spaces and the shared meanings of those spaces, symbols, signs, rituals, organizational messages, institutional logics, narratives, discourse, and ideology. The relationship between cognition and social settings has been a core concern of sociologists of culture (e.g., DiMaggio 1997; Cerulo 1997, 2006; Martin 2002; Mohr 1998). Many sociologists have explicitly called for an analysis of how individual-level elements of culture interact with supraindividual, environmental elements of culture. Culture, for DiMaggio (1997:274) "inheres not in the information [that individuals have], nor in the schemata [individual mental structures], nor in the symbolic universe [external symbolic environment], but in the interactions among them." In a similar vein, Lizardo (2017:110) calls for work that addresses the interface between personal and public forms of culture: "a key line of future work is to begin to theorize how dynamic enculturation, cultural activation, and cultural use processes link with dispositional, relational, and institutional/environmental mechanisms across settings to generate important phenomena of both theoretical and practical interest" (110). This chapter suggests ways in which culture researchers can take up this call.

Context affects implicit cognition in two ways: by shaping what concepts are *activated* in a situation and by shaping what implicit cognitive representations are *acquired* by individuals. Information that is stored in memory may become activated by thoughts related to that information, or by external stimuli associated with that information. When concepts are associated with each other in memory, often because they have been learned or experienced together, the activation of one leads to faster and more consistent activation of the other concept (Collins and Loftus 1975). A way of testing the relationship between implicitly stored information is through the use of priming, where exposure to some stimulus, whether conscious or not, activates related concepts such that they are more accessible to an individual. The activation of concepts guides how individuals interpret situations and how they understand which interpretations are appropriate for which contexts. Exposure to different types of primes can affect subsequent behavior (see Wheeler and DeMarree 2009, for a discussion of the psychological mechanisms posited as relevant to this process: direct activation of behavioral representations, goal activation, biases in person, situation, and self-perception).

The *acquisition* of implicit cognition refers to how individuals learn and store a complex network of associations in memory (e.g., Strauss and Quinn 1997). This diffuse network of stored associations influences how new information is perceived and evaluated (Smith 1998). These associations often take many, repeated instances to learn. Once encoded, they are relatively durable, such that they cannot be easily altered (see Lizardo et al. 2016, for more on the acquisition of implicit cognition). Acquisition and activation are closely related: at the neural level, learning is described by Hebb's rule, that neurons that "fire together, wire together" (Löwel and Singer 1992); the simultaneous activation of neurons leads to stronger connections between them, increasing the chance of activating together subsequently. Both activation and acquisition depend on the social, physical, and cultural environment. This observation resonates with existing work within sociology, especially by Bourdieu, regarding how location within a social field shapes associations, perceptions, physical actions, and how one carries one's body (e.g., Bourdieu 1990; Wacquant 2004).

One piece of evidence for this claim regarding the role of context in activation and acquisition of implicit cognition comes from what some have called a "replication crisis" in the fields of social and cognitive psychology, from which many methods for assessing implicit cognition are borrowed. The psychologist Brian Nosek and others spearheaded the Reproducibility Project, which exhorted colleagues to rerun 100 published experiments, some of which used implicit cognition measures, to assess the extent of the issue. Replicators found clear replication in only 39 percent of the replicated studies (Open Science Collaboration 2015; though see Gilbert et al. 2016, for a critique of these results). One attempt of the many that have been advanced to explain the high rate of nonreplication is particularly relevant for sociologists' purposes. Van Bavel et al. (2016) coded all of the reproduced studies for the extent to which the study depended on some *context* for its conceptualization. They identified context as related to time period or era (for example, before or after the Great Recession), widely circulating models (for example, the value of individualistic vs. collectivistic models of personhood), physical location (for example, rural vs. urban settings), or demographic characteristics (for example, a racially diverse setting vs. a predominantly white setting). They found that net of a number of controls, studies with greater contextual sensitivity (as assessed on a 5-point scale) were less likely to replicate. If we extrapolate a bit from these findings, we can use this as evidence regarding the importance of context, broadly defined, on a number of measures, including implicit cognition measures. We can add this result to those from another body of evidence within social and cognitive psychology that illustrates how context (for example, the race of experimenter, physical location, exposure to particular symbols) affects implicit cognition measures (see Shepherd 2011, for a review of these effects). These findings indicate the value of examining the role of context in shaping implicit cognition, and the activation of implicit cognition in particular.

I want to distinguish this approach to studying culture from what Vaisey (2008) characterizes as "Skinnerian"—a perspective that privileges the power of situations in shaping action and thus, he argues, relegates culture to a justificatory role rather than a motivational role in behavior. Assuming that cognition is fundamentally intertwined with the social, physical, and cultural environment is not the same as positing no role of cognition and interior mental states in action. Instead, the assumption that the external environment affects the activation and acquisition of cognitive concepts relies on a well-established literature in social and cognitive psychology that implicit cognition is instantiated within contexts (see Lizardo and Strand 2010). At the end of this chapter, I return to this premise to address the issue of the boundaries of this argument. In particular, I look to evidence regarding effects of context on implicit cognition over time, and what evidence about the noneffects of context on implicit cognition tell us about the interplay between this form of personal culture and context.

20.3 METHODS AND EVIDENCE

I now turn to a discussion of a set of findings and methods that can inform the study of the relationship between context and implicit cognition. The set of methods I review here is in no way comprehensive, and the selection is weighted toward areas in which there is some existing work on which culture researchers can build. Some of the methods described are well adapted to using implicit cognition measures, while others may lend insight into the processes by which context affects implicit cognition without using implicit measures. Implicit measures refer to a family of measures that have been developed to assess implicit cognition in an indirect manner. These measures include the Implicit Association Test (IAT), evaluative priming, the Go/No-Go Association Test, Sorting Paired Features Task, Extrinsic Affective Simon Task, Affect Misattribution Procedure, and others (see Nosek et al. 2011, or Uhlmann et al. 2012, for a more expansive list; see also Miles (this volume) for a review of some of these measures). Measures of implicit cognition need not themselves be implicit in the sense that respondents are not aware of what the measures are accessing. One of the tasks for sociologists using concepts of culture going forward is to articulate the types of explicit or declarative measures that can provide insight into traces of implicit cognition (see Miles this volume, or McDonnell 2014).

20.3.1 Acquisition of Implicit Cognition: Evidence from Project Implicit

We might use evidence regarding systematic differences between populations in implicit cognition measures as indicative of how individuals acquire implicit cognition and how context may affect that acquisition. To my knowledge, the only data on this comes from Project Implicit (http://www.projectimplicit.net/), which has been collecting information about various IATs online from individuals across the world since 1998. The website allows individuals to select and take different IATs and it records the results of those tests, along with demographic characteristics and location of participants based on their IP addresses. These IATs include tests of individual's implicit (below-awareness) evaluations (positive or negative) of, for example, black and white faces, old and young faces, fat and thin faces, gay and straight people, and disabled and abled people. Some of these IATs also assess implicit associations beyond simple positive-negative evaluations. For example, one IAT assesses implicit associations between males and females, and science and liberal arts, while another assesses implicit associations between black and white faces and harmless or harmful objects. Because participants select into participation, we cannot consider the results to be representative and we must be careful about the kinds of claims that can be made based on the data. Project Implicit participants are generally younger, more liberal, more educated, and more likely to be female than the US population overall (Xu et al. 2014). But we can use the information for broadly illustrative purposes.

The average score on the black-white IAT (which assesses how quickly an individual associates black or white faces with positive or negative words) varies by social groups. Men, individuals over 65, individuals who identify as strongly conservative, and whites all have higher average implicit measures of prowhite preference (Xu et al. 2014). Project Implicit data also suggests substantial variation by US state in average implicit measures of prowhite preference among white participants (see Figure 20.1).

As a test of the correlates of these state-based differences in racial implicit associations, Rae et al. (2015) aggregate data to state-level averages of the black-white IAT among white and black participants, separately (over 890,000 Project Implicit participants). They correlate the ratio of black to white residents in the state with these state-level black-white IAT measures. Even controlling for state education level, median income, percentage of US citizens, economic inequality, population density, political orientation, and whether the state was in the Confederacy, they find that a higher ratio of black to white residents is associated with stronger implicit measures of in-group preference for both white and black respondents. They replicate the results at the county level, and they note that the ratio of black to white residents at the county level is highly correlated with a measure of segregation. This work does not test the possible mechanisms underlying this effect, but the results suggest that processes of intergroup contact and the construction of intergroup threat (e.g., Blumer 1958; Riek et al. 2006) interact to shape systematic cognitive associations with racial groups. The correspondence between higher ratios of black to white residents and racial segregation at the county level suggests that negative outgroup racial meanings develop in the context of intergroup proximity without substantial contact, or, with systematically unequal contact. Sociologists might specify the mechanisms by which this type of social context may translate into systematic differences in implicit cognitive representations in the form of evaluations of racial groups.

Using Project Implicit data on implicit evaluations of overweight people, Marini et al. (2013) examine the role of national context in the sense of the national obesity rate on implicit beliefs about obesity, accounting for individual body mass index and individual identity. Using data from over 338,000 individuals in 71 countries over 4 years, they find that higher national rates of obesity are associated with more negative implicit evaluations of overweight people. They posit, but do not test, three mechanisms accounting for this effect: that a greater prevalence of obesity might prompt greater public discussion about it, increasing its stigma; that more obesity may prompt more public symbols in advertisements for gyms, healthy eating, and diet plans that emphasize slim bodies as ideal; that the association between thinness and social status is stronger, and obesity is thus more stigmatized, when the signal is more rare, as in countries with higher obesity rates. These mechanisms suggest different ways that the social and cultural environment might shape systematic differences in implicit cognitive representations in the form of evaluations of people based on weight.

Other research points to the possibility for change in implicit cognition in a population over time. Westgate et al. (2015) use Project Implicit data to examine change in implicit measures of preference for heterosexual individuals over homosexual individuals from 2006 to 2013 and find a reduction in the implicit measure of preference for heterosexual individuals of 13.4 percent over the period. They find greater declines by particular sub-populations: Hispanics, Whites, women, people who identify as politically liberal, and younger participants. They note that explicit measures of preference for heterosexuals declined by 26 percent over the same period. Again, we do not know what specific aspects of context affected change in implicit cognition measures, and how they affected some subpopulations differently than others, but the findings provide a starting place for further inquiry.

20.3.2 Laboratory Experiments

Existing work, mainly in psychological (vs. sociological) social psychology, uses experiments to manipulate aspects of the environment in order to assess the effect on implicit cognition. I have reviewed many of these studies elsewhere (see Shepherd 2011), but I present a selection of these studies as an example of the effects of the social, physical, and cultural context on implicit cognition. As the examples illustrate, the aspects of context that affect implicit cognition are broadly construed and merit further theorizing.

20.3.2.1 *Social Context*

A body of research demonstrates the effect of others on implicit measures of prejudice and suggests that social context affects the activation of implicit cognition (Sinclair et al. 2014). This work draws on shared reality theory (see Hardin and Higgins 1996), that people prefer, and are thus motivated, to share perceptions of the social world with others. When individuals want to affiliate with the person or persons they are interacting with, their beliefs and perspectives become more similar that person or persons. For example, white participants have lower implicit measures of bias when the experimenter is black, rather than white (Lowery et al. 2001). Further, when the likability of the experimenter was manipulated, white participants with a likable experimenter who was wearing an antiracism t-shirt, had lower implicit measures of prejudice than those who interacted with a less likable experimenter with an antiracism t-shirt (Sinclair et al. 2005). This "social tuning" effect was not observed when there was an antiracism poster on the wall, compared to on an individual's t-shirt, illustrating the distinctly social nature of the process (Lun et al. 2007). Other work finds that people pay more attention to and better remember external cultural symbols when they believe similar others are also paying attention to those symbols (e.g., Shteynberg 2010), though whether this is an implicit or explicit process is unclear.

20.3.2.2 *Physical Context*

In an exciting test of the effect of context on behavior, Berger et al. (2008) analyzed voting patterns for a 2000 Arizona initiative proposing to raise the state sales tax to increase funding for schools. Controlling for a variety of factors, they find that voters randomly assigned to vote in schools were more likely to support the initiative than those individuals assigned to vote in nonschool locations. They follow the analysis with a laboratory study where participants were shown either school-related images or nonschool location images, and find the same effect on voting preferences. They conclude that instead of simply activating proschool attitudes among those who already supported schools, exposure to school images primed school associations among all participants, regardless of their preexisting attitudes. They argue that stimuli in the physical and cultural (in the sense that schools carry a set of cultural and institutional meanings) environment altered voting behavior through activating particular sets of associations.

A study on the effect of where individuals grow up, and particularly the level of racial composition in those places, informs how we might think about the effect of place on the acquisition of implicit cognitive representations. Knowles and Peng (2005) examine the relationship between white students' implicit associations between themselves and being white using the IAT and the proportion of nonwhites in the zip code in which they primarily grew up. They found that these students were more likely to have implicit associations between themselves and being white, a measure of white identity, if they grew up in zip codes with a higher proportion of nonwhites. They also link higher scores on the implicit measure of white identity to more shame and embarrassment in reaction to a story about the lynching of black Americans. We can see this work as pointing to how physical context, in combination with social context, in the sense of opportunities for interracial interactions, informs the acquisition of implicit cognition.

20.3.2.3 *Cultural Context*

Experimental research on the effects of exposure to a symbol illustrates the potential effect of cultural context—public forms of culture—on implicit cognition. Ferguson and Hassin (2007) exposed research participants to an image of the American flag by asking them to place their signed consent form on a textbook with the image. Participants did not report seeing the flag image, indicating that they were exposed to the image beneath their conscious awareness. They then completed an implicit cognition measure, a word-stem completion task, related to concepts of war and aggression. They found that exposure to the flag activated war and aggression concepts, but only for those participants who regularly consumed the news. The effect was not mediated by participants' political orientation. They argue that exposure to the symbol of the flag, even beneath conscious awareness, increased the accessibility of concepts of aggression and war for news-consuming individuals.

This work is relevant to issues of both the activation of implicit cognition by the cultural environment (in this case, the symbol of the American flag) and the manner in which the cultural environment (in the form of news media) affects the acquisition of particular implicit representations. Presumably, those participants who regularly consume the news acquired particular representations, whether or not they had conscious access to them, between the US and aggressive acts abroad, in a way that those who did not regularly consume the news did not. Thus, the symbol of the US activated those representations for the news consumers and did not for the non–news consumers. There are a relatively small number of studies that primarily address heterogeneity in impact of primes that activate implicit cognitive representations based on different social groups (see Wheeler and Berger 2007, for an example based on gender). This is an area that merits further work.

20.3.3 Survey Experiments

Survey experiments provide an opportunity for culture researchers to examine the role of context on both the activation and acquisition of implicit cognition. Survey experiments use random assignment of participants to different conditions in order to examine the effects of treatment on participants' responses within the survey. These survey experiments can be conducted on nonrepresentative populations, which limits the generalizability of their conclusions, but they can also be conducted on nationally representative populations, as are experiments using the Time-sharing Experiments for the Social Sciences (TESS) platform (see Mutz 2011). Often, researchers use different vignettes across conditions to examine the effect of different information or different frames on participants' responses (see Jackson and Cox 2013, for a review). Existing survey experiments often posit, but do not directly test, an effect of a context or prime on implicit cognition.

Survey experiments have been widely used in other fields such as political science and psychology, which have been particularly interested in the effects of primes on explicitly reported attitudes (see Sniderman 2011; see Schuman and Bobo 1988, for work in sociology using survey experiments to examine racial attitudes). Public opinion researchers have rigorously examined the effect of survey design (including question wording, question order, and answer format) and the social context of survey administration (including the race of interviewer) on survey responses (e.g., Couper et al. 2004; Krosnick 1999; McDermott 2011; Schaeffer and Presser 2003; Schwarz and Hippler 1991; Schwarz and Strack 1991). For example, Deaton and Stone (2013) find that asking political questions directly before questions about overall well-being reduces reported levels of well-being the equivalent amount as an 89 percent reduction in income.

Culture and cognition researchers may adapt these insights for their own purposes. Survey experiments can capture a subset of or proxies for the types of supraindividual cultural forms researchers are interested in, particularly institutional logics, frames, narratives, discourses, and symbols as well as physical and social situational cues. They are, however, limited in their ability to capture other important elements of context. Survey experiments using nationally representative samples that explore heterogeneity in the effect of context on implicit cognition may also be able to inform researchers about differences between groups in implicit cognitive representations and in processes of the acquisition of implicit cognition. Survey experiments assessing the impact of context on implicit cognition may rely on the principles of implicit activation of concepts even if they do not directly measure implicit cognition, or they may use measures or proxy measures for assessing implicit cognition.

Survey experiments that do not use implicit cognition measures still rely on features of implicit activation. Survey manipulations make certain concepts, beliefs, or cognitive associations more accessible to respondents, thus shaping their responses (Tourangeau and Rasinski 1988). An example of this use of survey experiments, which does not directly measure implicit cognition, but which relies on the principle that contextual information structures what cognitive representations are accessible, is work by Pedulla and Thebaud (2015). These researchers provide participants with different information about the extent of supportive work–family policies across conditions, and examine participants' preferences for particular work–family relationship structures. They find more support for egalitarian relationship structures in the context of supporting work–family policies, demonstrating that preferences that are often treated as stable individual differences are in fact responsive to perceived institutional constraints, though the effects differ by gender and education. In a similar example, Marshall and Shepherd (2018) randomly assigned young women at a university to different frames for thinking about their futures (no frame, career-focused frame, or financial limitations frame) and examined the effect on their stated preferences about how many children they want to have and their ideal work-family configuration. Frames changed the desired family size and work–family configuration for women who were less religious, but not for women who were more religious. These examples suggest that researchers can use survey experiments in order to examine the effect of frames and contextual information on implicit cognition, and, importantly, to distinguish between individuals for whom frames and contextual information changes their responses and those for whom the information does not change their responses. Importantly, this latter concern points to systematic differences in the nature of implicit cognitive representations by social groups.

In another example of survey experiments that directly rely on increasing the salience of particular concepts, Williams et al. (2008) find that making participants' racial identity more salient to them by having them answer questions about their ethnic group led African American participants to report more contamination anxiety, a measure used to diagnose obsessive-compulsive disorder, compared to African American participants whose racial identity was not made salient, and compared to white participants. Making racial identity salient likely relies on implicit cognitive processes, as participants likely did not have conscious awareness that the racial identity questions were activating particular concepts for them. These effects also varied by regional location, where participants in the South reported higher contamination anxiety than those outside the South, regardless of race. The authors argue these differences are the result of different attitudes and practices about cleanliness, and responses to cleanliness-related racial stereotypes. This type of evidence can contribute to theorizing on the types of contextual information that impact implicit cognition.

Other survey experiments may employ implicit cognition measures or proxies for implicit cognition to examine the relationship between contextual information and implicit cognition. Researchers can use implicit cognition measures as outcome variables and examine the effect of vignettes, frames, or other context-specific information on implicit measures. For example, Pinkston (2015) uses a nationally representative sample to examine the effects of exposure to admired black individuals on IAT scores by race. He finds that the IAT scores for white participants are more susceptible to the presence of an admired black individual than are those of black participants. Pinkston refers to this as a racial malleability gap in implicit associations. This work points toward an analysis both of how contextual information (the presence of an admired black individual) shapes the activation of implicit cognition and how it may vary based on underlying differences in the acquisition of implicit cognitive representations, in this case, based on racial identity.

Researchers could also use implicit cognition measures to test proposed mechanisms in order understand the relationship between contextual primes and other outcomes. There is little work in this area, which presents a key opportunity for researchers. In one preliminary example, Shepherd and Marshall (2018) examine how different frameworks shape how participants report what keywords are relevant to their decisions about having children, where keywords are used as a proxy for the activation of implicit cognitive representations. Researchers can also build in response time measures in online surveys as a means of assessing how closely associated particular concepts are, with the idea that concepts that are closely associated or easily processed will result in lower response times than those that are less closely associated or easily processed.

Generally, survey experiment methodology provides many opportunities for culture and cognition researchers to develop empirical knowledge about the relationship between context and implicit cognition.

20.3.4 Implicit Cognition Measures in Natural Settings

Culture and cognition researchers can also adapt existing implicit cognition measures and methods that are usually constrained to laboratories for use in the field. Some of these adaptations are straightforward: migrating implicit cognition measures to online platforms or physical devices that can be used in the field. For example, work by researchers interested in the effect of context on implicit cognition regarding the environment adapted a version of the IAT (self-other/nature-built environment) for use on tablets, and administered the IAT to individuals going into zoos compared to individuals leaving zoos. They found that while there was no change in explicit reports of connectedness to nature between those entering and exiting the zoo, individuals had higher scores of implicitly measured connectedness with nature when leaving zoos than when entering (Bruni and Schultz 2010).

Other measures are more involved, but have the potential to yield exciting insights for culture and cognition researchers. Researchers have increasingly adopted the use of mobile devices to collect ecological momentary assessment (EMA) data to study a variety of social phenomena (Mehl and Conner 2012, Shiffman et al. 2008). Often, these studies use time-based prompts to request that respondents complete brief surveys several random times a day during waking hours (e.g., Dunton et al. 2014a, 2014b). In a novel approach, a team of health researchers has used implicit measures in EMA on mobile devices (see Waters et al. 2007; Waters et al. 2014; Waters and Li 2008; Waters et al. 2012). These researchers, who are primarily interested in linking implicit measures to tobacco- and drug-use relapse, have verified the utility of implicit measures on mobile devices. This research is valuable for two reasons. First, it allows for an assessment of the effect of the environment on implicit cognition measures in real time, and second, it allows for repeated testing within individuals, providing information on the extent to which the same individuals vary on implicit measures across time.

For example, Marhe et al. (2013) asked heroin-dependent participants in an addiction treatment center to carry around a mobile device for a week. These participants completed implicit cognition measures (the Stroop test of attentional bias and the IAT, assessing positive or negative associations with heroin) both at random times during the day and when they felt the temptation to use drugs. They found that greater attentional bias toward heroin and more positive implicit attitudes about heroin assessed at the times when participants felt temptation predicted drug-use relapses. Importantly for our purposes, they also conducted a within-subject analysis and found variation in attentional bias toward heroin increased before relapsing. This research provides proof of concept for culture researchers that measures of implicit cognition can vary within individuals.

In another example, Epstein et al. (2014) conducted a study in Baltimore where they gave mobile devices to twenty-seven opioid-dependent multiple drug users who were receiving methadone treatment. These participants were tracked over sixteen weeks and randomly prompted to complete mood, stress, and cravings measures three times per day. While these researchers used explicit measures, instead of implicit cognition measures, they also collected geolocation data (latitude, longitude, and altitude) and combined that with data on the extent of social disorder (e.g., condition of the buildings, presence of trash or graffiti, condition of sidewalks) in the city blocks participants traveled through. Thus, the researchers could begin to link subjective and emotional measures, as well as behavior (drug use), to physical locations characterized by social order or disorder. They found substantial variation in measures of mood, stress, and cravings based on physical surroundings. At both the neighborhood level and the census tract level, these researchers found, in contrast to their hypotheses, that greater social disorder in the environment was associated with lower ratings of drug cravings, negative mood, and stress. These researchers do not focus on within-individual variation in their measures, but their results suggest powerful effects of physical space on cognitive and emotional measures. While they do not assess the mechanisms linking social disorder to their results, their findings provide a starting point for examining the relevance of physical space to implicit cognitive processes.

Though the existing research that uses mobile devices to assess implicit cognition asks questions very different from the ones that most concern culture researchers, their experiences adapting implicit cognition measures for mobile devices are instructive. A key issue for adapting these measures is how much variation within individuals across time is due to environmental effects and how much is measurement error. These researchers note that there is more reaction time error on mobile devices, but they argue adequate information aggregated across observations can reduce measurement noise. Researchers using these measures need to account for large variation between subjects in baseline speed with implicit cognition measures that use reaction time; there is more variation between individuals for some implicit cognition measures (like the IAT) than others (like the Stroop test). These researchers estimate that about 50 percent of variance in IAT scores is due to within-individual variation across time and space compared to between-individual variation (Marhe et al. 2013).

As an example of the type of research that might be done using implicit measures in the field, Krivo et al. (2019) conducted research that links survey responses, geographic information, a mobile EMA survey, and IAT data in order to assess how individuals experience their social and physical world through their day, and how this is linked to forms of inequality. The integration of real-time explicit and implicit cognition assessments also allows for an examination of the mechanisms linking context and cognition in a way that standard retrospective interviews and survey methods cannot.

20.3.5 Methods for Assessing Feedback Effects

While the proposed set of methods I review here is in no way comprehensive, I want to finish by highlighting promising methods that address a fundamental theoretical concern: the extent of feedback between how context activates and leads to the acquisition of implicit cognition and the nature of that context itself. It is not enough to assume a unidirectional impact of context on implicit cognition; given how individuals' behaviors may change as a result of the acquisition and activation of implicit cognition, these behaviors themselves may feed back to shape the kinds of social and cultural cues that are available in the environment (for an articulation of the value of a process-based account of culture and cognition that highlights feedback effects, see Shepherd 2014). This is an important area of inquiry for culture and cognition researchers.

One example of this type of work uses transmission experiments to illustrate a feedback effect between implicit cognitive representations and what information is socially available in the world. In transmission experiments, researchers generally provide information to individuals and ask them to transmit the information to others, and then assess what information is transmitted and what is not transmitted. Individuals are more likely to transmit information that is consistent with existing patterns of implicit associations (or schematic representations), which shapes what kind of information is available for others to process (Hunzaker 2014, 2016; Lyons and Kashima 2001). This type of process is particularly clear when considering certain social media platforms, where individuals selectively share information available to them in their environments with others, which then affects what is available for others to consume. Hunzaker (2016) highlights the relevance of this process to the persistence of stereotypes, where "the selective transmission of schema-consistent information reinforces existing cultural biases, increasing the likelihood of receiving information that reaffirms cultural stereotypes and impeding the spread of information that might challenge or disconfirm them" (3). While current work does not examine which features of context shape the activation of implicit cognitive representations, like schemas, and thus what information is shared, the methods could easily be adapted to do so.

Another example of feedback effects is work that uses an agent-based modeling paradigm to illustrate the dynamic relationships between social context, implicit cognition, and the cultural environment. Shaw (2015) applies insights regarding implicit cognitive representations to examine the conditions under which shared meaning emerges in a collective using an agent-based modeling framework. The model assumes a strong social influence on implicit cognitive representations such that they are strengthened when an agent's interaction partner employs the same representation. The model produces results based on the structure of social ties: within interacting subgroups, over time, agents begin to consistently use the implicit cognitive representations of their neighbors. In 89 percent of the models, the systems did not converge to complete consensus, where each member used the same implicit cognitive representation. Most commonly, there was substantial variation in which implicit cognitive representation subgroups settled on. This model provides an account of how the social environment and the distribution of particular implicit cognitive representations among individuals, shapes the use (or activation) of particular implicit cognitive representations, which then changes what implicit cognitive representations are available and used in the social and cultural environment. These are promising methods for building models of culture that are sensitive to processes over time.

20.4 DISCUSSION

Human cognition is a dynamic process produced through interactions with the body and the external environment, and it may extend beyond the boundaries of an individual body (Robbins and Aydede 2009). Taking the dynamic and embedded nature of cognition seriously as part of culture redirects our analytical attention to nature of the social, physical, and cultural environment itself and to the processes involved in the interplay between implicit cognition and context. It suggests the need for a concerted and precise sensitivity to context. One task in front of cultural and cognition researchers is to build cumulative knowledge regarding the mechanisms linking the relationship between the social, physical, and cultural environment, and cognition. This may take the form of systematically testing whether and under what conditions particular elements of context shape the acquisition and activation of implicit cognition about some important area with behavioral implications. We may ask: What is the extent of variation in the activation of implicit cognition within a specific context across individuals and groups? How can we understand variation in the acquisition of cognitive structures when exposed to similar contexts across individuals and groups? What features of the social, physical, and cultural environment matter most to the acquisition and activation of implicit cognition? How do the effects of features of the environment on implicit cognition vary across time and the life course?

We might use examples of studies where context, in its multiple forms, did *not* result in changes in implicit cognition measures as a chance to illustrate some of these outstanding issues. One obvious issue, most relevant to studies that are concerned with the effects of context on the activation of implicit associations, is how long those effects last over time. In one study, researchers tested the effect of contextual interventions on multiple implicit measures of racial bias and uniformly found that the effects do not last longer than several hours to several days (Lai et al. 2016). In contrast, Weisbuch et al. (2009) find effects on implicit self-esteem over the course of a week, based on an initial interaction with a sympathetic experimenter. This discrepancy suggests that the domain of implicit cognitive representations (racial associations or evaluations of the self) may be relevant to the extent to which the effect of context on activation of implicit cognition persists over time.

A lack of effects of context on implicit cognition measures may give us information about the extent of malleability of implicit cognitive activation, or it may inform us about which features of the environment are relevant to cognition. In an example of a null effect of the cultural environment, Schmidt and Nosek (2010) use cross-sectional data from over 470,000 Project Implicit participants to examine the effect of the election of Barack Obama on implicit racial associations over a period of 2.5 years before and after the election. They find no effect of symbolic meaning of a black president on aggregate patterns of implicit racial associations in this dataset. It is unclear whether these null effects are due to the time frame that the researchers use (e.g., is a longer time frame needed to see widespread changes in implicit associations?) or whether exemplars at a national level, like a president, are themselves insufficient to shape the activation or acquisition of implicit racial associations. In another example, Bruni et al. (2015) fail to find an effect of certain elements of participation in an environmental program for children on implicit measures of connectedness to nature, prompting questions about whether the implicit cognitive representations of the environment and self are less malleable, whether effects might depend on age, whether aspects of the program were insufficient to shape implicit learning, or whether there was too much noise in the data.

One might argue that this evidence merely provides additional support for what we already know regarding the importance of dual-process theories of cognition, and the theoretical concepts, such as habitus, that are supported by this type of approach to cognition. Taking this perspective, we could conclude that the research and methods reviewed here provides tools that social scientists from various fields and subfields might employ in the service of developing more precise accounts of action, but it does not alter any theoretical pillars. I would argue, however, that the evidence presented here suggests two broader possible theoretical lessons for sociology. One theoretical lesson is that sociologists need to focus specifically on the mechanisms and processes within and across contexts relevant to social action. Drawing on pragmatist and symbolic interactionist traditions, sociologists across various subfields refer to the central importance of the role of context in understanding action. But we have yet to collectively identify and aggregate accounts of core processes and mechanisms involved in the translation of contexts to cognition and action. We can use the kind of research described in this chapter to be far more precise about, for example, the processes by which individuals acquire and deploy habitus across the life course, or the processes captured by the broad term, "socialization."

Beyond this, however, one might read the evidence presented here regarding the interaction of forms of cognition and social, physical, and cultural context, as providing support for a more radical reorientation within the field. Collins (2004) provides one such articulation of this reorientation, as he advances an account of interaction ritual chains that theorizes *situations* as the fundamental unit of analysis, and sees individuals as a product of chains of situations over time. Taking this kind of approach would move us away from conceptualizing of the mechanisms by which individuals and contexts interact, which still suggests the sovereignty, and perhaps primacy, of the individual, to studying situations and contexts primarily. As Collins (2004) puts it, "A situation is not merely the result of the individual who comes into it, nor even a combination of individuals.... Situations have laws or processes of their own; and that is what IR [interaction ritual] theory is about" (5). The body of work regarding the contextual nature of cognitive processes seems poised to contribute most to these last two theoretical approaches. Developing these theoretical approaches may yield valuable contributions to both theories of culture and theories of action.

Notes

I thank Andrew Miles for helpful comments on this chapter.

1. I sidestep nuances regarding the exact nature of those cognitive structures (e.g., associative networks, schemas, exemplars, parallel distributed processes; see Smith 1998). I should note, however, that models that posit a parallel distributed processing mechanism for memory—where cognition emerges from the activation of interconnected networks of neurons—elide this distinction between representations and process (see Conrey and Smith 2007; Rumelhart et al. 1986; Smith 1998).

References

Berger, Jonah, Marc Meredith, and S. Christian Wheeler. 2008. "Contextual Priming: Where People Vote Affects How They Vote." *Proceedings of the National Academy of Sciences* 105:8846–9.

Blumer, Herbert. 1958. "Race Prejudice as a Sense of Group Position." *Pacific Sociological Review* 1:3–7.

Bodenhausen, Galen V., and Javier R. Morales. 2013. "Social Cognition and Perception." pp. 225–46 in *Handbook of Psychology*, 2nd ed., Vol. 5, edited by I. Weiner, H. A. Tennen, and J. M. Suls. Hoboken, NJ: John Wiley and Sons.

Bourdieu, Pierre. 1990. *The Logic of Practice*. Stanford, CA: Stanford University Press.

Bruni, Coral M., and P. Wesley Schultz. 2010. "Implicit Beliefs about Self and Nature: Evidence from an IAT Game." *Journal of Environmental Psychology* 30:95–102.

Bruni, Coral M., Patricia L. Winter, P. Wesley Schultz, Allen M. Omoto, and Jennifer J. Tabanico. 2015. "Getting to Know Nature: Evaluating the Effects of the Get to Know Program on Children's Connectedness with Nature." *Environmental Education Research* 23:1–20.

Cerulo, Karen A. 1997. "Identity Construction." *Annual Review of Sociology* 23:385–409.

Cerulo, Karen A. 2006. *Never Saw It Coming: Cultural Challenges to Envisioning the Worst.* Chicago: University of Chicago Press.

Collins, Allan M., and Elizabeth F. Loftus. 1975. "A Spreading Activation Theory of Semantic Processing." *Psychological Review* 82:407–28.

Collins, Randall. 2004. *Interaction Ritual Chains.* Princeton, NJ: Princeton University Press.

Conrey, Frederica R., and Eliot R. Smith. 2007. "Attitude Representation: Attitudes as Patterns in a Distributed, Connectionist Representational System." *Social Cognition* 25:718–35.

Couper, Mick P., Tourangeau, Roger, Conrad, Frederick G., and Crawford, Scott D. 2004. "What They See Is What We Get: Response Options for Web Surveys." *Social Science Computer Review* 22(1):111–27.

Deaton, Angus, and Arthur A. Stone. 2013. "Do Context Effects Limit the Usefulness of Self-Reported Wellbeing Measures?" Research Program in Development Studies Working Paper #288.

DiMaggio, Paul. 1997. "Culture and Cognition." *Annual Review of Sociology* 23:263–87.

Dunton, Genevieve F., Eldin Dzubur, Keito Kawabata, Brenda Yanez, Bin Bo, and Stephen Intille. 2014a. "Development of a Smartphone Application to Measure Physical Activity Using Sensor-Assisted Self-Report." *Frontiers in Public Health* 2:1–13.

Dunton, Genevieve F., Jimi Huh, Adam Leventhal, Nathaniel Riggs, Donna Spruijt-Metz, Mary Ann Pentz, et al. 2014b. "Momentary Assessment of Affect, Physical Feeling States, and Physical Activity in Children." *Health Psychology* 33:255–63.

Epstein, David H., Matthew Tybruski, Ian M. Craig, Karran A. Phillips, Michelle L. Jobes, Massoud Vahabzadeh, et al. 2014. "Real-Time Tracking of Neighborhood Surroundings and Mood in Urban Drug Misusers: Application of a New Method to Study Behavior in Its Geographical Context." *Drug and Alcohol Dependence* 134:22–9.

Evans, Jonathan St. B. T. 2008. "Dual-Process Accounts of Reasoning, Judgment, and Social Cognition." *Annual Review of Psychology* 59:255–78.

Ferguson, Melissa, and Ran R. Hassin. 2007. "On the Automatic Association between America and Aggression for News Watchers." *Personality and Social Psychology Bulletin* 33:1632–47.

Gilbert, Daniel T., Gary King, Stephen Pettigrew, and Timothy D. Wilson. 2016. "Comment on 'Estimating the Reproducibility of Psychological Science.'" *Science* 351:1037.

Hardin, Curtis D., and E. Tory Higgins. 1996. "Shared Reality: How Social Verification Makes the Subjective Objective." pp. 28–84 in *Handbook of Motivation and Cognition: Foundations of Social Behavior*, Vol. 3, edited by R. Sorrentino and E. T. Higgins. New York: Guilford Press.

Hunzaker, Mary Beth Fallin. 2014. "Making Sense of Misfortune: Cultural Schemas, Victim Redefinition, and the Perpetuation of Stereotypes." *Social Psychology Quarterly* 77:166–84.

Hunzaker, Mary Beth Fallin. 2016. "Cultural Sentiments and Schema-Consistency Bias in Information Transmission." *American Sociological Review* 81:1223–50.

Jackson, Michelle, and David R. Cox. 2013. "The Principles of Experimental Design and Their Application in Sociology." *Annual Review of Sociology* 39:27–49.

Knowles, Eric D., and Kaiping Peng. 2005. "White Selves: Conceptualizing and Measuring a Dominant-Group Identity." *Journal of Personality and Social Psychology* 89:223–41.

Krivo, Lauren, Zaire Dinzey-Flores, Janne Lindqvist, and Hana Shepherd. 2019. "Developing an Application for Assessing Respondent Experiences of Their Surroundings in Real Time." National Science Foundation, Sociology Program. EAGER Grant.

Krosnick, Jon. 1999. "Survey Research." *Annual Review of Psychology* 50:537–67.

Lai, Calvin K., Allison L. Skinner, Erin Cooley, Sohad Murrar, Markus Brauer, Thierry Devos, et al. 2016. "Reducing Implicit Racial Preferences: II. Intervention Effectiveness across Time." *Journal of Experimental Psychology: General* 145:1001–16.

Lizardo, Omar. 2017. "Improving Cultural Analysis: Considering Personal Culture in Its Declarative and Nondeclarative Modes." *American Sociological Review* 82:88–115.

Lizardo, Omar, Robert Mowry, Brandon Sepulvado, Dustin S. Stoltz, Marshall A. Taylor, Justin Van Ness, et al. 2016. "What are Dual Process Models? Implications for Cultural Analysis in Sociology." *Sociological Theory* 34:287–310.

Lizardo, Omar, and Michael Strand. 2010. "Skills, Toolkits, Contexts and Institutions: Clarifying the Relationship between Different Approaches to Cognition in Cultural Sociology." *Poetics* 38:204–27.

Löwel, Siegrid, and Wolf Singer. 1992. "Selection of Intrinsic Horizontal Connections in the Visual Cortex by Correlated Neuronal Activity." *Science* 255:209–12.

Lowery, Brian S., Curtis D. Hardin, and Stacey Sinclair. 2001. "Social Influence Effects on Automatic Racial Prejudice." *Journal of Personality and Social Psychology* 5:842–55.

Lun, Janetta, Stacey Sinclair, Erin R. Whitchurch, and Catherine Glenn. 2007. "(Why) Do I Think What You Think? Epistemic Social Tuning and Implicit Prejudice." *Journal of Personality and Social Psychology* 93:957–72.

Lyons, Anthony, and Yoshihisa Kashima. 2001. "The Reproduction of Culture: Communication Processes Tend to Maintain Cultural Stereotypes." *Social Cognition* 19:372–94.

Marhe, Reshmi, Andrew J. Waters, Ben J. M. van de Wetering, and Ingmar H. A. Franken. 2013. "Implicit and Explicit Drug-Related Cognitions during Detoxification Treatment Are Associated with Drug Relapse: An Ecological Momentary Assessment Study." *Journal of Consulting and Clinical Psychology* 81:1–12.

Marini, Maddalena, Natarajan Sriram, Konrad Schnabel, Norbert Maliszewski, Thierry Devos, Bo Ekehammar, et al. 2013. "Overweight People Have *Low* Levels of Implicit Weight Bias, but Overweight Nations Have *High* Levels of Implicit Bias." *PLOS ONE.*

Marshall, Emily A., and Hana Shepherd. 2018. " Fertility Preferences and Cognition: Religiosity and Experimental Effects of Decision Context on College Women." *Journal of Marriage and the Family* 80:521–36.

Martin, John Levi. 2002. "Power, Authority, and the Constraint of Belief Systems." *American Journal of Sociology* 107:861–904.

McDermott, Monica. 2011. "Racial Attitudes in City, Neighborhood, and Situational Contexts." *Annals of the American Academy of Political and Social Science* 634:153–73.

McDonnell, Terence E. 2014. "Drawing Out Culture: Productive Methods to Measure Cognition and Resonance." *Theory and Society* 43:247–74.

Mehl, Matthias R., and Tamlin S. Conner, eds. 2012. *Handbook of Research Methods for Studying Daily Life.* New York: Guilford Press.

Miles, Andrew. 2019. "An Assessment of Methods for Measuring Automatic Cognition" (this volume).

Mohr, John W. 1998. "Measuring Meaning Structures." *Annual Review of Sociology* 24:345–70.

Mutz, Diana. 2011. *Population-Based Survey Experiments.* Princeton, NJ: Princeton University Press.

Nosek, Brian A., Carlee B. Hawkins, and Rebecca S. Frazier. 2011. "Implicit Social Cognition: From Measures to Mechanisms." *Trends in Cognitive Sciences* 15:152–9.

Open Science Collaboration. 2015. "Estimating the Reproducibility of Psychological Science." *Science* 349(6251):943–51.

Patterson, Orlando. 2014. "Making Sense of Culture." *Annual Review of Sociology* 40:1–30.

Pedulla, David S., and Sarah Thebaud. 2015. "Can We Finish the Revolution? Gender, Work-Family Ideals, and Institutional Constraint." *American Sociological Review* 80:116–39.

Pinkston, Kevin. 2015. "The Black-White Malleability Gap in Implicit Racial Evaluations: A Nationally Representative Study." *Journal of Social Psychology* 155:189–203.

Rae, James R., Anna-Kaisa Newheiser, and Kristina R. Olson. 2015. "Exposure to Racial Out-Groups and Implicit Race Bias in the United States." *Social Psychological and Personality Science* 6:535–43.

Riek, Blake M., Eric W. Mania, and Samuel L. Gaertner. 2006. "Intergroup Threat and Outgroup Attitudes: A Meta-Analytic Review." *Personality and Social Psychology Review* 10:336–53.

Robbins, Philip, and Murat Aydede. 2009. "A Short Primer on Situated Cognition." pp. 3–10 in *The Cambridge Handbook of Situated Cognition*, edited by P. Robbins and M. Aydede. Cambridge: Cambridge University Press.

Rumelhart, David E., Geoffrey E. Hinton, and James L. McClelland. 1986. "A General Framework for Parallel Distributed Processing." pp. 45–76 in *Parallel Distributed Processing: Explorations in the Microstructure of Cognition*. Volume 1: Foundations, edited by David E. Rumelhart, James.L. McClelland, and the PDP Research Group. Cambridge, MA: MIT Press.

Schacter, Daniel L. 1987. "Implicit Memory: History and Current Status." *Journal of Experimental Psychology: Learning, Memory, and Cognition* 13:501–18.

Schaeffer, Nora C., and Stanley Presser. 2003. "The Science of Asking Questions." *Annual Review of Sociology* 29:65–88.

Schmidt, Kathleen, and Brian A. Nosek. 2010. "Implicit (and Explicit) Racial Attitudes Barely Changed during Barack Obama's Presidential Campaign and Early Presidency." *Journal of Experimental Social Psychology* 46:308–14.

Schuman, Howard, and Lawrence Bobo. 1988. "Survey-Based Experiments on White Racial Attitudes toward Residential Integration." *American Journal of Sociology* 94:273–99.

Schwarz, Norbert, and Hans-Jürgen Hippler. 1991. "Response Alternatives: The Impact of Their Choice and Ordering." pp. 41–56 in *Measurement Error in Surveys*, edited by P. Biemer, R. Groves, N. Mathiowetz, and S. Sudman. Chichester, UK: Wiley.

Schwarz, Norbert, and Fritz Strack. 1991. "Context Effects in Attitude Surveys: Applying Cognitive Theory to Social Research." pp. 31–50 in *European Review of Social Psychology*, edited by M. Hewstone and W. Strobe. Chichester, UK: Wiley.

Shaw, Lynette. 2015. "Mechanics and Dynamics of Social Construction: Modeling the Emergence of Culture from Individual Mental Representation." *Poetics* 52:75–90.

Shepherd, Hana. 2011. "The Cultural Context of Cognition: What the Implicit Association Test Tells Us about How Culture Works." *Sociological Forum* 26:121–43.

Shepherd, Hana. 2014. "Culture and Cognition: A Process Account of Culture." *Sociological Forum* 29:1007–11.

Shepherd, Hana, and Emily A. Marshall. 2018. "The Implicit Activation Mechanism of Culture: A Survey Experiment on Associations with Childbearing." *Poetics* 69:1–14.

Shiffman, Saul, Arthur A. Stone, and Michael R. Hufford. 2008. "Ecological Momentary Assessment." *Annual Review of Clinical Psychology* 4:1–32.

Shteynberg, Garriy. 2010. "A Silent Emergence of Culture: The Social Tuning Effect." *Journal of Personality and Social Psychology* 99:683–89.

Sinclair, Stacey, and Andreana C. Kenrick, and Drew S. Jacoby-Senghor. 2014. "Whites' Interpersonal Interactions Shape, and Are Shaped by, Implicit Prejudice." *Policy Insights from the Behavioral and Brain Sciences* 1:81–7.

Sinclair, Stacey, Brian S. Lowery, Curtis D. Hardin, and Anna Colangelo. 2005. "Social Tuning of Automatic Racial Attitudes: The Role of Affiliative Motivation." *Journal of Personality and Social Psychology* 89:583–92.

Smith, Eliot A. 1998. "Mental Representation and Memory." pp. 391–445 in *Handbook of Social Psychology*, edited by D. Gilbert, S. Fiske, and G. Lindzey. New York: McGraw-Hill.

Sniderman, Paul M. 2011. "The Logic and Design of the Survey Experiment." pp. 102–114 in *Cambridge Handbook of Experimental Political Science*, edited by James Druckman et al. New York: Cambridge University Press.

Strauss, Claudia, and Naomi Quinn. 1997. *A Cognitive Theory of Cultural Meaning*. Cambridge: Cambridge University Press.

Tourangeau, Roger, and Kenneth A. Rasinski. 1988. "Cognitive Processes Underlying Context Effects in Attitude Measurement." *Psychological Bulletin* 103:299–314.

Uhlmann, Eric Luis, Keith Leavitt, Jochen I. Menges, Joel Koopman, Michael Howe, and Russell E. Johnson. 2012. "Getting Explicit about the Implicit: A Taxonomy of Implicit Measures and Guide for Their Use in Organizational Research." *Organizational Research Methods* 15:553–601.

Vaisey, Stephen. 2008. "Socrates, Skinner, and Aristotle: Three Ways of Thinking about Culture in Action." *Sociological Forum* 23:603–13.

Vaisey, Stephen. 2009. "Motivation and Justification: A Dual-Process Model of Culture in Action." *American Journal of Sociology* 114:1675–715.

Van Bavel, Jay J., Peter Mende-Siedlecki, William J. Brady, and Diego A. Reinero. 2016. "Contextual Sensitivity in Scientific Reproducibility." *Proceedings of the National Academy of Social Sciences* 113:6454–9.

Wacquant, Loic J. D. 2004. *Body and Soul: Notebooks of an Apprentice Boxer*. New York: Oxford University Press.

Waters, Andrew J., Reshmi Marhe, and I. H. A. Franken. 2012. "Attentional Bias to Drug Cues is Elevated before and during Temptations to Use Heroin and Cocaine." *Psychopharmacology* 219:909–21.

Waters, Andrew J., Brian L. Carter, Jason D. Robinson, David W. Wetter, Cho Y. Lam, and Paul M. Cinciripini. 2007. "Implicit Attitudes to Smoking are Associated with Craving and Dependence." *Drug and Alcohol Dependence* 91:178–86.

Waters, Andrew J., and Yisheng Li. 2008. "Evaluating the Utility of Administering a Reaction Time Task in an Ecological Momentary Assessment Study." *Psychopharmacology* 197:25.

Waters, Andrew J., Edwin H. Szeto, David W. Wetter, Paul M. Cinciripini, Jason D. Robinson, and Yisheng Li. 2014. "Cognition and Craving during Smoking Cessation: An Ecological Momentary Assessment Study." *Nicotine and Tobacco Research* 16:S111–18.

Weisbuch, Max, Stacey A. Sinclair, Jeanine L. Skorinko, and Collette P. Eccleston. 2009. "Self-Esteem Depends on the Beholder: Effects of a Subtle Social Value Cue." *Journal of Experimental Social Psychology* 45:143–8.

Westgate, Erin C., Rachel G. Riskind, and Brian A. Nosek. 2015. "Implicit Preferences for Straight People over Lesbian Women and Gay Men Weakened from 2006 to 2013." *Collabra: Psychology* 1(1), article 1.

Wheeler, S. Christian, and Jonah Berger. 2007. "When the Same Prime Leads to Difference Effects." *Journal of Consumer Research* 34:357–68.

Wheeler, S. Christian, and Kenneth G. DeMarree. 2009. "Multiple Mechanisms of Prime-to-Behavior Effects." *Social and Personality Psychology Compass* 3/4:566–81.

Williams, Monnica T., Eric Turkheimer, Emily Magee, and Thomas Guterbock. 2008. "The Effects of Race and Racial Priming on Self-Report of Contamination Anxiety." *Personality and Individual Differences* 44:746–57.

Xu, Kaiyuan, Brian Nosek, and Anthony G. Greenwald. 2014. "Psychology Data from the Race Implicit Association Test on the Project Implicit Demo Website." *Journal of Open Psychology Data* 2:e3.

CHAPTER 21

....

SOCIAL MINDSCAPES
AND THE SELF

the case for social pattern analysis

....

JAMIE L. MULLANEY

ALTHOUGH the field of cognitive sociology is relatively recent, its spirit is not; inquiry into the relationship between culture and cognition has long-standing roots in sociology, dating back to the works and traditions of some of the earliest sociological thinkers. In his recent book, Brekhus (2015) shows the diversity of the study of culture and cognition, identifying what he sees as at least five contemporary traditions[1] in the field, each with its own theoretical influences, assumptions, and methodologies. The question remains, then, as to *how* to study the relationship between culture and cognition, in short, how to "do" cognitive sociology. The chapters in this section of this edited volume grapple with this question and suggest, perhaps not surprisingly, that there are many possible answers, including a variety of quantitative and qualitative approaches. Here, I focus on one particular strain of cognitive sociology: Eviatar Zerubavel's social mindscapes tradition, also referred to as Rutgers School or culturalist cognitive sociology in other places (Brekhus 2007, 2015). In doing so, I examine the importance of social pattern analysis to work in this tradition in general and to identity research in particular.

In introducing what would become the social mindscapes/culturalist cognitive sociology (SM/CCS) tradition, Zerubavel called for "an altogether new vision of 'the mind' " (1997:1) in his groundbreaking book *Social Mindscapes: An Invitation to Cognitive Sociology*. This form of cognitive sociology would serve as a bridge between cognitive individualism, which highlights a more Romantic notion of the solitary, *individual* thinker, and cognitive universalism, popularized by cognitive science's quest to understand the mental hardware of the *human* thinker. Falling somewhere between these two perspectives, Zerubavel insisted that cognitive sociology could expand our "thinking about thinking" by stressing the *intersubjective* dimensions of the mind. In placing an emphasis on the coproduction of thoughts, Zerubavel invited an exploration into how social, cultural, and historical factors shape six key cognitive processes: perceiving, attending, classifying, assigning meaning, remembering, and reckoning the time (p. 21). This sociomental approach placed culture at the center of cognition, requiring scholars to take seriously "how culture mediates the natural in shaping how we perceive and organize our realities" (Brekhus 2007:450).

Social mindscapes/culturalist cognitive sociology did not arrive as a new substantive subfield of sociology; instead, practitioners envisioned it as a theoretical method or form of analytic literacy unto itself (Brekhus 2007:448–9; Nippert-Eng 1996). With SM/CCS, then, scholars could begin to better understand underexplored processes, such as how thought communities shape cognition, how cognitive socialization occurs, and how cognitive battles reflect an underlying politics of cognition (to name a few) *within any subfield* of sociology. In its focus on processes, however, SM/CCS also challenged scholars to think *across subfields*, to see, in a very Simmelian spirit, how cognitive forms transcend disciplinary content.

In the years since the publication of *Social Mindscapes*, a substantial amount of research has come out of this tradition. Zerubavel himself did not talk much about the area of identity, but many studies in this area have used an SM/CCS perspective to understand how individuals and groups perceive, create, maintain, and manage identities (Brekhus 2003; DeGloma 2014; Mullaney 2006). Much of this work has relied (both implicitly and explicitly) on the method of social pattern analysis (Zerubavel 2007). In what follows, I discuss how the SM/CCS tradition serves as a natural home for the growing literature on identity and how social pattern analysis (SPA) greatly enhances this work. While I review some of the existing identity research that makes use of this perspective and method throughout, in the final section of the chapter I narrow the focus to a specific area of contemporary identity research—virginity studies—as a way of demonstrating how SM/CCS and SPA together can greatly advance theoretical depth and understanding of identity processes.

21.1 SOCIAL PATTERN ANALYSIS

Although Zerubavel did not formalize social pattern analysis until his 2007 article in *Sociological Forum*, he introduced the foundations of this approach in his 1980 article "If Simmel Were a Fieldworker." In this early piece, Zerubavel discusses formal sociology and argues that many scholars have neglected the potential methodological implications to be gleaned from Simmel's tradition. In taking a Simmelian approach to field work (and research more broadly), formal sociologists prioritize patterns and forms over content and thus more closely resemble the geometrician, logician, or grammarian rather than the traditional ethnographer (1980:27–29). The formal sociologist (or "analytic fieldworker")—"motivated by the wish to know about [the social word] in *different ways*" rather than the desire to know more—would bear the task of entering the field with sensitizing concepts (29–30, emphasis original). Sensitizing concepts, Zerubavel claims, do not require rigid operationalization of variables or predictive hypotheses; instead, their purpose is to provide a cognitive orientation by establishing rough analytic foci or boundaries of perception for researchers. Rather than limiting data collection, Zerubavel insists that the use of such concepts enables "researchers to 'see' patterns they probably would have missed without them" and move toward the elimination of the artificial split between theory and methods in sociology (32).

Social pattern analysis, like cognitive sociology, challenges common-sense under-standings. Just as cognitive sociology calls into question the "natural" divisions or clas-sifications of the social world, SPA asks scholars to suspend their taken-for-granted research tendency to study cases that appear bound by time, space, and/or culture (Zerubavel 2007:133). Setting aside a focus on content, social pattern analysis demands that the researcher, in fact, disregard idiosyncrasies of situations and events and decon-textualize findings in order to allow formal patterns to emerge (131, 142). In requiring the researcher to be "omnivorous" in data collection by crossing traditional disciplinary boundaries of specialization, method, and scale, SPA relies heavily on the role of analogy (what Diane Vaughn called "Simmelarities") in order to observe common forms of sociation in what are thought to be dissimilar contexts (pp. 137–9).

In the process, SPA, then, does something even more brazen: it asks researchers to ignore or downplay the historical "evolution" of the discipline into specialized subfields. In the introduction to her book on becoming an "ex-," Ebaugh (1988)—which, inciden-tally uses SPA years before its formalization—writes at length about the theoretical losses that come with this shift toward increasing specialization over time. She laments,

> Most of us focus so narrowly on one limited aspect of the social world that we have lost sight of more general processes that describe human behavior regardless of the specific circumstances in which it is found. . . . We have "developed" and "matured" beyond our founders whose goals were to study and explicate the nuts and bolts of social life. However, in the process of academic specialization, we may be over-looking some very basic and fundamental realities that cut across disciplines and subspecialties. (14–15)

Of course, it would be easy to dismiss researchers who use SPA who defy fitting neatly into subdisciplinary fields as lacking organization, a charge Staudenmeier (2013:96) says was made of Simmel: flitting from topic to topic like a butterfly and crossing the bound-aries of time, space, and disciplines—practices some scholars view as suspect.

But this characterization misses the point of SPA. Social pattern analysis does not lack focus; it simply has a different analytic task. Unlike traditional ethnography, for exam-ple, where the final goal is a *thick description* and thin analysis of a particular social set-ting, SPA aims to produce a *thick analysis* across wide contexts (Brekhus 2007:458). Researchers using SPA choose sites by theme (rather than substance) and enter those settings with a clear analytic strategy. This method puts great faith in the researcher; it serves as an epistemological acknowledgement of our ability to find patterns based on our own trained attention as researchers to multiple social worlds—a risky "vote of confidence" or "license to generalize" for the researcher in an era where generalizing and thinking beyond one's case is often disparaged as a denial of the uniqueness of the specific groups we study.   (458)

In its aim for thick analysis, SPA, then, raises a high bar on researchers during even the earliest stages of projects by demanding a careful selection of sites.

21.2 Using SM/CCS and SPA in Identity Research

As an analytic approach that prioritizes form over content, the SM/CCS perspective and its method of social pattern analysis together invite researchers to challenge taken-for-granted assumptions in many areas of social life—as Zerubavel claims, to know in a different way. In this section, I suggest that identity research in particular can greatly benefit from both a social mindscapes/culturalist cognitive sociology lens and the methodological approach of social pattern analysis.

Inquiry into identity, of course, has not been the sole pursuit of sociologists: philosophers, psychologists, and thinkers across a variety of fields have explored personal and social understandings of the self and its processes. As a result, the methodological approaches to identity have ranged as well. While scholars have a long history of pondering and debating the nature of the self, there remains something uniquely important about identity in ways that were not always the case in previous eras. In her 2000 review of the then-current state of identity research, Judith Howard argues that, despite this long-standing interest in the self, identity is a fairly modern concern since, "when societies were more stable, identity was to a great extent assigned, rather than selected or adopted" (367).

This interest in identity is not just indicative of modern-day narcissism; as Jenkins (2008) suggests, identity and the process of identification matter greatly for two reasons. First, identification is a basic cognitive mechanism that people use to sort themselves and others. It is a " 'baseline' sorting that is fundamental to the organisation of the human world" (13). Even so, identification and identity are messy, ambiguous, and rarely predictive of human behavior. Furthermore, other scholars insist that the overuse of the term "identity" and its inability to capture the complexity of identification processes render it essentially useless as a social analytic concept. Rather than accept this death sentence for identity studies, Jenkins insists that scholars not throw out the identity baby with the murky bathwater of identification. This leads him to his second reason for keeping identity at the center of social science inquiry: identity matters not just to scholars but to the world outside academia. As he puts it, the "genie is already out of the bottle.... [Identity] features in a host of public discourses, from politics to marketing to self-help," and "denying ourselves one of its words of power is not good communications policy" (13). In keeping identity as a central focus of sociological inquiry, however, researchers must take seriously the dangers of a concept that potentially means everything and, as a result, nothing. Remembering that identity is ultimately about processes and working to unpack these processes are ways to move forward sociological perspectives on identity (14).

In its focus on general cognitive processes, the SM/CCS field of cognitive sociology serves as an ideal lens through which to explore identity. After all, identities arise out of and include all of the cognitive processes outlined by Zerubavel. We *perceive* attributes based on what we learn "counts"; we *attend* to these attributes according to ideas about their social weight (Mullaney 1999); we *classify* identities through the use of boundaries and labels; we *assign social and moral meanings* to identities. Identities also shape and are shaped by *memory* and *time* (Mead 1934; Vinitsky-Seroussi 1998).[2] In short, the "essence of self...is cognitive" (Mead 1934:173). But SM/CCS enhances the study of identity in an additional, critical way: it simultaneously advances some of the earlier traditions in identity research.

Much of the identity literature implicitly accepts the fundamental premises of symbolic interaction as starting points for understanding the self. These basic premises stress the importance of interaction and meaning in the construction of the self and highlight its fundamentally social nature. Mead (1934) in particular discussed the inherently social nature of the self, claiming that one has to be a member of a community to be a self, as it is only in acquiring language subsequently becoming an object to the self (through the process of taking the attitude of others) that the self appears. Furthermore, Mead claims, it is impossible to conceive of the self outside social situations since, even when alone, individuals interact with the self as if with others through a conversation of gestures. Strauss (1997) also stresses the importance of language in relation to identity and stated that it is not on the periphery of human action and identity since to define is to mark boundaries and "classification, knowledge, and value are inseparable" (25). Contemporary thinkers carry forward these ideas into their work. Jenkins (2008), for example, defines identity as "the human capacity—rooted in language—to know 'who's who.'" Like Strauss, he insists that, while categorization makes real social groupings and identities, these classifications are rarely neutral and always imply evaluation (12, 6).

Another foundational approach, social cognition theory (Fiske and Taylor 1991), focuses on how cognitive schema serve to organize identity classifications. Self-schema include "organized knowledge about one's self" in the form of "characteristics, preferences, goals, and behavior patterns" while group schema include "organized information about social positions and stratification statuses, such as gender, race, age, or class" (Howard 2000:368). Social cognition theory reveals the limits of human cognition by showing how individuals navigate the world as "cognitive misers" who engage in "streamlining information to manage the demands of everyday interaction." Using schema along the lines of social positions becomes one way of being cognitively efficient (368). Traditional social cognition theory, however, makes several key (and problematic) assumptions about identities, namely that they have "an intrinsic, essential content, defined by common origin or a common structure of experience, and often, both" (Howard 2000:385). Furthermore, it offers a limited view of the categories of identity and suffers from its implicit assumption of the "seeming obviousness of which dimensions become bases for categorizations" (386).

Identity research in sociology and related disciplines has followed along and borrowed from the lines of these traditions, investigating the meanings and experiences of politically salient collective identities or "standpoints." But, as Brekhus (2007) argues, sometimes the identities that matter are not the ones that sociologists have been trained to "naturally" see. While it is undeniable that, as standpoint theorists claim, "social marginality along these axes produces a unique perspective on the world," it is also the case that standpoints arise out of "membership in social categories that are not necessarily salient to sociologists or to social movements recognized by them" (455). In this regard, SM/CCS can enrich the study of identity, as it offers a way to "trouble" these commonsense assumptions about the most salient categories of identity. Also, SM/CCS introduces what Brekhus calls a "Simmelian-based standpoint theory that takes intersectionality seriously" along dimensions beyond traditional axes, such as race, class, and gender (459).

Social pattern analysis also plays a key role in facilitating thinking across nontraditional lines of thought communities. Rather than looking at identities of a particular type in terms of content (Republicans, vegans, or dancers), SPA demands that researchers imagine the ways in which identity processes unite individuals who seemingly have little else in common. In her work on "de-labelers," for example, Jenna Howard (2006) examines how individuals who previously defined themselves with particular disorder labels (individuals with eating disorders, bipolar diagnosis, or addiction struggles) navigated the recovery identity in the past. Suspending a focus on the symptomatic differences between these individuals allows Howard the chance to examine the temporal ambiguity of recovery identities, an ambiguity that she claims allows for the emergence of two types of trajectories, what she calls "expecting" and "accepting." De-labelers who placed themselves on an expecting trajectory in the past were forward-looking and hopeful toward their futures; the label served a stabilizing function in order to facilitate future change (312). Individuals on an accepting trajectory, in contrast, took on the label as an essential identity, imagining a future that was on level ground with the present. Using SPA through the lens of SM/CCS to examine recovery identities, Howard not only bridges identities seen as disparate and disconnected in other research; she also provides a starting point to explore other identities that may serve as an intermediate and remedial means to an end but are not necessarily related to recovery (308).

Just as the identities lumped together in social pattern analysis can cross contexts, they also need not share a common temporal ground. In her study of exes, for example, Ebaugh (1988) acknowledges that, while certain times better enable researchers to see the general process of role exit—especially when there is a lapse in time between roles (e.g., divorce) or when there is no subsequent culturally prescribed subsequent entrance (e.g., retirement)—the participants in her study experience a common exiting trajectory regardless of time spent in a former role. Similarly, although individuals moved through the stages at different paces, some of which involved time-related influences, all exes report following the path of having first doubts, seeking alternatives, and experiencing a turning point before entering the final stage of creating the "ex" role. By setting aside the content of the identity one is leaving, Ebaugh allows for a portrait of the sociologically unique process of exiting to emerge across a diverse sample of ex-nuns, transsexuals, divorcees, mothers without custody, retirees, ex-convicts, and former members of a wide range of occupations (physicians, dentists, police officers, teachers, mental health workers, and air traffic controllers). DeGloma (2014), too, reveals the underlying and common identity process in becoming an "awakener" by pulling together the narrative accounts of another seemingly disparate group from a variety of social/historical back-grounds (Zarathustra, Plato, the Buddha, present-day religious converts, war veterans, sexual abuse survivors). In describing how he analyzes and presents the data from a multitude of published formats, DeGloma states that he foregrounds the parts of the narratives that illustrate his themes while claiming that this approach does not amount to selective picking and choosing; instead, by "providing several substantively distinct autobiographical clips to illustrate each theme while actively pointing out what one story has in common with others allows...structural generalities that would otherwise be less clear" to emerge (28). One such structural generality in awakening narratives is that "darkness" and "falsehood" must define the past; in other words, awakeners detail the path of moving from a state of cognitive constraint to cognitive emancipation (73–74).

It is important to note that identity researchers who use SPA do not always highlight similarity at the expense of difference. While it is true that these researchers use an ana-lytic lens or focus that allows them to see the social divisions of the world in somewhat novel ways, they do not dismiss diversity in their samples. Just as Jenna Howard's de-labelers described their pasts using expecting or accepting trajectories, DeGloma's awakeners use two different narrative structures to account for their transformative moments that separate their pasts of falsehood from their current state of truth, which he identifies as the "sociomental express elevator" and the "sociomental staircase." Awakeners who describe their transformation in terms of the sociomental express elevator portray their transformations as rapid and without agency on their part; an external event triggers the truth so much so at times that the truth itself appears to have the agency (one informant describes being "slapped by the cold wave of memories"). In contrast to this transformation that is powerful, instantaneous, and momentous, the sociomental staircase description of an awakening details a step-by-step ascent where awakeners use "sociomental elimination" to rule out other possible truths as their con-sciousness transforms through their own agentic acts.

If, as Jenkins insists, scholars need to keep the focus on process when studying identity, then SPA appears well suited as a methodology for this area in that it places the "hows" (rather than the "whats") at the center of analysis. For example, the differences Howard (2006) and DeGloma (2014) note among their cases do not fall along tradi-tional lines that sociologists are trained to see, and a content-driven approach to identity would preclude the discovery of these differences. It is not the case, for example, that all Iraq veterans in DeGloma's sample tell the same awakening story (e.g., staircase model) nor do all former bulimics in Howard's research report the experience of the past (e.g., expecting trajectory). Using SPA within the areas of identity construction, transformation, and maintenance, then, allows researchers to explore the patterns in the cognitive processes highlighted by the SM/CCS perspective without assuming complete uniformity in how that occurs.

21.3 BAD FORM: WHEN CONTENT PREVAILS

In this section, I narrow the focus to one specific area of contemporary research—virginity—to show how the broad approach of SPA can open up new possibilities for a body of literature traditionally focused on identity content. I came to know these particularities about the research on virgins when I was invited to participate in a mixed method symposium on virginity in late adolescence and emerging adulthood. Given that I study neither virginity nor that specific period of the life course, I decided to explore whether and how my previous research on abstinence could contribute to the conversation. Having been trained in the Rutgers School under the mentorship of Zerubavel, my research on abstinence, perhaps not surprisingly, took a broad, social pattern analytic approach. Less interested in a given type of abstainer (such as virgins), and more concerned with how abstinence worked as a generic identity process, I explored how deliberate and intentional decisions to not do something (drive, eat certain foods, use drugs or alcohol, have sex, etc.) played out. Social pattern analysis allowed me to interrogate the formal aspects of abstinence (how people define, construct, and maintain identity) while suspending a focus on the content, that is, the particular types of abstinence or things they were not doing (Mullaney 2006).

In using this case, I do not mean to suggest, of course, that virginity is the only area of identity research that can benefit from SPA, nor do I take the presumptuous position that my own work is the sole answer to the limitations of this area of identity research. I simply offer it in the spirit of Zerubavel's quest to know things in different ways and to show one way in which the general method of SPA can offer different stories within particular (and specialized) areas of research. After identifying some of the limitations in the current literature on virginity, I argue that understanding virgin identity through SPA requires, somewhat paradoxically, a step away from sex altogether, moving beyond the boundaries of virginity (and perhaps even sexual abstinence altogether) by looking at how individuals construct identities based on deliberately not doing something.

21.3.1 Past and Persistent Limitations of Virginity Research

Earlier investigations into virginity and virgin identity suffered from the limitations of being extremely narrow in focus, both in their perspectives and samples. Specifically, this work neglected to look at individuals' subjective meanings of sex and virginity and often relied on samples made up of predominantly women, heterosexuals, and/or college students (Carpenter 2001). An extension of the lack of perspective from informants themselves, researchers often imposed their own implicit or explicit heteronormative bias in their starting assumption that the only type of sex that "counts" or leads to virginity loss is that involving a penis and vagina. The danger of using such narrow definitions, as Trotter and Alderson (2007:11) warn, is that they can contradict colloquial understandings of sex, which often include oral and anal sex.

Even when allowing for respondents to define virginity on their own terms, some research suggests a persistence of these narrow definitions among informants themselves. In Trotter and Alderson's (2007) analysis of university students' understanding of what counts as losing one's virginity, having sex, and counting someone as a sexual partner, results show that students have the narrowest definitions for what constitutes virginity loss, meaning that students perceive that there are acts that can count in the other categories but not constitute virginity loss. These findings, the researchers argue, demand that we cannot conflate virginity loss with or collapse it into other sexual experiences, especially since individuals may use these narrow definitions of virginity loss precisely in order to stay virgins.[3]

In recent years, there have been many good faith gestures to begin remedying some of these limitations of past research, mostly by (1) moving beyond the experiences and perspectives of women and individuals who identify as heterosexual[4] and (2) trying to honor and tap into subjective experiences/definitions rather than by measuring through predetermined measures set by researchers. A lot of the advances on this second front have been largely in part to Carpenter's sexual frames. Asking her informants to retrospectively reflect on their virginity loss, Carpenter finds that they frame it in one of three ways. First, the *virginity as gift* frame places an emphasis on virginity's "uniqueness, non-renewability, symbolic import, and status as an extension of the giver's self" (2005:58). Second, *virginity as process* involves the belief that virginity loss, like other transitions, would "increase their knowledge (about sexuality or themselves) and leave them feeling transformed." Under this frame, virginity loss is "an inevitable and desirable transition" (2001:133). Finally, when *virginity as stigma* is the perspective that virginity is an undesirable state, accompanied by the fear of the "ever-present possibility that their stigma could be discovered, exposed, and derided by others" (133).

Much of the work on virginity now relies on Carpenter's frames and allows for a better understanding of the connections between subjective meanings/cognitive frameworks and experiences (including the timing of sex, the choice of partner, etc.). For example, Humphreys (2013) suggests that the stigma frame is transitory and that individuals may be less likely to frame as such once they "get rid of" virginity. This raises the critical point made by Carpenter in her original research, that is, that frameworks may shift from pre– to post–virginity loss (674) or even within the period of pre–virginity loss (e.g., the stigma framework may only arise when individuals perceive themselves as behind "off track" from or "behind" their peers). Humphreys hints at a more ominous issue that continues to plague the virginity literature, however, when he notes that researchers still need to learn how these frameworks play out for those who have *not* yet experienced intercourse. In other words, as retrospective accounts, the research to date may be telling us more about individuals' *current* framework, not necessarily the ones they held when they were virgins.

In looking at the contemporary work on virginity, then, it appears that the research still suffers from three key limitations. First, despite efforts at improving definitional issues and an openness to understand subjective framings, there is still wide disagreement as to what virginity is and, therefore, who virgins are. A second limitation of virginity research is its peculiar temporal focus. With some exception, most of what we know about virginity comes after its loss. This might be an inconsequential, moot point were it not for the fact that research tells us that individuals (re)interpret events and how those events fit into their identities over their lifetimes (Carpenter 2001:128). The third and final issue is both temporal and definitional, as the focus in virginity research is often research on its loss. Sometimes the focus on loss makes sense, such as when trying to discern what allows (or prevents) adolescents saying "no" to sex, which is the focus of the pledging literature (Bearman and Bruckner 2001; Landor and Simons 2014). But even this literature often assesses perspectives on virginity at a point when individuals are no longer virgins, revealing little about virgin identities while they still exist.

21.3.2 Using Social Pattern Analysis in Virginity Research

What can we know about virginity and the virgin identity if definitions vary so widely and we are often asking about it and, in many ways, measuring it only after its loss? One way of knowing more is to break free from the content of virginity and to look at the form of abstinence, that is, how individuals construct, maintain, and narrate their identities based on not doing something. I want to focus on two main findings from my research with thirty-eight abstainers (Mullaney 2006) that I think can inform the work on virginity: the first has to do with how abstainers report doing their not-doing; the second has to do with how they tell their stories of abstinence.[5] I realize that some may critique that there is something fundamentally different about sexual abstinence. After all, we think that having sex once (however that is defined) permanently alters people in a way that eating meat or giving in to using technology does not. Perhaps that is the case. However, the advantage of using SM/CCS and SPA is that it asks, as a starting point, that we suspend these common-sense understandings (i.e., that virgins must be different from vegetarians, nondrivers, and people who do not smoke or that "real" virgins are different from individuals practicing celibacy for other reasons) in order to see what common ground unfolds.

Suspending a focus on content and understanding the "hows" of abstinence bear significant importance because abstinence is not about absence: it is deliberate, intentional, and performed. In interviewing abstainers, I discovered two dominant strategies, ones I labeled "fire walking" and "fence building." When fire walking, abstainers imagine the space between doing and not doing as vast, and they see how close to the fire they can get, so to speak, without getting burned. These individuals walk dangerously close to the fire for two main reasons: (1) they want to do a lot of related acts (such as having oral sex) while not "crossing the line" (that is, having intercourse), and thus staying a "virgin" or (2) they think that resisting temptation is a way to reaffirm the integrity of their abstinence, as they feel these encounters remind them of the importance of their abstinence. Fence building, on the other hand, is more protective, as it is based on a more cut-and-dried, rigid (and therefore more fragile) conceptualization of what it means to "do" and "not do." When fence building, often abstainers not only avoid the things from which they claim to abstain from; they also avoid tangential acts, as well, as they view these acts or things as potentially dangerous. Fences indicate a feeling that one cannot afford to err. At several points during an interview, one respondent used the phrase, "When in doubt, do without." This appears a general principle for many of the abstainers because, as this person tells me, when it comes to abstinence, "You'd rather be safe than sorry." Still, in the face of such principles arise glaring contradictions. Finding themselves engaging in acts that contradict their abstinence, individuals often rely on bracketing as a strategy to prevent such doings from "counting" or disrupting their otherwise abstinent practices. Bracketing allows individuals to make the statement that "I know that I'm doing something inconsistent, but it shouldn't be taken as such."

Another important insight from a formal SPA approach to abstinence (over a content-driven one) reveals that the stories told about abstinence appear to depend more on temporal location rather than on type of abstinence. In my research with abstainers, I found that understandings of abstinence depended on whether individuals had engaged in the act in the past and whether they intended to do so in the future. This led to the emergence of four types of abstainers, again based on formal temporal properties, not the content of the abstinence: those who had not engaged in the behavior in the past but would in the future ("waiters"), those who had not and did not plan to do so ("nevers"), those who were not engaged in the act currently but had before and would again ("time-outers") and those who decided to never again engage in a past act ("quitters"). While the common-sense logic of virginity research might encourage us to assume that all virgins would tell a similar story, this research suggests the possibility that someone who has not yet had sex (but plans to do so in the future) produces a narrative that is more similar to another type of "not-yet" abstinent identity than to someone else who is also a virgin but sees it as a "never-have-never-will" piece of identity (e.g., lifelong celibacy). These are not inconsequential differences, since narratives are important attempts to make sense of one's identity over time, and there are stark differences regarding the salience of abstinence depending on where people fall temporally.

How abstainers construct and maintain their identities can offer a fresh perspective on both how researchers study virginity and how they interpret their findings. Rigid definitions of virginity, particularly when imposed by researchers, encourage a discounting of a virgin identity when individuals engage in acts deemed "inconsistent" (e.g., oral sex). It is important to understand how individuals define and "do" this identity. For example, despite the counterintuitive nature of it, research shows that individuals *do* bracket when it comes to virginity and its loss, especially in the case of sexual acts that do not involve consent. Carpenter (2001) suggests that, while not all individuals agree on how to regard whether an act "counts" or not against one's virginity (132), consent does appear to be a key consideration.

Examining the strategies or the "hows" also requires that researchers engage in an act of resistance when it comes to studying youth and sex not characteristic of past work. On some level, SPA demands a political statement of sorts by saying researchers are not studying virginity due to beliefs about what is right or what young adults *should* be doing (or not doing). Instead, SPA potentially allows for a different story of virginity to emerge. It asks us to decontextualize findings—at least temporarily—in order to find general patterns.

At the most basic level, however, SPA demands that researchers recognize that not all virgins are the same, and that one-size-fits-all attempts to preserve virginity will fail. Virgins who adopt a stigma framework demonstrate the problem with a flattened approach to virginity. As Carpenter (2001) finds, many who adopt the stigma framework want to discard their virginity and may actually be involuntarily celibate (Humphreys 2013) and, therefore, very different from intentional abstainers. Consequently, researchers may learn more about this group by comparing them to people who hold other involuntary identities rather than those who are abstinent by choice (an altogether different avenue for SPA in this research).

Focusing on strategies of abstinence (fire walking and fence building) requires that researchers who may be starting from a moral interest in virginity (i.e., what individuals *should* be doing or not doing) take a step back and understand the hows and for what reasons people abstain. Some of these patterns, of course, will be temporal. Exploring the temporal dimensions of these identities expands the focus to sexual abstinence (or even abstinence in general) rather than limiting it to just virginity, which, after all, is only one type of sexual abstinence. It allows for a greater understanding of how sexual abstinence changes over the life course. This would be particularly beneficial when studying the experiences of emerging adults, many of whom may not be virgins but may be sexual abstainers. Finally, broadening the focus could also shape how we think about virginity pledging and the research surrounding it. As Landor and Simons (2014:1104) suggest, an all-or-nothing approach to pledging means there is no reason for individuals to abstain if they violate once (i.e., have sex), and so it may be important to highlight other forms of sexual abstinence that can occur post–virginity loss.

21.4 CONCLUSION

This chapter has argued for the inclusion of SPA in research that follows the SM/CCS tradition in general and explores identity processes in particular. In promoting a formal sociological imagination, the methodological approach of SPA extends the spirit of cognitive sociology by encouraging researchers to think and see across boundaries of time, space, and disciplinary training. As the example of the specific case of virgin identities shows, SPA, while not the only approach to understanding this identity, certainly opens up a different and complementary perspective to the ones offered by contemporary research.

As a final methodological consideration, it is worth noting that SPA need not start at the level of general comparisons but can, in fact, follow a content-driven study. When researchers adopt a formal sociological imagination, they can begin to project how their findings might extend beyond their individual cases. Two examples in the identity literature come to mind: Brekhus's (2003) work on suburban gays and Johnston's (2013) study on pagans.

In mapping the identity practices of suburban gay men, Brekhus (2003) finds that men fall into one of three types: "peacocks" or "lifestylers," who perform gay identity with high density and high duration regardless of setting; "chameleons" or "commuters," who turn gayness on and off in order to blend into the surrounding environment; and "centaurs" or "integrators," who always "do gayness" but at a low volume, as they believe it is simply one component of who they are. But Brekhus does not stop at gay suburbia. Claiming that "too often gay studies and queer theory have been ghettoized and their relevance to mainstream social theory ignored" (137), he begins to imagine how his three identity types might work in areas completely divorced from his research site. Using a wide range of data (newspapers, observation, letters to the editor, academic studies), Brekhus tests his findings through SPA in order to see whether "vegan peacocks, Christian chameleons, and soccer mom centaurs" look similar to those in gay suburbia.

Although she herself does not get to the stage of carrying out SPA, Johnston (2013), too, uses her findings from her research on practicing pagans to suggest how SPA could better inform conversion narratives that rely on a "rhetoric of continuity." Her site-specific work challenges the assumptions that awakening narratives are the only (and therefore authentic) models of conversion and that conversions require one to abandon all former sociomental affiliations (553, 568). Instead, the pagans she interviewed used three strategies to highlight continuity in the face of change: (1) accounting for previous inconsistent (here, religious) participation (2) using metaphors of coming home and (3) providing evidence of continuity from childhood (557). Johnston urges future research to explore these identity practices across contexts, since restricting analyses to specific groups may limit full understandings of social identity and may preclude new theoretical perspectives from emerging (570). To be sure, the claims made by pagans in Johnston's research echo those of many others claiming "authentic" identities, ranging from classic gender studies, such as Garfinkel's (1967) case of Agnes, to contemporary examples, such as straight-edge hardcore punks, who claim to have "always been" straight edge even before they had the subcultural awareness and language to identify it as such (Brekhus 2015; Williams 2006).

Whether beginning with a quest to uncover broad forms or using key findings to springboard into deeper waters to test patterns and processes across contexts, SPA serves as a valuable method in the study of culture and cognition. It offers the possibility to reinvigorate what Simmel believed to be the essence of sociology as a whole: a field that is not content-driven but is, instead, a "new method, an instrument of investigation" (Zerubavel 1980:26), a novel way of knowing.

NOTES

1. Brekhus identifies these orientations as: "1) a discourse, iconic, and neo-Durkheimian collective representations tradition; 2) symbolic interactionism; 3) Eviatar Zerubavel's social mindscapes (Rutgers School) tradition; 4) Ann Swidler's cultural toolkit tradition; and 5) an intersection with cognitive neuroscience and cognitive sociology tradition" (2015:9).
2. In his book *Culture and Cognition*, Brekhus (2015), in fact, identifies identity construction itself as an additional, seventh cognitive process.
3. Despite the downsides of limited, heteronormative definitions, there may be unintended positive consequences for certain demographics. Medley-Roth (2007) argues that heterosexual women in particular may benefit from defining virginity loss as tied to a specific act, such as intercourse, in that they can use it to abide by the sexual double standard, maintain virginity, and sexually bargain in other ways.
4. One study in particular, by Caron and Hinman (2013), does not break the heterosexual mold but does tip the gender scale by focusing exclusively on the experience of and the themes that emerge surrounding male virginity loss.
5. It is important to note that these reports occurred during times when individuals were actually abstaining and are not, like many of the data in the virginity literature, retrospective accounts.

REFERENCES

Bearman, Peter S., and Hannah Bruckner. 2001. "Promising the Future: Virginity Pledges and First Intercourse." *American Journal of Sociology* 106(4):859–912.

Brekhus, Wayne. 2003. *Peacocks, Chameleons, Centaurs: Gay Suburbia and the Grammar of Social Identity.* Chicago: University of Chicago Press.

Brekhus, Wayne. 2007. "The Rutgers School: A Zerubavelian Culturalist Cognitive Sociology." *European Journal of Social Theory* 10(3):448–64.

Brekhus, Wayne. 2015. *Culture and Cognition: Patterns in the Social Construction of Reality.* Malden, MA: Polity Press.

Caron, Sandra L., and Sarah P. Hinman. 2013. "'I Took His V-Card': An Exploratory Analysis of College Student Stories Involving Male Virginity Loss." *Sexuality and Culture* 17:525–39.

Carpenter, Laura M. 2001. "The Ambiguity of 'Having Sex': The Subjective Experience of Virginity Loss in the United States." *Journal of Sex Research* 38(2):127–39.

Carpenter, Laura M. 2005. *Virginity Lost: An Intimate Portrait of First Sexual Experiences.* New York: New York University Press.

DeGloma, Thomas. 2014. *Seeing the Light: The Social Logic of Personal Discovery.* Chicago: University of Chicago Press.

Ebaugh, Helen Rose Fuchs. 1988. *Becoming an Ex: The Process of Role Exit.* Chicago: University of Chicago Press.

Fiske, Susan T., and Shelley E. Taylor. 1991. *Social Cognition.* 2nd ed. New York: McGraw-Hill.

Garfinkel, Harold. 1967. *Studies in Ethnomethodology.* Englewood Cliffs, NJ: Prentice-Hall.

Howard, Jenna. 2006. "Expecting and Accepting: The Temporal Ambiguity of Recovering Identities." *Social Psychology Quarterly* 69(4):307–24.

Howard, Judith A. 2000. "Social Psychology of Identities." *Annual Review of Sociology* 26:367–93.

Humphreys, Terry P. 2013. "Cognitive Frameworks of Virginity and First Intercourse." *Journal of Sex Research* 50(7):664–75.

Jenkins, Richard. 2008. *Social Identity*. 3rd ed. New York: Routledge.

Johnston, Erin F. 2013. "'I Was Always This Way…': Rhetorics of Continuity in Narratives of Conversion." *Sociological Forum* 28(3):549–73.

Landor, Antoinette M., and Leslie Gordon Simons. 2014. "Why Virginity Pledges Succeed or Fail: The Moderating Effect of Religious Commitment versus Religious Participation." *Journal of Family Studies* 23:1102–13.

Mead, George Herbert. 1934. *Mind, Self, and Society from the Standpoint of a Social Behaviorist*. Chicago: University of Chicago Press.

Medley-Roth, Stephanie R. 2007. "'Am I Still a Virgin?': What Counts as Sex in 20 Years of Seventeen." *Sexuality and Culture* 11:24–38.

Mullaney, Jamie. 1999. "Making It 'Count': Mental Weighing and Identity Attribution." *Symbolic Interaction* 22(3):269–83.

Mullaney, Jamie. 2006. *Everyone is NOT Doing It: Abstinence and Personal Identity*. Chicago: University of Chicago Press.

Nippert-Eng, Christina E. 1996. *Home and Work: Negotiating Boundaries through Everyday Life*. Chicago: University of Chicago Press.

Staudenmeier, William J., Jr. 2013. "Alcohol-Related Windows on Simmel's Social World." pp. 95–123 in *Illuminating Social Life: Classical and Contemporary Theory Revisited*, 6th edition, edited by P. Kivisto. Los Angeles: SAGE.

Strauss, Anselm L. 1997. *Mirrors and Masks: The Search for Identity*. New Brunswick, NJ: Transaction.

Trotter, Eileah C., and Kevin G. Alderson. 2007. "University Students' Definitions of Having Sex, Sexual Partner, and Virginity Loss: The Influence of Participant Gender, Sexual Experience, and Contextual Factors." *Canadian Journal of Human Sexuality* 16(1–2):11–29.

Vinitsky-Seroussi, Vered. 1998. *After Pomp and Circumstance: High School Reunion as an Autobiographical Occasion*. Chicago: University of Chicago Press.

Williams, J. Patrick. 2006. "Authentic Identities: Straightedge Subculture, Music, and the Internet. *Journal of Contemporary Ethnography* 35(2):173–200.

Zerubavel, Eviatar. 1980. "If Simmel Were a Fieldworker: On Formal Sociological Theory and Analytical Field Research." *Symbolic Interaction* 3(2):25–34.

Zerubavel, Eviatar. 1997. *Social Mindscapes: An Invitation to Cognitive Sociology*. Cambridge, MA: Harvard University Press.

Zerubavel, Eviatar. 2007. "Generally Speaking: The Logic and Mechanics of Social Pattern Analysis." *Sociological Forum* 22(2):131–45.

....

CHAPTER 22

CHARTING THE EMERGENCE OF THE CULTURAL FROM THE COGNITIVE WITH AGENT-BASED MODELING

....

LYNETTE SHAW

THE emergence of social phenomena out of individual interactions has been a primary point of interest in sociology since Durkheim (1982). As foundational a premise as it is to the discipline, substantial disagreement nonetheless remains over exactly *how* the concept of emergence should be incorporated into our social explanations (Sawyer 2005:63–99). On one end, some have argued that directly unpacking the processes via which collective phenomena arise out of individual interactions, that is theorizing the so-called micro-to-macro transition (Coleman 1994), should be a central if not the primary concern in the development of social theory (Hedström and Swedberg 1998; Coleman 1994; Hedström and Ylikoski 2010). Others have contended that the complexities and contingencies of this transition entail that many social phenomena cannot be effectively reduced to individual behaviors and are thus better approached in a more holistic or realist fashion (Bhasker 1979; Archer 1995; Jepperson and Meyer 2011). These metatheoretical debates aside, when it comes to the actual practice of social research, many sociologists may pragmatically opt to avoid the conceptual stickiness of this transition and choose to either restrict their considerations to a single level of analysis or provide only the barest of sketches of how individual processes *might* relate to collective outcomes. As our interest continues to grow in connecting our models of culture to individual cognitive processing (Brekhus 2015; Cerulo 2010; Dimaggio 1997; Zerubavel 1997), however, the need to find more precise and effective methods for directly theorizing this transition will only become more pressing.

This chapter explores how one of the most important tools that has been developed to aid understanding of the emergence of macro-level phenomena from micro-level processes, agent-based modeling (ABM), might find new life in the context of cognitive sociology as a method for clarifying how individual cognition can give rise to the collective cultural processes that shape societies. This work undertakes this task by first briefly reviewing arguments for the ability of computer simulation, and ABM in particular, to provide social scientists with an alternative "symbol language" (Ostrom 1988) that overcomes major complexity barriers that have historically limited both verbal and mathematical models of social processes. The next part then drills more deeply into what the field of social simulation stands to gain from cognitive sociology and vice versa. Of specific interest in this section is cognitive sociology's potential ability to provide a set of *nonrational microfoundations* for the development of general, micro-to-macro social theory and the possible payoffs available to cognitive sociology for pursuing a stronger engagement with ABM. The final section then concludes with an overview of some of the resources available to those interested in getting started with ABM and a brief, high-level introduction to the logic of ABM design and some of the prevailing principles and practices of the field.

22.1 THE IMPLICATIONS OF AGENT-BASED MODELING FOR SOCIAL THEORY

The purpose of a model is to provide an abstract representation that is simpler, and thus more tractable, than the reality it seeks to represent. In order to articulate this representation, a system of symbols must necessarily be employed. As explored by Gilbert and Terna (2000), in the history of the social sciences, two primary "symbol languages" (Ostrom 1988) have been used. The first is natural language, that is, verbal accounts of objects or processes and their relationships to other objects or processes. The second class of models includes those that have been rendered in the symbolic language of mathematics. By and large, these types of models have largely been the province of the natural sciences, but notable examples within the social sciences exist, such as the differential equations of macroeconomic theory and models of social processes that are implicitly entailed in the application of demographic and regression analyses (see Abbott 1988, for a classic discussion of this issue).

It has been argued that the truly revolutionary advances in human computing has brought with it a new type of symbolic language, that of computer simulation (Ostrom 1988). While all simulations can hypothetically be represented in the form of an equation (Epstein 2006:54), this does not entail that it is the same symbol language of traditional mathematical models. To be sure, there are many instances in which computer simulations are used to numerically solve particularly formidable equations or explore complex mathematical models. Just as readily, however, computer simulations can be seen as an extension of natural language models that takes the series of steps or "rules" (Troitzsch 1998) posited as undergirding a particular process and translates them into a set of algorithms that can be executed at much larger scales and for many more iterations than any human could possibly hope to undertake through verbal elaboration alone. Especially in cases where the dynamics of interest are likely to contain endogenously arising feedbacks (i.e., nonlinearities) or major qualitative shifts in system behavior at certain scales or over long periods of time, computational modeling becomes an indispensable tool for clarifying our thinking and systematically testing our ideas in ways that cannot be accomplished through mathematical or verbal models alone.

Computer simulation is, in and of itself, an incredibly broad area containing a diversity of established modeling frameworks and approaches. The branch of simulation work most relevant to the present discussion, however, is specifically that of ABM. Agent-based modeling refers to a type of computational model in which a collection of autonomous, individual "agents" are given relatively simple sets of rules and are then allowed to interact with one another and their environment. Rather than developing an a priori, "top-down" specification of how macro-level forces interact with one another, the purpose of ABMs is to instead observe how the interactions of agents behaving according to these simple rules can, in a "bottom-up" fashion, lead to the *spontaneous emergence* of unexpected phenomena at the collective level (Macy and Willer 2002; Epstein and Axtell 1996; Sawyer 2005:145–69). The major benefit of ABM is that it allows us to *systematically* and *rigorously* demonstrate how individual processes generate complex, unexpected system-level behaviors. This property greatly increases the capacity for parsimony, clarity, and verifiability in social researchers' models of micro-to-macro processes than could be achieved through verbal elaboration alone. Furthermore, the flexibility of this modeling approach allows social researchers to escape the "trap of tractability" (Gilbert and Troitzsch 2005) by freeing her from the need to make the sort of strong and highly unrealistic assumptions, such as preference ordering or linear causal relationships, which are often required to make mathematical models analytically manageable.

In a nontrivial sense, ABM represents an approach to social theory development that works *with* complexity and processes of emergence, not against them. Specifically, it is a method that is extraordinarily well suited to overcoming the difficulties that have historically made it hard to close the "micro-to-macro gap" in our conceptualizations of the social world (Hedström and Ylikoski 2010). While we might be adept at intuiting how certain individual-level processes connect to large social forces, specifying exactly how the interactions of individuals aggregate into those phenomena is extremely hard and our attempts to trace them inevitably limited by our own cognitive capacities. Stated differently, on our own we lack the computational power necessary for the enormously complicated (and boring) task of working out how a multitude of simple interactions between individuals plays out across a large social system over a long period of time. In the face of such "complexity barriers," social theorists have taken any number of recourses, such as confining their scope of explanation to either more manageably small levels of group interactions (e.g., as is emphasized in symbolic interactionism

[Blumer 1969]) or to focusing primarily on the "structural" or macro-level features of societies (e.g., the approach commonly thought to typify structural-functionalism [Parsons 1951]). Still others have braved this area between the individual and collective in order to craft insightful, but nevertheless unavoidably complicated and convoluted, verbal explanations of the connection between individual and collective (e.g., Giddens's (1984) theorization of structuration and Habermas's (1984) voluminous expositions on communicative action). Alternatively, others have developed strikingly precise but nonetheless rigid mathematical models of the transition that are necessarily predicated on highly unrealistic assumptions about the individual (e.g., game-theoretic models based on the assumptions of rational choice theory—see Hechter and Kanazawa 1997 and Kroneberg and Kalter 2012, for overviews of applications within sociology). What ABM brings to the table is a means of *complementing*, not replacing, such existing approaches by providing a general tool that is custom built for crafting accessible, elegant descriptions of how simple individual processes can lead to emergent outcomes. It is this property that gives ABM an enormous degree of potential in the arena of cognitive sociology.

22.2 Cognitive Sociology, ABM, and the Promise of Nonrational Microfoundations for Sociological Theory

There have been many well-developed debates within sociology over the degree to which it is necessary to theorize the aforementioned transition from the individual to the social (see Sawyer 2005:63–99, for a masterful discussion of such debates). An unfortunate byproduct of the historical trajectory of these debates is that the concept of "methodological individualism" (Coleman 1994; Demeulenaere 2011), a concept that in its most general form refers to the theorizing of social phenomena in terms of the individual level processes that give rise to them, has become strongly coupled and even conflated with the concept of the "rational actor." In its strongest form, this rational actor is equivalent to the so-called *Homo economicus* that underlies the formal mathematical models favored in economics and is characterized by strong assumptions concerning individuals' self-interest, calculative capabilities, and access to "perfect" information. While there are numerous examples of this strong version of the rational actor and its associated game-theoretic models being applied in sociological contexts (Hechter and Kanazawa 1997), less rigidly specified iterations of him are found throughout many other sociological models that have sought to overcome the micro-to-macro gap (Demeulenaere 2011; Hedström 2005). In these "wider" cases, core assumptions are often relaxed in order to consider a more realistic version of the foundational actor.

Nonetheless, even in these more "boundedly rational" scenarios, there is still often a de facto emphasis on thinking about individuals in terms of their consciously available deliberative processes, intentional choices, and orientation toward increasing their own benefit.

For all the historical reinforcement of the relationship between the two, however, there is no fundamental reason why a microfoundational approach to social theory— that is, one which focuses on specifying processes at the individual level in a fashion that makes them amenable to *systematic and rigorous* elaboration into statements on collective outcomes—has to engage with any notion of rationality at all. The key requirements of using ABM as a platform for microfoundational theory are the identification of regular, relatively simple rules governing individuals' behaviors and an ability to specify how individuals' interactions with each other and/or their environment affect how those rules play out. The utility maximization of the rational actor is one such rule, and prior to the advent of ABM and computer simulation, it was one of the few theorizations of human behavior that seemed amenable to rigorous, systematic elaboration via formal, mathematical models. With the development of ABM and the establishment of computer simulation as a means of building social theory, however, the set of individual level processes that constitute potential candidates for our models of emergent social dynamics is greatly expanded. Realization of this point begins to make clear how some of the most exciting lines of future development in microfoundational theory may not come from further recasting of social processes into a rational actor type framework but, instead, through computational modeling of some of the distinctly *nonrational* individual-level processes that are suspected to undergird social life.

Cognitive sociology and the work currently being done under the heading of culture and cognition are ideally situated to make significant contributions in this area. Given its prevailing focus on the more perceptual and sense-making aspects of human cognition and the manner in which these processes constitute and are influenced by social context and interaction, sociologists working in this arena come preprepared with alternative theorizations of the individual that stand at the ready for further formalization into computational models of emergent cultural dynamics. Furthermore, as the connections between sociological theory and contemporary cognitive science research continue to tighten, we can only expect to encounter an ever-increasing number of opportunities for developing such models. This situation gives rise to a rich, and potentially highly generative, new field of social simulation research devoted to modeling the *nonrational microfoundations* of emergent social and cultural phenomena.

The key to making this transition will ultimately be in figuring out how to reformulate what we have learned about human cognition in social situations into sets of relatively simple rules that individual agents can follow in their interactions with one another. Attempting to translate the wildly intricate and complex nature of an individuals' cognitive processing into a set of simple procedures that small computer programs can run might seem like a dubious proposition to some. Of critical importance here, however, is realizing that the goal of this type of modeling is *not* the development of a full replication of the human brain, but a theoretical "carving of nature at its joints," wherein we seek to isolate and create simple models of just those particular aspects of the processes that we expect to be most relevant to the emergent social and cultural dynamics of interest.[1] Said otherwise, the priority rests on identifying which particular *cognitive mechanisms* might be usefully reconceptualized as *social mechanisms*[2] (Hedström and Swedberg 1998; Hedström and Ylikoski 2010; Demeulenaere 2011).

To give a tangible example of how such work might proceed, we can think about how connections proposed between the transmission of practices and mirror neurons (Lizardo 2007) might be reworked into a microfoundational/social mechanism theorization that is amenable to elaboration using ABM. The first priority of such a venture would be figuring out how the operation of individuals' mirror neuron systems (MNSs) might be effectively abstracted out into a set of rules that can be implemented by agents in an ABM. Fully representing the operation of even a single MNS would be an impossibly complex and computationally onerous task. However, in recognizing that it is the unconscious, implicit learning that the MNS induces which drives transmission and that repeated interaction and observation is likely required for developing the generalized representations of practical action that are likely to be of most of interest to sociologists (Lizardo 2007:330–32), the task of abstracting out a relatively simple set of rules becomes much more feasible. Specifically, it becomes clearer how we can conceive of the operation of MNSs as belonging to a broader class of social influence or social learning processes[3] wherein the general rule governing agents is that they "pick-up" the states or traits of other agents with whom they interact. Having identified this key resonance, we can then further develop our particular model of social influence to more specifically reflect the cognitive processes of interest. This might be accomplished by adding further modifications such as having agents develop generalized representations of only the most frequently observed elements of others' actions, giving agents the ability to infer what will happen next in an interaction based on previously developed representations, or linking the fidelity of the transmission process to frequency of observation. Once the baseline specification of the model has been established, additional variants of interest can also then be considered, such as allowing probabilistic alterations of the practice during the transmission process or giving agents the ability to creatively combine practices they have learned.[4]

What emergent collective outcomes would such a computational implementation produce? One of the main points of ABM is that it is not possible to definitively say at the outset what will be found without running the computational model itself. Given what is already known from similar models, however, it is possible to speculate on some of the things that might be gained through such a computational approach. The most foundational potential payoff is that such an implementation would likely be able to definitively demonstrate how individual-level transmission via the tacit learning of MNS is sufficient to account for a bottom-up establishment of collectively shared practices. In so doing, this ABM would help confirm the basic internal validity of the proposed model and strengthen the case for this cognitive mechanism being an important microfoundation for social processes. This basic validation of the initial conceptual model is only a beginning, however. Once a foundational model has been established and verified, it can then be used as a platform to explore a much wider range of other questions of related, substantive interest. To give just one example of such a modeling extension, one might decide to explore the effects of different social network structures between agents on the development of shared practices. Such investigations would potentially allow the modeler to gain further insight into how different interactional structures facilitate or inhibit changes to *habitus* and collective practice through time, impact how long communities of practice survive, or determine when there will be higher or lower levels of global variation in those collective practices.

This brief thought experiment of how a posited link between cognition and culture might be translated into an ABM offers just one example of how any number of other nonrational microfoundations might be computationally implemented. The potential usefulness and feasibility of using an ABM approach to connect individual-level processes of cognition to emergent cultural behavior is further borne out by a handful of other existing examples in the ABM literature that have undertaken comparable work, ranging from older models like those linking the psychology underlying "social impact theory" to public opinion patterns (Nowak et al. 1990) to more recent models that have explored using neurocognitive research to design rational agents with affective processing (Epstein 2013), the emergence of role relations and identity via individual "affect control" processes (Schröder et al. 2016), and the dynamics of social construction processes that arise from automatic sense-making via associative networks (Shaw 2015). Such models, hypothetical and actualized, demonstrate how a microfoundational social theory need not be synonymous with assumptions concerning individual-level rationality and helps clarify the manner in which ABM might serve as a critical tool for enabling cognitive sociology to take up the task of developing this class of nonrational, micro-to-macro theory. These examples also give an early indication of how in the hunt for the nonrational microfoundations undergirding emergent social phenomena, we may expect to find a variety of different cognitive processes on which to focus.[5]

22.3 MOTIVES FOR PURSUING THE DEVELOPMENT OF COGNITIVELY GROUNDED AGENT-BASED MODELS

This conversation on how cognitive sociology might make use of computational modeling naturally leads to another, broader discussion of what it stands to gain from doing so. Pursuing the development of cognitively grounded agent-based models is undoubtedly a pivot from the more qualitatively oriented and verbal forms of theory building that have historically predominated in the area. It is impossible to overstate the degree to which the thin, highly abstracted models required for ABM can only act as a complement to, not a substitute for, these established modes of theorizing. At the end of the day, these different approaches to theory do fundamentally different work. If not a replacement for existing practice then, what does cognitive sociology stand to gain from a greater incorporation of ABM into its methodological toolkit? There are a number of possible answers to this question, but in this context I focus on four arenas of particularly notable potential benefit to the development of theory in cognitive sociology: analytical leverage, generality, precision, and the development of new connections to existing fields of research.

22.3.1 Analytical Leverage

One of the chief benefits of pursuing computational amendments to the rich, verbally elaborated theories that predominate in cognitive and cultural sociology is that they potentially allow researchers to explain more with less. Consider, for instance, the difficulty of describing in words how a nexus of cognitive processing, interactional structures, feedback loops, and timing has given rise to the persistence and dominance of a given interpretive frame within a group. Such an explanation might very well require many pages, if not several chapters of a book, to thoroughly lay out. If the primary goal of a piece is to delve very deeply into the *particular* history of a *particular* group, this might be exactly what the researcher wants. If, however, a researcher has different or additional aspirations of being able to connect the processes playing out in that one case to other cultural processes more broadly, the explanatory workload can quickly become unwieldly (and the attention of the audience seriously overtaxed).

With a computational model at one's disposal, be it a general one that has been previously developed for the cognitive-cultural link of interest or a more richly specified one that is tightly coupled to the empirical facts of the particular case, one's analytical leverage is greatly increased. Use of an ABM allows one to easily draw a direct, clear line between relatively simple rules operating at the individual level to the collective phenomena being explained. In this particular example, for instance, it might be possible to forego a long verbal treatment of how this particular interpretative frame came to be established in order to more simply say that this particular case exhibited the type of "path-dependent" and "lock-in" processes which prior modeling has shown to be an inherent feature in the establishment of shared mental representations (Shaw 2015). Alternatively, the hypothetical researcher might choose to develop their own, empirically grounded variations of the aforementioned ABM in order to gain insight into a particular series of changes in interaction structures that lead to the specific observed outcome. Such an effort would cost more than just a reference to prior modeling work in terms of pages and audience attention, but it still might very likely be able to make the main points of the argument clear in a more efficient and potentially far more convincing way than could be achieved with a natural language description alone.

Stated more generally, ABM is often a much better tool for explaining certain aspects of emergent processes than verbal elaboration. Incorporating ABM as an additional tool in one's theoretical toolkit opens the door to the development of impressively parsimonious models that can do the same amount of analytical work in a few lines of code as many pages of dense text. The argument for pursuing such parsimony in explanation does not necessarily need to involve any appeal to it being an inherently preferable feature of theory. Instead, one needs only acknowledge the simple pragmatic point that using such models as complements to other modes of theorizing potentially saves researchers an enormous amount of time and explanatory effort. By investing in ABM as a tool for saying more with less, sociologists working at the intersection of cognition and culture are potentially freed up to spend more of their attention on bigger, more interesting aspects of their work.

22.3.2 Generality

Cognition and culture perspectives possess an innate capacity for generality. One of the very few features that has been true of every society is that they have been constituted by humans who have in common a set of fundamental cognitive capabilities and processes. This so-called psychic unity of mankind has been used as a strong argument for the validity and usefulness of rational-choice perspectives for the development of general social theory (Kiser and Hechter 1991; Coleman 1994) based on the presumption that all individuals have an innate disposition toward making choices in their own self-interest and the deliberative ability to do so. Given both the high variability across time and context of what individuals might actually consider to be in their own self-interest, as well as increasing bodies of evidence concerning how much of our behavior and thinking is determined outside of the arena of conscious thought or decision-making (Kahneman 2011; Bargh and Morsella 2008; Lizardo et al. 2016), there is a strong case to be made that the supposed universality of such microfoundations is ultimately dwarfed by that of other microfoundations that are based on deeper, more fundamental cognitive processes that are likely to operate much more consistently across time and place.[6]

Accordingly, it is not so much that ABM has the ability to make cognitively grounded social theory highly generalizable—that is a feature which is inherent to it. What this form of modeling can do, however, is provide an invaluable tool for developing transcendent statements on the sorts of social phenomena that are expected to spontaneously arise out of such universal, individual-level processes. Once established, such general statements can be subsequently applied and conditioned to better fit the particular cases under consideration. To extend the hypothetical example given earlier, if ABM can be used to clarify the "lock-in" dynamics of shared representations that *generally* arise from individual mental representation processes, this dynamic can subsequently be evoked as a causal explanation in the analysis of any number of particular instances in which shared meanings have emerged and then persisted in groups. In effect, ABM is an exceptionally efficient tool for establishing classes of highly general phenomena that individual researchers and theorists can subsequently apply or modify toward their own ends. This ability not only has the capacity to potentially enhance the explanatory reach of cognitive sociology but also gives it an uncommon opportunity to identify fundamental connections between seemingly disparate individual research cases.[7]

22.3.3 Precision

All theoretical elaboration inevitably entails the use of inferential leaps. This is especially true when theorists seek to verbally connect the individual to the collective level. Due in no small part to the necessity of paring down the immense complexity of the interdependencies involved in the transition from micro to macro to a level that can be expressed in words, audiences of such theorizations are unavoidably dependent on the validity of theorists' assumptions about how these different levels connect. Even in cases of the most seemingly well- reasoned and -supported inferential leaps, such links are prone to becoming conceptual black-boxes that resist analysis. This problem also arises for researchers attempting to adhere solely to rich descriptions of phenomena given that they often also must rely on implicit causal models of the connections between micro and macro, the opacity of which is only made more intense due to their lack of being openly stated.

One of the primary benefits of theoretical elaboration via ABM is the "glass box" (Wilensky and Rand 2015), which provides for exactly these emergent processes that are so difficult to capture verbally. Starting from a set of initial theoretical premises, the theorist develops her set of "rules" agents. Having set the stage in this fashion, she then essentially turns over the task of elaborating out the highly interdependent and complex process of how those individual processes subsequently lead to emergent, collective phenomena to the much larger computational capacity of her simulation. So translated, she is empowered to take on a much more thorough vetting of her proposed model and to pursue a much higher degree of precision her subsequent assertions. Of primary importance is the fact that she will actually be able to verify, in a fashion that others are able to also assess and confirm, that the individual processes in which she is interested are actually logically capable of generating the emergent macro-level phenomena she is attempting to explain. Having established this foundational plausibility, she and others can go on to explore how modifications of her model affect the outcomes of interest and in so doing, develop a more precise specification of the conditions under which her theoretical assertions should hold. These ABM-derived understandings can all then be subsequently translated back into her verbal depictions of her model on a much sounder and more transparent conceptual footing than would have been otherwise available.

22.3.4 Connections to Other Fields

A final motivation for incorporating ABM into cognitive sociology is the potential it has to create new connections between itself and other fields of study, both within and beyond the social sciences. In much the same way that network analysis may have begun as a primarily sociological endeavor but subsequently evolved far beyond that scope to inform research in everything from brains to the Internet, ABM has proven to be an immensely useful tool for clarifying the "transcendent" principles at play in self-organization and emergent orders across all scales of the natural and social world (Axelrod 2006). It has been able to accomplish this due to the ability of its models to provide what is essentially a common language through which researchers hailing from a host of different disciplines can identify and explore the commonalities between their extremely different arenas of substantive interest. Had they only been limited to field-specific jargon or specialized mathematical representations, it is arguable that these resonances would never have been made sufficiently obvious to have been discovered.

Agent-based modeling and the emergent dynamics it excels at demonstrating has already helped to established numerous points of fruitful exchange between the natural sciences and the social sciences. It is important to note that, historically, the enthusiasm for making such connections has led some to commit questionable acts of "violence to reality" (Weber 2015) in their eagerness to translate the complexities of the social world into models that resemble the much better behaved systems of physical reality. Nonetheless, it is exactly in this area that cognitive sociology's historical respect for nuance and the nonrational aspects of social life that cognitive-cultural ABMs have enormous amount to offer other fields. Especially given the centrality of sense-making to cognitive sociology and the growing engagement with "information theory" and classification dynamics in fields such as physics, machine learning, and artificial intelligence, there is a striking potential for *two-way* dialogues to become established via models focusing on the ways individuals take in information from an overwhelmingly complex environment and rework it into simplified, meaningful interpretations based on their past experiences. As such, pursuing connections between ABM and cognitive sociology holds a promise of making existing computational models of social processes better not only by deepening their fundamental assumptions about individuals but also by putting cognitive sociology into a position to both enrich and being enriched by a number of other disciplines.

22.4 Getting Started With ABM: Practical Resources and Basic Model Design

For all these potential advantages, a significant practical barrier to developing stronger relationships between ABM and cognitive sociology comes from the divergent methodological training researchers in the field tend to possess. Fortunately, a wealth of resources has already been developed to help researchers in general, and those in the social sciences in particular, develop competencies with ABM. Foundational texts such as *Complex Adaptive Systems* (Miller and Page 2007), *Generative Social Science* (Epstein 2006), and *Agent-Based Models* (Gilbert 2008) offer good overviews of both the philosophy that has motivated ABM and examples of the wide diversity of ways it has been applied to simulate social processes. Many universities also offer varying levels of coursework and workshops in ABM, both as a standalone methods classes and under specific disciplinary headings such as epidemiology, public policy, or ecology. There are also numerous introductory courses and guides available online, both for pay and for free and at various levels of formality (see for example the popular course offered through the Santa Fe Institute's Complexity Explorer series,[8] the tutorials made available through OpenABM,[9] and the *Online Guide for Newcomers to Agent-Based Modeling in the Social Sciences*[10] developed by Robert Axelrod and Leigh Tesfatsion).

For those of a more autodidactic bent, another common route for learning ABM is diving straight into a programming platform and using its associated tutorials and community resources to start practicing building one's own models. A wide array of free programming platforms and environments can be used for building ABMs. Among these, one of the most popular is that of NetLogo (Wilensky 1999), a free modeling environment built with a specific intention of making ABM accessible to those with little to no prior computer modeling or coding experience. Given the availability of an excellent accompanying textbook that also provides a comprehensive general introduction to ABM (Wilensky and Rand 2015) and the platform's streamlining of some of the more complicated design aspects of modeling such as model visualization and user-interface controls, NetLogo is often a strongly preferred option for researchers new to ABM. For those who have prior experience in other programming languages or would prefer to gain competencies with more generally applicable languages, an extensive variety of software toolkits and packages are also available. In the context of social science modeling specifically, the Java-based platforms of RePast (North et al. 2013) and MASON (Luke et al. 2005) have been popular options. For those familiar with R, packages such as RNetLogo and the NetLogo "R" extension provide ways of combining the functionality of R with the easy-to-use interface of NetLogo. Alternatively, another available approach for those experienced with R involves adopting a "roll your own" strategy that takes advantages of innate resonances between ABM and object-oriented programming to build one's models from scratch. Similarly, options in Python include building off of existing repositories such as the PyCX[11] (Sayama 2013) repository and building models that rely on a key conceptual linking between object class attributes and methods and agent-level variables and rule sets (Downey 2012).

In addition to acquiring the technical skills needed for the implementation of ABMs, a specific set of mental shifts is also required in order to be able to translate cognitive-cultural processes into a computational model design. As indicated previously, the most fundamental transition needed involves taking the first step of reworking cognitive mechanisms into social mechanisms. Getting into the brass tacks of an ABM design, however, requires this transition to be taken even further into developing a set of specifications of how the key elements of the model will look. Following after the excellent tutorials provided in (Macal and North 2010) and (Wilensky and Rand 2015) these elements can be divided as follows:

22.4.1 Agents

Agents are the autonomously functional programs (or objects) that represent individuals in the model. They are characterized by their individual states, usually expressed in terms of the values they have at a given moment for a defined set of *agent variables*, and rules governing how they will interact with other agents and their environment, usually expressed in terms of *agent methods* or *procedures*. In the context of cognitive sociology, the specification of agent states and rules are most likely to be derived from established understanding of real cognitive processes.

22.4.2 Environment

For some models, it may be important to be able to capture *nonsocial* or physical predicates and influences on agents' states and behaviors. Within the context of cognitive sociology, this might prove particularly important in attempts to model the emergent outcomes of embodied (Ignatow 2007; Lizardo 2007) and distributed (Martin 2010) cognition. Within the context of ABM, such nonsocial features are usually handled through specifying an environment in which agents are located and with which they can interact. Much as with the agents, every given part or "patch" in the environment can be imbued with its own set of variables/states and even procedures in those cases where nonstatic environments are expected to play a significant role (see Epstein and Axtell 1996, for classic examples of ABM that capture such dynamic interplays between social and environmental forces).

22.4.3 Interaction Topology

Regardless of whether the physical or otherwise nonsocially arising aspects of an environment are relevant to a given model, the structure of the "social environment" is an important consideration to take into account in any given agent-based model. Concordant with established understanding of the causal impact of social network structures in emergent social dynamics, the specification of who interacts with whom can have major impact on one's modeling results. Common options for interaction topology include "perfectly mixed" scenarios, where every agent has a probability of interacting with any other agent, situating agents on a lattice such that they only interact with their neighbors, and the use of any number of network structures in which ties reflect an interactional partnership between agents. In all cases, such decisions on inter-actional topology should be oriented toward faithfully reflecting the real substantive scenarios the researcher is interested in modeling.

22.4.4 Schedule

Schedule refers to the order of procedures that will be executed during each "time step" or turn of the model. This aspect of the model essentially captures the order of events that plays out during agents' interactions with each other and their local environment. Though this temporal aspect can be easy to overlook, a difference as small as having agents move first then interact with their environment or vice versus can profoundly affect what happens at the macro-level. Other considerations such as synchrony versus asynchrony, that is whether all agents go through their individual processes at the same time or in a staggered fashion, and relative time scales over which different processes play out are also important to keep in mind. For cognitive sociology models, this second issue of time scale is likely to be particularly relevant given the usual rapidity of cognitive processing vis-à-vis other environmental or social processes that might be occurring.

22.5 Practices and Principles of ABM

Beyond model implementation and design, there are also some foundational principles and practices that researchers entering into the arena of ABM do well to bear in mind. The first of these is the so-called KISS Principle of ABM: Keep It Simple and Stupid. A common temptation when one starts developing ABMs is to head straight into creating very complicated, elaborate models that include every feature one can think of as being potentially relevant to the processes of interest. Following this impulse, however, puts the modeler at risk of building something with so many moving parts that not even they can understand why the model does what it does. If one begins with a very complicated model that specifies a large number of interacting elements and rules, the task of confirming what exactly at the individual level is driving emergent behavior becomes much more difficult. In order to preserve the attractive "glass box" and parsimonious qualities of ABM, it is thus usually advisable to start with the most minimal and simplistic version of the model possible. Once one has developed a thorough understanding of how much can be accounted for with just that bare design, other additional layers of complication can then be added.

This principle of beginning simple and gradually increasing the design's complexity points to another fundamental tension in ABM that modelers should bear in mind— that of the balance between abstraction and concreteness. Successful ABMs have run the gamut between pure theory building and proof of concept models all the way to models built on raw empirical data that are used to formulate testable predictions of how real-world systems will behave. The decision of where a model should fall on this spectrum is ultimately driven by the modeler's intended purpose. If the goal is to be able to make general statements on the ability of simple cognitive mechanisms to account for a class of regularly observed features of social life, a more abstract model will likely be the best option. If instead the aim is to be able to explain or predict what will happen in a specific observable context, then there will necessarily need to be a much stronger coupling between the model and empirical observations, both in terms of model design and the use of real data in initializing the model. In these more concrete cases, it inevitable that model design is likely to end up being much more complicated than in the abstract case. Even here, however, the KISS principle holds and entails that modelers are likely to find great benefit by beginning with highly abstract, simple models of their system of interest, and then increasing the concreteness of it by using empirical data to iteratively "calibrate" and modify the model into increasingly realistic versions of itself.

A final set of considerations to be borne in mind is that of verification and validation (Wilensky and Rand 2015). Here, verification refers to the process of verifying the mapping between one's conceptual model and one's computational implementation of it. Translating ideas into code requires a surprisingly large number of judgment calls to be made, any set of which has the potential to create an unexpected amount of distance between the process one has proposed to model and the ABM that gets built. By proactively interrogating the connection between conceptual and computational models at both the level of individual design elements and emergent outcomes, and exploring how robust the model behavior proves to alternative design decisions, the modeler is best able to develop their case for having captured the processes they have set out to theorize. Whereas verification involves the mapping between ideas and computational implementation, validation involves confirming the connection between one's model and the outside world. This is obviously a critical piece of the process in situations where the aim is to develop concrete models. Even in scenarios involving highly abstract models, however, some degree of validation is still required in order to be able to make the claim that one's agent-based model has any bearing on the empirical processes of interest. Validation, especially for models not attempting to make concrete predictions about specific empirical contexts, is often achieved through a "pattern-matching approach" of demonstrating that the qualitative features of the model resemble the corresponding features of the real-world phenomena and dynamics it proposes to capture. This validation should take place at the level of both individual- and system-level behavior, with the ideal situation being one in which the modeler can further demonstrate pattern matches intermediate (i.e., meso) levels as well.

22.6 CONCLUSION

The goal of this chapter has been to articulate and motivate a computational approach to charting the emergence of cultural processes from individual cognition. Additionally, it has sought to offer readers a brief introduction to the conceptual shifts required to undertake this new direction of development and provide some practical resources for getting started with building one's own agent-based model. As a method for building theory that elegantly and transparently demonstrates how collective phenomena organically arise out of the interactions of individuals, ABM has already proven its usefulness in a wide diversity of disciplines.[12] In the context of social theory, the introduction of this "third symbol language" has created new potentials for the development of nonrational microfoundations which cognitive sociology is extremely well situated to take advantage of. At the end of the day, ABM can never replace the much richer modes of conceptual development and theorization that currently predominate in the field. It does, however, hold the capacity to become a powerful tool to help cognitive sociologists further their ability to understand and empirically study the relationship between individual cognition and collective cultural processes.

NOTES

1. The existence of the field of computational neuroscience acts as testament to both the feasibility and usefulness of developing simplified, computational models of the human brain.
2. Here, the term "social mechanisms" refers specifically to the concept as forwarded within the context of analytical sociology as individual-level causal processes that dynamically aggregate into social level outcomes and processes (i.e., microfoundations).
3. "Social influence" is a general term referring to an extremely broad class of models that pertain not only to other arenas of social dynamics, such as those involved in voting or opinion formation, but also to natural systems, the classic example of which being orientation of magnetic particles in a solid (Castellano et al. 2009). The identification of such fundamental resonances between extremely different types of systems is one of the major fruits born of ABM and complex systems research.
4. Such variants are a staple of a popular class of ABM class of models that use genetic algorithms (GA). The GA models have been used for everything from modeling species evolution to teaching computers to write their own programs (Mitchell 1998).
5. This realization mirrors established understanding of how the great majority of our cognitive processing occurs *outside* of conscious, deliberative view (Kahneman 2011; Bargh and Morsella 2008; Lizardo et al. 2016). We might have one general process of reasoning to consider when it comes to rational calculation, but when it comes to *unconscious and nonrational* drivers of human understanding and behavior, we encounter a veritable panoply of different mechanism to potentially consider.
6. Haidt's (2001) metaphor of the "rider and elephant" is extremely germane here. Conscious processing, as the "rider," may be able to steer the elephant, unconscious processing, in different directions, but it is ultimately unable to fundamentally alter its nature. The recognition of "metacognitive" abilities, wherein we can recognize the existence of unconscious cognitive processes and intervene strategically to redirect their course (e.g., making changes in one's environment in order to help break a bad habit), is likely to be a very important piece in explaining strategic cultural action in group contexts (e.g., as in the case of "framing" [Snow et al. 1986] in political movements). Ultimately, however, the fundamental principles of such automatic processing cannot be altered, only manipulated.
7. This orientation toward identifying more general classes of cognitive-cultural phenomena via the emergent dynamics that are expected to obtain across different specific instantiations of them bears a notable kinship with Zerubavel's (2007) work on generalization via social pattern analysis.
8. https://www.complexityexplorer.org/.
9. https://www.openabm.org/.
10. http://www2.econ.iastate.edu/tesfatsi/abmread.htm.
11. The PyCX repository was built as a complement to a technical but extremely thorough and well-written open access textbook on complex systems analysis and modeling (Sayama 2015).
12. For example, see overviews of ABM use in such diverse fields as ecology (Grimm and Railsback 2005), archeology (Barceló and Del Castillo 2016), cellular biology (Gorochowski 2016), and public health (Maglio and Mabry 2011).

Bibliography

Abbott, Andrew. 1988. "Transcending General Linear Reality." *Sociological Theory* 6(2):169–86.

Archer, Margaret. 1995. *Realist Social Theory: The Morphogenetic Approach*. New York: Cambridge University Press.

Axelrod, Robert 2006. "Agent-Based Modeling as a Bridge between Disciplines." pp. 1565–84 in *Handbook of Computational Economics, Vol. 2: Agent-Based Computational Economics*. Amsterdam: Elsevier.

Barceló, Juan, and Florencia Del Castillo. 2016. *Simulating Prehistoric and Ancient Worlds*. Cham, Switzerland: Springer International.

Bargh, John and Ezequiel Morsella. 2008. "The Unconscious Mind." *Perspectives on Psychological Science* 3(1):73–9.

Bhasker, Roy. 1979. *The Possibility of Naturalism*. New York: Routledge.

Blumer, Herbert. 1969. *Symbolic Interactionism: Perspective and Method*. Englewood Cliffs, NJ: Prentice-Hall.

Brekhus, Wayne. 2015. *Culture and Cognition*. Cambridge: Polity Press.

Castellano, Claudio, Santo Fortunato, and Vittorio Loreto. 2009. "Statistical Physics of Social Dynamics." *Reviews of Modern Physics*, 81(2):591–646.

Cerulo, Karen. 2010. "Mining the Intersections of Cognitive Sociology and Neuroscience." *Poetics* 28(2):115–32.

Coleman, James. 1994. *Foundations of Social Theory*. Cambridge, MA: Harvard University Press.

Demeulenaere, Pierre 2011. "Introduction." pp. 1–32 in *Analytical Sociology and Social Mechanisms*, edited by Pierre Demeulenaere. Cambridge: Cambridge University Press.

Dimaggio, Paul. 1997. "Culture and Cognition." *Annual Review of Sociology* 23(1):263–87.

Downey, Allen. 2012. *Think Complexity*. Sebastopol, CA: O'Reilly.

Durkheim, Émile. 1982. *The Rules of Sociological Method: And Selected Texts on Sociology and Its Method*. London: Macmillan.

Epstein, Joshua. 2006. *Generative Social Science: Studies in Agent-Based Computational Modeling*. Princeton: Princeton University Press.

Epstein, Joshua. 2013. *Agent Zero: Toward Neurocognitive Foundations for Generative Social Sciences*. Princeton: Princeton University Press.

Epstein, Joshua, and Robert Axtell. 1996. *Growing Artificial Societies: Social Science from the Bottom Up*. Washington, DC: Brookings Institute Press.

Giddens, Anthony. 1984. *The Constitution of Society: Outline of the Theory of Structuration*. Cambridge: Polity Press.

Gilbert, Nigel. 2008. *Agent-Based Models*. Thousand Oaks, CA: SAGE.

Gilbert, Nigel, and Pietro Terna. 2000. "How to Build and Use Agent-Based Models in Social Science." *Mind and Society* 1(1):57–72.

Gilbert, Nigel, and Klaus G. Troitzsch. 2005. *Simulation for the Social Scientist*. New York: Open University Press.

Gorochowski, Thomas. 2016. "Agent-Based Modelling in Synthetic Biology." *Essays in Biochemistry* 60(4):325–36.

Grimm, Volker, and Steven Railsback. 2005. *Individual-Based Modeling and Ecology*. Princeton Series in Theoretical and Computational Biology. Princeton: Princeton University Press.

Habermas, Jürgen. 1984. *The Theory of Communicative Action*. Vol. 2. Boston: Beacon Press.

Haidt, Jonathan. 2001. "The Emotional Dog and Its Rational Tail: A Social Intuitionist Approach to Moral Judgment." *Psychological Review* 108(4):814–34.

Hechter, Michael, and Satoshi Kanazawa. 1997. "Sociological Rational Choice Theory." *Annual Review of Sociology* 23(1):191–214.

Hedström, Peter. 2005. *Dissecting the Social: On the Principles of Analytical Sociology*. New York: Cambridge University Press.

Hedström, Peter, and Richard Swedberg 1998. "Social Mechanisms: An Introductory Essay." pp. 1–31 in *Social Mechanisms: An Analytical Approach to Social Theory*, edited by Peter Hedström and Richard Swedberg. Cambridge: Cambridge University Press.

Hedström, Peter, and Petri Ylikoski. 2010. "Causal Mechanisms in the Social Sciences." *Annual Review of Sociology* 36(1):46–67.

Ignatow, Gabriel. 2007. "Theories of Embodied Knowledge: New Directions for Culture and Cultural Sociology?" *Journal for the Theory of Social Behaviour* 37(2):115–35.

Jepperson, Ron, and John Meyer. 2011. "Multiple Levels of Analysis and the Limitations of Methodological Individualisms." *Sociological Theory* 29(1):54–73.

Kahneman, Daniel. 2011. *Thinking Fast and Slow*. New York: Farrar, Straus and Giroux.

Kiser, Edgar, and Michael Hechter. 1991. "The Role of General Theory in Comparative-Historical Sociology." *American Journal of Sociology* 97(1):1–30.

Kroneberg, Clemens, and Frank Kalter. 2012. "Rational Choice Theory and Empirical Research: Methodological and Theoretical Contributions in Europe." *Annual Review of Sociology* 38(1):73–92.

Lizardo, Omar. 2007. "'Mirror Neurons,' Collective Objects and the Problem of Transmission: Reconsidering Stephen Turner's Critique of Practice Theory." *Journal for the Theory of Social Behavior* 37(3):319–50.

Lizardo, Omar, Robert Mowry, Brandon Sepulvado, Dustin Stoltz, Marshall Taylor, Justin Van Ness, et al. 2016. "What Are Dual Process Models? Implications for Cultural Analysis in Sociology." *Sociological Theory* 37(4):287–310.

Luke, Sean, Claudio Cioffi-Revilla, Liviu Panait, Keith Sullivan, and Gabriel Balan. 2005. "MASON: A Multi-Agent Simulation Environment." *Simulation: Transactions of the society for Modeling and Simulation International* 81(7):517–27.

Macal, Charles M., and Michal J. North. 2010. "Tutorial on Agent-Based Modelling and Simulation." *Journal of Simulation* 4(3):151–62.

Macy, Michael M., and Robert Willer. 2002. "From Factors to Actors: Computational Sociology and Agent-Based Modeling." *Annual Review of Sociology* 28(1):143–66.

Maglio, Paul, and Patricia Mabry. 2011. "Agent-Based Models and Systems Science Approaches to Public Health." *American Journal of Preventative Medicine* 40(3):392–4.

Martin, John L. 2010. "Life's a Beach but You're an Ant, and Other Unwelcome News for the Sociology of Culture." *Poetics* 38(2):229–44.

Miller, John, and Scott Page. 2007. *Complex Adaptive Systems: An Introduction to Computational Models of Social Life*. Princeton: Princeton University Press.

Mitchell, Melanie. 1998. *An Introduction to Genetic Algorithms*. Cambridge, MA: MIT Press.

North, Michael J., Nicholson T. Collier, Jonathan Ozik, Eric Tatara, Mark Bragen, Charles M. Macal, et al. 2013. *Complex Adaptive Systems Modeling with Repast Simphony*. Heidelberg: Springer.

Nowak, Andrzej, Jacek Szamrej, and Bibb Latané. 1990. "From Private Attitude to Public Opinion: A Dynamic Theory of Social Impact." *Psychological Review* 97(3):362–76.

Ostrom, Thomas. 1988. "Computer Simulation: The Third Symbol Language." *Journal of Experimental Social Psychology* 24(5):381–92.

Parsons, Talcott. 1951. *The Social System*. Glencoe, IL: Free Press.

Sawyer, Keith. 2005. *Social Emergence: Societies as Complex Systems*. New York: Cambridge University Press.

Sayama, Hiroki. 2013. "PyCX: A Python-Based Simulation Code Repository for Complex Systems Education." *Complex Adaptive Systems Modeling* 1(1):1–10.

Sayama, Hiroki. 2015. *Introduction to the Modeling and Analysis of Complex Systems*. Geneseo, NY: Open SUNY Textbooks.

Schröder, Tobias, Jesse Hoey, and Kimberly Rogers. 2016. "Modeling Dynamic Identities and Uncertainty in Social Interactions: Bayesian Affect Control Theory." *American Sociological Review* 8(4):828–55.

Shaw, Lynette. 2015. "Mechanics and Dynamics of Social Construction: Modeling the Emergence of Culture from Individual Mental Representation." *Poetics* 52(1):75–90.

Snow, David, E. Burke Rochford, Steven Worden, and Robert Benford. 1986. "Frame Alignment Processes, Micromobilization, and Movement Participation." *American Sociological Review* 51(5):464–81.

Troitzsch, Klaus G. 1998. "Multilevel Process Modeling in the Social Sciences." pp. 20–36 in *Computer Modeling of Social Processes*, edited by W. B. G. Liebrand, A. Nowak, and R. Hegselmann. London: Sage.

Weber, Max. 2015. *On the Methodology of the Social Sciences*. Philadelphia: Lulu Press.

Wilensky, Uri. 1999. "NetLogo." Evanston, IL: Center for Connected Learning and Computer-Based Modeling, Northwestern University. http://ccl.northwestern.edu/netlogo/.

Wilensky, Uri, and William Rand. 2015. *Introduction to Agent-Based Modeling: Modeling Natural, Social, and Engineered Complex Systems with NetLogo*. Cambridge, MA: MIT Press.

Zerubavel, Eviatar. 1997. *Social Mindscapes: An Invitation to Cognitive Sociology*. Cambridge, MA: Harvard University Press.

Zerubavel, Eviatar. 2007. "Generally Speaking: The Logic and Mechanics of Social Pattern Analysis." *Sociological Forum* 22(2):131–45.

PART IV

....

THE SOCIOLOGY
OF PERCEPTION
AND ATTENTION

....

CHAPTER 23

SOCIOLOGY OF ATTENTION

fundamental reflections on a theoretical program

MARKUS SCHROER

EVEN though today "attention" is taken to be a key category for understanding contemporary modern society, and even though the term can look back on a long history in philosophy, psychology, and pedagogy (Crary 1999; Waldenfels 2004), sociology has yet to develop a systematic interest in the matter. This is remarkable insofar as there are indeed many references to the term—references made throughout the discipline's history by various sociologists such as Georg Simmel, Ferdinand Tönnies, Emile Durkheim, George Herbert Mead, Alfred Schütz, Thomas Luckmann, William Isaac Thomas, Max Scheler, Erving Goffman, Friedrich Tenbruck, Niklas Luhmann, Richard Münch, Zygmunt Bauman, and Alois Hahn. And yet its meaning—a couple of exceptions notwithstanding (see, e.g., Hahn 2001)—seems to be taken for granted.[1] Most of the time, it is mentioned only in passing, without further commenting on or clarifying its specific use. To date, sociology therefore still lacks a systematic and comprehensive treatment of the issue.

As I argue here, the concept of attention is essential to understanding the social. Without the individual's attention for the environment and without the environment's attention for the individual, human beings would simply be incapable of survival (Claessens 1980; Scheler 1973:144–7; Mead 2009). Let alone for reasons of self-preservation, human beings must be able to turn toward and react to impulses of the outside world, just as they need to be able to draw the attention of their fellow human beings. The heart of the matter therefore seemingly lies in the individual's ability to both pay and receive attention. And with numerous outside forces trying to exact their influence on this ability—striving to either optimize, govern, or otherwise control it—the meaning of attention always also takes on a social, cultural, and political dimension in addition to the more epistemological and psychological questions of perception. The questions relevant to a sociological perspective on attention—Why was this particular impression, event, or information selected and attended to and not another one? What exactly is the process of selection? According to which criteria was it selected? Who or what decides on what is selected? What happens to the other possibilities that were not realized?—cannot be answered with reference to biological, neurological, or psychological insights alone. Without a doubt, these are also of great significance and furthermore emphasize the necessarily interdisciplinary orientation of the field. However, there are always also social mechanisms at work when it comes to selecting certain phenomena, events, information, things, or people—mechanisms that vary historically and culturally. The topic of attention should therefore be placed at the center of sociological inquiry.

In order to underline my argument, I first deal with the term's origin and history by tracing the various ways in which it has been used. While today the term is more or less only used in the narrow sense of media attention (Franck 1998; Rötzer 1998; Beck and Schweiger 2001; Bleicher and Hickethier 2002; Pörksen and Krischke 2010; Bublitz 2010), I highlight its diverse meanings and sociologically relevant aspects (23.1). Second, I elaborate on a central terminological distinction—that between voluntary and involuntary attention—and then illustrate how closely the issue of attention is related to the question of the subject and its place in modern society. Although at the center of current sociological debates, this question has hitherto not been discussed in terms of attention. However, it can be argued that questions of modern subjectivity and of assessing contemporary society are part of the debate on whether it is the subject who determines what he or she pays attention to (voluntary attention), or whether it is the environment that forcefully steers attention from the outside (involuntary attention) (23.2). Third, I offer a genuinely sociological explanation for the often-quoted assertion that attention is a "scarce resource" or commodity (Luhmann 1983:67; Bauman 1991; Rötzer 1998; Goldhaber 1999/2000:79; Stiegler 2008:168) by showing how this scarcity can be accounted for by drawing on the concepts of modernization, individualization, mediatization, and technicalization. Furthermore it is argued that the "fight for attention" (Münch 1995:83; Rötzer 1998:72ff.; Franck 1998:14; Waldenfels 2004:255; Nolte 2005)—a phenomenon eminently significant to the understanding of contemporary society—can only be adequately explained if all of these factors are taken together (23.3). Fourth, I demonstrate that this fight for attention is not limited to the field of politics (see Nolte 2005), but characteristic of all social fields. Drawing on Pierre Bourdieu's notion of field (see Bourdieu 1993, 2006; Bourdieu and Wacquant 2004), I argue that, in each field, the struggle is about more than just the respective field-specific stakes: it is also about the investing and drawing of attention. The subsequent analysis of the fields of politics, economy, science, and art give evidence of the fact that the adage of the British philosopher George Berkeley (1710/1982) "Esse est percipi (et percipere)" ("To be is to be perceived and to perceive") holds even more true for the postmodern communication societies of our age than it did for the eighteenth century. The imperative that one has to draw attention to oneself if one does not want to be completely ignored or passed over (Münch 1991:17) radically applies only to contemporary society (23.4). The chapter closes with a brief summary of the argument and an outlook on the future tasks of a sociology of attention (23.5).

23.1 Origin, History and Meaning of the Term "Attention"

The term "attention" has had a rather fluctuating past. Findings of the term are scattered throughout the entire history of philosophy. It also features predominantly in psychology, pedagogy, and, as a more current development, in media and communication studies and neurosciences.[2] All of these findings could of course serve as resources from which to glean information as to the term's specific meaning. But since an exhaustive treatment of the many uses of the term would go beyond the scope of this paper (for an overview, see Neumann 1971; Assmann 2001; Crary 1999), only those meanings will be examined in further detail that are of sociological import. To this aim, the observation seems crucial that the word "attention" has an inherently social connotation: bestowing attention on others implies "actually giving them something instead of merely observing the facts" (Waldenfels 2004:263; my translation). From a sociological point of view, the following terminological pairs are the most relevant: attention and selection (23.1.1), attention and routine (23.1.2) and attention and absent-mindedness or dissipation (23.1.3).

23.1.1 Attention and Selection

The significance of attention as a phenomenon hinges on the assumption of an excess supply of possibilities that cannot be realized all at the same time. In a world conceived of as complex, attention decides on the impressions that get to enter our consciousness, which problems are to be dealt with, and which topics are to be taken up by the media— while also deciding on the ones that are to be left out. Attention therefore means *selection*. It is precisely because there is no general answer to the question of why one possibility takes precedence over the other that attention is an issue of sociological relevance. In each case, the selection process depends on who the actor is, in what kind of social situation he finds himself and on the field (politics, economy, science, religion) this situation is taking place in. Rather than being randomly distributed, attention is always turned to field-specific events. That attention as a phenomenon is inherently social in nature is furthermore manifested by the fact that societies, when compared both diachronically and synchronically, can be shown to vary not only in their respective foci of attention but also according to gender, profession, and milieu[3]: "In every society, the things women have to attend to differ from those of men, those of peasants from those of artisans, and those of priests from those of kings" (Hahn 2001:30; my translation). Also, the division of labor generates what might be called "special attentions"

(Hahn 2001:30; my translation) which account for differences between professionals and laypeople in terms of attention. While, on the one hand, the professional—due to years of training and experience—notices things which the layperson would simply overlook, the professional also, on the other, is prone to the proverbial "organizational blindness" which renders him unable to react to impulses from outside of his habitualized zone of special attention. Whichever criteria are applied, selection will always entail a wide range of possibilities not realized, actions not carried out, issues left unaddressed, and people not getting their turn. The sheer impossibility of simultaneously paying attention to all existing events, things, and people makes attention a rare commodity, and, by consequence, also accounts for the fact that from attention, competition ensues—competition in which there are winners and losers, for a gain in attention for A is a loss of attention for B.

Attention therefore generates potential for social conflict on account of the fact that it can only be bestowed successively. Whether it is in school, within the family, at meetings or party rallies, or in talkshows or seminars: in all of these situations the distribution of attention is virulent. In some cases, there is from the outset a stark difference in role allocation, as, for example, when only a few speakers (receiving all the attention) are faced with a large audience (paying all the attention). In others, the roles of speaker and audience are determined only as the situation runs its course.

To summarize: attention, as a phenomenon, derives its significance and meaning from the fact that not everything can be registered at the same time: "Harshly put, attention is a function of the circumstance that the mind cannot do everything at once, not even more than one thing at a time. […] Within a conceived field of things existing, the mind can only grasp and intentionally linger on one thing only, dissolving everything else into the background—and this is nothing other than a circumscription of attention" (Blumenberg 2002:198; my translation). The terms "selection" and "attention" are here used nearly synonymously. The mind can only occupy itself with a particular object at the expense of other objects, which, however, could also have been moved into the foreground. The distinction between foreground and background, which Blumenberg more or less explicitly draws on in order to elucidate the meaning of attention, nicely clarifies why Gaston Bachelard conceived of attention as a "magnifying glass" (Bachelard 1994:154) and also why Blumenberg takes recourse to a phenomenological formulation of the nature of perception and being-in-the-world which—from a system theoretical point of view—was rephrased as follows:

> It is a selection which does not eliminate that which is effectively not selected, but moves it into the background. You can come back to it. What is on the horizon can at any moment become the center of attention. Meaning is generated by steadfastly and sequentially bestowing attention, i.e., by focusing on this and not on that, but always bearing in mind that the direction can be changed and each bestowal principally revised.   (Hahn 2001:27, my translation)

It should therefore be noted that the concentration of attention on a particular topic, phenomenon, event, or person does not entail the permanent exclusion of all other topics, phenomena, events, or people. Exclusion is always situative and momentary—a contention that has been prominently argued by the postmodernist thinker Zygmunt Bauman, who holds that "[p]ostmodernity is weak on exclusion" (Bauman 1998:256), and which has also been taken up by Bruno Latour, who argues that, today, "[w]e can get rid of nothing and no one" (Latour 2005:40). Exclusion is only valid *until further notice*. What is being ignored at time *t*, will be taken under consideration again at time *t+1*. What has been excluded only a moment ago, can soon be included again (Latour 2004:196–7). The "work of inclusion and exclusion" (Latour 2004:194) is permanently being taken up again and therefore never finalized. However, this rather weak consolation of only being temporarily excluded can yet be categorically differentiated from the type of exclusion that perpetuates and consolidates itself. The sociologically relevant question that follows from this is why certain topics, phenomena, events and people are repeatedly being given preferential treatment. What mechanisms are at work here? The role of power cannot be underestimated in this regard and should invariably factor into a response to such questions.

Socialization and upbringing, acquired preferences in taste, and adopted patterns of perception are also important factors governing our attention (Schmidt 2001:187). We *learn* to pay attention to certain things while we fade out everything else. The infinite richness of potentially perceivable things is thereby reduced to a manageable amount that—while still substantive—does not put too great a strain on one's attentive capacities. To use the words of George Herbert Mead:

> The whole "intelligent process" of humans lies in "attention which is selective of certain types of stimuli. Other stimuli which are bombarding the system are in some fashion shunted off. [...] [O]ur attention is an organizing process as well as a selective process. [...] Our attention enables us to organize the field in which we are going to act.   (Mead 2009:25)

Habitually acquired and stabilized dispositions therefore provide the individual with relief from an overwhelming number of impressions and are therefore highly functional—a fact that impresses itself most vehemently when such routinized patterns break down.

23.1.2 Attention and Routine

In the previous section, it was established that there is no general answer to the question of what excites our attention because selection criteria vary according to society, context, social role, milieu, gender, socialization, and profession. Nonetheless, what is crucial is the fact itself of these factors having an impact on our disposition to pay attention. Attention cannot be generated or elicited at random. And while this insight generally holds true, there is, however, a strong candidate for an answer to the question of what, as a rule, draws our attention: the orientation toward the new. As was already observed by Immanuel Kant, "Through the new, to which the rare and that which has been kept hidden also belong, attention is enlivened. [...] Everyday life or the familiar extinguishes it" (Kant 2006:55). This insight—in Kant's time already widespread and often reiterated— has since become a well-established distinction made in nearly all treatises on attention: that between attention and routine. These two terms should not, however, be conceived as antagonistic, but rather as interdependent: "Foremost among the human capacities, according to Goethe, is attention. But it shares this primacy with habit, which from the outset vies with it for preeminence. All attentiveness has to flow into habit, if it is not to blow human beings apart, and all habits must be disrupted by attentiveness if it is not to paralyze the human being" (Benjamin 2005:592). This concept of a dialectical interplay between attention and routine, in which the necessity of routines as well as that of change are given equal emphasis, is also central to the action theory of Alfred (Schütz 1970). The phenomenological perspective, however, puts a much stronger focus on the building up of routines rather than on the intended disruption of the everyday familiar. In everyday life, the actor is only rarely faced with situations that cannot be dealt with using his acquired skill sets. Typical situations require typical action plans. What once was effective will continue to be effective. The attention afforded everyday routine activities therefore amounts to zero. It would be a waste of this scarce resource if such activities were to be carried out with high concentration. The taken-for-granted world can be put into question, however, and time-tested coping strategies may fail, necessitating a reorientation. In this case, attention is activated, adaption to the new situation is effectuated, and routines are built up again (Schütz and Luckmann 1973).

Following Kant, a distinction can be drawn between attention that the subject actively directs toward his or her environment and attention that is imposed on the subject. In the latter case, the subject cannot resist his or her attention being drawn because it is riveted almost automatically: "But it is an especially bad habit of our faculty of attention to fix itself directly, even involuntarily, on what is faulty in others: to fix one's eyes on a button missing from the coat of someone who is directly in front of us, or on gaps between his teeth, or to direct attention to a habitual speech defect, thereby confusing the other person and ruining the game not only for him but also for conversation" (Kant 2006:20). As Kant's observations illustrate, it is, first and foremost, deviation from the expected that captivates our attention, whereas everything routine and familiar is always in danger of going unnoticed. Accordingly, those who do not want to excite attention will be intent on remaining inconspicuous and on acting in conformity with expectations. Conversely, those who wish to call attention to themselves will violate rules and norms, confound expectations, and refuse to conform to convention. However, even deviance, intentional provocations, and violations of rules will eventually become familiar, the result being that a competition of ever more ostentatious behavior is set into motion: "the louder, the more attention-drawing and shocking, the better. [...] With public attention dulled and made blasé by diversion ever more plentiful and lurid, only shocks stronger than yesterday's shocks stand a chance of capturing it" (Bauman 1995:157). There are certainly many examples for this upward spiral of increasingly stronger shocks. The mass media's "preference for the extraordinary" (Luhmann 2000:19) awards every aberration from normalcy with the prospect of being reported. Displays of violence can be regarded as an "attention-grabber" (Luhmann 2000:18) par excellence.

And although there is plenty of evidence supporting this assumption of an escalation, the importance of contrast is nevertheless underestimated. Generally speaking, that which shows a marked difference to the conventional, familiar, common, and expected is also noticeable. The argument that only the increasingly loud, glaring, and shrill manifestations have a chance of being heard is one-sided insofar as more of the same thing— no matter how intensified—can also become tiresome. What is crucial in matters of attention is that an impression has to be markedly different from the previous one. It follows that the silent, the colorless, and the meek have a good chance of standing out in places where the loud, the glaring, and the shrill are predominant. Although this does not cancel out the logic of shocks trying to outdo each other, it nevertheless adds to it the possibility of placing counterpoints. Unmarred by this latter qualification, however, is the overall argument that when it comes to matters of attention, monotonous repetitions should by all means be avoided and an orientation toward that which has never been or happened before be adopted. In other words: attention requires a fixation on the new—a fixation that can be regarded as overall essential to modernity and its dynamics.

23.1.3 Attention and Absent-Mindedness or Dissipation

"Dissipation" and "absent-mindedness" are also prominent terms opposed to "attention." They signify distraction, a lapse of concentration, and a lack of focus on that which is relevant to a situation—all of which are usually deemed a social misbehavior and are sanctioned accordingly. In many social situations, giving the impression of letting the mind wander, of being easily distractible or of dreaming, means not meeting the expected requirement of being attentive. Interaction partners are led to believe that the absent-minded person does not pay the situation or the people in the situation the same amount of attention as they do and are therefore put in doubt of whether or not the occasion even warrants their attention. The absent-minded is therefore considered as someone who spoils the game and puts group cohesion and group activities at risk. In intimate relationships, this can have devastating consequences, for it is imperative that one should, without exception, be interested in all that concerns one's partner (Giddens 1993). Digressions of any kind, the slightest inattention such as directing one's gaze and thus one's interest in another direction can be regarded as an illegitimate indifference, the result often being a spoiled evening, serious conflict, or even a breakup— especially in the case of repeat offenders.

It is typical of social institutions to censure or disapprove of any lapse of attention. In schools, for instance, the lack of focus on a lesson's content is not interpreted as concentration on some other topic, but as a digression from the essential, as a reverie or as daydreaming. And of course it is still the teacher who gets to define what the essential is. There may be one case only in which absent-mindedness is not condemned, but downright cultivated and made part of one's self-presentation: that of the proverbial "scatterbrained professor," whose—sometimes calculated—blunderings are reinterpreted to indicate remoteness from the banalities of everyday life, a quality that in turn is a positive mark of the profession. Far from accusing the professor of lacking concentration, a sympathetic audience will rather accept this quirkiness of the notoriously absentminded professor as the price to be paid for the service to a higher calling (Algazi 2001). The intellectual's lapse in attention, unlike the student's, is deemed a pardonable "faux pas"—a phenomenon that gives further evidence to the fact that the judgments concerning attention-related behavior are always in some way related to the social status attributed to the person in question.

Respectively, the term "dissipation" can be interpreted as arising from the realization that excessive concentration poses a serious health risk and therefore requires compensation. In the case of the intellectual, going for a walk, music, or conversation are recommended (Algazi 2001). The masses, by contrast, are advised to visit variétés, theaters, and cinemas in order to alleviate the severe strain industrial work has put on their attention (Crary 1999) and to have a temporary "diversion"[4] from the exigencies of everyday life. However, the multiplication of possibilities for distraction has also given rise to critical voices which argue that therein lies the reason for the successive reduction of the subject's capability to be attentive. Lamenting the loss of the ability to focus one's attention is widespread and today manifests itself most prominently in the diagnosis of the so-called attention deficiency syndrome (ADS) or attention deficiency hyperactivity syndrome (ADHS)—a diagnosis that reproduces the already well-known reservations concerning television and computer games (Türcke 2012).

23.2 GIVING ATTENTION—WILLINGLY OR DUE TO FORCE: SUBJECT-CONSTITUTION IN THE DISCOURSE ON ATTENTION

The previous section's review of the different uses of the term "attention" and its counterparts has shown that attention is not an issue pertinent only to psychology such that sociology need not burden itself with it. Selection processes, routines, the orientation toward the new, and the criticism of dissipation in the name of concentrated attention as an idealized educational goal—all of these topics are sociological in nature. This section turns to another sociologically relevant dimension of the discourse on attention: it is shown that what is at stake in the debate on attention is the role of the subject itself. The discourse is marked by two opposing constructions of the subject that—as demonstrated—are inherently linked to diverging notions of attention.

On the one hand, attention is conceived of as a voluntary act or activity. Understood this way, the concept is closely related to those of "concentration" and "interest"—for example, as they are used by Wilhem Wundt, William James[5] (Kohn 1895/1999), Emile Durkheim (1997:239) and George Herbert Mead (2009:25). Attention is defined as a subject's deliberate and voluntary turn toward a certain thing. On the other hand, the concept of attention refers to a phenomenon that the subject has no control over and that has a power of its own. The assumption is that certain phenomena, events, and occurrences can impose themselves on our consciousness regardless of our will. According to this version, the subject is not at liberty to either attend to or ignore something. It is rather understood that there are stimuli so serious, impressive, or obtrusive that one simply *has* to fix one's attention on them—even if this is done unwillingly. One cannot help but notice that *the first version* adheres to the notion of a sovereign subject and to a bourgeois educational ideal according to which the subject, in the course of complex socialization and education processes, selects certain topics and activities and then learns to focus on them diligently without letting itself be distracted. Here attention is regarded as a virtue to be instilled by disciplinary means (Crary 1999; Ribot 1888/2007; Hagner 1998:278). The *second version* has time and again occasioned the lamentations of cultural criticism deploring the products of modern mass culture. These are accused of keeping the individual—an individual conceived of as extremely susceptible to manipulation—from following his or her own interests by downright forcing him or her to attend to them. Modern culture, in its search for the extraordinary, its fixation on everything that has never been seen or heard of before, its lust for sensation (Türcke 2002), turns out to be an *overwhelming* or *overpowering culture* in which the individual no longer gets to decide what he or she wants to pay attention to. Not only is this facet of the concept of attention often discussed in terms of the notion of "*Reizüberflutung*," that is, the onslaught of stimuli but also it is connoted with the suspicion of extensive manipulation.

The research literature refers to these two aspects of attention variously as "voluntary and involuntary," "active or passive," "artificial or natural" attention (Ribot 1888/2007; Scheler 1973):

> In practical life we discriminate between voluntary and involuntary attention. We call it voluntary if we approach the impressions with an idea in our mind as to what we want to focus our attention on. We carry our personal interest, our own idea into the observation of the objects. Our attention has chosen its aim beforehand, and we ignore all that does not fulfill this specific interest. [...] Through our voluntary attention we seek something and accept the offering of the surroundings only in so far as it brings us what we are seeking.   (Münsterberg 1916/2001:80)

As is suggested by Münsterberg, voluntary attention takes on the function of blinders. By fading out the various distractions our environment has in store for us, we determinedly steer toward that particular thing we have set our minds on. Münsterberg continues:

> It is quite different with the involuntary attention. The guiding influence here comes from without. The cue for the focusing of our attention lies in the events which we perceive. What is loud and shining and unusual attracts our involuntary attention. We must turn our mind to a place where an explosion occurs, we must read the glaring electric signs which flash up.   (Münsterberg 1916/2001:80)

Whether attention is depicted as coming from the inside or the outside plays an important role in the respective assessment of these two modes of attention. Münsterberg's assertion that "[t]he best does not come from without" (Münsterberg 1916/2001:79) is not only characteristic of the reservations concerning attention that is steered from the outside. It can rather be understood as a more general objection to any kind of external influence—an objection that is also shared by other authors such as David Riesman, who, in "The Lonely Crowd" (2001), argued against the "inner-directed type" of social character gradually being replaced by an "outer-directed" one. Characteristic of the first type is a self-disciplined and self-motivated personality who is guided in all his or her choices and endeavors by inner beliefs. The second type, by contrast, is anxiously oriented toward expectations coming from the outside. According to Riesman, it follows that, in the "age of other-directedness," autonomy and self-determination are in danger of being ousted by conformism and opportunism. The same concern was harbored by critical theorists, who feared the conformism of individuals yielding to outside constraints (Horkheimer and Adorno 2007). The list of examples could go on still further. What all of these examples have in common, however, is a concern with the fate of the modern individual and a fear of the modern subject degenerating into the proverbial puppet on the strings of social and cultural forces—a theme that lies at the heart of cultural criticism.

These few examples should suffice to illustrate how tightly the narrative of attention's decline is interwoven into the history of the modern individual. Involuntary attention progressively gains the upper hand over voluntary attention. Ironically, however, it is precisely the voluntary kind that the individual is in need of in order keep at bay the outside world with its many temptations. Voluntary and involuntary attention should therefore be conceived of not as complementary, but rather as competing systems of attention with one side trying to triumph over the other. The drama invoked by such scenarios can be accounted for in terms of what is at stake in these arguments, which is nothing less than the individual's freedom to choose, at will, what things to turn attention to. This point was emphasized not only by Late Enlightenment thinkers (Hagner 1998:276), but also by the pragmatist philosopher and sociologist George Herbert Mead, who conceived of the "human animal" as an "attentive animal" (Mead 2009:25) that selects and chooses among the many "stimuli which are bombarding the system" and separates them into those that are to be "shunted off" and those that get to enter into the organization of action: "Here we have the organism as acting and determining its environment. It is not simply a set of passive senses played upon by the stimuli that come from without. The organism goes out and determines what it is going to respond to, and organizes that world." (Mead 2009:25) As can be gleaned from this quote, Mead does not, in general, deny that humans are influenced by their environment (Mead 2009:25). He rather argues that—owing to the operation of attention—we are not completely at the environment's mercy, but to some degree able to shape it according to our own design. He tends to overestimate the organism's power of control, however, putting too much faith in voluntarism. If it were indeed the case that we are free to autonomously select the stimuli we respond to, then there would be no such thing as the onslaught of stimuli and all the concerns over the individual being overwhelmed would be unfounded. The following observation by Max Scheler would also be rendered incomprehensible: "'Passive attention', the imposition of objects with their qualities of attraction and repellence, presuppose at least the perception of the objects" (Scheler 1973:145). In other words: whether we are repelled or attracted by objects, in both cases they have already passed the borders of perception and thus impressed themselves on our consciousness.

Neurologists (Fischer 1996; Linke 1996) argue that the body is made up of various competing attention systems that—in the absence of a central authority—constantly grapple over which of the stimuli in any given situation warrants the first response by the respective system in charge. The fight for attention thus already takes place within the organism[6] and is not always resolved in favor of the subject, which—from the point of view of neurologists—is no longer the master of his own home: "What appears to be control is in actual fact the outcome of the competition between a variety of programs that all want to be executed. The most probable or the strongest stimulus then wins over all the others. It then only seems as if attention is directed towards something or as if one had decided upon something" (quoted in Rötzer 1998:92; my translation). By arguing that it only appears to us as if we were the ones deciding, Singer reveals the belief that it is the subject who actively and voluntarily directs his or her attention to be an illusion. However, instead of merely pitting this rather deterministic neurological view against Mead's optimism concerning the ability to steer one's attention, it should rather be noted that, in most cases, voluntary and involuntary attention cannot be sharply and distinctly differentiated. As Thomas Luckmann and Alfred Schütz have argued, there are only gradual differences between "forced attentiveness" (Schütz and Luckmann 1973:186) and "voluntary advertence" (Schütz and Luckmann 1973:190, 192–3).

It can therefore be argued, by way of conclusion, that the fight for attention is fought because of perception's fundamental and irrefutable selectivity. Human beings are always attentive to something, but their attention is fickle, unreliable, and uncontrollable—and precisely for these reasons it is contested and fought over. What makes attention worth fighting for is the individual's ability to bestow and also to withdraw it again. And this applies even in situations in which the steering of attention is not based on a conscious decision, but on the outcome of the organism's competing attention systems.

23.3 ATTENTION AS A SCARCE RESOURCE AND STATE OF EXCEPTION

Regardless of how different the varying concepts of attention may be, and no matter which opposing terms they are distinguished from, what seems to remain undisputed is that attention is of only temporary nature, a condition that cannot be made to last indefinitely (Ribot 1888/2007; Kohn 1895/1999; Dürr 2006; Tenbruck 1989:25). It is in this regard that attention is referred to as a "scarce resource." In addition to physiological, psychological, sensualistic, and neurological reasons for the scarcity of attention—all of which in some way or another have to do with individuals' abilities to focus on certain phenomena—there are also genuinely sociological reasons for attention becoming a scarce resource. In these sociological accounts, scarcity of attention can be generally understood as the lack of attention given to the individual and his actions by the other members of society, and the sociological reasons for this lack can be grouped into four main categories: (1) modernization, (2) individualization, (3) mediatization, and (4) technicalization.

1.   Modernization:

Throughout all of sociology's classical texts it is argued that modern society is of a new kind insofar as it is no longer based on the idea of an eternal, natural order, but on the idea of an open society whose order is not a given and therefore must be established (Tenbruck 1989:195ff.). A crucial modern experience is that of contingency: things do not have to be the way they are; they can be changed (Luhmann 1998; Makropoulos 1997). Modernization is furthermore described as a process of differentiation (Schimank 1996) that splits society into different microcosms—variously termed "value spheres," "social worlds," "provinces of meaning," "social systems," or "social fields"—fighting over which sphere gets to assume the leading role. As a consequence, the individual has more possibilities at his or her disposal for leading his or her life, a range of options that, in principle, could be interpreted as welcome opportunities, but instead are predominantly regarded as overwhelming to the individual. Taken in this sense, modernization can also be conceived of as an overall disruption of the established order of attention. The premodern concept of divine order and the membership in small social units (guilds, communities, cities, and so on) characteristic of premodern societies allow neither for the idea of a self-regulated attention nor for the notion of being overwhelmed by too many outside stimuli. The individual's attention is rather governed by the need for social integration and is thus directed toward the upholding of tradition, the defense against enemies, and communal life. And while there already is a differentiation of attention in the sense of people of different ages, gender, or status paying attention to different segments of the social world, the notion of a subject in need of optimal attention capabilities has not yet been conceived of. According to Jonathan Crary (1999:1–2), it was not until the nineteenth century that there emerged what he calls "the paradoxical intersection [...] between an imperative of concentrated attentiveness within the disciplinary organization of labor, education, and mass consumption and an ideal of sustained attentiveness as a constitutive element of a creative and free subjectivity." This paradoxical interplay between imperative and ideal comes to bear in the course of modernization processes and illustrates that attention—in modern times—was no longer perceived merely as a phenomenon, but rather as an imminent problem. It is only with the multiplication of opportunities for engaging one's attention that attention becomes the much talked of scarce resource.

2.   Individualization:

Nearly all of sociology's founding fathers argued in unison that modernization is accompanied by a process of individualization that dissolves traditional social bonds and allows the individual to enter into relationships of his or her own choosing (Schroer 2001). The assessment of this development, however, varies: whereas skeptical voices consider individualization to be a danger to social integration, others regard it as one of modernity's commendable accomplishments, arguing that individualization entails an increase in freedom for the individual that need not necessarily affect social cohesion. A third version—the mediating position between optimistic and pessimistic stances—is more sober in its assessment and views individualization as a process to be neither rejected nor endorsed, but as a mere byproduct of modernization as irreversible as modernization itself. Regardless, however, of these controversial evaluations, Durkheim, Simmel, and Weber are in agreement on the fact that modernity, compared with premodern social formations, allows the individual a far higher degree of self-determination. Modernization reduces social control (Durkheim 1997:239). In modern societies, "surveillance is irrevocably relaxed" (Durkheim 1997:241), whereas in premodern societies, "everyone's attention is constantly fixed upon what everyone else is doing" (Durkheim 1997:239). Durkheim thus interprets the reduction of attention as a lessening of social control, which in smaller social groups was felt far more strictly. Conversely, the individual's freedom increases in large and complex social groups and thus with the coming of modernity. Although quite similar in his diagnosis, Georg Simmel (1950) put a stronger focus on the downsides to individualization in the sense of the collective's reduced attention for the individual. Just like Durkheim, he argues that the individual is much less subjected to social control in the city than in the village. According to Simmel, however, the city not only allows for the individual "to hide in the crowd," and thereby escape the notice and curious stares of others. It also, conversely, makes it more difficult for individual to draw the attention of others. To Simmel, attention signifies more than just social control. It is also considered a form of taking notice, which is sought by the individual. Following Simmel, the ambivalence pertaining to the dwindling of attention people have for each other has its roots in the fact that, one the one hand, the modern individual has a need to belong and be immersed in a group, while, on the other, it also wants to stand out and be distinct from it.

Despite this difference of argument, both their accounts suggest that the modern individual no longer has at its disposal the attention of others and that it can therefore no longer be taken for granted. Both Simmel and Durkheim draw from this the conclusion of reduced social control, but only Simmel argues that now the individual has to fight for the attention of others. Modern city life "results in the individual's summoning the utmost in uniqueness and particularization, in order to preserve his most personal core. He has to exaggerate this personal element in order to remain audible even to himself." (Simmel 1950:422) My argument is based on the assumption that this necessity of having to make-oneself-heard and draw-attention-to-oneself has become ever more pressing in the course of ongoing modernization and individualization processes. Especially with regard to globalization and the way it increasingly confronts people not only with other people, but also with a growing number of things, problems, ways of life and information, it becomes more difficult for individual and collective actors to draw the attention needed for having their existence acknowledged.

3. Mediatization:

Another reason for attention becoming a scarce resource is the worldwide proliferation of the media. Among other things, modernity stands for the triumphal procession of the media, which have made it possible for communication to extend beyond face-to-face-situations (Thompson 1995; Wenzel 2001). In this sense, the media—by providing the means for distributing news across regional and national borders—are globalization's engine. With the help of the media, people do not have to limit their social relationships to their immediate environment, but can take up and maintain relationships at a distance. However, this means that people are also exposed to the relentless bidding of communications coming from all ends of the worlds. As Siegfried Kracauer put it, modern man endures an "antennal fate" (1995:333): "Since many people feel compelled to broadcast, one finds oneself in a state of permanent reciprocity" (Kracauer 1995:332). This theme of being overloaded with an unmanageable plethora of messages, as it is expressed by Kracauer, is central to the history of the media and puts the category of attention on the agenda: Karl W. Deutsch spoke of "attention overload" as "an element in the troubles of our driven and often shallow mass culture" and argued,

> attention and communication overload may force a frantic search for a privileged status for their own messages upon many people in a prosperous and economically equalitarian democracy. Unless its citizens turn into "status seekers", they must fear that they will lack the social status—that is, the priority accorded in the social system to the messages they send—and that their attractive, interesting, or influential contemporaries will simply have no time to pay attention to them. If this is true, an economic democracy may turn into a jungle of frustrated snobs, starved for attention.   (Deutsch 1966:162)

Without necessarily having to share Deutsch's conclusion at the end of the quote, it can be reasonably argued that contemporary society already closely resembles the condition outlined by Deutsch, considering the popularity of Internet platforms such as Facebook or YouTube (whose advertising slogan is "Broadcast Yourself!"), and of reality TV and talk shows, which are used by many a lay actor as a means to spread their words of wisdom. A growing number of senders are thus faced with millions of receivers who in turn have to decide on whom they are willing to bestow their not unlimited attention.

4. Technicalization:

As the French psychologist Théodule Ribot has argued, attention "is an exceptional, abnormal state" (Ribot 1888/2007:8; Hagner 1998). This holds even more true in an age in which social interactions are more and more mediated by technical artifacts. Far from being mere "silent valets," these artifacts should also be regarded as willful actors who are increasingly laying claim on our attention. The message propagated in Bruno Latour's social theory that "[h]umans are no longer by themselves" (Latour 1994:41) implies that we have to share attention not only with other subjects but also with objects. In a society in which eyes are no longer only turned on other people, but also—and increasingly so—toward monitors and in which face-to-screen-interactions in part replace face-to-face interactions (Knorr Cetina and Bruegger 2002), additional effort is required if one is to enter the perceptual field of others. What is characteristic for a "postsocial" society (Knorr Cetina 1997) is furthermore that technical artifacts (laptop, smartphone, MP3 player) are applied in order to reduce one's presence in face-to-face situations and thereby escape the unwanted attention of others. Paradoxically, the means for enabling communicating at a distance thus become a stronghold for the refusal to communicate in face-to-face situations.

Taken together, these four developments account for the fact that attention is becoming an ever-scarcer resource, for they all illustrate how an increase in the number of participants in communication requires attention to be ever more thinly dispersed among its recipients—inescapably leading to a full-fledged fight for attention.

23.4 SOCIAL FIELDS AND THE FIGHT FOR ATTENTION

The fight for attention can be observed in all social fields. Following George Berkeley's insight that "esse est percipi" (to be is to be perceived)—a maxim quoted several times by Pierre Bourdieu (1998a:14, 2003:106, 239)—each field can be understood as the interplay between attention focused on the currently prevailing topics, respective to each field, as well as the actors' search for attention for their own actions, decisions, activities, and practices. Thus, regardless of each respective field having its own functional principle ("Business is Business," "L'art pour l'art," and so on), it seems to be a principle common to all fields that actors strive for attention.

23.4.1 Politics

Politics is a field in which the fight for attention is considerably violent (Nolte 2005). It is a commonly held notion that politicians would go to any lengths to be invited to talk shows, to be interviewed by a news station, or to be quoted in newspaper articles. The strategy is to present oneself to the voters as an electable or reelectable politician, to signal to one's party colleagues that one is fit to take on higher responsibilities, and to show one's opponent that one is a competitor to be taken seriously. The formula that applies here is that it is always better to be met with protest than to be not heard at all. In a political system that is thoroughly media saturated, to be marked off in a survey as an "unknown" politician amounts to a near death sentence. Politicians are therefore dependent on being perceived. Newcomers, especially, have to try to distinguish themselves from the unknown mass of party members by coming up with original or provocative ideas. More established politicians, by contrast, can rely on their office as well as an already existing public image to be guaranteed the attention of the media. Regardless of a politician's relevance or fame, however, the media are, to a certain degree, manipulable: in accordance with the concept of *involuntary* attention, they have to turn their attention to events that particularly stand out: everything sensational and spectacular is guaranteed the media's attention. When it comes to votes, the politician is also dependent on the voter's *voluntary* attention, that is, on the voter bestowing his attention out of his own concern and motivation. But since this voluntary attention cannot easily be steered, politicians tend to take the detour of spectacular actions that will get the attention of the media in order to thereby reach their voters. The fact that media consultants are now a well-established feature of the political field underlines how crucial media appearance is. And yet politicians have to go beyond merely striving for attention. They themselves have to invest a high amount of attention: they have to diligently register and attend to their voters and their opinions just as they have to pay attention to the activities of their political opponents. They also have to take interest—in the sense of voluntary attention—in ongoing social developments in need of political solutions. Following Berkeley, it can therefore be argued that political existence consists of both perceiving and being perceived. And, last but not least, the phenomenon of "politics of attention" has to be noted in this context, the purpose of which is to draw attention to social groups that—on account of their low social status—otherwise would go unnoticed (Rancière 2002:41; my translation).

23.4.2 Economy

It is crucial for every company to attract the attention of potential customers. It is in no way sufficient to simply produce products and then wait for buyers. On the contrary: companies have to put all their effort into drawing the attention of as many consumers as possible to a product which they are supposed to buy. According to Werner Sombart, this business principle "may be enunciated as follows: search out the customer and attack him. [...] In practice it means that you set out to attract the customer's attention and to stir up within him the desire to purchase. You attract his attention by shouting in his ears, or catching his eye by loud, colored indicators" (Sombart 2001:87). Advertising, since the beginning of the industrial age, has the function of imposing, as obtrusively as possible, products on the customer. The demonstrative display of goods in shop windows, the running of ads in newspapers and magazines, colorful posters, brochures and leaf-lets, ever more intricate TV and Internet ads—all of these are efforts to draw the attention of customers. In the age of mass consumption, brands play an ever more important role (Hellmann 2003). Not only do they embody the promise of certain experiences and happiness but also they are a means to create an identity and express membership in life-style groups. In exchange for providing what can be termed a "filter for navigating [an] oversupply" in goods (Bolz 2002:129, my translation), the manufacturer of a brand-name product receives the loyalty of his consumers. In a world of chaos, brands pro-vide orientation. They also guarantee the attention of people: certain brands will involuntarily and inescapably attract the glances of others. And the economy, as well, not only has to attract but also invest attention by carefully observing market development, competitors, and pricing behavior.

23.4.3 Science

Attention also plays an important role in the field of science. Scientific endeavors are driven by the concern that, if left to their own devices, the things themselves will fail to draw the attention they deserve. It is from this assumption that scientific disciplines draw their legitimacy. According to Hans Blumenberg, raising attention is the formula for science's specific accomplishment: "Attention is drawn to those things of which it is assumed that they haven't yet been seen or not clearly enough seen" (Blumenberg 2006:183; my translation). Accordingly, the number of times authors of scientific texts announce that they wish to draw the reader's attention to this or that phenomenon are legion. What should be noted here is that in both Blumenberg's and Bauman's defini-tions the terms "attention/inattention" are equated or used in analogy to the terms "visibility/invisibility." It is characteristic of Western modernity that primacy is accorded the optical, which explains why these terms are so frequently used synonymously: bringing something to attention allows something previously invisible to become visi-ble. Science and art have this accomplishment in common. In contrast to the world of art, however, the scientific realm deems openly fighting for attention to be a form of ille-gitimate narcissism. And yet it can be argued that in an age of tight budgets and a global scale of competition, science, also, is under pressure to represent its results not only to a small-scale audience of scientists but also to a larger public.[7] The moving out of the ivory tower and into the media institutions is a result of this development—a development eyed with suspicion by many scientists who equate the inevitable popularization of knowledge with its banalization and who insinuate motives of vanity and being obsessed with one's image.

Pierre Bourdieu's work has contributed greatly toward showing that the scientific field, just like any other field, is dominated by struggles for social position and struggles of classification: "Intellectuals have interests, they want to be the best and the most extraordinary at all cost" (Bourdieu 1998b:28; my translation; see also Bourdieu 2006). The stakes are building a career, making a name for oneself, becoming the expert in one's field, recognition of one's accomplishments, and reputation: "Science is but a dance for attention. For what makes one a scientist is not only one's own amazement and curiosity. It is also the amazement evoked in other people; it is also trying to make other people take an interest in one's person" (Franck 1998:38; my translation). Scientists still cannot do without the awe for a certain object and its yet undiscovered characteristics. Receiving attention for their work and their person requires scientists to offer up attention themselves: attention for their objects of study as well as for their colleagues' findings. Perceiving and being perceived, the giving and receiving of attention, are therefore elementary in this field as well (Daston 2000).

23.4.4 Art

The fight for attention in the field of art begins, at the latest, with the demise of monarchical and feudal regimes that freed the artist from the constraints entailed in commissions and patronage. But this liberation also meant that the artist now lacked a regular income, making it necessary for him, if he wanted to survive, to attract the public's attention and therewith financially strong buyers. Instead of being reliant on the sponsorship and allowances of a patronizing court, the artist was now subjected to the laws of the market in which he had to sell his works. (Kris and Kurz 1995; Ruppert 1998) The emergence of art as an autonomous field brought with it the development of criteria on what counts as art. Abiding these rules and maintaining the established order ensured membership in the field. However, heightened attention is generated particularly by art that breaks with the traditional ways of viewing, interpreting, and reading it, by art that in some ways transcends the status quo and creates something new. This explains why the deliberate breaking of rules, the intentional deviation from established norms, the protest against old patterns and authorities is part of the history of modern art. Most of the works of modern art that are now revered and celebrated were once highly disputed objects, at risk of being banned or even destroyed. The image of the modern artist therefore draws on the notion of an independent individualist who adopts a critical stance toward society and takes on the role of outsider in order to be able to create his artwork free of any considerations regarding the tastes and preferences of the audience. The modern artist loathes nothing more than commissioned art in the sense of accommodating and agreeable art. The closer we get to contemporary society, the more we can observe the following trend: the artist—who, as a person, used to be nearly invisible—increasingly steps outside of his work and into public spotlight. In the public's perception, this self-presentation of the artist as person takes precedence over perception of his work. It has even been suggested that the artist Jeff Koons, for instance, "only has a body of artwork out of necessity, because, as an artist, one needs it in order to become famous and rich, but only in the way a race car driver needs a car" (Grasskamp 1995:163; my translation). The artwork itself is reduced to the status of mere instrument in the pursuit of fame. The artist no longer tries to turn the audience's attention on certain issues or phenomena, but on his person. He himself wants to be at the center of attention. What still applies, however, is the orientation toward that which has never been done before. As Helmuth Plessner has observed, artworks,

> like other products, have come to be subjected to the laws of rapid obsolescence and of accelerated consumption. In the ever mounting flood of supplies, new art objects attract attention only according to the degree of *shock* they produce. The influence of the "modernity business" on the artist is obvious: it induces him to withdraw into a region of pure aesthetics: *l'art pour l'art*. But as a consequence of this fact our society has to accept art not simply as l'art pour l'art, but as *le choc pour le choc*.
>
> (Plessner 1970:178–9)

A similar analysis could be done of the fields of sports, religion, and the media. The essential developments and mechanisms at work, however, can already be identified on the basis of the four examples given. Moreover, it was shown that the various meanings of the term "attention," as they were examined in the first section, are also relevant to the analysis of the fight for attention in social fields. By way of conclusion, the commonalities of all four social fields can be summarized as follows:

1. The *increase in efforts to be perceived*. As a result of strong competition, actors are increasingly under pressure to draw attention to themselves. Staging of all kinds is an attempt to enforce attention. What we therefore seem to be currently experiencing is a loss of confidence in voluntary attention in favor of involuntary attention.
2. The orientation toward the new. As a result of only the new and the striking attracting attention, actors enter into competition of trying to outdo each other in terms of originality and ostentatiousness. Something counts as new insofar as it runs counter to established routines and expectations.
3. The emergence of markets that enforce the search for the new and cause the practice of advertising to proliferate into all areas society.
4. The alignment of activities with the needs and requirements of the media. Politics, economy, science, and art are increasingly forced to organize their practices in light of media perception.
5. The emergence of star cultures. With the focus shifting more and more from issues to people, stars are beginning to populate all of the social fields.
6. Investing into spectacular architecture. Politics, economy, science, and art try to attain visibility on a global scale with the help of prestigious buildings built by star architects (for example the cupola of the Berlin Reichstag by Norman Foster, the Crystals Shopping Mall in Las Vegas by Daniel Libeskind and others, or the Guggenheim museum in Bilbao by Frank Gehry).
7. The orientation toward competitors. What are the others doing? Every politician, businessman, scientist, and artist has to know this. This orientation, again, offers evidence of the fact that the game is not only about the receiving of, but also about the paying of attention, about being perceived and perceiving, as was argued by Berkeley.

23.5 SUMMARY AND CONCLUDING REMARKS

The aim of this chapter was to demonstrate the relevance of the category "attention" for understanding the social. It was demonstrated that "attention" is not a term that can just as easily be dispensed with. Against the backdrop of neurological, psychological, and philosophical insights into the matter of attention, and drawing on both classical and current theories on this phenomenon, the chapter examined the term's respective meanings and elaborated on the genuinely sociological nature of certain questions and problems regarding attention. Drawing on the distinction between voluntary and involuntary attention, it argued that the (post)modern subject oscillates between being at liberty to bestow his attention at will and being forced to do so. Modernization, individualization, mediatization, and technicalization were then identified as sociological explanations for attention becoming a scarce resource and inducing a fight for attention, which then was traced throughout the social fields of politics, economy, science, and art. The concept of attention can therefore be argued to have tremendous heuristic value for examining current developments and changes in contemporary society. Its theoretical potential remains yet untapped, calling for not only a more comprehensive treatment of attention as a key sociological issue, but also for the systematic development of a sociological theory of attention towards which this article aims to be a first contribution.

NOTES

1. As William James put it: "Everyone knows what attention is" (James 2007:403).
2. It is therefore rather astounding that hardly any of these references can be found in Georg Franck's well-known study on the attention economy (1998). One reason for this could be that Franck is not concerned with developing a theory of attention, but rather with outlining the contemporary relevance of the phenomenon, which for Franck seems to lie entirely in the notion of attention having to be fought for.
3. The differentiation of attention according to social milieu was particularly emphasized by Max Scheler (1973:142–4).
4. According to Blumenberg, "distraction" is attention's "counter-phenomenon" (2002:199; my translation).
5. In the words of William James, "Millions of items of the outward order are present to my senses which never properly enter into my experience. Why? Because they have no *interest* for me. *My experience is what I agree to attend to.* Only those items which I *notice* shape my mind—without selective interest, experience is an utter chaos. Interest alone gives accent and emphasis, light and shade, background and foreground—intelligible perspective, in a word. It varies in every creature, but without it consciousness of every creature would be a gay chaotic indiscriminateness, impossible for us even to conceive" (James 1890/2007:402–3).

6. In Simmel's version, this insight is formulated as follows: "The physiological processes within our bodies offer the same picture of an unceasing struggle" (Simmel 2009, 443).

7. Not only scientists, but universities too fight for attention (Weingart 2005; Münch 2009).

REFERENCES

Algazi, Gadi. 2001. "Gelehrte Zerstreutheit und gelernte Vergesslichkeit." pp. 235–50 in *Der Fehltritt. Vergehen und Versehen in der Vormoderne*, edited by Peter von Moos. Cologne: Weimar; Vienna: Böhlau.

Assmann, Aleida. 2001. "Einleitung." pp. 11–23 in *Aufmerksamkeiten: Archäologie der literarischen Kommunikation VII*, edited byVon Aleida and Jan Assmann. Munich: Fink.

Bachelard, Gaston. 1994. *The Poetics of Space. The Classic Look at How We Experience Intimate Places*. Boston: Beacon Press.

Bauman, Zygmunt. 1991. *Intimations of Postmodernity*. London: Routledge.

Bauman, Zygmunt. 1995. *Life in Fragments. Essays in Postmodern Morality*. Oxford: Blackwell.

Bauman, Zygmunt. 1998. *Modernity and Ambivalence*. Cambridge: Polity.

Beck, Klaus, and Wolfgang Schweiger, eds. 2001. *Attention Please! Online-Kommunikation und Aufmerksamkeit*. Munich: Verlag Reinhard Fischer.

Benjamin, Walter. 2005. "Habit and Attentiveness." P. 592 in *Selected Writings. Volume 2, part 2: 1931–1934*, edited by Michael W. Jennings. Cambridge, MA: Harvard University Press.

Berkeley, George. 1710/1982. *A Treatise Concerning the Principles of Human Knowledge, Part 1*. Indianapolis: Hackett.

Bleicher, Joan K., and Kurt Hickethier, eds. 2002. *Aufmerksamkeit, Medien und Ökonomie*. Münster; Hamburg; London: Lit.

Blumenberg, Hans. 2002. *Zu den Sachen und zurück*. Frankfurt a. M.: Suhrkamp.

Blumenberg, Hans. 2006. *Beschreibung des Menschen*. Frankfurt a. M.: Suhrkamp.

Bolz, Norbert. 2002. *Das konsumistische Manifest*. Munich: Fink.

Bourdieu, Pierre. 1993. The Field of Cultural Production: Essays on Art and Literature. New York: Columbia University Press.

Bourdieu, Pierre. 1998a. On Television. New York: New Press.

Bourdieu, Pierre. 1998b. *Vom Gebrauch der Wissenschaft: Für eine klinische Soziologie des wissenschaftlichen Feldes*. Konstanz: UVK.

Bourdieu, Pierre. 2003. *Language and Symbolic Power*. Cambridge, MA: Harvard University Press.

Bourdieu, Pierre. 2006. *Science of Science and Reflexivity*. Cambridge: Polity Press.

Bourdieu, Pierre, and Loïc Wacquant. 2004. "The Logic of Fields." pp. 94–114 in *An Invitation to Reflexive Sociology*. Chicago: University of Chicago Press.

Bublitz, Hannelore. 2010. *Im Beichtstuhl der Medien: Die Produktion des Selbst im öffentlichen Bekenntnis*. Bielefeld: transcript.

Claessens, Dieter. 1980. *Das Konkrete und das Abstrakte: Soziologische Skizzen zur Anthropologie*. Frankfurt a. M.: Suhrkamp.

Crary, Jonathan. 1999. *Suspensions of Perception: Attention, Spectacle, and Modern Culture*. Cambridge, MA: MIT Press.

Daston, Lorraine. 2000. *Eine kurze Geschichte der wissenschaftlichen Aufmerksamkeit*. Munich: Carl Friedrich von Siemens Stiftung.

Deutsch, Karl W. 1966. *The Nerves of Government: Models of Political Communication and Control*. Glencoe, IL: Free Press of Glencoe.

Durkheim, Émile. 1997. *The Division of Labor in Society*. New York: Free Press.

Dürr, Georg Ernst. 1907/2006. *Die Lehre von der Aufmerksamkeit*. Leipzig: Elibron Classics.

Fischer, Burkhart. 1996. Aufmerksamkeit ist ein lebenswichtiges Auswahlverfahren: Burkhart Fischer im Gespräch mit Florian Rötzer. http://www.heise.de/tp/r4/artikel/2/2077/1.html (Accessed May 27, 2009).

Franck, Georg. 1998. *Ökonomie der Aufmerksamkeit: Ein Entwurf*. Munich; Vienna: Hanser.

Giddens, Anthony. 1993. *The Transformation of Intimacy: Sexuality, Love and Eroticism in Modern Societies*. Stanford, CA Stanford University Press.

Goldhaber, Michael. 1999/2000. "Ressource Aufmerksamkeit." pp. 78–83 in *Kunstforum International*, Bd. 148. Köln.

Grasskamp, Walter. 1995. "Kulturrevolution von oben: Auf Kaffeefahrt mit Jeff Koons." In *Der lange Marsch durch die Illusionen: Über Kunst und Politik*. Munich: Beck.

Hagner, Michael. 1998. "Aufmerksamkeit als Ausnahmezustand." pp. 273–94 in *Aufmerksamkeit.*, edited by N. Haas, H. J. Rheinberger, and R. Nägele. Eggingen: K. Isele.

Hahn, Alois. 2001. "Aufmerksamkeit." pp. 25–56 in *Aufmerksamkeiten*, edited by Aleida Assmann and Jan Assmann. Munich: Fink.

Hellmann, Kai-Uwe. 2003. *Soziologie der Marke*. Frankfurt a. M.: Suhrkamp.

Horkheimer, Max and Adorno, Theodor W. 2007. *Dialectic of Enlightenment: Philosophical Fragments*. Stanford, CA: Stanford University Press.

James, William 1890/2007. *The Principles of Psychology*. Vol. 1. New York: Cosimo Classics.

Kant, Immanuel. 2006. *Anthropology from a Pragmatic Point of View*. Cambridge: Cambridge University Press.

Knorr Cetina, Karin D. 1997 "Sociality with Objects: Social Relations in Postsocial Knowledge Societies." *Theory, Culture and Society* 14(4):1–30.

Knorr-Cetina Karin, and Ulf Bruegger. 2002. "Global Microstructures: The Virtual Societies of Financial Markets." *American Journal of Sociology* 107(4):905–50.

Kohn, Harry E. 1895/1999. *Zur Theorie der Aufmerksamkeit*. Hildesheim; Zürich; New York: zuerst Halle.

Kracauer, Siegfried. 1995. "Boredom." pp. 331–6 in *The Mass Ornament: Weimar Essays*. Cambridge, MA: Harvard University Press.

Kris, Ernst and Otto Kurz. 1995. *Die Legende vom Künstler: Ein geschichtlicher Versuch*. Frankfurt a. M.: Suhrkamp.

Latour, Bruno. 2004. *Politics of Nature. How to Bring the Sciences into Democracy*. Cambridge, MA: Harvard University Press.

Latour, Bruno. 1994. "On Technical Mediation—Philosophy, Sociology, Geneaology." *Common Knowledge* 3(2):29–64.

Latour, Bruno. 2005. "From Realpolitik to Dingpolitik, or How to Make Things Public." pp. 14–41 in *Making things public. Atmospheres of democracy*, edited by B. Latour and P. Weibel. Cambridge, MA; London; Karlsruhe: MIT Press; ZKM, Center for Art and Media in Karlsruhe.

Linke, Detlef. 1996. "Der letzte Mensch blinzelt. Ein Gespräch mit dem Hirnwissenschaftler Detlef Linke." http://www.heise.de/tp/artikel/2/2000/1.html.

Luhmann, Niklas. 1983. *Rechtssoziologie*. Opladen: Westdeutscher Verlag.

Luhmann, Niklas. 1998. "Contingency as Modern Society's Defining Attribute." pp. 44–62 in *Observations on Modernity*. Stanford, CA: Stanford University Press.

Luhmann, Niklas. 2000. *The Reality of the Mass Media*. Stanford, CA: Stanford University Press.

Makropoulos, Michael. 1997. *Modernität und Kontingenz*. Munich: Fink.

Mead, George Herbert. 2009. *Mind, Self, and Society: From the Standpoint of a Social Behaviorist*. Vol. 1. Chicago: University of Chicago Press.

Münch, Richard. 1991. *Dialektik der Kommunikationsgesellschaft*. Frankfurt a. M.: Suhrkamp.

Münch, Richard. 1995. *Dynamik der Kommunikationsgesellschaft*. Frankfurt a. M.: Suhrkamp.

Münch, Richard. 2009. *Globale Eliten, lokale Autoritäten: Bildung und Wissenschaft unter dem Regime von PISA, McKinsey&Co.* Frankfurt a. M: Suhrkamp.

Münsterberg, Hugo. 1916/2001. *Hugo Munsterberg on Film*. Hoboken, NJ: Taylor and Francis.

Neumann, Oskar. 1971. "Art. Aufmerksamkeit." pp. 635–45 in *Historisches Wörterbuch der Philosophie*, Vol. 1, edited by Joachim Ritter and Karlfried Gründer. Basel: AG Schwabe Verlag.

Nolte, Kristina. 2005. *Kampf um Aufmerksamkeit: Wie Medien, Wirtschaft und Politik um eine knappe Ressource ringen*. Frankfurt a. M.; New York: Campus.

Plessner, Helmuth. 1970. "The Social Conditions of Modern Painting." pp. 178–88 in *Aisthesis and Aesthetics*, edited by Erwin W. Straus and Richard M. Griffith. Pittsburgh, PA: The Fourth Lexington Conference on Pure and Applied Phenomenology.

Pörksen, Bernhard, and Wolfgang Krischke, eds. 2010. *Die Casting-Gesellschaft: Die Sucht nach Aufmerksamkeit und das Tribunal der Medien*. Cologne: Herbert von Halem.

Rancière, Jacques. 2002. *Das Unvernehmen: Politik und Philosophie*. Frankfurt a. M.: Suhrkamp.

Ribot, Théodule-Armand. 1888/2007. *The Psychology of Attention*. Whitefish, MN: Kessinger.

Riesman, David. 2001. *The Lonely Crowd: A Study of the Changing American Character*. New Haven, CT: Yale University Press.

Rötzer, Florian. 1998. *Digitale Weltentwürfe: Streifzüge durch die Netzkultur*. Munich: Carl Hanser.

Ruppert, Wolfgang. 1998. *Der moderne Künstler: Sozial- und Kulturgeschichte der kreativen Individualität in der kulturellen Moderne im 19. und 20. Jahrhundert*. Frankfurt a. M.: Suhrkamp.

Scheler, Max. 1973. *Formalism in Ethics and Non-Formal Ethics of Values: A New Attempt toward the Foundation of an Ethical Personalism*. Evanston, IL: Northwestern University Press.

Schimank, Uwe. 1996. *Theorien gesellschaftlicher Differenzierung*. Opladen: Leske + Budrich.

Schmidt, Siegfried. 2001. "Aufmerksamkeit: Die Währung der Medien." pp. 183–96 in *Aufmerksamkeiten*, edited by Aleida Assmann and Jan Assmann. Munich: Fink.

Schroer, Markus. 2001. *Das Individuum der Gesellschaft: Synchrone und diachrone Theorieperspektiven*. Frankfurt/M.: Suhrkamp.

Schütz, Alfred. 1970. *Reflections on the Problem of Relevance*. Edited by Richard M. Zaner. New Haven, CT; London: Yale University Press.

Schütz, Alfred, and Thomas Luckmann. 1973. *The Structures of the Lifeworld*. Vol. 1. Evanston, IL: Northwestern University Press.

Simmel, Georg. 2009. *Sociology: Inquiries into the Construction of Social Forms*. Vol. 1. Leiden; Boston: Brill.

Simmel. Georg. 1950. "The Metropolis and Mental Life." pp. 409–24 in *The Sociology of Georg Simmel*. Glencoe, IL: Free Press.

Sombart, Werner. 2001. *Economic Life in the Modern Age*. New Brunswick, NJ: Transaction.

Stiegler, Bernard. 2008. *Die Logik der Sorge: Verlust der Aufklärung durch Technik und Medien*. Frankfurt a. M.: Suhrkamp.

Tenbruck, Friedrich. 1989. *Die kulturellen Grundlagen der Gesellschaft: Der Fall der Moderne*. Opladen: Westdeutscher.

Thompson, John B. 1995. *The Media and Modernity: A Social Theory of the Media*. Stanford, CA: Stanford University Press.

Türcke, Christoph. 2002. *Erregte Gesellschaft: Philosophie der Sensation*. Munich: Beck.

Türcke, Christoph. 2012. *Hyperaktiv: Kritik der Aufmerksamkeitsdefizitkultur*. Munich: Beck.

Waldenfels, Bernard. 2004. *Phänomenologie der Aufmerksamkeit*. Frankfurt a. M.: Suhrkamp.

Weingart, Peter. 2005. *Die Wissenschaft der Öffentlichkeit: Essays zum Verhältnis von Wissenschaft, Medien und Öffentlichkeit*. Weilerswist: Velbrück.

Wenzel, Harald. 2001. *Das Abenteuer der Kommunikation: Echtzeitmassenmedien und der Handlungsraum der Hochmoderne*. Weilerswist: Velbrück.

CHAPTER 24

RISK, CULTURE, AND COGNITION

DAINA CHEYENNE HARVEY

FOR many researchers, risk is objective, fixed, and measurable (Gotham 2016). Social scientists, however, have long worked under the belief that risk is a social construction and is culturally determined (Douglas and Wildavsky 1983; Perrow 1984; Tierney 2014). In this chapter, I follow Wilkinson's use of the term "risk" (though see also others, especially Fischhoff et al. 1984; Gotham 2016; Tierney 2014), and thus the goal of the chapter is to review and map out the ways social actors perceive and make sense of hazards and conditions of threatening uncertainty (Wilkinson 2010:8). The first and most obvious way to achieve this is in providing findings to help clarify the differences between the scientific community, organizational actors, and individuals in the assessment of risks. As Freudenberg notes (1998), such a contribution is generally seen to lie in the area of risk perception, risk communication, and risk responsibility—all of which inherently involve a sociology of culture and cognition. The following section on risk and cognition explores in depth some of the key contributions in these three areas. The chapter ends with some observations on risk and cognition from ethnographic research on the long-term aftermath of Hurricane Katrina.

24.1 RISK AND COGNITION

The following sections focus on different types of mental actions in relation to risk.

24.1.1 Risk Perception

Studies on risk perception have rapidly increased in the last few decades (Cerulo 2006; Clarke and Short 1993; Clarke 1989, 2006 Dietz et al. 1989; Slovic 2000; Stallings 1990;

Tierney 1999, 2014). Most of these studies have demonstrated how risk is mediated by organizational frames and interests (Clarke 1989; Freudenburg 1993; Oreskes and Conway 2010; Perrow 1997; Vaughan 1996, 1999), scientific experts (Boehmer-Christiansen 1994; Rosa and Dietz 1998), and laypersons (Heimer 1988; Beamish 2001). Rather than focus on the individual or universal level, these studies situate the perception of risk firmly at the cultural level. Collectively these studies demonstrate that risk is thus best understood as the result of a local project and they complement work in the sociology of cognition that sees processes such as remembering, focusing, categorizing, and attending as the product of intersubjective associations (see Zerubavel 1997, for an overview). Here I review several important works on risk perception that focus on cultural level understandings of risk and that have helped shape approaches to studying disasters and hazards.

Early studies of the social construction of risk focused on the cognitive heuristics people use to make decisions about risk (Tversky and Kahneman 1974; Slovic et al. 1979). This work found that most of the time we use an automatic or fast way of thinking, which stresses habit, rather than a deliberate, slow way of thinking that emphasizes rationality. As I point out later in my discussion on how we cognitively process danger, when afraid or when we are reminded of extreme risk we typically resort to automatic ways of thinking. Here we resort to stereotypes and heuristics that bias us to typically underestimate risk and make us myopic when recalling dangerous situations.

While Slovic, Fischhoff, Lichtenstein, and others who based early work on risk perception on heuristics did not have access to more recent advancements in cognition, work on hot and cold cognition (DiMaggio 1997; Metcalfe and Mischel 1999) reveal that emotions also likely affect risk perception. Work here, particularly by Norgaard (2006, 2010, 2011), demonstrates that when a particular risk is emotionally salient, perhaps it challenges our understanding of who we think we are or how we perceive values, we are more likely to experience cognitive challenges to our sense of reality. Norgaard, using Lifton's (1993) concept of an "age of numbing," where we experience an ontological crisis because of the omnipresence of danger, explains that today we live in a "double reality" in which we simultaneously know and do not know about risk. For Norgaard this reality allows us to perceive risk, but we often fail to integrate understandings of risk into our everyday life, especially when that integration would present excessive cognitive demands. In her work on the risks associated with climate change in Norway, Norgaard (2011) demonstrates that while Norwegians may perceive risk, they use various cultural tools (Swidler 1986) to engage in, among other things, perspectival selectivity and selective attention, to limit the problems they associate with risk. Her subjects go to great lengths to avoid cognitive dissonance regarding their role in perpetuating risk and their positive self-esteem. Here social context is important, as culture helps explain why we might consider certain risks more thinkable than others.

Vaughan's (1996, 2002) classic work on risk perception (which I also discuss in the section on risk communication) highlights the role of risk and social context. Her work on the *Challenger* launch decision and subsequent disaster shows that while individuals repeatedly recognized the risk the defects in the rocket boosters posed, when in groups, they normalized the defects as an acceptable risk. Technological uncertainty became taken-for-granted. Likewise, changes in the rocket booster (from repeated use) occurred gradually, what Diamond (1995) has called "normality creep," so that small changes were thought of as normal. Had the change been sudden, it is more likely that scientists and engineers would have recognized the danger. Instead, the change in the booster was a weak signal. Secondly, as Vaughan (2002) points out, NASA's culture of production also had a cognitive consequence, namely that rule-following took precedence over other streams of information. Another cultural script at NASA that led to the disaster was the belief that technology is inherently messy. This skewed risk perception at NASA and accounted for why workers at NASA accepted defects in the O-rings.

To explain how we make sense of the external world, cognitive scientists note that we use various rules to mentally categorize concepts. One of these rules, "graded membership," has been shown to have an effect on how we perceive risk (Cerulo 2006). Cerulo (2006) notes that this particular aspect of human cognition privileges best-case examples and those objects near best cases and simultaneously distances us from anything less than the ideal. Thus we end up with what she calls "positive asymmetry"—"a way of seeing that foregrounds or underscores only the best characteristics and potentials of people, place, objects, and events" (2006:6). In terms of risk, Cerulo shows how we are culturally and cognitively wired to envision risk-free futures. We are just not really good at thinking about risk, so we tend not to perceive it (importantly she notes that those who do think about risk typically have to be resocialized to do so). Her work shows us that to consider risk we have to develop new evaluative practices and deviant ways of perceiving things. Reorienting ourselves to risk, however, can be difficult, as both Vaughan and Norgaard demonstrate.

Part of the difficulty in reconsidering risk can be explained by the concept of motivated cognition. Kahan (2007) explains that we often assume danger is inherent in activities or events that evoke fear, dread, anger, or disgust. Using Douglas and Wildavsky's (1983) work on a cultural theory of risk, Kahan et al. (2006; Kahan 2012) have found that our belief and understanding of risk depends on our worldview. Douglas and Wildavsky (1983) classify different preferences for the organization of society into "groups" and "grids." Using this group and grid system, Kahan et al. differentiate between individualists (who believe in a weak form of group life and maintain individual rights over collective rights) and solidarists (who place collective rights over individual rights) and between hierarchists (who prefer a social order based on consistent rankings of individuals by traditional classification systems of race, ethnicity, family name, etc.) and egalitarians (who believe that social order should be predicated on equal opportunity). Challenges to one's worldview thus engenders fear and a sense of danger. We are motivated to avoid danger or conduct we despair and thus are cognitively arranged to see challenges to these worldviews as risky.

These works on risk perception see risk as dependent on cultural categories. Risk, like culture, then is socially constructed and socially produced. Riskscapes (Morello-Frosch et al. 2001), risk objects (Hilgartner 1992), and risk frames (Auyero and Swistun 2009) all presuppose that as social actors we act in particular contexts with particular histories

(Beamish 2001:11). But cognition is essential to understanding why as members of particular cultures (subcultures) we therefore perceive or categorize risk in similar ways. Without grounding risk in the study of culture and cognition we essentially reify risk.

24.1.2 Risk Communication

Problems with risk perception are amplified by issues with risk communication (McCright and Shwom 2010). As Christakis and Fowler (2009) have demonstrated, we tend to trust information and communication from organizations and actors we tend to already agree with and distrust anything that comes from those social actors we regard with animosity (for risk in particular, see Kasperson and Kasperson 2005). Moreover, the ways in which some risks, particularly environmental risk, are often communicated, either with fear (Hulme 2009; Moser and Dilling 2007; O'Neill and Nicholson-Cole 2009) or guilt (Norgaard 2011) seem to make people either withdraw from discussions about risk or to dissuade them from any meaningful action that could be taken (Olaussin 2009). As Marx and Weber (2012) noted, while political science, economics, and applied science have aided us greatly in understanding why people do not make use of risk information, in order to understand the lack of overall action we need to look at the problem in terms of risk communication. In their work on *Flammable*, discussed in what follows, Auyero and Swistun focus on the production of "toxic uncertainty"—involving both everyday toxic routines and the "invisible elbows" (Tilly 1996) of neoliberal machinations between the government and industry (2009:6), that render one unsure about the risk of living in environmentally hazardous places. Here as elsewhere, mixed signals result in the confusion of risk communication. The work on risk communication has engaged the literature on cognition at times more clearly than risk perception as work on disasters have often stressed the failure for authorities to communicate hazards and dangers to the public.

As Tierney (2014:104) explains, communication is the basis for collective sense-making and yet, due to the features of organizations, risk communication is often unsuccessful. Her example of the failure of various agencies to communicate to the public and other government offices the threats posed by Osama bin Laden and al-Qaeda represents one of the largest communication failures of all time. Her work on the social roots of risk shows how communication blockages—involving multiple agencies, social actors, reams of documents, and different levels of government, resulted in an information breakdown. The failure of 9/11 is that sense-making simply did not take place.

Auyero and Swistun (2009) demonstrate the importance of risk communication for both perception and for collective action. In their study of Flammable, a shantytown in Argentina, they find that despite living in a toxic environment, residents also live with toxic uncertainty. Shell, one of a couple dozen corporate actors, sponsor sports teams, at times provide free health screenings, and promotes itself as a safe and responsible neighbor. It communicates to the public that it is socially responsible, while hiding its toxic assault on the community. The result is that some residents of Flammable believe Shell (i.e., why would they do all these goods things if they were bad), while others suspect that Shell is making them sick. The confusion is only compounded by the "discursive repertoire" of lawyers, doctors, activists, and state officials that continually send mixed signals (2009:81). Risk communication often involves structural conflicts in the communicative logic of risk (Beck 2009: 195). Decision makers have different priorities in communicating risk and at times avoid communication altogether. In Flammable, as with my work on New Orleans, discussed later, risk communication becomes noise (see also Vaughan 1996, 1999).

Most work on risk communication clearly demonstrates that the public typically lacks the information to make decisions regarding risk. Clarke's (1999) work on fantasy documents is an essential part of demonstrating how organizational rhetoric directed to the public who needs to be reassured about safety concerns has little grounding in reality. Clarke shows how in a number of situations fantasy documents communicate to the public that risk is manageable (or at least acceptable). For the lay public this means someone else is thinking about risk. Furthermore, these documents represent the conflict over communication strategies within and between organizations. The end result of this communication is that organizations tend to eventually believe their contingency plans for dealing with danger and forego opportunities to improve their plans, and perhaps more problematically, that they rarely try and improve on communication efforts with the public until a disaster occurs.

24.1.3 Responsibility for Risk

Finally, construction of potentially responsible agents affects perception of risk (Bickerstaff and Walker 2002; Kerr 2003). As Beck (1999) notes, there is in modern society a tendency to not hold individuals or institutions responsible for environmental problems. He uses the term "organized irresponsibility" to describe this tendency. Others have noted an increase in ambivalence toward moral or political discourses regarding environmental issues (Bickerstaff et al. 2008). Such irresponsibility and ambivalence, they find, limit social action regarding the management of risk. If there are no potentially responsible agents to assign blame for environmental degradation and misuse, then people do not perceive a problem. Much of the work discussed in what follows builds on both the European tradition of the risk society (Beck 1992; Giddens 1990; Luhmann 2003), which focuses on the central role that risk plays in structuring society, and the American tradition of seeing risk as an inevitable component of our reliance on modern technology (Erikson 1994; Perrow 1984).

The modern era is marked by what Erikson (1994) calls "a new species of trouble." In this time, danger is constant, it is, to use Erikson's phrase, a *persisting condition* (1994:229, emphasis in the original). What differentiates this trouble from others is that it has the potential to geometrically expand to affect others. The Great Recession thus originated from American banks creating highly risky mortgage-backed investments for Chinese investors, but ended up ruining Iceland's banking system, increasing the price of food throughout Latin America, and triggering real estate crises in Greece. Likewise, radiated organisms from the Fukushima Daiichi nuclear catastrophe have entered ocean currents and floated to the Pacific coast of the United States. We now live in an age where we are told polar ice sheets will likely melt in the next few hundred years and raise sea levels up to a few hundred feet or it could happen this century and sea levels might only rise 50 feet. Thinking about risk is pervasive while the absence of risk has become *unthinkable*.

But most of us do not think about risks on a daily basis. We place our trust in experts. As Wuthnow (2010) notes, most of what we know about risks is largely mediated to us by institutions responsible for protecting us. Our fear from extreme dangers, then, is largely managed through distributed cognition found in these organizations. These organizations interact to decide what counts as "acceptable risk" (Clarke 1989) and thus legitimate solutions to danger or disaster are dependent on which organizations are present. Understandings of risk then are simply a process of claims-making by organizations (Clarke 1989). Perception and communication of course still matter, but much of our attention toward danger is determined by who we see as legitimate risk actors.

Wuthnow explains that risk managers refer to reminders of potential risks as "bright lines" (2010:218). These lines are drawn in the proverbial sand, but they also become cognitive lines. We do not have to think about the risk until those responsible for protecting us let us know a line has been crossed. Responsible agents create and identify these lines for us. But our trust of these responsible agents depends heavily on the match between our cultural worldview and the worldview of the experts and organizations they represent. As noted above in the work of Kahan and others at the Cultural Cognition Project at Yale Law School, we tend to agree with those who share our worldview. Those who do not share our worldview we find less credible and ultimately doubt their risk assessments. There is a strong link between culture and credibility (Kahan 2007). We are biased toward those experts who share our cultural commitments. The challenge for us is that the risk society and the new species of trouble have appeared at the same time culture has propagated wildly different worldviews. And thus we now have unprecedented conflict among experts and organizations over how to protect society from extreme risks (Kahan 2007). This conflict among experts ultimately creates the dissensus we see today in society as we can find any expert that supports our cultural worldview and thus our understanding of peril. While we would like to think organizations assigned with protecting us are rational and, in our democracy, liberal and secular, the actuality is that we are cognitively constrained. Kahan (2007) calls this "cognitive illiberalism." He suggests that it not only involves arguments over facts about risk but also contests over whose understanding of the facts about risks are being distorted by one's cultural values. For Kahan the only solution is to admit that we have cognitive biases deeply rooted in our cultural worldviews.

24.2 Risk, Cognition, and Katrina

In the following sections, I extend some of the aspects of mental actions and risk discussed above to the long-term aftermath of Hurricane Katrina.

24.2.1 Chunking and Cognitive Consistency

In their studies of various businesses, Peters and Waterman find that, when faced with problems, successful managers engage in what they call "chunking" (1982). Chunking involves breaking down larger problems into smaller, simpler units. As Wuthnow (2010) notes, this process is extremely similar to "terror management," which enables activity rather than withdrawal. Terror management theory involves a cognitive mapping of the world where order is valued over chaos and ritual over impulsive behavior or anxiety (Greenberg et al. 1986; Lienard and Boyer 2006). Here, despite that the world may be literally falling apart, people look to build continuity and for familiarity for assurance that the world can be put back together. They use their established cultural worldview to provide relief from uncertainty and disorder (Rutjens et al. 2009).

In my ethnographic work on the long-term rebuilding of the Lower Ninth Ward in New Orleans, I found that people engaged in chunking in two ways. First and foremost, people cut up the postdisaster social world into doable parts. Chunking here becomes a way of putting one foot in front of the other; a way of making it through the day; it is a way of dealing with ontological risk. The second is perhaps more similar to what cognitive sociologists would look for in studies of boundary creation. *Here chunking is way to minimize or simply separate social phenomena into different categories.* It is a sense-making activity, often accomplished by placing time into different categories (here, most logically into pre- and post-Katrina, but see also Harvey 2015). It is a way to regain familiarity or certainty in places like the Lower Ninth Ward, where risk and danger reign. Both forms are indicative, however, of cognitive simplifying.

The clearest strategy of chunking that helped people get through the ordeal of living in the aftermath of Katrina was in gutting houses and rebuilding. While emotionally traumatic, gutting or demoing houses often provided some closure. As one resident said, it "gave us something to do, it kept us sane." In fact, a number of residents explained that the six- to nine-month wait they endured to begin gutting their homes was the most agonizing time in their lives.

While it might seem commonsensical to gut a house by going from room to room, there are actually other ways that are as logical. It would, for example, make more sense to remove the heaviest or largest items first or perhaps, in a lesson I quickly learned, the most toxic items. The handful of individuals I helped gut their homes, however, went from room to room, salvaging what they could, then removing items and sheetrock. What is more, the progress was calculated. Homes were rarely gutted in a linear manner, from one room to the next, but in a way suggestive of which rooms were of most importance (i.e., bedrooms first and bathrooms last).

Rebuilding and recovery involved chunking at both the micro and macro levels. At the micro level residents rebuilt homes, typically using the strategy just outlined—focusing on one room at a time. This was also used as a measure against the risk of running out of money, but many of those chunking simply saw their homes as individualized and separate spatial compartments. Thomas's home, for example, was an easy rebuild. It was a small house, approximately 850 square feet. But he did not want anyone to work on the house unless he was present, as he wanted to proceed room by room. When a new crew of volunteers showed up he would provide an orientation of the progress that had been made and let them know that "we do one room at a time." In this way he could exert control over the process and achieve some consistency in how he imagined the process.

Chunking was used as a strategy by Thomas and others mainly for cognitive consistency (Kruglanski and Freund 1983). Cognitive consistency is valued for its adaptive role in the regulation of uncertainty when decisive action and control are needed most (Swann 1987; Fiske & Taylor 1991; Webster & Kruglanski 1994); it is a way to maintain the logic of one's thought or way of thinking. Because the rebuilding and recovery phase proceeded at a torpid pace, particularly in the beginning, many residents years later still measured their progress with the early stages of resilience. Rebuilding a room at a time gave them the satisfaction that progress was being made without committing them to finishing their homes and thus exposing themselves to new uncertainties.

Field Note October 29, 2010: Doorbell or Sewage

> Working at Ms. Henrietta's house still. Darren came up to me and said he had promised the neighbors that while we worked on the house we could do a few small projects for them. And that by we he meant me. He pointed to the house on the corner of Dengiby and Charbonnet and told me the lady who lived there was having a couple of problems. The pipe connecting her waste water to the sewage was disconnected. It had been leaking for 3 1/2 years and was causing the house to sink on that side. I looked at Darren incredulously and said I don't really think I would know which pipe to fix, I haven't had much experience with plumbing. He laughed and said he was sure I'd figure out which pipe it was once I was under the house. He said the elderly lady, whom he called, momma—as he did all the elderly women, also had a broken doorbell and that this was particularly aggravating because she couldn't hear people knock on her door so she missed a lot of packages and visitors. I smiled and told "D" I would start with the doorbell. After a few hours I figured out that the only problem with the doorbell was that the wires were misconnected at the chime box. About that time "D" came inside and asked how I was making out. He jumped in to help and before long the bell chimed. He happily rang it 4–5 times and said that's us—which he always says when we fix something. I heard deep sobbing coming from the kitchen and looked over. Ms. Henrietta was holding on to the counter. She came over with her hand in front of her face and mouthed thank you several times. She steadied herself against the wall and said she had waited 3 1/2 years to hear that sound. Then she looked off into the living room, with a forlorn look, and said, only half-jokingly, I don't know what I'll do now. As if complaining or worrying about the doorbell had occupied most of her time which was suddenly freed. To which "D" replied, he still gotta fix the sewage. Ms. Henrietta smiled again.

Ms. Henrietta had chunked all of her problems onto her doorbell. It came to represent everything that had gone wrong with rebuilding, both her house and the community. Despite suffering from massive contractor fraud, subpar contracting work that had caused the house to noticeably shift (not the fault of leaky pipes), and a host of other problems, the doorbell not working had become the last thing to do, the last thing to consider in regard to Katrina. Afterward, the sewage now represented the unfulfilled promise of the doorbell.

Chunking likewise involved the creation of sharp temporal boundaries. The future, much like the past, was blurry because time had been broken into irregular pieces, with the present occupying most of the temporal space and the past and future banished to negligible amounts of space. Here uncertainty and confusion dominated and plans and possibilities were in a permanent state of abeyance because the present itself remained. Consider the following residents' statements in response to a query about what the neighborhood would be like in five to ten years:

> I don't know what the future will be like. I suppose kinda bad, mo', less like now. [Will it get better or worse] Who knows? You just don't know. I guess it'll look a lot like it does now.   (Derrick, black male, 50s)

> No clue. No idea. How could I know? You know, I wish I had a crystal ball, but I don't even think it does any good to think about it. It would just be frustrating. Like if you knew it was just going to be the same. What would that do for you? I don't like to worry about that.   (Theresa, white female, 50s)

From a cognitive economy perspective, chunking makes sense, as there are cognitive limitations on our ability to process information. Chunking perhaps makes even more sense in periods of extreme disruption when information and order are in flux. When peril is no longer the focus of our attention, but remains distal and highly accessible, what Wegner and Smart (1997) called "deep activation," the mechanisms we use to defend our worldview increases (Landau et al. 2011). Chunking is a cognitive strategy that is best understood as a form of cognitive simplifying. People have a strong need to organize large, seemingly unwieldy amounts of information into simplified cognitive models (Kahneman et al. 1982; Neuberg et al. 1997). In New Orleans, chunking allowed people facing peril to deal with uncertainty by taking steps toward simple and familiar ways of organizing their social world. As Simon (1957) notes, cognitive simplification is a type of bounded rationality. In situations of bounded rationality, cognitive biases and simplification dominate. The cognitive maps people make represent simple illustrations of us versus them and reveal the islands of meaning they create to process their social world. And while chunking and cognitive simplifying represent the predominant strategy, there are novel cognitive strategies that residents use to make sense of Katrina.

24.2.2 Immersing

A handful of studies have shown that under situations of extreme risk, people take the opportunity to examine the meaning of their life (McGregor 2004; McGregor et al. 2001). In some of these studies, uncertainty and reminders of constant peril led to higher scores on identity-seeking scales linked to searches for meaning. Threats cause us to seek out our identity and to pursue that identity with extreme focus. McGregor et al. (2001)

call this "compensatory conviction." Major social disruptions like Katrina require that people put their lives into perspective. Many of the residents spoke of "getting my house in order" and often did so with extreme conviction. A handful of residents were also willing to take on new risks or were open to novel avenues or paths for finding meaning. McGregor and Jordan (2007) note that in response to threats people develop extreme zeal for their passions and projects. I call this strategy of dealing with risk *immersing*. Residents who use immersing typically took on large projects, they headed up nonprofits, they created start-ups, they essentially became the stakeholders of the Lower Ninth Ward.

Mack, for instance, went from, in his words, "a thug," to a community leader. After Katrina he bought a large, rundown warehouse to pursue his hobby of rebuilding old cars. After a few months of sitting idle, however, he realized that the Village could be used for other purposes. At various times during the fourteen months I lived in the Ninth Ward, the Village was an after-school center where kids could play basketball or play on a computer, it was a job training center, a community garden or a place to learn about gardening, a place for piano restoration, a library, a farmer's market, it offered vol-unteer housing (up to eighty-three volunteers), had an apartment for rent, hosted an open mic night, it was a great place to watch Saints' games, and was the epicenter for a program called "Where's Your Neighbor?"—an attempt to document and locate all members of the Katrina Diaspora. And Mack was always looking for ways to extend the mission of the Village. For the most part, however, the Village served as the entry point for large groups of volunteers. Even volunteers who worked for other local nonprofits would eventually end up at the Village.

Mack immersed himself in the Village and all things Katrina to make sense of Katrina and deal with the dangers of the Lower Ninth Ward not surviving the post-Katrina reconstruction of New Orleans. The Village itself was a work in progress. Five years after beginning work on it, it remained unfinished. Mack's motivation was to avoid closure. There were blueprints on his office wall, renderings from some college's architectural students who had visited the Village to help gut houses in 2007. It depicted what looked like a bustling community center or small college campus (most of the people in the prints were white—which was odd given that the neighborhood had been over 90 percent black before the disaster) with a cafeteria and large classrooms. Mack, seeing me study it the first time I noticed it, said, "we're not there yet, getting there though, getting there."

Others also immersed. They started a locavore raw food company; one resident was trying to develop a soap factory; several ran legal, rebuild, or environmental nonprof-its—all of this in a neighborhood that had lost 75 percent of its population and only had three gas stations and one diner six years after Katrina. Only one who chose this strategy had worked in that particular area before. All were extremely protective of their opera-tions, what I call *risk projects*, and spent most of their time convincing others in the community that their particular project was key to the recovery of the neighborhood.

Landau et al. (2004) explain that danger is partly managed through efforts to main-tain one's self-esteem (see also, Baumeister 1982; Pyszczynski et al. 1999; Pyszczynski et al. 2004). Ongoing danger or the constant threat of peril can cause individuals to try to boost their self-esteem by making and maintaining favorable impressions on others (Steele et al. 1993). This can be done by appearing knowledgeable or intelligent or by trying to repair their integrity to enhance their self-worth (Landau et al. 2004; McGregor et al. 2001; Pyszczynski et al. 2004). As Rudman et al. (2007) note, people are able to recover from a threat in one domain by stressing their success or efforts in another domain. These compensatory cognitions are a way that those who engage in immersing deal with the disruption of Katrina; they channel problems in one domain (family, work, etc.) into a completely different area to maintain self-esteem and self-worth. Steele (1988) calls this the "fluid compensation" principle. As Heine et al. (2006) note, fluid compensation is most observable in feelings of uncertainty and in situations where individuals are reminded of risk. In part then, those who immerse are trying to enhance their self-worth by creating large, complex projects, often in areas unfamiliar to them so that they can avoid closure (Landau et al. 2004). Their respective risk projects take all of their cognitive focus so that they do not have to perceive or think about anything else.

Those who immersed continually put themselves in situations where flux was normative or required new ways of thinking. Lewin (1935), for instance, argues that when thinking about reality becomes difficult or intolerable, people often resort to fantastical thinking to crowd out negative thoughts. Likewise, as Kruglanski and Webster (1996) find, people with a low need for closure are more likely to explore other worldviews. Those who immersed themselves in large projects tended to avoid linear thinking and instead focused on multiple possible futures. Rather than proceeding from one project to the next, like those who used chunking as a strategy for moving on, those who were immersing sought multiple, creative avenues for arriving at the future. It was not that they did not care about the future, they just were not attached to any single way of getting there. In this way they tended both to be creative and to embrace what I call *cognitive mobility*. This mobility allowed them to contemplate and pursue multiple ways of perceiving problems and solutions and ultimately dealing with risk.

Those who immersed tended to see their projects as creative solutions to pressing problems and often talked about creativity as an important aspect of their life. In conversation with me, Jayla she spoke positively about creative thinkers not being wedded to a single point of view, but rather being able to maintain options.

> I just read an article, who was it? I think it was an old magazine, actually. An Oprah Winfrey magazine—what is it about?, about creativity, and it said that creative people tend to be less depressed or you know, because they're—they tend to be broader thinkers . . . are able to think about [a] kind of variety of solutions to problems where people who tend to be more depressed, are usually people who have only like one train of thought. Alright, you know very narrow thinking. You can only think of—one or two solutions. So that when—you know, when they get stuck, it's like that's it; they just get stuck and they are not able to step outside of that.   (Jayla, black female, 30s)

As Mack explained to a group of volunteers one day, "Old problems need new solutions." Vess et al. (2009) note that following reminders of danger, individuals who have a low need for structure are much more likely to be novelty seeking and consider novel interpretations of the world. Those who immersed saw themselves as radically changing not only themselves but also their neighborhoods.

In many ways, the risk projects were novel attempts to dramatize the condition of the neighborhood. The competition to promote their project became a competition in creativity. This linkage was facilitated by things like the participation in design charrettes for schools, parks, and community centers, and attendance at community symposiums where residents had an opportunity to vote on and voice concern with projects. While many residents resented the urban experimentation (Allen 2011; Lorenzen and Harvey 2016) that came to stand in for aid, those who engaged in immersion supported the creative offerings of others and eventually took up that creative impetus. In fact, the more creative their solution to the problem was, the more likely they saw themselves as succeeding.

Finally, those who immersed were extremely protective of their risk projects.

McGregor et al. (2009) discovered in a number of observations of neural patterns in experimentally manipulated conditions that simulated peril that activity in the brain emerged that mirrored antisocial defenses. Their subjects felt that their worldview was being threatened and alternated from being proud and trying to establish meaning to defending their worldview against various threats. To be sure many of those who immersed bounced back and forth between being highly social, interacting with volunteers, glad handing possible donors, trying to befriend the media, and being antisocial, blaming volunteers for the lack of success or progress, trying to sabotage the efforts of other nonprofits, refraining from any collaboration with other nonprofits, and avoiding people where possible.

24.3 CONCLUSION

Douglas and Wildavsky (1983) begin their seminal text on risk and culture by asking if we can ever really know the risks we face. I would argue that doing so would require a firm grounding in the sociology of culture and cognition. The approach undertaken here sees risk as stemming from the social order itself and from cultural beliefs and cognitive heuristics; micro, meso, and macro features of organizations; interorganizational fields; and the operation of political and socioeconomic forces at various scales (Tierney 2014). Risk is a collective construction. And yet the interaction between different systems might be too complex for us to ever completely understand risk (Perrow 1984).

In the immediate aftermath of Hurricane Katrina, the Bring New Orleans Back Commission and Mayor Ray Nagin decided to turn many predominantly minority neighborhoods into green spaces. This decision revealed a major cognitive limitation to understanding how people think about risk. While experts calculated that the Lower Ninth Ward was too risky to repopulate, residents of the neighborhood did not perceive their homes as part of a riskscape. People protested and moved back to their neighborhoods, rebuilding in a haphazard and potentially unsustainable manner. In the long term, Hurricane Katrina represents one of the best cases for understanding how bad we are at recognizing and making sense of risk (Daniels et al. 2006; Cole and Fellows 2008)

At best, by understanding the connections between risk and cognition we come to inhabit what Beck (2009) calls "risk communities." These communities have the ability to bind diverse peoples into "thought communities" (Zerubavel 1997). In these communities, mental models of risk connect us to the "other." These cognitive connections ultimately make us responsible for one another and creates what Tierney (2014) calls a "whole community" approach to managing risk and danger. In the long-term aftermath of Hurricane Katrina, much of the grassroots movements in marginalized neighborhoods was configured around creating whole-community approaches to understanding risk. In these communities, residents tried to convince others that to make their community viable (and hence not fail as a community), certain risks had to be understood and ameliorated. Whether it was rebuilding houses, attracting businesses, building schools or churches, or making the community safe, residents understood the necessity of the whole-community approach for securing a future for their neighborhood. This often involved meetings, where residents noted the importance of "getting right in their heads" (Harvey 2015). Here risk and reality were often openly discussed; the present paused, so that it could be deliberated on. Residents in the long-term aftermath of Katrina, particularly in places like the Lower Ninth Ward, were intimately familiar with how their landscape and power (including various forms of capital) interacted to produce risk. If Katrina did nothing else, it exposed risk, laid bare so that the rest of us might learn something. But here, as I have argued in this chapter, grounding risk in the sociology culture and cognition is key. Otherwise, we are likely to learn the wrong lessons.

REFERENCES

Allen, Barbara. 2011. " 'Laboratorization and the 'Green' Rebuilding of New Orleans's Lower Ninth Ward." pp. 225–44 in *The Neoliberal Deluge: Hurricane Katrina, Late Capitalism, and the Remaking of New Orleans*, edited by C. Johnson. Minneapolis: University of Minnesota Press.

Auyero, Javier, and Deborah Swistun. 2009. *Flammable: Environmental Suffering in an Argentine Shantytown*. New York: Oxford University Press.

Baumeister, Roy. F. 1982. "Self-Esteem, Self-Presentation, and Future Interaction: A Dilemma of Reputation." *Journal of Personality* 50:29–45.

Beamish, Thomas. 2001. "Environmental Threat and Institutional Betrayal: Lay Public Perceptions of Risk in the San Luis Obispo County Oil Spill." *Organization and Environment* 14(1):5–33.

Beck, Ulrich. 1992. *Risk Society: Towards a New Modernity*. London: SAGE.

Beck, Ulrich. 1999. "From Industrial Society to Risk Society: Questions of Survival, Social Structure and Ecological Enlightenment." *Theory, Culture and Society* 9(1):97–123.

Beck, Ulrich. 2009. *World at Risk*. Malden, MA: Polity Press.

Bickerstaff, Karen, Peter Simmons, and Nick Pidgeon. 2008. "Constructing Responsibilities for Risk: Negotiating Citizen–State Relationships." *Environment and Planning A* 40(6):1312–30.

Bickerstaff, Karen, and Gordon Walker. 2002. "Risk, Responsibility, and Blame: An Analysis of Vocabularies of Motive in Air-Pollution(ing) Discourses." *Environment and Planning A* 34: 2175–92.

Boehmer-Christiansen, Sonja. 1994. "Global Climate Protection Policy: The Limits of Scientific Advice Part 1." *Global Environmental Change* 4(2):140–59.

Cerulo, Karen A. 2006. *Never Saw It Coming: Cultural Challenges to Envisioning the Worst.* Chicago: University of Chicago Press.

Christakis, Nicholas, and James Fowler. 2009. *Connected: The Surprising Power of Our Social Networks and How They Shape Our Lives.* Boston: Little, Brown.

Clarke, Lee. 1989 *Acceptable Risk? Making Decisions in a Toxic Environment.* Berkeley: University of California Press.

Clarke, Lee. 1999. *Mission Impossible: Using Fantasy Documents to Tame Disaster.* Chicago: University of Chicago Press.

Clarke, Lee. 2006. *Worst Cases: Terror and Catastrophe in the Popular Imagination.* Chicago: University of Chicago Press.

Clarke, Lee, and James F. Short Jr. 1993. "Social Organization and Risk: Some Current Controversies." *Annual Review of Sociology* 19:375–99.

Cole, Terry, and Kelli Fellows. 2008. "Risk Communication Failure: A Case Study of New Orleans and Hurricane Katrina." *Southern Communication Journal* 73(3):211–28.

Daniels, Ronald, Donald Kettl, and Howard Kunreuther. 2016. *On Risk and Disaster: Lessons from Hurricane Katrina.* Philadelphia: University of Pennsylvania Press.

Diamond, Jared. 1995. "Easter's End." *Discover*, August. http://discovermagazine.com/1995/aug/eastersend543 (Accessed October 22, 2012).

Dietz, Thomas, Paul C. Stern, and Robert W. Rycroft. 1989. "Definitions of Conflict and the Legitimation of Resources: The Case of Environmental Risk." *Sociological Forum* 4:47–70.

DiMaggio, Paul. 1997. "Culture and Cognition." *Annual Review of Sociology* 23:263–87.

Douglas, Mary, and Aaron Wildavsky. 1983. *Risk and Culture: An Essay on the Selection of Technological and Environmental Dangers.* Berkeley: University of California Press.

Erikson, Kai. 1994. *A New Species of Trouble: The Human Experience of Modern Disasters.* New York: Norton.

Fischhoff, Baruch, Stephen R. Watson, and Chris Hope 1984. "Defining Risk." *Policy Sciences* 17(2): 123–39.

Fiske, Susan T., and Shelley Taylor. 1991. *Social Cognition.* New York: McGraw-Hill.

Freudenberg, William R. 1998. "Perceived Risk, Real Risk: Social Science and the Art of Probabilistic Risk Assessment." *Science* 242(4875): 44–9.

Freudenburg, William R. 1993. "Risk and Recreancy: Weber, the Division of Labor, and the Rationality of Risk Perceptions." *Social Forces* 71(4): 909–32.

Giddens, Anthony. 1990. *The Consequences of Modernity.* Stanford, CA: Stanford University Press.

Gotham, Kevin Fox. 2016. "Coastal Restoration as Contested Terrain: Climate Change and the Political Economy of Risk Reduction, a Case Study of Louisiana." *Sociological Forum* 31(S1): 787–806.

Greenberg, Jeff, Ton Pyszczynski, and Sheldon Solomon. 1986. "The Causes and Consequences of a Need for Self-Esteem: A Terror Management Theory." pp. 189–212 in *Public Self and Private Self*, edited by R. F. Baumeister. New York: Springer-Verlag.

Harvey, Daina Cheyenne. 2015. "Waiting in the Lower Ninth Ward in New Orleans: A Case Study on the Tempography of Urban Marginalization." *Symbolic Interaction* 38(4):539–56.

Heimer, Carol A. 1988. "Social Structure, Psychology, and the Estimation of Risk." *Annual Review of Sociology* 14:491–517.

Heine, Steven, Travis Proulx, and Kathleen Vohs. 2006. "The Meaning Maintenance Model: On the Coherence of Social Motivations." *Personality and Social Psychology Review* 10:88–110.

Hilgartner, Stephen. 1992. "The Social Construction of Risk Objects: Or, How to Pry Open Networks of Risk." pp. 39–53 in *Organizations, Uncertainties, and Risk*, edited by James F. Short and Lee Clarke. Boulder, CO: Westview Press.

Hulme, Mike. 2009. *Why We Disagree about Climate Change: Understanding Controversy, Inaction and Opportunity.* New York: Cambridge University Press.

Kahan, Dan M. 2007. "The Cognitively Illiberal State." 2007. *Stanford Law Review* 60(1):115–54.

Kahan, Dan M., Donald Braman, Paul Slovic, and John Gastil. 2006. "Fear and Democracy: A Cultural Evaluation of Sunstein on Risk." Yale Law School, Public Law Working Paper No. 100.

Kahan, Dan. M. 2012. "Cultural Cognition as a Conception of the Cultural Theory of Risk." pp. 723–59 in *Handbook of Risk Theory: Epistemology, Decision Theory, Ethics, and Social Implications of Risk*, edited by Sabine Roeser, Rafaela Hillerbrand, Per Sandin, and Martin Peterson. New York: Springer.

Kasperson, Jeanne X., and Roger E. Kasperson. 2005. *The Social Contours of Risk, Volume 1: Publics, Risk Communication and the Social Amplification of Risk.* London: Earthscan.

Kerr, Anne. 2003. "Rights and Responsibilities in the New Genetics Era." *Critical Social Policy* 23:208–26.

Kruglanski, Arie W., and Tallie Freund. 1983. "The Freezing and Unfreezing of Lay Inferences: Effects on Impressional Primacy, Ethnic Stereotyping, and Numerical Anchoring. *Journal of Experimental Social Psychology* 19:448–68.

Kruglanski, Arie W., and Donna M. Webster. 1996. "Motivated Closing of the Mind: 'Seizing' and 'Freezing.'" *Psychological Review* 103:263–83.

Landau, Mark J., Michael Johns, Jeff Grennberg, Tom Pyszczynski, Jamie Goldenberg, and Sheldon Solomon. 2004. "A Function of Form: Terror Management and Structuring the Social World." *Journal of Personality and Social Psychology* 87:190–210.

Landau, Mark, Spee Kosloff, and Brandon J. Schmeicheal. 2011. "Imbuing Everyday Actions with Meaning in Response to Existential Threat." *Self and Identity* 10:64–76.

Lewin, Kurt. 1935. *A Dynamic Theory of Personality.* New York: McGraw Hill.

Lienard, Pierre, and Pascal Boyer. 2006. "Precaution Systems and Ritualized Behavior." *Behavioral and Brain Sciences* 29:635–41.

Lifton, Robert Jay. 1993. *The Protean Self: Human Resiliency in an Age of Fragmentation.* New York: Basic Books.

Lorenzen, Janet, and Daina Cheyenne Harvey. 2016. "Forced In or Left Out: Experiencing Green from Community Redevelopment to Voluntary Simplicity and the Potential In-Between." pp. 263–74 in *Emergent Possibilities for Global Sustainability: Intersections of Race, Class and Gender*, edited by Phoebe Godfrey and Denise Torres. New York: Routledge.

Luhmann, Niklas. 2003. *Risk: A Sociological Theory.* Translated by Rhodes Barrett. New York: de Gruyter.

Marx, Sabine M., and Elke U. Weber. 2012. "Decision Making under Climate Uncertainty: The Power of Understanding Judgment and Decision Processes." pp. 99–128 in *Climate Change in the Great Lakes Region: Navigating an Uncertain Future*, edited by T. Dietz and D. C. Bidwell. East Lansing: Michigan State University Press.

McCright, Aaron, and Rachel Shwom. 2010. "Newspaper and Television Coverage." pp. 405–13 in *Climate Change Science and Policy*, edited by Stephen H. Schneider and Armin Rosencranz. Washington, DC: Island Press.

McGregor, Ian. 2004. "Zeal, Identity, and Meaning: Going to Extremes to Be One Self." pp. 182–99 in *Handbook of Experimental Existential Psychology*, edited by J. Greenberg, S. L. Koole, and T. Pyszczynski. New York: Guilford.

McGregor, Ian, and Christian H. Jordan. 2007. "The Mask of Zeal: Low Implicit Self-Esteem, and Defensive Extremism after Self-Threat. *Self and Identity* 6:223–37.

McGregor, Ian, Kyle Nash, and Michael Inzlicht, M. 2009. "Threat, High Self-Esteem, and Reactive Approach Motivation: Electroencephalographic Evidence. *Journal of Experimental Social Psychology* 45:1003–7.

McGregor, Ian, Mark Zanna, John Holmes, and Steven Spencer. 2001 "Compensatory Conviction in the Face of Personal Uncertainty: Going to Extremes and Being Oneself." *Personality Processes and Individual Differences* 80:472–88.

Metcalfe, Janet, and Walter Mischel. 1999. "A Hot-Cool System Analysis of Delay of Gratification: Dynamics of Willpower." *Psychological Review* 106(1):3–19.

Morello-Frosch, Rachel, Manuel Pastor, and James Sadd. 2001. "Environmental Justice and Southern California's 'Riskscape': The Distribution of Air Toxics Exposures and Health Risk among Diverse Communities." *Urban Affairs Review* 36(4):551–78.

Moser, Susanne C., and Lisa Dilling. 2007. *Creating a Climate for Change: Communicating Climate Change and Facilitating Social Change*. New York: Cambridge University Press.

Neuberg, Steven L., Nicole T. Judice, and Stephen G. West. 1997. "What the Need for Closure Scale Measures and What It Does Not: Toward Differentiating among Related Epistemic Motives." *Journal of Personality and Social Psychology* 72:1396–412.

Norgaard, Kari Marie. 2006. "'People Want to Protect Themselves a Little Bit': Emotions, Denial, and Social Movement Nonparticipation." *Sociological Inquiry* 76:372–96.

Norgaard, Kari Marie. 2010. *Cognitive and Behavioral Challenges in Responding to Climate Change*. Washington, DC: World Bank.

Norgaard, Kari Marie. 2011. *Living in Denial: Climate Change, Emotions and Everyday Life*. Cambridge, MA: MIT Press.

O'Neill, Saffron, and Sophie Nicholson-Cole. 2009. "'Fear Won't Do It' Promoting Positive Engagement with Climate Change through Visual and Iconic Representations." *Science Communication* 30(3):355–79.

Olaussin, Ulrika. 2009. "Global Warming-Global Responsibility? Media Frames of Collective Action and Scientific Certainty." *Public Understanding of Science* 18:421–36.

Oreskes, Naomi, and Erik M. Conway. 2010. *Merchants of Doubt: How a Handful of Scientists Obscured the Truth on Issues from Tobacco Smoke to Global Warming*. New York: Bloomsbury Press.

Perrow, Charles. 1984. *Normal Accidents: Living with High Risk Technologies*. New York: Basic Books.

Perrow, Charles. 1997. Organizing for Environmental Destruction." *Organizations and Environment* 10:66–72.

Peters, Thomas J., and Robert H. Waterman. 1982. *In Search of Excellence*. New York: Harper and Row.

Pyszczynski, Tom, Jeff Greenberg, and Sheldon Solomon. 1999. "A Dual-Process Model of Defense against Conscious and Unconscious Death-Related Thoughts: An Extension of Terror Management Theory." *Psychological Review* 106:834–45.

Pyszczynski, Tom, Jeff Greenberg, Sheldon Solomon, Jamie Arndt, and Jeff Schimel. 2004. "Why Do People Need Self-esteem? A Theoretical and Empirical Review." *Psychological Bulletin* 130:435–68.

Rosa, Eugene A., and Thomas Dietz. 1998. "Climate Change and Society: Speculation, Construction and Scientific Investigation." *International Sociology* 13:421–55.

Rudman, Laurie, Matthew Dohn, and Kimberly Fairchild. 2007. "Implicit Self-Esteem Compensation: Automatic Threat Defense." *Journal of Personality and Social Psychology* 93:798–813.

Rutjens, Bastiaan, Joop van der Pligt, and Frenk van Harreveld. 2009. "Things Will Get Better: The Anxiety Buffering Qualities of Progressive Hope." *Personality and Social Psychology Bulletin* 35:535–43.

Simon, Herbert 1957. *Models of Man: Social and Rational Mathematical Essays on Rational Human Behavior in a Social Setting.* New York: Wiley.

Slovic, Paul. 2000. *The Perception of Risk.* London: Earthscan.

Slovic, Paul, Baruch Fischhoff, and Sarah Lichtenstein. 1979. "Rating the Risks." *Environment* 21(3):14–39.

Stallings, Robert A. 1990. "Media Discourse and the Social Construction of Risk." *Social Problems* 37(1):80–95.

Steele, Claude M. 1988. "The Psychology of Self-Affirmation: Sustaining the Integrity of the Self." pp. 261–302 in *Advances in Experimental Social Psychology*, edited by L. Berkowitz. San Diego, CA: Academic Press.

Steele, Claude M., Steven J. Spencer, and Michael Lynch. 1993. "Self-Image Resilience and Dissonance: The Role of Affirmational Resources." *Journal of Personality and Social Psychology* 64:885–96.

Swann, William B. 1987. "Identity Negotiation: Where Two Roads Meet." *Journal of Personality and Social Psychology* 53:1038–51.

Swidler, Ann. 1986. "Culture in Action: Symbols and Strategies." *American Sociological Review* 51:273–86.

Tierney, Kathleen J. 1999. "Toward a Critical Sociology of Risk." *Sociological Forum* 14(2):215–42.

Tierney, Kathleen J. 2014. *The Social Roots of Risk: Producing Disasters, Promoting Resilience.* Stanford, CA: Stanford University Press.

Tilly, Charles. 1996. "Invisible Elbow." *Sociological Forum* 11(4):589–601.

Tversky, Amos, and Daniel Kahneman. 1974. "Judgment under Uncertainty: Heuristics and Biases." *Science* 185(4157):1124–31.

Vaughan, Diane. 1996. *The Challenger Launch Decision: Risky Technology, Culture, and Deviance at NASA.* Chicago: University of Chicago Press.

Vaughan, Diane. 1999. "The Dark Side of Organizations: Mistake, Misconduct, and Disaster." *Annual Review of Sociology* 25:271–305.

Vaughan, Diane. 2002. "Signals and Interpretative Work: The Role of Culture in a Theory of Practical Action." pp. 28–54 in *Culture in Mind: Toward a Sociology of Culture and Cognition*, edited by Karen A. Cerulo. New York: Routledge.

Vess, Matthew, Clay Routledge, Mark Landau, Jamie Arndt. 2009. "The Dynamics of Death and Meaning: The Effects of Death-Relevant Cognitions and Personal Need for Structure on Perception of Meaning of Life." *Journal of Personality and Social Psychology* 4:728–44.

Webster, Donna M., and Arie W. Kruglanski. 1994. "Individual Differences in Need for Cognitive Closure." *Journal of Personality and Social Psychology.* 67:1049–62.

Wegner, Daniel M., and Laura Smart. 1997. "Deep Cognitive Activation: A New Approach to the Unconscious." *Journal of Consulting and Clinical Psychology* 65:984–95.

Wilkinson, Iain. 2010. *Risk, Vulnerability and Everyday Life*. New York: Routledge.

Wuthnow. Robert. 2010. *Be Very Afraid: The Cultural Response to Terror, Pandemics, Environmental Devastation, Nuclear Annihilation, and Other Threats*. New York: Oxford University Press.

Zerubavel, Eviatar. 1997. *Social Mindscapes: An Invitation to Cognitive Sociology*. Cambridge, MA: Harvard University Press.

CHAPTER 25

CULTURAL BLIND SPOTS AND BLIND FIELDS

collective forms of unawareness

ASIA FRIEDMAN

25.1 WHAT IS A CULTURAL BLIND SPOT?

ANATOMICALLY, human beings have a structural blind spot in their field of vision where the optical nerve attaches. The term "blind spot" is also used colloquially to describe an area where a person's view is obstructed, for instance when using the side mirror while driving. This chapter elaborates the concept of *cultural blind spots*, which are not always visual (although they can be), and are not biological blockages of our ability to perceive something through the senses. Cultural blind spots cannot be seen or accessed in the brain or other anatomy; one must observe them in social life (Zerubavel 2015:8–9).

While sociologists have not previously theoretically elaborated the concept of a "cultural blind spot," some have used the term "blind spot" to convey the idea that a paradigm of thought ignores or obscures some other aspect or idea of possible interest (e.g., Athens 2002; Krysan and Bader 2009). In this vein, sociology as a discipline has been widely thought to have a biological blind spot, especially prior to the recent establishment of the sociology of the body and embodiment. Shilling, for example, argued "the body has historically been something of an 'absent presence' in sociology" (2003:17). Brekhus has similarly pointed out sociologists' "epistemological blindspotting of unmarked categories" (1998:39) due to the discipline's typical focus on studying marked populations.

Without using the term, many other sociologists have made observations about cognition and perception we might productively relate to the idea of "cultural blind spots." For example, there is a body of work in the sociology of gender that demonstrates that ingrained conceptions of gender as binary difference have limited researchers' ability to recognize biological similarities between males and females (Fausto-Sterling 2000 2012;

Fine 2011; Friedman 2013; Fujimura 2006; Jordan-Young 2011; Martin 1991; Moore 2007; Oudshoorn 1994). As I have argued elsewhere (Friedman 2013), we tend to visually perceive human bodies as "opposite sexes"—that is, as either male or female, rather than human—because hegemonic cultural discourses emphasize gender differences and sexual dimorphism much more than gender similarities and sex sameness. We therefore visually attend to the small number of bodily indicators of sex difference while the arguably much larger number of bodily details that better reflect our human commonalities form a cultural blind spot. Cerulo (2006) similarly highlights cultural blindness when she traces a "positive asymmetry" in contemporary American cultural thinking that makes it much easier for Americans to envision "best-case scenarios" than "worst-case scenarios."

If we expand the concept of a blind spot to our recollections of the past, research in the sociology of memory also finds that memories are structured as much by what is forgotten as what is recalled. Zerubavel (2003) examines the ways "mnemonic communities" shape their past, finding that some periods of history are heavily marked as important parts of the past to be commemorated and remembered, while others are comparatively mnemonically absent. In addition to marking, this "collective forgetting" (Schwartz 2009) also reflects the way memories of the past are attached to schemas of the present. As Brekhus explains, "part of highlighting the marked [...] involves forgetting the unmarked and discarding what does not fit into existing cognitive schemas" (Brekhus 2015:155).

A number of prominent social theorists also implicitly reference collective forms of unawareness, both sensory and cognitive, that we might understand as cultural blind spots. This includes Marx, whose treatment of ideology (and the later derivation of "false consciousness") addresses collective blind spots in the consciousness of the underclass regarding relations of domination and exploitation (Marx and Engels 1845–1849/1970), as well as Bourdieu, who describes habitus as unconsciously structuring "what is or is not to be seen" (Bourdieu 1984:86) and emphasizes that class-based preferences and perspectives feel like expressions of personal taste, but always involve "misrecognition" (1984:172) of their fundamental function of solidifying and naturalizing class boundaries. Foucault also broadly argues that when power is misunderstood as repressive, we are unable to perceive the characteristics of productive power he outlines (Foucault 1978). He further points out that silences, which we might include in the unattended, are part of the overall strategy of discursive power (1978:27). I would also include here Thomas Kuhn's observation that scientists perceive the exact same instruments and experimental materials differently under different historical "paradigms." As Kuhn describes:

> [A]fter the assimilation of Franklin's paradigm, the electrician looking at a Leyden jar saw something different from what he had seen before. The device had become a condenser, for which neither the jar shape nor glass was required [...]. Lavoisier [...] saw oxygen where Priestly had seen desophlostated air and where others had seen nothing at all.   (Kuhn 1962/1996:117)

One of Kuhn's fundamental points in tracing the rise and fall of scientific paradigms is to demonstrate that paradigms all include blind spots. Details that adherents of one paradigm cannot recognize are self-evident to adherents of another.

Although evocative, a blind spot is slightly imperfect as a metaphor for cultural blindness in that the term "spot" typically refers to something small and clearly bounded. This is the case in the examples of anatomical and automotive blind spots, for example, both of which imply that we are able to see most phenomena. However, it is often the case that we are blind to more than we see. Hence our cultural blind spots are frequently closer to blind "fields" or blind "zones." I continue to use the metaphor of a blind spot while pointing out examples of variation in the proportion of blindness to attention throughout.

Despite many evocative examples of cultural blind spots from a wide range of subfields and substantive contexts, sociologists have not previously developed the concept of a cultural blind spot in a theoretically focused way. There is, however, a rich conceptual foundation for a social theory of blind spots in research establishing thinking and perceiving as sociocultural processes (rather than only biological/universal or individual), as well as in studies of everyday life and the taken for granted, which point out that one characteristic of what is taken for granted is that we have trouble recognizing it. In particular, Zerubavel's work on the unattended (2015) and the taken for granted (2018) and Brekhus's work on the unmarked (1998) provide two of the most direct treatments of cultural blindness. The next section outlines this theoretical backdrop for the study of cultural blind spots, which points to two different cognitive processes that create blind spots—focusing and habituation.

25.2 THEORETICAL FOUNDATIONS FOR UNDERSTANDING CULTURAL BLIND SPOTS

Thinking and sensory perception are both social phenomena, reflecting the cultures and subcultures to which we belong, a point which cognitive sociologists have demonstrated by tracking variations and patterns in thought linked to social norms. From a sociological perspective, despite often feeling private and individual, our thoughts are usually similar in key aspects to those of the people that surround us. Yet this commonality does not necessitate the conclusion that particular ways of thinking are human universals deriving from biology. Rather, in addition to biological processes and individual idiosyncrasies, our thinking is culturally patterned, and examples of cognitive pluralism abound (Brekhus 2015; Zerubavel 1991, 1997, 2018).

The notion that perception is socially shaped underlies Mead's (1934) theories of the social self and intersubjectivity, particularly the concepts of "perspective taking" and the "generalized other." Shibutani similarly argues that it is "reference groups" that provide the basis for "the organization of the actor's experience. That is to say, it is a structuring of his perceptual field" (1955:563). Echoing Mead, Shibutani suggests that the social structuring of perception occurs through taking on "perspectives" provided by our reference groups:

> Perspective is an ordered view of one's world—what is taken for granted about the attributes of various objects, events, and human nature. It is an order of things remembered and expected as well as things actually perceived, an organized conception of what is plausible and what is possible; it constitutes the matrix through which one perceives his environment.   (1955:564)

The existence of social matrices for perception was also anticipated by Malinowski's (1929) observation that the Trobriand Islanders usually perceived children as resembling their father, even when he saw stronger resemblances to the mother. It is further supported by experimental research on cultural differences in sensory perception spanning at least half a century. For instance, Bagby (1957) found that when presented with two different images simultaneously, one depicting a scene from US American culture (such as a baseball game) and one depicting a comparable scene from Mexican culture (such as a bullfight), Mexicans and Americans selectively perceive the scene from their own culture. Other similar research demonstrates that people from India and people from the United States tend to recall different details of wedding ceremonies (Steffensen et al. 1979). Another perceptual "socio-attentional pattern" (2015:53) is greater "field independence" in Western observers. East Asians are more likely to attend to a broad perceptual field, while Westerners tend to center their attention on a focal object (Nisbett and Masuda 2003).

One of the key concepts for understanding how both cognition and perception vary across sociocultural contexts is attention. The social psychologists Arien Mack and Irvin Rock (1998:25–26) define attention as "the process that brings a stimulus to consciousness. It is, in other words, the process that permits us to notice something." Emphasizing that perception is both conscious and unconscious, Mack and Rock explicitly argue that there is no conscious perception without attention, including what they call "inattentional blindness." The term "inattentional blindness" is evocative of a blind spot, and usefully connects blind spots to patterns of attention. The one limitation of Mack and Rock's analysis of attention and blindness is that, while they insist that the meaning of the stimulus is the main determinant of whether attention is captured (xi, 229), they do not explore the ways that meanings—and therefore patterns of "inattentional blindness"—are socially defined and organized.

The sociology of attention, in contrast, analytically centers such cross-contextual differences in patterns of relevance (Zerubavel 2015:49). Directly using the terms "collective blind spots" and "cultural blind spots," for example, Zerubavel emphasizes both that attention is collective and attention's "inherently exclusionary nature" (2015:2):

> A sociology of attention [...] highlights our often-shared and therefore ultimately collective sense of relevance and concern, thereby reminding us that we actually notice and ignore things not only as individuals but also jointly, as parts of collectives.

As exemplified by the way various problems are collectively ignored, it thus also helps reveal our collective blind spots.   (Zerubavel 2015:9–10)

These social patterns of not noticing, or inattention, are—as Zerubavel suggests—the essence of cultural blind spots. Further, it is important to note that although the concepts of perspective and attention imply the possibility of perceptual choice or alternatives, "the actor himself is often unaware that there are alternatives" (Shibutani 1955:565) because of his or her embeddedness in one or more social groups. In light of this, we can broadly define cultural blind spots as *unconscious social patterns of inattention*.

Through his wide-ranging discussion of a huge number of different examples of selective attention, Zerubavel (2015) points to habituation and focusing as two distinct mechanisms for generating cultural blindness. Closely related to the concepts of the taken for granted, the background, and the unmarked, inattention due to habituation captures the way we are usually unaware of those things with which we are "overly familiar" (Zerubavel 2018:103–4, quoting Hawkes 1977:62). Focusing, on the other hand, results in blindness to everything that is not the focal object of our attention and to any information that challenges the boundaries or definition of the attended. I provide a more detailed treatment of blind spots due to habituation in the next section, and a discussion of blind spots due to focusing follows.

25.2.1 Habituation: The "Taken for Granted" as Cultural Blindness

The notion of the "taken for granted" includes varying levels of awareness, including total unawareness. Specifically, the familiarity of the taken for granted leads to inattention, as "we rarely notice that which is constantly around us" (Zerubavel 2015:27). Habituation is central to this form of blind spot in which "one is unable to notice something," as Wittgenstein 1953/(2009:56) put it, "because it is always before one's eyes." Schutz (1970:114–15) defines such gradations of awareness as explicitly social, arguing that we inherit a "ready-made guide to relevance" from our "ancestors, teachers, and authorities" that defines what we take for granted. He refers these domains of relevance as part of the "world taken for granted" by the group.

Schutz further points out those details we actively and clearly attend to are many fewer than those in the realm of the "taken for granted," to which we are so habituated we do not experience them at all. He describes this asymmetry of awareness as follows: "There is a relatively small kernel of knowledge that is clear, distinct, and consistent in itself. This kernel is surrounded by zones of various gradations of vagueness, obscurity, and ambiguity" (Schutz 1970:74). Invoking a similar asymmetry of attention in which the attended is much smaller than the unattended, the conceptual distinction between "figure" and "background" conveys that we are typically aware of only a small number of well-defined features of our perceptual field, while most of the technically present sensory information is indistinct and unnoticed (Schutz 1970:72–73). In light of this, cultural blindness due to habituation may be closer to a blind "field" than a blind "spot," as it encompasses much more than the attended. Garfinkel's concept of "background expectancies"—"a background of seen but unnoticed features of common discourse" (1964/1967:41)—and Goffman's distinction between "framed" and "unframed" activity (1974/1986) similarly draw on a figure/ground logic to convey that part of what makes up the taken for granted is an asymmetry of awareness between the attended and the unattended.

Another related concept necessary to understand the form of cultural blindness that results from the taken for granted and habituation is "unmarkedness." In his article calling on sociologists to study the unmarked, Brekhus (1998:35) defines "social marked-ness" as "the ways social actors actively perceive one side of a contrast while ignoring the other side as epistemologically unproblematic." We cognitively and perceptually attend to socially marked features, he argues, "while virtually ignoring and taking for granted unmarked features" (Brekhus 2015:25). Drawing on the figure/ground distinction, and again invoking the asymmetry between the attended and the unattended, he points out that "most of our social landscape blends into the unmarked background" (Brekhus 1998:35), and argues that both the discipline of sociology and culture at large tend to be inattentive to the unmarked. The unmarked can therefore be thought of as a cultural and disciplinary blind spot. Directly using the term "blind spot," in fact, Brekhus refers to this as "culture's epistemological blindspotting of unmarked categories" (39).

It is also important to note the role of unmarkedness and the taken for granted—and therefore of cultural blind spots—in the maintenance of power and privilege. The famil-iarity of the unmarked is a reflection of normativity, in which being unnoticed is a feature of cultural privilege. To be unmarked indicates that one fits within privileged, default categories, whereas to be marked is a sign of one's cultural marginality. In blindness due to habituation and taken for grantedness, then, the tacit social value is associated with what is unattended, rather than what is noticed. This is a difference from blind spots due to focusing, where the attended is what is socially valued, a point I further expand in the next section.

The cultural blindness that results from habituation and taken-for-grantedness is also likely in part due to it being cognitively processed automatically and subconsciously. "Dual-process" theories of cognition broadly posit that human cognition is composed of two qualitatively different kinds of processing. Type 1 thinking is correlated with auto-matic, fast, and largely unconscious processing, whereas Type 2 tends to be slower, more deliberate, and largely conscious (DiMaggio 1997; Evans 2008; Evans and Stanovich 2013; Kahneman 2011; Schwarz 1998; Vaisey 2009). Brekhus (2015:32) makes this connection explicitly, identifying automatic cognition as related to the blind spots of the unmarked and taken for granted:

> The unnoticed, unseen, taken-for-grantedness of unmarked categories and realities makes it likely that they are tied to cognitive efficiency and automatic cognition. People rarely deliberate or explicitly think about unmarked social categories unless

these are placed in a context with the marked that causes people to reflect upon the taken-for-grantedness of the unmarked.

The insight that the unmarked and the taken for granted are part of automatic rather than deliberate cognition has implications for how sociologists might approach studying cultural blind spots, which I address further on in the section on analytical strategies.

25.2.2 Focusing: Blindness to Ambiguity and Complexity

If habituation to the unmarked and the taken for granted represent one way of thinking about cultural blindness, the concepts of "focusing" and "typification" illustrate a somewhat different form of blind spot in which we are blind to socially irrelevant complexity, ambiguity, and anomaly, rather than the normative and taken for granted. As Schutz describes it, typification is a core part of our inherited stock of knowledge, a social structure of relevance that tells us "which facts or events have to be treated as substantially—that is, typically—equal (homogenous)" (1970:120). Treating two things as the same, of course, also requires ignoring any differences between them. That is to say, the very basis of our ability to "typify" something in the first place is socially shared blind spots. Any experience of "seeing as" implies picking out "relevant" sensory details that support the typification—and also not registering any ambiguous or contradictory information. Typification is therefore defined not only by relevance but also by blindness to the irrelevant, contradictory, and ambiguous; just as much as "rules of relevance" (Goffman 1961:25), then, rules of "tacit inattention" (Goffman 1955:219), or socially shared blind spots, are essential to our ability to think and perceive in categories. Typification's blind spots are not the taken for granted or unmarked, however, but information that complicates and makes problematic received ideas about what is relevant. This blindness to complexity is sociologically important and should be emphasized hand in hand with recognizing the invisible privilege of the unmarked.

Blindness to the taken for granted and blindness due to focusing are similar to the extent that both involve tacit inattention and are defined by social meanings and norms, yet they differ in at least two important respects. The first is that, unlike blind spots taking the form of the background or the unmarked, when we do not perceive ambiguous details when focusing or categorizing, it is not because these complicating details are so well accepted that they are taken for granted. Rather, the information inattended in focusing is what is threatening to the coherence of our social categories—and therefore to our sense of mental and social order. Goleman argues that this form of blind spot, which he refers to as a "lacuna," typically emerges to help us cognitively avoid anxiety-evoking information (Goleman 1985:107).

The power dynamics underlying these two forms of blind spots also differ, although both ultimately function to support hegemonic ideas. As alluded to earlier, the taken for granted reflects blindness to the privileged and the normative; in such cases, the inattended is afforded more social value than the attended, as it is unarticulated, generic, and "normalized without direct acknowledgement" (Brekhus 2015:26), while the attended (the marked category) is socially marginalized. In the case of blindness due to focusing, in contrast, the positive social valence is usually attached to the attended—which is also the socially "relevant"—and ambiguous or boundary-threatening details are unattended because they are culturally defined as insignificant, anomalous, or irrelevant. Thus while both forms of blind spots include a power dynamic, the alignment of attention, inattention, dominance, and marginality differs.

One final point of distinction relates to the ongoing tacit mental labor involved in focusing and typification. Whereas the taken for granted tends to be rather well defined and firmly established, focusing is a constant dynamic process of filtering out the ambiguous and irrelevant, involving subtle adjustments of attention to keep the necessary blind spots in place. Usually this processing is automatic and unconscious, but occasionally we become aware of ambiguity and experience a moment of deliberative thinking to address it, for instance when someone's gender presentation is ambiguous and we have to be more deliberate about categorizing them.

In summary, I have outlined two variations on cultural blind spots based on the extant sociological work touching on attention. Cultural blind spots generated by taken for grantedness and habituation are often unmarked and processed only through automatic thinking. Blind spots can also be generated by focused attention, which blinds us to the irrelevant and the ambiguous. Both types of blind spots contribute to sustaining differences in cultural value and privilege; however, this function manifests differently in each case. In blind spots due to focusing, social value is attached to the select information we attend, while the unattended is what is irrelevant, threatening, or marginalized. Habituation's blind spots, which come from social normativity and unmarkedness, are characterized by a positive social valuation of the unattended, which is the taken-for-granted and therefore unnoticed default or standard. In the next section, I suggest several strategies for revealing and examining cultural blind spots.

25.3   Cognitive and Analytical Strategies for Revealing Cultural Blind Spots

By definition, recognizing and analyzing cultural blind spots poses a challenge. In general, it is more difficult to notice absence than presence. As Zerubavel puts it, "unlike the marked, the unmarked is methodologically elusive, as absence is much more difficult to observe than presence. After all, acts of omission are harder to notice than acts of commission" (2018:14). In light of this, lacking positive evidence for those things we do not perceive (Zerubavel 2015:7) is the first obstacle to a study of cultural blind spots, and any effective analytic strategy must therefore focus on providing access to this information. Along with a lack of positive evidence, as previously discussed, both automatic processing and hegemonic social expectations provide additional resistance to recognizing cultural blind spots.

Despite these challenges, it is possible to cultivate a mindset of "observing the absences" (Zerubavel 2018:14). Both Garfinkel (1964/1967) and Schutz (1970), for example, argued that recognizing background expectancies and the taken for granted requires adopting a specific mental perspective. For Garfinkel, this is the mindset of a "stranger to the 'life as usual' character of everyday scenes" (1964/1967:37). Schutz similarly discusses a "special motive" required to make the taken for granted into the problematic, one that questions received notions of relevance (1970:116). Schutz further argues that only a "shock" can lead us to abandon the cognitive style of the paramount reality (254), and it was precisely the point of Garfinkel's breaching experiments to generate this kind of mental shock.

Zerubavel identifies a number of additional mental stances helpful for recognizing the background, the unmarked, and the unattended. He for instance argues that both "fuzzy" and "flexible" minded perspectives can help us to "unlump" and "unsplit" culturally taken-for-granted categories, which requires recognizing normally unnoticed cross-category similarities and within category differences (Zerubavel 1991). In other work, he also suggests that "multifocal attention," "open awareness," and "mindfulness" can cultivate awareness of absences (Zerubavel 2015:75–79). Taking a slightly different emphasis, Brekhus suggests adopting an "analytically nomadic" perspective so that "[i]n place of observing issues from a single fixed cultural viewpoint we can observe them from multiple perspectives, combining elements from each" (Brekhus 1998:47). Note that one key reason all of these proposed mental stances help reveal cultural blind spots is that they explicitly define attention and relevance as social rather than logical or natural. Broadly speaking, recognizing and problematizing cultural blind spots requires developing a sociology of attention (Zerubavel 2015:9–10).

In addition to emphasizing the social construction of attention and perception, each of these mindsets also critically performs "defamiliarization" (Shklovsky 1917/1965). Using the example of art, Shklovsky (1917/1965:12) describes the effect of defamiliarization as "to make the stone stony [...] to impart the sensation of things as they are perceived and not as they are known [...] to make objects unfamiliar." Defamiliarizing the structure of attention underlying our blind spots allows us to become aware of what was previously unnoticed. In order to open our awareness to the previously unattended, however, defamiliarization requires us to "remove the automation from perception" (Shklovsky 1917/1965:22). In other words, defamiliarization presupposes a conscious shifting—or "deautomatization" (Deikman 1966)—of attention. Deautomatization is "the undoing of a psychic structure permitting the experience of increased detail and sensation at the price of requiring more attention" (329). Deikman uses the examples of meditation and religious renunciation to illustrate the new dimensions of awareness, which he refers to as "perceptual expansion," available through increasing conscious, deliberative perception. Summarizing psychological research on dual-process theories of cognition, DiMaggio (1997:271–2) suggests three specific conditions that can help induce more deliberate cognition: Attention, motivation, and schema failure. In other words, when their attention is drawn to a problem, when inconsistencies disrupt a schema's unproblematic functioning, or when they are dissatisfied with the status quo, people can switch from automatic to deliberate cognition. In addition to adopting mindsets conducive to deautomatization and defamiliarization, there are specific analytic practices that sociologists can use to create some of these conditions, and thus the "attentional shifts" (Zerubavel 2018:89) necessary to bring the structure of our attention to consciousness.

One of the key analytic strategies of a sociology of attention is "reversing." Other terms for the strategy of reversing include "foregrounding," "marking the unmarked" (see Zerubavel, 2018:87–123), "figure-ground reversal" (Zerubavel 2015), and "reverse marking" (Brekhus 1998:43). The analytic power of reversing is to expand the boundaries of perception by effectively shifting our attention from the marked to the unmarked. Reversing in this manner challenges conventions of attention by bringing focus to the normally backgrounded, unmarked—and thus unseen—information. In expanding our attention to the unmarked, reversing also performs "semiotic subversion," eliminating "the semiotic asymmetry between the marked and the unmarked" (Zerubavel 2018:87).

Part of the privilege of the unmarked, as discussed already, is that it does not receive any special linguistic mark and therefore functions as a default norm. In light of this, language plays a key role in the strategy of reversal through foregrounding the unmarked by naming it. This was precisely the motivation for using the term "cisgender" to mark the category of individuals for whom biological sex and gender identity align in culturally normative ways, shifting cisgender—at least linguistically—from a default norm to a marked equivalent to transgender. Language can also create semiotic and attentional subversion through the opposite process—rather than marking the unmarked, unmarking the marked. Zerubavel (2018:117) describes unmarking the marked as follows:

> Marking and thereby "abnormalizing" what is conventionally taken for granted is but one way of subverting the fundamental semiotic asymmetry between the marked and the unmarked, yet such asymmetry can also be subverted by using the opposite cognitive tactic of unmarking and thereby normalizing what is conventionally considered "abnormal." Whereas marking the unmarked involves foregrounding, unmarking the marked involves the diametrically opposite act of backgrounding.

Linguistically, unmarking often requires removing qualifying adjectives or substituting neutral or unmarked terms for marked ones. For example, marked terms such as "chick lit" and "ethnic food" become unmarked by removing their qualifying adjectives and adding them to the unmarked categories "literature" and "food." As in these examples, linguistic unmarking prompts us to recognize and shift the boundaries of what is considered "normal" by drawing our attention to what was previously excluded. This elevated awareness of prior unawareness is an example of breaking the automaticity of attention. Returning to DiMaggio's (1997) argument that deliberate cognition replaces automatic cognition under certain conditions, specifically when our attention is drawn to a problem, or when inconsistencies disrupt a prior schema's unproblematic functioning, note that both unmarking the marked and marking the unmarked reveal and problematize the inadequacies of prior mental frameworks, leading—at least momentarily—to deautomatization.

A related but even more epistemologically radical analytic strategy for dislodging cultural blind spots is "marking everything" (Brekhus 1998:45). Rather than just reversing the figure and ground, marking everything is a strategy that destabilizes markedness (and the associated structure of our attention) by refusing the logical boundaries on which it rests. As Brekhus explains, "if we articulate entire continua with equal weight, there will be no negative spaces left. Since marking is relational, marking everything equally simultaneously leaves the entire continuum unmarked" (1998:45).

Each of these forms of reversal challenges conventions of attention by bringing focus to normally backgrounded, unmarked—and thus unseen—information. Such attentional shifts expand the scope of our attention, making our awareness fuller and more inclusive. Reversing also subverts taken-for-granted meanings, and requires us to reevaluate the boundaries of categories. All of these effects contribute to deautomatization, encouraging more deliberate modes of cognition that help us access the specificities of what we normally do not perceive due to our cultural blind spots.

Most of the analytic strategies I discuss are applicable to blind spots associated with habituation as well as those due to focusing because they work by disrupting norms of selective attention, which is the cognitive basis for both. Given their other distinct conceptual characteristics, however, different analytical strategies may be better suited to revealing one type of blind spot or the other. For example, the first strategy I discussed, reversing, is particularly well suited to analyzing blind spots associated with habituation and the taken for granted because the family of associated concepts (e.g., figure/ground, marked/unmarked) are all based on a conception of perception in which the attended and inattended are separated and spatially contiguous. Goffman's frame analysis (Goffman 1974/1986)—which focuses on the distinction between some "relevant" content (a painting, for instance) and that which it is not (the surrounding wall, everything outside of the picture frame)—is similarly based on a binary notion of attention in which details are either "in" or "out" of frame. As a way to analytically "flip" our attention and associated meanings, the strategy of reversing works well to disrupt blind spots due to habituation, unmarkedness, and being backgrounded or "out of frame." However, the blind spots associated with focusing have a somewhat different cognitive structure in which the attended and inattended are interwoven in the conceptual space *within* the attentional figure or foreground. In addition, while information that is out of frame, in the background, or part of the unmarked is more like a blind "field" than a blind "spot" since it is definitionally undefined and unbounded, and typically much larger than what is in frame or marked, the blind spots involved in focusing are proportionately smaller. Although reversing is still loosely applicable in such cases, another analytic strategy, filter analysis, may offer more targeted ways of teasing out the relevance structures involved in focusing.

Filter analysis uses the metaphor of a perceptual filter as an orienting guide for analytically noticing the previously inaccessible (DeGloma and Friedman 2005; Friedman 2013). The term "filter" invokes a mental "strainer" or "sieve" through which visual stimuli pass before they are consciously perceived, letting in culturally meaningful details while sifting out the culturally irrelevant. Filters in general function by allowing selected elements to pass through a set of holes while blocking others. Thinking in terms of filters thus specifically directs us to examine the question of which features or details pass through and are attended and, arguably more importantly, which are blocked by the filter and thus remain unnoticed. One of the virtues of Goffman's frame analysis is that it is based on a very evocative spatial image that effectively captures the way we focus on some details while ignoring others. The filter metaphor is similarly based on a concrete spatial image that provides a specific, useful guide for analysis, but also offers a number of further advantages for analyzing blind spots due to focusing. As mentioned already, in the frame metaphor, attention and inattention are represented as binary, fully separated, and spatially contiguous. Filter, in contrast, evokes the interweaving of the attended and inattended in the same conceptual space. The defining question of filter analysis—"what is being filtered out?"—for example, brings awareness to the processes of selective attention at work within the perceptual frame. Kelly Joyce's work on the complexities of "seeing" and "not seeing" when reading brain images is illustrative here, specifically radiologists' inattention to "artifacts" (aspects of the image attributable to the technology itself rather than the body being imaged) and "unidentified bright objects" (details that are not pathology but deviate from typical patterns of anatomy) (2008:64–66). While the concepts of "figure" and "ground" certainly apply to reading an MRI scan, most directly to show that what is outside of the imaged anatomy—the surrounding wall, any labels or other details in the margin of the image, or connected anatomy that is not the focus of the scan—should be ignored, artifacts and unidentified bright objects are small details *within* the image frame that are interpreted as irrelevant and inattended. In addition, as we have seen, the balance of attention and inattention implied in the metaphor of a frame is more closely reflective of "blind fields" than "blind spots." As again illustrated with the example of reading an MRI, a more narrowly defined blind *spot* within the boundaries of otherwise framed perceptual information may be better represented by the metaphorical blockages and holes of a filter.

One final analytic strategy for revealing cultural blind spots, particularly those rooted in sensory perception, is multisensory research, or studies that compare multiple modes of sensory perception or otherwise highlight rarely foregrounded perceptual realities. The broader cultural context for this strategy is what Jay (1993:48–49) refers to as Western cultural "ocularcentrism," where visual information is privileged and viewed as more "true" than other sensory information.[1] Given that visual information has disproportionately high truth status compared with the other senses, the visual likely plays an important role in the taken for granted (and therefore in cultural blind spots), which means that pursuing other sensory information can provide access to details and meanings that we are normally unable to access due to our subconscious overreliance on the visual. This is exemplified in my prior work (Friedman 2013) on the visual perception of male and female bodies as "different." I interviewed blind people about their sensory experiences of the human body in general and sex attribution in particular to clarify the extent to which the hegemonic understanding of sex is specifically "sex seen," as opposed to "sex sensed" more broadly. Based on these interviews, one of my central lines of argument is that dominant everyday conceptions of sex are based mostly on visual data and therefore exclude all the information available through the other senses, much of which conveys a great deal of ambiguity. More generally, in light of the social prominence of visual perception, I argue that sociologists can gain great insight into the social construction of reality by bracketing the visual, and exploring other modes of sensory perception.

25.4 CONCLUSION

While the general idea of social construction is basically axiomatic in sociology, there is room for much more research examining social construction as an active process. One particularly fruitful line of inquiry is to identify the cognitive and perceptual underpinnings of cultural processes. Here my emphasis has been "sociomental" (Zerubavel 1991, 1997) inattention as a mechanism of the social construction process, specifically socio-attentional patterns associated with taken-for-granted ways of thinking and the selective attention necessitated by focusing, which I used to theorize two variations of cultural blind spots.

The first, which is associated with taken for grantedness and habituation, connects inattention to privilege, unmarkedness, and normativity, capturing the way that we are blind to what we consider "normal" and "unremarkable." The second highlights the simplifying inattention required to maintain social categorization and meaning, emphasizing the way that the act of focusing involves blindness to ambiguous, contradictory, socially devalued, or irrelevant information. While the structure of attention in each case is slightly different, both types of blind spots provide insight into social construction as a process of excluding information, and both suggest analytic strategies for revealing the previously excluded. Given the lack of positive information, it is certainly more difficult to examine the inattended than that which we consciously perceive, but through cultivating mindsets conducive to "observing the absences" and applying the analytic strategies outlined earlier, which include reversing and filter analysis, it is possible to drive more analytic focus to this universe of unattended information underlying our experienced realities.

In a more applied sense, a focus on cultural blind spots can also help identify common ground in cultural conflicts and debates. By reconceptualizing such conflicts as "attentional battles" (Zerubavel 2015:57), or contests over what we should attend as relevant, it becomes possible to identify the shared beliefs and common ground that we become blind to when focusing on points of conflict. One example I am exploring in other research is the current conflict over mammography screening. Despite being the subject of an extensive research program spanning decades, mammography screening remains one of the most polarized topics in medicine. While points of disagreement typically guide research, debate, and media coverage on such conflicts, this focus on differences makes it difficult to recognize the substantial similarities in perspective. For example, almost all involved agree that mammography is beneficial to some extent, and that women age 50 to 75 should be screened at least every two years. More generally, the point is that thinking in terms of blind spots and patterns of attention can be useful in facilitating communication and understanding. The term "cultural blind spot" has been used in business in this vein, for example to describe barriers to cross-cultural communication and collaboration due to taken-for-granted norms and practices.[2]

Both sensory and cognitive forms of selective attention are foundational mechanisms of the social construction process. Despite this, and despite the presence of the unattended in social life as a consistent but often implicit theme in social theory, cultural blind spots have never previously been explicitly theorized. Analytically, examining cultural blind spots is aimed at expanding the boundaries of consciousness to bring awareness to the previously unconscious and unattended, and thus allowing for deliberate rather than automatic processing. In this way, studying cultural blind spots (and the sociology of attention more generally) may offer a perspective and set of analytic practices that can reveal how our unconscious biases and blind spots are organized, collectively shared, and ultimately changeable through shifting the structure of attention.

Notes

1. On cultural sensory hierarchies privileging vision, see also: Classen 1997; Classen et al. 1993; Howes and Classen 2014; Stoller 1984; Synnott 1993.
2. See, for example, http://nexgsd.org/research/case-stories/cultural-blind-spots/ and http://banksconsulting.net/CulturalBlindSpotsCountry.htm.

References

Athens, Lonnie. 2002. "'Domination': The Blind Spot in Mead's Analysis of the Social Act." *Journal of Classical Sociology* 2(1):25–42.

Bagby, James. 1957. "A Cross-Cultural Study of Perceptual Predominance in Binocular Rivalry." *Journal of Abnormal and Social Psychology* 54:331–4.

Bourdieu, Pierre. 1984. *Distinction: A Social Critique of the Judgment of Taste.* Cambridge, MA: Harvard University Press.

Brekhus, Wayne. 1998. "A Sociology of the Unmarked: Redirecting Our Focus." *Sociological Theory* 16(1):34–51.

Brekhus, Wayne. 2015. *Culture and Cognition: Patterns in the Social Construction of Reality.* Cambridge, England and Malden, MA: Polity.

Cerulo, Karen A. 2006. *Never Saw It Coming: Cultural Challenges to Envisioning the Worst.* Chicago: University of Chicago Press.

Classen, Constance. 1997. "Engendering Perception: Gender Ideologies and Sensory Hierarchies in Western History." *Body and Society* 3:1–19.

Classen, Constance, David Howes, and Anthony Synnott. 1993. *Aroma: The Cultural History of Smell*. New York: Routledge.

DeGloma, Thomas, and Asia Friedman. 2005. "Thinking with Socio-Mental Filters: Exploring the Social Structuring of Attention and Significance." Paper presented at the Annual Meeting of the American Sociological Association, Philadelphia, PA.

Deikman, Arthur J. 1966. "De-automatization and the Mystic Experience." *Psychiatry* 29:324–38.

DiMaggio, Paul. 1997. "Culture and Cognition." *Annual Review of Sociology* 23:263–87.

Evans, Jonathan St. B. T. 2008. "Dual-Processing Accounts of Reasoning, Judgment, and Social Cognition." *Annual Review of Psychology* 59:255–78.

Evans, Jonathan St. B. T., and Keith E. Stanovich. 2013. "Dual-Process Theories of Higher Cognition: Advancing the Debate." *Perspectives on Psychological Science* 8(3):223–41.

Fausto-Sterling, Anne. 2000. *Sexing the Body: Gender Politics and the Construction of Sexuality*. New York: Basic Books.

Fausto-Sterling, Anne. 2012. *Sex/Gender: Biology in a Social World*. New York: Routledge.

Fine, Cordelia. 2011. *Delusions of Gender: How Our Minds, Society, and Neurosexism Create Difference*. New York: Norton.

Foucault, Michel. 1978. *The History of Sexuality*. Vol. 1. New York: Vintage Books.

Friedman, Asia. 2013. *Blind to Sameness: Sexpectations and the Social Construction of Male and Female Bodies*. Chicago: University of Chicago Press.

Fujimura, Joan. 2006. "Sex Genes: A Critical Sociomaterial Approach to the Politics and Molecular Genetics of Sex Determination." *Signs* 32(1):49–82.

Garfinkel, Harold. 1964/1967. *Studies in Ethnomethodology*. Englewood Cliffs: Prentice Hall.

Goffman, Erving. 1955. "On Face-Work: An Analysis of Ritual Elements of Social Interaction." *Psychiatry: Journal for the Study of Interpersonal Processes* 18(3):213–31.

Goffman, Erving. 1961. "Fun in Games" in *Encounters: Two Studies in the Sociology of Interaction*. Indianapolis: Bobbs-Merrill.

Goffman, Erving. 1974/1986. *Frame Analysis: An Essay on the Organization of Experience*. Boston: Northeastern University Press.

Goleman, Daniel. 1985. *Vital Lies, Simple Truths*. New York: Simon & Schuster.

Hawkes, Terrence. 1977. *Structuralism & Semiotics*. Berkeley: University of California Press.

Howes, David, and Constance Classen. 2014. *Ways of Sensing: Understanding the Senses in Society*. London: Routledge.

Jay, Martin. 1993. *Downcast Eyes: The Denigration of Vision in Twentieth Century French Thought*. Berkeley and Los Angeles: University of California Press.

Jordan-Young, Rebecca. 2011. *Brain Storm: The Flaws in the Science of Sex Differences*. Cambridge, MA: Harvard University Press.

Joyce, Kelly. 2008. *Magnetic Appeal: MRI and the Myth of Transparency*. Ithaca, NY: Cornell University Press.

Kahneman, Daniel. 2011. *Thinking, Fast and Slow*. New York: MacMillan.

Krysan, Maria, and Michael D. M. Bader. 2009. "Racial Blind Spots: Black-White-Latino Differences in Community Knowledge." *Social Problems* 56(4):677–701.

Kuhn, Thomas. 1962/1996. *The Structure of Scientific Revolutions*. Chicago; London: University of Chicago Press.

Mack, Arien, and Irvin Rock. 1998. *Inattentional Blindness*. Cambridge, MA: MIT Press.

Malinowski, Bronislaw. 1929. *The Sexual Life of Savages in North Western Melanesia*. New York: Halcyon House.

Martin, Emily. 1991. "The Egg and the Sperm: How Science Has Constructed a Romance Based on Stereotypical Male-Female Roles." *Signs* 16(3):485–501.

Marx, Karl, and Friedrich Engels. 1845–1849/1970. *The German Ideology*. 3rd rev. ed. Moscow: Progress Publishers.

Mead, George Herbert. 1934. *Mind, Self, and Society from the Standpoint of a Social Behaviorist*. Edited by Charles W. Morris. Chicago: University of Chicago Press.

Moore, Lisa Jean. 2007. *Sperm Counts: Overcome by Man's Most Precious Fluid*. New York: New York University Press.

Nisbett, Richard, and Takahiko Masuda. 2003. "Culture and Point of View." *Proceedings of the National Academy of Sciences of the United States of America* 100(19):11163.

Oudshoorn, Nelly. 1994. *Beyond the Natural Body: An Archaeology of Sex Hormones*. London: Routledge.

Schutz, Alfred. 1970. *On Phenomenology and Social Relations: Selected Writings*, edited by Helmut R. Wagner. Chicago: University of Chicago Press.

Schwartz, Barry. 2009. "Collective Forgetting and the Symbolic Power of Oneness: The Strange Apotheosis of Rosa Parks." *Social Psychology Quarterly* 72(2):123–42.

Schwarz, Norbert. 1998. "Warmer and More Social: Recent Developments in Cognitive Social Psychology." *Annual Review of Sociology* 24:239–64.

Shibutani, Tamotsu. 1955. "Reference Groups as Perspectives." *American Journal of Sociology* 60:562–9.

Shilling, Chris. 2003. *The Body and Social Theory*. 2nd ed. Thousand Oaks, CA: SAGE.

Shklovsky, Viktor. 1965. "Art as Technique." pp. 3–24 in *Russian Formalist Criticism: Four Essays*, edited by Lee T. Lemon and Marion J. Reiss. Lincoln: University of Nebraska Press.

Steffensen, Margaret, Chitra Joag-Dev, and Richard C. Anderson. 1979. "A Cross-Cultural Perspective on Reading Comprehension." *Reading Research Quarterly* 15(1):10–29.

Stoller, Paul. 1984. "Sound in Songhay Cultural Experience." *American Ethnologist* 11:559–70.

Synnott, Anthony. 1993. *The Body Social: Symbolism, Self and Society*. London and New York: Routledge.

Vaisey, Stephen. 2009. "Motivation and Justification: A Dual-Process Model of Culture in Action." *American Journal of Sociology* 114(6):1675–715.

Wittgenstein, Ludwig. 1953/2009. *Philosophical Investigations*. 4th ed. Malden, MA: Wiley-Blackwell.

Zerubavel, Eviatar. 1991. *The Fine Line: Making Distinctions in Everyday Life*. New York: The Free Press.

Zerubavel, Eviatar. 1997. *Social Mindscapes: An Invitation to Cognitive Sociology*. Cambridge, MA: Harvard University Press.

Zerubavel, Eviatar. 2003. *Time Maps: Collective Memory and the Social Shape of the Past*. Chicago: University of Chicago Press.

Zerubavel, Eviatar. 2015. *Hidden in Plain Sight: The Social Structure of Irrelevance*. New York: Oxford.

Zerubavel, Eviatar. 2018. *Taken for Granted*. Princeton, NJ: Princeton University Press.

PART V

SOCIOCULTURAL FRAMES OF MEANING, METAPHOR, AND ANALOGY

CHAPTER 26

....

THE SACRED, PROFANE, PURE, IMPURE, AND SOCIAL ENERGIZATION OF CULTURE

....

DMITRY KURAKIN

THE problem of the social origins of thought—which legitimizes the very existence of cognitive sociology—even when recognized as such, is often presented in a shallow and simplified way. To admit that social pressure biases the original flow of thoughts among conformist individuals or that culture gives tools and accessories for self-sufficient cognition, means merely peeling the first layer of the onion and often leads to a "thin description" of social life. This shallow vision of the involvement of culture in cognition overlooks the fundamental nature of the social origins of the human mind and culture-cognition relations. It is much more important for sociologically sophisticated research to find out how the social and the individual, culture and cognition, meet in the human mind and how social life participates in individual thinking. In other words, in contrast to several contemporary approaches to cognition limiting culture to a subsidiary, fictional, or nonautonomous role, I argue that cognition cannot be treated adequately if culture is not seen as inherent to it.

The idea of culture is counterintuitive when it comes to cognition. The common sense implies that if there are individual cognitions and they can interact, then this interaction is derivative and secondary in relation to the existence of cognition. The idea of culture asserts the opposite; interrelations between cognitions are primary to its existence and thus must be seen as a forming an autonomous realm, with cognition as part of it. Meanwhile, some of the theories in sociology of culture and cognition virtually challenge this idea either by implying the insufficiency of culture (culture is fragmented and not self-consistent [Swidler 1986][1] and thus is not an autonomous realm); or by detaching cognition from culture and seeing it as a self-sufficient realm that only communicates with external reality of institutions and other contexts sometimes aggregately designated as culture or "cultural scaffolding" (Lizardo and Strand 2010); or by hollowing-out the idea of culture by means of its absorptive conflation with cognition in such constructions as "personal culture" (Lizardo 2017). What these different scenarios have in common is effective detaching cognition from culture, which is no longer seen as an internal environment of action.

One of the markers of such a detachment, which I multiply mention in this chapter, is a conceptual construction that I call the "informational theory of communication." It implies that any process of communication must be seen as an exchange of information. This vision presents any social interaction as an interchange of certain messages between addressants and addressees. Messages contain logically organized content, which might be stored and transferred; importantly, this content is information, containing a certain (quantifiable) number of distinctions. The information is governed by logical structure and is equal to itself. This vision contributes to a common-sense vision of cognition and makes the notion of culture virtually redundant.

The fundamentally sociological way to address the problem of the social origins of thought is to take the core of meaningful life as a starting point. By core, I mean a state in which human thought and culture are not yet even differentiated. It is not a coincidence that the most insightful sociologists who took culture seriously focused exactly on this state of indeterminacy to grasp its nature, and proceeded to see how culture and thought develop further and interact when they differ. Such was one thread of thought for Georg Simmel, who came to define culture as "the path of the soul to itself" (Simmel 1997:55). The meaning of this Aesopic formula is easy to unpack, keeping in mind Simmel's paradigm of meaningful life—the creation and perception of the object of art. In the time of creation, the fluid and subjective cognition is fused with the cultural object that is only yet about to emerge. The subjective and objective sides of the process are mutually constitutive and indistinguishable. When a cultural object is created, Simmel argues, the spirit and culture are separated, with the former returned to its intangible subjectivity and the latter solidified as an objective value. In the act of perceiving culture, however, the spirit is reengaged with culture, and the initial synthesis that is constitutive for both of them reemerges. Simmel's formula, thus, in effect means that it is only through engagements with culture that cognition can operate.

That means that, in the words of Clifford Geertz, culture is an "ingredient," not an "accessory," to human thought (Geertz 1973:83). While Simmel, with his renowned talent for sociological impressionism, got to the root and spirit of the problem, it was another founding father of sociology, Émile Durkheim, who developed an applicable sociological theory explaining relations between culture, thought, and social life. Like Simmel, he had been looking for an element where culture (or "collective representations") and thought (or "individual representations") originate within the "synthesis *sui generis*" (Durkheim 1974). Eventually he came to see the sacred/profane opposition to be the basic fact of every human society and the origin of culture and thought. The sacred objects and inherent rules that separate them from the mundane reality of ordinary, "profane" objects emerge and re-emerge within special social interactions, such as rituals; the sacred/profane boundaries, in turn, structure culture, perception and thought. Following Durkheim, both culture and cognition logically originate from this primary opposition. Locating an elementary process where culture and mind meet and understanding the corresponding sociological mechanisms reveals a sociological grammar of culture and thought—principles that structure and restructure culture as an inner environment of thought and action. In this chapter, I focus primarily on the late Durkheimian discovery of the sacred as a core of social life and human thought, and to the approaches in sociology that it inspired.

To illustrate the need for such theorizing, I briefly observe some examples that can draw social theorists toward the appreciation of a deep connection between culture and cognition. Thus, there are phenomena that obviously transcend the habitual addressant-addressee message transfer scheme I term "the informational theory of communication" and a flat semiotic picture of language as a set of tools for cognition. The examples of such transcendent phenomena are poetry, metaphor, and some genres and twists of plot, such as the tragedy. In these examples, insufficiency of the "cognition apart from culture" approaches manifests itself through the "missing mass" of emotional involvement: the effect of good poetry, bright metaphor, or Greek tragedy cannot be reduced to the content of the information they refer to; and can only be explained by means of special extralinguistic tools, which necessarily include an emotional dimension.

Poetry is a classic example of the insufficiency of explanation drawing on the informational theory of communication. If a verse is only a piece of information transferred through the text, and shaped by rhythm and rhyme, where does the great power of poetry come from? Following the aforementioned vision shared by Simmel, Durkheim, and Geertz, I assume that the disproportionate excess of emotional involvement by the reader points to the simple fact that what is happening in terms of the reader's cognition is not equal to what has been transferred within a message, but rather a synthesis of the same nature as that from which culture originates.[2]

Similarly, the power and effect of metaphor goes far beyond the transferred message about similarity between its principal and subsidiary subjects. There are various explanations for its salient emotional effect, but the very existence of this effect as the most intriguing feature of the metaphor was described as early as in the writings of Aristotle, who is known as its first theorist. Among the others, Paul Ricoeur argues that metaphor has an extrareferential nature and is a mechanism of meaning-making, rather than a simple transfer of information or a reference to already existing meanings. I will try to show further that the Durkheimian theory of the sacred can shed light on the sociological core of what is happening when we encounter such "centers of gravity" in the landscape of meanings.

In this chapter I argue that the Durkheimian theory of the sacred is a crucial yet not fully recognized source for cognitive sociology. It contains not only a theory of culture (which is acknowledged in contemporary sociology) but also a vision of culture–cognition relations. This has enabled the development of a number of useful sociological and anthropological theories. Durkheimian cultural sociology allows us to understand the crucial role the sacred/profane opposition plays in structuring culture, perception, and thought. Based on a number of theories, I also show how another opposition— between the pure and impure modes of the sacred, allows us to explain dynamic features of the sacred and eventually provides a basic model of social change. The importance of this latter opposition for explaining culture and thought is only growing under the conditions of modernity.

While explicating this vision and resultant opportunities for sociological analysis I also criticize some of the theories, approaches, and statements established within cognitive sociology. I argue, thus, that culture participates in cognition and is an intrinsic ingredient of the human mind. Culture is not an inconsistent and fragmented set of elements, as some sociologists imply to varying degrees (Lizardo 2017; Swidler 1986), but a system; and as such it is an inner environment for human thought and social action. This system, however, is governed not by formal logic, as some critics of the autonomy of culture presuppose, but by concrete configurations of emotionally charged categories, created and re-created in social interactions. This vision, in turn, overcomes the informational theory of communication, which functions as a sort of a common sense within cognitive science.

The chapter consists of four sections and a conclusion. The first section lays out the central argument, and explains the theoretical context and relevance of Durkheim's theory of the sacred for the problem of the social origins of human thought. The second section is dedicated to the emotional dimension of culture, which becomes obvious by virtue of the theory of the sacred. The third section shows how the Durkheimian theory of the sacred, having been developed and furthered within anthropological and cultural sociological theories, works in empirical realms. The last section deals with the often neglected problem of the ambiguity of the sacred, and the central role that the opposition of the pure and impure sacred plays in culture and thought. It closes with a series of empirical illustrations.

26.1 The Sacred as a Key Concept of Durkheimian Sociology

Sociology is a science inextricably bound up with modernity. By origin, it deals with a challenge brought by great changes in the life of human collectives, accompanied by the rise of industrialization and capitalism, an escalation of the intensity of social life in growing cities, changes in the structure of populations and in social classes, and a range of related issues. These changes made irrelevant the essentialist and simplified vision of basic forms of sociality that had been taken for granted for centuries. Correspondingly, some aspects of human life that were previously seen as profoundly individual unveiled their social nature. The change of perspective, fostered by modernity and driven by sociology, raised a whole new set of fundamental problems and even revealed some new areas of human experience. One central problem among these is the social origins of human thought. Dealing with this problem brought to light such processes and phenomena as rituals, social performances, socialization, total institutions, and many others, which, even when known before, could now be seen as having a distinct existential status.

Emile Durkheim, a founding father of sociology, spent most of his academic life dealing with this problem. He approached it from different angles, such as the division of labor, the difference between modern and premodern types of solidarity, social origins of the most intimate processes (such as committing suicide), and others. Starting with observing deep differences in the functioning of traditional and modern societies and in shaping the thought of the so-called primitives and modern people, he later came to see that it is rather what is common among these types of collectivities that was key to understanding the fundamental connection between the social and the individual. While at the beginning of this endeavor morality rather than cognition was seen by Durkheim as the central field of relation between the social and the individual, the development of the argument gradually shifted the focus from morality to cognition (Giddens 1986). Thought and cognitive order thus played a central role in Durkheim's solution to the problem of social solidarity. Its two key elements are the theory of the sacred and the sociological theory of knowledge (Durkheim 1995). It is therefore telling that Durkheim initially intended to title his main work "The Elementary Forms of Thought and Religious Life" (Lukes 1985:407).

Being a Cartesian methodologically, Durkheim anticipated resolving the problem of social solidarity by finding an "atom" of sociality, its elementary, nonreducible incarnation. He came to see the sacred as such an incarnation, and (broadly understood) religion as a primary (and thus eternal in its essence) form of social organization. In its different modes the sacred concentrates such mechanisms and principles as authority, hierarchy, cohesion, distinction, force, inference and other crucial features of the social; and the forms of sacredness along with their social orchestration stand behind the most important principles of social life and determine its design.

The structuring of social life, thought, and perception by the sacred/profane opposition can be traced in all spheres of social life, including the spatial and temporal zoning of collective interactions, social divisions, and human cooperation; in a word, it reveals itself at every level of social life. One can easily recognize it in every part of everyday experience, from the celebratory visualization of political power (think of "presidential suites," for one) to the intimate prioritizing of certain parts of the body over the others, which every person does in their own (but still essentially social) way. Following Durkheimians, the role of this opposition goes as far as, for example, the preeminence of the right hand as a major anthropological fact (Hertz 2009). If the argument for why exactly the right hand must be the main one nowadays looks dubious, the social causes of the very asymmetry maintain their relevance. Thus, if the very nature of social life, structured by the sacred/profane opposition, appoints deep differences between these two realms of experience, it inevitably must be embodied.[3]

Another part of the equation—the sociological theory of knowledge—asserts that concepts and even categories of knowledge are in fact collective representations. They are social in origin and enacted in the deep nature of the social—that is, correlative to basic principles of social communication, social-spatial and social-temporal interrelations, and the tie between the social and the individual. That means that concepts and categories, on the one hand, reflect universal conditions of human existence: that humans are mortal, they have a physical constitution enabling, in the context of Earth, certain modalities of their interactions, such as the adjustment of what George Herbert Mead called the manipulative zone, and many other conditions of human existence. Importantly, on the other hand, they are shaped by historically conditioned patterns of interactions and contingent social structures developed in particular cultures. Durkheim's view, thus, avoids the two extremes repeatedly mentioned by cognitive sociologists—individualism and universalism—in treating how the human mind operates (Brekhus 2015; Zerubavel 1997).

The link between social solidarity and thought plays a fundamental role in Durkheim's position, because instead of seeing certain cognitive conformity and an inclination toward cooperation as particular features of human cognition, he reconciles it with the nature of the social. Thus, following Durkheim's key hypothesis, the sacred and profane as two experiential spheres of life, existing in all known human societies, correspond to, represent, and enact the double nature of man, consisting of social and individual dimensions (Durkheim 1973). In other words, the social as such is enabled by the existence of the sacred/profane distinction, which brings it to life; it emerges and reproduces itself in the course of collective life through these two modes of observable reality.

Being human beings, which for Durkheim means "homo duplex," our thought is socially structured in many ways, the most fundamental of which is that which ascends to the primary opposition of the sacred and profane. If we then follow any sort of structural vision of culture, which implies that culture (or, in Durkheim's terms, a system of "collective representations") is a structured system, we must admit that this primary distinction structures all human thought and culture, being a distinction of the highest possible level.[4] That means that concrete cultural meanings are unavoidably defined by the tension between the sacred and profane, and thus reconstruction of particular (quite different) forms that this opposition takes in particular cultures and social groups is a necessary and a key step in the interpretation of meanings of social life.

"Homo duplex" is Durkheim's explicit anthropological picture of the human being, which means that his notorious sociologism in fact did not prevent him from avoiding a common sociological weakness, which became the major excuse (DiMaggio 2002; Lizardo and Strand 2010) for the continuing powerful cognitivist turn. Beginning with early work about the interrelation between individual representations (i.e., states of cognition) and collective representations (i.e., culture) (Durkheim 1974), he consequentially contributed to the problem of the nature of the human and eventually summarized his vision of the sociologically relevant cognitive construction of the human mind in his later work about the dualism of human nature (Durkheim 1973).

26.2 EMOTION AS A DIMENSION
OF CULTURE

It remains mostly unrecognized, but I argue that in the long run, Durkheim's theoretical move concerning emotions, which he used to resolve the problem of the social order based on the theory of the sacred and the sociological theory of knowledge, led to quite a specific and sociologically sophisticated understanding of culture. In opposition to structuralist or semiotic visions, which treat culture as a (more or less powerful) cybernetic-like system of distinctions, the Durkheimian view includes the crucial dimension of emotions.

Bringing emotions to the fore was driven both by theoretical necessity and empirical data. If the sacred and the profane are observable empirical realms, which are supposed to correspond to the social and the individual as the two basic levels of human nature, there must be mechanisms that bring this correspondence to life. Durkheim solved this problem by introducing the notion of "collective emotions," which, by definition, first have collective origins, that is, emerge in special sorts of collective interactions, and second, are extraordinarily intense—that is how individuals distinguish them from the moderate individual emotions they routinely deal with. The process of "effervescence,"— which describes special extraordinarily intense collective emotions, embracing individuals during rituals and marking certain involved objects as sacred—by superimposing the extraordinariness of these emotions onto observable reality, is the basic model Durkheim uses to introduce collective emotions.

The crucial consequence of this decision is that meanings (such as, for instance, the meaning of the sacred object in the aforementioned example of the effervescence) became connected with social interactions (ritual), and this connection is enabled by emotions. Emotions, thus, are intrinsically engaged in meaning-making in Durkheim's theorizing, and that gives culture a dimension that is absent in a purely semiotic perspective. This is important first because this dimension, as we will see later, takes part in structuring elements of culture (so that Durkheimians do not have to follow the oversimplified vision of logically structured culture so gloriously disgraced by Ann Swidler and some cognitive sociologists). And, second, because it shapes the vision of the connection between culture and cognition. This is, indeed, a very general view of the connection between culture and cognition; however it is sufficient for the advancement of cultural sociology with a special interest in cognition. Meanings are "meaningful" (and culture is effectual) because they are concerned with emotions. By comparison, a cybernetic system of systematically, mutually related elements is a flat, insufficient, and ultimately irrelevant model of culture.

In the realm of moral feeling, for example, any cultural distinctions would be senseless were they not evidenced by emotions. Empirically, this means that morally colored actions (that is, actions not neutral from the moral point of view) bring about strong emotions. This becomes evident in the case of the deviation from moral prescriptions. The same state of affairs is found in the sphere of aesthetics; beautiful and ugly are not mere semiotic codes attributed to observable objects of corresponding labels. This distinction is based on emotionally definite meanings. The very existence of the beautiful and the ugly as "cybernetic tokens" does not explain the striving for one of these extremes and disgust for the other, the emotionally intense admiration for the beautiful, nor intense aversion to the ugly. It may seem that the logical is not connected with the emotional, but it is not the case. Logically valid operations are not the realizations of an arbitrarily set system of distinctions. They impel themselves to any common-sensual individual.[5] The convincing power of logical proof and the role of mistakes in the procedure of the inference are connected with emotions that only seem to be nonnecessary or complementary. The same works for many other cognitive operations. Wayne Brekhus, for example, stresses the relevance of Durkheim's theory for such basic operations as distinguishing the marked from the unmarked and figure-background relations (Brekhus 2015). The social emphasis (or lack of emphasis) in these operations is revealed through emotional coloring. Similarly, Gabriel Ignatow advocates theories of embodied knowledge and criticizes seeing knowledge in terms of an "emotion-free information" (the vision corresponding to the informational theory of communication I criticize in this chapter) (Ignatow 2007:116).

Clifford Geertz was very clear about the prominent role of emotions and feelings in tying together mental life and culture. He wrote, "We are concerned not with solving problems, but with clarifying feelings" (Geertz 1973:81), and further, "the point is that in man neither regnant fields nor mental sets can be formed with sufficient precision in the absence of guidance from symbolic models of emotion. In order to make up our minds we must know how we feel about things; and to know how we feel about things we need the public images of sentiment that only ritual, myth, and art can provide" (Geertz 1973:82).

Meaningful life is emotionally marked off. We do not think and feel separately, these are deeply integrated processes. Every meaning has its emotional component, and is connected with other meanings not only by distinctions but also by means of emotions. Culture in general and particular meanings, thus, are not mere "information."

This vision contrasts sharply not just with many existing theories of culture but rather with the informational theory of communication as their conceptual underpinning, which is deeply integrated in both conceptual and commonsense thinking. The informational theory of communication popularized by the development of technology (and especially by the dominance of the "finite state machine" model) and partly by semiotics, distorted views of social communication and spread both into social sciences and into common sense.[6] Meanings are basically seen within this paradigm as pieces of information.

In Durkheimian logic, in opposition, meanings are established in concrete social interactions and gain different emotional colorings depending on dynamics within particular social landscapes and on relations with other meanings. It is not a logical order that makes culture structured (a position criticized by Swidler and others, who mistakenly inferred from this criticism the fragmented vision of culture), but rather relations, based on emotionally colored symbolic meanings, affected by (and affecting) actual social interactions. As opposed to elements in a cybernetic system, which are regulated by logical relations, cultural meanings are shaped by the tension between the sacred and the profane, and the other mechanisms related to this tension.

In other words, it is undeniable that there are situations when culture, understood as a formal-logical system, appears to be inconsistent and self-contradictory. For instance, Gordon Lynch, a Durkheimian cultural sociologist, describes an ongoing tension between the sacred form of the Irish Catholic nation, legitimizing the severe regime and abuse practices in the Irish industrial school system, and the sacrality of the care of children (Lynch 2012). While during most of the twentieth century the former has been a "dominant sacred form" and the latter a "subjugated sacred form," the public scandal around "systemic abuse and neglect of children" (Lynch 2012:54–86) within this school system concentrated a burst of collective emotions of indignation and has eventually overturned this hierarchy. This scandal, in turn, was partly enabled by changing contexts for meaning, such as "the emergence of a new, European, and cosmopolitan vision of the Irish nation" (Lynch 2012:85). This exemplifies that culture is indeed a system, but this system is governed not by the static laws of formal logic, but by emotionally charged categories, created and re-created in social interactions.

26.3 THE POWER OF THE SACRED: HOW DOES IT WORK IN THE FIELD?

26.3.1 The Sacred after Parsons

In spite of Durkheim's unquestioned authority as a classic of sociology, the most important and encompassing facets of his theoretical contribution—the theories of the sacred and sociological theory of knowledge—have barely been recognized in sociology for decades. Apart from such enclaves of academic landscape as the College de Sociologie (see, e.g., Caillois 1959; Hollier and Bataille 1988), these theories were tangentially dealt with until Talcott Parsons and some of his followers took them seriously. Without going into the details of this highly intriguing historical-sociological riddle, I only mention that the sociological mainstream was misled by Durkheim's conceptual vocabulary and his positivist image. It was hard indeed to foresee that a self-proclaimed rigorous positivist who scarcely employed the term "culture" in his writings was going to become the chief theorist of an interpretive cultural sociology.

It was Parsons who enabled such a reading of Durkheim in his "The Structure of Social Action" (Parsons 1937). This laid the groundwork for the first exemplary empirical studies that explicitly harnessed the power of the sacred/profane opposition, which appeared in a couple of decades. The first of these studies, chronologically, was the classical article of Edward Shils and Michael Young, "The Meaning of the Coronation" (Shils and Young 1953). Shils and Young, whose essay begins with a somewhat poetic formula, "[t]he heart has its reasons which the mind does not suspect" (Shils and Young 1953:63), show that there are deep sacred roots of collective life, which are rarely recognized by people but still govern their lives. These sacred foundations of social life—which, within this still structural-functionalist vision are exemplified by a set of values such as "generosity, charity, loyalty, justice in the distribution of opportunities and rewards, reasonable respect for authority, the dignity of the individual and his right to freedom" (Shils and Young 1953:65)—must be periodically "reaffirmed" by means of public rituals (such as coronation), so that their actual prominence remains undisturbed by the ambivalence emerging from human minds.

Importantly, this explanation explicitly bases itself on a vision of connection between cognition and culture. Addressing the psychoanalytic conception of Ernest Jones, Shils and Young argue that the human mind is highly ambivalent toward sacred symbols, so contact with the sacred in the form of ritual "makes the individual feel that he is in 'good relations' with the sacred, as well as safe from his own sacrilegious tendencies" (Shils and Young 1953:67).

In this early work the neo-Durkheimians thus take a position that, in the context of later debates in cognitive sociology, might be characterized as "structured culture and fragmented mind." I maintain that in spite of some obvious weaknesses in Shils and Young's argumentation, this formula reflects a solid cultural sociological perspective on the problem of culture-cognition relations.

A number of subsequent studies exploited the success of this study. For example, Robert Bellah built his famous theory of the civil religion, which found in contemporary American society basically the same symbolic mechanisms which Durkheim found in early religious forms (Bellah 1967). The sacred/profane opposition has been shown to govern political imagination, perception of power, nation, history, and social order. Shils himself created a sophisticated theory of the center and periphery, which elaborated on the spatial metaphor of the structuring power of the sacred/profane opposition (Shils 1975, 1988), and inspired a number of followers who developed their own studies, such as, for example, Shmuel Eisenstadt and Milton Singer (Eisenstadt 1988; Singer 1988).

These and a number of similar studies represent Durkheim's thesis on the eternity of the sacred at any level of societal development and exemplify his intention to apply the conceptual apparatus he developed based on simple, tribe-like communities—to the reality of complex, modern societies. What is important, however, is the way these theorists realized Durkheim's intention. Thus, the eternal sacred can take different forms in theorizing on modernity, such as "neotribalism" (Maffesoli 1996), specific forms of connection between culture and instincts (Caillois 1964), and an intrinsic principle of the "general economy" (Bataille 1991). In the Parsonian, neo-Durkheimian writings, however, the sacred takes the same shapes and structural forms as in a simple "totemic" tribe. This allowed some critics to reveal substantial weaknesses of the structural-functionalist reading of the theory of the sacred, pointing to the neglect of rituals of conflict (see, e.g., Lukes 1975:299–301) and to the overcentralized vision of the social order described by these authors (whereas multiple sources of power had been thematized in sociology since the 1950s (see, e.g., Riesman et al. 1950)).

26.3.2 Great Anthropological Insights

Interestingly enough, in the 1960s and 1970s the Durkheimian theory of the sacred had been read and applied in a much more fruitful way in another discipline—anthropology.[7] In her renowned "Purity and Danger," Mary Douglas built a model of cleanliness and dirt, and showed how this primary opposition reproduces itself at all the levels of human life, from the foundations of cultural order to micro-level perceptional attitudes. The same principle that governs religious restrictions on the consumption of pork in Judaism (pig as an element outside of symbolic classifications) (Douglas 1966:3), and informed the disgust with which eighteenth-century political economists evaluated the Poor Laws (which supposedly challenged the purity of the market system), is responsible for such everyday matters as, for example, the sense of being "uncozy" in dwellings that flout design conventions particular to different domestic zones (Douglas 1966:2).

The way in which symbolic classifications engage with social interactions affects the whole of social life. Analyzing two tribes inhabiting the same region of the Kasai River, Douglas shows how different principles of systematizing seasons of a year lead not only to different perceptions of the same weather but also to drastic consequences for the whole social organization and the effectiveness of its economy (Douglas 1975:234–38). The "grid and group" theory, developed by Douglas alongside the theory of purity and pollution, in turn, aims to describe modes of connection between the level of detail in symbolic classification and boundaries on the one hand and a social pressure regulating adherence to cultural prescriptions and penalizing violations on the other (Douglas 1996:4).

The power of symbolic classifications, so plausibly and multiply demonstrated by Douglas, shows how culture is a system, which ascends to the binary of the sacred and profane and changes concrete social interactions. It is neither a random collection of meanings nor a rigid set of elements connected by formal logic.

Another influential anthropologist, Victor Turner, created an enduring and widely applied theory of the rituals of passage (Turner 1969) drawing on both Durkheim and his contemporary Arnold van Gennep. In cultural theory this conception became a major (if not the main) model of cultural and social change. The substance and dynamics of the change, following Turner, are governed by two modes of relations between the sacred/profane opposition and the resultant symbolic system on the one hand, and social interactions and collective action on the other. These two modes are the "structure," a state of rule-following and respectful behavior toward cultural boundaries, and the "antistructure," a fluid state of violation of norms and taboos, which Turner also described with the term "liminality," addressing the uncertain, ambiguous, and a "threshold," "in-between" state of affairs.

26.3.3 The Sacred in Cultural Sociology

In the course of the "cultural turn," the Durkheimian theory of the sacred was repatriated into its native discipline of sociology along with the tremendous developments it attained within anthropology. Although there are a number of theories and approaches that integrated the Durkheimian theory of the sacred (see, e.g., Collins 2004, for one), I focus here only on the "strong program" of cultural sociology, because this approach follows Durkheim's crucial hypothesis in the most explicit and fundamental way (and the status of this theory, as I have explicated it previously, presupposes that it can only be validly followed in a complete way). So, in this particular context, this approach can be seen as a central tendency, an ideal type of Durkheimian cultural sociology, which most vividly reflects the virtues and developments that can be also seen among a number of other theories.

The "strong program" in cultural sociology is built around the thesis of the autonomy of culture, synthesizing the classical sociological conceptions of Max Weber and Emile Durkheim with a number of later developments in anthropology, literary theory, and philosophy, (Alexander and Smith 2003b, 2010). In particular, the Durkheimian theory of the sacred enables cultural autonomy, because the "grammar" of culture—its inner principles preventing it from being reduced to alien causations—is grounded in social interactions (in the same way as meanings of the sacred and profane emerge in rituals).

The sacred/profane opposition is used in the strong program approach as an origin of binaries that shape different spheres of social life. Thus, a major reconstruction of the codes of the civil sphere in the United States, performed by Jeffrey Alexander and Philip Smith (Alexander and Smith 2003a), not only described American political life as organized by such oppositions, as "autonomous/dependent," "reasonable/hysterical," "controlled/passionate," and others, but, importantly, provided the basis for a series of following studies, such as analysis of the Watergate scandal (Alexander 1988), studying the Holocaust as a cultural trauma, and others (Alexander 2003). These binaries serve as a system of axes of perception, within which particular events, actions, interactions, and intentions obtain their meanings.

Furthermore, this basic opposition can underlie more complex symbolic constructions and cultural mechanisms such as narratives and traumas. Thus, for example, Alexander showed that public perception of new technologies can be framed by a narrative of salvation, which, in turn, is structured by the symbolic opposition between wars, illnesses, and other disasters on the one hand, and the computer, a new miracle that promised rescue, on the other (Alexander 1992). The actual perception of emerging computers, thus, followed scenarios existing in culture and structured by the sacred/profane opposition.

In his major work on the Holocaust, Alexander showed that the whole symbolic construction of the perception of the Holocaust as the iconic trauma of modernity (and a frame of reference for perceiving future events) was enabled by the transition between two types of narratives. The first one, the "progressive narrative," was structured by the opposition between sacred American and allied soldiers and the impure Nazi;

importantly, it also had a temporal dimension oriented from the evil past to the sacred future, where the atrocities of the past were no longer possible. This narrative depicted the Holocaust as a terrible event that had been nevertheless overcome in the course of historical development—and because of that has not become a cultural trauma. The "tragic narrative," in contrast, does not have a temporal dimension, it exists in a static sacred time, similar to the time of myth.[8] The sacred pole (in its negative mode) of this narrative is the tragic event of the genocide itself. We see in this example that changing the sacred/profane foundations of the master narrative leads ultimately to a change in the perception not only of a single historic event, but of many other events, even history itself.

The sacred/profane opposition thus organizes culture by means of derived binaries and more complex symbolic constructions, such as narratives, traumas, dramas, and metaphors, creating emotionally charged meanings and frames of references governing perception. Up to this point I have referred to the static functioning of this opposition. Even when I described the processes of change, these changes were initiated not within the sacred/profane opposition itself, but rather by other parts of symbolic mechanisms, such as changing narratives. There is, however, a dynamic dimension of the sacred, which lies at its core.

26.4 Pure and Impure: Ambiguity of the Sacred as Its Dynamic Dimension

In contrast to its seemingly simplified "good versus bad" design, the concept of the sacred is in fact far more complicated. One sometimes ignored but in fact fundamental feature, recognized by the majority of theories of the sacred[9]—is the ambiguity of the sacred. As it was discovered by William Robertson Smith in the late nineteenth century, the sacred exists in two modes: the pure—graceful, benevolent, the most desired and virtuous, and the impure—threatening and horrifying (Robertson Smith 2002). The opposition between the pure and the impure is no less absolute than the sacred/profane opposition.[10] What is even more intriguing is that a pure sacred object under certain conditions turns impure and vice versa; and these transformations are by no means rare. For example, a corpse of someone recently deceased is treated as impure in many cultures; however, after a certain period of time it often becomes pure, sacred, and an object of piety. Similarly, sacred amulets can often consist of impure objects turned into pure mode. Furthermore, the majority of rituals include both modes of the sacred and employ their ability to turn into each other, and the rite of sacrifice is the most obvious example: the desired grace is derived from the evil of killing a living being. The very existence of the two modes of the sacred and its mutual ability to turn to its antipode under certain conditions is thus an established fact, described by many theories;

but building an explanation for these facts is a more difficult problem, which has found different resolutions in the history of the social sciences and philosophy.

I argue that the most appropriate resolution for sociological theory is to treat the impure as a result of the forbidden transgression of the sacred/profane boundary.[11] This view rests on the aforementioned theories of Mary Douglas and Victor Turner along with some of their readings within the strong program of cultural sociology, crucial works of Roger Caillois (Caillois 1959) and Rene Girard (Girard 2005), some elements of the approach of Georges Bataille (Bataille 1986), and Durkheim's own approach to the problem, described in a short section in "The Elementary Forms" (Durkheim 1995:412–17).

The transgression of the sacred/profane boundary (or other boundaries, derived from it), which leads to the emergence of the impure sacred, can happen through various scenarios, from direct violation of a taboo, to creating uncertainty concerning existing boundaries, to the injection of a symbolic element that does not fit within existing sacred/profane delineations.[12] Similar to the pure sacred, the impure sacred presents extremely intense emotions. One can easily imagine examples of this mechanism by recalling phenomena that challenge the clarity and solidity of any existing prominent binary, such as, for example, natural/artificial, adult/child, and male/female. Thus, for instance, sexual relations with children are treated as a severe violation of taboo and invoke intense emotions of disgust and anger because they call into question the rigidity of the adult/child opposition. The idea of a living being with more than two genetic parents often provokes rejections and initiates intense debate around the justifiability of such experiments because the natural/artificial boundary still lies at the core of modern culture, and these new technologies create an uncertainty concerning boundaries that are supposed to be clear. Similarly, persons transcending the duality of biological sex and social gender, such as transgender persons, transsexuals, and transvestites, are still considered as impure by some people. The amount of similar illustrations is virtually infinite, which gives perspective on the crucial importance of this basic symbolic mechanism for perception and social life.

Importantly, the substance and tone of intense emotions related to the transgression and the impure sacred, could be quite different. The paradigmatic illustrations provided by ethnographers often depict the impure as having to do with evil, or mere disgust or ugliness. However, the impure also causes pleasure and delight. The most telling example is the erotic. Thus, Bataille has shown that transgression of deeply rooted bodily boundaries lies at the core of the erotic (Bataille 1986). I believe this explains why, unlike humans, animals have sex but do not have an erotic realm.

A crucial consequence of the impure and transgression for culture, perception, and human mind is that they are responsible for the basic mechanism of social change. I mentioned earlier that Turner's theory of the rite of passage became the basic explanatory model for cultural change. Transgression, in turn, lies at the core of the most important phase of the rite—its liminal stage. In accordance with the Durkheimian theory of the sacred, which imparts the new symbolic order with legitimacy and plausibility, there is a need for super intense collective emotions. Transgression provides such collective emotions in a similar way with the "effervescence" described by Durkheim. That is why the liminal stage is the core of any rite of passage and hence any change in identity.

The pure and impure thus represent neither more nor less than the two logical options of dealing with the sacred/profane boundary: respective and transgressive. Dealing with the existing order with piety corresponds to the pure sacred mode, whereas challenging it in one way or another way corresponds to the impure mode of the sacred (Kurakin 2015:389). While the pure sacred is mostly responsible for the reproduction of the social order, the impure often corresponds with social change.

Rene Girard in his theory of the sacred and violence (which he understands extensively and which, in fact, might be seen as a synonym for "transgression") builds a model explaining how transgression might lead to change (Girard 2005). The substance of violence is "undifferentiation," an abolishment of cultural differences responsible for running the social order and human mind. It leads to what Turner calls liminality and antistructure, and produces a state of mind that is unbearable and almost indescribable (because language rests on differences, abolished by violence (Girard 2005:58–59). This explains why the role of the impure in social life is underestimated and the ambiguity of the sacred is often ignored in the social sciences. Following Girard, agony, as depicted by Greek tragedies, is the best available description of this state of culture and mind.

The unbalanced situation of disorder combined with the existence of these emotions leads to the creation of a renewed sacred order (which might be new, and might be a mere reproduction of the previous one)—a mechanism basically corresponding to Durkheim's "effervescence." Girard calls the process of creating new distinctions "mythical elaboration";[13] a narrative, based on renewed sacred/profane lineaments, emerges from the chaos and returns recognizable labels to characters and events, certainty to culture, and clarity to mind.

Importantly, in modernity, in the context of growing flexibility and "fluidity" of social life and the decline of major, stable forms of the sacred, such as religion, the impure, and transgression, come to the fore at all levels of social life. It is, thus, becoming most likely the most important symbolic mechanism, affecting perception, thought, and social life in general. It stands behind our culture and world order, but also energizes even the most micro-level perceptions and interactions. In the following section I provide several illustrations.

26.4.1 Illustrations

26.4.1.1 *Macro-Level*

The structures of the sacred/profane boundaries shape culture at all the levels of social life, from macro to micro; hence, the symbolic mechanism of transgression and the impure sacred must manifest its ubiquity as well. It is easy to see that this is exactly the case. At the macro-level, for example, we can see that the political world order and the deepest truth about what is right and what is wrong rests on traumatic events of the past, such as World War II and the Holocaust. This ultimately corresponds to a model of social change based on transgression. The hugely intense collective emotions, which are the only means of legitimizing a new order and making it deeply and widely believed at a personal level, are derived in these cases from unprecedented violence, crime, and horror.

26.4.1.2 *Metaphor*

My next example might seem disputable for many, but I believe it furthers knowledge of the social origins of basic cognitive operations. I argue that even if we turn to deep linguistic and cognitive mechanisms, which by all accounts underlie our thought and perception, and which are seemingly unrelated to social life, we can see that static and dynamic structures of the sacred shape them as well. The best example of such mechanism is probably the metaphor. If we go beyond descriptions of its linguistic mechanisms (a task achieved by scholars from Aristotle to Max Black) and address the question of why it is able to create such impressions and emotional effects, we will have to admit, following Paul Ricoeur, that separating metaphorical mechanisms from their peculiar emotional effects leads us to miss how metaphor actually works (Ricoeur 1978). Ricoeur placed the metaphor beyond theories of tropes and showed that classical rhetoric "only described the 'effect of sense' at the level of the word while it overlooked the production of this semantic twist at the level of sense" (Ricoeur 1978:146).

By drawing a similarity between two different objects, metaphor obviously creates a literal deviation, meaning that saying "a man is a wolf" is basically making a false statement. The standard way to see this is to presume that metaphor is creating a transfer in meaning. Ricoeur's innovation is that metaphor not only maintains tension between the old, literal, and the new, metaphorical meanings coexisting within metaphor (a feature that other researchers have also noticed, and which is sometimes called "stereoscopic vision") but that its whole effect depends on this tension.[14] Following Roman Jacobson, Ricoeur called this kind of speech strategy embedded in metaphor a "split reference," which means uncertainty in reference. The metaphor, then, works by means of a synthesis performed by means of productive imagination, which creates the "sameness" of the primary and subsidiary subjects of the metaphor "through" resisting an understanding of their difference. Metaphor, thus, should not be treated as a deviation in its own right, but rather as a way of overcoming deviation; "The metaphor is not the enigma but the solution of the enigma" (Ricoeur 1978:146). Understanding a metaphor, writes Ricoeur, "is grasping the dynamism in virtue of which a metaphorical utterance, a new semantic pertinence, emerges from the ruins of the semantic pertinence as it appears in a literal reading of the sentence" (Ricoeur 1984:x).

The process described by Ricoeur not only corresponds to the mechanism of cultural change based on transgression but also can be applied to the theory of the sacred. The transgression of the common-sense truth of literal meanings of words that happens within metaphor, like the liminal phase of the ritual of passage, is necessary to gain the emotional energy to legitimize a new order of meaning. The pleasure or delight we feel when meet a sharp metaphor (and this has been known as metaphor's basic feature from the times of Aristotle) not occasionally accompanies metaphor, but enables new meaning, just as ritual ecstasy enables the establishment of new roles and social structures. It "buys" our conviction and makes metaphorical meaning plausible. In other words, metaphor gains power and effect from uncertainty and ambiguity in exactly the same way and by the same token as any ritual of passage, and embraces the same type of dynamism as the transgression.[15]

26.4.1.3 *Micro-Level*

Meaning-making flows in the coordinate system of culture. This system consists of innumerable boundaries, each of which can be transgressed. Sometimes it leads to cultural change (I mentioned several examples earlier) whereas in other cases, as Georges Bataille has shown, it simply strengthens existing boundaries (or sometimes even reveals them, if they are implicit). For instance, in the case of the erotic, violation of social taboos and bodily boundaries evoke intense emotions, but the taboo remains valid (Bataille 1986); whereas in the case of fashion, novelty often rests on challenging the most settled conventions, which are abolished as a result. Fashion can also be connected to eroticism, which is also concerned with transgression. For instance, Jean Baudrillard has shown that fashion's fascination with erotism is based not on denudation but rather on the interplay of the body and the clothes. In this interplay, clothes transgress bodily boundaries by means of expressively disrupting its integrity, as in the case of a stocking top on the thigh[16] (Baudrillard 1993:101–2).

Irony and humor grow from the same source; or, more accurately, transgression plays an important role in creating a joke or an ironic commentary. I do not attempt to contribute to a general theory of humor in all its complexity, but some existing approaches only support my argument (for example by stressing the role of "incongruity" in humor; Fine 1983:160) that many successful jokes are based on the transgression of common sense. Slang seems to have a similar nature. Transgressing the boundaries of grammar, speech conventions, and decency makes slang so expressive. In fact, slang here is just an instance of stylistic "coolness," which largely rests on transgression. These examples show the widest spread of minor and major transgressions in social life; they powerfully energize culture and are responsible for a major part of emotional engagement they exert in people's minds.

26.5 CONCLUSION

In this chapter, I aimed to explicate the enormous role the sacred—in its different forms—plays in social life, and shaping perception and thought. This vision is based on Durkheim's theory of the sacred, which was substantially furthered within anthropology and cultural sociology, but the importance of which has not yet been fully acknowledged within sociology. The ubiquity of the sacred, which I tried to illustrate, cannot explain everything in the social world and human mind. In many particular processes it only helps to explain a certain aspect of what is happening, with the bulk of explanation yet to be built. However, in many cases, the application of the theory of the sacred enables us to recognize the previously neglected social nature of the problem or phenomenon.

When it comes to cognitive sociology, there is a growing misconception about culture within the field. Culture is seen as fragmented and disintegrated, so studying culture as a system can hardly contribute to the study of cognitive processes.[17] This misconception is based on a mistaken understanding of the "culture as a system" formula, which appears to be an easy target for criticism. The coherent vision of culture, which is often criticized, draws on the presupposition that it is formal logic that must connect elements of culture if it is to be seen as a system. Logical contradictions found between different elements of cultural complexes, therefore, are mistakenly seen as proof of the fragmented and inconsistent character of culture.

The theory of the sacred reveals different principles that provide culture with coherence and connect its elements. The sacred/profane opposition structures culture and thought by means of binaries, metaphors, narratives, and many other cultural complexes; and the opposition of the pure and impure sacred, based on the operation of transgression, is responsible for a dynamic dimension and represents a permanent source of change.

Culture is a system, but it is governed not by an abstraction of formal logic, but by concrete configurations of emotionally charged categories, created and re-created in social interactions. In other words, emotionally charged categories (primarily sacred/profane and subsequent binaries, alone and as part of more complicated mechanisms, such as narratives and metaphors) of social origin shape the grammar of culture instead of formal logic. The theory of the sacred, thus, contributes not only to returning culture to center stage but also to the sharpening of the sociological gaze within studies of cognition.

Notes

1. For example, Lizardo and Strand summarize these approaches stating, the "view of culture as largely external, 'fragmented,' 'contradictory,' 'weakly bounded' and 'contested' has become the *de facto* standard in contemporary discussions in cultural sociology" (Lizardo and Strand 2010:2).

2. This is somehow aligned with the vision of some of reflexive poets; for example, Joseph Brodsky, a Russian poet, an American essayist, and Nobel laureate, mentioned in an interview that the poet is a translator of metaphysical truth to earthly language whose ideal dialogue partner is not a man but an angel (from the "Interview with Joseph Brodsky" conducted by Giovanni Buttafava and published in *L'Expresso*, December 6, 1987).

3. How Hertz describes it: "To the right hand go honours, flattering designations, prerogatives: it acts, orders, and *takes*. The left hand, on the contrary, is despised and reduced to the role of a humble auxiliary: by itself it can do nothing; it helps, it supports, it *holds*" (Hertz 2009:89).

4. The often cited specification given by Durkheim: "In the history of human thought, there is no other example of two categories of things as profoundly differentiated or as radically opposed to one another. The traditional opposition between good and evil is nothing beside this one: Good and evil are two opposed species of the same genus, namely morals,

just as health and illness are nothing more than two different aspects of the same order of facts, life; by contrast, the sacred and the profane are always and everywhere conceived by the human intellect as separate genera, as two worlds with nothing in common" (Durkheim 1995:36).

5. In his earlier works, Durkheim paid special attention to the fact that insanity and crime became distinct only in the course of history (see, e.g., Durkheim 1933).

6. Cognitive cultural sociology is not an exception—it is sufficient to see how the structure of the most representative books about cognitive and cultural sociology follows the logic of the process of information processing (Cerulo 2002; Zerubavel 1997).

7. Nowadays this succession is well recognized (Alexander and Smith 2003b); it was not properly acknowledged at the time these prominent anthropological conceptions were built (Rothenbuhler 1992:66).

8. As Alexander describes it: "In this tragic narrative of sacred-evil, the Jewish mass killings become not an event in history but an archetype, an event out-of-time. As archetype, the evil evoked an experience of trauma greater than anything that could be defined by religion, race, class, region—indeed, by any conceivable sociological configuration or historical conjuncture. This transcendental status, this separation from the specifics of any particular time or space, provided the basis for psychological identification on an unprecedented scale" (Alexander 2003:52).

9. The only relevant exception is a theory of Giorgio Agamben, who explicitly rejects the conception of the ambiguity of the sacred (Agamben 1998).

10. Importantly, the notion of the impure should not be confused with the notion of the profane. The impure is the sacred, whereas the profane is its absolute opposite. In social life profane equals mundane and neutral, and is emotionally moderate. Although this confusion never happens among theorists of the sacred, it does happen within sociology (I analyzed this misinterpretation and its causes and consequences in detail in Kurakin 2015; see also (Riley 2005:275).

11. For more details about the problem of the ambiguity of the sacred and my version of its resolution and the alternative options within the theories of the sacred, see Kurakin (2015).

12. Mary Douglas explains why such different processes should be nevertheless seen as virtually same symbolic mechanism (Douglas 1966:47).

13. In this term "myth" is not set against "truth"; rather, it is seen as a socially established truth.

14. Ricoeur wrote, "The metaphor is alive as long as we can perceive, through the new semantic pertinence—and so to speak in its denseness—the resistance of the words in their ordinary use and therefore their incompatibility at the level of a literal interpretation of the sentence" (Ricoeur 1984:ix).

15. The individual character of the perception of metaphor should not misguide us. First, rituals can also be performed in solitude. Second, in both cases culture, as a collective product, provides a necessary environment for these mechanisms.

16. I am not following Baudrillard's deeper interpretation of erotization in fashion, based on its Freudian reading; in fact, in my explanation I substitute the Freudian phallocentric theory of castration anxiety with the theory of the sacred.

17. For example, Lizardo and Strand show that many approaches in cultural sociology and "postcultural" anthropology, including, most notably, the toolkit theory, insist that culture is not systematically organized or integrated, but rather "fragmented" and self-contradictory (Lizardo and Strand 2010:2).

References

Agamben, Giorgio. 1998. *Homo Sacer: Sovereign Power and Bare Life*. Translated by Daniel Heller-Roazen. Stanford, CA: Stanford University Press.

Alexander, Jeffrey C. 1988. "Culture and Political Crisis: Watergate and Durkheimian Sociology." pp. 187–224 in *Durkheimian Sociology: Cultural Studies*, edited by J. C. Alexander. Cambridge: Cambridge University Press.

Alexander, Jeffrey C. 1992. "The Promise of a Cultural Sociology: Technological Discourse and the Sacred and Profane Information Machine." pp. 293–323 in *Theory of Culture*, edited by R. Munch and N. J. Smelser. Berkeley: University of California Press.

Alexander, Jeffrey C. 2003. "On the Social Construction of Moral Universals: The 'Holocaust' from War Crime to Trauma Drama." pp. 27–84 in *The Meanings of Social Life: A Cultural Sociology*. Oxford: Oxford University Press.

Alexander, Jeffrey C., and Philip Smith. 2003a. "The Discourse of American Civil Society." pp. 121–54 in *The Meanings of Social Life: A Cultural Sociology*. New York: Oxford University Press.

Alexander, Jeffrey C., and Philip Smith. 2003b. "The Strong Program in Cultural Sociology: Elements of a Structural Hermeneutics." pp. 11–26 in *The Meanings of Social Life: A Cultural Sociology*. New York: Oxford University Press.

Alexander, Jeffrey C., and Philip Smith. 2010. "The Strong Program: Origins, Achievements, and Prospects." pp. 13–24 in *Handbook of Cultural Sociology*, edited by J. R. Hall, L. Grindstaff, and M. Lo. New York: Routledge.

Bataille, Georges. 1986. *Erotism: Death and Sensuality*. Translated by Mary Dalwood. San Francisco: City Lights Books.

Bataille, Georges. 1991. *The Accursed Share: An Essay on General Economy, Vol. 1: Consumption*. Cambridge, MA: Zone Books.

Baudrillard, Jean. 1993. *Symbolic Exchange and Death*. London: SAGE.

Bellah, Robert. N. 1967. "Civil Religion in America." *Daedalus* 96(1):1–21.

Brekhus, Wayne H. 2015. *Culture and Cognition: Patterns in the Social Construction of Reality*. Cambridge: Polity Press.

Caillois, Roger. 1959. *Man and the Sacred*. Translated by Meyer Barash. Glencoe, IL: Free Press.

Caillois, Roger. 1964. *Instincts et Société*. Paris: Gonthier.

Cerulo, Karen A., ed. 2002. *Culture in Mind: Toward a Sociology of Culture and Cognition*. New York; London: Routledge.

Collins, Randall. 2004. *Interaction Ritual Chains*. Princeton, NJ: Princeton University Press.

DiMaggio, Paul. 2002. "Why Cognitive (and Cultural) Sociology Needs Cognitive Psychology." pp. 274–82 in *Culture in Mind: Toward a Sociology of Culture and Cognition*, edited by K. A. Cerulo. New York; London: Routledge.

Douglas, Mary. 1966. *Purity and Danger: An Analysis of Concept of Pollution and Taboo*. London; New York: Routledge and Kegan Paul.

Douglas, Mary. 1975. "Environments at Risk." pp. 230–48 in *Implicit Meanings: Essays in Anthropology*. London; Boston: Routledge and Kegan Paul.

Douglas, Mary. 1996. *Natural Symbols: Explorations in Cosmology*. London: Routledge.

Durkheim, Emile. 1933. "Division of Labour In Society." Translated by W. D. Halls. Edited and with a new introduction by Steven Lukes. Palgrave Macmillan.

Durkheim, Emile. 1973. "The Dualism of Human Nature and Its Social Conditions." pp. 149–63 in *Emile Durkheim: On Morality and Society; Selected Writings*, edited by R. N. Bellah. Chicago; London: University of Chicago Press.

Durkheim, Emile. 1974. "Individual and Collective Representations." pp. 1–34 in *Sociology and Philosophy*. New York: Free Press.

Durkheim, Emile. 1995. *The Elementary Forms of Religious Life*. Translated and with Introduction by K. E. Fields. New York: The Free Press.

Eisenstadt, S. N. 1988. "Transcendental Vision, Center Formation, and the Role of Intellectuals." pp. 96–109 in *Center: Ideas and Institutions*, edited by L. Greenfeld and M. Martin. Chicago; London: University of Chicago Press.

Fine, Gary Alan. 1983. "Sociological Approaches to the Study of Humor." pp. 159–82 in *Handbook of Humor Research, Volume 1: Basic Issues*, edited by P. E. McGhee and J. H. Goldstein. New York; Berlin; Heidelberg; Tokyo: Springer-Verlag.

Geertz, Clifford. 1973. *The Interpretation of Cultures*. New York: Basic Books.

Giddens, Anthony. 1986. *Durkheim*. London: Fontana Press.

Girard, Rene. 2005. *Violence and the Sacred*. Translated by Patrick Gregory. London: Continuum.

Hertz, Robert. 2009. "The Pre-Eminence of the Right Hand: A Study in Religious Polarity." pp. 89–113 in *Death and the Right Hand*. Translated by Rodney and Claudia Needham. London; New York: Routledge.

Hollier, Denis, and Georges Bataille. 1988. *The College of Sociology (1937-39)*. Minneapolis: University of Minnesota Press.

Ignatow, Gabriel. 2007. "Theories of Embodied Knowledge : New Directions for Cultural and Cognitive Sociology?" *Journal for the Theory of Social Behaviour* 37(2):115–35.

Kurakin, Dmitry. 2015. "Reassembling the Ambiguity of the Sacred: A Neglected Inconsistency in Readings of Durkheim." *Journal of Classical Sociology* 15(4):377–95.

Lizardo, Omar. 2017. "Improving Cultural Analysis." *American Sociological Review* 82(1):88–115.

Lizardo, Omar, and Michael Strand. 2010. "Skills, Toolkits, Contexts and Institutions: Clarifying the Relationship between Different Approaches to Cognition in Cultural Sociology." *Poetics* 38(2):205–28.

Lukes, Steven. 1975. "Political Ritual and Social Integration." *Sociology* 9(2):289–308.

Lukes, Steven. 1985. *Emile Durkheim: His Life and Work. A Historical and Critical Study*. Stanford, CA: Stanford University Press.

Lynch, Gordon. 2012. *The Sacred in the Modern World: A Cultural Sociological Approach*. Oxford: Oxford University Press.

Maffesoli, Michel. 1996. *The Time of the Tribes: The Decline of the Individualism in Mass Society*. London: SAGE.

Parsons, Talcott. 1937. *The Structure of Social Action*. New York: The Free Press.

Ricoeur, Paul. 1978. "The Metaphorical Process as Cognition, Imagination, and Feeling." *Critical Inquiry* 5(1):143–59.

Ricoeur, Paul. 1984. *Time and Narrative*. Vol. 1. Translated by K. McLaughlin and D. Pellauer. Chicago; London: University of Chicago Press.

Riesman, D., R. Denney, and N. Glazer. 1950. *The Lonely Crowd: A Study of the Changing American Character*. New Haven, CT: Yale University Press.

Riley, Alexander T. 2005. "'Renegade Durkheimianism' and the Transgressive Left Sacred." pp. 274–302 in *The Cambridge Companion to Durkheim*. New York: Cambridge University Press.

Robertson Smith, W. 2002. *Religion of Semites*. London; New York: Transaction Publishers.

Rothenbuhler, Eric. W. 1992. "The Liminal Fight: Mass Strikes as Ritual and Interpretation." pp. 66–90 in *Durkheimian Sociology: Cultural Studies*, edited by J. C. Alexander. Cambridge; New York: Cambridge University Press.

Shils, Edward. 1975. *Center and Periphery: Essays in Macrosociology*. Chicago: University of Chicago Press.

Shils, Edward. 1988. "Center and Periphery: An Idea and Its Career, 1935–1987." pp. 250–82 in *Center: Ideas and Institutions*, edited by L. Greenfeld and M. Martin. Chicago; London: University of Chicago Press.

Shils, Edward, and Michael Young. 1953. "The Meaning of the Coronation." *Sociological Review* 1(2):63–81.

Simmel, Georg. 1997. "The Concept and Tragedy of Culture." pp. 55–74 in *Simmel on Culture: Selected Writings*, edited by D. Frisby and M. Featherstone. London: Sage.

Singer, Milton. 1988. "Symbolism of the Center, the Periphery, and the Middle." pp. 210–49 in *Center: Ideas and Institutions*, edited by L. Greenfeld and M. Martin. Chicago; London: University of Chicago Press.

Swidler, Ann. 1986. "Culture in Action: Symbols and Strategies." *American Journal of Sociology* 51:273–86.

Turner, Victor. 1969. *The Ritual Process: Structure and Anti-Structure*. Ithaca, NY: Cornell University Press.

Zerubavel, Eviatar. 1997. *Social Mindscapes: An Invitation to Cognitive Sociology*. Cambridge, MA; London: Harvard University Press.

CHAPTER 27

COGNITION AND SOCIAL MEANING IN ECONOMIC SOCIOLOGY

NINA BANDELJ AND CHRISTOFFER J. P. ZOELLER

IN 1985, Mark Granovetter published a classic piece on the embeddedness of economic action, a foundational statement for the new economic sociology. (The concerns of Marx, Weber, and Durkheim with political economy and the division of labor were central to the "old economic sociology.") For Granovetter (1985:481), examining embeddedness referred to "how economic action is embedded in structures of social relations," pronouncing the notion of "embeddedness" as the principal conceptual tool for economic sociologists. In 1990, Sharon Zukin and Paul DiMaggio edited one of the books that set the stage for the new economic sociology. *Structures of Capital* gathered contributions from some central figures of the then-emerging field, and examined how social forces shape the economy. In the introduction to the volume, Zukin and DiMaggio (1990) extended the notion of embeddedness to include four kinds of social forces that structure economic life. In addition to structural embeddedness encompassing the role of social relations as per Granovetter (1985), they also identified political embeddedness, cultural embeddedness, and cognitive embeddedness. Cognitive embeddedness was meant to encapsulate that economic reasoning can never be perfectly rational because of "the structured regularities of mental processes" (DiMaggio and Zukin 1990:16). The idea was to capture limits to economic rationality that result from the uncertainty and complexity of economic and social environments, and from the cost of information.

While research on structural embeddedness in economic sociology has flourished over the past three decades, with Granovetter's 1985 article cited over 34,000 times, the idea of cognitive embeddedness has had a much lesser following. Nevertheless, it would be incorrect to conclude that attention to cognitive processes, including classification, reasoning, framing, schemas, and knowledge structures has not been featured in sociological investigations of economic processes. These concerns are present, but under the guise of diverse theoretical perspectives that cross the fields of economic sociology, organizational studies, and behavioral economics.

The goal of this chapter is to review the literature on cognition and social meaning in economic sociology, with special attention to the case of money. In the first part of the essay, we discuss subfields related to economic sociology that have carved space for attention to the role of cognitive processes, including the institutional logics, conceptions of control, and classification/categorization perspectives. In the second part, we take up one central economic object, money, to compare and contrast the behavioral economics perspective on mental accounting with research on the social meaning of money and relational work perspective, which emphasizes how money's multiple meanings and forms influence the negotiation of social-economic relations.

27.1 Cognitive Embeddedness and Its Extensions

Based on the failures of neoclassical economic theory to explain divergent paths to macroeconomic success, variation in organizational forms, and heterogeneous individual rationality, Zukin and DiMaggio (1990) proposed a sociological framework to understand economic institutions and behavior that built off Granovetter's (1985) "embeddedness" approach. While Granovetter (1985) considers economic behavior as situated in social networks rather than conducted in abstract arms-length exchanges, Zukin and DiMaggio extend the concept of embeddedness to include cognitive structures. They identify "cognitive embeddedness" as "structured regularities of mental processes [that] limit the exercise of economic reasoning" (Zukin and DiMaggio 1990:15). Rather than following a universal rationality of means and ends, economic actors—individuals, firms, states—behave in boundedly rational ways.

Compared to the wide embrace of the concept of (structural) embeddedness in economic sociology (for reviews see Smelser and Swedberg 2005; Krippner and Alvarez 2007; Bandelj et al. 2017), researchers who took up the task to examine cognitive embeddedness are rare. Those who directly engage with this notion in economic sociology and organizational theory often treat cognitive embeddedness as a macro-level phenomenon, where cognitive models work as "social and collective large-scale processes of classification and categorization, or [as] public accounts that support and constitute meaningful organizational activity" (Dacin et al. 1999:329). In this literature, the establishment of cognitive frameworks is thought to dictate the nature of economic institutions and behavior, rather than merely reflecting them. For example, Kennedy (2008) points to the central role of media attention to new products for the eventual flourishing of these product markets. He argues that shared cognitive structures that media discourse helps to disseminate are crucial for actors to make sense of new markets. Investigating the case of the market for computer work-stations in the 1980s, Kennedy (2008) shows how levels of media coverage determined this industry's success to the extent that such coverage helped establish a reified cognitive model to legitimize this new industry. Similarly, in a study of the Scottish knitwear industry, Porac and colleagues (1995) find that what is actually a heterogeneous organizational landscape is held together by a shared conception of what constitutes an industry.

Cognitive orientations also matter for behavior within firms, by both enabling and constraining it. Le Breton-Miller and Miller (2009) compare family-run firms to explore the differences between family businesses with a strong "family orientation" and those without. They found that firms governed by ideals of family unity had significantly more executive power and profit for family members within them. But cognitive frameworks can also have constraining effects. In a comparison of for-profit and nonprofit social entrepreneurship, Kistruck and Beamish (2010) found that formerly nonprofit organizations were particularly resistant to entrepreneurial models because of their existing cognitive frameworks that focused on social value.

Other research has incorporated a focus on cognition, ideas, and cultural logics, without necessarily invoking the cognitive embeddedness concept. One such extension is work on how ideas matter in markets. For example, Somers and Block (2005:264) start with the premise that "even the most aggressive free market reforms do not disembed markets but simply re-embed them in different institutional arrangements." They focus on "ideational embeddedness" of markets and the role of "ideas, public narratives and explanatory systems by which states, societies, and political cultures construct, transform, explain, and normalize market processes." Their particular object of attention is the idea of market fundamentalism, and they show how a public discourse that assigned blame for poverty to the damaging effects of welfare's perverse incentives, at two vastly different historical points—the US 1996 Personal Responsibility and Work Opportunities Reconciliation Act, and the English 1834 New Poor Law—helped elevate market policies over existing welfare regimes. Others discuss how broader cultural logics underlie particular economic policies. For example, Dobbin (1994) shows that deep-seated ideas, or cultural logics, set a range of options that are available to and considered appropriate by policy makers. Thus, in his comparison of railroad policy in the United States, France, and Britain, Dobbin finds that policy makers drew on significantly different national conceptions of what is an efficient transportation system, and what constitutes industrial growth, with the United States, for instance, putting the protection of free markets front and center.

Cognitive models may also shape economic behavior into their image. Callon (1998:2) has argued that economic knowledge "performs, shapes, and formats the economy, rather than observing how it functions." In this vein, MacKenzie and Millo (2003) offer an account of derivatives trading at the Chicago Board of Exchange, detailing how the behavior of market participants changed due to the introduction of new pricing models. Rather than reflecting economic behavior as commonly conceived, in this case a theoretical pricing model actually changed market participants' behavior and aligned it with the model. As such, research on performativity points to a powerful role of mental models, as well as economic theories and technological tools, for performing the economy (cf. Garcia-Parpet 2007; Mackenzie et al. 2007).

Others have studied distributed cognition (Hutchins 1995) across multiple human beings and technological devices in financial markets (MacKenzie 2009). Hardie and

MacKenzie (2007) show that hedge fund traders rely on technical devices and on their colleagues and contacts at investment banks to make trading decisions. Along these lines, Beunza and Stark (2005:205) refer to trading rooms as "cognitive ecologies" because, they argue, these organizational spaces face two major cognitive challenges: to recognize opportunities and to recognize error. Beunza and Stark report how traders are able to extend their cognitive ecology beyond the trading room by using specialized quantitative techniques to gauge their competitors' models.

Further, economic sociologists have been interested in the relationship between cognition and emotion in economic transactions. Preda (2009b:35) conceptualizes cognition as "practical actions producing new representational knowledge...such as calculations, observations, classification, or narratives, among others," and argues that emotions aid decision-making in financial markets. In a study of online anonymous financial trading, where one could well expect emotions to be absent, Preda (2009a) finds that traders vocalize, cry, or curse, but these actions do not impede trading. Rather, these emotional displays help structure traders' cognitive processes, such as helping them pace themselves, focusing their attention, and helping them evaluate the situation. Bandelj (2009) highlights how emotional embeddedness, that is, emotional currents and their visceral and physical manifestations that emerge in economic interactions, complicates the rational means-ends logic of decision-making, so that actors engage in creative economic actions such as improvisation or situational adaptation rather than utility maximization.

Recent considerations of how perceptions of the future influence economic processes present yet another venue for incorporating cognition into the study of economy. Beckert (2016) provides a theoretical framework to examine how fictional expectations create an engine of capitalist dynamics because they help market actors deal with fundamental uncertainty about the economic future. This research program is concerned with the kind of cognitive models, but also calculative devices and business plans, actors use to imagine their economic future. With a focus on radical uncertainty that imposes limits on the possibility of forming rational expectations, the examination of imagined futures goes back to the central tenet of Zukin and DiMaggio's (1990) cognitive embeddedness notion, in that actors' perceptions (of the future) cannot be based purely on rational calculation of known factors, and that actors always have to contend with uncertainty and complexity of economic and social environments.

27.2 Theoretical Perspectives With a Cognitive Focus on the Economy

In this section we discuss approaches related to economic sociology that have carved space for attention to the role of cognitive processes, including the institutional logics, conceptions of control, and classification/categorization perspectives.

27.2.1 Institutional Logics

The "institutional logics" perspective has built from work within institutional theory, focusing on the symbolic, normative, and cognitive patterns of macro-institutions that structure behavior. In initial formulations, Friedland and Alford (1991) argued that society's predominant institutions—capitalism, the state, family, and religion—contain a central logic that is different from the others. Like other "new" institutional theories in sociology and organizational theory, this perspective pushes hard against individualist and rationalist models of economic behavior, arguing that rationality is socially constructed at the supraindividual level (Thornton and Ocasio 2008). Institutional logics are cognitive frameworks that allow actors to interpret power, interests, or resources (Thornton et al. 2012). Described as a metatheory, the institutional logics approach views the social world as an "interinstitutional system" made up of multiple, overlapping, and potentially competing institutions, each with its own logic (Thornton and Ocasio 2008:104).

The approach has been applied to a variety of empirical questions not limited to the economic realm. For example, Haveman and Rao (1997) looked at the development of thrifts, or small cooperative home-lending organizations in industrializing America to find that the rise of Progressivism as a dominant institutional logic helped establish stability in the thrift industry. Lounsbury (2007) examined change in mutual fund management through the lens of competing logics of trusteeship and performance. Shifting to a performance-based logic was an adaptive strategy that led to broader institutional change in the relationship between mutual funds and money managers. By contrast, in a study of microfinance organizations, Battilana and Dorado (2010) treat these as "hybrid" organizations that successfully lay claim to organizational forms that combine institutional logics of development and banking. Similarly, a study of the medical field shows that logics of care and science overlap in ways that are dynamic and politically contingent (Dunn and Jones 2010).

How do these logics change? Institutional change may be driven by "institutional entrepreneurs," who, while working with existing cognitive frameworks, still challenge institutional logics in a strategic and interest-driven manner (Clemens and Cook 1999). Greenwood and Suddaby (2006) show that change may be initiated by dominant actors, as in the case of organizational change driven by the "Big Five" accounting firms. A study of executive power consolidation in major corporations finds that CEOs have been able to gain power strategically within these organizations over existing institutional logics (Joseph et al. 2014). Full-fledged conflict between frames can be a primary driver of institutional change, however, actors may find strategies to manage this conflict (Reay and Hinings 2009). At the same time, institutional logics also allow actors to consciously mobilize or challenge dominant ideas (Thornton and Ocasio 2008).

We should note that in the context of a European tradition of economics of convention, the notion of "orders of worth" (Boltanski and Thévenot 1991, 1999, 2006) is similar to the institutional logics perspective. Orders of worth represent a cognitive or symbolic perspective on macro-institutions in the social world. From content analysis of texts used in managerial training in French corporations, Boltanski and Thévenot (1991) identify six "orders of worth," including civic, market, inspired, fame, industrial, and domestic. These are not associated with particular domains or institutions, but are thought to coexist in the same social space. The primary point of departure from French critical sociology is a stronger emphasis on the critical capacities of individuals (Jagd 2011). Rather than passively internalizing and routinizing dominant frameworks, actors are seen as continually able to critique and challenge them. While work in the field of institutional logics has emphasized political contention (e.g., Haveman and Rao 1997) or used a Gramscian approach to hegemony (e.g., Levy and Scully 2007), justification theory focuses significantly on orders of worth that challenge dominant ones. As actors are competent and willing to critique, orders of worth must be continually defended and upheld through contestation (Jagd 2011).

27.2.2 Conceptions of Control

The notion of conception of control was coined by Neil Fligstein (1993) in his study of the transformation of control in large enterprises. Fligstein defines "conceptions of control" as "understandings that structure perceptions of how a market works" (Fligstein 1996:658). These market-specific understandings allow actors to interpret the behavior of others, and reflect agreements of market competition (or cooperation) as well as organizational structure within a market or industry (Fligstein 1996). Conceptions of control are schemas that are not pregiven, but asserted by powerful actors to shape perceptions of market action in their favor, thus the emphasis on "control." For Fligstein, markets differ in how they are organized and how behavior is shaped within them, but these differences reflect power relations within markets. Rather than existing in a state of natural equilibrium, powerful economic actors (firms) must continuously shape market reality for their own survival (Fligstein 2002). Fligstein gives the example of the early automobile industry, where Henry Ford needed to establish a vision of national infrastructure to support his market position. Ford's vision was based on a technological conception of control that was as much social architecture as it was mechanical engineering (Fligstein 2002).

Fligstein traces the historical evolution of American corporations through various conceptions of control as firms attempted to consolidate their power internally, in markets, and vis-à-vis the state. In the late nineteenth century "direct control" predominated, where firms attempted to control their environment through cartelization and horizontal integration. When antitrust regulation made this impossible, successful manufacturing firms were able to control their market position through vertical integration of production and oligopolistic market structures, known as "manufacturing control." Squeezed by the Great Depression, firms were no longer able to compete through direct competition, but rather by creating and capturing markets untapped by competitors, initiating the "sales and marketing" conception of control. The modern era of financial control saw the most successful firms diversifying their production lines, and managing this diversification through strict financial criteria (Fligstein 1993).

Fligstein's work has inspired researchers to apply the notion of conceptions of control to various empirical sites, in particular as regards the spread of the shareholder conception of control. Associated with Fligstein's financial control, the move toward shareholder value has brought organizational changes favoring executive power, and changes in firms' relationships with various stakeholders, especially employees. For example, Ahmadijan and Robbins (2005) show how the influx of foreign ownership in Japanese industry has resulted in significant changes in the relationship of affected firms to traditional stakeholders in Japanese society. As the "financial" or "shareholder value" conception of control, associated with Anglo-American corporate governance, entered Japanese firms, traditional relationships with stakeholders deteriorated. Increasing "downsizing" marked this changing relationship. This transformation toward a shareholder value conception of control has been also explored elsewhere. Gunnoe (2016) documents the shift toward shareholder value in the US forestry industry, where the shareholder value conception of control has driven nonfinancial firms into financial activities. This has contributed to an increasing financialization of the economy, but also a firm structure that compensates executives handsomely through stock-price-driven bonuses.

The "shareholder value" conception of control is conceived of not only as an ideology (Gunnoe 2016) but also as something that changes the decision-making context for managers. These changes result in changing relations of power in the workplace at the expense of employees. Jung (2015) shows that the trend of corporate "downsizing" must be understood in this light, contributing to both income inequality and unemployment in the past three decades. In a broad study of US industries during the 1980s and 1990s, Goldstein (2012) points out that the shareholder conception of control, while driving increasing layoffs of employees, has also been accompanied by a significant rise in managerial salaries. Thus, conceptions of control are rarely politically neutral; they are organizing principles that determine how value is allocated among various actors within organizations and markets (Fligstein 1996). Moreover, the rise of the shareholder conception of control has been repeatedly linked to rising economic insecurity and stratification (Jung 2015, Cobb 2016). Notably, researchers also find that the transformation to a shareholder conception of control and its accompanying power relations have not delivered enhanced profitability and growth for firms (Fligstein and Shin 2007).

27.2.3 Classifications, Rankings, and Categories in the Economy

Classification systems are assumed to be important in structuring the cognition and action of those individuals who interact with them. A foundational argument here is that systems of classification correspond neither to objective universal principles nor to historical accident, but rather to psychological principles (Roach and Lloyd 1978). This observation has been applied to the study of the economy to provide an alternative to the universalizing tendencies of neoclassical economic theory. Categories allow actors to reduce uncertainty (Roach and Lloyd 1978), establish coherence in ambiguous circumstances (Lounsbury and Rao 2004), and facilitate shared understandings of these circumstances (Carruthers and Stinchcombe 1999).

The study of social categories in the economic field has focused on the structure of markets, pricing, and consumer demand, as well as a broader focus on the structure of institutional orders and organizational fields (Zhao 2008). The sociology of markets has benefited significantly from the application of social categories as an analytical tool. Rather than being constructed by market equilibria, product categories are constructed socially by market participants. Differentiating between producers and consumers in product markets, Koçak and colleagues (2014) argue that audiences in markets themselves shape the systems of categorization that producers use to shape their products. In a study of the stock market, Zuckerman (1999) identifies the role of public "critics" who influence and mediate the perceptions of market audiences regarding the conformity of products to conventional product categories. In a study of French and American wine markets, Zhao (2008) shows that the meaning of different classification systems is context-dependent.

From the categories/classification perspective, markets are viewed as a set of constructed classification systems that market participants must attempt to conform to. However, cognitive conformity is difficult to achieve and there are penalties for failure. For example, Hsu and colleagues (2009) examine the penalties for existing in-between or across multiple product categories. Examining the feature film industry, these authors find that audiences penalize products that do not fit neatly in a given category. Relatedly, producers who attempt to span industry categories find it more difficult to target audience expectations without the aid of clear genre, or category, schemas (Hsu et al. 2009). Zuckerman (2004) finds that stock market assets that defy standard classification experience more volatility due to this ambiguity. Emerging markets that fail to achieve mainstream recognition for a product category have less longevity than those that achieve such a market niche (Kennedy 2008). While a focus on classification often attempts to articulate a theory of market formation and order (e.g., Kocak et al. 2014), classification can also help us examine the potential for innovation and change. The study by Rao and colleagues (2005) of the French restaurant industry shows that actors may be able to shift categorization schemas in order to survive, when high-status actors initiate these changes.

A fruitful perspective that emphasizes classification and categories is a focus on commensuration (Porter 1995). Espeland and Stevens (1998) define commensuration as a process of comparison of different entities according to a common metric, such as rankings, ratios, or prices. It is a process of transforming qualities into quantities, to distill broad information into numbers that can be easily compared. Espeland and Sauder (2007) studied ranking of law schools, and developed a notion of reactivity, or actors changing their behavior because they are being measured and ranked. Likewise, Stevens (2007) described the admissions process at an elite college, and how the *U.S. News &*

World Report rankings influenced the decisions of students and administrators. With a broader focus on evaluation of merit, Lamont (2009) examined how experts in social sciences and humanities define excellence in fellowship and grant applications. A strong application of the idea of rankings in economic sociology concerns rating agencies, which produce and sell information to third parties to credit transactions and thus play a central role in debt markets (Poon 2005). Cohen and Carruthers (2009:1) refer to credit ratings as cognitive devices that investors and lenders use "to simplify and make sense of inherently ambiguous situations" (cf. Carruthers 2013). Rona-Tas and Hiss (2010) explore the role of credit-rating agencies such as Equifax, Experian, and TransUnion, which used a formalized scoring system to assess individuals in mortgage origination, and then how the rating systems like Moody's, S&P, and Fitch used those assessments in securitization, making an argument about how all these rating processes contributed to the subprime mortgage crisis in the United States.

Recently, the concept of classification has been applied to the question of social inequality. Fourcade and Healy (2013) coin the term "classification situations" to establish how classification impacts life chances for individuals. They focus on the proliferation and rising significance of credit-rating agencies that categorize ordinary consumers into evaluative categories of credit worthiness. In addition to establishing market order in credit markets, Fourcade and Healy (2013) argue that this classification has a significant impact on social stratification, where higher-risk categories of individuals are systematically discriminated against in credit transactions, and denied credit opportunities that other classes enjoy.

27.3 THE CASE OF MONEY: COGNITIVE, CULTURAL, AND RELATIONAL CONSIDERATIONS

In this second part of our chapter, we take up the case of money as a central instrument of economy. While classical economists proclaimed money as a neutral medium of exchange serving as a universal payment instrument, which emerged in response to the need for equivalence in economic exchange, scholars today persuasively demonstrate how cognitive, cultural, and relational factors shape the use of money and its role. The classical view of money as universal and easily movable from situation to situation is captured by the fungibility assumption. This fungibility assumption has been considered as a central defining feature of money that makes it so suitable as a general medium of exchange. However, research investigating the role of cognitive, cultural, and relational factors has launched challenges to the fungibility assumption. This has occurred both in the discipline of economics with the rise of behavioral economics and the theory of mental accounting, and in sociology, with attention to the social meaning of money and relational work. We review these perspectives in turn.

27.3.1 Behavioral Economics and Mental Accounting

Behavioral economics was inspired by groundbreaking work of Daniel Kahneman and Amos Tversky. Kahneman and Tversky (1979) used experimental work to establish that people are rather narrow in their focus of assessing alternative courses of action, and use heuristics to do so. For instance, changes in wealth or welfare seem to matter to people more than absolute wealth (McBride 2010). Or, when asked for a preference between gaining ten dollars and losing ten dollars, people have a strong preference for loss aversion, or a tendency to avoid losses more than favor acquiring gains (Tversky and Kahneman 1992).

Within the surge of behavioral economics (Frantz et al. 2016), Richard Thaler developed a concept of "mental accounting," or "a set of cognitive operations used by individuals and households to organize, evaluate, and keep track of financial activities" (Thaler 1999:183). What has become an influential view that informs policy makers on how individuals use their money, was initially conceived as a psychological perspective to amend microeconomic theory of consumer choice. Microeconomics typically regards choice as an outcome of objective valuations of price and product attributes (Thaler 2008). Using cognitive considerations of how people's minds operate, mental accounting suggests that individuals and groups, in fact, frame and perceive valuations in ways that deviate from the expectations of classical theory. For example, a ten-dollar discrepancy in price is perceived as diminishing in significance as the scale of numbers of the price increases (Thaler 2008). Cognitive and emotional processes routinely make valuations depart from a typical monetary utility function. As such, research in mental accounting highlights the principles by which money is treated differently depending on how it is presented, framed, and categorized cognitively. Prelec and Loewenstein (1998) show that different payment methods may mediate the "pain of paying." That is, a credit card purchase for example makes less of an impact on the mental sense of a household budget than an equivalent cash payment.

A key insight of mental accounting is that money is not perfectly fungible and is itself heterogeneous. The source of money may be a key distinction for individuals. Money earned through labor may be more psychologically difficult to spend than a "windfall" gained through a lottery (Kivetz 1999). Different forms or structures of payment facilitate more or less cognitive distance between the acts of payment and consumption (Gourville and Soman 1998).

In a recent statement, Jonathan Morduch (2017) challenges standard economic analyses of household choices that assume money's fungibility. In practice, Morduch argues, families often earmark money earned by a particular family member or generated from a particular job. He draws on evidence from the US Financial Diaries project that documents the frequency of earmarking in a sample of low- and moderate-income households in ten sites across America. Earmarking income for particular purposes generally leads to spending patterns that deviate from patterns delivered by household-level optimization with full fungibility. Murdoch's observations, from a behavioral economics perspective, come close to the investigations of the social meaning of money in sociology, which in fact, is an unusual transgression of otherwise firm disciplinary boundaries between sociology and economics.

27.3.2 The Social Meaning of Money and Relational Work

Mental accounting focuses on individuals' cognitive heuristics that prevent money from flowing as seamlessly from situation to situation as the fungibility assumption dictates. However, individuals are not evaluating their budgets and payments only as a matter of individual cognition. As Viviana Zelizer ([1994] 1997) famously pronounced, money has social meaning. One inspiration from the recognition of the meaning of money gravitates toward understanding its morality (Bandelj et al. 2017). Indeed, scholars remain deeply concerned about money's corrupting powers. For instance, the philosopher Michael Walzer proclaimed, "[m]oney is insidious, and market relations transform every social good into a commodity" (1983:119–20). Michael Sandel (2013) likewise worries about money's moral impact, especially when monetary concerns penetrate the world of intimate relations or human goods.

Others challenge the idea that money is immoral by default. In fact, as Fourcade and Healy (2007) argue, markets themselves are constituted by varying moralities, and markets are themselves moralizing entities. Indeed, even as concerns intimate social relations, Zelizer (2005) proposes that they be viewed as coconstituted by economic processes. For Zelizer, the spheres of money and intimacy are not hostile. Rather, people use appropriate payments for different social situations, taking the social meaning of money into account. For instance, Rene Almeling (2007) enters a controversial terrain of market exchange in eggs and sperm to find that in egg agencies, staff members use gendered meanings to talk about the money paid to women donors as a gift, while sperm bank staff consider payments to men donors to be compensation for a job well done. From the social meaning of money perspective, money is not singular, but multiple (Zelizer 1989). Similarly, in Haylett's study (2012) of egg donors and in vitro fertilization, the amount of money given to donors was interpreted as signaling quality of parenting; couples making bigger financial investments were regarded by egg donors as potentially better parents. In a context of religious ceremonies, Garcia (2014) elucidates how money in the form of tithes symbolizes trust that individuals have in religion and religious figures, and therefore, "a measure of faith" (Garcia, 2014:645), where more money means more trust. But meaning is not only attributed to actual payments. Lack of payment is considered consequential as well. Mears (2015) reports of women in VIP entertainment who engage in free labor for club promoters whose financial gains depend on women's presence at party venues. Instead of understanding their labor as work, women consider what they do as leisure, and their relationships to club promoters as friendships. In fact, they report feeling offended if actual payment (not gifts, drinks, or dinners) were to be offered in return for their party presence (Mears 2015).

Monetary differentiations come through forcefully in a study by Sykes and colleagues (2015) of the earned income tax credit (EITC) recipients. The authors examined the moral and relational significance of the EITC. For those receiving the EITC, the fact that it is not welfare but EITC signaled a more dignified transfer, making recipients feel that they belong to this country, rather than being discarded by it. Because it arrived in one big sum, and as part of a tax refund—rather than in small monthly increments from the welfare office—recipients were counting the days in anticipation for what felt like "Christmas" and were making plans about everything that they could potentially do with the money. While the EITC provided important financial relief to pay bills or pay off some debts, it was crucial for enhancing feelings of dignity and self-worth. Moreover, EITC recipients talked about how this money allows them some modest discretionary consumption for their family and treats for children. This signals that the social meaning of money does not exist outside of social relationships, and that the interpretations of the meaning of money are strongly coupled with relational considerations.

Indeed, the most recent advances in the sociology of money introduce the perspective of relational work (Bandelj et al. 2017). Zelizer (2005, 2012) coined the notion of relational work to capture that individuals negotiate appropriate matches between economic transactions, social relations, and media of exchange. Bandelj (2012, 2016) extended this formulation to suggest that relational work refers to how people form, negotiate, and sometimes dissolve economic relations, such as when closing an investment deal, hiring employees or looking for a job, making a sale or a purchase, or sending remittances overseas. For Bandelj, how relational work unfolds depends on negotiated meanings of money and relationships, as well as emotional valences that arise from the process of economic interaction with repercussions for (in)equality between exchange partners.

An integral part of relational work is relational—not simply mental—earmarking (cf. Wherry 2016 for relational accounting rather than mental accounting). Individuals who earmark their money are always situated in webs of meaningful relationships, and considerations of these relationships fundamentally reshape their earmarking processes. As Bandelj et al. (2017:7) illustrate with an example of a "college fund,"

> from a relational work perspective, people's reluctance to spend the money saved into their children's education funds transcends individual mental budgeting. These funds represent and reinforce meaningful family ties: the earmarking is relational. Suppose a mother gambles away money from the child's "college fund." This is not only a breach of cognitive compartments but involves a relationally damaging violation. Most notably, the mis-spending will hurt her relationship to her child. But the mother's egregious act is likely to also undermine the relationship to her spouse and even to family members or friends who might sanction harshly the mother's misuse of money.... These interpersonal dynamics thereby help explain why a college fund functions so effectively as a salient relational earmark rather than only a sacred or emotional cognitive category.

Researchers have started to substantiate how relational work plays out in various contexts. In a study of surrogate mothers, Berend (2016) finds that in the context of payments for surrogacy, surrogate mothers reference their action as altruistic giving, even when payment for surrogacy is normal and expected. But these women also express desire to create relationships with couples for whom they carry the baby. Lainer-Vos (2014) documents organizational efforts to create platforms of gift giving for the Jewish diaspora that reinforced ties to the home country. Organizational actors construed giving as a moral duty, in symbolic terms, but they also capitalized on the web of coethnic relations to engineer the timing and visibility of donations so as to generate generosity competitions among givers.

In these studies of relational work, meaning is well coupled with relations. However, there remains significant potential to integrate more strongly cognitive considerations into relational work. For instance, in her research on transnational brokered marriages in South Korea, Kim (2018) points to the central role of women's expectations for their ongoing relational work. Kim shows how women's expectations have transformed from initial consideration of transnational brokered marriage, during long-distance courtship with potential husbands arranged by brokers, to establishment of new families in their host country. Women's changing expectations reconfigured their relations with parents and siblings in the home country, with brokers who connected them with their husbands, and with husbands themselves. This, in turn, reformulated practices of payments that women engaged in, such as remittances and investments. Tracing the role of expectations is one concrete way of investigating directly the role of cognition in relational work.

27.4 CONCLUSION

In this chapter, we searched for ways in which preoccupations with cognitive models, schemata, and knowledge structures have entered sociological investigations of the economy. We started with the notion of cognitive embeddedness, coined by Zukin and DiMaggio (1990), who attempted to carve out space for attention to cognitive processes in economy, just as such space was occupied by investigations of structural, cultural, and political embeddedness. Indeed, it is not surprising that it was Paul DiMaggio who made a powerful early pronouncement about the relevance of cognition in economic processes, given his seminal statement on culture and cognition (DiMaggio 1997).

While economic sociologists have not coalesced around cognitive embeddedness as much as around other social forces, we have reviewed kindred perspectives that give insight into how cognitive structures operate to shape economy, including the institutional logics approach, conceptions of control studies, and the role of classification and categories in markets. In addition, investigations of ideational embeddedness and cultural logics undergirding economic policymaking, research in performativity of markets, and studies that look to how expectations about the future influence economic decision-making, all allude to the role of cognition in economy. These strands of research will continue to make contributions but would be well served to be more explicit about their cognitive focus and learn more directly from the advances in sociology of cognition.

Last but not least, we note that the distinction between cognitive embeddedness and other social foundations of economic behavior may be more analytical than empirical.

Dequech (2003) argues that Zukin and DiMaggio's (1990) original formulation of cognitive embeddedness can be read as having significant overlap with their other categories of embeddedness, particularly the cultural and structural. After all, cognitive frameworks are linked to culture and passed through social networks. There is potential for future research to explore these overlaps, and specify how not only single social factors—cognition, culture, power, or structures—but also relationships between social forces influence the economy. This is in line with the research on the social meaning of money and relational work, where cognitive considerations are infused with emotions, and worked out in negotiations of meaningful social relations.

References

Ahmadjian, Christina L., and Gregory Robbins. 2005. "A Clash of Capitalisms: Foreign Shareholders and Corporate Restructuring in 1990s Japan." *American Sociological Review* 70(3):451–71.

Almeling, Rene 2007. "Selling Genes, Selling Gender: Egg Agencies, Sperm Banks, and the Medical Market in Genetic Material." *American Sociological Review* 72(3):319–40.

Bandelj, Nina. 2009. "Emotions in Economic Action and Interaction." *Theory and Society* 38(4):347–66.

Bandelj, Nina. 2012. "Relational Work and Economic Sociology." *Politics and Society* 40(2):175–201.

Bandelj, Nina. 2016. "Thinking about Social Relations in Economy as Relational Work." pp. 227–51 in *Re-Imagining Economic Sociology*, edited by Patrik Aspers and Nigel Dodd. New York: Oxford University Press.

Bandelj, Nina, Tyler Boston, Julia Elyachar, Julie Kim, Michael McBride, Zaibu Tufail, et al. 2017. "Morals and Emotions of Money." pp. 39–56 In *Money Talks: Explaining How Money Really Works*, edited by Nina Bandelj, Frederick F. Wherry, and Viviana Zelizer. Princeton, NJ: Princeton University Press.

Bandelj, Nina, Frederick F. Wherry, and Viviana Zelizer. 2017. *Money Talks: Explaining How Money Really Works*. Princeton, NJ: Princeton University Press.

Battilana, Julie, and Silvia Dorado. 2010. "Building Sustainable Hybrid Organizations: The Case of Commercial Microfinance Organizations." *Academy of Management Journal* 53(6):1419–40.

Beckert, Jens. 2016. *Imagined Futures*. Cambridge, MA: Harvard University Press.

Berend, Zsuzsa. 2016. *The Online World of Surrogacy*. New York: Berghahn.

Beunza, Daniel, and David Stark. 2005. "Seeing through the Eyes of Others: Dissonance within and across Trading Rooms." pp. 203–20 In *The Oxford Handbook of the Sociology of Finance*, edited by Karin Knorr-Cetina and Alexandru Preda. New York: Oxford University Press.

Boltanski, Luc, and Laurent Thévenot. 1991. *De la justification: Les économies de la grandeur*. Paris: Gallimard.

Boltanski, Luc, and Laurent Thévenot. 1999. "The Sociology of Critical Capacity." *European Journal of Social Theory* 2(3):359–77.

Boltanski, Luc, and Laurent Thévenot. 2006. *On Justification: Economies of Worth*. Princeton, NJ: Princeton University Press.

Callon, Michel. 1998. *The Laws of the Markets*. Oxford: Blackwell.

Carruthers, Bruce. 2013. "From Uncertainty toward Risk: The Case of Credit Ratings." *Socio-Economic Review* 11(3):525–51.

Carruthers, Bruce, and Arthur Stinchcombe. 1999. "The Social Structure of Liquidity: Flexibility, Markets, And States." *Theory and Society* 28(3):353–82.

Clemens, Elisabeth, and James M. Cook. 1999. "Politics and Institutionalism: Explaining Durability and Change." *Annual Review of Sociology* 25(1):441–66.

Cobb, J. Adam. 2016. "How Firms Shape Income Inequality: Stakeholder Power, Executive Decision Making, and the Structuring of Employment Relationships." *Academy of Management Review* 41(2):324–48.

Cohen, Barry, and Bruce Carruthers. 2009. "Credit, Classification and Cognition: Credit Raters in 19th Century America." *SSRN Abstract* 1525626.

Dacin, M. Tina., Marc J. Ventresca, and Brent D. Beal. 1999. "The Embeddedness of Organizations: Dialogue and Directions." *Journal of Management* 25(3):317–56.

Dequech, David. 2003. "Cognitive and Cultural Embeddedness: Combining Institutional Economics and Economic Sociology." *Journal of Economic Issues* 37(2):461–70.

DiMaggio, Paul. 1997. "Culture and Cognition." *Annual Review of Sociology* 23(1):263–87.

DiMaggio, Paul, and Sharon Zukin. 1990. "Introduction." *Structures of Capital: The Social Organization of the Economy*. Cambridge: Cambridge University Press.

Dobbin, Frank. 1994. *Forging Industrial Policy: The United States, Britain, and France in the Railway Age*. New York: Cambridge University Press.

Dunn, Mary B., and Candace Jones. 2010. "Institutional Logics and Institutional Pluralism: The Contestation of Care and Science Logics in Medical Education, 1967–2005." *Administrative Science Quarterly* 55(1):114–49.

Espeland, Wendy, and Michael Sauder. 2007. "Rankings and Reactivity: How Public Measures Recreate Social Worlds." *American Journal of Sociology* 113(1):1–40.

Espeland, Wendy, and Mitchell Stevens. 1998. "Commensuration as a Social Process." *Annual Review of Sociology* 24:313–43.

Fligstein, Neil. 1993. *The Transformation of Corporate Control*. Cambridge, MA: Harvard University Press.

Fligstein, Neil 1996. "Markets as Politics: A Political-Cultural Approach to Market Institutions." *American Sociological Review* 61(4):656–73.

Fligstein, Neil. 2002. *The Architecture of Markets: An Economic Sociology of Twenty-First Century Capitalist Societies*. Princeton, NJ: Princeton University Press.

Fligstein, Neil, and Taekjin Shin. 2007. "Shareholder Value and the Transformation of the US Economy, 1984–2000." *Sociological Forum* 22(4):399–424.

Fourcade, Marion, and Kieran Healy. 2007. "Moral Views of Market Society." *Annual Review of Sociology* 33:285–311.

Fourcade, Marion, and Kieran Healy. 2013. "Classification Situations: Life-Chances in the Neoliberal Era." *Accounting, Organizations and Society* 38(8):559–72.

Frantz, Roger, Shu-Heng Chen, Kurt Dopfer, Floris Heukelom, and Shabnam Mousavi. 2016. *Routledge Handbook of Behavioral Economics*. London: Routledge.

Friedland, Roger, and Robert R. Alford. 1991. "Bringing Society Back In: Symbols, Practices and Institutional Contradictions." pp. 232–67 in *The New Institutionalism in Organizational Analysis*, edited by Walter Powell and Paul DiMaggio. Chicago: University of Chicago Press.

Garcia, Alfredo. 2014. "Relational Work in Economic Sociology: A Review and Extension." *Sociology Compass* 8(6):639–47.

Garcia-Parpet, Maria. 2007. "The Social Construction of a Perfect Market: The Strawberry Auction at Fontaines-en-Sologne." pp. 20–53 in *Do Economists Make Markets? On the Performativity of Economics*, edited by Donald Mackenzie, Fabian Muniesa, and Lucia Siu. Princeton, NJ: Princeton University Press.

Goldstein, Adam. 2012. "Revenge of the Managers: Labor Cost-Cutting and the Paradoxical Resurgence of Managerialism in the Shareholder Value Era, 1984 to 2001." *American Sociological Review* 77(2):268–94.

Gourville, John, and Dilip Soman. 1998. "Payment Depreciation: The Behavioral Effects of Temporally Separating Payments from Consumption." *Journal of Consumer Research* 25(2):160–74.

Granovetter, Mark. 1985. "Economic Action and Social Structure: The Problem of Embeddedness." *American Journal of Sociology* 91(3):481–510.

Greenwood, Royston, and Roy Suddaby. 2006. "Institutional Entrepreneurship in Mature Fields: The Big Five Accounting Firms." *Academy of Management Journal* 49(1):27–48.

Gunnoe, Andrew. 2016. "The Financialization of the US Forest Products Industry: Socio-Economic Relations, Shareholder Value, and the Restructuring of an Industry." *Social Forces* 94(3):1075–101.

Hardie, Ian, and Donald Mackenzie. 2007. "Constructing the Market Frame: Distributed Cognition and Distributed Framing in Financial Markets." *New Political Economy* 12(3):389–403.

Haveman, Heather, and Hayagreeva Rao. 1997. "Structuring a Theory of Moral Sentiments: Institutional and Organizational Coevolution in the Early Thrift Industry." *American Journal of Sociology* 102(6):1606–51.

Haylett, Jennifer. 2012. "One Woman Helping Another: Egg Donation as a Case of Relational Work." *Politics and Society* 40(2):223–47.

Hsu, Greta, Michael Hannan, and Özgecan Koçak. 2009. "Multiple Category Memberships in Markets: An Integrative Theory and Two Empirical Tests." *American Sociological Review* 74(1):150–69.

Hutchins, Edwin. 1995. *Cognition in the Wild*. Cambridge, MA: MIT Press.

Jagd, Soren. 2011. "Pragmatic Sociology and Competing Orders of Worth in Organizations." *European Journal of Social Theory* 14(3):343–59.

Joseph, John, William Ocasio, and Mary Hunter-Mcdonnell. 2014. "The Structural Elaboration of Board Independence: Executive Power, Institutional Logics, and the Adoption of CEO-Only Board Structures in US Corporate Governance." *Academy of Management Journal* 57(6):1834–58.

Jung, Jiwook. 2015. "Shareholder Value and Workforce Downsizing, 1981–2006." *Social Forces* 93(4):1335–68.

Kahneman, Daniel, and Amos Tversky. 1979. "Prospect Theory: An Analysis of Decision under Risk." *Econometrica* 47(2):263–92.

Kennedy, Mark T. 2008. "Getting Counted: Markets, Media, And Reality." *American Sociological Review* 73(2):270–95.

Kim, Julie S. 2018. "Payments and Intimate Ties in Transnationally Brokered Marriages." *Socio-Economic Review*. In press. https://dx.doi.org/10.1093/ser/mwx061.

Kistruck, Geoffrey, and Paul Beamish. 2010. "The Interplay of Form, Structure, and Embeddedness in Social Entrepreneurship." *Entrepreneurship Theory and Practice* 34(4):735–61.

Kivetz, Ran. 1999. "Advances in Research on Mental Accounting and Reason-Based Choice." *Marketing Letters* 10(3):249–66.

Koçak, Özgecan, Michael Hannan, and Greta Hsu. 2014. "Emergence of Market Orders: Audience Interaction and Vanguard Influence." *Organization Studies* 35(5):765–90.

Krippner, Greta, and Anthony Alvarez. 2007. "Embeddedness and the Intellectual Projects of Economic Sociology." *Annual Review of Sociology* 33:219–40.

Lainer-Vos, Dan. 2014. "Brothers' Keepers: Gift Giving Networks and the Organization of Jewish American Diaspora Nationalism." *Socio-Economic Review* 12(3):463–88.

Lamont, Michele. 2009. *How Professors Think: Inside the Curious World of Academic Judgment.* Cambridge, MA: Harvard University Press.

Le Breton-Miller Isabelle, and Danny Miller. 2009. "Agency vs. Stewardship in Public Family Firms: A Social Embeddedness Reconciliation." *Entrepreneurship Theory and Practice* 33(6):1169–91.

Levy, David, and Maureen Scully. 2007. "The Institutional Entrepreneur as Modern Prince: The Strategic Face of Power in Contested Fields." *Organization Studies* 28(7):971–91.

Lounsbury, Michael. 2007. "A Tale of Two Cities: Competing Logics and Practice Variation in the Professionalizing of Mutual Funds." *Academy of Management Journal* 50(2):289–307.

Lounsbury, Michael, and Hayagreeva Rao. 2004. "Sources of Durability and Change in Market Classifications: A Study of the Reconstitution of Product Categories in the American Mutual Fund Industry, 1944–1985." *Social Forces* 82(3):969–99.

Mackenzie, Donald. 2009. *Material Markets: How Economic Agents Are Constructed.* Oxford: Oxford University Press.

Mackenzie, Donald, and Yuval Millo. 2003. "Constructing a Market, Performing Theory: The Historical Sociology of a Financial Derivatives Exchange." *American Journal of Sociology* 109(1):107–45.

Mackenzie, Donald, Fabian Muniesa and Lucia Siu. 2007. *Do Economists Make Markets? On the Performativity of Economics.* Princeton: Princeton University Press.

McBride, Michael. 2010. "Money, Happiness, and Aspirations: An Experimental Study." *Journal of Economic Behavior and Organization* 74(3):262–76.

Mears, Ashley. 2015. "Working for Free in the VIP: Relational Work and the Production of Consent." *American Sociological Review* 80(6):1099–122.

Morduch, Jonathan. 2017. "Economics and the Social Meaning of Money." pp. 25–38 in *Money Talks: Explaining How Money Really Works*, edited by Nina Bandelj, Frederick Wherry, and Viviana Zelizer. Princeton, NJ: Princeton University Press.

Poon, Martha. 2005. "Rating Agencies." pp. 272–92 in *The Oxford Handbook of the Sociology of Finance*, edited by Karin Knorr-Cetina and Alexandru Preda. New York: Oxford University Press.

Porac, Joseph F., Howard Thomas, Fiona Wilson, Douglas Paton, and Alaina Kanfer. 1995. "Rivalry and the Industry Model of Scottish Knitwear Producers." *Administrative Science Quarterly* 40(2):203–27.

Porter, Theodore. 1995. *Trust in Numbers: The Pursuit of Objectivity in Science and Public Life.* Princeton: Princeton University Press.

Preda, Alexandru. 2009a. "Brief Encounters: Calculation and the Interaction Order of Anonymous Electronic Markets." *Accounting, Organizations And Society* 34:675–93.

Preda, Alexandru. 2009b. *Information, Knowledge, and Economic Life: An Introduction to the Sociology of Markets.* Oxford: Oxford University Press.

Prelec, Drazen, and George Loewenstein. 1998. "The Red and the Black: Mental Accounting of Savings and Debt." *Marketing Science* 17(1):4–28.

Rao, Hayagreeva, Phillipe Monin, and Rodolphe Durand. 2005. "Border Crossing: Bricolage and the Erosion of Categorical Boundaries in French Gastronomy." *American Sociological Review* 70(6):968–91.

Reay, Trish, and C. R. Hinings. 2009. "Managing the Rivalry of Competing Institutional Logics." *Organization Studies* 30(6):629–52.

Roach, Eleanor, and Barbara B. Lloyd. 1978. *Cognition and Categorization*. Hillsdale, NJ: Erlbaum.

Rona-Tas, Akos, and Stefanie Hiss. 2010. "The Role of Ratings in the Subprime Mortgage Crisis: The Art of Corporate and the Science of Consumer Credit Rating." pp. 115–55 in *Markets on Trial: The Economic Sociology of the U.S. Financial Crisis: Part A*, edited by Michael Lounsbury and Paul Hirsch. Research in the Sociology of Organizations, Vol. 30, Part A. Bingley: Emerald Group Publishing.

Sandel, Michael. 2013. *What Money Can't Buy: The Moral Limits of Markets*. New York: Farrar, Straus and Giroux.

Smelser, Neil, and Richard Swedberg. 2005. *The Handbook of Economic Sociology*. Princeton, NJ: Princeton University Press.

Somers, Margaret, and Fred Block. 2005. "From Poverty to Perversity: Ideas, Markets, and Institutions over 200 Years of Welfare Debate." *American Sociological Review* 70(2):260–87.

Stevens, Mitchell. 2007. *Creating a Class: College Admissions and the Education of Elites*. Cambridge, MA: Harvard University Press.

Sykes, Jennifer, Katrin Križ, Kathryn Edin, and Sarah Halpern-Meekin. 2015. "Dignity and Dreams: What the Earned Income Tax Credit (EITC) Means to Low-Income Families." *American Sociological Review* 80(2):243–67.

Thaler, Richard. 1999. "Mental Accounting Matters." *Journal of Behavioral Decision Making* 12:183–206.

Thaler, Richard. 2008. "Mental Accounting and Consumer Choice." *Marketing Science* 27(1):15–25.

Thornton, Patricia, and William Ocasio. 2008. "Institutional Logics." pp. 99–128 in *The Sage Handbook of Organizational Institutionalism*, edited by Royston Greenwood, Christine Oliver, Roy Suddaby, and Kerstin Sahlin. New York: SAGE.

Thornton, Patricia, William Ocasio, and Michael Lounsbury. 2012. *The Institutional Logics Perspective: A New Approach to Culture, Structure, and Process*. New York: Oxford University Press.

Tversky, Amos, and Daniel Kahneman. 1992. "Advances in Prospect Theory: Cumulative Representation of Uncertainty." *Journal of Risk and Uncertainty* 5(4):297–323.

Walzer, Michael. 1983. *Spheres of Justice: A Defense of Pluralism and Equality*. Oxford: Blackwell.

Wherry, Frederick F. 2016. "Relational Accounting: A Cultural Approach." *American Journal of Cultural Sociology* 4(2):131–56.

Zelizer, Viviana A. 1989. "The Social Meaning of Money: 'Special Monies.'" *American Journal of Sociology* 95(2):42–77.

Zelizer, Viviana A. [1994] 1997. *The Social Meaning of Money*. Princeton, NJ: Princeton University Press.

Zelizer, Viviana A. 2005. *The Purchase of Intimacy*. Princeton, NJ: Princeton University Press.

Zelizer, Viviana A. 2012. "How I Became a Relational Economic Sociologist and What Does That Mean." *Politics and Society* 40(2):145–74.

Zhao, Wubiao. 2008. "Social Categories, Classification Systems, and Determinants of Wine Price in the California and French Wine Industries." *Sociological Perspectives* 51(1):163–99.

Zuckerman, Ezra W. 1999. "The Categorical Imperative: Securities Analysts and the Illegitimacy Discount." *American Journal of Sociology* 104(5):1398–438.

Zuckerman, Ezra W. 2004. "Structural Incoherence and Stock Market Activity." *American Sociological Review* 69(3):405–32.

Zukin, Sharon and Paul DiMaggio. 1990. *Structures of Capital: The Social Organization of the Economy*. Cambridge: Cambridge University Press.

CHAPTER 28

....

SCIENTIFIC ANALOGIES AND HIERARCHICAL THINKING

lessons from the hive?

....

DIANE M. RODGERS

How does the image of a busy, cooperative hive of bees transition from a time-honored comparison to cooperative human industriousness only to later emerge as a contemporary example of individual competition and unemployed workers? The fate of the bee illustrates how humans think analogically within a social, cultural, and political context. Scientific analogies and their popularizing discourse have contributed to ideas of hierarchical social organization. However, these analogies use social concepts of structure that vary with time and place, and therefore also serve to change the dominant thinking about social order. I use the case of bees and other social insect analogies as described in scientific discourse as evidence of how analogical thinking is influenced by social patterns and also reinforces these patterns. However, because analogical reasoning is not a fixed, innate cognitive process it can best be explored through cognitive sociology. After generally defining the role of analogies in cognition, I turn to focus on scientific analogies and cognition, providing entomological examples in scientific writing. These entomological analogies have been systematically used from the nineteenth century onward to create and disseminate the ideas of hierarchical social organization, therefore offering a unique study on the cultural and political shaping of cognitive patterns.

28.1 ANALOGIES, METAPHORS, AND COGNITION

....

How significant are analogies and metaphors to cognition, and what is their relationship to each other? By using analogies, we attempt to clarify our understanding through familiar reference points or what the literature on analogical reasoning term a "base domain," and we use this to help explain a less familiar "target domain." Assumed qualities of one entity may be used as descriptors for another. A simple metaphor attempts to create a connection that evokes an image: "A nonreproductive female bee is a worker for the hive." Closely related would be a more cautious simile, "A female nonreproductive bee is *like* a worker for the hive." Both make a comparison; however, the metaphor is more direct in its transfer of qualities from base to target. The creation of complex analogies can include these metaphors in larger structural comparisons, as in this example of division of labor from Karl von Frisch:

> In a colony of bees division of labour is arranged as thoroughly as in a boot and shoe factory where a number of hands are employed, each in a different capacity: one for cutting the leather, another for stitching the cut out parts on a machine, a third for hammering nails in, and so on. Each one by keeping within the strictly limited range of certain activity requires a special skill. Something very similar takes place in the bee's workshop: here the various activities are distributed among various groups of bees to such an extent that even the foragers are subdivided into a group of nectar-collectors and one of pollen-collectors, each group devoting itself exclusively to its own particular task. (Frisch 1927/1953:14)

Frisch, a pioneer in entomology who discovered the "waggle dance" that serves to communicate foraging directions to "forager" honeybees in the hive by the "scouts," felt that analogies adequately expanded scientific observation by comparing the familiar with the unfamiliar (as he did by using human dance to explain bee communication). The unstated implication behind these analogies is that particular bee behaviors are observed by the scientist and could also be viewed by nonscientists as well. The insect behaviors are assumed to be universally observable, yet thought to require guided scientific interpretation, and this can be accomplished through the use of analogy.

Complex analogies express differences as well as similarities; but typically imply that there are enough points of connection structurally and that the connections are not just a figure of speech, or nonsensical. The analogous statement just quoted, on the division of labor in a hive, can be expanded to describe further connections between specific tasks, human and insect factories, or any number of things deriving from this seemingly simple initial comparison. There are debates and ongoing research on what makes analogies effective, in particular in the field of science education (Aubusson et al. 2006; Chiu and Lin 2005; Dagher 1995; Duit 1991; Duit et al. 2001). Analogies are used in everyday cognition by the public and in specialized ways by a wide array of disciplines (English 2004; Gazzinelli et al. 2010; Gentner and Jeziorski 1993; Holyoak and Thagard 1995; Holyoak et al. 2001; Meheus 2013).

Douglas Hofstader and Emanuel Sander (2001) believe analogy to be at the center of cognition, submerging metaphor under the larger category of analogy. Usha Goswami (2001:437), building from Holyoak and Thagard's (1995) work on analogies as "mental leaps" claims, "Analogical thinking lies at the core of human creativity. It has been argued that the very act of forming an analogy requires a kind of 'mental leap,' inasmuch as it necessitates seeing one thing as if it were another.... However, as well as being an important cognitive mechanism in creative thinking, analogy is the basis of much of our everyday problem solving."

Although metaphors have been critically explored for their influence in everyday life and specialized uses (Lakoff and Johnson 1980; Ortony 1993), analogies have been less of a direct focus outside of education and childhood development fields. Hofstadter and Sander (2013:135) believe that analogies are embedded in every aspect of our cognition yet, "the word 'analogy' is seldom heard in ordinary speech." Analogies have often been viewed as merely a useful tool that assists understanding of the unfamiliar target domain by comparing it to the more familiar base domain. Simple analogies used in testing, with the formulaic, A is to B as X is to Y, are not the concern of this chapter. Instead, I focus on the complex analogies and scientific analogies that use deeper structural relations. Both social science and the natural sciences have used complex analogies that are influenced by and influence the ways we think of the social structure. Therefore their use of metaphor and analogy takes on special significance for social patterns of cognition.

28.2 SCIENTIFIC THINKING/ SCIENTIFIC ANALOGIES

Eviatar Zerubavel notes that science provides a good case to analyze cognition. Scientists are shaped by social, cultural, and political contexts when making discoveries and practicing science.

> The way in which our perception is affected by our prior cognitive orientation is also quite evident in science. Even in the world of natural, "hard" science, what one observes is never totally independent of the particular "lens" through which it is mentally processed. Even seemingly objective scientific "facts," in other words, are affected by the particular mental filters through which scientists process what they observe in their heads. When scientists turn their telescopes and microscopes to the world around them, their minds are not *tabulae rasae* passively waiting to register the sensory impressions they are about to receive. Even astronomers and microbiologists do not simply observe the world "as it is." How they perceive it is always affected by their particular cognitive orientations prior to the actual act of observing it.   (Zerubavel 1997:25)

Despite periods of criticism about the use of analogy and metaphor for scientific thought, there has been a rich history of both in scientific discourse. Gentner and Jeziorski (1993) trace a shift in Western sciences from metaphors to complex analogies, noting, "there appear to have been significant historical changes in what has counted as the scientific use of analogy and metaphor" (448). Both metaphor and analogy are also still used together in contemporary scientific practice. The relationship between metaphors and complex analogies within the sciences has been well captured by Klamer and Leonard (1994):

> Analogy is an expanded metaphor; more precisely, analogy is sustained and systematically elaborated metaphor. Accordingly, in a scientific context, a metaphor becomes heuristic when it stimulates the construction of an analogical system. The mere coinage of a metaphor such as <human capital> does not make science. Science proceeds by taking a fertile metaphor and relentlessly articulating the nature of its subsidiary domains, probing the properties of that terrain, and testing the connections between that domain and the principal domain.
>
> (Klamer and Leonard 1994:35)

These scientific analogies can become what Kuhn (1962) describes as a part of "normal science," punctuated by paradigm shifts Kuhn identified as revolutions in scientific thought. Large paradigm shifts can also be explained by a shift in "mental lenses" according to Zerubavel's ideas on cognition (1997:26). The paradigms of science shape how we view the world for long periods of time, making these paradigms appear absolute during the time they are in place. Kuhn (1962) notes that a paradigm shift is not sudden, but as anomalies add up, a tipping point leads to the acceptance of a new way of thinking. Analogies are crucial in presenting paradigmatic beliefs as well as shifting those beliefs into new mental understandings in revolutionary ways or simply adding to their development. Holyoak et al. (2001) provide a solid example:

> At least two thousand years ago, the earliest recorded use of analogy to develop an enduring scientific theory produced the hypothesis that sound is propagated in the form of waves.... This abstraction continued to be developed over the course of centuries. At first simply a qualitative explanation of sound transmission, the wave theory was eventually given a mathematical formation. In the seventeenth century a wave theory of light was developed, by analogy with the wave theory of sound. The progression from highly specific, single-case analogies to more abstract concepts or schemas is one of the most powerful roles that analogy plays in cognition.   (6)

Mary Hesse (1966) identified very early on the significance of metaphor and analogies in science, claiming they are critical to scientific models and theory building. Hesse proposed that scientific analogies are more than simple comparisons between a familiar and unfamiliar domain, they also assume a connection to an overarching natural law or a universal correspondence. This is a critical component of the role that analogies have in cognition that link them to ideas of social order, making them appear universal and fixed. Although analogies are linked to creative thought, can existing analogies prevent seeing phenomena in a different light once the unfamiliar is linked to the familiar and accepted as a natural law? Hofstadter and Sander (2013:3) believe that "each concept in our mind owes its existence to a long succession of analogies made unconsciously over many years, initially giving birth to the concept and continuing to enrich it over the course of our lifetime."

One way to understand the influence of analogies on cognition is to examine the language we use in formulating them. Lakoff and Johnson (1980) made this explicit in discussing how to identify the power of metaphors on everyday thought:

> In most of the little things we do every day, we simply think and act more or less automatically along certain lines. Just what these lines are is by no means obvious. One way to find out is by looking at language. Since communication is based on the same conceptual system that we use in thinking and acting, language is an important source of evidence for what that system is like.   (3)

Zerubavel identifies language as a key to creating social meaning behind similarities and differences. Our "cognitive socialization" is facilitated by language distinguishing categories, and this happens in the various "thought communities" we are a part of (1996,1997). The use of analogous language to highlight similarities or differences is social and not simply a natural way the mind works. Language is learned and based on the context of the beliefs within any particular social structure. Words, metaphors, and analogies all contain social meanings that elucidate beliefs and values of any given social structure within a given time period. For instance, Lakoff and Johnson note that even words like "high" and "low" are not merely spatial, but reflect the values of a given culture depending on what priority and emphasis is placed on the terms as used in metaphoric systems (1980:15–19).

When it comes to scientific language, the influence of social meanings becomes submerged by the myth of the neutrality of science. Lynn Margulis cautions that ignoring these social meanings can be problematic. "Language can confuse and deceive. These antiquated terms—"blue-green algae," "protozoa," "higher animals," "lower plants," and many others—remain in use despite their penchant to propagate biological malaise and ignorance" (1998:55). The use of analogies by scientists, educators, and popularizers presents many possible downfalls. Metaphors or analogies in science can become literal, be incorrect, or both, creating limitations and misunderstandings (Duit et al. 2001; Kennedy 1992; Lewontin 1991; Margulis 1998). When it comes to anthropomorphic analogies between species, Lewontin (1991) suggests, "What happens is that human categories are laid on animals by analogy, partly as a matter of convenience of language, and then these traits are 'discovered' in animals and laid back on humans as if they had a common origin" (95–96). He notes that analogous similarities are not always indicative of actual similarities in either their biological or social purpose.

Taking into account culture and language, analogies can be productively analyzed through cognitive sociology and emphasizing awareness as to their influence can aid in rethinking them. As Wayne Brekhus (2015) states, "Analogical thinking can be oversimplified in ways that encourage us to see events in a given way and to not see them in other ways. Research in sociology of culture and cognition complicates understandings of meaning-making, metaphor, analogy, narrative, and discourse by showing the ways that these processes are often employed rather automatically without conscious deliberation and clear intent" (89–90). Examining analogies as socially created cognitive patterns questions the supposed naturalness of hierarchical social structures found in many scientific analogies.

28.3 SOCIAL INSECT ANALOGIES

Why is the case of social insect analogies a good one to highlight cognition and analogies, especially scientific analogies? Comparisons between social insect societies and human societies have been proposed by a wide variety of philosophers, scientists, naturalists, and the general public. The perceived qualities of ants, bees, wasps, and termites are considered highly social (eusocial) due to their reproductive division of labor, caste system, and care for young. In the Western science of the nineteenth and early twentieth centuries, the discipline of entomology became fully established and paid homage to the evolutionary lineage of social insects, often citing them as a model for humans. Charles Darwin used social insect analogies and elevated their mental faculties as compared to humans: "the brain of an ant is one of the most marvellous atoms of matter in the world, perhaps more marvellous than the brain of man (1871:140). Jean-Henri Fabre (1938), similar to many entomologists of the time, praised the productivity of social insects, "it is among the Hymenoptera that we find the busiest of insects, and some of them, such as the honeybee, the bumblebee, the wasp, and the ant, live in communities numbering many individuals" (89). Termites, within the order of Isoptera, are also social insects, but at times have been viewed as a "white ant" (Maeterlinck 1927; Marais 1937/1973). Fabre (1917) even referred to them as the "real ants" and claimed they were "noble workers" (10–11). The idea that social insect societies and behavior could be successfully used as a scientific analogy with human society was frequently offered in entomological literature. This was meant to offer a guide for many human behaviors and institutions by the comparison. As Vernon Kellogg claimed of ants:

> No insects are more familiar. They live in all lands and regions; they exist in enormous numbers; they are not driven away by the changes in primitive nature imposed by man's occupancy of the soil; they mine and tunnel his fields and invade his dwellings. And many things which man attempts they do more successfully than he does, and may be his teachers!   (Kellogg 1908:534)

And Maurice Maeterlinck includes the "Republics" of social insects:

> [I]t can scarcely be denied that the efforts of nature that we are now considering approximate to a certain ideal. This ideal—with which it is well that we should become acquainted so that we may discard certain hopes of ours that are dangerous or superfluous—is nowhere on this earth so clearly manifest as in the republics of…the bee, the ant and the termite.   (1927:186)

This is what makes the case of entomological analogies so fascinating. The work of these analogies ends up creating a "legitimating loop" between the field of social and natural, leading to a naturalizing outcome (Rodgers 2008). Our ideas about nature are filtered through the social ideas we have of it, but then we use those ideas as if they were unfiltered, natural, and a model or justification for inequalities within social structure or for their remedy. Systematic comparisons can become full-blown models that provide interlocking explanations for a wide variety of social institutions and practices. Analogies establish ideas about individuals, collectivities, and social structures. Social insects have been described as workers, queens, soldiers, nurses, farmers, slaves, and slave-makers. Their social structure has been framed alternately as a monarchy, as a democracy, as socialism, and as a caste system, and most often with a rigid division of labor and hierarchy. Allegedly inside the social insect societies the following actions occur: soldiers create bivouacs and military maneuvers, potential queens take marriage flights, farmers harvest crops, cows are tended by dairymen, workers labor for those higher up in the hierarchy. These terms also are applied to humans and human social structures, making it ripe for the complex shared analogies that attempt to explain the social order for both social insect and human societies. The dominant discourse created with these scientific analogies has tended to naturalize a hierarchical, specialized division of labor with queen as ruler over obedient workers. This however is anything but a natural pattern, as can be seen by contrary interpretations and paradigm shifts in the scientific views of these social structures.

The ideas about social order that became embedded into culture and discourse still inspire analogies for contemporary use either in agreement with past interpretations or the creation of new analogies. Terms that were created to express a hierarchical order and comparison to human social structure and behaviors that are hierarchical are still in use. For example, a 2013 article in *Insectes Sociaux* begins with several assumptions that continue to perpetuate analogies from the past: "Slave-making ants exploit the worker force of host colonies permanently and have to make recurrent raids in order to replenish the slave's stock" (Delattre et al. 2013:7). Other recent issues continue to use terms such as "queen," "workers," "drones," and "soldiers," which create caste system analogies. As plainly stated in the introduction of one contemporary article, "In social insects, the caste systems are based on reproductive division of labor, queens specialize in reproduction and workers primarily maintain the colony" (Matsuura and Yamamoto 2011). The division of labor within insect societies continues to be viewed as an analogous model that may explain the individual's relationship to society (Beshers and Fewell 2001). Hierarchical gender roles have a long tradition and the term "queen" is paired with an analogy to marriage, through descriptions of mating patterns as "nuptial flights" (Goodisman et al. 2000). Queens have a higher status over workers, and more recent portrayals of this hierarchical relationship have incorporated conflict into this analogy rather than strict obedience as in the past. Alaux et al. (2004:400) provide a vivid example: "The different putative ultimate causes of this efficient control by the queen are discussed, and we suggest a possible scenario of an evolutionary arms race that may occur between these two female castes." Evidently "sibling rivalry" also leads to competition within the hive, as "an agonistic encounter determines the egg-laying 'winner,' while the loser must resort to caring for her sister's offspring" (23). The notion of "dominance hierarchies" has been incorporated into the relationships within colonies. Other reproductive hierarchies and suppression of workers by queens or other competitive workers have been described as "policing" (Ratnieks 1988; Wenseleers et al. 2004). Building on the family analogy, studies of queenless workers or "orphaned worker bumblebees" focus on reproductive competition between siblings (Sibbald and Plowright 2013). In the new competitive hive some workers are "unemployed" or compared to temporary day workers (Rodgers 2012). Some ideas about social insects that were debated earlier in entomology, such as denying the role of the queen status as a ruler of a hierarchical society, have since reemerged. This has provided more analogies centered around self-organizing rather than hierarchical organization of society.

Analogies that encompass larger social systems show this contemporary shift. For example, Seeley (2010) creates a political analogy of honeybee society to a human political democratic system. In Seeley's "honeybee democracy" decision-making is created by workers in the hive and swarming behavior is attributed to new ideas of self-organizing rather than by direction from the queen. The new scientific understanding is shown to lead to new analogies.

> There is one common misunderstanding about the inner operations of a honeybee colony that I must dispel at the outset, namely that a colony is governed by a benevolent dictator, Her Majesty the Queen. The belief that a colony's coherence derives from an omniscient queen (or king) telling the workers what to do is centuries old, tracing back to Aristotle and persisting until modern times. But it is false. What is true is that a colony's queen lies at the heart of the whole operation, for a honeybee colony is an immense family consisting of the mother queen and her thousands of progeny.   (Seeley 2011:5)

Seeley proposes to provide "some practical lessons that we humans can learn from the bees for improving human group decision making, especially when the members of a group have common interests, as do the bees in a swarm" (119). Of course the interpretation of any "common interests" of bees creating either a democracy or a monarchy does not take into account what, if any, "political system" the honeybees have decided to adopt. Clearly, this is a shifting analogy that is used as a cognitive tool by humans in an effort to understand their own political systems.

"Thinking with insects" still seems to be viewed as a legitimate cognitive tool for not only entomology but also other disciplines, and has spurred new interdisciplinary directions. For instance Alan Kirman (1993), an economist, compared ants foraging to the process of humans choosing a restaurant to advance rational choice analysis. Gowdy and Krall (2016:1) believe some social insects and humans share a common origin that is driven by economics. This economic analogy assumes a shared social structure of, "complex division of labor, city-states, and an almost exclusive dependence on agriculture for subsistence."

Architecture, urban design, and planning have begun to look to social insects for new design strategies from termite mounds to beehives. For instance, insights from the published proceedings of an interdisciplinary conference on complexity, cognition, urban planning, and design include the following comparison to social insects: "Like a human city, the termite colony is a constructed environment that provides both habitation and the associated community infrastructure to support the comfort and sustenance of the inhabitants" (Turner 2016:116). The author continues to explain that termites have self-organizing features that should be modeled by humans in design and maintenance of physical structures. Interdisciplinary interest in biomimicry has brought forth a renewed interest in social insect analogies, specifically for human planning and design.

Termites were also the source of inspiration in identifying "stigmergy," a term coined by Pierre-Paul Grassé (1959). As Grassé describes it, the act of building a nest by individuals within a social insect colony relies on collective cues, creating a complex order seemingly without any direct oversight (1959). Some cognitive scientists have recently used this idea about social insects to understand human cognition and collective behavior (Susi and Ziemke 2001). Fields such as artificial intelligence and robotics have begun to apply social insect analogies based on the idea of stigmergy or "swarm intelligence" (Greiner 1988; Kennedy et al. 2001). Interdisciplinary teams of entomologists, computer scientists, and mathematicians are using these analogies in AI and computer simulations to create new algorithms from bee societies and ant societies for optimizing of systems, believing these societies to be models of efficiency (Bonabeau et al. 1999, 2000; Dorigo and Stützle 2004).

28.4 CHALLENGES TO THE UNIVERSALITY OF ANALOGIES

With the continued use and updating of scientific analogies using social insects, what caution might we take in regard to the universalizing of lessons from these comparisons? Despite the continuation of hierarchical structural analogies, there have also been challenges to these types of analogies, such as the shift to more self-organization. Since the beginning of entomology there have been disagreements as to how to interpret what was observed of insect social structure and behavior. Sometimes even disagreements on what was observed initially. "Even in science (which, more than any other cognitive framework, we tend to regard as a system of absolute truths) there is more than only one mental lens through which one can 'observe' things" (Zerubavel 1997:29). Scientists are not separate from the cultures they are born into and conduct science within. Science studies have long noted this effect of culture in the practice of science (Barnes and Shapin 1979; Hess 1995; Longino 1990; Pickering 1992). From the anthropological study of scientific laboratories and the social construction of scientific knowledge claims (Knorr-Cetina 1981; Latour and Woolgar 1979) to problematizing classification and boundary work (Bowker and Leigh Star 1999; Gieryn 1983; Leigh Star and Griesemer 1989) and cross-cultural approaches (Hess 1995) scientific ideas and practice have been viewed in the context of culture. Feminist scholars of science challenged the "view from nowhere" (Haraway 1989, 1991) and the need to identify the social location of scientists (Harding 1998).

Another aspect of cultural influence on scientific analogies is that scientific discourse is linked to social order discourse (Barnes and Shapin 1979; Farber 2000; Jasanoff 2004; Mirowski 1994; Rodgers 2008; Young 1985), which questions neutrality and can be connected to ideology (Aronowitz 1988; Hofstadter 1955; Lewotin 1991). We need to examine the involvement of analogy in the creation of this discourse. As Meheus (2013) claims, "strong analogies have an important heuristic function: they suggest a solution to the problem one is dealing with. In this case, however, the analogy itself provides reasons for accepting the solution" (26–27). An excellent example in challenging pre-conceived ideas and outcomes created from analogies can be found in the pioneering work of the entomologist Deborah Gordon (1989, 1999, 2010). Social insects have been defined by a hierarchical division of labor, in particular a reproductive division of labor relying on caste. Gordon questioned this dominant concept of caste for task allocation and the analogy it was based on:

> It may seem intuitively obvious that an organization that utilizes a division of labour based on permanently specialized individuals is inherently more efficient. But is it? Is an organization consisting of specialized individuals necessarily more efficient than one in which each individual is capable of a variety of tasks? This question suggests an analogy to human industry, from which the phrase "division of labor" is borrowed.   (1989:57)

In order to explain the task-switching behavior she observed in ant colonies that did not fit into analogies based on hierarchical division of labor, Gordon created a new analogy, one that "draws on the analogy between colonies and brains." She notes, "In both systems, relatively simple units (ants or neurons), using local cues, can achieve complex, global behavior" (1999:143). In this new model we do not see a "queen" ordering "workers" to enact particular tasks, but rather a self-organizing colony. This idea has become widely accepted, although as already discussed, concepts of hierarchy have crept back into self-organizing analogies (Camazine et al. 2001).

28.5 CROSS-CULTURAL INTERPRETATIONS

All models of social structures reflect social cognition that is influenced by any given culture at a particular time-period. Scientific analogies should be analyzed for cultural, social, and political differences. Zerubavel argues for cognitive sociology to use a comparative approach to accurately represent diversity between and within "thought communities" (1996, 1997). Even if one makes an argument that analogy is found in most cultures, the amount it is relied on and what assumptions are shared within analogies reveal cultural differences in cognition and analogies. As Gentner and Jeziorski (1993) note, "There are modern instances of cultures that possess the various forms of similarity, including analogy, but use them in a different distribution from current Western culture" (476). They are careful to point out that cultures are not homogeneous or static, however, and that differentiation occurs in Western cultures as well, using the case of the historic shift of analogy use in Western science. My examples of cross-cultural social insect analogies are taken from research within the subfield of ethnoentomology, and also assume a dynamic relation to analogical reasoning within every culture.

One example comes from Malawi, where bees are considered a nuisance by many people rather than as some moral guide (Morris 2006). The bee's reputation becomes centered around its problematic aspects, especially the: "continual invasion of bees into the houses and government offices in Zomba. Attacks from bees often hindered administrative work, and the public works department (PWD) was continually called in to clear buildings of what had been a troublesome pest—'a very disagreeable nuisance', as one administrator put it" (Morris 2006:100). These everyday encounters shape the discourse and any possible analogies that would be used. Unlike much of Western discourse, bees are not considered in a positive light or model; instead they are seen as a serious danger. "Several deaths of young children stung by a swarm of bees have been recorded from Malawi, and the newspapers regularly report bees attacking mourners at a funeral—which usually take place in a wooded graveyard (*manda*)—so that the ceremony has had to be abandoned" (Morris 2006: 99).

Bentley and Rodríguez (2001), in their case study of rural Honduran enthnoentomology, found that for rural Hondurans, social insects are not important because of their "socialness," rather they are deemed culturally important for their interactions with humans that may be deemed helpful or harmful. Bees that produce honey are important as food, but also some are known as causing pain from stings. Ants are also a source of potential pain from stings or bites. Similarly Gurung (2003:351) notes in the case study of Tharu farmers in Nepal, social insects are not even considered important enough by this group to seriously classify them with much distinction at all. The term "kiaraa" for insects includes a larger group of arthropods and any other creature that might be considered to cause "harm to crops, livestock or people." Ants are known only for their ability to pinch people, while bees are seen as useful for pollination only if researchers press for a beneficial aspect of insects. Social insects are not used in analogies to human society, and insects in general are mostly viewed as "harmful or a mistake in God's creation." Insects that are, according to Western classification, subsocial or solitary insects feature more prominently in the Nepalese rural culture: Fireflies, cicadas, and dung beetles appear in morality stories, while the Rice bug and praying mantis rise to the level of spiritual rituals because of the intensity of their perceived harmfulness (365).

Unlike Western scientific analogies of social insects, many cultures that do acknowledge the social aspect of insects do not feature a hierarchical ranking in the idea of social structure. One example is provided by Ellen (1993), who suggests that the Nuaulu of central Seram do not conceive of "deep hierarchies" in the animal social world. Ellen (1993) explains:

> The imagery of hierarchy, implying higher and lower, top and bottom, superior and inferior, with its technical associations of literate graphic representations and its social connotations of class and status, is absent from Nuaulu discourse on animal relationships.... It is neither appropriate as a *folk* representation of how the Nuaulu conceive the relationships between categories, nor does it adequately serve the purpose of comparison and generalisation from the ethnographic angle.   (89–90)

Another variation that occurs in analogies is that when hierarchy is present, it reflects the hierarchy within that particular culture. Darrel Posey's work on the idea of insects held by the Kayapó Indians who live in the states of Para and Mato Grosso in the Amazon of Brazil is a good example of this. The Kayapó distinguish social insects from other insects but they make distinctions among them as well that differ from Western descriptions. The term *ñy* includes termites, ants, wasps, and bees although they each have separate names as well. But the overarching term separates them from other animals because of their unique ability to be compared to humans, making them analogous, including elements of familial, political, and even physical attributes and behaviors. As Posey describes:

> The ñy or social insects are seen to be in a special relationship to man because of their communal nature. All ñy colonies [villages] are thought to have a chief... and be organized into family units just like the Kayapó. They are known to have warriors and the sounds of the movements are likened to Kayapó movements and singing.   (2002:89)

Posey elaborates on how these analogous roles are viewed: "To be good hunters...the Kayapó must know ants, just as they must know wasps to be brave and fearless warriors" (2002:92). The two most prominent social insects for the Kayapó are wasps and ants, as their behaviors are a model for certain roles within human social organization. Termites are seen as "worthless" because they are "weak" and "cowardly" and therefore, even though social, they are not role models (Posey 2002:92).

Analogies are created using perceived behaviors from observation, but this is social. Although size, description of behavior, and movement is important in Navajo classification, color and sex is not as important (Wyman and Bailey 1964:17). Without significant markers of color or sex it would be difficult for Navajo social insect analogies to create analogies that include queen, king, male drones, and nonreproductive females or slaves and slave-makers. Without distinctions of gender or color, gender and racial hierarchical analogies are not prevalent. Krause et al. (2010) suggest that the population in Roviana in the Western Solomon Islands do not even differentiate insects into their own category and do not have a separate word for them. This makes the idea of creating a particular group of insects such as social insects and creating analogies to humans with them to be completely out of the question. There are some names for particular insects that pose danger, which is similar to other populations. Costa-Neto (2000) also discusses the idea that the term "insect" may not compare to Western ideas of classification and that for many cultures the term insect is very inclusive and often negative. All of the cases presented illustrate terms and analogies that differ according to cultural beliefs and social structure. Analogies of social insects will be influenced by this variation in human social structure. This undermines the supposed naturalness and universality of hierarchical analogies.

28.6 CONCLUSION

We use a metaphor such as "busy as a bee" to express the perception that honeybees are industrious. We then extend this into a full-blown analogy to human society and find it reinforced by scientific discourse. This discourse shapes (and is shaped by) the mental processes of observation and interpretation. Watching bees flying, collecting pollen from flowers, creating honey in a hive, tending to pupae to encourage growth and survival; we may "see" industriousness because we value this trait in any given culture. Social insect analogies have been systematically employed in scientific discourse since the nineteenth century. These analogies play a legitimizing role in reinforcing social structures and most often have supported a hierarchical social structure in Western discourse. Although challenges have emerged to the dominant presentation of social insect analogies, hierarchy is still a persistent theme. Analogies need to be examined for their meanings, their directionality, and their limitations concerning both insect societies and human societies.

> Reifying the meaning of symbols essentially reduces them to mere indicators and therefore implies a readiness to give up the greatest advantage that being able to use symbols offers us. It basically means trading the cognitive freedom that typically comes with flexible-mindedness for the inevitably constrictive way of thinking promoted by the rigid mind. Given the virtually unlimited signifying potential of symbols, it also means a terrible waste of our distinctively human capacity to think creatively.   (Zerubavel 1997:80)

Analogies are not just simply a comparison from something familiar to understand something unfamiliar. As the case of social insects and scientific analogies illustrates, this tool of cognition can have a misleading or ideological influence on how we think about large social systems and the role of the individual within these social structures. Analogies and metaphors rely on assumptions and beliefs that are rooted in the cultural and social locations of those that create them. We can identify this context and exercise caution in attributing universality or any fixed quality to the analogies, even scientific analogies that have been previously viewed as neutral. If we acknowledge the limits of analogies and use them in a less constraining, less deterministic manner, this will allow us to think creatively about the natural and social world around us.

REFERENCES

Alaux, Cédric, Fabrice Savarit, Pierre Jaisson, and Abraham Hefetz. 2004. "Does the Queen Win It All? Queen-Worker Conflict over Male Production in the Bumblebee, Bombus terrestris." *Naturwissenschaften* 91(8):400–403.

Aronowitz, Stanley. 1988. *Science as Power: Discourse and Ideology in Modern Society.* Minneapolis: University of Minnesota Press.

Aubusson, Peter J., Allan G. Harrison, and Stephen M. Ritchie. 2006. *Metaphor and Analogy in Science Education.* Dordrecht, The Netherlands: Springer.

Barnes, Barry, and Steven Shapin, eds. 1979. *Natural Order: Historical Studies of Scientific Culture.* London: Sage.

Bentley, Jeffery W., and Gonzalo Rodríguez. 2001. "Honduran Folk Entomology." *Current Anthropology* 42(2):1–16.

Beshers, Samuel N., and Jennifer H. Fewell. 2001. "Models of Division of Labor in Social Insects." *Annual Review of Entomology* 46:413–40.

Bonabeau, Eric, Marco Dorigo, and Guy Theraulaz. 1999. *Swarm Intelligence: From Natural to Artificial Systems.* New York: Oxford University Press.

Bonabeau, Eric, Marco Dorigo, and Guy Theraulaz. 2000. "Inspiration for Optimization from Social Insect Behavior." *Nature* 406:39–42.

Bowker, Geoffrey C., and Susan Leigh Star. 1999. *Sorting Things Out: Classification and Its Consequences.* Cambridge, MA: MIT Press.

Brekhus, Wayne H. 2015. *Culture and Cognition: Patterns in the Social Construction of Reality.* Cambridge: Polity.

Camazine, Scott, Jean-Louis Deneubourg, Nigel R. Franks, James Sneyd, Guy Theraulaz, and Eric Banabeau. 2001. *Self-Organization in Biological Systems.* Princeton, NJ: Princeton University Press.

Chiu, Mei-Hung, and Jing-Wen Lin. 2005. "Promoting Fourth Graders' Conceptual Change of Their Understanding of Electric Current via Multiple Analogies." *Journal of Research in Science Teaching* 42(4):429–64.

Costa-Neto, Eraldo Medeiros. 2000. "The Significance of the Category "Insect" for Folk Biological Classification Systems." *Journal of Ecological Anthropology* 4:70–75.

Dagher, Zoubeida R. 1995. "Review of Studies on the Effectiveness of Instructional Analogies in Science Education." *Science Education* 79(3):295–312.

Darwin, Charles. 1871. *The Descent of Man.* New York: D. Appleton and Company.

Delattre O., N. Chaline, S. Chameron, E. Lecoutey, and P. Jaisson. 2013. "Opportunist Slave-Making Ants *Myrmoxenus ravouxi* Discriminate Different Host Species from a Non-Host Species." *Insectes Sociaux* 60:7–13.

Dorigo Marco, and Thomas Stützle 2004. *Ant Colony Optimization.* Cambridge, MA: MIT Press.

Duit, Reinders. 1991. "On the Role of Analogies and Metaphors in Learning Science." *Science Education* 5(6):649–72.

Duit, Reinders, Wolff-Michael Roth, Michael Komorek, and Jens Wilbers. 2001. "Fostering Conceptual Changes by Analogies—Between Scylla and Charybdis." *Learning and Instruction* 11:283–303.

Ellen Roy. 1993. *The Cultural Relations of Classification: An Analysis of Nuaulu Animal Categories from Central Seram*. Cambridge: Cambridge University Press.

English, Lyn D. 2004. "Mathematical and Analogical Reasoning in Early Childhood." pp. 1–22 in *Mathematical and Analogical Reasoning of Young Learners*, edited by L. D. English. New York: Routledge.

Fabre, Jean-Henri. 1917. *The Story-Book of Science*. Translated by Florence Constable Bicknell. New York: Century.

Fabre, Jean-Henri. 1938. *Marvels of the Insect World*. Edited, annotated, and translated by Percy F. Bicknell. New York: Appleton-Century.

Farber, Paul Lawrence. 2000. *Finding Order in Nature: The Naturalist Tradition from Linnaeus to E. O. Wilson*. Baltimore, MD: John Hopkins University Press.

Frisch, Karl von. 1927/1953. *The Dancing Bees*. New York: Harvest Book.

Gazzinelli, Maria F., Lucas Lobato, Leonardo Matoso, Renato Avila, Rita de Cassia Marques, Ami Shah Brown, et al. 2010. "Health Education through Analogies: Preparation of a Community for Clinical Trials of a Vaccine against Hookworm in an Endemic Area of Brazil." *PLoS Neglected Tropical Diseases* 4(7):e749.

Gentner, Dedre, and Michael Jeziorski. 1993. "The Shift from Metaphor to Analogy in Western Science." pp. 447–80 in *Metaphor and Thought*, 2nd ed., edited by A. Ortony. Cambridge: Cambridge University Press.

Gieryn, Thomas. 1983. "Boundary-Work and the Demarcation of Science from Non-Science: Strains and Interests in Professional Ideologies of Scientists." *American Sociological Review* 48(6):781–95.

Goodisman, Michael A. D., Christopher J. DeHeer, and Kenneth G. Ross. 2000. "Unusual Behavior of Polygyne Fire Ant Queens on Nuptial Flights." *Journal of Insect Behavior* 13(3):455–68.

Gordon, Deborah. 1989. "Caste and Change in Social Insects." pp. 56–72 in *Oxford Surveys in Evolutionary Biology*, Vol. 6, edited by P. H. Harvey and L. Partridge. Oxford: Oxford University Press.

Gordon, Deborah M. 1999. *Ants at Work*. New York: The Free Press.

Gordon, Deborah M. 2010. *Ant Encounters: Interaction Networks and Colony Behavior*. Princeton, NJ: Princeton University Press.

Goswami, Usha. 2001. "Analogical Reasoning in Children." pp. 437–70 in *The Analogical Mind: Perspectives from Cognitive Science*, edited by D. Gentner, K. James Holyoak, and B. N. Kokinov. Cambridge, MA: MIT Press.

Gowdy, John, and Lisi Krall. 2016. "The Economic Origins of Ultrasociality." *Behavioral and Brain Sciences* 39:e92. https://dx.doi.org/10.1017/S0140525X1500059X.

Grassé, Pierre-Paul. 1959. "La reconstruction du nid et les coordinations interindividuelles chez bellicositermes natalensis et cubitermes sp. La theorie de la stigmergie: essai d'interpretation du comportement des termites constructeurs." *Insectes Sociaux* 6:41–81.

Greiner, Russell. 1988. "Learning by Understanding Analogies." *Artificial Intelligence* 35(1):81–125.

Gurung, Astrid Björnsen. 2003. "Insects—A Mistake in God's Creation? Tharu Farmers' Perception and Knowledge of Insects: A Case Study of Gobardiha Village Development Committee, Dang-Deukhuri Nepal." *Agriculture and Human Values* 20:337–70.

Haraway, Donna. 1989. *Primate Visions: Gender, Race and Nature in the World of Modern Science*. New York: Routledge.

Haraway, Donna. 1991. *Simians, Cyborgs, and Women: The Reinvention of Nature*. New York: Routledge.

Harding, Sandra. 1998. *Is Science Multicultural? Postcolonialisms, Feminisms, and Epistemologies*. Bloomington: Indiana University Press.

Hess, David J. 1995. *Science and Technology in a Multicultural World: The Cultural Politics of Facts and Artifacts*. New York: Columbia University Press.

Hesse, Mary B. 1966. *Models and Analogies in Science*. Notre Dame, IN: University of Notre Dame Press.

Hofstadter, Douglas, and Emmanuel Sander. 2013. *Surfaces and Essences: Analogy as the Fuel and Fire of Thinking*. New York: Basic Books.

Hofstadter, Richard. 1955. *Social Darwinism in American Thought*. Boston: Beacon Press.

Holyoak, Keith, Dedre Getner, and Boicho Kokinov. 2001. "Introduction: The Place of Analogy in Cognition." pp. 1–19 in *The Analogical Mind: Perspectives from Cognitive Science*. Edited by D. Gentner, K. J. Holyoak, and B. N. Kokinov. Cambridge MA: MIT Press.

Holyoak, Keith J., and Paul Thagard. 1995. *Mental Leaps: Analogy in Creative Thought*. Cambridge, MA: MIT Press.

Jasanoff, Sheila, ed. 2004. *States of Knowledge: The Co-production of Science and Social Order*. New York; London: Routledge.

Kellogg, Vernon L. 1908. *American Insects*. New York: Henry Holt.

Kennedy James, Russell C. Eberhart, and Yuhui Shi. 2001. *Swarm Intelligence*. San Francisco: Morgan Kaufmann.

Kennedy, John S. 1992. *The New Anthropomorphism*. Cambridge: Cambridge University Press.

Kirman, Alan. 1993. "Ants, Rationality and Recruitment." *Quarterly Journal of Economics* 108(1):137–56.

Klamer Arjo, and Thomas C. Leonard 1994. "So What's an Economic Metaphor?" pp. 20–52 in *Natural Images in Economic Thought: "Markets Read in Tooth and Claw,"* edited by P. Mirowski. Cambridge: Cambridge University Press.

Knorr-Cetina, Karin D. 1981. *The Manufacture of Knowledge: An Essay on the Constructivist and Contextual Nature of Science*. Oxford: Pergamon Press.

Krause, Rachel J., Ismael Vaccaro, and Shankar Aswani. 2010. "Challenges in Building Insect Ethnobiological Classifications in Roviana, Solomon Islands." *Journal of Ethnobiology* 30 (2):313–25.

Kuhn, Thomas S. 1962. *The Structure of Scientific Revolutions*. Chicago: University of Chicago Press.

Lakoff, George, and Mark Johnson. 1980. *Metaphors We Live By*. Chicago: University of Chicago Press.

Latour, Bruno, and Steve Woolgar 1979. *Laboratory Life: The Social Construction of Scientific Facts*. Beverly Hills, CA: SAGE.

Leigh Star, Susan, and James Griesemer. 1989. "Institutional Ecology, 'Translations' and Boundary Objects: Amateurs and Professionals in Berkeley's Museum of Vertebrate Zoology, 1907–39." *Social Studies of Science* 19(3):387–420.

Lewontin, R.C. 1991. *Biology as Ideology*. New York: Harper Perennial.

Longino, Helen E. 1990. *Science as Social Knowledge: Values and Objectivity in Scientific Inquiry*. Princeton, NJ: Princeton University Press.

Maeterlinck, Maurice. 1927. *The Life of the White Ant*. New York: Dodd, Mead and Company.

Marais, Eugene. 1937/1973 *The Soul of the White Ant*. Middlesex, UK: Penguin Books.

Margulis, Lynn. 1998. *Symbiotic Planet: A New Look at Evolution*. New York: Basic.

Matsuura, K., and Y. Yamamoto. 2011. "Workers Do Not Mediate the Inhibitory Power of Queens in a Termite, Reticulitermes speratus (Isoptera, Rhinotermitidae)." *Insectes Sociaux* 58(4):513–18.

Meheus, Joke. 2013. "Analogical Reasoning in Creative Problem Solving Processes: Logico-Philosophical Perspectives." pp. 17–34 in *Metaphor and Analogy in the Sciences*, edited by F. Hallyn. Dordrecht: Springer.

Mirowski, Philip, ed. 1994. *Natural Images in Economic Thought: "Markets Read in Tooth & Claw."* Cambridge: Cambridge University Press.

Morris, Brian. 2006. *Insects and Human Life*. Oxford: Berg.

Ortony, Andrew, ed. 1993. *Metaphor and Thought*. 2nd ed. Cambridge: Cambridge University Press.

Pickering Andrew. 1992. *Science as Practice and Culture*. Chicago: University of Chicago Press.

Posey, Darrell A. 2002. *Kayapó Ethnoecology and Culture*. Edited by K. Plenderleith. London: Routledge.

Ratnieks, Francis L. W. 1988. "Reproductive Harmony via Mutual Policing by Workers in Eusocial Hymenoptera." *American Naturalist* 132(2):217–36.

Rodgers, Diane. 2008. *Debugging the Link between Social Theory and Social Insects*. Baton Rouge: Louisiana State University Press.

Rodgers, Diane. 2012. "Busy as a Bee or Unemployed? Shifting Scientific Discourse on Work." *Minerva* 50(1):45–64.

Seeley, Thomas. 2010. *Honeybee Democracy*. Princeton, NJ: Princeton University Press.

Sibbald, Emily D., and Catherine M. S. Plowright. 2013. "On the Relationship between Aggression and Reproduction in Pairs of Orphaned Worker Bumblebees (Bombus impatiens)." *Insectes Sociasux* 60(1):23–30.

Susi, Tarja, and Tom Ziemke 2001. "Social Cognition, Artefacts, and Stigmergy: A Comparative Analysis of Theoretical Frameworks for the Understanding of Artefact-Mediated Collaborative Activity." *Cognitive Systems Research* 2(4):273–90.

Turner, Scott. 2016. "Swarm Cognition and Swarm Construction: Lessons from a Social Insect Master Builder." pp. 111–27 in *Complexity, Cognition, Urban Planning and Design: Post-Proceedings of the 2nd Delft International Conference*, edited by J. Portugali and E. Stolk. Cham, Switzerland: Springer International Publishing.

Wenseleers Tom, Heikki Helantera, Adam Hart, and Francis L. W. Ratnieks 2004. "Worker Reproduction and Policing in Insect Societies: An ESS Analysis." *Journal of Evolutionary Biology* 17:1035–47.

Wyman Leland C., and Flora L. Bailey. 1964. *Navajo Indian Ethnoentomology*. University of New Mexico Publications in Anthropology Number 12. Albuquerque: University of New Mexico Press.

Young, Robert M. 1985. *Darwin's Metaphor: Nature's Place in Victorian Culture*. Cambridge: Cambridge University Press.

Zerubavel, Eviatar. 1996. "Lumping and Splitting: Notes on Social Classification." *Sociological Forum* 11:421–33.

Zerubavel, Eviatar. 1997. *Social Mindscapes: An Invitation to Cognitive Sociology*. Cambridge, MA: Harvard University Press.

CHAPTER 29

....

GETTING A FOOT
IN THE DOOR

*symbolism, door metaphors, and the
cognitive sociology of access*

....

STEPHANIE PEÑA-ALVES

DESPITE conventional notions of metaphors as fanciful linguistic devices that meet purely poetic ends, contemporary scholars across disciplines agree that metaphor is simultaneously a linguistic, cognitive, and cultural phenomenon (Gibbs 1997). Theoretical accounts abound to suggest that metaphorical projection is a tool of rational thought and thus central to human cognition (Lakoff and Johnson 1980; Johnson 1987), a tool of rhetorical persuasion and thus a central part of political life (Charteris-Black 2004), and a tool for the construction and maintenance of social reality and thus central to cultural systems of meaning (see Brekhus 2015:97–110). Cultural and cognitive sociologists have also looked beyond this wide-ranging utility and analyzed metaphors as products of these rational, political, and meaning-making efforts. As products, everyday metaphors emerge relative to particular communities, social contexts, and historical moments and they serve as discursive objects around which individuals act (Ignatow 2003, 2009; Winchester 2008; Cousineau 2014) and identify (Kato 2011) as members of social groups. Because this is relegated to the domain of cognitive linguistics, little scholarly attention is paid in sociology to the sociocognitive dynamics of *the metaphorical act*—that is, the ways culture shapes *the generic cognitive process* of metaphorical projection of a concrete idea or object onto abstract target realms. Whereas cognitive linguists tend to highlight the embodied, preconceptual basis of the metaphor process (Ortony 1979/1993; Johnson 1987; Lakoff and Johnson 1980), I argue cognitive sociology has much to offer our collective understanding of its cultural basis.

Likewise, the social issue of access in sociology is rarely treated as matter of social cognition. The first instinct in this area of research—logical and historically fruitful—has been to elucidate the social, political, and historical conditions governing access to various institutions and resources, be they citizenship, education, jobs, housing, health-care, or political participation, to name just a handful. However, lost in the pursuit of these determinants is the opportunity to explore how individuals conceptualize access as members of particular social groups, or more specifically, as thought communities (Fleck 1979; Zerubavel 1997), not to mention how they deploy those conceptualizations in meaningful and creative ways. To the extent that conceptualizations of access are patterned and their use strategic, they can reveal important sociocognitive dimensions of this important social phenomenon.

In this chapter, I analyze sociocultural frames of metaphor in the case of door metaphors to highlight the cognitive sociology of access. In so doing, I aim to broaden the scope of sociological inquiry on metaphor by bridging insights in cognitive linguistics and the cognitive sociology of relevance and social markedness. In addition, I attempt to foreground how cognitive sociology contributes knowledge to our larger sociological understandings of access, thus broadening the scope of the sociology of access to new cognitive terrain.

Spatially grounded access metaphors, such as door metaphors, are a generative empirical site for examining the ways culture shapes the sociocognitive process of metaphor. Moreover, a rich body of work in cognitive linguistics and sociology sets the stage for a deeper analysis of them. In what follows, I begin by outlining research that locates culture in the process of metaphorical projection, I then review relevant work on spatial metaphors of the built environment, and finally I combine formal and pragmatic analytic approaches to examine door metaphors and build on this cognitive sociology of metaphor.

Door metaphors, I argue, reveal two distinct sociomental processes. First, door metaphors involve mapping from the built environment only those elements we treat as culturally relevant and meaningful at doors while passively excluding myriad other elements of this source domain. Hence, this cognitive process and the metaphors that result are prestructured not just by embodied constraints in space but also by cultural constraints derived from the social activities of everyday life. Second, metaphor users construct door metaphors in strategic ways to shape the *metaphorical politics of access* in their targets. In establishing status relations between in and out and charting how one gains access to a given target—from out to in or in to out—users of door metaphors effectively politicize abstract target domains. Specifically, individuals can use door metaphors to plot deviant access, potentials of access, and culturally mediated access to a wide range of abstract realms.

Door metaphors complicate the experiential bases presumed to explain spatial metaphors, but they do so in a sociologically significant way, inviting us to examine cultural structures of thought and their roots in everyday spaces and uses in everyday speech.

29.1 Catching Culture in the Metaphorical Act

While sociological accounts of the cultural elements of metaphor tend to focus analytical attention on metaphor as part of the broader embodied cognitive structures of particular cultural groups (Ignatow 2003, 2009; Winchester 2008) or on metaphors as reflections of groups' worldviews and collective identities (Cousineau 2014; Kato 2011;

Rogers 2008; Santa Ana 2002), it is cognitive linguists who tend to examine the cultural elements of the metaphorical act itself. Tracing the correspondence between source and target domains of metaphors, these scholars outline the ways in which culture serves as the grounded basis for conceptually structuring abstract target domains. In their foundational analysis of metaphors in everyday speech, Lakoff and Johnson (1980) theorize the cultural elements of metaphor in this vein. While Lakoff and Johnson posit that a great many conceptual metaphors have a bodily basis with which all humans become schematically familiar—such as MORE IS UP and LESS IS DOWN,[1] which make metaphorical statements like "speeding *up*" and "slowing *down*" almost universally comprehensible—there are other classes of metaphors that are sourced from sociocultural phenomena and thus do not have a clear, or any, embodied basis. Take the conceptual metaphor TIME IS MONEY, which evokes the image of time as a quantifiable currency that social actors own and exchange. From this conceptual schema, one can make sense of phrases like "*giving* of one's time," "*getting* time off," "*buying* more time," or "*investing* time in," "*allocating* time for" and "*spending* time with others." Although money often manifests in some physical form like cash, coins, or credit card, the meaning of such metaphors is not reducible to the bodily experience with currency. Instead, these metaphors are understood in terms of social exchange relations, which are neither natural nor universal. Therefore, it is not the body, but culture that undergirds conventional understandings of TIME IS MONEY (Lakoff and Johnson 1980:9).

While it is firmly established that culture can and does serve as the conceptual ground of our everyday metaphors, how specific elements of a given culturally shaped source domain come to structure a target idea over and above other potential elements within that source is a hotly debated subject in metaphor studies (Davidson 1978). How, for instance, we know that TIME IS MONEY necessarily borrows from its source domain the activities and values of our system of economic exchange *and not* the physical characteristics of money itself is an important theoretical question. Holland and Quinn (1987) suggest that "cultural models" guide our tacit understandings of metaphors. "Presupposed, taken-for-granted" cultural models are presumed sequences of events or patterns of association within a given semantic realm; they are "models of the world widely shared by members of a society" (Holland and Quinn 1987:4). Internalized over time, these models become mental maps of ideas, meanings, and practices of a given domain, which ultimately steer individuals' thought, speech, and behavior toward the norms and values of their particular groups, as exemplified by these various metaphorical statements and popular images about marriage, like "*meshing with* one's partner," "*failing* one's partner" and "*working on* things," which reflect an American cultural model of marriage based on compatibility, success, and hard work (Quinn 1987).

Yu (2008) elaborates on the cultural model perspective by specifying how precisely they foster particular strains of metaphors: "cultural models function as a filter that lets certain elements from the source domain to be mapped onto the target domain while keeping others from getting through" (257). According to Yu, cultural preferences established by underlying models privilege some aspects of bodily experience in physical source domains, thus encouraging unique specifications of many otherwise universally understood metaphors. Such cultural filtering of embodied structures draws attention to the ways in which our understandings of metaphors are not inevitable or logical accomplishments, but rather are normatively hinged.

At the center of this debate is the issue of how individuals resolve inherent ambiguities in metaphorical mapping. The issue resembles a classic philosophical problem Wittgenstein identified with "ostensive definition," which is meant to "establish an association between the word and the thing," usually by way of pointing at and naming things in the physical world (1953:6). In such cases of ostension, if the meaning is not straightforward, the teacher must rely on other words within a language system to narrow down the meaning for the student. Analogously, with metaphors, the interpreter rarely relies on unambiguous associations of one literally defined domain to another, but rather on "commonplace associations" that effectively point them to specific elements within each domain to establish intended meaning (Black 1962). As Radman (1997) explains, understanding metaphors tends to require people to "[search] out possible interpretations within the semantic realm of a given world," in so doing evaluating "which property, of all the properties [a] predicate possesses, is the one which fits the metaphorical meaning in the proper way" (11–12). Literal meanings associated with a given source domain are, therefore, not the only meanings potentially relevant—if at all relevant—for a given metaphor. To understand, for instance, that the evocative metaphorical statement, "Misogynists are pigs," requires deducing first that of all the potential properties of pigs their status as animals is relevant, second that of all other potential properties one might map from the pig domain it is their dirty quality that is relevant, and still further one must deduce that the target object is not literally dirty in the soiled sense, but in the figurative moralistic sense. Although ambiguity pervades this metaphor, conventional *sociomental* steps can be taken to reach the social structures of relevance that shape its meaning. Establishing metaphorical meanings, therefore, suggests a *sociocognitive* mapping process of social structures of relevance and irrelevance (Zerubavel 2015a) from sociocultural source domains.

Applying a formal analytic approach to the study of attention, Zerubavel (2015a) argues that what we come to treat as relevant and irrelevant is internalized from attentional socialization within particular social groups. What we ultimately focus on and ignore in our phenomenal worlds is not a natural inevitability, therefore, but is rather taught to us and reinforced through norms, conventions, and traditions of attending, inattending, and disattending social reality. Crucially, this insight about social structures of relevance and irrelevance can be extended to the conceptual domain of metaphor. As evidenced in the "misogynists are pigs" example, what we treat as conceptually relevant and irrelevant in the source domains of pigs comes not from natural or universally recognized elements of pigness, but from how we, as members of Western, English-speaking thought communities, relate to pigs (and dirt) *culturally*. Deep social and historical roots undergird these social meanings and structures of relevance, ostensibly making this metaphorical statement immediately clear only to members of thought communities that share these roots. This centrality of the social group in both metaphorical mapping and understanding begs a deeper theoretical engagement from cognitive sociology.

29.2 Container and Passage Metaphors: The Metaphorical Politics of Access

> Doorknob: "Why it's simply impassable!"
> Alice: "Why, don't you mean impossible?"
> Doorknob: "No, I do mean impassable. Nothing's impossible!"
> —Lewis Carroll, *Alice's Adventures in Wonderland & Through the*
> *Looking-Glass*

Cognitive linguists have long recognized the pervasiveness of container metaphors in everyday speech, conceptual tools individuals use to ground abstract notions in the embodied experience of boundedness (Lakoff and Johnson 1980; Johnson 1987; Charteris-Black 2004). Using the human body, the homes and buildings that house such bodies, or the container generically conceived, individuals frequently describe spatial, temporal, and cultural realms as well as identity, emotions, and thoughts in terms of some form of physical containment. In US foreign relations rhetoric of the mid-twentieth century onward, for example, the modern nation-state is metaphorically framed as a container with political, economic, and cultural *perimeters* in need of *security* from *external threat* and *contamination* or from *leakage* of *internal contents* be they military intelligence, workforce personnel, or innovative scientific ideas (Chilton and Lakoff 1999). The sociologist Santa Ana (2002) explores a powerful instance of such container metaphors in media discourses on immigration in the late twentieth century. In this case, the United States is metaphorically framed as a house[2] whose *walls* are overrun by the powerful *tides* and consequent *flooding* of Latino immigration. Santa Ana uses these metaphors and other related imagery to argue that metaphors played an integral role in the passage of anti-immigrant policies.

In the vastly different substantive domain of emotional life, biological hearts can be thought of as containers protected by emotional *walls* that can *burst* with longing, sadness, or love (Kövecses 2003). Likewise, minds have *limits* that can be *blown* when *boundaries* of knowledge are *torn down* by novelty (Lakoff and Johnson 1980:27–28). Even classificatory categories, which have no concrete counterpart in the physical world, can be conceived of as containers *within* which some material and discursive objects can be *placed* and others conceptually *kept out* (Boot et al. 2012); as such, container metaphors are one method by which "islands of meaning" (Zerubavel 1991) are constructed in social reality, effectively containing meaningful groups of things whether such categorical walls have a natural logic or not. While a number of container types could be recruited to conceptually structure these various domains, according to cognitive linguists, the container that provides the ultimate "preconceptual" basis for understanding these metaphors is the human body, which establishes humans' most basic sense of "in" and "out" (Black 1962; Lakoff and Johnson 1980; Johnson 1987).

Often implied by container metaphors, but less often the central object of study in cognitive linguistic theory is *passage* across the boundaries of containers,[3] like the metaphorical passage so fruitfully analyzed in Santa Ana's case of the *tides* of Latino immigration. If a container can leak or be invaded and secured, then an opening or threshold of some kind is assumed, as is the flow of contents through or across them. Just as the bodily container fosters preconceptual knowledge of "in" and "out," it also provides the experiential basis for understanding *movement* from "in" to "out" and "out" to "in." Pathogens *enter* our bodies, waste *leaves* them, and we *pass* gas *out* of our bodies and *into* the air around us. Crossing, passage, transition, entering, and leaving are thus all experiences that have some universal bodily basis. Accordingly, *passage* and *threshold metaphors* figure prominently in metaphorical conceptualizations of a variety of abstract ideas from scholarly accounts of human cognition and the psyche[4] to everyday accounts of conceptual turning points, such as imminent success, demise, or change. In one of the earliest psychological accounts of consciousness, Freud frames the phenomenon in terms of containers and their thresholds, seeing instincts as flowing along "hallways," only entering the "room" of consciousness when pushing hard enough to cross its "threshold" (1917/1963:295–6). Respectively, threshold metaphors of conceptual turning points abound in everyday speech; a once-unknown Hollywood actor can be described as being on the *cusp* of greatness when approaching a conceptual threshold of fame, animals can be on the *verge* of extinction as their population numbers dwindle toward the ultimate threshold of zero, and progressive politics can usher societies toward a *threshold* of revolution. Such metaphors are understood almost intuitively on the basis of the bodily experience with containment, movement of things in and out of the bodily container, or also bodily movement across natural thresholds such as those where ocean meets land, forest meets clearing, or cliff meets fall.

Door metaphors stand out as a particularly unique class of threshold metaphors because their source domain, while undoubtedly physical and embodied, is imminently *social*. As such, there is more sociocultural nuance conceptually available for metaphorical mapping in this source domain compared with acultural thresholds like edges, cliffs, and clearings. In their source environment, doors do not merely establish openings along boundaries, they signify particular in-out relations between the sides of boundaries. They also serve as symbolic sites of *culturally mediated* passage for the containers in which they are embedded. Since doors are cultural hubs and thus sites of meaning-making and negotiation, access is not merely a matter of mustering enough natural force to pass through; rather, at doors, access and restriction are highly *conditional*, such that cultural rules govern who or what is considered in or out, who or what can pass or not, and the conditions under which someone or something can pass. Such conditionality makes a door an exceedingly political tool both materially on the ground and conceptually in the abstract. Take as examples the metaphorical constructions of spirituality, faith, bodies, and God in the Old Testament as *buildings* whose *doors* individuals must *knock on* in order to gain access (Charteris-Black 2004:202–4). Here, the selection of doors as a metaphorical source domain makes for a much more complex and much more political set of boundary relations in these abstract targets because it opens up the conceptual possibility to impose cultural conditions to access—here, knocks. Trivial as knocks might initially seem, they suggest a great deal about the social statuses of those implicated in an in-out relation. At the most basic level, the convention of knocking suggests that the knocker is "outside" and lacks "insider" status. Thus, to pass from out to in, outsiders are conventionally expected to respect the privacy of the insider by enacting a ritual knock. To appreciate the status-laden distinction here, consider by contrast the cultural absurdity of an individual knocking on her own office door before entering the empty room dedicated only to her or, to return to the Old Testament, an ostensibly almighty God knocking on His own door. Culturally speaking, neither conventions nor permissions are required to access a container one owns or controls. Thus, the inclusion of the concept of knocking in the biblical door metaphors above effectively *politicizes* the relation between the knockers and these spiritual buildings, or more formally, the relation between outsider and insider.

Whereas an acultural threshold only buys the metaphor user the conceptual potential for passage across a divide, the door buys the metaphor user the conceptual potential to additionally plot specific cultural rules and meanings of access and thereby establish *conditional passage* in the abstract. Such conditionality, therefore, makes doors tools for establishing a *metaphorical politics of access.* Moreover, since the built environment in which doors materially manifest is simultaneously spatial and sociocultural, one other theoretical conclusion is that understandings of door metaphors rely on *both* preconceptual embodied experience at thresholds and intersubjective knowledge about doors— their cultural meanings and the rules that govern movement across them—acquired through group membership.

I argue that culture shapes the metaphorical process of door metaphors in two senses then. First, social structures of relevance and irrelevance from particular social groups serve to prestructure the metaphorical mapping process such that only some conceptual elements in the source are treated as culturally relevant, while other elements are treated as irrelevant. Second, the metaphorical process is rendered a potentially political one to the extent that metaphor users leverage the access conditions of the culturally mediated built environment to strategically shape the boundary relations of their targets. In the analysis that follows, I explore each of these claims by applying a formal and pragmatic lens to the sociocognitive process of metaphorical projection.

29.3 A Formal and Pragmatic Approach

To analyze further the case of door metaphors, I draw on a Zerubavelian formal analytic approach to examine the generic ways in which culture shapes both the metaphorical process and its resulting metaphors by analyzing an eclectic range of metaphor cases and contexts of everyday life. Additionally, in the vein of Charteris-Black's critical metaphor analysis (1994), I apply a pragmatic lens to the cases I examine. While cognitive linguists tend to focus solely on the semantic relation between domains (see Ortony 1979/1993; Johnson 1987; Lakoff and Johnson 1980; Black 1962), Charteris-Black argues this leaves vital sociocultural contexts of use and of source domains unaccounted for. Moreover, he asserts that metaphors tend to be "incongruous linguistic representations" ultimately meant to influence opinions of the metaphor's audience (2004:21). Since part of the purpose of metaphor is to strategically persuade, capturing the "pragmatic criteria" of metaphors, or context of use, is important for analyzing the speaker's intentions. In the case of doors, social contexts shape how individuals interact with and use doors and cultural contexts shape how meaning is applied to them. Therefore, I deliberately attend to context to illustrate how meanings of and intentions behind door metaphors emerge in unambiguous ways from the context of their linguistic use and from the sociocultural contexts of doors in the built environment. A pragmatic approach, in contrast to the semantic, is devoted to this analytical dimension of context and, moreover, the *use* of words and objects in those contexts.

If my formal approach can be said to highlight the generic ways in which culture makes its way into the process of metaphorical projection, my pragmatic approach is what highlights the connection between door metaphor use and broader cultural and political ideas about access in the English-speaking context. Both are critical for establishing the dual sociomental processes I argue culture shapes.

29.4 THE FORMAL FEATURES OF DOORS METAPHORS

How individuals construct and understand door metaphors involves both embodied and cultural knowledge from the source domain of doors. In this section, I outline the formal features of the door source domain that emerge from this context-dependent knowledge and systems of relevance, starting first with the embodied, which serves as the foundation of any door metaphor, moving into the cultural, which serves as the modifiable structure of that basic form.

In the discussion of culturally shaped formal dimensions of the door source domain, I emphasize that while a great many features of the door metaphor source could be used to conceptually structure target domains it is ultimately the culturally relevant and socially marked dimensions of that source that are called on to metaphorically shape a given target realm. Of all the properties that could be relevant and meaningful at doors—the type of door, its height and weight, or whether it is open or closed, to name a few potential dimensions—only some properties appear in a regular fashion in door metaphors. That these particular dimensions constitute *generic* features of door metaphors, suggests common, moreover *shared*, ways of behaving toward and applying meaning to doors. That is, the formal cultural features of the door source domain suggest that door metaphor users share social structures of both relevance and irrelevance as well as markedness and unmarkedness.

29.4.1 Embodied Formal Features

As established in earlier sections, the embodied basis of door metaphors is derived from our preconceptual experience with containment and passage across thresholds. Thus, any door metaphor will include the basic elements of containers and thresholds. More specifically, every door metaphor features one or more containers and at least one door embedded in the boundary of a container. Such formal features set up the conceptual relation between in and out as well as the conceptual possibility of passage from one side of a boundary to another.

While door metaphors explicitly use the conceptual structure of a door to express some abstract politics of access, the importance of the containers in door metaphors should not be overlooked. Doors imply boundaries of some particular contained domain and thus, the abstract target containers to which doors lead in door metaphors—be they hearts, countries, or heaven, to name a random sample—represent substantive areas where access, as a social issue, matters or is at stake. While metaphors about doors to hearts, countries, and heaven each refer to boundary relations of substantively different realms, the commonality of doors across metaphorical cases suggests to us that the social phenomenon, if not problem, of access is germane to each of those metaphorically contained domains. Generally speaking, the containers referred to or implied by door metaphors can tell us a lot about where in social life access is relevant and important to the individuals and social groups who employ them.

29.4.2 Cultural Formal Features

In contrast to the embodied formal features of this metaphorical source domain—containers and thresholds—the culturally shaped formal features of door metaphors are derived from patterned interaction with and social marking of doors. Forms of cultural mediation in door metaphors, be they conventions, credentials, or gatekeeping, have roots in the goings-on of everyday boundary relations. Particular cultural meanings in door metaphors, like the significance of an open versus a closed door and a front versus back door, likewise have roots in the meaning-making and meaning–maintenance efforts of everyday life.

29.4.2.1 *Cultural Mediation at Doors*

At doors not all bodily experiences are created equal. While the containers that hold doors can be understood preconceptually based on a universal sense of "in," "out," and "through," the manner in which one comes to be inside, outside, or to pass through a particular container is often not natural, but contingent on a variety of cultural constraints be they rules, limits, requirements, or conventions. When seeking entry to privileged domains, for instance, one might need to offer certain social credentials to a gatekeeper, as exemplified by the doors of workplaces and schools that require identification cards to confirm social membership before granting passage. Similarly, access to other privileged containers require material credentials at doors, as is the case with "cover charges" at bars or proof of payment at ticketed performances. Still others might require symbolic credentials like secret passwords for entry to private events or meetings. In other cases, access is restricted even more selectively by requiring not a credential to a gatekeeper, but a physical key, whereby only the most privileged of that container can gain entry when its door is locked. There are other doors, however, at which access is easily granted with a conventional knock to honor the privacy of those within the room, as illustrated by knocks subordinates initiate at their bosses' office doors and the knocks children are encouraged to enact at the bedroom doors of their parents before entering.

Beyond the variety of cultural rules we tacitly adhere to at particular doors, we learn there are also temporal restrictions to access that qualify these rules still further, such that the very same bar door that required a cover charge the night before requires no material credential during "happy hour" the next day and the same convenience store door that required but a pull at noon requires a key at midnight. Likewise, rules and behavior change in different situational contexts, such that a boss's door can be passed through knockless, so to speak, when one is the boss herself, and the door at which one gave a password to a gatekeeper for one event is assumed accessible to all when a gatekeeper is not present. Thus, rules and behaviors can change at particular doors depending on who one is, to whom and what one seeks access, and when access is sought. In order to gain access one might need to negotiate with a gatekeeper, provide or embody a credential, or employ a culturally appropriate convention, contextually defined. Although it is taken for granted, this nuanced intersubjective knowledge shapes how we behave at doors and, for the purposes of metaphor, what we come to consider relevant at doors as potential metaphorical grounding devices.

29.4.2.2 *Symbolism at Doors*

In addition to the cultural shaping of behavior at doors, there are also ways in which social groups shape meaning at doors through social marking and symbolism. Doors carry a wealth of symbolic meaning because they are *marked semiotic objects*. Marked semiotic objects are objects that figure prominently—phenomenally and conceptually—against irrelevant, unremarkable counterparts or surroundings; they are considered special, exceptional, or strange features by virtue of social markedness, which is defined and its intensity measured with respect to particular groups and particular social contexts. As with all marked semiotic objects, doors have the quality of constituting a small proportion of their empirical dimension—fixed-feature space—relative to an unmarked majority—walls—and yet they garner substantially more attention and directed action from social actors (Zerubavel 2015b; Brekhus 1998; Waugh 1982), as the many ritualized behaviors at doors discussed earlier show. Therefore, as individuals approach a given building or room, their behavior, attention, and interpretations of the situation tend to be centered on doors. Moreover, particular features of doors can be more heavily marked than others; while changes to the color and material of a door are rarely accompanied with differences in meaning, the positions of doors—slightly open, wide open, closed without a lock, closed with a lock and unlocked, closed and locked—and the locations of doors—front, side, and back—come with critical symbolic distinctions, at least in the American cultural context.

The positions of doors, although physical distinctions, convey different cultural messages about the containers in which doors are found and the dynamics of access at those social thresholds. Depending on context, open doors can be symbolically inviting and welcoming, as is the case with the open door to a business during operating hours. Open doors can also convey the concepts of access and potential, as exemplified by the iconic open "door of opportunity." In other situational contexts, however, when the other side of a slightly open door is unknown or presumed dangerous, such doors can symbolize mystery, threat, or vulnerability, as illustrated by the heavy leveraging of such symbolism in American horror films (Rockett 1982). At the other end of the position spectrum, closed doors, too, are associated with context-dependent meanings and concepts. They can communicate temporary and permanent restriction, as evidenced by their strong symbolic presence in political discourse on migration (Chilton and Ilyin 1993) and they can also convey the concept of privacy (Schwartz 1968:746). Yet in other contexts, even closed and locked doors can symbolize the promising notion of opportunity when viewed against the conceptual backdrop of a daunting, definitive wall. Thus, beyond the material fact of their position, doors in their varying degrees of openness and closure convey myriad collectively understood meanings.

The locations of doors also carry differential symbolic weight in the source domain. Whereas front doors are conventionally considered appropriate points of entry, side and back doors are generally nontraditional and thus are socially marked. Back doors, in particular, signify less preferred, deviant, or even socially inferior means of entry, serving as access points only for those *unwelcome*, be they individuals lacking social privileges or deliberate transgressors. Although location has no functional bearing on the embodied experience of passing through doors, *socially marked* locations and the marked social statuses that accompany them shape the symbolic experience with doors in significant ways. To invoke the location of a door in metaphorical statements about access, therefore, is to conjure up culturally shaped mental associations imbued in doors by particular cultural communities on the ground. While cognitive linguists have examined the embodied basis for front and back distinctions such as these, which often manifest in TIME AS SPACE metaphors—"moving *ahead*" and "falling *behind*"' it is important to note here the deeply cultural, status-laden distinction between front, side, and back. Such distinctions in this semantic realm are not natural or embodied, but rather reflect sociosemiotic traditions (Zerubavel 2016) of applying meaning to our world, shared not by all groups, but by particular groups.

29.4.3 Resolving Ambiguity

Figure 29.1 summarizes the formal features of doors as metaphorical source domains, which constitute both the bodily basis and sociocultural basis for meaning in this complex semantic realm. At the most basic and universal level, door metaphors are built upon embodied experiences with containment and threshold crossing. All door metaphors, therefore, have at least the basic formal properties of a container and a threshold,

Embodied Formal Features	Modifiable Formal Features	Formal Modifiers
Container	Container*	

Door	Type**	Standard, hinged
		  Swinging
		  Screen
		  Automatic
		Sliding
		Revolving[i]

	Location	Front Side Back

	Position	Open
		  Continuous variable
		  ranging from
		  slightly open to
		  wide open
		Closed without lock
		Closed with lock
		  Unlocked
		  Locked

	Cultural Mediation	Conditions
		  Gatekeeper(s)
		    Individual
		    Collective
		    Symbolic
		  Credentials
		    Social
		    Material
		    Symbolic
		  Conventions
		    Knocking
		    Bowing[ii]

FIGURE 29.1 Formal Structure of the Door Metaphor Source Domain

* Since doors provide or do not provide access to some container, specifying the containers in a door metaphor is essentially specifying the metaphor's target domain. For example, specifying the container as OPPORTUNITY implies that the speaker is using the concreteness of a door to develop an access metaphor about the abstract idea of opportunity. The door is the source and opportunity is the target of metaphorical preojection.

** Door types can be specified further by physical dimensions of height, width, depth, and weight, color, and by attachments such as door bells, doorknobs, handles, handle bars, door closers, peep holes, and signs. I highlight *functional* types, which despite their physical dimensions and attachments which rely on the universal experience of "in" and "out" and transition between realms. Some door metaphors rely solely on the experiential, universally understood basis of these basic structures. Figurative actions like "erupting through a door," "crashing through a door," or "leaking through a door" draw from understandings of natural forces that inevitably give way to passage across thresholds out of and into any number of conceptual containers.

Examining the sociocultural context of the source domain of doors, on the other hand, suggests that the choices of metaphor users are prestructured not only by embodied preconceptual schemas but also by groups' social structures of relevance and irrelevance as well as markedness and unmarkedness. Such social structures give shape to an otherwise chaotic semantic realm, bringing some features of this source domain to the phenomenal and conceptual fore, while passively rendering a great many features of it conceptually irrelevant. As was the case with Holland and Quinn's cultural models (1987) and Yu's cultural filters (2008), so too in the case of door metaphors, sociocultural contexts intervene to constrain the possibilities of our everyday access metaphors.

In contrast to the door metaphors that draw only from the embodied formal properties of containers and thresholds, many other door metaphors are constructed on an ad hoc basis by *modifying* the culturally shaped formal properties of the source domain, a process similar to what Chilton and Ilyin term "particularization" (1993:13). Formal dimensions like the positions of the door—open, closed without a lock, unlocked, locked—the locations of the door—front, side, back—and the cultural conditions that

---

FIGURE 29.1 Continued

will necessarily impact movement. While most door metaphors imply a standard hinged door, other types could be called upon to establish different access relations in target domains.

[i] While I focus the discussion of metaphorical politics of access on the cultural elements of doors in built spaces, revolving door metaphors stand out as a particularly useful case of how modifying the type of door used in a door metaphor can yield substantially different meaning. Revolving door metaphors suggest bidirectional access, a funneling of people or things in and out and back in and out of the same two conceptual containers. The containers choices matter greatly for establishing the social status of actors in these metaphors. C. Wright Mills' 'revolving door' of the power elite, for example, was theorized to produce centralization of power by funneling elites in and out of core decision-making domains. It is no coincidence, therefore, that the actors implicated in the metaphor are elites since the containers of his metaphor are powerful domains. By contrast, consider the 'revolving door of prison,' conventionally used to capture the problem of recidivism. Since prison is a powerless domain, the actors metaphorically funneled in this metaphor are powerless, too. This metaphor, but in particular the choice of its revolving door, produces an evocative image of recidivists as trapped in a powerless condition.

[ii] Although this chapter is concerned with the American cultural context, it is worth acknowledging other cultural conventions that could constitute the formal structure of a door metaphor source domain in another context. The entry rituals of Japanese tearooms, for example, involve bowing reverently before entering a small knee-level high door – *nijiriguchi* – that is kept only partially open to incoming guests. The slightly open door sends the cultural message that guests are only conditionally welcome initially and, as a physical, but also normative necessity, they must humble themselves before entering the tearoom by bending over to clear the small doorway, in the process reverently bowing to the elders of the home (Knight 1981).

mediate access through the door—gatekeepers, credentials, and conventions—come to constitute the collectively held structure of relevance and meaning in the source domain, such that these dimensions are called on and modified over and above many other potential elements of the source. While some ambiguities of meaning may remain, analyzing the context of doors' use and meaning in everyday life takes us far in resolving ambiguity and the persistent question of what is likely to be projected from source to target domain when we use a given metaphor.

29.5 SHAPING THE METAPHORICAL POLITICS OF ACCESS

As the sociocultural context of doors shows, what might seem like purely functional differences in the formal structure of the door source domain—like the difference between an open door and a closed one or the difference in locating a door at the front versus the back of a building—slight material modifications in the door domain are often accompanied by substantial cultural differences of meaning. This suggests two distinct things. First, this suggests that social relations and cultural practice in the built environment—manifest in inscribed social structures of relevance and irrelevance, in sociosemiotic traditions of markedness, and in cultural conventions—constrain our conceptual world, paving mental paths toward specific *cultural forms of access*, while passively closing off paths to others. How we metaphorically structure access in abstract target domains not only is a sociomental act but also corresponds systematically to these prestructured cultural forms.

Second, the formal structure of the door source domain suggests that doors are uniquely suited to metaphorically capture abstract boundary relations in strategic ways. Given its modifiable form, individuals can deliberately and creatively configure the conceptual structure of the source domain, impose particular cultural meanings and rules to an abstract target realm, and thereby shape the *metaphorical politics of access* in that realm. The metaphorical act, therefore, involves a selective recruiting process of target-relevant properties from this experientially complex source domain; such *conceptual spotlighting*[5] draws the interpreter's attention to particular ways of conceptualizing access while excluding others.

Analyzing a handful of cases, I outline three cultural forms of access that derive systematically from particular configurations of the door source domain as well as the strategies implied by those metaphorical choices. In each door metaphor case, there is a container, or more than one container, and a threshold; however, there is also one or more modified formal properties of the source domain. Although a metaphor user may modify the type, location, and position of the door as well as the kind and degree of cultural mediation present in the grounded source domain, users do not necessarily select and modify all properties. On the contrary, I show that individuals are selective about the properties they recruit and modify to ground access in the target domain at hand and that those creative choices are tools for politicizing target domains in patterned ways.

29.5.1 Deviant Access

One way in which metaphor users can shape the politics of access in abstract target domains is by leveraging and modifying the location property of the door source domain. In modifying that dimension by specifying whether the door is located at the front, side, or back of the metaphorical container, metaphor users can culturally mark the metaphorical door of that target realm as a deviant means to access, in so doing implicating the metaphorical actor that seeks access that way. Such skewing of meaning from source to target is a metaphorical instance of "asymmetrical semiotization" (Zerubavel 2016). Back doors are culturally marked and thus stand in asymmetrical relation to front doors, which are unmarked and socially generic. Given the systematic relation between domains, marking the source necessarily marks the target, as evidenced here:

> The TPP is a horrible deal. It is a deal that is going to lead to nothing but trouble. It's a deal that was designed for China to come in, as they always do, through the back door and totally take advantage of everyone.
> — Donald Trump, Republican Presidential Debate (November 10, 2015)

In this complex door metaphor, Donald Trump conceptualizes the US economy as a metaphorical container and China as an actor that seeks deviant access to trade within it. By summoning the door location of all formal properties of the door source domain, and further by modifying that property, Trump adds semiotic asymmetry to the target realm, shaping the issue of access there in deviant terms. While specifying the location of a door should have no functional bearing on passage through doors, when particular meanings are applied to those locations, they can shape and in this case politicize social relations even in the abstract domain of international economic exchange.

Back door metaphors are also pervasive in the abstract domain of digital cryptography and cyber security. In this realm, container schemas like WEB AS NETWORK OF CONTAINERS or INTERNET AS HOME (Froomkin 1995) yield a variety of spatially grounded metaphorical terms including "fire*walls*," which establish virtual barriers between secure and unaccounted for networks (Oppliger 1997), "keys," which *lock in* cipher text in the process of data encryption, and "backdoors," which act as cloaked means of *invasion into* otherwise protected systems (Wysopal et al. 2010). Virtual backdoors are metaphors for deviant access because they are grounded on semiotic asymmetry in the source domain of doors. Although it is tempting to treat these metaphorical meanings as unambiguous, the foundation of that meaning is ultimately cultural.

29.5.2 Potentials of Access

Another cultural form of access individuals construct from the modifiable source domain of doors is the notion of potentials of access, which derive primarily from the formal property of door position. Take, for example, Barack Obama's use of door metaphor, which suggests that access to the abstract realm of opportunity might be a quantifiable and controllable measure of potential:

> The test was not, and never has been, whether the doors of opportunity are cracked a bit wider for a few. It was whether our economic system provides a fair shot for the many.
>> — President Barack Obama, Commemorative Speech for the
>> 50th Anniversary of the March on Washington (August 28, 2013)

Here, opportunity is conceptualized as a container and the door to opportunity is conceptualized as open. In this case, the open door is symbolically inviting, but given the allusion to the *scope* of that invitation, the metaphor suggests that the potential to access opportunity can be conceived of as disproportionately distributed. That is, potentials to access opportunity could reasonably vary based on social status. To accomplish this meaning, Obama draws from the physical properties of narrowness and wideness of an open door that can be modified in ways that correspond to symbolic shifts of meaning. Presumably, if the door is cracked open widely, it symbolizes greater access to opportunity and if the door is cracked open only slightly, it symbolizes lesser access to opportunity. Such leveraging of doors' positions thus is a tool for shaping politics of access in the abstract conceptual domain of opportunity.

Consider by symbolic contrast the lack of potential to access that can be mapped onto the domain of opportunity by summoning a *closed* door in statements like "slamming closed the door of opportunity." Such a door metaphor suggests the very same metaphorical container as the previous example, but builds into the source domain a closed door to suggest limits to potential. By leveraging the symbolic discontinuity closed doors establish in their source domain, a metaphor user can conceptually spotlight the ability to block off access.

29.5.3 Culturally Mediated Access

Finally, door metaphor users can politicize their various abstract target domains by introducing a form of cultural mediation at doors, be it a convention, a credential, or a gatekeeper. Gatekeeping is a particularly salient cultural form of access with metaphorical roots as far back as the Bible. Charteris-Black (2004) notes in his critical analysis of metaphors that "building metaphors" are pervasive in the Old and New Testaments. Take, for example, one passage in which the metaphor user constructs the metaphorical politics of access to the abstract domain of God's grace by introducing God as its gatekeeper:

So I say to you: Ask and it will be given to you; seek and you will find; knock and the door will be opened to you.

— Luke 11:9 (New International Version Bible)

Although there are a variety of source properties that could be used to structure this abstract realm, the ones selected and modified here are the most basic formal properties—container and threshold—and two sociocultural formal properties—door position and door mediation. Here, the metaphorical building is God's grace, it is fashioned with a door that is closed, thus communicating a block of access, the door is mediated exclusively by God, a symbolic gatekeeper, and will be opened only if the individual who seeks access solicits it with a ritual knock. The door metaphor is useful here not purely because of doors' instrumental functions to connect realms, but because gatekeeping and cultural conventions of knocking, otherwise irrelevant to the function of doors, are formal properties of the semantic realm of doors in our built environment that help describe the politics of access in this target domain. Such modifying of the cultural mediation feature in the source and projecting of cultural mediation on the target domain is yet another way in which doors can be used to shape metaphorical politics of access in the abstract.

29.6 TOWARD A COGNITIVE SOCIOLOGY OF ACCESS

While the concepts of cultural models (Holland and Quinn 1987) and filters (Yu 2008) appear to capture a similar phenomenon that I term cultural forms, the pragmatic approach I offer, which explicitly attends to sociocultural contexts in the source domain of the object leveraged for metaphor use, suggests a mechanism for the development of these socioculturally derived forms. Cultural forms, in other words, do not appear out of thin air. In this case of doors, cultural and social processes of meaning-making and practice among particular groups in the built environment shape this otherwise purely embodied metaphorical source domain. Rather than black-box the role of culture, I investigate how cultural forms might get their structure from the groups who create and maintain them through ritual and linguistic use. By examining varied sociocultural contexts in the source domain, I deduce formal generic features of this realm that emerge from social structures of both relevance and irrelevance as well as markedness and unmarkedness. By virtue of the role of these social structures of thought, of more general theoretical significance beyond the case of doors is that the process of metaphorical projection is distinctly *sociomental*.

As the analysis of target domains shows, access is not a singular notion, nor a universally defined one. Access is defined and organized by particular social groups and doors are powerful social tools for doing so. At the same time, how access is culturally defined and organized around doors on the ground is conceptually useful to individuals who seek not only to make sense of highly abstract realms, but to strategically politicize access and boundary relations within them. Only by applying a pragmatic lens to door use and metaphor use does it become clear that door metaphors do not simply establish conceptual relations between realms but also involve a sociomental process of shaping political boundary relations in various target domains.

Doors have been symbols of access since the earliest moments of human civilization. Janus, the Roman god of beginnings, ends, and transition was also the god of doors and gates, managing access and restriction of holy and imperial domains (Hamilton 1942). In ancient Egypt, "false doors" mediated the symbolic and presumed physical threshold between the dead and the living (Bard 1999). Doors have also been architecturally inscribed access points in institutional hierarchies for millennia (Stevenson Smith 1958/1998); doors—the multitudes through which one must pass to move through institutional hierarchies—continue to have salience today in the bureaucratic mode of modern societies. These deeply historical objects are simultaneously physical, social, and symbolic. But doors can also transcend their grounded sociospatial origins and serve as the conceptual foundation for shaping *abstract* politics of access through metaphor.

Moreover, access is a pervasive concern in social life. It is a phenomenon of critical importance in the domains of migration and immigration, education and healthcare, jobs and housing, and even interpersonal and inner life. If countries, neighborhoods, homes, jobs, thoughts, feelings, and ideas related to these domains can be metaphorically conceptualized as containers, then, social actors can use the rich semantic domains of doors to plot access to them. This encompassing substantive relevance of access coupled with the formal sociological insights provided here, suggest that boundary relations operate on deeply cognitive and generic levels. What is more, doors are just *one* conceptual tool of built spaces for establishing such boundary relations—buildings, homes, walls, windows, ceilings, floors, closets, drawers, and even curtains, mundane as they may seem, all do conceptual boundary setting for us of some kind. These reflections warrant a dedicated cognitive sociology of access that attends explicitly to the theoretical links between the built environment, language, culture, and thought. Mapping the conceptual and symbolic structure of our culturally marked and mediated spaces is important, therefore, if not only to appreciate these overlapping processes of culture and cognition more broadly but also to investigate the sociocognitive underpinnings of our ideas about access in these disparate substantive realms.

Notes

1. As is the style convention of the cognitive linguistic tradition, phrases that appear in all capital letters in this chapter refer to conceptual metaphors. Metaphorical statements appear in regular quotes.
2. Chilton and Ilyin (1993) offer another notable account of the metaphorical use of the house to contain nations. In the European political discourse of the 1980s, the house was used as an active building metaphor (as in the verb "to build") in some cases and as a container requiring the management of access and restriction in others.

3. Quinn 1991 is a notable exception. Quinn argues that containment metaphors have both embodied and sociocultural bases and, further, that containment and passage in and out of containers can also be thought of as events embedded in social relations and cultural contexts.

4. For threshold metaphors in psychological accounts of inner life in general, see Leary (1990) and Jager (1996). For threshold metaphors in psychological accounts of discrimination and perception see Corso (1956), and in accounts of consciousness, see Bruner and Fleisher Feldman (1990) and Freud 1917/1963.

5. I borrow the concept of spotlighting from Zerubavel (2015a), who describes it as a method of structuring phenomenal and moral attention by foregrounding a particular element against a presumed irrelevant "background." Here, I argue door metaphor users engage in conceptual spotlighting by drawing attention to some elements of the conceptual structure of access in the source domain and not others.

REFERENCES

Bard, Kathryn A. 1999. *Encyclopedia of the Archaeology of Ancient Egypt*. New York: Routledge.

Black, Max. 1962. *Models and Metaphors: Studies in Language and Philosophy*. Ithaca, NY: Cornell University Press.

Boot, Diane, Inge Pecher, and Saskia Dantzig. 2012. "Abstract Concepts: Sensory-Motor Grounding, Metaphors, and Beyond." pp. 217–48 in *The Psychology of Learning and Motivation*, edited by Brian H. Ross. Oxford: Elsevier.

Brekhus, Wayne. 1998. "Sociology of the Unmarked: Redirecting our Focus." *Sociological Theory* 16(1):34–51.

Brekhus, Wayne H. 2015. *Culture and Cognition: Patterns in the Social Construction of Reality*. Cambridge: Polity Press.

Bruner, Jerome, and Carol Fleisher Feldman. 1990. "Metaphors of Consciousness and Cognition in the History of Psychology." pp. 230–38 in *Metaphors in the History of Psychology*, edited by David E. Leary. Cambridge: Cambridge University Press.

Charteris-Black, Jonathan. 2004. *Corpus Approaches to Critical Metaphor Analysis*. New York: Palgrave MacMillan.

Chilton, Paul, and Mikhail Ilyin. 1993. "Metaphor in Political Discourse: The Case of the 'Common European House.'" *Discourse and Society* 4(1):7–31.

Chilton, Paul, and George Lakoff. 1999. "Foreign Policy by Metaphor." pp. 37–59 in *Language and Peace*, edited by Christina Schäffner and Anita L. Wenden. Amsterdam: Harwood Academic.

Corso, John F. 1956. "The Neural Quantum Theory of Sensory Discrimination." *Psychological Bulletin* 53(5): 371–93.

Cousineau, Matthew. 2014. "Discursive Resources in the Everyday Construction of Engineering." Dissertation, Columbia: University of Missouri.

Davidson, Donald. 1978. "What Metaphors Mean." *Critical Inquiry* 5(1):31–47.

Fleck, Ludwik. 1979. *The Genesis and Development of a Scientific Fact*. Chicago: University of Chicago Press.

Freud, Sigmund. 1917/1963. *The Standard Edition of the Complete Psychological Works of Sigmund Freud, Vol. 16. Introductory Lectures on Psycho-Analysis*, edited and translated by J. Strachey. London: Hogarth Press.

Froomkin, A. Michael. 1995. "Metaphor Is the Key: Cryptography, the Clipper Chip, and the Constitution." *University of Pennsylvania Law Review* 143(3):709.

Gibbs, Raymond W. 1997. "Taking Metaphor Out of Our Heads and Putting It into the Cultural World." pp. 145–66 in *Metaphor in Cognitive Linguistics*, edited by Raymond W. Gibbs Jr. and Gerard J. Steen. Amsterdam: John Benjamins.

Hamilton, Edith. 1942. *Mythology*. Boston; New York; London: Little Brown.

Holland, Dorothy, and Naomi Quinn, eds. 1987. *Cultural Models in Language and Thought*. New York: Cambridge University Press.

Ignatow, Gabriel. 2003. "'Idea Hamsters' on the 'Bleeding Edge': Profane Metaphors in High Technology Jargon." *Poetics* 31(1):1–22.

Ignatow, Gabriel. 2009. "Culture and Embodied Cognition: Moral Discourses in Internet Support Groups for Overeaters." *Social Forces* 88(2):643–69.

Jager, Bernd. 1996. "The Obstacle and the Threshold: Two Fundamental Metaphors Governing the Natural and Human Sciences." *Journal of Phenomenological Psychology* 27(1):26–48.

Johnson, Mark. 1987. *The Body in the Mind: The Bodily Basis of Meaning, Imagination, and Reason*. Chicago; London: University of Chicago Press.

Kato, Yuki. 2011. "Coming of Age in the Bubble: Suburban Adolescent's Use of a Spatial Metaphor as a Symbolic Boundary." *Symbolic Interaction* 34(2):244–64.

Knight, T. W. 1981. "The Forty-One Steps." *Environment and Planning B* 8(1):97–114.

Kövecses, Zoltán. 2003. *Metaphor and Emotion: Language, Culture, and Body in Human Feeling*. Cambridge; New York: Cambridge University Press.

Lakoff, George, and Mark Johnson. 1980. *Metaphors We Live By*. Chicago; London: University of Chicago Press.

Leary, David E., ed. 1990. *Metaphors in the History of Psychology*. Cambridge: Cambridge University Press.

Mills, C. Wright. 1956. *The Power Elite*. New York: Oxford University Press.

Oppliger, Rolf. 1997. "Internet Security: Firewalls and Beyond." *Communications of the ACM*. 40(5):94.

Ortony, Andrew. 1979/1993. "Metaphor, language, and thought." pp. 1–16 in *Metaphor and Thought*, edited by Andrew Ortony. Cambridge: Cambridge University Press.

Quinn, Naomi. 1987. "Convergent Evidence for a Cultural Model of American Marriage." pp. 173–92 in *Cultural Models in Language and Thought*, edited by Dorothy Holland and Naomi Quinn. New York: Cambridge University Press.

Quinn, Naomi. 1991. "The Cultural Basis of Metaphor." pp. 56–93 in *Beyond Metaphor: The Theory of Tropes in Anthropology*, edited by J. W. Fernandez. Standford, CA: Stanford University Press.

Radman, Zdravko. 1997. *Metaphors: Figures of the Mind*. Dordrecht: Kluwer Academic.

Rockett, W. H. 1982. "The Door Ajar: Structure and Convention in Horror Films That Would Terrify." *Journal of Popular Film and Television* 10(3):130–36.

Rodgers, Diane M. 2008. *Debugging the Link between Social Theory and Social Insects*. Baton Rouge: Louisiana State University Press.

Santa Ana, Otto. 2002. *Brown Tide Rising: Metaphors of Latinos in Contemporary American Public Discourse*. Austin: University of Texas Press.

Schwartz, Barry. 1968. "The Social Psychology of Privacy." *American Journal of Sociology* 73(6):741–52.

Stevenson Smith, W. 1958/1998. *The Art and Architecture of Ancient Egypt*. New Haven, CT; London: Yale University Press.

Waugh, Linda R. 1982. "Marked and Unmarked: A Choice between Unequals in Semiotic Structure." *Semiotica* 38(3/4):299–318.

Winchester, Daniel. 2008. "Embodying the Faith: Religious Practice and the Making of a Muslim Moral Habitus." *Social Forces* 86(4):1753–80.

Wittgenstein, Ludwig. 1953. *Philosophical Investigations*. Oxford: Blackwell.

Wysopal, Chris, C. Eng, and T. Shields. 2010. "Static Detection of Application Backdoors." *Datenschutz und Datensicherheit—DuD* 34(3):149–55.

Yu, Ning. 2008. "Metaphor from Body and Culture." pp. 247–68 in *The Cambridge Handbook of Metaphor and Thought*, edited by Raymond W. Gibbs Jr. Cambridge: Cambridge University Press.

Zerubavel, Eviatar. 1991. *The Fine Line: Making Distinctions in Everyday Life*. Chicago; London: Chicago University Press.

Zerubavel, Eviatar. 1997. *Social Mindscapes: An Invitation to Cognitive Sociology*. Cambridge, MA: Harvard University Press.

Zerubavel, Eviatar. 2015a. *Hidden in Plain Sight: The Social Structure of Irrelevance*. New York: Oxford University Press.

Zerubavel, Eviatar. 2015b. "Semiotic Asymmetry: A Sociological Perspective." Presentation at Annual Meeting of the American Sociological Association, Chicago, Illinois, August 2015.

Zerubavel, Eviatar. 2016. "The Marked and the Unmarked: Toward a Sociology of Cognitive Asymmetry." Presentation at Annual Meeting of the American Sociological Association, Seattle, Washington, August 2016.

PART VI

CATEGORIES, BOUNDARIES, AND IDENTITIES

CHAPTER 30

FOREGROUNDING AND BACKGROUNDING

the logic and mechanics of semiotic subversion

EVIATAR ZERUBAVEL

WHEN telling people that he was studying suburban gays, writes Wayne Brekhus, "I was often asked if I am gay. No one ever asked, however, if I was suburban" (2003:12), thereby tacitly revealing the far greater cultural salience attached to certain aspects of a person's identity than others. Yet why is being gay conventionally considered more culturally salient than being suburban? By the same token, why is the term "working mom" far more widely used than its nominally equivalent counterpart "working dad"? Answering such questions presupposes a fundamental semiotic distinction between *markedness* and *unmarkedness*.

In sharp contrast to the marked, which is explicitly accented, the unmarked remains essentially unarticulated (Brekhus 2003:14). As such, it resembles the default option on a computer menu. Effectively based on some *default assumption*, it is thus basically *taken for granted* (Zerubavel 2018).

Although unmarkedness is often associated with "normality" (and markedness with "abnormality" or "deviance"), these are not inherent qualities but products of unmistakably politicosemiotic processes of *normalization* and *abnormalization* (Foucault 1975/2003; Zerubavel 2018:44–50). By marking a particular type of person or behavior, we thus imply that it is somewhat "abnormal" and cannot therefore be assumed by default and taken for granted, thereby tacitly also attributing normality to what we leave unmarked.

Yet our sense of normality can also be subverted by drawing attention to what is "normally" assumed and thus taken for granted (Zerubavel 2015:82–89). That requires, of course, "abnormalizing" what is conventionally considered normal instead of taking it for granted.

30.1 Marking the Unmarked

What we mark or leave unmarked is often similar to what others around us do, thereby suggesting that those are more than just personal acts (Zerubavel 2018:21–24). Yet the choices we make in doing so are by no means universal (Zerubavel 2018:24–26). It is a *social* rather than some universal logic, for example, that leads us to consider being gay a particularly salient aspect of someone's identity while ignoring his suburbanness as essentially irrelevant. The distinction between markedness and unmarkedness is thus an unmistakably *sociocognitive* rather than strictly logical one.

It is thus as social beings rather than as individuals or as humans that we set most of our cognitive defaults. What we consider marked and unmarked (and therefore also what we do not or do take for granted) is ultimately a product of particular cognitive traditions and conventions that vary across cultures, among different subcultures, and across different social situations within a given society.

They also vary historically, with major shifts in what we consider "ordinary" (rather than "special" or "unusual") and thereby assume by default thus reflecting significant cultural shifts in the way we think (Zerubavel 2018:92–98). Such changes may occur spontaneously over time, yet they may also be a product of deliberate *semiotic subversion*.

There is a fundamental asymmetry (Waugh 1982; see also Brekhus 1996) between the culturally marked, which is semiotically "weighty" (see also Mullaney 1999), and the unmarked, which is not. Such *semiotic asymmetry*, however, is sometimes deliberately subverted through the use of a cognitive tactic specifically designed to alter the conventional relations between the two pans of the proverbial balance scale. Such a tactic involves *marking the conventionally unmarked* (Brekhus 1998:43–45) thereby making it semiotically weighty. It also implies making it explicit.

That requires, however, "educat[ing] the senses to *see the ordinary as extraordinary [and] the familiar as strange*," as the eighteenth-century poet Friedrich von Hardenberg, or Novalis, put it (Beiser 1998:294, emphasis added), since only when the familiar is "estranged" can we actively notice it. Noticing the unmarked, in other words, presupposes a cognitive process explicitly identified by Victor Shklovsky as *defamiliarization* or "estrangement" (1917/1965).

As a "conscious attempt to achieve a new look at the same old world," defamiliarization involves "distort[ing], invert[ing], or transpos[ing] the everyday ways of looking... which render the world a...familiar place" (Gordon 1961:34). In other words, it constitutes an effort to *notice what is habitually taken for granted* (which implies refraining from simply presuming what we habitually do) as well as *make the implicit explicit*.

That requires, of course, a more deliberative mode of cognizing (DiMaggio 1997:271–2) than our habitual, effectively automatic (Deikman 1966; see also Shklovsky 1917/1965) one. In other words, it presupposes a process of cognitive *deautomatization* (Deikman 1966:329; see also Shklovsky 1917/1965:11), which entails "problematizing" (Schutz 1932/1967:74) our taken-for-granted, default assumptions. Such deautomatization involves turning the proverbial spotlight on what we habitually ignore (Zerubavel 2006:65–68; Zerubavel 2015:82–89).

What we mark and therefore explicitly notice is proportionally smaller than what we leave unmarked and thereby tacitly ignore (Zerubavel 2015:23). The marked regions of our phenomenal world, in other words, receive glaringly disproportionate cultural attention relative to their size, whereas the typically larger unmarked ones receive hardly any notice at all (Brekhus 1996:518). Marking thus "strangles [our] awareness [by] limit[ing] us to seeing only a fraction of what there is to be seen" (Brown 1984:154–6). *Foregrounding* the unmarked, by contrast, expands it.

30.2 THE POLITICS OF FOREGROUNDING

Foregrounding plays a major role in the epistemically subversive process of *awareness raising* (Zerubavel 2006:64–68). A lexical marking of traditionally unmarked concepts, for instance, is an unmistakably political statement designed to challenge their presumed cultural redundancy and therefore semiotic superfluity.

As a semiotic *eye-opener* (Zerubavel 2006:65, 73–74; Zerubavel 2015:84), the act of *naming* helps foreground the conventionally unmarked (Brekhus 1998:45). The terms "carnism" and "speciesism," for example, are thus specifically designed to foreground and thereby challenge the presumed normality of the conventionally unnamed cultural opposites of vegetarianism and animal-rights activism. Using the term "asexuality" to signify "a lack of sexual attraction" and therefore the "rejection of sexual contact...as a necessary, fundamental, or innate component of...human experience" is likewise designed to challenge the presumed normality of sexual desire and thus "the equation of sexuality with wellbeing" (Brown 2014).

Along similar lines, consider also the semiotically subversive act of explicitly marking the notion of whiteness, as when using the term "historically white colleges" (Bonilla-Silva 2012) to foreground (and thereby tacitly challenge the presumed normality of) the culturally redundant and therefore semiotically superfluous counterpart of the conventional term "historically black colleges," or when Morgan Freeman, having been asked in an interview about Black History Month, sarcastically asked back, "Which month is *White* History Month?"[1] His allusion to the cultural presence of a "Black History Month" yet absence of a "White History Month" was clearly designed to foreground the asymmetrical tacit portrayal of "black American history" as something distinct, and thus separate, from "American history," yet "white American history" as effectively synonymous with it, thereby deeming the very notion of a "White History Month" culturally redundant and therefore semiotically superfluous. Such asymmetry, of course, tacitly also deems African Americans distinct from "ordinary," unmarked ones, thereby effectively *othering* them. By defying the pronouncedly asymmetrical distinction between "American" and "black American" history, Freeman thus challenged the tacit exclusion of African Americans from the unmarked category "American." By mockingly using the term "White History Month," he thus helped lay bare the conventionally presumed normality of whiteness in America.

Foregrounding whiteness also helps lay bare the glaring asymmetry whereby black criminals are often associated with "the black family" or "the ghetto underclass," whereas white ones are conventionally "afforded the privilege of individualization" (Wise 1999). As Tim Wise noted after the Columbine massacre, the fact that

> school killers have all been white lately has gone without mention in the media. Oh sure, we hear [that] all the shooters were boys; all the shooters used guns; all the shooters talked openly about violence; all the shooters played violent video games [yet] the racial similarities between the gun-lovin', trash-talkin', dark-clothes wearin', "Doom"-playin'…sacks of testosterone was irrelevant. While we can rest assured these kids would have been "raced" had they come from black "ghetto matri-archs"…it seems as though no one can see the most obvious common characteristic among them: namely, their white skin.   (Wise 1999)

In order to foreground the unmarked, marking it "abnormalizes" what is habitually assumed by default and thereby taken for granted, as exemplified by the semiotically subversive use of the term "vanilla sex" to signify what are conventionally considered "normal" sexual practices. By explicitly marking such practices, using this term thus defies their conventionally presumed normality. In sharp contrast to using, for example, the term "alternative sex," which implicitly genericizes sexual practices conventionally deemed "normal," it actually challenges their presumed genericity by the very act of naming them.

Furthermore, in so doing it tacitly also helps normalize conventionally "abnormal" behavior. By explicitly marking conventionally unmarked sexual practices, using the term "vanilla sex" thus effectively puts them on an equal semiotic footing with their conventionally marked "kinky" counterparts, thereby implicitly making the latter more culturally acceptable.

To further appreciate how marking the conventionally unmarked helps normalize the conventionally marked, consider also the use of the term "cisgender" to designate people whose gender identity matches their anatomical gender at birth. By effectively putting conventionally marked "trans" identities and conventionally unmarked "ordinary" ones on an equal semiotic footing, using such a term clearly helps normalize the former by subverting the latter's presumed normality and therefore also *cultural privilege of remaining unnamed.*

That is also true of using the terms "heterosexual" and "straight" to signify conven-tionally unmarked sexual "normality." Using such terms effectively defies the givenness and therefore axiomatic assumption of heterosexuality. In other words, they are clearly designed to challenge "the rhetorical opposition of what is…'natural' and what is 'derivative' or 'contrived' by demonstrating...that 'heterosexuality,' far from possessing a privileged status, must itself be treated as a dependent term" (Beaver 1981:115).

Along similar lines, by treating "ordinary" individuals as objects of explicit cultural attention, using terms such as "able-bodied," "sighted," or "neurotypicals" tacitly puts them on an equal semiotic footing with disabled ones. That is even more obvious in the case of using pronouncedly residual terms such as "non-blind" or "non-wheelies," let alone "non-disabled," which effectively transform conventionally unmarked "normals" into an explicitly marked population, thereby challenging their conventionally nonderivative, "basic," and thus taken-for-granted epistemic status.

Not only are conventionally unmarked "normals" marked as "able-bodied" (or simply "abled"), they are sometimes even *double-marked* by being labeled *temporarily abled* (Davis 1995:1, 7, 172), a term specifically designed to blur the conventional distinction between the "able-bodied" and the "disabled." As "a stark reminder that each of us stands vulnerable to the physical diminishments provoked by disease, accident, or simply the inevitable processes of aging" (Whitehead and Whitehead 2014:74), it tacitly defies the supposedly binary distinction between our conventional notions of able-bodiedness and disability. After all,

> [t]he fact is that most citizens will have some level of impairment....Most humans, as they age, will find themselves less able to see, hear, walk, or think so well as they did before. One disability activist recently spoke at a convention to "normal" people and said, "...Come back in twenty years and a lot of you will be with us!"
>
> (Davis 1995:xv)

Consider also, along these lines, the cultural emergence of the proverbial "straight white male." As Sally Robinson describes in *Marked Men* the recent fall of straight, white maleness from its traditional position as the very embodiment of conventional visions of normality (that is, as "a disembodied universality") to its current one as but "an embodied specificity" (Robinson 2000:25, 17),

> [w]hereas white male novelists, for example, might have until recently been read simply as "novelists," many might now find themselves categorically defined *as* white male novelists: they might find themselves *marked*, not read for their expression of a personal, individualized vision but, like women writers or African American writers, habitually read as the exemplars of a particularized—gendered and racialized—perspective.   (Robinson 2000:16)

Such semiotically subversive logic also led Jerry Falwell to name and thereby foreground the hitherto unmarked and therefore culturally invisible[2] social movement behind the post-1960s conservative backlash "The Moral Majority," and the Occupy Wall Street movement to use the term "The Ninety-Nine Percent" to explicitly foreground the hitherto unmarked millions of Americans effectively excluded from the pronouncedly marked income-earning category "The Top One Percent" (Gervis 2015).

30.3 ACADEMIC FOREGROUNDING

Yet the significance of foregrounding is more than just political. Indeed, it is often primarily intellectual. "The only true voyage of discovery," claimed Marcel Proust, "would be not to visit strange lands but *to possess other eyes*" (1923/2006:657, emphasis added), and scholarly innovation indeed involves generating intellectual novelties and not just factual ones (Zerubavel 1980:29–30, 32; see also Kuhn 1962/1970; Myers 2011).

In order to foreground the unmarked, however, it needs to be "othered," as exemplified by the deliberate feminist effort to turn visible the taken-for-grantedness of maleness, which led to the emergence in the 1980s of the field of men's (or masculinities) studies as part of a general intellectual assault on the presumed normality of maleness. Men, of course, had been studied long before that, yet not *as men*, whereas men's studies scholars try to make maleness explicit rather than merely implicit, let alone challenge its presumed normality.

The emergence of men's studies may have also inspired the analogous emergence in the 1990s of whiteness studies, yet another new academic field of inquiry explicitly challenging the presumed normality and therefore taken-for-grantedness of being white. Like men, whites, of course, had been studied long before that, yet not *as whites*. As Ruth Frankenberg, one of the early students of whiteness, reflected on the intellectual significance of foregrounding it,

> [m]y research engages whiteness [but] the statement "my research engages white-ness" could not have been made, meaningfully, at the time, around 1980, when I began the political inquiry that would lead me toward that work. This is so because, at that moment, the notion of "whiteness" was not present in the political or intel-lectual worlds of which I was a part.   (Frankenberg 2004:104, see also 112)

Effectively completing the cultural emergence of the tripartite proverbial straight white male, the 1990s also saw the beginning of a parallel intellectual assault on heteronormativ-ity. Like men and whites, heterosexuals, of course, had been studied long before that, yet not *as heterosexuals*, and books such as Jonathan Katz's *The Invention of Heterosexuality* (1995/2007), Hanne Blank's *Straight: The Surprisingly Short History of Heterosexu-ality* (2012), Louis-Georges Tin's *The Invention of Heterosexual Culture* (2008/2012), and James Dean's *Straights: Heterosexuality in Post-Closeted Culture* (2014) would have therefore been almost inconceivable before the 1990s. The deliberate effort to fore-ground the hitherto untheorized manner in which straightness has been culturally con-structed as a taken-for-granted, ordinary phenomenon clearly underlies such attempts to socioculturally contextualize heteronormativity's hegemonic grip on our minds.

As products of the 1980s and 1990s, the studies of maleness, whiteness, and straight-ness are parts of the same deliberate intellectual effort to "turn a critical eye on unmarked categories…that assume a normative…character in everyday life" (Heath 2013:564) and thereby challenge our fundamental conventional assumptions about the presumed normality of maleness, whiteness, and straightness. Harry Brod's underlying teaching philosophy explicitly underscores their inherent relatedness:

> I want my students to understand that men are gendered too.... To let the study of gender be equivalent to the study of women is to leave men as unmarked by gender and hence normatively human.... Once [students] have internalized this model, a study of race, for example, can no longer be mistaken solely for a study of people of color. Students will now come to see whites as being raced as well. Further... they come to see that the commonly posed question "What causes homosexuality?"... takes as norm and leaves uninterrogated the dominant category of heterosexuality.   (Brod 2002:166–7)

The intellectual quest to normalize conventionally marked, and often stigmatized, social identities (women, nonwhites, gays, and lesbians) has also inspired the effort to mark and thereby foreground the traditionally unmarked phenomenon of able-bodiedness rather than take it for granted. As Simi Linton explains her decision to refer to the able-bodied as "nondisabled,"

> [t]he use of *nondisabled*... is similar to the strategy of marking and articulating "whiteness." The assumed position in scholarship has always been the male, white, nondisabled [as] the default category.... [T]hese positions are not only presumptively hegemonic because they are the assumed universal stance, as well as the presumed neutral or objective stance, but also undertheorized. The nondisabled stance, like the white stance, is veiled.   (Linton 1998:13–14)

By the very act of opting to use this term, therefore, we can no longer remain blind to the "taken-for-granted background that goes about unnoticed.... It means to make the familiar practices of daily life that seem normal, and are often treated as if they are 'natural,' shine through in all their sociality" (Titchkosky 2003:19). Using it, in other words, allows us to remind ourselves that normality is but a cultural construct.

The quest to epistemically "abnormalize" the habitually taken for granted also led Edward Hall to foreground the hitherto untheorized (and therefore virtually unstudied) social organization of interpersonal distance and thereby establish the academic field of proxemics (Hall 1966; see also Zerubavel 1997:46). It likewise inspired Erving Goffman's studies of the conventionally taken-for-granted norms and rituals underlying face-to-face social interaction (1963, 1971), which effectively pioneered "the sociology of everyday life." The main goal of such a sociology is thus to make the familiar strange, which implies focusing one's scholarly gaze on what one habitually takes for granted:

> [T]he ordinary, mundane and "everyday" social world – the familiar – is made "strange" in order that it can be systematically analysed and explored. Hence taken-for-granted assumptions... are subjected to a sociological gaze... whereby "normal" and "expected" ways of doing things are problematized or questioned, and where familiar understandings of social life are challenged.   (Coffey 2004:21. See also Brekhus 1998)

Consider also, in this regard, Harold Garfinkel's breaching experiments (1964/1967). One of the foremost preconditions for taking something for granted is our ability to consider it routine rather than out-of-the-ordinary. When we encounter nonroutine phenomena, our sense of normality is therefore disrupted and our hitherto back-grounded tacit assumptions are suddenly thrust to the foreground. Instead of letting his subjects habitually "routinize" phenomenologically problematic situations, Garfinkel thus deliberately "problematized" for them ones that are conventionally considered routine, thereby actually making them more explicitly aware of what they were implicitly taking for granted.

30.4 Artistic Foregrounding

Activists and scholars, however, are not the only ones who try to foreground the conventionally unmarked. So, for that matter, do artists. After all, by "remov[ing] objects from the automatism of perception," art helps make them "unfamiliar" (Shklovsky 1917/1965:13, 12).

Consider, for example, poetry, aptly characterized by Novalis as "[t]he art...of making an object strange" (O'Brien 1995:317)—an idea further developed by Shklovsky, who viewed it as specifically designed

> to counteract the process of habituation encouraged by routine everyday modes of perception. We...cease to "see" the world we live in.... The aim of poetry is to reverse that process, to defamiliarize that with which we are overly familiar, to "creatively deform" the usual, the normal. (Hawkes 1977:62)

The role of poetry, in other words, is therefore to foreground by deautomatizing (Mukařovský 1932/1964:19). Lamenting the fact that "in consequence of the film of familiarity...we have eyes, yet not see," Samuel Coleridge, for example, thus praised its ability to "awake[n] the mind's attention from the lethargy of custom" (1817/1983, Vol. 2:7), while Percy Shelley noted that it "strips the veil of familiarity from the world" by "mak[ing] familiar objects be as if they were not familiar" (1840:58, 35).

Shklovsky's theory about the role of art in deautomatizing human perception (1917/1965:13) may have also inspired Bertolt Brecht's ideas about the playwright's ability to "estrange" the theater audience and thereby bring them to reflect on the taken for granted. Brecht's general approach to theater thus stressed its ability to "estrange the familiar, and problematise the self-evident" (Brooker 1994/2006:223):

> Before familiarity can turn into awareness *the familiar must be stripped of its inconspic-uousness [and] labelled as something unusual.* (Willett 1992:144, emphasis added)
>
> Characters and incidents from ordinary life...being familiar, strike us as more or less natural. Alienating them helps to make them seem remarkable to us. (140)

Indeed, Brecht characterized such "alienation effect" as a technique of presenting ordinary human occurrences as something that is not to be taken for granted. In other words, it involves "turning the object of which one is to be made aware, to which one's attention is to be drawn, *from something ordinary, familiar... into something peculiar, striking and unexpected*" (Willett 1992:143, emphasis added). Such foregrounding can also be done cinematically, as exemplified by films that specifically spotlight conventionally marginalized and therefore habitually ignored *background persons* (Zerubavel 2015:28–30) such as butlers (*The Butler*), housemaids (*The Help*), and backup singers (*20 Feet from Stardom*).

By the same token, artistic photographers often take pictures of their effectively unmarked, "ordinary" surroundings. They likewise often foreground the conventionally unmarked space between objects commonly referred to as "background" (Zerubavel 2015). As one photography professor would instruct his students: "Emphasize the negative space when taking a picture. Learn to see the interval between visual elements as figure. Position your camera in such a way as to make the interval between [objects] the integral part of your picture" (Zakia 2002:21).

Similarly, in drawing classes, students are often explicitly instructed to become aware of the unmarked, "background-like" spaces between conventionally marked, "thing-like" objects (Ehrenzweig 1953:28, 36). The art instructor Betty Edwards, for example, thus specifically trains her students to notice the shapes of the supposedly shapeless, "empty" spaces between pieces of furniture (1979:102–9, 1999:116–35). By the same token, effectively disputing the unmarked quality conventionally attributed to such "negative" spaces, fellow art instructor Carl Purcell insists that they be explicitly delineated (2010:141–2). Maurits Escher's, Rob Gonsalves's, and Sandro Del-Prete's spectacular efforts to portray such spaces as anything but empty (see, e.g., Zerubavel 2015:86–89, Plates 4, 5, and 6) are obvious products of such training.

30.5 COMIC FOREGROUNDING

Humor, too, offers a way of foregrounding taken-for-granted default assumptions. And it does so primarily by deautomatizing (Havránek 1932/1964:11) and thereby effectively problematizing what is conventionally presumed normal.

Consider, for example, the following excerpt from the article "Body Ritual among the Nacirema" published in 1956 by Horace Miner in the *American Anthropologist*:

> The Nacirema have an almost pathological horror of and fascination with the mouth, the condition of which is believed to have a supernatural influence on all social relationships. Were it not for the rituals of the mouth, they believe that... their friends [would] desert them, and their lovers reject them.... The daily body ritual performed by everyone includes a mouth-rite [that] involves a practice which strikes the uninitiated stranger as revolting. It was reported to me that the ritual consists of inserting a small bundle of hog hairs into the mouth, along with certain magical powders, and then moving the bundle in a highly formalized series of gestures. (Miner 1956:504)

It may have been the realization that *Nacirema* is *American* spelled backward that ultimately led Miner's readers to understand that they were actually reading an allegorical account of their own daily oral hygiene practices. The article, in other words, simply portrayed ordinary American health and cleanliness habits wittily featured as strange "Nacirema" rituals. At a time when anthropologists usually studied far-away, "exotic" cultures, none of those readers expected to read in the flagship journal of the American Anthropological Association about their own daily hygiene practices. By portraying the familiar and therefore taken-for-granted as "strange," Miner thus effectively exoticized it, thereby tacitly mocking the very idea of exoticism.

Comic foregrounding often involves the use of satirical as well as sarcastic forms of irony. Satire and sarcasm are thus used, for example, to mock the presumed normality of maleness. Ironic quips such as "Man, being a mammal, breast-feeds his young" and "Menstrual pain accounts for an enormous loss of manpower hours" (Martyna 1980:489) as well as "The University's four-man crews won in both the men's and women's divisions" (Fasold 1990:111), for instance, clearly subvert its conventionally presumed genericity. So does a cartoon featuring a little girl standing by a blackboard listing the terms *Stone Age Man*, *Bronze Age Man*, and *Iron Age Man* and asking the teacher: "Did they have women in those days?" (Romaine 1999:103).

Such discursive erasure of women (Ergun 2010:311) is spectacularly exemplified by people's response to a riddle about a fatal car accident in which a man dies on the spot and his son is rushed to the hospital, but upon seeing him there a startled surgeon exclaims: "I can't operate on my own son!" Arguably the simplest solution is that the surgeon is the boy's mother, yet, as I have learned watching many students to whom I have presented this riddle failing to solve it, people often have difficulty conjuring the image of a female surgeon, thereby tacitly revealing the conventional assumption that the term "surgeon" usually implies a man (see also Hofstadter 1982/1985:136–7; Reynolds et al. 2006:889).

The presumed normality of maleness is likewise mocked in a *New Yorker* (August 3, 2015:51) cartoon featuring an African American woman asking a librarian if they "have any books on the white-male experience," yet the cartoon clearly also targets the presumed normality of whiteness. So, indeed, does the term "ivorics" (the semiotic opposite of "Ebonics"), which, by foregrounding the traditionally unmarked "white, caucasian, or anglo manner of speaking,"[3] effectively subverts the conventional assumption that only nonwhites speak in a marked, "abnormal" manner.

By the same token, by parodying the way whites supposedly walk and talk, Richard Pryor (in his skit "White People Eat Quiet")[4] and Eddie Murphy (in his skit "White Like Me")[5] were clearly trying to subvert the glaring semiotic asymmetry whereby only nonwhites' behavior is conventionally considered abnormal, thereby tacitly challenging the presumed normality of whiteness. The semiotically subversive bite of such humor is likewise evident in Steve Martin's satirical allusion to the fact that, given the way we conventionally attach restrictive popular stereotypes primarily to marked identities, white actors' character repertoire is considerably wider than people of color's:

The biggest difficulty for me in being white is getting typecast in mostly white roles. When I first started I guess I should have done more black roles but one picture led to another and pretty soon I was known as a white person. I read for "The Wilt Chamberlain Story" and I was very good but they cast a less-experienced black person in the role. It's one of the things you have to live with as a white person in the United States.   (Davis 1993:180)

Consider also, along these lines, the comic subversion of heteronormativity, as exemplified by Charles Moser and Peggy Kleinplatz's satirical article "Does Heterosexuality Belong in the DSM?" which basically mocks the presumed normality of straightness (effectively featured as a psychosexual condition characterized by having "recurrent, intense sexually arousing fantasies, sexual urges, or behaviors involving sexual activity with an adult of the other sex" [2005:262]) with tongue-in-cheek statements such as the following:

Doubts and insecurities about making or keeping relationship commitments and subsequent attempts to save damaged or dysfunctional relationships appear to be common problems among heterosexuals.... [M]any individuals suffer endlessly in heterosexual relationships.   (Moser and Kleinplatz 2005:264)

Social or work contact can tempt [heterosexuals] to violate healthy boundaries and to engage in inappropriate sexual relationships (e.g. teacher-student, professional-client, employer-employee, adultery).   (264)

Such satirical critique of the presumed normality of heterosexuality also underlies the advice columnist Amy Dickinson's response to a mother who feels betrayed by her son's "decision to become" gay:

DEAR AMY: I recently discovered that my son...is a homosexual. We are part of a church group and I fear that if people in that group find out they will make fun of me for having a gay child. He won't listen to reason, and he will not stop being gay. I feel as if he is doing this just to get back at me.... Please help him make the right choice in life by not being gay.

DEAR BETRAYED: You could teach your son an important lesson by changing your own sexuality to show him how easy it is. Try it for the next year or so: Stop being a heterosexual to demonstrate to your son that a person's sexuality is a matter of choice.[6]

It likewise pervades Martin Rochlin's "Heterosexual Questionnaire,"[7] a tongue-in-cheek parody of diagnostic questionnaires conventionally targeting gays and lesbians. Effectively lampooning heteronormativity, it includes questions such as:

When and how did you first decide you were a heterosexual?

To whom have you disclosed your heterosexual tendencies? How did they react?

What do you think caused your heterosexuality?

Is it possible your heterosexuality is just a phase you may grow out of?

Why do you insist on flaunting your heterosexuality?

A disproportionate majority of child molesters are heterosexual men. Do you consider it safe to expose children to heterosexual male teachers, pediatricians, priests, or scoutmasters?

By effectively "reversing the gaze" (Seymour-Smith 2015:317), it is designed to turn one of our culture's most pervasive taken-for-granted assumptions on its head. As such, it perfectly exemplifies the cognitive phenomenon of *assumption reversal*.

30.6 BACKGROUNDING

Marking and thus "abnormalizing" what is conventionally taken for granted is but one way of subverting the fundamental semiotic asymmetry between the marked and the unmarked, yet such asymmetry can also be subverted by using the exact opposite cognitive tactic of *unmarking what is conventionally marked*, thereby making it semiotically "weightless." That implies broadening its conventional semantic scope and thereby referential potential by making it semiotically less restrictive and thus more inclusive. Whereas marking the unmarked involves foregrounding, unmarking the marked involves the diametrically opposite cognitive act of *backgrounding* (Zerubavel 2015:45–46), as manifested in attempts to "blend in" socially (Force 2010; Zerubavel 2015:27–44) or to "*neutralize*" people's accent through "accent-reduction" training in an effort to *genericize* their identity (Aneesh 2015:57–62).

The effort to genericize also underlies the semiotic attack on the pronominal *he*. Whether by substituting for it the pronoun *she*, replacing it with gender-neutral pronouns such as *they* (as in *if someone is born that way, they cannot help it*) or *ze*, or using *he* and *she* either alternately or randomly, the ultimate goal of such unmistakably subversive efforts is to challenge the presumed normality of maleness. That is also true of replacing traditional job titles such as *policeman, fireman*, and *salesman* by their gender-neutral equivalents *police officer, firefighter*, and *salesperson*.

Neutralizing or genericizing is also manifested in *unnaming* the conventionally marked, as exemplified by the removal of adjectives designed to narrow nouns' semantic scope and make them more specific. That explains, for example, the effort to "de-adjectivize" the term "gay marriage" or "same-sex marriage." As Liz Feldman has put it, "[i]t's very dear to me, the issue of *gay marriage. Or, as I like to call it: 'marriage.'* You know, because I had lunch this afternoon, not gay lunch. I parked my car; I didn't gay park it" (Harper 2012, accessed on June 11, 2016, emphasis added). Indeed, soon after the United States Supreme Court legalized same-sex marriage, a new slogan was born: "It's no longer gay marriage. It's just marriage."

30.7 FOREGROUNDING *AND* BACKGROUNDING

Although in opposite ways, both foregrounding and backgrounding, of course, are specifically designed to eliminate the semiotic asymmetry between the marked and the unmarked by renouncing the pronouncedly lopsided manner in which their referential scopes are conventionally delineated, thereby making the two pans of the proverbial scale semiotically symmetrical. Combining those two semiotically subversive acts together, however (as exemplified by the tweet "After this game, everyone better start calling it 'soccer' and 'men's soccer' "[8] posted after the US women's national soccer team won the 2015 World Cup Championship), allows us to nevertheless preserve that asymmetry yet in a topsy-turvy manner, thereby *simultaneously substituting the marked for the unmarked and vice versa.*

There is a formal dinner scene in Luis Buñuel's film *The Phantom of Liberty* in which all the chairs have been replaced by toilets, and the hosts and guests, casually lifting their dresses or dropping their pants, sit down and discuss body waste. One of the guests then pulls up his pants, asks to be excused from the table, and goes to a small room where, locking the door behind him, he sits down by himself and proceeds to eat. Effectively transposing the respective semiotic valences culturally attached to the acts of eating and defecating, the scene exemplifies the subversive act of turning the relations between the conventionally marked and the conventionally unmarked on their head (Brekhus 1998:43–45) by foregrounding the latter while at the same time backgrounding the former, thereby essentially switching them with each other.

Consider also in this regard Viviana Zelizer's allegorical portrayal of some imaginary domestic reward arrangements in the opening paragraph of a scholarly article about payments and social ties:

> Suppose for a moment that this is the year 2096. Let's take a look at American families.... "[H]ousewives" and "househusbands" receive monthly stipulated sums of money as salaries from their wage-earning spouses. Salaries are renegotiated yearly; fines imposed for sloppy cleaning, incompetent cooking, careless child care, or indifferent lovemaking. Midyear raises or cash prizes are awarded for exceptional performance. An arbitration board solves domestic financial disputes.... [C]hildren have a piecework scale for their various domestic responsibilities. Good report cards bring a bonus, and bad grades a deduction.   (Zelizer 1996:481–2)

Such portrayal of the family is symmetrically complemented by an equally satirical fantasy portrayal of the workplace, where employers reward exceptional performances by occasionally taking the worker out to dinner and a movie (Zelizer 1996:482). Effectively inverting the way reward is conventionally structured in the form of rationally systematized compensation at work and random "nice gestures" at home,

Zelizer thus challenges the presumed normality of our conventional, taken-for-granted systems of payment.

Along similar lines, consider also Esther Rothblum's satirical transposition of the respective semiotic valences culturally attached to romantic and platonic relationships by effectively reversing the conventional attribution of markedness and unmarkedness to lovers and friends. Envisaging a world where the latter are culturally marked and the former unmarked, Rothblum thus subverts the way we conventionally apply the label "significant others" only to lovers, as if their nonromantic counterparts are literally not deemed significant enough to warrant special cultural marking:

> [O]nce you have become part of a Friendship... [y]ou and your Friend will have an extravagant Friendship Commitment Ceremony that takes months to plan and to which you will invite all your lovers.   (Rothblum 1999:72)

> Friendliness is frowned upon in...situations in which you are expected to maintain a professional identity. If you spend too much time with one particular lover, people may wonder whether you are more than "just lovers" and suspect that you are "cheating" on your Friend. You can have fantasies of being friendly with lovers, but you're not supposed to "act on" these feelings without endangering your Friendship.   (72)

> Scores of how-to books...focus on ways to meet a Friend, to "work on" your Friendship, to keep your Friend from leaving you for another, or to keep a long-term Friendship from losing its spice. And everyone knows that the older you are when a Friendship ends, the harder it will be to enter into another Friendship because most people your age already have Friends and are thus "taken."   (73)

Such epistemically subversive spirit also underlies *Homoworld*, a short film that portrays an imaginary world where homosexuality is the norm and heterosexuality the exception (Butler 2004:15), and roadside billboards with slogans such as "Straight Bashing Is a Crime. Stomp Out Heterophobia" clearly mock the presumed normality of straightness, thereby subverting heteronormativity. And as the late comedian Mitch Hedberg mocked the way we conventionally "abnormalize" the natural form of corn by marking it:

> You know how they call corn on the cob "corn on the cob", right? But that's how it comes out of the ground, man. They should call that "corn". They should call every other version "corn *off* the cob"![9]

NOTES

1. https://www.youtube.com/watch?v=GeixtYS-P3s. Retrieved June 24, 2016.
2. On foregrounding the invisible and undiscussable, see also Zerubavel (2006:65–68, 2015:82–89).
3. http://www.urbandictionary.com/define.php?term=ivorics. Retrieved May 19, 2015.
4. https://www.youtube.com/watch?v=AOwVSgs3Gbg. Retrieved May 25, 2015.
5. http://www.rollingstone.com/tv/pictures/50-greatest-saturday-night-live-sketches-of-all-time-20140203/white-like-me-0201086. Retrieved May 26, 2015.
6. Dickinson (2013).

7. https://www.uwgb.edu/pride-center/files/pdfs/Heterosexual_Questionnaire.pdf. Retrieved June 27, 2015.
8. https://twitter.com/jaclynf/status/617835123317317632. Retrieved July 6, 2015.
9. http://en.wikipedia.org/wiki/Mitch_All_Together. Retrieved May 27, 2015. Emphasis added.

References

Aneesh, A. 2015. *Neutral Accent: How Language, Labor, and Life Become Global*. Durham, NC: Duke University Press.

Beaver, Harold. 1981. "Homosexual Signs: In Memory of Roland Barthes." *Critical Inquiry* 8:99–119.

Beiser, Frederick C. 1998. "A Romantic Education: The Concept of *Bildung* in Early German Romanticism." pp. 284–99 in *Philosophers on Education*, edited by Amélie O. Rorty. London: Routledge.

Blank, Hanne. 2012. *Straight: The Surprisingly Short History of Heterosexuality*. Boston: Beacon Press.

Bonilla-Silva, Eduardo. 2012. "The Invisible Weight of Whiteness." *Ethnic and Racial Studies* 35:173–94.

Brekhus, Wayne H. 1996. "Social Marking and the Mental Coloring of Identity: Sexual Identity Construction and Maintenance in the United States." *Sociological Forum* 11:497–522.

Brekhus, Wayne H. 1998. "A Sociology of the Unmarked: Redirecting Our Focus." *Sociological Theory* 16:34–51.

Brekhus, Wayne H. 2003. *Peacocks, Chameleons, Centaurs: Gay Suburbia and the Grammar of Social Identity*. Chicago: University of Chicago Press.

Brod, Harry. 2002. "Studying Masculinities as Superordinate Studies." pp. 161–75 in *Masculinity Studies and Feminist Theory: New Directions*, edited by Judith K. Gardiner. New York: Columbia University Press.

Brooker, Peter. 1994/2006. "Key Words in Brecht's Theory and Practice of Theatre." pp. 209–24 in *The Cambridge Companion to Brecht*, 2nd ed., edited by Peter Thomson and Glendyr Sacks. Cambridge: Cambridge University Press.

Brown, Lydia. 2014. "Reconnecting Disability and Asexuality." *Disability Intersections*, January 29. http://disabilityintersections.com/2014/01/reconnecting-disability-and-asexuality/ (Accessed July 19, 2015).

Brown, Tom. 1984. "Fill Your Senses, Light Up Your Life." *Reader's Digest*, August:153–6.

Butler, Catherine. 2004. "An Awareness-Raising Tool Addressing Lesbian and Gay Lives." *Clinical Psychology* 36:15–17.

Coffey, Amanda. 2004. *Reconceptualizing Social Policy: Sociological Perspectives on Contemporary Social Policy*. New York: Open University Press.

Coleridge, Samuel T. 1817/1983. *Biographia Literaria: Biographical Sketches of My Literary Life*. Princeton, NJ: Princeton University Press.

Davis, Lennard J. 1995. *Enforcing Normalcy: Disability, Deafness, and the Body*. London: Verso.

Davis, Murray S. 1993. *What's So Funny? The Comic Conception of Culture and Society*. Chicago: University of Chicago Press.

Dean, James J. 2014. *Straights: Heterosexuality in Post-Closeted Culture*. New York: New York University Press.

Deikman, Arthur J. 1966. "De-Automatization and the Mystic Experience." *Psychiatry* 29:324–38.

Dickinson, Amy. 2013. "Ask Amy: Parent Pressures Gay Son to Change." https://www.wash-ingtonpost.com/lifestyle/style/ask-amy-parent-pressures-gayson-to-change/2013/11/12/a46984d0-4815-11e3-bf0c-cebf37c6f484_story.html. (Accessed July 19, 2015).

DiMaggio, Paul. 1997. "Culture and Cognition." *Annual Review of Sociology* 23:263–87.

Edwards, Betty. 1979. *Drawing on the Right Side of the Brain: A Course in Enhancing Creativity and Artistic Confidence*. Los Angeles: J. P. Tarcher.

Edwards, Betty. 1999. *The New Drawing on the Right Side of the Brain*. New York: Jeremy P. Tarcher/Putnam.

Ehrenzweig, Anton. 1953. *The Psycho-Analysis of Artistic Vision and Hearing: An Introduction to A Theory of Unconscious Perception*. New York: Julian Press.

Ergun, Emek. 2010. "Bridging across Feminist Translation and Sociolinguistics." *Language and Linguistics Compass* 4:307–18.

Fasold, Ralph. 1990. *The Sociolinguistics of Language*. Cambridge: Blackwell.

Force, William R. 2010. "The Code of Harry: Performing Normativity in Dexter." *Crime, Media, Culture* 6:329–45.

Foucault, Michel. 1975/2003. *Abnormal: Lectures at the Collège de France 1974–1975*. New York: Picador.

Frankenberg, Ruth. 2004. "On Unsteady Ground: Crafting and Engaging in the Critical Study of Whiteness." pp. 104–18 in *Researching Race and Racism*, edited by Martin Bulmer and John Solomos. London: Routledge.

Garfinkel, Harold. 1964/1967. "Studies of the Routine Grounds of Everyday Activities." pp. 35–75 in *Studies in Ethnomethodology*. Englewood Cliffs, NJ: Prentice-Hall.

Gervis, Alexandra. 2015. "Bringing Forth the Background: Social Movements That Find Power in What We Take for Granted." Paper presented at the Annual Meeting of the Eastern Sociological Society, February, New York.

Goffman, Erving. 1963. *Behavior in Public Places: Notes on the Social Organization of Gatherings*. New York: Free Press.

Goffman, Erving. 1971. *Relations in Public: Microstudies of the Public Order*. New York: Basic Books.

Gordon, William J. 1961. *Synectics: The Development of Creative Capacity*. New York: Harper and Row.

Hall, Edward T. 1966/1969. *The Hidden Dimension*. Garden City: Anchor Books.

Harper, Robyn. 2012. "When I Get Married, Will It Be a 'Gay Marriage'?" http://www.huffing-tonpost.com/robyn-harper/marriage-quality_b_1572611.html (Accessed June 11, 2016).

Havránek, Bohuslav. 1932/1964. "The Functional Differentiation of the Standard Language." pp. 3–16 in *A Prague School Reader on Esthetics, Literary Structure, and Style*, edited by Paul L. Garvin. Washington, DC: Georgetown University Press.

Hawkes, Terence. 1977. *Structuralism and Semiotics*. Berkeley: University of California Press.

Heath, Melanie. 2013. "Sexual Misgivings: Producing Un/Marked Knowledge in Neoliberal Marriage Promotion Policies." *Sociological Quarterly* 54:561–83.

Hofstadter, Douglas R. 1982/1985. "Changes in Default Words and Images, Engendered by Rising Consciousness." pp. 136–58 in *Metamagical Themas: Questing for the Essence of Mind and Pattern*. New York: Basic Books.

Katz, Jonathan N. 1995/2007. *The Invention of Heterosexuality*. Chicago: University of Chicago Press.

Kuhn, Thomas S. 1962/1970. *The Structure of Scientific Revolutions*. Chicago: University of Chicago Press.

Linton, Simi. 1998. *Claiming Disability: Knowledge and Identity*. New York: New York University Press.

Martyna, Wendy. 1980. "Beyond the 'He/Man' Approach: The Case for Nonsexist Language." *Signs* 5:482–93.

Miner, Horace. 1956. "Body Ritual among the Nacirema." *American Anthropologist* 58:503–7.

Moser, Charles, and Peggy Kleinplatz. 2005. "Does Heterosexuality Belong in the DSM?" *Lesbian and Gay Psychology Review* 6:261–7.

Mukařovský, Jan. 1932/1964. "Standard Language and Poetic Language." pp. 17–30 in *A Prague School Reader on Esthetics, Literary Structure, and Style*, edited by Paul L. Garvin. Washington, DC: Georgetown University Press.

Mullaney, Jamie L. 1999. "Making It 'Count': Mental Weighing and Identity Attribution." *Symbolic Interaction* 22:269–83.

Myers, Robert. 2011. "The Familiar Strange and the Strange Familiar in Anthropology and Beyond." *General Anthropology* 18(2):1–9.

O'Brien, William A. 1995. *Novalis: Signs of Revolution*. Durham, NC: Duke University Press.

Proust, Marcel. 1923/2006. *Remembrance of Things Past, Vol. 2*. Hertfordshire: Wordworth Editions.

Purcell, Carl. 2010. *Your Artist's Brain*. Cincinnati: North Light Books.

Reynolds, David J., Alan Garnham, and Jane Oakhill. 2006. "Evidence of Immediate Activation of Gender Information from a Social Role Name." *Quarterly Journal of Experimental Psychology* 59:886–903.

Robinson, Sally. 2000. *Marked Men: White Masculinity in Crisis*. New York: Columbia University Press.

Romaine, Suzanne. 1999. *Communicating Gender*. Mahwah, NJ: Erlbaum.

Rothblum, Esther. 1999. "Poly-Friendships." *Journal of Lesbian Studies* 3:71–83.

Schutz, Alfred. 1932/1967. *The Phenomenology of the Social World*. Evanston, IL: Northwestern University Press.

Seymour-Smith, Sarah. 2015. "Qualitative Methods." pp. 316–32 in *The Palgrave Handbook of the Psychology of Sexuality and Gender*, edited by Christina Richards and Meg J. Barker. New York: Palgrave Macmillan.

Shelley, Percy B. 1840. "A Defence of Poetry." pp. 25–62 in *Essays, Letters from Abroad: Translations and Fragments, Vol.1*. Philadelphia: Lea and Blanchard.

Shklovsky, Victor. 1917/1965. "Art as Technique." pp. 5–24 in *Russian Formalist Criticism: Four Essays*, edited by Lee T. Lemon and Marion J. Reis. Lincoln: University of Nebraska Press.

Tin, Louis-Georges. 2008/2012. *The Invention of Heterosexual Culture*. Cambridge, MA: MIT Press.

Titchkosky, Tanya. 2003. *Disability, Self, and Society*. Toronto: University of Toronto Press.

Waugh, Linda R. 1982. "Marked and Unmarked: A Choice between Unequals in Semiotic Structure." *Semiotica* 38:299–318.

Whitehead, Evelyn E., and James D. Whitehead. 2014. *Fruitful Embraces: Sexuality, Love, and Justice*. Bloomington, IN: iUniverse.

Willett, John. 1992. *Brecht on Theatre: The Development of an Aesthetic*. New York: Hill and Wang.

Wise, Tim. "Blinded by the White: Race, Crime, and Columbine High." www.timwise. org/1999/06/blinded-by-the-white-race-crime-and-columbine-high/ (Accessed September 5, 2016).

Zakia, Richard D. 2002. *Perception and Imaging*. 2nd ed. Boston: Focal Press.

Zelizer, Viviana A. 1996. "Payments and Social Ties." *Sociological Forum* 11:481–95.

Zerubavel, Eviatar. 1980. "If Simmel Were a Fieldworker: On Formal Sociological Theory and Analytical Field Research." *Symbolic Interaction* 3(2):25–33.

Zerubavel, Eviatar. 1997. *Social Mindscapes: An Invitation to Cognitive Sociology*. Cambridge, MA: Harvard University Press.

Zerubavel, Eviatar. 2006. *The Elephant in the Room: Silence and Denial in Everyday Life*. New York: Oxford University Press.

Zerubavel, Eviatar. 2015. *Hidden in Plain Sight: The Social Structure of Irrelevance*. New York: Oxford University Press.

Zerubavel, Eviatar. 2018. *Taken for Granted: The Remarkable Power of the Unremarkable*. Princeton, NJ: Princeton University Press.

CHAPTER 31

WAR WIDOWS AND WELFARE QUEENS

the semiotics of deservingness in the US welfare system

BRITTANY PEARL BATTLE

FEW social problems have triggered more visceral and persistent debate than poverty in the United States, making this social issue a site for a particularly salient symbolic system in American culture. Contrasts occur at multiple levels across this symbolic system—between the "haves" and the "have-nots," "working moms" and "unemployed dads," and the "deserving poor" and the "undeserving poor." These distinctions are strongly attached to shared norms around poverty and are reflected broadly in descriptions and symbols of the "poor."[1] There is a breadth of literature examining categorical distinctions related to stratification more broadly; however, the cognitive relationship between "deservingness" and "undeservingness" merits more sociological attention. While most people have some sense of what it is to be normatively deserving or undeserving, there is less understanding of the constitutive processes that created and reinforced this conceptual distinction. I use a sociocognitive approach, drawing on analytical tools from a sociology of perception framework, to examine the normative social organization of deservingness in the American welfare system. I focus on social filters created by norms of poverty, welfare, and the family to explore how the deserving are differentiated from the undeserving. Using this theoretical framework, I create a conceptual model focusing on two dimensions of worth—morality and eligibility—by which deservingness is conceptualized along a continuum.

31.1 The Cultural Sociology of Deservingness and Undeservingness: Poverty and Welfare in the United States

Because of the attention on means-tested programs like TANF (Temporary Aid to Needy Families) and SNAP (Supplemental Nutrition Assistance Program, formerly the Food Stamps program), and to a lesser extent on entitlement programs like unemployment and disability insurance, there are several other government-sponsored programs that qualify as "welfare" but are often overlooked. In its definition, welfare refers to "financial or other assistance to an individual or family from a city, state, or national government" (Dictionary.com). In this way, because US Department of Agriculture and Federal Housing Administration mortgage assistance, public education, and tax subsidies provide financial and in-kind assistance, they are also relevant when discussing deservingness; therefore, I use this broader definition of welfare.

Although there is a wealth of literature discussing the ideological underpinnings of stratification systems (Huber and Form 1973; Tilly 1998; Massey 2007), these discussions often focus on categorical distinctions between the poor and the nonpoor, with much less discussion of distinctions made *among* the poor. The literature that examines deservingness as it relates to poverty also does not fully consider *how* these distinctions are made, often only referencing societal perceptions of the poor and their impact on policy (L. Appelbaum 2001; Reeskens and van Oorschot 2012; Aarøe and Petersen 2014). Other scholars have examined related concepts like "dependency" (Fraser and Gordon 1994), "welfare dependency" (O'Connor 2001), and the "underclass" (Gans 1995). In *The Undeserving Poor*, Michael Katz (1989, 2013) presents one of the most well-known and thorough histories of the categorization of the undeserving poor, but the discussion lacks a nuanced treatment of the sociocognitive dimensions of deservingness. Herbert J. Gans (1995) provides a detailed discussion of the development of deservingness, connecting the concept to the term "underclass," focusing on how the poor have been labeled over time. However, like Katz, Gans does not examine the sociocognitive dimensions of this social construct. Martin Gilens (1999) discusses Americans' perceptions of deservingness as a consequence of stereotypes held about African-Americans. Although this discussion provides context for the dynamics of deservingness, this analysis also lacks a treatment of this concept as a significant sociocultural phenomenon.

While important work on the development of social policy has often explicitly referenced or alluded to the significance of moral categories of worthiness (Skocpol 1992; Schneider and Ingram 2005), much less often have scholars grappled with the influence of culture as a fundamental focus of their theoretical framing in studying policy development. John Mohr's (1994) examination of early twentieth-century responses to poverty provides one valuable example analytically demonstrating the significance of cultural categories of deservingness in policies addressing poverty. Examining the categorical descriptions of clients in the 1907 New York City Charity Directory, Mohr (1994) conducts a blockmodel analysis to test the relationship between discourse roles and the treatment of the social identities included in the directory. In this analysis, Mohr (1994) grapples with questions of gender, perceived morality, and the achievement versus the ascription of statuses to investigate the services provided to different identities, including soldiers, mothers, working boys, immigrants, and the disabled. Mohr (1994) argues that these conceptual issues—morality, identity, role, and gender—were significant in the creation of a moral order governing the services offered to different categories of the poor.

Brian Steensland (2006) provides another prominent example of the impact of culture on policy outcomes, demonstrating that cultural categories of worthiness impact policy development through schematic, discursive, and institutional mechanisms. Analyzing archival and media records of the debates around the guaranteed annual income proposals in the 1960s and 1970s, Steensland (2006) argues that cultural categories of worth were significant in the political failure of these proposals. This project fills important gaps in the theoretical framing of policy development by addressing the import of culture in explaining policymaking processes. Steensland (2006) ultimately calls for "further exploring the constitutive nature of cultural categories rather than their particular contents" (1320). I attempt to respond to Steensland's call by investigating the cognitive mechanics of the conceptualization of deservingness and undeservingness. I build on these earlier works by exploring *how* these categories are constructed, creating a model that examines deservingness along a continuum to highlight the taken-for-granted cultural subtleties that shape perceptions of the poor.

31.2 RELEVANCE, FOCUS, AND FILTERS: SOCIOCOGNITION IN THE STUDY OF DESERVINGNESS

A sociology of perception framework is useful for examining how deservingness is conceptualized. From a sociocognitive standpoint, perception refers to social influences on the way that individuals perceive the world (Zerubavel 1997), both in sensory perception and thought. The sociology of perception is concerned with "the interpretive dimension of perception, since what we experience through our senses is normally 'filtered' through various interpretive frameworks" (Zerubavel 1997:23–24). In the study of public policy, perception is useful for examining the ways in which social issues are packaged. For example, Eviatar Zerubavel (1997) discusses the "'optical significance' of scientific revolutions," stating, "[t]hey are primarily cognitive upheavals that radically transform the way we 'look' at the world" and "[w]hile they may not always involve the discovery of any new facts, they do offer us new *mental lenses* through which old ones may be seen in a new way" (25–26). Similarly, the packaging of social issues may be used by politicians, the media, or the public to influence legislative agendas and secure support for policy changes by encouraging a new "look" at issues without necessarily presenting any new facts. In this way, examining the "mental lenses" related to deservingness is important in understanding how perceptions contribute to its conceptualization. This theoretical framework offers several analytical tools that are useful for examining the conceptualization of deservingness, including relevance (Zerubavel 2015), focus (Zerubavel 1997), and filters (Friedman 2013). Ultimately, in this analysis these tools help to reveal cultural interpretations related to issues of poverty, welfare, and the family, rather than the "objective reality" of these issues.

The sociocognitive underpinnings of cultural relevance, through attention and inattention, are valuable for the study of deservingness, because "not only does our social environment affect how we perceive the world; it also helps determine what actually 'enters' our minds in the first place" (Zerubavel 1997:35). Specifically, "[a]ttending something in a focused manner entails mentally disengaging it (as a 'figure') from its surrounding 'ground,' which we essentially ignore" (Zerubavel 1997:15). In this way, *mental focusing* helps to differentiate between the relevant and irrelevant by indicating what should be attended, as well as what should be disattended or deliberately ignored (Zerubavel 2015). Patterns of attention are shaped by morality, creating processes of *moral focusing* by demarcating the boundaries of "moral horizons" in that "any object we perceive as lying 'outside' this circle...is essentially considered morally irrelevant and, as such, does not even arouse our moral concerns" (Zerubavel 1997:39). As it relates to the study of deservingness, moral focusing around poverty, welfare, and the family is used to examine how some social issues and demographic characteristics are focused on while others are explicitly or implicitly ignored.

As a sociocognitive analytical tool, the *filter* (Friedman 2013) further helps to elucidate the impact of (dis)attention, focusing, and relevance on perception. The filter functions conceptually as a "mental strainer" or "sieve" that "let[s] in culturally meaningful details while sifting out the culturally irrelevant" (Friedman 2013:29). This tool "highlights what is seen *and* what is ignored because its metaphorical blockages and holes explicitly represent the dialectical relationship between attention and disattention" (Friedman 2013:29). As the filter is reflective of social norms (Friedman 2013), it is useful for exploring how culture impacts the development of social statuses. I use the filter to highlight how norms of poverty, welfare, and the family function to sift through culturally relevant and irrelevant factors to distinguish the deserving from the undeserving. *Mental weighing* (Mullaney 1999) is also critical for understanding how determinations are made in cases of disproportionate levels of morality and eligibility, the two dimensions of deservingness. In cases where one dimension is more outwardly weighty, the cultural relevance of the dimension can serve as a mental weight to balance out or reverse the relationship between the dimensions, contributing to the perceived deservingness or undeservingness of any given case or example. The use of these analytical tools elucidates the ways in which cognitive processes are at play in constructing categories of deservingness and undeservingness.

31.3 A Conceptual Model
of Deservingness

Deservingness has been the subject of diverse social scientific analysis, including examining perceptions of the deservingness of heart transplant recipients (O'Brien et al. 2014), of post–Hurricane Katrina FEMA aid recipients (Reid 2013), and of victims of violent crime (Lodewijkx et al. 2005). Some scholars have addressed deservingness related to poverty, examining how the media responds to Supplemental Security Income policy changes ending eligibility for elderly immigrants (Yoo 2001), how deservingness impacts the public's decisions about providing aid to the poor (L. Appelbaum 2001; Gilens 1999; Will 1993), how electoral competition impacts discretionary welfare spending (Barrilleaux and Bernick 2003), and under what conditions perceptions of particular groups translate into public policy (Nicholson-Crotty and Meier 2005). However, this work does not fully address the cognitive nuances that frame how distinctions are made between the deserving and the undeserving. In the context of the American welfare system, I suggest deservingness not only refers to an individual's eligibility to secure welfare benefits but also includes the individual's perceived worthiness of empathy, respect, care, and compassion or conversely of blame and guilt. Importantly, when discussing conceptualizations of deservingness, I focus on *normative perspectives* in the United States, as they are instrumental in legitimating the country's policy responses to poverty.

I present a conceptual model of deservingness that includes two dimensions, legality and morality, and highlights three filters, poverty, welfare, and the family. I explore perceptions of deservingness constructed through these dimensions and filters using descriptors and symbols (i.e., cases) of the poor. These cases represent cultural symbols of the poor, such as the "welfare queen," the "dependent poor," and "illegal aliens," as well as descriptive terms related to particular groups of the poor, such as "the elderly," "children," and "students." I chose both cases that are frequently referenced in discourse around poverty, welfare, and the family, and those that are not in order to illustrate the attention and focus on particular groups and issues, as well as the inattention to others.

To distinguish between the deserving and the undeserving, this symbolic system rests on formal legal criteria and informal norms of moral considerations. In this model, deservingness is a continuum along which cases are plotted. Essentially, legality and morality represent an x-y grid where the latter is plotted along the x (or horizontal) axis and the former is plotted along the y (or vertical) axis (see Figure 31.1). The positive values of both axes are conceptualized as "moral" and "legal" respectively, and the negative values as "immoral" and "illegal." The center of the model, representing the neutrality of both dimensions, is conceptualized as "amoral" (neither moral nor immoral) and "alegal" (either not explicitly legal or illegal, or fitting some criteria and not others). Higher levels of legality and morality represent higher levels of deservingness. The top right quadrant, where both components are high (highly moral and legal), represents extreme

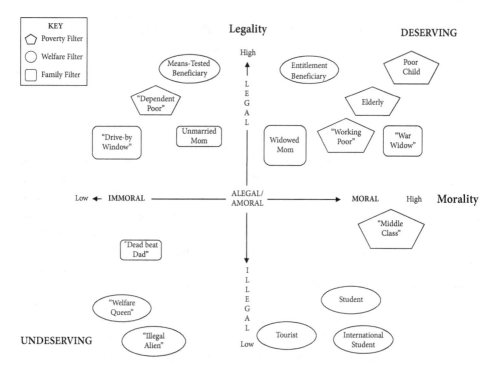

FIGURE 31.1 Conceptual Model of Deservingness.

deservingness. Conversely, the bottom left quadrant represents extreme undeservingness, where both components are low (highly immoral and illegal). Importantly, in this model, deservingness does not represent a simple dichotomy—descriptors and symbols of the poor may be more or less deserving based on their relative levels of legality and morality.

I position these cases in my conceptual model using multicontextual data, including federal and state legislation, political rhetoric, media coverage, popular culture, public opinion data, and academic research. This conceptual formal analytic approach allows for the exploration of general social patterns across diverse contexts (Zerubavel 2007). It is in the genericity of the patterns that this examination draws its analytical power in demonstrating the breadth and depth of deservingness as a sociological concept. These data were selected in a theme-driven (Zerubavel 2007) process of data collection, analytically focusing on the conceptualizations of worthiness and deservingness in my reading and analysis of varied pieces of multicontextual data. In this case, the diversity of these data allows for an examination of how values, mores, and norms around poverty, welfare, and the family across a wide range of contexts influence a collective understanding of legal and moral considerations.

Several concepts are relevant when determining an individual's or symbol's perceived level of morality, including family structure, employment, financial and social responsibility, and demographic factors. The examination of legality is drawn directly from welfare legislation, which outlines who may receive different benefits and under what conditions. Legal criteria for entitlement programs (e.g., Social Security and unemployment insurance) are notably different from means-tested programs (e.g., TANF and SNAP).

The most obvious difference is highlighted by the names of the respective programs in that the former represent assistance that individuals are entitled to, based on employment or other criteria, while the latter represent aid that may or may not be disbursed based on the financial circumstances of the individual and the state. For example, to be legally eligible to secure a VA home loan, an individual needs only to have been discharged from the armed services under a condition other than dishonorable and meet length of service requirements. However, to obtain TANF benefits, an individual must demonstrate financial hardship at a level determined by the state.

On its face, legality may appear to be a relatively objective measure; however, extensive changes to the eligibility criteria over time, and the diverse procedures of different states and municipalities, are indication of its subjectivity. For example, in 1913, a Wisconsin state statute mandating eligibility requirements for children receiving Aid to Dependent Children benefits said that the father had to be absent from the household and that the mother had to be of "*good moral character* and the proper person to have the custody and care" of the child (Wisconsin 1920). Today "good moral character" would never be explicitly mentioned as a formal legal criterion, but the influence of this construct is nevertheless present in legal criteria related to the conceptualization of deservingness.

The relationship between legality and morality is also an important consideration in this analysis. In some instances, legality is more heavily mentally weighed (Mullaney 1999) than morality, while in other cases the reverse is true. Specifically, when both dimensions are either extremely high or extremely low, legality and morality interact to create intense levels of deservingness and undeservingness respectively. However, when legality is extremely low and morality is relatively high, the former dimension is more salient and outweighs or overrides the latter, increasing the symbol's undeservingness. Similarly, when morality is extremely low and legality is relatively high, the former dimension is more salient also increasing undeservingness. Moderate levels on both dimensions result in higher relative deservingness.

This conceptual model of deservingness provides a more general framework for examining how cultural filters and weighing are used to delineate cultural worth and non-worth. These processes of sociocognitive politics create diverse conceptual categories that reinforce the assumed value of some groups over others. While the present analysis is examining distinctions made among groups of the poor in the United States, the conceptual tools employed here might also be used to develop models of worthiness in other contexts.

31.4 FROM WAR WIDOWS TO WELFARE QUEENS: DISTINGUISHING THE DESERVING FROM THE UNDESERVING

In the discussion that follows, I explore *how* distinctions are made in the American welfare system between the deserving and the undeserving. Ultimately, I suggest this system of classification rests on sociocognitive processes. While symbols are largely used to indicate deservingness and undeservingness, simple descriptive terms are also central to this discussion. I use both descriptors and symbols (identified using quotation marks to indicate their collective meaning) as cases of deservingness and undeservingness.

31.4.1 Poverty Filter

Norms related to poverty are central to the conceptualization of deservingness, particularly through ideas about dependency, work, and personal responsibility, which create a *poverty filter* separating the culturally relevant from the irrelevant to distinguish between the deserving and the undeserving. The concept of "dependency" is central to the poverty filter. Over time, dependence has shifted from being perceived as an unfortunate temporary position of the poor to a measure of the social ills associated with poverty. As Fraser and Gordon (1994) note, postindustrial dependency has been individualized, pathologized, and stigmatized. Prior to this time, poverty was a relatively expected condition, as most individuals were without great means of financial support. As higher income became more accessible and stable through factory work, poverty began to be viewed more as the result of individual characteristics, such as laziness, insolence, and vice, and less the result of structural conditions that prevented individuals from earning a living wage. This perspective has resulted in a stigma associated with being poor, so much so in fact that individuals now rarely describe themselves as poor, even when they in fact meet the criteria to be considered in poverty. In a 2012 Pew report, only 7% of respondents identified as belonging to the "lower class," despite the fact that nearly 16% of Americans were living in poverty in that year (Morin and Motel 2012; Bishaw 2013). The stigma associated with poverty makes seeking the financial assistance of the government more shameful. Therefore, when an individual or group is perceived as being part of the "dependent poor" (i.e., welfare-dependent) and not taking responsibility for their own well-being, their perceived deservingness is significantly impacted. By informing perceptions of poverty and the poor, stigma and shaming thus act as significant social influences on the cognitive mechanisms of deservingness, placing those who are stigmatized lower on the deservingness continuum.

Dependency, though criticized in adults, is viewed as "normal in the child" (Moynihan 1973:17) and therefore does not deem them undeserving. Poor children are perhaps perceived as the most deserving members of society, as the presumed innocence and associated morality of children are essentially universally agreed-on. While it is true that poor children are sometimes denied assistance by default when their parents are denied, it is unlikely that a child would be directly deemed undeserving. In fact, children are often legally eligible for benefits for which their parents are not, and the shift from Aid to Families with Dependent Children (AFDC) to TANF has actually resulted in an increase in "child-only" welfare cases, where members of the same family are perceived differently in terms of their deservingness (Moffitt 2003). In these instances, the mental distance between the parent and child is inflated to underscore the difference in deservingness between the two. While parent and child is one of the closest relationships individuals can have, here the two are perceived as separate units to be viewed and treated distinctly when it comes to their worthiness of aid.

Furthermore, the emotive function of the symbolism of the poor child is demonstrated by the frequency with which children are used in media campaigns to fundraise for organizations supporting the poor, which are intended to elicit strong feelings of concern, sympathy, compassion, guilt, and a desire to help. Through processes of moral focusing, where the hardships of poor children receive more collective attention via the frequent use of sentimental images to represent poverty, this group's perceived deservingness is sociocognitively influenced. Using this group of the poor to encourage sympathetic responses is an example of the packaging of this social issue and it impacts the sociocognitive lens through which poverty is perceived and deservingness is conceptualized. Accordingly, in a Google search of "campaigns for the poor," of the eight pages featuring actual campaigns in the top ten search results,[2] only two pages that had pictures on their homepage did not feature images of children. The Frontline documentary "Poor Kids" provides further context for the perceived deservingness of children. The documentary, which narrates the stories of several impoverished children, demonstrates the emotional strength of the symbolism connecting deserving poverty and children, as one *New York Daily News* review states, "Every so often the images in a TV show stay with you after the show ends. That happens with 'Poor Kids'" (Hinckley 2012). Moreover, it is the perceived deservingness of children, placing them at the top right of the continuum, that influences the much broader spectrum of welfare benefits provided nearly universally to children and not adults, including nutritional assistance, healthcare, and public education. It is not just the need for nutrition, healthcare, or education that is culturally relevant, but it is *who* has the need that is important.

Like the concept of dependency, the cultural construct of "work" is central to understanding how the poverty filter impacts the conceptualization of deservingness. In his 1996 remarks at the signing of welfare reform legislation, Clinton (1996) states, "More important, this Act is tough on work. Not only does it include firm but fair work requirements, it provides $4 billion more in child care than the vetoed bills—so that parents can end their dependence on welfare and go to work." In these remarks, a tough stance is taken to prevent parents from becoming dependent, defined as receiving welfare benefits for an extended period of time without contributing some level of work. The notion of not allowing welfare recipients to get something for nothing is so strongly valued that Clinton applauds spending *$4 billion* to provide child care so that welfare recipients with young children can go to work for their benefits. Poverty is packaged to encourage the perception that individuals may end their dependency through work, ignoring the fact that even individuals who work may not earn enough to be financially independent, influencing the mental lens through which individuals understand the issue of poverty.

Because of the focus on work, the "working poor" symbol is one representation of deservingness connected to poverty norms. The adjective "working" is important in indicating this cluster of the poor is not expecting something for nothing, but rather attempting to support themselves through paid work, but nevertheless requiring some government assistance. As work is tightly intertwined with morality (Weber 1905/2002), it is clear how describing a category of the poor as "working" underscores their moral posture, and moves them higher on the deservingness continuum. Insomuch as work provides financial stability and individuals are able to be responsible at least in part for their own well-being, the deservingness of the "working poor" reflects a cultural message about the importance of personal responsibility. The salience of work and independence inflates the cognitive distance between the "working poor" and just the "poor." Moreover, these factors push the "working poor" and the "dependent poor" further apart on the deservingness continuum, inflating the mental divide between those who exhibit "personal responsibility" and those who are "dependent." The perception that those who work are more responsible and independent, and are therefore more moral, is perceived as more relevant than the fact that both meet many of the legal criteria for means-tested benefits. While both the "working poor" and the just poor individuals face financial hardship, the former's participation in paid labor is more culturally relevant for their deservingness than the characteristics that both groups share or characteristics not considered at all, such as whether one resides in an urban or rural location.

In the case of the "working poor," the moral focus is on the contributions (i.e., work) this group makes, not on the assistance they need. While they may in fact be "dependent" on government aid to make ends meet, they are not considered "dependent" because of their paid labor. The perceived deservingness of the "working poor" is evidenced in the use of images of this group in the media to elicit sympathetic responses to poverty (Gilens 1999) and the moral boundaries that working-class men use to separate themselves from their unemployed counterparts (Lamont 2000). This perception of deservingness is also demonstrated by organizations focused on providing opportunities for the "working poor," such as The Working Poor Families Project. The initiative, funded by major philanthropic organizations, states on their website, "The goal of economic self-sufficiency remains an elusive dream for far too many working families" signifying that more must be done to help "working poor" families achieve financial stability. This moral focus indicates the salience of supporting the deserving "working poor" in pursuing personal responsibility and independence. *Paid* work is the culturally relevant factor separated from any other "form" of work including full-time education or training, or unpaid labor in the home. Post 1996 welfare reform, many states, rather than allow recipients to pursue education or training as an alternative to work, adopted "work-first" approaches that pushed beneficiaries to take any job that was available, making full-time students not legally eligible to access most welfare benefits despite the presumed morality of pursuing higher education or advanced training. Through the poverty filter, forms of work are sorted, only allowing paid work to pass through as relevant to one's deservingness and affecting the position of particular cases on the deservingness continuum.

The description of one group of the poor as "working" puts this subset closer to the "middle class," a group almost always identified as deserving because of their perceived strong commitment to work and self-sufficiency. One of the most consistently supported and favorably depicted groups in political rhetoric, media, popular culture, and public opinion, the "middle class" is a symbolic representation of the deserving. During election cycles, politicians from the right and left frequently reference the work they have done and are doing on behalf of the "middle class," work that is rarely if ever controversial in intent for the general public. While the "middle class" is typically not eligible for assistance traditionally viewed as welfare, they do benefit from many other programs that are included under a broader definition of welfare assistance, like mortgage subsidies and public education. And many benefits previously reserved for the poorest families, such as the Earned Income Tax Credit, have been expanded to be a "safety net" for more middle-income Americans, particularly during periods of economic recession, demonstrating that the legal criteria for welfare eligibility are expanding so that this group's deservingness now rests not only on moral considerations but also on legal ones.

The elderly are an additional example of the salience of poverty norms in perceptions of deservingness, highlighted by the system of entitlements that serves more than 38 million retirees and their families (The White House n.d.). Early distinctions between the able poor and the impotent poor, as well as the "relatives' responsibility" custom, underscore that the elderly have traditionally not been required to exhibit "personal responsibility" and have been viewed as deserving of assistance due to their inability to work and financially support themselves. In much the same way as the deservingness of children is constructed, dependency among the elderly is viewed as normal and expected, thereby not constituting a threat to their perceived morality and placing them high on the continuum of deservingness. Entitlement benefits for the elderly are often not even viewed as welfare, despite meeting the definition of the term. Even among Republicans, whose views on welfare are notoriously harsh, these entitlements are typically viewed as a right of deserving people. In the first Republican presidential debate of the 2016 election cycle, New Jersey Governor Chris Christie stated, "Social Security is meant to be—to make sure that no one who's worked hard, and played by the rules, and paid into the system, grows old in poverty in America" (Washington Post Staff 2015). In these remarks, entitlements are packaged as a right for those who have "done the right thing" and lived morally. Essentially, receiving an entitlement benefit is not viewed as the same as receiving a means-tested benefit, causing those who receive the former (i.e., entitlement beneficiaries) to be perceived as more deserving because they are not the recipients of "government hand-outs," like means-tested beneficiaries. In this way, seniors receiving Social Security Insurance benefits are perceived as deserving, even by those most critical of the welfare system. This divergence in the packaging of entitlement benefits as compared to means-tested benefits is an important cognitive mechanism for conceptualizing deservingness by providing a catalyst for differential perceptions of recipients of welfare.

31.4.2 Welfare Filter

Norms around the functions of welfare are also significant to the conceptualization of deservingness, specifically in the appropriate usage of welfare benefits, the ability to secure benefits, and the embodied practices of applying for and receiving benefits, creating a *welfare filter* that acts as a "mental strainer" to separate relevant from irrelevant factors and distinguish the deserving from the undeserving. The "welfare queen" is perhaps the most widely known symbol of the undeserving poor, used frequently in political rhetoric, media depictions, and popular culture, even having a Wikipedia page devoted to her. The term, made popular by then-presidential candidate Ronald Reagan as an argument in support of welfare reform, was based on a highly exaggerated story of a young African-American woman purported to be defrauding the welfare system. The moral focus on the immorality of the "welfare queen," not only in defrauding the welfare system (which makes her receipt of benefits "illegal"), but also in her lifestyle—being an unmarried, unemployed mother dependent on the government—influences her nearly universally agreed-on undeservingness. Like the poor child, the "welfare queen" elicits a similarly visceral response from the larger public. This emotional response—of disdain, contempt, and even hatred—is a result of the perceived immorality manifested through the assumed laziness, promiscuity, dishonesty, and irresponsibility of this symbol, rooted in notions of the pathology of poverty (à la Daniel Moynihan's 1965 "culture of poverty" argument) and is evidenced by the widespread pejorative references to the "welfare queen" in popular culture. In fact, the "welfare queen" is such a prevailing symbol that when interviewed on the fairness of the welfare system, poor women, "whom many would describe as welfare queens," separated themselves, "by asserting their positive roles as mothers," from the deviant "welfare queens" abusing the system (Gustafson 2011:152).

The embodied practices associated with applying for welfare benefits are also evidence of the distinction between the deserving and undeserving poor. In most states, to apply for TANF benefits, individuals are required to visit their local social services office, and in-person interviews with case workers are required in eight states, processes that can require several hours of wait time (Carroll 2014; Saul and Fox 2012). Excessive wait times for individuals seeking means-tested benefits highlight the low value placed on the lives of these welfare recipients, a process that has been described as "temporal domination" as a means of punishing the undeserving poor (Reid 2013). Comparatively, to access other benefits, many of which are not typically characterized as welfare, such as public education and mortgage assistance, individuals need only complete online forms or wait briefly for an appointment. In this way, "temporal domination," and effectively punishing one group in their attempts to secure welfare benefits, serves as a social influence on the conceptualization of deservingness by sending cultural cues about the worth and value of some groups of welfare recipients (i.e., means-tested beneficiaries) compared to other recipients (i.e., entitlement beneficiaries and recipients of nontraditional types of welfare).

Like that associated with poverty itself, the shame and stigma attached to the receipt of benefits also demonstrate how welfare norms are related to perceptions of deservingness. Importantly, the beneficiaries of means-tested aid are more often explicitly and implicitly required to identify themselves as recipients of welfare than are those receiving entitlement benefits. For example, several types of means-tested welfare benefits are used publicly, like SNAP benefits in which food is purchased using an Electronic Benefits Transfer (EBT) card or the use of Women, Infants, and Children (WIC) coupons. Others require individuals to explicitly identify themselves as recipients, as in the case of Section 8 housing subsidy beneficiaries, who must notify potential landlords of their status. Conversely, recipients of FHA mortgage loans or tax credits do not have to make public their receipt of these benefits.

The stigma of welfare is also demonstrated in the popular belief that the government spends too much on it. According to the General Social Survey, in 2014 half of Americans believed that the country spent too much on welfare (Smith et al. 2015). Conversely, more than 70 percent of Americans believed the government was spending too little to improve the nation's education system (Smith et al. 2015). This disparity indicates the perceptions of those benefits typically considered welfare compared to those that qualify as a government subsidy but are viewed as a right of Americans. Welfare is in fact so stigmatized that even those receiving benefits are critical of the system. The *New York Times* covers one individual who, despite receiving welfare benefits, "says that too many Americans lean on taxpayers rather than living within their means.... [He also] supports politicians who promise to cut government spending... [and] printed T-shirts for the Tea Party campaign of a neighbor" (B. Appelbaum and Gebeloff 2012). In this way, moral judgments of worthiness related to government expenditures inform the conceptualization of deservingness and impact the placement of these cases on the continuum of deservingness.

Moreover, the recipients of means-tested benefits face many rules and sanctions that regulate their lives. This approach to welfare includes "family cap" policies, which prevent children born to parents already receiving aid from becoming beneficiaries, and requirements that parents prove their children's immunizations are current. Single mothers are also required to name the father of their children and participate in the process of establishing paternity, in addition to signing over their child support payments to their home state as reimbursement for the aid they receive. Recipients additionally face sanctions for missing deadlines or appointments with case workers. Punitive regulations and sanctions are important social influences on the conceptualization of deservingness in providing additional mechanisms for reinforcing mental distinctions between groups of the poor. When some groups face sanctions, stigma, and temporal domination, while others do not, the cognitive lens though which poverty and welfare is normatively perceived and responded to is undoubtedly impacted. Essentially these processes not only influence the cognitive distinction between the deserving and the undeserving, but also act as functional differences in the actual treatment of the two groups. In this way, deservingness is not just semiotically conceptualized but also behaviorally enacted and thus reflected on the deservingness continuum.

Those groups deemed explicitly ineligible to receive welfare benefits (i.e., illegal) are also indicative of the salience of welfare norms to perceptions of deservingness. The undeservingness of those groups deemed completely ineligible to receive welfare benefits is so culturally taken for granted that they do not even come up in debates about welfare. For example, welfare reform in 1996 classified two categories of immigrants: (1) qualified immigrants, including lawful permanent residents, refugees, and other protected immigration statuses, who in most cases must wait five years before being eligible for benefits; and (2) nonqualified immigrants, including those in the country unlawfully, and some groups in the country lawfully, such as students and tourists, who are not legally permitted to receive benefits (Fortuny and Chaudry 2012). The discourse around immigration and the rights of immigrants has been a central feature of American political debate. While liberals and conservatives often disagree on whether immigrants lawfully in the country should receive welfare, there is less ambiguity around other groups of noncitizens' perceived deservingness. For example, "illegal aliens" are widely perceived as undeserving, not only due to their legislative illegality but also because of their perceived immorality. By entering the country without documentation, "illegal aliens" are frequently assumed to be immoral or even criminal. In this way, "illegal aliens," or those presumed to be in the country unlawfully, are strong symbolic representations of the undeserving.

Tourists and international students are also examples of the importance of welfare norms in conceptualizing deservingness. While the morality of tourists and international students is generally not in question, they are explicitly barred from accessing the welfare system. Though tourists may be elderly and international students may be widowed mothers, other groups typically deemed deserving, their lack of US citizenship ultimately overrides these and any other similarities, and deems them undeserving of assistance. In this way, the welfare filter separates the culturally relevant factors, citizenship or permanent residency, from all other irrelevant factors, such as marital status or age, for placement on the deservingness continuum for those groups. Importantly, it is unlikely that any significant attention would be placed on providing welfare benefits to these groups. Neither tourists nor international students enter into any debates around the expansion *or* reduction of the welfare system, indicating that their place as undeserving is so culturally normative as to not be focused on at all.

31.4.3 Family Filter

Norms around family structure are a significant influence on the conceptualization of deservingness. Factors such as marital status, the circumstances of childbirth, living arrangements, and gender roles related to caregiving and breadwinning are central components of both the legality and morality dimensions. American "family values" still place greater worth on "traditional" family dynamics, which include a heterosexual married couple living under the same roof as their children with a husband/father breadwinner and a wife/mother caregiver, making each of these factors important moral considerations. In addition, many legal criteria for means-tested welfare benefits are more favorable for parents living with their children, evidenced in the name Temporary Aid to Needy *Families*, not individuals. Moreover, welfare reform legislation states among its goals reducing out-of-wedlock pregnancies and increasing the number of two-parent households. These factors form a *family filter* that separates culturally relevant familial factors from the irrelevant to distinguish between the deserving and the undeserving.

Because of the strong symbolism of the poor child's deservingness, an adult's connection to children through parenthood often increases their own perceived deservingness.

This point is underscored by Theda Skocpol's (1992) conceptualization of the "maternal" welfare state highlighting that the focus was not on women, but rather on mothers; because children are deserving, the deservingness of women is in part defined through their roles as mothers. In a sense, the deservingness of the child is transferrable to the parent and elevates them on the deservingness continuum. Single men or women struggling financially are essentially promoted in their deservingness when they become fathers or mothers struggling to provide for themselves *and* their child. In this situation, the parental status of the individual is a more culturally relevant feature of their familial identity than others, like whether they have siblings or elderly parents, even if they are helping to financially support these other family members.

However, the value of parental status is also tied to other factors, including the marital status of the parent. For example, widowed mothers are typically considered the deserving poor, while unmarried mothers are typically considered less deserving. While both groups are technically "single mothers," the former group's perceived sexual chastity and personal responsibility means their motherhood is viewed as more legitimate and thereby more moral than the latter, distinguishing them as deserving. Inflating the mental distance between these two groups is a result of strong messages about the immorality of bearing children out-of-wedlock, as well as the compassion that should be felt for women whose male partners have died. The moral focus is placed on the circumstances of the birth of the child and on the relationship between the parents, indicating that these attributes are more culturally relevant than the poverty of the parent or simply being a parent. Focusing on these attributes over others inflates the cognitive distance between unmarried mothers and widowed mothers so that the latter are elevated on the deservingness continuum, while the former are classified as undeserving.

To extend this example, take the symbolic "war widow." Specifically, deservingness associated with the fact that the woman's husband died "serving" the country results from the cultural values of honor and patriotism, particularly related to the burden of poverty. The "war widow" is likely to be hailed as a heroine for supporting her husband's service and bearing the sacrifice of poverty as a result of his death. The "war widow" has been described as "a living symbol of patriotism. A reminder of the ultimate sacrifice of service" (Murphy 2015). Conversely, a woman whose gang-affiliated husband had been the victim of a drive-by shooting would very likely receive a fraction of the sympathy offered to the "war widow." This contrast highlights the complexity of the sociocognitive politics of deservingness and the hierarchies of cultural worth that are at play among the poor. Here, additional boundaries are created between groups that appear to be similar based on a dynamic set of cultural assumptions, creating a hierarchy within a hierarchy. In both instances, the male partner dies, contributing to the financial instability of the family; however, cultural norms contribute to very different responses to these two scenarios. Attentional precedence is placed on the moral conditions of the man's death, not marital status or meeting legal criteria (wherein both the "war widow" and "drive-by widow" are comparable). In much the same way that deservingness is transferable from child to parent, here the deservingness or undeservingness of the deceased partner is transferred to the woman. In the case of the "war widow," the woman benefits from the perceived morality of her husband's service, while in the case of the "drive-by widow," the woman suffers from the perceived immorality of her husband's gang affiliation. The moral condition of death is weighed more heavily than family structure (or any other factor) so much so that a woman who is the girlfriend or fiancé of a man killed in military service might still be classified as deserving despite not being legally eligible due to her marital status. In this way, the family filter separates the culturally relevant conditions and contexts of family life from the irrelevant to deem the "war widow" deserving and the "drive-by widow" undeserving.

The "war widow" might also be contrasted with the "deadbeat dad." The honor associated with the poverty of the former, and the blame associated with the poverty of the latter, is a result of cultural values of worthiness. The gender distinction between the female widow and the male dad highlight gendered notions of moral and acceptable need based on cultural messages about the desirability of the traditional male breadwinner and female caregiver family structure. Because hegemonic masculinity (Connell 1995) is in part defined by work and earning a living wage, men who are poor do not fit with cultural ideas about normative poverty and family structure. As women are "expected" to be secondary income-earners to their male partners, dominant ideologies around poverty are more tolerant of women who are poor. When women are not able to depend on the financial contributions of men, their poverty is seen as unavoidable. While the context of the absence of a male partner is quite important for their classification as deserving or undeserving, compassionate responses to poor women are more likely than to poor men, elevating their placement on the deservingness continuum.

Moreover, the legality and perceived morality, and thereby deservingness, of the "war widow" contrasted with that of the "deadbeat dad" is impacted by their relationship to parenthood. The "deadbeat dad" without custody of his children falls lower on the legality continuum because his relationship to parenthood does not involve the financial support of children in his household, and a single man would not constitute the "needy family" typically covered by TANF. While the "deadbeat dad" may qualify for some means-tested aid or other benefits such as the EITC, his benefit level would be lower than that of the poor "war widow" or even the "drive-by widow" who support their children in their homes. More importantly in this comparison, the perceived immorality and associated shame with being a "deadbeat" and not supporting one's children greatly impacts the "deadbeat dad's" deservingness. Not only is not supporting one's children viewed as immoral, it is also a criminal offense through child support enforcement legislation and considered a cause of the poverty of single mothers, demonstrated in part by the Deadbeat Parents Punishment Act passed in 1998 argued to be a means to keep single women and children from suffering from poverty. This legislation packages the poverty and hardship of single moms and children as directly related to fathers' financial shortcomings, instead of being the result of other economic or structural factors, influencing the perception of the deservingness of single moms and children, and also impacting the perception of the undeservingness of the "deadbeat dad." The financial hardships the "deadbeat dad" might be facing are culturally irrelevant to his perceived worth of compassion or assistance.

31.5 CONCLUSION

Scholars of culture and policy have created an important foundation demonstrating the significance of cultural categories of worth in the development of social welfare policy (Mohr 1994; Schneider and Ingram 2005; Steensland 2006). I build on these earlier works by exploring *how* these categories are conceptualized, offering a model of deservingness to highlight the taken-for-granted cultural subtleties that shape perceptions of the poor. Through sociocognitive processes of perception, relevance, focusing, and filtering, mental distinctions are created and mental distances are inflated between those considered deserving and those considered undeserving. Norms around poverty, welfare, and the family are central to understanding how the dimensions of deservingness—morality and legality—are socially constructed. These processes and norms function as the cognitive mechanisms necessary for the development and maintenance of this conceptual model of deservingness.

The distinction between deservingness and undeservingness is influenced by the cultural constructs of race, gender, and socioeconomic status; however, the conceptualization of deservingness has been able to persist over time precisely because it is not explicitly about these factors, but rather is coded through norms around legality and morality. Certainly race, gender, and socioeconomic disparities work in service of these symbols, evident in the fact that there is no equivalent "welfare king" to the "welfare queen" or that homeless women receive many more services than homeless men (HCH 2001) or that poor elderly minorities are less often depicted in media coverage of poverty than their white counterparts (Gilens 1999). However, in many instances other factors of morality and legality override racial, gender, and socioeconomic differences. For example, the "war widow" could be of any race and still be considered deserving as the perceived morality of patriotism and sacrifice is weighed more heavily than demographic characteristics. Similarly, while the "welfare queen" symbol was originally racialized through its attachment to the story of a African-American woman, it is now used more broadly to signify women who are perceived as immoral and defrauding the welfare system. Although racism, sexism, and classism are relevant to constructions of deservingness and undeservingness, these perspectives are more often manifested through sociocognitive processes that do not explicitly reference race, gender, or socioeconomic constructs. Racialized, gendered, and classed disparities in perceived deservingness typically align with perceptions of morality based on related stereotypes or bias. In this way, elucidating moral and legal considerations (regardless of their foundation) allows for a fuller and more accurate conceptualization of deservingness and undeservingness.

Potential variance in the determinations of particular cases as deserving or undeserving is another important consideration. While I examine *normative perspectives* about poverty, welfare, and the family, it is likely that there is divergence in perceptions of deservingness among particular groups of individuals. However, even among groups that do not perceive particular cases as deserving or undeserving, the model of deservingness built on conceptualizations of morality and legality is still effective for explaining their perceptions. For example, as a group, Catholics may not perceive the "dependent poor" as undeserving. This difference in perception is grounded in a divergence in norms of morality in that Catholic religious beliefs do not attach stigma and shame to poverty and extreme need. In fact, in the Catholic Church, poverty has been linked to being Christ-like. Pope Francis says, "And this is our poverty: the poverty of the flesh of Christ, the poverty that the Son of God brought us with His Incarnation" (Gregg 2013). In this way, the divergence in perceptions of deservingness originates in a poverty filter that does not perceive the poor through a sociocognitive lens of shame and stigma, but instead focuses on the morality of poverty. Similarly, some fathers' rights groups may not view "deadbeat dads" as immoral and therefore undeserving, or some family planning organizations may not view the out-of-wedlock parenthood of unmarried moms as immoral. In these cases, there is again a difference in moral focusing and relevance leading to a difference in the determinations of deservingness. In this way, the two dimensions of deservingness—morality and legality—are still applicable in distinguishing between the deserving and the undeserving in these cases. Ultimately, this conceptual model of deservingness highlights the ways this social construct is structured, maintained, and promulgated in order to better understand how some are perceived as worthy and others as unworthy. Moreover, this model allows for a broader understanding of how other conceptual categories of cultural worth and nonworth are created. Specifically, moral focusing, cultural filters, and mental weighing can be used to explore the sociocognitive dimensions of varied contexts of worth. This set of analytical tools and the conceptual model might be used to explore how worthiness and deservingness are conceptualized and then applied in diverse settings of decision-making and evaluation, such as promotion processes, award selections, and political nominations and elections. Ultimately, elucidating the cognitive underpinnings of morality and eligibility related to the cultural conceptualization of deservingness highlights the importance of understanding the cultural construction of categories and offers a framework for further exploration of the development of these categories and others in policymaking processes.

Notes

1. The terms "the poor" or "poor" are problematic for a number of reasons. In their contemporary usage, they have become, in many instances, pejorative terms used to demean low socioeconomic status individuals. Nevertheless, I have decided to use the terms in this chapter because of their historical and symbolic accuracy in capturing normative American approaches to poverty and welfare.
2. One top ten result was a Wikipedia page and one was an encyclopedia entry, both on Martin Luther King's Poor People's Campaign. The search was conducted on November 5, 2015, and returned a total of 98,700,000 results.

References

Aarøe, Lene, and Michael Bang Petersen. 2014. "Crowding Out Culture: Scandinavians and Americans Agree on Social Welfare in the Face of Deservingness Cues." *Journal of Politics* 76(3):684–97.

Appelbaum, Binyamin, and Robert Gebeloff. 2012. "Even Critics of Safety Net Increasingly Depend on It." *New York Times*. February 11. http://www.nytimes.com/2012/02/12/us/even-critics-of-safety-net-increasingly-depend-on-it.html?_r=0 (Accessed November 20, 2015).

Appelbaum, Lauren D. 2001. "The Influence of Perceived Deservingness on Policy Decisions Regarding Aid to the Poor." *International Society of Political Psychology* 22(3):419–42.

Barrilleaux, Charles, and Ethan Bernick. 2003. "Deservingness, Discretion, and the State Politics of Welfare Spending, 1990–96." *State Politics and Policy Quarterly* 3(1):1–22.

Bishaw, Alemayehu. 2013, September. "Poverty: 2000 to 2012." *American Community Survey Briefs*. Washington, DC: US Census Bureau. https://www.census.gov/prod/2013pubs/acsbr12-01.pdf (Accessed November 12, 2015).

Carroll, Emma M. 2014. "They Never Seem to Reason with You": Welfare, Sanctions, and the Double Bind of Black Women. Electronic thesis. https://etd.ohiolink.edu/ap/10?0::NO:10:P10_ETD_SUBID:97486 (Accessed November 1, 2015).

Clinton, William J. August 1996. "Statement on Signing the PRWORA of 1996." *The American Presidency Project*, edited by Gerhard Peters and John T. Woolley, http://www.presidency.ucsb.edu/ws/?pid=53,219 (Accessed November 5, 2015).

Connell, Raewyn W. 1995. *Masculinities*. Berkeley: University of California Press.

Dictionary.com. n.d. "Welfare." http://dictionary.reference.com/browse/welfare (Accessed October 5, 2015).

Fortuny, Karina, and Ajay Chaudry. 2012. *Overview of Immigrants Eligibility for SNAP, TANF, Medicaid, and CHIP*. Washington, DC: The Urban Institute. http://aspe.hhs.gov/basic-report/overview-immigrants-eligibility-snap-tanf-medicaid-and-chip (Accessed November 1, 2015).

Fraser, Nancy, and Linda Gordon. 1994. "Dependency" Demystified Inscriptions of Power in a Keyword of the Welfare State. *Social Politics* 1(1):4–31.

Friedman, Asia. 2013. *Blind to Sameness: Sexpectations and the Social Construction of Male and Female Bodies*. Chicago: University of Chicago Press.

Gans, Herbert J. 1995. *The War against the Poor: The Underclass and Antipoverty Policy*. New York: Basic Books.

Gilens, Martin. 1999. *Why Americans Hate Welfare: Race, Media, and The Politics of Antipoverty Policy*. Chicago: University of Chicago Press.

Gregg, Samuel. 2013. *Pope Francis on the True Meaning of Poverty*. Catholic Education Resource Center. http://www.catholiceducation.org/en/religion-and-philosophy/social-justice/pope-francis-on-the-true-meaning-of-poverty.html (Accessed February 1, 2016).

Gustafson, Kaaryn. S. 2011. *Cheating Welfare: Public Assistance and the Criminalization of Poverty*. New York: New York University Press.

Health Care for the Homeless Council (HCH) Clinicians' Network. June 2001. "Single Males: The Homeless Majority." *Healing Hands* 5(3).

Hinckley, David. 2012. TV review: "Frontline: Poor Kids." *New York Daily News*, November 20. http://www.nydailynews.com/entertainment/tv-movies/tv-review-frontline-poor-kids-article-1.1204558 (Accessed November 5, 2015).

Huber, Joan, and William Humbert Form. 1973. *Income and Ideology: An Analysis of the American Political Formula*. New York: The Free Press.

Katz, Michael. 1989. *The Undeserving Poor: From the War on Poverty to the War on Welfare*. New York: Pantheon Books.

Katz, Michael. 2013. *The Undeserving Poor: America's Enduring Confrontation with Poverty*. 2nd ed. New York: Oxford University Press.

Lamont, Michéle. 2000. *The Dignity of Working Men: Morality and the Boundaries of Race, Class, and Immigration*. Cambridge, MA; New York: Harvard University Press and Russell Sage Foundation.

Lodewijkx, Hein F. M., Erik W. de Kwaadsteniet, and Bernard A. Nijstad. 2005. "That Could Be Me (or Not): Senseless Violence and the Role of Deservingness, Victim Ethnicity, Person Identification, and Position Identification." *Journal of Applied Social Psychology* 35(7):1361–83.

Massey, Douglas S. 2007. *Categorically Unequal: The American Stratification System*. New York: Russell Sage Foundation.

Moffitt, Robert A. 2003. "The Temporary Assistance for Needy Families Program." In *Means-Tested Transfer Programs in the United States*, edited by R. A. Moffitt. Chicago: University of Chicago Press.

Mohr, John W. 1994. "Soldiers, Mothers, Tramps and Others: Discourse Roles in the 1907 New York City Charity Directory." *Poetics* 22:327–57.

Morin, Rich, and Seth Motel. 2012, September. "A Third of Americans Now Say They Are in the Lower Classes." In *Social and Demographic Trends*. Washington, DC: Pew Research Center. http://www.pewsocialtrends.org/2012/09/10/a-third-of-americans-now-say-they-are-in-the-lower-classes/ (Accessed November 12, 2015).

Moynihan, Daniel. 1965. *The Negro Family: The Case for National Action*. Washington, DC: Office of Policy Planning and Research, US Department of Labor.

Moynihan, Daniel. 1973. *The Politics of a Guaranteed Income: The Nixon Administrations and the Family Assistance Plan*. New York: Random House.

Mullaney, Jamie L. 1999. Making It "Count": Mental Weighing and Identity Attribution. *Symbolic Interaction* 22(3):269–83.

Murphy, Patricia. 2015, June 24. "Washington War Widows: It's OK to Move On." *KUOW*. http://kuow.org/post/washington-war-widows-its-ok-move (Retrieved October 31, 2015).

Nicholson-Crotty, Sean, and Kenneth J. Meier. 2005. "From Perception to Public Policy: Translating Social Constructions into Policy Designs." pp. 223–42 in *Deserving and Entitled: Social Constructions and Public Policy*, edited by A. L. Schneider and H. M. Ingram. Albany: State University of New York Press.

O'Brien, Geraldine M., Ngaire Donaghue, Iain Walker, and Clare A. Wood. 2014. "Deservingness and Gratitude in the Context of Heart Transplantation." *Qualitative Health Research* 24(12):1635–47.

O'Connor, Brendan. 2001. "The Intellectual Origins of 'Welfare Dependency.'" *Australian Journal of Social Issues* 36(3):221–36.

Reeskens, Tim, and Wim van Oorschot. 2012. "Disentangling the 'New Liberal Dilemma': On the Relation between General Welfare Redistribution Preferences and Welfare Chauvinism." *International Journal of Comparative Sociology* 53(2):120–39.

Reid, Megan. 2013. "Social Policy, 'Deservingness,' and Sociotemporal Marginalization: Katrina Survivors and FEMA." *Sociological Forum* 28(4):742–63.

Saul, Michael Howard, and Alison Fox. 2012. "Welfare Lines Overflow: Crowded Public-Assistance Centers Interrupt Services as Demand for Aid Grows." *Wall Street Journal*,

January 3. http://www.wsj.com/articles/SB10001424052970204720204577130950757135044 (Accessed October 20, 2015).

Schneider, Anne L., and Helen M. Ingram. 2005. *Deserving and Entitled: Social Constructions and Public Policy*. Albany: State University of New York Press.

Skocpol, Theda. 1992. *Protecting Soldiers and Mothers: The Political Origins of Social Policy in the United States*. Cambridge, MA: President and Fellows of Harvard College.

Smith, Tom W., Peter V. Marsden, Michael Hout, and Jibum Kim. 2015. *General Social Surveys, 1972–2014* [machine-readable data file]. Sponsored by National Science Foundation. Chicago: NORC at the University of Chicago [producer]; Storrs, CT: The Roper Center for Public Opinion Research, University of Connecticut [distributor].

Steensland, Brian. 2006. "Cultural Categories and the American Welfare State: The Case of Guaranteed Income Policy." *American Journal of Sociology* 111(5):1273–326.

The White House. n.d. "Seniors and Social Security." https://www.whitehouse.gov/issues/seniors-and-social-security (Accessed November 7, 2015).

Tilly, Charles. 1998. *Durable Inequality*. Berkeley: University of California Press.

Washington Post Staff. 2015, August 6. "Annotated Transcript: The Aug. 6 GOP Debate." *Washington Post*. https://www.washingtonpost.com/news/post-politics/wp/2015/08/06/annotated-transcript-the-aug-6-gop-debate/?utm_term=.9f06f1495c01 (Accessed December 15, 2017).

Weber, Max. 1905/2002. *The Protestant Ethic and the "Spirit" of Capitalism and Other Writings*. New York: Penguin Books.

Will, Jeffry A. 1993. "The Dimensions of Poverty: Public Perceptions of the Deserving Poor." *Social Science Research* 22(3):312–32.

Wisconsin, State Board of Control. 1920. "Law Providing Aid to Dependent Children (Mother's Pension Law)."

Yoo, Grace J. 2001. "Constructing Deservingness: Federal Welfare Reform, Supplemental Security Income, and Elderly Immigrants." *Journal of Aging and Social Policy* 13(4):17–34.

Zerubavel, Eviatar. 1997. *Social Mindscapes: An Invitation to Cognitive Sociology*. Cambridge, MA: Harvard University Press.

Zerubavel, Eviatar. 2007. "Generally Speaking: The Logic and Mechanics of Social Pattern Analysis." *Sociological Forum* 22(2):131–45.

Zerubavel, Eviatar. 2015. *Hidden in Plain Sight: The Social Structure of Irrelevance*. New York: Oxford University Press.

CHAPTER 32

PERCEIVING AND ENACTING AUTHENTIC IDENTITIES

J. PATRICK WILLIAMS

ONE assumption people in contemporary societies carry around is that some things are real or authentic, while other things are not. On the one hand, we go out of our way to find authentic Italian or Chinese food, we watch *Real Housewives* on TV, and we drink Coke because we have been told it is "the real thing." The notion of the real brings with it the idea that some things are not real and that we should constantly be vigilant of the difference between them. Thus we question the authenticity of Chinese cuisine if we see that the kitchen staff is not Asian. We fear that Louis Vuitton handbag or Rolex watch that seems like too good a deal online may be counterfeit. We buy some cool-looking clothes while second-hand shopping, only to find friends mocking us for "trying to be a hipster." Worse, we wonder whether we are living authentic lives, or whether contemporary living has somehow stripped us of that which makes us really us.

All of the above issues (and many more) point to the significance of authenticity in contemporary everyday life. Yet, how does one go about determining what is and is not authentic? As human beings, we do not define authenticity in a universal or generic way, but rather in myriad ways as members of social groups that are embedded in shared webs of signification (Fine and Fields 2008; Zerubavel 1997). Through culture and cognition, we develop and then use implicit sets of assumptions and understandings about reality, including what we judge to be authentic (DiMaggio 1997; Brekhus 2015).

While the literature on authenticity covers a diverse range of disciplines and topics, in this chapter I focus specifically on how the authenticity of identities is perceived and enacted. Because conceptions of authenticity are cultural rather than universal, it is impossible to discuss authentic identities in a way that is equally valid for all cultures or social groups (see Williams and Schwarz, forthcoming); I therefore rely on academic and lay discourses generated primarily in "the West." My explicit goals are twofold: first, to demonstrate the socially constructed nature of authenticity; and second to highlight the interrelated cognitive and cultural processes implicated in identity authentication. But first, we need to consider the history of self-authenticity and how identity authenticity differs from it.

32.1 CONCEIVING SELF AND AUTHENTICITY

Like "culture," the concept of authenticity is fraught with competing meanings and assumptions across the humanities and social sciences, with scholars in various disciplines often conceptualizing authenticity in noncomplementary or incompatible ways. Like common-sense lay conceptions, many academic theories and empirical studies treat issues of authenticity in objectivist terms, framing the differences between real and not-real as natural and unproblematic. There is a growing number of scholars, however, who conceptualize authenticity as something that is not self-evident, but rather culturally constructed and negotiated.

Modern concern with the authenticity of self sprouted from the philosophical soil of the European Enlightenment (Trilling 1972). From thinkers such as Descartes, who believed that the only thing that could be proven to be real was one's own consciousness, to Rousseau, who used the term "authenticity" to refer to the existential essence of human beings that was stripped away through living in societies, philosophers theorized the self as innate, self-evident, and agentic (Beer 2012). Subsequent continental philosophers further developed the idea of an authentic self under threat by social forces. For example, Nietzsche, like Rousseau, challenged the authority of society over the person, while Heidegger and Sartre theorized that individuals could and should embrace authentic selves rooted in personal responsibility and meaningful, autonomous engagement in the world.

From these philosophical ideas, generations of social scientists have implicitly linked self-authenticity to agency and autonomy, as well as to its tensions with external social forces. Trilling (1972:93) discussed authenticity in terms of "the peculiar nature of our fallen condition, our anxiety over the credibility of existence and of individual existence," as did Taylor (1994:30) when he wrote of common self-conceptions: "If I am not [true to myself], I miss the point of my life; I miss what being human is for *me*" (cited in Peterson 2011:9). Vannini (2008) found empirical evidence of such struggles among university professors who loathed participating in institutional governance because doing so, they said, felt untrue to their sense of self as researchers and/or teachers, and to the values, passions, and goals that accompanied such self-definitions. Many faculty in his study defined institutional service as "dirty work" and felt besieged by bureaucratic processes and structures. Vannini also showed how some professors not only engaged in institutional governance, but felt most authentic when doing so because such work gave them opportunities to act back on what they perceived to be injustices of the system.

In this way, authenticity research has implicitly maintained an emphasis on the true self as "an agent of structural and cultural resistance" set against social expectations, as well as something that can be lost and found (Vannini 2008:231; see also Vannini 2006).

Recent work in symbolic interactionism has bolstered views of a self that is authentic and in some ways separate from others and from the larger social world. Erickson (1995) argued that authenticity "highlights the importance of conceptualizing self in terms of meanings rather than identities" and that the self-concept "reflects individuals' subjective sense of their own feelings of authenticity" (135) in terms of "one's relationship to oneself" (124). Despite early interactionists' explication that the self-concept is always situated in social relations, interactionists have recently discussed authenticity as "a **self**-referential concept [that] does not explicitly include any reference to others" (124, emphasis in original), or as a search for people's "sense of *who they really are*" (McCarthy 2009:242, emphasis in original). This is a view reflective of psychological theories of self generally, where conceiving of a self "highly dependent on social interaction [is liable] for constructing a false sense of self that does not mirror one's authentic experiences" (Harter 1995:82). Unlike psychology, interactionism carries with it an implicit theoretical understanding of the self as a process and a product of society. Yet in writing, a noticeable amount of work textually reifies the self as something unique and distinct from social processes.

The autonomy of a core self, often buried or even "lost" within a person, found early support in Freud's psychology, which theorized one's sense of self as emerging out of harshness and cruelty imposed by the superego, a psychological structure that brought with it the propensity to see oneself negatively, for example as bad, pathetic, or weak. The superego itself, according to Freud, was formed from external (i.e., parental) sources experienced from infancy and thus represents a process through which social forces dominate a person's understanding of themselves. From these ideas, self-authenticity became linked to the struggle for agency and autonomy, and to "the moral process of establishing human accountability" vis-à-vis social structure (Turner 1976:991). This structural view of the self has dominated scientific and lay definitions of the self during the twentieth century, such that scholars have argued that "authentic subjectivity is to contemporary modernity [what] autonomous subjectivity [was] to early modernity" (Ferrara 1998:5).

By "authentic subjectivity," Ferrara refers to a growing condition in the West in which people accept not only the (objective) reality of authenticity but also the need to experience authenticity themselves, a need that is not only visible in philosophical treatises, but "in all manner of manuals, guides, therapeutic works and self-help surveys" as well (Giddens 1991:3). The problem arises, however, that the meaning of self-authenticity is neither universally agreed on nor easily achieved. In his study of tourism and performance, MacCannell (1973) noted a growing collective search for authentic experience, which he saw as an attempt to replace the perceived lack of meaning in people's lives. He argued that many people traveled to experience "primitive" cultures for example, whose members maintained deep, so-called authentic connections with their social, spiritual, and physical environments. Social commentators have for the last several decades argued that such feelings of "personal meaninglessness has become a fundamental…problem" in late modernity (Arnould and Price 2003:140). In this discourse, globalization is seen as having fundamentally influenced the construction of selfhood by removing traditional references and introducing new technologies and relational forms that de/recontextualize people's selves and identities (Gergen 1991). As a response, individuals increasingly seek out meaningful cultural and personal narratives through which to make sense of themselves, others, and the social world in which they live. Seeing self-realization discourses as reactions to an increasing dependence on instrumental relationships and alienation via the rationalization of labor, "authenticity becomes understood as a managerialist guise for dealing with the self-alienation caused by modern work, a means of dealing palliatively with…disenchantment" (Bell and McArthur 2014:368).

32.2 From True Selves to Authentic Identities

While the authenticity of self has kept scholars' attention for centuries, the study of authentic identities has a much shorter history. To be clear, self and identity are not synonymous. Weigert and Gecas (2003:268) contend that self "becomes as self does and others respond.…Self is aware, knows, feels, decides and so forth," while identity refers to that aspect of "self defined by self or other…Identities are…defined objects, stable for the time being, that function as objects and instances of a category." Identities come into being as individuals announce themselves, place others, or get placed as social objects or members of social categories, all of which happens in situations. As Stone (1962:93) noted, an identity casts the individual "in the shape of a social object by the acknowledgement of his participation or membership in social relations." In short, identities are those aspects of self that we or others name in situations, and which are often objectified through social relations such as roles or memberships in groups or categories.

Like the self, identity has undergone significant theorization since its earliest use. Identity has been conceived of in many ways, including as a cognitive structure, as a self-reflexive process, as a social achievement, and as a political or ideological construct, among others. It has been broken down into analytical types, measured in terms salience and centrality, and theorized to be both a cause and an effect vis-à-vis cognition, emotion, and behavior. As Howard (2000:367) notes, in earlier times "identity was not so much an issue; when societies were more stable, identity was to a great extent assigned, rather than selected or adopted. In current times, however, the concept of identity increasingly carries the full weight of the need for a sense of who one is." Howard goes on to review social cognitive and interactionist perspectives on identity, linguistic and temporal features of identity construction, the main social bases on which identities are formed, such as ethnicity and sexuality, as well as identities' conflictual, intersectional, and fluid dimensions.

From a strict social constructionist perspective, all identities are products of social interaction and meaning-making and thus there are no such things as authentic identities. Rather, individuals and groups engage cognitively and interactively in the process of identifying themselves and others, and in doing so create, enact, and enforce boundaries between identities defined as real or not. In this sense, authenticity is an evaluative concept, with different groups establishing their own methods for defining and assessing the authenticity of any particular identity or identity performance. As mentioned earlier, however, authenticity tends to be taken as objectively real in everyday life, in part due to the cognitive-miserly ways in which people process identity-relevant information (Fiske and Taylor 2013). To conceive of one's or another's identity as (in)authentic requires that people have in mind not only categories for authentic and inauthentic but also clear boundaries between those identity categories as well as methods for perceiving, enacting and/or assessing identities in ways that conform to whatever normative definitions of authenticity are salient at any given moment. Gilovich and Savitsky (1996) argued that various heuristics—"judgmental shortcuts that generally get us where we need to go" (48)—enable people to make basic assumptions about the realness or validity of phenomena in the world around them, including identities. Using such heuristics, people decide what makes a "real" woman, a "real" Native American, or whatever (see Garfinkel 1967; Jacobs and Merolla 2017), while ignoring contradictory (i.e., nonrepresentative) information that would complicate their reasoning. To describe the links between such cognitive-miserly/heuristic processes and cultural definitions of authenticity, I now turn to a discussion of how identity categories are constructed, reified, and discursively managed.

32.2.1 Ethnicity and Authenticity

Ethnicity is a useful identity type to begin with because of the extent to which societies have historically taken it as an essential rather than arbitrary aspect of who a person is. The social-psychological literature is rich with studies that investigate the cognitive, affective, and behavioral implications of everyday understandings of ethnicity. Within discursive psychology and interactionist sociology, studies have examined how ethnic sameness/difference is established during communication about or with ethnic others. For example, Varjonen, Arnold and Jasinskaja-Lahti (2013) explored the complex dynamics of identification among ethnic Finns who emigrated from Russia to Finland in the late 2000s. Analyzing focus group data among ethnically homogeneous participants, the authors identified a repertoire of "intergroup relations" through which individuals construct their and others' ethnic identities. Down under, Italian-born Australians construct their "Italian-ness" through comparisons with various ethnonational out-groups (Sala et al. 2010), while on the island of Thrace ethnic Greeks distinguish themselves as trustworthy from "shifty" and ethnically dissimilar Muslims living on the island (Evergeti 2011). Language-oriented research on ethnic identities often focuses on social interaction as the process through which ethnicities are made relevant or real.

Traditionally, this realness would have referred to people's taken-for-granted conceptions of ethnic categories, measured in terms of similarity to others who share the same ethnicity and difference from those in ethnic outgroups. To the extent individuals believe in the realness of ethnicity, they will have developed strategies to authenticate individuals who are ethnically similar, while categorizing those dissimilar to themselves as ethnic outsiders.

Measuring one's identity in terms of similarity and difference was the hallmark of social identity theory, which emerged from experimental social psychological research on the use and function of social categorizations, schema, and social comparisons (Hogg and Abrams 1988; Tajfel 1974; Turner 1975). Social identity theory sought the cognitive basis on which individuals labeled themselves and others as members of identity categories, as a corrective to prior social-psychological research that had tended to treat identities as epiphenomenal to intergroup conflict (Tajfel and Turner 2004). Since the early days of social identity theory however, research has increasingly argued that relying on rigid conceptions of identity categories rooted in similarity and difference is problematic. In Varjonen et al.'s (2013) study mentioned earlier, the researchers found that ethnic Finns talked about themselves primarily as Finns while living as minorities in Russia, but relevant self-identifications became more diverse once they emigrated to Finland, and participants even problematized what it meant to be Finnish. Other reasons for rethinking the rigidness of identity categories abound. Brekhus (2015), for example, noted the extent to which people today actively identify across multiple membership categories, formal organizations, and informal networks simultaneously. This occurs in two broad ways: "either by bringing their many affiliations together to form one multiply-influenced and socially networked self (multidimensionality) or by balancing their affiliations across time and space, shifting the salience and competing attributes and foregrounding and performing different selves across different social networks and social contexts (mobility)" (128). Thus, ethnicity becomes one of many negotiable identity categories that individuals invoke in everyday life.

Whereas Brekhus focuses on movement beyond rigid binary conceptions of insider/outsider identities, Bucholtz and Hall (2005) take a different approach by reorienting scholarship toward a set of relational tactics of identification, reframing social identity theory's binary cognitive schema of similarity/difference into three interactional tactics (also binaries), which they intend to highlight the distinctly interactional versus cognitive nature of identity work. Like social identity theorists, Bucholtz and Hall (2005) maintain the core idea of relationality—that is, the notion that "identities always acquire social meaning in relation to other available identity positions" (598). While the sameness versus difference axis of relationality is key to understanding the boundaries between groups, they argue that focusing only on perceptions of similarity and difference oversimplifies and even ignores some of the intricate interactional processes that constitute the process of identification.

Weninger and Williams (2017) demonstrate how these relational tactics enable the process of place-based authentication in their study of two ethnic identity groups—Hungarians and Romanians—discursively battling over rights to a third identity, one that is authentically Transylvanian. Following Bucholtz and Hall (2004, 2005), Weninger and Williams first reframe similarity/difference as adequation/distinction to highlight how individuals selectively emphasize or downplay both similarities and differences in support of their efforts to position themselves and others in interaction. Adequation suggests that the similarity among group members "is not complete, but sufficient" (Bucholtz and Hall 2004:494), and the same interpretive shift applies to distinction. Their data show how adequation and distinction go hand-in-hand: Hungarians and Romanians regularly adequated themselves with European-ness, distinguished themselves from Asian-ness, adequated the other with Asian-ness, and distinguished the other from European-ness by invoking history, moral discourse, and wordplay. At the turn of the millennium, when the data were produced, establishing an authentic European identity was important for many people in both nations.

Bucholtz and Hall discuss two additional sets of intersubjective tactics: verification/ denaturalization and authorization/illegitimation (see Weninger and Williams 2017:186, note 1). Acts of verification confirm the "realness" of a social identity, while denaturalization highlights processes through which social identity claims are de-essentialized. This is an important distinction from early social identity theory, which deemphasized instances in which people failed to align with categorical identities. Weninger and Williams use denaturalization to explore how both Hungarians and Romanians sought to prevent each other from attaining an authentic Transylvanian identity. In their sample, members of both ethnic categories were quick to denaturalize the others' claim to Transylvanian-ness, but were either unable or unwilling to recognize that their own tactics of verification as Transylvanians were equally rhetorical. In the third pair of relational tactics, authorization refers to the process of affirming or imposing identities through ideological structures, while illegitimation has to do with the dismissal or marginalization of identities through the same structures. The authors highlight how individuals discursively aligned their own ethnicity with European moral and institutional authorities such as the EU and NATO, while creating distance between the other and those same institutions as a way of legitimating their own claims as rightful heirs of a European land and identity.

32.2.2 Essentialism and Authentication

The previous examples highlight the interactional nature of authentic identity construction. The ways in which ethnic groups characterize themselves and each other fit well with Zerubavel's (1997:78) claim that, despite the cultural and cognitive nature of identities, we often disregard their conventional nature, "thereby basically reifying them." Likewise, regardless of sociological insights into multidimensionality, mobility, and relationality, a significant amount of research on identity authenticity continues to involve essentialist notions, particularly in psychology. Like reification, essentialism is a mundane practice through which individuals and groups simplify identity categories and implicitly firm up the boundaries that separate them.

To essentialize an identity means to define it in inherent, self-evident terms rather than see it as a social product or project. When people essentialize, they work cognitively and interactionally to clarify boundaries between identities and the people attached to them. Essentializing identity may be a logical outcome of essentializing the self. As discussed earlier in terms of rationalist philosophy, the West has a long history of conceiving the individual self as essential, autonomous, and unique. Mead (1934) long ago pointed out that individuals learn to take themselves as objects and thus to situate themselves in relation to others. From earliest childhood, individuals see the world from their own subjective standpoints, but also learn to accept that others define them as objects and label them in essentialist sorts of ways as well. Thus people not only essentialize themselves as unique subjective entities, they also essentialize aspects of their and others' identities.

Like the study from Central Europe mentioned earlier, a host of studies from multiple contexts confirm lay conceptions of essentialism and authenticity, which "still [have] a strong influence on the dynamics of racial and ethnic groups in contemporary life" (Warikoo 2007:390). Carter (2003) showed how African American youth in New York essentialize types of music, ways of walking, and styles of speaking as a means of authenticating "black" identity, while Jackson (2005) highlighted a similar process with experiences of poverty. As Tuan (1999:106) shows, third- and higher-generation Asian Americans find themselves in an "authenticity dilemma," not accepted as really American by whites (who see them as foreigners), nor as really Asian by more recent Asian immigrants to the United States (who see them as "watered down" Asians who have lost their cultural roots). And in her study of the Indian diaspora, Maira (1999) found youth confrontations around essentialist versus constructivist notions of language use, religiosity, and sexuality, including both heteronormativity and intra-ethnic romance.

The process of essentializing is cultural and differs pragmatically among various groups, networks, and subcultures. Brekhus (2003) showed how some homosexual men engaged in "identity lifestyling," whereby the term "gay" became an idealized category associated with specific sets of attributes and characteristics, which these men oriented toward as a way of distinguishing themselves from the straight world. The emphasis on the boundary between who one is and who one is not is also evident in terms of what people do versus do not do. The men in Becker's (1963) and Sutter's (1966) studies, for example, authenticated their own superiority vis-à-vis mainstream "square" society partly in terms of their drug use. In the opposite direction, adherents of the abstinence-based straightedge subculture identify themselves as superior to those who use recreational drugs or engage in casual sex. Essentializing the intentions or behaviors of outsiders serves as a foil against which a subcultural identity develops and sustains its moral force and coherence (Copes and Williams 2007; Mullaney 2006).

Once members of a particular group define certain characteristics of an identity as "authentic," they then use those characteristics to distinguish among persons and identities, past and present (Cornell and Hartmann 1998:94). This process refers not only to cases in which (assumed) homogeneous groups police boundaries but also among groups with clearly mixed membership and heritage. Shenk's (2007) analysis of peer talk among bilingual Mexican American college students focused explicit attention on interactional negotiations of who are and are not "real" members of particular ethnic identity categories. She illustrates how purity of bloodline, purity of nationality, and degree of Spanish proficiency function as ideological constructs and are invoked by interlocutors in bids to negotiate cultural authenticity, what she calls "authentication moves." Similarly, Warikoo (2007) showed that, in multiethnic contexts, there are still dominant definitions of racial/ethnic authenticity against which individuals are assessed; those who do not measure up are sanctioned or marginalized. The findings in these studies fit conceptually with Bucholtz and Hall's (2005) tactics of verification/denaturalization and authorization/illegitimation.

All this suggests that identity-authentication may be a generic social process, though with individuals and groups assigning pragmatically relevant criteria and methods to the authentication process itself. Thus, Brekhus's (2003) "identity lifestyling" can be understood against two other identity strategies among homosexual men, "identity commuting," whereby men entered and exited idealized gay social spaces and networks, and "identity integration," in which homosexual men rejected the idea of a totalizing gay identity category in preference for a more fluid, multidimensional self-conception. Individuals who subscribe to each identity strategy are likely to see their preferred strategy as authentic and other strategies as not. That would certainly be the case if I were to apply Brekhus's strategies to my own research on self-identifying straightedge youths (Williams 2006) and their extensive arguing over whether their subcultural identity was to be understood in terms of membership within the oppositional hardcore punk subculture from which straightedge emerged (i.e., "identity lifestyling"), or whether a personal commitment to abstinence could be integrated alongside separate, nonoppositional identities and going concerns (i.e., "lifestyle integration"). After observing hundreds of conversations over a couple of years, I found that almost everyone involved defined themselves as essentially authentic. However, the hardcore music scenesters were adamant that they were the only authentic straightedgers, while those who came to the identity from outside the music scene—often through the Internet—believed that anyone who subscribed to certain key subcultural values and lifestyle practices could rightfully claim the identity.

32.3 AUTHENTICATING SOCIAL IDENTITIES

When cognitive anthropologists say that categories are revealed lexically within interacting groups (Boster 2005), they mean that social cognition can be empirically studied through language use. Symbolic interactionism as a sociological tradition has long focused on the interactive mechanisms through which people produce reality, social relations, and identities. Within as well as beyond symbolic interactionism, the extensive research literatures on subcultures and deviance show that members of oppositional and/or marginal groups establish and maintain identity categories through "semantic dimensions...a two-valued set that is used to conceive of and evaluate aspects of language use" (Seitel 1974:51). These semantic dimensions function as symbolic boundaries between authentic insiders and everyone else, including inauthentic "poseurs" or "wannabes" within a subcultural group, as well as outsiders. In his study on hip-hop authenticity, McLeod (1999) discusses six such dimensions that emerged from interview data with hip-hop artists: being true to oneself versus following mass trends, being black versus white, supporting underground versus commercial actors, acting masculine versus feminine or effeminate, coming from the streets versus the suburbs, and being able to connect one's participation back to an "old school" versus a mainstream commodified version of hip-hop. As mentioned earlier, I also noted two strategies for identity authentication in my study of a subcultural internet forum (Williams 2006), though those strategies were sometime conflictive rather than complementary: being active in local hardcore music scenes and maintaining a personal commitment to sub-cultural values and norms, and identity. It is important not to take for granted that the men "keepin' it real" in McLeod's research were black, working-class, masculine, old-school independent artists, while in my research there was a mixture of self-identifying subculturalists coming from both inside and outside the hardcore straightedge music scene. Had McLeod interviewed white or middle-class or effeminate rappers, his find-ings would likely have been very different. Subcultural individuals typically construct authenticity around criteria to which they themselves conform.

Research suggests that authenticity discourses are a major concern among subcultur-alists and are highly salient when oppositional cultural identities are marginalized or threatened by dominant or popular cultural forces (Copes et al. 2008; Force 2009; Larsson 2013; Lewin and Williams 2009; Mullaney 2012). Within such subcultures, mul-tiple and even contradictory strategies of identity authentication may co-occur within a group as interactional situations may make different identities more or less appropriate or salient (Sandberg 2009). This is evident in an interview-based study of members of a criminal street culture who admitted to regular crack cocaine use. One the one hand, interviewees took pains to construct distinct boundaries that separated themselves as "hustlers" (a high-value, respected identity in street culture) from other crack cocaine users, whom they defined as "crackheads" (a stigmatized identity) in five distinguishing ways (Copes et al. 2008). First, hustlers maintained their personal hygiene and displayed their monetary success through clothing, cars, and such, while crackheads forgot them-selves and their public image. Second, hustlers kept control of personal assets or suc-cessfully scammed assets from others, while crackheads were willing to lose everything to stay high. Third, hustlers displayed self-control in front of others, while crackheads often acted nervous, afraid, or paranoid, especially in ambiguous situations. Fourth, hustlers did not allow their drug use to negatively affect their overall prosperity in the street economy, while crackheads became incapable of managing themselves, or even surviving on the streets. Fifth, hustlers had the courage and will to face difficult situa-tions, while crackheads were unable to make tough choices to protect themselves.

Interviewees articulated these identity distinctions through stories about themselves and their lives on the street. They also narrated how they ("hustlers") would trick or abuse other men on the street ("crackheads") for profit or fun to substantiate in their own and others' minds their authenticity as masters of street culture and economy. Yet the stories these men told (Copes et al. 2008:265–6) also suggested an ugly, violent self that lurked beneath the hustler rhetoric. This potentially stigmatized self was further exposed through the total institutional setting in which the interviews occurred, and through their talk about interactions with victims. Thus in addition to narrating an authentic hustler identity, they also engaged in salvaging work to distinguish themselves from authentically violent individuals (Hochstetler et al. 2010). As in their hustler narratives, they constructed binary semantic pairs with clear and unambiguous boundaries (Alexander and Smith 1993). For example, they described how, unlike authentically violent associates who searched out and enjoyed violence, these men first sought to avoid violence, only inflicting harm when they were "forced" into it by situational constraints, such as when victims decided to defend themselves. Further, they explained how they tried to minimize the violence they inflicted, for example by incapacitating victims instead of killing them or by exiting situations in which children or pregnant women were at risk. In short, they described themselves as individuals *doing* violence and contrasted this with associates who were guilty of *being* violent people (see also Widdicombe and Wooffitt 1990).

32.4 CONCLUSION

In this chapter, I have mapped out some of the contours of authenticity in relation to identity and identification. I began by distinguishing between self-authenticity, which is phenomenological and self-referential (often pitting the individual self against the external physical and social world), and identity authenticity (what I have elsewhere called social authenticity), which focuses explicitly on the discursive processes through which social identities are invoked or enacted in situations. I explored the roles that categorization and essentialism play in framing identity authenticity, and then went on to exemplify some of the processes and criteria through which authentic identities are constructed and assessed across many different studies.

The emphases on categories, criteria, and their socially constructed nature raise questions about the auspices within which authenticity is perceived and enacted, the links between authenticity and authority, and ultimately the socially constructed nature of authenticity itself. First, under what auspices are authenticity discourses produced? As Gubrium and Holstein (2009:123) note, "everyday authenticity relates to the audiences and circumstances of the work involved. If authenticity is interactionally produced, it materializes under particular *auspices*—the interpretive expectancies, resources, and preferences that surround authenticity work." This idea helps clarify why authentication seems to be a generic social process, while allowing for semantic and substantive variety of authenticity discourses among various (types of) identity groups and contexts. Elsewhere I have taken up this issue and argued that analyses of authentication should take situations and audiences into careful account (Williams 2013). This would help explain why it is, for example, people sometimes put immense effort into establishing the authenticity of their social identities, while at other moments they put as much effort into avoiding being placed into seemingly obvious identity categories (Widdicombe 1998).

Second, who has the ability or capacity to define and sustain authentic identity discourses and criteria? In an early study of American punks, Fox (1987) constructed a typology of punk identity, with "hardcore" punks occupying the subcultural center, and increasingly less authentic identities forming concentric rings, from "softcore" to "preppie" punks and eventually to outsiders. The problem with such a typology is to be found in the sampling procedure used. Fox relied on information from key informants and interviewees, who appear to be the same individuals that she eventually placed in the "real" punk category. It is not surprising to find that those she interviewed constructed themselves as authentic punks, while those she did not interview—and who were dissimilar to the "hardcore" punks in terms of class and aesthetics, and who were not close friends with Fox's informants—were labeled as less authentic or as outsiders. Her work, like McLeod's (1999), is therefore useful in terms of identifying the semantic dimensions for authenticity, but problematic to the extent that it fails to articulate the authorial nature of social authenticity claims (Williams and Copes 2005).

To paraphrase van Leeuwen (2005:396), the study authenticity should be concerned more with the moral authority involved in its representation than with its truth or reality. He goes on to link the idea of representations of authenticity to power: "social control rests on control over the representation of reality which is accepted as the basis for judgement and action" (Hodge and Kress 1988:147; cited in van Leeuwen 2005:396). Identity authenticity discourses are instances of the politics of identity representation in everyday life, and recognition of this provides opportunities for further study of authenticity's significance. Here we can appreciate the innovativeness of scholars like Hannerz (2015), who spent time asking his informants who they thought were *inauthentic* members of the subcultural groups he studied. Moving from one informant to the next, Hannerz repeatedly found that those individuals labeled as inauthentic were able to articulate their own identity authenticity, and able to point out others, whom they believed were inauthentic instead.

Third, is authenticity really real or is it a social creation? I have shown how identity authenticity is socially constructed, while also supporting the idea that authenticity is typically real to the people who invoke it, and thus real in its coneuences. From an everyday folk perspective, social identities have essential qualities and characteristics; they seem always there and always meaningful. As I noted earlier, some disciplines, especially psychiatry and psychology, still operate under assumptions about an essential self. Other disciplines such as business (e.g., Gilmore and Pine 2007) managerial sciences (e.g., Avolio and Gardner 2005; Beverland 2005) and areas of the humanities (e.g., Levy 2011; Young 2001) also continue to write as if real selves and authentic experiences/behaviors were unproblematic. From the perspective taken in this chapter, such identities are constructions of interpersonal interaction, whose meanings are further diffused via mass and social media discourse (Altheide 2000; Williams and Ho 2016). As Babbie (1998), Zerubavel (1997) and others have noted, discussions about truth and reality have a cultural basis, with what is defined as "true" or "real" being collectively (if only implicitly) agreed on. Sociologists need simply to recognize "that human beings do have concepts of authenticity and the important thing is to see how they arrive at these definitions without being judgmental in terms of what is authentic or not" (Beer 2012:51).

I have focused specifically on identity authenticity in this chapter and thus have not included any discussion of scholarship on the perceived authenticity of cultural objects more generally. Researchers from several (inter)disciplinary fields are following lines of inquiry like those described here, primarily in terms of theorizing how individuals go about constructing definitions of and boundaries around the things they consider authentic. Examples include work in social science (Vannini and Williams 2009), artistic production and performance (Dibben 2009; Peterson 1997), tourism (Cole 2007), consumerism (Atencio et al. 2013; Carroll and Wheaton 2009), ethics (Agich 2015), education (Weninger 2017), and literature (Kádár 2016), among others. Some of this scholarship at least implicitly recognizes that authentication practices are both cognitive and cultural processes linked together in mutually reinforcing ways. Scholarship on identity authenticity can fruitfully avoid theories rooted in realist ontologies and instead develop theories that recognize the collectively created, contingent and negotiated nature of meanings that circulate in everyday life.

References

Agich, George J. 2015. "Authenticity." pp. 1–7 in *Encyclopedia of Global Bioethics*, edited by Hank ten Have. New York: Springer.

Alexander, Jeffrey C., and Philip Smith. 1993. "The Discourse of American Civil Society: A New Proposal for Cultural Studies." *Theory and Society* 22(2):151–207.

Altheide, David L. 2000. "Identity and the Definition of the Situation in a Mass-Mediated Context." *Symbolic Interaction* 23(1):1–27.

Arnould, Eric J., and Linda L. Price. 2003. "Authenticating Acts and Authoritative Performances." pp. 140–63 in *The Why of Consumption: Contemporary Perspectives on Consumer Motives, Goals, and Desires*, edited by Srinivasan Ratneshwar, David G. Mick, and Cynthia Huffman. London: Routledge.

Avolio, B. J., and Gardner, W. L. 2005. "Authentic Leadership Development: Getting to the Root of Positive Forms of Leadership." *Leadership Quarterly* 16(3):315–38.

Babbie, Earl. 1998. *Observing Ourselves*. Long Grove, IL: Waveland Press.

Becker, Howard S. 1963. *Outsiders: Studies in the Sociology of Deviance*. New York: Free Press.

Beer, Sean. 2012. "Philosophy and the Nature of the Authentic." pp. 47–52 in *The Routledge Handbook of Cultural Tourism*, edited by Melanie Smith and Greg Richards. New York: Routledge.

Bell, Emma, and McArthur. 2014. "Visual Authenticity and Organizational Sustainability." pp. 365–78 in *Routledge Companion to Visual Organization*, edited by Emma Bell, Samantha Warren, and Jonathan Schroeder. New York: Routledge.

Beverland, Michael. 2005. "Brand Management and the Challenge of Authenticity." *Journal of Product and Brand Management* 14(7):460–1.

Boster, James S. 2005. "Categories and Cognitive Anthropology." pp. 91–118 in *Handbook of Categorization in Cognitive Science*, edited by Henri Cohen and Claire Levebvre. Amsterdam: Elsevier.

Brekhus, Wayne H. 2015. *Culture and Cognition: Patterns in the Social Construction of Reality*. Cambridge: Polity.

Brekhus, Wayne H. 2003. *Peacocks, Chameleons, Centaurs: Gay Suburbia and the Grammar of Social Identity*. Chicago: University of Chicago Press.

Bucholtz, Mary, and Kira Hall. 2004. "Theorizing Identity in Language and Sexuality Research." *Language in Society* 33(4):469–515.

Bucholtz, Mary, and Kira Hall. 2005. "Identity and Interaction: A Sociocultural Linguistic Approach." *Discourse Studies* 7(4–5):585–614.

Carroll, Glenn R., and Dennis R. Wheaton. 2009. "The Organizational Construction of Authenticity: An Examination of Contemporary Food and Dining in the U.S." *Research in Organizational Behavior* 29:255–82.

Carter, Prudence L. 2003. "'Black' Cultural Capital, Status Positioning, and Schooling Conflicts." *Social Problems* 50(1):136–55.

Cole, Stroma. 2007. "Beyond Authenticity and Commodification." *Annals of Tourism Research* 34(4):943–60.

Copes, Heith, Andy Hochstetler, and J. Patrick Williams. 2008. "'We Weren't Like No Regular Dope Fiends': Negotiating Hustler and Crackhead Identities." *Social Problems* 55(2):254–70.

Copes, Heith, and J. Patrick Williams. 2007. "Techniques of Affirmation: Deviant Behavior, Moral Commitment, and Subcultural Identity." *Deviant Behavior* 28(2):247–72.

Cornell, Stephen E., and Douglas Hartmann. 1998. *Ethnicity and Race: Making Identities in a Changing World*. Thousand Oaks, CA: Pine Forge Press.

Dibben, Nicola. 2009. "Vocal Performance and the Projection of Emotional Authenticity." pp. 317–34 in *Ashgate Research Companion to Popular Musicology*, edited by Derek B. Scott. Farnham, UK: Ashgate.

DiMaggio, Paul D. 1997. "Culture and Cognition." *Annual Review of Sociology* 23(1):263–87.

Erickson, Rebecca J. 1995. "The Importance of Authenticity for Self and Society." *Symbolic Interaction* 18(2):121–44.

Evergeti, Venetia. 2011. "Discrimination and Reaction: The Practical Constitution of Social Exclusion." *Symbolic Interaction* 34(3):377–97.

Ferrara, Alessandro. 1998. *Reflective Authenticity: Rethinking the Project of Modernity*. London: Routledge.

Fine, Gary A., and Corey D. Fields. 2008. "Culture and Microsociology: The Anthill and the Veldt." *Annals of the American Academy of Political and Social Science* 619(1):130–48.

Fiske, Susan T., and Shelley E. Taylor. 2013. *Social Cognition: From Brains to Culture*. Thousand Oaks, CA: Sage.

Force, William R. 2009. "Consumption Styles and the Fluid Complexity of Punk Authenticity." *Symbolic Interaction* 32(4):289–309.

Fox, Kathryn J. 1987. "Real Punks and Pretenders: The Social Organization of a Counterculture." *Journal of Contemporary Ethnography* 16(3):344–70.

Garfinkel, Harold. 1967. *Studies in Ethnomethodology*. Englewood Cliffs, NJ: Prentice Hall.

Gergen, Kenneth J. 1991. *The Saturated Self: Dilemmas of Identity in Contemporary Life*. New York: Basic Books.

Giddens, Anthony. 1991. *Modernity and Self-Identity: Self and Society in the Late Modern Age.* Stanford, CA: Stanford University Press.

Gilmore, James H., and B. Joseph Pine. 2007. *Authenticity: What Consumers Really Want.* Cambridge, MA: Harvard Business Press.

Gilovich, Thomas, and Kenneth Savitsky. 1996. "Like Goes with Like: The Role of Representativeness in Erroneous and Pseudoscientific Beliefs." *Skeptical Inquirer* 20(2):34–40.

Gubrium, Jaber F., and James A. Holstein. 2009. "The Everyday Work and Auspices of Authenticity." pp. 121–38 in *Authenticity in Self, Culture and Society*, edited by Phillip Vannini and J. Patrick Williams. Farnham, UK: Ashgate.

Hannerz, Erik. 2015. *Performing Punk.* New York: Palgrave.

Harter, Susan. 1995. "The Person Self in Social Context: Barriers to Authenticity." pp. 81–105 in *Self and Identity: Fundamental Issues*, edited by Richard D. Ashmore and Lee Jussim. New Brunswick, NJ: Rutgers University Press.

Hochstetler, Andy, Heith Copes, and J. Patrick Williams. 2010. "'That's Not Who I Am': How Offenders Commit Violent Acts and Reject Authentically Violent Selves." *Justice Quarterly* 27(4):492–516.

Hodge, Robert I. V., and Gunther R. Kress. 1988. *Social Semiotics.* Cambridge: Polity.

Hogg, Michael A., and Dominic Abrams. 1988. *Social Identifications: A Social Psychology of Intergroup Relations and Group Processes.* New York: Routledge.

Howard, Judith A. 2000. "Social Psychology of Identities." *Annual Review of Sociology* 26:367–93.

Jackson, John L. 2005. *Real Black: Adventures in Racial Sincerity.* Chicago: University of Chicago Press.

Jacobs, Michelle R., and David M. Merolla. 2017. "Being Authentically American Indian: Symbolic Identity Construction and Social Structure among Urban New Indians." *Symbolic Interaction* 40(1):63–82. doi: https://dx.doi.org/10.1002/symb.266.

Kádár, Judit Á. 2016. "The Problem of Authenticity in Contemporary American 'Gone Indian' Stories." pp. 64–73 in *Routledge Companion to Native American Literature*, edited by Deborah L. Madsen. New York: Routledge.

Larsson, Sussanna. 2013. "'I Bang My Head, Therefore I Am': Constructing Individual and Social Authenticity in the Heavy Metal Subculture." *Young* 21(1):95–110.

Levy, Neil. 2011. "Enhancing Authenticity." *Journal of Applied Philosophy* 28(3):308–18.

Lewin, Philip, and J. Patrick Williams. 2009. "The Ideology and Practice of Authenticity in Punk Subculture." pp. 65–83 in *Authenticity in Self, Culture and Society*, edited by Phillip Vannini and J. Patrick Williams. Aldershot, UK: Ashgate.

MacCannell, Dean. 1973. "Staged Authenticity: Arrangements of Social Space in Tourist Settings." *American Journal of Sociology* 79(3):589–603.

Maira, Sunaina. 1999. "Ideologies of Authenticity: Youth, Politics, and Diaspora." *Amerasia Journal* 25(3):139–49.

McCarthy, E. Doyle. 2009. "Emotional Performance as Dramas of Authenticity." pp. 241–56 in *Authenticity in Self, Culture and Society*, edited by Phillip Vannini and J. Patrick Williams. Aldershot, UK: Ashgate.

McLeod, Kembrew. 1999. "Authenticity within Hip-Hop and Other Cultures Threatened with Assimilation." *Journal of Communication* 49(4):134–50.

Mead, George. H. 1934. *Mind, Self and Society.* Chicago: University of Chicago Press.

Mullaney, Jamie L. 2006. *Everyone is NOT Doing It: Abstinence and Personal Identity*. Chicago: University of Chicago Press.

Mullaney, Jamie L. 2012. "All in Time: Age and the Temporality of Authenticity in the Straight-Edge Music Scene." *Journal of Contemporary Ethnography* 41(6):611–35.

Peterson, Anders. 2011. "Authentic Self-Realization and Depression." *International Sociology* 26(1):5–24.

Peterson, Richard A. 1997. *Creating Country Music: Fabricating Authenticity*. Chicago: University of Chicago Press.

Sala, Emanuela, Justine Dandy, and Mark Rapley. 2010. "'Real Italians and Wogs': The Discursive Construction of Italian Identity among First Generation Italian Immigrants in Western Australia." *Journal of Community and Applied Social Psychology* 20(2):110–24.

Sandberg, Sveinung. 2009. "Gangster, Victim, or Both? The Interdiscursive Construction of Sameness and Difference in Self-Presentations." *British Journal of Sociology* 60(3):523–42.

Seitel, Peter. 1974. "Haya Metaphors for Speech." *Language in Society* 3(1):51–67.

Shenk, Petra S. 2007. "'I'm Mexican, Remember?' Constructing Ethnic Identities via Authenticating Discourse." *Journal of Sociolinguistics* 11(2):194–220.

Stone, Gregory. 1962. "Appearance and Self." pp. 88–118 in *Human Behavior and Social Process: An Interactionist Approach*, edited by Arnold Rose. Boston: Houghton Mifflin.

Sutter, Alan G. 1966. "The World of the Righteous Dope Fiend." *Issues in Criminology* 2:177–222.

Tajfel, Henri. 1974. "Social Identity and Intergroup Behavior." *Social Science Information* 13(2):65–93.

Tajfel, Henri, and John C. Turner. 2004. "The Social Identity Theory of Intergroup Behavior." pp. 276–93 in *Political Psychology: Key Readings*, edited by John T. Jost and Jim Sidanius. New York: Psychology Press.

Taylor, Charles. 1994 "The Politics of Recognition." pp. 25–73 in *Multiculturalism*, edited by Amy Guttman. Princeton, NJ: Princeton University Press.

Trilling, Lionel. 1972. *Sincerity and Authenticity*. Cambridge, MA: Harvard University Press.

Tuan, Mia. 1999. "Neither Real Americans nor Real Asians? Multigeneration Asian Ethnics Navigating the Terrain of Authenticity." *Qualitative Sociology* 22(2):105–25.

Turner, John C. 1975. "Social Comparison and Social Identity: Some Prospects for Intergroup Behavior." *European Journal of Social Psychology* 5(1):5–34.

Turner, Ralph H. 1976. "The Real Self: From Institution to Impulse." *American Journal of Sociology* 81(5):989–1016.

van Leeuwen, Theo. 2005. "What Is Authenticity"? *Discourse Studies* 3(4):392–7.

Vannini, Phillip 2006. "'Dead Poets' Society: Teaching, Publish-or-Perish, and Professors' Experience of Authenticity." *Symbolic Interaction* 29(2):235–58.

Vannini, Phillip 2008. "Symbolic Spaces in Dirty Work: Authenticity as Resistance." *Studies in Symbolic Interaction* 30:229–54.

Vannini, Phillip, and J. Patrick Williams, eds. 2009. *Authenticity in Self, Culture and Society*. Aldershot, UK: Ashgate.

Varjonen, Sirkku, Linda Arnold, and Inga Jasinskaja-Lahti. 2013. "'We're Finns Here and Russians There': A Longitudinal Study on Ethnic Identity Construction in the Context of Ethnic Migration." *Discourse and Society* 24(1):110–34.

Warikoo, Natasha K. 2007. "Racial Authenticity among Second Generation Youth in Multiethnic New York and London." *Poetics* 35(6):388–408.

Weigert, Andrew J., and Viktor Gecas. 2003. "Self." pp. 267–88 in *Handbook of Symbolic Interactionism*, edited by Larry T. Reynolds and Nancy Herman-Kenny. New York: Rowman & Littlefield.

Weninger, Csilla. 2017. "Problematising the Notion of 'Authentic School Learning': Insights from Student Perspectives on Media/Literacy Education." *Research Papers in Education* 33(2):239–54. doi: https://dx.doi.org/10.1080/02671522.2017.1286683

Weninger, Csilla, and J. Patrick Williams. 2017. "The Interactional Construction of Social Authenticity: 'Real' Identities and Inter-Group Relations in a Transylvania Internet Forum." *Symbolic Interaction* 40(2):169–89.

Widdicombe, Sue. 1998. "'But You Don't Class Yourself': The Interactional Management of Category Membership and Non-Membership." pp. 52–70 in *Identities in Talk*, edited by C. Antaki and S. Widdicombe. London: Sage.

Widdicombe, Sue, and Robin Wooffitt. 1990. "'Being' versus 'Doing' Punk: On Achieving Authenticity as a Member." *Journal of Language and Social Psychology* 9(4):257–77.

Williams, J. Patrick. 2006. "Authentic Identities: Straightedge Subculture, Music, and the Internet." *Journal of Contemporary Ethnography* 35(2):173–200.

Williams, J. Patrick. 2013. "Authenticity and the Dramaturgical Self." pp. 93–107 in *The Drama of Social Life: A Dramaturgical Handbook*, edited by Charles Edgley. Aldershot, UK: Ashgate.

Williams, J. Patrick, and Heith Copes. 2005. "'How Edge Are You?' Constructing Authentic Identities and Subcultural Boundaries in a Straightedge Internet Forum." *Symbolic Interaction* 28(1):67–89.

Williams, J. Patrick, and Samantha Xiang Xin Ho. 2016. "'Sasaengpaen' or K-Pop Fan? Singapore Youths, Authentic Identities, and Asian Media Fandom." *Deviant Behavior* 37(1):81–94. doi: http://dx.doi.org/10.1080/01639625.2014.983011.

Williams, J. Patrick, and Kaylan C. Schwarz. (Forthcoming). *Studies in the Social Construction of Identity and Authenticity*. London: Routledge.

Young, James O. 2001. "Authenticity in Performance." pp. 452–61 in *Routledge Companion to Aesthetics*, edited by Berys Nigel Gaut and Dominic Lopes. London: Routledge.

Zerubavel, Eviatar. 1997. *Social Mindscapes: An Invitation to Cognitive Sociology*. Cambridge, MA: Harvard University Press.

CHAPTER 33

....

COGNITIVE MIGRATIONS
a cultural and cognitive sociology of personal transformation[1]

....

THOMAS DEGLOMA AND ERIN F. JOHNSTON

33.1 COGNITIVE MIGRATIONS AND NARRATIVE IDENTITY WORK

IN this chapter, we explore the ways that individuals account for *cognitive migrations* (DeGloma 2014a:148)—significant changes of mind and consciousness that are often expressed as powerful discoveries, transformative experiences, and newly embraced worldviews. Whether individuals articulate these developments as conversions (Snow and Machalek 1983), awakenings (DeGloma 2010, 2014a), or self-actualizations (Johnston 2013), they typically involve an active embrace of new modes of thinking and acting in the world and an equally active, whether explicit or implicit, rejection of other (prior) ways of being. Cognitive migrations can, but do not necessarily, align with other forms of self-change. They are analytically distinct, for example, from entry into or exit from social roles (e.g., changes in occupation; becoming a parent) or social groups (e.g., joining a new organization) and from behavioral and personality changes (e.g., quitting smoking; becoming less anxious). Instead, cognitive migrations draw our attention to changes in an individual's worldview—including one's self-understanding and the meanings one attributes to broadly relevant issues, events, and experiences.

Peter L. Berger and Thomas Luckmann (1966:156–63) pioneered the discussion of such profound transformations of mind with their theory of "alternations," which they described as cases "in which the individual 'switches worlds'" (156–7). Alternations involve the dismantling of one "nomic structure," or structure of social laws, in favor of another.[2] For Berger and Luckmann, a new (commonly, though not necessarily, religious) ideology "provides the indispensable plausibility structure for the new reality" (158). More, "the alternating individual disaffiliates himself," they argue, "from his previous world and the plausibility structure that sustained it, bodily if possible, mentally if not" (159). A core part of this process involves "nihilating" the past "by subsuming it under a negative category occupying a strategic position in the new legitimating apparatus" (160).

Berger and Luckmann's work draws our attention to alternations as a general type of personal transformation and highlights the "biographical rupture" central to such experiences. However, their theory of alternations neglects to fully examine how individuals reflexively constitute themselves in the world (how they actively make and know their selves as agentic characters situated in relation to others) as they create, interpret, and express their sociomental reorientations. More, this seminal work fails to illuminate the dynamic ways that individuals perform their personal transformations for themselves and others, defining various broadly relevant experiences and situations in the process. Much more is needed to grasp the relationship between the individual dimensions of such transformative experiences and the broader social and cultural environments in which those seemingly personal experiences become meaningful.

Like Berger and Luckmann's concept of alternations, our concept of cognitive migrations refers to the ways individuals switch (move between) sociomental reference groups.[3] However, we specifically develop this notion to argue the following set of inter-related points. First, cognitive migrations take autobiographical form, which is to say they manifest as the narrative identity work (Ibarra and Barbulescu 2010) of individuals who undergo them.[4] Second, such narrative identity work provides a reflexive foundation for an individual's understanding of self and identity in relation to other possible selves and identities—for seeing oneself as a relationally situated character. Third, individuals who articulate cognitive migrations use the culturally coded plot structure at the root of their narrative identities to express their allegiance to a new sociomental community. They thereby take on new cognitive norms and identity-defining conventions while rejecting potential alternatives, locating themselves within a broader *sociomental field*. Thus, developing the issue of reflexivity mentioned earlier, such individuals know who they are, not just as a function of their social position in the world, but as a function of their dynamic relation to other social positions (cf. Martin 2003:40). We use the spatial metaphor of cognitive *migrations* to explicitly draw attention to the broader sociomental field in which such radical changes of mind take place. Finally, such narrative identity work links self-understandings to the often-contested meanings of broadly relevant issues, events, and experiences; when individuals account for their migrations, they also advance claims that reach well beyond their personal lives. We now briefly address each of these points and discuss the concepts central to our analytic framework before moving on to illustrate different types of cognitive migrations with case studies from our respective areas of research.

*   *   *   *   *   *   *   *

Cognitive migrations involve narrative identity work insofar as the individuals who undergo them create and recreate their selves as emplotted subjects (as the main protagonists) in an evolving autobiographical story about personal transformation. While there is now a rich tradition in the social sciences (e.g., Bruner 1986; Gergen and

Gergen 1997; Davis 2005a) and in the study of religious conversion (e.g., Snow and Machalek 1983; Stromberg 1993; Jindra 2011) that regards narrative as a foundation of self and identity, the concept of "narrative identity" (Ricoeur 1988, 1991; Somers 1992, 1994; Ezzy 1998. See also Kerby 1991; Gergen and Gergen 1997) specifically highlights the significance of *plot* to the definition of self, and recognizes emplotment as central in the relation of self to others. The plot of an individual's life story refers to the ways that individuals selectively string a series of events together to create a coherent picture of the self (Ricoeur 1992; Zerubavel 2003; Davis 2005b) as an integrated entity or "intelligible whole" (Ochs and Capps 2009:206) that has evolved over time and projects into the future. In short, our selves (and our identities) take story form and are emergent in storytelling activity. Cognitive migrations, as a form of self-change, are accomplished in, and sustained through, the act of storytelling.

From this perspective, our selves become meaningful as characters in the stories we tell, to ourselves and to others, about who we are, about how we have arrived at our current situations, and about our beliefs, aims, and objectives in the world (see also Frank 1995, 2000; Vinitzky-Seroussi 1998). Thus, narrative identity work requires self-reflexivity (Ezzy 1998). As Mead (1934) argued, our capacity to critically reflect on ourselves—to experience ourselves as we experience others—gives us a sense of our social position in the world; just as we think of and ascribe identity to others, we think of ourselves as socially defined and situated character-like beings. More, our ability to reflect on our past selves as distinct from our present thinking, reflecting, and storytelling selves is at the core of our capacity to experience self-change over time (DeGloma 2014a:127–49). Such a capacity—indeed, a central characteristic of human consciousness—facilitates what Margaret Somers (1994:617) refers to as "historicity and relationality"; it allows individuals to craft and express their identities as stories in such a way that they locate themselves in time and space.

When individuals undergo cognitive migrations, they use the plot structure of their autobiographical stories to express allegiance to a particular sociomental community (whether formally defined or not) in a complex and pluralistic social environment. Thus, they mark their position in a broader sociomental field that includes a multiplicity of communities, each with their respective cognitive norms, perspectives, and identity frameworks.[5] Further, their stories reveal a situated perspective on the relations among communities, helping to construct boundaries between competing perspectives.[6] For example, when religious converts account for their new affiliations (Winchester 2015; Johnston 2013), or when contemplative Catholics describe their spiritual journeys (Johnston 2015), they draw on the narrative templates and shared rhetorics made available in their new sociomental communities not only to construct and express a sense of personal authenticity but also to position themselves in relation to others who hold different (and often competing) perspectives on the nature of religious truth, or the meaning of spiritual personhood. Thus, individual self-understanding is intimately tied up with collective boundary-work; self-narratives reflect and construct relationships not only between the self and others but also among sociomental communities in the broader cultural context.

At another level, communities often compete directly with one another over the correct definition of morally or politically salient issues, experiences, or situations (both ongoing and in the past). When individuals align their autobiographical stories with the collective claims of a particular sociomental community, they simultaneously reject the perspectives and positions of other, contending camps.[7] Individuals who undergo cognitive migrations use their narrative identities not only as a way of situating and defining their selves but also to shape broadly relevant meanings. For example, when antiwar activist veterans describe their experiences at war (Snyder 2014; DeGloma 2014a, 2015; Flores 2016), when various individuals describe embracing a new sexual orientation, or when former Hasidic Jews account for their rejection of the orthodoxy (Footsteps 2015; Davidman 2015), they are each ascribing meaning to contentious issues, events, and situations that loom much larger than any individual's personal experiences. Thus, the meanings of culturally relevant events and shared experiences, situated in contentious dynamics, often come to life at the level of personal reflection; they are frequently at the core of individuals' narrative identity work.

We see cognitive migrations as analytically distinct aspects of personal (self) change that are inseparably connected to broader social tensions and cultural competitions. These phenomena are ideal for observing and analyzing how acts of self-articulation fuse individual experiences and identities to socially shared meanings and cultural discourses positioned in broader pluralistic (and often competitive) sociomental fields. Drawing from our respective areas of research, we analyze several distinct cases in which individuals account for major sociomental developments in their lives. In the process, we identify and outline three ideal typical forms of cognitive migration, elucidating the plot structure, key metaphors, and unifying logics underlying each. Despite their differences, all of the cases we discuss involve individuals who have undergone a significant sociomental reorientation; they develop new conceptions of self (often seeing their new ways of being as more authentic or "true," attribute new meanings to socially relevant issues, events, and experiences, and, in the process, recast their relationships to the broader social environment.

33.2 COGNITIVE MIGRATION PATTERNS: THE SOCIAL FORMULAE OF PERSONAL TRANSFORMATION

We now briefly discuss three ideal typical patterns of cognitive migration, or formulae underlying the narrative identity work at the core of personal discovery and transformation. These are the awakening, the self-actualization, and the ongoing quest. Viewing cognitive migrations as a particularly salient form of narrative identity work, we make a strong argument about the social foundations of cognition by linking the achievement and definition of an emplotted self to collective identities and meanings rooted in the dynamic relations among sociomental communities.

33.2.1 Awakenings: Personal Discoveries and Cultural Contentions

In September of 2012, California Governor Jerry Brown signed a bill making it illegal to practice sexual "conversion" or "reparative" therapy on individuals under 18 years of age (Levs 2012). New Jersey soon followed with similar legislation and, more recently, the Obama administration expressed federal support for such a measure (Liptak and Serfaty 2015). The issue of sexual reparative therapy has been politically salient and highly contentious in recent years, but the controversy concerning this practice stems back to a May 1973 convention of the American Psychiatric Association (APA) at which hundreds of people gathered to witness a highly charged debate over whether the APA should continue to consider homosexuality to be a psychiatric disorder (Bayer 1981:125–6; DeGloma 2014b:79–91). At this debate, the well-known reparative therapists Irving Bieber and Charles Socarides defended the conventional psychiatric view (rooted in a psychoanalytic logic) that homosexual behavior is symptomatic of underlying (repressed) problems (unresolved conflicts) in need of treatment.[8] They were faced by psychiatrists and others affiliated with a growing and increasingly vocal gay pride movement who sought to undermine the very logic of sexual "repair," arguing that the practice is unscientific and overwhelmingly harmful. Rather than treating problems, they claimed, sexual reparative therapy creates them.

In the wake of its May 1973 convention, the APA voted to remove homosexuality from the *Diagnostic and Statistical Manual of Mental Disorders*.[9] However, various psychotherapists and religious counselors continue to treat homosexuality as a mental disorder and work to "cure" their patients of homosexual inclinations (see, e.g., Cohen 2006; Nicolosi 2009; Chambers 2009). Many such practitioners are affiliated with umbrella groups such as the National Association for Research and Therapy of Homosexuality (NARTH) and Exodus International. Further, various conservative public advocacy institutions such as the Family Research Council (FRC) advance policy positions (e.g., Sprigg 2014a, 2014b) that provide public and political support for the sexual reparative perspective, often working to undermine legislative efforts to ban sexual reparative therapy and to oppose the gay pride agenda in general (see FRC 2016). The FRC states,

> Family Research Council believes that homosexual conduct is harmful to the persons who engage in it and to society at large, and can never be affirmed. It is by definition unnatural, and as such is associated with negative physical and psychological health effects. [...] Sympathy must be extended to those who struggle with unwanted same-sex attractions, and every effort should be made to assist such persons to overcome those attractions, as many already have.   (FRC 2016)[10]

While a number of factors have fueled the more recent political, legal, and moral scrutiny of sexual reparative therapy (leading to legislative efforts to ban such practices), one factor of central significance is the development and mobilization of communities of individuals who identify as "ex-gay survivors" or "exexgay" (see also DeGloma 2014a). Many of these individuals once embraced the promise and/or perspective of sexual reparative therapy but have since rejected it, now embracing their homosexual orientations in various ways. They tell what DeGloma (2014a) calls awakening stories. Expressing the collective perspective and sentiment of this sociomental community, the homepage of the Beyond Ex-Gay movement reads,

> Beyond Ex-Gay is an online community and resource for those of us who have survived ex-gay experiences. So often healing comes through community and through sharing our stories and experiences with each other. Our kinship in this journey gives us the opportunity to hear each other deeply, particularly in a world that sometimes scoffs at the many things we have done to change or contain our same-sex attractions and gender differences. Many of us have found healing, wholeness and understanding through facing our pasts. This is your space to connect with other survivors, read survivor narratives and to share your own.   (Beyond Ex-Gay 2016a)[11]

By telling their stories in public venues, ex-gay survivors use their personal awakening narratives to take a stand in current debates over the character and consequences of sexual reparative therapy, the nature of human sexuality, and the myriad political and legal concerns that stem from these contentious issues. Aligned with other individuals and groups associated with the broader gay pride movement, such as the Human Rights Campaign (HRC 2016), ex-gay survivors use their autobiographical accounts to weigh in on an increasingly salient moral and political dispute.

For example, after years struggling with various forms of religious sexual reparative therapy, Paul writes,

> Ironically (since "de-conversion"), I now have my 'miracle' after 35 years of tortuous struggle. When I stopped believing in a God who does not accept my attraction to men, something in me changed. I was able to accept that part of myself. I've found friends for the first time in my life, gay and straight, who know me, accept me and even love me for who I am. [...] I had spent my life trying to kill a part of myself, but my instinct was to live. Once I stopped trying to kill my attraction to the same sex, that part of me became content to just be. [...] I discovered what I needed all along was simple acceptance. I am no longer alone. I am no longer living a lie or acting in a way that damages me or others.   (Paul's story 2016)

While Paul's story centers on the achievement of personal authenticity, he also uses the plot at the foundation of his autobiographical account—a plot which is also at the core of the Beyond Ex-Gay community's cooperative narrative identity work—to weigh in on broadly relevant issues concerning the moral and scientific legitimacy of sexual "repair" and the "truth" about human sexuality more generally. Whereas proponents of sexual reparative therapy link homosexual behavior to unresolved inner wounds that lead individuals into a life of falsehood and despair, and link reparative therapeutic intervention to truth, healing, and authenticity (e.g., Chambers 2009:41–65), ex-gay survivors such as Paul invert the moral and emotional coding of the ex-gay narrative. In other words, these individuals perform their cognitive migrations to associate sexual reparative therapy with harm (in Paul's words, "trying to kill a part of" one's self) and link the acceptance of same-sex attraction with truth and healing ("no longer living a lie or acting in a way that damages me or others"). Told in a public venue, Paul uses his personal awakening story to take a stand in a conflict between sociomental communities.

Likewise, Darlene Bogle, Michael Bussee, and Jeremy Marks, all former leaders of various ex-gay ministries, performed a public apology[12] to the same political and moral purpose when they wrote,

> As former leaders of ex-gay ministries, we apologize to those individuals and families who believed our message that there is something inherently wrong with being gay, lesbian, bisexual, or transgender. Some who heard our message were compelled to try to change an integral part of themselves, bringing harm to themselves and their families. Although we acted in good faith, we have since witnessed the isolation, shame, fear, and loss of faith that this message creates. We apologize for our part in the message of broken truth we spoke on behalf of Exodus and other organizations.
>
> (Bogle et al. 2007)

By issuing a public apology for their past views and actions, Darlene, Michael, and Jeremy undermine the "truth" and legitimacy of their prior sociomental position and embrace a new sociomental standpoint with regard to this contentious moral and political issue. As they perform this apology, they engage in narrative identity work to recode sexual reparative therapy (now associated with "bringing harm [...] isolation, shame, fear, and loss of faith" as well as "broken truth") and indict their formerly embraced community.

By using their autobiographical stories to take a stand in this controversy, Beyond Ex-Gay affiliates stand opposed to the official position of NARTH, the FRC, and other groups. Such individuals present their self-stories to public audiences as a way of defining their "true" selves and their broadly relevant social situations, establishing their sociomental standpoint with one community in dynamic and contentious relation to others. While groups like Beyond Ex-Gay highlight the cognitive migrations of those who once embraced and now reject sexual reparative therapy, groups like NARTH and Exodus International highlight those of individuals who once embraced their homosexuality and now embrace a "repaired" heterosexual worldview and lifestyle (see also DeGloma 2014a). This cultural battle, while deeply personal for many of those who share their autobiographical stories, plays out in the social realms of psychology, law, public policy, popular media, and more.

When individuals tell awakening stories, they link the self (self-understandings) to cultural/collective meanings in a multifarious and often contentious environment. Such major cognitive developments take form as autobiographical performances that individuals use to take a stand on matters of cultural controversy.[13] As with the case of the Beyond Ex-Gay community, such performed narrative identity work expresses the diametric opposition of two sociomental camps. It expresses conflicts and tensions of the broader sociomental field. By advancing the outlook of one group and simultaneously rejecting and undermining others, individuals who use such a story formula typically work to define socially relevant events, experiences, and general issues of public concern—both for themselves and others.[14] Thus, they reinforce boundaries between competing groups, separating them according to a personal narrative of change over time, thereby emplotting the distinctions between them with a logic of personal (autobiographical) development.

33.2.2 Self-Actualizations: Autobiographical Continuity and Situated Authenticity

> The contents of the tape had simply given me permission to accept a part of my own psyche that I had denied for years—and then extend it. Like most Neo-Pagans, I never converted in the accepted sense. I simply accepted, reaffirmed, and extended a very old experience. I allowed certain kinds of feelings and ways of being back into my life.
>
> —Margot Adler, *Drawing Down the Moon*, p. 20

In contrast to the awakening narrative described earlier, which depicts a radical break with a past version of self, the narratives of Pagan practitioners like Margot Adler, quoted in the epigraph, construct "an image of a temporally continuous self and an innate, embodied Pagan identity" (Johnston 2013:550). In learning about Paganism, practitioners claim they discovered a label and a community that both reflects and legitimates an identity that was always present, albeit previously muted or unrealized. Their stories draw on a *rhetoric of continuity* and suggest, more or less explicitly, that being Pagan is simply "part of [their] DNA" (Johnston 2013:560–61). The plot structure and cultural coding of this ideal typical narrative template *downplays* differences between the past and present through the construction of an underlying true self, which is simultaneously affirmed and more fully actualized as a result of the storyteller's exposure to the community and its associated beliefs and practices.[15]

In adopting the Pagan identity, adherents like Adler have undergone an important cognitive migration. They join a new sociomental community, and, in doing so, embrace new cognitive norms and frameworks for interpreting their selves, their experiences, and the broader social world. However, Pagans' accounts construct a sense of continuity by explicitly referencing past experiences and events that serve to affirm, for themselves and others, that they were *always* Pagan. In Adler's account, for example, she describes a time when, as a child, she first learned about Greek mythology. Her story emphasizes the deep interest and inherent feelings of connection she had with the Greek gods and goddesses. She recalls, "I remember entering into the Greek myths as if I had returned to my true homeland." This experience is then given new meaning in light of her Pagan identity. She notes, "What were these fantasies of gods and goddesses? What was their use, their purpose? I *see them now* as daydreams used in the struggle toward my own becoming" (Adler 1986:16, emphasis added). Just as transsexuals "scan their biographies for evidence of a differently gendered 'true self'" (Mason-Schrock 1996:176), Pagans select and reinterpret past experiences, presenting them as evidence of a continuous Pagan identity (see Johnston 2013:561–3). In adhering to these autobiographical norms, practitioners claim an authentic Pagan identity and express allegiance to their newly embraced sociomental community.

The emphasis on self-continuity underlying this narrative identity work, however, not only conveys personal authenticity for the storyteller but also reflects and helps construct the collective identity and shared beliefs of the larger Pagan community, situating adherents vis-à-vis culturally relevant others in the broader sociomental (and in this case, religious) field. More specifically, the "foregrounding" (Winchester 2015) of self-continuity is part of a broader cultural claim, made by those within the community, that Pagans, unlike other religious adherents, do not "convert" (Adler 1979; Ezzy and Berger 2007). In *Drawing Down the Moon*, quoted earlier, Adler opens the second chapter, "A Religion without Converts," as follows:

> How do people become Neo-Pagans? This question assumes great importance when we consider that Neo-Pagan groups rarely proselytize and certain of them are quite selective. There are few converts. In most cases, word of mouth, a discussion between friends, a lecture, a book, or an article provide the entry point. But these events merely confirm some original, private experience, so that the most common feeling of those who have named themselves Pagans is something like, "*I finally found a group that has the same religious perceptions I always had.*" A common phrase you hear is, "*I've come home*," or, as one woman told me excitedly after a lecture, "I always knew I had a religion, I just never knew it had a name."   (Adler 1979:14)

In Adler's personal account, which follows these introductory remarks, she explicitly contrasts her experience of "becoming Pagan" with the prototypical experience of "conversion." "Converts," she suggests, join religious groups in which they are passive vessels, internalizing a worldview imposed on them from the outside in the process. She, however, claims not to have undergone such a conversion in joining the Pagan community; instead, she simply embraced a label—*naming* herself Pagan—which reflects an identity she always had.[16] Throughout, Adler uses her personal account to make a broader cultural claim about the character of Paganism vis-à-vis other religious options. Her rhetorical emphasis on self-continuity not only supports her claims to an authentic Pagan identity but also simultaneously serves to define and differentiate Paganism from competing groups and perspectives in the broader sociomental field.

In the awakening narrative template described earlier, the storyteller constructs two selves—past and present—which serve as symbolic representations of two competing sociomental communities. The temporal distinction between these two selves is then used to reinforce boundaries between the two groups, and to indict the former community through metaphoric contrasts (DeGloma 2014a:127–49). The self-actualization narrative, however, performs boundary-work through its very emphasis on continuity. In rejecting the prototypical "awakening narrative," Pagans are simultaneously rejecting an approach to religious life that, they argue, requires individual passivity and the acceptance of religious dogma through "conversion." This narrative identity work—centered on a rhetoric of continuity—helps "secure the distinctiveness of [the] group" and fends "off comparisons that would submerge it into some broader category" (Gallagher 1994:860). It both constructs and reflects the "contrast and opposition" (Adler 1979) Pagans describe between themselves and (what they perceive to be) more authoritarian forms of religious life. Their individual accounts help establish the group's relative uniqueness and positionality, securing a distinct collective narrative identity in the process. In this case, however, it is not a temporal distinction between an "old" self and a "new" self, but rather the foregrounding of continuity relative to change that helps reinforce the boundaries between competing groups in the broader sociomental field.

The ideal typical formula underlying Pagan narrative identity work also helps articulate and advance key differences between the Pagan worldview and that of other religious groups. The emphasis on autobiographical continuity and personal "fit," for example, complements Pagan practitioners' epistemological stance on religious truth (see also Beckford 1978). The self-actualization is articulated as a resonance between the community's beliefs and practices and the individual's deepest, most authentic self—as finding one's *personal* truth. This emphasis on a situated personal authenticity suggests that there are multiple, equally valid approaches to accessing (personal) religious truth. Moreover, because the individual's current affiliation with the Pagan community is not premised in the rejection of any prior affiliation, many Pagans continue to dabble in their old religious traditions, crafting, for example, syncretic versions of a Pagan-Jewish practice. The narrative emphasis on *personal* truth rather than *objective* truth gives the storyteller flexibility to maintain some affiliation with prior sociomental traditions. Adler and others argue that this sociomental freedom is what sets the "Neo-Pagan resurgence" apart from other new religious movements of the 1960s and 1970s, and is tied to the fact that the "Neo-Pagan religious framework is based on a polytheistic outlook—a view that allows differing perspectives and ideas to coexist" (Adler 1979:23). Pagan adherents' self-narratives, therefore, not only construct personal self-understanding but also simultaneously make broader cultural claims about the nature of the self and of religious truth.

All cognitive migrations involve both continuity and change (see Flores 2016). The foregrounding of continuity or change, then, "is a product of rhetorical selection and filtering that aligns individual narratives with norms of discourse" (Johnston 2013:564) in the new sociomental community. For many individuals, Adler's book is one of the first sources of information on Pagan beliefs and practices they encounter. Her personal story and its interpretation then serve to transmit the conventional patterns of "telling the story of becoming" in the wider community (Mayer and Gründer 2010:401; Rosenwald and Ochberg 1992). In embracing these autobiographical norms, practitioners' accounts reflect and reinforce the collective identity and shared beliefs of the community, establishing both the storyteller's and the group's identity and sociomental standpoint in relation to relevant out-groups in the broader sociomental field.

33.2.3 Quests: Migrations as Continuous Becomings

> […] every day is a journey, and the journey itself is home.
>
> —Matsuo Bashō, "The Narrow Road to the Interior," p. 1

> We have a direction, not a destination. We are going East, but you can't get East. You can only go East.
>
> —Ramdas[17]

An increasing number of individuals in the United States describe their religious and spiritual lives as an active and open-ended pursuit of personal development and spiritual formation (Roof 1999; Batson 1976). This orientation toward religious life manifests and is made concrete in the adoption of a shared narrative template—the *ongoing quest* (see Johnston 2015). This form of narrative identity work draws explicitly on the metaphor of the "quest" (or "journey"), along with a unifying logic of progressive attainment, to unite disparate experiences into a story of continuous and *ongoing* personal growth. Both retrospective and prospective, the past, present, and future are provided a sense of coherence through a teleological account of movement toward an ultimate and *ever-elusive* goal.[18] In contrast to the narratives described previously, this ideal typical narrative form describes "an *ongoing* process of self-transformation rather than a completed process" (Johnston 2015:85). In describing their personal transformations as open-ended, such individuals thereby position themselves as *aspirants* who continue to inhabit the liminal space between the old self and the ideal self, or between darkness and light.

While spiritual practitioners who adopt a "quest orientation" (Baston 1976) do not necessarily abandon their former affiliations, they do adopt a new identity framework and perspective on religious life (see Johnston 2015). It is only through immersion in a new sociomental community—usually in the form of classes and training programs— that newcomers learn to see themselves as individuals on a spiritual journey, and to view religious life as a process of continuous formation. Drawing on the community's autobiographical norms, however, participants "emplot" this shift in orientation (the cognitive migration into a quest orientation) not as a dramatic self-transformation (or "rebirth") nor as the validation of an always-already present true self, but rather as another step forward—albeit a particularly large one—on a longer and continuous path of personal development. The cognitive migration is tied into an overarching "progressive" plot structure (LaRossa and Sinha 2006), one in which the slope of change described within the narrative is positive.

The progressive nature of this narrative template is both retrospective and prospective. On the one hand, not only the cognitive migration, but all past events and experiences, no matter how disparate or seemingly contradictory, are integrated into a coherent narrative arc by articulating the role they played in facilitating personal growth. At the same time, the quest narrative is marked by a "looking forward to" discourse (LaRossa and Sinha 2006:446), based on the underlying sentiment that there is always more to learn and additional ways to grow and develop. Aadesh, an Integral Yoga teacher, for example, used the image of the goddess of knowledge to describe this aspect of spiritual formation. He notes that she is "always pictured holding a book...a scroll, something [...] even the source of all knowledge and all the art is constantly learning." It is the same way with the spiritual journey, he continued: "There is no end. It's infinite. There is so much more we can learn. It never ends."[19] Unlike the narrative forms described earlier, those who embrace a quest narrative do not claim that they have discovered *the* truth nor do they claim to have found their true selves, but rather describe themselves as actively working toward the achievement of these ideals.

From this perspective, being a spiritual seeker is defined not by embodying a set of characteristics, but by continuous and concerted efforts to develop a set of idealized dispositions (Johnston 2015). This narrative template constructs the storyteller as a perpetual student or aspirant (Thornborrow and Brown 2009), and ties authentic spiritual personhood to a forward-looking and continuous desire for "something more." Johnston (2015:39–44), for example, finds that whenever the participants she spoke with—at both a yoga studio and a Catholic spiritual center—described forms of personal progress, they almost always immediately followed these claims with references to how far they remained from their goals. Practitioners, regardless of their degree of proficiency or the number of years they had been practicing, described themselves as being at the same general location on their spiritual journeys. This position was defined by several key characteristics. Practitioners (1) were consciously aware of being on a spiritual journey or quest, (2) were putting in conscious and explicit effort toward their spiritual formation, (3) felt they had made some progress, but (4) described themselves as still far from their aspired-to selves.

While many of the metaphors used to describe this process of cognitive migration, such as a "journey" or an "unveiling" (see DeGloma 2014a:116; Johnston 2015:45), are also sometimes found in awakening and self-actualization narratives, these templates construct the individual at a very different structural position. When awakeners and self-actualizers draw on journey metaphors, their narratives "portray their current autobiographical community as the culminating point of their quest, the 'truth' or 'home' that they discovered at the end of their arduous 'path'" (DeGloma 2014a:118). Drawing on the metaphor of the staircase used by DeGloma (2014a:110–21), awakeners and self-actualizers depict their present selves as having made it to the top of the staircase, where they are reflecting backward on the journey that brought them there. Those who adopt the ongoing quest narrative, however, describe themselves as somewhere on the staircase itself, and imagine themselves as occupying this position perpetually.

Moreover, for awakeners, the journey—as a time of liminality and uncertainty—was often characterized by "cognitive anxiety and distress" (DeGloma 2014a:115). For questers, however, being in a liminal space of ongoing formation is a source of pride and satisfaction.

In fact, embracing the ambiguity and uncertainty that marks this space is part of what distinguishes this form of narrative identity work from others. As Bashō's quote at the beginning of this section illustrates, these individuals come to see the liminal space itself as "home." Spiritual aspirants learn to accept the fact that they are unlikely to ever make it to the landing. While, for example, Siddhārtha Gautama's journey to Enlightenment serves as an example of an awakening narrative (see DeGloma 2014a:119–21), most spiritual seekers who follow Siddhārtha embrace the questing character of Siddhārtha's story but will never claim its conclusion for themselves, assuming instead that they will not (at least not in this lifetime) achieve "Enlightenment."

By embracing the plot structure and cultural coding of the quest narrative template, spiritual practitioners express allegiance to their new sociomental community. More than this, however, the quest narrative communicates broader visions of what it means to be a "good," "authentic," and "mature" religious person. The Contemplative Catholics studied by Johnston (2015), for example, described the developmental process underlying their own stories of spiritual formation not only as more broadly applicable but also as *ideal*. The ultimate goal of their journeys—which they referred to as a state of "Christ-consciousness"—was seen not only as a personal ideal but also as one that all mature religious persons ought to be actively seeking to embody. Because of this belief, practitioners hoped to change Catholicism from the inside, encouraging other adherents to grow spiritually by adopting a contemplative—process and future-oriented—approach to their religious lives. Barbara, for example, noted that "the problem with a lot of our Catholics today is the fact that most of them still have an *eighth-grade mentality* [regarding] what their Catholicism is all about, they're still in a *child-like*" orientation. Barbara suggests that the typical Catholic is stuck where he has always been—"not having moved forward"—and because of this cannot possibly have the same level of appreciation for the Mass or for their faith, more broadly, as she does.[20]

Barbara's account weaves together her personal experience of shifting religious orientations with broader claims about the process and nature of spiritual maturation. The depiction of her personal cognitive migration as developmental and ongoing marks her as a member of the "contemplative" community, and serves to differentiate her from other Catholics (and non-Catholics). Moving beyond personal resonance, however, Barbara also claims that her new approach to religious life—as more active and reflexive—represents an objectively more authentic and ideal way of being religious. She positions herself as farther along the spiritual journey than other Catholics, who remain stuck in an "eighth grade mentality." In embracing this narrative template, practitioners like Barbara actively demarcate their collective approach from other available options in the "spiritual marketplace" (Roof 1999) as well as in the broader sociomental field. Their narrative identity work portrays a sense not only of difference, but of distinction (Burri 2008). As with narratives of self-actualization, by deploying a specific plot structure, questers not only express allegiance to a particular sociomental community but also draw boundaries between themselves and others while advancing community-based definitions of reality.

33.3 Conclusion

Cognitive migrations involve significant sociomental reorientations, including changes in how individuals give meaning to their selves, to their experiences, and to a range of culturally salient issues. As such, these experiences present a problem for the construction and performance of coherent selves. Because our identities are social accomplishments grounded in complex "webs of interlocution" (Taylor 1989:39), individuals must account for these changes in ways that make sense, to themselves and to others, in order to reestablish a sense of self-continuity and accomplish authenticity (see also Ibarra and Barbulescu 2010). As narrative identity work, cognitive migrations must take form as socially patterned and acceptable stories.

In this chapter, we have outlined three ideal typical narrative formulae that provide different structural foundations for emplotting cognitive migrations: awakenings, self-actualizations, and ongoing quests. Awakeners emplot their cognitive migrations as a transformational rebirth: they explicitly reject a prior sociomental framework that was fundamental to who they once (thought they) were and adopt a new way of seeing who they are in relation to the world. Alternatively, self-actualizers emplot their cognitive migrations as a moment of self-recognition: they discovered a label and community that validated and affirmed their truest and most authentic self, effectively downplaying the extent of their sociomental reorientation. Finally, questers emplot their cognitive migrations as an important—and perhaps particularly large—step forward in a continuous and ongoing journey of personal transformation. Despite important differences in the underlying plot structure, rhetorics, and unifying logics, each ideal typical narrative template serves to re-establish narrative coherence by tying together disparate experiences into an intelligible and meaningful story.

However, the ways in which individuals emplot these experiences reflects more than just a need for coherence. Narratives of cognitive migration are not merely descriptive but also constitutive (Winchester 2015; Ricoeur 1988); these stories are practices of identity formation and acts of meaning-making. On the one hand, in adhering to one or another set of autobiographical norms, individuals use their stories to express allegiance to a particular sociomental community and help constitute their identities as members. On the other hand, these personal accounts are also means through which individuals make broader social and cultural claims, articulating and justifying a particular position on morally salient and controversial issues. As individuals craft their accounts of cognitive migration according to the conventions and shared logics of a particular sociomental community, they reinforce the collective identity and shared beliefs of that community, establishing not only the storyteller's but also the group's identity and sociomental standpoint in relation to other communities in the broader sociomental field.

In this way, cognitive migrations illuminate the dynamic interconnections between acts of self-articulation, on the one hand, and broader systems of meaning and cultural discourses, on the other. As our analysis here suggests, self-narratives both reveal and help constitute the discursive struggles over meaning and truth among diverse perspectives in a pluralistic, and often contentious, sociomental field. This perspective suggests that cognitive sociologists ought to be aware of the structures and dynamics of fields in order to explore how our socially situated mindsets, rooted in communities, exist in relation to and often in competition with other possible perspectives. Such an approach calls our attention to the connections between autobiographical and collective dimensions of meaning, bridging the concerns of symbolic social psychology and cultural sociology to advance a multidimensional and relational cognitive sociology.

NOTES

1. Both authors contributed equally to this chapter.
2. We must also note Max Weber's undeniable influence on this general line of thought. Weber's (1915/1946) discussion of purifying and rationalizing "spheres of values" in the modern world provides a launching point for a sociological analysis of the proliferation of different and competing sociomental communities. See also Zerubavel (1997) on socio-mental communities and sociomental pluralism. See also DeGloma (2014a).
3. See Shibutani (1955) for a cognitive perspective on reference groups. See also Zerubavel (1997) on sociomental communities and DeGloma (2014a) and Medley-Rath (2016) on autobiographical communities.
4. For foundational discussions of narrative identity, see Ricoeur (1988, 1991); Somers (1992, 1994); Ezzy (1998). Ibarra and Barbulescu (2010:137) "introduce the term *narrative identity work* to refer to social efforts to craft self-narratives that meet a person's identity aims." Developing a "process model" that takes into account both interactive dynamics and cultural resources, Ibarra and Barbulescu address the ways individuals navigate "work role transitions," viewing these as "key occasions for narrative identity work" (136). We expand on this concept by considering the more general cultural and cognitive implications of narrative identity work when individuals undergo more thorough personal transformations. On autobiographical work, see Frank (2000), Davis (2005a), and DeGloma (2014a).
5. Somers (1994) provides a cogent "relational and historical approach" (607) that links narrative identity to "relational setting," arguing that "people construct identities (however multiple and changing) by locating themselves or being located within a repertoire of emplotted stories" (614) and notes, "it is emplotment that allows us to construct a *significant* network or configuration of relationships" (617).
6. Here we adapt Bourdieu's (1984:170) point that "the habitus is both the generative principle of objectively classifiable judgments and the system of classification of these practices." While Bourdieu was concerned with the ways individual dispositions and judgments reflect and recreate structural class distinctions, we take a strong approach to culture (Alexander and Smith 1993), arguing that culture structures identities and the relations among them, on the one hand, *and* agents use their identities in storied form to define and reinforce cultural distinctions and contentions, on the other. See also Martin (2003:38–40) on "a phenomenology of intersubjectivity."
7. See DeGloma (2015) on the alignment of autobiographical narratives with community claims. See also Fligstein and McAdam (2011), who argue that meso-level fields of dialogue and contention are embedded in "the broader environment" that is made up of "complex

webs of other fields" (8) where contests focused on different issues play out and "different actors in different positions will vary in their interpretation of events and respond to them from their own point of view" (4).

8. See, for example, Bieber et al. (1962); Socarides (1968, 1978).
9. See Bayer (1981) for an extended discussion.
10. When no publication date is provided for stories and statements published online, we cite the most recent retrieval date.
11. The Beyond Ex-Gay movement was started by Peterson Toscano and Christine Bakke-O'Neill. The two met in 2005 and launched the Beyond Ex-Gay website in 2007, the same year that the first and only "Ex-Gay Survivor Conference" took place in Irvine, California (serving as a counter-conference to the "Exodus Freedom Conference" occurring in the same area) (see Beyond Ex-Gay 2016b). While in-person meetings played a significant role in this community's history, the rise of Internet communications technology has facilitated movement development and mobilization and has undoubtedly spurred individuals to tell their personal awakening stories in public venues.
12. See DeGloma (2014a:138–41) on "apologetic metanoia."
13. On social performance more generally, see Alexander (2006).
14. Notably, we act as audience to our own accounts. As Alexander and Mast (2006:13) suggest, performances are also "occasions in which we tell a story about ourselves *to ourselves.*" From the perspective of C. Wright Mills (1959/2000), such actors often reimagine "personal troubles" to be "public issues."
15. A similar narrative form has been found in other groups, as well (Mason-Schrock 1996; Lewis 2010; Zuckerman 2011; Winchester 2015).
16. In doing so, Adler constructs "conversion" as a belief-centered experience. She argues, "*belief* has never seemed very relevant to the Neo-Pagan movement," relaying that she "was never asked to *believe* in anything" (20) during her involvement with this community. Yet, despite claims that Paganism is free of "dogma" and "doctrine," Adler goes on to describe a set of common beliefs—the "Pagan Worldview"—held by members of the Pagan community including animism, pantheism, and polytheism (Adler 1986:24–28).
17. Audio file (June 2012), recorded by Erin F. Johnston during her time as a participant observer at a 200-hour teacher training program in Integral Yoga. Ramdas was the instructor for a meditation workshop given as a part of this training program. All participants gave their consent to be recorded.
18. Johnston (2015), for example, finds that the process of divinization—or becoming "like God"—structures and gives meaning to the past and present, as well as projecting forward into the future, for participants at both a yoga studio and a Catholic spiritual center.
19. Interview with Johnston (2015).
20. Interview with Johnston (2015).

References

Adler, Margot. 1979/1986. *Drawing Down the Moon: Witches, Druids, Goddess-Worshippers, and Other Pagans in America Today.* Boston: Beacon Press.

Alexander, Jeffrey C. 2006. "Cultural Pragmatics: Social Performance between Ritual and Strategy." pp. 29–90 in *Social Performance: Symbolic Action, Cultural Pragmatics, and Ritual,* edited by Jeffrey C. Alexander, Bernhard Giesen, and Jason L. Mast. Cambridge: Cambridge University Press.

Alexander, Jeffrey C., and Jason L. Mast. 2006. "Introduction: Symbolic Action in Theory and Practice: The Cultural Pragmatics of Symbolic Action." pp. 1–28 in *Social Performance: Symbolic Action, Cultural Pragmatics, and Ritual*, edited by Jeffrey C. Alexander, Bernhard Giesen, and Jason L. Mast. Cambridge: Cambridge University Press.

Alexander, Jeffrey C., and Philip Smith. 1993. "The Discourse of American Civil Society: A New Proposal for Cultural Studies." *Theory and Society* 22(2):151–207.

Bashō, Matsuo. 1694/1991. *The Narrow Road to the Interior*. Translated by Sam Hamill. Boston: Shambhala Publications.

Batson, C. Daniel. 1976. "Religion as Prosocial: Agent or Double Agent?" *Journal for the Scientific Study of Religion* 15(1):29–45.

Bayer, Ronald. 1981. *Homosexuality and American Psychiatry: The Politics of Diagnosis*. New York: Basic Books.

Beckford, James A. 1978. "Accounting for Conversion." *British Journal of Sociology* 29(2):249–62.

Berger, Peter L., and Thomas Luckmann. 1966. *The Social Construction of Reality: A Treatise in the Sociology of Knowledge*. New York: Doubleday.

Beyond Ex-Gay. 2016a. Website. http://www.beyondexgay.com/ (Accessed January 20, 2016).

Beyond Ex-Gay. 2016b. "History." http://www.beyondexgay.com/history.html (Accessed January 23, 2016).

Bieber, Irving, Harvey J. Dain, Paul R. Dince, Marvin G. Drellich, Henry G. Grand, Ralph H. Gundlach, et al. 1962. *Homosexuality: A Psychoanalytic Study*. New York: Basic Books.

Bogle, Darlene, Michael Bussee, and Jeremy Marks. 2007. "Apology from Former Ex-Gay Leaders." http://beyondexgay.com/article/apology.html (Accessed January 21, 2016).

Bourdieu, Pierre. 1984. *Distinction: A Social Critique of the Judgement of Taste*. Cambridge, MA: Harvard University Press.

Bruner, Jerome.1986. *Actual Minds, Possible Worlds*. Cambridge, MA: Harvard University Press.

Burri, Regula Valérie. 2008. "Doing Distinctions: Boundary Work and Symbolic Capital in Radiology." *Social Studies of Science* 38(1):35–62.

Chambers, Alan. 2009. *Leaving Homosexuality: A Practical Guide for Men and Women Looking for a Way Out*. Eugene, OR: Harvest House.

Cohen, Richard. 2006. *Coming Out Straight: Understanding and Healing Homosexuality*. Winchester, VA: Oakhill Press.

Davidman, Lynn. 2015. *Becoming Unorthodox: Stories of Ex-Hasidic Jews*. Oxford; New York: Oxford University Press.

Davis, Joseph E. 2005a. *Accounts of Innocence: Sexual Abuse, Trauma, and the Self*. Chicago: University of Chicago Press.

Davis, Joseph E. 2005b. "Victim Narratives and Victim Selves: False Memory Syndrome and the Power of Accounts." *Social Problems* 52:529–48.

DeGloma, Thomas. 2007. "The Social Logic of 'False Memories': Symbolic Awakenings and Symbolic Worlds in Survivor and Retractor Narratives." *Symbolic Interaction* 30(4):543–65.

DeGloma, Thomas. 2010. "Awakenings: Autobiography, Memory, and the Social Logic of Personal Discovery." *Sociological Forum* 25(3):519–40.

DeGloma, Thomas. 2014a. *Seeing the Light: The Social Logic of Personal Discovery*. Chicago: University of Chicago Press.

DeGloma, Thomas. 2014b. "The Unconscious in Cultural Dispute: On the Ethics of Psychosocial Discovery." pp. 77–97 in *The Unhappy Divorce of Sociology and Psychoanalysis: Diverse Perspectives on the Psychosocial*, edited by Lynn Chancer and John Andrews. London: Palgrave Macmillan.

DeGloma, Thomas. 2015. "The Strategies of Mnemonic Battle: On the Alignment of Autobiographical and Collective Memories in Conflicts over the Past." *American Journal of Cultural Sociology* 3(1):156–90.

Ezzy, Douglas. 1998. "Theorizing Narrative Identity: Symbolic Interactionism and Hermeneutics." *Sociological Quarterly* 39(2):239–52.

Ezzy, Douglass, and Helen A. Berger. 2007. "Becoming a Witch: Changing Paths of Conversion in Contemporary Witchcraft." pp. 41–55 in *The New Generation Witches: Teenage Witchcraft in Contemporary Culture*, edited by Hannah E. Johnston and Peg Aloi. Aldershot, UK; Burlington, VT: Ashgate.

Family Research Council (FRC). 2016. "Homosexuality." http://www.frc.org/homosexuality (Accessed January 20, 2016).

Fligstein, Neil, and Doug McAdam. 2011. "Toward a General Theory of Strategic Action Fields." *Sociological Theory* 29(1):1–26.

Flores, David. 2016. "From Prowar Soldier to Antiwar Activist: Change and Continuity in Narratives of Political Conversion among Iraq War Veterans." *Symbolic Interaction* 39(2):196–212.

Footsteps. 2015. Website. http://footstepsorg.org/ (Accessed December 2015).

Frank, Arthur W. 1995. *The Wounded Storyteller: Body, Illness, and Ethics.* Chicago: University of Chicago Press.

Frank, Arthur W. 2000. "Illness as Autobiographical Work: Dialogue as Narrative Destabilization." *Qualitative Sociology* 23:135–56.

Gallagher, Eugene V. 1994. "A Religion without Converts? Becoming a Neo-Pagan." *Journal of the American Academy of Religion* 62(3):851–67.

Gergen, Kenneth J., and Mary M. Gergen. 1997. "Narratives of the Self," pp. 161–84 in *Memory, Identity, Community: The Idea of Narrative in the Human Sciences*, edited by Lewis P. Hinchman and Sandra K. Hinchman. Albany: State University of New York Press.

Human Rights Campaign (HRC). 2016. Retrieved January 25, 2016. http://www.hrc.org/resources/therapeutic-fraud-prevention-act?_ga=1.161685244.1735848677.1453731417.

Ibarra, Herminia, and Roxana Barbulescu. 2010. "Identity as Narrative: Prevalence, Effectiveness, and Consequences of Narrative Identity Work in Macro Work Role Transitions." *Academy of Management Review* 35(1):135–54.

Jindra, Ines W. 2011. "How Religious Content Matters in Conversion Narratives to Various Religious Groups." *Sociology of Religion* 72(3):275–302.

Johnston, Erin F. 2013. "'I Was Always This Way…': Rhetorics of Continuity in Narratives of Conversion." *Sociological Forum* 28(3):549–73.

Johnston, Erin F. 2015. "Learning to Practice, Becoming Spiritual: Spiritual Disciplines as Projects of the Self." PhD dissertation, Department of Sociology, Princeton University.

Kerby, Anthony Paul. 1991. *Narrative and the Self.* Bloomington; Indianapolis: Indiana University Press.

LaRossa, Ralph, and Cynthia B. Sinha. 2006. "Constructing the Transition to Parenthood." *Sociological Inquiry* 76(4):433–57.

Levs, Josh. 2012. "California Governor OKs Ban on Gay Conversion Therapy, Calling It 'Quackery.'" http://www.cnn.com/2012/10/01/us/california-gay-therapy-ban/index.html (Accessed January 20, 2016).

Lewis, James Roger. 2010. "Fit for the Devil: Toward an Understanding of 'Conversion' to Satanism." *International Journal for the Study of New Religions* 1(1):117–38.

Liptak, Kevin, and Sunlen Serfaty. 2015. "White House Seeks Ban on Gay and Gender Identity Conversion Therapies." http://www.cnn.com/2015/04/08/politics/white-house-seeks-ban-on-gay-conversion-therapies/ (Accessed January 20, 2016).

Martin, John Levi. 2003. "What Is Field Theory?" *American Journal of Sociology* 109(1):1–49.

Mason-Schrock, Douglas. 1996. "Transsexuals' Narrative Construction of the 'True Self.'" *Social Psychology Quarterly* 59(3):176–92.

Mayer, Gerhard, and René Gründer. 2010. "Coming Home or Drifting Away: Magical Practice in the Twenty-First Century—Ways of Adopting Heterodox Beliefs and Religious Worldviews." *Journal of Contemporary Religion* 25(3):395–418.

Mead, George Herbert. 1934/1967. *Mind, Self, and Society: From the Standpoint of a Social Behaviorist*. Chicago; London: University of Chicago Press.

Medley-Rath, Stephanie. 2016. "'Tell Something About the Pictures': The Content and the Process of Autobiographical Work Among Scrapbookers." *Symbolic Interaction* 39(1):86–105.

Mills, C. Wright. 1959/2000. *The Sociological Imagination*. Oxford: Oxford University Press.

Nicolosi, Joseph. 2009. *Shame and Attachment Loss: The Practical Work of Reparative Therapy*. Downers Grove, IL: InterVarsity Press.

Ochs, Elinor, and Lisa Capps. 2009. *Living Narrative: Creating Lives in Everyday Storytelling*. Cambridge, MA: Harvard University Press.

Paul's story. 2016. http://www.beyondexgay.com/narratives/paul.html (Accessed January 20, 2016).

Ricoeur, Paul. 1988. *Time and Narrative*, Vol. 3. Chicago: University of Chicago Press.

Ricoeur, Paul. 1991. "Narrative Identity." *Philosophy Today* 35(1):73–81.

Ricoeur, Paul. 1992. *Oneself as Another*. Chicago: University of Chicago Press.

Roof, Wade Clark. 1999. *Spiritual Marketplace: Baby Boomers and the Remaking of American Religion*. Princeton, NJ: Princeton University Press.

Rosenwald, George C., and Richard L. Ochberg, eds. 1992. *Storied Lives: The Cultural Politics of Self-Understanding*. New Haven, CT; London: Yale University Press.

Shibutani, Tamotsu. 1955. "Reference Groups as Perspectives." *American Journal of Sociology* 60(6):562–9.

Snow, David A., and Richard Machalek. 1983. "The Convert as a Social Type." *Sociological Theory* 1:259–89.

Snyder, Justin. 2014. "'Blood, Guts, and Gore Galore:' Bodies, Moral Pollution, and Combat Trauma." *Symbolic Interaction* 37(4):524–40.

Socarides, Charles W. 1968. *The Overt Homosexual*. New York: Grune and Stratton.

Socarides, Charles W. 1978. *Homosexuality*. New York and London: Jason Aronson.

Somers, Margaret R. 1992. "Narrativity, Narrative Identity, and Social Action: Rethinking English Working-Class Formation." *Social Science History* 16(4):591–630.

Somers, Margaret R. 1994. "The Narrative Constitution of Identity: A Relational and Network Approach." *Theory and Society* 23(5):605–49.

Sprigg, Peter. 2014a. "Protect Client and Therapist Freedom of Choice Regarding Sexual Orientation Change Efforts." Family Research Council website. http://www.frc.org/soce-therapyban (Accessed December 19, 2017).

Sprigg, Peter. 2014b. "Truth Matters in Ex-Gay Debate." Family Research Council blog. http://www.frcblog.com/2014/08/truth-matters-ex-gay-debate/ (Accessed January 21, 2016).

Stromberg, Peter G. 1993. *Language and Self-Transformation: A Study of the Christian Conversion Narrative*. Cambridge: Cambridge University Press.

Taylor, Charles. 1989. *Sources of the Self: The Making of Modern Identity*. Cambridge, MA: Harvard University Press.

Thornborrow, Thomas, and Andrew D. Brown. 2009. "'Being Regimented': Aspiration, Discipline and Identity Work in the British Parachute Regiment." *Organization Studies* 30(4):355–76.

Vinitzky-Seroussi, Vered. 1998. *After Pomp and Circumstance: High School Reunion as an Autobiographical Occasion*. Chicago: University of Chicago Press.

Weber, Max. 1915/1946. "Religious Rejections of the World and Their Directions." pp. 323–59 in *From Max Weber: Essays in Sociology*, edited by H. H. Gerth and C. Wright Mills. New York: Oxford University Press.

Winchester, Daniel. 2015. "Converting to Continuity: Temporality and Self in Eastern Orthodox Conversion Narratives." *Journal for the Scientific Study of Religion* 54(3):439–60.

Zerubavel, Eviatar. 1997. *Social Mindscapes: An Invitation to Cognitive Sociology*. Cambridge, MA: Harvard University Press.

Zerubavel, Eviatar. 2003. *Time Maps: Collective Memory and the Social Shape of the Past*. Chicago: University of Chicago Press.

Zuckerman, Phil. 2011. *Faith No More: Why People Reject Religion*. New York: Oxford University Press.

PART VII

TIME AND MEMORY

CHAPTER 34

......

THE EXPERIENCE OF
TIME IN ORGANIZATIONS

......

BENJAMIN H. SNYDER

For sociologists, time is not a universal property of the cosmos but a product of social institutions and can therefore have diverse expressions (Bergson 1913; Elias 1994; Hubert 1999; Mead 1981; Schutz 1967; Sorokin and Merton 1937). Time is multiple and multidimensional (Adam 1990). It varies with social context and comprises myriad dimensions, such as duration, timing, tempo, sequence, articulation, and synchronization. Formal and complex organizations, the main focus of this chapter, are one of the major social structures influencing all of these dimensions of temporality. Organizations surround individuals with schedules, deadlines, timetables, and development schemes and introduce processes and task flows that shape individuals' experience of the rhythms and trajectories of life.

In this chapter, I present a framework for understanding organizational temporality that brings many strands of disparate research together. First, I discuss two major structures that shape temporality in general—timescapes and time maps—grounding these concepts in philosophical, developmental psychological, and sociological theories of time. Then, I focus mainly on scholarship about work and workplaces, examining research that is both explicitly and implicitly about time. I trace out a dominant theme in the literature about how organizational temporal structures shape experiences of freedom and domination.

34.1 TEMPORAL COGNITION

......

Across many disciplines, research on temporality works from a core distinction between two kinds of time, which I refer to as event time and abstract time (Adam 1990:30). Understanding how these concepts are rooted in philosophy and psychology helps to highlight the unique contributions of sociological approaches to temporality.

34.1.1 Philosophical Perspectives

The philosopher James McTaggart (1993) argued that time is fundamentally divided into what he called the A-series and B-series. The A-series is the concrete, event-based and "tensed" experience of time. It is the experience of time flowing from a moment that was, to a moment that is, to a moment that will be (Gell 2001:151). The A-series grasps the sense of time as a flow of sequenced occurrences, which, when perceived from a particular vantage point, constitutes an event (Adam 1990:20). This sense of event time is what we talk about when we say that time feels like it is flowing fast or slow, staccato or legato, is full and intense or empty and unstimulating.

The B-series, by contrast, is the abstract, event-independent, and "tenseless" experience of time, a kind of container or line on which tensed experiences of time can be objectively sequenced and ordered (Adam 1990:20). The B-series allows us to discuss the relationships and distances among A-series experiences as they occur "in" time using terms like "before" and "after" (Gell 2001:151). So, where I may have the A-series experience "I *was* eating breakfast, now I *am* eating lunch, and I *will* eat dinner," I can also understand this experience in the more abstract terms of the B-series: "I eat lunch *after* breakfast but *before* dinner." Putting the two notions of time together allows us to make complex temporal statements that bounce back and forth between the flow of events and the ordering of events in time.

34.1.2 Developmental Psychological Perspectives

Developmental psychologists have shown that young children initially cognize time in terms of their engagement with context-specific events (the A-series, event time) (Cromer 1971; Weist 1989). They cannot engage in "temporal decentering"—the ability to "adopt a temporal perspective on an event from a point in time that may not coincide with the time of the event itself or with the present time" (McCormack and Hoerl 2008:91). Young children cannot think about events as occurring within an abstract timeline, thus, they "have no way of grasping... that events that are currently taking place would have been in the future from the perspective of a point of time in the past and will be in the past from the perspective of a point of time in the future" (McCormack and Hoerl 2008:92).

Teresa McCormack and Christoph Hoerl (2008) suggest that between the ages of three and five children add to their event-based experience of time a further ability to cognize time as event-independent (the B-series, abstract time). The child can think not just about a sequence of occurrences that make up the flow of time, but also imagine a generic point along an abstract timeline that can contain events with which they may have no actual involvement at the moment of speaking about them.

Though it receives less attention in the psychological literature, children seem to gain their facility with both event time and abstract time through interaction with adults who provide a "scaffolding" for temporal cognitions using clocks, schedules, routines, games, conversations, and the like (Fivush, Haden, and Reese 2006; Hudson 2006). These activities typically involve both tensed and tenseless language, and thus cue children to develop ever greater competence with forms of temporal cognition.

34.1.3 Sociological Perspectives

In sociology, the distinction between event time (A-series) and abstract time (B-series) is treated in a substantially different way. As Alfred Gell (2001:154) notes,

> A-series temporal considerations apply in the human sciences because agents are always embedded in the context of a situation about whose nature and evolution they entertain moment-to-moment beliefs, whereas B-series temporal considerations also apply because agents build up temporal "maps" of their world and its penumbra of possible worlds.

Event time and abstract time describe two ways in which social context influences both the moment-to-moment flow of action and the mapping of that action within a world of possible trajectories. Societies develop more event-based and/or more abstract systems of time reckoning, which function as a scaffolding that gives clues about and cues for "normal" action. This occurs not just during childhood development but also throughout one's entire life. Whereas the social scaffoldings that shape temporal cognition receive only limited attention in philosophy and psychology, then, they are central to sociology.

Sociologists have focused on two types of temporal scaffolding—timescapes and time maps—which roughly reflect the A-series and B-series of time respectively. "Timescape"—a term developed by Barbara Adam (1995, 1998, 2004)—refers to the intersection in a specific place of multiple rhythmic processes, which span from the macro-scale of the cosmos and social structures to the micro-scale of individual and biological rhythms. The cycles of the sun, routines, habits, task flows, deadlines, schedules, timetables, alarms, instructions, turn-taking, gestures, body rhythms, and the like, all have time (event time) living within them because they are processes that unfold to their own rhythms (Lefebvre 2013). When they intersect in different ways in different contexts, a timescape is produced. Timescapes give a situation "its specific temporal profile, which is unique to the context in question" (Adam 2003:96).

Timescapes are embedded in another class of temporal structures, which Eviatar Zerubavel (2003) calls "time maps" (see also Gell 2001:235–39). Zerubavel introduced this term to analyze collective memory and the social shaping of the past. For him, time maps are "conventional schematic formats that help us mentally string past events into coherent, culturally meaningful historical narratives" (Zerubavel 2003:7). If the meaning of events "lies in the way they are situated in our minds vis-à-vis other events," then time maps tell us which events to situate and in what patterns (Zerubavel 2003:12).

Though Zerubavel focuses on memory and the past, time maps also apply to the future, a line of thought that has been taken up most forcefully by Ann Mische (2009; see also Cerulo 2006; Tavory and Eliasoph 2013). As with memory, societies provide time maps of "projectivity"—the future-oriented aspects of meaning-making and action, such as expectations, anticipations, predictions, and plans.

We can think of time maps, then, as cultural representations of the abstract, B-series of time, which allow us to "navigate in time, that is, in order to know how to act in a timely manner" (Gell 2001:236). They provide a cognitive line or surface on which both past events and anticipated future events can be emplotted into a narrative. As Zerubavel (2003:7) documents, the shape of this line can take many forms, "linear versus circular, straight versus zigzag, legato versus staccato, unilinear versus multilinear." Military and educational careers, for example, are stepwise and staccato time maps that feature "discrete historical episodes separated from one another by pronounced breaks marking abrupt, rapid changes" (Zerubavel 2003:35).

In the next sections, I bring this discussion to bear on organizational life, focusing particularly on workplaces. Work organizations build temporal scaffoldings—such as task procedures and career paths—that map on to the two dimensions of time and shape the ways people experience them.

34.2 Organizational Timescapes

The main ways organizations structure timescapes, and thus the experience of event time, is through scheduling, timetabling, the setting of task procedures, and project deadlines (Bluedorn 2002; Fine 1996; Hall 1984; Zerubavel 1979). These techniques discipline actors' bodies and minds so that when they expend energy at work they do so in coordination with the rhythms of the organization.

34.2.1 Time Discipline

Time discipline is the extent to which an individual conforms to the rhythms of a social group (Glennie and Thrift 1996). It is a primary way organizations generate coordinated social action and an important mechanism of power. The ability to control social rhythms constrains the individual's capacity to act in ways that might go against organizational goals, such as efficiency and profit.

Historically, clock time has been one of the most important ways in which organizations discipline members and gain control over timescapes (Adam 2004:127). The use of clock time-based schedules can be found as early as the thirteenth century in the Benedictine monastic tradition (Snyder 2013; Zerubavel 1980), but their greatest impact has been in the realm of industrial labor (Postone 1996), expanding rapidly in the Fordist era under the direction of Frederick Winslow Taylor and his program of time-and-motion study (Braverman 1974; Burawoy 1979; Roy 1959).

The social analysis of industrial clock time discipline is most closely associated with the influential 1967 essay "Time, Work Discipline, and Industrial Capitalism," by the historian E. P. Thompson. Thompson argues that burgeoning capitalist modes of organizing, such as the putting-out system and the factory system, introduced a new form of work discipline into England between the sixteenth and nineteenth centuries, which fundamentally transformed work timescapes. Where earlier agricultural, craft, and guild laborers followed what Thompson calls a "task-oriented" time, in which work tasks are given the time they need to take, later wage laborers were coerced by capitalists and cultural elites to conform to rigid clock-based rhythms in order to increase efficiency and consolidate power in the owning class. This organizational innovation, Thompson argues, had an important impact not only on work but also on English working-class culture. "By the 1830s and 1840s," Thompson (1967:91) writes, "it was commonly observed that the English industrial worker was marked off…by his regularity, his methodical paying-out of energy, and perhaps also by a repression…of the capacity to relax in the old, uninhibited ways."

Thompson's thesis that premodern work timescapes were relatively leisurely, spontaneous, and unconcerned with time, and modern ones are sped up, rigid, and time obsessed has come under intense scrutiny by other labor historians (Stein 1995), especially Paul Glennie and Nigel Thrift (1996, 2009). They argue that Thompson conflates several dimensions of time, thus creating the impression that there is only one form of time discipline—modern, clock-based—which emerged out of a relatively undisciplined and clock ignorant premodern Europe. Reconstructing the history and concept of time discipline, Glennie and Thrift (1996, 2009) argue that, not only was there a great deal of clock time fluency and awareness in Europe prior to the rise of capitalism but also the concept of time discipline is much richer than Thompson assumes. People can be disciplined to share the same rhythms of action (standardization), they can be disciplined to take on highly repetitive and routinized rhythms (regularity), or they can be disciplined to smoothly connect their actions with others (coordination) (Glennie and Thrift 1996:285–6). Some organizational contexts, such as a Fordist factory floor, will encourage all three types of time discipline, but others may focus on only one or two dimensions. Premodern agricultural work, for example, may not have been very standardized or coordinated, but that does not make it any less time intensive or disciplined in terms of regularity. Glennie and Thrift's critique suggests that researchers should open up to the multiplicity of the temporal world when thinking about time discipline, rather than focus too narrowly on obvious forms of time like clocks and schedules.

Explorations of time discipline in postindustrial, team-based, and virtual workplaces have provided an opportunity to do just that (Hassan 2003; Hassan and Petranker 2007; Whipp et al. 2002). Heejin Lee and Jonathan Liebenau (2002), for example, argue that the introduction of virtual work environments has created new time disciplines that are less clock- and schedule-oriented but no less time intensive. They argue that virtual environments encourage diversification rather than standardization, irregularity rather than regularity, and require more complex skills of coordination than in the spatially fixed workplaces of industrial organizations (Lee and Liebenau 2002:137). Because there are very few physical restrictions on when and where virtual work can be done, they note, the boundaries between work and nonwork spaces become blurred. It thus makes less sense for organizations to use scheduling systems that require workers to be in a particular place at a particular time (though see Poster 2007:77). As a result, Lee and Liebenau (2002:135) argue, virtual workers "are always on—that is, available any time." While they may be physically free to roam, they are still mentally tied to work, thus requiring the discipline to know when to "switch off."

Other research has documented how the intense concentration required of digital work, in particular, can generate a kind of absorbing "flow" state that makes it difficult for workers to disengage, thus encouraging a (seemingly) self-induced overwork (Zaloom 2006). Moreover, workers are often aware that their digital activity can be tracked and monitored remotely by their employers, thus further encouraging them to remain glued to their screens (Sewell and Taskin 2015). The timescapes of virtual work environments, then, have transformed the conditions of discipline, control, and autonomy.

34.2.2 The Time Squeeze

Discussions of organizational life today often refer to a pervasive complaint that time is becoming accelerated, squeezed, and scarce (Rosa and Scheuerman 2009; Schor 1993; Wajcman 2015). Scholars use the term "time pressure" to capture this cluster of sentiments. In the United States, time pressure is experienced regularly by over a quarter of the adult population (Galinsky and Galinsky 2001), and has risen substantially since the 1960s, especially among women (Robinson and Godbey 1997; Hochschild 1997; Mattingly and Sayer 2006). It is now considered a leading cause of stress in many developed countries (Jacobs and Gerson 2004; Sauter et al. 1999).

A major effort has been made to account for time pressure by looking for evidence of an objective "time scarcity" problem using time diaries—detailed logs of how many hours people allocate to different tasks. Are people working more hours, taking less leisure time, and therefore justifiably pressed for time? Evidence for widespread time scarcity has been mixed (Robinson 1990; Robinson and Godbey 1997; Schor 1993, 2000). Some studies indicate that it has arisen among specific groups of workers, such as single mothers, dual-earner couples, and highly educated professionals (Bianchi et al. 2006; Clarkberg and Moen 2001; Jacobs and Gerson 2001). However, the link between objective time scarcity and subjective time pressure is complex and unclear. Mattingly and Sayer (2006) find that, though a gender divide in leisure time has emerged since the widespread movement of women into the labor force, with women now having less leisure time than men, even women who do have more leisure time today than in the recent past still report rising rates of time pressure. Leisure time appears to have a leisurely effect for men but not for women (see also Bittman and Wajcman 2000).

Indeed, studies consistently find that women feel more time pressure than their male counterparts independently of the objective structure of their time (Taylor et al. 2006).

Another set of explanations focuses on dimensions of time other than duration— most importantly synchronization and density. More so than the duration of work activities, scholars point to the rise of a chaotic rhythm to work as organizations have moved to a 24/7 basis. Harriet Presser (2003), for example, finds that nearly two-fifths of American workers have a nonstandard work schedule (something other than 9–5, Monday-to-Friday), and the majority of them do not choose these arrangements. As I discuss more later, in industries as diverse as retail, food service, and transportation, these "nonstandard" workers are asked to be "on call" in case employers decide to ramp up or push down hours in order to match changes in demand (Halpin 2015). Because many of the organizations that require a steady supply of nonstandard workers lie in traditionally feminine industries, such as service work, these arrangements especially affect women.

In an interview study of suburban households in Britain, Dale Southerton and Mark Tomlinson (2005) find that people's complaints about feeling rushed and pressed for time often have less to do with issues of time scarcity and more to do with problems of coordination that arise from the lack of standardized work rhythms in the community (see also Southerton 2003). People who work nonstandard schedules find it difficult to align with those on regular schedules, such as school children. They rush to get "on beat" with family and friends who have more predictable lives. From this perspective, then, time pressure is more about a desynchronized timescape than about not having "enough" time (Lambert 2012; Lesnard 2008, 2009).

In her account of the rising double burden on women in paid work *The Time Bind*, Arlie Hochschild (1997) provides yet another perspective on women's outsized feelings of time pressure. She shows that time pressure can result from a sense that time is too emotionally intense. Competing demands on one's attention and energy, such as work deadlines and children's need for attention, require a sense of urgency that makes time feel too full and compressed. This is made all the more prevalent by the sense that care requires a relaxed and leisurely emotional state, to which the constant juggling of career and family does not lend itself (Blair-Loy 2003). The problem is not necessarily that women have too little time—though Hochschild (2005) also makes this argument—but that the day is filled with a sense of urgency that makes it seem as if nothing is being given its "proper time" (Southerton and Tomlinson 2005:233).

These alternative accounts of the time squeeze suggest that women's feelings of time pressure are indeed objective, not just because many have real time scarcities but also because the pacing, sequencing, timing, and cultural valuation of women's time tends to get more disrupted than men's by the double burden of choreographing both work and home timescapes.

Finally, another body of research, which focuses less on gender, points to the role of information communications technologies (ICTs) in creating a texture to time that feels accelerated and exhausting (Agger 1989; Rosa and Scheuerman 2009; Virilio 1997; Wajcman 2015). These ICTs create an entirely new kind of time—dubbed variously "timeless time" (Castells 1996), "instantaneous time" (Urry 2000), "chronoscopic" time (Hassan 2003), or "immediacy" (Tomlinson 2007)—because of their unprecedented capacity to collapse time and space. The local and the global can be experienced simultaneously in "real time" because ICTs operate at speeds so fast that the human senses simply cannot detect the time it takes for a signal to travel from point to point. This contributes to the sense that we are living in an age of accelerating, incessant, and unstoppable change (Gleick 2000). Though people may spend just as much or even less (clock) time working as they did in the past, it may be that the technologies with which they work—digital screens, e-mail, chat applications, and so forth—create another kind of time that generates a sense of urgency and rush (Wajcman 2008).

34.2.3 Workplace Flexibility

Scheduling is the most common form of temporal scaffolding in organizations (Zerubavel 1979, 1980, 1981). It is the chief means by which organizations "give" time to or "take" time away from workers, thus shaping their experience of temporal control. A key term in discussions of temporal control is "flexibility"—the degree to which organizational timescapes can shift and accommodate workers' and/or employers' changing needs.

Scholars distinguish between two types of scheduling flexibility—"organizational flexibility" and "worker flexibility" (Dastmalcian and Blyton 2001). Organizational flexibility refers to "the degree to which organizational features incorporate a level of flexibility that allows them to adapt to changes in their environment" (Dastmalcian and Blyton 2001:1). This refers to things like just-in-time production systems, which allow the employer to ramp production up or down on short notice in order to match fluctuations in demand (Sewell and Wilkinson 1992); numerical flexibility, which involves the rapid hiring and firing of workers through the use of downsizing and short-term contracts (Kalleberg 2009); and various forms of lean production, in which processes are incessantly updated with an eye toward continual improvement (Graham 1995).

Researchers generally find that organizational flexibility creates a pernicious unpredictability to the flow of time for workers, which makes it difficult for them to coordinate their lives and make a steady or even knowable income (Bell and Tuckman 2002; Golden 2015; Lambert 2012). For example, in a study of a high-end catering company that mainly employs undocumented Mexican immigrants, Brian Halpin (2015) discusses the use of "mock schedules," which are meant to create a lean and flexible workforce through the spontaneous manipulation of the number of workers and timing of work, such as cutting workers early from shifts. The schedules are "mock" because, though they are posted publicly, they are so contingent and revisable that they are not really schedules at all. The company boldly emblazons "subject to change without notice" at the bottom of its publicly posted schedules (Halpin 2015:428). This creates a catch-22 for workers. They must maintain total availability because work can be arranged in a variety of erratic patterns that may change from week to week, yet employers can also alter this "plan" in mid-flight, thus leaving workers unexpectedly underemployed (Lambert 2012).

Like other scholars (for example Smith and Neuwirth 2008), Halpin finds that the purposeful insecurity of this just-in-time flexibility is "mystified" through a number of organizational practices, such as ensuring that the same workers are not subjected to shift cutting every week. The company "spreads the pain" of flexibility across the workforce, thereby concealing exploitation beneath a veneer of fairness (Halpin 2015:433). Thus, many of the undocumented workers Halpin meets think of their employers as providing a good place to work, which treats them fairly. Indeed, among workers who are far less structurally insecure than undocumented immigrants, such as students and parents of small children whose spouse is securely employed, a hyperflexible and unpredictable schedule might actually facilitate their ability to set time aside for study or care, thus making their lack of control over work time seem like control over other domains of time (CIPD 2013). The relationship between lack of control over time and worker subjectivity, then, can be inflected by other factors in a worker's timescape, such as her wider structural vulnerability, comparisons with other companies she has worked for, or the degree to which she can control the timing of nonwork responsibilities.

"Worker flexibility," sometimes called "flextime," is "the degree to which workers are able to make choices to arrange core aspects of their professional lives, particularly regarding where, when, and for how long work is performed" (Hill et al. 2008:151). This includes things like customized start and end times, customized work weeks, the choice to work at home, or the option to pause and resume employment for life events without penalty (Altman and Golden 2007:314). This type of flexibility "primarily emphasizes individual agency" (Hill et al. 2008:152) and helps prevent employees from being punished "for working to their own rhythms" (Moen et al. 2011:407). It is typically considered a more humane kind of flexibility because it gives control over time to workers (Grzywacz et al. 2008).

As was the case with organizational flexibility, however, the relationship between worker flexibility and subjective experience can look very different in certain timescapes. In a study of stockbrokers, for example, Mary Blair-Loy (2009) finds that the stresses of intense client contact and the 24/7 nature of the work are actually exacerbated by having *too much* flexibility. Brokers who can set their own schedules and work remotely, she observes, end up working all the time because they encounter few fixed temporal boundaries. Brokers with more traditionally rigid schedules, by contrast, experience less spillover of their work into nonwork domains. "When occupational responsibilities and client expectations potentially invade every block of time," Blair-Loy (2009:281) comments, "it is bureaucratic scheduling rigidity...that allows brokers to have a daily set period of time in which they are *not* working." In short, while worker flexibility breaks down pernicious temporal boundaries for most people (Moen et al. 2011), in certain circumstances it may remove helpful temporal boundaries (Barley and Kunda 2004; Heritage 2014). The complex intersections of temporal patterns can create diverse timescapes such that the sources of discontent in one context can be the solutions to discontent in another.

34.3 Organizational Time Maps

Organizational time maps consist of things like employment contracts, careers, hierarchies, hiring and firing policies, leave policies, and promotion and retirement plans. These structures provide a framework for understanding work events "in" time (the abstract, B-series of time). They scaffold workers' capacity to emplot their work experiences into a narrative, thus allowing them to see whether their investments of energy today and in the past will pay off in the future or have simply been a "waste of time." While the things that constitute time maps have received a great deal of attention in the literature, they have rarely been discussed explicitly as forms of temporality (though see Epstein et al. 1998; Moen and Roehling 2004; Sennett 2000, 2006; Standing 2013; Sweet et al. 2007). However, this research can be easily interpreted in such terms. In addition to qualities like duration, pacing, sequencing, and rhythm, time maps primarily shape the *trajectories* of organizational time.

34.3.1 The Bounded Career and Conformity

The career is the most prominent example of an organizational time map (Zerubavel 1979:9–11, 2003:34). To an earlier generation of sociologists, the career referred to the "bounded career"—an internal labor market with preplanned pathways of promotion that resides within a single company (Lasch 1979; Packard 1962; Riesman 1967; Whyte 1965). In America, the bounded career concept emerged out of the planning departments of early twentieth-century manufacturing organizations, which had until then focused mainly on improving the efficiency of labor processes (Gilbreth and Gilbreth 1916). Rather than coerce workers to be efficient through clock time discipline, the career would invite them to consent to time discipline in exchange for increased security and a clear pathway to seniority (Burawoy 1979). As Peter Cappelli (1999:131) notes, the bounded career relied on a different understanding of worker motivation, a "happy worker model," which was meant to replace the "frightened worker" model of the Fordist factory system. It shifted the focus of time discipline from the "stick" of the clock to the "carrot" of promotion, and from the shorter time horizon of hourly shifts to the longer time horizon of years of seniority (Snyder 2013). It is unclear just how widespread the bounded career was in practice (Cappelli 1999:113–14), but the idea that hard work will reap the reward of security took on a kind of mystique in many developed countries, especially in the context of male-dominated white-collar work (Moen and Roehling 2004).

It was among male white-collar workers that the bounded career seemed to weigh most heavily psychologically. Between the 1920s and 1960s, a vociferous critique of the bounded career emerged, which pegged it as creating a culture of conformity. Popular novels like Sinclair Lewis's 1922 *Babbit*, John P. Marquand's 1949 *Point of No Return*, and

Sloan Wilson's 1955 *The Man in the Gray Flannel Suit*, were matched by widely read sociological studies like Jonathan Riesman's (1967) *The Lonely Crowd* and William Whyte's (1965) *The Organization Man*. These critics argued that the bounded career made the trajectory of men's lives too stable and predictable, preventing them from expressing themselves as creative and entrepreneurial individuals (Hamilton and Wright 1986). As Whyte (1965:16) put it, "It is not the evils of organizational life that puzzle [the Organization Man], *but its very beneficence*. He is imprisoned in brotherhood."

Discontent with the bounded career may seem surprising, especially given the fact that the sources of economic security that Organization Men enjoyed have been deeply eroded in the twenty-first century. Their complaints become clearer, however, when we consider the bounded career as a form of the B-series of time. In the B-series, time is "a stable field, rather than a process of becoming, and we have the idea that events 'happen' only because we 'encounter' them in a particular causal order, not because time itself actually progresses from future to present to past" (Gell 2001:155). Where A-series time is dynamic and unfolding, B-series time is static and spatial. Overly rigid and pre-planned organizational time maps, then, magnify this stagnant quality of the B-series. They make it seem as if one is encountering life events already preformed as they arrive, rather than participating in their creation.

34.3.2 The Boundaryless Career and Precarity

Since the 1970s, a number of transformations in work have led to the introduction of new kinds of time maps, such as the increasing use of short-term, temporary, and casual employment contracts, often referred to as "casualization" (Cappelli 1995; Kalleberg 2009; Standing 2008). Much as organizational flexibility does to event time, these arrangements aim to give organizations, rather than workers, more control over abstract time. They provide firms with greater control over timing by creating a nimble labor supply that can provide just the right amount of labor at just the right time for the organization (Cappelli 1999). For workers, however, casualization fragments the B-series of time by presenting them with multiple lines of progression that are only partial, fuzzy, and discontinuous (Sennett 2000). Rather than Organization Men, then, casual firms invite workers to see themselves as a "company of one" (Lane 2011), to be more entrepreneurial (Smith 2001), and to self-construct their own "boundaryless" careers (Arthur and Rousseau 1996). These careers do not carry the same promise of security through seniority, but they also do not chain workers to a single company for life.

A widely documented implication of this transformation is a rising sense of uncertainty, unpredictability, and insecurity, which has been dubbed by scholars as "precarity" (Kalleberg 2009, 2011; Standing 2011, 2013). Unlike discontent with the bounded career, which involved a sense of alienating submission to a preplanned life, discontent with the casual firm involves a sense of frustration with an inability to plan at all (Barley and Kunda 2004; Lane 2011; Pugh 2015; Sennett 2000; Sharone 2014; Smith 2001; Snyder 2016b). Richard Sennett (2006:53) likens it to the difference between anxiety and dread.

"Anxiety attaches to what might happen; dread attaches to what one knows will happen. Anxiety arises in ill-defined conditions, dread when pain or ill-fortune is well defined." The dread of bounded careers, then, seems to be giving way to the anxiety of boundary-less careers.

Yet alongside this pervasive sense of anxiety, scholars have also noted that in place of a narrative of security workers often construct a narrative of entrepreneurial individualism that may feel deeply gratifying, at least in the short term (Lane 2011; Pugh 2015; Sharone 2014; Smith 2001; Snyder 2016b). Being precariously employed requires constant vigilance of unforeseeable risks, but that is also precisely where some workers locate their sense of dignity. Ofer Sharone (2007), for example, finds this is particularly the case among American white-collar professionals, who draw on self-help literature and an ethos of defiant positivity to embrace precarious employment as an invigorating challenge that reveals their core identities as entrepreneurs (see also Snyder 2016a). Though the casualization of organizational time maps has fragmented abstract time, then, workers still find ways to construct narratives that can fuse fragmented timelines into something meaningful.

34.4 CONCLUSION

Organizations shape the experience of time by scaffolding humans' inherent capacity to cognize time as both a subjective flow and an objective line, as something we create through interaction and something we encounter as already given in the world. Research on organizational temporalities reflects this dichotomy, with some researchers focusing on timescapes—the flow of daily life—and some focusing on time maps—the ordering of lifelines in time. A central concern in the literature has been the relationship between the rigidity or flexibility of these structures and feelings of freedom and domination. This relationship is remarkably complex. The very same temporal structures that create freedom in one context may create a sense of domination in another.

While early research on organizational temporalities was rather narrowly focused on obvious forms of time, such as clocks and schedules, the field has finally begun to come to terms with the multidimensionality and multiplicity of times, just as many scholars had hoped (Adam 2006). We can no longer say that a nuanced analysis of time is missing in the study of organizational life (Ancona and Chong 1996). Yet there remains a great deal of discontinuity between areas of research. Those focused on timescape concerns, such as the sense of rush and pressure that so many workers feel, rarely discuss exactly how this links to time map concerns, such as the sense that organizational trajectories are fragmented and precarious (though see Snyder 2016b). Future research might examine more directly the mechanisms that link the two dimensions of time and how the intersections of different combinations of timescapes and time maps shape experience.

Yet even this minor corrective points to a deeper issue. Timescape/time map is a rather blunt analytical dichotomy laid over what is actually a complex, fluid, and inter-connected experience of temporality. This reflects a more general dominance in social theories of time by, as Barbara Adam (1990:153) describes it, a tradition of "Cartesian dualism," which, she argues, has hindered our ability to "understand time as an immense synthesis rather than an abstraction." In attempting to capture the dynamism of organi-zational life, the timescape/time map dualism actually lends itself to a rather abstract, static, and reified conception of temporality, grounding it in the spatial imagery of "scapes" and maps. Perhaps ironically, such a framework is good at accounting for tem-poral stabilities—repetition, structured movement, trajectory—but tells us less about temporal instability and therefore social change itself. Beyond refining this framework, then, there remains the need for innovative theories that transcend overly dualistic and static accounts of temporality. Fortunately, relatively untapped theoretical resources abound that could aid in such an effort, such as Gilles Deleuze's (1994) philosophy of time, Henri Lefebvre's (2013) and Susan Langer's (1953) meditations on rhythm, Niklas Luhmann's (1988) theory of autopoietic systems, John Hall's (2009) apocalyptic theory of social temporalities, or Robin Wagner-Pacifici's (2017) theory of events. Each of these contributions attempts to break out of the timescape/time map dualism in different ways and signals possible new perspectives on time in organizations.

REFERENCES

Adam, Barbara. 1990. *Time and Social Theory*. New York: Polity Press.

Adam, Barbara. 1995. *Timewatch: The Social Analysis of Time*. New York: Polity.

Adam, Barbara. 1998. *Timescapes of Modernity: The Environment and Invisible Hazards*. New York: Routledge.

Adam, Barbara. 2003. "When Time Is Money: Contested Rationalities of Time in the Theory and Practice of Work." *Theoria: A Journal of Social and Political Theory* 102:94–125.

Adam, Barbara. 2004. *Time*. Malden, MA: Polity Press.

Adam, Barbara. 2006. "Time." *Theory, Culture, and Society* 23(2–3):119–26.

Agger, Ben. 1989. *Fast Capitalism: A Critical Theory of Significance*. Chicago: University of Illinois Press.

Altman, Morris, and Lonnie Golden. 2007. "The Economics of Flexible Work Scheduling: Theoretical Advances and Contemporary Paradoxes." pp. 313–42 in *Workplace Temporalities*, Vol. 17: *Research in the Sociology of Work*, edited by B. A. Rubin. New York: Elsevier.

Ancona, Deborah G., and Chee Chong. 1996. "Entrainment: Pace, Cycle, and Rhythm in Organizational Behavior." pp. 251–84 in *Research in Organizational Behavior*, Vol. 18, edited by B. Staw and T. Cummings. Greenwich, CT: JAI Press.

Arthur, Michael B., and Denise M. Rousseau. 1996. *The Boundaryless Career: A New Employment Concept for a New Organizational Era*. New York: Oxford University Press.

Barley, Stephen R., and Gideon Kunda. 2004. *Gurus, Hired Guns, and Warm Bodies: Itinerant Experts in a Knowledge Economy*. Princeton, NJ: Princeton University Press.

Bell, Emma, and Alan Tuckman. 2002. "Hanging on the Telephone: Temporal Flexibility and the Accessible Worker." pp. 115–25 in *Making Time: Time and Management in Modern*

Organizations, edited by R. Whipp, B. Adam, and I. Sabelis. New York: Oxford University Press.

Bergson, Henri. 1913. *Time and Free Will: An Essay on the Immediate Data of Consciousness*. New York: Macmillan.

Bianchi, Suzanne M., John P. Robinson, and Melissa A. Milkie. 2006. *Changing Rhythms of American Family Life*. New York: Russell Sage Foundation.

Bittman, M., and J. Wajcman. 2000. "The Rush Hour: The Character of Leisure Time and Gender Equity." *Social Forces* 79(1):156–89.

Blair-Loy, Mary. 2003. *Competing Devotions: Career and Family among Women Executives*. Cambridge, MA: Harvard University Press.

Blair-Loy, Mary. 2009. "Work without End? Scheduling Flexibility and Work-to-Family Conflict among Stockbrokers." *Work and Occupations* 36(4):279–317.

Bluedorn, Allen C. 2002. *The Human Organization of Time: Temporal Realities and Experience*. Stanford, CA: Stanford University Press.

Braverman, Harry. 1974. *Labor and Monopoly Capital*. New York: Monthly Review Press.

Burawoy, Michael. 1979. *Manufacturing Consent: Changes in the Labor Process under Monopoly Capitalism*. Chicago: University of Chicago Press.

Cappelli, Peter. 1995. "Rethinking Employment." *British Journal of Industrial Relations* 33(4):563–602.

Cappelli, Peter. 1999. *The New Deal at Work: Managing the Market-Driven Workforce*. Boston, MA: Harvard Business School Press.

Castells, Manuel. 1996. *The Rise of the Network Society*. Cambridge, MA: Blackwell.

Cerulo, Karen A. 2006. *Never Saw It Coming: Cultural Challenges to Envisioning the Worst*. Chicago: University of Chicago Press.

Chartered Institute of Personnel Development (CIPD). 2013. *Zero-Hours Contracts: Myth and Reality*. London: Chartered Institute of Personnel Development.

Clarkberg, Marin, and Phyllis Moen. 2001. "Understanding the Time Squeeze: Married Couples' Preferred and Actual Work-Hour Strategies." *American Behavioral Scientist* 44(7):1115–36.

Cromer, R. F. 1971. "The Development of the Ability to Decenter in Time." *British Journal of Psychology* 62:353–65.

Dastmalcian, A., and P. Blyton. 2001. "Workplace Flexibility and the Changing Nature of Work: An Introduction." *Canadian Journal of Administrative Sciences* 18(1):1–4.

Deleuze, Gilles. 1994. *Difference and Repetition*. New York: Columbia University Press.

Elias, Norbert. 1994. *Time: An Essay*. Cambridge, MA: Blackwell.

Epstein, Cynthia Fuchs, Carroll Seron, Bonnie Oglensky, and Robert Saute. 1998. *The Part-Time Paradox: Time Norms, Professional Life, Family and Gender*. New York: Routledge.

Fine, Gary Alan. 1996. *Kitchens: The Culture of Restaurant Work*. Berkeley: University of California Press.

Fivush, R., C. A. Haden, and E. Reese. 2006. "Elaboration on Elaborations: The Role of Maternal Reminiscing Style in Cognitive and Socioemotional Development." *Child Development* 77:1568–88.

Galinsky, Ellen, and Bond Galinsky. 2001. *Feeling Overworked: When Work Becomes Too Much*. New York: Families and Work Institute.

Gell, Alfred. 2001. *The Anthropology of Time: Cultural Constructions of Temporal Maps and Images*. New York: Berg.

Gilbreth, Frank B., and Lillian M. Gilbreth. 1916. "The Three Position Plan of Promotion." *Annals of the American Academy of Political and Social Science* 65:289–96.

Gleick, James. 2000. *Faster: The Acceleration of Just about Everything*. New York: Vintage.

Glennie, Paul, and Nigel Thrift. 1996. "Reworking E.P. Thomson's 'Time, Work Discipline, and Industrial Capitalism.'" *Time and Society* 5(3):275–99.

Glennie, Paul, and Nigel Thrift. 2009. *Shaping the Day: A History of Timekeeping in England and Wales 1300–1800*. New York: Oxford University Press.

Golden, Lonnie. 2015. *Irregular Work Scheduling and Its Consequences*. Washington, DC: Economic Policy Institute.

Graham, Laurie. 1995. *On the Line at Subaru-Isuzu: The Japanese Model and the American Worker*. Ithaca, NY: ILR Press.

Grzywacz, J. G., D. S. Carlson, and S. Shulkin. 2008. "Schedule Flexibility and Stress." *Community, Work and Family* 11:199–214.

Hall, Edward T. 1984. *The Dance of Life: The Other Dimension of Time*. New York: Anchor Books.

Hall, John R. 2009. *Apocalypse: From Antiquity to the Empire of Modernity*. New York: Polity.

Halpin, Brian W. 2015. "Subject to Change without Notice: Mock Schedules and Flexible Employment in the United States." *Social Problems* 62:419–38.

Hamilton, Richard F., and James D. Wright. 1986. *State of the Masses: Sources of Discontent, Change and Stability*. New York: Aldine.

Hassan, Robert. 2003. *The Chronoscopic Society: Globalization, Time and Knowledge in the Network Economy*. New York: Peter Lang.

Hassan, Robert, and Jack Petranker, eds. 2007. *24/7: Time and Temporality in the Network Society*. Stanford, CA: Stanford University Press.

Heritage, Stuart. 2014. "Flexible Working Hours Are the Dream ... but Not If You Can't Switch Off." *The Guardian*, July 1. http://www.theguardian.com/commentisfree/2014/jul/01/flexible-working-hours-dream-switch-off?CMP=fb_gu (Accessed November 28, 2014).

Hill, E. Jeffrey, Joseph G. Grzywacz, Sarah Allen, Victoria L. Blanchard, Christina Matz-Costa, Sandee Shulkin, and Marcie Pitt-Catsouphes. 2008. "Defining and Conceptualizing Workplace Flexibility." *Community, Work and Family* 11(2):149–63.

Hochschild, Arlie Russell. 1997. *The Time Bind: When Work Becomes Home and Home Becomes Work*. New York: Henry Holt.

Hochschild, Arlie Russell. 2005. "On the Edge of the Time Bind: Time and Market Culture." *Social Research* 72(2):339–54.

Hubert, Henri. 1999. *Essay on Time: A Brief Study of the Representation of Time in Religion and Magic*. London: Durkheim Press.

Hudson, J. A. 2006. "The Development of Future Time Concepts through Mother-Child Conversation." *Merrill-Palmer Quarterly* 52:70–95.

Jacobs, Jerry A., and Kathleen Gerson. 2001. "Overworked Individuals or Overworked Families? Explaining Trends in Work, Leisure, and Family Time." *Work and Occupations* 28(1):40–63.

Jacobs, Jerry A., and Kathleen Gerson. 2004. *The Time Divide: Work, Family, and Gender Inequality*. Cambridge, MA: Harvard University Press.

Kalleberg, Arne L. 2009. "Precarious Work, Insecure Workers: Employment Relations in Transition." *American Sociological Review* 74:1–22.

Kalleberg, Arne L. 2011. *Good Jobs, Bad Jobs: The Rise of Polarized and Precarious Employment Systems in the United States, 1970s to 2000s*. New York: Russell Sage Foundation.

Lambert, Susan J. 2012. "When Flexibility Hurts." *New York Times*, September 20. http://www.nytimes.com/2012/09/20/opinion/low-paid-women-want-predictable-hours-and-steady-pay.html.

Lane, Carrie. 2011. *A Company of One: Insecurity, Independence, and the New World of White-Collar Unemployment*. Ithaca, NY: Cornell University Press.

Langer, Susanne K. 1953. *Feeling and Form*. London: Routledge and Kegan Paul.

Lasch, Christopher. 1979. *The Culture of Narcissism: American Life in an Age of Diminishing Expectations*. New York: W. W. Norton.

Lee, Heejin, and Jonathan Liebenau. 2002. "A New Time Discipline: Managing Virtual Work Environments." pp. 126–39 in *Making Time: Time and Management in Modern Organizations*, edited by R. Whipp, B. Adam, and I. Sabelis. New York: Oxford University Press.

Lefebvre, Henri. 2013. *Rhythm Analysis: Space, Time and Everyday Life*. New York: Bloomsbury Academic.

Lesnard, Laurent. 2008. "Off-Scheduling within Dual-Earner Couples: An Unequal and Negative Externality for Family Time." *American Journal of Sociology* 114(2):447–90.

Lesnard, Laurent. 2009. *The Dislocated Family*. Paris: PUF.

Luhmann, Niklas. 1988. "The Autopoiesis of Social Systems." pp. 172–92 in *Sociocybernetic Paradoxes*, edited by F. Geyer and J. Van der Zouwen. London: SAGE.

Mattingly, Marybeth J., and Liana C. Sayer. 2006. "Under Pressure: Gender Differences in the Relationship between Free Time and Feeling Rushed." *Journal of Marriage and Family* 68:205–21.

McCormack, Teresa, and Christoph Hoerl. 2008. "Temporal Decentering and the Development of Temporal Concepts." *Language Learning* 58(1):89–113.

McTaggart, J. M. E. 1993. "The Unreality of Time." pp. 23–34 in *The Philosophy of Time*, edited by L. P. Robin and M. Murray. Oxford: Oxford University Press.

Mead, George Herbert. 1981. *The Philosophy of the Present*. Edited by A. E. Murphy. Chicago: University of Chicago Press.

Mische, Ann. 2009. "Projects and Possibilities: Researching Futures in Action." *Sociological Forum* 24(3):694–704.

Moen, Phyllis, Erin L. Kelly, Eric Tranby, and Qinlei Huang. 2011. "Changing Work, Changing Health: Can Real Work-Time Flexibility Promote Health Behaviors and Well-Being?" *Journal of Health and Social Behavior* 52(4):404–29.

Moen, Phyllis, and Patricia Roehling. 2004. *The Career Mystique: Cracks in the American Dream*. New York: Rowman and Littlefield.

Packard, Vance. 1962. *The Pyramid Climbers*. London: Longmans, Green.

Poster, Winifred Rebecca. 2007. "Saying 'Good Morning' in the Night: The Reversal of Work Time in Global ICT Service Work." pp. 55–112 in *Workplace Temporalities*, Vol. 17: *Research in the Sociology of Work*, edited by B. A. Rubin. New York: Elsevier.

Postone, Moishe. 1996. *Time, Labor, and Social Domination: A Reinterpretation of Marx's Critical Theory*. New York: Cambridge University Press.

Presser, Harriet B. 2003. *Working in a 24/7 Economy: Challenges for American Families*. New York: Russell Sage Foundation.

Pugh, Allison J. 2015. *The Tumbleweed Society: Working and Caring in an Age of Uncertainty*. New York: Oxford University Press.

Riesman, David. 1967. *The Lonely Crowd: A Study of the Changing American Character*. New Haven, CT: Yale University Press.

Robinson, John P. 1990. "The Time Squeeze." *American Demographics* 12(2):30–33.

Robinson, John P., and Geoffrey Godbey. 1997. *Time for Life: The Surprising Ways Americans Use Their Time*. University Park: Pennsylvania State University Press.

Rosa, Hartmut, and William E. Scheuerman. 2009. *High-Speed Society: Social Acceleration, Power, and Modernity*. University Park: Pennsylvania State University Press.

Roy, Donald F. 1959. "'Banana Time': Job Satisfaction and Informal Interaction." *Human Organization* 18:158–68.

Sauter, Steven et al. 1999. *Stress…at Work*. NIOSH. http://www.cdc.gov/niosh/docs/99-101/.

Schor, Juliet B. 1993. *The Overworked American: The Unexpected Decline of Leisure*. New York: Basic Books.

Schor, Juliet B. 2000. "Working Hours and Time Pressure: The Controversy about Trends in Time Use." pp. 70–80 in *Working Time: International Trends, Theory, and Policy Perspectives*, edited by L. Golden and D. M. Figart. New York: Routledge.

Schutz, Alfred. 1967. *The Phenomenology of the Social World*. Evanston, IL: Northwestern University Press.

Sennett, Richard. 2000. *The Corrosion of Character: The Personal Consequences of the New Capitalism*. New York: W. W. Norton.

Sennett, Richard. 2006. *The Culture of the New Capitalism*. New Haven, CT: Yale University Press.

Sewell, Graham, and Laurent Taskin. 2015. "Out of Sight, Out of Mind in a New World of Work? Autonomy, Control, and Spatiotemporal Scaling in Telework." *Organization Studies* 36(11):1507–29.

Sewell, Graham, and B. Wilkinson. 1992. "'Someone to Watch over Me': Surveillance, Discipline, and the Just-In-Time Labour Process." *Sociology* 26(2):271–89.

Sharone, Ofer. 2007. "Constructing Unemployed Job Seekers as Professional Workers: The Depoliticizing Work-Game of Job Searching." *Qualitative Sociology* 30:403–16.

Sharone, Ofer. 2014. *Flawed System/Flawed Self: Job Searching and Unemployment Experiences*. Chicago: University of Chicago Press.

Smith, Vicki. 2001. *Crossing the Great Divide: Worker Risk and Opportunity in the New Economy*. Ithaca, NY: Cornell University Press.

Smith, Vicki, and Esther B. Neuwirth. 2008. *The Good Temp*. Ithaca, NY: ILR Press.

Snyder, Benjamin H. 2013. "From Vigilance to Busyness: A Neo-Weberian Approach to Clock Time." *Sociological Theory* 31(3):243–66.

Snyder, Benjamin H. 2016a. "The Disruptables." *Hedgehog Review* 18(1):46–57.

Snyder, Benjamin H. 2016b. *The Disrupted Workplace: Time and the Moral Order of Flexible Capitalism*. New York: Oxford University Press.

Sorokin, Pitirim A., and Robert K. Merton. 1937. "Social Time: A Methodological and Functional Analysis." *American Journal of Sociology* 42(5):615–29.

Southerton, Dale. 2003. "'Squeezing Time': Allocating Practices, Coordinating Networks and Scheduling Society." *Time and Society* 12(1):5–25.

Southerton, Dale, and Mark Tomlinson. 2005. "'Pressed for Time': The Differential Impacts of a 'Time Squeeze.'" *Sociological Review* 53(2):215–39.

Standing, Guy. 2008. "Economic Insecurity and Global Casualisation: Threat or Promise?" *Social Indicators Research* 88(1):15–30.

Standing, Guy. 2011. *The Precariat: The New Dangerous Class*. London: Bloomsbury Academic.

Standing, Guy. 2013. "Tertiary Time: The Precariat's Dilemma." *Public Culture* 25(1):5–23.

Stein, Jeremy. 1995. "Time, Space, and Social Discipline: Factory Life in Cornwall, Ontario, 1867-1893." *Journal of Historical Geography* 21(3):278–99.

Sweet, Stephen, Phyllis Moen, and Peter Meiksins. 2007. "Dual Earners in Double Jeopardy: Preparing for Job Loss in the New Risk Economy." pp. 437–61 in *Workplace Temporalities*, Vol. 14, edited by B. A. Rubin. New York: Elsevier.

Tavory, Iddo, and Nina Eliasoph. 2013. "Coordinating Futures: Toward a Theory of Anticipation." *American Journal of Sociology* 118(4):908–42.

Taylor, Paul, Cary Funk, and Peyton Craighill. 2006. *Who's Feeling Rushed? (Hint: Ask a Working Mom)*. Washington, DC: Pew Research Center.

Thompson, E. P. 1967. "Time, Work-Discipline, and Industrial Capitalism." *Past and Present* 38:56–97.

Tomlinson, John. 2007. *The Culture of Speed: The Coming of Immediacy*. London: SAGE.

Urry, Jonathan. 2000. *Sociology beyond Societies: Mobilities for the Twenty-First Century*. London: Routledge.

Virilio, Paul. 1997. *Open Sky*. London: Verso.

Wagner-Pacifici, Robin. 2017. *What Is an Event?* Chicago: University of Chicago Press.

Wajcman, Judy. 2008. "Life in the Fast Lane? Towards a Sociology of Technology and Time." *British Journal of Sociology* 59(1):59–77.

Wajcman, Judy. 2015. *Pressed for Time: The Acceleration of Life in Digital Capitalism*. Chicago: University of Chicago Press.

Weist, R. M. 1989. "Time Concepts in Language and Thought: Filling the Piagetian Void from Two to Five Years." pp. 63–118 in *Time and Human Cognition: A Life-Span Perspective*, edited by I. Levin and D. Zakay. Amsterdam: Elsevier.

Whipp, Richard, Barbara Adam, and Ida Sabelis, eds. 2002. *Making Time: Time and Management in Modern Organizations*. New York: Oxford University Press.

Whyte, William H. 1965. *The Organization Man*. New York: Penguin.

Zaloom, Caitlin. 2006. *Out of the Pits: Traders and Technology from Chicago to London*. Chicago: University of Chicago Press.

Zerubavel, Eviatar. 1979. *Patterns of Time in Hospital Life: A Sociological Perspective*. Chicago: University of Chicago Press.

Zerubavel, Eviatar. 1980. "The Benedictine Ethic and the Spirit of Modern Scheduling: On Schedules and Social Organization." *Sociological Inquiry* 50(2):157–69.

Zerubavel, Eviatar. 1981. *Hidden Rhythms: Schedules and Calendars in Social Life*. Berkeley: University of California Press.

Zerubavel, Eviatar. 2003. *Time Maps: Collective Memory and the Social Shape of the Past*. Chicago: University of Chicago Press.

CHAPTER 35

....

SILENCE AND COLLECTIVE MEMORY*

....

VERED VINITZKY-SEROUSSI
AND CHANA TEEGER

WHAT role does silence play in collective memory? Most immediately, when we think of silence, we think of forgetting and amnesia, not memory (Connerton, 2008). To remember the past, it seems, we must recount and recollect it. It comes as no surprise, therefore, that when nations, collectives, or individuals wish to ensure that certain events, eras, and people are remembered, they quite naturally turn to words and images. What can be heard, seen, and touched has become the cornerstone of memory. Scholars of collective memory have thus focused much attention on the form and content of historical representations. In terms of form, they have examined rituals, historical museums, monuments, memorials, textbooks, films, curricula, and much more. In terms of content, scholars have paid attention to the words, images, and narratives that have filled these forms. Other researchers have focused on what Olick (1999) has called "collected memories": aggregated individual-level recollections of the collective past. These researchers, too, have focused on talk by attending to the socially patterned ways in which individuals recall (Schuman and Scott 1989) and deploy (Teeger 2014) the collective past.

But what about those events and people about which individuals and institutions keep silent? While silence is a difficult domain to investigate empirically (Zerubavel 2006), scholars of collective memory have quite naturally taken note of what is missing and not talked about in representations of the past. In this way, they have drawn attention to distortions in what had hitherto been perceived as the truth about the past (e.g., Ben-Yehuda 1995) and to processes through which people and events were excluded from collective memory (e.g., Stora 2006; Piterberg 2006; Choi 2001; Yoneyama 1999; Prost 1999; Aguilar 1999; Sturken 1991; Ehrenhaus 1989). Underpinning these studies is an assumption that silence is invariably related to forgetting, while talk is tightly coupled with remembering. This assumption has been shared by a variety of groups who have

* This chapter reproduces parts of our 2010 *Social Forces* paper, entitled "Unpacking the Unspoken: Silence in Collective Memory and Forgetting." We thank SF for granting us the permission to do so.

mobilized around the silencing of aspects of the past in a variety of mnemonic spaces (see, e.g., Gutman 2015; Zolberg 1998; Scott 1996; Young 1993; Wagner-Pacifici and Schwartz 1991).

In what follows, we elaborate on our earlier work (Vinitzky-Seroussi and Teeger 2010) to offer a broader understanding of the role of silence in collective memory and forgetting. We show that, while silence often reflects desires at forgetting and amnesia, it can also be used to promote memory.[1] Conversely, we demonstrate how talk can be used to enhance forgetting. We distinguish between two types of silence: overt and covert. Overt silences are those types of silences that we quite normally think of. They are literal silences characterized by a complete absence of any narrative or speech and are thus usually quite easy to detect. Covert silences, on the other hand, are silences that inhere within speech. These are silences that are veiled by much mnemonic talk and as such are harder to decipher and identify. Both types of silence (overt and covert) can be used as mechanisms through which to enhance either memory or forgetting.

We begin by describing these different dimensions of silence. Specifically, we distinguish between the function and form of silence. In terms of the former, we identify how silence can be used to enhance either memory or forgetting. In terms of the latter, we distinguish between overt and covert silences. In other words, we identify four types of silence: (1) overt silence in the domain of memory, (2) overt silence in the domain of forgetting, (3) covert silence in the domain of memory, and (4) covert silence in the domain of forgetting. Having outlined this typology, we discuss how each of these forms of silence can be broken. These processes highlight how, like memory, silence is a process rather than a thing (Olick 2016) and can be unstable, mutable and unpredictable (Zelizer 1995).

35.1 OVERT AND COVERT SILENCES

Our analysis of the various forms and functions of silence is undoubtedly located within a contemporary social and political era where groups, sectors, and entire nations are expected to recognize and confront their postheroic pasts (Schwartz and Schuman 2005) and to examine their shameful histories and embarrassing moments (Olick 2007). For reasons that are beyond the scope of this chapter, celebrating a mythic and heroic past and ignoring "difficult pasts" (Wagner-Pacifici and Schwartz 1991; Vinitzky-Seroussi 2002) seems to have become less and less legitimate. As such, keeping completely silent about certain issues is increasingly becoming a nonoption for many nations (or, at the very least, an option with a high domestic and international political price-tag attached). This has not, however, meant that commemorative activities around these pasts are wholeheartedly embraced. Today, as in the past, certain constituencies do not wish to remember and acknowledge certain pasts, especially if such memories bring up issues of accountability and guilt. However, unlike in the past, these groups often cannot simply withdraw into a complete and collective silence around these pasts. How then do groups and/or nations who wish to forget the past, or at the very least not to talk about it, do so in a context where this is less and less acceptable (and, in some cases, where they are legislatively forced to "remember")? Furthermore, how do groups who do wish to remember the past do so while minimizing conflict with other groups who do not wish to recollect its shameful aspects?

We show how covert silences can become a mechanism for dealing with difficult, traumatic, and shameful pasts. Unlike overt silences, which are characterized by a complete lack of speech, covert silences are veiled by much mnemonic talk. As such, they can become a particularly effective tool for (1) remembering the past while minimizing its potentially conflictual elements or (2) forgetting the past while presenting the appearance of memory. Before elaborating how such covert silences can be used to promote either memory or forgetting, we turn to the types of silence we most immediately think of: overt silences characterized by a complete absence of speech. We show how, like covert silences, such overt and literal silences can be used to enhance not only forgetting, but also memory.

35.1.1 Overt Silences in the Domain of Forgetting

An intuitive understanding of silence brings our attention to literal and overt silences that are characterized by a complete absence of mnemonic talk and are aimed at promoting forgetting. Forgetting, of course, is an inescapable element in remembering. Schudson puts it succinctly when he states, "[m]emory is distortion since memory is invariably and inevitably selective. A way of seeing is a way of not seeing, a way of remembering is a way of forgetting, too" (1997:348). As many have pointed out, in any recollection of the past, certain elements are always highlighted while others are ignored (e.g., Crane 2000; Winter & Sivan 1999; Brink 2000). Memory, like narrative, is "constructed around its own blind spots and silences" (Brink 2000:37). In other words, the ability to remember, to speak of, or to commemorate one thing, may implicitly be predicated on the ability to forget, sideline, and keep silent on others.

Time may play a role in demarcating those topics that become silenced as other, more recent histories take mnemonic center stage. As witnesses pass away or grow old and collectives grow apathetic or disinterested, certain topics, events, and people may recede from memory and become veiled in silence.[2] Still, overt silences are often far from benign and may reflect real desires to mute certain aspects of the past in order to (re)present its other aspects in specific ways, often more favorable to those in power (Yoneyama 1999; Trouillot 1995; Spillman 1994; Sturken 1991, 1997). In this sense, the narration of certain memories and the silencing of others can be conceptualized as the attempts of those with power to set the limits on what is speakable or unspeakable about the past.

We see these types of overt silences, for example, in Japanese silence about the forced sexual abuse of Korean women during World War II (Sand 1999), as well Turkey's silence about the Armenian genocide (Akçam 2010). Such silences can also be seen in the reconstruction of national identities following civil war. The Balkans provide a clear example. There, in the process of history revisionism following the ethnic wars of the

1990s, history textbooks erased traces of common Yugoslav identity and replaced it with new constructions of ethnonational identities (Pavasovic Trost 2018). Focusing on the same region but moving from nation-building to international impression management, Rivera (2008) documents how Croatia engaged in a type of stigma management by omitting any mention of war and reinventing itself as a tourist destination.

35.1.2 Overt Silences in the Domain of Memory

Overt silences are not, however, only about forgetting. On the contrary, in many social and national contexts, the most sacred ritual begins with a moment of silence. This silence is intentional, purposive, and planned in advance, and its raison d'être is commemoration. The aim of such moments of silence is introspection and reflection on that which is commemorated. These moments interrupt the usual flow of time, of gestures and bodily movements, of speech, and of thoughts. There is probably no text that can perform a similar commemorative function by inscribing itself on one's body so powerfully.

Memorial ceremonies for individuals who have passed often contain a moment of silent reflection. Such moments are also commonly integrated into commemorative events that are organized in the aftermath of natural disasters and unexpected tragedies. Such moments of silence were observed following 9/11 in the US, the 2005 tube and bus bombings in London, and the 2004 Asian tsunami, to name but a few examples.[3]

Such moments of silence can also be repeated annually during national memorial days and ceremonies. Holocaust Remembrance Day in Israel presents one such example. There, a one-minute siren is heard across the country at 10 a.m. every memorial day. Even on the highway, it is in no way uncommon to see people stopping their cars, stepping onto the road and standing still until the siren is over (see Young 1993). The annual reenactment of the moment of silence is so powerful that individuals often find that when the siren sounds, they stand still, keep silent, and contemplate the day even if the demarcated moment finds them alone in their homes or offices. The structured moment of silence thus becomes something that is difficult to ignore or sidestep. Borrowing from Durkheim (1964) and Foucault (1977), one could say that the regulated and ritualized moment of silence becomes the ultimate manifestation of social control in that it comes to be internalized without external surveillance, creating "docile bodies" disciplined in the act of memory.

35.1.3 Covert Silence in the Domain of Memory

Schudson (1997:355) has argued that in an "effort not only to report the past but to make it interesting, narratives simplify." Part of this simplification is the result of commercial considerations which seek to "make an account of the past palatable to all tastes—hence, bland and uncontroversial" (354). Commercial considerations, however, are not the only motivation for inducing audiences. Agents of memory are often motivated by a variety of reasons to sideline certain troubled aspects of the past recounted in order to enable broader collectives to participate in a memory that otherwise may be hard to share. Thus, within commemorative activities and narratives, certain issues come to be ignored and silenced in the aim of memory. Sometimes this silencing involves complete sidelining of the aspects of the narrative. Other times, the silencing is more subtle and is manifest, for example, through issues that are hinted at but not explored. Such covert silences can facilitate more peaceful transitions between regimes (Knutsen 2015) and curtail the eruption of conflict over representations of shameful and contested pasts.

The South African transition to democracy, for example, is often hailed as a model for how to remember shameful pasts without reigniting conflict in the present (Goldstone 2000). Critical scholarship on the South African Truth and Reconciliation Commission highlights how, in addressing the country's apartheid past, certain elements were silenced and sidelined. Significantly, the focus on individual victims and perpetrators allowed white South Africans to join black South Africans in incredulity at the gross human rights violations that had been committed in their name during the apartheid regime (Posel 2002). The everyday structural dimensions of apartheid were deemed outside of the Commission's purview, and the topic of beneficiaries was silenced. Similar mnemonic strategies have been found in contemporary South African high schools as teachers grapple with the dilemma of how to talk about the country's apartheid past without creating micro-interactional conflict between black and white students (Teeger 2015). These processes are not dissimilar from those identified by Kampf (2009) in his analysis of the discursive strategies that allow politicians to acknowledge past wrongs while avoiding responsibility (see also Brown 2015).

Covert silences in the domain of memory are often the result of political compromise. These silences are not about a complete denial of the past. Rather, they are about avoiding difficult aspects of the past that persist into the present. They enable broader collectives to participate in mnemonic activities but they do so at the expense of depth, accountability, and context. In many ways, they allow for a memory of the past that keeps the past firmly in the past while covertly remaining silent on aspects of the past that evoke issues of guilt, shame, and responsibility in the present.

35.1.4 Covert Silences in the Domain of Forgetting

Complete silence about the past is one way through which collectives may try to forget the past. Others, however, develop sophisticated mechanisms through which to attempt to effect forgetting, some of which carry the appearance of commemoration. This is often a result of the fact that, while certain groups find commemorating particular people or events to be unacceptable or uncomfortable for a variety of reasons, keeping totally silent on these issues is increasingly being perceived as illegitimate within the broader society. Moreover, agents of memory are often aware of potential criticism that may be raised against them if they fail to mention certain elements of the past and thus preemptively respond to these potential criticisms by incorporating difficult aspects of the past in ways that minimize their impact (Teeger and Vinitzky-Seroussi 2007). Such covert silences are not easily identifiable and thus not easily critiqued, as they are covered and hidden by much mnemonic talk.

Yitzhak Rabin commemorations provide a good illustration of this type of silence. In 1995, Rabin—who was the Israeli prime minister at the time—was assassinated by a right-wing religious Jew. In 1997, the state legislated a national memorial day on the date of assassination. Most Israeli state schools interpreted the new law as one that required a memorial ceremony (Vinitzky-Seroussi 2001). For reasons that are beyond the scope of this chapter, the requirement "to remember" posed challenges for state-religious schools. These schools coped with this challenge by merging the ceremony for Rabin with other events (a memorial day for a biblical matriarch and a prayer for rain).

While a generalized day focused on many individuals or events may have many financial, commercial and logistical advantages (as is the case in the United States with Presidents Day), it may also threaten the ability to concentrate on a specific individual or event. The uniqueness of any one event or person may be diminished such that all the events and people who share the commemorative time and space may become inter-changeable or forgotten altogether. Moreover, when a specific day dedicated to a specific person is expanded to include more events and people, hierarchies of importance begin to be constructed as decisions are made about the allocation of commemorative space and time.

In the case of Rabin commemorations, state religious schools created cacophonous commemorations that exhibited so much mnemonic stimulation that the uniqueness and content of Rabin's commemoration was lost (Vinitzky-Seroussi 2009). Covert silence—silence that is hidden in much commemorative talk—can be an extremely sophisticated mechanism through which to effect collective amnesia about certain issues, people, or events. Amplification, in short, is not always about hearing better, and silence itself may be facilitated and escorted by much noise.

35.2 BREAKING THE SILENCE: CONCLUDING REMARKS

The notion of silencing the past and thus burying specific events is not new. But, in a world that demands talk and memory even about pasts that contain embarrassing moments, human rights violations, shameful events, and little to be proud about, silence may conquer a new position and social space. Most immediately, silence is connected in our mind with forgetting while talk is tied to remembrance. In this chapter, however, we elaborated on how silence can also be part of the language of remembrance and talk can be found in the language of forgetting.

At the extremes of memory and forgetting, we find two types of overt silence. The first, in the domain of memory, is heavily ritualized, bounded, short, and clearly defined in relation to particular memories. This kind of silence is perhaps the highest official honor that can be granted to the past. The second is silence in the domain of forgetting. Here, the silence does not exist in a clearly demarcated time or space and often represents deliberate processes of muting and erasure.

In between these extremes of literal silence, we find covert silences: Silences that are contained within, and disguised by, much mnemonic talk. First, there are covert silences in the domain of memory. These are used by agents of memory who give up on aspects of the historical narrative so as to enlarge the potential mnemonic audience, and thus to enhance memory, albeit a selective and partial one. The second kind of covert silence is used strategically by groups who do not want to remember but who are expected to commemorate. Cacophonous commemorations where a mnemonic time and space is shared with many other issues, become an effective mechanism of promoting forgetting through much talk.

All the forms of silence that we identify can be broken. Overt silences in the domain of memory can be broken by groups and individuals who refuse to stop what they are doing, refrain from speaking and contemplate the memories demanded by the moment of silence. Less directed ways of breaking these types of silence can occur when individuals impatiently wait for the moment of silence to be over so that they can return to their routine (see Brown 2012). Overt silences in the domain of forgetting can be broken when, for a variety of reasons, nations are forced to confront and acknowledge their shameful and traumatic pasts. These silences can also be challenged on the more micro level as individuals and communities continue to talk about pasts that have been silenced in the public domain (Zerubavel 2006; Sasson-Levy and Lomsky-Feder 2018; Whitlinger 2015). In addition, the archive remains a repository of memory that can be tapped as a resource to break the silence (Assman 2008). Silence, even in the domain of forgetting, is not necessarily the same as deletion (Dessingué and Winter 2015).

Like overt silences, covert silences can also be broken. In the domain of memory, the covert silencing of certain aspects of the past can be broken by groups and individuals who refuse to compromise on the historical narrative in the name of consensus. In the domain of forgetting, covert silences can be broken by audiences who somehow managed to pay attention in the context of cacophonous commemorations and begin to interrogate and inquire about the sprinklings of mnemonic talk that were offered in the hope of being forgotten. The processes of breaking the silence highlight how silence at one level of analysis (e.g., the institutional level) might be challenged by talk at another level of analysis (e.g., the individual level), creating a dynamic interplay between memory and forgetting.[4] Memory and forgetting, talk and silence, all have the potential for contestation.[5]

Forgetting, as we have illustrated, can be achieved by silence, but it can also be achieved by much talk. Inversely, memory may be achieved by much talk, but it may also be enhanced through silence. In this chapter we have shown how silence should be understood as a socially embedded construct used for different ends by different collectives. Furthermore, we have suggested that silence is a broad concept, one that includes a variety of mechanisms enabling both forgetting and remembering. In a world that still believes that some past events and people should be remembered, addressing the role of silence may in fact be the key for understanding not only collective amnesia but also collective memory.

Notes

1. A similar argument has been recently made in the psychological literature on individual-level recall. Drawing on experimental lab studies, Stone et al. (2012) document how, under certain conditions, silence (or suppression) can counterintuitively enhance memory.
2. It is worth noting that the relationship between time and this type of silence is not always linear, as interested parties may rediscover buried and forgotten histories. See, for example, the recovery of the story of Masada after 2000 years of silence (Ben Yehuda 1995; Zerubavel 1995)
3. See Brown(2012) and Allen and Brown (2011) for a discussion of evolving role of moments of silences in commemorative events and rituals.
4. These challenges can take place in face-to-face interaction, but they can also occur through new media, as Xu (2017) demonstrates in his discussion of online challenges to official silences. Furthermore, it is important to note that even at the institutional level, different commemorative sites have been shown to give rise to different narratives that highlight, and silence, various aspects of the past (Vinitzky-Seroussi 2002; Simko 2012).
5. For a discussion of the shape that such contestations can take in terms of "mnemonic battles," see DeGloma (2015).

References

Aguilar, Paloma. 1999. "Agents of Memory: Spanish Civil War Veterans and Disabled Soldiers." pp. 84–103 in *War and Remembrance in the Twentieth Century*, edited by Jay Winter and Emmanuel Sivan. Cambridge: Cambridge University Press.

Akçam, Taner. 2010. "Facing History: Denial and the Turkish National Security Concept." pp. 151–8 in *Confronting Genocide*, edited by René Provost, and Payam Akhavan. New York: Springer.

Allen, Matthew J., and Steven D. Brown. 2011. "Embodiment and Living Memorials: The Affective Labor of Remembering the 2005 London Bombings." *Memory Studies* 4(3):312–27.

Assman, Aleida. 2008. "Canon and Archive." pp. 97–106 in *Cultural Memory Studies: An International and Interdisciplinary Handbook*, edited by Astrid Erll and Ansgar Nunning. Berlin: De Gruyter.

Ben-Yehuda, Nachman. 1995. *The Masada Myth*. Madison: University of Wisconsin Press.

Brink, Andre. 2000. "Stories of History: Reimagining the Past in Post-Apartheid Narrative." pp. 29–42 in *Negotiating the Past: The Making of Memory in South Africa*, edited by Sarah Nuttal and Carli Coetzee. Cape Town, South Africa: Oxford University Press.

Brown, Kate Pride. 2015. "Guarding the Memory of the National Guard: Strategies of Avoidance in Official Historiography." *Memory Studies* 8(3):313–27.

Brown, Steven D. 2012. "Two Minutes of Silence: Social Technologies of Public Commemoration." *Theory and Psychology* 20(2):234–52.

Choi, Chungmoo. 2001. "The Politics of War Memories toward Healing." pp. 395–409 in *Perilous Memories: The Asia-Pacific War(s)*, edited by T. Fujitani, Geoffrey M. White, and Lisa Yoneyama. Durham, NC: Duke University Press.

Connerton, Paul. 2008. "Seven Types of Forgetting." *Memory Studies* 1(1):59–71.

Crane, Susan A., ed. 2000. *Museums and Memory*. Stanford, CA: Stanford University Press.

DeGloma, Thomas. 2015. "The Strategies of Mnemonic Battle: On the Alignment of Autobiographical and Collective Memories in Conflicts over the Past." *American Journal of Cultural Sociology* 3(1):156–90.

Dessingué, Alexandre, and Jay M. Winter, eds. 2015. *Beyond Memory: Silence and the Aesthetics of Remembrance*. New York: Routledge.

Durkheim, Emile. 1964. *The Rules of Sociological Methods*. Glencoe, IL: The Free Press.

Ehrenhaus, Peter. 1989. "Commemorating the Unwon War: On Not Remembering Vietnam." *Journal of Communication* 39(1):96–107.

Foucault, Michel. 1977. *Discipline and Punish: The Birth of the Prison*. New York: Random House.

Goldstone, Richard. 2000. "Foreword." pp. viii–xiii in *Looking Back, Reaching Forward: Reflections on the Truth and Reconciliation Commission of South Africa*, edited by C. Villa-Vicencio and W. Verwoerd. Cape Town, South Africa: Cape Town University Press.

Gutman, Yifat. 2015. "Looking Backward to the Future: Counter-Memory as Oppositional Knowledge-Production in the Israeli-Palestinian Conflict." *Current Sociology* 65(1): 54–72.

Kampf, Zohar. 2009. "Public (Non-) Apologies: The Discourse of Minimizing Responsibility." *Journal of Pragmatics* 41(11):2257–70.

Knutsen, Ketil. 2015. "Strategic Silence: Political Persuasion between the Remembered and the Forgotten." pp. 125–40 in *Beyond Memory: Silence and the Aesthetics of Remembrance*, edited by Alexandre Dessingué, and Jay M. Winter. New York: Routledge.

Olick, Jeffrey K. 1999. "Collective Memory: The Two Cultures." *Sociological Theory* 17(3):333–48.

Olick, Jeffrey K. 2007. *The Politics of Regret: On Collective Memory and Historical Responsibility*. New York: Routledge.

Olick, Jeffrey K. 2016. *The Sins of the Fathers: Germany, Memory, Method*. Chicago: University of Chicago Press.

Pavasovic Trost, Tamara. 2018. "Ruptures and Continuities in Ethno-National Discourse: Reconstructing the Nation through History Textbooks in Serbia and Croatia." *Nations and Nationalism* 24(3): 716–40.

Piterberg, Gabriel. 2006. "Can the Subaltern Remember? A Pessimistic View of the Victims of Zionism." pp. 177–200 in *Memory and Violence in the Middle East and North Africa*, edited by Ussama Makdisi and Paul A. Silverstein. Bloomington: Indiana University Press.

Posel, Deborah. 2002. "The TRC Report: What Kind of History? What Kind of Truth?" pp. 147–72 in *Commissioning the Past: Understanding South Africa's Truth and Reconciliation Commission*, edited by D. Posel and G. Simpson. Johannesburg, South Africa: Witwatersrand University Press.

Prost, A. 1999. "The Algerian War in French Collective Memory." pp. 161–76 in *War and Remembrance in the Twentieth Century*, edited by Jay Winter and Emmanuel Sivan. Cambridge: Cambridge University Press.

Rivera, Lauren A. 2008. "Managing 'Spoiled' National Identity: War, Tourism, and Memory in Croatia." *American Sociological Review* 73(4):613–34.

Sand, Jordan. 1999. "Historians and Public Memory in Japan: The Comfort Women Controversy." *History and Memory* 11(2):117–26.

Sasson-Levy, Orna, and Edna Lomsky-Feder. 2018. *Israeli Soldiers and Citizenship: Gendered Encounters with the State*. New York: Routledge.

Schudson, Michael. 1997. "Dynamic of Distortion in Collective Memory." pp. 346–64 in *Memory Distortion*, edited by Daniel. L. Schacter. Cambridge, MA: Harvard University Press.

Schuman, Howard, and Jacqueline Scott. 1989. "Generations and Collective Memories." *American Sociological Review* 54(3):359–81.

Schwartz, Barry, and Howard Schuman. 2005. "History, Commemoration and Belief: Abraham Lincoln in American Memory 1945–2001." *American Sociological Review* 70(2):183–203.

Scott, Shaunna L. 1996. "Dead Work: The Construction and Reconstruction of the Harlan Miners Memorial." *Qualitative Sociology* 19:365–93.

Simko, Christina. 2012. "Rhetorics of Suffering: September 11 Commemorations as Theodicy." *American Sociological Review* 77(6):880–902.

Spillman, Lyn. 1994. "Imagining Community and Hoping for Recognition: Bicentennial Celebrations in 1976 and 1988." *Qualitative Sociology* 17(1):3–28.

Stone, Charles B., Alin Coman, Adam D. Brown, Jonathan Koppel, and William Hirst. 2012. "Toward a Science of Silence the Consequences of Leaving a Memory Unsaid." *Perspectives on Psychological Science* 7(1):39–53.

Stora, Benjamin. 2006. "The Algerian War in French Memory: Vengeful Memory's Violence." pp. 151–74 in *Memory and Violence in the Middle East and North Africa*, edited by Ussama Makdisi and Paul A. Silverstein. Bloomington: Indiana University Press.

Sturken, Marita. 1991. "The Wall, the Screen, and the Image: The Vietnam Veterans Memorial." *Representations* 35:118–42.

Sturken, Marita. 1997. *Tangled Memories: The Vietnam War, The AIDS Epidemic, and the Politics of Remembering*. Berkeley: University of California Press.

Teeger, Chana. 2014. "Collective Memory and Collective Fear: How South Africans Use the Past to Explain Crime." *Qualitative Sociology* 37(1):69–92.

Teeger, Chana. 2015. "'Both Sides of the Story': History Education in Post-Apartheid South Africa." *American Sociological Review* 80(6):1175–200.

Teeger, Chana, and Vered Vinitzky-Seroussi. 2007. "Controlling for Consensus: Commemorating Apartheid in South Africa." *Symbolic Interaction* 30(1):57–78.

Trouillot, Michel-Rolph. 1995. *Silencing the Past: Power and the Production of History*. Boston: Beacon Press.

Vinitzky-Seroussi, Vered. 2001. "Commemorating Narratives of Violence: The Yitzhak Rabin Memorial Day in Israeli Schools." *Qualitative Sociology* 24(2):245–68.

Vinitzky-Seroussi, Vered. 2002. "Commemorating a Difficult Past: Yitzhak Rabin's Memorials." *American Sociological Review* 7:30–51.

Vinitzky-Seroussi, Vered. 2009. *Yitzhak Rabin's Assassination and the Dilemmas of Commemoration*. New York: SUNY Press.

Vinitzky-Seroussi, Vered, and Chana Teeger. 2010. "Unpacking the Unspoken: Silence in Collective Memory and Forgetting." *Social Forces* 88(3):1103–22.

Wagner-Pacifici, Robin, and Barry Schwartz. 1991. "The Vietnam Veterans Memorial: Commemorating a Difficult Past." *American Journal of Sociology* 97:376–420.

Whitlinger, Claire. 2015. "From Countermemory to Collective Memory: Acknowledging the 'Mississippi Burning' Murders." *Sociological Forum* 30(1):648–70.

Winter, Jay, and Emmanuel Sivan, eds. 1999. *War and Remembrance in the Twentieth Century.* Cambridge: Cambridge University Press.

Xu, Bin. 2017. "Commemorating a Difficult Disaster: Naturalizing and Denaturalizing the 2008 Sichuan Earthquake in China." *Memory Studies* 11(3):483–97.

Yoneyama, Lisa. 1999. *Hiroshima Traces: Time, Space and the Dialectics of Memory.* Berkeley: University of California Press.

Young, James E. 1993. *The Texture of Memory.* 1993. New Haven, CT: Yale University Press.

Zelizer, Barbie. 1995. "Reading the Past against the Grain: The Shape of Memory Studies." *Critical Studies in Mass Communication* 12:214–39.

Zerubavel, Eviatar. 2006. *The Elephant in the Room: Silence and Denial in Everyday Life.* New York: Oxford University Press.

Zerubavel, Yael. 1995. *Recovered Roots: Collective Memory and the Making of Israeli National Tradition.* Chicago: University of Chicago Press.

Zolberg, Vera 1998. "Contested Remembrance: The Hiroshima Exhibit Controversy." *Theory and Society* 27(4):565–90.

Name Index

Subject Index

A

affordances 71–2, 161–6, 276–7
affect misattribution procedure (AMP) 344–5,
    348–50, 371
agent-based modeling (ABM) 18, 380, 403–18
    analytical leverage of 410
analogy, in cognitive thought 9, 527–39
    cross–cultural variation in 535–7
    and metaphor 9, 528–30
    social insect 526–7, 531–8
assimilation 305, 309, 311–13, 315
attention 2–3, 6–8, 35–7
    as cognitive coordination process 57, 246
    competition for 439–43
    definition 470
    in dual-process models 5, 31, 169, 171,
        184n.8, 195–6, 287, 435, 491–2
    in mass and social media 438–9,
        508–9, 546
    inattention, disattention, selective attention
        5–7, 10, 261–2, 427–30, 450, 467–74, 587–8
    filter metaphor for 472–3, 588
    influenced by positioning 90, 260–1
    influenced by social class 273–6, 427–8
    linguistic markers of 6, 250, 261–2
    related to novelty 430–1, 472–3
    related to sensory apparatus 478–9
    related to social power 426–9, 468, 472–4,
        593, 599–600
    related to working memory 6–7, 195–6,
        287–8
    role in creating metaphors 544, 559
    social construction of 6–8, 35–7, 95, 373,
        392, 429
    to risk and danger 454
    voluntary or involuntary 426–7, 432–3
    within thought communities 5–7, 31,
        439–43, 470

attentional bias 378
attentional norms 36–7, 431–2, 434–5
authenticity 9–10, 400, 606–15, 625,
    628–32, 636
authentication 612–17

C

C-system 171
carnal sociology 68, 87, 116, 121, 127–9, 132
    carnal ethnography 121–3, 128–31, 143–4
categorization
    automatic 234
    social/cultural 9–10, 146–7, 392–3, 479,
        586, 591, 596
    embodied 65–6
    evaluative 392
    identity 392–3
    risk 451–2
chunking 455–7, 459
classification 9
    as embodied practice 71–2
    as intersubjective cultural practice 192–3
    as part of public culture 18, 32–5
    cross-cultural variation in 495, 536–8
    in implicit association testing 345
    in artificial intelligence and machine
        learning 413
    in economic sociology 496, 508–9, 513–15
    in public policy 597–601
    in science 535
    methods of studying 433
    of identities and individuals 196–7, 392–3,
        492, 597–8
    primary forms of 115, 495
    related to knowledge 392
    related to value/evaluation 392, 451, 537–8,
        597–601
    rules and norms for 36, 514